RELIGION IN THE SOVIET UNION

GARLAND REFERENCE LIBRARY
OF SOCIAL SCIENCE
(VOL. 659)

RELIGION IN
THE SOVIET UNION
A Bibliography, 1980–1989

Boris Korsch

GARLAND PUBLISHING, INC. • NEW YORK & LONDON
1992

Library of Congress Cataloging-in-Publication Data

Korsch, Boris.
    Religion in the Soviet Union : a bibliography, 1980-1989 / Boris Korsch.
        p.   cm. — (Garland reference library of social science ; vol. 659)
    Includes index.
    ISBN 0-8240-7096-8
    1. Soviet Union—Religion—Bibliography. 2. Atheism—Soviet Union—
Bibliography. I. Title. II. Series: Garland reference library of social science ; v. 659.
Z7757.S65K67 1992
[BL940.S65]
016.2'00947—dc20   92-10129
                                                                           CIP

Printed on acid-free, 250-year-life paper
Manufactured in the United States of America

With love to my wife Shuly,
My daughters Shifra and Tzvia,
My grandsons Gilly, Shai and Ori-Basil.

CONTENTS

PREFACE

Religion and Atheism as reflected in publications published under the auspices of the Communist Party of the Soviet Union (CPSU), the Soviet government, different party-state agencies and both censored and uncensored religious publications, sponsored by the various denominations in the USSR, are the subject of this bibliography.

This comprehensive bibliography covers ten years (1980-1989) of important events in the realm of Religion and Atheism in the Soviet Union, showing continuity in the anti-religious and pro-atheist stand and the change of strategy and approach in these matters.

The aim of this study is to present Soviet religious policies as illustrated by propaganda in a socio-political and ideological context, framed in accordance with the CPSU and Soviet government objectives of the moment. It covers Soviet publications from a wide range of disciplines: socio-political, ideological, theoretical, natural sciences, jurist, philosophical, psychological, pedagogical, medical, biological, musical, military, arts, publicistic and methodological, demonstrating the unity and homogeneity of party-government inspired attitudes up to 1987, when the Gorbachevite press changed its tone.

The bibliography includes books, pamphlets, articles in journals, reviews, dissertations, censored and uncensored religious publications. Each item is listed only once. A translation of the item from Russian or another language is cited with bibliographical information only if published in a different year or by a different publishing house from the original edition. Languages of translations are only mentioned if published by the same publishing house as the original edition.

The English translations, of the titles are given in square brackets. All translations are mine except those marked by an asterisk (*) denoting a publisher's translation. Titles are translated as close as possible to Russian - even vocally - (narodniki-narodnics, kontseptsiia-concept, aktual'naia-actual). For long titles, given as political slogans, I have tried to express their spirit. I preferred Perestroika to Reconstruction, considering it to be a word which has passed into the English language; "uniatstvo" is translated as the Uniate Church and "studencheskaia molodezh'" as students. Administrative, legal territorial divisions of the Soviet Union (Okrug, Oblast', Raion) are rendered in Russian. Soviet bibliographical series descriptions are not standardized and are given as in original forms.

This compilation is intended as a guide for researchers and students whose field of study is the USSR, its nationalities and its religious policies in general and different separate religious denominations, sects, cults and paganism in particular. It will also, I hope, provide a source of information for theologians, journalists and other public and political figures concerned with the CPSU and Soviet government ideology, attitudes and policies toward these subjects, and will lead the reader to sources which otherwise he would not discover.

This bibliography lists writings on Religion in general; on the "Marxist-Leninist" approach to Religion and Atheism; on separate religious denominations propagated in the USSR and abroad; on theoretical and methodological problems of "scientific atheism"; anti-religious works and atheistic education in the Soviet Union and abroad, non-Marxist atheism, freethinking, philosophy, psychology and sociology of Religion; religious philosophical and theological literature.

To avoid uncertainty, I only enumerate those publications on Judaism with titles clearly mentioning the subject, despite the fact that it is common knowledge that Judaism is linked with nearly all the numerous books and articles on Zionism and the State of Israel which have been published in the Soviet Union during the years covered by this bibliography. (See my *Publications on Judaism, Zionism and the State of Israel, 1984-1988*. An Annotated Bibliography. (New York: Garland, 1990).

The bibliography is arranged by authors and titles of collections, except for reviews, which are arranged separately by author of the work reviewed preceded by an asterisk. Titles of reviewed books are, where possible, abbreviated. The second author's initial is given in square brackets only when his identity was certainly established.

The listings were compiled from the holdings of the major libraries of the Hebrew University of Jerusalem campuses and Soviet National Bibliographies: *Knizhnaia letopis'. Osnovnoi vypusk; Knizhnaia letopis'. Dopolnitel'nyi vypusk. Knigi i broshiury; Knizhnia letopis'. Dopolnitel'nyi vypusk. Avtoreferaty disertatsii; Letopis' retsenzii; Letopis' zhurnal'nykh statei; Ezhegodnik knigi SSSR; Novye knigi v SSSR; INION Data Base; Novaia sovetskaia inostrannaia literatura po obshchestvennym naukam. Blizhnii i Srednii Vostok. Afrika; Problemy Ateizma i Religii*, and *Nezavisimyi Bibliograf* No 4. Spravochnik periodicheskogo samizdata. Moskva; and from A.I. Suetnov's listings in his "Samizdat: Novyi istochnik bibliografirovaniia" *Sov. bibl.* 2 (1989): 31.

ACKNOWLEDGMENTS

I would like to take the opportunity of thanking those colleagues and friends in Israel who in various ways have provided me with assistance: Suzan-Sarah Cohen, Raya Gotfreund, Felina Rozin, Maya Ulanovskaia and Shlomo Goldberg and his staff of The Jewish National and University Library, Hebrew University of Jerusalem; Ginette Avram of the Marjorie Mayrok Center for Soviet and East European Research, Hebrew University of Jerusalem; Nina Bibichkova of the Center for Research and Documentation of East-European Jewry, Hebrew University of Jerusalem; Prof. Arye Levin and Dr. Shaul Migron, Hebrew University of Jerusalem; Ruth Tweig and Louis Kaplan, and to Shosh Shahar, the patient lady behind the Laser.

Among those who have extended their assistance from abroad, I should like to mention, with gratitude, Dr Christine Thomas, Head of the Slavic and East European Department of The British Library.

I would like to thank the Ruth Kahan-Eber Foundation for its generous grant which made possible the publication of this book.

My gratitude is also expressed to the Leah Goldberg Fund for Russian and Slavic Studies of the Hebrew University of Jerusalem for its grant which made possible the preparation of the manuscript for publication.

At Garland Publishing, Inc. I am grateful to Phyllis Korper, my editor, for her supportive enthusiasm.

To all I wish to express my deepest appreciation.

Jerusalem-London-Jerusalem   B.K.
November 1989 - July 1991

INTRODUCTION

Religion was and is a permanent problem of the Soviet regime, having endured all the fluctuating CPSU policies - from most rigorous repressions to sporadical relaxations and vice versa.

It is not the scope of this introduction to enumerate and elaborate on CPSU ideological resolutions where "religious prejudices" are strongly condemned, where the struggle against religion and in favor of atheistic education was urged, in accordance with Lenin's precept that religion could "under no circumstances" be regarded from the party's point of view "as a private matter". All resolutions have a common denominator: a vigorous ideological struggle against religion resulting in one single outcome, bans or restrictions on religious organizations, communities and believers.

Ambiguity, ambivalence and nominality of CPSU religious policies become clear with the beginning of the Soviet regime when, in spite of constitutional promises of freedom of worship and religion, believers were deprived of those rights guaranteed by the Constitution. It is worthy of note that the Constitution of 1918 recognized freedom of both religious and anti-religious propaganda, but only security organs had the authority and power of determining what was religious propaganda and what was anti-revolutionary propaganda, thus allowing a wide range of freedom of interpretation in favor of the CPSU. An amendment of the constitution adopted on May 22, 1929 permitted freedom of religious worship and of anti-religious propaganda, as distinct from the above mentioned previous right to both religious and anti-religious propaganda. Restriction on religious propaganda was re-enacted in the 1936 Constitution, which in 1977 gave the right to religious worship or atheistic propaganda - a play of formulations and interpretations. Another vivid example is the repeated decisions of the CPSU Congresses or Plenary Sessions of the Central Committee, especially those taken at the Sixteenth Congress (1930) underlining that the practice of closing of churches "bears no relationship to the policy of our party". The instruction to stop mockery of religion and the administrative closing of churches is fictitiously disguised as the overall voluntary wish of the population, permitting "churches to be closed only in accordance with the wishes of the predominant majority" of the population.[1]

Often issues of resolutions and directives requiring opposition to manifestations of religious belief and improvement of atheistic education are an implicit admission of failure, as witnessed nowadays.

There is vast literature on Soviet legislation on religion and CPSU resolutions in this realm. I limit myself only with continuity and changes in politics of religion and stages within the context of the bibliography, elucidating the content of the enumerated items. A change, if it exists, cannot be analysed without a demonstration of continuity, to be appraised both against and compared with it. General, repetitive similarity in Soviet publications on religion and atheism will be compared against the nature of time and the needs of the moment.

By a decree of January 23, 1918 the church was separated from state and school, in 1929 a Law on Religious Associations was promulgated, secretly amended in 1962, revised in 1975, revealing and incorporating previous secret decrees. At last after lengthy and heated debates in October 1990 the "Law of the Union of Soviet Socialist Republics: On Freedom of Conscience and Religious Organizations" was adopted.[2]

Enumerated in the bibliography are publications which demonstrate the stages through which the CPSU and Soviet government had to undergo to arrive at the 1990 Law, the most liberal toward religion since the existence of the USSR.

Twists and turns in CPSU religion policies were and are framed in accordance with the objectives of the party at that moment, in its economic, political, internal and foreign situation. Stalin's concessions to the Russian Orthodox Church and other recognized religious communities during WWII (1941) in exchange for participation in the war effort marked the authorization of changes in party policies toward religion. Convinced that further concessions to religion would strengthen independent control over the thinking and behaviour of the believer, Khrushchev in 1954 revived the harsh campaign against religion. A vigorous anti-religious propaganda and administrative harassment of religious bodies started. This campaign was, as usual, ideologicaly motivated by the July 7 and November 10, 1954 CPSU CC resolutions "Concerning Serious Errors in Scientific-Atheistic Propaganda and Measures for its Improvement" and "On Errors in Conducting Scientific-Atheistic Propaganda among Population".[3] Between 1959-1964 Khrushchev intended to eliminate religious organized life, closing places of worship, resorting to arrests and other coercive methods. A short description of "Religious Prisoners" in Soviet concentration camps[4] during the Khrushchev and Brezhnev era is most informative and horrific in depicting the sadistic behaviour of camp authorities, reminiscent of sufferings of believers in A.I. Solzhenitsyn's "One Day in the Life of Ivan Denisovich" during Stalin's regime of terror. A policy of persecution of religion was pursued, but attenuated by post-Khrushchev leadership up to the 1970s, when the old system of persecution and arrests become daily practice. The Party Statute ratified at Gorbachev's XXVIIth CPSU Congress in 1986 obliged party members to lead "a decisive struggle... against religious prejudices... foreign to the socialist way of life".[5]

Glasnost has changed the social atmosphere in the Soviet Union, sanctioning public disclosure and criticism of abuse of power as a prerequisite of perestroika.

Channels for expressing controlled feelings of discontent have been opened, with the proviso that doubt not be cast on the correctness of CPSU politics toward religion. Socialism should not be undermined, answers should be sought "within the boundaries of socialism".[6] The desire for change has always existed in a state of gestation and was only awaiting a chance to emerge into the open.

The Marxist-Leninist position of the CPSU toward religion did not change, the struggle being both obligatory and necessary. The question was discussed as to appropiate tactics to be undertaken to change from crude primitive harassment of believers, to respect for their feelings. This approach was facilitated by Gorbachev's declaration that "Believers are Soviet people, working people, patriots, and they have full rights to express their opinions with dignity".[7] The pro-Gorbachev press began a campaign in 1987 against the abuse of believers' legal rights, depicting them as results of Stalin's personality cult and the previous command-administrative system.[8] It demanded the introduction of "new thinking" into "scientific-atheistic" propaganda, a basic perestroika in atheistic work representing a subtle approach in the form of dialogues between Marxists and believers. On the other hand, the clergy, believers and laity, following the advent of glasnost, voiced their protests against the humiliated status and retrictions imposed upon religion in the Soviet Union. Paradoxically the interests of both sides coincided - from two extremely different points of view and expectations. Pro-Gorbachev circles and especially the intelligentsia, aware of a large percentage of believer's among the population, sought steps to improve their standing with Gorbachev and at the same time, by appropriate tactics to eradicate the believers feelings of alienation within Soviet society, thus facilitating the decrease of religious influences and achieving the desired goal of the CPSU - dying out of religion "in the interests of socialism".[9] Believers, however, received concessions, using the "new thinking" approach and taking an active part in state affairs, hoping to steer matters in the direction of their own interests by enlarging parishes, expanding churches and their activities, increasing religious publications and the dissemination of religious feelings thereby raising social prestige, strengthening its position and independence. No doubt such a climate and the two-way pressure - from above and below - paved the way for the new law on religion, just reflecting the prevailing political atmosphere. As O. Osipov remarked the "law" and not "life" must be changed when they "contradict one another".[10]

Religious institutions have social, political and economic elements and for this reason some denominations in pre-Gorbachev time, and now all, are officially tolerated. The situation in religious politics in the Soviet Union was, and now to a lesser degree, is complex. Some religious faiths, under certain circumstances, are more tolerated than others. Sometimes the untolerated exchange place with previously tolerated. The common policy toward all of them is the CPSU and Soviet government warning against politicization of religion. Conferring different statuses, keeping religious bodies under stringent control, the CPSU uses them as a potential policy tool and manipulates them to its policies of today. So it was during Stalin's regime, when organized religious associations participated in Communist party sponsored "movements and campaigns for Peace" was "initiated" in May 1952 the "Conference of all Churches and Religions Associations in the USSR for the Defence of Peace".[11] This policy continues. Soviet intervention in Hungary (1956), in Czechoslovakia (1968) and in Afghanistan (1980) was endorsed by the Moscow Patriarchate.[12] More vivid examples are for instance, during the negotiations on nuclear armament, when religious bodies in the Soviet Union organized an International Conference "Religious Personalities for Salvation of the Holy Gift of Life from Nuclear Catastrophe" in Moscow, May 10-14, 1982. The Soviet propaganda publishing house "Novosti" [News] issued thousands of copies of booklets on this Conference in a multitude of languages for dissemination all over the world.[13] Soviet intervention in Middle Eastern affairs was endorsed by a special session "For the Peace and Justice in Near East" in the Armenian Echmiadzhinsk monastery in 1987.[14] Religious organizations are mobilized for the home front as well. For Gorbachev's campaign against alcoholism a conference on "The Church and Overcoming of Alcoholism and Drug Addiction" was organized by the Ministry of Health of the USSR and Moscow Patriarchate.[15] The political journal "New Time" published an interview with Pasha-zade al-Islam Allakhshukov, Chairman of the Spiritual Administration of Moslems in the Caucasus on the problem of "Believers for Peace",[16] and the journal "Religion in USSR" published an account by Mufti Talgat Tadzhuddin on the Islamic International Conference "Prophet Muhammad's Appeal - for Peace and Social Justice".[17] Under the auspices of the Soviet authorities the Baptists organized a Conference of the European Federation of Baptists on "Christian Responsibility in the Contemporary World" (Moscow, Feb. 10-12, 1987);[18] the Fifth Conference of Christians of USSR and Japan[19] took place in Minsk (1987) and Khambo-lama Gaadan points out that Mongolian Buddhists are against nuclear war.[20]

Gorbachev's praising of religious bodies for their struggle against nuclear arms and support of his home and foreign policies, as underlined by "we have a common history, one Fatherland and one future",[21] was the penultimate step towards the culmination point of his approach toward religion, changed since 1987, with the new Law on Religion. 1987 perestroika in religious politics was preceded by small concessions "foretold" by the permission given to Danilov Monastery in May 1985 to ring its bells.

Gorbachev's perestroika toward religion as during the Brezhnev era[22] demands to convince and not to coerce believers.[23] The continuity persists in formulations. Change in Brezhnev's time was mere words; in Gorbachev's era, words accompanied by deeds. Glasnost divulged and criticized the poor state of affairs of religion in the Soviet Union. It repudiated all previous solemn declarations that the "USSR is the first state of freedom of conscience"[24] and points out that only now is it on the way to such a freedom,[25] consolidated by social guarantees.[26]

No wonder that perestroika is welcomed by religious communities, especially by the previously most persecuted, such as the Old Believers,[27] regarding it as "ice that has begun to break". Seventh Day Adventists manifest their solidarity with Gorbachev.[28] Baptists analysed "Religion and Politics" in a special TV programme[29] and it is even praised by the Head of the Polish Catholic Church Cardinal W. Glemp.[30] The clergy claim that the church needs perestroika,[31] analyse the state of the church in the USSR under perestroika,[32] welcome the change of climate and express satisfaction that the authorities "remembered" that believers as well "are conscious-minded".[33]

From small concessions given to recognized religious bodies since 1985, authorities throughout 1987 permitted more functional steps toward greater freedom of religion. Judaism which was singled out by the CPSU and Soviet authorities for more intensive suppression and discrimination than any other religion legally allowed to exist[34] was permitted to restore the Jewish ritual bath at the Leningrad synagogue and for a Kosher restaurant to be opened by the Moscow synagogue. Discriminated Islam, legalized in 1943, started to open a multitude of Moslem organizations,[35] and a Moslem spiritual administration.[36] Evangelical Christian-Baptists came into the open with statistical data and facts about their community.[37] In December 1989 the Ukrainian Catholic Church (Uniate) banned since 1946 emerged from the underground and Protestants were allowed to import Bibles from abroad. Political, literary, historical, professional dailies and journals became accessible to clergy. Articles on and around the Millennium Anniversary of the introduction of Christianity into Rus' and advocacy of perestroika policies toward religion were simultaneously published for home and foreign use.[38] Gorbachev's declaration is paraphrased by Filaret, Metropolitan of Kiev "One History, one Fatherland".[39] The "Holy History of the Old and New Testament", which was published in 1868 was allowed to be serialized[40] and Biblical sayings appeared in the periodical "Timber Industry".[41] Special collections such as *Veruiushchii v usloviiakh perestroiki* [The Believer under Perestroika] were published and an exhibition on "Christianity in the Orient" was opened in Moscow.[42]

Perestroika in politics of religion, as in all other realms of Soviet life, criticizes "mistakes" and "distortions of party line", acknowledges "constructive" achievements of the past and instructs their adoption and adaptation to the newly created situation and conditions. This approach of ideological continuity and change in method is well expressed in a most authoritative unsigned article, published by the leading CPSU ideological-theoretical organ *Kommunist.*[43] This historiographic, ideological, philosophical article-analysis of 70 years of party religious politics is based on Lenin's precepts: religion is incompatible in the USSR and appropriate means have to be used in the anti-religious struggle. The distinguished factor of this article is the similarity between the argument of the above-mentioned resolution of the CC of the CPSU of Nov. 10, 1954 and other similar such arguments in forbidding "abusive attacks against clergy and believers... depicted as not deserving political confidence" and violation of their rights.[44] Such wording goes back to 1925 when the League of the Militant Godless was created and "advised" to conduct its anti-religious work in a "skillfuly" Leninist way, without sharp insults and ridiculing "the feelings of the sincerely believing part of the population...".[45] The importance of continuity of anti-religious struggle is stressed in this pragmatic article by its endorsing the activity of the League of Militant Godless, Khrushchev's rigorous anti-religious struggle and accusing Stalin of "turning off the road" of atheistic propaganda in the post-war years.[46] The article demands only a change of approach because the 1918 decree is "the basis" for all legislation on the inter-relationship of the Soviet authorities and religious associations.[47] In other words "new arguments in an old dispute".[48]

The CPSU cannot abandon its struggle against religion, as such a step would not only denote deviation from Leninism, but an admission of erroneous party policies since the creation of the USSR. The party can never err. Resolutions on politics of religion were taken within the authoritarian Marxist-Leninist precepts, and they can not be denied. Personality cults, rash decisions, stagnation and actions based on wishful thinking, boasting and empty words, bureaucratism and dogmatism bristle in the article as causes for deviation and distortion of the Party's Leninist line in its "ideological struggle with religion".[49] From the classics of Marxism-Leninism, Lenin is always singled out and manoeuvred to accommodate the CPSU leadership in power at that moment. It was so under Brezhnev's "Real Socialism,"[50] and it is so now under Gorbachev's Glasnost and Perestroika.[51] In both cases Lenin's scientific atheistic legacy has a life-asserting character.[52]

Scientific atheistic education has to be disseminated in accordance with the decisions of the latest Party Congress, Plenary decision or the leaders' last declaration; only they are correct, updated and meet the requirements of today. In this field continuity reigns. The role of the libraries in atheistic education of the population in the light of the XXVIIth Party Congress was the topic of special organized seminars in Odessa[53] and Samarkand in 1988.[54] Endorsing Party statutes (March 1986) on the obligatory struggle against "religious prejudices", seminar participants subtly softened their decisions "in the light of" Gorbachev's (April 1988) declaration to the Patriarch of Moscow which stated that the differing depths of world outlooks between believers and non-believers are not an obstacle to collaboration.

Of prime importance was the equipping of students with sound knowledge of scientific atheism, to estrange them from religious influences. A differentiated approach toward students continues as during the years of Gorbachev's predecessors. Brezhnev used a permanently active Republican Seminar of atheist-lecturers in the RSFSR[55] for updating the actual needs of atheistic propaganda, and the All-Union Conferences of Teachers of Scientific Atheism debated the problems of further perfection in teaching scientific atheism in different educational institutions.[56] Special seminars on scientific atheist schooling in certain disciplines were active: for student-physicists,[57] medical students,[58] and geographers.[59] The role of chemical knowledge was taken into consideration in forming a scientific world outlook for students[60] and an analysis of the religiosity of young technical engineers was undertaken.[61] The problems of atheistic education of sportsmen[62] and of sport and religious organizations[63] are studied as well as the specific nature of teaching "Fundamentals of Scientific Atheism" in universities of art[64] and the shaping of atheistic convictions of students of humanities.[65] In para-military work among the civilian population, aspects of interrelation of military-patriotic and atheistic upbringing of youth[66] are taken into consideration. A special approach for the atheistic upbringing of youth in the Soviet Republics of Middle Asia is outlined[67] and psychological aspects of the theory and practice of atheistic education are considered.[68] Use of belles-lettres in atheistic work[69] as well as the atheistic potential of Russian literature[70] is recommended. Children's atheistic upbringing is not neglected but diversified: "Mysteries" of religion,[71] in the illustrated children's encyclopedia "Scholars to Schoolpupils"; text-books of atheistic essays,[72] illustrated riddles on religion, published in the serial "I Want to Know",[73] or illustrated stories on the church's antipopular essence, where believers are portrayed as "depraved people".[74]

Scientific atheistic education continuously embraces all aspects of Soviet society. Coercive and liberal multiple CPSU decisions are used, but they have not repaid the Party's investment, by harvesting envisaged results in Soviet life. Soviet society became over-saturated, could absorb no more and the systematic anti-religious pressure gave adverse results. Religious beliefs gained ground in the last twenty years - especially in the Soviet European peripheral and Asian Republics - and the growth of religious consciousness is marked among the younger age brackets. Since the 80s the enrollment in the three Russian Orthodox theological seminaries and in the two belonging to the Roman Catholic Church in the Baltic Republics has increased. The facts speak for themselves. The warning that "clericalism counts on youth"[75] became the first issue on the agenda.

Sociological research of the level of religiosity and dissemination of atheism [ateizatsii] among university students[76] gave poor results and the *Agitator* propaganda organ of the CPSU pointed to the need to strengthen the atheistic education in schools and universities.[77]

Since political indoctrination and current information in the USSR are identical, the steady and sometimes massive stream of anti-religious messages and aggresiveness of their tone pursued an absolute discrediting of religion and a demonstration of the rule of unanimity in CPSU propaganda against it. With Gorbachev came a change - in both tone and unanimity - due to the polarization process in the Party's leadership attitude to the "New Thinking" approach in its religious politics. Part of the CPSU leadership, apparatchiks and obstinate bureaucrats, fearful for their position and power, constitute the political conservatism. Using obfuscation and obstructionism under the disguise of "theoretical resistance", they do their utmost to maintain and preserve previous religious politics. Their headlong attacks on religion continue. It is distressing. On the other side pro-Gorbachev dailies and other publications favourably depict believers, in accordance with their leader's approach, which is a reassuring process and leads to its institutionalization - promulgation of the Law on Religion. Articles and collections of A. Nezhnyi, the foremost defender of believers' legal rights, focus on the hard working monastic life[78] or on conflicts between believers and malpractices of local officials.[79] The anti-religious monthly *Nauka i religiia* [Science and religion] tolerates friendly descriptions on monasteries and monasticism[80] and even an article by Ch. Kavaliauskas, Lithuanian senior priest of the Ionish parish, in which he explains the reasons why he believes in the resurrection of Christ.[81] Opposition replications accompany Gorbachevite publications. The most vivid example is the use of "recollections" of former theologians and clergy[82] or "critical analysis of clerical radio-propaganda".[83] Formulation of the titles of anti-Gorbachevite publications presupposes the acceptance of the facts warding off any possible contradiction, such as "Anti-Sovietism under the Banner of 'Defence of Religion'"[84] or dissemination of the influence of contemporary Western religious ideology on Soviet youth and on the necessity of strengthening anti-religious work among "Today's God-Seekers".[85]

The implementation of the policy of perestroika in the realm of religion is apparent in spite of opposition. The Church of Evangelist Christian-Baptists, denounced in 1987 together with Adventists and Pentecosts, as belonging to the religious extremism in the USSR and means for overcoming them were outlined,[86] already in 1988 organized in Moscow a special seminar for its young clergy.[87] Perestroika's goodwill toward catholicism is underlined,[88] and the role of the Head of the Armenian Church, Catholicos Vazgen I in the normalization of international relations inside the Soviet Union is praised.[89] While CPSU politics fluctate, pragmatism gains over ideological theories. It all depends on the interests and needs of the present leader at that time and on certain circumstances. A glance at the Party's pejorative attributes toward the Uniate Church throws light on the extent of its vacillations. The Uniate Church, accused of subversive activity on Soviet territories during WWII,[90] being in the service of fascism and imperialist reaction,[91] was doomed to complete failure.[92] Its way to treachery and disgrace[93] is described in 1987, and in 1988 its being in the service of Anti-Communism[94] was underlined. By December 1989 it was recognized by Soviet authorities, not without the blessings of the CPSU.

The Russian Orthodox Church, the largest religious body in the USSR, was always under stringent control of the CPSU and Soviet authorities. Even during the last decade, in spite of receiving some concessions, especially since 1983, it was accused of cultivation of religious mysticism.[95] Its age-old sins of "reactionary and anti-popular activity" during Russia's first revolution of 1905-1907 are brought to mind[96] and in 1986 the "Anti-humanity" of its teachings and practices was outlined.[97] Nevertheless the International Symposium on the role of the Russian Orthodox Church in the history of Russia between the Xth-XVIIth Centuries, held in Florence (April 1988), was attended by a Soviet delegation.[98] Intent to rehabilitate is felt in a positive description of the role of military priests in the history of Russian army.[99]

Judaism, the most persecuted, discriminated and humiliated religion, officially recognized by the Soviet authorities, up to the present is omitted from the Soviet classification number (4) on "Atheism and Religion". "Judaism" can be found under many classifications categories, appertaining to nationality and bourgeois reactionary nationalism as linked with Zionism, Imperialism, Fascism, Genocide, the desire for domination over all non-Judaic nations, loyal to centres outside the Soviet Union.[100] In other words a religion of unreliable outsiders. At the same time signs of some concessions toward Judaism are evident. A delegation representing the All American Council of Rabbis visited their coreligionists[101] and the Order of Friendship of People was conferred upon Adol'f Shaevich, the Chief Rabbi of Moscow for his peacemaking activity.[102] A clear, initial statement of the need to include Judaism into the "New Thinking" appeared only in February 1989. Two officials of the Soviet Academy of Sciences, S. Rogov and V. Nosenko demanded, in a long article dealing with Antisemitism in the USSR, that Judaism be "scientifically" criticized along Leninist precepts, but without insulting the feelings of Jewish believers.[103] The monthly *Nauka i religiia* published a short article on the Jewish holiday Khanuca in October 1989, in memory of the resumption in 165 B.C. of divine services in the Temple of Jerusalem.[104] In the same year the Moscow Choral Synagogue was allowed to publish the "Mishna" in Hebrew.[105]

This new approach towards Judaism is not of the same extent as that conferred upon other denominations. It has a different connotation. It is not accompanied by publications praising its activities as is the case when other religious bodies and communities are made public. Neither articles by nor interviews with Jewish religious dignitaries have seen light in Soviet newspapers or journals, as is common with representatives of other previously severely criticized faiths.

Until 1941 the CPSU and Soviet authorities attempted to suppress Islam. After the Nazi invasion into the USSR this policy was revised and in 1943 it was legalized. Harsh treatment and discrimination, aside from periodic interludes, were the trademark of the authorities toward Islam. The lion's share of anti-publications up to the present have been devoted to Islam, not taking into consideration the disproportionate quantity of publications against Judaism, linked with Zionism and the State of Israel, in the various languages into which they were translated. In spite of all concessions conferred upon Islam and its integration since 1956 with Soviet Middle Eastern policy, it is still under criticism, because the Islamic authorities convert Islam-religion into an Islam-political tool. Publications trying to discredit Islam in Soviet public opinion, especially in the Soviet Asian republics, point out Moslem-nationalist distortions of the Socialist way of life,[106] enumerating features of Moslem religious survivals.[107] Islam is described as a tool in the service of Anti-Communism and Anti-Sovietism[108] and Islam's harmful consequences and its reactionary essence are outlined.[109] Now in 1989 Islam is accused of juvenile delinquency in Kazan[110] and of the self-cremation of Tajik women.[111] Dissemination of inimical Moslem religious literature from abroad into Tajikistan and Uzbekistan is revealed.[112]

Since the 1960s the Soviet regime has started to use opinion polls, surveys and round table discussions for the analysis of attitudes towards current problems. However, such experimentation with public opinion declined during Brezhnev's years of stagnation. Now, under Gorbachev it is developing rapidly and the results are made public.

Lectures, question and answer sessions and individual talks with believers were used in the anti-religious struggle. Under Gorbachev a new style of round table discussions has evolved, where directly involved parties are taking part, and not as before, where the participants were called to formally endorse decisions made by the Party's different echelons. In the round table on "Common security and moral-ethical values" scientific experts and theologians representing Christianity, Buddhism, Hinduism, Judaism and Islam disussed the problem of religious peacemaking activity in the nuclear era;[113] sociologists and clergy met at a round table organized by the journal *Vek XX i mir* on "Church and Society - Contemporaneity and Prognosis for the Future".[114] A special round table discussion was organized by the Academy of Social Sciences of the CPSU Central Committee on the problem of freedom of conscience in general and on interrelations between the Russian Orthodox Church and the state, particularly[115] where high ranking party specialists and theologians took part. The necessity of a dialogue and collaboration of Marxists and believers in the struggle for peace and progress[116] is time and again underlined as well as the problem of State-Church collaboration.[117]

Now as never before, with the advent of glasnost, the disparity between the reality of the situation of religious bodies in the USSR and officially depicted conditions, is too clear to require elaboration. Very sensitive to public opinion from abroad and the governments on whose good will the Soviet government depends for international loans and commerce, it does its utmost to change the unfavourable image. In order to affirm the existence of freedom of worship in the Soviet Union, the CPSU and the Soviet government have since Khrushchev's regime aimed to create and demonstrate facts. In 1975 the Soviet Union, together with another 34 states, ratified the Helsinki Act providing inter alia freedom of worship. With the consent of the Soviet authorities, church dignitaries attended various international conferences, representing their denominations, reassuring the participants, by their mere presence, of the existing Freedom of Conscience in the Soviet Union, thus contributing their share to Soviet foreign policy. Promoting Soviet interests in Africa and Asia, the Soviet Section of the Christian World

Confederation attended Conferences in Zambia, Zimbabwe, Angola and Ghana in February 1981.[118] In Colombo the Soviet religious delegation was active in theological consultations on the "Theological basis for cooperation with living religions for peace and justice."[119] Another Soviet delegation representing the World Council of Churches and the World Moslem Congress again attended a Conference of Christians and Moslems in Colombo (March 20-April 1, 1982).[120] A Soviet Christian delegation visited Japan in November 1981 on a mission of peace and friendship;[121] another went to India on the occasion of the 70th anniversary of the restoration of the Syrian Orthodox Church in the Orient.[122] The first pilgrimage of representatives of the Krishna Society from the USSR to India was advertised by the journal *New Time* disseminated all over the world.[123]

Another fact demonstrating the existence of freedom of worship and peaceful coexistence of different faiths in the Soviet Union is the possibility given to religious bodies to initiate international conferences on themes according to Soviet policies of the moment and to play host to foreign religious delegations. The Society of Soviet-Indian Friendship received Indian participants of the World Conference on "Religious Personalities for the Salvation of the Holy Gift of Life from Nuclear Catastrophe" on May 14, 1982[124] and Banddido Khamba lama Erdyneer, the Chairman of the Spiritual Administration of Buddhists in the USSR was awarded the Order of Friendship of People.[125] During 11-19 May, 1987 the Second International Scientific Church Conference on "Theology and Spirituality" took place in Moscow. Its delegations from abroad called "to follow the blessed" example of the Russian Orthodox Church's appeal for peace.[126] Another International First Conference on "Theologians and Publicists call for Peace" was organized in Moscow on 10-13 January, 1988.[127]

Thirdly, "Western falsifications" on the condition and status of the religion in the USSR are exposed, by dissemination of specially published booklets in foreign languages all over the world. A published book in the Soviet Union confers status on a certain topic. Massive publication has as its goal the strengthening of the current leader's politics and the consolidation of his authority. The Soviet publishing industry is called upon to take action on every current topic and to build up mass-produced literature around it. It is therefore manipulated to always pursue the practical goals of the moment. Thus, a torrent of widely and easily accessible low-priced booklets is issued in thousands of copies. The carefully controlled publishing house "Novosti" specializing in dissemination of Soviet propaganda abroad, embellishes the image of the situation of religious and national problems in the Soviet Union with a flow of specially illustrated literature. Moslem freedom of worship in the USSR is widely depicted in European, Asian and African languages.[128] Booklets on the Catholic church in the USSR are often published in several editions intended for states practising Catholicism.[129] One of many booklets on the "prosperous" situation of Soviet Jewry and Judaism carries an eloquent title "Without falsity...: Essays on the Life of Soviet Jews", published mainly in European languages.[130] In sharp contrast a publication on discrimination against Jews living in the USA[131] was put out by Novosti for dissemination in Europe and America.

Taking into consideration that aspirations of church dignitaries engender centrifugal tendencies, pro-Gorbachev circles try to appease them and prefer to introduce controlled changes to spontaneous demands from below. In this realm Gorbachevite publications try to kill two birds with one stone: appeasing and providing theoretical foundation for such a change in attitude toward religion. The published and planned publications for 1990 obviously demonstrate this trend. Under the auspices of Leningrad State University, the Leningrad Metropolitan See, the Research-Information Centre, Archives of the USSR Academy of Sciences-Leningrad section, and the North-Western Bible Commission a collection of archive material was published in 1990 by the Commission for the scientific edition of the Slavonic Bible (The Russian Bible Commission), 1915-1929.[132] A new serial "Publitsistika perestroiki" [Journalism of Perestroika] endows religion with a role in moral purification of Soviet society.[133] A collection denoting active movement in the Christian world in the anti-imperialist struggle for peace, democracy and social progress[134] is due to be published in 1990 by Moscow Politizdat. A monograph will analyse modernist tendencies of traditional and new religions and the impact of rising social and scientific-technical progress.[135] An illustrated scientific history of the Russian church is promised[136] and a reliable guide to Russian hagiology[137] will be published by "Kniga".

There is a concentration of doctoral dissertations with nearly identical titles, around CPSU efforts to strengthen atheistic education of workers and students in the 1980s,[138] an admission of the Party's failure in the struggle against "religious prejudices" and that of "Scientific Atheist" precepts, based on Marxist-Leninst predictions. Religion thrives on persecution. The CPSU confesses its perpetual perplexity and concern over stubborn persistence of religious attachments all over the Soviet Union. The above mentioned pragmatic article in *Kommunist* bluntly admits that "millions of believers of various faiths" in the Soviet Union "is not a vexing blunder of history, it's reality". It vindicates by "historical unprecedented circumstances, that the church could find its place in socialist society, not waiving its religious dogma, nor deceiving the trust either of the believers or of the state". The article prepares the party's opinion for Gorbachev's forthcoming meeting with Orthodox dignitaries pointing out that "churches in the USSR look, in their own spiritual fund, for values in keeping with humanist ideals of socialism, revealing loyalty and solidarity with the programme aims of Soviet society".[139]

Authoritative testimony to the strength of religious attachments in the Soviet Union are continuously published providing material for lecturer-atheists on the motives of preservation and features of manifestations of religiousness in Soviet contemporary conditions,[140] on religion in Soviet society and means for overcoming it,[141] and how to use the theory of the socialist way of life to study the reasons of religious preservation under socialism.[142]

The Soviet Moslem republics arouse the anxiety of the Moscow authorities to Islam's tenaciousness. Special literature is dedicated to the peculiarities of Moslem religiosity and prejudices,[143] on the necessity of knowledge of the religious situation in the region,[144] and sociological research is being conducted on the state of religiosity and atheistic education in regions of traditional dissemination of Islam.[145]

The Marxist-Leninist fallacy that the dying out of religion is possible is evident after more than 70 years of "Socialist" experience in the Soviet Union. Soviet authorities have tried up to and including 1989 to cut it both ways. Literature on the groundlessness of the myth of religious revival in the USSR[146] and failure of atheistic education[147] is disseminated. In this way contradictory literature, on one side admitting to religion striking root, on the other denying of its revival, was born and the failure of prognosis surfaced.

Evidence that attests to the lull on the onslaught against religion is fair. The year 1989 signifies the end of an era and the beginning of a new one in the realm of religion in the Soviet Union. No one can guarantee the permanence of this "New Thinking". Lessons of past Soviet history leave enough ground for uncertainty in the continuity of this Gorbachevite religious policy. Even Gorbachev may have a change of heart, as we have witnessed before. If no reversal of this policy occurs, religion will without doubt progress. If it will occur, religion will survive as it has during the last 70 years, and no return to the black years will be possible.

I would like to end my introduction by an unexpected quirk of fate. N.S. Krushchev, who during 1959-1964 closed more than 14000 Orthodox churches, in addition to other Christian, Jewish and Moslem places of worship, found his last repose in the Novodevichyi Monastery burial grounds, later closed by Brezhnev to stop pilgrimages by the Soviet people to the tomb of his predecessor.[148]

NOTES

1. *Kommunisticheskaia partiia Sovetskogo Soiuza v rezoliutsiiakh i resheniiakh s'ezdov, konferentsii i plenumov TsK* [The Communist Party of the Soviet Union in Resolutions and Decisions of the Congresses, Conferences and Central Committee Plenary Meetings]. 7th ed. (Moscow, 1954). vol. II, pp. 670-671.

2. *Pravda*, Oct. 9, 1990. P. 4.; *Izvestiia*, Oct. 9, 1990. P. 3.
   For a comprehensive analysis of the law see: Stephen J. Roth "The New Soviet Law on Religion". *Soviet Jewish Affairs* Vol. 20, 2-3 (1990): 27-37.

3. "O krupnykh nedostatkakh v nauchno-ateisticheskoi propagande i merakh ee uluchsheniia". *Voprosy ideologicheskoi raboty* (M., 1961). Pp. 62-65.
   "Ob oshibkakh v povedenii nauchno-ateisticheskoi propagandy sredi naseleniia". *Pravda*, Nov. 11, 1954.

4. A. Marchenko. *My Testimony* (New-York: Dutton, [1969]), 189-191.

5. *Ustav Kommunisticheskoi partii Sovetskogo Soiuza* [Statute of the Communist Party of the Soviet Union]. (M., Politizdat, 1986).

6. "Prakticheskimi delami uglubliat' perestroiku" [With Practical Deals to Extend the Perestroika]. *Pravda*, July 15, 1987. P. 2.

7. "Vstrecha General'nogo Sekretaria TsK KPSS M.S. Gorbacheva s Patriarkhom Moskovskim i vseia Rusi" [The Meeting of the General Secretary of the CC of the CPSU with Moscow and All Russia Patriarch]. *Pravda*, April 30, 1988. P. 1.

8. See item 4704.

9. See item 1435.

10. See item 3295.

11. R.A. Bauer; A. Inkeles; C. Kluckhohn. *How Soviet System Works. Cultural, Psychological and Social Themes* (New York: Vintage, 1956), 71.

12. Jane Ellis. *The Russian Orthodox Church:* A Contemporary History. (Bloomington: Indiana University Press, 1986), 273.

13. See item 3719.

14. See item 4767.

15. "Sovmestnoe soveshchanie Minzdrava SSSR i Moskovskoi Patriarkhii 'Tserkov' i preodolenie alkogolizma i narkomanii'" *Mosk. pravda*, Nov. 19, 1989.

16. See item 3368.

17. See item 3041.
18. "Kommiunike o Mezhdunarodnoi konferentsii 'Khristianskaia otvetstvennost' v sovremennom mire'" *Religiia v SSSR* 1 (1987): GN 1-GN 2.
19. "Khristiane SSSR v Iaponii vstretilis' na 'zemle soten malen'kikh Khirosim'" *Religiia v SSSR* 6 (1987): VP 1.
20. Khambo-lama Gaadan. "Splochennymi usialiiami poborot' beznravstvennost' i beschestnost'" *Religiia v SSSR* 2 (1987): KhG 1 - KhG 3.
21. *Pravda,* Apr. 30, 1988.
22. See item 485.
23. See item 2708.
24. See item 433.
25. See item 3093.
26. See item 4342.
27. Alimpii staroobradcheskii Arkhiepiskop Moskovskii i Vseia Rusi. "Led tronulsia, nastupaet vesna!" *Religiia v SSSR* 1 (1986): AA 1 - AA 3.
28. See item 1672.
29. See item 630.
30. See item 1479.
31. See item 2112.
32. Aleksandr arkhiepiskop Dmitrovskii. "Ruskaia Pravoslavnaia Tserkov' v novykh istoricheskikh usloviiakh" [Russian Orthodox Church under New Historical Conditions]. *Zhurn. Mosk. patriarkhii* 11 (1987): 4-7.
33. Sergii. "Vspomnili, chto u nas est' sovest' ..." *Sots. obespechenie* 2 (1990): 23-26.
34. Boris Korsch. *Soviet Publications on Judaism, Zionism and the State of Israel, 1984-1988.* An Annotated Bibliography. (New York: Garland, 1990). xxxix, 126 pp.
35. See item 3082.
36. See item 2466.
37. See item 4182.
38. See items 978, 1264-1270, 1853, 3437-3438, 4641.
39. *Trud,* June 5, 1988.
40. "Popul. rus. izlozhenie Biblii" *Lit. Rossiia* serialized from Oct. 6, 1989.
41. "Kladez' mudrosti. Bibleiskie izrecheniia" *Les. prom-st.* Serialized from Nov. 25-30, 1989.
42. *Narody Azii i Afriki* 1 (1989): 145.
43. See item 4200.
44. *Pravda,* Nov. 11, 1954.
45. As quoted in M. Fainsod *Smolensk under Soviet Rule* (New York: Vintage, 1963), 432.
46. Note 43, p.119.
47. Ibid, p. 115.

48. See item 3275.
49. Note 43, p. 121.
50. See item 205.
51. Note 43, pp. 115-116, 118.
52. See item 216.
53. See item 4631.
54. *Bibliotekar'*, 8 (1988): 21.
55. See item 2853.
56. See item 2448.
57. See item 3008.
58. See item 2124.
59. See item 1032.
60. See item 3763.
61. See item 330.
62. See item 2465.
63. See item 2621.
64. See item 4503.
65. See item 4053.
66. See item 4889.
67. See item 3872.
68. See item 2881.
69. See item 3054.
70. See item 3546.
71. See item 2427.
72. See item 3290.
73. See item 2696.
74. See item 2839.
75. See item 1338.
76. See item 4157.
77. See item 3544.
78. See item 3160.
79. See item 3159.
80. See items 2513-2514.
81. See item 2005.
82. See items 493, 971, 1848, 1906, 3292.
83. See item 2388.
84. See item 4580.
85. See item 1050.
86. See item 460.
87. See item 4164.
88. See item 4403.
89. See item 3146.

90.   See item 1040.
91.   See item 1037.
92.   See items 4557, 5610.
93.   See item 4581.
94.   See item 4751.
95.   See item 1537.
96.   See item 4505.
97.   See item 4356.
98.   See item 3803.
99.   V.V. Sergeev. "Podnimalis' v ataku s krestom" [They Went in to the Attack with Crosses]. *Sov. patriot,* Oct. 29, 1989.
100.   V. Begun. *Sionizm i iudaizm* [Zionism and Judaism]. (Minsk: Znanie BSSR, 1972).
101.   See item 1634.
102.   See item 1855.
103.   S. Rogov; V. Nosenko. "Chto skazal 'A' i chto skazal 'B' [What Said "A" and What Said "B"]. *Sovetskaia kul'tura,* Feb. 9, 1989. P. 6.
104.   See item 2511.
105.   See item 5805.
106.   See item 248.
107.   See item 658.
108.   See item 4364.
109.   See items 980, 4569.
110.   See item 2510.
111.   See item 2548.
112.   See item 5838.
113.   See item 5848.
114.   See item 1019.
115.   See item 2113.
116.   See item 1388.
117.   See item 5854.
118.   "Kommiunike o poseshchenii delegatsii KhMK Afriki" *Zhurn. Mosk. patriarkhi* 4 (1981): 34-35.
119.   A. Kravchenko. "Bogoslovskaia konsul'tatsiia Aziatskoi KhMK v Kolombo" *Zhur. Mosk. patriarkhii* 2 (1981): 51-52.
120.   Konferentsiia khristiian i musul'man v Kolombo" *Zhurn. Mosk. patriarkhii* 6 (1982): 67.
121.   Vladimir, arkhiepiskop Krasnodarskii i Kubanskii. "S missiei mira i druzhby v Iaponii" *Zhurn. Mosk. patriarkhii* 4 (1982): 41-42.
122.   Na tserkovnykh torzhestvakh v Indii" *Zhurn. Mosk. patriarkhii* 12 (1982): 123.

123. See item 1794.
124. "V obshchestve sovetsko-indiiskoi druzhby" *Zhurn. Mosk. patriarkhii* 8 (1982): 45.
125. See item 3651.
126. E. Speranskaia. "II Mezhdunarodnaia nauchnaia tserkovnaia konferentsiia v Moskve. 11-18 maia 1987 goda" *Zhurn. Mosk. patriarkhii* 11 (1987): 17-21.
127. A. Kozha, "Sotrudnichestvo bogoslovov i publitsistov" *Religiia v SSSR* Ak 1 - Ak 3.
128. See items 1180, 3081.
129. See item 4479.
130. *Bez fal'shi:* Ocherki o zhizni Sov. evreev. [Introd.: S. Zivs]. (M.: Raduga, 1985).
131. A. Konstantinov; Iu. Andreev. *Evrei v SShA:* Glazami amerikantsev. (M.: Novosti, 1985).
132. *Komissiia po nauchnomu izdaniiu Slavianskoi Biblii (Russkaia Bibleiskaia komissiia)* [Comp.: K.I. Logachev]. (L.: LGU, 1990).
133. *Religiia i obshchestvo:* Tserkov' v SSSR, rol' religii v nravstv. ochishchenii obshchestva. [Comp.: M. Kondrat'ev]. (M.: Novosti, 1990). (Publitsistika perestroiki). In English. Published also in French, German, Latvian and Spanish.
134. V. Debren'kov; A. Radugin. *Khristianskaia teologiia i revoliutsiia. V poiskakh novogo myshleniia* [Christian Theology and Revolution]. (M.: Politizdat, 1990). [Novie knigi - 12 (1989): 7].
135. E. Babosov. *Sovremennyi religioznyi modernizm* [Contemporary Religious Modernism]. ([Minsk]: Belarus', 1990).
136. N. Nikol'skii. *Istoriia russkoi tserkvi* ([Minsk]: Belarus', 1990).
137. G. Fedotov. *Sviatye Drevnei Rusi.* ([M.]: Kniga, 1991). [Novye knigi - 23 (1990): 16].
138. See items 5434, 5522, 5534, 5663, 5688.
139. Note 43, pp. 122-123.
140. See item 3277.
141. See item 3715.
142. See item 1005.
143. See item 4585.
144. See item 2509.
145. See item 4199.
146. See items 700, 5639.
147. See item 1495.
148. *Soviet Analyst* Vol. 16. 25 (1985): 7.

Religion in the Soviet Union

BIBLIOGRAPHIES AND REFERENCE WORKS

1   Akhmadeeva, A.G.; Valeeva, N.A. *Problemy nauchnogo ateizma*. Rek. bibliogr. ukaz. [Problems of Scientific Atheism. Recommended Bibliographical Guide]. Ufa: 1982. 76 pp. (Otd. propagandy i agitatsii Bashk. obkoma KPSS, Bashk. resp. b-ka im. N. K. Krupskoi).

2   Andriashvili, R.I. *Metodicheskie ukazaniia po teme 'Islam i ego osnovnye napravleniia'* [Methodical Instructions on the Subject "Islam and its Basic Trends". Tbilisi: Izd-vo Tbil. un-ta, 1988. 128 pp. In Georgian. Bibl.: p. 126.

3   Andrienko, L.A. "Kul'tura, isskustvo, religiia: Krat. bibliogrf." [Culture, Art, Religion: Short bibliography]. *Vopr. nauch. ateizma* 30 (1982): 326-329.

4   Andrienko, L.A. "Literatura po nauchnomu ateizmu, izdannaia v SSSR v 1976-1980 gg." [Scientific-Atheistic Literature Published in USSR in 1976-1980]. *Vopr. nauch. ateizma* 29 (1982): 273-300.

5   Arsenkin, V.K. *Krizis religioznosti i molodezh'*: Metodol. aspekty issled. [Religiosity Crisis and Youth: Methodological Aspects of Research]. M.: Nauka, 1984. 264 pp.

6   *Ateisticheskaia propaganda sredstvami samodeiatel'nogo teatra*: (Metod. rekomendatsii) [Atheistic Propaganda by the Means of Amateur Theatre]. M.: VNMTsNTIKPR, 1984. 19 pp. Bibl.: pp. 12-19. [Vsesoiuz. nauch.-metod. tsentr nar. tvorchestva i kul't.-prosvet. raboty, Gos. tsentr. teatr. b-ka.].

7   *Ateisticheskie motivy v khudozhestvennoi literature* Bibliogr. ukaz. lit. [Atheistic Motifs in Belles-Lettres: Bibliographical Guide of Literature]. Comp.: N. N. Chernenko. Odes. gos. nauch. b-ka im. A. M. Gor'kogo. Odessa: 1988. 114 pp. Name index: pp. 108-113.

8   *Ateisticheskii entsiklopedicheskii slovar'* [Encyclopedia of Atheism]. Ed.: M.A. Usmanov. Tashkent: Gl. red. Uzb. sov. entsikl., 1988. 478 pp. In Uzbek.

9   *Ateisticheskii slovar'* [Dictionary of Atheism]. Ed.: M.P. Novikova. M.:
    Politizdat, 1983. 559 pp. Three 2nd revised and enlarged editions were
    published in: 1984 (511pp.); 1985 (512 pp.); 1986 (511 pp.). For reviews
    see items 4935-4936.

10 *Ateisticheskoe vospitanie*: Sprav. dlia ideol. aktiva [Atheistic Education:
    Reference Book for Ideological Activists]. Comp.: V.A. Bashkalova; I.S.
    Golodnenko; V.A. Zots. M.: Politizdat, 1983. 175 pp.
    Published also in:
    Tashkent: Uzbekistan, 1985. 189 pp. In Uzbek.
    Erevan: Aiastan, 1986. 195 pp. In Armenian.
    Alma-Ata: Kazakhstan, 1986. 181 pp. In Kazakh.

11 *Ateisticheskoe vospitanie trudiashchikhsia* (Bibliogr. spisok) [Atheistic
    Education of Workers (Bibliographical list)]. Comp.: M.N. Ustinova; M.A.
    Ustinova. Kiev: GRB UkSSR, 1980. 19 pp. In Ukrainian.

12 *Ateisticheskoe vospitanie v SSSR*. Bibliogr. ukaz. kn. i st. na rus. iaz. za
    1983-1987 (Mai) gg. [Atheistic Education in USSR. Bibliographical Guide
    of Books and   Articles published in Russian in 1983-1987]. Comp.: G.P.
    Manchkha; V.A. Fokeev; Ed.: L.G. Golubeva. M., 1988. 113 pp. Name
    and title index: pp. 102-113.

13 *Ateizm, religiia i sovremennaia ideologicheskaia bor'ba*: Rek. bibliograf. ukaz.
    [Atheism, Religion and the Contemporary Ideological Struggle: Recommen-
    ded Bibliographical Guide]. Comp.: P. L. Kaushanskii; L.F. Tsukanova.
    Kiev: Politizdat, 1988. 46 pp. Author and title index: pp. 41-45.

14 *Ateizm i religiia*: Voprosy i otvety [Atheism and Religion: Questions and
    Answers]. [Annual]. M.: Politizdat, 1985-
    1985 / Comp.: V. M. Kuveneva. 208 pp.
    1986 / Comp.: A. Akhmedov. 256 pp.
    1987 / Comp.: V. M. Kuveneva. 255 pp.
    Published also in:
    Frunze: Kyrgyzstan, 1987. 204 pp. In Kirghiz.
    Erevan: Aiastan, 1988. 198 pp. In Armenian.
    Ashkhabad: Turkmenistan, 1988. 234 pp. In Turkmen.

15 *Baptistskii zhurnal*: Vchera i segodnia [Baptist Journal: Yesterday and Today].
    Kiev: "Znanie" UkSSR,   1989. (V pomoshch' lektoram, propagandistam
    nauch. ateizma].
    No.1. Comp.: P.V. Rusin. 57 pp.

16   Belousov, Ia.P. *Obzomaia retsenziia na materialy, izdannye oblastnymi*
     organizatsiiami obshchestva "Znanie" Kazakhskoi SSR po voprosam
     ateisticheskogo vospitaniia [Survey Review of Material Published by the
     Regional Organizations of the Society "Znanie" [Knowledge] Kazakh SSR
     on Atheistic Education]. Alma-Ata: Znanie KazSSR, 1984. 23 pp.

17   Belov, O.A.; Il'inskaia, S.P. *Formirovanie u molodezhi nauchno-ateisticheskogo*
     mirovozzreniia. Bibliogr. ukaz. lit. [Forming Youth's Atheistic World Out-
     look. Bibliographic Guide of Literature]. M.: [S.n.], 1981. 43 pp.

18   Boremchuk, E.S.; Gorot', O.V. *Siloi ubezhdeniia*: Nauch.-ateist. propaganda v
     oblasti. Bibliogr. ukaz. [By power of Persuasion: Scientific-Atheistic
     Propaganda in Oblast'. Bibliographical Guide]. Lutsk: [S.n.], 1982. 32 pp.
     (Volyn. Gos. obl. nauch. b-ka). In Ukrainian.

19   Borovishki, V. "Zaboty bolgarskikh ateistov" [Anxieties of Bulgarian Atheists].
     Nauka i religiia 12 (1984): 52-53.

20   Bubnov, N.Iu. "Pisaniia russkikh staroobriadtsev" [Writings of Russian
     Old-Believers]. *Istoriografiia obshchestvennoi mysli dorevoliutsionnogo Urala.*
     Sverdlovsk, 1988. Pp. 113-119.

21   Bulanin, D.M. "Katalog knig kirillovskoi pechati XVI - XVII vekov Muzeia
     istorii religii i ateizma v Leningrade" [Catalog of Books in Cyrillic Printing
     of XVIth-XVIIth Centuries in the Leningrad Museum of the History of
     Religion and Atheism]. *Nauchno-ateisticheskie issledovaniia v muzeiakh.* L.:
     1987. Pp. 90-107.

22   Chernov,M. *K 1000-letiiu vvedeniia khristianstva na Rusi* [On the Occasion of
     the Thousandth Year of the Introduction of Christianity into Rus']. M.:
     Tsentr. dom. nauch. ateizma, Goskominturist SSSR. Gl. upr. propagandy i
     inform., 1988. 97 pp. (V pomoshch' propagandistam i aktivu rabotaiush-
     chim s gruppami inostr. turistov). Bibl.: p. 96.

23   Chubar, B. "Kakim viditsia nebo iz kosmosa" [How Heaven is Seen from the
     Cosmos]. *V mire knig* 3 (1981): 57-58.

24   Danil'chenko, R. " Put' k istine" [The Way to Truth]. *Bibliotekar'* 6 (1980):
     21--21.

25   Derkevits, Z.P. *Nagliadnye sredstva po nauchnomu ateizmu* [Visual Aids for
     Scientific Atheism]. Riga: Znanie Latv SSR, 1980. 69 pp. Bibl.: 16-17.

26 Derkevits, Z.P.; Kudriashov, G.E. "Nagliadnye sredstva k spetskursam po istorii religii i ateizma" [Visual Aids for Special Courses on the History of Religion and Atheism]. *Problemy istorii religii i ateizma*. Cheboksary, 1981. Pp. 125-128.

27 Dzhegutanov, E. "S samykh pervykh nomerov..." [From the First Issues...]. *Nauka i religiia* 3 (1980): 18-20.

28 Emeliakh, L.I. "Novye istoricheskie trudy o vvedenii khristianstva na Rusi (1985-pervaia polovina 1987 g.)" [New Historical Works on the Introduction of Christianity into Rus' (1985-Early 1987)]. *Russkoe pravoslavie i ateizm v otechestvennoi istorii*. L., 1988. Pp. 5-50.

29 Ermakova, D. "Otrazhaia zhizn'" [Reflecting Life]. *Nauka i religiia* 12 (1982): 53-55.

30 Ermakova, D. "Tribuna znanii i opyta" [Journal of Knowledge and Experience]. *Nauka i religiia* 5 (1984): 53-54.

31 Ezhova, A. "Po stranitsam 'Ateizmusa'" [Over the Pages of "Ateizmus"]. *Nauka i religiia* 9 (1985): 55-56.

32 Fel'man, A. "V bor'be za nauchnoe mirovozzrenie" [The Struggle for Scientific World Outlook]. *Nauka i religiia* 2 (1981): 52-54.

33 Fel'man, A. "V teorii i na praktike" [Theory and Practice]. *Nauka i religiia* 1 (1983): 49-51.

34 Fel'man, A. "Vystupaia vo vtoroe desiatiletie" [Entering the Second Decade]. *Nauka i religiia* 3 (1985): 55-57.

35 Gadel'shina, N.A.; Lensu, M.Ia. *Metodicheskie rekomendatsii po ispol'-zovaniiu materialov XXVI s'ezda KPSS v kurse 'Osnovy nauchnogo ateizma'* [Methodical Recommendations for the Use of Materials of the XXVIth CPSU Congress in the Course "Fundamentals of Scientific Atheism"]. Minsk: BGU, 1981. 30 pp.

36 Gal'perin, B.I. *Religioznyi ekstremizm: Kto est' kto* [Religious Extremism: Who Is Who]. Kiev: Politizdat Ukrainy, 1989. 133 pp. Annot. bibl.: pp. 129-132.

37 Gordienko, N. "Neobkhodimye izdaniia" [Necessary Publications]. *Nauka i religiia* 6 (1982): 26-27.

38 Gorovaia, O.V.; Terent'ev, A.A. "Spravochnik-opredelitel' ikonograficheskikh obrazov severnogo buddizma" [Reference Guide of Iconographic Images of Northern Buddhism]. *Nauchno ateisticheskie issledovaniia v muzeiakh*. Ch. 1. L., 1987. Pp. 107-132.

39 Gul'chinskii, V.I. "Bibliia v sovremennom mire" [Bible in the Contemporary World]. *Sov. bibliogr.* 3 (1989): 65-71.

40 Iastrebov, *I.B. Vatikan i politika voiny i mira* [Vatican and the Policy of War and Peace]. Vil'nius: Znanie, 1987. 18 pp.

41 *Ideologicheskaia bor'ba i kontrpropaganda*: Kat. lit. po vopr. polit. oblicheniia klerik. antikommunizma [Ideological · Struggle and Counterpropaganda: Catalog of Literature on the Problem of Political Exposure of Clerical Anti-Communism]. Kiev: Znanie UkSSR, 1984. 25 pp. (V pomoshch' ideol. aktivu / O-vo "Znanie" UkSSR).

42 Innokentii. "K bibliografii bibleisticheskoi literaturyi [Bibliography of Biblical Literature]. *Sov. bibliogr.* 3 (1989): 71-72.

43 Iskanderov, R. "Novye knigi dlia sovetskikh musul'man" [New Books for Soviet Moslems]. *Religiia v SSSR* 1 (1987): BM 1-BM 2.

44 *Islam*: Krat. sprav. [Islam: Concise Reference Book]. Ed.: E.M. Primakov. M.: Nauka, 1983. 159 pp. 2nd enlarged ed., 1986. 139 pp.
    Published also in:
    Ashkhabad: Turkmenistan, 1988. 161 pp. In Turkmen. Bibl.: pp. 156-157. Subject index: pp. 159-160.
    Alma-Ata: Kazakhstan, 1988. 192 pp. In Kazakh.
    Baku: Azernesher, 1989. 158 pp. In Azerbaijan.

45 *Islam*: Osnovnye napravleniia, techeniia, sekty, istoricheskaia khronologiia, prazdniki [Islam: Main Trends, Tendencies, Sects, Historical Chronology, Holidays]. Ed.: V.V. Peskov. M.: Znanie, 1988. 31 pp. (V pomoshch' lektoru). Bibl.: p. 30.

46 *Islam*: Slov. ateista [Islam: Atheist's Dictionary]. [A.V. Avksent'ev, et al.; Introduction by G.V. Miloslavskii, et al]. M.: Politizdat, 1988. 254 pp.

47 *Islam*: Spravochnik [Islam: Reference Book]. Ed.: M.A. Usmanov. [Comp.: M.M. Khairullaev]. Tashkent: Izd-vo lit. i iskusstva, 1986. 208 pp. In

Uzbek. Republished: Tashkent: Gl. red. Uzb. sov. entsikl., 1987. 208 pp. In Uzbek.

48   *Islam i problemy ateisticheskogo vospitaniia*: (Met. rekomendatsii). [Islam and Problems of Atheistic Education (Methodical Recommendations)]. Comp.: V.P. Kochneva. Alma-Ata, 1988. 21 pp.

49   *Islam v Povolzh'e i na Urale* [Islam on the Volga and the Urals]. Prepared by R.I. Sultanov. Ufa: "Znanie", Sektsiia po propagande nauch.-ateist. znanii, 1989. 28 pp. Bibl.: pp. 26-27.

50   *Istoricheskie i filosofskie problemy pravoslaviia na Rusi v rabotakh sovetskikh uchenykh*: Ref. sb. [Historical and Philosophical Problems of Orthodoxy in Rus' in the Works of Soviet Scientists: Ref. Coll.]. Ed.: B.A. Lapshov; Iu.P. Zuev. AN SSSR. INION, Akad. obshchestv. nauk pri TsK KPSS. In-t nauch. ateizma. M., 1987. 138 pp. (Ser. Problemy metodologii istorii).

51   Ivanchikova, L.A. *Nauka protiv religii*: Rek. ukaz. lit. [Science against Religion: Recommended List of Literature]. M.: [S.n.], 1981. 42 pp.

52   Ivanenko, S. "Nravstvennye tsenosti ateizma" [Moral Values of Atheism]. *Bibliotekar'* 12 (1981): 47-50.

53   *K 1000-letiiu vvedeniia khristianstva na Rusi*: Rek. spisok lit. [On the Occasion of the Thousandth Year Anniversary of the Introduction of Christianity into Rus': Recommended List of Literature]. Ed.-comp.: G.G. Stel'mashok. M., 1988. For: 1986-1987. 20 pp.

54   *K 1000-letiiu vvedeniia khristianstva na Rusi*: (Sprav.-analit. material) [On the Occasion of the Thousandth Year Anniversary of Introduction of Christianity into Rus': (Reference-Analytical Material)]. [Comp.: M. Chernov]. M: Znanie, 1988. 97 pp. (V pomoshch' propagandistam i aktivu, rabotaiushchim s gruppami inostr. turistov / Vsesoiuz. o-vo "Znanie", Tsentr. Dom nauch. ateizma). Bibl.: p. 96.

55   "Kak sostavit' plan raboty" [How to Make up a Working Plan]. *Nauka i religiia* 9 (1982): 8-10.

56   *Kak voznik islam?*: (Metod. rek. lektoram i propagandistam) [How Islam arose?: (Methodical Recommendations for Lecturers and Propagandists)]. Comp.: R.I. Sultanov. Ufa: Znanie, 1989. 35 pp.

57 *Karmannyi slovar' ateista* [Atheist's Pocket Dictionary]. Comp.: Iu.A. Bakhnykin; M.S. Belenkii; A.V. Belov. Ed.: M.P. Novikova. 3rd revised and enlarged ed. M.: Politizdat, 1981. 280 pp.
4th ed., 1983. 270 pp.
5th ed., 1985. 270 pp. For review see item 5086.
6th ed., 1986. 270 pp.
7th ed., 1987. 270 pp.
Published also in:
Kishinev: Kartia Moldoveniaske, 1982. 310 pp. In Moldavian.
Erevan: Aiastan, 1983. 306 pp. In Armenian.
Baku: Azerneshr, 1987. 305 pp. In Azerbaijan.
Alma-Ata: Kazakhstan, 1988. 287 pp. In Kazakh.
Dushanbe: Irfan, 1988. 287 pp. In Tajik.

58 Khupka, G. "Deistvennyi pomoshchnik" [Efficient Assistant]. *Nauka i religiia* 5 (1981): 53-54.

59 Komissarova, T.G. "Rol' bibliografii v istorii kitaiskogo buddizma" [The Role of Bibliography in the History of Chinese Buddhism]. *Pis'mennye pamiatniki Vostoka, 1978-1979.* M., 1987. Pp. 218-233.

60 Korepanova, N.A.; Terent'ev, A.A. "Spravochnik-opredelitel' ikonograficheskikh obrazov severnogo buddizma" [Reference-Descriptory Guide of Iconographic Images of Northern Buddhism]. *Nauchno-ateisticheskie issledovaniia v muzeiakh.* L., 1988. Pp. 110-146. Bibl.: pp. 111-112.

61 Krasnikov, N.P. *Kriticheskii obzor sotsial'no-eticheskogo soderzhaniia 'Zhurnala Moskovskoi patriarkhii' za 1979-1980 gg.* [Critical Review of the Socio-Ethical Contents of the "Journal of Moscow Patriarchate" for 1979-1980]. M.: [S.n.], 1981. 48 pp.

62 Krasnov, A.P. "Obzor literatury, posviashchennoi priniatiiu khristianstva na Rusi" [Review of Literature Dedicated to the Adoption of Christianity in Rus']. *Prepodavanie istorii v shk.* 4 (1988): 79-82.

63 *Kratkii ateisticheskii slovar'* [Short Atheistic Dictionary]. [Comp.: G. Akmyradov; Y. Akmyradov; G. Aknyiazov, et al.]. Ashkhabad: Turkmenistan, 1985. 143 pp. In Turkmen.

64 Lavrik, E. "Slovatskaia nov'" [Slovakian Virgin Soil]. *Nauka i religiia* 2 (1980): 57-58.

65   "Literatura po nauchnomu ateizmu, izdannaia v SSSR v 1981-1983 gg."
     [Literature on Scientific Atheism Published in USSR in 1981-1983]. Comp.:
     L.A. Andrienko. *Vopr. nauch. ateizma* 31 (1983): 296-305.

66   Malakhova, I.A. *Novye tendentsii v ideologii i deiatel'nosti khristianskogo
     sektanstva* [New Tendencies in the Ideology and Activity of Christian
     Sectarianism]. M.: Znanie RSFSR, 1980. 39 pp. (V pomoshch' lektoru /
     O-vo "Znanie" RSFSR, Nauch-metod. sovet po propagande nauch.
     ateizma).

67   Martynova, E.N.; Terebeichik, N.G. *Aktual'nye problemy nauchnogo ateizma i
     religii*: Bibliogr. ukaz. [Actual Problems of Scientific Atheism and Religion:
     Bibl. Guide]. L'vov: L'vov. nauch. b-ka, 1982. 178 pp. In Ukrainian and
     Russian.

68   "Materialy k 'Bogoslovsko-tserkovnomu slovariu'" [Material for 'Church-
     Theological Dictionary']. *Bogoslovskie trudy.* M., 1988. Pp. 321-336.

69   Mel'nikova, E.I. *Ateisticheskoe vospitanie molodezhi*: Rek. ukaz. lit. [Youth's
     Atheistic Upbringing: Guide of Recommended Literature]. Odessa: OGNB,
     1980. 24 pp.

70   *Metodicheskie rekomendatsii dlia chteniia problemnoi lektsii po kursu
     nauchnogo ateizma na temu 'Religiia kak sotsial'noe iavlenie'* [Methodical
     Recommendations for Reading the Problematic Lecture on "Religion as a
     Social Appearance" in the Course on Scientific Atheism]. Comp.: A.N.
     Gudyma. Kiev, 1987. 63 pp., chart.

71   *Metodicheskie rekomendatsii po ispol'zovaniiu materialov ustnogo narodnogo
     tvorchestva v ateisticheskoi propagande:* V pomoshch' propagandistu nauch.
     ateizma [Methodical Recommendations for the Use of Oral Material of
     People's Art in Atheistic Propaganda: Aid for Propagandist of Scientific
     Atheism]. Comp.: A.G. Bakanurskii; E.G. Primak; Sci. ed.: Iu.A. Dmitriev.
     Kiev: Znanie, Resp. dom nauch. ateizma, 1987. 35 pp. Bibl.: pp. 33-34.

72   *Metodicheskie rekomendatsii po ispol'zovaniiu proizvedenii drevnerusskogo
     izobrazitel'nogo iskusstva v ateisticheskoi propagande* [Methodical
     Recommendations for the Use of Old Russian Fine Arts in Atheistic
     Propaganda]. Prepared by: V.I. Ul'ianovskii. Kiev: Znanie UkSSR, Dom
     nauch. ateizma, 1987. Pt. 1. 41 pp. Pt. 2. 52 pp. Bibl.: pp. 41-45.

73 *Metodicheskie rekomendatsii po kriticheskomu analizu soderzhaniia religioznykh propovedei:* V pomoshch' propagandistu nauch. ateizma [Methodical Recommendations for Critical Analysis of the Content of Religious Sermons: Aid for the Propagandist of Scientific Atheism]. Prepared by: V.G. Kalashnikov; T.I. Didenko. Kiev: Znanie UkSSR, Dom nauch. ateizma, 1987. 36 pp. Bibl.: p. 35.

74 *Metodicheskie rekomendatsii po kritike netraditsionnykh religii:* V pomoshch' propagandistu nauch. ateizma [Methodical Recommendations for Criticism of Non-Traditional Religions: Aid for the Propagandist of Scientific Atheism]. Sci. ed.: N.R. Novichenko. Kiev: Znanie UkSSR, Res. Dom nauch. ateizma, 1988. 35 pp. Bibl.: pp. 33-34.

75 *Metodicheskie rekomendatsii po organizatsii ideino-vospitatel'noi raboty s posledovateliami baptisma* [Methodical Recommendations for Organization of Ideological-Educational Work among the Followers of Baptism]. Prepared by: V.E. Elenskii. Kiev: Znanie UkSSR, Resp. Dom nauch. ateizma, 1989. 23 pp. Bibl.: p. 22.

76 *Metodicheskie rekomendatsii po organizatsii i provedeniiu ateisticheskoi raboty sredi posledovatelei katolitsizma* [Methodical Recommendations for Organization and Conducting Atheistic Work among Followers of Catholicism]. Prepared by: N.N. Kozachishin; L.M. Krasovskaia. Kiev: Znanie UkSSR, Resp. Dom nauch. ateizma, 1987. 27 pp. (V pomoshch' propagandistu nauch. ateizma). Bibl.: pp. 25-26.

77 *Metodicheskie rekomendatsii po osveshcheniiu istokov ateizma i svobodomysliia vostochnoslavianskikh narodov v ateisticheskoi propagande:* V pomoshch' propagandistu nauch. ateizma [Methodical Recommendations in Atheistic Propaganda for Elucidating the Sources of Atheism and Free-Thinking of the Eastern Slav Peoples: Aid for the Propagandist of Scientific Atheism]. Prepared by: L.B. Piliavets; Sci. ed.: T.S. Golichenko. Kiev: Znanie UkSSR, Resp. Dom nauch. ateizma, 1988. 36 pp. Bibl.: pp. 34-37.

78 *Metodicheskie rekomendatsii po podgotovke i provedeniiu lektsii i besed o vvedenii khristianstva na Rusi:* V pomoshch' propagandistu nauch. ateizma [Methodical Recommendations for Preparation and Conducting Lectures and Discussions on the Introduction of Christianity into Rus': Aid for the Propagandist of Scientific Atheism]. Prepared by: A.V. Shuba; Iu.M. Efremov. Kiev: Znanie UkSSR, Resp. Dom nauch. ateizma, 1988. 37 pp.

79   *Metodologicheskie voprosy sovetskogo islamovedeniia:* Temat. sb. nauch. tr.
      [Methodological Problems of Soviet Studies of Islam: Thematic Collection
      of Treatises]. [Ed.: G.I. Mustafaev]. Baku: Azerb. un-t, 1884. 90 pp. Part
      of the text in Azerbaijan.

80   *Mifologicheskii slovar'* [Mythological Dictionary]. Comp.: M.N. Botvinnik;
      M.A. Kogan; M.B. Rabinovich; B.P. Seletskii. Minsk: Universitetskoe, 1989.
      255 pp., illus.

81   *Mify narodov mira*: Entsiklopediia [Myths of Peoples of the World:
      Encyclopaedia]. In 2 vols. Ed.: S.A. Tokarev. M.: Sov. entsiklopediia,
      1980. V. 1. A-K. 1980. 671 pp., illus. V. 2. K-Ia. 1982. 718 pp., illus.
      Index: pp. 689-718. Republished as 2nd ed., 1987. For reviews see items
      5164-5174.

82   *Nauchnyi ateizm. Istoriia religii i ateizma:* Nauch. popul. publ. v LatvSSR
      1970-1980 [Scientific Atheism. History of Religion and Atheism:
      Popular-Scientific Publications in Latv SSR 1970-1080]. Comp.: A.P. Ozola.
      Riga: In-t filosofii i prava, 1984. 117 pp.

83   *NTR, ateizm i religiia.* Rek. bibliogr. ukaz. [NTR, Atheism and Religion:
      Guide of Recommended Bibliogr.]. Comp.: K.L. Blazhevich; P.L. Kaushan-
      skii. Kiev: Politizdat Ukrainy, 1986. 22 pp.

84   *O religii islama* [On Islamic Religion]. Kazan': [S.n.], 1981. 33 pp. In Tatar.
      For review see item 5195.

85   *Obzor nauchno-ateisticheskoi literatury* [Review of Scientific-Atheistic Litera-
      ture]. L.: Znanie RSFSR.
      Vyp. 18. 1982. / G.D. Kalinicheva. 19 pp.

86   *Obzor nauchno-ateisticheskoi literatury izdatel'stva RSFSR* [Review of Scientific-
      Atheistic Literature of RSFSR's Publishing Houses]. M.: Goskomizdat, Gl.
      red. massovo-polit. lit., 1981. 18 pp.

87   *Obzor periodicheskikh izdanii russkoi pravoslavnoi tserkvii* [Review of Periodi-
      cal Publications of the Russian Orthodox Church]. Prepared by: N.R. Novi-
      chenko. Kiev: Znanie UkSSR, Resp. Dom nauch. ateizma, 1988. 25 pp.

88   *Organizatoru ateisticheskogo vospitaniia molodezhi*: Tez. dokl. na seminare-
      soveshchanii, Apr. 1983 g. [For the Organizer of Youth's Atheistic

Upbringing: Theses of Lectures at Seminary-Conference, April 1983]. Ed.: I.I. Enikeev. Omsk, [S.n.], 1983. 63 pp.

89 *Organizatsiia i metodika ateisticheskogo vospitaniia* [Organization and Methodics of Atheistic Education]. [V.V. Vrublevskaia; V.I. Garadzha; R.P. Zolotareva]. M.: Politizdat, 1986. 303 pp. Bibl.: pp. 295-300. Published also in:
Ashkhabad: Turkmenistan, 1989. 342 pp. In Turkmen. Bibl: pp. 332-339. For review see item 5202.

90 *Otvechaem veruiushchim*: Spravochnik [We Reply to Believers: Reference Book]. [I.I. Brazhnik; S.M. Vozniak; P.F. Darmanskii]. Kiev: Politizdat Ukrainy, 1984. 112 pp.

91 Pitirim mitropolit Volokolamskii i Iur'evskii. "Ob izdatel'skoi deiatel'nosti Russkoi Pravoslavnoi Tserkvii" [Publication Activity of the Russian Orthodox Church]. *Religiia v SSSR* 11 (1988): 1-28.

92 *Pravoslavie*: Slov. ateista [Orthodoxy: Atheist's Dictionary]. [I.F. Belenkin, et al]. M.: Politizdat, 1988. 272 pp. For review see item 5231.

93 *Protestantizm*: Slov. ateista [Protestantism: Atheist's Dictionary]. [K.L. Blazhenov, et al]. M.: Politizdat, 1990. 319 pp.

94 *Protestantizm i politika*: Ref. sb. [Protestantism and Politics: Ref. Collection]. Ed.: N.N. Razumovich. M.: INION AN SSSR, 1988. 108 pp. (Ser.: Kritika burzhuaz. ideologii, reformizma i revizionizma).

95 *Protestantskie organizatsii v SSSR*: (Sotsial. oblik, ideologiia, polit. pozitsiia, propovedn. deiatel'nost') [Protestant Organizations in USSR: (Social Aspect, Ideology, Political Position, Preaching Activity)]. [Ed.: G.S. Lialina]. M.: AON, 1989. 150 pp.

96 *Rabota bibliotek po propagande ateisticheskoi i estestvenno-nauchnoi literatury*: bibliogr. ukaz. [Libraries' Work for Propagandising of Atheistic and Scientific Literature: Bibliographical Guide]. Comp.: G.V. Ustiuzhanina; Ed.: M.L. Desenko. Odessa: OGNB, 1987. 39 pp.

97 *Religioznaia propoved' segodnia* [Religious Preaching Today]. Kiev: Znanie UkSSR, 1989. Vyp. 2. Sci. ed.: V.D. Bondarenko. 38 pp.

98   *Religioznye prazdniki v 1989-1993 godakh* [Religious Holidays in 1989-1993].
      [Comp.: D.Ia. Sibirichev; K.N. Kononova]. M.: Znanie, 1989. 20 pp. (V
      pomoshch' lektoru, propagandistu, organizatoru ateist. raboty / Vsesoiz.
      o-vo "Znanie", Tsentr. Dom nauch. ateizma). Bibl.: pp. 19-20.

99   Roshchin, A.M. "Ob izuchenii istorii russkogo antireligioznogo svobodomysliia
      i ateizma: Kritiko-bibliogr. ocherk" [On the Study of the History of
      Russian Antireligious Free-Thinking and Atheism: Critical-Bibliographical
      Essay]. *Russkoe pravoslavie i ateizm v otechestvennoi istorii.* L., 1988. Pp.
      146-154.

100   *Rukopisi Arkhangel'skogo sobraniia*   [Manuscripts of Archangel Collection].
      Comp.: A.A. Amosov. L.: Nauka. Leningr. otd-nie. 1989. 326 pp. Index:
      pp. 272-325.

101   "Russkie i inostrannye istochniki o 'kreshchenii Rusi'" [Russian and Foreign
      Sources on the "Christening of Rus'"]. *"Kreshchenie Rusi" v trudakh
      russkikh i sovetskikh istorikov.* M., 1988. Pp. 271-306.

102   *Russko-Kirgizskii slovar' terminov po ateizmu* [Russian-Kirghiz Dictionary of
      Terms on Atheism]. [Comp.: M. Abdyldaev; E. Maanaev]. Frunze: Ilim,
      1988. 136 pp. Bibl.: pp. 3-4.

103   Sakalauskas, I. "Ateisticheskie trudy Antanasa Metelenisa. K stoletiiu so dnia
      rozhdeniia" [Antanas   Metelenis' Atheistic Works. Centenary of his
      Birthday]. *Ateistines minties raida lietuvoje.* Kaunas, 1988. Pp. 69-75. In
      Lithuanian. Summary in Russian.

104   Savchenko, L. "Ateisticheskaia propaganda v molodezhnoi pechati" [Atheistic
      Propaganda in Youths' Press]. *Molodezh. Religiia. Ateizm* M., 1988. Vyp.
      4. Pp. 169-182.

105   Sharifov, V.; Khushkadamov, D. *Slovar'-spravochnik ateista* [Atheist's
      Dictonary-Reference Book]. Dushanbe: Irfon, 1985. 192 pp. In Tajik. For
      review see item 5287.

106   Sheimukhambetova, G. "Intellektual'naia situatsiia na srednevekovom
      Blizhnem i Srednem Vostoke" [Intellectual Situation in Near and Middle
      East in the Middle Ages]. *Filosofiia stran Azii i Afriki*: Problemy
      noveishei istoriografii. M., 1988. Pp. 3-35.

107   Shpazhnikov, G.A. *Religii stran Afriki*: Spravochnik [Religions of African Countries: Reference Book]. M.: Nauka, 1981. 365 pp., map. Bibl.: pp. 319-344. Geogr. index: pp. 346-363.

108   Shpazhnikov, G.A. *Religii stran Iugo-Vostochnoi Azii:* Spravochnik [Religion of Countries of South-Eastern Asia: Reference Book]. M.: Nauka, 1980. 247 pp., map. Bibl.: pp. 229-245. For review see item 5291.

109   Sibirichev, D.Ia. *Ateisticheskie izdaniia* (Annot. ukaz. lit., izd. v 1985-1986 gg.). [Atheistic Publications: (Annotated Guide of Literature published in 1985-86.)]. V pomoshch' propagandistu i organizatoru ateist. raboty. M.: Znanie, Tsaentr. Dom nauch. ateizma, 1988. 80 pp.

110   *Slovar'-spravochnik po islamu i ateizmu* [Dictionary-Reference Book on Islam and Atheism]. [Comp.: Ia.G. Abdullin; Sh.Sh. Abilov et al]. 2nd revised and enlarged ed. Kazan': Tatar. kn. izd-vo, 1981. 198 pp. In Tatar.

111   *Slovar' dlia veruiushchikh i neveruiushchikh* [Dictionary for Believers and Unbelievers]. M.: Progress, [1989]. 622 pp. In English. Russian ed. was published under the title: '*Ateisticheskii slovar*'.

112   *49 voprosov i otvetov ob islame* [49 Questions and Answers about Islam]. Tashkent: Fan, 1988. 108 pp. Bibl.: pp. 105-107.

113   *Spravochnik ateista* [Atheist's Reference Book]. [Comp.: A.S. Onishchenko et al]. Kiev: Nauk. dumka, 1986. 520 pp.

114   Stashevskii, M. *Gosudarstvo i religioznye ob'edineniia v Evropeiskikh sotsialisticheskikh stranakh*: Spravochnik [The State and Religious Unions in European Socialist Countries: Reference Book]. Transl. from Polish and Russian. Tallin: Eesti raamat, 1985. 175 pp. In Estonian. Title of Russian ed.: '*Sotsialisticheskoe gosudarstvo i religioznye ob'edineniia*'.

115   Stetskevich, M.S. "Tserkov' i gosudarstvo v evropeiskikh stranakh sotsializma" [The Church and State in European Socialist Countries]. *Muzei v ateisticheskoi propagande*. L., 1986. Pp. 52-72.

116   *100 otvetov veruiushchim*: Popul. spravochnik [100 Answers to Believers: Popular Reference Book]. Ed.: V.A. Mezentseva. 2nd revised. ed. M.: Politizdat, 1980. 440 pp. For reviews see items 5302-5303.
       Published also in:

Cheboksary: Chuvash. kn. izd-vo, 1982. 318 pp. In Chuvash.
Kishinev: Kartia Moldoveniaske, 1983. 379 pp. In Moldavian.

117   Suiarko, V.A. *Izuchenie materialov XXVI S'ezda KPSS v kurse nauch. ateizma:* Metod. rekomendatsii [The Study of Materials of the XXVIth Congress of the CPSU in the Course on Scientific Atheism: Method. Recommendations]. Kiev: Vishcha shk., Izd-vo pri Kiev. un-te, 1982. 27 pp. (V pomoshch' prepodavateliu-obshchestvovedu). Bibl.: p. 25.

118   Trofimova, Z.P. "Obzor zhurnala 'Religioznyi gumanizm'" [Review of the Journal 'Religious Humanism']. *Religii mira.* M., 1989. Pp. 229-239.

119   Uspenskaia, G.P. *Religiia i sovremennost':* Bibliogr. ukaz. [Religion and Contemporaneity: Bibliogr. Index]. Odessa: OGNB, 1980. 30 pp.

120   *Vvedenie v izuchenie Ganchzhura i Danchzhura* [Introduction into the Teachings of Ganchjura and Danchjura]. Ed.: R.E. Pubaev. Novosibirsk: Nauka. Sib. otd-nie, 1989. 198 pp. Bibl.: pp. 163-193. Annot. bibl.: pp. 143-162.

121   Zadorozhniuk, I.E. "Novye raboty po psikhologii religii" [New Works on the Psychology of Religion]. *Psikhol. zhurnal* T. 9, 6 (1988): 159-163.

MARXISM-LENINISM ON RELIGION AND ATHEISM

122   Akhmedov, A. "Pod flagom islama" [Under the Flag of Islam]. *Argumenty.*
       1981. M., 1981, Pp. 5-38.

123   Akhmedov, A. "V obshchem khore antikommunizma: O nekotorykh islam-
       skikh 'teoriiakh', prizvannykh oprokinut' uchenie marksizma-leninizma" [In
       the Common Chorus of Anti-Communism: On Some Islamic "Theories"
       Calling for Overturning the Teaching of Marxism-Leninism]. *Nauka i
       religiia* 1 (1982): 56-59.

124   Baimuradov, N. *Leninskii printsip svobody sovesti i ego osushchestvlenie v
       Tadzhikistane* [Leninist Principles on the Freedom of Conscience and its
       Implementation in Tajikistan]. Ed.: R.M. Madzhidov. Dushanbe: Donish,
       1980. 100 pp. For review see item 4957.

125   Balaev, M.A. V.I. Lenin o sviazi religii i politiki v klassovom obshchestve
       [V.I. Lenin on the Connection of Religion and Politics in Class Society].
       Izv. AN. AzSSR. Ser. istorii, filosofii i prava. 2 (1989): 91-98. In Azer-
       baijan. Summary in Russian.

126   Biletskii, O.V. "Lenin o roli deiatel'noi sushchnosti cheloveka v preodolenii
       religioznogo mirovozzreniia" [V.I Lenin on the Role of Man's Active
       Nature in Overcoming the Religious World-Outlook]. *Vopr. ateizma* 16
       (1980): 107-114.

127   Birger, B; Matveeva, I. "Leninskie idei ateisticheskogo vospitaniia trudiash-
       chikhsia" [Leninist Ideas on the Atheistic Education of Workers]. *Kom-
       munist Tatarii* 10 (1981): 84-88.

128   Dzhabbarov, I. "Leninskoe atesticheskoe nasledie i religiia na sovremennon
       etape" [Leninst Atheistic Heritage and Religion in Contemporary Period].
       Kommunist Uzbekistana 4 (1983): 47-55.

129   Emeliakh, L.I. "Kritika V.I. Leninym religii" [V.I. Lenin's Criticism of
       Religion]. *Vech. sred. shk.* 2 (1983): 35-38.

130   Emilov, Iv.N. *Marksistsko-leninskoe obrazovanie i ateisticheskoe vospitanie naseleniia* [Marxist-Leninist Cognizance and Atheistic Education of the Population]. Makhachkala: Dag. kn. izd-vo, 1984. 30 pp. (Sots. obraz zhizni i religiia).

131   Eryshev, A.A.; Kirsanova, V.P. *Tvorcheskoe razvitie KPSS leninskikh idei o preodolenii religii* [CPSU Creative Development of Leninist Ideas on Overcoming of Religion]. Kiev: Znanie UkSSR, 1983. 47 pp. (Ser. 5 "Nauchno-ateisticheskaia" / O-vo "Znanie" UkSSR; No 2). In Ukrainian. Bibl.: pp. 46-47.

132   Gabidzashvili, O. "K. Marks o sotsial'noi prirode religii" [K. Marx on the Social Nature of Religion]. *Kommunist Gruzii* 7 (1983): 73-76.

133   Galechka, T. *Ateizm, teologiia, revizionism: Kritich. analiz revizionist. fal'sifikatsii marksistsko-leninskogo ateizma* [Atheism, Theology, Revisionism: Critical Analysis of Revisionist Falsifications of Marxist-Leninist Atheism]. Kiev: Politizdat Ukrainy, 1980. 181 pp. In Ukrainian.

134   Gapochka, M.P. *Materializm protiv fideizma:* Leninskie printsipy kritiki fideizma i sovremennost' [Materialism against Fideism: Leninist Principles of Critique of Fideism and Contemporaneity]. M.: Politizdat, 1980. 191 pp.

135   Garadzha, V.I. "K marksistskomu ponimaniiu roli religii i tserkvi v istoricheskom protsesse" [Marxist Understanding the Role of Religion and Church in the Historical Process]. *Vopr. nauch. ateizma* 37 (1988): 3-7.

136   Golovei, V.M. *Izuchenie proizvedenii klassikov marksizma-leninizma v kurse osnov nauchnogo ateizma v vuze* [Study of the Works of the Classics of Marxism-Leninism in the Course on Fundamentals of Scientific Atheism in Institutions of Higher Education]. L'vov: Vishcha. shk. Izd-vo pri L'vov. un-te, 1984. 95 pp. (Ateist. b-chka studenta). In Ukrainian.

137   Golovei, V.M. "Ob izuchenii studentami trudov klassikov marksizma-leninizma [v kurse nauchnogo ateizma] [On Students' Studies of the Works of the Classics of Marxism-Leninism (in the Course on Scientific Atheism)]. *Vopr. ateizma* 20 (1084): 10-13.

138   Gomeniuk, A.P. "Leninskie zavety i voprosy ateisticheskoi propagandy sredi molodezhi" [Leninist Legacy and Problems of Atheistic Propaganda among Youth]. *Vopr. ateizma* 16 (1980): 88-95.

139 Gortopan, N.A. "K. Marks i F. Engel's ob utverzhdaiushchei funktsii ateizma" [K. Marx and F. Engels on the Asserting Function of Atheism]. *Ocherki po istorii filosofii.* Kishinev, 1980. Pp. 33-39.

140 *Gumanizm marksistskogo ateizma* [Humanism of Marxist Atheism]. [Comp.: K. Sapunova]. M.: Znanie, 1981. 64 pp. (Novoe v zhizni, nauke, tekhnike. Ser. "Nauch. ateizm": No 8). Bibl.: p. 63.

141 Guzenkov, V.A.; Riazantseva, L.F. "Kritika F. Engel'som feierbakhovskoi 'religii' liubvi - faktor razvitiia filosofskogo i nravstvennogo samosoznaniia studentov" [F. Engels' Criticism of Feuerbach's "Religion" of Love - Development Factor of Students' Philosophical and Moral Self-consciousness]. *Vopr. obshchestv. nauk* Vyp. 74 (1988): 114-121.

142 Iakovlev, V.[G]. "K. Marks, F. Engels, V.I. Lenin ob ateisticheskom vospitanii" [K. Marx, F. Engels, V.I. Lenin on Atheistic Education]. *Part. zhizn' Kazakhstana* 5 (1983): 49-52.

143 Iakovlev, V.G. "V.I. Lenin o reaktsionnoi sushchnosti religioznogo mistitsizma" [V.I. Lenin on Reactionary Essence of Religious Mysticism]. Materialisticheskaia dialektika i sovremennost'. Alma-Ata, 1980. Pp. 152-164.

144 Iarmalavichius, Iu.Iu. *Leninskaia natsional'naia politika i razvitie nauchnogo ateizma* [Leninist National Policy and the Development of Scientific Atheism]. Vil'nius: Znanie LitSSR, 1982. 22 pp. (Material dlia lektora / O-vo "Znanie" LitSSR). In Lithuanian. Bibl.: p. 22.

145 Ignatenko, A. "Videt' sotsial'nuiu sut' iavleniia" [To See the Social Essence of the Occurrence]. *Nauka i religiia* 11 (1981): 60-61.

146 Ipatov, A.N. "Leninskie idei ob otnoshenii k kul'turnomu naslediiu i nauchno-atesticheskoe vospitanie" [Leninist Ideas on the Attitude towards Cultural Heritage and Scientific-Atheist Education]. *Vopr. Ateizma* 16 (1980): 74-81.

147 Ivanov, A. "'S samykh razlichnykh storon...': Leninskie printsipy ateist. propagandy v dokumentakh partii" ["From Various Aspects...": Leninist Principles of Atheistic Propaganda in Party Documents]. *Nauka i religiia* 4 (1980): 5-8.

148 Kalinin, Iu.A.; Il'nykh, N.I. "Osveshchenie kategorii 'religioznoe otchuzhdenie' v rabotakh L. Feierbakha i K. Marksa" [Interpretations of Categories "Religious Alienation" in L. Feuerbach's and Marx's Works]. *Probl. filosofii* 63 (1984): 29-36.

149 Kalinin, Iu.A.; Khar'kovshchenko, E.A. "Metodologicheskie osnovy kritiki religii v rabote F. Engel'sa 'Liudvig Feierbakh i konets klassicheskoi nemetskoi filosofii" [Methodological Foundations of Religions' Criticism in F. Engels' work "Ludwig Feuerbach and the End of German Classical Philosophy"]. *Filos. probl. sovremen. estestvoznaniia* 65 (1987): 102-108.

150 Khimchenko, A.G. "Znachenie leninskogo ateisticheskogo nasrediia dlia resheniia problem proiskhozhdeniia religii" [The Importance of Leninist Atheistic Legacy for the Resolution of the Problems of the Origin of Religion]. *Vopr. ateizma* 16 (1980): 136-141.

151 Khobriankina, T.N. "V.I. Lenin o klassovom kharaktere religiozno-politicheskikh dvizhenii" [V.I. Lenin on the Class Character of Religious-Political Movements]. *Kritika religioznoi ideologii i problemy ateisticheskogo vospitaniia.* M., 1982. Pp. 17-23.

152 Khusanov, S.Kh. "Klassiki marksizma-leninizma o roli estestvenno-nauchnykh znanii v bor'be s religioznym mirovozzreniem" [Classics of Marxism-Leninism on the Role of Natural-Sciences in the Struggle with the Religious World Outlook]. *Aktual'nye voprosy formirovaniia nauchno-materialisticheskogo mirovozzreniia trudiashchikhsia.* Tashkent, 1989. Pp. 98-102.

153 Kolodnaia, A.I.; Kolodnyi, A.N. "Znachenie leninskikh metodologicheskikh printsipov dlia otsenki ateisticheskogo nasrediia ukrainskikh progressivnykh myslitelei" [The Importance of Leninist Methodological Principles for Evaluation of the Atheistic Legacy of Ukrainian Progressive Thinkers]. *Vopr. ateizma* 16 (1980): 50-58.

154 Kolubabov, N.S.; Nikonov, K.I. "Sviaz' prepodavaniia nauchnogo ateizma s prepodavaniem marksistsko-leninskoi fillosofii" [Correlation of Teaching Scientific Atheism with the Teaching of Marxist-Leninist Philosophy]. *Prepodavanie nauchnogo ateizma v vuze.* M., 1988. Pp. 62-89.

155 Krasovskaia, L.M. "Leninskaia kritika nrastvennykh kontseptsii katolitsizma" [Leninist Criticism of the Moral Conceptions of the Catholicism]. *Vopr. ateizma* 17 (1981): 56-63.

156   Kryvelev, I.A. "Leninizm i nekotorye aktual'nye voprosy religievedeniia i ateisticheskoi propagandy" [Leninism and Some Actual Problems of the Study of Religion and Atheistic Propaganda]. *Leninizm i problemy etnografii.* L., 1987. Pp. 198-214.

157   Kuchinskii, S.A. *Marksistsko-leninskii ateizm i nravstvennoe vospitanie* [Marxist-Leninist Atheism and Moral Education]. L.: Znanie RSFSR, 1982. 16 pp. (V pomoshch' lektoru / O-vo "Znanie" RSFSR, Leningr. org.). Bibl.: p.16.

158   Kuchinskii, S.A. "Sootnoshenie marksistskogo i religioznogo aspektov sotsial'nogo gumanizma" [Correlation of Marxist and Religious Aspects of Social Humanism]. *Vopr. nauch. ateizma* 35 (1986): 82-96.

159   Kuchkarov, A. "Leninskie printsipy ateisticheskogo vospitaniia" [Leninist Principles of Atheistic Education]. *Kommunist Uzbekistana* 4 (1985): 51-57.

160   Lapkin, K.I.; Khairullaev, M.M. "F. Engel's o nekotorykh aspektakh islama i svobodomysliia" [F. Engels on Some Aspects of Islam and Freethinking]. *Obshchestv. nauki v Uzbekistane* 4 (1988): 41-45.

161   "Leninskoe ateisticheskoe nasledie i sovremennost'" [Leninist Atheistic Heritage and Contemporaneity]. Comp.: N.G. Lukasheva et al. *Aktual'-nye problemy izucheniia istorii religii i ateizma* L., 1980. Pp. 3-24.

162   Livshits, G.M. *Kritika idealizma i religii soratnikami K. Marksa i F. Engel'sa* [Criticism of Idealism and Religion by Companion-in-Arms of K. Marx and F. Engels]. Minsk: Nauka i tekhnika, 1984. 232 pp. Bibl.: pp. 230-231.

163   Livshits, G.M. *Kritika idealizma i religii v trudakh G.V. Plekhanova* [Criticism of Idealism and Religion in G.V. Plekhanov's Writings]. Minsk: Vysheish. shkola, 1981. 304 pp. Bibl.: pp. 290-294. Annot. bibl.: pp. 243-289. Name, titles and terms index: pp. 295-303.

164   Livshits, G.M. *Kritika idealizma i religii v trudakh K. Marksa i F. Engel'sa* [Criticism of Idealism and Religion in the Writings of K. Marx and F. Engels]. Minsk: Nauka i tekhnika, 1982. 351 pp. Annot. bibl.: pp. 311-341. Name, titles and terms index: pp. 342-350.

165   Livshits, G.M. *Kritika V.I. Leninym idealizma i religii* [V.I. Lenin's Criticism of Idealism and Religion]. Minsk: Nauka i tckhnika, 1983. 280 pp. Bibl.: pp. 276-279.

166   Lugashov, V.A. "Preodolenie religii i dal'neishee razvitie natsional'nykh otnoshenii v svete marksistsko-leninskogo ucheniia" [Overcoming of Religion and Subsequent Development of National Relationships in the Light of Marxist-Leninist Teachings]. *K. Marks i F. Engel's o voprosakh sotsial'noi dialektike.* Frunze, 1983. Pp. 105-111.

167   Makhmudov, P.G. "V.I. Lenin i ateisticheskoe vospitanie molodezhi" [V.I. Lenin and Youth's Atheistic Upbringing]. *Aktual'nye voprosy ateisticheskogo vospitaniia molodezhi.* Baku, 1988. Pp. 17-27. In Azerbaijan. Summary in Russian.

168   Mamedov, M.; Akhmadov, A. "Preemstvennost' leninskikh printsipov nauchno-ateisticheskogo vospitaniia" [Continuity of Leninist Principles of Scientific-Atheistic Education]. *Kommunist Azerbaidjana* 1 (1987): 93-97.

169   Midzhidov, R.M.; Abdullaev, Sh. "Burzhuazno-klerikal'noe izvrashchenie marksistskogo ateizma" [Bourgeois-Clerical Distortion of Marxist Atheism]. *Izv. AN TadzhSSR.* Otd-nie obshchestv. nauk 3 (1983): 30-33. Summary in Tajik.

170   Mikutskas, P. "Pervye marksisty Litvy o gnoseologicheskikh istokakh religii" [Lithuanian First Marxists on Gnoseological Sources of Religion]. *Ateistines minties raida lietuvoje.* Kaunas, 1988. Pp.: 76-92. In Lithuanian. Summary in Russian.

171   Mitrokhin, L. "Ateisticheskoe nasledie Engel'sa" [Engels' Atheistic Legacy]. *Nauka i religiia* 8 (1985): 10-14; 9 (1985): 17-21; 10 (1985): 20-24; 11 (1985): 17-21.

172   Mitrokhin, L.N. "Poniaitie religii u K. Marksa" [K. Marx's Meaning of Religion]. *Vopr. filosofii* 8 (1983): 44-58. Summary in English: p. 173.

173   Morina, L.G. "Znachenie leninskogo printsipa edinstva filosofii i estestvoznaniia v bor'be s bogoslovskimi popytkami soedinit' nauku i religiiu" [Importance of Leninist Principle of the Unity of Philosophy and Natural Sciences in the Struggle with Theological Attempts to Unite Science and Religion]. *Aktual'nye problemy ateisticheskogo vospitaniia i kritika religioznoi ideologii.* M., 1983. Pp.: 21-25.

174 Nesterchuk, V.P. "Marksizm o stanovlenii i razvitii nauchno-ateisticheskogo mirovozzreniia (Nekotorye aspekty)" [Marxism on the Formation and Development of a Scientific-Atheistic World Outlook (Some Aspects)]. *Izv. AN AzSSR.* Ser. istorii, filosofii i prava 1 (1986): 104-109. Summary in Azerbaijan.

175 Nikishov, S.I. *Leninskoe ateisticheskoe nasledie i sovremennost'* [Lenin's Atheistical Legacy and Contemporaneity]. M.: Znanie, 1980. 13 pp.

176 Nikishov, S.[I]. "Leninskoe nasledie i sovremennost'" [Leninist Legacy and Contemporaneity]. *Nauka i religiia* 4 (1982): 13-15.

177 Nikishov, S.[I]. "Opiraias' na leninskoe ateisticheskoe nasledie" [Guided by Leninist Atheistic legacy]. *Agitator* 11 (1980): 37-39.

178 *O religii i tserkvii: Sb. vyskazyvanii klassikov marksizma-leninizma, dokumentov KPSS i Sov. gosudarstva* [On Religion and Church: Collection of Statements by Marxist-Leninist Classicists, CPSU and Soviet State Documents]. 2nd enlarged. Ed. M: Politizdat, 1981. 176 pp. Published also in: Minsk: Belarus', 1983. 128 pp. Annot. bibl. pp. 121-125. For review see 5194.

179 Oganiants, B.G. "Leninskii printsip voinstvuiushchego materializma i formirovanie nauhno-ateisticheskogo mirovozzreniia" [Leninist Principle of Militant Materialism and Formation of a Scientific-Atheistic World Outlook]. *Obshchestvennoe soznanie i voprosy formirovaniia nauchnogo mirovozzreniia* M., 1980. Pp: 98-122.

180 Ognevaia, E.V. "V.I. Lenin ob otnoshenii partii i gosudarstva k religii" [V.I. Lenin on the Party and State Attitude towards Religion]. *Vopr. ateizma* 16 (1980): 34-41.

181 Okhrimenko, Iu.M. "Ateisticheskii kharakter sovetskogo obraza zhizni kak organicheskaia sostavnaia chast' realizatsii leninskogo plana postroeniia sotsializma" [Atheistic Character of Soviet Way of Life as Organic Component of the Realisation of Leninist Plan for Building of Socialism]. *Vopr. ateizma* 17 (1981): 43-49.

182 Okulov, A.F. *Leninskoe ateisticheskoe nasledie i sovremennost'* [Leninist Atheistic Legacy and Contemporaneity]. M.: Politizdat, 1986. 128 pp. Bibl.: pp. 123-127. For reviews see items 5197-5198.

183   Ovsienko, F.G. "Pol'skaia religiovedcheskaia problematika na stranitsakh sovetskikh izdanii" [Polish Problematics of the Study of Religion in the Pages of Soviet Publications]. *Katolicheskaia tserkov' v PNR v 80-kh godakh.* M., 1988. Pp. 184-193.

184   Pashchik, Iu.B. *Stanovlenie ateizma K. Marksa i F. Engel'sa* [K. Marx and F. Engels' Realization of Atheism]. M.: Mysl', 1983. 173 pp. Annot. bibl.: pp. 168-172. For reviews see items 5220-5221.

185   Patsukova, L.A. "Analiz evoliutsii katolitsizma v rabotakh latinoamerikanskikh marksistov" [Analysis of Evolution of Catholicism in the Writings of Latino American Marxists] *Nekotorye filosofskie i sotsial'no-politicheskie problemy marksizma-leninizma.* M., 1987. Pp. 123-128.

186   Pavlov, A. "V.I. Lenin, KPSS ob ateisticheskom vospitanii trudiashchikhsia i voinov Sovetskikh Vooruzhennykh Sil" [V.I. Lenin, CPSU on Atheistical Education of Workers and Soldiers of the Soviet Armed Forces]. *Voen. -ist. zhurn.* 12 (1984): 44-48.

187   Pechiura, P. "Lenin i ateisticheskii gumanizm" [Lenin and Atheistic Humanism]. *Kommunist.* Vil'nius 9 (1981): 96-99.

188   Pishchik, Iu.B. *Marksizm ob istoricheskoi prirode religii* [Marxism on Historical Nature of Religion]. Kiev: Vishcha. shk., 1983. 104 pp. (Ateist. b-chka studenta).

189   *Problemy ateizma i kritiki religii v trudakh K. Marksa i F. Engel'sa* [Problems of Atheism and Criticism of Religion in K. Marx and F. Engels' Works]. [Ed.: R.T. Rashkova]. L.: GMIRIA, 1983. 155 pp.

190   Rekuts, I.F. *Ateisticheskoe nasledie soratnikov V.I. Lenina: Iskusstvo i religiia* [Atheistic Legacy of V.I. Lenin's Companion-in-Arms: Art and Religion]. Minsk: Belarus', 1985. 129 pp. Annot. bibl.: pp. 126-128.

191   Saenko, N.I. "Marksistsko-leninskaia filosofiia - metodologicheskaia osnova ateisticheskogo vospitaniia" [Marxist-Leninst Philosophy - Methodological Basis of Atheistic Education]. *Vopr. ateizma* 16 (1980): 82-88.

192   Saidov, Z.Kh.; Makhlin, I.I. *Marksizm-leninizm o vliianii religii na obshchestvennyi progress* [Marxism-Leninism on Religion's Influence on Social Progress]. Tashkent: Uzbekistan, 1986. 40 pp. (Ser. "Marksizm-leninizm"; No 13). In Uzbek.

193 Sapelkina, E.V. "Marksistskoe uchenie o cheloveke i sovremennyi katolicheskii antropologizm" [Marxist Teaching about Man and Contemporary Catholic Anthropology]. *Vopr. ateizma* 25 (1989): 124-131.

194 Seliverstova, N.A. "Leninskaia teoriia otrazheniia kak metodologicheskaia osnova kritiki religii" [Leninist Reflection Theory as Methodological Basis of Criticism of Religion]. *Voprosy filosofii i sotsiologii.* L., 1980. Pp. 92-96.

195 Shchedrin, V.K. "V.I. Lenin o printsipakh dialektiko-materialisticheskogo miroponimaniia kak filosofskom obosnovanii nauchnogo ateizma" [V.I. Lenin on Principles of Dialectical-Materialistic World-Outlook as the Philosophical Substantiation of Scientific Atheism]. *Vopr. ateizma* 16 (1980): 11-17.

196 Shinkaruk, V.I. "Nekotorye metodologicheskie problemy marksistskogo osveshcheniia istorii dukhovnoi kul'tury i religii" [Some Methodological Problems of Marxist Interpretation of the History of Spiritual Culture and Religion]. *Otechestvennaia obshchestvennaia mysl' epokhi Srednevekov'ia.* Kiev., 1988. Pp. 17-28.

197 Sitnova, L.I. "Ideologicheskaia platforma dialoga marksistov i khristian" [Ideological Platform of Marxists and Christian Dialogue]. *Kritika religioznoi ideologii i problemy ateisticheskogo vospitaniia.* M., 1982. Pp. 58-67.

198 Skibitskii, M.M. *O vere i neverii:* (Mysli o religii i ateizme) [On Faith and Unbelief: (Thoughts on Religion and Atheism)]. M.: Politizdat, 1982. 239 pp.

199 Smolinskii V.I. "V.I. Lenin o razrushenii religioznogo soznaniia v protsesse ateisticheskogo vospitaniia" [V.I. Lenin on Destruction of Religious Consciousness in the Process of Atheistic Education]. *Vopr. ateizma* 16 (1980): 102-107.

200 Spevakovskii, A.B. *Dukhi obortni demony i bozhestva ainov* [Spirits, Werewolfs, Demons and Ainus Deities]. M.: Nauka, 1988. 205 pp., illus. Summary in English. Bibl.: pp. 178-189. Annot bibl.: pp. 175-177. Indices: pp. 192-203.

201 Stepinskii, M.A. "Gumanism marksistsko-leninskogo ateizma i ateisticheskoe vospitanie molodezhi" [Humanism of Marxist-Leninist Atheism and

Youth's Atheistic Upbringing]. *Nauch. tr. / Kurskii ped. in-t*   1982, T. 219, pp. 92-106.

202   Stetsenko, A.K. "Marksizm i dinamika sovremennogo razvitiia levykh techenii khristianskoi demokratii v Tsentral'noi Amerike" [Marxism and Dynamics of Contemporary Development of Leftist Trends of Christian Democracy in Central America]. *Velikii Oktiabr' i Latinskaia Amerika.* M., 1987. Pp. 44-45.

203   Suiarko, V.A. "Klassiki marksizma-leninizma o prekhodiashchem kharaktere religii" [Classics of Marxism-Leninism on Transient Character of Religion]. *Vopr. ateizma* 20 (1984): 90-98.

204   Suiarko, V.A. "Leninskie printsipy propagandy i vnedrenie sovetskoi obriadnosti" [Leninist Principles of Propaganda and Indoctrination of Soviet Ceremonial]. *Vopr. ateizma* 21 (1985): 20-25.

205   Suiarko, V.A. "Utverzhdenie leninskikh ateisticheskikh printsipov v usloviiakh real'nogo sotsializma" [Confirmation of Leninist Atheistic Principles in Conditions of Real Socialism]. *Vopr. ateizma* 16 (1980): 42-49.

206   Sukhikh, A.A. "Kritika osnovnykh napravlenii burzhuazno-klerikal'noi fal'sifikatsii marksistsko-leninskogo ateizma" [Critique of Basic Directions of Bourgeois-Clerical Falsifications of Marxist-Leninist Atheism]. *Vopr. ateizma* 17 (1981): 49-56.

207   Tancher, V.K. "Leninskoe ateisticheskoe nasledie" [Leninist Atheistic Legacy]. *Vopr. ateizma* 16 (1980): 3-11.

208   Timofeev, V.D *Leninskie printsipy politiki v otnoshenii religii, tserkvi, veruiushchikh.* [Leninist Principles of Politics in Relation to Religion, Church, Believers]. M.: Znanie, 1987. 64 pp. (Novoe v zhizni, nauke, tekhnike. Ser.: Nauch ateizm; 1987, 12). Bibl.: pp. 63-64.

209   Tishchenko, V.I. "Lenin i aktual'nye problemy nauchnogo ateizma" [V.I. Lenin and Actual Problems of Scientific Atheism]. *Biologiia v shk.* 2 (1984): 10-15.

210   Titov, N. "Leninskie printsipy otnosheniia k tserkvi, veruiushchim i molodezhnoe dvizhenie" [Leninist Principles of Relation towards Church, Believers and Youth Movement]. *Molodezh' i molodezhnye organizatsii v politicheskoi sisteme sotsialisticheskogo obshchestva.* M., 1988. Pp. 257-269.

211 Utkin, A.I. "Marksizm-leninizm ob otnosheniiakh utopicheskogo sotsializma i religii" [Marxism-Leninism on Attitudes of Utopian Socialism and Religion]. *Vopr. ateizma* 16 (1980): 58-66.

212 Varichev, E.S. "Rol' ateisticheskoi propagandy v leninskom plane kul'turnoi revoliutsii" [Role of Atheistic Propaganda in Leninist Plan for Cultural Revolution]. *Tr. / NII kul'tury* 102 (1981): 70-78.

213 Vorontsov, G.V. *Leninskie printsipy svobody sovesti* [Leninist Principles of Freedom of Worship]. L.: Lenizdat, 1980. 70 pp. (V pomoshch' propagandistu nauch. ateizma). Bibl.: pp. 68-69.

214 *Zakon, religiia, tserkov':* Sb. vyskazyvanii klassikov marksizma-leninizma, dokumentov KPSS, Kompartii Uzbekistana, Pravitel'stva SSSR i UzSSR o religii i ateizme [Law, Religion, Church: Collection of Statements on Religion and Atheism by Classics of Marxism- Leninsm, Documents of the CPSU, Uzbekistan Communist Party, government of the USSR and UzSSR]. [Comp.: P.S. Krivosheev et al]. Tashkent: Uzbekistan, 1987. 150 pp. Published also in Uzbek.

215 Zhabborov, I. *Leninskoe ateisticheskoe nasledie i sovremennost'* [Leninist Atheistic Legacy and Contemporaneity]. Tashkent: Znanie, 1984. 30 pp. (V pomoshch' lektoru / O-vo "Znanie" UzSSR). In Uzbek.

216 *Zhizneutverzhdaiushchii kharakter leninskogo ateisticheskogo naslediia* [Life-Asserting Character of Lenin's Atheistic Legacy]. [Comp.: T.V. Glavak; V.I. Garadzha, V.K. Tancher]. Kiev: Vishcha shk., 1983. 179 pp.

217 Zmeev, Iu.N. "F. Engel's i nekotorye voprosy estestvennonauchnogo obosnovaniia ateizma" [F. Engels and some Questions of Natural-Scientific Substantiation of Atheism]. *Filos. probl. sovremen. estestvoznaniia* 65 (1987): 108-112.

218 Zots, V.A. "Leninskie ateisticheskie zavety i molodezh'" [Leninist Atheistic Legacies and Youth]. *Vopr. ateizma* 19 (1983): 3-10.

219 Zots, V.A. "Vypolniaia leninskie ateisticheskie zavety" [Fulfilling Leninist Atheistic Legacies]. *Kommunist Ukrainy* 4 (1982): 69-77.

SOVIET PUBLICATIONS ON RELIGION AND ATHEISM
(1980-1989)

220   *A.N. Radishchev i dekabristy:* Iz ateist. naslediia pervykh rus. revoliutsionerov [A.N. Radishchev and Decembrists: From Atheistic Legacy of the First Russian Revolutionaries]. [Comp.: L.B. Poliakov; Introduction by A.D. Sukhov, pp. 3-24]. M.: Mysl', 1986. 269 pp. (Nauch.-ateist. b-ka). Annot. bibl.: pp. 241-256. Name index: pp. 257-263.

221   Abaev, N.V. "Aktual'nye zadachi buddologicheskikh issledovanii v BION" [Actual Tasks of Buddhist Researches in BION]. *Tsybikovskie chteniia.* Ulan-Ude, 1989. Pp. 5-7.

222   Abaev, N.V. "Arkhaichnye formy religioznoi teorii i praktiki v chan-buddizme" [Archaic Forms of Religious Theory and Practice of Ch'an-Buddhism]. *Buddizm i srednevekovaia kul'tura narodov Tsentral'oi Azii.* Novosibirsk, 1980. P.p. 156-176.

223   Abaev, N.V. *Chan-buddizm i kul'tura psikhicheskoi deiatel'nosti v srednevekovom Kitae* [Ch'an-Buddhism and the Culture of Psychical Activity in Medieval China]. Novosibirsk: Nauka. Sib. otd-nie, 1983. 125 pp. Bibl.: pp. 114-124. For reviews see items 4902-4903.

224   Abaev, N.V. *Chan-buddizm i kul'turno-psikhologicheskie traditsii v srednevekovom Kitae* [Ch'an-Buddhism and Cultural-Psychological Traditions in Medieval China]. 2nd revised. and enlarged ed. Novosibirsk: Nauka. Sib. otd- nie, 1989. 273 pp. Bibl.: pp. 257-272. For reviews see items 4904-4905.

225   Abaev, N.V. "Chan' (dzen)-buddizm i u-shu" [Ch'an (Zen) Buddhism-and Wy-Shu]. *Narody Azii i Afriki* 3 (1981): 62-74.

226   Abaev, N.V. "Kitaiskii buddizm: Traditsii i sovremennost'" [Chinese Buddhism: Traditions and Contemporaneity]. *Nauka i religiia* 1 (1981): 57-60.

227   Abaev, N.V. Kontseptsiia 'prosvetleniia' v "Makhaiana-shraddkhotpa'da-
      shastre" [The Conception of "Enlightnment" in "Mahayana-Sraddhotpada -
      Sastra"]. *Psikhologicheskie aspekty buddizma.* Novosibirsk, 1986. Pp. 23-46.

228   Abaev, N.V. "D.T. Sudzuki i ku'turnoe nasledie Dzen (Ch'an)-buddizma na
      Zapade" [Sudtzuki and Zen (Ch'an) Buddhism's Cultural Heritage in the
      West]. *Narody Azii i Afriki* 6 (1980): 176-186.

229   Abaev, S. *Ateisticheskoe vospitanie v usloviiakh perestroiki* [Atheistic
      Education under Perestroika]. Nukus: Karakalpakstan, 1989. 73 pp.

230   Abaev, S. *Ateizm i vospitanie novogo cheloveka* [Atheism and Education of
      the New Man]. Nukus: Karakalpakstan, 1982. 79 pp. Bibl.: pp. 78-79. For
      review see item 4906.

231   Abaev, S. *Ateizm v Karakalpakstane:* Opyt i probl. [Atheism in Karakal-
      pakstan: Experience and Problems]. Tashkent: Fan, 1987. 156 pp.

232   Abaev, S. *Nauchno-ateisticheskoe vospitanie na novom etape* [Scientific-
      Atheistic Education on a New Stage]. Tashkent: Uzbekistan, 1981. 32 pp.
      (Ser. "Marksizm-Leninizm" No 14). In Uzbek.

233   Abaev, S. "Periodizatsiia ateizma v Karakalpakstane" [Division into Periods
      of Atheism in Karakalpakstan]. *Vestn. Karakalp. fil. AN UzSSR* 3 (1980):
      91-93. Summary in English.

234   Abaev, S. *Velikii Oktiabr' i razvitie ateizma v Karakalpakii* [The Great
      October and the Development of Atheism in Karakalpak]. Nukus:
      Karakalpakstan, 1984. 75 pp. In Karakalpak.

235   Abaeva, L.L. "Kuznechnyi kul't u mongoloiazychnykh narodov" [Blacksmith's
      Cult of Mongolian Speaking Peoples]. V *Mezhdunarodnyi kogress mongo-
      lovedov* (Ulan-Bator, sentiabr', 1987). M., 1987. 3. Arkheologiia, kuyl'tura,
      etnografiia, filologiia. Pp. 3-12. Bibl.: pp. 11-12.

236   Abaeva, L.L. "Modernistskie tendentsii v sovremennom buddizme" [Moder-
      nist Tendencies in Contemporary Buddhism]. *Metodologicheskie aspekty
      izucheniia istorii dukhovnoi kul'tury Vostoka.* Ulan-Ude, 1988. Pp. 80-95.

237   Abaeva, L.L. "O vliianii buddizma na traditsionnuiu obriadnost' buriat"
      [Buddhism's Influence on Buriat Traditional Ritual]. *III Vsesoiuznaia*

konferentsiia vostokovedov "Vzaimodeistvie i vzaimovliianie tsivilizatsii kul'tur na Vostoke". M., 1988. T. 2. Pp. 3-4.

238 Abaeva L.L. "Problema traditsionnosti i variativnosti v izuchenii lokal'nykh kul'tov mongol'skikh narodov" [Problem of Traditionalism and Variability in the Study of Local Cults of Mongol Peoples]. *Tsybikovskie chteniia.* Ulan- Ude, 1989. Pp. 12-13.

239 Abakeliia, N.K. "Kosmologicheskie simvoly v Zapadnoi Gruzii" [Cosmological Symbols in Western Georgia]. *Materialy po etnografii Gruzii.* Tbilisi, 1987. T. 23. Pp. 237-244. In Georgian. Summary in Russian.

240 Abakeliia, N.K. "Kul't boga-iunoshi v Zapadnoi Gruzii: ('Tar-Chabukvi') [Cult of the Youth-God in Western Georgia ("Tar-Chabukvi")]. *Istoriko-etnograficheskie shtudii.* Tbilisi, 1988. Ch. 3. Pp. 129-139. In Georgian. Summary in Russian.

241 Abakeliia, N.K. "Obraz sv. Georgiia v zapadnogruzinskikh religioznykh verovaniiakh" [The Image of St. George in West Georgian Beliefs]. *Sov. etnografiia* 5 (1988): 86-93.

242 Abbasov, A. "Sotsial'naia priroda i politicheskaia napravlennost' 'islamskogo sotsializma'" [Social Nature and Political Trend of "Islam's Socialism"]. *Kommunist Azerbaidzhana* 4 (1985): 92-98.

243 Abbasov, Sh. *Nauchnye osnovy ateisticheskogo vospitaniia* [Scientific Foundations of Atheistic Education]. Tashkent: Uzbekistan, 1981. 24 pp. (Ser. "Marksizm-Leninizm"; No 7). In Uzbek.

244 Abbyldaev, M. *Formirovanie ateisticheskogo mirovozzreniia* [Forming Atheistic World Outlook]. Frunze: Kyrgyzstan, 1982. 100 pp. (B-chka ateista). In Kirghiz.

245 Abdukhalikov, S. "Tipy narushenii sovetskogo zakonodatel'stva o religioznykh kul'takh v usloviiakh sovershenstvovaniia sotsializma i puti ikh predotvrashcheniia" [Types of Transgressions of Soviet Legislation on Religious Cults in Conditions of Perfection of Socialism and Ways for Averting Them]. *Rol' sotsial'no-ekonomicheskikh faktorov v formirovanii lichnosti kommunistiheskogo tipa v usloviiakh sovershenstvovaniia sotsializma.* Tashkent, 1988. Pp. 50-57.

246   Abdullaev, G.B. et al. *Estestvoznanie protiv idealizma i religii* [Natural Sciences against Idealism and Religion]. Makhachkala: Dag. kn. izd-vo, 1982. 238 pp. Bibl.: pp. 227-237. For review see item 4907.

247   Abdullaev, Kh.A. "Ateisticheskoe vospitanie uchashchikhsia" [Atheistic Education of Pupils]. *Sov. pedagogika* 2 (1988): 49-51.

248   Abdullaev, M.[A]. "Kritika musul'mansko-natsionalisticheskikh izvrashchenii sotsialisticheskogo obraza zhizni" [Criticism of Moslem-Nationalist Distortions of Socialist Way of Life]. *Sov. Dagestan* 6 (1981): 31-35.

249   Abdullaev, M.A. "Vazhnyi istochnik srednevekovogo sufizma" [Important Source of Medieval Sufism]. *Vopr. filosofii* 7 (1986): 82-90. Summary in English, p. 173.

250   Abdullaev, Sh. "Kritika bogoslovskikh fal'sifikatsii marksizma" [Criticism of Theological Attempts at Falsification of Marxism]. *Kompleksnyi podkhod v ateisticheskom vospitanii.* Dushanbe, 1988. Pp. 70-87. Bibl.: pp. 86-87.

251   Abdullaev, Sh. *Nauchno-tekhnicheskaia revoliutsiia i islam* [Scientific-Technical Revolution and Islam]. Dushanbe: Irfon, 1984. 45 pp. In Tajik. Annot. bibl.: pp. 43-44.

252   Abdullaeva, M. "Nastupatel'no vesti ateisticheskuiu rabotu" [To Wage an Offensive Atheistic Work]. *Part. zhizn'.* Tashkent. 2 (1987): 81-84.

253   Abdulloev, Sh. *Deistvitel'nost' i islam* [Reality and Islam]. Dushanbe: Irfon, 1984. 20 pp. In Tajik.

254   Abdulloev, Sh. "Vliianie NTR na 'traditsionnuiu kul'turu' i ee otrazhenie v ideologii sovremennogo islama" [The Influence of NTR on "Traditional Culture" and its Reflection in the Ideology of Contemporary Islam]. *Respublikanskaia nauchno-teoreticheskaia konferentsiia molodykh uchenykh i spetsialistov TadzhSSR.* Dushanbe, 1982. Sektsiia obshchestv. nauk: Istoriia, filosofiia. Pp. 59-60.

255   Abdurakhmanov, O. *Konets 'proroka' dzunglei* [The End of Jungles' "Prophet"]. Tashkent: Esh gvardiia, 1987. 111 pp. In Uzbek.

256   Abdurasulova, T. *Islam i zhenshchiny-uzbechki* [Islam and Uzbek Women]. Tashkent: Uzbekistan, 1986. 24 pp. (B-ka ateista). In Uzbek.

257   Abdurasulova, T. *Zhenshchiny uzbechki - nositeli ateisticheskikh ubezhdenii*
       [Uzbek Women - Carriers of Atheistic Convictions]. Tashkent: Znanie
       UzSSR, 1980. 25 pp. (V pomoshch' lektoru / O-vo "Znanie" UzSSR. Ser.
       Obshchestv.-politicheskaia). In Uzbek.

258   Abdusamedov, A. [I]. "Gazeta i aesticheskoe vospitanie" [Newspaper and
       Atheistic Education]. *Part. zhizn'*. Tashkent. 8 (1986): 90-93.

259   Abdusamedov, A.I. *Metodika lektsionnoi propagandy po nauchnomu ateizmu*
       [Method of Propaganda by Lectures on Scientific Atheism]. Tashkent:
       Uzbekistan, 1982. 31 pp. (Ser. "Lektor. masterstvo": No 13). In Uzbek.

260   Abdusamedov, A.I. *Nauchnyi ateizm* [Scientific Atheism]. Tashkent: Ukit-
       uvchi, 1987. 214 pp. In Uzbek.

261   Abdusamedov, A.I. *Sotsial'nyi progress i islam* [Social Progress and Islam].
       Tashkent: Uzbekistan, 1984. 152 pp. In Uzbek.

262   Abdusamedov, A.I. *Sovremennaia ideologocheskaia bor'ba i religiia* [Contem-
       porary Ideological Struggle and Religion]. Tashkent: Znanie UzSSR, 1983.
       23 pp. (V pomoshch' lektoru / O-vo "Znanie" UzSSR. Ser. "Obshchest-
       venno-politicheskaia").

263   Abdusamedov, A.I.; Shamukhamedov, Sh.Sh. *Uraza:* (Proickhozhdenie,
       sushchnost', vred). [(Origin, Essence, Harm)]. Tashkent: Znanie UzSSR,
       1985. 19 pp. (V pomoshch lektoru / O-vo "Znanie" UzSSR. Ser. Obsh-
       chestv.-polit.). In Uzbek.

264   Abdyldaev, M.K. *Obychai na vesakh vremeni* [Custom on the Scale of
       Time]. Frunze: Kyrgyzstan, 1988. 52 pp. (B-chka ateista). In Kirghiz.
       Annot. bibl.: p. 51.

265   Abdyldaev, S.A. *Ateisticheskoe vospitanie kak sostavnaia chast' kommu-
       nisticheskogo vospitaniia* [Atheistic Education as Component Part of
       Communist Upbringing]. Frunze: Mektep, 1986. 29 pp. In Kirghiz.

266   Abdyldaev, S.A. *Ateisticheskoe vospitanie molodezhi* [Atheistic Upbringing of
       Youth]. Frunze: Mektep, 1982. 64 pp. In Kirghiz.

267   Abdyldaev, S.A. *Religiia i novaia zhizn'* [Religion and New Life]. Frunze"
       Kyrgyzstan, 1984. 56 pp. (B-chka ateista). In Kirghiz.

268   Ablova, A.R.; Zhuravlev, A.P.; Krapman, R.L. "Muzykal'nye kul'tovye
       pamiatniki Fennoskandii" [Finno-Scandia's Musical Religious Monuments].
       *XI Vsesoiuznaia konferentsiia po izucheniiu istorii, ekonomiki, literatury i
       iazyka Skandinavskikh stran i Finliandii.* M., 1989. I. Pp. 180-181.

269   Abramian, L.A. "Besedy u dereva" [Talks by the Tree]. *Sov. etnografiia* 5
       (1988): 121-131.

270   Abramov, A.I. "Gegel' i slavianofily ob otnoshenii filosofii k religii" [Hegel
       and Slavophiles on the Attitude of Philosophy toward Religion].
       Aktual'nye problemy istorii russkoi filosofii XIX veka. M., 1987. Pp. 48-81.

271   Abrorov, Kh. "'Sviatye mesta'. Mify i real'nost'" ["Holy Places". Myths and
       Reality]. *Kommunist Tadzhikistana* 3 (1989): 67-72.

272   Abrosimov, V.S.; Kobetskii, V.D. "Problemy metodologii i metodiki ateist-
       icheskogo vospitaniia v vysshei shkole" [Methodological and Methodical
       Problems of Atheistic Education in Advanced School]. *Vestn. Leningr.
       un-ta.* Ser. 6, Istoriia KPSS, nauch. kommunizm, filosofiia, pravo 4 (1987):
       31-40. Summary in English.

273   Abrosimov, V.S.; Kobetskii, V.D.; Savel'ev, S.N. "Sovershenstvovanie
       podgotovki spetsialistov nauchnogo ateizma na filosofskom fakul'tete
       Leningradskogo universiteta" [Perfection of the Preparation of Specialists
       of Scientific Atheism in the Faculty of Philosophy of the Leningrad
       University]. *Aktual'nye vopr. metodiki prepodavaniia obshchestv. nauk i
       kom. vospitaniia studentov* 5 (1987): 51-57.

274   Abu Khamid-al-Gazali. "Voskreshenie nauk o vere" [Resurrection of Sciences
       about Faith]. *Narody Azii i Afriki* 6 (1986): 194-198. For review see item
       4908.

275   Abutidze, A.V.; Bibiluri, T.I.; Maisurashvili, N.N. "Rannekhristianskii
       mogil'nik Akhali Armazi" [Ahali Armazi's Early Christian Burial Ground].
       Soobshch. AN GSSR. Tbilisi, 1988. T. 131. No 3. Pp. 653-656. In
       Georgian. Summaries in English and Russian.

276   Adrianova, N. "K komu i kak my obrashchaemsia" [To Whom and How we
       Appeal]. *Nauka i religiia* 4 (1980): 16-18.

277   Adrianova, N. "Kogda i gde vesti besedu ateistu?" [When and Where the Atheist should Lead a Discussion]. *Nauka i religiia* 6 (1980): 20-23.

278   Adrianova, N. "V chem glavnyi kriterii?" [What is the Main Criterion]. *Nauka i religiia* 8 (1980): 13-14.

279   "Advaita i purva-mimansa. Kommentarii Shankary na chetvertuiu sutru Badaraiany" [Advaita and Purva-Mimansa. Sankara's Commentary on the Fourth Sutra of Badarayana]*.Transl. from Sanskrit, introd. and commentaries by N.V. Isaeva. *Narody Azii i Afriki* 5 (1985): 101-118. Summary in English, p. 221.

280   Afanas'eva, V.K. "Predanie, etiologicheskii mif i mifologema v shumerskoi literature" [Legend, Aetiological Myth and Mythology in Sumeric Literature]. *Zhizn' mifa v antichnosti* M., 1988. Ch. I. Pp. 27-45.

281   *Aforizmy starogo Kitaia* [Ancient China's Aphorisms]. Ed.: I.S. Lisevich. M.: Nauka, 1988. 192 pp. Bibl.: pp. 166-167. Name index: pp. 189-191.

282   Agaev, I. "Allegoricheskoe tolkovanie religioznykh dogm i uchenie o sootnoshenii very i znania v entsiklopedii 'Chistykh brat'ev'" [Allegorical Interpretation of Religious Dogmas and Learning on Correlation of Faith and Knowledge in "Pure Brothers" Encyclopaedia]. *Dokl. AN AzSSR.* T. 41. 4 (1985): 68-72. Summary in Azerbaijan and English.

283   Agaev, I.A.; Dodikhudoev, Kh.D. "Kontseptsiia religii v rannem ismailisme" [The Conception of Religion in Early Ismailism]. *Izv. AN TadzhSSR.* Ser. Filosofiia, ekonomika, pravovedenie. 2 (1989): 47-52. Summary in Tajik.

284   Agaev, S.L. "Rukholla Musavi Khomeini" [Ruholla Musavi Khomeini]. *Vopr. istorii* 6 (1989): 79-100.

285   Agakov, V.G. "O roli astronomii v formirovanii materialisticheskogo mirivozzreniia" [The Role of Astronomy in Forming Materialistic World Outlook]. *Problemy istorii religii i ateizma.* Cheboksary, 1981. Pp. 38-54.

286   Agapova, N.G. "Metodologicheskie osnovy teorii ateisticheskogo vospitaniia v svete reshenii XXVI s'ezda KPSS" [Methodological Fundamentals of the Theory of Atheistic Education in the Light of the XXVIth CPSU Congress Resolutions]. *Aktual'nye problemy ateisticheskogo vospitaniia i kritika religioznoi ideologii.* M., 1983. Pp. 3-7.

287   Agasieva, E.A. "Nekotorye aspekty islama v Turtsii" [Some Aspects of Islam in Turkey]. *Islam v istorii i sovremennost'.* Baku, 1981. Pp. 56-64.

288   Aglarov, M.A. "Iazycheskoe sviatilishche na vershine gory Bakhargan" [Pagan Sanctuary on the Peak of Bahargan Mountain]. *Mifologiia narodov Dagestana.* Makachkala, 1984. Pp. 36-42.

289   Aidinian, R.M. "Poniatie religii i genesis religiozno-misticheskikh predstavlenii" [Concept of Religion and Genesis of Religious Mystical Notions]. *Kategorii istoricheskikh nauk.* L., 1988. Pp. 144-171.

290   Aimova, G.N. *Aktivnost' ateista* [Atheist's Activity]. Alma-Ata: [S.n.], 1984. 20 pp.

291   Aimova, G.N. *Ateisicheskoe vospitanie molodezhi* [Atheistic Upbringing of Youth]. Alma-Ata: Kazakhstan, 1984. 128 pp.

292   Aimova, G.N. "Nekotorye voprosy metodologii analiza problemy formirovaniia nauchno-materialisticheskogo ateisticheskogo mirovozzreniia molodezhi" [Some Questions of Methodological Analysis of Problems of Shaping Youth's Scientific-Materialist Atheistic World Outlook]. *Vestn. AN KazSSR.* 2 (1986): 67-72.

293   Aimova, G.N. *Rabota po formirovaniiu y molodezhi ateisticheskikh ubezhdenii* [Work for Shaping Youth's Atheistic Convictions]. Alma-Ata: Znanie KazSSR, 1982. 46 pp.

294   Aitbaev, O. "Rol' nauchno-ateisticheskogo vospitaniia v aktivizatsii chelovecheskogo faktora" [Role of Scientific-Atheistic Education in Activization of Human Factor]. *Problemy aktivizatsii chelovecheskogo faktora v usloviiakh sovershenstvovaniia sotsializma.* Karaganda, 1988. Pp. 76-82.

295   Aivazian, K.V. "Kul't Grigorii Armianskogo, 'armianskaia vera' i 'armianskaia eres' v Novgorode (XIII-XVI vv.)" [The Cult of Gregory the Armenian, "Armenian Faith" and "Armenian Heresy" in Novgorod [XIIIth- XVIth C.)]. *Russkaia i armianskaia srednevekovye literatury* L., 1982. Pp. 255-332.

296   Aivazova, N.V. *Puti povysheniia kachestva i effektivnosti nauchno-ateisticheskoi propagandy* [Ways to Increase the Quality and Effectiveness of Scientific-Atheistic Propaganda]. M.: Znanie RSFSR, 1982. 47 pp. (V pomoshch' lektoru / O-vo "Znanie" RSFSR, Nauch.-metod. sovet po propagande nauch. ateizma).

297 Aivazova, N.[V]. "S pozitsii trebovatel'nosti" [From the Position of Exactingness]. *Nauka i religiia* 8 (1981): 15-17.

298 Akhadov, A.F. *Islam v pogone za vekom* [Islam in Pursuit of the Century]. M.: Politizdat, 1988. 80 pp. Published also in: Tashkent: Uzbekistan, 1989. 84 pp. (B-chka ateista). In Uzbek.

299 Akhadov, A.F. *Sovremennyi shiizm i osobennosti ego proiavleniia* [Contemporary Shiism and Features of its Manifestations]. M: Znanie, 1980. 19 pp. (V pomoshch' lektoru).

300 Akhadov, A.N. *Svoboda sovesti. Ateizm i zakon* [Freedom of Worship. Atheism and Law]. Baku: Azerneshr, 1989. 183 pp. In Azerbaijan.

301 Akhmadov, S. *V poiske effektivnykh putei ateisticheskoi raboty* [In the Search of Effective Ways of Atheistic Work]. Dushanbe: Irfon, 1986. 77 pp. In Tajik.

302 Akhmadzhoizoda, A. "O probleme tak nazyvaemoi musul'manskoi kul'tury" [On the Problem of so - called Moslem Culture]. *III Vsesoiuznaia konferentsiia vostokovedov "Vzaimodeistvie i vzaimovliianie tsivilizatsii kul'tur na Vostoke".* M., 1988. T. 1. Pp. 3-4.

303 Akhmedov, A. *Islam v sovremennoi ideino-politicheskoi bor'be* [Islam in Contemporary Ideological-Political Struggle]. M.: Politizdat, 1985. 240 pp. Published also in: Tashkent: Uzbekistan, 1986. 296 pp. In Uzbek. For review see item 4909.

304 Akhmedov, A. *Sotsial'naia doktrina Islama* [Islam's Social Doctrine]. M.: Politizdat, 1982. 270 pp. Published also in: Ashkhabad: Turkmenistan, 1986. 289 pp. In Turkmen. For reviews see items 4910-4912.

305 Akhmedov, B.A. "Zhitiia musul'manskikh 'sviatykh' kak istoricheskii istochnik" [Lives of Moslem "Saints" as Historical Source]. *Istochnikovedcheskie razyskaniia, 1985.* Tbilisi, 1988. Pp. 207-214.

306 Akhmedov, M.M.; Agabekov, Dzh.G. "Rol' religioznogo i traditsionnogo v razvitii sovremennogo turetskogo obshchestva" [The Role of Religiosity and Tradition in the Development of Contemporary Turkish Society]. *Aktual'nye problemy sovremennoi Turtsii.* Baku, 1988. Pp. 17-48.

307   Akhmedov, S. "Ateizm v sisteme dukhovnoi kul'tury" [Atheism in the System of Spiritual Culture]. *Izv. AN TadzhSSR*. Otd-nie obshchestv. nauk 1 (1985): 94-99. Summary in Tajik.

308   Akhmedov, S. *Vliianie kul'turnoi revoliutsii na formirovanie nauchno-ateisticheskogo mirovozzreniia trudiashcikhsia* [The Influence of the Cultural Revolution in Forming Workers' Scientific-Atheistic World Outlook]. Dushanbe: Donish, 1987. 110 pp. Annot. bibl.: pp. 101-109.

309   Akhmedzhanov, B. "Lozh' i kleveta na sluzhbe klerikal'nogo antikommunizma" [Lie and Slander in the Service of Clerical Anti-Communism]. *Kommunist Uzbekistana* 1 (1986): 84-86.

310   Akhmedzhanov, R.M. "Tekhnicheskie sredstva obucheniia i ateisticheskoe vospitanie studencheskoi molodezhi" [Technical Means of Study and Atheistic Upbringing of Students]. *Problemy formirovaniia nauchno-ateisticheskogo mirovozzreniia v sotsialisticheskom obshchestve*. Samarkand, 1980. Pp. 78-85.

311   Akhtamon, A.; Leshchinskii, V. "O fal'sifikatsii burzhuaznymi ideologami polozheniia musul'man v SSSR" [On Bourgeois Ideologists' Falsifications about the Moslems' Position in USSR]. *Kommunist Uzbekistana* 12 (1983): 85-87.

312   Akhunbabaev, Kh.G. "Domashnie khramy rannesrednevekovogo Samarkanda" [Home Temples of Early Medieval Samarkand]. *Gorodskaia kul'tura Baktrii-Tokharistana i Sogda*. Tashkent, 1987. Pp. 10-21.

313   Akhundov, M.D. "Prostranstvo i vremia: Ot mifa k nauke" [Space and Time: From Myth to Science]. *Priroda* 8 (1985): 53-64.

314   Akhundova, N.Ch. "Ob organizatsii 'Islamskii front' v Sirii" [On "Islamic Front" Organization in Syria]. *Problemy sovremennoi sovetskoi arabistiki*. Erevan, 1988. Vyp. I. Pp. 82-86.

315   Akhunzianov, T. "Obogoshchaia dukhovnyi mir cheloveka" [Enrichment of Man's Spiritual World]. *Nauka i religiia* 4 (1984): 4-7.

316   Akimova, O.A. "Ispol'zovanie antichnykh istochnikov v 'Istorii arkhiepiskopov Salony i Splita'" [The Use of Ancient Sources in the "History of Archbishops of Salon and Split"]. *Sov. slavianovedenie* 3 (1981): 65-73.

317   Akimushkin, O.F. "K istorii formirovaniia fonda musul'manskikh rukopisei Instituta vostokovedeniia AN SSSR" [History of Organization of Moslem Manuscripts Fund of the Institute of Oriental Studies at the Academy of Sciences of the USSR]. *Pis'mennye pamiatniki Vostoka, 1978-1979.* M., 1987. Pp. 9-27.

318   Akinchits, I.I. "Molodoi protestant segodnia" [Young Protestant Today]. *Veruiushchii v usloviiakh perestroiki* M., 1989. Pp. 94-111.

319   Akinchits, I.I. "Osobennosti nravstvennogo soznaniia molodogo veruiu-shchego" [Peculiarities of the Moral Consciousness of the Young Believer]. *Vopr. nauch. ateizma* 35 (1986): 213-234.

320   Akinchits, I.I. *Porosl' otrezannoi vetvi* [Shoots of Cut Off Branch]. M.: Mol. gvardiia, 1985. 224 pp.

321   Akinchits, I.I. "Smysl' zhizni i nravstvennyi ideal sektantskoi molodezhi" [The Meaning of Life and Moral Ideal of Sectarian Youth]. *Nauchnyi ateizm: Ideal i mirovozzrenie.* Perm', 1988. Pp. 58-66.

322   Akinchits, I.I. "Sotsial'no-psikhologicheskaia kharakteristika molodykh posledovatelei protestantizma" [Socio-Psychological Description of Young Followers of Protestantism]. *Protestantskie organizatsii v SSSR.* M., 1989. Pp. 68-83.

323   Akinchits, I.I.; Filist, G.M. *Ateisticheskie besedy s uchashchimisia* [Atheistic Talks with Pupils]. Minsk: Nar. asveta, 1985. 158 pp.

324   Akmuradov, A. *Kollektiv i ateisticheskoe vospitanie* [The Collective and Atheistic Education]. Ashkhabad: Turkmenistan, 1980. 67 pp. In Turkmen.

325   Akmuradov, K. *Ateisticheskoe vospitanie sel'skogo naseleniia na sovremennom etape* [Villagers' Atheistic Education in the Contemporary Stage]. Ashkhabad: Ylym, 1985. 119 pp. Annot. bibl.: pp. 115-118. For review see item 4913.

326   Aknazarov, Kh.Z. *Osobennosti islama v Kazakhstane* [Islam's Features in Kazakhstan]. Alma-Ata: Znanie, 1986. 33 pp. In Kazakh.

327   Aknazarov, Kh.Z.; Seitzhanov, T.S. *Nekotorye voprosy ateisticheskogo vospi-taniia naseleniia* [Some Problems of the Population's Atheistic Education]. Alma-Ata: Znanie KazSSR, 1984. 18 pp. In Kazakh.

328   Akopian, G.Kh. *Iz istorii armianskoi ateisticheskoi mysli* [History of Armenian Atheistic Thought]. Erevan: Aiastan, 1983. 151 pp. In Armenian.

329   Akopian, G.Kh. *Nekotorye voprosy ateisticheskogo vospitaniia* [Some Problems of Atheistic Education]. Erevan: Aiastan, 1988. 280 pp. In Armenian.

330   Akpian, G.B. "Analiz religioznosti nekotoroi chasti v inzhenerno-tekhnicheskoi molodezhi v usloviiakh obshchego krizisa religii" [Analysis of the Religiosity of Some Sections of Engineer-Technical Youth in the Conditions of Common Religion's Crisis]. *Vopr. filosofii* 2 (1982): 141-156. Summary in Armenian.

331   Aktsorin, V.A. "Istoriko-geneticheskie sviazi finno-ugarskikh plemen po dannym mifologii" [Historic-Genetic Ties of Finno-Ugric Tribes According to Mythology]. *Vopr. mariiskogo fol'klora i iskusstva* 2 (1980): 13-27.

332   "Aktual'na li ateisticheskaia propaganda?" [Is Atheistic Propaganda Topical?]. *Kommunist Tatarii* 4 (1988): 84-86.

333   *Aktual'nye problemy ateisticheskogo vospitaniia i kritika religioznoi ideologii* [Actual Problems of Atheistic Education and Critique of Religious Ideology]. [Ed: N.A. Pashkova]. M.: Izd-vo MGU, 1981. 80 pp. Vyp. 6. Published also under editorship of N.K. Dmitrieva, M.: Izd-vo MGU, 1983. 54 pp.

334   *Aktual'nye problemy ateizma i kritiki religii* [Actual Problems of Atheism and Critique of Religion]. [Ed.: E.A. Lekhner]. M.: MOPI, 1985. 120 pp.

335   *Aktual'nye problemy izucheniia istorii religii i ateizma* [Actual Problems of Study of History of Religion and Atheism]. [Ed.: A.M. Leskov]. L.: GMIRIA, 1980. 165 pp.
Published also under editorship of Ia.Ia. Kozhurin, M.: GMIRIA, 1981. 158 pp., illus., and in 1982, 164 pp.

336   *Aktual'nye problemy kritiki religii i formirovaniia ateisticheskogo mirovozzreniia* [Actual Problems of Critique of Religion and the Forming of an Atheistic World Outlook]. Ed.: M.V. Bagabov. Makhachkala: DGU, 1982. 160 pp.

337   *Aktual'nye problemy nauchnogo ateizma* [Actual Problems of Scientific Atheism]. Ed.: V.D. Timofeev; E.G. Filimonov. M.: AON, 1986. 171 pp.

338 *Aktual'nnye problemy obespecheniia effektivnosti nauchno-ateisticheskoi raboty* [Actual Problems of Ensuring the Effectiveness of the Scientific-Atheistic Work]. [Ed.: G.E. Kudriashov]. Cheboksary: ChGU, 1986. 129 pp.

339 *Aktual'nye problemy teorii i praktiki nauchnogo ateizma* [Actual Problems of Theory and Practice of Scientific Atheism]. Ed.: M.P. Novikova; F.G. Ovsienko. M.: Izd-vo MGU, 1985. 239 pp. Annot. bibl.: pp. 225-238.

340 *Aktual'nye problemy teorii nauchnogo ateizma* [Actual Problems of Theory of Scientific Atheism]. [Ed.: I.A. Besedin]. M.: INION, 1983. 259 pp.

341 *Aktual'nye voprosy ateisticheskogo vospitaniia* [Actual Problems of Atheistic Education]. Ed.: S.B. Dorzhenov. Frunze: KGU, 1980. 97 pp.

342 *Aktual'nye voprosy ateisticheskogo vospitaniia na sovremennom etape* [Actual Problems of Atheistic Education in Contemporary Stage]. [Comp.: N.A. Trofimchuk]. M.: Znanie, 1986. 64 pp. (Novoe v zhizni, nauke, tekhnike. Nauch. ateizm; 12/1986). Bibl.: p. 61.

343 *Aktual'nye voprosy nauchnogo ateizma i istorii religii* [Actual Problems of Scientific Atheism and History of Religion]. [Ed.: G.A. Martirosov]. Grodno: GrGU, 1985. 115 pp.

344 *Aktual'nye voprosy nauchnogo ateizma i kritiki religii* [Actual Problems of Scientific Atheism and Critique of Religion]. Minsk: Vysheish. shkola, 1980. 135 pp.

345 *Aktual'nye zadachi ateisticheskogo vospitaniia Molodezhi v svete reshenii XXVII KPSS i ianvarskogo (1987 g.) Plenuma TsK KPSS* [Actual Problems of Youth's Atheistic Education in the Light of XXVIIth Congress of the CPSU and CPSU CC January (1987) Plenum]. [Ed.: G.Kh. Akopian]. Erevan: Izd-vo Erev. gos. un-ta, 1987. 52 pp.

346 Akulov, I.B.; Maliuk, O.P. *Mastera klevety* [Masters of Slander]. Kiev: Politizdat Ukrainy, 1981. 72 pp. In Ukrainian.

347 Alapaev, O. *Ateisticheskoe vospitanie i 'svoboda sovesti'* [Atheistic Education and "Freedom of Worship"]. Frunze: Kyrgyzstan, 1988. 93 pp. (BA: B-chka ateista). In Kirghiz.

348 Alapaev, O. *Religiia i ateisticheskoe vospitanie molodezhi* [Religion and Youth's Atheistic Upbringing]. Frunze: Mektep, 1985. 85 pp. In Kirghiz. Bibl.: pp. 83-84.

349 Alapaev, O. *Religiia i ee vred* [Religion and its Harmfulness]. Frunze: Mektep, 1980. 100 pp. In Kirghiz.

350 Al'bedil', M.F. "K rekonstruktsii mifologicheskoi semantiki protoindiiskikh tekstov" [Reconstruction of Mythological Semantics of Protoindian Texts]. *Literatura i kul'tura drevnei i srednevekovoi Indii.* M., 1987. Pp. 11-25. Bibl.: pp. 24-25.

351 Aleinik, R. "Ateizm Fridrikha Feierbakha" [Friedrick Feuerbach's Atheism]. *Nauka i religiia* 2 (1983): 30-32.

352 Alekseev, A.A. "Proekt tekstologicheskogo issledovaniia kirillo-mefo-dievskogo perevoda Evangeliia" [Project of Textual Research of Cyrillic-Mephodian Translation of the Gospel]. *Sov. slavianovedenie* 1 (1985): 82-94.

353 Alekseev, G.M. "Iz opyta ateisticheskoi raboty v g. Cheboksary" [Experience of Atheistic Work in Cherboksar]. *Problemy istorii religii i ateizma.* Cheboksary, 1980. Pp. 108-112.

354 Alekseev, N.A. *Rannie formy religii tiurkoiazychnykh narodov Sibirii* [Early Forms of Religion of the Turkic Language People of Siberia]. Novo-sibirsk: Nauka. Sib. otd-nie, 1980. 317 pp., illus. For review see item 4916.

355 Alekseev, N.A. *Shamanizm tiurkoiazychnykh narodov Sibirii* [Shamanism of the Turkic Language People of Siberia]. Novosibirsk: Nauka. Sib. otd-nie, 1984. 233 pp., illus. Bibl.: pp. 226-232.

356 Alekseev, V. "Neozhidannyi dialog: O vstreche Stalina s rukovodstvom pravoslavnoi tserkvi" [Unexpected Dialogue: Stalin's Meeting with Leader-ship of the Orthodox Church]. *Agitator* 6 (1989): 41-44.

357 Alekseev, V.; Brushlinskaia, O. "Strana molodykh" [The Country of the Young]. *Nauka i religiia* 7 (1984): 2-5.

358 Alekseev, V.A. *Ateisticheskoe vospitanie molodezhi* [Atheistic Upbringing of Youth]. M.: Znanie RSFSR, 1989. 39 pp. Bibl.: pp. 37-38.

359   Alekseev, V.A. "Komsomol'skaia periodicheskaia pechat' - propagandist nauchno-ateisticheskikh znanii" [Komsomol Periodical Press - Propagandist of Scientific-Atheistic Knowledge]. *Akual'nye problemy nauchno-ateisticheskogo vospitaniia molodezhi.* M., 1987. Pp. 29-44.

360   Alekseev, V.A. "O kharaktere antireligioznogo dvizheniia v SSSR v 20--30-e gody" [On the Character of the Antireligious Movement in USSR in the 20-30s]. *Nauchnyi kommunizm* 2 (1989): 98-103.

361   Alekseev, V.A. "Ot kakogo 'opyta' segodnia otkazyvaiutsia" [What "Experience" is Turned Down Today]. *Polit. obrazovanie* 9 (1989): 93-97.

362   Alekseev, V.A. "'Pravaia oppozitsiia' i bor'ba s religiei" ["The Rightist Opposition" and the Struggle against Religion]. *Agitator* 5 (1989): 41-44.

363   Aliev, A.G. *Dukhovnaia kul'tura i religiia* [Spiritual Culture and Religion]. Baku: Azerneshr, 1981. 91 pp. In Azerbaijan.

364   Aliev, A.G. *Dukhovnyi progress lichnosti i ateizm* [Individual's Spiritual Progress and Atheism]. Baku: Znanie AzSSR, 1980. 64 pp. (V pomoshch' lektoru / O-vo "Znanie" AzSSR). In Azerbaijan. Bibl.: p. 64.

365   Aliev, A.G. *Nauchnoe poznanie i religioznaia vera* [Scientific Cognition and Religious Belief]. Baku: Azerneshr, 1989. 134 pp. In Azerbaijan.

366   Aliev, A.G. "Zametki o sufiiskom ordene Sukhraverdiiia [Remarks on Sufist Order Suhrawardiyya]. *Islam v istorii narodov Vostoka.* M., 1981. Pp. 154-159. Annot. bibl.: pp. 158-159.

367   Aliev. A.K. "Sblizhenie i razvitie natsii i narodnostei SSSR - vazhnoe uslovie ateisticheskogo vospitaniia" [Rapprochement and Development of USSR Nations and Nationalities - Important Condition of Atheistic Education]. *Vopr. nauch. ateizma* 26 (1980): 36-50.

368   Aliev, R.Ia. "Alzhir i Egipet: Islam i puti razvitiia" [Algeria and Egypt: Islam and Ways of Development]. *Aktual'nye problemy sovremennoi Afriki.* M., 1988. Vyp. 2. Pp. 80-87.

369   Aliev, R.Ia. "Islam kak komponent natsionalizma" [Islam as a Component of Nationalism]. *Sovetskoe vostokovedenie.* M., 1988. Pp. 284-292.

370   Aliev, R.Ia. *Islam v kontseptsiiakh 'natsional'nogo sotsializma'* [Islam in
       Conceptions of "National Socialism"]. Baku: Elm, 1987. 161 pp. For
       review see item 4917.

371   Aliev, R.Ia. "Predposylki svetskogo podkhoda Iemenskoi sotsialisticheskoi
       partii NDRI k islamu" [Pre-condition of Secular Approach to Islam of
       Yemen Socialist Party NDRI]. *Problemy zarubezhnogo Vostoka: Istoriia i
       sovremennost.* Baku., 1988. Pp. 70-82.

372   Aliev, R.Ia.; Mamedov, A.M. *Islam i natsional'no-osvoboditel'noe dvizhenie v
       arabskikh stranakh* [Islam and National-Liberation Movement in Arab
       Countries]. Baku: Elm, 1986. 75 pp. In Azerbaijan.

373   Aliev, R.M. *Ateisticheskoe vospitanie, obriady, traditsii* [Atheistic Education,
       Rites, Traditions]. Baku: Znanie AzSSR, 1984. 40 pp. V pomoshch' lekto-
       ru / O-vo "Znanie" AzSSR). In Azerbaijan.

374   Aliev, S. "Islam i politika" [Islam and Politics]. *Aziia i Afrika segodnia* 12
       (1981): 5-9.

375   Aliev, V.M.; Isaev, N.M. "Rol' ateisticheskogo nasledija azerbaidzhanskikh
       prosvetitelei v ateisticheskom vospitanii molodezhi" [The Role of Atheistic
       Heritage of Azerbaijanian Educators in Atheistic Upbringing of Youth].
       Aktual'nye voprosy ateisticheskogo vospitaniia molodezhi. Baku., 1988. Pp.
       46-62. In Azerbaijan. Summary in Russian.

376   Alieva, B.A. "Interpretatsiia sotsial'no-nravstvennykh aspektov nauki v
       musul'manskoi mysli" [Interpretation of Science's Social-Moral Aspects in
       Moslem Thought]. *Aktual'nye problemy kritiki religii i formirovaniia
       ateisticheskogo miriovozzreniia.* Makhachkala, 1982. Pp. 77-88.

377   Alieva, B.A. *Sovremennyi islam i nauka* [Contemporary Islam and Science].
       M.: Znanie, 1981. 64 pp. (Novoe v zhizni, nauke, tekhnike. Ser. "Nauch.
       ateizm"; No 3). Bibl.: pp. 61-63.

378   Alimarin, S.; Barabashev, A. "'Put' voina': Karlos Kastaneda i ego uchenie"
       ["Warrior's Way": Carlos Castaneda and His Teaching]. *Nauka i religiia*
       10 (1988): 40-46.

379   Alimbaev, A.A. *Ateizm sovetskogo rabochego klassa* [Atheism of Soviet
       Workers Class]. Alma-Ata: Kazakhstan, 1985. 113 pp. For review see
       item 4918.

380   Alimbaev, A.A. *Molodym - ateisticheskuiu ubezhdennost'* [To Young People - Atheistic Conviction]. M.: Politizdat, 1980. 55 pp. (B-ka ateista).

381   Alimova, D.A. "K istoriografii ateisticheskogo vospitaniia zhenshchin v respublikakh Srednei Azii (60-80-e gody) [Historiography of Atheistic Education of Women in Middle Asian Republics (60s-80s)]. *Obshchestv. nauki v Uzbekistane* 6 (1986): 38-42.

382   Alimova, D.A.; Savurov, M.D. *Voprosy ateisticheskogo vospitaniia mass* [Problems of Atheistic Education of Masses]. Tashkent: Uzbekistan, 1989. 39 pp. (Marksizm-leninizm; No 7). In Uzbek.

383   Alizade, Z.M.M. "Religiia v mirovozzrenii Nagiba Makhfuza" [Religion in Naguib Makhfuz's World Outlook]. *Problemy zarubezhnogo Vostoka: Istoriia i sovremennost'.* Baku, 1988. Pp. 215-228.

384   Al'miasheva, L.N. *Na putiakh k dukhovnoi svobode* [On the Means to Spiritual Freedom]. Saransk: Mordov. kn. isd-vo, 1983. 77 pp. Bibl.: p. 76.

385   Alpeeva, T.M. *Religiia i sovremennaia ideologicheskaia bor'ba* [Religion and the Contemporary Ideological Struggle]. Minsk: Znanie BSSR, 1980. 19 pp. (Material v pomoshch' lektoru / Pravl. o-va "Znanie" BSSR, Nauch.-metod. sovet po propagande nauch. ateizma). Bibl.: pp. 18-19.

386   Altybaev, M. "Slovo otzovetsia v serdtse" [The Word will Repercusse in the Heart]. *Part. zhizn'.* Tashkent, 6/7 (1982): 167-170.

387   Altynov, M.A. *Ateizm i sotsialisticheskaia kul'tura* [Atheism and Socialist Culture]. Tashkent: Fan, 1984. 94 pp. Bibl.: pp. 88-93.

388   Altynov, M.A. *Tvorcheskoe razvitie nauchnogo ateizma* [Creative Development of Scientific Atheism]. Tashkent: Uzbekistan, 1984. 44 pp. (Marksizm-leninizm; No 9). In Uzbek.

389   Amanturlin, Sh.B. *Predrassudki i sueveriia, ikh preodolenie* [Prejudices and Superstitions, Their Overcoming]. Alma-Ata: Kazakhstan, 1985. 124 pp.

390   Amir'iants, I.A. "Etnicheskie protsessy v Perednei Azii v nachal'nyi period rasprostraneniia islama" [Ethnic Processes in the Western Asia during the Initial Period of Islam's Dissemination]. *Istoricheskaia dinamika rasovoi i etnicheskoi differentsiatsii naseleniia Azii.* M., 1987. pp. 180-183.

391   Amirkhanov, R.M. "Ob etapakh razvitiia svobodomysliia" [Stages in Development of Freethinking]. *Iz istorii formirovaniia i razvitiia svobodomysliia v dorevoliutsionnoi Tatarii.* Kazan', 1987. Pp. 3-6.

392   Amogolonova, D.D. "Ideologocheskoe znachenie Bkhagavadgity - pamiatnika dukhovnoi kul'tury Indii" [Ideological Importance of Bhagavad Gita - Monument of India's Spiritual Culture]. *Metodologicheskie aspekty izucheniia istorii dukhovnoi kul'tury Vostoka.* Ulan-Ude, 1988. Pp. 133-143.

393   Amogolonova, D.D. "K voprosu ob izuchenii psikhologocheskikh aspektov aiurvedy" [Problems of Studying the Psychological Aspects of Ayur-Veda]. *Psikhologicheskie aspekty buddizma.* Novosibirsk, 1986. Pp.104-109

394   Amogolonova, D.D. "M.K. Gandi i khalifatskoe dvizhenie Indii" [M.K. Ghandi and India's Caliphate Movement]. *V Vsesoiuznaia shkola molodykh vostokovedov.* M., 1989. T. 3. Pp. 11-13.

395   Anarbaev, A. "Sotsial'naia aktivnost' lichnosti: Nravstvennoe znachenie i ateisticheskii potentsial" [Individual's Social Activity: Moral Importance and Atheistic Potential]. *Vopr. nauch. ateizma* 35 (1986): 162-180.

396   Andashev, Kh.; Shukurov, Sh. *Mezhdunarodnye sviazi sovetskikh musul'man* [Soviet Moslems' International Relations]. M.: Novosti, 1983. 48 pp., illus. In Arabic.
      Published also by Novosti in: Dari (56 pp., illus.), English (52 pp., illus.), French (55 pp., illus.), Pushtu (79 pp., illus.).

397   Andre-Vensan, F. *Za podlinnuiu teologiiu osvobozhdeniia* [For a Genuine Theology of Liberation]. M.: INION, 1989. 20 pp.

398   Andreev, A.P. "Bor'ba s religioznym ponimaniem otvetstvennosti cheloveka - vazhnyi element povysheniia sotsial'noi aktivnosti veruiushchikh pri sotsializme" [The Struggle with Religious Conception of Man's Responsibility - Important Element in Promoting Believer's Social Activity under Socialism]. *Chelovecheskii faktor i uskorenie nauchno-ateisticheskogo progressa.* Ufa, 1987. Pp. 124-131. Bibl.: pp. 130-131.

399   Adreev, A.P. "Ob integral'nom znachenii kategorii potrebnosti v postroenii predmeta issledovaniia v nauchnom ateizme" [On Integral Importance of the Category of Necessity in Composing Research in the Realm of Scientific Atheism]. *Marksistsko-leninskaia filosofiia i integratsionnye protsessy v nauke.* Tiumen', 1981. Pp. 23-28.

400 Andreev, A.P. "Sotsial'nye posledstviia nauchno-tekhnicheskoi revoliutsii pri sotsializme i izmenenie soznaniia veruiushchikh" [Social Consequences of Scientific-Technical Revolution under Socialism and Change of Believers' Consciousness]. *Formirovanie kommunisticheskikh obshchest- vennykh otnoshenii i sotsial'nye problemy burno razvivaiushchikhsia regionov.* Tiumen', 1981. Pp. 92-97.

401 Andreev, I.L. "Islam i ideinaia bor'ba v osvobodivshikhsia stranakh" [Islam and Ideloogical Struggle in Liberated Countries]. *Problemy mirivogo revoliutsionnogo protsessa.* M., 1982. Vyp. 2. Pp. 194-215.

402 Andreev, M.V. "Katolicheskaia tserkov' i sotsial'naia zhizn' na Afrikanskom kontinente" [Catholic Church and Social Life in the African Continent]. *Vopr. nauch. ateizma* 36 (1987): 110-124.

403 Andreev, M.V. *Kritika ideologii sovremennogo klerikalizma* [Criticism of Ideology of Contemporary Clericalism]. M.: Znanie, 1982. 63 pp. (Novoe v zhizni, nauke, tekhnike. Nauch. ateizm; 11). Bibl.: p. 54.

404 Andreev, M.V. *Marksisty i khristiane:* Dialog [Marxists and Christians: A Dialogue]. M.: Politizdat, 1983. 64 pp. (B-ka atista). For review see item 4919.

405 Andreev, M.V. "Novye tendentsii antikommunizma v sovremennom katolit-sizme (1958-1987)" [New Tendencies of Anti-Communism in Contempo-rary Catholicism (1958-1987)]. *Burzhuaznaia sovetologiia i propaganda.* M., 1987. Pp. 98-119. Bibl.: pp. 118-119.

406 Andreev, M.V. *Politika klerikal'nogo antikommunizma:* (Vatikan, 1917-1987) [Policy of Clerical Anti-Communism: (Vatican, 1917-1987)]. M.: Znanie, 1987. 64 pp. (Novoe v zhizni, nauke tekhnike. Nauch. ateizm; 10/1987). Bibl.: p. 63.

407 Andreev, V. "Pod znakom ognia i tigra?" [Under the Sign of Fire and Tiger?]. *Nauka i religiia* 12 (1985): 59-61.

408 Andreev, V.F. "Novyi spisok 'Semisobornoi rospisi' Novgoroda" [New Manuscript Copy of Novgorod's "Semisobor Register"]. *Novgor. ist. sb.* 3 (1989): 219-223.

409 Andreeva, E.V. *Zhestokii put'* [Cruel Way]. Trans. from Russian by S. Pasteenne. Vil'nius: Vaga, 1980. 309 pp., illus. In Lithuanian.

410   Andreeva, O.V. "Anglo-amerikanskaia burzhuaznaia istoriografiia polozheniia
       pravoslavnoi tserkvi v SSSR" [Anglo-American Bourgeois Historiography
       on the Position of the Orthodox Church in the USSR]. *Vopr. nauch.
       ateizma* 37 (1988): 287-299.

411   Andreeva, O.V. "Kontseptsiia 'gosudarstvennogo ateizma' v sovremennoi
       anglo-amerikanskoi burzhuaznoi istoriografii" [The Conception of "State
       Atheism" in Contemporary Anglo-American Bourgeois Historiography].
       Zarubezhnaia istorigrafiia sotsial'no-politicheskogo razvitiia SSSR. M., 1989.
       Pp. 75-84.

412   Andrianov, N.P. "Ateisticheskoe vospitanie v sisteme tekhnikumov" [Atheistic
       Education in   Technical Colleges]. *Aktual. vopr. metodiki prepodavaniia
       obshchestv. nauk i kom. vospitaniia studentov.* L., 1987. Vyp. 5. Pp.
       94-100.

413   Andrianov, N.P. *Ateizm i emotsional'nyi mir lichnosti* [Atheism and the
       Individual's Emotional World]. L.: Znanie RSFSR, 1982. 16 pp. (V
       pomoshch' lektoru / O-vo "Znanie" RSFSR, Leningr. org.).

414   Andrianov, N.P. *Ateizm v razvitom sotsialisticheskom obshchestve* [Atheism in
       Developed Socialist Society]. L.: Lenizdat, 1980. 62 pp. (V pomoshch'
       propagandistu nauch. ateizma). Bibl.: pp. 60-61.

415   Andrianov, N.P. *Obraz zhizni - tvorchestvo:* Sotsial.-gumanist. tsennost'
       ateizma [Way of Life - Creative Work: Socio-Humanist Value of
       Atheism]. L.: Lenizdat, 1984. 128 pp., illus. For review see item 4920.

416   Andrianov, N.P. *Sovetskii obraz zhizni i ateisticheskoe vospitanie* [Soviet Way
       of Life and Atheistic Education]. M.: Politizdat, 1981. 64 pp. (B-ka
       ateista).
       Published also in:
       Frunze: Mekter, 1982. 76 pp. In Kirghiz.

417   Andrianov, N.P.; Makarenia, A.A. *Estestvennonauchnye osnovy ateisticheskoi
       propagandy* [Natural Scientific Fundamentals of Atheistic Propaganda]. L.:
       Znanie RSFSR. Leningr. org. Dom nauch. ateizma, 1988. 32 pp. Bibl.: p.
       32. (V pomoshch' lektoru).

418   Andrianov, N.P.; Markin, L.V. *Aktual'nye voprosy ateisticheskogo vospitaniia*
       [Actual Problems of Atheistic Education]. L.: Znanie RSFSR, 1984. 20
       pp. (V pomoshch' lektoru / O-vo "Znanie" RSFSR, Leningr. org.}.

419   Andrianov, N.P.; Nikonov, K.I. *Aktual'nye voprosy ateisticheskogo vospitaniia v svete reshenii XXVI s'ezda KPSS:* [Actual Problems of Atheistic Education in the Light of the Resolutions of the XXVIth CPSU Congress]. M.: Znanie, RSFSR 1982. 40 pp. (V pomoshch' lektoru / O-vo "Znanie" RSFSR, Nauch.-metod. sovet po propagande nauch. ateizma).

420   Andriashvili, R.I. *Dogmatika i sotsial'noe uchenie islama* [Dogmatics and Islam's Social Teaching]. Tbilisi: Metsniereba, 1984. 80 pp. In Georgian. Summary in Russian.

421   Andriashvili, R.I. *Musul'manskie bytovye traditsii v Gruzii i puti ikh preodoleniia* [Moslem Social Traditions in Georgia and Means of Overcoming them]. Tbilisi: Sabchota Sakartvelo, 1988. 108 pp. In Georgian.

422   Andriashvili, R.I. *Perezhitki islama v Gruzii* [Islam's Survivals in Georgia]. Tbilisi: Sabchota Sakartvelo, 1983. 141 pp. In Georgian. For review see item 4921.

423   Andriashvili, R.I. *Sovremennyi islam* [Contemporary Islam]. Tbilisi: Znanie GSSR, 30 pp. (Nauch ateizm / O-vo "Znanie" GSSR; No 10). In Georgian.

424   Andriiauskas, A.A. "Problema degumanizatsii kul'tury i iskusstva v kontseptsii 'khristianskogo gumanizma' N. Berdiava" [The Problem of Dehumanization of Culture and Art in N. Berdiaev's Conception of "Christian Humanism"]. *Filos. nauki* 3 (1988): 42-50.

425   Andriushenko, M.T. "Ob otnoshenii very k znaniiu v svete razvitiia nauki" [On Faith's Attitude toward Knowledge in the Light of Development of Science]. *Problemy metodologii nauki.* Irkutsk, 1984. Pp. 15-23.

426   Andronova, V.P. "Khristianskie nizovye obshchiny-novaia forma sotsial'nogo protesta veruiushchikh" [Christian Lower Communities-New Form of Believers Social Protest]. *Latin. Amerika* 11 (1984): 17-30.

427   Andronova, V.P. "'Narodnaia tserkov' v Latinskoi Amerike" ["Popular Church" in Latin America]. *Vopr. nauch. ateizma* 36 (1987): 79-95.

428   Androsov, V.P. "Dialektika rassudochnogo poznaniia v tvorchestve Nagardzhuny" [Dialectics of Rational Cognition in Nagarjuna's Creative Work].

Ratsionalisticheskaia traditsiia i sovremennost'. M., 1988. Kn. 1. Pp. 46-74.

429   Androsov, V.P. "Shantarakshita i proniknovenie indiiskogo buddizma v Tibet" [Shantarakshita and Penetration of Indian Buddhism into Tibet]. *Narody Azii i Afriki* 5 (1981): 112-120.

430   Andrushkevich, O.V. "Buddizm makhaiany o problemakh beskonechnosti i bespredel'nosti" [Mahayana's Buddhism on the Problems of Endlessness and the Boundless]. *Tsybikovkie chteniia.* Ulan-Ude, 1989. Pp. 8-10.

431   Anichas, I.[Iu]. "Ocherednoi kompromiss" [Next Compromise]. *Nauka i Religiia* 3 (1981): 32-33.

432   Anichas, I.[Iu]. *Sotsialisticheskoe gosudarstvo i religioznye kul'ty* [Socialist State and Religious Cults]. Kaunas: Shviesa, 1981. 123 pp. In Polish.

433   Anichas, I.Iu. *SSSR - pervoe gosudarstvo svobody sovesti* [USSR - The First State of Freedom of Worship]. Vil'nius: Znanie LitSSR, 1983. 19 pp. (Material dlia lektora / O-vo "Znanie" LitSSR). In Lithuanian. Bibl.: p. 19.

434   Anichas, I.Iu.; Machiulis, I.I. *Evoliutsiia katolitsizma v SSSR* [Evolution of Catholicism in USSR]. M.: Znanie, 1983. 64 pp. (V pomoshch' lektoru / Vsesoiuz. o-vo "Znanie", sektsiia ateist. vospitaniia).

435   Anichas, I.[Iu].; Machiulis, I.[I]. "Pod natiskom zhizni" [Under Life's Pressure]. *Nauka i religiia* 2 (1980): 29-30.

436   Anisimov, E. "'Novye' bogi, 'novye' idoly. Tseli starye" ["New" Gods, "New" Idols. Goals-Old]. *Molodoi kommunist* 11 (1981): 64-69.

437   Anisimov, E. "Reshaia postavlennye zadachi" [Solving Raised Problems]. *Nauka i religiia* 10 (1981): 8-9.

438   Anisimov. E.I. "Tserkovnaia i podatnaia reformy Petra I" [Peter Ist Church and Tax Reforms]. *Vopr. nauch. ateizma* 37 (1988): 163-172.

439   Anisimoov, S.F.; Gurev, G.A. *Problema smysla zhizni v religii i ateizme* [The Problem of the Meaning of Life in Religion and in Atheism]. M.: Znanie, 1981. 64 pp. (Novoe v zhizni, nauke, tekhnike. Ser. "Nauch. ateizma"; No 6). Bibl.: p. 63.

440 Annanurov, M. "Religioznye perezhitki, sviazannye s doislamskimi verovaniia-mi" [Religious Survivals, Connected with Pre Islamic Beliefs]. *Izv. AN TSSR.* Ser. obshchestv. nauk 3 (1980): 10-15. Summary in English.

441 *Antikommunisticheskaia sushchnost' uniatsko-natsionalisticheskoi fal'sifikatsii istorii ukrainskogo naroda* [Anti Communist Essence of Uniate- Nationalist Falsificatiions of the History of the Ukrainian People]. Ed.: P.L. Iarotskii. Kiev: Vishcha. shk., 1984. 191 pp. In Ukrainian. For review see item 4922.

442 Antoniuk, S.M.; Chistiakov, O.O. "Obshchestvenno-politicheski krizis v Pol'she i katolicheskaia tserkov' (1980-1981)" [Socio-Political Crisis in Poland and the Catholic Church (1980-1981)]. *Vopr. novoi i noveishei istorii.* Kiev, 1989. Vyp. 35. Pp. 40-47.

443 Antonov, A.P.; Solomka, A.P. *Pod prikrytiem very* [Under the Cover of Faith]. Donetsk: Donbas, 1985. 56 pp.

444 Antonov, V.; Akhmedov, A. "Gadanie ili predvidenie?: Zemnye korni sverkh'estestvennogo" [Divination or Foresight?: Supernatural's Earthly Roots]. *Nauka i religiia* 7 (1981): 40-43.

445 Antonova, O.[A]. "Edinstvennoe chudo: Ateizm i muz. iskusstvo" [The Only Miracle: Atheism and Musical Art]. *Nauka i religiia* 5 (1985): 17-19.

446 Antonova, O.A. *Katolitsizm i iskusstvo, XX v.* [Catholicism and Art, XXth C.]. M.: Mysl', 1985. 175 pp., illus. Bibl.: pp. 168-174.

447 Antonova, O.A. "Mesto i rol' muzykal'nogo iskusstva i religii v kul'turno-istoricheskom protsesse" [Place and Role of Musical Art and Religion in the Cultural-Historic Process]. *Vopr. nauch. ateizma* 30 (1982): 78-94.

448 Antonova, O.A. *Sovremennoe zarubezhnoe iskusstvo o khristianskom gumanizme* [Contemporary Foreign Art on Christian Humanism]. M.: Znanie, 1989. 62 pp. (Novoe v zhizni, nauke, tekhnike. Ser.: Nauch. ateizm; 1989, 9).

449 *Apokrify drevnikh khristian* [Ancient Christian Apocryphy]. [Ed.: A.F. Okulov]. M.: Mysl', 1989. 336 pp. (Nauch.-ateist. b-ka). For review see item 4923.

450   *Apostoly dvulikogo Ianusa: Religiia i tserkov' v arsenale ideol. diversantov*
      [Apostles of the Twofaced Janus: Religion and Church in Arsenal of
      Ideological Saboteurs]. Rostov n/D: Kn. izd-vo, 1986. 156 pp.

451   Aptekman, D.M. *Ateisticheskii potentsial sovetskogo obriada i prazdnika*
      [Atheistic Potential of Soviet Ceremonial and Holiday]. M.: Znanie
      RSFSR. Sektsia propagandy nauch. ateizma, 1987. 41 pp. Bibl.: p. 41.

452   Aptekman, D.M. *Ateisticheskoe vospitanie : usloviia i printsipy peres- troiki:*
      [Atheistic Education: Conditions and principles of Perestroika]. M.:
      Znanie. Tsentr. dom nauch. ateizma, 1988. 60 pp.

453   Aptsiauri, N.K. *Istochnikovedcheskie voprosy rasprostraneniia khristianstva na
      Kavkaze* [Problems of the Study of Sources on Dissemination of Christi-
      anity in the Caucasus]. Tbilisi: Izd-vo Tbil. un-ta, 1987. 55 pp. In
      Georgian.

454   *Arabskii Koran* [Arab Koran]. Ufa, 1989. 576 pp. In Arabic.

455   Ardzinba, V.G. "K istorii kul'ta zheleza i kuznechnogo remesla" [History of
      the Cult of Iron and Blacksmith's Profession]. *Drevnii Vostok:
      etnokul'turnye sviazi.* M., 1988. Pp. 263-306. Bibl.: pp. 301-306.

456   Aref'ev, M.A. "Svobodomyslie i ateizm russkikh revoliutsionerov-narodnikov"
      [Freethinking and Atheism of Russian Revolutionary-Populists].
      Sotsial'no-filosofskie aspekty kritiki religii. L., 1987. Pp. 28-44.

457   *Areopagiticheskie razyskaniia* [Investigations in Areopagitika]*. [Comp.: D.
      Sumbadze]. Tbilisi: Izd-vo Tbil. un-ta, 1986. 225 pp., illus. In Georgian.
      Summary in English.

458   Arestov, V.N. "Antiobshchestvennaia sushchnost' religioznogo ekstremizma"
      [Antisocial Essence of Religious Extremism]. *Vopr. ateizma* 25 (1989):
      30-36.

459   Arestov, V.N. *Baptizm bez maski:* Kritika ideologii i praktiki sovrem.
      baptizna [Baptism Without Mask: Criticism of Ideology and Practice of
      Contemporary Baptism]. Khar'kov: Vishcha shk. Izd-vo pri Khar'k. un-te,
      1983. 121 pp. Bibl.: pp 116-119. Name index: pp. 119-120.

460   Arestov, V.N. *Religioznyi ekstremizm:* Soderzh., prichiny i formy proiavleniia,
      puti preodoleniia [Religious Extremism: Content, Reasons and Manifes-

tation Forms, Ways of Overcoming]. Khar'kov: Vishcha shk. Izd-vo pri Khar'k. un-te, 1987. 149 pp. Bibl.: pp. 145-147.

461 Arestov, V.N. *Zhizn' vo lzhi:* Dokum. publitsist. ocherki o relig. ekstremizme [Life in Lie: Documentary-Publicistic Essays on Religious Extremism]. Khar'kov: Prapor, 1983. 86 pp.

462 Arestov, V.N.; Shudrik, I.A. *Iad s dostavkoi na dom:* 'Netradits. religii' v sisteme ideol. diversii imperializma [Home Delivery of Poison: "Nontraditional Religions" in Imperialist System of Ideological Diversions]. Khar'kov: Prapor, 1986. 123 pp. Bibl.: pp. 116-117. Annot. bibl.: pp. 111-115. For review see item 4924.

463 *Argumenty* [Arguments]. M.: Politizdat. Published since 1980, under editorship of P.M. Komarov (1980-1981) and V.I. Garadzha (1982-1989). For reviews see items 4925-4926.

464 Aripov, M.K. *Sotsialnyi ideal islama:* Mify i real'nost' [Islam's Social Ideal: Myths and reality]. Tashkent: Uzbekistan, 1988. 118 pp. Bibl.: pp. 113-117. For review see item 4927.

465 Arkhiepiskop Sinaiskii Damian. "SSSR - strana otkrytosti i mira" [USSR - Country of Openness and Peace]. *Religiia v SSSR.* M., 1987. No 9.

466 Arkun, M. "Lichnost' v islame" [Individual in Islam]. *Sotsiol. issled.* 2 (1989): 103-111.

467 Arnaut, E.K. *Doiti do serdtsa kazhdogo* [To reach Everyone's Heart]. Kishinev: Kartia Moldoveniaske, 1988. 156 pp. Bibl.: pp. 153-155.

468 Aroian, G. "Sotsial'naia spravedlivost' i formirovanie nauchno-ateisticheskogo mirovozzreniia" [Social Justice and Forming Scientific- Atheistic World Outlook]. *Po lenin. puti.* Erevan, 9 (1988): 46-53.

469 Aroian, Ts.Ts. *K svetu* [To Light]. Erevan: Aiastan, 1984. 47 pp. In Armenian.

470 Arsen'ev, V.A.; Danilov, V.I. *Baptisty-raskol'niki - kto oni?* [Baptists-Schismatics - Who are They?]. Khar'kov: Prapor, 1980. 88 pp. Published also as 2nd enlarged ed., 1983. 94 pp.

471   Arsenkin, V.K. "Pochemu sushestvuiut lozhnye orientiry?" [Why Do False
       Reference Points Exist?]. *Molodoi kommunist* 7 (1987): 55-63.

472   Artem'ev, A.I. *Obshchina. Sem'ia. Veruiushchii* [Community. Family.
       Believer]. Alma-Ata: Znanie KazSSR, 1989. 41 pp.

473   Artemova, O.Iu. *Prescribed deception in traditional magic:* (Based on data
       pertaining aboriginal Australia). [Proc. of the] 12th Intern. congr. of
       anthropol. a. ethnological sciences. Zagreb, Yugoslavia, July 24-31, 1988.
       Moskow: Nauka, 1988. 9 pp. Bibl.: pp.8-9.* Russian title: "Verit li koldun
       v svoiu magiiu?".

474   Artikov, V.A. *Effektivnost' ateisticheskoi propagandy* [Effectiveness of
       Atheistic Propaganda]. Tashkent: Uzbekistan, 1982. 80 pp. (B-ka ateista).
       In Uzbek.

475   Artiukh, A.A. "O iazyke ikonopisi" [The Language of Icon-Painting]. *Filos. i
       sotsiol. mysl'* 3 (1989): 34-35.

476   Artiukhov, E.; Ostal'skii, A. "Brat'ia-musul'mane na sluzhbe reaktsii"
       [Moslem-Brotherhood in the Service of Reaction]. *Nauka i religiia* 2
       (1981): 62-63.

477   Artiunova, L.M. "Puti uskoreniia protsessa nauchno-ateisticheskogo
       mirovozzrenia zhenshchin [Ways to Quicken the Forming Process of
       Women's Scientific-Atheistic World Outlook]. *Formirovanie dukhovnoi
       kul'tury lichnosti v usloviiakh uskoreniia sotsial'no-ekonomicheskogo
       razvitiia.* Tashkent, 1988. Pp. 67-72.

478   Artsruni, G.A.; Kalashin, A.G. *Vnedrenie sotsialisticheskoi obriadnosti -
       vazhnyi faktor ateisticheskogo vospitaniia* [Introduction of Socialist
       Ceremonial - Important Factor of Atheistic Education]. Erevan: Znanie
       ArmSSR, 1984. 36 pp. (V pomoshch' lektoru / O-vo "Znanie" ArmSSR).
       (Reshenie iiun'skogo (1983) Plenuma - v zhizn'). In Armenian. Bibl.: p.
       36. In Uzbek.

479   Artykov, A.[A]. *Kritika fal'sifikatsii polozheniia islama i musul'man v
       Uzbekistane* [Criticism of Falsifications on the Position of Islam and
       Moslems in Uzbekistan]. Tashkent: Znanie UzSSR, 1981. 23 pp. (V
       pomoshch' lektoru / O-vo "Znanie" UzSSR. Ser. obshchestv.-
       politicheskaia). In Uzbek.

480   Artykov, A.[A]. *Sovetskaia intelligentsiia i ateisticheskoe vospitanie* [Soviet Intelligentsia and Atheistic Education]. Tashkent: Uzbekistan, 1984. 31 pp. (Ser. "Marksizm-leninizm"; No 7). In Uzbek.

481   Arutiunov, S.A.; Zhukovskaia, N.L. *'Sviatye' relikvii: Mif i deistvitel'nost'* ["Holy" Relics: Myth and Reality]. M.: Politizdat, 1987. 109 pp., illus. (Besedy o mire i cheloveke).

482   Arutiunov, S.[A].; Zhukovskaia, N.L. "Turinskaia plashchanitsa: Otpechatok tela ili tvorenie khudozhnika?" [Turin's Shroud of Christ: Body Print or Painter's Creation?]. *Nauka i religiia* 9 (1984): 18-23.

483   Arzhanukhin, V.V. "Kritika pravoslavnogo i religiozno-filosofskogo idealov ratsional'nosti" [Criticism of Orthodox and Religious-Philosophical Ideals of Rationality]. *Nauchnyi ateizm: ideal i mirovozzrenie*. Perm', 1988. Pp. 74-82.

484   Arzhanukhin, V.V. *Russkaia dukhovnaia kul'tyra i pravoslavnoe bogoslovie* [Russian Spiritual Culture and Orthodox Theology]. L.: Znanie RSFSR, 1984. 17 pp. (V pomoshch' lektoru / O-vo "Znanie" RSFSR, Leningr. org.). Bibl.: p. 17.

485   Arzuev, U.; Normatov, K. "Umenie ubezhdat'" [Ability to Convince]. *Agitator* 13 (1980): 50-53.

486   Ashin, B.A. "Anglo-amerikanskaia burzhuaznaia istoriografiia vzaimoot-noshenii sovetskogo gosudarstva i russkoi pravoslavnoi tserkvi v 1921-1922 godakh" [Anglo-American Bourgeois Historiography on Interrelation of the Soviet State and the Russian Orthodox Church in 1921-1922]. *Zarubezhnaia istoriografiia sotsial'no-politicheskogo razvitiia SSSR* M., 1989. Pp. 64-75.

487   Ashirov, N. *Islam i natsii* [Islam and Nations]. Alma-Ata: Kazakhstan, 1982. 168 pp. In Kazakh.

488   Ashirov, N. *Nravstvennye poucheniia sovremennogo islama* [Moral Precepts of Contemporary Islam]. Alma-Ata: Kazakhstan, 1982. 81 pp. In Uigur.

489   Ashirov, N.; Ismailov, Kh.I. *Kritika antisovetskoi fal'sifikatsii polozheniia islama i musul'man v SSSR* [Critique of the Anti-Soviet Falsifications on the Position of Islam and Moslems in USSR]. M.: Znanie, 1982. 64 pp. (Novoe v zhizni, nauke, tekhnike. Ser. "Nauch. ateizm"; 4). Bibl.: p. 63.

Published also in:
Alma-Ata: Kazakhstan, 1984. 64 pp., in Kazakh, and in 1985, 85 pp., in Uigur.

490   Ashrafian, K.[Z]. "Nirankari" [Nirankari]. *Aziia i Afrika segodnia* 4 (1981): 59-62.

491   Ashrafian, K.Z. *Religiia v sovremennoi obshchestvenno-politicheskoi zhizni Indii* [Religion in Contemporary Socio-Political Life in India]. M.: Nauka, 1982. 7 pp. Bibl.: p. 7.

492   Ashrafian, K.Z. "Sikkhizm v obshchestvennoi zhizni Indii (XVI - nachalo 80-kh godov XX v.)" [Sikhism in Social Life in India (XVIth - early 80s XXth C.)]. *Religii mira*. 1986. M., 1987. Pp. 100-119.

493   Asildinov, A. "Esli ty ne posadish' iabloniu..." [If You Will Not Plant an Apple-tree...]. *Nauka i religiia* 2 (1982): 35-39.

494   Asliddinov, S. "Religiia i molodezh'" [Religion and Youth]. *Problemy formirovaniia nauuchno-ateisticheskogo mirovozzreniia v sotsialisticheskom obshchestve*. Samarkand, 1980. Pp. 41-44.

495   Astakhova, V.G. *Sotvorenie ili evoliutsiia?* [Creation or Evolution?]. M.: Politizdat, 1981. 95 pp., illus. (Besedy o mire i cheloveke). Published also in:
Kishinev: Kartia moldoveniaske, 1983. 95 pp., illus., in Moldavian.

496   *Astrologicheskii pomoshchnik '1990* [Astrological Aid for 1990]. [Comp.: Edda and Eduard Paukson]. [Tallinn]: Profsoiuz rabotnikov kul'tury ESSR, [1989?]. 117 pp., illus. In Estonian.

497   Ataniiazov, S. "Ob ispol'zovanii toponimicheskikh materialov v bor'be s religioznymi perezhitkami" [The Use of Toponymical Materials in the Struggle with Religious Survivals]. *Izv. AN TSSR*. Ser. obshchestv. nauk 1 (1985): 71-75. Summary in English.

498   *Ateisticheskaia propaganda v mnogotirazhnoi pechati* [Atheistic Propaganda in Large Editioned Press]. Comp.: B. Mar'ianov. M.: Znanie, 1984. 8 pp.

499   *Ateisticheskie chteniia* [Atheistic Readings]. M.: Politizdat. Published since 1966.
Vyp. 11. 1980. 97 pp., illus.

[Vyp.] 12. 1982. 95 pp., illus.
Vyp. 13. 1984. 95 pp., illus.
Vyp. 14. 1985. 103 pp., illus.
Vyp. 15. 1986. 111 pp., illus.
Vyp. 16. 1986. 111 pp., illus.
Vyp. 18. 1989. 111 pp., illus. For review see item 4934.

500   *Ateisticheskie chteniia* [Atheistic Readings]. M.: Politizdat, 1981. 302 pp.,
       illus. Published also in 1988, 343 pp., illus.; 1989, 343 pp., illus.

501   *Ateisticheskie ocherki* [Atheistic Essays]. [Ed.: O.D. Leonova]. Petrozavodsk:
       Kareliia, 1983. 126 pp. (V pomoshch' propagandistu).

502   *Ateisticheskie traditsii russkogo naroda* [Atheistic Traditions of the Russian
       People]. [Ed.: L.I. Emeliakh]. L.: GMIRIA, 1982. 160 pp.

503   "Ateisticheskoe obrazovanie uchitelei i vospitanie uchashchikhsia" [Teacher's
       Atheistic Education and Pupils Upbringing]. *Sov. pedagogika* 3 (1989):
       41-46.

504   *Ateisticheskoe vospitanie* [Atheistic Education]. M., Znanie. (V pomoshch'
       agitatoru i politinformatoru; Ser. 5).
       Vyp. 2-3. *Religiia v arsenale antikomunizma* [Religion in the Arsenal of
       Anti Communism]. 1981. 48 pp. Bibl.: pp. 46-47.
       Vyp. 4. *Rol' sotsialisticheskoi obriadnosti v preodolenii religioznykh traditsii
       i obychaev* [The Role of Socialist Ceremonials in Overcoming Religious
       Traditions and Customs]. 1981. 16 pp.
       Vyp. 5-6. *Sovetskoe zakonodatel'stvo o religioznykh kul'takh* [Soviet
       Legislation on Religious Cults]. 1981. 30 pp.
       Vyp. 7. *Katolitsizm v sovremennom mire* [Catholicism in Contemporary
       World]. 1981. 16 pp.
       Vyp. 8. *Ateisticheskoe vospitanie v trudovom kollektive* [Atheistic Education
       in Labour Collective]. 1982. 16 pp. Bibl.: p. 15.
       Vyp. 9. *Gumanizm marksistskogo ateizma* [Humanism of Marxist
       Atheism]. 1983. 16 pp.

505   *Ateisticheskoe vospitanie*: Formy i metody [Atheistic Education: Forms and
       Methods]. M.: Znanie, 1981. 64 pp. (Novoe v zhizni, nauke, tekhnike.
       Ser. "Nauchnyi ateizm"; No 10). Bibl.: pp. 64. For review see item 4937.

506   *Ateisticheskoe vospitanie*: Poisk, problemy [Atheistic Education: Search, Problems]. [Comp.: V.G. Gutsu]. Kishinev: Kartia moldoveniaske, 1988. 343 pp. For Reviews see items 4938-4939.

507   *Ateisticheskoe vospitanie*: Soderzhanie, formy i metody [Atheistic Education: Content, Forms and Methods]. [Ed.: A.S. Onishchenko et al]. Kiev: Politizdat Ukrainy, 1989. 288 pp. (Aktual. probl. kom. vospitaniia: APKV). Annot. bibl.: pp. 284-286.

508   *Ateisticheskoe vospitanie: Voprosy i otvety* [Atheistic Education: Questions and Answers]. [Comp.: V.M. Kuveneva]. M.: Politizdat, 1983. 256 pp. For reviews see items 4940-4941.

509   *Ateisticheskoe vospitanie naseleniia* [Atheistic Education of Population]. [Comp.: E.N. Kozik; E.V. Proka]. Kishinev: Kartia moldoveniaske, 1987. 201 pp. In Moldavian.

510   *Ateisticheskoe vospitanie shkol'nikov* [Atheistic Upbringing of Schoolboys]. Ed.: R.M. Rogova. M.: Prosveshchenie, 1986. 192 pp. For review see item 4942.

511   *Ateisticheskoe vospitanie shkol'nikkov*: Materialy seminara, proved. v g. Moskve 14 Maia 1987 g. [Atheistic Upbringing of Schoolboys: Seminary materials, Moscow, 14th May 1987]. [Ed.: O.G. Budnaia; V.G. Lebedeva]. M.: [S.n.], 1987. 68 pp. Bibl.: pp. 66-67.

512   *Ateisticheskoe vospitanie shkol'nikov*: Uch. posob. dlia uchitelia [Atheistic Upbringing of Schoolboys: Teacher's Text Book]. Ed.: R.M. Rogova. Frunze: Mektep, 1988. 206 pp. In Kirghiz.

513   *Ateisticheskoe vospitanie v truduvom kollektive* [Atheistic Education in Labour Collective]. [Comp.: N.V. Aivazova]. M.: Profizdat, 1984. 80 pp. (B-chka profsoiuz. aktivista; 4). Bibl.: pp. 76-79.

514   *Ateisticheskoi rabote - effektivnost'* [Effectiveness in Atheistic Work]. [Comp.: I.I. Semenov]. Cheboksary: Chuvash. kn. izd-vo, 1986. 125 pp.

515   *Ateisticheskomu vospitaniiu - delovitost' i konkretnost'*: Opyt. Razmyshleniia. Problemy [Efficiency and Concreteness in Atheistic Education: Trial. Reflections. Problems]. [Comp.: A.E. Vlasenko]. Rostov n/D: Kn. izd-vo, 1980. 207 pp.

516   *Ateisty Kubani rasskazyvaiut...* [Kuban's Atheists Recount...]. [Comp.: P.M. Stepanov]. Krasnodar: Kn. izd-vo, 1983. Kn. 1. 1983. 191 pp.; Kn. 2. 1988. 180 pp. For review see item 4943.

517   *Ateisty za rabotoi* [Atheists at Work]. [E.Ia. Komissarova et al]. Cheliabinsk: Iuzh.-Ural. kn. izd-vo, 1985. 121 pp.

518   *Ateizm, religiia i ideologicheskaia bor'ba* [Atheism, Religion and Ideological Struggle]. [Ed.: A. Gaidis et al]. Vil'nius: Mintis, 1985. 116 pp. (Ideol. bor'ba v sovrem. mire). In Lithuanian. Nauch.-ateist. lit. Bibl.: p. 115.

519   *Ateizm i dukhovnaia kul'tura* [Atheism and Spiritual Culture]. Ed.: V.A. Zots. Kiev: Vishcha shk., 1985. 437 pp. Name index: pp. 428-435. For review see item 4944.

520   *Ateizm i dukhovnyi mir sovetskogo cheloveka* [Atheism and Spiritual World of the Soviet Man]. Compil.: E.V. Asimov. M.: Znanie, 1983. 63 pp. (Novoe v zhizni, nauke, tekhnike. Nauch. ateizm; 12). Bibl.: p. 62.

521   *Ateizm i nauchno-ateisticheskoe vospitaniie* [Atheism and Scientific- Atheistic Education]. Ed.: A.I. Abdusamedov. Tashkent: TashGU, 1985 [1986], 87 pp.

522   *Ateizm i obshchestvennyi progress* [Atheism and Social Progress]. [B.A. Lobovik et al]. Kiev: Politizdat Ukrainy, 1981. 152 pp. In Ukrainian.

523   *Ateizm i religiia: Voprosy i otvety* [Atheism and Religion: Questions and Answers]. Comp.: V.M. Kuveneva. M.: Politizdat, 1988. 1988/Alekseev, V.A. et al. 208 pp.

524   *Ateizm i religiia v Buriatii* [Atheism and Religion in Buriat]. Ulan-Ude: Buriat. kn. izd-vo, 1986. 80 pp.

525   *Ateizm i religiia v Litve* [Atheism and Religion in Lithuania]. [Comp.: I. Machiulis]. Vil'nius: Mintis, 1985. 224 pp. In Lithuanian. Bibl.: pp. 222-223. For review see item 4945.

526   *Ateizm i sotsialisticheskaia kul'tura* [Atheism and Socialist Culture]. [Ed.: V.S. Solov'ev et al]. Ioshkar-Ola: Mariiskoe kn. izd-vo, 1982. 112 pp.

527   *Ateizm i sovremennost'* [Atheism and Contemporaneity]. [Ed.: I. Machiulis et al]. Vil'nius: Mintiis, 1983. 157 pp. In Lithuanian.

528   *Ateizm v kommunisticheskom vospitanii* [Atheism in Communist Education].
      Ed.: S. Redzhepov; A. Khonydov. Ashkhabad: Ylym, 1986. 135 pp. Annot.
      bibl.: 132-134. In Turkmen.

529   *Ateizm v SSSR:* Stanovlenie i razvitie [Atheism in USSR: Formation and
      Development]. Ed.: A.F. Okulov. M.: Mysl', 1986. 238 pp. For reviews
      see items 4946-4948.

530   Atoev, K. "Religioznaia situatsiia v sovremennom Afganistane" [Religious
      Situation in Contemporary Afghanistan]. *Voprosy teorii i praktiki
      nauchnogo ateizma.* M., 1988. Pp. 197-219.

531   Avdeeva, L. "Ramadan v Irane" [Ramadan in Iran]. *Nauka i kul'tura* 4
      (1985): 61.

532   Averichev, E.P. "Osobennosti formirovaniia ateisticheski orientirovannogo
      obshchestvennogo mneniia na sele". [Structural Features of Atheistic
      Orientated Public Opinion in the Village]. *Nauchnyi ateizm i obshchest-
      vennoe mnenie.* M., 1987. Pp. 113-129.

533   Averintsev, S.[S]. "Khristianstvo - vek trinadtsatyi" [Christianity - Thirteenth
      Century]. *Nauka i religiia* 6 (1988): 38.

534   Averintsev, S.S. "Novyi zavet" [New Testament]. *V mire knig* 11 (1988):
      23-24.

535   Averintsev, S.S. "Spetsifika obraza raia v siriiskoi literature" [Specificity of
      the Image of Paradise in Syrian Literature]. *Problemy istoricheskoi poetiki
      literatur Vostoka.* M., 1988. Pp. 138-151. Bibl. p. 151.

536   Averintsev, S.S. "Vizantiia i Rus': Dva tipa dukhovnosti" [Byzantium and
      Rus': Two Types of Spirituality]. *Novyi mir* 7 (1988): 210-220; 9 (1988):
      227-239.

537   Avksent'ev, A.V. *Islam na Severnom Kavkaze* [Islam in Northern Caucasus].
      2nd revised. and enlarged ed. Stavropol': Kn. izd-vo, 1984. 287 pp. Annot.
      bibl.: pp. 281-286. For review see item 4949.

538   Avksent'ev, A.V.; Mavliutov, R.R. *Kniga o Korane* [The Book on the
      Koran]. 2nd revised ed. Stavropol': Kn. izd-vo, 1984. 191 pp. Bibl.: pp.
      189-190. Published also in:

Cherkesk: Stavrop. kn. izd-vo. Karachaevo-Cherkes. otd-nie, 1985. 215 pp., in Karachaev and in 1986. 204 pp., in Kabardino-Circassian. For reviews see items 4950-4951.

539 Avshalumova, L.[Kh]. "Chto nam nuzhno" [What Do We Need]. *Sov. Dagestan* 1 (1988): 31-32.

540 Avshalumova, L.Kh. *Kritika iudaizma i sionizma* [Critique of Judaism and Zionism]. Makhachkala: Dag. kn. izd-vo, 1986. 173 pp. Annot. bibl.: pp. 166-172.

541 Avtandilian, A.N. "Dlia formirovaniia ubezhdennykh ateistov" [For Shaping Convinced Atheists]. *Vestn. vyssh. shk.* 1 (1983): 60-64.

542 Azarenko, S.A. "Mifologicheskii aspekt liubvi kak fenomena kul'tury" [Mythological Aspect of Love as a Cultural Phenomenon]. *Otnoshenie cheloveka k irratsional'nomu.* Sverdlovsk, 1989. Pp. 251-276.

543 Azevedo, K.de. "Evoliutsiia brazil'skoi tserkvi" [Evolution of the Brazilian Church]. *Latin. Amerika* 9 (1980): 82-86.

544 Azhibekova, K.A. *Osobennosti ateisticheskogo vospitaniia molodezhi v usloviiakh NTR* [Features of Atheistic Upbringing of Youth under Conditions of NTR]. Frunze: Kyrgyestan, 1988. 81 pp. (BA: B-chka ateista). Annot. bibl.: pp. 79-80.

545 Azikuri, N.E. "'Kotori' kak ritual'nyi khleb v Tusheti" ["Kotori" as Ritual Bread in Tushet]. *Materialy po etnografii Gruzii.* Tbilisi, 1987. T. 23. Pp. 216-223. In Georgian. Summary in Russian.

546 Azimov, A.V. *V nachale* [At the Beginning]. Trans. from English by V. Babenko; Vl. Gakova. M.: Politizdat, 1989. 374 pp., illus. Excerpts from this book were serialized in *Nauka i religiia* 7 (1987)-10 (1988).

547 Azizov, S.A. "Nekotorye obriady agrarnogo tsikla u narodov Iuzhnogo Dagestana v XIX- nach.XX v." [Some Rituals of Agrarian Cycle of South Daghestan Peoples in XIXth - early XXth C.]. *Kalendar' i kalendarnye obriady narodov Dagestana.* Makhachkala, 1987. Pp. 71-74.

548 Azizova, Z.S. "Iz ateisticheskogo naslediia S. Agamali ogly" [S. Agamali Ogly's Atheistic Heritage]. *Dokl/AN AzSSR.* T. 41. 12 (1985): 77-78. Summary in Azerbaijan and English.

549   Babakhan, Sh. "Kak bylo obrazovano dukhovnoe upravlenie musul'man Srednei Azii i Kazakhstana" [How Moslem's Spiritual Administration was Formed in Middle Asia and Kazakhstan]. *Religiia v SSSR* 10 (1987): ISh 1-ISh 2.

550   Babakhan, Sh. "Kak zhivut musul'mane v Sovetskom Soiuze" [How Moslems Live in Soviet Union]. *Religiia v SSSR* 7 (1987): MB 1-MB 2.

551   Babakhan, Sh. "Velikii Oktiabr' i musul'mane" [The Great October and Moslems]. *Religiia v SSSR* 9 (1987): ISh 1-ISh 3.

552   Babakhan, Z.I. *Islam i musul'mane v Strane Sovetov* [Islam and Moslems in the Land of Soviets]. M.: Progress, 1980. 182 pp., illus. In English.
       Published also by Progress in Dari (1980. 215 pp., illus.) and Bengali (1984. 176 pp., illus.).

553   Babakhanov, Sh.Z. *Mufti Ziia ed-Din Khan i ego ideinoe nasledie* [The Mufti Zyya ed-Din Khan and His Ideological Legacy]. M.: Vneshtorgizdat, 1986. 318 pp. in Arabian pagination, illus. In Arabic.

554   Babii, A.I. "Pravoslavie v istorii Moldavii: Domysly i fakty" [Orthodoxy in the History of Moldavia: Conjectures and Facts]. *Izv. AN MSSR.* Ser. Obshchestv. nauk 1 (1988): 49-58.

555   Babii, A.I. *Pravoslavie v Moldavii:* Istoriia i sovremennost' [Orthodoxy in Moldavia: History and Contemporaneity]. Kishinev: Kartia moldoveniaske, 1988. 85 pp. For review see item 4952.

556   Babii, A.I. et al. *Preodolenie religii i utverzhdenie ateizma v Moldavskoi SSR* [Prevailing. over Religion and Confirming Atheism in Moldavian SSR]. Kishinev: Shtiintsa, 1983. 196 pp. For review see item 4953.

557   'Babii, A.[I].; Ganenko, A. "Vazhnoe zveno atesticheskogo vospitaniia trudiashchikhsia" [Important Link of Workers Atheistic Education]. *Kommunist Moldavii* 6 (1980): 27-33.

558   Babii, M.A. "Nesostoiatel'nost' 'sovetologicheskoi' kontseptsii 'ateistic-heskogo gosudarstva'" [Groundlessness of "Sovietologic" Conception of "Atheistic State"]. *Vopr. nauch. ateizma* 27 (1981): 212-231.

559   Babinov, Iu.A. "Nesostoiatel'nost' burzhuazno-klerikal'nykh izvrashchenii dukhovnoi kul'tury sotsialisticheskogo obshchestva" [Groundlessness of

Bourgeois-Clerical Distortions of Socialist Society's Spiritual Culture]. *Vopr. nauch. ateizma* 73 (1988): 120-126.

560   Babosov, E.M. *Istina i bogoslovie* [Truth and Theology]. Minsk: Belarus', 1988. 416 pp. Annot. bibl.: pp. 391-397. Subject and name index: pp. 398-415. For reviews see item 4954-4955.

561   Babasov, E.M. *Nauchno-tekhnicheskaia revoliutsiia i utverzhdenie ateisticheskogo mirovozzreniia* [Scientific-Technical Revolution and Affirmation of the Atheistic World Outlook]. M.: Znanie, 1982. 64 pp. (Novoe v zhizni, nauke , tekhnike. Nauch. ateizm; 2). Bibl.: p. 63. For review see item 4956.

562   Babasov, E.[M]. "O chem govoriat issledovaniia: Na ateist. temy" [What Researches Point To: On Atheistic Themes]. *Agitator* 6 (1984): 37-39.

563   Babosov, E.M. "Propaganda nauchno-materialisticheskikh vzgliadov sredi naseleniia" [Propaganda of Scientific-Materialist Views Among the Population]. *Vopr. nauch. ateizma* 34 (1986): 44-58.

564   Babosov, E.M.; Prokoshina, E.S. "Real'nyi sotsializm i utverzhdenie ateisticheskoi ubezhdennosti" [Real Socialism and Consolidation of Atheistic Conviction]. *Nauch. ateizm i ateist. vospitanie* 1 (1983): 12-25.

565   Badrul Alam Khan. "Islam v Narodnoi Respublike Bangladesh " [Islam in the Popular Republic of Bangladesh]. *Filosofskaia i obshchestvennaia mysl' stran Azii i Afriki.* M., 1981. Pp. 142-154.

566   Bagirli, R. "Krepit' sviaz' ateisticheskoi propagandy s zhizn'iu" [To Strengthen the Connection of Atheistic Propaganda with Life]. *Kommunist Azerbaidzhana* 10 (1983): 42-47.

567   Bagranovskii, A.E. "Religioznye otnosheniia v strukture obshchestvennykh otnoshenii" [Religious Attitudes in the Structure of Social Relations]. *Molodezh' i tvorchestvo:* Sotsial'no-filosofskie problemy. M., 1988. Ch. 3. Pp. 290-292.

568   Bagrov, N.V. "Effekt vzaimodeistviia" [Effect of Interaction]. *Vopr. nauch. ateizma* 29 (1982): 55-70.

569   Bai, O. "Zemnye dela tserkvi: Beseda s molodym mitropolitom Rus. pravoslav. tserkvi" [Church's Earthly Affairs: Conversation with the Young

Metropolitan of the Russian Orthodox Church]. *Novoe vremia* 24 (1988): 26.

570   Bai, O; Podshibiakin, V. "Russkie staroobriadtsy" [Russian Old-Believers]. *Novoe vremia* 33 (1988): 48.

571   Baialieva, T.D. *Religioznye perezhitki u kirgizov i ikh preodolenie* [Religious Survivals among Kirghiz and their Overcoming]. Frunze: Ilim, 1981. 101 pp., illus.

572   Baiburtian, A.V. "Deiatel'nost' missionerov ordena karmelitov sredi armianskogo naseleniia Irana (XVII v.) [Activity of Missionaries of Carmelite Order among Iran's Armenian Population (XVIIth C.]. *Vestn. obshchestv. nauk* / AN ArmSSR. Erevan, 1988. Pp. 51-61. In Armenian. Summary in Russian.

573   Baidin, V.I. "Ural'skoe staroobriadchestvo kontsa XVII - serediny XIX v. v dorevoliutsionnoi i sovetskoi istoriografii" [Urals Old Belief at the end of XVIIth - middle XIXth C. in Prerevolutionary and Soviet Historiography]. *Istoriografiia obshchestvennoi mysli dorevoliutsionnogo Urala.* Sverdlovsk, 1988. Pp. 43-50.

574   Baidin, V.I.; Shashkov, A.T. "Istoricheskie sochineniia Ural'skikh staroobriadtsev XVIII - XIX vv." [Historical Works of Urals Old Believers of the XVIIIth -XIXth Centuries]. *Istoriografiia obshchestvennoi mysli dorevoliutsionnogo Urala.* Sverdlovsk, 1988. Pp. 4-9.

575   Baikabilova, R. *XXVI s'ezd KPSS o povyshenii effektivnosti i deistvennosti ateisticheskogo vospitaniia* [XXVIth CPSU Congress on Raising the Effectiveness and Efficacy of Atheistic Education]. Tashkent: Znanie UzSSR, 1982. 24 pp. (V pomoshch' lektoru / O-vo "Znanie" UzSSR. Ser. obshchestv.--politicheskaia). In Uzbek.

576   Baimuradov, N. "Svoboda sovesti: Kak ee ponimat'?" [Freedom of Worship: How to Comprehend It]. *Kommunist Tadzhikistana* 1 (1987): 57-61.

577   Baimurzaev, A.B. *Formirovanie sotsialisticheskogo pravosoznaniia narodov Dagestana* [Formation of Socialist Sense of Justice by Daghestan Peoples]. Makhachkala: Dag. kn. izd-vo, 1984. 139 pp.

578   Baipakov, K.M. "Kul't ognia na Syrdar'e" [The Cult of Fire in Syrdar]. *Izv. AN KazSSR.* Ser. obshchestv. nauk 5 (1987): 51-61.

579 Bairamov, E.Z. *S chem idesh' k liudiam?* [With what are you Going to the People?]. M.: Sovetskaia Rossiia 1988. 141 pp.

580 Bairamov, E.Z. *V otvete za cheloveka:* Zametki propagandista ateizma [Be Answerable for Man: Remarks of a Propagandist of Atheism]. M.: Politizdat, 1983. 80 pp. (B-ka ateista).

581 Bairamov, E.Z. *Zabroshennye chetki:* Razgovor po dusham s posledovateliami islama [Abandoned Rosaries: Heart-to-Heart Talk with Followers of Islam]. M.: Politizdat, 1985. 189 pp. For review see item 4958.

582 Bairamsakhatov, N. "Ateisticheskoe vospitanie molodezhi: Sostoianie i napravleniia" [Youth's Atheistic Upbringing: Condition and Direction]. *Turkmenistan kommunisti* 6 (1987): 18-24. In Turkmen.

583 Bairamsakhatov, N. *Dukhovnaia kul'tura naroda i ateizm* [Peoples' Spiritual Culture and Atheism]. Ashkhabad: Turkmenistan, 1981. 223 pp.

584 Bairamsakhatov, N. *Pravda ob islame* [The Truth about Islam]. Ashkhabad: Turkmenistan, 1988. 397 pp. In Turkmen.

585 Bakaev, Iu.N. "Antireligioznaia rabota v Sibirskoi derevne (1920-1929 gg)" [Antireligious Work in Siberian Village (1920-1929)]. *Kul't. razvitie Sov. Sib. derevni.* Novosibirsk, 1980. Pp. 62-75

586 Bakaev, Iu.N. *Voprosy nauchnogo ateizma v kurse istorii KPSS* [Problems of Scientific Atheism in the CPSU History Course]. Khabarovsk: Kn. izd-vo, 1988. 160 pp. Bibl.: pp. 158-159.

587 Bakaeva, E.P. "Kalendarnye prazdniki kalmykov: Problemy sootnosheniia drevnikh verovanii i lamaizma (XIX-nachale XX vv.)" [Kalmyk's Calendar Holidays: Problems of Correlation of Ancient Beliefs and Lamaism (XIXth-early XXth C.)]. *Voprosy istorii lamaizma v Kalmykii.* Elista, 1987. Pp. 71-87.

588 Bakanurskii, A.G. *Antiklerikal'nye traditsii ukrainskogo folklora* [Anti Clerical Traditions of Ukrainian Folklore]. Kiev: Znanie UkSSR, 1988. 48 pp. (Ser. 5. Nuachno-Ateisticheskaia / O-vo "Znanie" UkSSR; No 12). Bibl.: pp. 47-48. In Ukrainian.

589 Bakanurskii, A.G. "Kritika protestantskogo modernizma na primere 'teologii igry' Kharveia Koksa" [Critique of Protestant Modernism on Example of Harvey Cox's "Theology of Festivity"]. *Vopr. ateizma* 18 (1982): 120-127.

590 Bakanurskii, A.G. *Pravoslavnaia tserkov' i skomoroshestvo* [Orthodox Church and Buffoonery]. M.: Znanie, 1986. 63 pp. (Novoe v zhizni, nauke, tekhnike. Nauch. ateizm; 5/1986).

591 Bakanurskii, G.L. *Bibleiskie dogmy i politicheskie spekuliatsii:* Sionist. klerikalizatsiia iudaizma [Biblical Dogmas and Polical Speculations: Zionist Clericalization of Judaism]. Kiev: Znanie UkSSR, 1985. 49 pp. (Ser. V "Naucno-ateisticheskaia" / O-vo "Znanie" UkSSR; No 6). Annot. bibl.: p. 49.

592 Bakanurskii, G.L. *Iudeiskii klerikalizm - orudie antikommunizma* [Judaic Clericalism - an Anti Communist Tool]. Kiev: Politizdat Ukrainy, 1985. 41 pp.

593 Bakanurskii, G.L. *Iudeisko-sionistskii soiuz i prava cheloveka* [Judeo-Zionist Union and the Rights of Man]. Kiev: Znanie UkSSR, 1981. 48 pp. (Nauch.-ateist. ser. O-vo "Znanie" UkSSR; No 6). Bibl.: p. 48.

594 Bakanurskii, G.L. "Kritika iudeiskogo klerikalizma i sionizma" [Criticism of Judaic Clericalism and Zionism]. *Prepodavanie nauchnogo ateizma v vuze.* M., 1988. Pp. 143-158.

595 Bakanurskii, G.L. *Krizis i modernizatsiia iudaizma* [Crisis and Modernization of Judaism]. M.: Znanie, 1980. 64 pp. (Novoe v zhizni, nauke, tekhnike. Ser. "Nauch. ateizm"; No 2).

596 Bakanurskii, G.L. *Lozhnye doktriny, reaktsionnaia politika: Kritika soiuza iudeiskoi religii i sionizma* [False Doctrines, Reactionary Policy: Critique of the Union of Judaic Religion and Zionism]. Odessa: Maiak, 1982. 240 pp. Bibl.: pp. 231-239. For reviews see item 4959-4960.

597 Bakanurskii, G.L. *Reaktsionnyi al'ians: Iudeiskii klerikalizm i sionizm* [Reactionary Alliance: Judaic Clericalism and Zionism]. M.: Znanie, 1988. 64 pp. (Novoe v zhizni, nauke, tekhnike. Ser. "Nauch. ateizm"; 3/1988). Bibl.: p. 63.

598 Bakanurskii, G.[L]. "Sionizatsiia iudaizma" [Zionisation of Atheism]. *Nauka i religiia* 1 (1981): 53-56.

599 Bakanurskii, G.[L]. "Spekuliruia na vetkhozavetnykh dogmakh" [Speculating on Old Testament's Dogmas]. *Nauka i religiia* 8 (1983): 28-31.

600 Bakhrushin, S. "K voprosu o kreshchenii Kievskoi Rusi" [On the Question of the Baptism of Kievan Rus']. *Khriastianstvo i Rus'*. M., 1988. Pp. 31-46.

601 Bakhtiiarova, L.I. "Velikii Oktabr' i sotsial'naia baza massovogo ateizma" [The Great October and Social Basis of Mass Atheism]. *Trudy konferentsii molodykh uchenykh Akademii nauk "Velikii Oktiabr' i sovremennost'*: Aktual'nye problemy obshchestvovedeniia". Baku, 1988. Pp. 15-16.

602 Bakhtin, G.T.; Dem'ianov, A.I. "Rol' sotsiologicheskikh issledovanii v formirovanii ateisticheskoi ubezhdennosti studentov [Role of Sociological Researches in Forming Students' Atheistic Conviction]. *Aktual. vopr. metodiki prepodavaniia obshchestv. nauk i kom. vospitaniia studentov* 5 (1987): 100-108.

603 Bakradze, A.T. *Kritika russkoi religioznoi filosofii XIX-XX vekov* [Critique of Russian Religious Philosophy of the XIXth–XXth Centuries]. Tbilisi: Metsniereba, 1982. 187 pp.

604 Baktimirova, N.N. *Buddiiskaia sangkha v nezavisimoi Kampuchii* [Buddhist Sangha in Independent Kampuchea]. M.: Nauka, 1981. 181 pp. Annot. bibl.: pp. 160-171. Name and geographical index: pp. 178-180.

605 Bakusev, V.M. "Nekotorye aspekty svobodomysliia Ekkharta" [Some Aspects of Eckhart's Free Thinking]. *Kritika religioznoi ideologii i problemy ateisticheskogo vospitaniia* M., 1982. Pp. 67-75.

606 Balagushkin, E.G. *Kritika ideologii i praktiki sovremennogo krishnaizma* [Criticism of Ideology and Practice of Contemporary Krishnaism]. M.: Znanie, 1984. 64 pp. Bibl.: p. 64. Annot. bibl.: p. 63.

607 Balagushkin, E.G. *Kritika sovremennykh netraditsionnykh religii:* Istoki, sushchnost', vliianie na molodezh' Zapada [Criticism of Contemporary Non Traditional Religions: Sources, Essence, Influence on Western Youth]. M.: Izd-vo MGU, 1984. 286 pp. Bibl.: pp. 280-284. For review see item 4961.

608 Balagushkin, E.G. "Neoorientalizm: religiozno-misticheskie kul'ty i ideinye iskaniia Zapada [Neo-Orientalism: Religious-Mystical Cults and Western's Ideological Quests]. *Vopr. nauch. ateisma* 32 (1985): 103-125.

609 Balagushkin, E.G. *Netraditsionnye religii v kapitalisticheskikh stranakh Zapada i ikh vliianie na molodezh'* [Non Traditional Religions in Capitalist Countries of the West and Their Influence on Youth]. M.: Izd-vo MGU, 1980. 103 pp. Bibl. pp. 100-102.

610 Balagushkin, E.[G]. "Stavka na mistiku i okkul'tizm" [Counting on Mysticism and Occultism]. *Molodezh'. Religiia. Ateizm.* 4 (1988): 40-63.

611 Balakireva, R.S. et al. *Rol' trudovykh kollektivov v formirovanii ateisticheskoi ubezhdennosti molodezhi* [Role of Working Collectives in Forming Atheistic Conviction of Youth]. Kiev: Znanie UkSSR, 1983. 47 pp. (Ser V "Nauchno-ateisticheskaia" / O-vo "Znanie" UkSSR; No 7). In Ukrainian. Bibl.: p. 46. Annot. bibl.: pp. 44-45.

612 Balandin, R.K. *Chudo ili nauchnaia zagadka?: Nauka i religiia o Turin. plashchanitse* [Miracle or Scientific Riddle?: Science and Religion on Shroud of Torino]. M.: Znanie, 1989. 64 pp. (Novoe v zhizni, nauke, tekhnike. Znak voprosa; 1'89).

613 Balashov, Dm. "Tysiacheletie: Razmyshleniia po povodu" [Millenium: Reflections on the Occasion]. *Znamia* 8 (1988): 170-174.

614 Balevits, Z.V. *Katolicheskaia tserkov' v Latvii* [Catholic Church in Latvia]. 2nd enlarged ed. Riga: Avots, 1981. 101 pp. In Latvian.

615 Balevits, Z.[V]. "Katolitsizm na rasput'e" [Catholicism at the Cross-roads]. *Kommunist Sov. Latvii* 3 (1980): 93-96.

616 Balevits, Z.V. *Pravoslavnaia tserkov' v Latvii* [Orthodox Church in Latvia]. Riga: Avots, 1987. 160 pp. In Latvian.

617 Balevits, Z.[V]. "Razoblachenie ideologicheskikh diversii imperializma, osushchestvliaemykh pod flagom klerikalizma [Exposure of Imperialism's Ideological Diversions Implemented under the Guise of Clericalism]. *Kommunist Sov. Latvii* 12 (1984): 78-84.

618 Ballod, I.Ia. *Ia pomogu tebe* [I will Help You]. M.: Sov. Rossiia, 1989. 128 pp.

619   Bal'sis, A. "Rol' nauchnogo ateizma v obshchestve" [The Role of Scientific Atheism in Society]. *Kommunist.* Vil'nius 11 (1983): 29-38.

620   Baltanov, R.G. "Ateizm - eto utverzhdenie cheloveka" [Atheism - Is Affirmation of the Person]. *Kommunist Tatarii* 4 (1989): 51-57.

621   Baltanov, R.[G]. "Logicheskie aspekty nuchno-ateisticheskoi propagandy" [Logical Aspects of Scientific-Atheistic Propaganda]. *Kommunist Tatarii* 10 (1980): 75-82.

622   Baltanov, R.[G]. "Psikhologicheskie i pedagogicheskie aspekty ateisticheskogo vospitaniia" [Psychological and Pedagogical Aspects of Atheistic Education]. *Kommunist Tatarii* 11 (1983): 74-80.

623   Baltanova, G.R. "Aktual'nye problemy ateisticheskogo vospitaniia studentov v raionakh traditsionnogo rasprostraneniia islama" [Actual Problems of Atheistic Education of Students in Regions of Islam's Traditional Dissemination]. *Aktual'nye problemy nauchno-atesticheskogo vospitaniia molodezhi.* M., 1987. Pp. 95-98.

624   Baltanova, G.R. "Ateizm kak utverzhdenie bytiia cheloveka" [Atheism as Confirmation of Man's Existence]. *Dukhovnyi mir sovremennogo cheloveka.* M., 1987. Pp. 120-122.

625   Baltanova, G.[R]. "Islam i sovremennaia ideologicheskaia bor'ba" [Islam and Contemporary Ideological Struggle]. *Kommunist Tatarii* 8 (1986): 89-92.

626   Baltanova, G.R. "Problema 'musul'manskogo vozrozhdeniia' v sovremennom burzhuaznom islamovedenii" [Problem of "Moslem Renaissance" in Contemporary Bourgeois Study of Islam]. *Aktual'nye problemy ateisticheskogo vospitaniia i kritika religioznoi ideologii.* M., 1983. Pp. 48-52.

627   Balycheva, M.B. "Nravstvennaia tsennost' ateisticheskoi ubezhdennosti lichnosti" [Moral Value of Person's Atheistic Conviction]. *Vopr. nauch. ateizma* 35 (1986): 127-146.

628   Balycheva, M.B. "Vliianie ateisticheskoi ubezhdennosti na nravstvennost' cheloveka" [Influence of Atheistic Conviction on Man's Morality]. *Kritika religioznoi ideologii i problemy ateisticheskogo vospitaniia.* M., 1982. Pp. 10-16.

629   Bank, L.G. *Za prosveshchenie dlia trudiashchikhsia: Bor'ba protiv burzhuaz natsionalizma i klerikalizma v oblasti prosveshcheniia na zapadno-ukrainskikh zemliiakh do vossoedineniia ikh s Sov. Ukrainoi* [For Workers Education: Struggle Against Bourgeois Nationalism and Clericalism in Realm of Education in Western Ukrainian Lands Before their Reunion with Soviet Ukraine]. L'vov: Vishcha shk. Izd-vo pri L'vov. un-te, 1983. 192 pp. In Ukrainian.

630   "Baptisty vystupaiut po sovetskomy televideniiu" [Baptists Appear on Soviet Television]. *Religiia v SSSR* 6 (1987): IV 1-IV2.

631   Barabanov, N.D. "Bor'ba vnutri vizantiiskoi tserkvi na rubezhe XIII-XIV vv." [Struggle Inside Byzantine Church on the Threshold of XIIIth-XIVth Centuries]. *Antichnyi i srednevekovyi gorod.* Antich. drevnost' i sred. veka. Sverdlovsk, 1981. Pp. 141-156.

632   Barabash, Iu. "Bogoslov? Mistik? Ateist?" [Theologian? Mystic? Atheist?]. *Nauka i Religiia* 2;3; 4 (1988): 36-38.

633   Baranets, A.A. "Protivorechiia khristianskikh khiliasticheskikh dvizhenii" [Contradictions of Christian Chiliastic Movements]. *Vestn. Mosk. un-ta.* Ser. 7. FilosofiiaA (1980): 57-66.

634   Barashenkov, V. "Sud'by Vselennoi" [Fates of the Universe]. *Nauka i religiia* 10 (1988): 5-7.

635   Barmenkov, A.I. *Svoboda sovesti v SSSR* [Freedom of Worship in USSR]. M.: Progress, 1983. 181 pp. In English.
       Published also in:
       M.: Mysl', 1986. 224 pp. For review see item 4962.

636   Barna Sharkadi Nad'. "Gosudarstvo i tserkov' v VNR" [State and Church in Hungarian Popular Republic]. *Argumenty, 1987.* M., 1987. Pp. 115-127.

637   Bartikian, R. "O sviaziakh monastyria Grigoriia Pakuriana s Armeniei [XI-XII vv.]" [On Relations of Gregory Pakurian's Monastery with Armenia (XIth-XIIth C.)]. *Vestn. obshchestv. nauk* 6 (1988): 52-56. Summary in Armenian.

638   Barysh, Iu.P. "Bibleiskaia apokaliptika kak ideinaia baza khristianskoi eskhatologii" [Biblical Apocalyptics as Ideological Basis of Christian

Eschaetology]. *Ob'ektivnoe i sub'ektivnoe v obshchestvennom razvitii.* Vladivostok, 1981. Pp. 80-86.

639   Barzdaitis, I.I. *Obshchestvennaia rol' religii* [Social Role of Religion]. Vil'nius: Mintis, 1981. 189 pp. Bibl.: pp. 173-188. For review see item 4963.

640   Barzdaitis, I.I. *Traditsii ateizma v Litve (Konets XIX v. - nach. XX v.)* [Tradition of Atheism in Lithuania (End XIXth C.- early XXth C.]. Vil'nius: Mintis, 1980. 166 pp. In Lithuanian. Bibl.: pp. 153-165. For review see item 4963.

641   Basaev, S.E. "Problemy preodoleniia individual'noi religioznosti v Buriatii" [Problems of Overcoming Individual Religiosity in Buriat]. *Aktual'nye problemy nauchno-ateisticheskogo vospitaniia molodezhi.* M., 1987. Pp. 154-159.

642   Bashirov, D.D. "Usilenie islamskogo faktora v obshchestvenno-politicheskoi zhizni Egipta v 70-e gody" [Strengthening of Islamic Factor in Egypt's Socio-Political Life in the 70s]. *Zarubezhnyi Vostok: istoriia i sovremennost'.* M., 1988. Pp. 137-146.

643   Bashirov, L.A. "Sovetskii obraz zhizni i preodolenie religioznykh perezhitkov" [Soviet Way of Life and Overcoming Religious Survivals]. *Vopr. nauch. ateizma* 26 (1980): 149-164.

644   Basilov, V.N. *Izbranniki dukhov* [Chosen by Spirits]. M.: Politizdat, 1984. 208 pp., illus. For reviews see item 4964-4968.

645   Basilov, V.N.; Khoppal, M. "Sovetsko-vengerskii simpozium 'Sravnitel'noe izuchenie rannikh form religii'" [Soviet-Hungarian Symposium "Comparative Study of Religion's Early Forms"]. *Sov. etnografiia* 1 (1983): 143-148.

646   Basinova, D.A. "Ispol'zovanie nagliadnykh sredstv obucheniia v protsesse prepodavaniia nauchnogo ateizma" [Use of Visual Teaching Aids in the Process of Teaching Scientific Atheism]. *Aktual'nye vopr. metodiki prepodavaniia obshchestv. nauk i kom. vospitanie studentov* 5 (1987): 115-123.

647   Bataitis, S.P. *Krest bez raspiatogo* [Cross without the Crucified]. Kaunas: Shviesa, 1987. 182 pp. In Lithuanian.

648 Batalov, E. "Vid s serediny mosta" [View from the Middle of the Bridge]. *Novoe vremia* 50 (1988): 3-7.

649 Batsashi, Ts.N. *Etnoreligioznye protsessy v Severo-Vostochnoi Anatolii* [Ethno Religious Processes in North-Eastern Anatolia]. Tbilisi: Metsniereba, 1988. 80 pp. Bibl.: pp. 70-79. In Georgian. Summary in Russian.

650 Batser, M.I. "Reformatsionnye tendentsii v russkom raskole XVII-XVIII vv." [Reformative Tendencies in Russian Schism in XVIIth-XVIIIth C.]. *Filos. i sotsiol. mysl'.* Kiev. 7 (1989): 93-102.

651 Batueva, L. "Kliuch-gorod na beregakh Slavuticha" [Key-town on the Banks of Slavutich]". *Nauka i religiia* 6 (1985): 39-42.

652 Batunskii, M.A. "O nekotorykh novykh tendentsiiakh v istoriografii pervon-achal'nogo islama; [Some new Tendencies in Historiography of the Primary Islam]. *Narody Azii i Afriki* 6 (1987): 143-153.

653 Batyreva, S.G. "Kalmytskaia natsional'naia shkola kul'tovoi skul'ptury i zhivopisi" [Kalmyk National School of Ecclesiastical Sculpture and Painting]. *Voprosy itorii lamaizma v Kalmykii.* Elista, 1987. Pp. 40-57.

654 Batyrov, Sh.[B]. *Kul'turno-tekhnicheskii uroven' truzhenikov sela i ateisticheskoe vospitanie* [Villagers' Cultural-Technical Level and Atheistic Education]. Tashkent: Uzbekistan, 1980. 30 pp. (Ser. "Marksizm-leninizm"; No 12).

655 Batyrov, Sh.B.; Kolemasova, N.Kh. *Sprashivaiut - otvechaem* [They Ask - We Answer]. Tashkent: Esh gvardiia, 1983 (published in 1984). 39 pp. (Metod. pomoshch' molodym lektoram i kom. aktivu / TsK LKSM Uzbekistana, Lektor. gruppa).

656 Bazarbaev, Zh. "Malye religioznnye gruppy i voprosy ateisticheskogo vospi-taniia" [Small Religious Groups and Problems of Atheistic Education]. *Vestn. Karakalp. fil. AN UzSSR* 4 (1988): 52-57.

657 Bazarbaev, Zh. "Perestroika i ateisticheskaia rabota" [Perestroika and Atheistic Work]. *Kommunist Kirgizstana* 10 (1987): 56-60.

658 Bazarov, A.B. "Osobennosti musul'manskikh religioznykh perezhitkov: Po dannym oprosa v Samark. oblasti" [Features of Moslem Religious

Survivals: On Data of Referendum in Samarcand Region]. *Sotsial. issled.* 2 (1982): 172-173.

659 Bazarov, M. "Trudovaia aktivnost' sel'skikh truzhenikov kak faktor preodoleniia religioznykh predrassudkov" [Villagers Labour Activity as Factor of Overcoming Religious Prejudices]. *Problemy formirovaniia nauchno-ateisticheskogo mirovozzreniia v sotsialitischeskom obshchestve.* Samarkand, 1980. Pp. 4-10.

660 Bazarov, O.B. et al. *Osnovy nauchnogo ateizma* [Fundamentals of Scientific Atheism]. Tashkent: Ukituvchi, 1984. 231 pp. In Uzbek.

661 Bazhenova, G.S. "O nekotorykh aspektakh bor'by kazakhskikh prosvetitelei protiv vostochnogo klerikalizma" [Some Aspects of Kazakhs Educators' Struggle against Oriental Clericalism]. *Aktual'nye probl. istorii filosofii narodov SSSR* 9 (1981): 48-53.

662 Begun, V.Ia. *Rasskazy o 'detiakh vdovy'* [Tales about "Widow's Children"]. Minsk: Nauka i tekhnika, 1983. 112 pp. Bibl.: pp. 109-111. For review see item 4969.

663 Begunov, Iu.K. "K voprosu o tserkovno-politicheskikh planov Grigoriia Tsamblaka" [On the Question of Gregory Tsamblac's Church-Political Plans]. *Sov. Slavianovedenie* 3 (1981): 57-64.

664 Beilis, V.A. *Islam i traditsionnye religii v Tropicheskoi Afrike* [Islam and Traditional Religions in Tropical Africa]. M.: INION, 1983. 54 pp. Bibl.: pp. 51-54.

665 Beilis, V.A. *Traditsiia v sovremennykh kul'turakh Afriki* [Tradition in Africa's Contemporary Cultures]. M.: Nauka, 1986. 248 pp. Bibl.: pp. 239-245. Summary in English.

666 Bekmetov, E. "Ateisticheskoe vospitanie - zhivoe, tvorcheskoe delo" [Atheistic Education - Living, Creative Act]. *Part. zhizn'.* Tashkent. 8 (1983): 85-88.

667 Bekmetov, E. *My - ateisty* [We - Atheists]. Tashkent: Esh gvardiia, 1981. 69 pp. (V pomoshch' propagandistu). In Uzbek.

668 Bekmetov, E. *Trudovoi kollektiv i ateisticheskoe vospitanie* [Working Collective and Atheistic Education]. Tashkent: Uzbekistan, 1985. 56 pp. (B-ka ateista). In Uzbek.

669 Bekov, K. *Mukhammad Shakuristani - istorik filosofii* [Muhammad Shakuristani - Historian of Philosophy]. Dushanbe: Donish, 1987. 118 pp. Bibl.: pp. 103-117.

670 Bektemirova, N. "Novyi etap v istorii buddizma v Kampuchii" [New Stage in the History of Buddhism in Kampuchea]. *Aziia i Afrika segodnia* 10 (1981): 58-59.

671 Belenko, T.I. "Istoki klerikal'nykh stereotipov o polozhenii veruiushchikh v SSSR" [Sources of Clerical Stereotypes on the Situation of Believers in USSR]. *Vopr. ateizma* 25 (1989): 65-71.

672 Belenko, T.I. "Nesostoiatel'nost' pravoslavno-bogoslovskoi otsenki vvedeniia kristianstva na Rusi" [Groundlessness of Orthodox-Theological Appraisal of Introduction of Christianity into Rus']. *Vopr. ateizma* 22 (1986): 3-10.

673 Beletskaia, A. "Ot konfrontatsii k sotrudnichestvu" [From Confrontation to Collaboration]. *Nauka i religiia* 11 (1981): 54-56.

674 Beliaev, V.P. *Ia obviniaiu!* [I Accuse!]. M.: Politizdat, 1980. 160 pp. Published also as 2nd enlarged ed., 1984. 224 pp., and in: Kiev: Politizdat Ukrainy, 1980. 154 pp. In Ukrainian. For reviews see items 4970-4971.

675 Beliakova, E.V. "K istorii uchrezhdeniia avtokefalii russkoi tserkvi" [History of the Establishment of Russian Autocephalous Church]. *Rossiia na putiakh tsentralizatsii.* M., 1982. Pp. 152-156.

676 Beliakova, E.[V]. "Pravoslavnaia apologetika v svete nauchnoi kritiki" [Orthodox Apologetics in the Light of Scientific Criticism]. *Nauka i religiia* 12 (1983): 38-39.

677 Beliakova, O.V. "Boginia Neit - pokrovitel'nitsa faraona" [Goddess Neit - Pharaoh's Patroness]. *Vest. Mosk. un-ta.* Ser. 8 . Istoriia 2 (1983): 65-73.

678 Belik, A.A. "Psikhologiia religii E. Fromma i A. Maslou" [E. Fromm's and A. Maslow's Psychology of Religion]. *Religii mira.* M., 1989. Pp. 214-228.

679 Belikova, G. "Obshchenie, obshchnost', obshchina..." [Relations, Commune, Community...]. *Nauka i religiia* 2 (1983): 41-44.

680 Belimov, A.F. *Ateisticheskoe vospitanie naseleniia* [Atheistic Education of the Population]. Frunze: Kyrgyzstan, 1981. 71 pp. (B-chka ateista). In Kirghiz.

681 Belkina, T.L. *Kul'tura i religiia* [Culture and Religion]. Kishinev: Znanie MSSR, 1980. 22 pp. (Materialy v pomoshch' lektoru / O-vo "Znanie" MSSR. Ser. "Obshchestv.-polit. nauki") (Znaniia-narodu).

682 Belousov, S.R. "Konfutsianstvo i modernizatsiia Kitaia" [Confucianism and Modernization of China]. *Probl. Dal'nego Vostoka* 5 (1989): 104-116.

683 Belov, A. "Khrista radi iurodivye" ["God's Fool" for the Sake of Christ]. *Nauka i religiia* 6 (1984): 42-45.

684 Belov, A. "Khristianskoe sektantstvo" [Christian Sectarianism]. *Agitator* 9 (1982): 43-46.

685 Belov, A. "Klerikal'nyi antikommunizm" [Clerical Anti-Communism]. *Nauka i religiia* 6 (1982): 18-21.

686 Belov, A. "V chem vred 'pedagogiki' khristianskogo sektanstva" [How the "Pedagogy" of Christian Sectarianism is Harmful]. *Vospitanie shkol'nikov* 1 (1981): 28-32.

687 Belov, A. "Zhenskie imena v sviattsakh" [Female Names in Church Calendars]. *Nauka i religiia* 3 (1984): 42-44.

688 Belov, A.; Miller, I. "Dve zhizni Frantsiska Assizkogo" [Two Lives of Francis of Assisi]. *Nauka i religiia* 10 (1985): 42-46.

689 Belov, A.N.; Shadiev, K.K. *K fal'sifikatsii polozheniia Islama v respublikakh Srednei Azii i zadachi kontrpropagandy* [On Falsifications of Islam's Situation in Middle Asia and Problems of Counter Propaganda]. Tashkent: Esh gvardiia, 1987. 27 pp.

690 Belov, A.V. *Klerikal'nyi antikommunizm:* Ideologiia, politika, propaganda [Clerical Anti-Communism: Ideology, Policy, Propaganda]. M.: Politizdat, 1987. 256 pp. (Kritika burzhuaz. ideologii i revizionizma). For review see item 4972.

691   Belov, A.V. *Kogda zvoniat kolokola* [When the Bells Toll]. 2nd revised and enlarged ed. M.: Sov. Rossiia, 1988. 252 pp. Index: pp. 243-250.

692   Belov, A.V. *Ne delai sebe kumira: Besedy o religii i znanii* [Don't Make an Idol for Yourself: Discussions about Religion and Knowledge]. M.: Mol. gvardiia, 1984. 175 pp., illus. For reviews see items 4973-4974.

693   Belov, A.V. *O Rozhdestve Khristovom* [On Christmas]. 3rd revised and enlarged ed. Perm': Kn. izd-vo, 1983. 90 pp. (B-chka "Razgovory po dusham"). Published also as 2nd ed. in Kishinev: Kartia moldoveniaske, 1988. 109 pp., in Moldavian.

694   Belov, A.V. *Ot rozhdestva Khristosa:* Ateist. ocherki [From Christmas: Atheistic Essays]. M.: Det. Lit., 1981. 143 pp., illus.

695   Belov, A.V. *Sovremennaia ideologicheskaia bor'ba i religiia* [Contemporary Ideological Struggle and Religion]. Tbilisi: Znanie GSSR, 1984. 32 pp. In Georgian.

696   Belov, A.[V]. "Starets Serafim" [Elderly Monk Seraphim]. *Nauka i religiia* 3 (1982): 27-29.

697   Belov, A.V. *Sviatye bez nimbov* [Saints Without Nimbuses]. M.: Sov. Rossiia, 1983. 213 pp., illus. For review see item 4975.

698   Belov, A.V. *Ulybka drakona* [The Smile of the Dragon]. Kazan': Tatar. kn. izd-vo, 1982. 105 pp. In Tatar.

699   Belov, A.V.; Karpov, A.D. *Pod flagom antisovetizma* [Under the Banner of Anti-Sovietism]. M.: Znanie, 1980. 63 pp. (Novoe v zhizni, nauke tekhnike. Ser. "Nauch. ateizm"; No 11).

700   Belov, A.V. et al. *Mif o 'religioznom vozrozhdenii' v SSSR* [Myth on the "Renaissance of Religion" in the USSR]. M.: Znanie, 1983. 64 pp. (Novoe v zhizni, nauke, tekhnike. Nauch. ateizm; 3). Bibl.: p. 57.

701   Belov, O.A.; Zelenkov, B.I. "Nekotorye voprosy ateisticheskogo vospitaniia molodezhi" [Some Problems of Youth's Atheistic Upbringing]. *Vopr. nauch. ateizma* 29 (1982): 162-172.

702   Berar, P. *Religiia v sovremennom mire* [Religion in the Contemporary World]. Tallin: Eesti raamat, 1983. 119 pp. In Estonian.

703   Berdiaev, N. "Khistianstvo i antisemitizm: Relig. sud'ba evreistva" [Christianity and Antisemitism: Religious Fate of Jewry]. *Druzhba narodov* 10 (1989): 205-213.

704   Berdiaev, N.A. "'O religioznom znachenii L'va Tolstogo'" ["On Religious Importance of Leo Tolstoy]. *Vopr. lit.* 4 (1989): 269-274.

705   Berdyshev, G.D. *Nauka i religiia o smerti i bessmertii* [Science and Religion about Death and Immortality]. Kiev: Znanie UkSSR, 1986. 49 pp. (Ser. 5, Nauchno-atesticheskaia / O-vo "Znanie" UkSSR; No 2).

706   Bereishin, L.V. "Na praktike ateisticheskogo vospitaniia molodezhi v Grodnenskoi oblasti" [From the Practice of Youth's Atheistic Upbringing in the Grodno Region]. *Aktual'nye problemy nauchno-ateisticheskogo vospitaniia molodezhi.* M., 1987. Pp. 50-55.

707   Berezkin, Iu.E. *Golos d'iavola sredi snegov i dzhunglei:* Istoki drev. religii [Devil's Voice Amidst Snow and Jungles: Sources of Ancient Religions]. L.: Lenizdat, 1987. 172 pp., illus. (Razum poznaet mir). Bibl.: pp. 170-171. For review see item 4976.

708   Berezovskaia, O.A. "Kritika obosnovaniia idei boga vo frantsuzkom persona-lizme" [Criticism of Basing the Idea of God in French Individualism]. *Aktual'nye problemy ateisticheskogo vospitaniia i kritika religioznoi ideologii.* M., 1981. Pp. 62-68.

709   Berezovskaia, O.A. "Kritika personalistskoi kontseptsii nauchnogo poznaniia" [Criticism of Individual Conception of Scientific Knowledge]. *Kritika religioznoi ideologii i poblemy ateisticheskogo vospitaniia.* M., 1982. Pp. 75-83.

710   Berezovskaia, V.F. "Opyt tipologii neoinduistskikh relogioznykh organizatsii" [Typology Experience of Neohinduist Religious Organizations]. *V Vseso-iuznaia shkola molodykh vostokovedov.* M., 1989. T. 3. Pp. 5-11.

711   Berzin, E.O. *Chemu uchil Zaratushtra?* [What Did Zaratushtra Teach?]. Tashkent: Uzbekistan, 1987. 23 pp. (Beseda o nauke; No 17). In Uzbek.

712   *Besedy o mirovozzrenii* [Talks About World Outlook]. [Comp.: A. Gailene]. Vil'nius: Mintis, 1984. In Lithuanian.
       [Book] 1. 1984. 239 pp.
       [Book] 2. Comp.: A. Ribalis. 1986. 247 pp.

713   *Besedy po voprosam mirovozzreniia* [Talks on the Questions of World
      Outlook]. Vil'nius: Mintis. Published since 1977. In Lithuanian.
      No 4. [Comp.: F. Latsrinaites]. 1980. 143 pp.
      No 5. [Comp.: F. Latsrinaites]. 1981. 103 pp.

714   Bespal'chii, V.F. *Trud i religiia* [Work and Religion]. Kiev: Nauk. dumka,
      1981. 207 pp. (Nauch.-popul. lit.). In Ukrainian. Bibl.: pp. 205-206.

715   Bespamiatnykh, N.N. "K voprosu o kritike sovremennoi katolicheskoi
      antropologii" [Problem of Criticism of Contemporary Catholic Anthro-
      pology]. *Aktual'nye problemy nauchno-ateisticheskogo vospitaniia molodezhi.*
      M., 1987. Pp. 162-166.

716   Bespamiatnykh, N.N. "Ob ateisticheskom kharaktere sotsialisticheskogo
      obraza zhizni" [On Atheistic Character of Socialist Way of Life]. *Nauch.
      ateizm i ateist. vospitanie* 1 (1983): 25-30.

717   Bespamiatnykh, N.N. "Sovremennaia ideologicheskaia bor'ba i modernizatsiia
      neotomistskoi antropologii" [Contemporary Ideological Struggle and
      Modernization of Neothomist Anthropology]. *Dialektika sotsialnykh
      protsessov: XXVII s'ezd KPSS o bor'be sovremennykh idei.* Minsk, 1988.
      Pp. 150-166.

718   Bessonov, M.N. *Kritika burzuazno-klerikal'nykh izmyshlenii po povodu 1000-
      letia vvedeniia khristianstva na Rusi* [Criticism of Bourgeois-Clerical
      Fabrications on the Occasion of 1000th Year of Introduction of Chris-
      tianity into Rus']. M: Znanie, 1988. 27 pp.

719   Bessonov, M.N. "Raskol'niki iz Dzhordanvillia" [Dissenters from Jordanville].
      Argumenty, 1987. M., 1987. Pp. 11-28.

720   Bessonov, M.N. "Russkaia pravoslavnaia tserkov' i 1000-letie 'kreshcheniia
      Rusi'" [Russian Orthodox Church and 1000th Anniversary of "Baptism of
      Rus'"]. *Pravoslavie v Karelii.* Petrozavodsk, 1987. Pp. 3-24.

721   Bessonova, S.S. *Religioznye predstavleniia skifov* [Scythians' Religious
      Notions]. Kiev: Nauk. dumka, 1983. 138 pp., illus. (Arkheologiia). Bibl.:
      pp. 121-135.

722   Bestuzhev-Lada, I. "Begstvo iz raia" [Flight from Paradise]. *Nauka i religiia* 4
      (1986): 4-7.

723 Bestuzheva, S.; Iurtaev, V. "Molodezh' i religiia na sovremennom Vostoke" [Youth and Religion in Today's Orient]. V *Vsesoiuznaia shkola molodykh vostokovedov.* M., 1989. T. 3. Pp. 112-116.

724 Bezklubenko, S.D. *Muzy na lozhe Prokrusta* [Muses on Procrustes Bed]. Kiev: Mistetsvo, 1988. 197 pp., illus. Bibl.: pp. 190-194.

725 Bezklubenko, S.D. *Sokrushenie idolov* [The Shattering of Idols]. Kiev: Politizdat Ukrainy, 1989. 255 pp., illus. Bibl.: pp. 251-254.

726 Bezrogov, V.G. "Mifologicheskie predstavleniia o korole na nachal'nykh etapakh stanovleniia korolevskoi vlasti v Irlandii" [Mythological Notions about a King in the First Stages of Creation of a Kingdom in Ireland]. *Kul'tura srednikh vekov i novogo vremeni.* M., 1987. Pp. 42-50. Bibl.: pp. 47-50.

727 Biazrova, T.T. "K voprosu zakonomernostiakh formirovaniia i razvitiia drevnerusskogo svobodumysliia" [On the Problem of Legality of Forming and Developing Old Russian Freethinking]. *Dukhovnyi mir sovremennogo cheloveka.* M., 1987. Pp. 177-180.

728 Bibikova, O. "Musul'mane v Kitae" [Moslems in China]. *Aziia i Afrika segodnia* 2 (1985): 60-61.

729 "Bibleiskaia kniga 'Sud'i'" [The Book of "Judges"]. Introd. and trans. by I.Sh. Shifman. *Narody Azii i Afriki* 3 (1989): 117-127; 4 (1989): 93-106.

730 "Bibliia i aparteid" [Bible and Apartheid]. *Novoe vremia* 3 (1989): 17.

731 Bicheldei, K.A. "Rol' i znachenie religioznoi mysli v stanovlenii i razvitii dukhovnosti" [Role and Importance of Religious Thought in the Making and Developing Spirituality]. *Tsybikovskie chteniia.* Ulan-Ude, 1989. Pp. 26-27.

732 Biderman, G.; Lange, E. *Kritika religii v nemetskoi klassike - osushche-stvennyi istochnik nauchnogo ateizma* [Criticism of Religion in German Classics - Important Source of Scientific Atheism]. Tbilisi: Izd-vo Tbil. un-teta, 1982. 96 pp. In Georgian. Annot. bibl.: pp. 78-95.

733 Biiukov, M.I. "Ob ateisticheskom vospitanii v mnogonatsional'nom raione" [Atheistic Education in Multi-National Region]. *Problemy ateisticheskogo vospitaniia v usloviiakh Karachaevo-Cherkesii.* Cherkessk, 1979. Pp. 41-49.

734   Biletskaia, L.V. "Kategoriia very v religioznom i nauchno- materialist-
       icheskom mirovozzrenii" [The Category of Faith in the Religious and
       Scientific-Materialist Outlook]. *Vopr. ateizma* 17 (1981): 91-98.

735   Biletskaia, L.V. "Kritika pravoslavnoi kontseptsii sootnosheniia very i
       ubezhdeniia v religioznom mirovozzrenii" [Criticism of Orthodox
       Conception of Correlation of Faith and Conviction in Religious World
       Outlook]. *Vopr. ateizma* 22 (1986): 113-119.

736   Biskup, A.V. *Ateizm v bor'be s uniatskimi fal'sifikatorami* [Atheism in the
       Struggle with Uniates Falsificators]. L'vov: Vishcha shk. Izd-vo pri L'vov.
       un-te, 1984. 142 pp. In Ukrainian.

737   Biskup, A.V. *Propovedniki vrazhdy* [Preachers of Enmity]. L'vov: Kameniar,
       1986. 70 pp. In Ukrainian.

738   Bivol, V.G.; Lysenko V.M. "Antiobshchestvennyi kharakter mirovozzren-
       cheskogo vozdeistviia netraditsionnykh religii" [Antisocial Character of
       Non Traditional Religions on World Outlooks' Influences]. *Filos. vopr.
       meditsiny i biologii* 18 (1986): 110-116.

739   Blagova, T.I. "Feministskaia teologiia i religioznyi modernizm" [Feminist
       Theology and Religious Modernism]. *Vestn. Mosk. un-ta.* Ser. 7. Filosofiia
       5 (1984): 75-82.

740   Blagova, T.[I]. "Padcheritsy bozh'i" [God's Step-Daughters]. *Nauka i religiia*
       3 (1982): 56-58.

741   Blagova, T.[I]. "Tupiki feminizma" [Deadlocks of Feminism]. *Nauka i religiia*
       3 (1984): 61-62.

742   Blakhnitska, I.; Ershna, Ia.; Shidlovski, P. "Sotsial'nyi smysl kontseptsii
       'poliak-katolik'" [Social Essence of the Concept "Catholic-Pole"]. *Nauch.
       dokl. vysh. shkoly. Filos.* nauki 5 (1980): 118-125.

743   Blavatskaia, E.P. "Tainaia Doktrina" [Secret Doctrine]. *Nauka i religiia* 1
       (1989): 42-47; 2 (1989): 30-42. Published also in *Raduga* 7 (1989): 152-
       158.

744   Blinova, E.P.; Blagoeva, T.I.; Shaidulina, L.I. "Musul'manskie ideologi o
       polozhenii zhenshchiny na Arabskom Vostoke" [Moslem Ideologists on

Woman's Position in Arab Orient]. *Ideino-politicheskaia bor'ba i nekotorye problemy zhenskogo dvizheniia.* M., 1981. Pp. 194-220.

745 Bliumenfel'd, L. "Razmyshlenie o nauke i o religii v stikhakh i proze" [Reflections on Science and Religion in Verses and Prose]. *Nauka i religiia* 10 (1989): 60-62.

746 Bliumkhen, S.I. "Filosofsko-religioznye predstavlenie epokhi Chzhou: Ot totema k kul'tu Neba" [Philosophical - Religious Notions of Chou Epoch: From Totem to the Cult of Nebo]. *Deviatnadtsataia nauchnaia konferentsiia "Obshchestvo i gosudarstvo v Kitae".* M., 1988. ch. 2. Pp. 30-37.

747 Bluzmanas, P. *Sovremennaia polemika predstavitelei nauki i religii po voprosu ob evoliutsii zhizni* [Contemporary Polemics of Science and Religion Representatives on the Problem of Life's Evolution]. Vil'nius: Znanie LitSSR, 1981. 17 pp. (Material dlia lektora / O-vo "Znanie" LitSSR). In Lithuanian.

748 Bobokhanova, Z.M. "Individual'naia rabota s veruiushchimi" [Individual Work with Believers]. *Kompleksnyi podkhod v ateisticheskom vospitanii* Dushanbe, 1988. Pp. 88-97. Bibl.: p. 97.

749 Bobosadykova, G.B. "O sovershenstvovanii form i metodov ateisticheskoi raboty" [Perfection of Forms and Methods of Atheistic Work]. *Vopr. nauch. ateizma* 3 (1983): 193-205.

750 Bodrov, V.N. "Nesostoiatel'nost' neokhristianskoi interpretatsii prirody sotsial'nogo zla" [Baselessness of Neochristian Interpretation of the Nature of Social Evil]. *Kritika religioznoi ideologii i problemy ateisticheskogo vospitaniia.* M., 1982. Pp. 35-42.

751 Bogachuk, A.I. *Vremia zhit': Ocherki* [Time to Live: Essays]. Donetsk: Donbas, 1988. 175 pp.

752 Bogdanenko, R.V. "Nauchno-tekhnicheskii progress v sotsialisticheskom obshchestve kak faktor sekuliarizatsii" [Scientific-Technical Progress in Socialist Society as Factor of Secularization]. *Voprosy teorii i praktiki nauchnogo ateizma.* M., 1988. Pp. 3-28.

753 Bogdanov, A. "Astrologicheskii pir vo vremia chumy" [Astrological Feast in Plague's Time]. *Nauka i religiia* 10 (1988): 57-60.

754 Bogemskii, S. "'Sud nad sobstvennoi sovest'iu'" ["Trial on One's Own Conscience"]. *Nauka i religiia* 9 (1987): 55-56.

755 Bogomolov, A.S. "Ekzistentsial'naia dialektika" [Existentialist Dialectics]. *Idealisticheskaia dialektika v XX stoletii.* M., 1987. Pp. 27-47.

756 Bogomolov, G.I.; Buriakov, Iu.F. "Kul'tovye pomeshcheniia pri zhilykh domakh s gorodishcha Kanka" [Religious Locations in Dwelling Houses in Kanka]. *Istoriia mater. kul'tury Uzbekistana.* 21 (1987): 76-88.

757 Bogoslovskii, E.S. "O vostanovlenii mnogobozhiia v Egipte posle smerti Amenkhotpa IV" [Restoration of Polytheism in Egypt after the Death of Amenophist IV]. *Pis'mennye pamiatniki i problemy istorii kul'tury narodov Vostoka.* M., 1987. Ch. 1. Pp. 62-66.

758 Boiko, M.S.; Starovoit, I.S. *Ateizm i religiia v usloviiakh NTR* [Atheism and Religion under the Conditions of NTR]. Kiev: Politizdat Ukrainy, 1985. 95 pp. Annot. bibl.: pp. 90-94.

759 Bois, M. *Zoroastriitsy. Verovaniia i obychai* [Zoroastrians. Beliefs and Customs]. [Transl. from English]. M.: Nauka, 1987. 302 pp., illus. Published also as 2nd revised ed. in 1988. Translated from *Zoroastrians /* Mary Boyce (London, 1979). For review see item 4977.

760 Bokarev, P.I. *Pochemu nekotorye nashi sovremenniki veriat v boga* [Why Some of Our Contemporaries Believe in God]. M.: Znanie RSFSR, 1980. 32 pp. (V pomoshch' lektoru / O-vo "Znanie" SFSR, Nauch.-metod sovet po propagande nauch. ateizma). Bibl.: pp. 31-32.

761 Bokov, Kh.Kh. "Ne sniat s povestki dnia" [Not to Remove from the Agenda]. *Nauka i religiia* 11 (1983):2-6.

762 Boldizhar, M.N. *Antinarodnaia deiatel'nost' uniatskoi tserkvi* [Antipopular Activity of Uniate Church]. L'vov: Vishcha shkola. Izd-vo pri L'vov. un-te, 1980. 199 pp. In Ukrainian.

763 Boldizhar, M.N. *Besslavie* [Infamy]. Uzhgorod: Karpati, 1981. 118 pp. In Ukrainian.

764 Boldizhar, M.N. "Kritika burzhuazno-klerikal'nykh fal'sifikatsii antiklerikal'nogo dvizheniia sredi molodezhi Zakarpat'ia v 20-30-e gody" [Criticism of Bourgeois-Clerical Falsifications on Anticlerical Movement

among Transcarpathian Youth in the 20s-30s]. *Vopr. ateizma* 19 (1983): 114-117.

765   Boldizhar, M.N. *Kto i zachem obeliaet istoriiu unii* [Who is Whitewashing the History of the Uniate Church and Why]. Uzhgorod: Karpati, 1985. 160 pp. In Ukrainian.

766   Boldizhar, M.N. *Uniatstvo: pravda istorii i izmyshleniia fal'sifikatorov* [Uniatism: Historical Truth and Falsifiers' Fabrications]. L'vov: Vishcha shk. Izd-vo pri L'vov. un-te, 1988. 143 pp. In Ukrainian.

767   Bolotin, I.S. *Kritika antikommunisticheskik kontseptsii sovremennogo religioznogo natsionalizma* [Criticism of Anti-Communist Conception of Contemporary Religious Nationalism]. M.: Znanie, 1984. 63 pp. (Novoe v zhizni, nauke, tekhnike. Nauch. ateizm; 7). Bibl.: p. 62.

768   Bolotin, I.S. *Tupiki klerikal'nogo natsionalizma* [Impasses of Clerical Nationalism]. M.: Politizdat, 1987. 110 pp. (B-ka ateista). For reviews see items 4978-4979.

769   Bolotin, I.S.; Kuznetsova, I.V. "Kritika klerikal'nogo natsionalizma v kurse nauchnogo ateizma" [Criticism of Clerical Nationalism in the Course on Scientific Atheism]. *Tezisy dokladov i vystuplenii na Vsesoiuznoi konferentsii "Nauchnye osnovy kritiki nemarksistskikh kontseptsii v kursakh obshchestvennykh distsiplin", 12-15 okt. 1988 g.* Odessa, 1988. Pp. 89-90.

770   Bolotov, M.K. *Podkhod - individual'nyi: Formy i metody ateist. raboty* [Method of Approach: Forms and Methods of Atheistic Work]. Ustinov: Udmurtiia, 1986. 89 pp. Bibil.: p. 88.

771   Bol'shakov, O.G. *Istoriia khalifata. T. I. Islam v Aravii, 570-633.* [History of the Caliphate. V. I. Islam in Arabia, 570-633]. M.: Nauka, 1989. 312 pp.

772   Bol'shakov, O.G. "Sueveriia i moshennichestva v Bagdade XII-XIII vv." [Superstitions and Swindling in Baghdad XIIth-XIIIth C.]. *Islam: Religiia, obshchestvo, gosudarstvvo.* M., 1984. Pp. 144-148.

773   Bondarenko, Iu.[Ia]. "Astrologiia - za i protiv" [Astrology - Pro and Con]. *Nauka i religiia* 2 (1989): 59-62; 3 (1989): 27-29.

774   Bondarenko, Iu.Ia. *Ideia sud'by: Korni i evoliutsiia* [Concept of Destiny: Roots and Evolution]. M.: Znanic, 1989. 64 pp. (Novoe v zhizni, nauke, tekhnoke. Nauch. ateizm; 5 /1989).

775   Bondarenko, V.D. *Evoliutsiia sovremenngo pravoslavnogo bogosloviia* [Evolution of Contemporary Orthodox Theology]. Kiev: Znanie UkSSR, 1988. 48 pp. (Ser. 5. Nauch.-ateist. /O-vo "Znanie" UkSSR; No 4). In Ukrainian. Annot. bibl.: p. 47.

776   Bondarenko, V.D. *Sovremennoe pravoslavie: tendentsii evoliutsii* [Contemporary Orthodoxy: Evolution's Tendencies]. Simferopol': Tavriia. 1989. 176 pp.

777   Bondarenko, V.D. "Sushchnost' pravoslavno-bogoslovskoi kontseptsii 'sotsial'-nogo sluzheniia'" [The Essence of Orthodox-Theological Conception of "Social Service"]. *Aktual'nye problemy nauchno-ateisticheskogo vospitaniia molodezhi.* M., 1987. Pp. 123-128.

778   Bondarenko, V.D.; Eleseev, V.E. *Na vesakh zhiznennoi pravdy* [On the Scales of Life's Truth]. Donetsk: Donbas, 95 pp.

779   Bondarenko, V.D. et al. *Religioznaia obshchina v sovremennom obshchestve* [Religious Community in Contemporary Society]. Kiev: Politizdat Ukrainy, 1988. 127 pp. Annot. bibl.: pp. 125-126.

780   Bongard-Levin, G.M. "Budda molchit..." [Buddha is Silent...]. *Nauka i religiia* 7 (1989): 38-42.

781   Bongard-Levin, G.M. *Drevneindiiskaia tsivilizatsiia: Filosofiia, nauka, religiia* [Ancient Indian Civilization: Philosophy, Science, Religion]. M.: Nauka, 1980. 333 pp. Bibl.: pp. 330-332. For reviews see items 4980-4981.

782   Bongard-Levin, G.M.; Karpiuk, S.G. "Svedeniia o buddizme v antichnoi i rannekhristiankoi literature" [Information on Buddhism in Ancient and Early Christian Literature]. *Drevniaia Indiia:* Ist.-kul't. sviazi. M., 1982. Pp. 42-52. Annot. bibl.: pp. 51-52.

783   Bonkheffer, D. "Soprotivlenie i pokornost'" [Resistance and Obedience]. *Vopr. filosofii* 10 (1989): 106-167; 11 (1989): 90-162.

784   *Bor'ba Iugo-Zapadnoi Rusi i Ukrainy protiv ekspansii Vatikana i unii (X-nach. XVII v.)* [Struggle of South-Western Rus' and Ukraine against

Vatican and Uniate Church's Expansion (Xth-early XVIIth C.)]. [Comp.: E.A. Griniv et al]. Kiev: Nauk. dumka, 1988. 288 pp. In Ukrainian. Name index: pp. 269-287.

785 *Bor'ba za novyi obshchestvennyi byt i rozhdenie sovetskoi bezreligioznoi obriadnosti* [Struggle for a New Social Way of Life and the Birth of Soviet Nonreligious Ceremonial]. M.: Znanie, Tsentr. Dom nauch. ateizma, 1988. 39 pp.

786 Boriskin, V.M. *Ateizm i tvorchestvo* [Atheism and Creative Work]. Saransk: Mordov. kn. izd-vo, 1986. 118 pp. Annot. bibl.: pp. 111-117. For review see item 4982.

787 Borisoglebskii, L. "'Sviatye' iz Solt-Leik-Siti" ["Saints" from Salt-Lake-City]. *Nauka i religiia* 3 (1982): 62-63.

788 Borisov, L. "Rasprostranenie islama prodolzhaetsia?" [Spreading of Islam Continues?]. *Nauka i religiia* 12 (1984): 54-57.

789 Borisov, N.[S]. *Russkaia tserkov' v politicheskoi bor'be XIV-XV vekov* [Russian Church in Poltical Struggle of XIVth-XVth Centuries]. M.: Izd-vo MGU, 1986. 207 pp. Name index: pp. 198-206. For reviews see items 4983-4984.

790 Borisov, N.S. *Tserkovnye deiateli srednevekovoi Rusi XIII-XVII vv.* [Church Dignitaries of Medieval Rus' of XIIIth-XVIIth C.]. M.: Iz-vo MGU, 1988. 200 pp. Annot. bibl.: pp. 195-199.

791 Borkhes, Kh.L. "Buddizm" [Buddhism]. *Ateisticheskie chteniia* 18 (1989): 98-106.

792 Borovskii, Ia.E. *Mifologicheskii mir drevnikh kievlian* [Mythological World of Ancient Inhabitants of Kiev]. Kiev: Nauk. dumka, 1982. 104 pp., illus. (Nauch.-popul. lit.). Bibl.: p. 103.

793 Borshchevskii, N.Iu. "Evoliutsiia iaponskoi 'novoi religii' tenrike" [Evolution of Japanese "New Religion" Tenri-kyo]. *Sotsial'no-filosofskie aspekty kritiki religii.* L., 1988. Pp. 63-80.

794 Borunkov, Iu.F. "Mirovozzrencheskoe znachenie ateizma" [World Outlook's Importance of Atheism]. *Prepodavanie Nauchnogo ateizma v vuze.* M., 1988. Pp. 215-222.

795   Borunkov, Iu.F. *Nesovmestimost' nauchnogo i religioznogo poznaniia* [Incompatibility of Scientific and Religious Cognition]. M.: Znanic, 1982. 64 pp. (Novoe v zhizni, nauke, tekhnike. Nauch. ateizm; 12). Bibl.: p. 63.

796   Borutskii, S.T. "Utverzhdenie sovetskikh prazdnikov i obriadov - effectivnoe sredstvo ateisticheskogo vospitaniia trudiashchikhsia" [Assertion of Soviet Holidays and Ceremonials - Effective Means of Atheistic Education of Workers]. *Vopr. ateizma* 21 (1985): 79-84.

797   Botnar', I.F. "Rol' islamskogo faktora v politicheskoi zhizni Turtsii" [The Role of the Islamic Factor in Turkey's Political Life]. *Vestn. Mosk. un-ta.* Ser. 13, Vostokovedenie 3 (1987): 30-38.

798   Bovaev, B.E. "Klerikal'naia publitsistika Kalmykii kontsa XIX-nachala XX vv. o roli lamaistskogo dukhovenstva" [Kalmyk's Clerical Writings Late XIXth early XXth C. about the Role of Lamaist Clergy]. *Voprosy istorii lamaizma v Kalmykii.* Elista, 1987. Pp. 122-131.

799   Bragin, G.M. "Ob obydennoi forme okkul'tizma" [Ordinary Form of Occultism]. *Otnoshenie cheloveka k irratsional'nomu.* Sverdlovsk, 1989. Pp. 130-142.

800   Braichevskii, M.Iu. *Utverzhdenie khristianstva na Rusi* [Assertion of Christianity in Rus']. Kiev: Nauk. dumka, 1988. 261 pp. In Ukrainian. Summary in English. Bibl.: pp. 229-255. Published also in: 1989, 296 pp., in Russian. Bibl.: pp. 270-293.

801   Braiovich, S.M. "Vozvrahchaiutsia li bogi?" [Do Gods Come Back?]. *Aktual'nye problemy marksistskoi filosofii v zarubezhnykh stranakh.* M., 1987. Pp. 91-101.

802   Brandt, Iu. "Nekotorye razmyshleniia otnositel'no pozitsii khristianskikh i musul'manskikh krugov v osvoboditel'nom dvizhenii na siriisko-livanskoi territorii v period do pervoi mirovoi voiny" [Some Reflections Concerning the Position of Christian and Moslem Circles in Liberation Movement on Syrian-Lebanese Territory Before the First World War]. *Arabskie strany: Istoriia i sovremennost'* (sotsial., ekon. i pol. probl.). M., 1981. Pp. 12-20.

803   Braslavskii, L.Iu. "Evoliutsiia sotsial'no-eticheskikh pouchenii v staroobriadchestve i khristianskom sektantstve" [Evolution of Socio-Ethical

Preaching of Old Belief and Christian Sectarianism]. *Problemy istorii religii i ateizma.* Cheboksary, 1981. Pp. 116-124.

804 Braslavskii, L.Iu. "K voprosu genezisa staroobriadchestva i khristianskogo sektantstva na territorii sovremennoi Chuvashii v doreformennye gody (XVII-pervaia polovina XIX v.)." [Problem of the Origin of Old Belief and Christian Sectarianism on the Territory of Today's Chuvash in Pre Reform Years (XVIIth-early XIXth C.)]. *Problemy istorii religii i ateizma.* Cheboksary, i980. Pp. 57-63.

805 Braslavskii, L.Iu. *Protestantskie sekty v Chuvashii* [Protestant Sects in Chuvash]. Cheboksary: Chuvash. kn. izd-vo, 1988. 95 pp. In Chuvash.

806 Braslavskii, L.Iu. *Staroobriadchestvo i khristianskoe sektantstvo v Chuvashii* [Old Belief and Christian Sectarianism in Chuvash]. Cheboksary: Chuvash. kn. izd-vo, 1984. 96 pp.

807 Braslavskii, L.Iu. "Uchet novykh tendentsii v sovremennom sektantstve - vazhnoe uslovie povysheniia effektivnosti ateisticheskoi raboty" [Taking into Account the New Tendencies in Contemporary Sectarianism - Important Condition of Increasing the Effectiveness of Atheistic Work]. *Aktual'nye problemy obespecheniia effektivnosti nauchno-ateisticheskoi raboty.* Cheboksary, 1986. Pp. 90-97.

808 Braslavskii, L.Iu.; Gurova, T.G. "Praktika studentov v Gosudarstvennom muzee istorii religii i ateizma" [Student's Practice in the State Museum of History of Religion and Atheism]. *Muzei v ateisticheskoi propagande.* L., 1986. Pp. 47-51.

809 Brazhnik, I. "Na universitetskoi osnove" [On University Basis]. *Nauka i religiia* 11 (1981): 13-14.

810 Brazhnik, I. "Religioznyi ekstremizm: popranie prav veruiushchikh" [Religious Extremism: Suppression of Believers' Rights]. *Nauka i religiia* 1 (1981): 17-19.

811 Brazhnik, I.I. *Ateizm i svoboda sovesti* [Atheism and Freedom of Worship]. Kiev: Rad. shk., 1985. 96 pp. In Ukrainian.

812 Brazhnik, I.I. "O klassovoi sushchnosti polozheniia 'religiia - chastnoe delo grazhdanina'" [Class Essence of the Attitude Toward "Religion - Citizen's Private Affair]. *Vopr. ateizma 16 (1980): 17-24.*

813   Brazhnik, I.I. *Pravo. Religiia. Ateizm: Pravovoe soderzh. nauch. ateizma* [Law.
       Religion. Atheism: Legal Content of Scientific Atheism]. Kiev: Nauk.
       dumka, 1983. 206 pp. For reviews see items 4985-4986.

814   Brazhnik, I.I. "Pravovoe soderzhanie nauchnogo ateizma i formirovanie
       politicheskoi kul'tury grazhdan" [Legal Content of Scientific Atheism and
       Shaping Citizens' Political Culture]. *Vopr. ateizma* 17 (1981): 11-19.

815   Brazhnik, I.I. *Problemno-profiliruiushchee prepodavanie nauchnogo ateizma*
       [Problematic-Typical Teaching of Scientific Atheism]. Kiev: Vishcha skola.
       Izd-vo pri Kiev. un-te, 1980. 67 pp.

816   Brazhnik, I.I. *Sektantstvo i sektanty: ot proshlogo k sovremennosti*
       [Sectarianism and Sectarians: From the Past to Contemporaneity]. Kiev:
       Znanie UkSSR, 1989. 46 pp. (Ser. 5 Nauchno-ateisticheskaia / O-vo
       "Znanie" UkSSR; No 7}. In Ukrainian.

817   Brazhnik, I.I. *Vzaimosviaz' pravovogo i ateisticheskogo vospitaniia* [Correlation
       of Legal and Atheistic Education]. Kiev: Znanie UkSSR, 1982. 47 pp.
       (Ser. 5 "Nauchno-ateisicheskaia" / O-vo "Znanie" UkSSR; No 12). In
       Ukrainian. Bibl.: pp. 44-46.

818   Brechak, I.M. *Kritika religioznoi kontseptsii proiskhozhdeniia cheloveka*
       [Critique of the Religious Concept of the Origin of Man]. M.: Znanie,
       1980. 64 pp. (Novoe v zhizni, nauke, tekhnike. Ser. "Nauch. ateizm"; No
       10).

819   Brechak, I.M. *Proiskhozhdenie cheloveka: mify i fakty* [The Origin of Man:
       Myths and Facts]. Kiev: Znanie UkSSR, 1985. 48 pp. Ser. V "Nauchno-
       ateisticheskaia" / O-vo "Znanie" UkSSR; No 5). In Ukrainian.

820   Brenman, R.A. *Iudaizm i sionizm v sovremennoi ideologicheskoi bor'be*
       [Judaism and Zionism in Contemporary Ideological Struggle]. Kiev:
       Znanie UkSSR, 1981. 32 pp. (Ser. 5 "Nauchno-ateistickeskaia" / O-vo
       "Znanie" UkSSR; No 1). Bibl.: p. 32. In Ukrainian.

821   Briantseva, V.N. *Mify Drevnei Gretsii i muzyka* [Ancient Greece Myths and
       Music]. 3rd ed. M.: Muzyka, 1988. 44 pp., illus.

822   Brikovskis, V. "Perestroika: mnenie litovskogo katolika" [Perestroika: Opinion
       of a Lithuanian Catholic]. *Religiia v SSSR* 8 (1987): VB 1.

823 Britvin, V.G. et al. "Formirovanie nauchno-ateisicheskoi ubezhdennosti u molodezhi" [Shaping Youth's Scientific-Atheistic Conviction]. *Vopr. nauch. ateizma* 26 (1980): 191-204.

824 Brodskaia, E. "Spasenie mira po professoru Uaitu" [Professor White's View on the Salvation of the World]. *Nauka i religiia* 8 (1980): 36-37.

825 Brudzin'ski, V. "Ioann XXIII i vatikanskaia kontseptsiia mira" [John XXIIIrd and the Vatican's Conception of the World]. *Kritika sovremennoi katoli-cheskoi i protestanskoi teologii.* M., 1989. Pp. 65-92.

826 Brushlinskaia, O. "'Ia chuvstvuiu pravdu vashego dvizheniia'" ["I Feel the Truth of Your Movement"]. *Nauka i religiia* 11 (1987): 5-8.

827 Brushlinskaia, O. "Ostalsia neraskaiannym..." [Remained Unrepentant...]. *Nauka i religiia* 6 (1988): 42-46.

828 Brushlinskaia, O.; Zhernevskaia, I. "Sviaz' vremen: Gos. muzeiu istorii religii i ateizma - 50 let" [The Bond of Times: Fiftieth Anniversary of the State Museum of History of Religion and Atheism]. *Nauka i religiia* 1 (1983): 2-9.

829 Brykina, G.A. "Idoly iz Kairagacha i nekotorye voprosy verovanii u drevnikh fergantsev" [Idols from Kairagach and some Questions on the Beliefs of the Ancient Ferghans]. *Pamiatniki kul'tury: Novye otkrytiia. Ezhegodnik,* 1980. L., 1981. Pp. 507-521.

830 Bubiakov, S.B.; Kosianchuk, A.S. *Grazhdanskie obiazannosti i religioznaia vera* [Civic Duties and Religious Faith]. Kiev: Politizdat Ukrainy, 1980. 76 pp. (Besedy s veruiushchimi).

831 Bublik, S.A. "Rol' patrioticheskogo vospitaniia v formirovanii ateisticheskikh ubezhdenii" [The Role of Patriotic Education in Forming Atheistic Convictions]. *Vopr. ateizma* 18 (1982): 55-61.

832 Bublik, S.A.; Dubovenko, N.F. "Partiinost' nauchnogo ateizma i ee burz-huazno-klerikal'naia fal'sifikatsiia" [Party Spirit of Scientific Atheism and its Bourgeois-Clerical Falsification]. *Vopr. ateizma* 25 (1989): 50-58.

833 Bubnova, M.A. "Srednevekovye kladbishcha Pamira X-XI vv." [Pamir's Medieval Cemeteries Xth-XIth C.]. *Pamirovedenie* 2 (1985): 140-160.

834   Bubnovich, A.V. "O programmno-tselevom podkhode k upravleniiu formiro-
         vaniem nauchno-ateisticheskogo mirovozzreniia lichnosti" [Special Purpose
         Programme of Approach for Directing the Forming of the Individual's
         Scientific-Atheistic   Outlook].   *Aktual'nye   problemy   istoricheskogo
         materializma.* Alma-Ata, 1982. Pp. 139-151.

835   *Buddizm: istoriia i kul'tura* [Buddhism: History and Culture]. M.: Nauka,
         1989. 227 pp. Part of the text in Tibetan.

836   *Buddizm, gosudarstvo i obshchestvo v stranakh Tsentral'noi i Vostochnoi Azii
         v srednie veka* [Buddhism, State and Society in Central and Eastern Asian
         Countries in the Middle Ages]. Ed.: G.M. Bongard-Levin. M.: Nauka,
         1982. 317 pp. (Kul'tura narodov Vostoka. Materialy i issled.). For review
         see item 4987.

837   *Buddizm i gosudarstvo na Dal'nem Vostoke* [Buddhism and the State in the
         Far East]. Ed.: L.P. Deliusin. M.: Nauka, 1987. 228 pp.

838   *Buddizm i literaturno-khudozhestvennoe tvorchestvo narodov Tsentral'noi Azii*
         [Buddhism and Belles Lettres of the Peoples of Central Asia]. Ed.: R.E.
         Pubaev. Novosibirsk: Nauka. Sib. otd-nie, 1985. 127 pp.

839   *Buddizm i srednevekovaia kul'tura narodov Tsentral'noi Azii* [Buddhism and
         Medieval Culture of Peoples of Central Asia]. [Ed.: K.M. Gersimova et
         al.]. Novosibirsk: Nauka. Sib. otd-nie, 1980. 177 pp. For reviews see items
         4988-4989.

840   *Buddizm i traditsionnye verovaniia narodov Tsentral'noi Azii* [Buddhism and
         Traditional Beliefs of Peoples of Central Asia]. [Ed.: K.M. Gerasimova et
         al]. Novosibirsk: Nauka. Sib. otd-nie, 1981. 185 pp., illus. For review see
         item 4988.

841   *Buddizm v SSSR* [Buddhism in USSR]. M.: Novosti, 1988. 31 pp. In
         English.

842   *Budni ateista* [Atheist's Weekdays]. [Comp.: Kh. Kiaen]. Tallin: Eesti raamat,
         1985. 96 pp., illus. In Estonian.

843   Budov, A.I. "Mezhdu veroi i neveriem" [Between Faith and Unbelief].
         Molodoi kommunist 8 (1980): 45-48.

844   Budov, A.I. *Religioznye illiuzii na poroge zhizni* [Religious Illusions at Life's Threshold]. Kishinev: Kartia moldoveniaske, 1983. 172 pp., illus. In Moldavian. For reviews see items 4990-4991.

845   Budov, A.I. "Tsennosti ateizma" [Values of Atheism]. *Molodoi kmmunist* 11 (1981): 55-59.

846   Buevskii, A. "Tserkov' i Velikii Oktiabr'" [Church and the Great October]. *Religiia v SSSR* 3 (1987): AB 1-AB 4.

847   Bukhert, B.G. "Chislennost' i sotsial'nyi sostav staroobriadtsev Nizhegorod-skogo kraia po itogam perepisei pervoi poloviny XVIII v." [Numbers and Social Structure of Old Believers in Nijninovgorod Krai According to the Results of the Census of the early XVIIIth C.]. Publitsistika i istori-cheskie sochineniia perioda feodalizma. Novosibirsk, 1989. Pp. 126 - 131.

848   Bukin, B.R. *Ateisticheskomu vospitaniiu - kompleksnyi podkhod* [A Complex Approach to Atheist Education]. L.: Lenizdat, 1980. 47 pp. (V pomoshch' propagandistu nauch. ateizma).

849   Bukina, I.N. "Nauchno-tekhnicheskaia revoliutsiia i religioznaia orientatsiia lichnosti" [Scientific-Technical Revolution and Religious Orientation of the Individual]. *Nauchno-tekhnicheskaia revoliutsiia i lichnost'*. L., 1982. Pp. 85-95.

850   Bukina, T.M. "Vzgliady E. Diurkgeima na religiiu" [E. Durgheims' Views on Religion]. *Aktual'nye problemy ateisticheskogo vospitaniia i kritika religioznoi ideologii*. M., 1981. Pp. 49-56.

851   Bukina T.N.[sic!] "Sotsiologiia E. Diurkgeima kak teoreticheskii istochnik Sovremennoi burzhuaznoi sotsiologii religii" [E. Durgheims' Sociology as Theoretical Source of the Contemporary Bourgeois Sociology of Religion]. *Kritika religioznoi ideologii i problemy ateisticheskogo vospitaniia*. M., 1982. Pp. 42-51.

852   Bukovich, D.M. et al. *Uniia na sluzhbe reaktsii: Pravosudie uniat. tserkvi* [Uniate Church in the Service of Reaction: Justice of Uniate Church]. Uzhgorod: Karpati, 1980. 128 pp. In Hungarian.

853   Bulambaev, Zh.A. *Stikhii, vnushavshie strakh* [Elementals, Suggesting Fear].
        Alma-Ata: Kazakhstan, 1986. 62 pp., illus. (Uchenye beseduiut s
        veruiushchimi). Bibl.: p. 61.

854   Bulatova, A.G. "Prazdniki letnego kalendarnogo tsikla u dargintsev (XIX-
        nach. XX v.)". [Holidays of the Dargin Summer Cycle Calendar (XIXth-
        early XXth C.)]. *Kalendar' i kalendarnye obriady narodov Dagestana.*
        Makhachkala, 1987. Pp. 47-63.

855   Bulgakov, S. "Intelligentsiia i religiia" [Intelligentsia and Religion]. *Nauka i
        religiia* 11 (1989): 24-29.

856   Bulgakov, S. "Karl Marks kak religioznyi tip" [Karl Marx as a Religious
        Type]. *Kuban'* 11 (1989): 60-68. Reprint from *Mosk. ezhenedel'nik.* 1906.
        No 22-25.

857   Bunechko, I.G. *Vospityvat' grazhdanina i truzhenika* [To Educate a Citizen
        and Toiler]. Kiev: Znanie UkSSR, 1987. 48 pp. (Ser. 5,
        Nauchno-ateisticheskaia / O-vo "Znanie" UkSR; No 4). In Ukrainian.

858   Buniat-zade, Z.A.; Badirbeili, R.F. "Khram ognia Ateshgiakh v opisanii
        poliakov (XIXth v.)" [Ateshghyah Temple of Fire Described by Poles
        (XIXth C.)]. *Dokl. AN AzSSR.* T. 38. 8 (1982): 49-52. Summaries in
        Azerbaijan and English.

859   Burduli, M.I. "Verovaniia, sviazannye s psikho-nervnymi zabolevaniiami i
        magiko-religioznye ritualy v Svaneti" [Beliefs Linked with Psycho-Nervous
        Illnesses and Magic-Religious Ritual in Svanetia]. *Istoriko- etnograficheskie
        shtudii.* Tbilisi, 1988. Ch. 3. Pp. 110-116. In Georgian. Summary in
        Russian.

860   Buriakovskii, A.L.; Smirnov, M.Iu. "Kritika vzgliadov sovremennoi khris-
        tianskoi teologii na sotsial'nye konflikty v usloviiakh kapitalizma" [Critique
        of Contemporary Christian Theologic Views on Social Conflicts under
        Capitalism]. *Vestn. Leningr. un-ta.* Ser. 6. Istoriia KPSS, nauch. kommu-
        nizm, filosofiia , pravo 2 (1987): 103-105. Summary in English.

861   Burikhodzhaev, M.[Ia] *Iskusstvo i ateisticheskoe vospitanie* [Art and Atheistic
        Education]. Tashkent: Uzbekistan, 1980. 37 pp. (Ser. "Marksizm-leninizm";
        No 3). In Uzbek.

862 Burikhodzhaev, M.Ia. "Literatura i formirovanie ateisticheskoi kul'tury nashego sovremennika" [Literature and the Forming of the Atheistic Culture of Our Contemporary]. *Aktual'nye voprosy formirovaniia nauchno-materialisticheskogo mirovozzreniia trudiashchikhsia.* Tashkent, 1989. Pp. 126-130.

863 Burkhanov, Sh.Sh.; Gusarov, V.I. *Sovetskaia vlast' i islam* [Soviet Regime and Islam]. M.: Novosti, 1984. 48 pp. In English.
Published also by Novosti in: Dari, French and Pushtu.

864 Burkov, V.V. *Pod maskoi 'khristianskoi liubvi'* [Under the Mask of "Christian Love"]. L.: Lenizdat, 1983. 64 pp. (Sov. deistvitel'nost' i mify burzhuaz. propagandy).

865 Burkova, G.A. *K kritike filosofskikh osnov krishnaizma* [Criticism of Philosphical Foundations of Krishnaism]. Ioshkar-Ola, 1988. 10 pp. Bibl.: p. 10.

866 Bushenieks, A.A. *Antiklerikalizm i ateizm v Latvii nakanune i vo vremia revoliutsii 1905 goda* [Anticlericalism and Atheism in Latvia on the Eve and During the 1905 Revolution]. Riga: Znanie LatvSSR, 1980. 26 pp. (Material v pomoshch' lektoru / O-vo "Znanie" LatvSSR, Nauch.-metod. sovet po propagande nauch. ateizma) (Znanie narodu). In Latvian. Bibl.: pp. 24-26.

867 Bushmanis, G. *Kritika teologicheskikh dokazatel'stv bytiia boga* [Critique of the Theological Proofs of God's Existence]. Riga: Znanie LatvSSR, 1980. 27 pp. (Material v pomoshch' lektoru / O-vo "Znanie" LatvSSR, Nauch.-metod. sovet po propagande nauch. ateizma). (Znanie narodu). In Latvian. Annot. in Russian. Bibl.: p. 26.

868 Bushmanis, G.G. "Otchuzhdenie v religiozno-ideologicheskom mirovozzrenii" [Alienation in Religious-Idealistic World Outlook]. *Problemy istorii religii i ateizma.* Cheboksary, 1980. Pp. 37-43.

869 Busygina, M.V. *Ateizm i formirovanie politicheskoi kul'tury lichnosti* [Atheism and the Forming of the Political Culture of the Individual]. Kiev: Znanie UkSSR, 1987. 48 pp. (Ser. 5 Nauchno-ateisticheskaia / O-vo "Znanie" UkSSR; No 11). Annot. bibl.: p. 48.

870   Busygina, M.V. "Vospitanie politicheskoi kul'tury v protsesse ateisticheskoi propagandy" [Education of Political Culture in the Process of Atheistic Propaganda]. *Vopr. ateizma* 24 (1988): 49-53.

871   Butene, F.K. *Obnovlenie katolitsizma* [Renovation of Catholicism]. Vil'nius: Znanie LitSSR, 1982. 25 pp. (Material dlia lektora / O-vo "Znanie" LitSSR). In Lithuanian. Bibl.: p. 25.

872   Butene, R.K. *Biografiia bez lichnosti* [Biography Without Personality]. Vil'nius: Mintis, 1984. 254 pp. (Besedy s veruiushchimi). In Lithuanian. Bibl.: pp. 248-251.

873   Butikov, G.P. "Khudozhestvennyi muzei v nauchno-ateisticheskom vospitanii" [Museum of the Arts in Scientific-Atheistic Education]. *Muzei v ateisticheskoi propagande.* L., 1980. Pp. 40-50.

874   Butinova, M.S. "O sozdanii ekspozitsii 'Religiia pervobytnogo obshchestva' v Leningradskom muzee istorii religii i ateizma" [On the Layout of Exhibition of "Religion in Primitive Society" in the Leningrad Museum of the History of Religion and Atheism]. *Muzei v ateisticheskoi propagande.* L., 1981. Pp. 54-72.

875   Butinova, M.S. "Religiia pervobytnogo obshchestva" [Religion of the Primitive Society]. *Muzei istorii religii i ateizma.* Putevoditel'. L., 1981. Pp. 27-43.

876   Butinova, M.S. "Traditsii i innovatsii v religii narodov Okeanii" [Traditions and Innovations in the Religion of Peoples of Oceania]. *Nauchno-ateisticheskie issledovaniia v muzeiakh.* L., 1987. Pp. 7-33.

877   Buzova, N.G. "Filosofskaia modernizatsiia idei boga v teologii P. Tillikha" [Philosophical Modernization of the Idea of God in P. Tillichs' Theology]. *Kritika religioznoi ideologii i problemy ateisticheskogo vospitaniia.* M., 1980. Pp. 61-68.

878   Bychko, A.K. *U istokov khristianskogo irratsionalizma* [By the Sources of Christian Irrationalism]. Kiev: Politizdat Ukrainy, 1984. 140 pp. Annot. bibl.: pp. 132-137. Name index: pp. 138-139.

879   Bychko, B.I.; Grabovskii, S.I.; Koval', M.D. "K voprosu o spetsifike mifologicheskogo mirovospriiatiia Kievskoi Rusi" [On the Problem of the Specific in the Mythological World Perception of the Kievan Rus']. *Probl. filosofii* 54 (1981): 136-141.

880   Bychkov, A.M. "Pravo na blagodeianie" [Right to Good Deed]. *Novoe vremia* 22 (1988): 46-47.

881   Bykovskii, A. "Urodlivyi simbioz" [Ugly Symbiosis]. *Zhurnalist* 4 (1989): 9-14.

882   Bysku, F.[A]. "Ateisticheskoe vospitanie molodykh rabochikh" [Atheistic Education of Young Workers]. *Kommunist Moldavii* 5 (1984): 36-41.

883   Bysku, F.A. *Ateisticheskoe vospitanie rabotaiushchei molodezhi* [Atheistic Education of Working Youth]. Kishinev: Shtiintsa, 1985. 115 pp. Summaries in English and French. Annot. bibl.: pp. 111-112.

884   Chakhava, M. *Narod, bog i zakon* [People, God and Law]. Tbilisi: Merani, 1989. 125 pp., illus. In Georgian. Part of the text in Russian.

885   Chakhkiev, D.Iu. "O sotsial'nom i konfessial'nom statute vladel'tsev vaina-khskikh boevykh bashen s krestami-'golgofami'" [Social and Confessional Statute of Owners of Fighting Towers with "Calvary"- Crosses]. *Etnografiia i voprosy religioznykh vozzrenii chechentsev i ingushei v dorevoliutsionnyi period.* Groznyi, 1981. Pp. 52-57.

886   Chanchibaeva, L.V. "Kratkii obzor izucheniia religioznykh verovanii u altaitsev" [Short Review of the Study of Religious Beliefs of the Altai People]. *Voprosy istorii Gornogo Altaia.* Gorno-Altaisk, 1980. Pp. 132-141.

887   Chechulin, A.A. "Obshchenie veriushchikh kak faktor sokhraneniia i vospro-izvodstva religioznykh perezhitkov" [Relations Among Believers as a Factor of Preservation and Reproduction of Religious Survivals]. *Nauchnyi ateizm, religiia i sovremennost'.* Novosibirsk, 1987. Pp. 161-188.

888   Chedavichius, A.M. *Sotsial'naia priroda religioznogo chuvstva* [Social Nature of Religious Feelings]. Vil'nius: Mintis, 1984. 292 pp. In Lithuanian. Name index: pp. 288-290.

889   Chekal', L.A. "Kompensatsionnaia funktsiia religii" [Religion's Compensatory Function]. *Filos. i sotsiol. mysl'* 2 (1989): 119-122. Summary in English, p. 136.

890   Chekal' L.A. "Nesostoitel'nost' sovremennykh burzhuaznykh interpretatsii sotsial'noi prirody religioznogo soznaniia" [Ungroundlessness of Contem-porary Bourgeois Interpretations of the Social Nature of Religious Cons-ciousness]. *Vopr. ateizma* 25 (1989): 105-112.

891 Chekodanova, K.K. "Izmenenie vnutrennego mira lichnosti i stanovlenie ateisticheskogo soznaniia" [Change of Individual's Inner World and Coming into Being of Atheistic Consciousness]. *Muzei v ateisticheskoi propagande.* L., 1986. Pp. 31-46.

892 Chekodanova, K.K. "Otnoshenie k kul'turnomu naslediiu Drevnei Rusi i ateisticheskaia propaganda" [Attitude to Cultural Heritage of the Ancient Rus' and Atheistic Propaganda]. *Muzei v ateisticheskoi propagande.* L., 1980. Pp. 59-73.

893 Chekuolis, A. "Litva: Dialog s katolicheskim dukhovenstvom" [Lithuania: Dialogue with Catholic Clergy]. *Religiia v SSSR* 9 (1987): ACh 1-ACh 6.

894 Chelko, Ia. "Ekho Oktiabria" [Echo of October]. *Nauka i religiia* 11 (1987): 57.

895 Chelko, Ia. "Khristianskaia tserkov' i revoliutsionnye peremeny v Chekhoslovakii v kontse 40-kh godov" [Christian Church and Revolutionary Changes in Czechoslovakia at the End of the 40s]. *Vopr. nauch. ateizma* 36 (1987): 208-220.

896 Chemiakina, A.V. "Vliianie nauchno-tekhnicheskoi revoliutsii na religiiu" [The Influence of Scientific-Technical Revolution on Religion]. *Nauka i razvitie obshchestvennykh otnoshenii.* Sverdlovsk, 1980. Pp. 55-57.

897 Chemiakina, A.V.; Tronina, G.I.; Chenyshkova, Z.E. "Sotsial'nyi progress i osobennosti modernizatsii religioznoi ideologii v sovremennuiu epokhu" [Social Progress and Features of Modernization of Religious Ideology in Contemporary Epoch]. *Chelovek i sotsal'nyi pogress.* Izhevsk, 1982. Pp. 163-165.

898 Cherednichenko, T.V. "Religiia i religioznost' v sovremennoi kul'ture" [Religion and Religiosity in Contemporary Culture]. *Dukhovnaia zhizn' obshchestva i struktura obshchestvennogo soznaniia.* M., 1988. Pp. 56-71.

899 Chernetsov, A.V. "Amulety-zmeeviki i problema 'dvoeveriia'" [Amulets-Serpentines and the Problem of "Twofaith"]. *Vopr. nauch. ateizma* 37 (1988): 74-88.

900 Cherniak, E.B. *Nevidimye imperii: Tainye obshchestva starogo i novogo vremeni na Zapade* [Invisible Empires: Secret Societies of the Old and

New Times in the West]. M.: Mysl', 1987. 272 pp., illus. Bibl.: pp. 252-270.

901 Cherniak, I.Kh. "Bibleiskaia filologiia Lorentso Vally i erazmov perevod Novogo zaveta" [Laurence Valla's Biblical Philology and Erasmus Translation of the New Testament]. *Erazm Rotterdamskii i ego vremia.* M., 1989. Pp. 59-66.

902 Cherniak, L. "Pod sen'iu sviatykh darov" [Under the Protection of Holy Gifts]. *Nauka i religiia* 7 (1982): 41-45.

903 Cherniak, V.A. "Opyt interval'nykh sotsiologicheskikh issledovanii ateizma rabochego klassa" [Experience of Interval Sociological Researches of Atheism of the Workers Class]. *Vopr. nauch. ateizma* 26 (1980): 178-190.

904 Cherniak, V.A. *Sotsiologiia ateizma i istoricheskii materializm* [Sociology of Atheism and Historical Materialism]. Alma-Ata: Kazakhstan, 1989. 176 pp.

905 Cherniakhovskii, A. "Za gran'iu nauki: Est' li zhizn' posle smerti?" [Beyond Science's Verge: Is There Life After Death?]. *Nauka i religiia* 2 (1980): 18-22.

906 Chernii, A.M. *Ateisticheskoe vospitanie molodezhi: Opyt i problemy* [Atheistic Upbringing of Youth: Experience and Problems]. Kiev: Znanie UkSSR, 1981. 47 pp. (Ser. 5 "Nauchno-ateisticheskaia" / O-vo "Znanie" UkSSR; No 6). Bibl.: p. 46.

907 Chernii, A.M. *Ateisticheskoe vospitanie na sele* [Atheistic Education in the Village]. Kiev: Politizdat Ukrainy, 1981. 104 pp. In Ukrainian.

908 Chernii, A.M. *Ot neveriia do vysot ateisticheskoi kul'tury* [From Unbelief up to the Heights of Atheistic Culture]. Kiev: Znanie UkSSR, 1984. 47 pp. (Ser. 5 "Nauchno-ateisticheskaia" / O-vo "Znanie" UkSSR; No 2). In Ukrainian. Bibl.: p. 46. Annot. bibl.: p. 45.

909 Chernii, A.V. *Religiia i ateizm v ideologicheskoi bor'be* [Religion and Atheism in Ideological Struggle]. M.: [S.n.], 1979 (dated 1980). 35 pp. (V pomoshch' koms. aktivu, lektoram, dokladchikam, propagandistam / TsK VLKSM. B-chka "Probl. ideol. bor'by na sovrem. etape"). Bibl.: p. 34.

910   Chernopiatov, M.P.; Vasil'ev, A.V. "Pravoslavnaia tserkov'" [Othodox Church]. *Brat. vestnik* 3 (1988): 47-55.

911   Chernov, M.I. "Russkaia pravoslavnaia tserkov': Proshloe i nastoiashchee" [Russian Orthodox Church: Past and Present]. *Sov. pedagogika* 6 (1988): 114-122.

912   Chernov, M.I. "Sotsial'nye aspekty 1000-letnego iubileia 'kreshcheniia Rusi'" [Social Aspects of the 1000th Year Jubilee of "Christening of Rus'"]. *Sov. pedagogika* 5 (1988): 109-117.

913   Chernysheva, N.A. "Znachenie kompleksnogo vospitaniia v povyshenii sotsial'noi aktivnosti lichnosti" [The Importance of All-Embracing Education in Raising Individual's Social Activity]. *Kritika religioznoi ideologii i problemy ateisticheskogo vospitaniia.* M., 1980. Pp. 26-33.

914   Chernysheva, O.V. "Religioznye i patsifistskie organizatsii v shvedskom antivoennom dvizhenii" [Religious and Pacifist Organizations in Swedish Anti-War Movement]. *Severnaia Evropa.* M., 1988. Pp. 97-127.

915   Chernysheva, O.V. "Sotsial'naia politika sovremennoi Shvedskoi tserkvi" [Social Policy of Contemporary Swedish Church]. *Skandinavskii sbornik* Tallin, 1988. T. 32. Pp. 34-49.

916   Chernysheva, O.V. "Svobodnotserkovnoe dvizhenie v sovremennoi Shvetsii" [Freechurch Movement in Contemporary Sweden]. *XI Vsesoiuznaia konferentsiia po izucheniiu istorii, ekonomiki, literatury i iazyka Skandinavskikh stran i Finliandii.* M., 1989. [T]. 1. Pp. 20-21.

917   Chernysheva. O.V.; Komarov, Iu.D. "Tserkov' skandinavskikh stran vo vtoroi polovine XX v." [Church of Scandinavian Countries in the second half of XXth C.]. *XI Vsesoiuznaia konferentsiia po izuchenii istorii, ekonomiki, literatury i iazyka Skandinavskikh stran i Finliandii.* M., 1989. [T]. 1. Pp. 6-7.

918   Chernysheva, O.V., Komarov, Iu.D. *Tserkov' v skandinavskikh stranakh* [Church in Scandinavian Countries]. M.: Nauka, 1988. 177 pp., illus. (Nauch.-popul. lit. Ser. "Istoriia i sovremennost'").

919   Chernyshkova, Z.E. "Ideia boga v russkoi filosofii nachala XX veka" [The Idea of God in Russian Philosophy early XXth Century]. *Otnoshenie cheloveka k irratsional'nomu.* Sverdlovsk, 1989. Pp. 117-129.

920   Chertikhin, V.E. *V poiskakh raia i ada* [In the Search of Paradise and
       Hell]. M.: Politizdat, 1980. 88 pp., illus. (Besedy o mire i cheloveke).
       Published also in:
       Kishinev: Kartia moldoveniaske, 1981. 112 pp. In Moldavian.
       Dushanbe: Irfon, 1983. 91 pp. illus. In Tajik.

921   Chertkov, A.[B]. "Kak otvechat' na voprosy posle lektsii" [How to Answer
       Questions After the Lecture]. *Nauka i religiia* 12 (1983): 15-16.

922   Chertkov, A.B. *Otvety na voprosy posle ateisticheskoi lektsii* [Answers to
       Questions After Atheistic Lecture]. M.: Znanie, 1988. 64 pp. (Novoe v
       zhizni, nauke, technike. Nauch. ateizm; 2 /1988). Bibl: p. 63.

923   Chertkov, A.B. *Pravoslavnaia filosofiia i sovremennost'*: Kritich. analiz
       'metafiziki vseedinstva' i ee roli v ideologii sovremen. pravoslaviia
       [Orthodox Philosophy and Contemporaneity: Critical Analysis of
       "Metaphysics of Allunity" and Its Role in Ideology of Contemporary
       Orthodoxy]. Riga: Avots, 1989. 364 pp. Bibl.: pp. 353-362.

924   Chertkov, A.B. "Uluchshat' nauchno-ateisticheskoe vospitanie" [To Improve
       Scientific-Atheistic Education]. *Kommunist Sov. Latvii* 10 (1986): 78-84.

925   Chesterton, G.K. "Frantsisk Assizkii" [Francis of Assisi]. *Vopr. filosofii* 1
       (1989): 83-128.

926   Chibirov, L.A. *Drevneishie plasty dukhovnoi kul'tury osetin* [Ancient Layers of
       Osetins Spiritual Culture]. Tskhinvali: Iryston, 1984. 217 pp. Name,
       geographical, mythic cults and subject indices: pp. 207-216. For reviews
       see items 4992-4993.

927   Chigrinskaia, L.F. "Kritika vzgliadov pravoslavnykh bogoslovov na ekologi-
       cheskie problemy" [Critique of Orthodox Theologians' Views on Ecolo-
       gical Problems]. *Voprosy filosofii i sotsiologii*. L., 1980. Pp. 107-110.

928   Chigrinskaia, L.F. "Zadachi ateisticheskogo vospitaniia v tekhnicheskikh
       vuzakh" [Tasks of Atheistic Upbringing in Technical Institutions of Higher
       Education]. *Aktual. vopr. metodiki prepodavaniia obshchestv. nauk i kom.
       vospitaniia studentov* 5 (1987): 79-85.

929   Chigrinskii, M.F. "O verovaniiakh aborigenov Taivana" [On Beliefs of
       Taiwan's Aboriginals]. *Strany i narody Vostoka* 25 (1987): 165-178. Bibl.:
       pp. 176-178.

930   Chigrinskii, M.F. "Zapadnye missionery na Taivane (XVII-XIX vv.)"
       [Western Missionaries in Taiwan (XVIIth-XIXth C.)]. *Deviatnadtsataia
       nauchnaia konferentsiia "Obshchestvo i gosudarstvo v Kitae".* M., 1988. Ch.
       2. Pp. 132-137.

931   Chinchaladze, A. *Religiia i ideologicheskaia bor'ba na sovremennom etape*
       [Religion and Ideological Struggle in Contemporary Stage]. Tbilisi: Znanie
       GSSR, 1980. 32 pp. In Georgian. Bibl.: p. 32.

932   "Chitateli o turinskoi plashchanitse: Obzor pisem i neobkhodimye
       utochaeniia" [Readers About the Shroud of Torino: Review of Letters
       and Necessary Elaborations]. *Nauka i religiia* 9 (1985): 28-34.

933   Chkadua, R.M. "Rol' obshchestva 'Znanie' GSSR v propagande nauchnogo
       ateizma" [The Role of Society "Knowledge" GSSR in the Propaganda of
       Scientific Atheism]. *Istoriia religii i ateisticheskaia propaganda.* Tbilisi,
       1987. Kn. 11. Pp. 12-24. In Georgian. Summary in Russian.

934   Chkhartishvili, I.N. *Antireligioznaia bor'ba v Gruzii vo vtoroi polovine XIX v.*
       [Anti-Religious Struggle in Georgia in the second half of XIXth C.].
       Tbilisi: Metsniereba, 1982. 126 pp. In Georgian. Summary in Russian.

935   Chkhartishvili, I.N. *Antireligioznye vozzreniia gruzinskikh prosvetitelei (vtoraia
       polovina XIX i nach. XX v.)* [Antireligious Outlook of Georgian
       Enlighteners (Second half of XIXth and early XXth C.)]. Tbilisi:
       Metsniereba, 1988. 78 pp.

936   Chkhartishvili, I.N. "Antireligioznye vzgliady publitsistov gazety 'Droeba'"
       [Antireligious Views of the Journalists of the Newspaper "Droeba"]. *Iz
       istorii religii i ateizma v Gruzii.* Tbilisi, 1988. Pp. 33-59. In Georgian.
       Summary in Russian.

937   Chkartashvili, I.N. "Gruzinskaia pressa II-i poloviny XIX i nachala XX vv. o
       roli prosveshcheniia v bor'be s sueveriiami" [Georgian Press of the Late
       XIXth and Early XXth C. on the Role of Enlightenment in the Struggle
       with Superstitions]. *Istoriia religii i ateisticheskaia propaganda.* Tbilisi, 1987.
       Kn. II. Pp. 94-101. In Georgian. Summary in Russian.

938   Chmykhov, N.A. "Kompromiss khristianstva s iazychestvom" [Christianity's
       Compromise with Heathenism]. *Otechestvennaia obshchestvennaia mysl'
       epokhi Srednevekov'ia.* Kiev, 1988. Pp. 106-114.

939 Chueva, I.P. *Problema cheloveka v sovremennom pravoslavii* [The Problem of Man in Contemporary Orthodoxy]. L.: Znanie RSFSR, 1980. 22 pp. (V pomoshch' lektoru / O-vo "Znanie" RSFSR, Leningr. org.).

940 Chugasian, L.B.-V. "Nersisian. Armianskie illiustrirovannye evangeliia" [Nersisian. Armenian Illustrated Gospels]. *Ist.-filol. zhurn.* 1 (1989): 238-241. In Armenian.

941 Chukhina, L.A. *Chelovek i ego tsennostnyi mir v religioznoi filosofii:* Kritich. ocherk [Man and His Valuable Universe in Religious Philosophy: Critical Essay]. Riga: Zinane, 1980. 288 pp. Name index: pp. 286-287. For reviews see items 4994-4996.

942 Chukovenkov, Iu.A. *Individual'naia ateisticheskaia rabota* [Individual Atheistic Work]. M.: Sov. Rossiia, 1988. 127 pp. Bibl.: pp. 125-126.

943 Chukovenkov, Iu.[A]. "Individual'naia ateisticheskaia rabota: Metod. sovety" [Individual Atheistic Work: Methodical Advices]. *Agitator* 2 (1982): 55-57.

944 Chkovenkov, Iu.A. *Individual'naia rabota s veruiushchimi: Voprosy metodiki i organizatsii* [Individual Work with Believers: Problems of Methodics and Organization]. M.: [S.n.], 1983. 39 pp. (Metod. material v pomoshch' lektoru / Mosk. obl. org. o-va "Znanie" RSFSR, Nauch. metod. sovet po propagande nauch. ateizma). Bibl.: pp. 37-38.

945 Chukovenkov, Iu.A. "Predmet, struktura i metod pravoslavnoi antropologii" [Object, Structure and Method of Orthodox Anthropology]. *Vopr. nauch. ateizma* 37 (1988): 252-270.

946 Chulaki, M. "Vechnoe bespokoistvo dukha" [Eternal Spirit's Anxiety]. *Nauka i religiia* 12 (1988): 21-22.

947 Chumicheva, O.V. "Novye materialy po istorii solovetskogo vosstaniia" [New Material on the History of Solovetsk Insurrection]. *Publitsistika i istoricheskie sochineniia perioda feodalizma.* Novosibirsk, 1989. Pp. 58-76.

948 Churlanova, P.K. "Vperedi-bol'shaia rabota" [Ahead-Important Task]. *Nauka i religiia* 2 (1988): 8-10.

949 Chutkerashvili, N.I. *Ateisticheskoe vospitanie molodezhi* [Atheistic Education of Youth]. Tbilisi: Metsniereba, 1986. 76 pp. In Georgian. Annot. bibl.: pp. 73-75.

950   Chutkerashvili, N.I *Osobennosti proiavleniia religioznosti sredi molodezhi i puti bor'by s nimi* [Manifestation Features of Youth's Religiousness and Ways of Struggle Agaist Them]. Tbilisi: Metsniereba, 1980. 47 pp. (Traditsiia i sovremennost'; 3). In Georgian.

951   Chutkerashvil, N.I. *Prichiny sushchestvovaniia religioznykh perezhitkov i puti ikh preodoleniia* [Causes of Existence of Religious Survivals and Ways to Overcome Them]. Tbilisi: Znanie GSSR, 1981. 30 pp. (O-vo "Znanie" GSSR; No 11). In Georgian.

952   Chuzhikova, N.D. "Kritika burzhuazno-klerikal'noi fal'sifikatsii ateisticheskogo vospitaniia v SSSR" [Critique of Bourgeois-Clerical Falsification about Atheistic Education in USSR]. *Aktual'nye problemy ateisticheskogo vospitaniia i kritika religioznoi ideologii.* M., 1981. Pp. 17-26.

953   Chyngyshbaeva, G. *Formy i metody ateisticheskogo vospitaniia uchashchikhsia* [Forms and Methods of Atheistic Upbringing of Pupils]. Frunze: Mektep, 1987. 87 pp. In Kirghiz.

954   *D.I. Pisarev ob ateizme, religii i tserkvi* [D.I. Pisarev on Atheism, Religion and Church]. Comp.: E.I. Rozenberg. M.: [S.n.], 1984. 53 pp. For review see item 4997.

955   *Da skroetsia t'ma!* [Keep Back Darkness!]. [Comp.: V.N. Kuznetsov]. Erevan: Aiastan, 1980. 391 pp. In Armenian.

956   Dadabaeva, S.Iu. "Voprosy povysheniia effektivnosti ateisticheskogo vospitaniia" [Problems of Increasing Effectiveness of Atheistic Education]. *Kompleksnyi podkhod v ateisticheskom vospitanii.* Dushanbe, 1988. Pp. 6-18. Bibl.: p. 18.

957   Dadybaeva, K.D. "Ateisticheskoe znachenie ustnogo tvorchestva kirkizkogo naroda" [Atheistic Importance of Oral Creation of Kirghiz People]. *Sotsial'no-eticheskie problemy povysheniia effektivnosti ateisticheskogo vospitaniia v mnogonatsional'nom regione.* Frunze, 1987. Pp. 26-34.

958   Dagdanov, G.B. "Sotsial'no-psikhologicheskie aspekty sistemy tsigun v Kitae" [Socio-Psychological Aspects of Tzugun System in China]. *Psikhologicheskie aspekty buddizma.* Novosibirsk, 1986. Pp. 110-120.

959   Dagvadorzh, D. "Rost ateizma v MNR" [Increase of Atheism in Mongolian People's Republic]. *Stroitel'stvo sotsializma i utverzhdenie nauchno-*

materialisticheskogo, ateisticheskogo mirovozzreniia (v regionakh rasprostraneniia lamaizma). M., 1981. Pp. 145-157.

960   Dandamaev, M.A. "Gosudarstvo i religiia na drevnem Blizhnem Vostoke: Dokl. podgot. k XVI MKIN" [State and Religion in Ancient Near East: Papers prepared for the XVIth World Congress of Historical Sciences]. *Vestn. drev. istorii* 2 (1985): 3-9. Summary in English.

961   Danielian, R.S. "Iz istorii deiatel'nosti protestantskikh missionerov v Osmanskoi imperii (konets XIX - nachalo XX v.)" [History of Protestant Missionaries' Activity in Ottoman Empire (end XIXth - early XXth C.)]. *Strany i narody Blizhnego i Srednego Vostoka.* Erevan, 1989. 15. Pp. 138-157. In Armenian. Summary in Russian.

962   Daniialov, M. "Zarubezhnye avtory o polozhenii religii v Dagestane" [Foreign Authors on Status of Religion in Dagestan]. *Sov. Dagestan* 2 (1987): 74-77.

963   Danil'chenko, R.N. *Ateisticheskoe vospitanie - vazhnyi faktor utverzhdeniia kommunisticheskoi morali* [Atheistic Education - Important Confirmation Factor of Communist Morals]. M.: Znanie, 1987. 64 pp. (Novoe v zhizni, nauke, tekhnike. Nauch. ateizm; No 6).

964   Danil'chenko, R.[N]. "Zhemchuzhina gorodov volzhskikh" [The Pearl of Volga's Towns]. *Nauka i religiia* 1 (1983): 39-41.

965   Danil'chenko, R.N. *Problema lichnosti v sovremennom khristianstve* [The Problem of Personality in Contemporary Christianity]. M.: Znanie, 1980. 64 pp. (Novoe v zhizni, nauke, tekhnike. Ser. "Nauch. ateizm"; No 8).

966   Danilova, M.; Tazhurizina, Z. "Kul'tura i mirovozzrenie: Problemy i diskussii" [Culture and World Outlook: Problems and Discussions]. *Nauka i religiia* 10 (1982): 19-22.

967   Darkevich, V.P. "Tserkov' i iazycheskie igrishcha" [Church and Pagan Festivals]. *Ateisticheskie chteniia* 18 (1989): 84-97.

968   Darmanskii, P.F. *Chemu uchat 'zapovedi bozh'i'* [What Do "God's Commandments" Teach]. Kiev: Znanie UkSSR, 1988. 47 pp. (Ser. 5, Nauch.-ateist. / O-vo "Znanie" UkSSR; No 1). In Ukrainian.

969 Darmanskii, P.F. *Novaia zhizn' - novye obriady* [New Life - New Ceremonials]. Kiev: Politizdat Ukrainy, 1984. 87 pp. (Ser. "Besedy s veruiushchimi"). In Ukrainian.

970 Darmanskii, P.F. *Sviashchennaia akva vite* [Holy Aqua Vitae]. Kiev: Politizdat Ukrainy, 1988. 102 pp. (Ser. "Besedy s veruiushchimi"). In Ukrainian.

971 Darmanskii, P.F. *Za ikonostasami altarei* [Behind Altars' Iconostasises]. Kiev: Politizdat Ukrainy, 1989. 263 pp., illus. In Ukrainian.

972 Darmanskii, P.F. *Zemnye istochniki 'sviashchennogo pisaniia'* [Worldly Sources of "Holy Scripture"]. Kiev: Molod', 1985. 183 pp., illus. In Ukrainian.

973 Dashiev, D.B. "Nekotorye sotsial'no-psikologicheskie aspekty kul'ta nastavnika (po tibetskim istochnikam)" [Some Socio-Psychological Aspects of Perceptor's Cult (by Tibetan Sources)]. *Psikhologicheskie aspekty buddizma.* Novosibirsk, 1986. Pp. 137-143.

974 Dashtseveg, B. "Reshenie 'lamskogo voprosa' v MNR" [Solution of the "Lama Problem" in Mongolian People's Republic]. *Stroitel'stvo sotsializma i utverzhdenie nauchno-materialisticheskogo, ateisticheskogo mirovozzre- niia.* M., 1981. Pp. 41-51.

975 Dausinas, M. *Moi put' k ateizmu* [My Way to Atheism]. Vil'nius: Mintis, 1984. 54 pp. (Besedy s veruiushchmi). In Lithuanian.

976 David mitropolit Sukhumskii i Abkhazskii. "Ne mogu ostavat'sia bezuchastnym k 'bogosloviiu osvobozhdeniia'" ["I Can Not Remain Unconcerned Towards 'Theology of Liberation'"]. *Religiia v SSSR* 4 (1987): BK1 -BK4.

977 David mitropolit Sukhumskii i Abkhazskii. *Osvobodit' ugnetennykh ot okov* [To Free Oppressed from Fetters]. M.: Novosti, 1988. 63 pp., illus. In English.
Published also by Novosti in: French, Spanish and Portuguese.

978 David mitropolit Sukhumskii i Abkhazskii. *Zhit' radi mira i spravedlivosti* [To Live for Peace and Justice]. M.: Novosti, 1986. 104 pp., illus. In English.
Published also by Novosti in: Italian and Spanish. Additional English ed. was published in 1988.

979 David-Neel', A. "Pobezhdaiushchie stuzhu [Conquerors of Frost]. *Nauka i religiia* 11 (1989): 56-57.

980 Davitadze, G.Z. *Islam, ego vrednye posledstviia* [Islam, Its Harmful Consequences]. Batumi: Sabchota Adzhara, 1985. 94 pp. In Georgian.

981 Davletshin, K.D. *Natsii i islam* [Nations and Islam]. Kazan': Tatar. kn. izdvo, 1986. 199 pp.

982 Davletshin, K.D. *Sotsialisticheskii obraz zhizni i svoboda sovesti* [Socialist Way of Life and Freedom of Worship]. Kazan': Tatar. kn. izd-vo, 1984. 129 pp. In Tatar.

983 Davliatov, M. "Ideologicheskaia nesostoiatel'nost' 'islamskogo faktora'" [Ideological Groundlessness of the "Islamic Factor"]. *Kommunist Tadzhikistana* 8 (1986): 81-88.

984 Davliatov, M. "Modernizatsia sotsial'no-politicheskoi kontseptsii sovremennogo islama" [Modernization of Socio-Political Conception of Contemporary Islam]. *Kommunist Tadzhikistana* 6 (1985): 79-85.

985 Davydenko, A.Iu. "K voprosu ob usilenii pozitsii kommunalistskikh i religioznoobshchinnykh sil v profsoiuznom dvizhenii nezavisimoi Indii" [On the Problem of Strengthening the Position of Communal and Religious Communities Forces in the Trade Union Movement of Independent India]. *Zarubezhnyi Vostok: Istoriia i sovremennost'* M., 1988. Pp. 70-84.

986 Davydova, N. "'Tod katkhin' v Tailande" ["Tod Kathin" in Thailand]. *Aziia i Afrika segodnia* 2 (1983): 60-61.

987 Dediukhin, B. "Serdtsa sokrushennye: Rasskazy iz zhizni sovremen. monastyrei" [Distressed Hearts: Life Stories From Contemporary Monasteries]. *Volga* 6 (1989): 166-182; 7 (1989): 144-159; 8 (1989): 138-162; 9 (1989): 162-177.

988 Deitsev, S.E. "1000-letnii iubilei Ruskoi pravoslavnoi tserkvi i sovremennoe sotsial'no-politicheskoe razvitie" [1000th Anniversary of Russian Orthodox Church and Contemporary Socio-Political Development]. *Sov. gosudarstvo i pravo* 2 (1989): 127-128.

989 Dekonis, B.K. "K voprosu ob istokakh ateisticheskoi mysli v Litve" [On the Problem of Soures of Atheistic Thought in Lithuania]. *Ateistines minties*

raida lietuvoje. Kaunas, 1988. Pp. 14-24. In Lithuanian. Summary in Russian.

990   Deksnis, B.Iu. *Gumanizm, katolitsizm i sovremennost'* [Humanism, Catholicism and Contemporaneity]. Vil'nius: [S.n.], 1981. 25 pp. (Material v pomoshch' lektoru / Muzei ateizma LitSSR). In Lithuanian. Bibl.: pp. 24-25.

991   Deksnis, B.[Iu]. *Gumanizm i katolitsizm* [Humanism and Catholicism]. Vil'nius: Mintis, 1980. 166 pp. In Lithuanian.

992   Deksnis, B.[Iu]. "Issledovanie filosofii i mirovozzreniia klerikal'nogo antikommunizma" [Study of Philosophy and World Outlook of Clerical Anti-Communism]. *Uchen. zap. vuzov LitSSR.* Problemy. 36 (1987): 120-121.

993   *Del'tsy ot religii, ili O tom, kak zhuliki i samozvantsy ispol'zuiut v kachestve kompan'onov Allakha, Khrista, Iegovu i drugikh bogov* [Smart Operators of Religion, or About how Swindlers and Impostors use it in the Capacity of Companions of Allah, Christ, Jehovah and other Gods]. [Comp.: V. Efimov]. Tashkent: Esh gvardiia, 1988. 143 pp., illus.

994   Demchenkova, N.M. "Sovershenstvovanie organizatsionnoi struktury nauchno-ateisticheskoi raboty (1971-1980)" [Perfection of Organizational Structure of Scientific-Atheistic Work (1971-1980)]. *Vopr. istorii KPSS* 18 (1987): 105-110.

995   Demenchonok, E.V. "Chelovek i ego mir v 'teologii osvobozhdeniia'" [Man and His World in "Theology of Liberation"]. *Problema cheloveka v sovremennoi religioznoi i misticheskoi literature.* M., 1988. Pp. 89-101.

996   Dem'ianov, A.I. "Pravoslavnyi veruiushchi v sem'e, obshchine, trudovom kollektive" [Orthodox Believer in Family, Community, Labour Collective]. *Veruiushchii v usloviiakh perestroiki.* M., 1989. Pp. 27-48.

997   Dem'ianov, A.I. *Religioznost': tendentsii i osobennosti proiavleniia* [Religiosity: Tendencies and Peculiarities of its Manifestation]. Voronezh: Izd-vo Voronezh. un-ta, 1984. 184 pp. Bibl.: pp. 180-183. For review see item 4998.

998   Demidchik, A.E. "K voprosu o 'demokratizatsii' egipetskoi religii posle krusheniia Drevnego tsarstva" [On the Problem of "Democratization" of

Egyptian Religion after the Collapse of the Ancient Kingdom]. *Tezisy konferentsii aspirantov i molodykh nauchnykh sotrudnikov.* M., 1987. T. 1. Pp. 13-16.

999 Demidchik, A.E. "Neskol'ko zamechanii o 'vzaimootnosheniiakh' egiptian s bozhestvom v nachale II tysiachiletiia do n.e." [Some Remarks about Egyptian "Interrelations" with Deity at the beginning of IInd Century B.C.]. *Drevnii i srednevekovyi Vostok.* M., 1988. Ch. I. Pp. 65-89.

1000 Demidov, S.[M]. "'Chernyi kamen' Kaaby" ["The Black Stone" of Caaba]. *Iunost'.* Ashkhabad. 8 (1989): 51-55.

1001 Demidov, S.M. *Legendy i pravda o 'sviatykh' mestakh* [Legends and Truth About "Holy" Places]. Askhabad: Ylym, 1988. 134 pp. Annot. bibl.: pp. 129-133.

1002 Demidova, G.M.; Geletko, M.V. "Bibleiskii i koranicheskii mify o sotvorenii pervogo cheloveka" [Biblical and Koran Myths about the Creation of the First Man]. *Uchen. zap. Leningr. un-ta, 1984.* No 414. Ser. vostokoved. nauk. vyp. 26. Pp. 142-148.

1003 Demin, A. "Kreshchenie Rusi i drevnerusskaia lieratura" [Baptism of Rus' and Old Russian Literature]. *Vopr. lit.* 7 (1988): 167-188.

1004 Demin, I.L. "Rol' pravomusul'manskoi ideologii v sovremennom Afganistane" [The Role of Moslem Legislative Ideology in Contemporary Afghanistan]. *Aktual'nye problemy stran Blizhnego i Srednego Vostoka.* M., 1988. Ch. 2. Pp. 3-9.

1005 Demin, M.P. "O metodologii primeneniia teorii sotsialisticheskogo obraza zhizni dlia izucheniia prichin sokhraneniia religii v usloviakh sotsializma" [On Methodology of Application of the Theory of Socialist Way of Life for Studying the Reasons of Religion's Preservation under Socialism]. *Vestn. AN KazSSR* 5 (1983): 63-70.

1006 Demin, M.P. *Sotsialisticheskii obraz zhizni i ateisticheskoe vospitanie* [Socialist Way of Life and Atheistic Education]. Alma-Ata: Znanie KazSSR, 1984. 22 pp.

1007 Denisenko, M.S. "Iazyk i religioznaia ideologiia" [The Language and Religious Ideology]. *Filosofiia i iazyk.* Kiev, 1987. Pp. 106-108.

1008   Denisov, P.V. "Razvitie nauchno-ateisticheskoi mysli v Chuvashskoi ASSR"
       [Development of Scientific-Atheistic Thought in Chuvash ASSR]. *Tr./NII
       iaz., lit., istorii i ekonomiki pri Sovete Ministrov Chuvash. ASSR.* 1980, vyp.
       100, Pp. 70-86.

1009   Denisova, E.V. "Raskol sredi sviashchennikov-deputatov v I i II Gosudars-
       tvennykh dumakh (1906-1907 gg.)" [Split Among Priests-Deputies of the
       Ist and IInd State Dumas (1906-1907)]. *Russkoe pravoslavie i ateizm v
       otechestvennoi istorii.* L., 1988. Pp. 133-145.

1010   Deriugin, S.V. "Katoliki i marksisty: Ot dialoga k sotrudnichestvu" [Catholics
       and Marxists: From Dialogue to Collaboration]. *Lat. Amerika* 2 (1988):
       7-15.

1011   Deriugin, S.V. "Miatezhnyi iezuit" [Rebellious Jesuit]. *Lat. Amerika* 3 (1987):
       55-61.

1012   Derosh-Nobl'kur, K. "Mertvogo imia nazvat'..." [To Call the Name of the
       Dead...]. *Ateisticheskie chteniia.* M., 1988. Pp. 99-107.

1013   Detchuev, B.V. "V tridtsatye gody" [In the 30s]. *Nauka i religiia* 4 (1989):
       38-41.

1014   "Deti iz probirki" [Test-tube Children]. *Nauka i religiia* 3 (1988): 20-21.

1015   Deviatova, S.V. "O spetsifike khristianskoi traktovki nauchno-tekhnicheskogo
       progressa" [Specific Character of Christian Interpretation of Scientific-
       Technical Progress]. *Nauchno-tekhnicheskii progress: metodologiia, ideolo-
       giia, praktika.* M., 1989. Pp. 214-219.

1016   Deviatova, S.V. "Osobennosti kritiki sovremennoi religioznoi ideologii"
       [Peculiarities of Critique of Contemporary Religious Ideology]. *Tezisy
       dokladov i vystuplenii na Vsesoiuznoi nauchno-metodicheskoi konferentsii
       "Nauchnye osnovy kritiki nemarksistskikh kontseptsii v kursakh
       obshchestvennykh distsiplin", 12-15 okt. 1988 g.* Odessa, 1988. Pp. 115-116.

1017   Devrishbekov, S.-A.; Abdullaev, G.B.; Ismailov, A.Sh. *Chelovek, religiia,
       vremia* [Man, Religion, Time]. Makhachkala: Dag. kn. izd-vo, 1987. 132
       pp., illus. Bibl.: pp. 127-128.

1018   D'iakonova, N.V.; Rudova, M.L. "Tysiacherukii Avalokiteshvara iz Turfana" [Thousandhanded Avalokiteshvara from Turfan]. *Konferentsiia "Iskusstvo i kul'tura Mongolii i Tsentral'noi Azii".* M., 1981. Pp. 41-42.

1019   Dialog vo blago otechestva [Dialogue for the Good of Fatherland]. *Vek XX i mir* 7 (1988): 40-48.

1020   Diatlov, A.; Dalmatov, V. "'U nas obshchaia istoriia i odno budushchee'" [We have a Common History and One Future]. *Rodina* 1 (1989): 82-84.

1021   Diatropov, P.D. "Rasprostranenie khristianstva v Khersonese Tavricheskom v IV-VI vv. n.e." [Dissemination of Christianity in Tauridan Khersoness in IVth-VIth C. A.D.]. *Antichnaia grazhdanskaia obshchina.* M., 1986 . Pp. 127-151. Annot. bibl.: pp. 143-150.

1022   Dimukhametova, S.A.; Chagin, G.N. "Izuchenie kul'tury i byta staroobriadcheskogo naseleniia Verkhokam'ia" [Study of Culture and Way of Life of Old Beliefs Inhabitants of Upperkama]. *Muzei v ateisticheskoi propagande.* L., 1986. Pp. 5-18.

1023   Diumezil', Zh. *Verkhovnye bogi indoevropeitsev* [Indo-Europeans' Supreme Gods]. Transl. from French. M.: Nauka, 1986. 234 pp. Bibl.: p. 5-7. Annot. bibl.: pp. 208-230.

1024   Diusenbin, Zh. *Nesviatost' 'sviatykh'* [Unholiness of "Saints"]. Alma-Ata: Kazakhstan, 1980. 56 pp. In Kazakh.

1025   Dmitrenko, P. "Esli sporit', to chestno" [If to Argue, then Honestly]. *Agitator* 23 (1989): 20-22.

1026   Dmitrev, A. "Petr I i tserkov'" [Peter the First and the Church]. *Khristianstvo i Rus'.* M., 1988. Pp. 82-92.

1027   Dmitriev, I. "Nekotorye aspekty ideologii obshchestva 'Khodzhatie' [Some Ideological Aspects of "Hodjatie" Society]. *Vsesoiuznaia shkola molodykh vostokovedov.* M., 1989. T. 3. Pp. 15-18.

1028   Dmitriev, M. "Belorusskii skeptik XVI veka" [Belorussian Sceptic of the XVIth Century]. *Nauka i religiia* 4 (1984): 48-49.

1029 Dmitrieva, L.M. "Kollektivizm kak sredstvo preodoleniia religioznoi otchuzhdennosti lichnosti" [Collectivism as Means for Overcoming Personal Religious Estrangement]. *Problemy dukhovnoi zhizni sotsialisticheskogo obshchestva.* Omsk, 1984. Pp. 104-109.

1030 Dmitrieva, N. "O znachenii kreshcheniia Rusi dlia iskusstva" [On Importance of Baptism of Rus' for Arts]. *Dekor. iskusstvo SSSR* 6 (1988): 20-25.

1031 Dmitrieva, N.K. "Netraditsionnye religii i kul'ty" [Non -Traditional Religions and Cults]. *Inform. materialy / AN SSSR. Filos. o-vo SSSR* 6 (1988): 41-53.

1032 Dmitrieva, N.K. "Rol' kursa nauchnogo ateizma v mirovozzrencheskoi zakalke spetsialistov-geografov" [Role of Scientific Atheistic Course in Tempering the World Outlook of Specialists-Geographers]. *Metodologiia Geografii:* teoriia, praktika, prepodavanie. M., 1986. Pp. 141-144.

1033 Dmitrieva, N.K. "Vsesoiuznoe soveshchanie zaveduiushchikh kafedrami nauchnogo ateizma" [All Union Conference of Heads of Chair of Scientific Atheism]. *Nauch. dokl. vyssh. shkoly.* Filos. nauki 4 (1980): 165-167.

1034 Dmitrieva, N.K.; Chernyheva, N.A. "Sotsial'nyi i gnoseologicheski analiz poniatiia 'klerikalizm'" [Social and Gnosiological Analysis of the Notion "Clericalism"]. *Filos. nauki* 8 (1987): 106-109.

1035 Dmitrieva, T.N. "K metodologii izucheniia religioznykh verovanii po arkheologicheskim istochnikam Kamennogo veka" [Methodology of Study of Religious Beliefs by Archeological Sources of the Stone Age]. *Aktual'nye problemy izucheniia istorii religii i ateizma* L., 1980. Pp. 87-98.

1036 Dmitrieva, T.N. "Problema proiskhozhdeniia religii v sovetskoi literature dovoennogo perioda" [Problem of Religion's Provenance in Soviet Pre-war literature]. *Muzei v ateisticheskoi propagande.* L., 1988. Pp. 6-24.

1037 Dmitruk, K.E. *Obrechennye:* Burzhuaz.-natsionalist. i uniat. provokatory na sluzhbe fashizma i imperialist. reaktsii [Doomed: Bourgeois-Nationalist and Uniate Provocateurs in the Service of Fascism and Imperialist Reaction]. L'Vov: Kameniar, 1981. 327 pp. In Ukrainian.

1038 Dmitruk, K.E. *Pravda istorii i izmyshleniia fal'sifikatorov:* Po povodu odnogo tserkov. iubileia [Historical Truth and Falsifiers Concoctions: On Occasion of a Church Anniversary]. Kiev: Znanie UkSSR, 1985. 48 pp. (Ser. 5 "Nauchno-ateisticheskaia" / O-vo "Znanie" UkSSR; No 9). In Ukrainian. Bibl.: pp. 47-48.

1039 Dmitruk, K.E. *S krestami i trezubtsem* [With Crosses and Trident]. M.: Politizdat, 1980. 224 pp., illus.

1040 Dmitruk, K.E. *Svastika na sutanakh* [Swastika on Soutanes]. Kiev: Politizdat UkSSR, 1981. 172 pp., illus. In English.

1041 Dmitruk, K.E. *Uniatskie krestonostsy:* vchera i segodnia [Uniate Crusaders: Yesterday and Today]. M.: Politizdat, 1988. 381 pp., illus.

1042 "Do i posle ekskursii" [Before and After Excursion]. *Nauka i religiia* 6 (1984): 8-10.

1043 "Do i posle lektsii" [Before and After Lecture]. *Nauka i religiia* 11 (1981): 14-15.

1044 Dobren'kov, V.I. *Sovremennyi protestantskii teologicheskii modernizm v SShA:* Ego zamysly i rezul'taty [Contemporary Protestant Theological Modernism in USA: Its Intentions and Results]. M.: Izd-vo MGU, 1980. 248 pp. Bibl.: pp. 245-247. For reviews see items 4999-5001.

1045 Dobrik, V.F. "Vse nachinaetsia s cheloveka" [Everything Starts with Man]. *Nauka i religiia* 9 (1986): 2-3.

1046 Dobruskin, M.E. "Obshchee i osobennoe v reshenii religioznogo voprosa v sotsialisticheskikh stranakh" [Common and Particular in Solution of Religious Problem in Socialist Countries]. *Vopr. nauch. ateizma* 27 (1981): 116-132.

1047 Dobruskin, M.E. *Religiia i ateizm v evropeiskikh sotsialisticheskikh stranakh* [Religion and Atheism in European Socialist Countries]. M.: Nauka, 1986. 188 pp. (Nauch.-popul. lit). (Ser. "Ateizm i religiia"). For review see item 5002.

1048 Dobrzhanskii, V.F. *Bruklinskaia shkola litsemeriia* [Brooklin's School of Hypocrisy]. Uzhgorod: Karpati, 1986. 104 pp. In Ukrainian.

1049   Dodoboeva, S.Iu. *XXVI s'ezd KPSS i zadachi ateisticheskogo vospitaniia* [XXVIth CPSU Congress and Problems of Atheistic Education]. Dushanbe: Irfon, 1984. 22 pp. In Tajik.

1050   Doev, A.[B]. "Sovremennye bogoiskateli" [Today's God-Seekers]. *Kommunist Kirgizstana* 7 (1987): 87-91.

1051   Doev, A.B. "XXVII s'ezd KPSS ob amoralizme religioznogo ekstremizma" [XXVIIth CPSU Congress on Amoralism of Religious Extremism]. *Sotsial'no-eticheskie problemy povysheniia effektivnosti ateisticheskogo vospitaniia v mnogonatsional'nom regione.* Frunze, 1987. Pp. 3-16.

1052   Doev, A.B. "Islam v Kirgizii: mify i real'nost'" [Islam in Kirghizia: Myths and Reality]. *Kritika burzhuaznykh fal'sifikatsii sovremennoi deistvitel'nosti Sovetskogo Kirgizstana.* Frunze, 1988. Pp. 203-223.

1053   Doev, A.B. "Obshchiny protestanskogo tolka na territorii Kirgizskoi SSR" [Protestant Communities in Kirghiz SSR]. *Protestantskie organizatsii v SSSR.* M., 1989. Pp. 120-125.

1054   Doev, A.B. *Sovremennye iudaizm i sionizm* [Contemporary Judaism and Zionism]. Frunze: Kyrgyzstan, 1983. 68 pp.

1055   Doktorov, V.G. *Katolitsizm segodnia:* Nekotorye vopr. ideologii [Catholicism Today: Some Questions of Ideology]. Minsk: Belarus', 1984. 47 pp. Annot. bibl.: p. 46.

1056   Doktorov, V.G. *'Nebesnye khraniteli' khristian* [Christians' "Celestial-Custodians"]. Minsk: Belarus', 1989. 78 pp.

1057   Dolgova, V.S. *Oglianis' v razdum'e:* Ateist. ocherki [Thoughtfully Take a Look At: Atheistic Essays]. M.: Politizdat, 1984. 78 pp. (B-ka ateista). Published also in:
Kishinev: Kartia moldoveniaske, 1986. 133 pp. In Moldavian.

1058   Dolgova, V.S. *Sobiraemsia u kamina* [We Gather by Fire-Side]. M.: Mosk. rabochii, 1987. 78 pp. (Besedy o religii).

1059   Dolia, V.E. *Illiuziia dukhovnosti:* O prevratnom kharaktere relig. mirovo-zzreniia [Spirituality's Illusion: Perverse Character of Religious World Outlook]. L'vov: Vishcha shk. Izd-vo pri L'vov. un-te, 1985. 224 pp. Annot. bibl.: pp. 216-223.

1060 Dolia, V.E. *Problema svobody v ateizme i religii* [The Problem of Freedom in Atheism and Religion]. M.: Znanie, 1980. 64 pp. (Novoe v zhizni, nauke, tekhnike. Ser. "Nauch. ateizm"; No 5).

1061 Dolin, A.A. "Legendarnyi monastyr', ili traditsii ushu" [Legendary Monastery, or Usu Traditions]. *Probl. Dal. Vostoka* 6 (1988): 171-181.

1062 Donini, A. "Ia - vash chitatel'!" [I am your Reader!]. *Nauka i religiia* 9 (1980): 12-15.

1063 Donini, A. *U istokov khristianstva* [By Christianity's Sources]. Riga: Zinatne, 1984. 320 pp. illus. In Latvian.
Published also as 2nd ed., M.: Politizdat, 1989, 365 pp., illus. Translated from "Storia del Cristianesimo" / Ambrogio Donini (Milano, 1977).

1064 Dordzhieva, G.Sh.; Oglaev, Iu.O.; Ubushnevz, S.I. "Lamaistskaia tserkov' v Kalmykii. Nachal'nyi etap sovetskoi istoriografii problemy: 1917-1937 gg." [Lamaism in Kalmyk: Initial Stage of Soviet Historiography of the Problem 1917-1937]. *Voprosy istorii lamaizma v Kalmykii*. Elista, 1987. Pp. 100-121.

1065 Doroguntsova, N.S. *Sovetskaia obriadnost' kak faktor ateisticheskogo vospitaniia* [Soviet Ceremonial as Factor of Atheistic Education]. Kiev: Znanie UkSSR, 1982. 14 pp. (B-chka v pomoshch' lektoru "Probl. nauch. ateizma" / O-vo "Znanie" UkSSR). In Ukrainian.

1066 Doroshenko, E.[A]. "Iran: Musul'manskie (shiitskie) traditsii i sovremennost'" [Iran: Moslem (Shiite) Traditions and Contemporaneity]. *Aziia i Afrika segodnia* 8 (1980): 59-61.

1067 Doroshenko, E.[A]. "Shiitskoe dukhovenstvo v Irane" [Shiite Clergy in Iran]. *Nauka i religiia* 9 (1983): 54-56.

1068 Doroshenko, E.A. *Shiitskoe dukhovenstvo v sovremennom Irane* [Shiite Clergy in Contemporary Iran]. M.: Nauka, 1985. 229 pp. Summary in English. Bibl.: pp. 217-226. For reviews see items 5003 - 5004.

1069 Doroshenko, E.A. *Zorooastriitsy v Irane: Ist.-etnogr. ocherk* [Zoroastrians in Iran: Historic-Ethnographic Essay]. M.: Nauka, 1982. 133 pp. Annot. bibl.: pp. 119-132.

1070 Doroshenko, T.A. "A.I. Gertsen i ateisticheskaia traditsiia" [A.I. Herzen and Atheistic Tradition]. *Kritika religioznoi ideologii i problemy ateisticheskogo vospitaniia.* M., 1980. Pp. 94-100.

1071 Dorzhenov, S.B. *Islam i natsional'nye otnosheniia* [Islam and National Relations]. Alma-Ata: Znanie KazSSR, 1985. 47 pp. In Kazakh.

1072 Dorzhenov, S.B. *Islam segodnia* [Islam Today]. Frunze: Kyrgyzstan, 1980. 167 pp. (B-ka ateista). In Kirghiz.

1073 Dorzhenov, S.B. *Islam, veruiushchie i zhizn'* [Islam, Believers and Life]. Alma-Ata: Kazakhstan, 1985. 149 pp. In Kazakh.

1074 Dorzhiev, Zh.D. "Propaganda ateizma v Aginskom buriatskom natsional'nom okruge Chitinskoi oblasti" [Propaganda of Atheism in Aghint Buriat National Okrug of Chitin Oblast']. *Stroitel'stvo sotsializma i utverzhdenie nauchno-materialisticheskogo, ateisticheskogo mirovozzreniia (v regionakh rasprostraneniia lamaizma).* M., 1981. Pp. 166-172.

1075 *Drevnegruzinskii perevod 'Zhitiia Ioanna Zlatousta' i ego osobennosti* [Ancient Georgian Translation of "The Life of John Zlatoust" and its Peculiarities]. Text prepared for publication by R.V. Gvaramiia. Tbilisi: Metsniereba, 1986. 192 pp. In Georgian. Summaries in French and Russian.

1076 *Drevnie obriady, verovaniia i kul'ty narodov Srednei Azii* [Ancient Rites, Beliefs and Cults of Middle Asia Peoples]. Ed.: V.N. Basilov. M.: Nauka, 1986. 208 pp., illus. For review see item 5005.

1077 Dubianskii, A. "Khramy na kolesakh" [Temples on Wheels]. *Aziia i Afrika segodnia* 1 (1983): 58-59.

1078 Dubianskii, A. "Shestilikii Skanda" [The Six-Faced Skanda].* *Aziia i Afrika segodnia* 4 (1985): 57-59.

1079 Dubina, A.I. ...*Pozhnesh' sud'bu* [...Will Reap Fate]. Kiev: Politizdat Ukrainy, 1982. 51 pp. (Besedy s veruiushchimi). In Ukrainian.

1080 Dubovenko, N.F. "Usilenie ateisticheskogo vospitaniia rabochei molodezhi" [Strengthening Atheistic Upbringing of Working Youth]. *Vopr. ateizma* 18 (1982): 78-84.

1081 Dubrovskaia, D.V. "Pervye iezuity v Kitae. Matteo Richchi - missioner, kitaeved [First Jesuits in China. Matteo Ricci - Missionary, Sinologist]. *Dvadtsataia nauchnaia konferentsiia "Obshchestvo i gosudarstvo v Kitae".* M., 1988. Ch. 2. Pp. 177-181.

1082 Dubrovskii, A. "Informatsionnye banki molchat" [Information Jars Keep Silence]. *Nauka i religiia* 9 (1985): 35.

1083 Dubrovskii, E.; Zybkovets, V. "Odin iz stareishikh" [One of the Oldest]. *Nauka i religiia* 3 (1983): 18-22.

1084 Dudarenok, S.M. *Ateizm v sotsialisticheskom obshchestve:* Probl. teorii i metodologii [Atheism in Socialist Society: Problems of Theory and Methodology]. Vladivostok: Izd-vo Dal'nevost. un-ta, 1988. 163 pp.

1085 Dudarenok, S.M. "Chelovek kak ob'ekt ateisticheskogo vospitaniia" [Man as Object of Atheistic Education]. *Chelovek: opyt kompleksnogo issledovaniia.* Vladivostok, 1988. Pp. 145-152.

1086 Dudarenok, S.M. "Izmenenie sotsial'noi struktury sotsialisticheskogo obshchestva kak ob'ektivnyi faktor formirovaniia atesticheskogo mirovozzreniia" [Change of Social Structure of Socialist Society as Objective Factor of Forming Atheistic Outlook]. *Chelovek kak ob'ekt filosofskogo i sotsiogumanitarnogo poznaniia.* Vladivostok, 1988. Pp. 72-84.

1087 Dudarenok, S.M. "O sushchnosti poniatiia 'nauchnyi ateizm'" [Essence of the Notion "Scientific Atheism"]. *Vestn. Leningr. un-ta, 1983.* No 23. Ekonomika, filosofiia, pravo. Vyp. 4. Pp. 82-84. Summary in English.

1088 Dudkin, V.Ia.; Furmanov, M.R. *Kritika novykh tendentsii burzhuaznoi filosofskoi apologetiki religii* [Critique of New Tendencies of Bourgeois Philosophical Apologetics of Religion]. M.: Znanie, 1987. 64 pp. (Novoe v zhizni, nauke, tekhnike. Nauch. ateizm; 4/1987). Bibl.: p. 61.

1089 Dugarov, R.N. "Religioznoe ulozhenie XVI v. 'Arban buiany tsaaz'" [XVIth Century "Arban Buyan Saaz" Religious Code]. *Kul'tura Mongolii v srednie veka i novoe vremia (XVI-nachalo XX v.).* Ulan-Ude, 1986. Pp. 115-121.

1090 Duisenbin, Zh. *Nauka i islam o proiskhozhdenii cheloveka* [Science and Islam on the Origin of Man]. Alma-Ata: Znanie KazSSR, 1962. 18 pp. In Kazakh.

1091   *Dukhovenstvo i politicheskaia zhizn' na Blizhnem i Srednem Vostoke v period feudalizma* [The Clergy and Political Life in the Near and Middle East in the Period of Feudalism]. Ed.: G.F. Kim et al. M.: Nauka, 1985. 213 pp.

1092   Duluman, E.K. *Besedy s veruiushchimi po aktual'nym voprosom* [Talks with Believers on Topical Problems]. Kiev: Znanie UkSSR, 1982. 47 pp. (Ser. 5 "Nauchno-ateisticheskaia" / O-vo "Znanie" UkSSR; No 7). In Ukrainian. Bibl.: p. 45.

1093   Duluman, E.K. *'Blagochestivye' vymysly i istoricheskaia deistvitel'nost': Pravda o priniatii khristianstva na Rusi* ["Pious" Fabrications and Historical Reality: Truth About the Conversion to Christianity in Rus']. Kiev: Znanie UkSSR, 1988. 48 pp. (Ser. 5. Nauch.-ateist. / O-vo "Znanie" UkSSR; No 5). In Ukrainian.

1094   Duluman, E.K. *Krizis religii v sovremennykh usloviiakh* [Crisis of Religion in Contemporary Conditions]. Kiev: Vishcha shk. Izd-vo pri Kiev. un-te, 1982. 64 pp. (Ateist. b-chka studenta). Bibl.: pp. 62-63.

1095   Duluman, E.K; Glushak, A.S. *Vvedenie khristianstva na Rusi: legendy, sobytiia, fakty* [Introduction of Christianity into Rus': Legends, Events, Facts]. Simferopol': Tavriia, 1988. 184 pp.

1096   Duluman, E.K.; Kolodnyi, A.N. *Individual'naia rabota s veruiushchimi* [Individual Work with Believers]. Kiev: Znanie UkSSR, 1981. 48 pp. (Ser. 5 "Nauchno-ateisticheskaia" / O-vo "Znanie" UkSSR; No 12). In Ukrainian. Bibl.: p. 47.

1097   Duluman, E.K.; Zaglada, A.A. "Metodologicheskaia nesostoiatel'nost' obosnovaniia religioznogo mirovozzreniia" [Methodological Groundlessness of Substantiation of the Religious Outlook]. *Vopr. ateizma* 23 (1987): 74-81.

1098   Duluman, E.K. et al. *Nauchno-tekhnicheskaia revoliutsiia i formirovanie ateisticheskogo mirovozzreniia* [Scientific-Technical Revolution and Forming Atheistic Outlook]. Kiev: Nauk. dumka, 1980. 311 pp.

1099   Dumitriu, D.O. *Sushchnost' ideologii i deiatel'nosti sovremennogo piatidesiatnichestva* [The Essence of Ideology and Activity of the Contemporary Pentecostal Movement]. Kishinev: Znanie MSSR, 1983. 19 pp. (Material v pomoshch' lektoru / O-vo "Znanie" MSSR). In Moldavian. Bibl.: p. 19.

1100 Dundulene, P.V. *Iazychestvo v Litve* [Paganism in Lithuania]. Vil'nius: Mintis, 1989. 165 pp. In Lithuanian. Bibl.: pp. 160-163.

1101 Dundulene, P.V. *Ptitsy v drevnikh litovskikh verovaniakh i v iskusstve* [Birds in Ancient Lithuanian Beliefs and in the Art]. Vil'nius: M-vo. vyssh. i sred. spets. obrazovaniia LitSSR, 1982. 96 pp., illus., maps. In Lithuanian.

1102 Durdyeva, G. "Vovlechenie v obshchestvenno-poleznyi trud - odno iz uslovii ateisticheskogo vospitania zhenshchin-turkmenok" [Involvement in Public-Useful Work - is one of Condition of Atheistic Education of Turkmen-Women]. *Izv. AN TSSR.* Ser. obshchestv. nauk 2 (1981): 23-27. Summary in Turkmen.

1103 Durdyeva, Ia. "Vliianie 'islamskogo faktora' na razvitie mezhnatsional'nykh otnoshenii" [Influence of "Islam's Factor" in the Development of International Relations]. *Rol' sredstv massovoi informatsii v sovershenstvovanii mezhnatsional'nykh otnoshenii.* M., 1989. Ch. 2. Pp. 68-74.

1104 Durdyeva, T.V. "Rol' ob'ektivnykh uslovii i sub'ektivnogo faktora v povyshenii effektivnosti ateisticheskoi raboty" [The Role of Objective Conditions and Subjective Factor in Increasing Effectiveness of Atheistic Work]. *Voprosy teorii i praktiki nauchnogo ateizma.* M., 1988. Pp. 74-95.

1105 Durdyeva, T.V. "Rol' ob'ektivnykh uslovii v povyshenii effektivnosti ateisticheskoi raboty" [The Role of Objective Conditions in Increasing Effectiveness of Atheistic Work]. *Aktual'nye problemy nauchno-ateisticheskogo vospitaniia molodezhi.* M., 19887. Pp. 74-77.

1106 Dush Santush, E. "Tserkov' i kapitalisticheskii obraz myshleniia na severe Portugalii: Konkretnyi primer" [Church and Capitalist Way of Thinking in Northern Portugal: A Concrete Exemple]. *Stanovlenie kapitalizma v Evrope.* M., 1987. Pp. 190-197.

1107 Dussel', E. "Tserkov' v Latinskoi Amerike: Opyt interpretatsii" [Church in Latin America: Interpretation Experience]. *Latin. Amerika* 5 (1989): 45-58; 6 (1989): 56-67.

1108 Dvornichenko, A.M. *Drevnerusskoe obshchestvo i tserkov'* [Ancient Russian Society and the Church]. L.: Znanie RSFSR, 1988. 32 pp. (V pomoshch' lektoru / O-vo "Znanie" RSFSR, Leningr. org.). Bibl.: p. 31.

1109   Dvornichenko, L.P.; Bezarova, G.I. "Samostoiatel'naia rabota studentov po izucheniiu proizvedenii K. Marksa, F. Engel'sa, V.I. Lenina, materialov XXVII s'ezda KPSS v formirovanie nravstvenno-esteticheskoi kul'tury i ateisticheskoi ubezhdennosti studencheskoi molodezhi" [Students' Independent Work for study of the works of K. Marx, F. Engels, V.I. Lenin, materials of the XXVIIth CPSU Congress and Forming Moral-Aesthetic Culture and Atheistic Conviction of Students]. *Vopr. obshchestv. nauk.* M., 1988. Vyp. 74. Pp. 57-62.

1110   Dyiachkov, M.V. "Iazykovaia traditsiia v dvukh drevnikh khristianskikh tserkvakh Afriki" [Lingual Tradition in Two Ancient African Churches]. *Afrika: Kul'tura i obshchestvo.* M., 1989. Pp. 46-50.

1111   Dzalilov, M.F.; Mamedov, A.A. *Povedenie, moral' i religiia* [Behaviour, Morals and Religion]. Baku: Znanie AzSSR, 1981. 50 pp. (V pomoshch' lektoru / O-vo "Znanie" AzSSR). Bibl.: p. 55.

1112   Dzekunov, M.E. *Obshchestvennyi dolg i religiia* [Social Duty and Religion]. Kiev: Znanie UkSSR, 1981. 46 pp. (Ser. 5 "Nauchno-atesticheskaia" / O-vo "Znanie" UkSSR;   No 11). In Ukrainian. Bibl.: p. 45.

1113   Dzhabbarov, I. "Aktual'nye problemy ateisticheskogo vospitaniia" [Actual Problems of Atheistic Education]. *Kommunist Uzbekistana* 6 (1980): 48-55.

1114   Dzhabbarov, I. "K dukhovnoi svobode" [To Spiritual Freedom]. *Nauka i religiia* 12 (1980): 6-9.

1115   Dzhabbarov, I. *Obraz zhizni, traditsii i nravstvennost'* [Way of Life, Traditions and Morality]. Tashkent: Uzbekistan, 1983. 112 pp. (B-ka ateista). In Uzbek.

1116   Dzhabbarov, I. *Ot nevezhestva k massovomu ateizmu* [From Ignorance to Mass Atheism]. Tahkent: Esh gvardiia, 1984. 127 pp., illus. In Uzbek. For review see item 5006.

1117   Dzhabbarov, I.M. *Bogi, sviatye i liudi: Nauch.-popul. ateist. skazaniia* [Gods, Saints and People: Scientific-Popular Atheistic Stories]. Tashkent: Esh gvardiia, 1985. 144 pp. In Uzbek. For review see item 5006.

1118   Dzhabbarov, I.M. *Dukhovnyi mir: nevezhestvo i sovershenstvo* [Spiritual World: Ignorance and Perfection]. Tashkent: Uzbekistan, 1988. 391 pp., illus. In Uzbek. For review see item 5007.

1119 Dzhabbarov, S.I. *Mify i legendy Korana* [Koran's Myths and Legends]. Tashkent: Fan, 1986. 54 pp. In Uzbek.

1120 Dzhabbarova, M.K. *Ateisticheskoe vospitanie molodezhi* [Youth's Atheistic Upbringing]. Dushanbe: Irfon, 1986. 127 pp.

1121 Dzhabbarova, M.[K]. "Nekotorye problemy ateisticheskogo vospitaniia molodezhi" [Some Problems of Youth's Atheistic Upbringing]. *Kommunist Tadzhikistana* 1 (1985): 85-89.

1122 Dzhabbarova, M.K. "Nekotorye rezul'taty issledovaniia otnosheniia molodezhi k ateizmu i religii" [Some Findings of Research of Youth's Attitudes toward Atheism and Religion]. *Vopr.nauch. ateizma* 34 (1986): 167-174.

1123 Dzhabbarova, M.K. *Puti preodoleniia religioznykh perezhitkov v razvitom sotsialisticheskom obshchestve* [Ways of Overcoming Religious Survivals in Developed Socialist Society]. Dushanbe: Irfon, 1984. 21 pp. In Tajik.

1124 Dzhalabadze, N.G. "O prirode bozhestva 'Adgilis Deda'" [The Nature of the Deity 'Adghilis Deda']. *Istoriko-etnograficheskie shtudii.* Tbilisi, 1988. Ch. 3. Pp. 140-147. In Georgian. Summary in Russian.

1125 Dzhalabadze, N.G. "O religioznm sinkretizme ('Adgilis deda - Gvtisshobeli')" [Religious Syncretism ("Adghilis Deda - Gvtisshobeli")]. *Istoriia religii i ateisticheskaia propaganda.* Tbilisi, 1987. Kn. II. Pp. 75-84. In Georgian. Summary in Russian.

1126 Dzhalalov, M.A. *V teni islama* [In Islam's Shadow]. Tashkent: Esh gvardiia, 1987. 104 pp. (Priroda. Obshchestvo. Chelovek).

1127 Dzhalilov, M.F. *Byt, traditsii i ateisticheskoe vospitanie* [Way of Life, Traditions and Atheistic Education]. Baku: AzINKh, 1983. 104 pp. In Azerbaijan.

1128 Dzhalilov, M.F. *Nauchno-tekhnicheskaia revoliutsiia i ateisticheskoe mirovozzrenie* [Scientific-Technical Revolution and Atheistic World Outlook]. Baku: Azerneshr, 1982. 105 pp. In Azerbaijan.

1129 Dzhalilov, M.F.; Mamedov, A.A. *Ateizm i nravstvennoe vospitanie* [Atheism and Moral Education]. Baku: Maarif, 1988. 12 pp. In Azerbaijan.

1130 Dzhanybaeva, R.[M]. "Situatsiia vnosit korrektivy: O nekotorykh probl. ateist. vospitaniia v Kirgizii" [Situation Introduces Amendments: Some Problems of Atheistic Education in Kirghiz]. *Kommunist Kirgizstana* 3 (1989): 30-33.

1131 Dzhanybaeva, R.M. "Sotsialisicheskaia demokratiia i osushchestvlenie svobody sovesti" [Socialist Democracy and Realization of Freedom of Conscience]. *Demokratiia i distsiplina v usloviiakh sovershenstvovaniia sotsializma.* Frunze, 1989. Pp. 127-136.

1132 Dzhavadova, G.; Israfilov, V. "Voprosy ateisticheskogo vospitaniia shkol'noi molodezhi" [Problems of Atheistic Upbringing of Schoolboys]. *Aktual'nye voprosy ateisticheskogo vospitaniia molodezhi.* Baku, 1988. Pp. 39-45. In Azerbaijan. Summary in Russian.

1133 Dzhavliev, T.K. *Priroda, chelovek i religiia* [Nature, Man and Religion]. Tashkent: Fan, 1986. 173 pp. In Uzbek.

1134 Dzhumaev, A. "Vechno zhivaia muzyka" [Always Living Music]. *Nauka i religiia* 11 (1980): 30-32.

1135 Dzhumanazarov, B.S. "K voprosu o printsipe laitsizma v Turetskoi respub-like" [On the Problem of Laicism in Turkish Republic]. *Akual'nye proble-my stran Blizhnego i Srednego Vostoka.* M., 1988. Ch. I. Pp. 10-24.

1136 Dzhumanazarov, B.S. "Voennyi perevorot 12 sentiabria 1980 g. i printsip laitsizma v Turtsii" [September 12, 1980 Military Overturn and the Principle of Laicism in Turkey]. *V Vsesoiuznaia shkola molodykh vostokovedov.* M., 1989. T. 3. Pp. 41-42.

1137 Dzhurabaev, T. "Poka neubeditel'no, ili Kak osveshchaet voprosy ateist-icheskogo vospitaniia gazeta 'Kommunizm sari'" [For the Time Being Unconvincing, or How the Newspaper "Kommunizm sari" Elucidates the Problem of Atheistic Education]. *Kommunist Tadzhikistana* 3 (1988): 87-88.

1138 Dzukaeva, Z.N. "'Bog-otets' ili 'bog-mat'" ["God-Father" or "God-Mother"]. *SShA. Ekonomika, politika, ideologiia* 8 (1989): 59-61.

1139 Dzutsev, Kh.V. "Vliianie mirovozzreniia na religioznuiu aktivnost' individa" [The Influence of the World Outlook on Individual's Religious Activity]. *Kratkoe soderzhanie dokladov i soobshchenii I nauchno-prakticheskoi konfe-rentsii Severo-Osetinskogo filiala Severo-Kavkazskogo otdeleniia*

Sovetskoi sotiologicheskoi assotsiatsii AN SSSR "Nekotorye voprosy sotsiologii Severnoi Osetii", 24-25 noiabria 1988 g. g. Ordzhonikidze. Ordzhonikidze, 1988. Pp. 13-16.

1140 Edel'man, A.I. *Komu sluzhit 'bogoizbrannost'* [Whom Serves "Godchosenness". Uzhgorod: Karpati, 1985. 160 pp.

1141 Edel'man, A.I. *Kritika bogoslovsko-filosofskikh spekuliatsii sionizma* [Criticism of Zionist Theologic-Philosophical Speculations]. Kiev: Znanie UkSSR, 1980. 48 pp. (Ser. 5 "Nauchno-ateisticheskaia" / O-vo "Znanie" UkSSR; No 8). In Ukrainian. Bibl.: pp. 46-47.

1142 *Edinstvo i mnogoobrazie form, sredstv i metodov ateisticheskogo vospitaniia* [Unity and Variety of Forms, Means and Methods of Atheistic Education]. [Comp.: V.P. Kopp]. M.: Znanie, 1985. 62 pp. (Novoe v zhizni, nauke, tekhnike. Nauch. ateizm; No 7). Bibl.: p. 7.

1143 "Edinstvo protivopolozhnstei" [Unity of Contrasts]. *Kommunist Tadzhikistana* 5 (1989): 44-50.

1144 Efendieva, R.P. "Nekotorye predstavleniia o smerti i ee prichinakh u azerbaidzhantsev XIX - nachala XX vv." [Some Notions on Death and Its Causes by Azerbaijanians in XIXth - Early XXth C.]. *Materialy nauchnoi konferentsii.* Baku, 1989. Pp. 54-56.

1145 Efendieva, R.P. "O perezhitkakh nekotorykh doislamskikh verovanii v pogrebal'nykh obriadakh azerbaidzhantsev" [Relics of Some Pre Islamic Beliefs in Azerbaijanians Funeral Ceremonies]. *Dokl. AN AzSSR.* T. 43. 5 (1987): 78-81.

1146 *Effektivnost' ateisticheskogo vospitaniia* [Effectiveness of Atheistic Education]. [Comp.: V. Virtmane]. Riga: Avots, 1980. 215 pp. In Latvian.

1147 *Effektivnost' ateisticheskogo vospitaniia* [Effectiveness of Atheistic Education]. [Comp.: A.F. Trai'ko]. L'vov: Kameniar, 1984. 78 pp. In Ukrainian.

1148 Efimova, L.M. "Islam v istorii i sovremennom mire" [Islam in History and in Contemporary World]. *Novaia i noveishaia istoriia* 3 (1981): 161-171.

1149 Efimova, L.[M]. "Osobennosti islamskoi religioznosti" [Peculiarities of Islamic Religiosity]. *Aziia i Afrika segodnia* 11 (1988): 55-58.

1150 Efimova, L.M. *Sovremennyi islam i politika na zarubezhnom Vostoke* [Contemporary Islam and Politics in Foreign Orient]. M., 1986. 84 pp. Bibl.: p. 83.

1151 Efrosman, A. "Kak Dionisii Malyi vychislil datu rozhdeniia Khrista" [How Dionysius the Younger Calculated the Date of Christ's Birthday]. *Nauka i religiia* 12 (1987): 50-52.

1152 Egamberdiev, N.U.; Nuriddinov, M.N. *Moral', povedenie i religiia* [Morals, Conduct and Religion]. Tashkent: Uzbekistan, 1985. 29 pp. (Vopr. kom. morali; No 12). In Uzbek.

1153 Egamberdyev, Z.; Egamberdieva, Z. *Nauka i religioznye predrassudki* [Science and Religious Prejudices]. Tashkent: Uzbekistan, 1981. 16 pp. (Besedy o nauke; 17). In Uzbek.

1154 Eganian, G.M. *Rol' dukhovenstva v obshchestvenno-politicheskoi zhizni Irana (1953-1978 gg.)* [Role of the Clergy in Iran's Socio-Political Life (1953-1978)]. Erevan: Izd-vo AN ArmSSR, 1987. 221 pp. Bibl.: pp. 208-220. In Armenian.

1155 Egorkin, V.G.; Grebel'nikov. Iu.G. "Psikhologiia religioznogo fanatizma i ee vliianie na soznanie molodezhi" [Psychology of Religious Fanaticism and Its Influence on Youth's Cosciousness]. *Teoreticheskie voprosy formirovaniia soznaniia sovetskoi molodezhi*. Barnaul, 1987. Pp. 122-131. Bibl.: p. 131.

1156 Eingorn, I.D. *Ocherki istorii religii i ateizma v Sibirii (1917-1937 gg.)* [Studies of History of Religion and Atheism in Siberia (1917-1937)]. Tomsk: Izd-vo Tom. un-ta, 1982. 225 pp. For reviews see items 5008-5009.

1157 Ekhatamm, V.; Shevelev, V. "Ostrov na more lezhit..." [Island Lies on the Sea..]. *Nauka i religiia* 11 (1985): 6-11.

1158 Ekk, L. *V poiskakh sviatoi matushki-Rusi* [In the Search of Holy Mother-Rus']. M.: Progress, [1988]. 187 pp., illus. (Svidetel'stva ob SSSR). In English.

1159 *Ekspansionistskie tendentsii v ideologii i politike i zadachi ateisticheskoi raboty* [Expansionist Tendencies in Ideology and Politics and the Tasks of Atheistic Education]. [Comp.: B. Deksnis et al]. Vil'nius: Znanie LitSSR, 1988. 35 pp. In Lithuanian.

1160 *Eksportery dukhovnogo nasiliia* [Exporters of Spiritual Violence]. [M.I. Gaikovskii et al]. L'vov: Kameniar, 1982. 120 pp. In Ukrainian.

1161 Elenskii, V.E. *Iudeiskii klerikalizm i sionizm* [Judaic Clericalism and Zionism]. Kiev: Vishcha shk., 1988. 113 pp. (Ateist. b-chka studenta).

1162 Elenskii, V.E. *Sovremennyi protestantizm: dinamika, protsessy, tendentsii* [Contemporary Protestantism: Dynamics, Processes, Tendencies]. Kiev: Znanie UkSSR, 1989. 47 pp. (Ser. 5, Nauchno-ateisticheskaia / O-vo "Znanie" UkSSR; No 12). In Ukrainian.

1163 Elfimova, T.V. "Rol' sotsial'no-kul'turnogo progressa v preodolenii religio-znykh verovanii" [Role of the Socio-Cultural Progress in Overcoming Religious Beliefs]. *Aktual'nye problemy ateisticheskogo vospitaniia i kritika religioznoi ideologii.* M., 1983. Pp. 16-20.

1164 Eliade, M. *Kosmos i istoriia:* Izbr. raboty [Cosmos and History: Selected Works]. Transl. from English and French. M.: Progress, 1987. 312 pp. (Dlia nauch. b-k). Annot. bibl.: pp. 282-298. Subject and name index: pp. 299-310. For review see item 5010.

1165 Elizarenkova, T.Ia. "Pamiati Oktiabriny Fedorovny Volkovoi" [In the Memory of Volkova, Oktiabrina Fedorovna]. *Narody Azii i Afriki* 2 (1989): 209-210.

1166 Elizarova, M.M. "Vetkhozavetnaia apokrificheskaia literatura i kumranskie nakhodki" [Old Testament Apocryphal Literature and Qumran Finds]. *Palest. sb.* 28 (1986): 62-68.

1167 Elkanidze, M.M. "Buddizm v sisteme sotsial'no-politicheskikh otnoshenii obshchestva" [Buddhism in the System of Society's Socio-Political Relations]. III *Vsesoiuznaia konferentsiia vostokovedov "Vzaimodeistvie i vzaimovliianie tsivilizatsii kul'tur na Vostoke".* M., 1988. T. I. Pp. 87-88.

1168 Elkanidze, M.M. "O roli buddizma v sisteme religioznykh predstavlenii drevnelankiiskogo obshchestva" [Buddhism's Role in the System of Religious Conception of Ancient Lankist Society]. *Istoriia i filologiia drevnego i srednevekovogo Vostoka.* M., 1987. Pp. 42-50.

1169 Elkanidze, M.M. "Otnosheniia mezhdu buddiiskoi sangkhoi i tsarskoi vlast'iu
      v drevnelankiiskom obshchestve v III v. do n.e. - IV v. n.e." [Relations
      Between Buddhist Sankhya and Regal Power in Ancient Lankist Society
      in IIIrd C. BC - IVth C. AD]. *Istoriia i filologiia drevnego i srednev-*
      ekovogo Vostoka. M., 1987. Pp. 51-63.

1170 Elkanidze, M.M. "Problema rasprostraneniia buddizma na Lanke" [The
      Problem of Dissemination of Buddhism in Lanka]. *Buddizm. Istoriia i*
      kul'tura. M., 1989. Pp. 104-118.

1171 El'port, M.S. "'Moral'noe bol'shinstvo': propaganda i deiatel'nost'" ["Moral
      Majority": Propaganda and Activity]. *Ateisticheskie chteniia.* M., 1988. Pp.
      241-250.

1172 El'port, M.S. "'Politicheskaia teologiia' kak sovremennaia forma proiavleniia
      krizisa khristianstva" ["Political Theology" as Contemporary Form of
      Disclosure of the Crisis of Christianity]. *Filosofskii analiz iavlenii*
      dukhovnoi kul'tury: Teoret. i ist. aspekty. M., 1984. Pp. 70-76.

1173 El'port, M.S. "'Poiticheskaia teologiia' kak sovremennoe religiozno-
      sotsial'noe iavlenie" ["Political Theology" as Current Religious-Social
      Occurrence]. *Vestn. Mosk. un-ta. Ser. 7. Filosofiia.* 1 (1984): 64-73.

1174 Embulaeva, L.S. "Grazhdanskaia pozitsiia veruiushchikh v usloviiakh
      perestroiki" [Believers Civic Position under Perestroika]. *Protestantskie*
      organizatsii v SSSR. M., 1989. Pp. 18-38.

1175 Emeliakh, L.I. *Ateisticheskie traditsii sovetskogo naroda* [Atheistic Traditions
      of the Soviet People]. L.: Znanie RSFSR, 1980. 20 pp. (V pomoshch'
      lektoru / O-vo "Znanie" RSFSR, Leningr. org.). Bibl.: pp. 4-5.

1176 Emeliakh, L.I. "Khristianizatsiia Rusi" [Rus' Conversion to Christianity].
      Religii mira, 1986. M., 1987. Pp. 193-229.

1177 Emeliakh, L.I. "Velikii Oktiabr' i ateizm narodnykh mass" [The Great
      October and Atheism of National Masses]. *Sotsial'no-filosofskie aspekty*
      kritiki religii. L., 1987. Pp. 5-27.

1178 Emeliakh, L.I. *'Zagadki' khristianskogo kul'ta* ["Mysteries" of Christian
      Religion]. L.: Lenizdat, 1985. 189 pp., illus. For review see item 5011.

1179   Emets, I.P. "Ateisticheskoe vospitanie vazhneishii aspekt ideino- politicheskoi raboty bibliotek Belorusskoi SSR" [Atheistic Education is Most Important Aspect of Ideologic-Political Work of Belorussian SSR Libraries]. *Vopr. bibliografovedeniia i bibliotekovedeniia* 7 (1986): 14-21.

1180   Emin, L. *Musul'mane v SSSR* [Moslems in USSR]. M.: Novosti, 1983. 79 pp., illus. In Pushtu.
       Published also by Novosti in 1984 in Dari, English, French and Turkish; in 1986 in Arabic, English, French and Spanish.

1181   Erasov, B.[S]. "Chto za religioznoi obolochkoi: Nekotorye kharakter. cherty relig. protsessov na Vostoke" [What is Behind Religious Cover: Some Characteristic Traits of Religious Processes in Orient]. *Nauka i religiia* 8 (1980): 56-59.

1182   Erasov, B.S. "Vliianie massovogo soznaniia na aktivizatsiiu islama" [The Influence of Mass Consciousness on Activization of Islam]. *Vopr. nauch. ateizma* 31 (1983): 51-65.

1183   Erasova, I.[A]. "'Afrikanizatsiia' khristianskoi tserkvi" ["Africanization" of Christian Church]. *Aziia i Afrika segodnia* 12 (1986): 55-57.

1184   Erasova, I.V.[Sic].[A]. "Katolicheskaia tserkov' protiv marksizma-leninizma" [Catholic Church against Marxism-Leninism]. *Rasprostranenie marksizma-leninizma v Afrike*. M., 1987. Pp. 300-307.

1185   Erasova, I.A. "Katolitsizm i afrikanskaia intelligentsiia" [Catholicism and African Intelligentia]. *Puti evoliutsii i obshchestvennaia rol' sovremennoi afrikanskoi intelligentsii: poiski, tendentsii, perspektivy*. M., 1988. Pp. 222-227.

1186   Erasova, I.A. *Vatikan v sovremennoi Afrike: Ideologiia i politika* [Vatican in Contemporary Africa: Ideology and Politics]. M.: Nauka, 1989. 136 pp. Summary in English. Bibl.: pp. 130-134.

1187   Eremeev, D.[E]. "Islam - ideologiia mnogokladnogo obshchestva" [Islam - Ideology of Many-Structural Society]. *Aziia i Afrika segodnia* 7 (1984): 26-29.

1188   Eremeev, D.[E]. "Islam i politicheskaia bor'ba v Turtsii" [Islam and Political Struggle in Turkey]. *Aziia i Afrika segodnia* 10 (1981): 17-20.

1189   Eremeev, D.E. "Iz opyta sotsiologicheskogo analiza Korana" [From the Experience of Sociological Analysis of Koran]. *Vestn. Mosk. un-ta.* Sr. 13, Vostokovedenie. 2 (1988): 30-40.

1190   Eremeev, D.E. "Sotsial'nye faktory ranneislamskogo dvizheniia" [Social Factors of the Early Islamic Movement]. *Religii mira.* M., 1989. Pp. 121-132.

1191   Eremeev, D.[E]. "Zhenshchina i islam: Vzgliad etnografa" [Woman and Islam: Ethnographer's View]. *Aziia i Afrika segodnia* 1 (1989): 51-55; 2 (1989): 58-62.

1192   Eremenko, V.P. *Istoricheskaia rol' khristianstva: real'nost' i mify* [Christianity's Historical Role: Reality and Myths]. Kiev: Znanie UkSSR, 1989. 47 pp. (Ser. 5, Nauchno-ateisticheskaia / O-vo "Znanie" UkSSR; No 4). In Ukrainian.

1193   Eremenko, V.P. "Kriticheskii analiz pravoslavno-bogoslovskoi interpretatsii roli religii v sovremennykh usloviiakh" [Critical Analysis of Orthodox-Theological Interpretation of Religion's Role in Contemporary Conditions]. *Dialektika material'noi i dukhovnoi sfer sotsializma v protsesse uskoreniia sotsial'no-ekonomicheskogo razvitiia obshchestva.* Dnepropetrovsk, 1987. Pp. 55-63.

1194   Eremenko, V.P. *Mistika v pravoslavii* [Mysticism in Orthodoxy]. Kiev: Vishcha shk., 1986. 81 pp. (Ateist. b-chka studenta).

1195   Eremenko, V.P. "Preodolenie misticheskikh sueverii i predrassudkov - vazhnyi faktor vyrabotki zhiznennoi pozitsii sovetskogo cheloveka" [Overcoming of Mythical Superstitions and Prejudices - Important Factor of Producing Active Vital Position of the Soviet Man]. *Dukhovnaia sfera sotsialisicheskogo obraza zhizni i sovremennaia ideologicheskaia bor'ba.* Dnepropetrovsk, 1981. Pp. 77-82.

1196   Eremenko, V.P. *V poiskakh istoricheskoi istiny* [In the Search of Historical Truth]. Dnepropetrovsk: Promin', 1989. 222 pp.

1197   Eremenko, V.P. "Vospitanie istoriei v usloviiakh perestroiki i 1000-letnego iubileia Russkoi pravoslavnoi tserkvi" [Education by History under Perestroika and 1000th Jubilee of Russian Orthodox Church]. *XXVII S'ezd KPSS i Problemy Formirovaniia Kommunisticheskoi ubezhdennosti studentov v usloviiakh perestroiki vysshei shkoly.* Dnepropetrovsk, 1988. Pp. 153-161.

1198 Eremenko, V.P. "Vyrabotka ateisticheskoi ubezhdennosti - uslovie formirovaniia vsestoronne razvitoi lichnosti" [Forming Atheistic Conviction - Condition for Shaping a Thoroughly Developed Personality]. *Nauchnye osnovy formirovaniia garmonicheskoi razvitoi lichnosti.* Dnepropetrovsk, 1983. Pp. 124-129.

1199 Eres'ko, M.N. "Kontseptsiia religioznogo simvolizma Mirche Eliade" [Conception of Religious Symbolism of Mirce Eliade]. *Aktual'nye problemy ateisticheskogo vospitaniia i kritika religioznoi ideologii].* M., 1983. Pp. 30-34.

1200 Eres'ko, M.N. "Religioznyi modernizm v bor'be s sovremennoi naukoi" [Religious Modernism in the Struggle with Contemporary Science]. *XXVII s'ezd KPSS o roli fundamental'noi nauki v uskorenii nauchno-tekhnicheskogo protsessa.* Ufa, 1986. Pp. 96-102.

1201 Eres'ko, M.N. "Spetsifika religioznogo simvola" [Specificity of Religious Symbol]. *Vest. Mosk. un-ta.* Ser. 7. Filosofiia 1 (1983); 60-70.

1202 Ergashev, F. *XXVII s'ezd KPSS i formirovanie ateisticheskogo mirovozzreniia molodezhi* [XXVIth CPSU Congress and Forming Youth's Atheistic Outlook]. Tashkent: Znanie UzSSR, 1983. 20 pp. (V pomoshch' lektoru / O-vo "Znanie" UzSSR. Ser. obshchestv.-politicheskaia). In Uzbek.

1203 Erkomaishvili, V.I. *Vera v rok i ee otritsatel'nye posledstviia* [Belief in Fate and Its Negative Consequences]. Tbilisi: Izd-vo Tbil. un-ta, 1984. 127 pp. In Georgian.

1204 Ermakov, M.E. "Bazovye ideologemy populiarnogo kitaiskogo budizma" [Basic Ideologic Points of Popular Chinese Buddhism]. *Dvadtsataia nauchnaia konferentsiia "Obshchestvo i gosudarstvo v Kitae".* M., 1989. Ch. I. P. 93.

1205 Ermakov, M.E. "Buddiiskii deiatel' v predstavlenii ofitsial'nogo kitaiskogo istoriografa" [Buddhist Dignitary in Presentation of Official Chinese Historiographer]. *Buddizm i gosudarstvo na Dal'nem Vostoke.* M., 1987. Pp. 109-129.

1206   Ermakov, M.E. "Zhizneopisanie - zhitie" [Biography - Life]. *Pis'mennye pamiatniki i problemy istorii kul'tury narodov Vostoka: XXII godich. nauch. ses.* LO IV AN SSSR. M., 1989. Ch. I. Pp. 105-110.

1207   Ermakov, N.M. *Razum zovet k zhizni* [Reason Calls to Life]. Minsk: Belarus', 1987. 112 pp. In Belorussian.

1208   Ermakov, S.A. "Obriad kak forma vyrazheniia dukhovnogo mira cheloveka" [Ceremony as a Form of Expression of Man's Spiritual World]. *Dukhovnyi mir sovremennogo cheloveka.* M., 1987. Pp. 127-130.

1209   Ermakova, L.M. "Ritual'nye i kosmologicheskie znacheniia v rannei iaponskoi poezii" [Ritual and Cosmological Significances in Early Japanese Poetry]. *Arkhaicheskii ritual v folklornykh i ranneliteraturnykh pamiatnikakh.* M., 1988. Pp. 61-82. Bibl.: pp. 81-82.

1210   Ermaliuk, Iu.[K]. "Chem skoree uiasnim etu mysl'..." [The Sooner we will Understand This Thought...]. *Zhurnalist* 9 (1988): 29-31.

1211   Ermaliuk, Iu.K. *Deviat' 'retseptov' schast'ia:* Besedy o novozavet. zapovediakh blazhenstva [Nine "Prescriptions" of Happiness: Talks About New Testament's Commandments of Bliss]. Minsk: Universitetskoe, 1987. 60 pp.

1212   Ermaliuk, Iu.K. *K dukhovnomu osvobozhdeniiu* [To Spiritual Liberation]. Minsk: Belarus', 1988. 145 pp.

1213   Ermaliuk, Iu.K. *Mesto v zhizni* [Place in Life]. Minsk: Belarus', 1983. 62 pp., illus.

1214   Ermaliuk, Iu.[K]. "Za 'ostrymi' uglami: Pochemu 'buksuiut kolesa' ateist. vospitaniia?" [Behind "Sharp" Corners: Why "Skid the Wheels" of Atheistic Education?] *Kommunist Belorussii* 3 (1988): 55-61.

1215   Ernashvili, Zh.G. *Drevneishie sotsial'no religioznye instituty gornykh raionakh Gruzii* [Ancient Socio-Religious Institutes in Mountainous Districts of Georgia]. Tbilisi: Metsniereba, 1982. 197 pp. In Georgian. Summary in Russian.

1216   Ershov, A.A.; Khal'zov, V.N. "Ateisticheskoe vospitanie studencheskoi molodezhi - vazhnoe sredstvo aktivizatsii chelovecheskogo faktora" [Atheistic Education of Students - Important Means for Activization of

Human Factor]. *Sotsial'nye problemy aktivizatsii chelovecheskogo faktora.* Cheboksary, 1988. Pp. 121-125.

1217 Ershov, G.G. "Sistema ateisticheskogo vospitaniia studentov v meditsinskom vuze" [The System of Atheistic Education of Medical Students]. *Aktual. vopr. metodiki prepodavaniia obshchestv. nauk i kom. vospitaniia studentov.* L., 1987. Vyp. 5. Pp. 68-75.

1218 Ershov, G.G. *Smysl zhizni i sotsial'noe bessmertie cheloveka* [Purport of Life and Human Social Immortality]. L.: Lenizdat: 1981. 56 pp. (B-chka molodogo ateista). Bibl.: p. 55.

1219 Ershov, I.M. "Formirovanie atesticheskoi ubezhdennosti lichnosti razvitogo sotsializma v protsesse ee sotsial'nogo tvorchestva" [Shaping Atheistic Conception of Personality of the Developed Socialism in the Process of Its Social Creative Work]. *Vopr. ateizma* 19 (1983): 32-37.

1220 Ershov, I.M. "Tvorcheskaia aktivnost' lichnosti v sfere nravstvennykh otnoshenii" [Creative Activity of Personality in the Sphere of Moral Relations]. *Vopr. nauch. ateizma* 35 (1986): 148-161.

1221 Ershov, I.M. "Tvorcheskaia deiatel'nost' i mirovozzrenie lichnosti: Ateist. aspekt" [Creative Activity and Personality's World Outlook: Atheistic Aspect]. *Vopr. ateizma* 23 (1987): 15-21.

1222 Ershov, I.M.; Vlasenko, G.G. "Kritika teologicheskoi kontseptsii tvorchestva" [Criticism of Theological Conception of Creative Work]. *Tezisy dokladov i vystuplenii na Vsesoiuznoi nauchno-metodicheskoi konferentsii "Nauchnye osnovy kritiki nemarksistskikh kontseptsii v kursakh obshchestvennykh distsiplin", 12-15 okt. 1988* g. Odessa, 1988. Pp. 103-105.

1223 Ershov, P.M. "Ateisticheskaia kniga kak faktor utverzhdeniia nauchnogo ateizma" [Atheistic Book as Affirmation Factor of Scientific Atheism]. *Izv. AN MSSR. Ser. obshchestv. nauk* 1 (1983): 32-41.

1224 Ershov, V.P. "Dukhovnyi mir pravoslavnogo veruiushchego: 80-e gody" [Spiritual World of Orthodox Believer: in the 80s]. *Pravoslavie v Karelii.* Petrozavodsk, 1987. Pp. 102-123.

1225 Ershov, V.P. *Rodniki poznaniia* [Springs of Knowledge]. M.: Politizat, 1981. 72 pp. (B-ka ateista). For reviews see items 5012-5013.

1226   Ershov, V.P. *Skazka-lozh', da v nei namek* [Fairy Tale-a Lie, But with a Hint]. Petrozavodsk: Kareliia, 1988. 157 pp., illus. Bibl.: pp. 155-156.

1227   Ershov, V.P. *Zrimoe slovo* [Visible word]. M.: Politizdat, 1987. 96 pp. (B-ka ateista).

1228   Eryshev, A.A. *Sotsializm - obshchestvo tvortsov sobstvennoi sud'by:* K 70-letiiu Velikoi Okt. sots. revoliutsii [Socialism - Society of Creators of Their Own Fate: On the Occasion of 70th Anniversary of the Great October Socialist Revolution]. Kiev: Znanie UkSSR, 1987. 48 pp. (Ser. 5, Nauchno-ateisticheskaia / O-vo "Znanie" UkSSR; No 12). Annot. bibl.: Pp. 46-47.

1229   Esbergenov, Kh.E.; Nurmukhamedova, I.M. "Obriady, sviazannye s bezdet-nost'iu u karakalpakov i ikh otmiranie v usloviiakh sotsializma" [Karakalpak Rites Related to Childlessness and Their Withering Away under Socialism]. *Vestn. Karakalp. fil. AN UzSSR.* Nukus, 4 (1988): 57-61.

1230   Esitashvili, Sh.A. *Vzaimootnsheniia mifologii i religii po gruzinskim istochnikam* [Interrelation of Mythology and Religion by Georgian Sources]. Tbilisi: Metsniereba, 1985. 91 pp. In Georgian. Summary in Russian.

1231   *Estestvoznanie v bor'be s religioznym mirovozzreniem* [Natural Sciences in the Struggle with Religious World Outlook]. Eds.: M.D. Akhundov; L.B. Bazhenov. M.: Nauka, 1988. 244 pp.

1232   *Etika i ritual v traditsionnom Kitae* [Ethics and Ritual in Contemporary China]. [Ed.: L.S. Vasil'ev]. M.: Nauka, 1988. 331 pp., illus. Name index and titles of papers: pp. 324-329.

1233   Etingof, O.E. "Vizantiiskaia ikonografiia 'oplakivaniia' i antichnyi mif o plodorodii kak spasenii" [Byzantine Iconography of "Lamentation" and Ancient Fertility Myth as Salvation]. *Zhizn' mifa v antichnosti.* M, 1988. Ch. I. Pp. 256-265.

1234   *Etnografiia i voprosy religioznykh vozzrenii chechentsev i ingushei v dorevoliutsionnyi period* [Etnography and Problems of Religious Outlooks of Chechens and Ingush in Pre-Revolutionary Period]. Ed.: V.B. Vinogradov. Groznyi: ChIIISF, 1981. 103 pp., illus.

1235 "Evangelie ot Marka" [Mark's Gospel]. *Narody Azii i Afriki* 6 (1989): 112-124.

1236 Evgen'ev, D. "Ashura - traurnaia dekada shiitov" [Ashura Shiites Decade of Mourning]. *Aziia i Afrika segodnia* 9 (1985): 60-61.

1237 Evgen'ev, D. "Islam i alkogol'" [Islam and Alcohol]. *Aziia i Afrika segodnia* 10 (1986): 56-58.

1238 Evgen'ev, V. "Russkie na gore Afon" [Russians on the Mount of Athos]. *Nauka i religiia* 6 (1988): 61-62.

1239 Evsiukov, V.V. *Mifologiia kitaiskogo neolita* [Mythology of China's neolithic age]*. Novosibirsk: Nauka. Sib. otd-nie, 1988. 128 pp., illus. (Istoriia i kul'tura vostoka Azii). Annot. bibl.: pp. 110-127. For review see item 5014.

1240 Evsiukov, V.V. *Mify o mirozdanii* [Myths About the Universe]. M.: Politizdat, 1986. 112 pp., illus. (Besedy o mire i cheloveke).
Published also in:
Tashkent: Uzbekistan, 1988. 128 pp., illus. In Uzbek.
Kishinev: Kartia moldoveniaske, 1988. 171 pp., illus. In Moldavian.

1241 Evsiukov, V.V. *Mify o vselennoi* [Myths About the Universe]. Novosibirsk: Nauka. Sib. otd-nie, 1988. 177 pp., illus. (Ser. "Iz istorii mirovoi kyl'tury"). Bibl.: pp. 170-176.

1242 Ezhov, A.F. *Islam na sluzhbe reaktsii i antikommunizma* [Islam in the Service of Reaction and Anti-Communism]. Tashkent: Uzbekistan, 1986. 38 pp. (Ser. "Marksizm-leninizm"; No 6). In Uzbek.

1243 Faiazov, M.F. *Nesovmestimost' kommunisticheskoi i religioznoi morali* [Incompatibility of Communist and Religious Morality]. Tashkent: Uzbekistan, 1986. 30 pp. (Ser. "Marksizm-leninizm"; No 4). In Uzbek.

1244 Fakhrutdinova, N.Z. "'Religioznyi faktor' v politicheskoi bor'be v Afrike" ["Religious Factor" in Political Struggle in Africa]. *Afrika v sovremennom mire*. M., 1989. Pp. 111-122.

1245 Fartukhova, G.V. *Sotsial'naia otvetstvennost' lichnosti i ateizm* [Person's Social Responsibility and Atheism]. M.: Politizdat, 1980. 56 pp. (B-ka ateista).

1246 Fartushnyi, A.A. *Klerikal'nyi antikommunizm na sluzhbe imperializma* [Clerical Anti-Communism in the Service of Imperialism]. L'vov: Vishcha shk. Izd-vo pri L'vov. un-te, 1983. 87 pp. (Ateist. b-chka studenta).

1247 Fartushnyi, A.A. *Politika v sutane:* Molodezhi o sotsial. sushchnosti klerikal. antikommunizma [Politics in Soutane: To Youth on Social Essence of Clerical Anti-Communism]. Kiev: Molod' 1988. 142 pp. Annot. bibl.: pp. 134-137.

1248 Fatulla-ogly, A. "Nekhitrye tainy sviatykh mogil" [Simple Secrets of Holy Graves]. *Nauka i religiia* 5 (1980): 31-35.

1249 Fatulla-ogly, A. "Shiitskii kul't segodnia" [Shiites Cult Today]. *Nauka i religiia* 9 (1985): 24-27.

1250 Fatulla-ogly, A. "Shiity segodnia" [Shiites Today]. *Nauka i religiia* 5 (1981): 36-39.

1251 Favorskii, A. "Islam i osvoboditel'naia bor'ba" [Islam and Struggle of Liberation]. *Gorizont* 10 (1981): 26-29.

1252 Fedchin, V.S. "Sootnoshenie material'nogo i ideal'nogo v pravoslavnoi ideologii" [Correlation of the Material and Ideal in Orthodox Ideology]. *Osnovnoi vopros filosofii i dialektika teoreticheskogo poznaniia.* Irkutsk, 1980. Pp. 50-57.

1253 Fedorov, E.V. "Obraz shamana v molodykh sibirskikh literaturakh" [Shaman's Image in Young Siberian Literature]. *Poliarnaia zvezda.* 3 (1988): 114-118.

1254 Fedorova, I.P. "Opyt ateisticheskoi propagandy na materialakh Permskoi khudozhestvennoi galerei" [Experience of Atheistic Propaganda on Materials of Perm's Art Gallery]. *Muzei v ateisticheskoi propagande.* L., 1986. Pp. 18-22.

1255 Fedosik, V.A. "Deiatel'nost' Soiuza voinstvuiushchikh bezbozhnikov BSSR v 1933-1941 godakh" [The Activity of the League of the Militant Godless of BSSR in 1933-1941]. *Nauch. ateizm i ateist. vospitanie* 1 (1983): 118-127.

1256 Fedosik, V.A. *Kritika bogoslovskikh kontseptsii sushnosti khristianskogo katekhumenata* [Criticism of Theological Conceptions of the Essence of Christian Catechism]. Minsk: Nauka i tekhnika, 1983. 87 pp.

1257 Fedosik, V.A. *Tserkov' i gosudarstvo:* Kritika bogosl. kontseptsii [The Church and the State: Criticism of Theological Conceptions]. Minsk: Nauka i tekhnika, 1988. 205 pp. For review see item 5015.

1258 Fedosik, V.A. *V sladkoglasii pesnopenii liturgii* [Sweetvoiced Singing of Liturgy]. Minsk: Nauka i tekhnika, 1985. 70 pp.

1259 Fedotov, G. "Sviatye Drevnei Rusi" [Saints of the Ancient Rus']. *Nashe nasledie* 4 (1988): 45-53.

1260 Fedotova, L.F. "O edinstve internatsional'nogo i ateisticheskogo vospitaniia" [On the Unity of International and Atheistic Education]. *K voprosu ob internatsionalizatsii obshchestvennoi zhizni v usloviiakh razvitogo sotsializma.* Ordzhonikidze, 1981. Pp. 110-118.

1261 Feierbakh, F. "Religiia budushchego" [Religion of the Future]. *Vopr. nauch. ateizma* 29 (1982): 258-272.

1262 Felikov, B.Z. "Rasprostranenie induizma i buddizma v amerikanskom obshchestve" [Spreading of Hinduism and Buddhism in American Society]. *SShA. Ekonomika, politika, ideologiia* 8 (1985): 32-43.

1263 Fesiun, A.G. "Psikhologicheskie aspekty ucheniia Kukaia" [Psychological Aspects of Kukai's Teaching]. *Psikhologicheskie aspekty buddizma.* Novosibirsk, 1986. Pp. 120-130.

1264 Filaret, mitropolit. "Dni i veka" [Days and Centuries]. *Novoe vremia* 23 (1988): 46-47.

1265 Filaret, mitropolit. "Liubit' cheloveka" [To Love Human Being]. *Ogonek* 22 (1988): 14-16.

1266 Filaret, mitropolit. "Russkaia Pravoslavnaia tserkov' i ee vneshnie sviazi" [Russian Orthodox Church and Its Foreign Relations]. *Mirovaia ekonomika i mezhdunar. otnosheniia* 6 (1988): 70-78.

1267 Filaret, mitropolit. "Tysiacheletie" [Millennium]. *Mezhdunar. zhizn'* 5 (1988): 50-55.

1268 Filaret, mitropolit. "Tysiacheletie kreshcheniia Rusi" [Millennium of Baptism of Rus']. *Sov. potreb. koop.* 6 (1988): 10-12.

1269   Filaret, mitropolit. "1000-letie kreshcheniia Rusi - vydaiushcheesia sobytie
         otechestvennoi i mirovoi istorii" [1000th Anniversary of Baptism of Rus' -
         Outstanding Event of Home and World History]. *Voprosy istorii* 5
         (1988): 102-110.

1270   Filaret, mitropolit. "Znamenatel'naia vekha istorii: K 1000-letiiu vved.
         khristianstva na Rusi" [Significant Landmark of History: On the Occasion
         of Thousandth Anniversary of Introduction of Christianity into Rus'].
         Sovety nar. deputatov 6 (1988): 114-117.

1271   Filatov, S.B. "Amerikanskii katolitsizm i Vatikan" [American Catholicism and
         Vatican]. *SShA. Ekonomika, politika, ideologiia* 10 (1980): 119-125.

1272   Filatov, S.B. "Pravoslavie na amerikanskoi pochve" [Orthodoxy on American
         Ground]. *SShA. Ekonomika, politika, ideologiia* 10 (1981): 101-109.

1273   Filatov, S.[B]. "Tserkov' i reiganomika" [The Church and Reagan Econo-
         mics]. *Nauka i religiia* 1 (1988): 55-57.

1274   Filatova, P.[I]. "Na osnove tesnogo edinstva" [On the Basis of Close Unity].
         Kommunist Tadzhikistana 6 (1986): 84-87.

1275   Filatova, P.I. *Rol' trudovogo kollektiva v ateisticheskom vospitanii* [The Role
         of the Working Collective in Atheistic Education]. Dushanbe: Irfon, 1984.
         27 pp. In Tajik.
         Published also in:
         Kompleksnyi podkhod v ateisticheskom vospitanii. Dushanbe, 1988. Pp.
         19-30.

1276   Filimonov, E.G. *Aktual'nye voprosy ateisticheskogo vospitaniia* [Actual
         Problems of Atheistic Education]. M.: Znanie RSFSR, 1985. 40 pp. (V
         pomoshch' lektoru / O-vo "Znanie" RSFSR. Nauch.-metod. sovet otd-niia
         po propagande nauch. ateizma. Bibl.: p. 39.

1277   Filimonov, E.G. "Aktual'nye zadachi atesticheskogo vospitaniia molodezhi"
         [Actual Tasks of Atheistic Upbringing of Youth]. *Aktual'nye problemy
         nauchno-ateisticheskogo vospitaniia molodezhi.* M., 1987. Pp. 7-16.

1278   Filimonov, E.G. *Ateisticheskoe vospitanie na etape sovershenstvovaniia
         razvitogo sotsializma* [Atheistic Education in the Stage of Perfection of
         Developed Socialism]. M.: Znanie, 1985. 64 pp. (Novoe v zhizni, nauke,
         tekhnike. Nauch. ateizm; No 8). Bibl.: p. 54.

1279 Filimonov, E.G. *Khristianskoe sektantstvo i problemy ateisticheskoi raboty* [Christian Sectarianism and the Problems of Atheistic Work]. Kiev: Politizdat Ukrainy, 1981. 183 pp. Annot. bibl.: pp. 176-182. For review see item 5016.

1280 Filimonov, E.[G]. "Krizis very i religioznyi ekstremizm" [Crisis of Faith and Religious Extremism]. *Nauka i religiia* 2 (1980): 26-28.

1281 Filimonov, E.[G]. "Nekotorye voprosy ateisticheskogo vospitaniia" [Some Questions of Atheistic Education]. *Agitator* 22 (1983): 32-34.

1282 Filimonov, E.[G]. "Religioznyi ekstremizm: ideologicheskaia i sotsial'naia sushchnost'" [Religious Extremism: Ideological and Social Essence]. *Nauka i religiia* 8 (1984): 18-22.

1283 Filimonov, E.G. *Sotsial'naia i ideologicheskaia sushchnost' religioznogo ekstremizma* [Social and Ideological Essence of Religious Extremism]. M.: Znanie, 1980. 20 pp. (V pomoshch' lektoru).

1284 Filimonov, E.G. *Sotsial'naia i ideologicheskaia sushchnost' religioznogo ekstremizma* [Social and Ideological Essence of Religious Extremism]. M.: Znanie, 1983. 63 pp. (Novoe v zhizni, nauke, tekhnike. Nauch. ateizm; 8). Bibl.: p. 54. Annot, bibl.: pp. 52-53.

1285 Filimonov, E.[G]. "V chem sushchnost' religioznogo ekstremizma?" [What is the Essence of Religious Extremism?]. *Agitator* 9 (1987): 57-59.

1286 Filimonov, E.[G]. "Vospityvat' ateistov" [To Educate Atheists]. *Kommunist Azerbaidzhana* 2 (1988): 62-66.

1287 Filipovich, A.I. "K voprosu o strukture religioznogo soznaniia" [The Structure Issue of Religious Consciousness]. *Vopr. ateizma* 18 (1982): 91-98.

1288 Filipovich, A.I. "Osveshchenie problem smysla zhizni v [vuzovskom] kurse 'Osnovy nauchnogo ateizma'" [Illumination of Problems of the Meaning of Life in the [University] Course "Fundamentals of the Scientific Atheism"]. *Vopr. ateizma* 20 (1984): 127-132.

1289 Filipovich, L.A. *Filosofsko-eticheskii analiz pravoslavno-bogoslovskoi kontseptsii nravstvennykh kachestv cheloveka* [Philosophic-Ethical Analysis of Orthodox-Theological Conceptions of Human Being's Moral Values]. Kiev: AN UkSSR, 1989. 28 pp. Bibl.: pp. 26-28.

1290 Filippov, B.[A]. "Ioann Pavel II: politicheskii portret" [John Paul II: Political Portrait]. *Nauka i religiia* 2 (1989): 12-20.

1291 Filippov, B.A. "Ioann Pavel II, politik i chelovek" [John Paul II, Politician and Human Being]. *Mirovaia ekonomika i mezhdunar. otnosheniia* 11 (1989): 100-105.

1292 Filippov, L. "Mezhdu razumom i veroi" [Between Reason and Faith]. *Nauka i religiia* 1 (1980): 30-33.

1293 Filippova, A.R. "Ideologicheskaia funktsiia prepodavaniia nauchnogo ateizma v vuze" [Ideological Function of Reading Scientific Atheism in Institution of Higher Education]. *Vopr. ateizma* 20 (1984): 30-38.

1294 Filippova, M.I. *Obshchestvennye funktsii islama v sovremennom amerikanskom islamovedenii* [Islam's Social Functions in Contemporary American Studies of Islam]. M.: Nauka, 1989. 148 pp. Bibl.: pp. 130-146.

1295 Filippova, M.I. "Otsenka amerikanskimi uchenymi 'islamskogo faktora' v mezhdunarodnykh otnosheniiakh (nachalo 80-kh godov)" [Appreciation by American Scientists of the "Islamic Factor" in Internationl Relations (early 80s)]. *"Islamskii faktor" v mezhdunarodnykh otnosheniiakh v Azii (70-e - pervaia polovina 80-kh gg)*. M., 1987. Pp. 14-28.

1296 Filippova, M.I. "Sovremennye tendentsii izucheniia islama v anglo-amerikan-skom burzhuaznom vostokovedenii 50 - 70-kh godov" [Contemporary Tendencies of Study of Islam in Anglo-American Bourgeois Oriental Studies in 50s - 70s]. *Aktual'nye problemy ideologii i kul'tury stran Vostoka*. M., 1982. Pp. 39-53.

1297 Filist, G.M. "Dinamika sotsial'no-demograficheskikh protsessov v protes-tantskikh obshchinakh Bretskoi oblasti" [Dynamics of Socio-Demographical Processes in Protestant Communities in Brest Oblast]. *Protestantskie organizatsii v SSSR*. M., 1989. Pp. 84-92.

1298 Filist, G.M. "K voprosu o putiakh proniknoveniia khristianstva na Rus'" [On the Means of Christianity's Penetration into Rus']. *Vopr. nauch. ateizma* 37 (1988): 30-49.

1299 Filist, G.[M]. "O 'kreshchenii' Beloi Rusi" [On "Baptism" of White Rus']. *Neman* 9 (1988): 169-173.

1300   Filist, G.M. *Urbanizatsiia i sektantstvo* [Urbanisation and Sectarianism].
       Minsk: Belarus', 1986. 128 pp. Annot. bibl.: pp. 125-127.

1301   Filist, G.M. *Vvedenie khristianstva na Rusi: predposylki, obstoiatel'stva,*
       posledstviia [Introduction of Christianity into Rus': Preconditions,
       Circumstances, Consequences]. Minsk: Belarus', 1988. 254 pp. Annot.
       bibl.: pp. 245-253. For reviews see items 5017-5018.

1302   Filonenko,   N.V.   *Kritika   bogoslovskikh   kontseptsii   obshchestvenno-*
       istoricheskogo razvitiia [Criticism of Theological Conceptions of
       Socio-Historical Development]. Kiev: Znanie UkSSR, 1984. 47 pp. (Ser. 5
       "Nauchno-ateisticheskaia" / O-vo "Znanie" UkSSR; No 3). In Ukrainian.
       Bibl.: pp. 45-46.

1303   Filonenko,   N.V.   "Nesostoiatel'nost'   bogoslovskikh   idei   'neprekhodia-
       shchego' znacheniia pravoslaviia" [Groundlessness of Theological Ideas of
       "Untransient" Importance of Orthodoxy]. *Vopr. ateizma* 22 (1986): 127-133.

1304   Filonenko, N.V. *Pravoslavie v poiskakh istoricheskogo samoopravdaniia*
       [Orthodoxy in the Search of Historical Self-justification]. Kiev: Znanie
       UkSSR, 1987. 48 pp. (Ser. 5, Nauchno-ateisticheskaia / O-vo "Znanie"
       UkSSR; No 10. In Ukrainian. Bibl.: pp. 47-48.

1305   Filonenko, N.V. *Sotsial'nyi ideal - real'nyi i mnimyi* [Social Ideal - Real and
       Imaginary]. Kiev: Politizdat Ukrainy, 1981. 135 pp. In Ukrainian.

1306   Filonenko, N.V.; Rebkalo, V.A. *Pravoslavie i sovremennost'* [Orthodoxy and
       Contemporaneity]. Kiev: Vishcha shk., 1982. 87 pp. (Ateist. b-chka
       studenta). Bibl.: p. 86.

1307   *Filosofiia. Religiia. Kul'tura:* Krit. analiz sovrem. burzhuaz. filosofii
       [Philosophy. Religion. Culture: Critical Analysis of Contemporary
       Bourgeois Philosophy]. Ed.: G.M. Tavrizian. M.: Nauka, 1982. 397 pp.
       Name and subject index: pp.388-397. For reviews see items 5019-5020.

1308   *Filosofiia i religiia na zarubezhnom Vostoke, XX v.* [Philosophy and Religion
       in Foreign Orient, XXth C.]. M.: Nauka, 1985. 272 pp. For reviews see
       items 5021-5022.

1309   *Filosofskie i sotsial'nye aspekty buddizma* [Philosophical and Social Aspects
       of Buddhism]. [Eds.: M.T. Stepaniants et al]. M.: [S.n.], 1989. 189 pp.

1310 *Filosofskie kontseptsii katolitsizma* [Philosphical Conceptions of Catholicism].
[Comp.: B. Kuzmitskas]. Vil'nius: Mintis, 1986. 174 pp. In Lithuanian.
Summaries in Russian and English. For review see item 5023.

1311 *Filosofskie problemy ateizma* [Philosophical Problems of Atheism]. [Ed.: D.
Gegeshidze]. Tbilisi: Metsniereba, 1989. 144 pp. In Georgian. Summary in
Russian.

1312 *Filosofskie problemy istorii svobodomysliia i ateizma* [Philosophical Problems
of the History of Freethinking and Atheism]. [Ed.: V.N. Sherdakov]. M.:
[S.n], 1986. 77 pp.

1313 *Filosofskie voprosy buddizma* [Philosophical Problems of Buddhism]. [Ed.:
V.V. Mantatov]. Novosibirsk: Nauka. Sibir. otdnie, 1984. 124 pp. For
reviews see items 5024-5025.

1314 *Filosofskoe nasledie musul'manskogo mira i sovremennaia ideologicheskaia
bor'ba:* Nauch. analit. obzor [Philosophical Heritage of Moslem World
and Contemporary Ideological Struggle: Scientific Analytical Review].
[A.V. Sagadeev]. M.: INION, 1987. 51 pp. (Ser. "Sovremen. probl. sotsial.
razvitiia i ideologii stran Azii, Afriki i Latin. Ameriki" / AN SSSR,
INION). Bibl.: pp. 46-51.

1315 Fil'shtinskii, I. "Pamiatnik arabskoi slovesnosti" [Monument of Arabic
Literature]. *Nauka i religiia* 12 (1980): 27-30.

1316 Finogenova, S.I. "Kul't Demetry na Bosfore po arkheologicheskim dannym"
[Demeter Cult in Bosphorus According to Archeological Data]. *Tezisy
dokladov nauchnoi sessii, posviashchennoi itogam raboty Gosudarstvennogo
muzeia izobrazitel'nykh iskusstv im. A.S. Pushkina. 1987.* M., 1988. Pp.
13-15.

1317 Fishevskii, Iu.K. "Idti dal'she, dobivat'sia bol'shego" [To Go Further, To
Achieve More]. *Nauka i religiia* 7 (1982): 4-8.

1318 Fishevskii, Iu.[K]. "Na uroven' sovremennykh zadach [On the Level of
Contemporary Tasks]. *Nauka i Religiia* 11 (1983): 7-9.

1319 Fletcher, U. "Sovetskie veruiushchie" [Soviet Believers]. *Sotsiol. issled.* 4
(1987): 28-35.
Published also in:
Argumenty M., 1988. Pp. 59-72.

1320 Florenskii, P. "Ikonostas" [Iconostasis]. *Dekor. iskusstvo* 6 (1988): 26-37.

1321 Florenskii, P. "Khramovoe deistvo kak sintez iskusstva" [Temple Ritual as Synthesis of Art]. *Str-vo i arkhitektura Moskvy* 6 (1988): 17-20.
Published also in: *Sov. muzei* 4 (1989): 65-69
Vestn. Mosk. un-ta. Ser. 7. Filosofiia. 2 (1989): 58-66
Prepodavanie chertorii v shk. 5 (1989): 15-19.

1322 Florenskii, P.V. "Sviashchennik Pavel Florenskii: real'nosti i simvol" [The Priest Pavel Florenskii: Realities and Symbol]. *Lit. Rossiia* 21 (1989): 21.

1323 Floria, N.I. *Pravda ob ateizme i religii v SSSR* [Truth on Atheism and Religion in USSR]. Kishinev: Znanie MSSR, 1983. 25 pp. (Znaniia narodu / O-vo "Znanie" MSSR). Bibl.: p. 25. In Moldavian.

1324 Foigel', A.M. "Ateisticheskoe vospitanie v usloviiakh nauchno-tekhnicheskoi revoliutsii pri sotsializme [Atheistic Education in Conditions of Scientific-Technical Revolution under Socialism]. *Problemy dukhovnoi zhizni sotsialisticheskogo obshchestva.* Omsk, 1984. Pp. 71-87.

1325 Foigel', A.M. "Gnoseologicheskie korni religii i sovershenstovanie ateisticheskogo vospitaniia" [Gnosiological Roots of Religion and Perfection of Atheistic Education]. *Sotsial'no ekonomicheskie problemy razvitogo sotsializma.* Tomsk, 1981. Pp. 82-90.

1326 Foigel', A.M. "Individual'naia rabota s veruiushchimi" [Individual Work with Believers]. *Aktual'nye problemy obespecheniia effektivnosti nauchno-ateisticheskoi raboty.* Cheboksary, 1986. Pp. 84-90.

1327 Foigel', A.M. *Individual'naia rabota s veruiushchimi* [Individual Work with Believers]. M.: Znanie, 1988. 64 pp. (Novoe v zhizni, nauke, tekhnike. Nauch. ateizm; 5/1988). Bibl.: p. 62.

1328 Foigel', A.[M]. "Opyt vospitaniia veruiushchikh" [Experience in the Education of Believers]. *Agitator* 19 (1988): 58-60.

1329 Foigel' A.M. *Put' k serdtsu i razumu* [The Way to Heart and Reason]. Omsk: Kn. izd-vo, 1989. 111 pp. (V pomoshch' ateistu).

1330 Fokina, L.A. "Istoricheskaia obuslovlennost' khristianizatsii Drevnei Rusi" [Historical Conditionality of Ancient Rus' Conversion to Christianity]. *Molodezh' i tvorchestvo: sotsial'no-filosofskie problemy.* M., 1988. Ch. 1. Pp. 69-72.

1331 Fomenko, A.K. "Ateisticheskoe vospitanie kak sredstvo aktivizatsii chelovechcskogo faktora" [Atheistic Education as Means of Activization of Human Factor]. *Vopr. ateizma* 24 (1988): 24-29.

1332 Fomenko, A.K. *Kak ponimat' dukhovnuiu svobodu* [How to Understand Spiritual Freedom]. Kiev: Politizdat Ukrainy, 1985. 72 pp. (Ser. "Besedy s veruiushchimi). In Ukrainian. Bibl.: pp. 69-71.

1333 Fomenko, A.K. "Kritika pravoslavnoi kontseptsii kriteriia tsennosti cheloveka" [Criticism of Orthodox Criterion of Human Value]. *Vopr. ateizma* 17 (1981): 123-130.

1334 Fomenko, A.K. "Nauchno-ateisticheskooe vospitanie - odno iz sredstv utverzhdeniia tsennosti cheloveka razvitogo sotsializma" [Scientific-Atheistic Education - One of the Means of Assertion of Human Value of the Developed Socialism]. *Dukhovnaia sfera sotsialisticheskogo obraza zhizni i sovremennaia ideologicheskaia bor'ba.* Dnepropetrovsk, 1981. Pp. 72-77.

1335 Fomenko, A.K. *Nesovmestimost' kommunisticheskoi i khristianskoi morali* [Incompatibility of Communist and Christian Morals]. Kiev: Znanie UkSSR, 1980. 20 pp. (B-chka v pomoshch' lektoru "Nravstv. vospitanie novogo cheloveka / O-vo "Znanie" UkSSR).

1336 Fomenko, A.K. *Nesovmestimost' kommunisticheskoi nravstvennosti i religiia* [Incompatibility of Communist Morals and Religion]. Kiev: Znanie UkSSR, 1980. 48 pp. (Ser. V "Nauchno-ateisticheskaia" / O-vo "Znanie" UkSSR; No 12). Bibl.: p. 48.

1337 Fomenko, A.K.; Fomenko, I.A. *Otnoshenie khristianstva k zhenshchine, sem'e, detiam* [Christianity's Attitude Towards Woman, Family, Children]. Kiev: Znanie UkSSR, 1983. 48 pp. (Ser. V "Nauchno-ateisticheskaia" / O-vo "Znanie" UkSSR; No 6). Bibl.: pp. 45-46. Annot. bibl.: pp. 44-45.

1338 Fomichenko, V.V. *Klerikalizm: stavka na molodezh'* [Clericalism: Counts on Youth]. Simferopol': Tavriia, 1988. 192 pp., illus.

1339 Fomichenko, V.V. *Klerikal'nyi antikommunizm v sisteme ideologicheskikh diversii* [Clerical Anti-Communism in the System of Ideological Diversion]. Simferopol': Tavriia, 1984. 81 pp.

1340 Fomichenko, V.V. *Kritika ideologii i praktiki sovremennogo katolitsizma* [Criticism of Ideology and Practice of the Contemporary Catholicism].

Kiev: Znanie UkSSR, 1982. 48 pp. (Ser. "Nauchno-ateisticheskaia" / O-vo "Znanie" UkSSR; No 1). Bibl.: p. 47.

1341 Fomichenko, V.V. *Kritika sotsial'noi filosofii sovremennogo katolitsizma* [Criticism of Social Philosophy of the Contemporary Catholicism]. Kiev: Vishcha shk. Izd-vo pri Kiev. un-te, 1983. 81 pp. (Ateist. b-chka studenta). Bibl.: pp. 78-80.

1342 Fomichenko, V.V. *Problema cheloveka i sovremennyi klerikal'nyi anti-kommunizm* [Human Problem and Contemporary Clerical Anti-Communism]. Kiev: Politizdat Ukrainy, 1982. 165 pp. Annot. bibl.: pp. 158-164.

1343 Fomichenko, V.V. *Sovremennyi Vatikan: dukhovnaia kul'tura ili eskalatsiia antikommunizma?* [Contemporary Vatican: Spiritual Culture or Escalation of Anti-Communism?]. Kiev: Znanie UkSSR, 1988. 47 pp. (Ser. 5, Nauchno-ateisticheskaia / O-vo "Znanie" UkSR; No 10). In Ukrainian. Annot. bibl.: pp. 145-46.

1344 Fomichev, S.A. *Komediia A.S. Griboedova 'Gore ot uma': Kommentarii* [A.S. Griboedov's Comedy "The Misfortune of Being Wise": Commentaries]. M.: Prosveshchenie, 1983. 207 pp. Bibl.: pp. 204-207. Annot. bibl.: pp. 202-203.

1345 Fomin, V.N. *Mirovozzrenie i sovershenstvovanie lichnosti: Kritika khristian. vozzrenii na nravstv. samosovershenstvovanie* [World Outlook and Perfection of Personality: Criticism of Christian Outlook on Moral Self-perfection]. Kiev: Znanie UkSSR, 1985. 48 pp. (Ser. 5 "Naucho-ateisticheskaia" / O-vo "Znanie" UkSSR; No 4). In Ukrainian. Bibl.: pp. 45-46. Annot. bibl.: pp. 44-45.

1346 Fomkin, M.S. "O religioznoi situatsii v Anatolii XIII-XIV vv." [Religious Situation in Anatolia of XIIIth-XIVth C.]. V *Vsesoiuznaia shkola molodykh vostokovedov.* M., 1989. T. I. Pp. 81-83.

1347 *Formirovanie materialisticheskogo mirovozzreniia i aktivnoi zhiznennoi pozitsii sovetskogo cheloveka v svete reshenii XXVI s'ezda KPSS* [Forming Materialistic World Outlook and Active Vital Position of the Soviet Man in the Light of XXVIth CPSU Congress Resolutions]. Briansk: Uprpoligrafizdat, 1981. 43 pp.

1348 *Formirovanie nauchno-ateisticheskogo mirovozzreniia v usloviiakh sotsial'nogo i tekhnicheskogo progressa* [Forming Scientific-Atheistic World Outlook in Conditions of Social and Technical Progress]. Ed.: G.S. Doroshenko. M: [S.n.], 1985. 147 pp.

1349 Formirovat' ateisticheskuiu ubezhdennost' [To Form Atheistic Conviction]. *Komunist Tadzhkistana* 3 (1988): 69-79.

1350 Frezer, D.D. *Fol'klor v Vetkhom zavete* [Folklore in the Old Testament]. Transl. from English and comment.: S.A. Tokareva. 2nd revised ed. M.: Politizdat, 1985. 511 pp., illus. (B-ka ateist. lit.). Republished in 1986 and 1989.

1351 Frezer, D.D. *Zolotaia vetv'* [The Golden Bough]. M.: Politizdat, 1980. 831 pp. (B-ka ateist. lit.). Translated from: *The Golden Bough* / Frazer, J.G. (London, 1923). Subject and mytholog. name index: pp. 821-828. Published as 2nd ed., in 1983, 703 pp., illus. and in 1986.
Published also in:
Erevan: Aiastan, 1989, 879 pp. In Armenian. Index: pp. 869-877.
For reviews see items 5027-5031.

1352 Froianov, I.Ia. *Istoricheskie usloviia kreshcheniia Rusi* [Historical Conditions of Baptism of Rus']. L.: Znanie RSFSR. Leningr. org., Leningr. Dom nauch. ateizma, 1988. 32 pp. Bibl.: p. 31.

1353 Froianov, I.Ia.; Dvornichenko, A.Iu.; Krivosheev, Iu.V. "Vvedenie khristianstva na Rusi i iazycheskie traditsii" [Introduction of Christianity into Rus' and Heathen Traditions]. *Sov. etnografiia* 6 (1988): 25-34.

1354 Frolov, K.V. "Za gran'iu nauki - nauka..." [Beyond the Verge of Science -Science...]. *Nauka i religiia* 12 (1988): 6-8.

1355 Frolova, E.A. "Nauka i islam: Nekotorye filos. aspekty ikh vzaimootnoshenii" [Science and Islam: Some Philosophic Aspects of Their Interrelations]. *Metodologicheskie problemy izucheniia istorii filosofii zarubezh- nogo Vostoka.* M., 1987. Pp. 117-134. Bibl.: pp. 133-134.

1356 Fromm, E. *Psikhoanaliz i religiia* [Psychoanalysis and Religion]. Vil'nius: Mintis, 1981. 144 pp. In Lithuanian.

1357 Furman D.E. *Religiia i sotial'nye konflikty v SShA* [Religion and Social Conflicts in USA]. M.: Nauka, 1981. 256 pp. Bibl.: pp. 248-255.

Published also in:
M.: Progress, 1984, 254 pp. In English. Bibl.: pp. 244-251. Name index: pp. 252-254. For reviews see items 5032-5035.

1358 Furman D.E. "Tendentsii razvitiia massovogo religioznogo soznaniia v SShA" [Tendencies of Development of Mass Religious Consciousness in USA]. *Sotsial. issled.* 4 (1985): 137-144.

1359 Furman, D.E. et al. *Religiia v politicheskoi zhizni SShA (70-e - nach. 80-kh gg.)* [Religion in the Political Life of USA (70s - early 80s)]. M.: Nauka, 1985. 225 pp. For reviews see items 5036-5039.

1360 Furov, V.G. *Gran' naslediia* [Aspects of Legacy]. M.: Sov. Rossiia, 1985. 175 pp., illus.

1361 Fursenko, V.M. "Khristianin i rodina" [Christian and Fatherland]. *Nauka i religiia* 4 (1989): 27-29.

1362 Fursin, I.I. "Sotsialisticheskaia i religioznaia obriadnost' - protivopolozhnye tipy prakticheski-dukhovnogo osvoeniia mira" [Socialist and Religious Ceremonial - Opposite Types of Practical-Spiritual Mastering of the World]. *Vopr. ateizma* 21 (1985): 40-47.

1363 Furtseva, L.R. "Rannie shkoly Khinaiany v istorii buddizma" [Early Hinayana Schools in the History of Buddhism]. *III Vsesoiuznaia konferentsiia vostokovedov "Vzaimodeistvie i vzaimovlianie tsivilizatsii kul'tur na Vostoke.* M., 1988. T. I. Pp. 136-139.

1364 Gabdullin, B.G. *Vzgliady kazakhskikh prosvetitelei na religiiu:* (Shamanism, islam, ateizm, deizm, antiklerikalizm) [Views of Kazakh Educators on Religion: (Shamanism, Islam, Atheism, Deism, Anticlericalism)]. Alma-Ata: Kazakhstan, 1988. 103 pp. In Kazakh.

1365 Gabidzashvili, O.D. *Religiia kak sotsial'noe iavlenie* [Religion as Social Occurrence]. Tbilisi: Sabchota Sakartvelo, 1987. 223 pp. In Georgian.

1366 Gabidzashvili, O.D. *Voprosy sotsiologii religii* [Problems of Sociology of Religion]. Tbilisi: Metsniereba, 1984. 78 pp. In Georgian. Summary in Russian.

1367 Gabinskii, G.A. *Bozhestvennoe otkrovenie i chelovecheskoe poznanie* [Divine Revelation and Human Cognition]. M.: Politizdat, 1989. 127 pp., illus. (Besedy o mire i cheloveke).

1368 Gabinskii, G.A. "Ratsionalizm kak faktor razvitiia ateisticheskogo soznaniia" [Rationalism as Factor of Development of Atheistic Consciousness]. *Vopr. nauch. ateizma* 30 (1982): 30-45.

1369 Gabinskii, G.A. *V poiskakh chuda: Besedy o mire i chekoveke* [In the Search of Miracle: Discussions about the World and Man]. Riga: Avots, 1981. 83 pp. In Latvian.
Published also in:
Kishinev: Kartia moldoveniaske, 1981, 124 pp. (Nauka i religiia). In Moldavian.

1370 Gabinskii, G.[A].; Lobachev, V. "Pokushenie na chudo" [Attempt on Miracle]. *Nauka i religiia* 1 (1987): 12-16.

1371 Gabriel', G.; Sofyina, K. "Novaia ekspozitsiia Muzeia istorii religii i ateizma" [New Exposition of the Museum of History of Religion and Atheism]. *Dekor. iskusstvo SSSR* 1 (1982): 30-31.

1372 Gabuniia, G.R. "Sotsial'naia sushchnost' sufizma" [Social Essence of Sufism]. *Aktual'nye problemy kritiki religii i formirovaniia ateisticheskogo mirovozzrenia.* Makhachkala, 1982. Pp. 27-35.

1373 Gadaev, V.Iu. *Dorogoi istiny* [On the Way of Truth]. Groznyi: Chech.-Ing. kn. izd-vo, 1982. 80 pp.

1374 Gadaev, V.Iu. *Za chastokolom miuridskikh propovedei* [Beyond the Fence of Miurid Sermons]. Groznyi: Chech.-Ing. kn. izd-vo, 1987. 56 pp.

1375 Gadzhiev, G. "Komu na ruku nasha lozh'" [Whom Does Our Lie Serve]. *Sov. Dagestan* 2 (1988): 16-18.

1376 Gadzhiev, S.M. *Koran bez chudes* [Koran Without Miracles]. Makhachkala: Dag. kn. izd-vo, 1982. 96 pp.

1377 Gaer, E.A. *The passing away of the deceased man's soul into the next world-buni:* (The example of shamans' rituals).* M., Nauka, 1988. 13 pp.

1378 Gaev, G.I. "Khristianstvo i iazycheskaia kul'tura" [Christianity and Pagan Culture]. *Ateisticheskie chteniia.* M., 1988. Pp. 303-309.

1379 Gagarin, Iu.V. "Ochagi staroobriadchestva na russkom severe v kontse XVII-XVIII vv." [Old-Beliefs Centre in Northern Russia Late XVIIth-XVIIIth C.]. *Agramye otnosheniia i istoriia krest'ianstva Evropeiskogo Severa Rossii (do 1917 goda).* Syktyvkar, 1981. Pp. 99-107.

1380 Gagloeva, Z.D. "Okhota v verovaniiakh i obychaiakh osetin i svanov" [The Hunting in the Beliefs and Customs of Osetins and Svans]. *Izvestiia AN GSSR.* Iugo-Oset. NII. Tbilisi, 1987. Vyp. 31. Pp. 49-57.

1381 Gagulashvili, I.Sh. "Mifologicheskii obriad smerti v gruzinskom folklore" [Mythological Image of Death in Georgian Folklore]. *Byt i kul'tura Iugo-Zapadnoi Gruzii.* Tbilisi, 1988. 15. Pp. 100-105. In Georgian. Summary in Russian.

1382 Gaibov, S. "Opisanie religii narodov v 'Nukhbat ad-dakhr fi adzhaib al-barr va l-bakhr' Shams ad-Dani ad-Dimashki" [Description of Peoples Religion in "Nuhbat al-dahr fi ajaib al-barr wal-bahr" Shams al-Din al-Dimashqi]. *III Vsesoiuznaia konferentsiia vostokovedov "Vzaimodeistvie i vzaimov-liianie tsivilizatsii kul'tur na Vostoke".* M., 1988. T. 2. Pp. 73-74.

1383 Gaidash, O.N. "Metodologicheskii analiz problemy cheloveka v nauchnom ateizme" [Methodological Analysis of the Human Problem in Scientific Atheism]. *Molodezh' i tvorchestvo: sotsial'no-filosofskie problemy.* M., 1988. Ch. 3. Pp. 295-297.

1384 Gaidash, O.N. "Problema sushchnosti cheloveka v ateizme i religii" [The Problem of Human Essence in Atheism and Religion]. *Dukhovnyi mir sovremennogo cheloveka.* M., 1987. Pp. 122-124.

1385 Gaidis, A.[A]. "Antiklerikal'naia deiatel'nost' P. Vilunasa v gody tsarskoi vlasti" [P. Vilunas' Anticlerical Activity During Tsar's Power]. *Ateistines minties raida lietuvoje.* Kaunas: 1988. Pp. 41-47. In Lithuanian. Summary in Russian.

1386 Gaidis, A.[A]. *Evoliutsiia katolicheskogo klerikal'nogo antikommunizma* [Evolution of Catholical Clerical Anti-Communism]. Vil'nius: Znanie LitSSR, 1981. 38 pp. (Material dlia lektora / O-vo "Znanie" LitSSR). In Lithuanian.

1387 Gaidis, A.A. *Katolicheskii klerikal'nyi antikommunizm* [Catholic Clerical Anti-Communism]. Vil'nius: Mintis, 1982. 311 pp. Summary in English. Bibl.: pp. 287-305. For review see item 5040.

1388 Gaidis, A.[A]. "Neobkhodimost' dialoga i sotrudnichesva marksistov i khristian v bor'be za mir i sotsial'nyi progress" [Necessity of Dialogue and Collaboration of Marxists and Christians in the Struggle for Peace and Social Progress]. *Nekotorye aspekty filosofskogo ponimaniia cheloveka.* Vil'nius, 1988. Pp. 120-125.

1389 Gaidis, A.A. *Religiia i politicheskii klerikalizm* [Religion and Political Clericalism]. Vil'nius: Mintis, 1987. 97 pp. (Popul. b-ka. Besedy o filosofii). In Lithuanian.

1390 Gaidis, A.A. "Spekuliatsii na nravstvenno-eticheskoi problematike kak sredstvo ideologicheskikh aktsii katolicheskogo klerikal'nogo antikommunizma" [Speculations on Moral-Ethical Problematics as Means of Ideological Actions of Catholic Clerical Anti-Communism]. *Vopr. nauch. ateizma* 35 (1986): 274-285.

1391 Gaigalaite, A.I. *Ionas Ragauskas* [Ionas Ragauscas]. Kaunas: Shviesa, 1989. 112 pp., illus. In Lithuanian.

1392 Gaigalaite, A.[I]. *Reaktsionnaia rol' katolicheskoi tserkvi v istorii Litvy* [Reactionary Role of Catholic Church in the History of Lithuania]. Vil'nius: Znanie LitSSR, 1980. 34 pp. (Material dlia lektora / O-vo "Znanie" LitSSR). Bibl.: pp. 33-34.

1393 Gaikovskii, M.I. *Reaktsionnaia deiatel'nost' pravoslavnoi tserkvi na Severnoi Bukovine (1918-1940)* [Reactionary Activity of Orthodox Church in Northern Bukovina (1918-1940)]. Kiev: Nauk. dumka, 1984. 135 pp. In Ukrainian.

1394 Gainullin, N. "Kharidzhity" [Haridjite]. *Nauka i religiia* 9 (1982): 34-37.

1395 Galdanova, G.R. *Dolamaistskie verovaniia buriat* [Pre-Lamaist Beliefs of Buriat]. Novosibirsk: Nauka. Sib. otd-nie, 1987. 115 pp. Bibl.: pp. 105-114.

1396 Galerkina, O. "O nekotorykh proiavleniiakh kul'turnoi obshchnosti narodov 'khristianskogo' i 'musul'manskogo' Vostoka" [Some Manifestations of Cultural Community of Peoples of "Christian" and "Moslem" Orient].

Vtoroi mezhdunar. simpoz. po arm. iskusstvu. Erevan, 1981. T. 3. Pp. 336-343.

1397 Galiakbarov, R.R. *Ugolovnia otvetstvennost' za posiagate'stva na lichnost' i prava grazhdan pod vidom ispol'neniia religioznykh obriadov* [Criminal Responsibility for Infringement Upon Individual and Citizens' Rights under the Pretence of Fulfilment of Religious Rites]. Omsk: Omskaia vyssh. shkola militsii, 1981. 76 pp. Bibl.: p. 73.

1398 Galin, V. "Otvergaia mech" [Rejecting the Sword]. *Novoe vremia* 49 (1987): 34-35.

1399 Galitskaia, I.A. "Ateisticheskoe vospitanie v shkole" [Atheistic Upbringing in School]. *Sov. pedagogika* 6 (1988): 15-19.

1400 Galitskaia, I.[A]. "Nekotorye voprosy ateisticheskogo vospitaniia molodezhi" [Some Problems of Atheistic Upbringing of Youth]. *Polit. samoobrazovanie* 4 (1983): 108-115.

1401 Gal'perin, B.I. "Ateizm - eto sozidanie cheloveka" [Atheism - Is Man's Creation]. *Filos. i sotsiol. mysl'* 11 (1989): 51-57. Summary in English, p. 127.

1402 Gal'perin, B.[I]. "Baptizm i revoliutsiia" [Baptism and Revolution]. *Nauka i religiia* 11 (1987): 55-56.

1403 Gal'perin, B.[I]. "Baptizm i samoderzhavie" [Baptism and Autocracy]. *Nauka i religiia* 10 (1987): 53-55.

1404 Gal'perin, B.I. *Mozhno li verit' Biblii?* [Is it Possible to Believe in the Bible?]. Frunze: Kyrgyzstan, 1982. 92 pp. (B-chka ateista. BA). In Kirghiz.

1405 Gal'perin, B.I. "Soderzhanie i priemy religioznogo vozdeistviia na detei i molodezh' v baptistskikh obshchinakh i sem'iakh" [The Content and Methods of Religious Influence on Children and Youth in Baptist Communities and Families]. *Protestantskie organizatsii v SSSR.* M., 1989. Pp. 51-67.

1406 Gal'perin, B.[I]. "Ssylaias' na Bibliiu" [Referring to Bible]. *Nauka i religiia* 7 (1980); 29-32.

1407   Gal'perin, B.I.; Litovchenlo, N.N. *Sovremennyi militarizm i klerikalizm* [Contemporary Militarism and Clericalism]. Kiev: Znanie UkSSR, 1986. 47 pp. (Ser. 5, Nauchno-ateisticheskaia / O-vo "Znanie" UkSSR; No 5). In Ukrainian. Bibl.: pp. 46-47.

1408   Gal'perin, B.I.; Zazulin, A.N. "Ateisticheskoe vospitanie v trudovom kollektive" [Atheistic Education in Working Collective]. *Vopr. nauch. ateizma* 29 (1982): 71-83.

1409   Gal'vidis, Iu. *Formy i kul'tury drevnikh verovanii* [Forms and Cultures of Ancient Beliefs]. Vil'nius: Mintis, 1980. 71 pp. (Malaia ateist. ser.). In Lithuanian.

1410   Gamagelian, M.G. *Predannost' delu prosveshcheniia* [Devotion to Enlightenment]. Erevan: Lus, 1986. 297 pp. In Armenian.

1411   Gambashidze, N.S. "Rozhdestvo v Ertso-Tianeti" [Christmas in Ertso-Tianet]. *Materialy po etnografii Gruzii.* Tbilisi, 1987. T. 23. Pp. 195-201. In Georgian. Summary in English.

1412   Ganikhanova, E.E. "Obraz Iisusa Khrista v sovremennoi arabskoi poezii" [The Image of Jesus Christ in Arab Contemporary Poetry]. *V Vsesoiuznaia shkola molodykh vostokovedov.* M., 1989. T. I. Pp. 104-105.

1413   Gapanovich, V.F.; Tsarenkov, L.A. *Vcherashnii i segodniashnii den' uniatskoi tserkvi* [Yesterday's and Today's of the Uniate Church]. Minsk: Belarus', 1985. 97 pp. In Belorussian.

1414   Gapochka, I.M.; Gribachev, V.N. *Rostom s goru Vashington* [Height in the Size of Mount Washington]. M.: Molodaia gvardiia, 1987. 190 pp., illus. (Imperializm: Sobytiia, fakty, dokumenty).

1415   Gapochka, M.P. "Uroki bogostroitel'stva" [The Lessons of Godstructuring]. *Vopr. nauch. ateizma* 25 (1980): 186-204.

1416   Garadzha, V.[I]. "Ateizm i sovremennaia ideologicheskaia bor'ba" [Atheism and Contemporary Ideological Struggle]. *Agitator* 21 (1983): 30-33.

1417   Garadzha, V.I. "Bezrazlichie? Net, mirovozzrencheskaia nezrelost'" [Indifference? No, World Outlook's Immaturity]. *Molodoi kommunist* 7 (1986): 37-42.

1418   Garadzha, V.[I]. "Chto esli boga net?" [What if There is no God?]. *Rodina* 8 (1989): 20.

1419   Garadzha, V.I. "Kliuchevye problemy nauchnogo ateizma" [Key Problems of Scientific Atheism]. *Nauka i religiia* 2 (1986): 11-13.

1420   Garadzha, V.[I]. "Na uroven' trebovanii zhizni" [Abreast of Life's Requirements]. *Nauka i religiia* 1 (1988): 10-12.

1421   Garadzha, V.I. *Nauchnaia i khristianskaia interpretatsiia istorii* [Scientific and Christian Interpretation of History]. M.: Znanie, 1980. 64 pp. (Novoe v zhizni, nauke, tekhnike. Ser. "Nauch. ateizm"; No 6).

1422   Garadzha, V.I. "Nauchnyi ateizm v svete zadach sovershenstvovaniia sotsializma" [Scientific Atheism in the Light of Tasks of Perfection of Socialism]. *Vopr. nauch. ateizma* 34 (1986): 6-25.

1423   Garadzha, V.[I]. "Pereosmyslenie" [Reinterpretation]. *Nauka i religiia* 1 (1989): 2-5.

1424   Garadzha, V.[I]. "Prometeev ogon'" [Promethean Fire]. *Avrora* 2 (1984): 124-130.

1425   Garadzha, V.I. "V interesakh sotsializma: Beseda o vzaimootnosheniiakh gosudarstva i tserkvi" [In the Interests of Socialism: Talk on State and Church Interrelations]. *Molodoi kommunist* 8 (1988): 28-35.

1426   Garadzha, V.I. "B razvitie dialoga" [For Development of the Dialogue]. *Nauka i religiia* 7 (1987): 20-22.

1427   Garntsev, M.A. "Ot Bonaventury k D. Skotu: k kharakteristiki avgustinianstva vtoroi poloviny XIII-nachala XIV v." [From Bonaventura to D. Scott: On Characteristics of Augustinian of the Late XIIIth-Early XIVth C.]. *Srednie veka*. M., 1988. Vyp. 51. Pp. 94-115.

1428   Garshkaite, R. "S. Matulaitis o vozniknovenii i razvitii idei boga" [S. Matulaitis on the Origin and Development of the Idea of God]. *Ateistines minties raida lietuvoje,* Kaunas, 1988. Pp. 93-99. In Lithuanian. Summary in Russian.

1429   Gartsev, I.A. *Rezul'taty i posledstviia missionerskoi deiatel'nosti amerikanskikh obshchestv v blizhnevostochnykh stranakh v kontse XIX- nachale XX vv.*

[Results and Consequences of Missionary Activity of American Societies in Near Eastern Countries Late XIXth-Early XXth C.]. L: [S.n.], 1988. 17 pp. Bibl.: pp. 16-17.

1430   Gasanov, A. *Bor'ba azerbaidzhanskikh prosvetitelei protiv islama (vtoraia polovina XIX v.-nach. XX v.)* [The Struggle of Azerbaijani Enlighteners against Islam (Late XIXth C.-Early XXth C.)]. Baku: Iazychy, 1983. 224 pp. In Azerbaijan.

1431   Gasanov, Sh.G. "O nekotorykh formakh ateisticheskoi raboty v dagestanskom aule v pervye gody Sovetskoi vlasti" [On Some Forms of Atheistic Work in Daghestan Aul in the First Years of Soviet Power]. *Sotsializm i kul'turnyi progress narodov Dagestana.* Makhachkala, 1987. Pp. 20-33. Bibl.: pp. 32-33.

1432   Gasanov, T.B. "Kommentarii k nekotorym koranicheskim stikham o zaprete vina" [Commentaries on Some Koran Verses on Prohibition of Wine]. *Izv. AN AzSSR.* Ser. istorii, filosofii i prava 4 (1988): 62-65. Summary in Azerbaijan.

1433   Gasanova, E.Iu. "Ispol'zovanie islama v ideologii natsionalizma v Turtsii" [The Use of Islam in Nationalist Ideology in Turkey]. *Sovetskoe vostoko-vedenie.* M., 1988. Pp. 312-319.

1434   Gavrilin, A.V. "Rol' pravoslavnogo dukhovenstva v perekhode latyshskikh i estonskikh krest'ian v pravoslavie v 1845-1848 godakh" [The Role of Orthodox Clergy in Conversion of Latvian and Estonian Peasants into Orthodoxy in 1845-1848]. *Izv. AN LatvSSR* 11 (198): 40-51.

1435   Gavrilov, V.M. "Taina sostradaiushchei teologii" [Secret of Compassionate Theology]. *Latin. Amerika* 5 (1988): 5-11.

1436   Gavriushin, N. "Padut li sem' pechatei?: Apokalipsis v relig. i svetskom soznanii: neskol'ko granei vechnoi temy" [Will the Seven Seals Fall?: Revelation in Religious and Secular Consciousness: Several Grains of an Eternal Theme]. *Nauka i religiia* 11 (1988): 37-39.

1437   Gazdeliani, E.K. "Proiskhozhdenie nekotorykh religioznykh terminov v svanskom" [The Origin of Some Religious Terms in Svain]. *Etimologicheskie razyskaniia.* Tbilisi, 1988. Pp. 67-72. In Georgian. Summary in Russian.

1438 Gazhos, V. "Adventizm pered litsom sovremennykh problem" [Adventism in the Face of Contemporary Problems]. *Kommunist Moldavii* 12 (1983): 62-66.

1439 Gazhos, V.; Tabunshchik, F. "Vopreki istoricheskoi pravde" [In Spite of Historical Truth]. *Kommunist Moldavii* 5 (1988): 69-76.

1440 Gazibaev, Kh. *Bor'ba s religioznymi i natsionalisticheskimi perezhitkami* [The Struggle with Religious and Nationalist Survivals]. Tashkent: Uzbekistan, 1988. 22 pp. (Besedy o nauke; No 15). In Uzbek.

1441 "Gde pasut'sia 'troianskie koni'? ili O tesnoi sviazi natsionalizma i klerikalizma" [Where 'Trojan Horses' Graze? or On the Tight Bond of Nationalism and Clericalism]. *Dary danaitsev*. Minsk, 1987. Pp. 191-278.

1442 Geche, G. *Bibleiskie istorii* [Biblical Stories]. M.: Politizdat, 1988. 367 pp., illus. (B-ka ateist. lit.). Name index: pp. 357-363. Transl. from Hungarian *Bibliai tortenetek* / Gecse, G. (Budapest, 1985).
Published also in: 1989, 318 pp., illus. from Hungarian ed. of 1989.

1443 Gegeshidze, D.V. *Ateizm, religiia, sovremennost'* [Atheism, Religion, Contemporaneity]. Tbilisi: Sabchota Sakartvelo, 1982. 183 pp. In Georgian.

1444 Gegeshidze, D.V. *Beseda po voprosam ateizma i religii* [Talk on the Problems of Atheism and Religion]. Tbilisi: Sabchota Sakartavelo, 1988. 162 pp. In Gerogian.

1445 Gegeshidze, D.V. *Kritika bogoslovskoi kontseptsii roli i mesta khristianstva v istorii Gruzii* [Critique of Theological Conception of Christianity's Role and Place in the History of Georgia]. Tbilisi: Metsniereba, 1986. 103 pp. Bibl.: pp. 99-102. In Georgian. Summary in Russian.

1446 Gegeshidze, D.V. *Kritika burzhuazno-klerikal'noi fal'sifikatsii polozheniia religii i tserkvi v Gruzii* [Critique of Bourgeois-Clerical Falsifications on the Position of Religion and Church in Georgia]. Tbilisi: Sabchota Sakart-velo, 1986. 133 pp. In Georgian.

1447 Gegeshidze, D.V. *Kritika teiarovskoi kontseptsii vzaimootnoshenii nauki i religii* [Critique of Teilhardian Conception of Interrelations of Science and Religion]. Tbilisi: Metsniereba, 1981. 78 pp. In Georgian. Summary in Russian.

1448 Gegeshidze, D.V. *Modernizm i deiatel'nosti sovremennoi gruzinskoi tserkvi* [Modernism and Activities of the Contemporary Georgian Church]. Tbilisi: Znanie GSSR, 1983. 32 pp. (Nauch. ateizm / O-vo "Znanie" GSSR; 7). In Georgian.

1449 Gegeshidze, D.[V]. "Moral'no-psikhologicheskaia obstanovka i religioznost' naseleniia" [Moral-Psychological Situation and Population's Religiosity]. *Kommunist Gruzii* 6 (1984): 59-63.

1450 Gegeshidze, D.[V]. "Sovremennyi religioznyi modernizm i zadachi nauchno-ateisticheskoi propagandy" [Contemporary Religious Modernism and Problems of Scientific-Atheistic Propaganda]. *Kommunist Gruzii* 5 (1982): 84-92.

1451 Geiushev, R.B. *Khristianstvo v Kavkazkoi Albanii* [Christianity in Caucasian Albanyi]. Baku: Elm, 1984. 192 pp., illus. Summaries in Azerbaijan and English. Annot. bibl.: pp. 157-168.

1452 Geletiuk, P. "Na sluzhbe Iegovy" [In the Service of Jehovah]. *Nauka i religiia* 1 (1983): 36-39; 2 (1983): 45-47.

1453 Gel'fman, T.M. "Fond iudaizma v GMIRiA" [Fund of Judaism in GMIRA]. *Muzei v ateisticheskoi propagande.* L., 1980. Pp. 74-91.

1454 Gel'fman, T.M. "Voprosy istorii iudaizma v muzeinoi eksponatsii" [Problems of the History of Judaism in Museums' Exhibits]. *Muzei v ateisticheskoi propagande.* L., 1988. Pp. 103-118.

1455 Gel'vetsii, K.A. *Schast'e* [Happiness]. M.: Sov. Rossiia, 1987. 480 pp. (Khudozh. i publitsist. b-ka ateista).

1456 Gemuev I.N.; Sagalaev, A.M. *Religiia naroda mansi: Kul'tovye mesta, XIX-nach. XX v.* [Religion of the People of Mansi: Worship Places, XIXth-Early XXth C.]. Novosibirsk: Nauka. Sib. otd-nie, 1986. 192 pp. illus.

1457 Georgievskii, A.B.; Orlov, S.A. *Kontseptsiia bozhezstvennogo tvoreniia zhivogo i sovremennaia ideologicheskaia bor'ba* [The Conception of Divine Creation of Living and Contemporary Ideological Struggle]. L.: Znanie RSFSR, Leningr. org. Leningr. Dom nauch. ateizma, 1988. 32 pp. Bibl.: p. 31.

1458 Gerasimchuk, A.A. *Chelovek i priroda:* Kritika relig.-idealist. interpretatsii ekol. probl. [Man and Nature: Criticism of Religious-Idealistic Interpretation of Ecological Problems]. Kiev: Vishcha shkola. Izd-vo pri Kiev. un-te, 1981. 144 pp. Annot. bibl.: p. 136-143. For review see item 5045.

1459 Gerasimenko, V.K. *Budni ateistov* [Atheists' Week-Days]. M.: Politizdat, 1983. 64 pp. (B-ka ateista).

1460 Gerasimenko, V.[K]. "Ispol'zuia novye vozmozhnosti" [Using New Possibilities]. *Agitator* 7 (1988): 57-58.

1461 Gerasimov, Iu.N.; Rabinovich, V.I. *Zodchestvo i pravoslavie* [Architecture and Orthodoxy]. M.: Mosk. rabochii, 1986. 65 pp. (Besedy o religii).

1462 Gerasimov, O. "Puteshestvie v Mekku i Medinu [Journey to Mecca and Medina]. *Nauka i religiia* 7 (1980): 56-58.

1463 Gerasimova, K.M. "Buddizm i ontologiia traditsionnykh verovanii" [Buddhism and Ontology of Traditional Beliefs]. *III Vsesoiuznaia konferentsiia vostokovedov "Vzaimodeistvie i vzaimovliianie tsivilizatsii kul'tur na Vostoke"*. M., 1988. T. I. Pp. 79-81.

1464 Gerasimova, K.M. "Mongol'skaia obriadovaia literatura kak istochnik istoricheskoi informatsii" [Mongolian Ceremonial Literature as Source of Historical Information]. *V Mezhdunarodnyi kongress mongolovedov (Ulan-Bator, sentiabr' 1987)*. M., 1987. I. Istoriia, ekonomika. Pp. 19-27.

1465 Gerasimova, K.M. "Nekotorye osobennosti preodoleniia lamaizma v sovremennykh usloviiakh" [Some Features of Overcoming Lamaism in Contemporary Conditions]. *Stroitel'stvo sotsializma i utverzhdenie nauchno-materialisticheskogo, ateisticheskogo mirovozzreniia (v regionakh rasprostraneniia lamaizma)*. M., 1981. Pp. 104-118.

1466 Gerasimova, K.M. "O sootnoshenii v obriadovykh tekstakh doktrinal'nogo i populiarnogo urovnei buddiiskoi ideologii" [Correlation in Ritual Texts of Doctrinal and Popular Levels of Buddhist Ideology]. *Tsybikovskie chteniia*. Ulan-Ude, 1989. Pp. 36-38.

1467 Gerasimova, K.M. *Traditsionnye verovaniia tibetsev v kul'tuvoi sisteme lamaizma* [Tibetans Traditional Beliefs in the Religious System of Lamaism]. Novosibirsk: Nauka. Sib. otd-nie, 1989. 319 pp. Bibl.: pp. 277-297.

1468 Germanovich, A.; Medvedko, L. "'Vozrozhdenie islama' ili probuzhdenie naroda?" ["Islam's Renaissancc" or People's Awakening]. *Nauka i religiia* 7 (1982): 56-59.

1469 Gills, N.A. *Bessmertie: illiuzii i deistvitel'nost'* [Immortality: Illusions and Reality]. Riga: Znanie LatvSSR, 1983. 29 pp. (Materialy v pomoshch' lektoru / O-vo "Znanie" LatvSSR, Nauch.-metod. sovet po propagande nauch. ateizma). (Znanie - narodu). Bibl.: pp. 28-29. In Latvian.

1470 Gimadeev, R.A. "O nekotorykh vostochnykh i grecheskikh sootvetstviiakh predstavleniiam Irodota o bozhestve" [On Some Oriental and Greek Appropriate Ideas to Herodotus Conceptions of Divine]. *Drevnii i srednevekovyi Vostok.* M., 1988. Ch. I. Pp. 98-109.

1471 Gimatudinov, M.Kh. "Islam v sovremennoi ideologicheskoi bor'be" [Islam in the Contemporary Ideological Struggle]. *Aktual'nye problemy istoricheskogo materializma.* Alma-Ata, 1982. Pp. 126-139.

1472 Giorgadze, D.G. *Pogrebal'nye i traurnye obriady v Gruzii* [Funeral and Mourning Rituals in Georgia]. Tbilisi: Metsniereba, 1987. 108 pp. In Armenian. Bibl.: pp. 96-106.

1473 Gladkaia, T.V. "Nesostoiatel'nost' burzhuazno-klerikal'nykh otsenok polozheniia religii i tserkvi v SRV" [Groundlessness of Bourgeois-Clerical Estimation of the Situation of Religion and Church in SRV]. *Vopr. ateizma* 25 (1989): 78-85.

1474 Gladkaia, T.V. "Razvitie printsipov svobody sovesti pri sotsializme" [The Development of Principles of Freedom of Conscience under Socialism]. *Vopr. ateizma* 24 (1988): 115-122.

1475 Gladunets, V. "Koordinaty raia" [Paradise's Coordinates]. *Nauka i religiia* 1 (1989): 28-29.

1476 Gladysh, I. "Ravnodushnykh ne byvaet" [Indifferents Do Not Exist]. *Nauka i religiia* 6 (1981): 12-13.

1477 Glagolev, V.S. *Religioznyi modernizm i kul'tura* [Religious Modernism and Culture]. M.: Znanie, 1988. 64 pp. (Novoe v zhizni, nauke, tekhnike. Nauch. ateizm; 4 / 1988).

1478 Glavon', K. "Eticheskie aspekty v teorii nauchnogo ateizma" [Ethical Aspects in the Theory of Scientific Atheism]. *Vopr. nauch. ateizma* 35 (1986): 24-33.

1479 Glemp, I. "Prostor dlia nesushchikh dobro" [Space for Carriers of Good Deed]. *Novoe vremia* 26 (1988): 41.

1480 Globa, P.; Globa, T. "Goroskop Stalina" [Stalin's Horoscope]. *Nauka i religiia* 11 (1989): 45-46; 12 (1989): 16-19. To be continued.

1481 Glomozda, K.E. *'Kreshchenie Rusi' v kontseptsiiakh sovremennoi burzhuaznoi istoriografii* ["Baptism of Rus'" in Conception of Contemporary Bourgeois Historiography]. Kiev: Nauk. dumka, 1988. 168 pp. Annot. bibl.: pp. 143-166.

1482 Glushak, A.S. "Kritika religioznoi interpretatsii vvedeniia khristianstva na Rusi" [Criticism of Religious Interpretation of Introduction of Christianity into Rus']. *Vopr. ateizma* 22 (1986): 10-16.

1483 Glushak, A.S. "Religioznyi modernizm i nekotorye problemy nauchno-ateisticheskogo vospitaniia molodezhi" [Religious Modernism and Some Problems of Scientific-Atheistic Upbringing of Youth]. *Vopr. ateizma* 19 (1983): 107-114.

1484 Gogebashvili, Ia.S. *Bibleiskaia istoriia.* [Biblical History]. Lagerlef, S. *Legendy o Khriste.* [Legends about Christ]. Tbilisi: Merani, 1989. 333 pp., illus. In Georgian.

1485 Gogoberishvili, V.G. *Problemy religii v usloviiakh nauchno-tekhnicheskoi revoliutsii* [Problems of Religion under Scientific-Technical Revolution]. Tbilisi: Metsniereba, 1989. 108 pp. In Georgian. Summary in Russian. Bibl.: pp. 107-108.

1486 Gogochuri, Kh.G. *K marksistskoi kritike religiozno-ekzistentsialisticheskogo ponimaniia spetsifike filosofskogo znaniia* (Na prim. filosofii N.A. Berdiaeva) [Marxist Critique of Religious-Existentialist Understanding of Specificity of Philosophical Knowledge: (On the Example of N.A. Berdiaev's Philosophy)]. Tbilisi: Metsniereba, 1980. 124 pp. In Georgian. Summary in Russian.

1487 Gogova, F.I. "K voprosu o neobkhodimosti internatsional'nogo i ateisticheskogo vospitaniia" [On the Problem of Necessity of International and

Atheistic Education]. *Sotsial'no-eticheskie osnovy internatsional'nogo vospitaniia.* Ordzhonikidze, 1985. Pp. 120-122.

1488   Gol'bakh, P.A. *Galereia sviatykh* [Gallery of Saints]. Erevan: Aiastan, 1986. 415 pp., illus. In Armenian.
Published also in:
Kiev: Politizdat Ukrainy, 1987. 335 pp.

1489   Gol'bakh, P.A. *Karmannoe bogoslovie* [Pocket Theology]. Kiev: Politizdat Ukrainy, 1980. 192 pp., illus. In Ukrainian.
Published also in:
Erevan: Aiastan, 1982. 287 pp., illus. In Armenian.

1490   Gol'bakh, P.[A]. "O religioznoi morali" [On Religious Morals]. *Vopr. nauch. ateizma* 27 (1981): 309-321.

1491   Gol'danskii, V. "Nauka svoe slovo skazala" [Science Had Its "Say"]. *Nauka i religiia* 6 (1989): 12.

1492   Goldenberg, M.[A]. "Genotsid imenem iakhve" [Genocide in the Name of Yahweh]. *Nauka i religiia* 6 (1983): 61-63.

1493   Goldenberg, M.A. *Ideologiia sovremennogo iudaizma i sionizma* [The Ideology of Contemporary Judaism and Zionism]. M.: Znanie, 1980. 15 pp. (V pomoshch' lektoru).

1494   Goldenberg, M.A. *Iudaizm i 'izbrannyi narod'* [Judaism and "The Chosen People"]. Kishinev: Kartia moldoveniaske, 1981. 110 pp. (Nauka i religiia).

1495   Goldenberg, M.[A]. "Oshibka kardinala Keniga" [Cardinal Koenig's mistake]. *Molodoi kommunist* 8 (1980): 49-53.

1496   Goldenberg, M.[A]. "Paradoksy krizisa" [Paradoxes of Crisis]. *Nauka i religiia* 7 (1980): 50-52.

1497   Goldenberg, M.A. "Printsip svobody sovesti i ego klerikal'nye interpretatory" [The Principle of Freedom of Conscience and Its Clerical Interpreters]. *Vopr. nauch. ateizma* 27 (1981): 232-250.

1498   Goldenberg, M.[A]. "Protiv fal'sifikatsii polozheniia religii v SSSR" [Against Falsification on Religion's Standing in the USSR]. *Nauka i religiia* 10 (1984): 26-30.

1499 Goldenberg, M.A. "Religioznaia opora sionizma" [Religious Support of Zionism]. *Argumenty. 1981.* M., 1981. Pp. 96-116.

1500 Goldenberg, M.[A]. "Terrorizm vo slavu Iakhve" [Terrorism to the Glory of Yahweh]. *Nauka i religiia* 3 (1982): 59-61.

1501 Goldenberg, M.[A]. "Veruiushchie protiv sionizma" [Believers against Zionism]. *Nauka i religiia* 8 (1982): 60-63.

1502 Goldenberg, M.A.; Tabakaru, D.N. "Ateizm sotsialisticheskogo obraza zhizni i ego burzhuazno-klerikal'naia interpretatsiia" [Atheism of Socialist Way of Life and Its Bourgeois-Clerical Interpretation]. *Sotsialisticheskii obraz zhizni i sovremennaia bor'ba idei.* Kishinev, 1989. Pp. 67-88.

1503 Gol'din, B.Ia.; Krisbaeva, T.E. "O nekotorykh problemakh nauchno-ateisticheskogo vospitaniia na sovremennom etape" [Some Problems of Atheistic Education in the Contemporary Stage]. *XXVII s'ezd KPSS i voprosy aktivizatsii chelovecheskogo faktora.* Tashkent, 1987. Pp. 95-103.

1504 Golenchenko, G.Ia. "Novye pis'mennye istochniki o deiatel'nosti russkikh eretikov v Belorussii i Litve vo vtoroi polovine XVI v." [New Written Sources on the Activity of Russian Heretics in Belorussia and Lithuania Late XVIth C.]. *Istoriia knigi, knizhnogo dela, i bibliografii v Belorusii.* Minsk, 1986. Pp. 148-168.

1505 Goliak, V.A. *Trud - faktor utverzhdeniia nauchno-ateisticheskoi ubezhdennosti* [Labour - Affirmation Factor of Scientific-Atheistic Conviction]. Kiev: Znanie UkSSR, 1985. 47 pp. (Ser. 5 "Nauhno- ateisticheskaia" / O-vo "Znanie" UkSSR; No 7). In Ukrainian. Annot. bibl.: pp. 46-47.

1506 Golichenko, T.S. "O znachenii kul'ta roda v slavianskom mifologicheskom mirovozzrenii" [On the Meaning of the Cult of Birth in Slavonic Mythological Outlook]. *Chelovek i istoriia v srednevekovoi filosofskoi mysli russkogo, ukrainskogo i belorusskogo narodov.* Kiev, 1987. Pp. 12-20.

1507 Golichenko, T.S. "Slavianskaia mifologiia i antichnaia kul'tura" [Slavonic Mythology and Ancient Culture]. *Otechestvennaia obshchestvennaia mysl' epokhi Srednevekov'ia.* Kiev, 1988. Pp. 92-100.

1508 Golobutskii, P.V. *Pravoslavie: Kreshchenie Rusi - pravda i vymysly* [Orthodoxy: Baptism of Rus' - Truth and Fabrications]. Kiev: Politizdat Ukrainy, 1981. 78 pp. (Besedy s veruiushchimi). In Ukrainian.

1509 Golobutskii, P.V. *Vvedenie khristiantva na Rusi - pravda i vymysly* [Introduction of Christianity into Rus' - Truth and Fabrications]. 2nd reviscd and enlarged ed. Kiev: Politizdat Ukrainy, 1987. 95 pp. (Ser. "Besedy s veruiushchimi"). In Ukrainian.

1510 Golodnenko, I. "V edinom komplekse vospitaniia" [In a Single Complex of Education]. *Nauka i religiia* 3 (1984): 8-11.

1511 Golovei, V.M.; Shanaida, V.I. "Kritika khristianskogo tolkovaniia semeinobrachnykh otnoshenii" [Criticism of Christian Interpretation of Family-Conjugal Relations]. *Vopr. ateizma* 17 (1981): 136-143.

1512 Golovko, A.B. "Khristianizatsiia vostochnoslavianskogo obshchestva i vneshniaia politika Drevnei Rusi v IX-pervoi treti XIII veka" [Conversion to Christianity of Eastern Slavonic Society and Foreign Policy of Ancient Rus' in IXth-Early XIIIth C.]. *Vopr. istorii* 9 (1988): 59-71.

1513 Golovko, B.M. "Preemstvenost' i osobennosti prepodavaniia kursa nauchnogo ateizma v pedinstitute" [Continuity and Peculiarities of Teaching the Course of Scientific-Atheism in Pedagogical Institute]. *Vopr. ateizma* 20 (1984): 52-60.

1514 Golovko, N.V. "V poiskakh dialoga: Sovrem. zarubezh. teologi o probl. nravstvennosti" [In the Search of a Dialogue: Contemporary Foreign Theologians on the Problem of Morality]. *Nauka i religiia* 6 (1981): 56-58.

1515 Golubeva, E.V. "Zarubezhnaia istoriografiia o politizatsii katolicheskoi tserkvi na Filippinakh" [Foreign Historiography on Politization of the Catholic Church in the Philippines]. *Istochnikovedenie i istoriografiia stran Vostoka: uzlovye problemy teorii.* M., 1988. Vyp. I. Pp. 87-92.

1516 Golubinskii, E.E. "'Khristianstvo v Rossii ot nachala gosudarstva do sv. Vladimira'" ["Christianity in Russia from the Origin of the State up to St. Vladimir"]. *Pamiatniki Otechestva* 1 (1988): 152-160.

1517 Golubtsova, E.S. "Gosudarstvo i religiia v antichnom mire" [State and Religion in the Ancient World]. *Vestn. drev. istorii* 2 (1985): 10-15. Summary in English.

1518 Golubtsova, E.S. "Iazycheskie i khristianskie motivy v ideologii sel'skikh zhitelei Maloi Azii" [Pagan and Christian Motives in the Ideology of

Villagers of Asia Minor]. *Kul'tura i obshchestvennaia mysl'*. M., 1988. Pp. 17-28.

1519 Golynets, G.K. "K istorii ural'skoi ikonopisi XVIII-XIX vekov" [History of Urals Icon-Painting of XVIIIth-XIXth Centuries]. *Iskusstvo* 12 (1987): 61-68.

1520 Gomboeva, A.Sh. "Simvolicheskie izobrazheniia planet na buddiskikh ikonakh" [Symbolic Images of Planets on Buddhist Icons]. *Tsybikovskie chteniia*. Ulan-Ude, 1989. Pp. 39-41.

1521 Gomeniuk, A.P.; Kulik, V.S. "Klassovoe vospitanie studentov v protsesse izucheniia kursa nauchnogo ateizma" [Class Education of Students in the Process of Study of the Course of Scientific Atheism]. *Vopr. ateizma* 20 (1984): 38-45.

1522 Gopchenko, P.G. *Sotsial'nyi progress i bogoslovskie utopii* [Social Progress and Theological Utopias]. Odessa: Maiak, 1980. 103 pp.

1523 Goran, V.P. "Sovremennyi kreatsionizm i nauka" [Contemporary Creation and Science]. *Nauchnyi ateizm, religiia i sovremennost'*. Novosibirsk, 1987. Pp. 75-90.

1524 Gordienko, E.A. "Bol'shoi ikonostas Sofiiskogo sobora (po pis'mennym istochnikam)" [The Great Iconostasis of Sophia's Cathedral (Based on Written Sources)]. *Novgor. ist. sb.* 2 (1984): 211-229.

1525 Gordienko, N.S. *Ateizm i religiia v sovremennoi bor'be idei:* Kritika klerikal. antikommunizma [Atheism and Religion in Contemporary Struggle of Ideas: Criticism of Clerical Anti-Communism]. L.: Lenizdat, 1982. 175 pp. Bibl.: pp. 173-174. For reviews see items 5048-5050.

1526 Gordienko, N.[S]. "Deistvitel'nost' oprovergaet domysly" [The Reality Refutes Conjectures]. *Nauka i religiia* 5 (1983): 58-60.

1527 Gordienko, N.S. "Evoliutsiia bogoslovskoi interpretatsii vvedeniia khristianstva na Rusi" [Evolution of Theological Interpretation of the Introduction of Christianity into Rus']. *Russkoe pravoslavie i ateizm v otechestvennoi itorii*. L., 1988. Pp. 50-69.

1528 Gordienko, N.S. *Evoliutsiia russkogo pravoslaviia (20-80-e gg. XX st.).* [Evolution of Russian Orthodoxy (20s-80s of XXth C.)]. M.: Znanie,

1984. 64 pp. (Novoe v zhizni, nauke, tekhnike. Nauch. ateizm; 1). Bibl.: p. 63.

1529 Gordienko, N.S. *Evoliutsiia sovremennogo pravoslaviia* [Evolution of Contemporary Orthodoxy]. M.: Znanie, 1980. 16 pp. (V pomoshch' lektoru).

1530 Gordienko, N.S. *Kak sformirovalsia kul't blazhennoi Ksenii* [How the Cult of the Blessed Xenia was Formed]. L.: Znanie RSFSR. Leningr. org., 1989. 21 pp. Bibl.: p. 21.

1531 Gordienko, N.S. *'Kreshchenie Rusi': fakty protiv legend i mifov* ["Baptism of Rus'": Facts Against Legends and Myths]. L.: Lenizdat, 1984. 287 p. Bibl.: pp. 282-286. Republished in 1986, and serialized in *Nauka i religiia* as from Jan. 1984. For reviews see item 5051-5052.

1532 Gordienko, N.S. *Mirovozzrencheskaia otsenka protsessa khristianizatsii Drevnei Rusi* [World Outlook's Estimation of the Process of Conversion to Christianity of the Ancient Rus']. M.: Znanie RSFSR, 1984. 40 pp. (V pomoshch' lektoru / O-vo "Znanie" RSFSR, Nauch.-metod. sovet otd-niia po propagande nauch. ateizma). Bibl.: p. 39.

1533 Gordienko, N.S. *Mistika na sluzhbe sovremennogo pravoslaviia* [Mysticism in the Service of Contemporary Orthodoxy]. M.: Znanie, 63 pp. (Novoe v zhizni, nauke, tekhnike. Ser. "Nauch. ateizm"; No 1). Bibl.: p. 62.

1534 Gordienko, N.S. *Osnovy nauchnogo ateizma* [Foundations of Scientific Atheism]. M.: Prosveshchenie, 1988. 304 p. For review see item 5053.

1535 Gordienko, N.S. "Pamiati tovarishcha. Glubokii issledovatel', uchennyi-novator" [In the Memory of a Comrade. Profound Researcher, Scientist-Innovator]. *Vopr. nauch. ateizma* 34 (1986): 258-269.

1536 Gordienko, N.S. *Pravoslavnye sviatye: kto oni?* [Orthodox Saints: Who are They?]. Kiev: Politizdat Ukrainy, 1983. 292 pp. In Ukrainian.

1537 Gordienko, N.[S]. "S pozitsii mistitsizma" [From the Position of Mysticism]. *Nauka i religiia* 11 (1980): 24-27; 12 (1980): 24-26.

1538 Gordienko, N.S. *Sovremennoe russkoe pravoslavie* [Contemporary Russian Orthodoxy]. L.: Lenizdat, 1987. 304 pp., illus. Bibl.: pp. 301-303. Republished in 1988. For reviews see items 5054-5055.

1539   Gordienko, N.S. "Voprosy profilizatsii kursa 'Osnovy nauchnogo ateizma' v vuze: Iz opyta raboty kaf. nauch. ateizma Leningr. ped. in-ta" [Problems of Profilisation of the Course "Fundamentals of Scientific Atheism" in University: From the Experience of the Work of the Chair of Scientific Atheism of the Leningrad Pedagogical Institute]. *Aktual'nye vopr. metodiki prepodavaniia obshchestv. nauk i kom. vospitaniia studentov* 5 (1987): 44-51.

1540   Gordienko, N.S. *Vvedenie khristianstva na Rusi: domysly burzhuazno-klerikal'noi propagandy* [Introduction of Christinity into Rus': Conjectures of Bourgeois Clerical Propaganda]. M.: Znanie, 1987. 64 pp. (Novoe v zhizni, nauke, tekhnike. Nauch. ateizm; 2/1987). Bibl.: p. 59.

1541   Gordienko, N.S.; Kobrin, V.M. "Pereosmyslenie: za i protiv" [Re-Interpretation: Pro and Con]. *Nauka i religiia* 8 (1989): 5-9.

1542   Gordienko, N.S.; Komarov, P.M. *Obrechennye: O rus. emigrant. psevdotserkvi* [Doomed: On Russian Emigrant Pseudo-Church]. L.: Lenizdat, 1988. 208 pp., illus.

1543   Gordienko, N.S.; Kurochkin, P.K. "Osnovnye osobennosti evoliutsii religii i tserkvi v usloviiakh sotsialisticheskogo obshchestva" [Main Features of the Evolution of Religion and Church under Socialist Society]. *Vopr. nauch. ateizma* 25 (1980): 223-243.

1544   Gordienko, N.S.; Novikov, M.P. *Sovremennaia ideologicheskaia bor'ba i religiia* [Contemporary Ideological Struggle and Religion]. M.: Znanie RSFSR, 1980. 40 pp. (V pomoshch' lektoru / O-vo "Znanie" RSFSR, Nauch. -metod. sovet po propagande nauch. ateizma). Bibl.: p. 39.

1545   Gordon, D.S. "Biologiia i religiia" [Biology and Religion]. *Problemy istorii religii i ateizma*. Cheboksary, 1981. Pp. 30-37.

1546   Gordon-Polonskaia, L.R. *Religiia v politicheskoi zhizni razvivaiushchikhsia stran Azii i Afriki:* [Religion in the Political Life of the Developing Countries of Asia and Africa]. M.: Nauka, 1982. 9 pp. In English and French.

1547   Goregliad, V.N. "Vzaimovliianie raznykh religioznykh sistem v srednevekovoi i sovremennoi Iaponii" [Reciprocal Influence of Different Religious Systems in Medieval and Today's Japan]. *III Vsesoiuznaia konferentsiia vostokovedov* "*Vzaimodeistvie i vzaimovliianie tsivilizatsii kul'tur na Vostoke*". M., 1988. T. 2. Pp. 81-82.

1548 Gorelkina, O.D. "K voprosu o magicheskikh predstavleniiakh v Rossii XVIII v." [On the Problem of Magical Conceptions in Russia of the XVIIIth C.]. *Nauchnyi ateizm, religiia i sovremennost'*. Novosibirsk, 1987. Pp. 289-305.

1549 Gorelov, A. "Optina pustyn': opyt voskhozhdeniia: Tserkov. moral' i sovremen. obshchestvo" [Optina Pustyn Monastery: The Experience of Ascent: Church Morals and Today's Society]. *Novoe vremia* 47 (1989): 42-43.

1550 Goremyshkina, V.I. *V poiskakh istiny o rannem khristianstve* [In Search of Truth About the Early Christianity]. Minsk: Belarus', 1989. 95 pp. Bibl.: pp. 86-94.

1551 Goreva, N. "'Tserkov' v SSSR osushestvliaet svoiu missiiu v blagopriiatnykh usloviiakh'" [The Church in the USSR Accomplishes Its Mission in Favourable Conditions]. *Religiia v SSSR* 7 (1987): NG 1-NG 2.

1552 Gorfunkel', A.Kh. "Erazm i ital'ianskaia eres' XVI v." [Erasmus and the Italian Heresy in the XVIth C.]. *Erazm Rotterdamskii i ego vremia*. M., 1989. Pp. 197-205.

1553 Gorgliad, V. "Omotoke - 'uchenye velikogo kornia' [Omotokyo-"Scientists of the Great Root"]. *Aziia i Afrika segodnia* 7 (1980): 56-59.

1554 Goriacheva-Tikhomirova, I. "Svoboda sovesti" [Freedom of Conscience]. *Bibliotekar'* 9 (1983): 42-44.

1555 Gorkun, A.P. "O modernistskikh tendentsiiakh v sovremennom russkom pravoslavii" [On Modernist Tendencies in Today's Russian Orthodoxy]. *Mirovozzrencheskie i ideologicheskie problemy v istorii filosofii*. Novosibirsk, 1983. Pp. 81-97.

1556 *Goroskopy: Druidov, zapadnyi zodiakal'nyi, vostochnyi iaponskii, kitaiskii* [Horoscopes: Of Druids, Western Zodiacal, Oriental Japanese, Chinese]. Makhachkala: Dag. kn. izd-vo, 1989. 119 pp.

1557 Gorovoi, V.N. *Obriadnost' v zerkale vremeni* [Rites in the Mirror of Time]. Dnepropetrovsk: Promin', 1988. 78 pp.

1558 Gorovoi, V.N. *Religioznaia obriadnost': tendentsii izmenenii i puti preodoleniia* [Religious Rites: Tendencies of Change and Ways of Overcoming]. Kiev: Znanie UkSSR, 1985. 32 pp. (Ser. 5. "Nauchno-ateisticheskaia" / O-vo "Znanie" UkSSR; No 3). In Ukrainian.

1559 Gorskii, V.L. *Adventizm: istoriia i sovremennost'* [Adventism: History and Contemporaneity]. Kiev: Znanie UkSSR, 1987. 58 pp. (Ser. 5, Nauchno-ateisticheskaia / O-vo "Znanie" UkSSSR; No 7). In Ukrainian.

1560 Gorskii, V.S. "Problema tselostnosti mira i filosofskoi kul'ture Kievskoi Rusi i drevnei Bolgarii" [The Problem of World Integrity in Philosophical Culture of Kievan Rus' and Ancient Bulgaria]. *U istokov obshchnosti filosofskikh kul'tur russkogo, ukrainskogo i bolgarskogo narodov.* Kiev, 1983. Pp. 42--57. Bibl.: pp. 56-57.

1561 Gorskii, V.S. "'Sredinnyi sloi' kartiny mira v kul'ture Kievskoi Rusi" ["The Middle Layer" of the World Picture in the Culture of Kievan Rus']. *Otechestvennnaia obshchestvennaia mysl' epokhi Srednevekov'ia.* Kiev, 1988. Pp. 169-176.

1562 Gortopan, N.A. *Mirovozzrencheskaia rol' nauchnogo ateizma* [The World Outlook's Role of Scientific Atheism]. Kishinev: Znanie MSSR, 1983. 27 pp. (Material v pomoshch' lektoru / O-vo "Znanie" MSSR). In Moldavian. Bibl.: p. 27.

1563 Goshevskii, V.O. "Kritika P.L. Lavrovym 'khristianskogo sotsializma'" [P.L. Lavrov's Criticism of "Christian Socialism"]. *Sotsial'no-filosofskie aspekty kritiki religii.* L., 1987. Pp. 55-71.

1564 Gosudarev, A.A. "Teoreticheskoe opravdanie melkoburzhuaznoi revoliutsionnosti v uchenii A.A. Bogdanova i v bogostroitel'stve" [Theoretical Justification of Petty-Bourgeois Religiosity in A.A. Bogdanov's Teachings and in Godbuilding]. *Filosofiia i osvoboditel'noe dvizhenie v Rossii.* L., 1989. Pp. 195-205.

1565 Gotsiridze, G.Sh. *Musul'manskii prazdnik 'Mokharram' v Tbilisi* [Moslem Holiday "Muharram" in Tbilisi]. Tbilisi: Metsniereba, 1988. 63 pp., illus. (Traditsiia i sovremennost'. No 24). In Georgian. Summary in Russian.

1566 Gozheva, N.A. "Ikonografiia obraza Buddy v laosskoi skul'pture" [Iconography of Buddha in Laos Sculpture]. *Ku'tura i iskusstvo narodov Vostoka.* M., 1987. Pp. 26-28.

1567   Gracheva, G.N. *Traditsionnoe mirovozzrenie okhotnikov Taimyra* [Traditional World Outlook of Taimir Hunters]. L.: Nauka. Leningr. otd-nie, 1983. 173 pp., illus. Bibl.: pp. 158-171.

1568   Grazhdan, V.D. *Verouchenie i moral' piatidesiatnikov* [Dogma and Morals of Pentecosts]. M.: Znanie, 1989. 63 pp. (Novoe v zhizni, nauke, tekhnike. Nauch. ateizm; 7/1989). Bibl.: p. 60.

1569   Grekov, A.P. *Freski tserkvi Spasa Preobrazheniia na Kovaleve* [Frescoes of the Church of Transfiguration of the Saviour in Kovalev]. M.: Iskusstvo, 1987. 95 pp., illus.

1570   Grekova, T.I. *Ateizm i meditsina* [Atheism and Medicine]. L.: Znanie RSFSR, 1984. 32 pp. (V pomoshch' lektoru / O-vo "Znanie" RSFSR, Leningr. org.). Bibl.: pp. 31-32.

1571   Grekova, T.I. *Bolezn' i smert' - zlo ili blago?: Vzgliad nauki i religii* [Illness and Death - Evil or Blessing: The View of Science and Religion]. M.: Politizdat, 1983. 93 pp., illus. (Besedy o mire i cheloveke).
Publised also in:
Kishinev: Kartia moldoveniaske, 1984. 119 pp. In Moldavian
Frunze: Kyrgystan, 1984. 97 pp., illus. (B-chka ateista), In Kirghiz. For review see item 5056.

1572   Grekova, T.[I]. "Dva sluzheniia doktora Voino-Iosenetskogo" [Doctor's Voino-Iosenetski Two Devotions]. *Nauka i religiia* 8 (1986): 12-19.

1573   Grekova, T.I. *Meditsina i religiia* [Medicine and Religion]. L.: Znanie RSFSR, 1982. 16 pp. (V pomoshch' lektoru / O-vo "Znanie" RSFSR, Leningr. org.).

1574   Grene, F. "Nekotorye zamechaniia o korniakh zoroastrizma v Srednei Azii" [Some Remarks on Roots of Zoroastrianism in Middle Asia]. *Vestn drev. istorii* 1 (1989): 170-171.

1575   Griaznevich, P.A. "Koran v Rossii (izuchenie, perevody i izdaniia)" [Koran in Russia (Studies, Translations and Publications]. *Islam: Religiia, obshchestvo, gosudarstvo.* M., 1984. Pp. 76-82.

1576   Griaznevich, P.A. "Problemy izucheniia istorii vozniknoveniia islama" [Problems of Study of the History of the Origin of Islam]. *Islam: Religiia, obshchestvo, gosudarstvo.* M., 1984. Pp. 5-18.

1577 Grigas, K.I. "Iazychestvo i khristianstvo v razvitii narodnogo miroosh-chushcheniia" [Paganism and Christianity in the Development of People's Disposition]. *Tr. AN LitSSR.* Ser.: Obshchestv. nauki 1 (102) (1988): 134-143. In Lithuanian. Summary in Russian.

1578 Grigorenko, A.Iu. *Fideizm i nauka* [Fideism and Science]. M.: Znanie, 1983. 64 pp. (Novoe v zhizni, nauke, tekhnike. Nauch. ateizm; 10). Bibl.: p. 63. Annot. bibl.: pp. 61-62.

1579 Grigorenko, A.Iu. *Koldovstvo pod maskoi nauki* [Witchcraft under the Mask of Science]. M.: Znanie, 1988. 63 pp. (Novoe v zhizni, nauke, tekhnike. Nauch. ateizm; 8/1988). Bibl.: p. 63.

1580 Grigorenko, A.Iu. *Raznolikaia magiia* [Different Faced Magic]. M.: Sov. Rossiia, 1987. 191 pp. Bibl.: pp. 186-189.

1581 Grigorenko, A.Iu. *Son razuma rozhdaet chudovishch:* Kritich. ocherki o mistike i irratsionalizme [Sleep of Reason Gives Birth to Monsters: Critical Essays on Mysticism and Irrationalism]. L.: Lenizdat, 1986. 176 pp., illus. Bibl.: p. 175.

1582 Grigorenko, V.T.; Iagimshchak, V.M. "Vlianie idei Velikogo Oktiabria na bor'bu molodezhi Zapadnoi Ukrainy protiv klerikalizma" [Influence of the Ideas of the Great October on Western Ukrainian's Youth Struggle against Clericalism]. *Vestn. L'vov. politekhn. in-ta.* 216 (1987): 40-44.

1583 Grigor'ev, V.I. "Problema evoliutsii traditsionnykh kul'turnykh tsennostei v islame" [The Problem of Evolution of Traditional Cultural Values in Islam]. *Filosofskaia i obshchestvennaia mysl' stran Azii i Afriki.* M., 1981. Pp. 114-124.

1584 Grigor'eva, I.V. "Sotsialisticheskii obraz zhizni, ego obriady i traditsii" [Socialist Way of Life, Its Ceremonial and Traditions]. *Problemy formirovaniia nauchno-ateisticheskogo mirovozzreniia v sotsialisticheskom obshchestve.* Samarkand, 1980. Pp. 60-65.

1585 Grigor'eva, Z. "Khoroshaia organizatsiia - zalog uspekha" [Good Organization - Token of Success]. *Nauka i religiia* 11 (1981): 19-21.

1586 Grigulevich, I. "I snova Chernyi kontinent" [And Again the Black Continent]. *Gorizont* 19 (1982): 35-39. Published also in: *Nauka i religiia* 8 (1982): 54-56.

1587 Grigulevich, I.R. *Inkvizitsiia* [Inquisition]. 3rd ed. M.: Politizdat, 1985. 448 pp., illus. (B-ka ateis. lit.). Annot. bibl.: pp. 438-446.
Published also in:
Tallin: Eesti raamat, 1981. 445 pp., illus. In Estonian. For review see item 5057.

1588 Grigulevich, I.R. *Istoriia inkvizitsii* [History of the Inquisition]. M.: Progress, 1980. 414 pp., illus.

1589 Grigulevich, I.R. *Katolicheskaia tserkov' i osvoboditel'noe dvizhenie v Latinskoi Amerike* [Catholic Church and Liberation Movement in Latin America]. M.: Progress, 1984. 510 pp. (Probl. razvivaiushchikhsia stran). In Spanish.

1590 Grigulevich, I.R. "Kongress istorikov" [Historians' Congress]. *Nauka i religiia* 1 (1981): 27-28.

1591 Grigulevich, I.R. *Latinskaia Amerika: tserkov' i revoliutsionnoe dvizhenie, 1960 - nachalo 1980-kh godov* [Latin America: Church and Revolutionary Movement, 1960-Early 1980s]. M.: Nauka, 1988. 174 pp. Summaries in English, French and Russian. Bibl.: pp. 168-171.

1592 Grigulevich, I.R. *Papstvo. Vek XX* [Papacy. XXth Century]. 2nd enlarged ed. M.: Politizdat, 1981. 532 pp., illus.
Published also in:
Vil'nius : Mintis, 1982. 358 pp., illus. In Lithuanian.
M.: Progress, 1982. 356 pp. In Spanish.
M.: Progress; Leipzig: Urania, 1984. 266 pp. In German.
Budapest: Izd-vo im. Koshuta; Uzhgorod: Karpati, 1986. 341 pp., illus. In Hungarian.
Riga: Avots, 1986. 413 pp., illus. In Latvian.
Kiev: Politizdat Ukrainy, 1988. 544 pp., illus. In Ukrainian.

1593 Grigulevich, I.R. *Proroki 'novoi istiny': Ocherki o kul'takh i sueveriiakh sovrem. kapitalist. mira* [Prophets of "The New Truth": Essays on Cults and Superstitions of Today's Capitalist World]. M.: Politizdat, 1983. 303 pp., illus.
Published also in:
Erevan: Aiastan, 1989, 295 pp., illus. In Armenian. For review see item 5058.

1594 Grigulevich, I.R. "Religiia, rasizm i rasovaia diskriminatsiia" [Religion, Racialism and Racial Discrimination]. *Rasy i obshchestvo*. M., 1982. Pp. 279-302.

1595 Grigulevich, I.R. *Tserkov' i oligarkhiia v Latinskoi Amerike, 1810-1959* [The Church and Oligarchy in Latin America, 1810-1959]. M.: Nauka, 1981. 327 pp., illus. For reviews see item 5059-5060.

1596 Grika, E.V. *Ateisticheskoe vospitanie sel'skoi molodezhi* [Atheistic Upbringing of Village Youth]. Kiev: Politizdat Ukrainy, 1982. 104 pp. In Ukrainian.

1597 Grinin, E.A. *Bruklin na razdorozh'e* [Brooklin on the Crossroad]. Kiev: Znanie UkSR, 1980. 46 pp. (Se. 5 "Naucno-ateisticheskaia" / O-vo "Znanie" UkSSR; No 7). In Ukrainian. Bibl.: pp. 43-45.

1598 Grishanov, L.K. *O schast'e podlinnom i mnimom* [On Real and Imaginary Happiness]. Kishinev: Kartia moldoveniaske, 1986. 186 pp. Annot. bibl.: pp. 183-185.

1599 Grishanov, L.[K].; Belkina, T. "Kul'tura i religiia: problema vzaimosviazi i ee fal'sifikatsia" [Culture and Religion: Problem of Interrelation and Its Falsification]. *Kommunist Moldavii* 10 (1986): 70-76.

1600 Grishanov, L.K.; Voronov, D.A. *Zhizn', smert', bessmertie* [Life, Death, Immortality]. Kishinev: Shtiintsa, 1987. 218 pp. In Moldavian.

1601 Grishina, E.A. "Mirovozzrencheskie orientatsii molodoi intelligentsii i sovremennyi mistitsizm" [Young Intelligentsia's World Outlook Orientations and Contemporary Mysticism]. *Dukhovnye tsennosti sovetskoi molodezhi*. M., 1988. Pp. 130-137.

1602 Grishina, E.A. "Sovremennyi neomistitsizm" [Contemporary Neomysticism]. *Aktual'nye problemy nauchno-ateisticheskogo vospitaniia molodezi*. M., 1987. Pp. 178-184.

1603 Grishka, A. "Nauka i religiia: Iz istorii ateist. mysli v starom Vil'n. un-te" [Science and Religion: History of Atheist Thought in the Old Vilnius University]. *Kommunist*. Vil'nius. 8 (1984): 58-64.

1604 Gritsov, A.A. "U istokov svobody sovesti" [By the Sources of Freedom of Conscience]. *Nauka i religiia* 4 (1980): 30-32. Published also in:

Vopr. nauch. ateizma 27 (1981): 5-24.

1605 Griunebaum, G.E fon. *Klassicheskii islam*: ocherk istorii, 600-1258 [Classical Islam: Historical Essay, 600-1258]. M.: Nauka, 1988. 216 pp. Bibl.: pp. 194-198. Annot. bibl.: pp. 199-204. Name, dynasties, geographic and ethnographic index: pp. 205-215. Transl. from: *Classical islam* / G.E. von Grunebaum (London, 1970).

1606 Griunebaum, G.E. fon. *Osnovnye cherty arabo-musul'manskoi kul'tury* [Main Traits of Arab-Moslem Culture]. M.: Nauka, 1981. 227 pp. Index: pp. 220-226.

1607 Gromov, M.N. "Obraz Sofii Premudrosti v kul'ture drevnei Rusi" [The Image of Sophia of Divine Wisdom in the Culture of Ancient Rus']. *Otechestvennaia obshchestvennaia mysl' epokhi Srednevekov'ia.* Kiev., 1988. Pp. 114-119.

1608 Gromyko, M.M. "Dukhovnaia kul'tura russkogo, ukrainskogo i belorusskogo krest'ianstva XVIII-XIX vv.: predmet i problemy issledovaniia" [Spiritual Culture of Russian, Ukrainian and Belorussian Peasantry of the XVIIIth-XIXth C.: Subject and Problems of Research]. *Istoria, kul'tura, etnografiia i fol'klor slavianskikh narodov.* M., 1988. Pp. 180-196.

1609 Grushevoi, G.V. "K voprosu o traditsiiakh svobodomysliia v obshchestvennoi mysli Belorussii XVI-XVIII vv." [Problem of Freethinking Traditions in Social Thought of Belorussia of the XVIth-XVIIIth C.]. *Otechestvennaia obshchestvennaia mysl' epokhi Srednevekov'ia.* Kiev, 1988. Pp. 274-281.

1610 Grusman, V.M. "Propaganda ateizma v ekspozitsiiakh Gosudarstvennogo muzeia etnografii narodov SSSR" [Propaganda of Atheism in Expositions of the State Ethnographical Museum of the Peoples of the USSR]. *Muzei v ateisticheskoi propagande.* L., 1980. Pp. 30-39.

1611 *Gruzinskaia versiia apokraficheskoi knigi Nikodima* [Georgian Version of Nicodime's Apocrypha]. Text prepared for publication by Ts.I. Kurtsikidze. Tbilisi: Metsniereba, 1985. 91 pp. In Georgian. Summaries in German and Russian.

1612 Gryniv, E.A. "Vozdeistvie sotsial'nykh protsessov na soznanie i povedenie sovremennogo veruiushchego" [The Influence of Social Processes on the Consciousness and Behaviour of the Contemporary Believer]. *Protestantskie organizatsii v SSSR.* M., 1989. Pp. 39-50.

1613 Gubin, V.D. "Nekotorye problemy filosofii buddizma i ikh vliianie na sovremennuiu burzhuaznuiu filosofiiu" [Some Problems of Buddhism's Philosophy and Their Influence on Contemporary Bourgeois Philosophy]. *Filosofskaia i obshchestvennaia mysl' stran Azii i Afriki.* M., 1981. Pp. 155-169.

1614 Gubman, B.L. *Krizis sovremennogo neotomizma:* Kritika neotomist. kontseptsii [Crisis of the Contemporary Neothomism: Critique of Neothomist Conception]. M.: Vissh shk., 1983. 143 pp. Bibl.: pp. 137-142.

1615 Gubman, B.L. "Ob osobennostiakh sovremennoi khristianskoi filosofii istorii" [On Peculiarities of Contemporary Christian Philosophy of History]. *Filosofiia i mirovozzrenie.* M., 1988. Pp. 69-85.

1616 Gubman, B.L. *Sovremennaia katolicheskaia filosofiia: chelovek i istoriia* [Contemporary Catholic Philosophy: Man and History]. M.: Vyssh. shk., 1988. 190 pp. For review see item 5061.

1617 Gudavichius, E. "Politicheskaia problema priniatiia khristianstva Litvoi" [Political Problem of Conversion to Christianity by Lithuania]. *Lieituvos istorijos metrastis* Vilnius, 1988. Pp. 14-22. In Lithuanian. Summary in Russian.

1618 Gudman, L. "Znak Devy" [The Sign of Virgo]. *Nauka i religiia* 8 (1989): 40-43; "Znak Vesov" [The Sign of Libra]. 9 (1989): 20-21; "Znak skorpiona" [The Sign of Scorpio]. 10 (1989): 48-50; "Znak Strel'tsa" [The Sign of Sagittarius]. 11 (1989): 30-31; "Znak Kozeroga" [The Sign of Capricorn]. 12 (1989): 14-16.

1619 Gudozhnik, I.G. "Zapadnoe missionerstvo i polticheskaia kul'tura livanskogo obshchestva" [Western Missionary Work and Political Culture of Lebanese Society]. V *Vsesoiuznaia shkola molodykh vstokovedov.* M., 1989. T. 3. Pp. 47-49.

1620 Gudyma, A.N. "Ispol'zovanie spetsial'nykh uprazhnenii po ateizmu kak sposob aktivizatsii poznavatel'noi deiatel'noti studentov" [Utilization of Special Exercises on Atheism as Means of Activization of Students Cognitive Activity]. *Vopr. ateizma* 20 (1984): 14-19.

1621 Gudyma, A.N. *Pravda zhizni i illiuzii very* [Life's Truth and Faith's Illusions]. L'vov: Kameniar, 1981. 102 pp. In Ukrainian.

1622   Gudyma, A.N. *Religiia i chelovecheskoe dostoinstvo* [Religion and Human
       Dignity]. Kiev: Znanie UkSSR, 1987. 48 pp. (Ser. 5, Nauchno-ateistiches-
       kaia / O-vo "Znanie" UkSSR; No 9). In Ukrainian. Bibl.: pp. 47-48.

1623   Gugutishvili, M.G. "Nekotorye osobennosti ateisticheskogo vospitaniia na
       sovremennom   etape   razvitiia   sotsialisticheskogo   obshchestva"   [Some
       Features of Atheistic Education in the Contemporary Stage of Develop-
       ment of Socialist Society]. *Iz istorii religii i ateizma v Gruzii.* Tbilisi, 1988.
       Pp. 3-11. In Georgian. Summary in Russian.

1624   Gukova, S.N. "Kosmograficheskii traktat Evstratiia Nikeiskogo" [Eustathius of
       Nicaea Cosmographical Treatise]. *Vizant. vremennik.* 1986. T. 47. Pp.
       145-156.

1625   Gulbiani, N.L. *Formirovanie mirovozzreniia molodezhi i zadachi ateisti-
       cheskogo vospitaniia* [Forming of Youth's World Outlook and the Tasks
       of Atheistic Education]. Tbilisi: Sabchota Sakartvelo, 1985. 108 pp. In
       Georgian.

1626   Gulbiani, N.[L]. "Za deistvennost' antireligioznoi propagandy" [For Effective
       Antireligious Propaganda]. *Kommunist Gruzii* 11 (1986): 66-68.

1627   Guliaev, V.I. "Bogi drevnikh maiia" [The Gods of Ancient Mayas]. *Ateisti-
       cheskie chteniia* M., 1988. Pp. 209-222.

1628   Guliev, O.Kh. "K voprosu o metodicheskikh printsipakh izucheniia islama v
       sovetskom islamovedenii" [On the Problem of Methodical Principles of
       Study of Islam in Soviet Studies of Islam]. *Islam v istorii i sovremennostii.*
       Baku, 1981. Pp. 65-70.

1629   Gulyga, A. "Otdelit' ateizm ot gosudarstva" [To Separate Atheism from the
       State]. *Rodina* 8 (1989): 65.

1630   *Gumanizm i religiia* [Humanism and Religion]. [Ed.: R.T. Rashkova]. L.:
       GMIRIA, 1980. 154 pp. For review see item 5062.

1631   Guranovskii, Ia. "Problema 'obnovleniia khristianskoi ideologii' v sovre-
       mennom mire" [Problem of "Renewal of Christian Ideology" in Contem-
       porary World]. Transl. from Polish. *Nauch. dokl. vyssh. shkoly.* Filos.
       nauki 1 (1980): 123-132.

1632 Gurevich, A.Ia. "Dukh i materiia. Ob ambivalentnosti povsednevnoi srednevekovoi religioznosti" [The Spirit and the Matter. On Ambivalency of Daily Medieval Religiosity]. *Kul'tura i obshchestvennaia mysl'*. M., 1988. Pp. 117-123.

1633 Gurevich, A.Ia. *Kul'tura i obshchestvo srednevekovoi Evropy glazami sovremennikov* [Culture and Society in Medieval Europe in the Eyes of Contemporaries]. M.: Iskusstvo, 1989. 367 pp., illus. Summary in English.

1634 Gurevich, G. "Amerikanskie ravviny v gostiakh u edinovertsev v SSSR" [American Rabbis Guests of Co-religionists in USSR]. *Religiia v SSSR* 6 (1987): n.m.

1635 Gurevich, P.S. *Beskhramovye Bogi* [Templeless Gods]. L.: Lenizdat, 1984. 134 pp. (Mify i real'nost' na frontakh ideol. bor'by).

1636 Gurevich, P.[S]. "Epikureistvo i zhertvennost'" [Epicureanism and Sacrificial]. *Nauka i religiia* 12 (1988): 23.

1637 Gurevich, P.[S]. "Eshche raz o 'prozreniiakh drevnikh' i slepote sovremennikov" [Again on "Recovery of Sight of the Ancients" and Blindness of Contemporaries]. *Nauka i religiia* 6 (1987): 42-45.

1638 Gurevich, P.[S]. "Komy siiaiut kupola" [Who Shines Cupolas]. *Rodina* 3 (1989): 80-82.

1639 Gurevich, P.[S]. "Materiia i karma" [Matter and Karma]. *Nauka i religiia* 10 (1989): 21-22.

1640 Gurevich, P.S. *Le mysticisme aujourd'hui: Origines et manifestations.* * Transl. from Russian by A. Gaillard; L. Larionova. M.: Progress, 1988. 304 pp. Indices: pp. 296-303.
Published also in:
Tallin: Periodika, 1987, 111 pp. (B-ka "Looming"; No 19-21). In Estonian.

1641 Gurevich, P.[S]. "Mistitsizm - orudie dukhovnogo zakabaleniia mass" [Mysticism - Tool of Spiritual Enslavement of Masses]. *Aziia i Afrka segodnia* 1 (1986): 18-21. Summary in English, Suppl., p. 5.

1642 Gurevich P.S. *Mistitsizm protiv cheloveka* [Mysticism against Man]. M.: Znanie, 1987. 64 pp. (Novoe v zhizni, nauke, tekhnike-Molodezhnaia; 6/ 1987). Bibl.: p. 63.

1643 Gurevich, P.S. *Netraditsionnye religii na Zapade i vostochnye religioznye kul'ty*
      [Nontraditional Religions in the West and Oriental Religious Cults]. M.:
      Znanie, 1985. 64 pp. (Novoe v zhizni, nauke, tekhnike. Nauch. ateizm; 9).
      Bibl.: p. 63. Name index: p. 63.

1644 Gurevich, P.[S]. "Novye 'proroki' starogo otkroveniia" [New "Prophets" of the
      Old Revelations]. *Nauka i religiia* 4 (1986): 58-61.

1645 Gurevich, P.S. *'Novye religii' i bor'ba idei:* Tochka zreniia sov. sotsiologii
      ["New Religions" and the Struggle of Ideas: Point of View of Soviet
      Sociology]. M.: Novosti, 1984. 84 pp. (Dva mira-dve ideologii). In
      Spanish.
      Published also by Novosti, 1985 in: English, French and German.

1646 Gurevich, P.[S]. "Religioznoe vozrozhdenie ili nravstvennye iskaniia?" [Reli-
      gious Revival or Moral Strivings?]. *Nauka i   religiia* 7 (1989): 15-17.

1647 Gurevich, P.[S]. "Sokhranit li   sebia chelovek?" [Will Man Preserve
      Himself?]. *Nauka i religiia* 7 (1988): 18-19.

1648 Gurevich, P.S. "Sovremennye evangel'skie 'kul'ty' v burzhuanykh stranakh"
      [Contemporary Evangelic "Cults" in Bourgeois Countries]. *Vopr. nauch.
      ateizma* 32 (1985): 78-102.

1649 Gurevich, P.S. *Sovremennye vnekonfessional'nye religioznye organizatsii na
      Zapade* [Contemporary Extra-Confessional Religious Organizations in the
      West]. M.: Znanie, 1983. 64 pp. (Novoe v zhizni, nauke, tekhnike. Nauch.
      ateizm; 2). Bibl.: p. 63.

1650 Gurevich, P.S. *Sovremennyi mistitsizm: istoki i sovremenost'* [Mysticism of
      Today: Origins and Contemporaneity]. M.: Progress, 1988. 304 pp., illus
      In French. Index: pp. 296-303.

1651 Gurevich, P.S. *Spaset li messiia?: 'Khristomaniia' v zap. mire* [Will Messiah
      Save?: "Christomania" in the Western World]. M.: Politizdat, 1981. 272
      pp.

1652 Gurevich, P.S. *Vozrozhden li mistitsizm?:* Kritich. ocherki [Is Mysticism
      Revived?: Critical Essays]. M.: Politizdat, 1984. 302 pp. illus.
      Published also in:
      Riga: Avots, 1988, 395 pp. In Latvian.
      Erevan: Aiastan, 1989. 394 pp. in Armenian. For review see item 5063.

1653 Gur'ianova, N.S. *Krest'ianskii antimonarkhicheskii protest v staroobria-
dcheskoi eskhatologicheskoi literature perioda pozdnego feodalizma* [Peasant
Anti-Monarchist Protest in Old Beliefs Eschatological Literature of the
Late Feudalist Period]. Novosibirsk: Nauka. Sib. otd-nie, 1988. 188 pp.
Bibl.: pp. 153-181. Name index: pp. 182-187. Suppl.: Old Beliefs
Eschatological Works.

1654 Gur'ianova, N.S. "Staroobriadcheskie sochineniia XVIII-nachala XIX v. o
dogmate nemoleniia za gosudaria v fedoseevskom soglasii" [Old-Beliefs
Works of the XVIIIth-Early XIXth C. about the Dogma of Phedoseevs'
Consent Not to Pray for the Sovereign]. *Issledovaniia po istorii
obshchestvennogo soznaniia epokhi feodalizma v Rossii.* Novosibirsk, 1984.
Pp. 75-86.

1655 Gurov, Iu.S. *Formirovanie ateisticheskoi ubezhdennosti u molodezhi* [Forming
of Youth's Atheistic Conviction]. M.: Znanie RSFSR, 1984. 31 pp. (V
pomoshch' lektoru / O-vo "Znanie" RSFSR, Nauch.-metod. sovet otd-niia
po propagande nauch. ateizma). Bibl.: p. 29. Filmstrip : p. 30.

1656 Gurov, Iu.S. "Metodologicheskoe znachenie kategorii 'mirovozzrencheskii
indifferentizm v voprosakh ateizma i religii'" [Methodological Importance
of Category of the "World Outlook's Indifference to the Questions of
Atheism and Religion"]. *Kategorii dialektiki i ikh metodologicheskaia i
mirovozzrencheskaia funktsii.* Cheboksary, 1983. Pp. 110-116.

1657 Gurov, Iu.S. "Nekotorye metodologicheskie i konkretno-sotsiologicheskie
problemy issledovaniia mirovozzrencheskogo indifferentizma v voprosakh
ateizma i religii" [Some Methodological and Specific-Social Problems of
Research of World Outlook's Indifference to the Questions of Atheism
and Religion]. *Problemy istorii religii i ateizma.* Cheboksary, 1980. Pp.
142-152.

1658 Gurov, Iu.S. *Ot bezrazlichiia - k ubezhdennosti:* Aktual. probl. ateist.
vospitaniia molodezhi [From Indifference - To Conviction: Actual
Problems of Youth's Atheistic Upbringing]. Cheboksary: Chuvash. kn.
izd-vo, 1982. 112 pp. For review see item 5064.

1659 Gurov, Iu.S. *Ot znaniia - k ubezhdeniiu* [From Knowledge - To Conviction].
M.: Sov. Rossiia, 1988. 64 pp.

1660 Gurov, Iu.S. "Povyshenie urovnia nauchnogo upravleniia protsessom formirovaniia nauchno-materialisticheskogo mirovozzreniia v sovremennykh usloviiakh" [To Increase the Level of Scientific Direction by Forming Scien-

tific-Materialist Outlook in Contemporary Conditions]. *Formirovanie kommunisticheskoi ubezhdennosti i aktivnoi zhiznennoi pozitsii sovetskikh liudei.* Irkutsk, 1980. Pp. 131-138.

1661   Gurov, Iu.S. "Problema otsenki sushchnosti i perspektiv cheloveka v marksizme i khristianstve" [Evaluation Problem of Man's Essence and Perspectives in Marxism and Christianity]. *Istoriia khristianizatsii narodov Srednego Povolzh'ia. Kriticheskie suzhdeniia i otsenka.* Cheboksary, 1988. Pp. 109-115.

1662   Gurov, Iu.S. "Rol' trudovogo kollektiva v preodolenii mirovozzrencheskogo indifferentizma i formirovanii ateisticheskoi ubezhdennosti molodykh rabochikh" [The Role of Working Collective in Overcoming World Outlook's Indifference and Forming Atheistic Conviction of Young Workers]. *Trudovoi kollektiv i razvitie lichnosti.* Cheboksary, 1981. Pp. 100-112.

1663   Gurov, Iu.S. "Sotsialisticheskii obraz zhizni i problemy ateisticheskogo vospitaniia molodezhi" [Socialist Way of Life and Problems of Youth's Atheistic Upbringing]. *Problemy istorii religii i ateizma.* Cheboksary, 1981. Pp. 83-91.

1664   Guseinov, G.B. *Mesto i rol' islama v sotsial'noi politicheskoi zhizni sovremennogo Irana* [Place and Role of Islam in Social Political Life of Contemporary Iran]. Baku: Elm, 1986. 203 pp. Annot. bibl.: pp. 192-202.

1665   Guseinov, G.[B].; Mamedov, A. "Politizatsiia islama i ideologicheskaia bor'ba" [Politicization of Islam and Ideological Struggle]. *Kommunist Azerbaidzhana* 11 (1988): 84-88.

1666   Guseinov, R.A. "Siriiskii istochnik VIII veka o religioznykh ucheniiakh na Kavkaze i v sopredelenykh regionakh" [Syrian Source of the VIIIth Century about Religious Studies in Caucasus and Contiguous Regions]. *Aktual'nye problemy izucheniia i izdaniia pis'mennykh istoricheskikh istochnikov.* Tbilisi, 1982. P. 32.

1667   Gusev, V.E. "Slavianskii obriad provodov vesny" [Slavonic Ritual of Seeing Off of Spring]. *Istoriia, kul'tura, etnografiia i fol'klor slavianskikh narodov.* M., 1988. Pp. 196-208.

1668   Gus'kov, P. "Zhertvy na chuzhom altare. Ocherki" [Victims on a Strange Altar. Essays]. *Stavropol'e* 5 (1985): 66-79.

1669 Gutnova, E.V. "Kharakternye cherty krest'ianskikh utopii zapadnoevro-peiskogo srednevekov'ia" [Characteristic Features of Peasant Utopias of Western European Middle Ages]. *Istoriia sots. uchenii.* M., 1988. Pp. 176-194.

1670 Gutsu, V.; Elenskii, V. "Aktualizatsiia vospitatel'noi raboty sredi molodezhi" [Actualization of Educational Work Among Youth]. *Kommunist Moldavii* 1 (1989): 49-55.

1671 Gvaladze, L.E. "Arabskaia i gruzinskaia versii 'Muchenichestva sviatogo Vavily'" [Arab and Georgian Versions of "St. Vavila's Martyrdom"]. *Semitolog. shtudii* 3 (1987): 66-72.

1672 "I my za peremeny" [We Are for Change]. *Religiia v SSSR* 6 (1987): MV 1-MV 2.

1673 *I nastal den'* [The Day Came]. Comp.: V.K. Gerasimenko. Simferopol': Tavriia, 1985. 63 pp.

1674 "I za sud'bu svoego Otechestva... Rus. pravosl. tserkov' torzhestvenno otmechaet 1000-let. iubilei Khreshcheniia Rusi" [For the Fate of One's Own Fatherland... Russian Orthodox Church Solemnly Marks the 1000th Year Jubilee of Baptism of Rus']. Prepared by O. Bai et al. *Novoe vremia* 25 (1988): 5-6.

1675 *Ia ateist: 25 otvetov na vopr. 'Pochemu vy ateist?'* [I Am an Atheist: 25 Answers on the Question "Why You Are an Atheist?"]. [Comp.: V. Zybkovets]. M.: Politizdat, 1980. 190 pp., illus.
Published also in:
Riga: Avots, 1982. 213 pp. In Latvian.
Kishinev: Kartia Moldoveniaske, 1928. 179 pp., illus. In Molduavian. For reviews see items 5065-5066.

1676 *'Ia veriu v razum!..': Narodniki revoliutsionery ob ateizme i religii* ["I Believe in Reason!"..: Narodniks-Revolutionaries on Atheism and Religion]. [Comp.: M.A. Aref'ev]. L.: Lenizdat, 1989. 240 pp., illus. Bibl.: pp. 238-240.

1677 Iablokov, I.N. *Religiia: Sushchnost' i iavleniia* [Religion: Essence and Occurrence]. M.: Znanie, 1982. 64 pp. (Novoe v zhizni, nauke, tekhnike. Ser. "Nauch. ateizm"; No 1). Bibl.: p. 64. For review see item 5067.

1678   *Iadovity tuman* [Poisoned Mist]. Comp.: B.V. Prokhorov; V.F. Aleksirov.
       Frunze: Kyrgyzstan, 1985. 65 pp., illus.

1679   Iagodzin'skii, Ia. "Vatikan i ekumenicheskoe dvizhenie. Ekumenizm v
       Pol'she" [Vatican and Ecumenical Movement. Ecumenism in Poland].
       Katolicheskaia tserkov' v PNR v 80-kh godakh. M., 1988. Pp. 129-161.

1680   Iakas, P. *Chego katolichestvo ne dalo Litve?* [What Catholicism Did Not
       Give Lithuania?]. Vil'nius: Mintis, 1986. 36 pp. (Besedy s veruiushchimi).
       In Lithuanian. For review see item 5068.

1681   Iakentaite, L. "Kriticheskii ocherk filosofii katolicheskogo modernizma"
       [Critical Essay on Philosophy of Catholic Modernism]. *Uchenye zap. vuzov
       LitSSR.* Problemy 36 (1987): 121-123.

1682   Iakh'ev, Sh.B. *Islam i sovremennost'* [Islam and Contemporaneity]. Tashkent:
       Uzbekistan, 1985. 28 pp. (Marksizm-leninizm; No 8). In Uzbek.

1683   Iakhshilikov, D. *Sotsial'nyi progress i ateizm* [Social Progress and Atheism].
       Tashkent: Fan, 1986. 54 pp. In Uzbek.

1684   Iakhshilikov, D. *Tekhnicheskii progress i ateisticheskoe vospitanie* [Technical
       Progress and Atheistic Education]. Tashkent: Uzbekistan, 1984. 30 pp.
       (Ser. "Marksizm-leninizm"; No 8). In Uzbek.

1685   Iakhshilikov, Zh. "Nauchno-tekhnicheskii progress i ego vliianie na
       formirovanie nauchno-ateisticheskogo mirovozzreniia trudiashchikhsia"
       [Scientific-Technical Progress and Its Influence on Forming Workers
       Scientific-Atheistic Outlook]. *Problemy formirovaniia nauchno-
       ateisticheskogo mirovozzreniia v sotsialisticheskom obshchestve.* Samarkand,
       1980. Pp. 11-16.

1686   Iakovenko, A.V. "Kritika A.M. Gor'kim idei khristianskogo gumanizma"
       [A.M. Gorky's Criticism of the Idea of Christian Humanism]. *Nauch.
       ateizm i ateist. vospitanie* 1 (1983): 84-97.

1687   Iakovlev, A. "Plakun-trava, plyvushchaia naprotiv vody" ["Purple Loosestrife
       Flowing in Defiance of Water"]. *Druzhba narodov* 12 (1984): 210-222.

1688   Iakovlev, E.G. *Iskusstvo i mirovye religii* [Art and World's Religions]. 2nd
       revised and enlarged ed. M.: Vysh. shk., 1985. 287 pp., illus.

1689 Iakovlev, E.G. "Istoricheskaia tipologiia khudozhestvenno-religioznogo obraza prirody" [Historical Typology of Art-Ecclesiastical Image of Nature]. *Filos. nauki* 9 (1988): 55-61.

1690 Iakovlev, E.G. "Mif, religiia i iskusstvo v sovremennom burzhuaznom obshchestve" [Myth, Religion and Art in Contemporary Bourgeois Society]. *Vest. Mosk. un-ta.* Ser. 7, Filosofi-ia 6 (1988): 23-30.

1691 Iakovlev, Ia.A. "Kul'tovye mesta XIX v. - nachala XX v. na territorii Tomskoi oblasti" [Worship Sites of the XIXth-Early XXth C. on the Territory of Tomsk Province]. *Pamiatnki istorii, arkheologii i arkhitektury Sibiri.* Novosibirsk, 1989. Pp. 35-53.

1692 Iakovlev. N.N. "I oni vozvodiat svoi sionmormony" [They Raise Their Own Zionmormons]. *V mire knig* 12 (1986): 52-55.

1693 Iakovlev, N.N. *Religiia v Amerike 80-kh: Zametki amerikanista* [Religion in America of the 80s: Notes of a Specialist in American Studies]. M.: Politizdat, 1987. 192 pp.

1694 Iakovlev, N.N. "Vera po-amerikanski" [Faith American Way]. *Argumenty. 1987.* M., 1987. Pp. 129-147.

1695 Iakovlev, O.V. *Istoki i sushchnost' khristianskogo smireniia* [Sources and Essence of Christian Humbleness]. Alma-Ata: Znanie KazSSR, 1984. 38 pp.

1696 Iakovlev, V.G. *Kritika bogoslovsko-teologicheskikh dokazatel'stv bytiia boga* [Critique of the Divine-Theological Proofs on God's Existence]. Alma-Ata: Znanie KazSSR, 1980. 36 pp.

1697 Iakovleva, M.P. "Religioznoe soznanie i russkaia pravoslavnaia tserkov'" [Religious Consciousness and Russian Orthodox Church]. *Pravoslavie v Karelii.* Petrozavodsk, 1987. Pp. 124-143.

1698 Iakubenok, L. "Nepal'skii fenomen" [Nepal's Phenomenon]. *Nauka i religiia* 1 (1986): 62-63.

1699 Iakubov, T. "Na uroven' trebovanii vremeni" [Abreast of Time's Demands]. *Kommunist Kirgizstana* 7 (1987): 53-57.

1700   Iallop, D. *Kto ubil papu rimskogo?* [Who Killed the Pope?]. Transl. from
       English. M.: Progress, 1986. 308 pp., illus.
       Published also in:
       Vil'nius: Mintis, 1987. 272 pp. In Lithuanian.

1701   Ianborisov, V.R. "O kul'te konia u turkmen" [Turkmen's Worship of Horse].
       Nauchno-ateisticheskie issledovaniia v muzeiakh. L., 1988. Pp. 104-110.

1702   Ianchenko, L.V. "Ateisticheskoe obuchenie i vospitanie uchashchikhsia
       pedagogicheskogo uchilishcha" [Atheistic Teaching and Upbringing of
       Pupils of Pedagogical College]. *Vopr. ateizma* 20 (1984): 60-66.

1703   Ianchenko, L.V. "Kriticheskii analiz tserkovnogo iskusstva v ateisticheskoi
       propagande" [Critical Analysis of Ecclesiastic Art in Atheistic Propa-
       ganda]. *Vopr. ateizma* 23 (1987): 55-62.

1704   Ianchenko, L.V. *Kritika esteticheskoi kontseptsii sovremennogo pravoslaviia*
       [Critique of Aesthetical Concept of Contemporary Orthodoxy]. Kiev:
       Znanie UkSSR, 1986. 48 pp. (Ser. 5, Nauchno-ateisticheskaia / O-vo
       "Znanie" UkSSR; No 8). Annot. bibl.: p. 47.

1705   Ianchenko, L.V. "Metodika nauchnogo analiza tserkovnogo iskusstva v
       ateisticheskoi propagande sredi molodezhi" [Method of Scientific Analysis
       of the Ecclesiastic Art in Atheistic Propaganda among Youth]. *Aktual'nye
       problemy nauchno-ateisticheskogo vospitaniia molodezhi.* M., 1987. Pp.
       78-81.

1706   Iangutov, L.E. *Iz istorii formulirovaniia shkol kitaiskogo buddizma* [From the
       History of Formulation of Schools of Chinese Buddhism]. Novosibirsk:
       [S.n.], 1983. 6 pp.

1707   Iangutov, L.E. *Filosofskoe uchenie shkoly khuaian'* [Philosophical Teaching of
       the Huayan School]. Novosibirsk: Nauka. Sib. otd-nie, 1982. 142 pp., illus.
       Annot. bibl.: pp. 117-128. Name, terms and titles indices: pp. 137-141.

1708   Iangutov, L.E. "Ob issledovaniiakh po buddizmu v Institute obshchestvennykh
       nauk BF SO AN SSSR" [On Researches of Buddhism in the Institute of
       Social Sciences BF SO AN USSR]. *Filosofiia stran Azii i Afriki:* Problemy
       noveishei istoriografii. M., 1988. Pp. 169-182.

1709   Iangutov, L.E. "Psikhologicheskie aspekty ucheniia o 'spasenii' v kitaiskom
       buddizme" [Psychological Aspects of the Teaching on "Salvation" in

Chinese Buddhism]. *Psikhologicheskie aspekty buddizma.* Novosibirk, 1986. Pp. 11-22.

1710 Ianin, V. "Mirskaia istoriia tserkovnogo prazdnika: Zagadka Znamen. ikony" [Secular Story of Church's Holiday: Mystery of the Famous Icon]. *Nauka i religiia* 8 (1984): 34-37.

1711 Ianin, V. "Staraia skhema" [Old Scheme]. *Nauka i religiia* 3 (1989): 4.

1712 Ianovskaia, S.P. "Analiz stepeni nauchnosti ateisticheskikh vozzrenii studencheskoi molodezhi" [Analysis of the Extent of the Scientific Character of Students' Atheistic Outlook]. *Aktual. vopr. metodiki prepodavaniia obshchestv. nauk i kom. vospitaniia studentov* 5 (1987): 108-115.

1713 Iansen, E. "Svetskoe i tserkovnoe v mirovozzrenii estonskogo krest'ianstva (pervaia polovina XIX veka)" [Secular and Ecclesiastical in Outlook of Estonian Peasantry (Early XIXth Century)]. *Religooni ja ateismi ajaloost eestis* 3 (1987): 192-220. In Estonian. Summary in Russian.

1714 Ianshina, E.M. "Rol' obshchestvennykh dvizhenii VIII-III vv. do n.e. v formirovanii konfutsianstva v Kitae" [The Role of Social Movements in the VIIIth-IIIth Centuries B.C. in Forming of Confucianism in China]. *Obshchestvennye dvizheniia i ikh ideologiia v doburzhuaznykh obshchestvakh Azii* M., 1988, Pp. 34-43.

1715 Iaremchuk, D. "Muzei i ateisticheskoe vospitanie" [Museum and Atheistic Education]. *Agitator* 19 (1982): 59-61.

1716 Iarkov, O.V. "Nesostoiatel'nost' musul'manskogo religioznogo natsionalizma" [Groundlessness of Moslem Religious Nationalism]. *Dialektika sistemnokompleksnogo podkhoda v internatsional'nom vospitanii molodezhi.* Alma-Ata, 1988. Pp. 66-70.

1717 Iarmysh, G.G. "Sotsializm i khristianskie kontseptsii cheloveka" [Socialism and Christian Conceptions of Human Being]. *Vopr. ateizma* 23 (1987): 98-105.

1718 Iaroshevskii, T.M. "Sotsial'naia doktrina katolitsizma i problemy sotrudnichestva marksistov i veruiushchikh v PNR" [Catholicism's Social Doctrine and Problems of Cooperation of Marxists and Believers in Polish People's Republic]. *Vopr. nauch. ateizma* 36 (1987): 221-232.

1719 Iaroslavskii, E.M. *Bibliia dlia veruiushchikh i neveruiushchikh* [The Bible for Believers and Nonbelievers]. 3rd ed. Kiev: Politizdat Ukrainy, 1982. 324 pp., illus. In Ukrainian. Published also in: Kishinev: Kartia moldoveniaske, 1985. 371 pp., In Moldavian.

1720 Iaroslavskii, E.M. *Kak rodiatsia, zhivut i umiraiut bogi i bogini* [How Gods and Goddeses are Born, Live and Die]. 4th ed. Kiev: Politizdat Ukrainy, 1983. 246 pp., illus. In Ukrainian.

1721 Iarotskii, P.L. *Evoliutsiia sovremennogo iegovizma* [Evolution of the Contemporary Jehovism]. Kiev: Politizdat Ukrainy, 1981. 143 pp. Annot. bibl.: pp. 138-142.

1722 Iarotskii, P.L. *Ideinyi krakh sovremennogo klerikalizma i ego modifikatsii* [Ideological Failure of the Contemporary Clericalism and Its Modifications]. Kiev: Znanie UkSSR, 1982. 49 pp. (Ser. 5 "Nauch. ateisticheskaia" / O-vo "Znanie" UkSSR; No 2). Bibl.: p. 48. In Ukrainian.

1723 Iarotskii, P.L. *Klerikal'nyi antisovetizm: sistema ideologicheskikh diversii* [Clerical Anti-Sovietism System of Ideological Diversions]. Kiev: Politizdat Ukrainy, 1984. 303 pp.

1724 Iarotskii, P.L. "Konets sveta perenositsia..." [The End of the World is Postponed...]. *Nauka i religiia* 4 (1986): 36-38.

1725 Iarotskii, P.L. "Oblik sovremennogo veruiushchego, osobennosti perstroiki ideinovospitatel'noi, ateisticheskoi raboty" [The Aspect of Contemporary Believer, Features of Perestroika of Ideologic-Educational, Atheistic Work]. *Protestantskie organizatsii v SSSR*. M., 1989. Pp. 3-17.

1726 Iarotskii, P.L. *Sovremennyi politicheskii klerilalizm* [Contemporary Political Clericalism]. Kiev: Znanie UkSSR, 1988. 48 pp. (Ser. 5, Nauchno-ateisticheskaia / O-vo "Znanie" UkSSR; No 3). Annot. bibl.: p. 48.

1727 Iarotskii, P.L.; Utkin, A.I. "Uniatskaia tserkov': pravda istorii i sovremennost'" [The Uniate Church: Historical Truth and Contemporaneity]. *Pod znamenem leninizma* 23 (1988): 72-77.

1728 Iarovnkova, R.T. "Osobennosti ispol'zovaniia funktsii religii v formirovanii religioznogo mirovozzreniia" [Features of Utilization of the Functions of Religion in Forming Religious World Outlook]. *Nauchnyi ateizm, religiia i sovremennost'*. Novosibirsk, 1987. Pp. 188-196.

1729 Iartys', A.V.; Sysliuk, Ia.G. "Ateisticheskii potentsial sovetskoi trudovoi obriadnosti" [Atheistical Potential of Soviet Working Ceremonial]. *Vopr. ateizma* 24 (1988): 35-42.

1730 Iashin, P.P. *Ideologiia i praktika evangel'skikh khristian-baptistov* [Ideology and Practice of Evangelical Christian-Baptists]. Khar'kov: Prapor, 1981. 88 p. Published also as 2nd enlarged ed. in 1984, 119 pp., bibl.: pp. 117-118.

1731 Iashin, P.P. "Konstitutsionnyi printsip svobody sovestiosnova pravovogo regulirovaniia deiatel'nosti religioznykh organizatsii v SSSR" [Constitutional Principle of Freedom of Worship - Basis of Legal Regulation of the Activity of Religious Organizations in USSR]. *Probl. sots. zakonnosti* 22 (1988): 95-100.

1732 Iashin, V.V. "Russkaia pravoslavnaia tserkov' i antivoennoe dvizhenie" [Russian Orthodox Church and Anti-War Movement]. *Vopr. nauch. ateizma* 32 (1985): 251-266.

1733 Iasin'ski, E. "Formy i metody vozdeistviia katolicheskoi tserkvi na molodezh' PNR" [Forms and Methods of Influence of Catholic Church on Youth of Polish Peoples Republic]. *Katolicheskia tserkov' v PNR v 80-kh godakh.* M., 1988. Pp. 70-102.

1734 Iastrebov, I.B. "Kritika katolicheskoi interpretatsii prav cheloveka i svobody sovesti" [Criticism of Catholic Interpretation of the Rights of Man and Freedom of Worship]. *Vopr. nauch. ateizma* 28 (1981): 59-70.

1735 Iastrebov, I.B. *Kritika sotsial'noi doktriny sovremennogo katolitsizma* [Criticism of Social Doctrine of Contemporary Catholicism] M.: Znanie, 1985. 64 p. (Novoe v zhizni, nauke, tekhnike. Nauch. ateizm; 1). Bibl.: p. 64.

1736 Iastrebov, I.[B]. "Novoe myshlenie i katolitsizm" [New Thinking and Catholicism]. *Kommunist.* Vil'nius. 4 (1989): 35-41.

1737 Iastrebov, I.B. *Sotsial'naia filosofiia katolitsizma v XX veke* [Catholicism's Social Philosophy in the XXth Century]. Kiev: Vyshcha shk., 1988. 190 pp. Bibl.: pp. 186-189. Published also in:
Vil'nius: Mintis, 1988, 175 pp., with an add. sub-title: "Istoki i tendentsii" [Sources and Tendencies].

1738   Iatsenko, V.B. "Zhertvoprinnoshenie - ideia zhizni i svobody" [Sacrifice - Idea of Life and Freedom]. *V Vsesoiuznaia shkola molodykh vostokovedov.* M., 1989. T. I. Pp. 191-193.

1739   Iaunishkis, B.F. *Bez illiuzii* [Without illusions]. Transl. from Lithuanian. Kaunas: Shviesa, 1983. 203 pp. In Polish.

1740   Iaunishkis, B.F. *Malen'kaia taina* [A Small Mystery]. Kaunas: Shviesa, 1980. 91 pp. In Polish.

1741   Iaunishkis, B.F. *Posledniaia ispoved'* [The Last Confession]. [Transl. from Russian]. Riga: Avots, 1984. 303 pp., port. In Latvian. Published also in: Tbilisi: Ganatleba, 1985, 208 pp. In Georgian.

1742   Iazberdiev, A. "Sasanidskii kanon Avesty i istoriia zapisi ego tekstov" [The Sasanid Canon of the Avesta and the History of Recording of Its Texts]. *Izv. AN TSSR. Ser. obshchestv.nauk* 1 (1987): 26-37. Bibl.: pp. 36-37. Summary in English.

1743   Iazykovich, V.R. "O kharaktere nravstvenno-psikhologicheskogo vozdeistviia protestantizma na veruiushchikh" [On the Character of Moral-Psychological Influence of Protestantism on Believers]. *Nauch. ateizm i ateist. vospitanie* 1 (1983): 70-77.

1744   Ibadullaev, N. "Ot zhizni neotdelima" [Inseparable from Life]. *Nauka i religiia* 4 (1989): 20-21.

1745   Ibragim, T.K. "O kalame kak 'ortodoksal'noi filosofii islama': Kritika odnogo lozhnogo stereotipa" [On Kalam as "Orthodox Philosophy of Islam": Critique of one False Stereotype]. *Narody Azii i Afriki* 3 (1986): 205-212.

1746   Ibragimov, I.; Toktosunova, A. "Protiv ideologii i politiki klerikal'nogo antikommunizma" [Against the Ideology and Policy of Clerical Anti-Communism]. *Kommunist Kirgistana* 2 (1989): 87-92.

1747   Ibragimov, N. "Kul't 'sviatykh' v islame po arabskim istochnikam XII-XIV vv. (arabskaia narodnaia sira i 'Puteshestvie' Ibn Battuty)" [The Cult of "Saints" in Islam by Arab Sources of the XIIth-XIVth C. (Arab Popular Sira and "The Journey" of Ibn Battuta)]. *Islam v istorii narodov Vostoka.* M., 1981. Pp. 170-176.

1748 Ibragimov, Sh. *Pamiatniki kul'tury i ateizma* [Monuments of Culture and Atheism]. Tashkent: Uzbekistan, 1984. 32 p. (Ser. "Marksizm-leninizm"; No 4). In Uzbek.

1749 Ibragimova, N. *Ateisticheskoe vospitanie po mestu zhitel'stva* [Atheistic Education by Place of Residence]. Tashkent: Uzbekistan, 1986. 38 pp. In Uzbek.

1750 *Ideino-filosofskoe nasledie Ilariona Kievskogo* [Ideologic-Philosophical Heritage of Ilarion of Kiev]. [V 2 ch]. [Ed.: A.A. Bazhenova]. M., [S.n.], 1986. (Pamiatniki filos.-estet. mysli Drev. Rusi).

1751 *Ideologiia russkogo pravoslaviia: Kritich. analiz* [The Ideology of Russian Orthodoxy: Critical Analysis]. [Ed.: B.A. Lobovik]. Kiev: Politizdat Ukrainy, 1986. 197 pp., illus. In Ukrainian. Annot. bibl.: pp. 186-195.

1752 *Iegovizm* [Jehovism]. [Ed.: M.Ia. Lensu.] Minsk: Nauka i tekhnika, 1981. 134 pp. Bibl. (1960-1979): pp. 131-133.

1753 Iettmar, K. *Religii Gindukusha* [The Religions of Hindu Kush]. Transl. from German. M.: Nauka, 1986. 524 pp., illus. Bibl.: pp. 485-504. Index : pp. 505-521.

1754 Ignatenko, A.A. "Boeviki, prishedshie iz proshlogo: (Islam. religioz.-polit. ekstremizm v arab. stranakh)" [Militants Arrived from the Past: (Islamic Religious-Political Extremism in Arab Countries)]. *Ateisticheskie chteniia* 17 (1988): 48-64.

1755 Ignatenko, A.A. *Khalify bez khalifata. Islam. nepravitel'stv. relig.-polit. org. na Blizhnem Vostoke: istoriia, ideologiia, deiatel'nost'* [Caliphs Without Chalifates: Islamic Nongovernmental Religious Political Organizations in the Near East: History, Ideology, Activity]. M.: Nauka, 1988. 207 pp. Annot. bibl.: pp. 183-194.

1756 Ignatenko, A.A. "O tipologii islamskikh nepravitel'stvennykh religiozno-politicheskikh organizatsii na Blizhnem Vostoke" [Typology of Islamic Nongovernmental Religious-Political Organizations in the Near East]. *Problemy sovremennoi sovetskoi* arabistiki. Erevan, 1988. Vyp. I. Pp. 97-103.

1757 Ignatenko, A.A. "Politika gosudarstvennogo terrorizma i islamskie nepravitel'-stvennye religiozno-politicheskie organizatsii na Blizhnem Vostoke"

[Politics of State Terrorism and Islamic Nongovernmental Religious-Political Organizations in the Near East]. *"Islamskii faktor" v mezhdunarodnykh otnosheniiakh v Azii (70-e-pervaia polovina 80-kh gg.).* M., 1987. Pp. 48-59.

1758   Ignatenko, A.A. "Problemy razvitiia arabo-musul'manskoi obshchestvenno-politicheskoi mysli srednevekov'ia: Metodol. aspekt" [Problems of Development of Arab-Moslem Socio-Political Thought of the Middle Ages: Methodological Aspect]. *Metodologicheskie problemy izucheniia istorii filosofii zarubezhnogo Vostoka.* M., 1987. Pp. 155-181. Bibl.: pp. 178-181.

1759   Ignatenko, A.A. "Srednevekovye 'poucheniia vladykam' i problematika vlasti" [The Middle Ages "Sermons for Sovereigns" and Problematics of Power]. *Sotial'no-politichskie predstavleniia v islame: Istoriia i sovremennost'.* M., 1987. Pp. 21.44. Annot. bibl.: pp. 37-41.

1760   *Ignat'ev, I.P. Kritika sovremennogo neomistisizma* [Criticism of Contemporary Neomysticism]. L.: Znanie RSFSR, Leningr. org. Leningr. Dom nauch. ateizma, 1988. 106 pp.

1761   Ignat'ev, I.P. "Sotsial'no-psikhologicheskie aspekty kritiki psevdovostochnykh kul'tov" [Socio-Psychological Aspects of Criticism of Pseudo Oriental Cults]. *Sotsial'no-filosofskie aspekty kritiki religii.* L., 1988. Pp. 87-100.

1762   Ignatovich, A.[N]. "Buddizm v Iaponii" [Buddhism in Japan]. *Aziia i Afrika segodnia* 2 (1982): 35-36.

1763   Ignatovich, A.N. *Buddizm v Iaponii: Ocherk rannei istorii* [Buddhism in Japan: Essay of Early History]. M.: Nauka, 1987. 317 pp. Bibl.: pp. 283-295. Index: pp. 296-315. Republished in 1988. For review see item 5069.

1764   Ignatovich, A.N. "'Desiat' stupenei bodkhisattvy'" ["Ten Steps of Bodhisattva"]. *Psikhologocheskie aspekty buddizma.* Novosibirsk, 1986. Pp. 69-90.

1765   Ignatovich, A.N. "Sostav i natsional'nye sily nitirenovskogo dvizheniia" [Social Structure and National Strength of Nichiren Movement]. *Vestn. Mosk. un-ta. Vostokovedenie* 1 (1981): 3-13.

1766   Ignatovich, A.N. "Ucheniia o teokraticheskom gosudarstve v iaponskom buddizme" [Studies About Theocratic State in Japanese Buddhism]. *Buddizm i gosudarstvo na Dal'nem Vostoke.* M., 1987. Pp. 146-179.

1767 Ikhshilov, D. "Nauchno-tekhnicheskii progress i ateisticheskoe vospitanie sel'skikh truzhenikov Uzbekistana" [Scientific-Technical Progress and Atheistic Education of Uzbekistan Villagers]. *Obshchestvennye Nauki v Uzbekistane* 9 (1982): 39-41.

1768 Ikhshilov, D. "Perezhitki drevnikh verovanii i puti ikh preodoleniia" [Survivals of Ancient Beliefs and Ways of Surmounting Them]. *Sov. Dagestan* 4 (1981): 28-31.

1769 Il'enkov, E. "Kosmologiia dukha: Rol' mysliashchei materii v sisteme mirovogo vzaimodeistviia" [Cosmology of the Spirit: The Role of Thinkable Matter in the System of World Interaction]. *Nauka i religiia* 8 (1988): 4-7.

1770 Il'iasov, I. *Dogmaty islama i deistvitel'nost'* [Islam's Dogmas and Reality]. Alma-Ata: Kazakhstan, 1983. 32 pp. In Uigur.

1771 Il'in, V.A. "Polemika s anabaptizmom v anglikanskoi publitsistike XVI veka" [Controversy with Anabaptism in Anglican Socio-Political Journalism of the XVIth Century]. *Obshchestvo i gosudarstvo v drevnosti i srednie veka.* M., 1984. Pp. 94-113.

1772 Il'in, V.V. "Astrologiia: rol' i mesto v sisteme drevnei kul'tury" [Astrology: Role and Place in the System of Ancient Culture]. *Istoriko-astronomicheskie issledovaniia* 19 (1987): 123-138. Bibl.: p.138.

1773 Il'in, V.V. "'Astrologiia - tshchetnaia nauka'" ["Astrology - Futile Science"]. *Zemlia i Vselennaia* 6 (1989): 24-29.

1774 Inadze, M.P. "Rol' khramovykh tsentrov v sotsial'no-politicheskoi zhizni drevnekolkhidskogo obshchestva" [Role of Temple Centres in Socio-Political Life of Ancient Chaldean Society]. *Voprosy istorii narodov Kavkaza.* Tbilisi, 1988. Pp. 65-90.

1775 Indriksons, A. *Put' k istine: Vospominaniia i razmyshleniia byvshego sviashchennika i uchitelia* [The Way to Truth: Recollections of a Former Priest and Teacher]. Riga: Avots, 1985. 176 pp. In Latvian.

1776 *Induizm: traditsii i sovremennost'* [Hinduism: Traditions and Contemporaneity]. [Eds.: A.D. Litman; R.B. Rybakov]. M.: Nauka, 1985. 281 pp.

1777   Innokentii, igumen. "Bibliia v sovremennom mire" [The Bible in Contemporary World]. *Sov. bibliogr.* 3 (1989): 65-71.

1778   Innokentii, ieremonakh. "Tysiacheletnii put' russkoi khristianskoi kul'tury" [Thousand Years of Russian Christian Culture]. *Lit. Kirgizstan* 5 (1988): 101-108.

1779   Inzhievskii, Iu.F.; Riabikov, V.M. *Pravoslavnye prazdniki* [Orthodox Feasts]. 2nd ed. Kiev: Poltizdat Ukrainy, 1986. 81 pp. (Besedy s veruiushchimi). In Ukrainian.

1780   Inzhievkii, Iu.F.; Riabikov, V.M. *Religioznye prazdniki pravoslaviia* [Religious Feasts of Orthodoxy]. Kiev: Politizdat Ukrainy, 1981. 80 pp. (Besedy s veruiushchimi). In Ukrainian.

1781   Ioann, ieremonakh. "Vizantinizm, slaviane i Rossiia" [Byzantinism, Slavs and Russia]. *Vopr. isorii* 8 (1989): 54-75.

1782   Iofan, N.A.; Scmcntsova, E.L. "Drevnii mif i ego izobrazitel'nye voploshcheniia v doantichnom i antichnom Sredizemnomor'e" [Ancient Myth and Its Depictive Representation in Preancient and Ancient Mediterranean Region]. *Zhizn' mifa v antichnossti* M., 1988. Ch. I. Pp. 46-59.

1783   Ionova, A.[I]. "Doktriny, dogmaty, zhizn': Obshchestv. problematika v sovrem. islame" [Doctrines, Dogmas, Life: Social Problematics in Contemporary Islam]. *Nauka i religiia* 4 (1981): 60-61.

1784   Ionova, A.I. *Islam v Iugo-Vostochnoi Azii: problemy sovremennoi ideinoi evoliutsii* [Islam in South-Eastern Asia: Problems of Contemporary Ideological Evolution]. M.: Nauka, 1981. 264 pp. Bibl.: pp. 239-257. Index of moslem terms and names: pp. 257-263. For reviews see items 5070-5071.

1785   Ionova, A.I. "Islam v sovremennoi mezhdunarodnoi politike. Podkhod sovetskikh uchenykh (70-80-e gody)" [Islam in Contemporary International Politics. Soviet Scientists Approach (70s-80s)]. *"Islamskii faktor" v mezhdunarodnykh otnosheniiakh v Azii (70-e-pervaia polovina 80-kh gg.).* M., 1987. Pp. 3-13.

1786   Ionova, A.I. *Izuchenie sovetskimi uchenymi islama na zarubezhnom Vostoke (1970-1982):* 31-i Mezhdunar. kongr. po gumanit. naukam v stranakh Azii i Afriki, 31 avg. - 7 sent. 1983 g., Tokio-Kioto. Sektsiia 5.A [Study by

Soviet Scientists of Islam in Foreign Orient (1970-1982): 31st International Congress of Humanities in Asian and African Countries, 31st Aug. - 7th Sep. 1983. Tokyo-Kyoto. M.: Nauka, 1983. 32 pp. In English. Bibl.: pp. 14-32.

1787 Ionova, A.I. "O sovremennoi musul'manskoi traktovke problem sobstvennosti, kapitala, i truda" [Contemporary Moslem Interpretation of Problems of Property, Capital and Labour]. *Sotsial'no-politicheskie predstavleniia v islame: Istoriia i sovremennost'.* M., 1987. Pp. 81-97.

1788 Ionova, A.[I]. "Sovremennyi islam: sektantstvo kak forma sotsial'nogo protesta" [Contemporary Islam: Sectarianism as a Form of Social Protest]. *Aziia i Afrika segodnia* 2 (1981): 57-60.

1789 Iordanskii, V.B. "Sviashchennye chisla v mifologii i obriadnosti narodov Tropicheskoi Afriki" [Sacral Numbers in Mythology and Rites of Peoples of Tropical Africa].* *Narody Azii i Afriki* 1 (1989): 87-97.

1790 Iovasha, L. *Lichnost' i professiia* [Personality and Profession]. Kaunas: Shviesa, 1981. 247 pp. In Lithuanian. Bibl.: pp. 240-244.

1791 Ipatov, A.N. "Khristianstvo i russkaia kul'tura" [Christianity and Russian Culture]. *Nauchnyi ateizm, religiia i sovremennost'.* Novosibirsk, 1987. Pp. 125-147.

1792 Ipatov, A.N. *Pravoslavie i russkaia kul'tura* [Orthodoxy and Russian Culture]. M.: Sov. Rossiia, 1985. 128 pp., illus.

1793 Ipatov, A.[N]. "Pravoslavie i russkaia ku'tura: Vymysly i deistvitel'nost'" [Orthodoxy and Russian Culture: Fabrications and Reality]. *Nauka i religiia* 6 (1985): 43-45; 9 1985): 38-41.

1794 Irodov, S. "Pervoe palomnichestvo: Sov. krishnaity v Indii" [The First Pilgrimage: Soviet Krishnaites in India]. *Novoe vremia* 19 (1989): 39.

1795 Isaenko, A.V. *Ekstremisty-baptisty i ikh posledovateli* [Baptists-Extremists and Their Followers]. Ordzhonikidze: Ir, 1988. 72 pp. Bibl.: pp. 70-71.

1796 Isaenko, A.V. "Sotsial'naia sushchnost' religioznogo ucheniia angliiskikh puritan XVI veka" [Social Essence of Religious Teaching of English

Puritans of the XVIth Century]. *Izv. Sev-Kavk. Nauch. tsentra vyssh. shkoly. Obshchestv. nauki* 1 (1981): 39-44.

1797   Isaev, I.A. "Retsidiv teokraticheskoi utopii: tserkov' i feodal'naia gosudarstvennost' v raskole" [Reccurence of Theocratical Utopia: Church and Feudal State System in Schism]. *Istoriko-pravovye voprosy vzaimootnoshenii gosudarstva i tserkvi v istorii Rossii*. M., 1988. Pp. 110-119.

1798   Isaeva, N.V. "Polemika Shankary s sarvastivadoi" [Sankara's Polemics with Sarvastivadin Sect]. *Ratsionalisticheskaia traditsiia i sovremennost'*. M., 1988. Kn. I. Pp. 150-165.

1799   Isaeva, N.V. "Shankara i buddisty v 'Kommentarii na "Brakhma Sutru'" [Sankara and Buddhists in "Commentaries to 'Brahma Sutra'"]. *Buddizm. Istoriia i kul'tura*. M., 1989. Pp. 44-57.

1800   Isaia ieremonakh. "N.P. Kondakov i ego issledovaniia na Sinae" [N.P. Kondakov and His Researches in Sinai]. *Bogoslovskie trudy* 28 (1987): 262-267. Bibl.: p. 271.

1801   Isaian, T.S. *Religiia i sovremennaia ideologicheskaia bor'ba* [Religion and Contemporary Ideological Struggle]. Erevan: Znanie ArmSSR, 11981. 36 pp. (V pomoshch' lektoru / O-vo "Znanie" ArmSSR). In Armenian.

1802   Ishchenko, I.S.; Ishchenko, S.I. *Iz plena sueverii: Zametki ob ateist. vospitanii voinov* [From the Captivity of Superstitions: Remarks on Atheistic Education of Soldiers]. M.: Voenizdat, 1989. 127 pp.

1803   Ishmukhametov, Z.A. *Islam i ego ideologiia* [Islam and Its Ideology]. Kazan': Tatar. kn. izd-vo, 1983. 207 pp. In Tatar.   Bibl.: pp. 205-206.

1804   Isidor, arkhiepiskop. "U nas odno Otechestvo, obshchie zaboty" [We have one Motherland, Common Concerns]. *Kuban'* 5 (1989):   41-49.

1805   Isiev, D.A. "K voprosu o verovaniiakh uigurskogo naroda" [On the Problem of Beliefs of Uigur People]. *Voprosy istorii i kul'tury uigurov*. Alma-Ata, 1987. Pp. 121-137.

1806   *Iskusstvo i religiia v istorii filosofii* [Art and Religion in the History of Philosophy]. Ed.: V.G. Shtiuka. Kishinev: Shtiintsa, 1980. 147 pp. Summaries in English, French and German. Annot. bibl.: pp. 138-143. For reviews see items 5073-5074.

1807 *Islam: problemy ideologii, prava, politiki i ekonomiki* [Islam: Problems of Ideology, Law, Politics and Economics]. [Ed.: A.I. Ionova]. M.: Nauka, 1985. 279 pp. For review see item 5075.

1808 *Islam: Proiskhozhdenie, istoriia i sovremenost'* [Islam: Origin, History and Contemporaneity]. Comp.: G.M. Kerimov. M.: Znanie, 1984. 63 pp. (Novoe v zhizni, nauke, tekhnike. Nauch. ateizm; 11). Bibl.: p. 61.

1809 *Islam: Religiia, obshchestvo, gosudarstvo* [Islam: Religion, Society, State]. [Eds.: P.A. Griaznevich; S.M. Prozorov]. M.: Nauka, 1984. 232 pp. Annot. bibl.: pp. 229-231.

1810 *Islam: ubezhdennost' i mirovozzrenie* [Islam: Conviction and World Outlook]. Tahkent: Uzbekistan, 1988. 134 pp., illus. In Uzbek.

1811 *Islam i ateizm v voprosakh i otvetakh* [Islam and Atheism in Questions and Anwers]. [Ed.: A. Kuchkarov]. Tashkent: Uzbekistan, 1986. 253 pp. Published also: in 1987, 271 pp., in Uzbek.

1812 *Islam i problemy natsionalizma v stranakh Blizhnego i Srednego Vostoka* [Islam and Problems of Nationalism in Near and Middle Eastern Countries]. Ed.: Iu.V. Gankoavskii. M.: Nauka, 1986. 237 pp.

1813 *Islam i sovremennaia ideologicheskaia bor'ba* [Islam and Contemporary Ideological Struggle]. Sci. ed.: B.B. Abdullaev. Makhachkala: DGU, 1985. 152 pp.

1814 *Islam i sovremennost'* [Islam and Contemporaneity]. [Ed.: T.A. Stetskevich]. L.: GMIRIA, 1985. 143 pp.

1815 *Islam v istorii i sovremennosti [Islam in History and Contemporaneity]. [Ed.: G.I. Mustafaev]. Baku: AzGU, 1981. 92 pp. In Azerbaijan.*

1816 *Islam v istorii narodov Vostoka* [Islam in the History of Peoples of Orient]. [Eds.: I.M. Smilianskaia; S.Kh. Kiamilev]. M.: Nauka, 1981. 197 pp. For review see item 5076.

1817 *Islam v politicheskoi zhizni stran sovremennogo Blizhnego i Sredngo Vostoka* [Islam in Political Life of Contemporary Near and Middle Eastern Countries]. [Ed.: N.O. Oganesian]. Erevan: Izd-vo AN ArmSSR, 1986. 229 pp. For review see item 5077.

1818 *Islam v respublikakh Sovetskogo Vostoka: formy proiavleniia* [Islam in Republics of Soviet Orient: Forms of Manifestations]. [Comp.: K.Sh. Sulembaev]. Alma-Ata: [S.n.], 1987. 133 pp. In Kazakh.

1819 *Islam v sovremennoi politiki stran Vostoka (konets 70-kh-nach. 80-kh gg. XX v.)* [Islam in Contemporary Politics of Countries of the Orient (Late 70s-Early 80s of the XXth C.)]. [Ed.: R. Polonskaia]. M.: Nauka, 1986. 279 pp. (Puti razvitiia osvobodivshikhsia stran Vostoka). Bibl.: pp. 261-272. Name and term index: pp. 273-277. For review see item 5078.

1820 *Islam v SSSR: Osobennosti protsessa sekuliarizatsii v resp. sov. Vostoka* [Islam in the USSR: Peculiarities of the Secularization Process in the Republics of the Soviet Orient]. Ed.: E.G. Filimonov. M.: Mysl' 1983. 173 pp. For review see item 5079.

1821 *Islam v stranakh Blizhnego i Srednego Vostoka* [Islam in the Near and Middle Eastern Countries]. [Ed.: Iu.V. Gankovskii]. M.: Nauka, 1982. 238 pp.

1822 *Islam v Zapadnoi Afrike* [Islam in Western Africa]. [Ed.: A.M. Vasil'ev]. M.: Nauka, 1988. 268 pp. Summary in English. Bibl.: pp. 248-257.

1823 *'Islamskii faktor' v mezhdunarodnykh otnosheniiakh v Azii (70-e -pervaia polovina 80-kh godov)* ["Islamic Factor" in International Relations in Asia (70s-Early 80s)]. Ed.: L.R. Polonskaia. M.: Nauka, 1987. 191 pp.

1824 Ismailov, A.[Sh]. "Islamskii fideizm segodnia" [Islamic Fideism Today]. *Nauka i religiia* 8 (1982): 56-58.

1825 Ismailov, A.Sh. "Nesostoiatel'nost' nekotorykh aspektov modernizatsii islamskogo miroponimaniia" [Groundlessness of Some Aspects of Modernization of Islamic World Outlook]. *Aktual'nye problemy kritiki religii formirovaniia ateisticheskogo mirovozzreniia.* Makhachkala, 1982. Pp. 99-108.

1826 Ismailov, Kh. "Otvet proritsateliam" [Answer to Soothsayers]. *Nauka i religiia* 1 (1980): 40-43.

1827 Ismailov, Sh.A. "Rol' trudovogo kollektiva v internatsionalistskom i ateisticheskom vospitanii" [Role of Labour Collective in Internationalist and Atheistic Education]. *Vopr. nauch. ateizma* 26 (1980): 22-35.

1828 Ismatov, B. *Antieligioznye vzgliady tadzhikskikh myslitelei* [Antireligious views of Tajik Thinkers]. Dushanbe: Irfon, 1988. 128 pp. In Tajik.

1829 *Ispol'zovanie muzeinykh kollektsii v kritike buddizma* [Use of Museum Collections in Criticism of Buddhism]. Ed.: T.A. Stetske- vich. L.: GMIRIA, 1981. (Publ. in 1982). 175 pp., illus.

1830 "Istina rozhdaetsia v spore" [Truth is Borne in Dispute]. *Nauka i religiia* 11 (1987): 44-50.

1831 *Istochnikovedenie i istoriografiia istorii buddizma:* Strany Tsentr. Azii [Study of Sources and Historiography of the History of Buddhism: Countries of the Central Asia]. Ed.: R.E. Pubaev. Novosibirsk: Nauka. Sib. otd-nie, 1986. 124 pp.

1832 *Istoriia i teoriia ateizma* [History and Theory of Atheism]. Univ. textbook. [G.L. Bakanurskii et al.] Tbilisi: Izd-vo Tbil. un-ta, 1980. 419 pp. In Georgian.
Published also in:
Erevan: Izd-vo Erev. un-ta, 1985, 431 pp. In Armenian. 2nd ed.: M.: Mysl', 1982. 476 pp. Reprinted as 3rd ed.: in 1987. For review see item 5080.

1833 *Istoriia khristianizatsii narodov Srednego Povol'zh'ia:* Kritich. suzhdeniia i otsenka [History of Conversion to Christianity of the Peoples of the Middle Volga: Critical Opinion and Appraisal]. Cheboksary: ChGU, 1988. 123 pp.

1834 *Istoriia kitaiskoi filosofii* [History of Chinese Philosophy]. Transl. from Chinese by V.S. Taskina. M.: Progress, 1989. 552 pp. Name index: pp. 548-550.

1835 *Istoriia religii i ateisticheskaia propaganda v Gruzii* [History of Religion and Atheistic Propaganda in Georgia]. Formerly *Voprosy istorii religii i ateizma v Gruzii.* See item No 4718.

1836 "Istoriia shkoly tibetskogo buddizma Sak'ia v 'Dumbta-shelchzhi-melon'" [History of Tibetan Buddhist School Sa - Skya in "Grub - Mtha' Shel - Gyi Me Long"].* Transl. from Tibetan by R.N. Krapivina. *Narody Azii i Afriki* 1 (1988): 117-128. Summary in English, p. 221.

1837 *Istoriko-pravovye voprosy vzaimootnoshenii gosudarstva i tserkvi v istorii Rossii* [Historic-Legal Problems of Interrelation of State and Church in Russia's History]. Ed.: I.A. Isaev; O.A. Omel'chenko. M.: [S.n.], 1988. !69 pp.

1838 Itkin, S.M. *Ateisticheskomu vospitaniiu deistvennost'* [Effectiveness to Atheistic Education]. Saransk: Mordov. kn. Izd-vo, 1984. 110 pp.

1839 Iukhas, I. "Katolitsizm v Vengrii: ego analiz i kritika" [Catholicism in Hungary: Its Analysis and Criticism]. *Nekotorye filosofskie i sotsial'no-politicheskie problemy marksizma-leninizma.* M., 1987. Pp. 96-100.

1840 Iulina, N.S. *Teologiia i filosofiia v religioznoi mysli SShA XX veka* [Theology and Philosophy in Religious Thought of USA in the XXth Century]. M.: Nauka, 1986. 161 pp. For review see item 5081.

1841 Iunusova, D.[M]. *Edinstvo nravstvennogo i ateisticheskogo vospitaniia zhenshchin* [Unity of Moral and Atheistic Education of Women]. Tashkent: Znanie UzSSR, 1982. 27 pp. (V pomoshch' lektoru / O-vo "Znanie" UzSSR. Ser. obshchestv.-politicheskaia). In Uzbck. Bibl.: p. 27.

1842 Iunusova, D.M. *V avangarde ateisticheskogo vospitaniia* [In Vanguard of Atheistic Education]. Tashkent: Uzbekistan, 1986. 16 pp. (B-ka Ateista). In Uzbek.

1843 Iuraskina, T.I. "Kritika ponimaniia intuitsii v khristianskoi kontseptsii poznaniia" [Criticism of Understanding of Intuition in Christian Concept of Cognition]. *Kritika religioznoi ideologii i problemy ateisticheskogo vospitaniia.* M., 1980. Pp. 48-54.

1844 Iur'ev, M. "Esli by voskres Nostradamus" [If Only Nostradamus were Risen from the Dead]. *Nauka i religiia* 10 (1981): 56-57.

1845 Iurginis, Iu.[M]. "Katolicheskaia tserkov' i iskusstvo" [Catholic Church and Art]. *Litva lit.* 10 (1987): 138-161.

1846 Iurginis, Iu.M. *Khristianstvo Litvy: Issled. sotsial. i kul't. razvitiia feodal. o-va* [Lithuania's Christianity: Research of Social and Cultural Development of Feudal Society]. Vil'nius: Mokslas, 1987. 334 pp. In Lithuanian. Name and geographical index: pp. 323-333.

1847 Iurgins, Iu.M. *Mucheniki i sviatye: legendy i deistvitel'nost'* [Martyrs and Saints: Legends and Reality]. Vil'nius: Mintis, 1984. 69 pp. (Besedy s veruiushchhimi). In Lithuanian. Bibl.: pp. 67-68.

1848 Iushan, L.G. *Ispoved' byvshego veruiushchego* [Confession of a Former Believer]. Kishinev: Kartia moldoveniaske, 1983. 80 pp. In Moldavian. Published also as 2nd ed. in 1985, 78 pp.

1849 Iushin, E.A. "Anglo-amerikanskaia burzhuaznaia istoriografiia vzaimoot-noshenii Sovetskogo gosudarstva i russkoi pravoslavnoi tserkvi v 1921-1922 godakh" [Anglo-American Bourgeois Historiography on Interrelations of Soviet State and Russian Orthodox Church in 1921-1922]. *Zarubezhnaia istoriografiia sotstial'no-politicheskogo razvitiia SSSR.* M., 1989. Pp. 64-75.

1850 Iushkiavichius, B. *Ateisticheskaia mysl' v tvorchestve Iu. Martsinkiavichiusa* [Atheistical Thought in Iu. Martsinkiavichius' works]. Vil'nius: Znanie LitSSR, 1984. 18 pp. (Material dlia lektora / O-vo "Znanie" LitSSR). In Lithuanian.

1851 Iusupov, P.[S]. "O nekotorykh takticheskikh polozheniiakh dvizheniia 'Brat'ev-musul'man'" [Some Tactical Positions of "Moslem-Brotherhood" Movement]. *Torzhestvo razuma.* Dushanbe, 1988. Pp. 172-177. Bibl.: pp. 176-177.

1852 Iusupov, P.S. "'Shakhada' i 'islamskaia revoliutsiia' v rabotakh dukhovenstva Irana i 'Brat'ev-musul'man'" ["Shahada" and "Islamic Revolution" in the Works of Iran Clergy and "Moslem-Brotherhood"]. *V Vsesoiuznaia shkola molodykh vostokovedov.* M., 1989. T. 3. Pp. 21-24.

1853 Iuvenalii, mitropolit. "V predverii 1000-letia" [On the Threshold of 1000th years]. *Novoe vremia* 15 (1988): 42-43.

1854 Ivakin, A.A. *Chto takoe schast'e* [What Happiness Is]. Alma-Ata: Kazakhstan, 1985. 69 pp., illus. (Uchenye beseduiut s veruiushchimi). For review see item 5082.

1855 Ivakin, L. "Ravvin Afol'f Shaevich nagrazhden ordenom Druzhby narodov [Rabbi Afol'f Shaevich Awarded the Order of Friendship of Peoples]. *Religiia v SSSR* 10 (1987): LI 1 - LI 2.

1856 Ivanchenko, A.V. *Vospityvat' ateistov* [To Educate Atheists]. Kiev: Molod', 1985. 167 pp. In Ukrainian. Bibl.: pp. 161-166.

1857 Ivanchenko, R.G. *Privideniia lavrskikh peshcher* [Ghosts of Lavra's Caves].
      2nd enlarged and revised ed. Kiev: Veselka, 1984. 133 pp., illus. Title of
      the 1st ed. *Teni lavrskikh peshcher* [Shadows of Lavra's Caves]. In
      Ukrainian.

1858 Ivanchuk, N.V. "Vina: ee mesto i rol' v marksistskoi i religioznoi ideologii"
      [The Guilt: Its Place and Role in Marxist and Religious Ideologies].
      Otnoshenie cheloveka k irratsional'nomu. Sverdlovsk, 1989. Pp. 222-238.

1859 Ivanenko, S.[I]. "Klerikal'nye passazhi" [Clerical Passages]. *Kommunist
      Kirgizstana* 5 (1988): 70-75.

1860 Ivanenko, S.[I]. "Religioznoe soznanie i sotsialisticheskaia deistvitel'nost'"
      [Religious Consciousness and Socialist Reality]. *Kommunist Sov. Latvii* 1
      (1985): 88-95.

1861 Ivanenko, S.I. "Evoliutsiia otnosheniia russkogo pravoslaviia k prosveshcheniiu
      i nauchnomu znaniiu" [Evolution of Russian Orthodoxy's Attitude Toward
      Enlightenment and Scientific Knowledge]. *Vopr. nauch. ateizma* 37 (1988):
      271-286.

1862 Ivanenko, S.I. "K voprosu o poniatii 'religioznaia vera'" [On the Problem of
      Concept of "Religious Faith"]. *Vopr. nauch. ateizma* 26 (1980): 283- 296.

1863 Ivanenko, S.I. "Kritika sovremennykh religioznykh vozzrenii na nauchno-
      tekhnicheskii progress" [Criticism on Contemporary Religious Outlook on
      Scientific-Technical Progress]. *Molodezh' i nauchno-tekhnicheskii progress.*
      M., 1982. Pp. 97-98.

1864 Ivanenko, S.I. *Nauka i pravoslavie* [Science and Orthodoxy]. M.: Mosk.
      rabochii, 1984. 93 pp. (Besedy o religii).

1865 Ivanenko, S.I. *Nauchnoe znanie i krizis pravoslaviia* [Scientific Knowledge
      and Crisis of Orthodoxy]. M.: Znanie RSFSR. Sektsiia propagandy nauch.
      -ateist. znanii, 1988. 45 pp. Bibl.: p. 44.

1866 Ivanenko, S.I. *Progress nauki i sovremennoe pravoslavie* [Science's Progress
      and Contemporary Orthodoxy]. M.: Znanie, 1988. 63 pp. Bibl.: p. 62.

1867 Ivanenko, S.I.; Pushnenkova, N.K. "Ateisticheskaia rabota v sel'skom raione"
      [Atheistic Work in Rural Region]. *Aktual'nye problemy nauchno-ateisti-
      cheskogo vospitaniia molodezhi.* M., 1987. Pp. 82-86.

1868 *Ivano-Frankovskii muzei istorii religii i ateizma* [Ivan-Franko's Museum of History of Religion and Atheism]. N.G. Povkh et al. Uzhgorod: Karpati, 1982. 79 pp., illus. In Ukrainian and Russian.

1869 Ivanov, A.T. "Religioznost' kak forma sub'ektivnosti" [Religiosity as a Form of Subjectivity]. *Dukhovnyi mir sovremennogo cheloveka.* M., 1987. Pp. 125-127.

1870 Ivanov, B.V.; Grusman, V.M. *Rol' sovetskoi obriadnosti v ateisticheskom vospitanii molodezhi].* [The role of Soviet Ceremonial in Atheistic Upbringing of Youth]. L.: Znanie RSFSR, 1985. 15 pp. (V pomoshch' lektoru / O-vo "Znanie" RSFSR, Leningr. org.).

1871 Ivanov, I. "Tenrike" [Tenri-kyo]. *Nauka i religiia* 1 (1981): 81-62.

1872 Ivanov, N. "Sotsial'nye aspekty traditsionnogo islama" [Social Aspects of Traditional Islam]. *Aziia i Afrika segodnia* 3 (1982): 7-10.

1873 Ivanov, V.V. "Farisei ili sviatoi?" [Pharisee or a Saint?]. *Pravoslavie v Karelii.* Petrozavodsk, 1987. Pp. 85-96.

1874 Ivanov, Viach. Vs. "Antichnoe pereosmyslenie arkhaicheskikh mifov" [Ancient Reinterpretation of Archaic Myths]. *Zhizn' mifa v antichnosti.* M., 1988. Ch. I. Pp. 9-26.

1875 Ivanova, I.I. "Islamskaia revoliutsiia v Irane i protsess islamizatsii v Turtsii" [Islamic Revolution in Iran and Process of Islamisation in Turkey]. *III Vsesoiuuznaia konferentsiia vostokovedov "Vzaimodeistvie i vzaimovliianie tsivilizatsii kul'tur na Vostoke".* M., 1988. T. 2. Pp. 102-104.

1876 Ivanova, I.I. "Rol' Turtsii v musul'manskom mire i politika Zapada" [Turkey's Role in Moslem World and Politics of the West]. *"Islamskii faktor" v mezhdunarodnykh otnosheniiakh v Azii (70-e - pervaia polovina 80-kh gg.).* M., 1987. Pp. 141-147.

1877 Ivanova, O.V. "Konferentsiia 'Vvedenie khristianstva u narodov Tsentral'noi i Vostochnoi Evropy. Kreshchenie Rusi'" [Conference on "Introduction of Christianity by the Peoples of Central and Eastern Europe. Baptism of Rus']. *Sov. slavianovedenie* 6 (1987): 121-123.

1878 Ivashchenko, Iu.F. "K spetsifike religioznykh predstavlenii naseleniia Bosfora v rannevizantiiskoe vremia" [Specifics of Religious Notions of the

Population of Bosphorus in Early Byzantine Times]. *Problemy issledovanii antichnykh gorodov*. M., 1989. Pp. 51-52.

1879   Ivonin, Iu.M. *Khristianstvo v Udmurtii: Istoriia i sovremennost'* [Christianity in Udmurt: History and Contemporaneity]. Ustinov: Udmurtiia, 1987. 114 pp. Annot bibl.: pp. 107-113.

1880   *Iz istorii formirovaniia i razvitiia svobodomysliia v dorevoliutsionnoi Tatarii* [History of Forming and Development of Free-Thinking in Prerevolutionary Tatar]. [Ed.: R.M. Amirkhanov]. Kazan': IIaLI, 1987. 121 pp.

1881   *Iz istorii religii i ateizma v Estonii* [History of Religion and Atheism in Estonia]. Tallin: Eesti raamat. In Estonian. Vyp. 3. [Comp.: Iu. Kivimiae]. 1987. 302 pp. Summaries of articles in Russian and German. Name and subject index: pp. 285-301.

1882   *Iz istorii religii i ateizma v Gruzii* [History of Religion and Atheism in Georgia]. Formerly *Voprosy istorii i ateizma v Gruzii*. See item 4718.

1883   *Iz opyta ateisticheskogo vospitaniia* [Experience of Atheistic Education]. [Ed.: V.B. Tsybikzhapov]. Ulan-Ude: Buriat. kn. izd-vo, 1983. 49 pp.

1884   *Iz opyta nauchno-ateisticheskoi raboty v Moskovskoi oblasti* [Experience of Scientific-Atheistic Work in Moskow's Oblast]. [Prepared by E.A. Durmanova]. M.: Znanie, 1985. 22 pp. (V pomoshch' propagandistu i organizatoru ateist. raboty / Vsesoiuz. o-vo "Znanie", Tsentr. Dom nauch. ateizma). Bibl.: pp. 21-22.

1885   *Iz opyta raboty Samarkandskogo oblastnogo Doma nauchnogo ateizma* [Work Experience of the House of Scientific Atheism of the Samarcand Oblast]. M.: Znanie, 1985. 15 pp. (V pomoshch' propagandistu i organizatoru ateist. raboty / Vsesoiuz. o-vo "Znanie", Tsentr. Dom nauch. ateizma).

1886   *Iz plena lozhnykh predstavlenii* [From Captivity of False Notions]. Ed.: F.S. Manasypov. Kazan': Tatar. kn. idz-vo, 1986. 127 pp.

1887   Izimbetov, T. *Ateizm, religiia i sotsial'naia zhizn'* [Atheism, Religion and Social Life]. Nukus: Karakalpakstan, 1981. 331 pp. In Karakalpak.

1888 Izimbetov, T. *Genezis i evoliutsiia islama* [Genesis and Evolution of Islam]. Nukus: Karakalpakstan, 1985. 215 pp., illus. In Karakalpak. Annot. bibl.: pp. 202-213.

1889 Izimbetov, T. "Islam i natsional'nye traditsii, obriady i obychai" [Islam and National Traditions, Rituals and Customs]. *Kommunist Uzbekistana* 9 (1984): 70-76.

1890 Izimbetov, T. *Modernizatsiia islama pri kapitalizme* [Modernization of Islam under Capitalism]. Nukus: Karakalpakstan, 1987. 167 pp. In Karakalpak. Annot. Bibl.: pp. 159-166.

1891 Izimbetov, T. *Prichiny i sushchnost' modernizatsii islama pri sotsializme* [The Motives and Essence of Modernization of Islam under Socialism]. Nukus: Karakalpakstan, 1988. 231 pp. In Karakalpak. Bibl.: pp. 218-229.

1892 *Izuchenie materialov XXVII s'ezda KPSS v kurse osnov nauchnogo ateizma* [Study the Materials of XXVIIth Congress of the CPSU in the Course of Fundamentals of Scientific Atheism]. [V.K. Tancher et al]. Kiev: Vishcha shk. Izd-vo pri Kiev. gos. un- te, 1987. 54 pp. (XXVII s'ezd KPSS). (V pomoshch' prepodavateliu obshchestv. nauk). Bibl.: pp. 52-53.

1893 *K mysliam i chuvstvam: Ateist. vospitanie: opyt, problemy, razmyshleniia* [Towards Thoughts and Feelings: Atheistic Education, Experience, Problems, Reflections]. [Comp.: T.N. Andreeva]. L.: Lenizdat, 1988. 137 pp.

1894 *K zhizni, k svetu* [Towards Life, Towards Light]. [Comp.: Ia. Nemesh]. Uzhgorod: Karpati, 1983. 70 pp. In Hungarian.

1895 Kabanov, A.M. "Chan'skii ritual" [Ch'an Ritual]. *Etika v traditsionnom Kitae.* M., 1988. Pp. 236-255. Bibl.: pp. 254-255.

1896 Kabanov, A.M. "Eisai - rodonachal'nik dzen v Iaponii" [Eisai - ancestor of Zen in Japan]. *Pis'mennye pamiatniki i problemy istorii kul'tury narodov Vostoka: XV godich. nauch. sessiia LO IV AN SSSR.* M., 1981. Ch. I(I). Pp. 93-98.

1897 Kabanov, A.M. "Formirovanie sistemy 'godzan' ('piati monastyrei') i biurokratizatsiia dzen-buddizma" [Forming of the system of "Gozan" ("Five Monasteries") and Zen-Buddhism's Bureaucratisation]. *Buddizm i gosudarstvo na Dal'nem Vostoke.* M., 1987. Pp. 180-203.

1898 Kabanov, A.M. "Kul't bozhestva Vinaiaki v kitaiskom buddizme" [Deity's Vinayaka Cult in Chinese Buddhism]. *Deviatnadtsataia nauchnaia konferentsiia "Obshchestvo i gosudarstvo v Kitae"*. M., 1988. Ch. I. Pp. 168-173. Bibl.: pp. 172-173.

1899 Kabo, V.R. "Pervonachal'nye formy religii" [Primary Forms of Religion]. *Religii mira, 1986.* M., 1987. Pp. 136-154.

1900 Kabo, V.R. "Sovremennaia amerikanskaia etnografiia i proiskhozhdenie religii" [Contemporary American Ethnography and the Origin of Religion]. *Etnologiia v SShA i Kanade.* M., 1989. Pp. 258-271.

1901 Kadanchik, G.E. "Razvitie nauchno-ateisticheskoi mysli v Belorussii (1946-1976 gody)" [Development of Scientific-Atheistic Thought in Belorussia (1946-1976)]. *Nauch. ateizm i ateist. vospitanie* 1 (1983): 138-149.

1902 Kaigorodova, G.A. *Doiti do kazhdogo* [To Reach Everyone]. Alma-Ata: Kazakhstan, 1986. 56 pp.

1903 Kairis, Iu. *Posledniaia 'Ave Mariia'* [The Last "Ave Maria"]. Vil'nius: Mintis, 1988. 151 pp., illus. (Besedy s veruiushchimi). In Lithuanian.

1904 Kaiumov, A.P. *Epokha i obriady* [The Epoch and Rituals]. Tashkent: Uzbekistan, 1986. 22 pp. (B-ka ateista). In Uzbek.

1905 *Kak byla kreshchena Rus'* [How Rus' was Baptized]. M.: Politizdat, 1988. 383 pp. Publ. also as 2nd ed., 1989, 320 pp. Suppl.: Narodnyi Prirodnyi calendar'. For review see item 5083.

1906 *Kak prekrasen etot mir, posmotri:* Rasskazy liudei, v proshlom veruiushchikh, o tom, kak oni obreli materialist. mirovozzrenie, stali aktivnymi uchastnikami kom. str-va [Look, How Beautiful This World Is: Stories of People, Formerly Believers, as how they Found Materialistic Outlook, Become Active Participants of Building of Communism]. [Comp.: V.L. Novoselov]. Donetsk: Donbass, 1980. 108 pp.

1907 Kakhk, Iu. "Khristianstvo, nauka i protsessy nad ved'mami v XVII veke" [Christianity, Science and Witch-hunt in XVIIth Century]. *Religiooni ja ateismi ajaloost eestis* 3 (1987): 145-171. In Estonian. Summary in Russian, pp. 259-261.

1908 "Kakim byt' zakonu o svobode sovesti?" [How the Law of Freedom of Conscience Should be]. *Nauka i religiia* 2 (1989): 6-8.

1909 Kalachev, B.F.; Poliakov, S.P. "Bytovoi islam" [Everyday Islam]. *Molodoi kommunist* 2 (1989): 31-38.

1910 Kalaganov, A.[N]. "Pozitivnoe i negativnoe v ateisticheskoi propagande" [Positive and Negative in Atheistic Propaganda]. *Kommunist Tatarii* 5 (1988): 53-60.

1911 Kalaganov, A.N. "O sovershenstvovanii raboty s propagandistami ateizma" [Perfection of the Work with Propagandists of Atheism]. *Vopr. nauh. ateizma* 29 (1982): 43-54.

1912 Kalashnikov, M.F. "Ideal: Sushchnost', struktura, funktsii" [Ideal: Essence, Structure, Functions]. *Nauchnyi ateizm: ideal i mirovozzrenie.* Perm', 1988. Pp. 5-20.

1913 Kalashnikov, M.F. "Razvitie massovogo ateizma v SSSR" [Development of Mass Atheism in USSR]. *Problemy istorii religii i ateizma.* Cheboksary, 1980. Pp. 64-68.

1914 Kalashnikov, M.F.; Kurochkin, P.K. *Formirovanie nauchno-materialisticheskogo mirovozzreniia molodezhi* [Forming Youth's Scientific-Materialistic World Outlook]. M.: Znanie, 1981. 64 pp. (Novoe v zhizni, nauke, tekhnike. Ser. "Nauch. ateizm"; No 9). Bibl.: p. 63.

1915 Kalashnikov, V.L. *O religii i natsional'nykh otnosheniiakh:* Vopr. i otvety [Religion and National Relations: Questions and Answers]. M.: Znanie RSFSR. Sektsiia propagandy nauch. ateizma, 1989. 46 pp. Bibl.: pp. 44-45.

1916 Kalbi Khisham ibn Mukhammad, al. *Kniga ob idolakh* [The Book on Idols]. Transl. from Arabic, introduction and remarks by Vl.V. Polosina. M.: Nauka, 1984. 64 pp. (Pamiatniki pis'mennosti Vostoka; 68). Sumamry in English. Bibl.: pp. 52-55. Annot. bibl.: pp. 40-50.

1917 *Kalendar' ateista* [Atheist's Calendar]. Comp.: V.A. Zots. Kiev: Politizdat Ukrainy, 1982. 398 pp., illus. In Ukrainian.

1918 Kalinicheva, Z.V. *Ateizm kak faktor formirovaniia kommunisticheskoi lichnosti* [Atheism as Formation Factor of Communist Personality]. L.: Znanie

RSFSR. Leningr. org., 1982. 16 pp. (V pomoshch' lektoru / O-vo "Znanie" RSFSR, Leningr. org.).

1919   Kalinicheva, Z.V. *"Kristal nebes mne ne pregrada dole..."* [Crystal of Heaven is No More an Obstacle for Me]. L.: Lenizdat, 1986. 191 pp., illus.

1920   Kalinicheva, Z.V. *Politika i religiia* [Politics and Religion]. L.: Znanie RSFSR, 1984. 32 pp. (V pomoshch' lektoru / O-vo "Znanie" RSFSR, Leningr. org.). Bibl.: p. 32.

1921   Kalinin, Iu.A. *Kritika filosofsko-idealisticheskikh osnov sovremennogo pravoslaviia* [Criticism of Philosophical-Idealistic Fundamentals of Contemporary Orthodoxy]. Kiev: Vishcha shk. Izd-vo pri Kiev. gos. un-te, 1987. 130 pp. (Ateist. b-ka studenta).

1922   Kalinin, Iu.A. "Kritika filosofskogo obosnovaniia mirovozzrencheskikh osnov pravoslaviia" [Criticism of Philosophical Basis of World Outlook Fundamentals of Orthodoxy]. *Vopr. ateizma* 22 (1986): 58-64.

1923   Kalinin, Iu.A. "Kritika idealisticheskoi apologii v sovremennom russkom pravoslavii" [Criticism of Idealistic Apologia in Contemporary Russsian Othodoxy]. *Vopr. ateizma* 20 (1984): 106-113.

1924   Kalinin, Iu.A. *Kritka religiozno-idealisticheskoi kartiny mira* [Criticism of Religious-Idealistic World's Image]. Kiev: Vishcha shk. Izd-vo pri Kiev. un-te, 1982. 55 pp. (Ateist. b-ka studenta). Bibl.: pp. 51-54.

1925   Kalinin, Iu.A. *Modernizatsiia ideologii sovremennogo russkogo pravoslaviia* [Modernization of Ideology of Contemporary Russian Orthodoxy]. Kiev: Znanie UkSSR, 1983. 47 pp. (Ser. 5 "Nauchno-ateisticheskaia" / O-vo "Znanie" UkSSR; No 4). In Ukrainian. Bibl.: pp. 45-47.

1926   Kalinin, Iu.A. *Modernizm russkogo pravoslaviia* [Modernism of Russian Orthodoxy]. Kiev: Politizdat Ukrainy, 1988. 77 pp. Annot. bibl.: pp. 73-76.

1927   Kalinin, Iu.A. "Osobennosti modernistskikh tendentsii v ideologii sovrmennogo pravoslaviia" [Peculiarities of Modernist Tendentiousness in Ideology of Contemporary Orthodoxy]. *Vopr. ateizma* 17 (1981): 130-136.

1928   Kalinin, Iu.A.; Karasevich, A.A. "Preodolenie religioznykh perezhitkov-vazhnyi faktor stanovleniia sovetskoi obriadnosti" [Overcoming of Religious

Survivals - Important Factor of Coming into Being of Soviet Ceremonial]. *Vopr. ateizma* 21 (1985): 54-59.

1929 Kalinin, Iu.A., Marchenko, A.V. "Znachenie kritiki neokhristianstva dlia praktiki ateisticheskogo vospitaniia" [Importance of Criticism of Neochristianity for the Practice of Atheistic Work]. *Vopr. ateizma* 23 (1987): 105-112.

1930 Kalinin, Iu.A.; Novokhatskaia, L.P. "Nekotorye voprosy ateisticheskogo vospitaniia v usloviiakh sovershenstvovaniia sotsialisticheskogo oobshchestva" [Some Problems of Atheistic Education under Conditions of Perfection of Socialist Society]. *Vopr. nauch. kommunizma* 69 (1987): 69-74.

1931 Kalinin, Iu.A.; Saukh, P.Iu. "Nesostoiatel'nost' religiozno-idealisticheskikh traktovok gumanizma" [Groundlessness of Religious-Idealistic Interpretations of Humanism]. *Probl. filosofii* 53 (1981): 129-135.

1932 Kalinin, V.N. *Sovetskoe zakonodatel'stvo o svobode sovesti i religioznykh organizatsiiakh* [Soviet Legislation on Freedom of Worship and Religious Organizations]. M.: Znanie, 1989. 63 pp. (Novoe v zhizni, nauke tekhnike. Ser.: Nauch. ateizma; 1989, 1).

1933 Kalmykov, I.Kh. "Narodnaia meditsina i religiia u adygov" [Popular Medicine and Religion by Adygeis]. *Voprosy arkheologii i traditsionnoi etnografii Karachaevo-Cherkesii.* Cherkessk, 1987. Pp. 129-141.

1934 Kalmykov, I.Kh. "Sledy religioznykh vozzrenii v kalendarnoi sisteme adygov" [Traces of Religious Outlooks in Adygeis Calendar System]. *Problemy ateisticheskogo vospitaniia v usloviiakh Karachaevo-Chekesii.* Cherkessk, 1979. Pp. 96-103.

1935 Kalmykov, S.K. "Neomisticheskie kul'ty i ideologicheskaia bor'ba" [Neomystical Cults and Ideological Struggle]. *Voprosy teorii i praktiki nauchnogo ateizma.* M., 1988. Pp. 119-138.

1936 Kamalov, T.R. "Sotsial'naia rol' religii v kontekste obshchestvenno-politicheskikh vzgliadov F. Amirkhana kak proiavlenie svobodomysliia" [Social Role of Religion in the Context of F. Amirhan's Socio-Political Views as Manifestation of Free Thinking]. *Iz istorii formirovaniia i razvitiia svobodomysliia v dorevoliutsionnoi Tatarii.* Kazan', 1987. Pp. 91-96.

1937   Kameisha, B.I. "K istorii religioznogo sektantstva v Zapadnoi Belorussii" [History of Religious Sectarianism in Western Belorussia]. *Nauch. ateizm i ateist. vospitanie* 1 (1983): 127-1137.

1938   Kamilov, Ch. *Nekotorye voprosy organizatsii ateisticheskogo vospitaniia* [Some Problems of Organization of Atheistic Education]. Dushanbe: Irfon, 1983. 62 pp. In Tajik. Bibl.: pp. 61-62.

1939   Kandareli, T.R. "Problema ateizma v filosofii Dzh. Santaiany" [The Problem of Atheism in G. Santayana's Philosophy]. *Soobshch. AN GSSR* T. 131. 3 (1988): 633-636. Summaries in English and Georgian.

1940   Kant, I. *Religiia v predelakh tol'ko razuma* [Religion within the Limits of Pure Reason Only]. Tbilisi: Ganatleba, 1989. 246 pp. (Vydaiushcheisia liudi o religii i ateizme). In Georgian. Annot. bibl.: pp. 231-238. Index: pp. 239-244.

1941   Kanterov, I.Ia. "Katolitsizm: novye formy bor'by s ateizmom" [Catholicism: New Forms of Struggle with Atheism]. *Vopr. nauch. ateizma* 34 (1986): 60-78.

1942   Kanterov, I.Ia. *Klerikalizm-ideologiia dukhovnogo nasiliia* [Clericalism-Ideology of Spiritual Coercion]. M.: Pedagogika, 1986. 190 pp., illus. (Imperializm: Sobytiia, fakty, dokumenty). Bibl.: pp. 187-189.

1943   Kanterov, I.Ia. *Klerikalizm segodniia* [Clericalism Today]. M.: Znanie, 1988. 64 pp. 1988. (Novoe v zhizni, nauke, tekhnike. Nauch. ateizm; No 6). Bibl.: pp. 63-64.

1944   Kanterov, I.Ia. *Kriticheskii analiz klerikal'nykh fal'sifikatsii nauchnogo ateizma* [Critical Analysis of Clerical Falsifications of Scientific Atheism]. M.: Znanie, 1983. 64 pp. (Novoe v zhizni, nauke, tekhnike. Nauch. ateizm; 1).

1945   Kanterov, I.Ia. "Poslesobornyi katolitsizm i ateizm" [Postsynod Catholicism and Atheism]. *Vopr. nauch. ateizma* 28 (1981): 71-88.

1946   Kanterov, I.[Ia].; Skibitskii, M. "Vse li iasno v 'dele Galileia'?" [Is Everything Clear in "The Case of Galileo"?]. *Nauka i religiia* 5 (1982): 25-30; 6 (1982): 39-40.

1947 Kapitonov, K. "S Koranom - v bol'shuiu politiku" [With Koran - Into Great Politics]. *Novoe vremia* 2 (1989): 20-22.

1948 Kapranov, V.A. *Illiuzii khristianskogo gumanizma* [Illusions of Christian Humanism]. L.: Znanie RSFSR, 1983. 19 pp. (V pomoshch' lektoru / O-vo "Znanie" RSFSR, Leningr. org.). Bobl.: pp. 18-19.

1949 Kapranov, V.A. *Nravstvennoe soderzhanie nauchnogo ateizma* [Moral Content of Scientific Atheism]. L.: Znanie RSFSR. Leningr. org., 1989. 19 pp.

1950 Kapranov, V.A. "Real'nye istoki religioznogo ideala" [Real Sources of Religious Ideal]. *Nauchnyi ateizm: ideal i mirovozzrenie.* Perm', 1988. Pp. 139-147.

1951 Kapto, A.S. "Nravstvennyi potentsial ateisticheskogo vospitaniia" [The Moral Potential of Atheistic Education]. *Vopr. nauch. ateizma* 32 (1985): 15-34.

1952 Kapto, A.[S]. "S pozitsii ateizma" [From the Position of Atheism]. *Sovety nar. deputatov* 12 (1984): 21-28.

1953 Kapustin, B.G. "Osnovnye napravleniia istoricheskoi evoliutsii sotsial'nykh islamskikh uchenii" [Basic Directions of Historical Evolution of Islam's Social Teachings]. *Islam: problemy ideologii, prava, politiki i ekonomiki.* M., 1985. Pp. 26-44. Bibl.: pp. 41-44.

1954 Kapustin, B.[G]. "Sotsial'noe uchenie islama: kontseptsii i deistvitel'nost'" [Islam's Social Teaching: Conceptions and Reality]. *Pamir* 7 (1982): 69-74.

1955 Kapustin, N.S. *Osobennosti evoliutsii religii* [Peculiarities of Religion's Evolution]. M.: Mysl', 1984. 222 pp. Annot. bibl.: pp. 206-221. For reviews see items 5084-5085.

1956 Kapustin, N.S. "Spetsifika religioznogo sinkretizma" [Specific Character of Religious Syncretism]. *Izv. Sev.-Kavk. nauch. tsentra vyssh. shkoly. Obshchestv. nauki* 1 (1988): 93-101.

1957 Kapustina, M.I. "Kritika kontseptsii pravoslaviia kak osnovy russkoi kul'tury" [Criticism of Conception of Orthodoxy as Foundations of Russian Culture]. *Russkoe pravoslavie i ateizm v otechestvennoi istorii.* L., 1988. Pp. 69-80.

1958 Kara-Murza, A.A. "U istokov sovremennoi afro-khristianskoi kul'tury v Ekvatorial'noi Afrike" [By Sources of the Contemporary Afro-Christian Culture in Equatorial Africa]. *Narody Azii i Afriki* 6 (1988): 39-48.

1959 Karachaily, I. *Voprosy ateisticheskoi raboty i bor'by s perezhitkami* [Problems of Atheistic Work and Struggle with Survivals]. Cherkessk: Stavrop. kn. izd-vo. Karachaevo-Cherkes. otd-nie, 1984. 174 pp., port. Includes list of authors' works, pp. 164-173.

1960 Karagodin, A.I. "Kalmytskoe dukhovenstvo v XVII-pervoi polovine XIX vv." [Kalmyk Clergy in XVIIth-Early XIXth C.]. *Voprosy istorii lamaizma v Kalmykii.* Elista, 1987. Pp. 5-23.

1961 Karaianu, I. "Sredi 'bozh'ikh detei'" [Among "God's Children"]. *Nauka i religiia* 3 (1983): 40-43; 4 (1983): 41-43.

1962 Karamyshev, Kh.G. *Ateisticheskoe vospitanie:* opyt, problemy [Atheistic Education: Experience, Problems]. Ufa: Bashk. kn. izd-vo, 1984. 113 pp., illus. In Bashkir.

1963 Karamysheva, N. "V tiskakh khanzhestva i litsemeriia" [In the Clutches of Hypocrisy and Dissimulation]. *Nauka i religiia* 2 (1981): 57-59.

1964 Karasevich, A.A. "Ateisticheskaia napravlennost' sotsialisticheskikh obriadov" [Atheistic Trends of Socialist Ceremonials]. *Dukhovnye tsennosti kak predmet filosofskogo analiza.* M., 19885. Pp. 109-113.

1965 Kargaldaev, T. *Internatsionalizm i ateizm* [Internationalism and Atheism]. Frunze: Kyrgyzstan, 1985. 72 pp. (B-chka ateista. BA). In Kirghiz.

1966 Kar'iakhiarm, T. "Voprosy tserkovnoi reformy v Pribaltike (nachalo XX veka 1916 god)" [Problems of Church Reform in Baltic Region (Early XXth Century-1916)]. *Religiooni ja ateismi ajaloost eestis.* 3 (1987): 221-249. In Estonian. Summary in Russian, pp. 264-266.

1967 Karimov, A. "Osobennosti ateisticheskogo vospitaniia v usloviiakh moderni-zatsii islama" [Peculiarities of Atheistic Education under Conditions of Modernization of Islam]. *Vopr. ateizma* 23 (1987): 62-67.

1968 Karimov, D.; Tsoi, G. "Ateisticheskoe vospitanie - eto prezhde vsego zabota o cheloveke" [Atheistic Education - First of All Means Concern for Man's Welfare]. *Kommunist Uzbekistana* 7 (1988): 61-68.

1969 Karimov, D.; Tsoi, G. "Po novomu stroit' ateisticheskuiu rabotu" [Construct Atheistic Work by New Methods]. *Kommunist Uzbekistana* 3 (1989): 32-38.

1970 Karimov, I. *Sredstva ateisticheskogo vospitaniia* [Means of Atheistic Education]. Tashkent: Uzbekistan, 1984. 32 pp. (Vopr. kom. morali; No 5). In Uzbek.

1971 Karimskii, A.M. *Teologiia istorii i real'nost': k kritike protestantskoi eskhatalogii* [Theology of History and Reality: Critique of Protestant Eschatology]. M.: Znanie, 1985. 64 pp. (Novoe v zhizni, nauke, tekhnike. Nauch. ateizm; 10). Bibl.: p. 63.

1972 Karly, D.D. *Islam-ideologiia klassovogo obshchestva* [Islam-Ideology of Class Society]. Ashkhabad: Znanie TSSR, 1980. 23 pp. (V pomoshch' lektoru / O-vo "Znanie" TSSR). Bibl.: p. 22.

1973 Karly, D.D. *Vliianie sotsialisticheskoi dukhovnoi kul'tury na ateisticheskoe vospitanie molodezhi* [Influence of Socialist Spiritual Culture on Youth's Atheistic Upbringing]. Ashkhabad: Znanie TSSR, 1982. 25 pp. (V pomoshch' lektoru / O-vo "Znanie" TSSR). Bibl.: pp. 24-25.

1974 Karmysheva, B.Kh. "K voprosu o kul'tovom znachenii konnykh igr v Srednei Azii" [On the Problem of Religious Importance of Horses Games in Middle Asia]. *Proshloe Srednei Azii*. Dushanbe, 1987. Pp. 231-242.

1975 Karpov, N.B. *Ateisticheskie i antiklerikal'nye idei v tvorchestve G.I. Uspenskogo* [Atheistic and Anticlerical Ideas in G.I. Uspenskii's Works]. Tula: Priok. kn. iz-vo, 1982. 89 pp., port. Bibl.: pp. 87-88. Annot. bibl.: pp. 84-86. For review see item 5087.

1976 Karpovich, N.M. *Induizm v Nepale: traditsii i sinkretizm* [Hinduism in Nepal: Traditions and Syncretism]. M.: Nauka, 1986. 11 pp. Bibl.: pp. 10-11. (Paper at 32nd International Congress on Asiatic and North African Researches-Hamburg, 1986). In English.

1977 Karpovskii, E.M. *My - ateisty: Sov. obraz zhizni i religiia* [We - Atheists: Soviet Way of Life and Religion]. Gor'kii: Volgo-Viat. kn. izd-vo, 1983. 127 pp. Annot. bibl.: pp. 121-126.

1978 Kartsev, E.F.; Nekrasov, S.M. "Rol' vneauditornykh form raboty v ateisticheskom vospitanii studentov" [Role of Extra Auditorium Working

Forms in Atheistic Education of Students]. *Aktual. vopr. metodiki prepodavaniia obshchestv. nauk i kom. vospitaniia studentov* 5 (1987): 133-136.

1979 Kasatkin, S. "Gotovias' k besede" [Preparing for a Talk]. *Agitator* 5 (1982): 59-60.

1980 Kasavin, I.T. "Shaman i ego praktika" [Shaman and His Practice]. *Priroda* 11 (1988): 78-85.

1981 Kashinskaia, L.V. "Ateisticheskaia propaganda v molodezhnoi pechati: problemy, poiski, resheniia" [Atheistic Propaganda in Youth Press: Problems, Quests, Decisions]. *Aktual'nye problemy molodezhnoi pechati.* M., 1988. Pp. 65-84.

1982 Kashuba, M.V. *Antikommunizm sovremennogo uniatstva* [Anti-Communism of the Contemporary Uniate Church]. Kiev: Znanie UkSSR, 1981. 48 pp. In Ukrainian. Bibl.: p. 47.

1983 Kashuba, M.V. "Istolkovanie otechestvennoi istorii deiateliami Kievo-Mogilianskoi akademii v bor'be protiv unii" [Interpretation of Fatherland History by Members of Kiev-Moghilian Academy in the Struggle against Uniate Church]. *Chelovek i istoriia v srednevekovoi filosofskoi mysli russkogo, ukrainskogo i belorusskogo narodov.* Kiev, 1987. Pp. 140-147.

1984 Kasperavichius, M. "Khristianskie demony Nila" [Christian Demons of the Nile]. *Nauka i religiia* 1 (1981): 38-39.

1985 Kasperavichius, M. "Religioznaia simvolika drevnego mira i khristianstvo" [Religious Symbolism of the Ancient World and Christianity]. *Nauchno-ateisticheskie issledovaniia v muzeiiakh.* L., 1988. Pp. 71-87.

1986 Kassirskii, I.A. "Vospominaniia o professore V.F. Voino-Iasenetskom" [Reminiscences on Professor V.F. Voino-Iasenetskii]. *Nauka i Religiia* 5 (1989): 76-89, port.

1987 Kasymov, P. "Meditsinskaia nauka protiv religioznykh predrassudkov" [Medical Science against Religious Prejudices]. *Med. zhurn. Uzbekistana* 4 (1986): 7-9.

1988 Kasymov, S.K. *Religiia - vrag zdorov'ia* [Religion - Enemy of Health]. Tashkent: Meditsina UzSSR, 1988. 31 pp. In Uzbek.

1989 Kataev, A.A. "Edinstvo i vzaimosviaz' idealov v ateisticheskom i interna-tsional'nom vospitanii" [Unity and Intercommunication of Ideals in Atheistic and International Education]. *Nauchnyi ateizm: ideal i mirovo-zzrenie.* Perm', 1988. Pp. 129-139.

1990 Kataev, A.A. "Religiia kak prevrashchennaia forma kul'tury" [Religion as a Converted Form of Culture]. *Izv. Sev.-Kavk. nauch. tsentra vyssh. shk.* Obshchestv. nauki 1 (1983): 60-62.

1991 Katamidze, V.I. *Vstrechi v Baku:* Islam. forum glazami zhurnalista [Meetings in Baku: Islamic Forum in Journalist's Eyes]. Transl. from Russian. M.: Novosti, 1987. 63 pp., illus. In English and Turkish.
Published also in 1988 in Arabic, Persian and Pushtu.

1992 *Katolicheskaia filosofiia segodnia* [Catholic Philosophy Today]. Ed.: E.V. Demenchonok. M.: IFAN, 1985. 142 pp.

1993 *Katolicheskaia tserkov' v Litve v 1917-1940 gg.* [Catholic Church in Lithuania in 1917-1940]. Collection of Documents. Vil'nius: Mintis, 1986. 259 pp. In English.

1994 *Katolicheskaia tserkov' v PNR v 80-kh godakh* [Catholic Church in Polish People's Republic in the 80s]. [Ed.: L.N. Velikovich et al.]. M.: AON, 1988. 225 pp.

1995 "Katolichestvo i Rus': Papskie poslaniia rus. kniaz'iam i dukhovenstvu Pribaltiki v XIII v." [Catholicism and Rus': Papal Epistles to Russian Princes and Clergy of the Baltics in XIIIth C.]. Transl. from Latin and commentaries by N. Daragan. *Nauka i religiia* 6 (1988): 38-41.

1996 *Katolitsizm i sovremennaia ideologicheskaia bor'ba* [Catholicism and Contemporary Ideological Struggle]. [Comp.: V. Kuzmitskas]. Vil'nius: Mintis, 1988. 183 pp. In Lithuanian.

1997 *Katolitsizm i svobodomyslie v Latinskoi Amerike v XVI-XXvv.* (Dokumenty i materialy) [Catholicism and Free Thinking in Latin America in XVIth-XXth Centuries. (Documents and Materials)]. [Ed.: I.R. Grigulevich]. M.,: Nauka, 1980. 296 pp. Bibl. at the end of articles. Name index: pp. 291-292. For review see item 5088.

1998 *Katolitsizm v Belorussii: traditsionalizm i prisposoblenie* [Catholicism in Belorussia: Traditionalism and Adaptation]. Eds.: A.S. Maikhrovich; E.S.

Prokoshina. Minsk: Nauka i tekhnika, 1987. 240 pp. For reviews see items 5089-5090.

1999   Kauniatskis, I. *Prelat Ol'shauskas: Dokum. ocherk* [Prelate Ol'shauskas: A Documentary Essay]. 3rd ed. Vil'nius: Vega, 1984. 253 pp. In Lithuanian.

2000   Kaurkin, R.V. "'Bogokhul'nye' dela i razvitie klassovoi bor'by v Rossii v XVIII veke" ["Blasphemeous" Matters and Development of Class Struggle in Russia in XVIIIth Century]. *Ideologiia i kul'tura feodal'noi Rossii.* Gor'kii, 1988. Pp. 75-82. Bibl.: p. 82.

2001   Kaushanskii, P.L. *S pretenziei na istinu: O vzgliadakh i deiatel'nosti ekstremistov ot baptizma* [To Lay Claim on Truth: On Views and Activities of Baptist Extremists]. Odessa: Maiak, 1988. 247 pp. Annot. bibl.: pp. 238-246.

2002   Katsura, A. "Misticheskie kul'ty i ekologicheskii pessimizm" [Mystical Cults and Ecological Pessimism]. *Inostr. lit.* 6 (1985): 199-202.

2003   Kaurdakov, L.G.; Nagumanov, A.B. *Dolgoia doroga v tumane:* Reportazh iz baptist. obshchiny [Long Way in the Mist: Reporting from Baptist Community]. Novosibirsk: Kn. izd-vo, 1986. 168 pp.

2004   Kavaliauskas, Ch. "O krivom zerkale" [On Distorting Mirror]. *Nauka i religiia* 10 (1987): 39-40.

2005   Kavaliauskas, Ch. "Pochemu ia veruiu v Voskresenie Khristovo" [Why I Believe in Resurrection of Christ]. *Nauka i religiia* 1 (1989): 22-27.

2006   Kavun, V.V. *Internatsional'noe i ateisticheskoe vospitanie: tselenapravlennost' i effektivnost'* [International and Atheistic Education: Purposefulness and Effectiveness]. Kiev: Znanie UkSSR, 1983. 32 pp. (Ser. V "Nauchno-ateisticheskaia" / O-vo "Znanie" UkSSR; No 8). In Ukrainian. Bibl.: pp. 31-32. Annot. bibl.: pp. 30-31.

2007   Kazakova, N.A. "Nestiazhatel'stvo i eresi" [Ungreediness and heresies]. *Vopr. nauch. ateizma* 25 (1980): 62-79.

2008   Kazantseva, M.G. "Ob izuchenii muzykal'noi kul'tury staroobriadchestva na Urale" [Study of Musical Culture of Old Belief in Urals]. *Istoriografiia obshchestvennoi mysli dorevoliutsinnogo Urala.* Sverdlovsk, 1988. Pp. 98-102.

2009 Kazlauskene, P. *Kogda prisedaet chert* [When the Devil Squats]. Vil'nius: [S.n.], 1981. 263 pp., illus. In Lithuanian.

2010 Keiper, F.B.Ia. *Trudy po vediiskoi mifologii* [Works on Vedas Mythology]. Transl. from English. M.: Nauka, 1986. 196 pp. (Issled. po fol'kloru i mifologii Vostoka). For review see item 5091.

2011 Keniia, R.I. *Osobennosti dekorativnogo ubranstva okladov evangelii v Gruzii* [Peculiarities of Decorative Attire of Gospels Setting Frame in Georgia]. Tbilisi: Metsniereba, 1983. 16 pp. Annot. bibl.: pp. 14-16. Published also in English.

2012 Kenin-Lopsan, M.B. *Obriadovaia praktika i fol'klor tuvinskogo shamanstva, konets XIX-nach. XX v.* [Ceremonial Practice and Folklore of Tuva's Shamanism, Late XIXth-Early XXth]. Novosibirsk: Nauka. Sib. otd-nie, 1987. 164 pp. Annot. bibl.: pp. 152-159. For review see item 5092.

2013 Kerechanin, V.M. "O spetsifike individual'noi raboty sredi veruiushchikh-katolikov" [On the Specific Character of Individual Work among Believers-Catholics]. *Vopr. nauch. ateizma* 28 (1981): 238-244.

2014 Kerimov, G.M. "Aktivizatsiia islama v stranakh Blizhnego i Srednego Vostoka" [Activization of Islam in the Countries of Near and Middle East]. *Vopr. nauch. ateizma* 33 (1985): 265-274.

2015 Kerimov, G.M. *Islam i ego vliianie na obshchestvenno-politicheskuiu zhizn' narodov Blizhnego i Srednego Vostoka* [Islam and Its Influence on Socio-Political Life of the Peoples of Near and Middle East]. M.: Znanie, 1982. 63 pp. (Novoe v zhizni, nauke, tekhnike. Ser. "Nauch. ateizm"; 10). Bibl.: p. 62.

2016 Kerimov, G.[M]. "Kak islam otnositsia k iskusstvu?" [How Does Islam Regard Art?]. *Nauka i religiia* 4 (1980): 41-42.

2017 Kerimov, G.M. *Pozitsiia musul'manskogo dukhovenstva v sobytiiakh na Blizhnem i Srednem Vostoke* [The Position of Moslem Clergy in Near and Middle Eastern Events]. M.: Znanie, 1980. 12 pp. (V pomoshch' lektoru).

2018 Kerimov, G.M. "Problemy voiny i mira v islame" [Problems of War and Peace in Islam]. *Vopr. nauch. ateizma* 31 (1983): 148-162.

2019 Kerimov, G.M. *Shariat i ego sotsial'naia sushchnost'* [Sharia and Its Social Essence]. Baku: Azerneshr, 1987. 222 pp. In Azerbaijan. Bibl.: pp. 217-220.

2020 Kerimov, G.M. *Uchenie islama o gosudarstve i politike* [Islam's Teaching on State and Politics]. M.: Znanie, 1986. 63 pp. (Novoe v zhizni, nauke, tekhnike. Nauch. ateizm; 11/1986). Bibl.: p. 53.

2021 Kerimov, V. "A. Khomiakov protiv I. Kireevskogo" [Khomyakov against I. Kireyevsky]. *Nauka i religiia* 1 (1989): 12-14.

2022 Kerov, V.L. *Narodnye vosstaniia i ereticheskie dvizheniia vo Frantsii v kontse XIII-nachale XIV veka* [Popular Uprisings and Heretical Movements in France in the Late XIIIth-Early XIVth Centuries]. M.: Izd-vo Un-ta druzhby narodov, 1986. 136 pp., illus. Bibl.: pp. 118-134.

2023 Khachatrian, A.S. "O poniatii 'ideologiia tserkvi'" [On the Concept of "Ideology of the Church"]. *Dukhovnye tsennosti kak predmet filosofskogo analiza.* M., 1985. Pp. 113-116.

2024 Khchaturov, K.A. *'Eretiki' i inkvizitory* ["Heretics" and Inquisitors]. M.: Sov. Rossiia, 1988. 128 pp. (Po tu storonu). For reviews see items 5093-5095.

2025 Khachaturov, K.A. "Kto popiraet bibleiskie zapovedi?" [Who Tramples Upon Biblical Commandments?]. *Lat. Amerika* 6 (1988): 13-24.

2026 Khachaturov, K.[A]. "Miatezhnaia tserkov'" [Rebellious Church]. *Mezhdunar. zhizn'* 3 (1988): 73-80.

2027 Khachaturov, K.A. "Protestanty vmesto katolikov?" [Protestants Instead of Catholics?]. *Lat. Amerika* 10 (1987): 19-33.

2028 Khachaturova, K.I. "Ateisticheskie ubezhdeniia kak faktor formirovaniia mirovozzreniia lichnosti" [Atheistical Convictions as Forming Factor of Person's World Outlook]. *Aktual'nye problemy ateisticheskogo vospitaniia i kritika religioznoi ideologii.* M., 1981. Pp. 3-10.

2029 Khachaturova, K.I. "Znachenie ateisticheskikh ubezhdenii dlia preodoleniia mirovozzrencheskogo indifferentizma molodezhi" [The Importance of

Atheistic Convictions for Overcoming of Youth's Outlook of Indifferentism]. *Kritika religioznoi ideologii i problemy ateisticheskogo vospitaniia.* M., 1982. Pp. 3-10.

2030 Khaddur, I. "Islam i ego rol' v protsesse obshchestvennogo razvitiia" [Islam and Its Role in the Process of Social Development]. *Tsivilizatsiia: teoriia, istoriia i sovremennost'.* M., 1989. Pp. 89-104.

2031 Khadzhiev, Ia. *Utverzhdaia ateisticheskoe mirovozzrenie* [Acknowledging Atheistic World Outlook]. Ashkhabad: Turkmenistan, 1988. 208 pp. Annot. bibl.: pp. 199-207.

2032 Khaidarova, M.S. "Istoriia rasprostraneniia norm musul'manskogo prava v Srednei Azii" [History of the Dissemination of Norms of Moslem Law in Middle Asia]. *Izv. AN TadzhSSR.* Ser.: filosofiia, ekonomika, pravove-denie. Dushanbe. 4 (1988): 56-62. Summary in Tajik.

2033 Khaints, K. "O kharaktere religioznykh sistem pri dinastii Akhemenidov" [On the Nature of Religious Systems under Achaemenian Dynasty]. *Iz istorii drevnego mira i srednevekov'ia.* M., 1988. Pp. 31-44.

2034 Khakuashev, E.T. *Novoe vremia - novye obychai* [New Times-New Customs]. Nal'chik: El'brus, 1984. 158 pp. Published also as 2nd revised and enlarged ed., 1987. 169 pp.

2035 Khalidov, A.B. "Islam i arabskii iazyk" [Islam and Arabic]. *Islam: Religiia, obshchestvo , gosudarstvo* M., 1984. Pp. 69-75.

2036 Khalikova, E.A. *Musul'manskie nekropoli Volzhskoi Bulgarii X-nachala XIII v.* [Volga-Kama Bulgaria's Moslem Necropolis of the Xth-early XIIIth C.]. Kazan': Izd-vo Kazan. un-ta, 1986. 160 pp., illus.

2037 Khalilova, Kh. "Religioznost' zhenshchin-uzbechek i puti ee preodoleniia" [Religiosity of Uzbek-Women and Ways of Overcoming It]. *Problemy formirovaniia nauchno-ateisticheskogo mirovozzreniia v sotsialisticheskom obshchestve.* Samarkand, 1980. Pp. 37-41.

2038 Khalmirzaev, A. *Tsentr ateisticheskogo vospitaniia* [The Center of Atheistical Education]. Tashkent: Uzbekistan, 1980. 37 pp. (Ser. "Ku'tura"; No.7). In Uzbek.

2039   Khal'zov, V.I. "Vybor ob'ekta i osnovnye printsipy ateisticheskoi deiatel'nosti"
       [Choice of Object and Basic Principles of Atheistic Activity]. *Aktual'nye
       problemy obespecheniia effectivnosti nauchnoi ateisticheskoi raboty.*
       Cheboksary, 1986. Pp. 39-48.

2040   Khal'zov, V.I. "Vzaimodeistvie esteticheskoi i kul'tovoi funktsii ikon v
       religioznom komplekse" [Reciprocity of Aesthetical and Worship Functions
       of Icons in Religious Complex]. *Problemy istorii religii i ateizma.*
       Cheboksary, 1980. Pp. 31-37.

2041   Khamruni, S. "Osobennosti razvitiia svobodomysliia v arabskoi kul'ture
       VIII-IX vv." [Peculiarities of Freethinking Development in Arab Culture
       of the VIIIth-IXth Centuries]. *Dukhovnye tsennosti kak predmet filoso-
       fskogo analiza.* M., 1985. Pp. 133-138.

2042   Khanbabaev, K.M. "Nesostoiatel'nost' islamskoi kontseptsii svobody voli"
       [Groundlessness of Islamic Conception of Freedom of Will]. *Aktual'nye
       problemy kritiki religii i formirovaniia ateisticheskogo mirovozzreniia.*
       Makhachkala, 1982. Pp. 67-76.

2043   Kharakhorkin, L.R.; Krendeleva, L.A. *Ateizm i religiia v epokhu nauchno-
       tekhnicheskoi revoliutsii* [Atheism and Religion in the Epoch of Scientific-
       Technical Revolution]. L.: Znanie RSFSR. Leningr. org., 1988. 17 pp.

2044   Kharazov, V. "Al'bina, Iuozas i... bogoroditsa" [Albina, Joseph and... the
       Virgin]. *Nauka i religiia* 3 (1982): 24-27.

2045   Kharazov, V. "Chudesa v Grusheve" [Miracles in Grushka]. *Nauka i religiia*
       5 (1988): 21-24; 6 (1988): 46-49.

2046   Kharazov, V. "Delo o pravde i zakone" [The Matter of Truth and Law].
       Nauka i religiia 1 (1989): 6-10.

2047   Kharazov, V. "Zdes' i seichas..." [Here and Now...]. *Nauka i religiia* 6
       (1987): 26-29; 7 (1987): 16-20; 8 (1987): 24-28; 9 (1987): 42-44.

2048   Kharchev, K.M. "Garantii svobody" [The Guarantees of Freedom]. *Nauka i
       religiia* 11 (1987): 21-23.

2049   Kharchev, K.[M]. "Religiia, tserkov', veruiushchie" [Religion, Church,
       Believers]. *Agitator* 12 (1988): 37-40.

2050 Kharchev, K.M. "Sovest' svobodna" [Conscience is Free]. *Ogonek* 21 (1988): 26-28.

2051 Kharchev, K.[M]. "Sovetskoe gosudarstvo i tserkov'" [Soviet State and the Church]. *Religiia v SSSR* 10 (1987): KKh 1-KKh 6.

2052 Kharchev, K.[M]. "Svoboda sovesti i sovetskii zakon" [Freedom of Conscience and Soviet Law]. *Religiia v SSSR* 3 (1987): KKh 1-KKh 2.

2053 Kharitonov, V.P. "Nekotorye problemy ateisticheskogo vospitaniia studencheskoi molodezhi tekhnicheskogo vuza" [Some Problems of Atheistic Education of Students of Technical Institute of Higher Education]. *Teoretiko-metodologicheskie problemy formirovaniia kommunisticheskogo mirovozzreniia.* Iaroslavl', 1987. Pp. 55-60.

2054 Khark, E.S. *Estonskaia evangelicheskaia liuteranskaia tserkov' segodnia* [Estonian Evangelist Lutheran Church Today]. Tallin: Periodika, 1982. 71 pp., illus. In English. Published also in Estonian and German.

2055 Khar'kovshchenko, E.A. "Kritika kul'turologicheskoi apologetiki bogoiskatel'stva" [Criticism of Standard of Logical Apologetics of God Seeking]. *Vopr. ateizma* 25 (1989): 98-105.

2056 Khasanov, A. *Novye obriady i ateisticheskoe vospitanie* [New Rituals and Atheistical Education]. Tashkent: Uzbekistan, 1984. 104 pp. (B-chka ateista). In Uzbek.

2057 Khazratkulov, M. *Doislamskie verovaniia* [Pre Islamic Beliefs]. Dushanbe: Irfon, 1986. 124 pp. In Tajik. Bibl.: pp. 115-123. For review see item 5096.

2058 Khazratkulov, M. *Sufizm* [Sufism]. Dushanbe: Maorif, 1988. 126 pp. In Tajik.

2059 "'Khel'sinki-87' o svobode sovesti v SSSR" ["Helsinki 87" on Freedom of Conscience in USSR]. *Religiia v SSSR* 7 (1987): NG 1-NG 2.

2060 Khermann, Kh. *Savonarola: Eretik iz San-Marko* [Savonarola: Heretic from San-Marco]. Transl. from German: N.A. Savinkova; V.V. Chernysheva. M.: Progress, 1982. 296 pp., illus., port. Bibl.: pp. 290-295. Annot. bibl.: pp. 281-289.

2061 Khiuttner, E.; Khegenbert, Z.; Broda, R. "Reshenie religioznogo voprosa v Germanskoi Demokraticheskoi Respublike" [Answer to the Religious Question in the German Democratic Republic]. *Vopr. nauch. ateizma* 27 (1981): 161-173.

2062 Khmurchik, A.G. "Perestroika i ateizm" [Perestroika and Atheism]. *Nauka i religiia* 11 (1988): 2-3.

2063 Khobriankina, T.N. "Ob oshibochnykh otsenkakh religii v sovremennoi publitsistike" [On Erroneous Estimation of Religion in Contemporary Journalism]. *Kritika religioznoi ideologii i problemy ateisticheskogo vospitaniia.* M., 1980. Pp. 88-93.

2064 Khodzhamuradov, I. *Trudovye traditsii i ateisticheskoe vospitanie* [Working Traditions and Atheistical Education]. Tashkent: Uzbekistan, 1982. 40 pp. (Ser. "Marksizm-leninizm"; No. 13).

2065 Khommel', Kh. 'Akill-bog' [Achilles-God]. *Vestn. drev. istorii* 1 (1981): 53-76. Summary in English.

2066 Khorobor, A. "Cherez proshloe k budushchemu" [Through the Past to the Future]. *Molodezh'. Religiia. Ateizm.* 4 (1988): 5-24.

2067 Khoroshev, A.S. "Batyevshchina i tserkovnaia propoved' neprotivleniia" [Batyevshchina and Church Sermon of Non-resistance]. *Vopr. nauch. ateizma* 37 (1988): 131-139.

2068 Khoroshev, A.S. "Khristianizatsiia Rusi po arkheologicheskim dannym" [Conversion to Christianity of Rus' According to Archeological Data]. *Priroda* 7 (1988): 68-76.

2069 Khoroshev, A.S. *Politicheskaia istoriia russkoi kanonizatsii (XI-XVI vv.).* [Political History of Russian Canonization (XIth-XVIth Centuries)]. M.: Izd-vo MGU, 1986. 206 pp. Bibl.: p. 193. Name index: pp. 194-205.

2070 Khoruzhii, S. "V chem naznachenie khrama?" [What's the Purpose of the Temple?]. *Rodina* 8 (1989): 36.

2071 Khrapova, N.Iu. "Osobennosti formirovaniia religioznogo soznaniia razlichnykh sotsial'no-ekonomicheskikh grupp altaitsev: Analiz deiatel'nosti Alt. dukhov. missii (1830-nach. XX v.)" [Forming Features of Religious Consciousness of Different Socio-Economical Altai Groups: Analysis of the Activity of Altai Ecclesiastical Mission (1830-Early XXth C.)]. *Teoriia i metodologiia formirovaniia soznaniia.* Barnaul, 1985. Pp. 77-87.

2072 *Khrestomatiia po istorii ateizma Litvy: Kritika religii, svobodomyslie i ateizm v Litve* [Reader on the History of Atheism of Lithuania: Criticism of Religion, Free-thinking and Atheism in Lithuania]. [Comp.: L. Vileitene]. Vil'nius: Mintis, 1988. 632 pp. In Lithuanian. For review see item 5097.

2073 *Khristianstvo i ego sotsial'naia funktsiia v Litve* [Christianity and Its Social Function in Lithuania]. [Ed.: V. Lazutka]. Vil'nius: Mintis, 1986. 319 pp. In Lithuanian. Summaries in English and Russian. For reviews see items 5098-5099.

2074 *Khristianstvo i Rus'* [Christianity and Rus']. [Ed.: P. Fedoseev]. M.: Nauka, 1988. 176 pp. (Ser. "Sov. religiovedenie"; 2). Published also in English and French.

2075 *Khristianstvo i tserkov' v Rossii feodal'nogo perioda* [Christianity and Church in Feudal Russia]. [Ed.: N.N. Pokrovskii]. Novosibirsk: Nauka. Sib. otd-nie, 1989. 366 pp., illus. Bibl.: pp. 73-76.

2076 Khromova, K.Kh. "Kritika kontseptsii 'islam kak absoliutnaia tsennostnaia orientatsiia' sovremennogo iranskogo filosofa Sainda Khoseina Nasra" [Criticism of Conception of "Islam as Absolute Valuable Orientation" of the Contemporary Iranian Philosopher Saind Khosein Nasr]. *Problemy etiki v filosofskikh ucheniiakh stran Vostoka.* M., 1986. Pp. 116-128.

2077 Khrshanovskii, V.A. "Pozdneantichnye pogrebeniia na nekrople Ilurata" [Late Antique Burials in Ilurat Necropolis]. *Nauchno-ateisticheskie issledovaniia v muzeiakh.* L., 1988. Pp. 16-27.

2078 Khrshanovskii, V.A. "Problema otnosheniia khristianstva k antichnomu kul'turnomu naslediiu v russkoi i sovetskoi istoriografii XIX-XX vekov" [The Problem of Christianity's Attitude Towards Ancient Cultural Heritage in Russian and Soviet Historiography of the XIXth-XXth Centuries]. *Problemy formirovaniia svetskoi kul'tury v Zapadnoi Evrope.* L., 1987. Pp. 106-124.

2079 Khrustalev, Iu. "Shirokii diapazon sredstv" [Broad Range of Means]. *Nauka i religiia* 8 (1980): 11-12.

2080   Khudbkhoi, P. "Koe chto o novoi 'islamskoi nauke'" [Something on New "Islamic Science"]. *Mir nauki* T. 33, 3 (1989): 19-23.

2081   Khunich, D. "K voprosu o sushchnosti dialoga mezhdu marksistami i khristianami" [On the Problem of the Essence of Dialogue Between Marxists and Christians]. *Velikii Oktiabr', ego vliianie na obshchestvennyi progress i sovremennost'.* M., 1988. Pp. 77-81.

2082   Khusein-Zade, M.Sh. "Iazycheskie verovaniia sredi fellakhov Egipta" [Heathen Beliefs Among Egypt's Fellahs]. *Sb. dokl. I Vsesoiuznoi nauch. konf. molodykh vostokovedov.* Tbilisi, 1981. Pp. 81-92.

2083   Khushvakhtov, Kh. "Predshestvennik religioznogo reformizma v Egipte Sheikh at-Takhtavi" [Sheikh al-Tahtavy - Predecessor of Religious Reformism in Egypt]. *Problemy arabskoi klassicheskoi i sovremennoi literatur.* Dushanbe, 1989. Pp. 105-109.

2084   Khutsishvili, L.K. "Sviatilishche sv. Georgiia v sele Birkiani" [St. George's Sanctuary in Birkian Village]. *Kavk. etnogr. sb.* Tbilisi, 1988. T. 7. Pp. 60-65.

2085   Khutsishvili, M.N. *Sotsial'no-politicheskaia pozitsiia Gruzinskoi pravoslavnoi tserkvi (XIX-XX vv.)* [Socio-Political Position of the Georgian Orthodox Church (XIXth-XXth Centuries)]. Tbilisi: Metsniereba, 1987. 248 pp. In Georgian. Summary in Russian.

2086   Khuzhamuradov, I.R. *Problemy sekuliarizatsii v regionakh rasprostraneniia islama* [Problems of Secularization in Regions of Islamic Dissemination]. Tashkent: Tashk. un-t., 1981. 20 pp.

2087   Khuzhamuradov, I.R. *Sotsialisticheskii obraz zhizni i ateisticheskoe vospitanie* [Socialist Way of Life and Atheistic Education]. Tashkent: Uzbekistan, 1984. 23 pp. (Besedy o nauke; No 16). In Uzbek.

2088   Khuzhamuradov, I.R. *Sushchnost' sekuliarizatsii sovremennogo islama* [The Essence of Secularization of Contemporary Islam]. Tashkent: Uzbekistan, 1987. 24 pp. (Besedy o nauke; No 12). In Uzbek.

2089   Khuzhamuradov, I.R.; Muksimov, A.M. *Svobodnoe vremia i ateisticheskoe vospitanie* [Spare Time and Atheistic Education]. Tashkent: Uzbekistan, 1988. 30 pp. (Marksizm-leninizm; No 4). In Uzbek.

2090 Khvedelidze, M.G. "Dva poniatiia vechnosti v kosmogoniiakh drevnego Egipta" [Two Concepts of Eternity in Cosmogonies of Ancient Egypt]. *Meroe* 3 (1985): 239-242. Summary in English, pp. 274-275.

2091 Khvedelidze, M.G. "Problema 'boga' v izuchenii drevneegipetskoi religii" [Problem of "God" in Study of Ancient Egyptian Religion]. *Kavk. -Blizhnevost. sb.* 7 (1984): 35-48. Summary in English, pp. 171-172.

2092 Khydyrov, T.Kh. "Novye sovetskie prazdniki i obriady - deistvennoe sredstvo ateisticheskogo vospitaniia trudiashchikhsia" [New Soviet Holidays and Ceremonies - Effectual Means of Atheistic Education of Workers]. *Izv. AN TSSR.* Ser. obshchestv. nauk 3 (1985): 91-93.

2093 Khzhanovskii, K. "Katolicheskaia tserkov' v PNR. Struktura. Apparat." [Catholic Church in Polish People's Republic. Structure. Apparatus.]. *Katolicheskaia tserkov' v PNR v 80-kh godakh.* M., 1988. Pp. 5-19.

2094 Khzhanovskii, K. "Otnoshenie katolicheskoi tserkvi k antisotsialisticheskim silam v pol'skoi derevne v period obshchestvenno-politicheskogo krizisa nachala 80-kh godov" [Attitude of Catholic Church Toward Antisocialist Forces in Polish Village during Socio-Political Crisis Early 80s]. *Katolicheskaia tserkov' v PNR v 80-kh godakh.* M., 1988. Pp. 47-70.

2095 Kiamilev, S.Kh. "K interpretatsii koranicheskikh terminov *kogst i adl'*" [On interpretation of Koran Terms Cogst and Adel]. *Sotsial'no-politicheskie predstavleniia v islame: Istoriia i sovremennost'.* M., 1987. Pp. 98-107.

2096 Kichanova, I. [M]. "Formirovanie nauchnogo mirovozzreniia" [Forming Scientific Outlook]. *Kommunist.* Vil'nius 4 (1982): 25-30.

2097 Kichanova, I.M. "Kritika burzhuazno-klerikal'nykh iskazhenii morali sotsialisticheskogo obshchestva" [Criticism of Bourgeois-Clerical Distortions of the Morals of Socialist Society]. *Vopr. nauch. ateizma* 35 (1986): 256-273.

2098 Kichanova, I.M. "Osvoenie trudiashchimisia-veruiushchimi sotsial'no-nravstvennykh tsennostei sotsialisticheskogo obshchestva" [Assimilation of Socio-Moral Values of the Socialist Society by Workers-Believers]. *Vopr. nauch. ateizma* 35 (1986): 181-195.

2099 Kichanova, I.M. *Svetit putevodnaia zvezda* [Guiding Star Shines]. M.: Mol. gvardiia, 1987. 222 pp., illus. For review see item 5103.

2100   Kichanova, I.[M]. "Za krasotu dukhovnoi zhizni" [For the Beauty   of
       Spiritual Life]. *Kommunist.* Vil'nius. 8 (1985): 47-52.

2101   Kichanova, I.M. "Znachenie problemy tsennostei dlia teorii i praktiki
       ateisticheskogo vospitaniia" [The Importance of the Problem of Values for
       the Theory and Practice of Atheistic Education]. *Vopr. nauch. ateizma* 35
       (1986): 108-126.

2102   Kiknadze, Z.G. *Besedy o Biblii* [Talks About the Bible]. Tbilisi: Metsniereba,
       1989. 190 pp. (Nauch.-popul. ser. "Blik"). In Georgian.

2103   Kikodze, G.M. *Propovedi Episkopa Imeretii Gavriila, proiznesennye im v
       1860-1870 godakh* [Bishop Imeretii Gavriil's Sermons Delivered by Him in
       1860-1870]. Tbilisi: Sabchota Sakartvelo, 1989. T. I. - XVI, 544 pp., illus.,
       portr.

2104   Kikvidze, Ia.A. *Zemledelie i zemledel'cheskii kul't v drevnei Gruzii*
       [Agriculture and Agricultural Cult in Ancient Georgia]. Transl. from
       Georgian by N.A. Mshvidobadze. Tbilisi: Metsniereba, 1988. 269 pp., illus.
       Bibil.: pp. 250-260.

2105   Kimelev, Iu.A. *Sovremennaia zapadnaia filosofiia religii* [Contemporary
       Western Philosophy of Religion]. M.: Mysl', 1989. 286 pp. Bibl.: pp.
       276-284.

2106   Kimelev, Iu.A.; Poliakova, N.L. *Nauka i religiia* [Science and Religion]. M.:
       Nauka, 1988. 175 pp. (Nauch.-popul. lit. Ser.: Ateizm i religiia). For
       review see item 5104.

2107   Kin, Ts.I. *Alkhimiia i real'nost':* Bor'ba idei v sovrem. it. kul'ture [Alchemy
       and Reality: Struggle of Ideas in Contemporary Italian Culture]. M.: Sov.
       pisatel', 1984. 399 pp., port.

2108   Kirabaev, N.S. "Islam i filosofiia" [Islam and Philosophy]. *Filosofskaia i
       obshchestvennaia mysl' stran Azii i Afriki.* M., 1981. Pp. 124-134.

2109   Kirabaev, N.S. *Sotsial'naia filosofiia musul'manskogo Vostoka (Epokha
       srednevekov'iia)* [Social Philosophy of the Moslem Orient (In the Middle
       Ages)]. M.: Izd-vo Un-ta druzhby narodov, 1987. 175 pp. For review see
       item 5105.

2110 Kirikov, O.I. "Kriticheskii analiz modernistskogo istolkovaniia pravoslavnoi dogmatiki" [Critical Analysis of Modernist Interpretation of Orthodox Dogmatics]. *Vopr. ateizma* 22 (1985): 99-105.

2111 Kirill, arkhiepiskop. "Utverzhdaia prioritet dukhvnogo ..." [Asserting Spiritual Priority...]. *Teatr* 6 (1988): 24-29.

2112 Kirill, arkhiepiskop Smolenskii i Kaliningradskii. "Tserkvi nuzhna perestroika" [The Church Needs Perestroika]. *Novoe vremia* 36 (1989): 42-43.

2113 Kirill, arkhiepiskop Smolenskii i Viazemskii. "Zakony i ubezhdeniia" [Laws and Beliefs]. *Nauka i religiia* 6 (1989): 6-8.

2114 Kirillin, V.M. "Simvolika chisel v drevnerusskikh skazaniiakh XVI v." [Symbolism of Numbers in Old Russian Tales of the XVIth C.]. *Estestvennonauchnye predstavleniia Drevnei Rusi.* M., 1988. Pp. 76-111.

2115 Kirillina, S.A. "Evoliutsiia egipetskikh sufiiskikh bratstv (XIX-nachalo XX v.) [Evolution of Egyptian Sufist Brotherhoods (XIXth-Early XXth C.)]. *Islam: problemy ideologii, prava, politiki i ekonomiki.* M., 1985. Pp. 172-190.

2116 Kirillina, S.A. *Islam v obshchestvennoi zhizni Egipta (vtoraia polovina XIX-nach. XX v.)* [Islam in Egypt's Social Life (Late XIXth-Early XXth C.)]. M.: Nauka, 1989. 203 pp. Bibl.: pp. 193-202.

2117 Kirillov, R.S. "Utverzhdenie massovogo ateizma v sovetskoi Chuvashii v period postroeniia sotsializma" [Assertion of Mass Atheism in Soviet Chuvash in the Period of Construction of Socialism]. *Problemy istorii religii i ateizma.* Cheboksary, 1980. Pp. 68-80.

2118 Kirinenko, M.G. *Svoboda sovesti v SSSR* [Freedom of Conscience in USSR]. M.: Iurid. lit., 1985. 198 pp. For review see item 5106.

2119 Kiriushko, N.I. "Ateisticheskoe obshchestvennoe mnenie o novoi obriadnosti" [Atheistic Public Opinion about the New Ritual]. *Vopr. ateizma* 18 (1982): 44-50.

2120 Kiriushko, N.I. *Ateizm i razvitie sotsialisticheskoi kul'tury* [Atheism and Development of Socialist Culture]. Kiev: Znanie UkSSR, 1983. 49 pp. (Ser. V "Nauchno-ateisticheskaia" / O-vo "Znanie" UkSSR; No 1). Annot. bibl.: pp. 47-48.

2121 Kiriushko, N.I. *Rol' ateizma v kul'turnom razvitii lichnosti* [The Role of Atheism in Cultural Development of Personality]. Kiev: Znanie UkSSR, 1980. 48 pp. (Ser. 5 "Nauchno-ateisticheskaia" / O-vo "Znanie" UkSSR; No 9). In Ukrainian. Bibl.: p. 47.

2122 Kiriushko, N.I.; Rybachuk, N.F. *Ateizm, trud, kul'tura* [Atheism, Labour, Culture]. Kiev: Nauk. dumka, 1981. 246 pp.

2123 Kirk, G.M. "Eta razdelennaia vzaimosviaz'" [This Shared Intercommunication]. *Argumenty, 1987.* M., 1987. Pp. 175-178.

2124 Kirpichenko, A.A.; Protas, R.N.; Khobotov, G.A. "Gotovim propagandistov ateizma" [We Prepare Propagandists of Atheism]. *Vesti vysh. shkoly* 4 (1982): 51-53.

2125 Kiselev, S.P. *Vospityvat' ateistov* [To Educate Atheists]. M.: Sov. Rossiia, 1986. 80 pp.

2126 Kiselev, V.B. "Sovershenstvovanie prepodavaniia nauchnogo ateizma kak mirovozzrencheskaia problema" [Perfection of Teaching Scientific Atheism as World Outlook's Problem]. *Mirovozzrencheskaia napravlennost' uchebnogo protsessa v pedagogicheskom vuze.* M., 1987. Pp. 62-68.

2127 Kishkovskii, L. "Pravoslavnye v Amerike" [Orthodoxes in America]. *Novoe vremia* 49 (1989): 42-43.

2128 Kislova, A.A. "Tserkov' i rabstvo v SShA (pervaia polovina XIX v.)" [The Church and Slavery in USA (Early XIXth C.)]. *Amer. ezhegodnik.* M., 1988. Pp. 63-84.

2129 Kislova, O.P. *Ateizm i sovremennaia ideologicheskaia bor'ba* [Atheism and Contemporary Ideological Struggle]. Tashkent: Uzbekistan, 1986. 39 pp. (Ser. "Marksizm-leninizm"; No 7). In Uzbek.

2130 Kislova, O.P. *Obshchestvennoe mnenie - sredstvo ateisticheskogo vospitaniia* [Public Opinion - Means of Atheistic Education]. Tashkent: Uzbekistan, 1982. 31 pp. (Ser. "Marksizm-leninizm"; No 9). In Uzbek.

2131 Kislova, O.P. "Organizatsiia nauchno-ateisticheskoi propagandy v klube" [Organization of Scientific Atheistic Propaganda in the Club]. *Sb. nauch. tr. Tashk. un-t* 649 (1980): 36-46.

2132 Kizilov, O. "Chto znachit byt' ateistom?" [What Does It Mean to be an Atheist?]. *Vech. sred. shk.* 6 (1983): 28-30.

2133 Kizima, M.P. "Puritanizm i amerikanskie mify" [Puritanism and American Myths]. *Vopr. nauch. ateizma* 36 (1987): 32-56.

2134 Klassen, P.I. *O mennonitstve i mennonitakh* [On Mennonitism and Mennonites]. Alma-Ata: Kazakhstan, 1989. 96 pp. In German. Bibl.: pp. 95-96.

2135 Kleandrova, V.M. "Iz istorii vzaimootnoshenii gosudarstva i tserkvi v Rossii" [History of State and Church Interrelation in Russia]. *Vopr. nauch. ateizma* 37 (1988): 152-162.

2136 *Klerikal'nyi antisovetizm: sistema ideologicheskikh diversii* [Clerical Anti Sovietism: System of Ideological Diversions]. [Ed.: P.L. Iarotskii]. Kiev: Politizdat Ukrainy, 1984. 303 pp. (Kritika ideologii i politiki antikommunizma). Annot. bibl.: pp. 289-301.

2137 Klervoskii, B. "O blagodati i svobode voli" [On Abundance and Freedom of Will]. *Sred. veka* 45 (1982): 265-303.

2138 Kliashtornyi, S. "Drevnetiurskaia religiia: problemy rekonstruktsii i genezisa" [Old Turkic Religion: Problems of Reconstruction and Genesis]. *Inform. biull. / Mezhdunarod. assots. po izucheniiu kul'tur Tsentr. Azii.* M., 1987. Vyp. spets. Pp. 45-53.

2139 Klibanov, A.I.; Mitrokhin .L.N. "Istoriia i religiia" [History and Religion]. *Kommunist* 12 (1987): 91-98.

2140 Klibanov, A I.; Mitrokhin, L.N. *Kreshchenie Rusi: istoriia i sovremennost'* [Baptism of Rus': History and Contemporaneity]. M.: Znanie, 1988. 64 pp. (Novoe v zhizni, nauke, tekhnike. Nauch. ateizm; 9/1988).

2141 Klibanov, A.[I].; Mitrokhin, L.[N]. "Novye podkhody k izucheniiu religii" [New Approaches Toward the Study of Religion]. *Religiia v SSSR* 8 (1987): AK 1-AK 7.

2142 Klibanov, A.I.; Mitrokhin, L.N. "Religiia kak predmet nauki" [Religion as Object of Science]. *Religii mira.* M., 1989. Pp. 5-34.

2143   Klim, V. "Protsess politicheskoi i ideologicheskoi differentsiatsii khristian i
       ikh uchastie v bor'be za mir" [Political and Ideological Process of
       Differentiation of Christians and Their Participation in the Struggle for
       Peace]. *Vopr. nauch. ateizma* 36 (1987): 24-31.

2144   Klimov, V.V. *Uniatskie klerikaly protiv sovetskoi kul'tury* [Uniate Church
       Clericals Against Soviet Culture]. Kiev: Znanie UkSSR, 1986. 47 pp. (Ser.
       5, Nauch.-ateist. / O-vo "Znanie" UkSSR; No 3). In Ukrainian. Bibl.: pp.
       46-47.

2145   Klimov, V.V. *Uniatstvo - iaryi vrag ukrainskoi kul'tury* [Uniate Church Ardent
       Enemy of Ukrainian Culture]. Kiev: Znanie UkSSR, 1981. 46 pp. (Ser. 5,
       " Nauchno-ateisticheskaia" / O-vo "Znanie" UkSSR; No 10). In Ukrainian.
       Bibl.: pp.45-46.

2146   Klimova, A.V. *Antiklerikalizm kak obshchestvennoe dvizhenie* [Anticlericalism
       as Social Movement]. Kiev: Vishcha shk., 1986. 87 pp. (Ateist. b-chka
       studenta).

2147   Klimova, A.V. "Ereticheskie dvizheniia i svobodomyslie" [Heretical Move-
       ments and Freethinking]. *Kritika religioznoi ideologii i problemy
       ateisticheskogo vospitaniia.* M., 1982. Pp. 23-29.

2148   Klimova, A.V. "Sushchnost' poniatiia 'antiklerikalizm'" [The Essence of the
       Concept of "Anticlericalism"]. *Kritika religioznoi ideologii i problemy
       ateisticheskogo vospitaniia.* M., 1980. Pp. 105-112.

2149   Klimovich, L.I. *Kniga o Korane, ego proiskhozhdenii i mifologii* [Book about
       Koran, Its Origins and Mythologies]. M.: Politizdat, 1986. 270 pp.
       Published also as 2nd enlarged ed., 1988, 286 pp., illus., name and
       subject index: pp. 272-284. For review see item 5107.

2150   Kliubuvna, A.; Kliuba, E. "Buddizm v Shri Lanke" [Buddhism in Sri Lanka].
       Transl. from Polish by T. Trifonova. *Ateisticheskie chteniia.* M., 1988. Pp.
       189-193.

2151   Kliuchevskii, V.O. *Drevnerusskie zhitiia sviatykh kak istoricheskii istochnik*
       [Oldrussian Lives of the Saints as Historic Source]. M.: Nauka, 1988. IV,
       512 pp., port. Bibl.: pp. 494-497. Index: pp. 467-470.

2152 Kliuev, B.I. "Ideologiia indusskogo vozrozhdenchestva" [The Ideology of Hindu Renaissance]. *Obshchestvennaia mysl' Indii.* M., 1989. Pp. 118-154.

2153 Kliuev, B.[I]. "Islam v Indii" [Islam in India]. *Aziia i Afrika segodnia* 2 (1986): 14-17. Summary in English, suppl., pp. 3-4.

2154 Kliuev, B.I. "Obshchina sikkhov (70-e gody)" [Sikhs' Community (in 70s)]. *Religiia i obshchestvennaia zhizn' v Indii.* M., 1983. Pp. 99-144. Annot. bibl.: pp. 142-144.

2155 Kliuev, B.I. "Propovedniki i 'bogocheloveki': Vzlet i padenie 'verouchitelia' Bkhagvana Shri Radzhnisha" [Preachers and "God-Men": The Rise and the Fall of Bhagvana Shri Rajnisha "Apologist"]. *Indiia, 1987.* M., 1988. Pp. 199-213.

2156 Klochkov, V.V. *Sotsialisticheskoe gosudarstvo, pravo i religioznye organizatsii* [Socialist State, Law and Religious Organizations]. M.: Znanie, 1984. 64 pp. (Novoe v zhizni, nauke, tekhnike. Nauch. ateizm; 2).

2157 Klochkov, V.[V]. "Svoboda veroispovedaniia v SSSR: burzhuano-propagandistskie vymysly i deistvitel'nost'" [Freedom of Religion in USSR: Bourgeois-Propagandist Fabrications and Reality]. *Sots. zakonnost'* 3 (1988): 26-29.

2158 Klochkov, V.V. *Zakon i religiia: Ot gos. religii v Rossii k svobode sovesti v SSSRA* [Law and Religion: From State Religion in Russia to the Freedom of Conscience in USSR]. M.: Politizdat, 1982. 160 pp.
Published also by Progress, 1985, 184 pp., in Portuguese.

2159 Klor, O. "Problemy sotrudnichestva marksistov i khristian v GDR" [Problems of Cooperation of Marxists and Christians in GDR]. *Vopr. nauch. ateizma* 36 (1987): 191-200.

2160 Knabe, G.S. "Rimskii mif i rimskaia istoriia" [Roman Myth and Roman History]. *Zhizn' mifa v antichnosti.* M., 1986. Ch. 1. Pp. 241-252.

2161 "Kniga o prirode veshchei" [The Book about the Nature of Things]. Transl. from Latin and commentaries by T.Iu. Borodai. *Vopr. istorii estestvoznaniia i tekhniki* 1 (1988): 139-152.

2162 *Knigi Vetkhogo zaveta* [Books of the Old Testament]. Tbilisi: Metsniereba, 1989 - (Pamiatniki drevnegruz. lit.). In Georgian.

Vyp. I: *Bytie, iskhod.* [Genesis, Exodus]. 1989. 640 pp.

2163   Knokhe, Kh. *Bog posle sumerek idolov* Ekumen. otvety na maniiu progressa, polit. ideologiiu i materializm [Gott nach Götzendämerung]. M.: AN SSSR. INION, 1988. 22 pp. [Synopsis].

2164   Knysh, A.D. "Nekotorye problemy izucheniia sufizma" [Some Problems of Study of Sufism]. *Islam: Religiia, obshchestvo, gosudarstvo.* M., 1984. Pp. 87-95. Annot. bibl.: pp. 94-95.

2165   Kobelianskaia, L.S. *Smysl zhizni: dve tochki zreniia* [The Meaning of Life: Two Points of View]. Kiev: Politizdat Ukrainy, 1989. 112 pp.

2166   Kobelianskaia, L.S. "Smysl zhizni ateisticheski zreloi lichnosti i realizatsiia kommunisticheskogo ideala" [The Meaning of Life of Atheistic Mature Personality and Realization of Communist Ideal]. *Vopr. ateizma* 24 (1988): 90-95.

2167   Kobelianskaia, L.S. "Smysl zhizni cheloveka - aktual'naia problema teorii nauchnogo ateizma" [The Essence of Man's Life - Actual Problem of the Theory of Scientific Atheism]. *Vopr. ateizma* 20 (1984): 120-127.

2168   Kobetskii, V.D. "Voprosy sovershenstvovaniia metodicheskogo rukovodstva ateisticheskim vospitaniem studentov v vuze" [Problems of Perfection of Methodical Guidance of Atheistic Education of Students in Institution of Higher Education]. *Aktual. vopr. metodoki prepodavaniia obshchestv. nauk i kom. vospitaniia studentov* 5 (1987): 136-141.

2169   Kobishchanov, Iu.M. *Istoriia rasprostraneniia islama v Afrike* [History of Dissemination of Islam in Africa]. M.: Nauka, 1987. 223 pp. Summary in English. Bibl.: pp. 206-215. For review see item 5108.

2170   Kobishchanov, Iu.M. "Natsionalisticheskie religiozno-ideologicheskie sistemy v Afrike" [Nationalistic Religious-Ideological Systems in Africa]. *Religii mira: Istoriia i sovremennost'.* Ezhegodnik. 1982. M., 1982. Pp. 120-140.

2171   Kobishchanov, Iu.[M]. "Religiia i etnicheskie problemy v Afrike" [Religion and Ethnic Problems in Africa]. *Aziia i Afrika segodnia* 3 (1981): 55-56, 59.

2172   Kobo, V.R. "U istokov religii" [By the Sources of Religion]. *Priroda* 3 (1984): 51-60.

2173 Kobzev, A.I. "Buddizm, konfutsianstvo i zapadnye politekonomiia i sotsiologiia" [Buddhism, Confucianism and Western Political Economy and Sociology]. *Filosofskie osnovaniia teorii mezhdunarodnykh otnoshenii* 1 (1987): 95-124. Bibl.: pp. 121-124.

2174 Kobzev, A.I. "Poniatiino-teoreticheskie osnovy konfutsianskoi sotsial'noi utopii" [Conceptional-Theoretical Foundations of Confucian Social Utopia]. *Kitaiskie sotsial'nye utopii* M., 1987. Pp. 58-103.

2175 Kochan, I.G. *Teni vcherashnego dnia* [Yesterday's Shadows]. Kiev: Politizdat Ukrainy, 1983. 236 pp., illus. In Ukrainian.

2176 Kocharli F.K. "Voinstvuiushchii ateist: K 175-letiiu so dnia rozhdeniia M.F. Akhundova" [Militant Atheist: M.F. Ahunda's 175 Birthday Anniversary]. *Izv. AN AzSSR.* Ser. istorii, filosofii i prava 2 (1988): 3-12.

2177 Kochetov, A.N. *Buddizm* [Buddhism]. 2nd revised ed. M.: Nauka, 1983. 177 pp. (Nauch.-ateist. ser.).

2178 Kochetov, A.N. *Iskusstvo i religiia* [Art and Religion]. M.: Znanie, 1984. 63 pp. (Novoe v zhizni, nauke, tekhnike. Nauch. ateizm; 9). Bibl.: p. 60.

2179 Kochetov, A.N. *Kritika mirovozzrencheskikh osnov buddizma* [Criticism of Buddhism's World Outlook Foundations]. M.: Znanie, 1980. 64 pp. (Novoe v zhizni, nauke, tekhnike. Ser. "Nauch. ateizm; No 3).

2180 Kochetov, A.N. "O tak nazyvaemoi 'teorii poznaniia' buddizma. Mesto buddizma v sovremennoi ideologicheskoi bor'be" [On So-Called Buddhism's "Theory of Knowledge". Buddhism's Place in Contemporary Ideological Struggle]. *Sotsial'naia otvetstvennost' uchenykh i ideologicheskaia bor'ba: istoriia i sovremennost'* M., 1989. Pp. 53-73.

2181 Kochetov, A.N. "Protivonauchnyi kharakter predstavlenii buddizma o mire" [Antiscientific Character of Buddhism's Conception about the World]. *Stroitel'stvo sotsializma i utverzhdenie nauchno-materialisticheskogo, ateisticheskogo mirovozzreniia (v regionakh rasprostraneniia lamaizma).* M., 1981. Pp. 89-103.

2182 Kochiev, K.K. "K voprosu o perezhitkakh kul'ta barana u osetin" [The Problem of Survival of the Cult of Ram by Ossets]. *Izvestiia - Akad. nauk GSSR. Iugo-Oset. NII* 32 (1988): 71-79.

2183 Kochiev, K.K. "Tutyr - vladyka volkov" [Tutyr - Master of Wolves]. *Izvestiia - Akad. nauk GSSR. Iugo-Oset. NII* 31 (1987): 58-65.

2184 Kogan, L.N. "Stanovlenie problemy vechnosti v domarksistskoi mysli i sovremennaia bogoslovie" [Creating the Problem of Eternity in Premarxist Thought and Contemporary Theology]. *Otnoshenie cheloveka k irratsional'nomu.* Sverdlovsk, 1989. Pp. 39-66.

2185 Koita, K.K. *Razgovor nachistotu o katolitsizme* [Open Talk About Catholicism]. Minsk: Belarus', 1985. 127 pp. Annot. bibl.: pp. 123-126.

2186 Koita, K.K. *V poiskakh istiny* [In the Search of Truth]. Minsk: Belarus', 1982. 158 pp.

2187 Koita, K.K.; Kalkun, V.R. *Religioznye obriady i ikh vred* [Religious Rituals and their Harm]. Minsk: Belarus', 1981. 30 pp. (San. znaniia - v massy).

2188 Kokhan, M.B. "Otrazhenie v dereviannoi rez'be obshchinnykh domov religioznykh vozzrenii i prazdnestv v'etnamskoi obshchiny" [Reflections of Religous Outlooks and Festivities of Viet-Nam Community in Wooden Carvings of Communal Houses]. *Nauch. soobshch. / Muzei iskusstva narodov Vostoka* 16 (1982): 47-64.

2189 Koks, Kh. "V poiskakh sovetskogo Khrista" [In the Search of Soviet Christ]. *Nauka i religiia* 7 (1989): 12-17.

2190 Kolemasova, N.Kh. *Khristianskoe sektantstvo v Uzbekistane* [Christian Sectarianism in Uzbekistan]. Tashkent: Uzbekistan, 1986. 46 pp. (B-chka ateista).

2191 Kolemasova, N.Kh. *Kritika fal'sifikatsii vvedeniia khristianstva na Rusi* [Criticism of Falsification of the Introduction of Christianity into Rus']. Tashkent: Znanie UzSSR, 1988. 26 pp. (B-chka "Aktual. vopr. ateist. vospitaniia").

2192 Kolemasova, N.Kh. *Krizisnye iavleniia khristianskogo sektantstva v Uzbekistane* [Crisis Occurrences in Christian Sectarianism in Uzbekistan]. Tashkent: Znanie UzSSR, 1981. 27 pp. (V pomoshch' lektoru / O-vo "Znanie" UzSSR. Ser. obshchestv.- politicheskaia). Bibl.: p. 27.

2193 Kolemasova, N.Kh. "Protestantskie obshchiny v Uzbekistane" [Protestant Communities in Uzbekistan]. *Protestantskie organizatsii v SSSR.* M., 1989. Pp. 112-119.

2194 Kolemasova, N.Kh. *Vospityvat' ateisticheskuiu ubezhdennost'* [Educate Atheistic Conviction]. Tashkent: Uzbekistan, 1984. 32 pp. (Marksizm-leninizm; No 2). In Uzbek.

2195 Kolesnik, N.A.; Furov, V.G. *Grazhdanstvennost' i religioznaia vera* [Civic Spirit and Religious Faith]. Kiev: Politizdat Ukrainy, 1985. 118 pp.

2196 Kolenikov, A.I. "Dve versii dogovora Mukhammada s khristianami Nadzhrana" [Two Versions of Muhammad's Pact with Nadjran Christians]. *Palest. sb.* 28 (1986): 24-34. Summary in English.

2197 Kolesnikov, A.I. "Zaroastriitsy i khristiane v gosudarstve Sasanidov" [Zoroastrians and Christians in the State of Sassanians]. *III Vsesoiuuznaia konferentsiia vostokovedov "Vzaimodeistvie i vzaimovliianie tsivilizatsii kul'tur na Vostoke".* M., 1988. T. I. Pp. 23-25.

2198 Kolesnikova, A.P. *Oprokinutoe nebo:* Sb. ateist. ocherkov [Overturned Heaven: Collection of Atheistic Essays]. Voronezh: Tsentr.-Chernozem. kn. izd-vo, 1987. 142 pp., illus. For review see item 5109.

2199 Koliadich, T.M.; Kapitsa, F.S. "Tysiacheletnii put' russkoi kul'tury" [Millennial Road of Russian Culture]. *Lit. v shk.* 4 (1988): 17-18.

2200 Kolodnyi, A.N. *Ateisticheskaia ubezhdennost' lichnosti* [Atheistic Conviction of Individual]. Kiev: Vishcha shk. Izd-vo. pri Kiev. un-ta, 1983. 152 pp. For review see item 5110.

2201 Kolodnyi, A.N. *Ateisticheskaia zrelost' i ee urovni* [Atheistic Maturity and Its Levels]. Kiev: Znanie UkSSR, 1984. 47 pp. (Ser. 5 "Nauchno-ateisticheskaia" / O-vo "Znanie" UkSSR; No 4). In Ukrainian. Bibl.: pp. 45-46.

2202 Kolodnyi, A.N. *Ateizm kak forma mirovozzrencheskogo znaniia i samosoznaniia lichnosti* [Atheism as a Form of World Outlook's Knowledge and Individual's Selfconsciousness]. Kiev: Nauk. dumka, 1984. 159 pp. In Ukrainian. Bibl.: pp. 154-158.

2203   Kolodnyi, A.N. "Ateizm kak vyrazhenie sotsial'nogo optimizma lichnosti sotsialisticheskogo obshchestva" [Atheism as Expression of Social Optimism of Individual of Socialist Society]. *Vopr. ateizma* 18 (1982): 22-29.

2204   Kolodnyi, A.N.; Kolodnaia, A.I. "Metodologicheskaia nesostoiatel'nost' popytok adaptirovaniia nauchnogo ateizma v ramkakh teologii" [Methodological Groundlessness of Attempts of Adaptation of Scientific Atheism within Theology's Frames]. *Vopr. ateizma* 25 (1989): 58-65.

2205   Kolodnyi, A.N.; Kolodnaia, A.I. "Organicheskoe edinstvo obrazovaniia i ateisticheskogo vospitaniia" [Organic Unity of Education and Atheistic Upbringing]. *Vopr. ateizma* 24 (1988): 60-65.

2206   Kolodnyi, A.N.; Kondratik, L.I. *Ateizm - poznannaia istina* [Atheism - Cognized Truth]. Kiev: Znanie UkSSR, 1987. 47 pp. (Ser. 5, Nauchno-ateisticheskaia / O-vo "Znanie" UkSSR; No 2). In Ukrainian. Annot. bibl.: p. 46.

2207   Kolodnyi, A.N.; Kondratik, L.I. "Sotsial'no-ekonomicheskie osnovaniia masso-vogo ateizma v usloviiakh sotsializma" [Socio- Economical Grounds of Mass Atheism under Socialism]. *Vopr. ateizma* 23 (1987): 8-15.

2208   Kolosnitsyn, V.I. *Religioznoe otchuzhdenie* [Religious Alienation]. Sverdlovsk: Izd-vo Ural. un-ta, 1987. 181 pp.

2209   Koltuniuk, S.V. *Kul'tura. Ateizm. Lichnost'* [Culture. Atheism. Individual]. Kiev: Politizdat Ukrainy, 1988. 141 pp., illus. Annot. bibl.: pp. 139-140.

2210   Komar, V.I. "Intelligentsiia i islamskie dvizheniia v Tunise" [Intelligentsia and Islamic Movements in Tunisia]. *Puti evoliutsii i obshchestvennaia rol' sovremennoi afrikanskoi intelligentsii: poiski, tendentsii, perspektivy.* M., 1988. Pp. 217-222.

2211   Komarov, Iu.; Korolev, V. "Svoboda sovesti i ateisticheskoe vospitanie" [Freedom of Conscience and Atheistic Education]. *Kommunist Tatarii* 6 (1983): 88-93.

2212   Komarov, V.N. *Ateizm i nauchnaia kartina mira* [Atheism and Scientific Image of the World]. Kaunas: Shviesa, 1984. 144 pp. (V mire znanii). In Lithuanian.

2213 Komarov, V.N. *Byt' mudrom bez boga!...* [To be Wise without God!...]. M.: Mosk. rabochii, 1986. 240 pp. (Iunost' tvoi bol'shoi mir). Published also in: Taskent: Uzbekistan, 1989. 264 pp. In Uzbek.

2214 Komarov. V.N. *Neprimirimoe protivostoianie: Besedy so starsheklassnikami o nauke i religii* [Irreconcilable Confrontation: Talks with Senior Pupils on Science and Religion]. M.: Pedagogika, 1988. 192 pp.

2215 Komarov, V.N.; Panovkin, B.N. *Chelovek poznaiushchii* [Cognizant Man]. M.: Mosk. rabochii, 1983. 220 pp., illus.

2216 Komarova, E.I.; Stavskaia, N.R. "O sootnoshenii otrazhatel'noi i tvorcheskoi funktsii nauhnoi deiatel'nosti i kritika religiozno-idealisticheskikh kontseptsii" [On Correlation of Reflective and Creative Functions of Scientific Activity and Criticism of Religious-Idealistic Conceptions]. *Kritika sovremennykh religiozno- idealisticheskikh kontseptsii.* M., 1979. Pp. 3-18.

2217 Komen, A.I. "U istokov" [By the Sources]. *Pamiatniki Otechestva* 1 (1988): 60-62.

2218 Komissarova, E.[Ia]. "Obshchee delo" [A Common Pursuit]. *Nauka i religiia* 1 (1985): 15-16.

2219 Komissarova, E.Ia. et al. *Vazhnoe zveno sistemy ateisticheskogo vospitaniia* [Important Link in the System of Atheistic Education]. M.: Znanie RSFSR, 1983. 38 pp. (V pomoshch' lektoru / O-vo "Znanie" RSFSR, Nauch.-metod. sovet po propagande nauch. ateizma).

2220 "Kommunizm i khristianstvo" [Communism and Christianity]. *Inostr. lit.* 5 (1989): 203-204.

2221 "Kompleksnaia programma issledovanii 'Rol' religii v istorii i sovremennom mire'" [Over-all Programme of Research "The Role of Religion in History and in the Contemporary World"]. *Vopr. istorii* 6 (1989): 173-184.

2222 *Kompleksnyi podkhod v ateisticheskom vospitanii* [All Embracing Approach in Atheistic Education]. Ed.: S.Iu. Dadabaeva. Dushanbe: Donish, 1988. 127 pp.

2223 *Komu eto vygodno?* [For Whom is it Advantageous?]. Comp.: N.A. Zabere-zh'ev. Kiev: Politizdat Ukrainy, 1980. 141 pp.

2224 Kondakchian, R.P. *Turtsiia: vnutrennaia politika i islam* [Turkey: Home Policy and Islam]. Erevan: Izd-vo AN ArmSSR, 1983. 238 pp. Bibl.: pp. 217-237.

2225 Kondrat'ev, E.D. "K voprosu ob ideinykh istokakh sovremennykh pravoslavnykh kontseptsii nauki" [On the Problem of Ideological Sources of Contemporary Orthodox Conceptions of Science]. *Problemy istorii religii i ateizma.* Cheboksary: 1980. Pp. 16-30.

2226 Kondrat'ev, E.D. "Kritika popytok sovremennykh bogoslovov primirit' nauku i religiiu" [Criticism of Contemporary Theologians' Attempts to Reconcile Science and Religion]. *Problemy istorii religii i ateizma.* Cheboksary, 1981. Pp. 3-19.

2227 Kondrat'ev, E.D. "Problemy sovershenstvovaniia ateisticheskogo vospitaniia v trodovom kollektive v svete reshenii XXVII s'ezda KPSS" [Problems of Perfection of Atheistic Education in Labour Collective in the Light of Decisions of the XXVIIth Congress of the CPSU]. *Aktual'nye problemy obespecheniia effectivnosti nauchno-ateisticheskoi raboty.* Cheboksary, 1986. Pp. 4-11.

2228 Kondrat'ev, S.V. "Problema religioznogo i politicheskogo edinstva v traktatakh F. Becona" [Problem of Religious and Political Unity in F. Bacon's Treatises]. *Problemy sotsial'noi istorii i kul'tury srednikh vekov.* L., 1986. Pp. 23-33.

2229 Kondratik, L.I. "Sotsial'no-gumanisticheskoe soderzhanie ateisticheskogo vospitaniia" [Socio-Humanist Content of Atheistic Education]. *Vopr. ateizma* 24 (1988): 95-101.

2230 Kondratov, A.M.; Shilik, K.K. *Kak rozhdaiutsia mify XX veka* [How Myths of the XXth Century are Born]. L.: Lenizdat, 1988. 176 pp. (Razum poznaet mir).

2231 Kondrina, M.A. "Osnovnye etapy razvitiia sufizma v Sudane (XV-XX vv.) [Basic Stages of Development of Sufism in Sudan (XVth-XXth C.)]. *V Vsesoiuznaia shkola molodykh vostokovedov.* M., 1989. T. 3. Pp. 18-21.

2232 Koniaev, P.G. *Ateisticheskoe znachenie nauchnogo poznaniia Vselennoi* [Atheistic Significance of Scientific Cognition of the Universe]. M.: Zanie RSFSR, 1984. 38 pp. (V pomoshch' lektoru / O-vo "Znanie" RSFSR. Nauch.-metod. sovet otd-niia po propagande nauch.-ateizma). Bibl.: pp. 36-37.

2233 Konik, V.[V]. "'Bozh'i poslanniki' ishchut posledovatelei" ["God's envoys" Search for Followers]. *Nauka i religiia* 8 (1982): 40-42.

2234 Konik, V.V. *Illiuzii svidetelei Iegovy* [Illusions of Jehovah's Witnesses]. M.: Sov. Rossiia, 1981. 176 pp.

2235 Konik, V.V. *Svoboda sovesti i ee lzhezashchitniki* [Freedom of Conscience and Its False Defenders]. M.: Mol. gvardiia, 1986. 175 pp., illus. Annot. bibl.: pp. 172-174.
Published also in:
Baku: Giandzhlik, 1988. 175 pp. In Azerbaijan.
Kishinev: Kartia Moldoveniaske, 1988. 178 pp., illus. In Moldavian.

2236 Konikov, B.A. "O nekotorykh storonakh verovanii i iskusstva taezhnogo naseleniia Priirtysh'ia epokhi srenevekov'ia" [Some Features of Beliefs and Art of Taiga Population by Irtysh in the Middle Ages]. *Problemy proiskhozhdeniia i etnicheskoi istorii tiurkskikh narodov Sibiri.* Tomsk., 1987. Pp. 185-202.

2237 *Konkretno, tvorcheski, effektivno* [Concrete, Creative, Effective]. M.: Mosk. rabochii, 1986. 285 pp.

2238 Konorov, V.I. *Mistika i okkul'tizm na sluzhbe ideologov 'nekonservativnoi vol'ny'* [Mysticism and Occultism in the Service of Ideologists of "Free Neoconservatism"]. M.: Znanie, 1985. 64 pp. (Novoe v zhizni, nauke, tekhnike. Ser. "Nauch. ateism"; No 5). Bibl.: pp. 63-64.

2239 Konopel'ko, G.G. *Zdravokhranenie i ateisticheskoe vospitanie trudiashchi-khsia* [Public Health and Worker's Atheistic Education]. Kiev: Znanie UkSSR, 1980. 48 pp. (Ser. 5 "Nauchno-ateisticheskaia"; No 4).

2240 Konoplitskaia, M.B.; Shovkovaia, E.Ia. *Chervonogradskii filial L'vovskogo muzeia istorii religii i ateizma:* Putevoditel' [Chervonograd Branch of Lvov's Museum of History of Religion and Atheism: Guide]. L'vov: Kameniar, 1987. 37 pp., illus. In Ukrainian. Summary in Russian.

2241   Konovalov, A.V. "Kazakhskaia mantika" [Kazakh Prediction]. *Nauchno-
       ateisticheskie issledovaniia v muzeiakh.* L., 1988. Pp. 87-104.

2242   Konovalov, B.N. *Ateisticheskoe vospitanie - na nauchnuiu osnovu* [Atheistic
       Education - On Scientific Basis]. Kiev: Znanie UkSSR, 1985. 48 pp. (Ser.
       V "Nauchno-ateisticheskaia" / O-vo "Znanie" UkSSR; No 12). Annot.
       bibl.: pp. 47-48.

2243   Konovalov, B.N. "Ateizm v sotsialisticheskom obshchestve" [Atheism in
       Socialist Society]. *Vopr. ateizma* 25 (1980): 244-266.

2244   Konovaloov, B.N. *Kompleksnyi podkhod v nauchno-ateisticheskom vospitanii*
       [All-Embracing Approach in Scientific-Atheistic Education]. M.: Znanie,
       1982. 63 pp. (Novoe v zhizni, nauke, tekhnike. Nauch. ateizm; 8). Bibl.:
       p. 62.

2245   Konovalov, B.N. "Mnogogrannost' ateizma" [Many Sides of Atheism].
       Molodoi Kommunist 8 (1981): 30-34.

2246   Konovalov, B.[N]. "Soiuzu voinstvuiushchikh bezbozhnikov - 60 let" [Sixtieth
       Anniversary of the League of Militant Atheists]. *Nauka i religiia* 12
       (1985): 19-20.

2247   Konovalov, B.N.; Abdusamedov, A.I. *Ateisticheskoe vospitanie na sovreme-
       nnom etape* [Atheistic Education in the Contemporary Stage]. Tashkent:
       Uzbekistan, 1980. 37 pp. (Ser. "Kul'tura"; No 13). In Uzbek.

2248   Konovalova, N.S. "Katolicheskaia ierarkhiia o putiakh preodoleniia
       strukturnogo krizisa" [Catholic Hierarchy about the Ways to Surmount
       the Structural Crisis]. *Latinskaia Amerika 80-kh godov: Tendentsii
       obshchestv. razvitiia.* M., 1988. Pp. 55-70.

2249   "Konservativen li bog?. Politicheskii fundamentalizm v Soedinennykh
       Shtatakh Ameriki" [Is God Conservative?. Political Fundamentalism in the
       United States of America]. *Argumenty, 1987.* M., 1987. Pp. 165-174.

2250   Konzhukova, N.Z.; Erasova, I.A. "'Boitsy tserkvi' na sluzhbe antiko-
       mmunizma" ["Church's Militants" in the Service of Anti-Communism].
       Antikommunizm v strategii i taktike imperializma v Afrike. M., 1987. Pp.
       60-76.

2251 Kopaleishvili, G.Sh. "Mir zemnoi ('samzeo') i zagrobnyi mir ('suleti') v religioznykh verovaniakh pshavov i khevsur" [Earthly World ("Samzeo") and the Next World ("Suleti") in Religious Beliefs of Pshav and Hevsur]. *Materialy po etnografii Gruzii.* Tbilisi, 1987. T. 23. Pp. 208-215. In Georgian. Summary in Russian.

2252 Kopanitsa, M.M. *'Sotial'naia etika' v russkom pravoslavii* ["Social Ethics" in Russian Orthodoxy]. Kiev: Znanie UkSSR, 1982. 46 pp. (Ser. 5 "Nauchno-ateisticheskaia" / O-vo "Znanie" UkSSR; No 11). In Ukrainian. Bibl.: pp. 43-45.

2253 Kopanitsa, M.M. *Sovremennye sotsial'nye kontseptsii russkogo pravoslaviia* [Contemporary Social Conceptions of Russian Orthodoxy]. Khar'kov: Vyshcha shk. Izd-vo pri Khar'k. gos. un-te, 1988. 144 pp. Annot. bibl.: pp. 139-143.

2254 Kop'eva, E.S. "Pervobytnaia mifologiia i religiia: problemy genezisa [Primitive Mythology and Religion: Problems of Genesis]. *Vestn. Mosk. un-ta.* Ser. 7. Filosofiia 2 (1984): 69-77.

2255 Koppel', O. "Afganistan: Revoliutsiia i islam" [Afghanistan: Revolution and Islam]. *Liudina i svit* 8 (1987): 47-51. In Ukrainian.

2256 Korabel'nik, N.M. "Nekotorye voprosy sotsial'no-eticheskogo ucheniia Chaitan'i" [Some Questions on Socio-Ethical Teachings of Chaitanya]. *Obshchestvennaia mysl' Indii.* M., 1989. Pp. 204-217.

2257 *Koran.* [Koran]. Transl. by I.Iu. Krachkovskii. [Ed.: V.I. Beliaev]. 2nd ed. M.: Nauka, 1986. 727 pp., illus. Annot. bibl.: pp. 698-721.

2258 Korbo, Kh. "Preodolevaia nasledie kolonializma" [Surmounting the Legacy of Colonialism]. *Nauka i religiia* 1 (1980): 54-57.

2259 Korcheva, Z.G.; Iashin, P.P. *Sovetskoe zakonodatel'stvo o religioznykh kul'takh* [Soviet Legislation on Religious Cults]. Khar'kov: Vishcha shk. Izd-vo pri Khar'k. un-te, 1985. 119 pp. (Ateist. b-chka studenta). Bibl.: pp. 112-118).

2260 Koretskii, D.; Shamaro, A. "'Sviataia' Nastia" ["The Saint" Nastia]. *Nauka i religiia* 3 (1984): 45-50.

2261 Kormysheva, E.E. *Religiia Kusha* [The Religion of Kusch]. M.: Nauka, 1984. 264 pp. Bibl.: pp. 249-258. Summary in English.

2262   Kornetov, G.B. "U istokov pedagogicheskoi teorii v drevnem Kitae: voprosy vospitaniia v uchenii Konfutsiia" [By the Sources of Pedagogical Theory in Ancient China: Problems of Education in Confucius' Teachings]. *Ocherki istorii shkoly i pedagogicheskoi mysli drevnevego Srednevekovogo Vostoka.* M., 1988. Pp. 46-57. Bibl.: pp. 56-57.

2263   Kornev, V.I. *Buddizm - religiia Vostoka* [Buddhism - Religion of the Orient]. M.: Znanie, 1990. 64 pp. (Novoe v zhizni, nauke, tekhnike. Ateizm i religiia: istoriia, sovremennost'; 2/1990). Index of Buddhist terms: pp. 62-63.

2264   Kornev, V.I. *Buddizm i ego rol' v obshchestvennoi zhizni stran Azii* [Buddhism and Its Role in Social Life of Asian Countries]. M.: Nauka, 1983. 248 pp. Summary in English. Bibl.: pp. 231-242. Index of Buddhist terms: pp. 243-245.

2265   Kornev, V.I. *Buddizm i obshchestvo v stranakh Iuzhnoi i Iugo-Vostochnoi Azii* [Buddhism and Society in Southern and South-Eastern Asian Countries]. M.: Nauka, 1987. 220 pp. Index of Buddhist terms: pp. 213-215. Summary in English.

2266   Kornev, V.[I]. "Buddizm i sovremennaia nauka" [Buddhism and Contemporary Science]. *Aziia i Afrika segodnia* 12 (1988): 54-58. Summary in English, Suppl.: p. 6.

2267   Kornev, V.I. "K izucheniiu buddizma" [On Studying Buddhism]. *Vopr. istorii* 6 (1981): 76-90. Summary in English: p. 190.

2268   Kornev, V.I. "VII Konferentsiia Mezhdunarodnoi assotsiatsii po izucheniiu buddizma" [VIIth Conference of International Association for Study of Buddhism]. *Narody Azii i Afriki* 1 (1986): 139-142.

2269   Korneva, L.S. "Voobrazhenie i religioznoe soznanie" [Imagination and Religious Consciousness]. *Problemy dukhovnoi zhizni sotsialisticheskogo obshchestva.* Omsk, 1984. Pp. 58-71.

2270   Korolev, V. "Aktual'na li ateisticheskaia propaganda?" [Is Atheistic Propaganda Actual?]. *Kommunist Tatarii* 4 (1988): 84-86.

2271   Korolev. V. "Vzaimosviaz' internatsional'nogo i ateisticheskogo vospitaniia" [Correlation of International and Atheistic Education]. *Kommunist Tatarii* 10 (1987): 70-75.

2272 Korotkaia T.P. *Religioznaia filosofiia v Belorussii nachala XX veka:* kriticheskii analiz [Religious Philosophy in Belorussia Early XXth Century: Critical Analysis]. Minsk: Nauka i tekhnika, 1983. 108 pp.

2273 Korovikov, A.V. "Seiid Kutb - ideolog islamskogo ekstremizma" [Sayyid Kutb - Ideologist of Islamic Extremism]. *Religii mira, 1986.* M., 1987. Pp. 120-135.

2274 Korsunkiev, Ts.K. "O prepodavanii gumanitarnykh i estestvenno- nauchnykh distsiplin v kalmytskikh monastyrskikh shkolakh: XIX - nachalo XX vv." [On Teaching Humanities and Natural Sciences in Kalmyk Monastic Schools: XIXth - Eearly XXth C.]. *Voprosy istorii lamaizma v Kalmykii.* Elista, 1987. Pp. 88-99.

2275 Korytin, G.Ia. *Chto takoe sekty: ikh ideologiia i politika* [What Are Sects: Their Ideology and Policy]. Baku: Azernesher, 1987. 134 pp.

2276 Korzheva, K.P. "Problemy pervokhristianstva v sovetskoi istoriografii" [Problems of Prime Christianity in Soviet Historiography]. *Vopr. istorii* 1 (1982): 67-81. Summary in English: p. 190.

2277 Korzun, M.S. "K voprosu o sotial'noi roli religii v Drevnei Gretsii" [On the Problem of the Social Role of Religion in Ancient Greece]. *Vestn. Belorus. un-ta.* Ser. 3, Istoriia, filosofiia, nauch. kommunizm, ekonomika, pravo. 2 (1989): 16-18.

2278 Korzun, M.S. *Russkaia pravoslavnaia tserkov' na sluzhbe ekspluatatorskikh klassov, X v. - 1917 g.* [Russian Orthodox Church in the Service of the Exploiter Classes, Xth. C. - 1917]. Minsk: Belarus', 1984. 255 pp. Bibl.: pp. 251-252. For reviews see items 5111-5112.

2279 Korzun. M.S. *Russkaia pravoslavnaia tserkov', 1917-1945 gg: Izmenenie sotsial.-polit. orientatsii i nauch. nesostoiatel'nost' veroucheniia* [Russian Orthodox Church, 1917-1945: Change of Socio-Political Orientation and Scientific Groundlessness of Dogma]. Minsk: Belarus', 1987. 111 pp. Bibl.: p. 110. Annot. bibl.: pp. 107-109.

2280 Kosarev, V. "Chas pribytiia... chas otbytiia" [Time of Arrival... Time of Departure]. *Kodry* 4 (1988): 3-22.

2281 Kosedovskii, Ia. "Katolicheskaia tserkov' i rabochii klass PNR" [Catholic Church and the Working Class of Polish People's Republic]. *Katolicheskaia tserkov' v PNR v 80-kh godakh*. M., 1988. Pp. 20-47.

2282 Kosenko, V.P. *Kompromissy sovremennykh bogoslovov* [Compromises of Contemporary Theologians]. Alma-Ata: Kazakhstan, 1987. 108 pp.

2283 Kosenko, V.P.; Zyrianov, V.F. *Rekomendatsii po ateisticheskomu vospitaniiu naseleniia* [Recommendations on Atheistic Education of Population]. Alma-Ata: Znanie KazSSR, 1983. 26 pp.

2284 Koshbakhteev, A.R. "Ideologicheskie ustanovki neoreligioznykh kul'tov Zapada" [Ideological Purposes of Western Neoreligious Cults]. *Sbornik trudov Respublikanskoi nauchno-prakticheskoi konferentsii molodykh uchenykh i spetsialistov (12-14 aprelia 1989 g.)*. Dushanbe, 1989. Sektsiia "Obshchestvennye nauki".

2285 Koshkarian, M.S. "Khristianskii spiritualizm v Italii (1945-68) i istoriko-filosofskaia traditsiia" [Christian Spiritualism in Italy (1945-68) and Historic-Philosophical Tradition]. *Respublikanskaia nauchno-teoreticheskaia konferentsiia molodykh uchenykh i spetsialistov po obshchestvennym naukam, posviashchennaia 70-letiiu VLKSM: Riga, 24-25 noiab. 1988 g.* Riga, 1988. Pp. 88-89.

2286 Kosidovskii, Z. *Bibleiskie skazaniia* [Biblical Legends]. Erevan: Aiastan, 1980. 551 pp., illus. In Armenian.
Published also in:
M.: Politizdat, 1987. 463 pp., illus (5th ed.).
Tallin: Eesti raamat, 1988, 334 pp., ilus. In Estonian.

2287 Kosidovskii, Z. "Istoki khristianstva" [Sources of Christianity]. Transl. from Polish. *Nauka i religiia* 10 (1984): 46-50.

2288 Kosidovskii, Z. *Skazaniia evangelistov* [Evangelist Gospels]. Kiev: Politizdat Ukrainy, 1981. 260 pp. In Ukrainian; 2nd ed. 1985, 262 pp.
Published also in:
Riga: Zinatne, 1982. 352 pp. In Latvian.
Vil'nius: Vaga, 1984. 389 pp., illus. In Lithuanian; 2nd ed. by Vituris, 1985.
M.: Politizdat, 1987. 256 pp., illus. 4th ed.

2289 Kosolapova, O.R. "Rol' obshchestvennogo mneniia v ateisticheskom vospitanii" [The Role of Public Opinion in Atheistic Education]. *Dukhovnye tsennosti kak predmet filosofskogo analiza.* M., 1985. Pp. 103-108.

2290 Kosova, N.A. "Kriticheskii ocherk psikhologii religii v SShA" [Critical Essay of Psychology of Religion in USA]. *Vopr. psikhologii* 3 (1981): 158-162.

2291 Kosova, N.A. "Sotsial'no-psikhologicheskie osobennosti veruiushchego" [Believers' Socio-Psychological Features]. *Psikhol. zhurnal* v. 3, 1 (1982): 151-152.

2292 Kostareva, S.B. "Ob osobennostiakh funktsionirovaniia protestantskikh obshchin Omskoi oblasti" [Functions and Features of Protestant Communities of Omsk Oblast]. *Protestantskie organizatsii v SSSR.* M., 1988. Pp. 144-148.

2293 Kostenko, N.A. *Ateizm i nravstvennost'* [Atheism and Morals]. M.: Mysl' 1982. 175 pp. For reviews see items 5113-5115.

2294 Kostenko, N.A. "Nauchnyi ateizm i ego rol' v formirovanii soznaniia lichnosti" [Scientific Atheism and Its Role in Forming Individual's Consciousness]. *Nauchnyi ateizm, religiia i sovremennost'.* Novosibirsk, 1987. Pp. 7-26.

2295 Kostenko, N.[A]. "Pered soboi i obshchestvom" [In the Face of Oneself and Society]. *Nauka i religiia* 11 (1981): 8-9.

2296 Kostenko, N.A. "Religiia i ateizm v sovremennoi ideologicheskoi bor'be" [Religion and Atheism in Contemporary Ideological Struggle]. *Osobennosti ideologicheskoi bor'by v sovremennykh usloviiakh.* Novosibirsk, 1985. Pp. 120-134.

2297 Kostiuchenko, V.S. "Filosofiia Shankary i neovedantizm" [Sankara's Philosophy and Neovedantism]. *Obshchestvennaia mysl' Indii.* M., 1989. Pp. 153-178.

2298 Kostiuchenko, V.S. *Klassicheskaia vedanta i neovedantizm* [Classical Vedanta and Neovedantism]. M.: Mysl' 1983. 272 pp., illus. Annot. bibl.: pp. 245-271.

2299   Kosukha, P.I. "Ateisticheskoe vospitanie i dukhovnyi mir molodogo pokoleniia" [Atheistic Upbringing and Young Generation's Spiritual World]. *Vopr. ateizma* 19 (1983): 17-26.

2300   Kosukha, P.I. *Differentsirovannyi podkhod v ateisticheskoi rabote s veruiushchimi* [Differential Approach in Atheistic Work with Believers]. Kiev: Znanie UkSSR, 1983. 16 pp. (B-chka v pomoshch' lektoru "Probl. nauch. ateizma" / O-vo "Znanie" UkSSR). In Ukrainian.

2301   Kosukha, P.I. *Nauchnyi ateizm i dukhovnyi mir molodezhi* [Scientific Atheism and Youth's Spiritual World]. Kiev: Znanie UkSSR, 1982. 46 pp. (Ser. 5 "Nauch.-ateisticheskaia" / O-vo "Znanie" UkSSR; No 8). Bibl.: p. 48. Annot bibl.: pp. 46-48.

2302   Kosukha, P.I. *Nauchnyi ateizm v sisteme dukhovnykh tsennostei sotsializma* [Scientific Atheism in the System of Spiritual Values of Socialism]. Kiev: Vishcha shk., 1983. 73 pp. (Ateist. b-chka studenta).

2303   Kosukha, P.I. *Religiia v planakh antikommunizma* [Religion in the Plans of Anti Communism]. Kiev: Politizdat Ukrainy, 1980. 88 pp. In Ukrainian.

2304   Kotliar, I. "Siloi kollektivnogo mneniia" [By Force of Collective Opinion]. *Kommunist Belorussii* 9 (1986): 60-66.

2305   Kotliar, N.F. "Iazychestvo i khristianstvo: smena formatsii - smena religii" [Heathenism and Christianity: Change of Structure - Change of Religion]. *Kommunist Ukrainy* 6 (1988): 68-77.

2306   Kotliar, N.F. *Vvedenie khristianstva v Kievskoi Rusi i ego posledstviia* [Introduction of Christianity into Kievan Rus' and Its Consequences]. Kiev: Znanie UkSSR, 1985. 48 pp. (Ser. 5 "Nauchno-ateisticheskaia" / O-vo "Znanie" UkSSR; N 8). In Ukrainian. Annot. bibl.: pp. 47-48.

2307   Kotov, O.V.; Rogachev, M.B. 'V boga ne veriu...': *Molodezh': religiia i ateizm* ["I Don't Believe in God...": Youth: Religion and Atheism]. Syktyvkar: Komi kn. izd-vo, 1984. 93 pp., illus. Bibl.: pp. 90-92.

2308   Kotov, O.V.; Rogachev, M.B.; Shabaev, Iu.P. "Religioznye obriady i molodezh'" [Religious Rituals and Youth]. *Aktual'nye problemy nauchno-ateisticheskogo vospitaniia molodezhi*. M., 1987. Pp. 141-146.

2309 Koval', A.D.; Konechnaia, T.G. "Novye podkhody v rabote s veruiushchimi" [New Approaches in the Work with Believers]. *Veruiushchii v usloviiakh perestroiki.* M., 1989. Pp. 112-126.

2310 Kovalenko, A.P. *Suggestivnost' iskusstva, religiia, ateizm* [Suggestiveness of Art, Religion, Atheism]. Kiev: Znanie UkSSR, 1989. 31 pp. (Ser. 5, Nauchno-ateisticheskaia / O-vo "Znanie" UkSSR; No 11). In Ukrainian.

2311 Kovalev, V.I. "Sotsial'no-psikhologicheskie mekhanizmy formirovaniia religioznykh potrebnostei individa" [Socio-Psychological Mechanisms of Formation of Religious Needs of the Individual]. *Kritika religioznoi ideologii i problemy ateisticheskogo vospitaniia.* M., 1980. Pp. 55-61.

2312 Koval'skii, N.A. *Imperializm. Religiia. Tserkov'.* [Imperialism. Religion. Church.]. M.: Politizdat, 1986. 271 pp. For reviews see items 5116-5118.

2313 Koval'skii, N.A. "Kommunisticheskoe dvizhenie v stranakh Zapada i religioznye sily" [Communist Movement in Western Countries and Religious Forces]. *Vopr. nauch. ateizma* 33 (1985): 85-104.

2314 Koval'skii, N.A. "Vatikan: 'Kak prodvigat'sia vpered...?'" [Vatican: "How to Advance...?"]. *Latin. Amerika* 9 (1980): 40-51.

2315 Koval'skii, N.A.; Ivanova, I.M. *Katolitsizm i mezhdunarodnye otnosheniia* [Catholicism and International Relations]. M.: Politizdat, 1989. 270 pp. Bibl.: pp. 258-269.

2316 Kovel'man, A.B. *Ritorika v teni piramid* [Rhetoric under the Shadow of Pyramids]. M.: Nauka, 1988. 192 pp., illus. (Ser. Po sledam ischznuvshikh kul'tur Vostoka). Bibl.: pp. 161-184.

2317 Kovnatskii, E.P. *Istina glazami veruiushchego i ateista* [The Truth in the Eyes of Believer and Atheist]. Groznyi: Chech.-Ing. kn. izd-vo, 1988. 56 pp.

2318 Kovnatskii, E.P. *Iudaizm i sionizm* [Judaism and Zionism]. Groznyi: Chech.-Ing. kn. izd-vo, 1985. 64 pp.

2319 Kovynev, V.M.; Pasika, V.M. "Katolicheskoe uchenie o cheloveke i sovremennost'" [Catholic Teaching About the Man and Contemporaneity]. *Vopr. nauch. ateizma* 28 (1981): 143-162.

2320 Kozachishin, N.N. *Novye popytki - starye tseli* [New Attempts - Old Goals]. L'vov: Kameniar, 1985. 80 pp. In Ukrainian.

2321 Kozachishin, N.N.; Matiukhina, A.A. *'Vostochnaia politika' Vatikana* [Vatican's "Oriental Policy"]. L'vov: Kameniar, 1989. 70 pp. In Ukrainian.

2322 Kozachishin, N.N.; Simonchik, A.N. *Vopreki vole naroda* [In Spite of People's Will]. L'vov: Vishcha shk. Izd-vo pri L'vov. un-te, 1984. 63 pp. (Ateist. b-chka studenta). In Ukrainian.

2323 Kozak, T.D. *Ateizm i sotsial'naia aktivnost' lichnosti* [Atheism and Individual's Social Activity]. Kiev: Znanie UkSSR, 1983. 16 pp. (B-chka v pomoshch' lektoru "Probl. nauch. ateizma" / O-vo "Znanie" UkSSR). In Ukrainian.

2324 Kozarzhevskii, A.Ch. *Istochnikovedcheskie problemy rannekhristianskoi literatury* [Problems of Study of Sources of Early Christian Literature]. M.: Izd-vo MGU, 1985. 146 pp. For review see item 5119.

2325 Kozarzhevskii, A.Ch. "A.I. Vvedenskii i obnovlencheskii raskol v Moskve" [A.I. Vvedenskii and Reform Split in Moscow]. *Vest. Mosk. un-ta.* Ser. 8, istoriia 1 (1989): 54-66.

2326 Kozhemiakin, G. "Ateisticheskii tsentr" [Atheistic Centre]. *Agitator* 16 (1981): 57-59.

2327 Kozhevnikov, A.V. "O propagande ateizma v muzeiakh pod otkrytom nebom" [Propaganda of Atheism in Open Air Museums]. *Muzei v ateisticheskoi propagande.* L., 1986. Pp. 23-31.

2328 Kozhin, P.M. "Partiia i religioznye organizatsii: problema nachal'nogo etapa stroitel'stva sotsializma" [The Party and Religious Oganizations: Problem of Initial Stage of Building of Socialism]. *Problema stroitel'stva sotsializma v Kitaiskoi Narodnoi Respublike v Svete reshenii XIII s'ezda Kommunisticheskoi partii Kitaia.* M., 1989. Pp. 201-207.

2329 Kozhokin, M.M. *Khristiansko-demokraticheskoe dvizhenie v burzhuaznoi Pol'skoi Respublike (1918-1926 gg.)* [Christian-Democratic Movement in Polish Bourgeois Republic (1918-1926)]. M: [S.n.], 1989. 198 pp. Bibl.: pp. 175-198.

2330 Kozhurin, Ia.[Ia]. "Muzei i ateisticheskoe vospitanie" [Museum and Atheistic Education]. *Agitator* 21 (1985): 58-60.

2331 Kozhurin, Ia.Ia. "Rol' muzeev v ateisticheskoi propagande" [The Role of Museums in Atheistic Propaganda]. *Vopr. nauch. ateizma* 34 (1986): 212-223.

2332 Kozhurin, Ia.Ia.; Savel'ev, S.N. "Bogoiskatel'stvo i pravoslavnyi modernizm" [God-Seeking and Orthodox Modernism]. *Sotsial'no-filosofskie aspekty kritiki religii.* L., 1987. Pp. 81-95.

2333 Kozik, P.Z. "K voprosu o razvitii khristianstva vo II-III vv." [On the Issue of Development of Christianity in the IInd-IIIrd C.]. *Vopr. ateizma* 19 (1983): 118-131.

2334 Kozik, P.Z. *Rannee khristianstvo: vymysly i deistvitel'nost'* [Early Christianity: Falsehoods and Reality]. Kiev: Vishcha shk., 1987. 113 pp. Bibl.: pp. 108-112.

2335 Kozin, A.P. *Religioznye verovaniia v svete nauchnoi medetsiny* [Religious Beliefs in the Light of Scientific Medicine]. Kiev: Zdorov'ia, 1983. 54 pp. For review see item 5120.

2336 Kozlenko, V.N.; Chernyshov, A.V. "Aktivizatsiia ateisticheskoi raboty studentov" [Activization of Students' Atheistic Work]. *Vopr. ateizma* 23 (1987): 49-54.

2337 Kozlov, B. "Svoboda sovesti i bessovestnaia lozh'" [Freedom of Conscience and Unscrupulous Lie]. *Novoe vremia* 5 (1985): 23-24.

2338 Kozlovskii, Iu.B. "Konfutsianskie shkoly: filosofskaia mysl' i avtoritarnye traditsii" [Confucian Schools: Philosophic Thought and Authoritarian Traditions]. *Narody Azii i Afriki* 3 (1987): 67-77.

2339 Kozlovskii, Iu.B. "Osobennosti razvitiia mysli v konfutsianskikh shkolakh drevnosti i srednevekov'ia" [Features of Thought Development in Confucian Ancient and Medieval Schools]. *Filos. nauki.* 6 (1988): 51-61.

2340 Kozlovskii, V.P. "Vl.S. Solov'ev ob antinomiiakh srednevekovogo religioznogo mirovozzreniia" [Vl.S. Solov'ev on Antinomies of Medieval Religious Outlook]. *Otechestvennaia obshchestvennaia mysl' epokhi Srednevekov'ia.* Kiev, 1988. Pp. 67-77.

2341   Kraliuk, P.M. "Mesto sotsinianstva v kul'turno-prosvetitel'skom protsesse na Ukraine v pervoi polovine XVII st." [The Place of Sotsinian Movement in Cultural-Enlightenment Process in Ukraine in the Early XVIIth C.]. *Otechestvennaia obshchestvennaia mysl' epokhi Srednevekov'ia*. Kiev, 1988. Pp. 269-274.

2342   Kramar, P.P. "Nesostoiatel'nost' religioznoi kontseptsii truda i tvorchestva" [Groundlessness of Religious Conception of Labour and Creative Work]. *Vopr. ateizma* 18 (1982): 127-134.

2343   Kramar, P.P.; Chernyshev, V.S. *Nauchnyi ateizm: filosofsko-mirovozzrencheskoe obosnovanie* [Scientific Atheism: On Philosophic - Outlook Basis]. Kiev: Vishcha shk., 1989. 81 pp. (Ateist. b-chka studenta).

2344   Krapivina, R.N. "Raniaia istoriia tibetskogo roda Kon i vosniknovenie shkoly tibetskogo buddizma Sachzhaba" [Early History of Tibetan Clan Kon and the Rise of School of Tibetan Sachjab Buddhism]. *Pis'mennye pamiatniki i problemy istorii kul'tury narodov Vostoka: XV godich. nauch. sessiia LO IV AN SSSR*. M., 1981. Ch. I(I), Pp. 109-115.

2345   Krasikov, A. "Bez prava na ravnodushie: Rus. pravoslav. tserkov' i bor'ba za mir" [Not Entitled to Indifference: Russian Orthodox Church and the Struggle for Peace]. *Nauka i religiia* 6 (1988): 15.

2346   Krasikov, A.A. *Akkreditirovan v Vatikane: Zametki sov. zhurnalista* [Accredited in Vatican: Notes of a Soviet Journalist]. M.: Novosti, 1988. 100 pp., illus. In Spanish. Published also in Italian.

2347   Krasikov, A.[A]. "Ioann Pavel II" [John Paul II]. *Ekho planety* 20 (1988): 20-24.

2348   Krasiuk, V.F. "Dialektika formirovaniia ateisticheskogo mirovozzreniia na urovne obydennogo soznaniia" [Dialectics of Forming Atheistic Outlook on the Level of Ordinary Consciousness]. *Nauch. ateizm i ateist. vospitanie* 1 (1983): 31-40.

2349   Krasnikov, A.N. "Kritika transtsendental'nogo [kanadskogo katolika] Bernarda Lonergana" [Criticism of Transcendental [of Canadian Catholic] Bernard Lonerghan]. *Aktual'nye problemy ateisticheskogo vospitaniia i kritika religioznoi ideologii*. M., 1983. Pp. 25-29.

2350 Krasnikov, A.N. "Priroda religioznogo dogmatizma" [The Nature of Religious Dogmatism]. *Kriticheskii analiz nenauchnogo znaniia.* M., 1989. Pp. 91-107.

2351 Krasnikov, A.N.; Popov, A.S. "Razvitie ateisticheskoi ubezhdennosti studentov vo vneuchebnoi vospitatel'noi rabote" [Development of Atheistic Conviction of Students in Extracurricular Educational Work]. *Prepodavanie nauchnogo ateizma v vuze.* M., 1988. Pp. 202-214.

2352 Krasnikov, N.P. *Evoliutsiia sotsial'no-eticheskikh vozzrenii Russkogo pravoslaviia* [Evolution of Socio-Ethical Outlooks of Russian Orthodoxy]. M.: Znanie, 1986. 64 pp. (Novoe v zhizni, nauke, tekhnike. Nauch. ateizm; 3). Bibl.: pp. 60-61.

2353 Krasnikov, N.P. "Kritika sovremennykh bogoslovskikh istolkovanii roli pravoslaviia v istorii Rossii" [Criticism of Contemporary Theological Interpretations of the Role of Orthodoxy in the History of Russia]. *Vopr. nauch. ateizma* 37 (1988): 237-250.

2354 Krasnikov, N.P. *Moral' bez budushchego:* (Nravstv. progress, ateizm, religiia) [Morals without Future: (Moral Progress, Atheism, Religion)]. M.: Mosk. rabochii, 1984. 94 pp. (Besedy o religii).

2355 Krasnikov, N.P. *Pravoslavnaia etika: proshloe i nastoiashchee* [Orthodox Ethics: The Past and Present]. M.: Politizdat, 1981. 96 pp. For reviews see items 5121-5122.

2356 Krasnikov, N.P. *Russkoe pravoslavie: istoriia, sovremennost'* [Russian Orthodoxy: History, Contemporaneity]. M.: Mosk. rabochii, 1988. 77 pp. (Ser. "Pozitsiia"). Annot. bibl.: 71-76.

2357 Krasnikov, N.P. *Sotsial'no-eticheskie vozzreniia russkogo pravoslaviia v XX veke* [Socio-Ethical Views of Russian Orthodoxy in the XXth Century]. Kiev: Vyshcha shk., 1988. 179 pp. Bibl.: pp. 172-178.

2358 Krasnikov, N.P. "Sotsial'no-eticheskii aspekt religioznogo reformatorstva kontsa XIX - nachala XX v." [Socio-Ethical Aspect of Religious Reformation Late XIXth - Early XXth C.]. *Vopr. nauch. ateizma* 26 (1980): 206-222.

2359 Krasnikov, N.P.; Stepin, K.K. *Istoriia, kul'tura i ateisticheskoe vospitanie* [History, Culture and Atheistic Education]. M.: Znanie RSFSR, 1981. 39

pp. (V pomoshch' lektoru / O-vo "Znanie" RSFSR, Nauch.-metod. sovet po propagande Nauch. ateizma). Bibl.: pp. 37-38.

2360   Krasnodembskaia, N.[G]. "Buddizm: idealy i real'nost'" [Buddhism: Ideals and Reality]. *Aziia i Afrika segodnia* 7 (1985): 58-61. Summary in English, suppl.: p. 5.

2361   Krasnodembskaia, N.[G]. "Buddizm: istoki, idei, dogmy" [Buddhism: Origins, Ideas, Dogmas]. *Aziia i Afrika segodnia* 6 (1985): 58-61.

2362   Krasnodembskaia, N.G. *Traditsionnoe mirovozzrenie singalov: (Obriady i verovaniia)* [Traditional World Outlook of Singals: (Rites and Beliefs)]. M.: Nauka, 1982. 213 bibl., illus. Bibl.: pp. 203-212.

2363   Krasnov, A.V. *Iz t'my k svetu* [From Darkness to Light]. Ioshkar-Ola: Mariiskoe kn. izd-vo, 1986. 82 pp. In Mari.

2364   Krasnov, A.V. *Kak i zachem voznikla religiia* [How and Why Religion Arose]. Ioshkar-Ola: Mariiskoe kn. izd-vo, 1984. 79 pp., illus. In Mari.

2365   Krasnov, A.V. *Kul'tura i religiia* [Culture and Religion]. Ioshkar-Ola: Mariiskoe kn. izd-vo, 1988. 86 pp. In Mari.

2366   Krasovskaia, L.M. "Nesostoiatel'nost' sotsial'no-eticheskikh kontseptsii sovremennogo katolitsizma" [Groundlessness of Socio-Ethical Conceptions of the Contemporary Catholicism]. *Vopr. ateizma* 18 (1982): 99-106.

2367   Krasovskaia, L.M.; Stetsenko, V.I. "Kritika katolicheskikh klerikal'nykh istolkovanii nravstvennoi tsennosti nauchnogo ateizma" [Criticism of Catholic Clerical Interpretation of Moral Values of Scientific Atheism]. *Vopr. ateizma* 25 (1989): 85-92.

2368   Krasovskaia, L.M.; Stetsenko, V.I. "Osobennosti kritiki nravstvennykh konseptsii katolitsizma v protsesse prepodavaniia nauchnogo ateizma" [Features of Criticism of Moral Conceptions of Catholicism in the Teaching Process of Scientific Atheism]. *Tezisy dokladov i vystuplenii na Vsesoiuznoi nauchno-metodicheskoi konferentsii "Nauchnye osnovy kritiki nemarksistskikh kontseptsii v kursakh obshchestvennykh distsiplin", 12-15 okt. 1988 g.* Odessa, 1988. Pp. 109-110.

2369 Kraus, K.N. "Molites' za Reigena, kogda vy molites' za missii!" [Pray for Reagan, When You Pray for Mission!]. *Argumenty, 1987.* M., 1987. Pp. 185-187.

2370 Kravchenko, I.I. *Kritika religioznykh kontseptsii burzhuaznogo obshchestva* [Criticism of Religious Conceptions of Bourgeois Society]. M.: Znanie, 1982. 64 pp. (Novoe v zhizni, nauke, tekhnike. Ser. "Nauch. kommunizm"; 6). Bibl.: p. 61.

2371 Kravchenko, I.I. "Sovremennoe nauchnoe poznanie i krizis religii" [Contemporary Scientific Knowledge and Crisis of Religion]. *Vopr. nauch. ateizma* 26 (1980): 89-108.

2372 Kravchuk, L.[M]. "Ateisticheskaia rabota v novykh usloviiakh" [Atheistic Work under New Conditions]. *Pod znamenem leninizma* 6 (1988): 12-20.

2373 Kravchuk, L.[M]. "Konkretno, tvorcheski, effektivno" [Concrete, Creative, Effective]. *Nauka i religiia* 6 (1985): 2-5.

2374 Kravchuk, L.M. "Novye grani ateisticheskogo vospitaniia [New Verges of Atheistic Education]. *Kommunist Ukrainy* 5 (1989): 17-27.
Published also in: *Kommunist Belorussii* 9 (1989): 38-45.

2375 Kravchuk, L.[M]. "Umelo i deistvenno vesti ateicheskoe vospitanie" [To Conduct Atheistic Education Skillfully and Effectively]. *Part. zhizn'* 10 (1982): 56-60.

2376 Kravtsova, M.E. "Obriad 'prepodneseniia kubkov' (shi dian') i ofitsial'naia ideologia Shesti dinastii" [The Ceremony of "Presentation of Goblets" (Si Dyan) and Official Ideology of the Six Dynasties]. *Deviatnadtsataia nauchnaia konferentsiia "Obshchestvo i gosudarstvo v Kitae".* M., 1988. Ch. I. Pp. 147-152.

2377 Krest'ianinov, V.F. *Aktivnaia zhiznennaia pozitsiia i ateisticheskoe vospitanie* [Active Vital Position and Atheistic Education]. L.: Znanie RSFSR, Leningrd. org., 1980. 16 pp. (V pomoshch' lektoru / O-vo "Znanie" RSFSR, Leningr. org.). Bibl.: p. 16.

2378 Krest'ianinov, V.F. "Vospityvat' ubezhdennykh ateistov" [To Educate Convinced Atheists]. *Aktual'. vopr. metodiki prepodavaniia obshchestv. nauk i kom. vospitaniia studentov* 5 (1987): 75-79.

2379   Krianev, Iu.V. "Ekumenicheskie kontseptsii cheloveka" [Man's Ecumenical Conceptions]. *Filosofiia: istoriia i sovremennost'* M., 1988. Pp. 101- 107.

2380   Krianev, Iu.V. *Khristianskii ekumenizm* [Christian Ecumenism]. M.: Politizdat, 1980. 159 pp.
       Published also in:
       M.: Progress, 1982. 246 pp. In English. For review see item 5123.

2381   Krianev, Iu.[V].; Pavlova, T. "'Kreshchenie Rusi': fakty i in- terpretatsii" ["Christening of Rus'": Facts and Interpretations]. *Kommu- nist* 12 (1989): 124-127.

2382   Krichevtsova, N.E. "Ispovedal'nyi zhanr v evropeiskoi kul'ture i khristianskaia kontseptsiia cheloveka" [Confessional Genre in European Culture and Christian Conception of Man]. *Otnoshenie cheloveka k irratsional'nomu.* Sverdlovsk, 1989. Pp. 289-310.

2383   Krimus, Iu.V. *Nesostoiatel'nost' baptistskoi kontseptsii 'obshchestva budushchevo'* [Groundlessness of Baptist Conception of "Society of the Future"]. Kiev: Znanie UkSSR, 1983. 32 pp. (Ser. 5 "Nauchno- ateisticheskaia" / O-vo "Znanie" UkSSR; No 11). Bibl.: p. 32. Annot. bibl.: p. 31.

2384   Krinichnaia, N.A. *Korreliatsiia arkhetipov individa, kollektiva i prirody v mifologii* [Correlation of Archetypes of Individual, Group, and Nature in Mythology]. Petrozavodsk: KFAN SSSR, 1986. 41 pp.

2385   Krishtopa, S.I. *Ateisticheskaia napravlennost' nravstvennykh tsennostei obshchestva razvitogo sotsializma* [Atheistic Trend of Moral Values of Society of Developed Socialism]. Kiev: Znanie UkSSR, 1981. 47 pp. (Ser. 5 "Nauchno-ateisticheskaia" / O-vo "Znanie" UkSSSR; No 8). In Ukrainian. Bibl.: p. 45.

2386   Krishtopa, S.I.; Krishtopa, V.I. *Ateisticheskaia napravlennost' nravstvennykh tsennostei sotsialisticheskogo obshchestva* [Atheistic Trend of Moral Values of Socialist Society]. Kiev: Nauk. dumka, 1987. 177 pp. Annot. bibl.: pp. 168-176.

2387   *Kriterii istiny* [Criterions of Truth]. Comp.: A.A. Minailenko. L'vov: Kameniiar, 1986. 100 pp. In Ukrainian.

2388 *Kriticheskii analiz klerikal'noi radiopropagandy* [Critical Analysis of Clerical Radiopropaganda]. Kiev: Znanie UkSSR. Resp. dom nauch. ateizma, 1989- (V pomoshch' lektoram, propagandistam nauch. ateizma). Vyp. 1. Prepared by V.V. Fomichenko. 35 pp.

2389 *Kriticheskii analiz nenauchnogo znaniia* [Critical Analysis of Unscientific Knowledge]. [Ed.: I.T. Kasanin]. M.: [S.n.], 1989. 145 pp.

2390 *Kriticheskii analiz ponimaniia obshchestva i lichnosti v pravoslavii* [Critical Analysis of Conception of Society and Individual in Orthodoxy]. Ed.: V.A. Bespiatnykh. Kazan': Izd-vo Kazan. un-ta, 1985. 94 pp. Annot bibl.: pp. 85-92.

2391 *Kritika burzhuazno-klerikal'noi falsifikatsii politiki KPSS i sovetskogo gosudarstva v otnoshenii religii i tserkvi* [Criticism of Bourgeois- Clerical Falsifications of CPSU and Soviet State's Policies in Relation to Religion and Church]. [Comp.: V.G. Lukasheva]. L.: Znanie RSFSR, Leningr. org., 1982. 16 pp. Bibl.: p. 16.

2392 *Kritika filosofskoi apologii religii* [Criticism of Philosophical Apology of Religion]. Ed.: B.A. Lobovik. Kiev: Nauk. dumka, 1985. 278 pp.

2393 *Kritika ideologii i praktiki netradisionnykh kul'tov i neomistitsizma* [Criticism of Ideology and Practice of Nontraditional Cults and Neomysticism]. [Comp.: A.A. Chechulin]. Novosibirsk: [S.n.], 1989. 121 pp.

2394 *Kritika katolicheskoi i uniatskoi ideologii v ateisticheskoi propagande* [Criticism of Catholic and Uniate Church Ideology in Atheistic Propaganda]. [Ed.: A.V. Iartys']. L'vov: [S.n.], 1985 -
Ch. 1. *Kritika ideologii i deiatel'nosti sovremennogo katolitsizma* [Criticism of Ideology and Activity of Contemporary Catholicism]. 1985. 75 pp.
Ch. 2. *Kritika ideologii i antinarodnoi deiatel'nosti zarubezhnykh ostatkov uniatstva* [Criticism of Ideology and Antipopular Activity of Remainders Uniates from Abroad]. 1985. 35 pp.
Ch. 3. *Osobennosti ateisticheskoi raboty sredi katolikov i veruiushchikh iz chisla byvshikh uniatov* [Features of Atheistic Work Among Catholics and Believers, Former Uniates]. 1985. 47 pp.

2395 "Kritika novykh tendentsii v sovremennoi khristianskoi ideologii" [Criticism of New Tendencies in the Contemporary Christian Ideology]. A. L. Buriakovskii et al. *Ideologicheskaia bor'ba i molodezh'*. L., 1987. Pp. 136-145.

2396 *Kritika religioznoi ideologii i problemy ateisticheskogo vospitaniia* [Criticism of
      Religious Ideology and Problems of Atheistic Education]. M.: Izd-vo
      MGU.
      Vyp. 5. 1980. 113 pp. Ed.: N.K. Dmitrieva.
      Vyp. 7. 1987. 97 pp. Ed.: N.A. Pashkova.

2397 *Kritika sovremennoi katolicheskoi i protestantskoi teologii* [Criticism of Con-
      temporary Catholic and Protestant Theology]. [Ed.: F.G. Ovsienko]. M.:
      AON, 1989. 134 pp.

2398 *Kritika   sovremennykh   religiozno-idealisticheskikh   kontseptsii* [Criticism of
      Current Religious-Idealistic Conceptions]. [Ed.: V.I. Plekhov]. M.: [S.n.],
      1979 (Publ. 1980). 112 pp.

2399 *Kritika vneveroispovedenykh form religii (very v sud'bu, gadaniia, znakharstva)*
      [Criticism of Extra Denomination Forms of Religion (Beliefs in Fate,
      Fortune-Telling, Sorcery)]. L.: Leningr. org. o-va "Znanie" RSFSR, 1985.
      19 pp. Bibl.: p. 18.

2400 Kriuchkov, N.I.; Mikhailov, T.M. *Preodolenie religioznykh perezhitkov Buriatii*
      [Overcoming Religious Survivals of Buriat]. Ulan-Ude: Buriat. kn. izd-vo,
      1987. 143 pp. Bibl.: pp. 141-142. Annot. bibl.: pp. 131-137. For review see
      item 5124.

2401 Krivitskii, V.V. "O znachenii obraza konia i povozki v religii i iskusstve
      drevnego Kavkaza" [On the Meaning of the Image of Horse and Carriage
      in the Religion and Art of Ancient Caucasus]. *Izv. Akad. nauk GSSR.*
      Iugo-Oset. NII. Tbilisi, 1987. Vyp. 31. Pp. 66-73.

2402 Krivonosov, V.T; Makarov, B.A. *Arkhitekturnyi ansambl' Borisoglebskogo*
      monastyria [Architectural Harmony of the Borisgleb Monastery]. M.:
      Iskusstvo, 1987. 199 pp., illus. Summary in English. Bibl.: p. 190.

2403 Krivosheev, Iu.B. *Religiia vostochnykh slavian nakanune kreshcheniia Rusi*
      [Religion of Oriental Slavs on the Eve of Baptism of Rus']. L.: Znanie
      RSFSR. Leningr. org. Leningr. Dom nauch. ateizma, 1988. 32 pp. Bibl.:
      p. 32.

2404 Krivov, M.V. "Apocalypse of pseudo-methodius of Patara as a source on
      history of Ethiopia"* *Proceedings of the ninth International congress of*
      Ethiopian studies, Moscow, 26-29 Aug. 1986. Moscow, 1988. Pp. 111-117.

2405 *Krizis sovremennoi khristianskoi apologetiki* [Crizis of the Contemporary Christian Apologetics]. M.: Znanie, 1981. 64 pp. (Novoe v zhizni, nauke, tekhnike. Ser. "Nauch. ateizm"; No 12}. Bibl.: p. 63.

2406 Krotov, G.A.; Timofeev, V.I. *'Sviatoe delo'* ["Holy Cause"]. M.: Sov. Rossiia, 1987. 124 pp. (Po tu storonu).

2407 Kruglov, A.[A]. "Issledovanie katolitsizma belorusskimi uchenymi" [Research of Catholicism by Belorussian Scientists]. *Ateistines minties raida lietuvoje.* Kaunas, 1988. Pp. 119-127. Bibl.: pp. 125-127.

2408 Kruglov, A.A. *My i religiia* [We and Religion]. Minsk: Belarus', 1984. 96 pp. Annot. bibl.: p. 92.

2409 Kruglov, A.A. *Osnovy nauchnogo ateizma* [Fundamentals of Scientific Atheism]. Minsk: Belarus', 1983. 319 pp. Annot. bibl.: pp. 313-316.

2410 Kruglov, A.A. *Razvitie ateizma v Belorussii (1917-1987 gg)* [Development of Atheism in Belorussia (1917-1987)]. Minsk: Belarus', 1989. 367 pp. Bibl.: pp. 334-357. Name and subject index: pp. 357-366.

2411 Kruglov, A.A. "Razvitie i propaganda nauchnogo ateizma" [Development and Propaganda of Scientific Atheism]. *Vestn. Belorus. un-ta.* Ser. 3. Istoriia, filosofiia, nauch. kommunizm, ekonomika, pravo 3 (1981): 19-23.

2412 "Kruglyi stol: 1000-letie khristianizatsii Rusi" [The Round Table: Millennium of Baptism of Rus']. *Sov. slavianovedenie* 6 (1988): 10-75.

2413 Kruzhilin, Iu. "Dlia vsekh, krome nishchikh dukhom: Razmyshleniia o religii i ateizme" [To All, Except Poor in Spirit: Reflections on Religion and Atheism]. *Zvezda Vostoka* 7 (1985): 121-127.

2414 Krylova, S.E. "K voprosu o tserkovnoi reforme v Anglii vo vtoroi polovine XII v." [On the Question of Church Reform in England Late XIIth C.]. *Sotsial'no-politicheskie otnosheniia v Zapadnoi Evrope (srednie veka - novoe vremia).* Ufa, 1988. Pp. 3-11.

2415 Krystev, K. "Po puti dukhovnogo osvobozhdeniia" [On the Way of Spiritual Liberation]. *Nauka i religiia* 9 (1980): 55-58.

2416   Krystev, K. "Vzaimootnosheniia mezhdu gosudarstvom i tserkv'iu v Narodnoi
        Respublike Bolgarii" [Interrelations Between the State and Church in
        People's Republic of Bulgaria]. *Vopr. nauch. ateizma* 36 (1987): 178-190.

2417   Kryvelev, I. "Bol'she vzyskatel'nosti" [More Demanding]. *Kommunist.* Vil'nius.
        7 (1984): 69-74.

2418   Kryvelev, I. *Khristos: mif ili deistvitel'nost'?* [Christ: Myth or Reality?]. M.:
        Obshchestv. nauki i sovremennost', 1987. 143 pp. (Ser. Sov. religiovedenie
        / AN SSSR; No 1). For reviews see items 5125-5126.

2419   Kryvelev, I. "Pervorodnyi grekh i sud'by chelovechestva" [Original Sin and
        the Fortunes of Humanity]. *Nauka i religiia* 6 (1985): 28-31.

2420   Kryvelev, I. "Religiia - istochnik i garant nravstvennosti?" [Religion - Source
        and Guarantor of Morality?]. *Rodina* 8 (1989): 53.

2421   Kryvelev, I. "V otvet na otkliki" [Answer to Comments]. *Nauka i religiia* 12
        (1982): 40-41.

2422   Kryvelev, I. "Veruiu... veruiu..." [I Belive... I Believe...]. *Nauka i religiia* 8
        (1983): 37-39.

2423   Kryvelev, I. "Vo chto zhe veruet pravoslavnyi episkop?: Moia polemika s
        Vladimirom-Vasiliem Rodzianko [In What does the Orthodox Bishop
        Believe?: My Polemics with Vladimir-Vasily Rodzianko]. *Nauka i religiia* 4
        (1984): 56-58.

2424   Kryvelev, I.A. *Bibliia: istoriko-kriticheskii analiz* [The Bible: Historic- Critical
        Analysis]. M.: Politizdat, 1982. 255 pp., illus. For reviews see items
        5127-5128.

2425   Kryvelev, I.A. "Bibliia v svete nauchnogo analiza" [The Bible in the Light of
        Scientific Analysis]. *Nauka i religiia* 7 (1981): 34-38; 8 (1981): 30-35; 9
        (1981): 22-28; 10 (1981): 38-43; 11 (1981): 29-32; 12 (1981): 43-48; 1
        (1982): 26-32; 2 (1982): 40-45.

2426   Kryvelev, I.A. *Istoriia religii:* Ocherki: V 2 t. [History of Religion]. 2nd
        revised. ed. M.: Mysl', 1988. T. I. 1988. 446 pp., illus. Bibl.: pp. 444-446.
        T. 2. 1988. 383 pp.

2427 Kryvelev. I.A. O *'Tainakh' religii* [On Religion's "mysteries"]. M.: Pedagogika, 1981. 104 pp., illus. (B-chka Det. entsiklopedii "Uchenye shkol'niku"). Published also in: Kishinev: Lumina, 1985. 107 pp., illus. In Moldavian.

2428 Kryvelev, I.A. "Ob istoriko-religioznykh vzgliadakh Dzh. Frezera" [On J. Frazer's Historic-Religious Views]. *Sov. etnografiia* 2 (1982): 141-147.

2429 Kryvelev, I.A. "Religiia kak obshchestvennoe iavlenie" [Religion as Social Phenomenon]. *Religii mira, 1986.* M., 1987. Pp. 5-16.

2430 Krzhenek, F. "O marksistskom ponimanii protsessa sekuliarizatsii" [On Marxist Conception of the Process of Secularization]. *Vopr. nauch. ateizma* 26 (1980): 269-282.

2431 Kublanov, M. "Chetyre 'interpoliatsii'" [Four "Interpolations"]. *Nauka i zhizn'* 1 (1980): 124-130.

2432 Kubrak, V.N.; Nikolaev, N.M. *Vospityvaia ateistov* [Educating Atheists]. Iuzhno-Sakhalinsk: Dal'nevost. kn. izd-vo. Sakhalin. ot-nie, 1984. 48 pp. Bibl.: pp. 43-44.

2433 Kuchin'ska, A. "Otnoshenie k tserkvi i religii v pol'skom rabochem dvizhenii (1882-1914 gg.)" [Attitude toward Church and Religion in Polish Workers Movement (1882-1914)]. *Vopr. nauch. ateizma* 36 (1987): 295-314.

2434 Kuchinskii, S.A. *Ateizm i nravstvennyi ideal* [Atheism and the Moral Ideal]. L.: Lenizat, 1981. 56 pp. (B-chka molodogo ateista). Bibl.: p. 55. For review see item 5129.

2435 Kuchinskii, S.A. "Antigumanizm khristianskogo ucheniia o 'grekhovnosti' cheloveka" [Antihumanism of Christian Teaching About Man's "Sinfulness"]. *Gumanizm i religiia.* L., 1980. Pp. 55-72.

2436 Kuchinskii, S.A. *Chelovek moral'nyi* [Moral Person]. M.: Politizdat, 1987. 271 pp., illus. (Lichnost'. Moral'. Vospitanie: Ser. khudozh.-publitsist. i nauch.-popul. izd.). For review see item 5130.

2437 Kuchinskii, S.A. "K voprosu o poniatii 'religioznaia moral'" [The Issue of the Notion of "Religious Moral"]. *Sotsial'no-filosofskie aspekty kritiki religii.* L., 1980. Pp. 12-22.

2438   Kuchko, L.T.   "Iazikovye priemy izvrashcheniia ateisticheskogo soznaniia sovetskikh liudei" [Lingual Devices of Distortion of Atheistic Consciousness of Soviet People]. *Filosofiia i iazyk.* Kiev, 1987. Pp. 109-114.

2439   Kudriashov, G.E.   "Aktual'nye problemy istorii religii i ateizma i zadachi ateistov regiona" [Actual Problems of History of Religion and Atheism and the Tasks of Regional Atheists]. *Problemy istorii religii i ateizma.* Cheboksary, 1980. Pp. 3-15.

2440   Kudriashov, G.E. *Krizis religii* [The Crisis of Religion]. Cheboksary: Chuvash. kh. izd-vo, 1981. 112 pp.

2441   Kudriashov, G.E.   "Nauchnoe planirovanie ateisticheskoi raboty - vazhnoe uslovie povysheniia ee effektivnosti" [Scientific Planning of Atheistic Work - Important Condition of Increasing Its Effectiveness]. *Aktual'nye problemy obespecheniia effektivnosti nauchno-ateistichskoi raboty.* Cheboksary, 1986. Pp. 11-18.

2442   Kudriashov, G.E.   "Nauchnye osnovy spetsializatsii studentov vuza po istorii religii i ateizma" [Scientific Foundations of Specialization of University Students in the History of Religion and Atheism]. *Problemy istorii religii i ateizma.* Cheboksary, 1981. Pp. 54-67.

2443   Kudriashov, G.E.   "Pravoslavnaia khristianizatsiia nerusskikh narodov" [Conversion to Orthodoxy of Non Russian People]. *Vopr. nauch. ateizma* 25 (1980): 151-169.

2444   Kudriavtsev, A.V.   "Kontseptsiia 'islamskogo resheniia' blizhnevostochnoi problemy" [The Conception of "Islamic Solution" of the Neareastern Problem]. *"Islamskii faktor" v mezhdunarodnykh otnosheniiakh v Azii (70-e - pervaia polovina 80-kh gg.).* M., 1987. Pp. 77-87.

2445   Kudriavtsev, A.V.   "Kontseptsiia 'islamskogo resheniia' Iusefa al'-Kardavi" [The Conception of "Islamic Solution" of Yusuf al-Kardawi]. *Islam: problemy ideologii, prava, politiki i ekonimiki.* M., 1985. Pp. 240-247.

2446   Kudriavtsev, A.V.   "Musul'manskii mir i palestinskaia problema" [Moslem World and the Palestinian Problem]. *Konferentsiia molodykh uchenykh "Arabskii mir: ekonomika, politika, ideologiia".* M., 1987. Pp. 69-73.

2447   Kudriavtsev, O.F.   "Sobstvennost' kak nravstvenno-pravovaia problema v ideologii khristianskogo srednevekov'ia (do Fomy Akvinskogo)" [Property as Moral-Legal Problem in the Ideology of Medieval Christianity (up to Thomas Aquinas)]. *Kul'tura i obshchestvennaia mysl'*. M., 1988. Pp. 76-86.

2448 Kufakova, N.D. "O dal'neishem sovershenstvovanii prepodavaniia nauchnogo ateizma v vysshikh i srednikh spetsial'nykh uchebnykh zavedeniiakh v svete reshenii XXVI s'ezda partii i iiunskogo (1983 g.) Plenuma TsK KPSS" [Further Perfection of Teaching Scientific Atheism in High and Middle Special Educational Institutions in the Light of the Resolution of the XXVIth Party Congress and June (1983) Plenum of the CPSU CC]. *Vestn. Mosk. un-ta.* Ser. 7. Filosofiia 6 (1984): 85-87.

2449 Kufakova, N.D.; Nemirovskaia, L.Z. "Ob osnovnom priznake religioznogo soznaniia" [About Basic Indication of Religious Consciousness]. *Vestn. Mosk. un-ta.* Ser. 7. Filisofiia 1 (1988): 84-90.

2450 Kufakova, N.D.; Sokurenko, E.G. "Ekologicheskie problemy v ekumeni-cheskoi interpretatsii" [Ecological Problems in Ecumenical Interpretations]. *Vestn. Mosk. un-ta.* Ser. 7. Filosofiia 4 (1985): 80-89.

2451 Kufakova, N.D.; Sokurenko, E.G. "Global'nye problemy sovremennosti v uchebnom kurse 'Osnovy nauchnogo ateizma'" [Global Problems of Contemporaneity in the Course "Fundamentals of Scientific Atheism"]. *Prepodavanie nauchnogo ateizma v vuze.* M., 1988. Pp. 111-121.

2452 Kukharenko, N.P.; Mal'tsev, Iu.S. "K simvolike izobrazheniia kresta v Srednei Azii" [On the Symbolism of Representation of the Cross in Middle Asia]. *III Vsesoiuznaia konferentsiia vostokovedov "Vzaimodeistvie i vzaimovliianie tsivilizatsii kul'tur na Vostoke".* M., 1988. T. 2. Pp. 26-27.

2453 Kukulenko, P.K. *Za schast'e zemnoe* [For Mundane Happiness]. Kiev: Politizdat Ukrainy, 1980. 192 pp., illus. In Ukrainian.

2454 Kukushkin, A.V. "Nekotorye metodologicheskie problemy issledovaniia religioznogo soznaniia" [Some Methodological Problems of Research of Religious Consciousness]. *Metodologicheskie problemy sovremennoi nauki.* Iaroslavl', 1980. Pp. 144-152.

2455 Kukushkin, A.V. "Opredeliaiushchii priznak religii i ego metodologicheskoe znachenie" [Determinative Indicator of Religion and Its Methodological Importance]. *Aktual'nye metodologicheskie problemy nauchnogo poznaniia.* Iaroslavl', 1982. Pp. 88-97.

2456 Kukushkin, V.D. "Nekotorye metodologicheskie voprosy preodoleniia religioznosti v SSSR" [Some Methodological Problems of Overcoming Religiosity in USSR]. *Aktual'nye metodologicheskie problemy nauchnogo poznaniia.* Iaroslavl', 1982. Pp. 97-107.

2457 Kukushkin, V.D. "Nekotorye voprosy informatsionnogo obespecheniia upravleniia v protsesse preodoleniia religioznosti" [Some Problems of Securing Information for Directing the Process of Overcoming Religiosity]. *Razvitoi sotsializm. Problemy teorii i upravleniia.* Iaroslavl', 1985. Pp. 86-97.

2458 Kulakov, M.P. "Tochka zreniia religioznogo deiatelia" [From the Point of View of a Religious Activist]. *Nauka i religiia* 12 (1988): 14-15.

2459 Kulbakhtin, N.M.; Sergeev, Iu.N. "Religioznaia politika tsarizma v Bashkirii v XVIII v." [Religious Policy of Tsarism in Bashkir in the XVIIIth C.]. *Sotsial'no-ekonomicheskoe razvitie i klassovaia bor'ba na Iuzhnom Urale i v Srednem Povol'zhe.* Ufa, 1988. Pp. 34-43.

2460 Kulebiakin, E.V.; Kossov, A.Iu. "O dialektike ob'ektivnykh i sub'ektivnykh faktorov vospitaniia ateisticheskoi ubezhdennosti v trudovom kollektive" [On Dialectics of Objective and Subjective Factors of Education of Atheistic Conviction in Working Collective]. *Ob'ektivnoe i sub'ektivnoe v obshchestvennom razvitii.* Vladivostok, 1981. Pp. 166-174.

2461 Kulemzin, V.M. *Chelovek i priroda v verovaniiakh khantov* [Man and Nature in the Beliefs of Khant]. Tomsk: izd-vo Tom. un-ta, 1984. 192 pp. Bibl.: pp. 179-188.

2462 Kulemzin, V.M. "Ob izobrazhenii umershikh u severnykh khantov" [Representation of the Deceased of Northern Khant]. *Problemy etnogeneza i etnicheskoi istorii aborigenov Sibiri.* Kemerovo, 1986. Pp. 79-84.

2463 Kuliev, N.K. *Islam i ateizm* [Islam and Atheism]. Ashkhabad: Turkmenistan, 1982. 63 pp. In Turkmen. Bibl.: pp. 57-62.

2464 Kuliev, N.K. *O stanovlenii i razvitii massovogo ateizma v Sovetskom Turkmenistane* [Formation and Development of Mass Atheism in Soviet Turkmenistan]. Ashkhabad: Znanie TSSR, 1984. 28 pp. (V pomoshch' lektoru / O-vo "Znanie" TSSR, Resp. Dom nauch. ateizma).

2465 Kulinkovich, K.A. "Sport i religiia" [Sport and Religion]. *Teoriia i praktika fiz. kul'tury* 7 (1981): 43-45.

2466 Kul'sharipov, M.M. "Otkrytie dukhovnogo upravleniia musul'man v Ufe" [Opening of Ecclesiastical Administration of Moslems in Ufa]. *Sotsial'no-ekonomicheskoe razvitie i klassovaia bor'ba na Iuzhnom Urale i v Srednem Povolzh'e.* Ufa, 1988. Pp. 43-47.

2467 *'Kul'tura. Religiia. Ateizm.'* Nauch. prakt. konf. 24-26.11.86. Vil'nius. Tezisy. ["Culture. Religion. Atheism." Scientific-Practical Conference 34-26.11.86. Vil'nius. Thesises]. Vil'nius: [S.n.], 1986. 80 pp. In Lithuanian.

2468 Kulygina, G.A. "Kategoriia 'sostoianie' v analize nravstvennogo soznaniia sovremennogo veruiushchego" [Category "Condition" in Analysis of Moral Consciousness of Contemporary Believer]. *Filosofskii status poniatiia sostoianiia i ego metodologicheskoe znachenie.* Saransk, 1981. Pp. 124-129.

2469 Kurbanmamadov, A. *Esteticheskaia doktrina sufizma* [Aesthetic Doctrine of Sufism]. Dushanbe: Donish, 1987. 108 pp. Bibl.: pp. 96-108.

2470 Kurbanov, A.D. *Ateisticheskoe vospitanie molodezhi* [Atheistic Upbringing of Youth]. Baku: Giandzhlik, 1982. 198 pp. In Azerbaijan.

2471 Kurbanov, A.D. *Religiia na sluzhbe antikommunizma* [Religion in the Service of Anti Communism]. Baku: Znanie AzSSR, 1983. 67 pp. (V pomoshch' lektoru / O-vo "Znanie" AzSSR). In Azerbaijan. Bibl.: pp. 65-66.

2472 Kurbanov, A.Sh. "Obshchesovetskie i progressivnye natsional'nye traditsii, kak faktor formirovaniia ateisticheskoi ubezhdennosti molodezhi v usloviiakh perestroiki" [All-Soviet and Progressive National Traditions as Forming Factor of Youth's Atheistic Conviction under Perestroika]. *Sbornik trudov Respublikanskoi nauchno-prakticheskoi konferentsii molodykh uchenykh i spetsialistov (12-14 aprelia 1989 g.).* Dushanbe, 1989. Sektsiia "Obshchestvennye nauki". Pp. 44-47.

2473 Kurbanov, Kh. "Sufiiskaia kontseptsiia 'universal'nogo cheloveka' v tvor-chestve Ibn Arabi (XII v.)" [Sufist Conception of "Universal Man" in Ibn Arabi's Works (XIIth C.)]. *Respublikanskaia nauchno-teoreticheskaia konferentsiia molodykh uchenykh i spetsialisov TadzhSSR.* Dushanbe, 1982. Sektsiia filologii i vostokovedeniia. Pp. 85-87.

2474 Kurbanov, M.; Kurbanov, G. "Sviataia prostota" [Holy Simplicity]. *Sov. Dagestan* 4 (1987): 36-38.

2475 Kurbanov, S.Sh. *Obrazovanie i religiia* [Education and Religion]. Tashkent:
      Uzbekistan, 1980. 127 pp. In Uzbek.

2476 Kurbatov, G.L., et al. *Khristianstvo. Anichnost'. Vizantiia. Drevniaia Rus'*
      [Christianity. Antiquity. Byzantium. Ancient Rus']. L.: Lenizdat, 1988. 334
      pp., illus.

2477 Kurdgelashvili, Sh.N. "Vzaimosviaz' i vzaimozavisimost' natsional'nogo, tradi-
      tsionnogo i religioznogo faktorov v ofitsial'noi ideologii Liviiskoi Dzhama-
      khirii" [Intercomunication and Interdependency of National, Traditional
      and Religious Factors in the Official Ideology of Libyan Jamahiri]. *III
      Vsesoiuznaia konferentsiia vostokovedov "Vzaimodeistvie i vzaimovliianie
      tsivilizatsii kul'tur na Vostoke"*. M., 1988. T. 2. Pp. 121-122.

2478 Kurganskaia, V.D. "'Novoe religioznoe soznanie' i ofitsial'noe pravoslavie:
      konfrontatsiia v bor'be za veruiushchikh i tserkov' (nachalo XX v.) ["New
      Religious Consciousness" and Official Orthodoxy: Confrontation in the
      Struggle for Believers and Church (Early XXth C.)]. *Vestn. Mosk. un-ta.*
      Ser. 7, Filo- sofiia 6 (1986): 47-57.

2479 Kurochkin, P.[K]. "Funktsii nashei raboty" [Functions of Our Work]. *Nauka i
      religiia* 11 (1980): 13-16.

2480 Kurochkin, P.K. *K voprosu o predmete nauchnogo ateizma* [On the Issue of
      the Topic of Scientific Atheism]. M.: Znanie, 1980. 16 pp. (V pomoshch'
      lektoru).

2481 Kurochnik, P.K. "Problemy nauchnogo ateizma v svete reshenii XXVI s'ezda
      KPSS" [Problems of Scientific Atheism in the Light of the Resolutions of
      the XXVIth Congress of CPSU]. *Vopr. nauch. ateizma* 28 (1981): 3-20.

2482 Kurochkin, P.[K]. "Ubezhdennost'" [Conviction]. *Nauka i religiia* 1 (1980):
      2-4.

2483 Kuroedov, V.[A]. "La législation soviétique sur la religion et la liberté de
      conscience"* *Istina* P.: 1987. T. 32. N. 1/2 Pp. 20-31.

2484 Kuroedov, V.A. *Religiia i tserkov' v Sovetskom gosudarstve* [Religion and
      Church in Soviet State]. M.: Politizdat, 1981. 263 pp. Republished in
      1982, 263 pp.
      Published also in:
      M.: Progress, 1983. 167 pp., illus. In Spanish.

M.: Progress, 1984. 165 pp., illus. In Arabic.
Alma-Ata: Kazakhstan, 1984. 274 pp. In Kazakh.
2nd enlarged ed. was published under the title *Religiia i tserkov' v sovetskom obshchestve* [Religion and Church in Soviet Society]. M.: Politizdat, 1984. 256 pp.
Kazan': Tatar. kn. izd-vo, 1985, 272 pp. In Tatar.
M.: Progress, [1986]. 177 pp., illus. In French.
Kishinev: Kartia Moldoveniaske, 1986. 183 pp. In Moldavian. For reviews see items 5131-5139.

2485   Kuroedov, V.A. *Religiia i tserkov' v SSSR* [Religion and Church in USSR]. M.: Novosti, 1982. 67 pp., illus. Published in: Danish, Dutch, English, Finnish, Italian, Norwegian and Swedish.

2486   Kuroedov, V.A. *Sovetskoe gosudarstvo i tserkov'* [Soviet State and the Church]. Tallin: Eesti raanat, 1981. 70 pp.

2487   Kurov, M.N. "Ateisticheskii potentsial vuzovskogo kursa nauhnogo ateizma" [Atheistic Potential of Institutes of Higher Education Course on Scientific Atheism]. *Aktual. vopr. metodiki prepodavaniia obshchestv. nauk i kom. vospitania studentov.* L., 1987. Vyp. 5. Pp. 19-28.

2488   Kurov, M.N. "Problema svobody sovesti v dorevoliutsionnoi Rossii" [Problem of Freedom of Conscience in Pre-Revolutionary Russia]. *Vopr. nauch. ateizma* 27 (1981): 252-272.

2489   Kurpakova, L.P. "Religiia i tserkov' v FRG" [Religion and Church in FRG]. *Vopr. nauch. ateizma* 29 (1982): 204-217.

2490   Kurtik, G. *Teoriia protsessii v srednevekovoi indiiskoi i rannei islamskoi astronomii* [Theory of Procession in the Medieval Indian and Early Islamic Astronomy].* M.: [S.n.], 1987. 32 pp. Bibl.: pp. 29-32. Summary in English.

2491   Kusaev, V. "Protest mysliashchego uma" [Protest of the Thinking Mind]. *Nauka i religiia* 4 (1980): 37-39.

2492   Kushleiko, V. "Vremia iskat': Ob osobennostiakh ateist. propagandy v sovrem. usloviiakh" [Time to Seek: On Peculiarities of Atheistic Propaganda in Contemporary Conditions]. *Bibliotekar'* 9 (1983): 44-47.

2493   Kushmatov, A. *Stupeni zrelosti* [Levels of Maturity]. Dushanbe: Irfon, 1988.
       62 pp. In Tajik.

2494   Kushmatov. A. *Vozniknovenie i sushchnost' mazarov* [Mazar's Origin and
       Essence]. Dushanbe: Irfon, 1985. 38 pp. In Tajik.

2495   Kuskov, V.V. "Vvedenie khristianstva na Rusi i drevnerusskaia literatura"
       [Introduction of Christianity into Rus' and Ancient Russian Literature].
       Vestn. Mosk. un-ta. Ser. 9, Filologiia 4 (1988): 12-18.

2496   Kutaliia, G.M. *Pedagogicheskie vzgliady Martina Liutera* [Martin Luther's
       Pedagogical Views]. Tbilisi: Izd-vo Tbil. un-ta, 1982. 128 pp. In Georgian.
       Summary in Russian.

2497   Kutsenok, B.M. *Emotsii i religiia* [Emotions and Religion]. Kiev: Politizdat
       Ukrainy, 1982. 103 pp. Annot. bibl.: pp. 100-102.

2498   Kutsenok, B.M. *Psikhiatriia i religiia* [Psychiatry and Religion]. Kiev: Znanie
       UkSSR, 1980. 48 pp. (Ser. 5 "Nauchno-ateisticheskaia" / O-vo "Znanie"
       UkSSR; No 6). Bibl.: p. 48.

2499   Kuvakin, V.A. *Filosofiia Vl. Solov'eva* [Vl. Soloviev's Philosophy]. M.:
       Znanie, 1988. 64. (Novoe v zhizni, nauke, tekhnike. Ser. Filosofiia: 1988,
       8). Bibl.: p. 45-48.

2500   Kuvakin, V.A. *Religioznaia filosofiia v Rossii:* Nach. XX v. [Religious
       Philosophy in Russia: Early XXth C.]. M.: Mysl', 1980. 309 pp. Bibl.: pp.
       298-303. Name index: pp. 304-307. For reviews see items 5140-5142.

2501   Kuveneva, V.M. *Kritika revizionistskoi fal'sifikatsii nauchnogo ateizma*
       [Criticism of Revisionist Falsification of Scientific Atheism]. Kiev:
       Politizdat Ukrainy, 1983. 159 pp. Annot. bibl: pp. 151-158.
       Published also as 2nd enlarged and revised ed., in 1988, 198 pp. (Vopr.
       ideol. bor'by i kontrpropagandy).

2502   Kuziev, A.A. *Urbanizatsiia i ateizm* [Urbanization and Atheism]. Tashkent:
       Uzbekistan, 1982. 29 pp. (Ser. "Marksizm-leninizm"; No 4). In Uzbek.

2503   Kuz'menko, N.N. "Sovremennyi mistitsizm kak vyrazhenie bezdukhovnosti"
       [Contemporary Mysticism as Expression of Unspirituality]. *Dukhovnyi mir
       sovremennego cheloveka.* M., 1987. Pp. 134-136.

2504 Kuz'min, A.G. "'Kreshchenie Rysi': kontseptsii i problemy" ["Baptism of Rus'": Conceptions and Problems]. *"Kreshchenie Rusi" v trudakh russkikh i sovetskikh istorikov.* M., 1988. Pp. 3-56.

2505 Kuz'min, A.G. *Padenie Peruna: Stanovlenie khristianstva na Rusi* [The Fall of Perun: Coming into Being of Christianity in Rus']. M.: *Mol. gvardiia,* 1988. 240 pp., illus. Bibl.: pp. 235-240. For reviews see items 5143-5144.

2506 Kuz'min, A.G. "Priniatie khristianstva na Rusi" [Conversion to Christianity in Rus']. *Vopr. nauch. ateizma* 25 (1980): 7-35.

2507 Kuz'min, A.G. "Tserkov' i svetskaia vlast' v epokhu Kulikovskoi bitvy" [The Church and Lay Power During the Batlle of Kulikovo]. *Vopr. nauch. ateizma* 37 (1988): 90-99.

2508 Kuz'min, B.V. "Formirovanie ateisticheskoi ubezhdennosti rabotaiushchei molodezhi" [Forming of Atheistic Conviction of Working Youth]. *Vopr. ateizma* 19 (1983): 79-86.

2509 Kuz'mina, Iu. "Chtoby ateizm vyrastal iz znaniia" [May Atheism Grow Up from Knowledge]. *Nauka i religiia* 9 (1989): 19.

2510 Kuz'mina, Iu. "Kazan'. Takie dela" [Kazan. Such Deeds]. *Nauka i religiia* 8 (1989): 49-53.

2511 Kuz'mina, Iu. "Khanuka" [Hanuka]. *Nauka i religiia* 10 (1989): 18-19.

2512 Kuz'mina, Iu "Po Khorezmu - bez putevoditelia" [Along Khorezm - Without a Guide]. *Nauka i religiia* 1 (1988): 5-9.

2513 Kuz'mina, Iu. "Ushla v Monastyr'..." [She Went into a Monastery ...]. *Nauka i religiia* 3 (1988): 45-48.

2514 Kuz'mina, Iu. "V chuzhoi monastyr'" [In a Strange Monastery]. *Nauka i religiia* 6 (1989): 31-33.

2515 Kuz'mina, L.P. "Generic diversity of the shamanic folklore among the peoples of Siberia"* *Traces of the Central Asian culture in the North.** Helsinki, 1986. Pp. 139-148. Bibl.: pp. 147-148.

2516 Kuz'mishchev, V. "Solntsepoklonniki Tauantinsuiiu" [Sunworshippers of Tuantinsu]. *Nauka i religiia* 1 (1982): 38-42; 3 (1982): 41-44.

2517   Kuzmitskas,   B.Iu.   *Filosofskie   kontseptsii   katolicheskogo   modernizma*
       [Philosophical Conceptions of Catholic Modernism]. Vil'nius: Mintis, 1982.
       208 pp. Bibl.: pp. 202-207. For review see item 5145.

2518   Kuzmitskas, B.Iu. "Ot modernizma k neortodoksii" [From Modernism to
       Neoorthodoxy]. *Kommunist.* Vil'nius. 9 (1986): 54-58.

2519   Kuznetsov, A.A. *Istina protiv zabluzhdenii i fal'sifikatsii* [Truth against
       Delusions and Falsifications]. L.: Lenizdat, 1981. 59 pp. (B-chka
       molodogo ateista). Bibl.: p. 58.

2520   Kuznetsov, A.A. "Nekotorye aspekty sotsiologii religii v trudakh Maksa
       Vebera" [Some Aspects of Sociology of Religion in Max Weber's Works].
       Sotsial'no-filosofskie aspekty kritiki religii. L., 1980. Pp. 57-64.

2521   Kuznetsov, A.A. *Nravstvennaia tsenost' ateizma* [Moral Value of Atheism].
       L.: Znanie RSFSR, 1981. 20 pp. (V pomoshch' lektoru / O-vo "Znanie"
       RSFSR, Leningr. org.).

2522   Kuznetsov, B.I. "Iavliaetsia li Shenrab, osnovatel' religii bon, istoricheskoi
       lichnost'iu?" [Is Shenrap, Founder of Religion Bon, a Historical
       Personality?]. *Vostokovednye issledovaniia v Buriatii.* Novosibirsk, 1981. Pp.
       92-95.

2523   Kuznetsov, B.I. "O termine 'dkharma'" [About the Term "Dharma"].
       *Istochnikovedenie i tekstologiia pamiatnikov srednevekovykh nauk v stranakh
       Tsentral'noi Azii.* Novosibirsk, 1989. Pp. 192-199.

2524   Kuznetsov, B.I. "Osnovnye idei rannego buddizma (buddiiskaia   shkola
       Makhasangika)" [Main Ideas of the Early Buddhism (Buddhist School of
       Mahasanghika)]. *Uchen. zap. Leningr. un-ta.* No 405, 1981. Ser.
       vostokoved. nauk. Vyp. 24., Pp. 143-152.

2525   Kuznetsov, Iu. "Rastushchaia rol' islama" [The Growing Role of Islam].
       Aziia i Afrika segodnia 7 (1989): 29-30.

2526   Kuznetsov, L.M. 'Sviataia' *mafiia* [The "Holy" Mafia]. M.: Znanie, 1989. 64
       pp. (Novoe v zhizni, nauke, tekhnike. Nauch. ateizm; 10/1989).

2527   Kuznetsov, V. "O rasprostranenii khristianstva v Alanii" [On Dissemination
       of Christianity in Alania]. *Lit. Osetiia* 12 (1988): 178-183.

2528 Kuznetsov, V.N. *Ateisticeskie vzgliady Deni Didro* [Atheistic Views of Denis Diderot]. M.: Znanie, 1984. 64 pp. (Novoe v zhizni, nauke, tekhnike. Nauch. ateizm; 4). Bibl.: p. 63.

2529 Kuznetsov, V.S. "Sin'khaiskaia revoliutsiia i kitaiskaia musul'manskaia obshchina" [Sinhaist Revolution and Chinese Moslem Community]. *"Obshchestvo i gosudarstvo v Kitae".* M., 1988. Ch. 3. pp. 75-78.

2530 Kuznetsova, V.V. "Aktual'nye problemy prepodavaniia nauchnogo ateizma" [Actual Problems of Teaching Scientific Atheism]. *Inform. materialy / AN SSSR.* Filos. o-vo SSSR. 1 (1988): 48-50.

2531 Kvasov, G.G. "O sovershenstvovaniia prepodavaniia nauchnogo ateizma i ateisticheskogo vospitaniia v vysshikh uchebnykh zavedeniiakh" [Perfection of Teaching Scientific Atheism and Atheistic Education in High Educational Institutions]. *Prepodavanie nauchnogo ateizma v vuze.* M., 1988. Pp. 3-14.

2532 Kychanov, E.I. "Gosudarstvennyi kontrol' za deiatel'nost'iu buddiskikh obshchin v Kitae v period Tan-Sun (VII-XIII vv.)" [State Control over the Activity of Buddhist Communities in China of Tang-Tsun Period (VIIth-XIIIth C.)]. Buddizm i gosudarstyo na Dal'nem Vostoke. M., 1987. pp. 71-90.

2533 Kychanov, E.I. "Gosudarstvo i buddizm v Si Sia (982-1227)" [State and Buddhism in Hsi-Hsia (982-1227)]. *Buddizm i gosudarstvo na Dal'nem Vostoke.* M., 1987. Pp. 130-145.

2534 Labazov, V.V., Simonov, N.V. "Ispol'zovanie kraevedeniia v ateisticheskom vospitanii molodezhi" [Utilization of the Study of Local Lore in Atheistic Education of Youth]. *Aktual'nye problemy nauchno- ateisticheskogo vospitaniia molodezhi.* M., 1987. Pp. 61-64.

2535 Ladzari, A.K. *Pravoslavnaia tserkov' v SSSR: Kak ia otkryl religiiu v Rossii* [Orthodox Church in USSR: How I Discovered Religion in Russia]. M.: Novosti, 1984. 88 p., illus. (SSSR glazami inostrantsev). In English. Published also in: Portuguese and Spanish.

2536 Lagover, Iu. "Mladshii brat Moskvy" [Moscow's Younger Brother]. *Nauka i religiia* 5 (1983): 28-31.

2537 Lakis, Iu.Iu. "Bor'ba protiv natsionalisticheskoi i klerikal'nnoi ideologii" [Struggle against Nationalist and Clerical Ideologies]. *Vopr. teorii i praktiki ideol. raboty* 19 (1987): 248-265.

2538 *Lamaizm v Buriatii XVIII-nachala XX veka: Struktura i sotsial. rol' kul'tovoi sistemy* [Lamaism in Buriat in the XVIIIth-Early XXth C.: Structure and Social Role of the Religious System]. [Ed.: V.V. Mantatov.]. Novosibirsk: Nauka. Sib. otd-nie, 1983. 235 pp. Annot. bibl.: pp. 223-233. For review see item 5146.

2539 Lamont, K. *Illiuziia bessmertiia* [Illusion of Immortality]. 2nd ed. M.: Politizdat, 1984. 286 pp., illus. (B-ka ateist. lit.). For review see item 5147.

2540 Landa, R.; Malashenko, A. "Islam v Alzhire: vchera i segodnia" [Islam in Algeria: Yesterday and Today]. *Nauka i religiia* 2 (1984): 60-63.

2541 Lapshov, B.A.; Khalevinskii, I.V. "Mukhammed: Ot mifa - k cheloveku" [Muhammad: From Myth - to Human Being]. *Vopr. istorii* 5 (1984): 78-91.

2542 Lapshov, B.A.; Khalevinskii, I.V. "Ob istoricheskikh usloviiakh vozniknoveniia islama i nekotorykh osobennostiakh islamskogo dvizheniia sovremennosti" [On Historical Conditions of Islam's Origin and Some Features of Islamic Movement of the Present Time]. *Obshchestv. nauki v Uzbekistane* 4 (1982): 21-33. Summary in Uzbek.

2543 Lapshov, B.A.; Khalevinskii, I.V. "Stanovlenie rannego islama" [Formation of the Early Islam]. *Vopr. istorii* 11 (1982): 107-119.

2544 Larichev, V.E. *Mudrost' zmei: Pervobyt. chelovek. Luna i Solntse* [Serpent's Wisdom: Primitive Man. Moon and Sun]. Novosibirsk: Nauka. Sib. otd-nie, 1989. 272 pp. (Ser.: Istoriia nauki i tekhniki).

2545 Laskovaia, M.P. *Khristianskaia religiia v nashi dni* [Christian Religion in Our Days]. M.: Mosk. rabochii, 1981. 110 pp. (Besedy o religii). Annot bibl.: pp. 106-109.

2546 Latifov, D. "Ateisticheskaia rabota i novoe myshlenie" [Atheistic Work and New Thought]. *Kommunist Tadzhikistana* 11 (1988): 70-78.

2547 Latifov, D. "V propagande nauchnogo ateizma ukhodit ot stereotipov [To Depart from Stereotypes in the Propaganda of Scientific Atheism]. *Part. zhizn'* 17 (1989): 30-33.

2548 Latifov, D.; Makhmadov, M. "Chto tolknulo ikh v ogon'?" [What Pushed Them Into Fire?]. *Kommunist Tadzhikistana* 4 (1989): 68-73.

2549 Latypova, P.F. "K voprosu o vospitanii i formirovanii ubezhdennogo internatsionalista i soznatel'nogo ateista v mnogonatsional'nom kollektive" [On the Problem of Education and Shaping Convinced Internationalist and Conscious Atheist in a Multinational Group]. *Formirovanie sotsial'noi zrelosti studenta.* Sverdlovsk, 1987. Pp. 96-103.

2550 Latysheva, E. "'I starym bredit novizna'?" ["And Old People Dream of Novelty"?]. *Nauka i religiia* 6 (1989): 4-5.

2551 Latysheva, V.A. "K istorii kul'tov naseleniia khersonesskoi khory" [History of Cults of the Population of Chersonesus Heracleotica]. *Problemy issledovanii antichnykh gorodov.* M., 1989. Pp. 65-67.

2552 Laukaitite, R. "Iz sotsial'noi deiatel'nosti monashestv v Litve v 1919-1940 gg." [Social Activity of Monasticism in Lithuania in 1919-1940]. *Nauch. tr. vuzov LitSSR. Istoriia* 29 (1988): 88-101. In Lithuanian. Summary in Russian.

2553 Laukhina, V.V. "O teoreticheskikh istokakh istoriko-filosofskikh kontseptsii russkogo teizma kontsa XIX-nachala XX v." [Theoretical Origins of Historic-Philosophical Conceptions of Russian Theism at the End of XIXth-Early XXth C.]. *Problemy filosofii* 74 (1987): 112-120.

2554 Laurinchiukas, A. "Tam, za gorizontom" [There, Beyond the Horizon]. *Nauka i religiia* 1 (1981): 40-41.

2555 Laverychev, V.Ia. "Krupnaia burzhuaziia i staroobriadcheskie organizatsii v dorevoliuytsionnoi Rossii" [Big Bourgeoisie and Old Belief Organizations in Pre Revolutionary Russia]. *Vopr. nauch. ateizma* 37 (1988): 202-208.

2556 Lavrov, P.L. *O religii* [On Religion]. [Comp.: A.I. Volodin]. M.: Mysl', 1989. 415 pp. (Nauch.-ateist. b-ka). Annot. bibl.: pp. 336-385. Name and mythological name index: pp. 386-414.

2557 Lazarev, E. "Egipet i Rus': solnechnaia sviaz'" [Egypt and Rus': Solar Link]. Nauka i religiia 6 (1989): 40-42.

2558 Lazarev, E. "Izvechnye tainy bytiia" [Age-Long Secrets of Being]. Nauka i religiia 7 (1988): 46-49.

2559 Lazarev, E. "Tibetskoe skazanie ob Iisuse" [Tibetan Tale About Jesus]. Nauka i religiia 7 (1989): 59-60.

2560 Lazarev, E. "Znamia Graalia" [The Banner of Graal]. Nauka i religiia 12 (1987): 56-62.

2561 Lazutka, V.A. Natsionalizm i katolitsizm [Nationalism and Catholicism]. Vil'nius: Znanie LitSSR, 1984. 23 pp. (Material dlia lektora / O-vo "Znanie" LitSSR). In Lithuanian. Bibl.: pp. 21-22.

2562 Lebed', G.E. "Formirovanie ateisticheskoi ubezhdennosti sovetskogo cheloveka" [Forming Atheistic Conviction of Soviet Man]. Vopr. ateizma 18 (1982): 50-55.

2563 Lebedenko, V. "Vazhnyi uchastok ideologicheskogo vlianiia" [Important Section of Idelogical Influence]. Part. zhizn' Kazakhstana 1 (1983): 53-55.

2564 Lebedev, A.A. "'Posledniaia religiia'" ["The Last Religion"]. Vopr. filosofii 1 (1989): 35-55.

2565 Lebedev, A.A. "Raskryvat' dukhovnyi potentsial ateizma" [To Reveal the Spiritual Potential of Atheism]. Nauka i religiia 7 (1988): 2-4.

2566 Lebedev, A.A.; Tsvetkov, V.A. Glavnyi faktor: Sots.-ekon. izmenenia kak faktor preodoleniia relig. perezhitkov [The Main Factor: Socio-Economical Changes as Factor of Overcoming Religious Relics]. M.: Politizdat, 1987. 95 pp. (B-ka ateista).

2567 Lebedev, A.A.; Tsvetkov, V.A. V bor'be za cheloveka [Struggle for the Human Being]. Tula: Priok. kn. izd-vo, 1984. 97 pp. Annot. Bibl.: p. 96.

2568 Lebedev, E.A.; Ionova, A.I. "Rol' islama v proshlom i nastoiashchem" [The Role of Islam in the Past and Today]. Narody Azii i Afriki 1 (1981): 164.

2569 Lebedev, G. "Nakanune Rus' X veka" [On the Eve of Xth Century Rus']. Znanie - sila 7 (1988): 35-42. [2nd article].

2570 Lebedev, L.L. "Tainy drevnikh ikon" [Secrets of the Ancient Icons]. *Nauka i religiia* 10 (1988): 61-64; 12 (1988): 61-64; 3 (1989): 60-63.

2571 Lebedev, S.N. "Traditsionnye formy sovremennogo dzen-buddizma" [Traditional Forms of Today's Zen-Buddhism]. *Kritika religioznoi ideologii i problemy ateisticheskogo vospitaniia.* M., 1980. Pp. 82-88.

2572 Lebedev, V.[G]. "Dialog" [Dialogue]. *Nauka i religiia* 5 (1989): 60-61.

2573 Lebedev, V.G. *Dialogi: Besedy ateista s veruiushchimi o 'sviatykh pis'makh'* [Dialogues: Atheist's Talks with Believers about "Holy Writs"]. M.: Znanie, 1988. 36 pp.

2574 Lebedev, V.I. *Dukhi v zerkale psikhologii* [Spirits in the Mirror of Psychology]. M.: Sov. Rossiia, 1987. 224 pp., illus.

2575 Lebedev, V.I. *Obshchenie s bogom ili...* [Relations with God or ...]. M.: Politizdat, 1986. 112 pp. (Besedy o mire i cheloveke).

2576 Lebedeva, I.L. "Religioznoe vliianie baptistskoi sem'i na podrastaiushchee pokolenie i puti ego preodoleniia" [Religious Influence of Baptist Family on the Growing Generation and Ways of Surmounting it]. *Obraz zhizni sem'i i formirovanie novogo cheloveka.* Gor'kii, 1987. Pp. 65-78. Bibl.: p. 78.

2577 Leibin, V.M. "Vera ili razum?" [Faith or Reason?]. *Vopr. filosofii* 8 (1988): 126-132.

2578 Leikin, S.F. "Traditsii narodnykh ereticheskikh sekt i ideologiia vosstaniia ikhetuanei" [Traditions of Popular Heretical Sects and the Ideology of Insurrection of Yhetyan]. *Dvenadtsataia nauchnaia konferentsiia "Obshchestvo i gosudarstvo v Kitae".* M., 1989. Ch. I. Pp. 171-174.

2579 Leitsalu, I.; Sakaluskene, M. *Rol' sotsialisticheskoi obriadnosti v dukhovnoi zhizni sovetskogo obshchestva* [The Role of Socialist Ceremonial in the Spiritual Life of Soviet Society]. M.: Znanie. Tentr. Dom nauch. ateizma, 1989. 51 pp.

2580 *Lektsionnaia ateisticheskaia propaganda: opyt i problemy* [Atheistic Propaganda Method Based on Lectures: Experience and Problems]. [Comp: S.I. Ivanenko]. M.: Znanie, 1984. 40 pp.

2581 Lelekov, L.A. "Izuchenie Avesty v shvedskoi orientalistke" [Study of Avesta in Swedish Orientalism]. *Narody Azii i Afriki* 4 (1982): 166-175.

2582 Lelekov, L.A. "O simvolizme pogrebal'nykh oblachenii" [Symbolism of Funeral Vestments]. *Skifo-sibirskii mir: Iskusstvo i ideologiia.* Novosibirsk, 1987. Pp. 25-31.

2583 Lelekov, L.A.; Raevskii, D.S. "Inokul'turnyi mif v grecheskoi izobrazitel'noi traditsii" [Foreign Cultural Myth in Greek Decorative Tradition]. *Zhizn' mifa v antichnosti.* M., 1988. Ch. I. Pp. 215-226.

2584 Lemeshko, L.G. "Nekotorye ateisticheskie aspekty mirovozzrencheskoi podgotovki studentov v tekhnicheskikh vuzakh" [Some Atheistic Aspects of the World Outlook Preparation of Students in Technical Institutions of Higher Education]. *Aktual. vopr. metodiki prepodavaniia obshchestv. nauk i kom. vospitaniia studentov* 5 (1987): 86-94.

2585 Lensu, M.Ia. *Metodologiia i metodika ateisticheskogo vospitaniia* [Methodology and Methods of Atheistic Education]. Minsk: Belarus', 1985. 142 pp. Annot. bibl.: pp. 138-141.

2586 Lensu, M.[Ia].; Matias, D. "Partiinost' i gumanizm nauchnogo ateizma" [Party Spirit and Humanism of Scientific Atheism]. *Kommunist Belorussii* 8 (1987): 80-87.

2587 Lensu, M.Ia.; Platonov, R.P. *Nekotorye problemy sovershenstvovaniia ateisticheskogo vospitaniia* [Some Problems of Perfection of Atheistic Education]. Minsk: Znanie BSSR, 1983. 24 pp. (Material v pomoshch' lektoru / Pravl. o-va "Znanie" BSSR). Bibl.: p. 24.

2588 Lentin, V.N. "K voprosu o sushchnosti klerikal'nykh peredach 'Golosa Ameriki'" [On the Question of the Essence of Clerical Transmissions of "The Voice of America"]. *Vopr. ateizma* 25 (1989): 23-30.

2589 Lentin, V.N. "Molodezh' kak ob'ekt klerikalizma" [Youth as Object of Clericalism]. *Tezisy dokladov i vystuplenii na Vsesoiuznoi nauchno-metodicheskoi konferentsii "Nauchnye osnovy kritiki nemarksistskikh kontseptsii v kursakh obshchestvennykh distsiplin", 12-15 okt. 1988 g.* Odessa, 1988. Pp. 95-96.

2590 Lentina, E.V. "Nekotorye osobennosti burzhuazno-klerikal'noi propagandy na sovetskuiu molodezh'" [Some Features of Bourgeois-Clerical Propaganda on Soviet Youth]. *Molodezh' i tvorchestvo: sotsial'no-filosofskie problemy.* M., 1988. Ch. 3. Pp. 293-295.

2591 Leonov, A.F. "Stanovlenie i razvitie buddiiskoi sistemy vospitaniia i obrazovaniia v srednevekovom Nepale" [Formation and Development of Buddhist System of Upbringing and Education in Medieval Nepal]. *Ocherki istorii shkoly i pedagogicheskoi mysli drevnego i srednevekovogo Vostoka.* M., 1988. Pp. 92-103. Bibl.: pp. 102-103.

2592 Leonov, G.A. "Relikvii iz lamaistskikh skul'ptur i obriad osveshcheniia v lamaizme" [Relics from Lamaist Sculptures and Ritual of Sanctification in Lamaism]. *V Mezhdunarodnyi kongress mongolovedov (Ulan Bator, sentiabr', 1987).* M., 1987. 3. Arkheologiia, kul'tura, etnografiia, filologiia. Pp. 99-107.
Published also in:
Tr. Gos. Ermitazha, T. 27 (1989): 117-131. Summary in English, p. 155.

2593 Leonova, T.A. "Nachal'nyi etap formirovaniia antipapskogo zakonodatel'stva v Anglii XIV v." [Initial Stage of Forming Anti-Papal Legislation in England of the XIVth C.]. *Sotsial'no-politicheskie otnosheniia v Zapadnoi Evrope (srednie veka-novoe vremia).* Ufa, 1988. Pp. 11-24.

2594 Lepekhov, S.Iu. "Psikhologicheskie problemy v 'Khridaia-sutre'" [Psychological Problems in "Hridaya-Sutra"]. Novosibirsk, 1986. Pp. 90-103

2595 Lepekhov, S.Iu. "Razvitie filosofsko-psikhlogicheskikh vozzrenii buddizma ot khinaiany do pozdnei makhaiany" [Development of Philosophic-Psychological Outlook of Buddhism from Hinayana to Late Mahayana]. *Metodologicheskie aspekty izucheniia istorii dukhovnoi kul'tury Vostoka.* Ulan-Ude, 1988. Pp. 96-107.

2596 Leshan, V. "Ekskursii, kotorykh zhdut" [Expected Excursions]. *Nauka i religiia* 3 (1980): 17-18.

2597 Leshan, V.E. "K sotsial'no-psikhologichskomu portretu veruiushchego-sektanta" [Socio-Psychological Portrait of Believer-Sectarian]. *Vopr. nauch. ateizma* 34 (1986): 203-211.

2598 Leshan, V.E. *Liki khristianskogo sektantstva* [Faces of Christian Sectarianism]. Kiev: Politizdat Ukrainy, 1988. 207 pp. Annot. bibl.: pp. 201-206.

2599   Leshan, V.E. *O chem govoriat v propovediiakh* [What They Talk About in Sermons]. Kiev: Znanie UkSSR, 1985. 49 pp. (Ser. V "Nauch.-ateisticheskaia" / O-vo "Znanie UkSSR; No 10).

2600   Leshchenko, V.Iu. "K voprosu o genezise i sotsial'noi sushchnosti religioznykh zapretov" [On the Problem of Genesis and Social Essence of Religious Bans]. *Aktual'nye problemy izucheniia istorii religii i ateizma.* L., 1980. Pp. 98-115.

2601   Leshchenko, V.Iu. "O perezhitkakh traditsionnykh verovanii u evenkov" [On Survival of Evenk's Traditional Beliefs]. *Nauchno-ateisticheskie issledovaniia v muzeiakh.* L., 1987. Pp. 34-50.

2602   Leshchinskii, A.N. "Genezis i evoliutsiia traditsionnoi pravoslavnoi kontseptsii kultury" [Genesis and Evolution of Traditional Orthodox Conception of Culture]. *Vopr. nauch. ateizma* 30 (1982): 120-134.

2603   Lesnu, M.Ia. "Vzaimodeistvie printsipov i metodov - metodologicheskaia osnova edinstva teorii i praktiki ateisticheskogo vospitaniia" [Reciprocity of Principles and Methods - Methodological Basis of Unity of Theory and Practice of Atheistic Education]. *Nauch. ateizm i ateist. vospitanie* 1 (1983): 40-49.

2604   Lev (episkop Tashkentskii i Sredneaziatskii). "Diktuet zhizn'" [Life Dictates]. *Nauka i religiia* 11 (1989): 21-23.

2605   Levashova, T.V. "Nasledniki Nostradamusa" [Nostradamus' Heirs]. *Priroda i chelovek* 12 (1989): 46-50.

2606   Levchenko, N.I. "Negritianskaia metodistskaia tserkov' v antirabovladel'-cheskom dvizhenii SShA" [Negro Methodist Church in USA Antislavery Movement]. *Amerikanskii ezhegodnik, 1987.* M., 1987. Pp. 196-209.

2607   Levchenko, M.V. "Kreshchenie Rusi pri Vladimire" [Baptism of Rus' under Vladimir]. *"Kreshchenie Rusi" v trudakh russkikh i sovetskikh istorikov.* M., 1988. Pp. 107-138.

2608   Levin, E.M. "K probleme sud'by v kul'ture Kievskoi Rusi" [On the Problem of Fate in the Culture of Kievan Rus']. *Otechestvennaia obshchestvennaia mysl' epokhi Srednevekov'ia.* Kiev, 1988. Pp. 100-106.

2609 Levin, Z.I. *Islam i natsionalizm v stranakh zarubezhnogo Vostoka* [Islam and Nationalism in the Countries of the Foreign Orient]. M.: Nauka, 1988. 223 pp. Bibl.: pp. 217-222.

2610 Levina, V.N. "Problemy profilizatsii prepodavaniia kursa 'Osnovy nauchnogo ateizma' v meditsinskom vuze'" [Problems of Outlining the Teaching of the Course "Foundations of Scientific Atheism" in Medical Institution of Higher Education]. *Vopr. ateizma* 2 (1984): 76-84.

2611 Lezin, Z.I. "Umma i arabskii natsionalizm" [Umma and Arab Nationalism]. *Sotsial'no-politicheskie predstavleniia v islame: Istoriia i sovremennost'*. M., 1987. Pp. 108-116.

2612 Lialina, G. "'Odno iz nesomnennykh prav cheloveka'" ["One of Undoubted Rights of Man"]. *Nauka i religiia* 6 (1989): 8-9.

2613 Lidov, A.M. "Obraz 'Khrista-arkhiereia' v ikonograficheskoi programme Sofii Okhridskoi" [The Image of "Christ-Bishop" in Iconographical Layout of Sophia from Ohrid]. *Vizantiia i Ruus'*. M., 1989. Pp. 65-90.

2614 Lidova, N.R. "Protoinduizm. K postanovke problemy" [Proto Hinduism. Formulation of a Problem]. *V Vsesoiuznaia shkola molodykh vostoko-vedov*. M., 1989. T. I. Pp. 128-129.

2615 Likhachev, D.S. "Kreshchenie Rusi i gosudarstvo Rus'" [Baptism of Rus' and the State Rus']. *Novyi mir* 6 (1988): 249-258.

2616 Lillienfel'd, F. fon. "V poiskakh ideala" [In the Search of Ideal]. *Vopr. Lit.* 6 (1989): 186-198.

2617 Lisavtsev, E.I. *Religiia i bor'ba idei v sovremennom mire* [Religion and the Struggle of Ideas in the Contemporary World]. M.: Znanie, 1981. 64 pp. (V pomoshch' lektoru. B-chka "Aktual. probl. sovrem. ideol. bor'by"). Republished in 1982 by Moscow Znanie in the Ser. (Novoe v zhizni, nauke, tekhnike. Nauch. ateizm; 9).

2618 Lisichkin, V.M. *Ideologiia i politika sovremennogo russkogo pravoslaviia* [Ideology and Politics of the Contemporary Russsian Orthodoxy]. Minsk: Belarus', 1984. 80 pp. Annot. bibl.: pp. 78-79.

2619 Lisichkin, V.M. "Modernistskie tendentsii v ideologii pravoslavnoi tserkvi" [Modernist Trends in the Ideology of the Orthodox Church]. *Nauch. ateizm i ateist. vospitanie* 1 (1983): 60-70.

2620 Lisichkin, V.M. "Prisposablivaias' k novym realiiam: Ob ideologii i politike sovremen. pravoslaviia" [Adaptations to New Realities: Ideology and Policy of Contemporary Orthodoxy]. *Kommunist Belorussii* 5 (1986): 76-82.

2621 Lisitsyn, B.A. *Sport i religioznye organizatsii* [Sport and Religious Organizations]. M.: Fizkul'tura i sport, 1985. 81 pp., illus.

2622 Lisovenko, N.A. *Chelovek i mir ego tsennostei* [Man and His World of Values]. Kiev: Znanie UkSSR, 1984. 47 pp. (Ser. 5 "Nauchno-ateisticheskaia" / O-vo "Znanie" UkSSR; No 11). In Ukrainian. Bibl.: p. 47.

2623 Lisovenko, N.A. "Religiia i problema tsennostnogo otnosheniia cheloveka k miru" [Religion and the Problem of Valuable Attitude of Man Toward the World]. *Vopr. ateizma* 20 (1984): 113-120.

2624 Litavrin, G.G. "Religiia i politika v Bolgarii nakanune i v period utverzhdeniia khristianstva (VIII - konets IX v.)" [Religion and Politics in Bulgaria on the Eve and in the Period of Assertion of Christianity (VIIIth - Late IXth C.)]. *Istoriia, kul'tura, etnografiia i fol'klor slavianskikh narodov.* M., 1988. Pp. 82-100.

2625 Litavrin, G.[G.]; Floria, B.[N]. "Khristianizatsiia stran Tsentral'noi, Iugo-Vostochnoi Evropy i Drevnei Rusi" [Conversion to Christianity of Countries of Central, South-Eastern Europe and Ancient Rus']. *Obshchestv. nauki* 2 (1989): 199-216.

2626 Litavrin, G.G.; Floria, B.N. "Priniatie khrisianstva narodami Tsentral'noi i Iugo-Vostochnoi Evropy i kreshchenie Rusi" [Adoption of Christianity by the People of Central and South-Eastern Europe and Baptism of Rus']. *Sov. slavianovedenie* 4 (1988): 60-67. Bibl.: p. 67.

2627 Litvinskii, B.A. "Monastyrskaia zhizn' vostochnoturkestanskoi sangkhi. Buddiiskie tseremonii" [Monastic Life of Eastern-Turkestan Sangha. Buddhist Rituals]. *Buddizm. Istoriia i kul'tura.* M., 1989. Pp. 169-189.

2628 Litvinskii, B.A. "Protoiranskii khram v Margiane" [Proto Iranian Temple in Marghian]. *Vestn. drev. istorii* 1 (1989): 177-179.

2629 Liubarskene, Z. "Voprosy vzaimosviazi nravstvennosti i religii v rabotakh Ionasa Ragauskasa" [Problems of Intercommunication of Morality and Religion in Johannes Ragauskas' Works]. *Ateistines minties raida lietuvoje.* Kaunas, 1988. Pp. 108-118. In Lithuanian. Summary in Russian.

2630 Liubarskii, Ia.N. "Zamechaniia o Nikolae Mistike v sviazi s izdaniem ego sochinenii" [Remarks on Nikolas the Mystic in Connection with the Publication of His Works]. *Vizant. vremennik.* 1986. T. 47. Pp. 101-108.

2631 Liutter, G. "K voprosu o sotsial'noi orientatsii evangelicheskoi tserkvi v usloviiakh sotsializma" [The Problem of Social Orientation of Evangelical Church under Socialism]. *Vopr. nauch. ateizma* 36 (1987): 201-207.

2632 Liutter, G. "Sovremennaia protestantskaia teologiia v FRG" [Contemporary Protestant Theology in FRG]. *Vopr. nauch. ateizma* 26 (1980): 223-236.

2633 Livshits, G.M. "Kritika bogoslovskoi i burzhuaznoi interpretatsii dannykh kumranskikh tekstov" [Criticism of Theological and Bourgeois Interpretations of Data of the Qumran Texts]. *Vopr. istorii* 8 (1981): 92-99.

2634 Livshits, G.M. *Ocherki po istorii ateizma v SSSR, 20-30-e gody* [Essays on the History of Religion in USSR, 20s-30s]. Minsk: Nauka i tekhnika, 1985. 215 pp. Bibl. of G.M. Livshits' treatises: pp. 203-209. Bibl.: pp. 210-214.

2635 Livshits, G.M. *Religiia i tserkov' v istorii obshchestva* [Religion and Church in the History of Society]. Minsk: Vysheish. shkola, 1980. 351 pp. Bibl.: pp. 325-335. Annot. bibl.: pp. 313-324. Name index: pp. 336-350.

2636 Livshits, R.L. "Miloserdie i sostradanie" [Mercy and Compassion]. *Otnoshenie cheloveka k irratsional'nomu.* Sverdlovsk, 1989. Pp. 277-288.

2637 Livshits, V.A.; Steblin-Kamenskii, I.M. "Protozoroastrizm" [Proto Zoro-astrianism]. *Vestn. drev. istorii* 1 (1989): 174-176.

2638 Lobachev, V. "Kommentarii v predelakh, dopustimykh neznaniem nashim" [Commentaries Within the Bounds of Our Permissible Ignorance]. *Nauka i religiia* 1 (1989): 26-27.

2639   Lobachev, V. "Ravnoapostol'naia" [Alike Apostolic]. *Nauka i religiia* 3 (1988): 5-6.

2640   Lobachev, V.K.; Pravotorov, V.F. *Tysiacheletie russkogo pravoslaviia* [Thousandth Anniversary of Russian Orthodoxy]. M.: Novosti, 1988. 117 pp., illus. In English. Published also in: Amharian, Greek and Italian.

2641   Lobashkov, A.M. *Istoriia ssyl'nogo kolokola* [History of the Exiled Bell]. Iaroslavl': Verkh. Volzh. kn. izd-vo, 1988. 48 pp., illus. Bibl.: pp. 46-47.

2642   Lobazov, P.; Batiuk, I. "Nauchnyi ateizm - zadachi prepodavaniia" [Scientific Atheism - Teaching Tasks]. *Nauka i religiia* 1 (1985): 17.

2643   Lobazov, P.K.; Bevziuk, N.P. "O tendentsii religioznosti v SSSR" [Tendencies of Religiosity in USSR]. *Tezisy dokladov i vystuplenii na Vsesoiuznoi nauchno-metodicheskoi konferentsii "Nauchnye osnovy kritiki nemarksistskikh konteptsii v kursakh obshchestvennykh distsiplin", 12-15 okt. 1988 g.* Odessa, 1988. Pp. 91-92.

2644   Lobovik, B.A. "K postanovke voprosa gnoseologichesikh korniakh religii" [On Formulation of the Question of Gnosiology of the Roots of Religion]. *Vopr. ateizma* 16 (1980): 25-34.

2645   Lobovik, B.A. *Religiia kak sotsial'noe iavlenie* [Religion as a Social Occurrence]. Kiev: Vishcha shkola, 1982. 96 pp. (Ateist. b-chka studenta).

2646   Lobovik, B.A. *Religioznoe soznanie i ego osobennosti* [Religious Consciousness and Its Peculiarities]. Kiev: Nauk. dumka, 1986. 247 pp. For review see item 5148.

2647   Lobovik, B.A.; Filonenko, N.V. "Sotsial'no-politicheskaia orientatsiia i mirovozzrencheskie pozitsii sovremennogo russkogo pravoslaviia" [Socio-Political Orientation and World Outlook Positions of Contemporary Russian Orthodoxy]. *Vopr. ateizma* 23 (1987): 87-92.

2648   Lobovik, B.A.; Kobelianskaia, L.S. *Nauchnyi ateizm o smysle zhizni cheloveka* [Scientific Atheism on the Meaning of Man's Life]. Kiev: Znanie UkSSR, 1983. 48 pp. (Ser. V "Nauchno-ateisticheskaia" / O-vo "Znanie" UkSSR; No 12). Bibl.: pp. 46-47.

2649 Lobovik, B.A.; Shadurskii, V.G. *Religioznoe soznanie i zdravyi smysl* [Religious Consciousness and Common Sense]. Kiev: Znanie UkSSR, 1986. 49 pp. (Ser. 5, Nauchno-ateisticheskaia / O-vo "Znanie" UkSSR; No 4).

2650 Lobytsyna, M. "Russkie masony" [Russian Masons]. *Nauka i religiia* 7 (1988): 44-45.

2651 Logashova, B.R. "Vliianie islama na etiket u turkmen Irana" [Influence of Islam on Etiquette of Turkmen of Iran]. *Etiket u narodov Perednei Azii.* M., 1988. Pp. 164-179.

2652 Loginov, A.V. "Etnologicheskie podkhody v amerikanskom religievedenii" [Ethnologic Approaches in American Study of Religion]. *Etnologiia v SShA i Kanade.* M., 1989. Pp. 241-257.

2653 Lokk, D. et al. *Angliiskoe svobodomyslie* [English Freethinking]. M.: Mysl' 1981. 301 pp., port. (Nauch.-Ateist. b-ka). Annot. bibl.: pp. 278-299.

2654 Lokshin, A. "Zemnaia plot' drevnikh simvolov: Iz istorii iudeiskogo kul'turnogo iskusstva" [Earthly Flesh of Ancient Symbols: History of Judaic Cultural Art]. *Nauka i religiia* 8 (1989): 62-64.

2655 Lomsadze, Sh.V. *Mikhail Tamarashvili i gruzinskie katoliki* [Mikhail Tamarashvili and Georgian Catholics]. Tbilisi: Sobchata sakartvelo, 1984. 258 pp., illus. In Georgian. Summary in Russian.

2656 Lopatkin, A.R. "Politicheskaia bor'ba vokrug konkordata Iugoslavii s Vatikanom" [Political Struggle Around Yugoslavian Concordat with Vatican]. *Vopr. nauch. ateizma* 36 (1987): 162-176.

2657 Lopatkin, R.A. "Nekotorye problemy sotsiologicheskogo izucheniia obshchestvennogo mneniia po voprosam religii i ateizma" [Some Problems of Sociological Study of Public Opinion on Questions of Religion and Atheism]. *Nauchnyi ateizm i obshchestvennoe mnenie.* M., 1987. Pp. 3-15.

2658 Lopatkin, R.A. *Sotsialisticheskaia obriadnost' i ateisticheskoe vospitanie* [Socialist Ceremonial and Atheistic Education]. M.: Znanie, 1980. 9 pp. (V pomoshch' lektoru).

2659 Lopukhova, O.B. "Kul't siriiskoi bogini na Delose" [Cult of Syrian Goddess of Delos]. *Tretii Vsesoiuznyi simpozium po problemam ellinisticheskoi kul'tury na Vostoke, Mai 1988 g.* Erevan, 1988. Pp. 43-44.

2660 Lopyrev, M.V. "K voprsu ob osobennostiakh individual'noi raboty s veruiushchei molodezh'iu" [On the Problem of Features of Individual Work with Believing Youth]. *Aktual'nye problemy nauchno-ateisticheskogo vospitaniia molodezhi.* M., 1987. Pp. 128-131.

2661 Loseva, I.N. "Mifologiia i religiia" [Mythology and Religion]. *Vopr. nauch. ateizma* 30 (1982): 46-60.

2662 Loseva, I.N. "Razlichenie mifologii i religii kak form obshchestvennogo soznaniia" [Distinction of Mythology and Religion as Forms of Social Consciousness]. *Izv. Sev.-Kavk. nauch. tsentra vyssh. shk. Obshchestv. nauki* 1 (1983): 46-51.

2663 Loukotka, I. "Svoboda sovesti i ee garantii v sotsialisticheskoi Chekhoslovakii" [Freedom of Conscience and Its Guarantees in Socialist Czechoslovakia]. *Vopr. nauch. ateizma* 27 (1981): 174-186.

2664 Lozan, M.N. *Nauka i religiia o proiskhozhdenii cheloveka* [Science and Religion on the Origin of Man]. Kishinev: Lumina, 1987. 71 pp., illus. In Moldavian.

2665 Lozinskii, S.G. *Istoriia papstva* [History of Papacy]. M.: Politizdat, 1986. 382 pp., illus. (B-ka ateist. lit). Subject index: pp. 378-381.

2666 Lubenskii, V.Ia. *Prozrenie: Dokum. ocherki* [Insight: Documentary Essays]. Khar'kov: Prapor, 1980. 144 pp. In Ukrainian.

2667 Lubenskii, V.Ia. *Vozvrashchennoe schast'e* [Returned Happiness]. Kiev: Politizdat Ukrainy, 1989. 107 pp. (Besedy s veruiushchimi). In Ukrainian.

2668 Lubskii, V.I. "Formirovanie nauchno-ateisticheskoi ubezhdennosti studentov-zaochnikov v protsesse prepodavaniia kursa 'Osnovy nauchnogo ateizma'" [Forming Scientific-Atheistic Conviction of External Students in the Process of Teaching "Foundations of Scientific-Atheism"]. *Vopr. ateizma* 20 (1984): 24-30.

2669 Lubskii, V.I. *Kritika religioznykh kontseptsii voiny i mira* [Criticism of Religious Conception of War and Peace]. Kiev: Vishcha shk. Izd-vo pri Kiev. un-te, 1985. 78 pp. (Ateist. b-chka studenta). Annot. bibl.: pp. 75-77.

2670 Lubskii, V.I. "Modernizatsiia pravoslavnykh kontseptsii voiny i mira" [Modernization of Orthodox Conception of War and Peace]. *Vopr. ateizma* 23 (1987): 92-98.

2671 Lubskii, V.I. *Problemy voiny i mira v sovremennoi religioznoi ideologii* [The Problems of War and Peace in Contemporary Religious Ideology]. Kiev: Znanie UkSSR, 1980. 18 pp. (B-chka v pomoshch' lektoru "Problemy nauch. ateizma" / O-vo "Znanie" UkSSR). In Ukrainian. Bibl.: p. 18.

2672 Lubskii, V.I.; Gorbachenko, T.G. "Rol' bibliotek v formirovanii nauchno-materialisticheskogo mirovozzreniia shkol'nikov" [Libraries' Role in Forming Scientific-Materialist World-Outlook of Schoolboys]. *Vopr. ateizma* 23 (1987): 43-49.

2673 Luchshev, E.M. "Problemy religii i morali v sovremennoi publitsistike" [Problems of Religion and Morals in Contemporary Journalism]. *Sotsial'no-filosofskie aspekty kritiki religii* L., 1988. Pp. 20-42.

2674 Luchsheva, Z.A. "Kritika revoliutsionnymi demokratami slavianofil'skoi kontseptsii roli pravoslaviia v istorii Rossii" [Criticism by Revolutionary Democrats of Slavophil Conception of the Role of Orthodoxy in the History of Russia]. *Russkoe pravoslavie i ateizm v otechestvennoi istorii* L.,1988. Pp. 91-107.

2675 Luchsheva, Z.A. "Kritika revoliutsionnymi demokratami sotsial'no-eticheskikh vozzrenii predstavitelei religioznoi filosofii" [Criticism by Revolutionary Democrats of Socio-Ethical Outlook of the Representatives of Religious Philosophy]. *Sotsial'no-filosofskie aspekty kritiki religii.* L., 1987. Pp. 44-55.

2676 Luchsheva, Z.A. "Problemy nauchno-tekhnicheskoi revoliutsii v interpretatsii ideologov protestantskogo modernizma" [Problems of Scientific-Technical Revolution in Interpretation of Ideologists of Protestant Modernism]. *Aktual'nye problemy izuchenia istorii religii i ateizma.* L., 1980. Pp. 32-39.

2677 Lukach, I. "Putem dialoga i sotrudnichestva" [By Way of Dialogue and Cooperation]. *Nauka i religiia* 8 (1980): 53-55.

2678 Lukach, I. *Puti bogov: K tipologii religii, predshestvovavshikh khristianstvu* [The Ways of Gods: Typology of Religions, Predecessors of Christianity]. M.: Politizdat, 1984. 248 pp.

2679 Lukach, I. "Svoboda sovesti i politika v oblasti religii i tserkvii v
      sotsialisticheskoi Vengrii" [Freedom of Conscience and Politics in the
      Realm of Religion and Church in Socialist Hungary]. *Vopr. nauch.*
      ateizma 27 (1981): 151-160.

2680 Lukasheva, N.G. "Ovladenie navykami kritiki klerikal'nogo antikommunizma -
      vazhnaia zadacha formirovaniia ateisticheskoi ubezhdennosti studentov"
      [Mastery of Skills of Criticism of Clerical Anti-Communism - Important
      Task in Shaping Atheistic Conviction of Students]. *Aktual. vopr.*
      metodiki prepodavania obshchestv. nauk i komm. vospitaniia studentov 5 (1987):
      28-35.

2681 Lukashik, N.I. *K voprosu o prirode i kharaktere sovremennykh religiozno-*
      politicheskikh dvizhenii v razvivaiushchikhsia stranakh [On the Problem of
      Nature and Character of Contemporary Religious-Political Movements in
      Developing Countries]. Iaroslavl': Iarosl. politekhn. in-t., 1982. 15 pp.

2682 Lukina, N.V. "Kul'tovye mesta khantov r. Niurol'ki" [Places of Worship of
      Khants by the River Niurol']. *Voprosy etnokul'turnoi istorii Sibirii.* Tomsk,
      1980. Pp. 92-99.

2683 Lukoianov, A.K. "Eksport 'islamskoi revoliutsii': teoriia i praktika" [Export
      of "Islamic Revolution": Theory and Practice]. *"Islamskii faktor" v*
      mezhdunarodnykh otnosheniakh v Azii (70-e - pervaia plovina 80-kh. gg.).
      M., 1987. Pp. 114-123.

2684 Lukshaite, I. *Radikal'noe napravlenie reformatsii v Litve* [Radical Trend of
      Reformism in Lithuania]. Vil'nius: Mokslas, 1980. 134 pp., illus. Bibl.: pp.
      126-133.

2685 Lukshaite, I. "Raz'iasnenie prichin vozniknoveniia i porazheniia Reformatsii v
      litovskoi burzhuaznoi i emigrantskoi istoriografii" [Explanation of Reasons
      of the Rise and Defeat of Reformation in Lithuanian Bourgeois and
      Emigrant Historiography]. *Burzuazinit koncepciju lietuvos istorijos*
      klausimais kritika. Vil'nius, 1987. Pp. 25-44. In Lithuanian.

2686 Lunacharskii, A.V. *Religiia i prosveshchenie* [Religion and Enlightenment].
      M.: Sov. Rossiia, 1985. 542 pp. (Khudozh. i publitsit. b-ka ateista). Annot.
      bibl.: pp. 494-541.

2687 Lunin, B.V. "Sotsial'no-ekonomicheskie i politicheskie aspekty islam-
      ovedcheskogo naslediia V.V. Bartol'da i sovremennost'" [Socio-Economical

and Political Aspects of V.V. Barthold Legacy of Islamic Studies and Contemporaneity]. *Obshchestv. nauki v Uzbekistane* 12 (1988): 44-52.

2688 Luparev, G.P. *Pravosoznanie veruiushchikh i ego osobennosti* [Believers' Sense of Justice and Its Features]. Alma-Ata: Kazakhstan, 1989. 208 pp.

2689 Lushkova, T.N. "Pozitsiia tserkvi po problemam obshchestvennogo razvitiia" [Position of the Church on the Problem of Social Development]. *Problemy razrabotki kontseptsii sotsialisticheskoi orientatsii i nekotorye aspekty ee realizatsii na sovremennom etape.* M., 1989. Pp. 109-111.

2690 Lysenko, V.G. "Darshana, anvikshiki i dkharma: filosofiia i religiia v Indii" [Darshana Anvikshika and Dharma: Philosophy and Religion in India]. *Meodologicheskie problemy izucheniia istorii filosofii zarubezhnogo Vostoka.* M., 1987. Pp. 94-116.

2691 Lysenko, V.M. "Vliianie religioznogo verovaniia na deiatel'nost' cheloveka" [Influence of Religious Belief on the Activity of Man]. *Filos. vopr. meditsiny i biologii* 17 (1985): 124-128.

2692 Lytkin, V.V. "O nekotorykh problemakh kritiki khristianstva v nasledii K.E. Tsiolkovskogo" [Some Problems of Criticism of Christianity in the Legacy of K.E. Tsiolkovskii]. *Nauchno-ateisticheskie issledovaniia v muzeiakh.* L., 1987. Pp. 71-79.

2693 *L'vovskii muzei istorii religii i ateizma* [Lvov museum of religion and atheism history].* L'vov: Kameniar, 1988. 96 pp., illus. Summary in English.

2694 Machianskas, F.[P]. "Kapsukasa protiv klerikalizma" [Kapsukas against Clericalism]. *Kommunist.* Vil'nius. 2 (1983): 22-31.

2695 Machianskas, F.P. *Obshchestennye vzgliady V. Kapsukasa: Kritika filos., sotsial.-polit. i ideol. kontseptsii klerikalizma* [Social Views of V. Kapsukas: Criticism of Philosophy, Socio-Political and Ideological Conceptions of Clericalism]. Vil'nius: Mintis, 1987. 195 pp. In Lithuanian. Bibl.: pp. 190-194. For review see item 5149.

2696 Machianskas, F.P. *Sto zagadok po religii* [Hundred Riddles on Religion] 2nd revised and enlarged ed. Vil'nius: Vituris, 1985. 417 pp., illus. (Khochu znat'). In Lithuanian.

2697   Machiulis, I.[I]. *Nauchno-ateisicheskaia propaganda v sovremennykh usloviiakh* [Scientific-Atheistic Propaganda in Contemporary Conditions]. Vil'nius: Znanie LitSSR, 1980. 22 pp. (Material dlia lektora / O-vo "Znanie" LitSSR). In Lithuanian. Bibl.: pp. 21-22.

2698   Machiulis, I.[I]. "Nauchnoe mirovozzrenie dolzhno byt' tselostnym" [Scientific World Outlook Should be Integral]. *Kommunist.* Vil'nius. 11 (1988): 69-73.

2699   Machiulis, I.I. "Obnovlencheskie tendentsii v katolicheskoi tserkvi" [Renovated Tendencies in Catholic Church]. *Vopr. nauch. ateizma* 28 (1981): 105-123.

2700   Machiulis, I.[I]. "Pastyri 'domashnego kostela" [Pastors of "Domestic Roman Catholic Church"]. *Nauka i religiia* 4 (1985): 32-34.

2701   Machiulis, I.[I]. "Zhizn' diktuet izmeneniia" [Life Dictates Changes]. *Nauka i religiia* 10 (1980): 24-27.

2702   Madar, M. "Protsessy nad ved'mami v Estonii v XVI-XVII vekakh" [Witch Hunt in Estonia in the XVIth-XVIIth Centuries]. *Religiooni ja ateismi ajalost eestis* 3 (1987): 123-145. In Estonian. Summary in Russian.

2703   Madzhidov, R.M. "Metodologicheskie problemy sekuliarizatsii" [Methodological Problems of Secularization]. *Izv. AN TadzhSSR.* Ser.: Filosofiia, ekonomika, pravovedenie. 1 (1987): 3-9. Summary in Tajik.

2704   Madzhidov, R.M. "Modernistskie tendentsii v islame v usloviiakh sotsializma" [Modernist Tendencies in Islam under Socialism]. *Vopr. nauch. ateizma* 31 (1983): 222-240.

2705   Madzhidov, R.M. *Sotsialisticheskii obraz zhizni i ateizm* [Socialist Way of Life and Atheism]. Dushanbe: Irfon, 1984. 30 pp. In Tajik.

2706   Madzhidov, R.M. "Sushchnost' modernizatsii islama i ee kritika v praktike ateisticheskoi raboty" [The Essence of Islam's Modernization and Its Criticism in the Practice of Atheistic Work]. *Kompleksnyi podkhod v ateisticheskom vospitanii.* Dushanbe, 1988. Pp. 45-69. Bibl.: pp. 66-69.

2707   Madzhidov, R.M. "Svoboda sovesti v SSSR: stranitsy istorii" [Freedom of Conscience in USSR: Pages of History]. *Izv. AN TadzhSSR.* Ser.: Filosofiia, ekonomika, pravovedenie 4 (1988): 68-72.

2708 Madzhidov, R.[M]. "Ubezhdat', a ne prinuzhdat'" [To Convince, not to Coerce]. *Kommunist Tadzhikistana* 4 (1989): 63-67.

2709 Madzhidov, R.[M].; Rakhimov, A. "Sushchnost' modernizatsii islama v sovremennykh usloviiakh" [Essence of Modernization of Islam in Contemporary Conditions]. *Kommunist Tadzhikistana* 2 (1988): 76-82.

2710 Madzhister, S. *Politika Vatikana v Italii, 1943-1978* [The Policy of Vatican in Italy, 1943-1978]. Transl. from Italian. Ed.: N.A. Koval'skii. M.: Progress, 1982. 335 pp. Annot. bibl.: pp. 286-325. Name, parties and organizations index: pp. 326-334.

2711 Magnai, Zh. "Kriticheskii analiz moral'nykh pouchenii lamaizma" [Critical Analysis of Moral Preachings of Lamaism]. *Stroitel'stvo sotsializma i utverzhdenie nauchno-materialisticheskogo, ateisticheskogo mirovozzreniia (v regionakh rasprostraneniia lamaizma)*. M., 1981. Pp. 73-88.

2712 Magomedova, M.A. "Obriady vyzvaniia dozhdia u dargintsev (XIX-nach.XX v.)" [Ritual for Calling for Rain by Dargints]. *Kallendar' i kalendarnye obriady narodov Dagestana*. Makhachkala, 1987. Pp. 89-98.

2713 Maikhrovskii, Ia. "Deiatel'nost' Instituta religiovedeniia Iagellonskogo universiteta" [Activity of the Institute for the Study of Religion at the Jagellon University]. *Religii mira, 1986.* M., 1987. Pp. 262-265.

2714 Maiorov, G.G. *Tsitseron i antichnaia filosofiia religii* [Cicero and Ancient Philosophy of Religion]. M.: Znanie, 1989. 63 pp. (Novoe v zhizni, nauke, tekhnike. Ser.: Filosofiia; 1989, 8).

2715 Maisiuk, A.V. "Religiia, veruiushchie i perestroika" [Religion, Believers and Perestroika]. *Problemy aktivizatsii chelovecheskogo faktora v usloviiakh sovershenstvovaniia sotsializma.* Karaganda, 1988. Pp. 68-76.

2716 Maisiuk, A.V. "Sotsial'nye tsennosti sotsialisticheskogo obshchestva v krivom zerkale religioznogo mirovozzreniia" [Social Values of Socialist Society in Distorting Mirror of Religious World Outlook]. *Kul'tura i sotsial'nye tsennosti lichnosti v sotsialisticheskom obshchestve.* Karaganda, 1987. Pp. 97-104.

2717 Makarenko, V.P. "Izuchenie obshchestvennogo mneniia molodezhi po vopro-sam ateizma i religii - aktual'naia zadacha obshchestvennykh sotsiologi-cheskikh ob'edinenii" [The Study of Youth Public Opinion on Questions

of Atheism and Religion - Actual Task of Public Sociological Unions].
*Problemy razvitiia obshchestvennykh sotsiologicheskikh ob'edinenii pri
komitetakh komsomola: opyt, problemy.* M., 1987. Pp. 85-93.

2718 Makarenko, V.P. *Vera, vlast' i biurokratiia: Kritika sotsiologii M. Vebera*
[Faith, Power and Bureaucracy: Criticism of M. Weber's Sociology].
Rostov n/D: Izd-vo Rost. un-ta, 1988. 301 pp. Bibl.: pp. 297-298.

2719 Makarenko, V.P. "Vzaimodeistvie nravstvennogo i ateisticheskogo vospitaniia
v protsesse formirovaniia dukhovnogo mira molodykh zhenshchin-
rabotnits" [Interaction of Moral and Atheistic Education in the Forming
Process of Spiritual World of Young Women-Workers]. *Aktual'nye
problemy nauchno-ateisticheskogo vospitaniia molodezhi.* M., 19887. Pp.
87-91.

2720 Makarov, N.A. "Kamen' Antoniia Rimlianina" [Rock of the Roman
Antonius]. *Novgor. ist. sb.* 2 (1984): 203-210.

2721 Makatov, I.[A]. "Aktivno perestraivat' ateisticheskuiu rabotu" [Actively to
Reform Atheistic Work]. *Kommunist Uzbekistana* 6 (1988): 58-65.

2722 Makatov, I.A. "Religioznoe vliianie v semeino-rodstvennykh otnosheniiakh i
ego preodolenie" [Religious Influence in Family-Relative Relations and Its
Overcoming]. *Vopr. nauch. ateizma* 31 (1983): 241-250.

2723 Makatov, I.A. "Sootnoshenie natsional'nogo i religioznogo v traditsiiakh
narodov Severnogo Kavkaza" [Correlation of National and Religious in
Traditions of Peoples of Northern Caucasus]. *Voprosy sovershenstvovaniia
natsional'nykh protsessov v SSSR.* Tashkent, 1987. Pp. 186-197.

2724 Makhin, V.[A]. "Ostrye problemy na 'kruglom stole'" [Sharp Problems on
"The Round Table"]. *Nauka i religiia* 10 (1982): 38-39.

2725 Makhin, V.A. *Prikryvaias' imenem boga* [Covering Oneself with the Name of
God]. M.: Sov. Rosiia, 1982. 54 pp.

2726 Makhkamov, K.M. "Nazrevshie problemy" [Ripen Problems]. *Nauka i religiia*
3 (1987): 2-4.

2727 Makhmudov, P.G. *Ateisticheskaia propaganda v kommunisticheskom vospitanii*
[Atheistic Propaganda in Communist Education]. Baku: Azerneshr, 1983.
91 pp. In Azerbaijan.

2728 Makhmudov, P.G. *Est' li religioznye chudesa?* [Do Religious Miracles Exist?]. Baku: Azerneshr, 1987. 55 pp. (B-chka ateista). In Azerbailan.

2729 Maksimchuk, P.P. *Pressa SSSR v bor'be protiv klerikal'nogo antikommunizma* [The Press of the USSR in the Struggle against Clerical Anti Communism]. Kiev: Nauk. dumka, 1986. 151 pp. Annot. bibl.: pp. 140-150. In Ukrainian.

2730 Maksimenko, V.I. "Magribinskie uchenye o politizatsii Islama: Abdalla Larui" [Magreb Scientists on Politicization of Islam: Abdullah Larui]. *Istochnikovedenie i istoriografiia stran Vostoka: uzlovye problemy teorii* 1 (1988): 36-38.

2731 Maksimova, I.V. "Mladshie bogi rimskogo panteona u pozdnikh zapadnykh apologetov" [Junior Gods of Roman Pantheon and Late Western Apologists]. *Problemy issledovanii antichnykh gorodov.* M., 1989. Pp. 70-71.

2732 Maksimova, N.A. *Kak podgotovit' i prochitat' lektsiiu na temu 'Religiia i iskusstvo'* [How to Prepare and Read a Lecture on "Religion and Art"]. Minsk, Znanie BSSR, 1982. 22 pp. (Material v pomoshch' lektoru / Pravl. o-va "Znanie" BSSR. Nauch.-metod. sovet po propagande nauch. ateizma). Bibl.: pp. 21-22. Film stripe: p. 22.

2733 Maksimova, N.A. "Problema svobody v neokhristianstve" [The Problem of Freedom in Neochristianity]. *Nauch. ateizm i ateist. vospitanie* 1 (1983): 109-118.

2734 Maksumova, F.A. *Islamskoe religioznoe soznanie i ideologicheskaia bor'ba v arabskikh stranakh* [Islamic Religious Consciousness and Ideological Struggle in Arab Countries]. M.: Vyssh. koms. shk. pri TsK VLKSM, 1987. 35 pp. Bibl.: p. 34.

2735 Malakhova, I.A. *Anatomiia religioznoi very* [The Anatomy of Religious Faith]. M.: Politizdat, 1980. 48 pp. (B-ka ateista). Published also in: Erevan: Aiastan, 1985. 71 pp. In Armenian.

2736 Malakhova, I.A. *Ideologiia i etika evangel'skikh khristian-baptistov na sovremennom etape: Zadachi, formy i metody ateist. raboty* [Ideology and Ethics of Evangelical Christian-Baptists in Contemporary Stage: Tasks, Forms and Methods of Atheistic Work]. M.: Znanie, Tsentr. Dom nauch. ateizma, 1988. 23 pp.

2737 Malakhova, I.[A]. "Na uroven' aktual'nykh zadach" [On the Level of Actual Tasks]. *Nauka i religiia* 6 (1984): 4-5.

2738 Malakhova, I.A. "Religioznaia potrebnost': Poniatie i sushchnost" [Religious Need: Notion and Essence]. *Vopr. nauch. ateizma* 26 (1980): 297- 308.

2739 Malakhova, I.A. *Sovremennyi baptizm: ideologiia i deiatel'nost'* [Contemporary Baptism: Ideology and Activity]. M.: Znanie, 1987. 64 pp. (Novoe v zhizni, nauke, tekhnike. Nauch. ateizm; 9/1987). Bibl.: pp. 57-58.

2740 Malakhova, I.[A.].; Timofeev, V. "Diskussiia v Smolenitsakh" [Discussion in Smoljanovtsi]. *Nauka i Religiia* 2 (1984): 58-59.

2741 Malakhovskaia, M.L. "'Adagii' Erazma i katolicheskaia tsenzura XVI-XVII vv." [Erasmus' "Adagia" and Catholic Censorship XVIth-XVIIth C.]. *Erazm Rotterrdamskii i ego vremia.* M., 1989. Pp. 227-235.

2742 Maliavin, V.V. "Budizzm i kitaiskaia traditsiia" [Buddhism and Chinese Tradition]. *Etika i ritual v traditsionnom Kitae.* M., 1988. Pp. 256-273. Bibl.: pp. 272-273.

2743 Maliavin, V.V. "K opredeleniiu poniatiia narodnoi religii i traditsionnoi tsivilizatsii" [Definition of the Concept of People's Religion and Traditional Civilization]. *Sov. etnografiia* 1 (1988): 27-39. Summary in English.

2744 Maliavin, V.V. "Sinkreticheskie religii v Kitae v XX v.: traditsionnoe i posttraditsionnoe". [Syncretic Religions in China of XXth C.: Traditional and Post Traditional]. *Religii mira.* M., 1989. Pp. 107-120.

2745 Maliavin, V.[V]. "V potemkakh 'istinnogo sveta'" [In the Darkness of the "True Light"]. *Aziia i Afrika segodnia* 9 (1984): 60-61. Summary in English, suppl. p. 6.

2746 Malich, A.A. "Religioznaia ideologiia v svete problemy sootnosheniia nauki i ideologii i formirovanie voinstvuiushchego ateizma" [Religious Ideology in the Light of the Problem of Correlation of Science and Ideology and Forming Militant Atheism]. *Formirovanie aktivnoi zhiznennoi pozitsii liudei razvitogo sotsializma.* Tallin, 1982. Pp. 136-144.

2747 Malinin, Iu.P. "Rukopis' 'Tolkovaniia na psalmy' P. Abeliara v sobranii Gosudarstvennoi Publichnoi biblioteki im. M.E. Saltykova-Shchedrina" [P.

Abelard's Manuscript "Interpretations of Psalms" in the Collection of M.E. Saltykov-Shchedrin State Public Library]. *Muzei v ateisticheskoi propagande.* L., 1980. Pp. 112-115.

2748 Malinovkin, S.N. *Ot religii k ateizmu* [From Religion to Atheism]. Gor'kii: Volgo-Viat. kn. izd-vo, 1987. 96 pp., illus.

2749 Malinovskii, T.I. *Besedy o prirode* [Talks About Nature]. Kishinev: Kartia moldoveniaske, 1981. 102 pp., illus. (Nauka i religiia). In Moldavian.

2750 Malinovskii, T.I. *Mir zvezd* [The World of Stars]. Kishinev: Kartia Moldoveniaske, 1984. 94 p. (Nauka i religiia). In Moldavian.

2751 Malinovskii, T.I. *Stroenie Vselennoi* (The Structure of the Universe]. Kishinev: Kartia Moldoveniaske, 1987. 112 pp. (Besedy s veruiushchimi). In Moldavian.

2752 Malinovskaia, L.N. *Zhitie u mutnoi vody: O sektakh i sektantakh* [The Life by Troubled Waters: On Sects and Sectarians]. Khabarovsk: Kn. izd-vo, 1985. 63 pp.

2753 Malov, V. *Pis'ma o morali* [Letters on Morals]. M.: Sov. Rossiia, 1984. 88 pp.

2754 Mal'tsev, G.P. "Missionerskaia deiatel'nost' Russkoi pravoslavnoi tserkvi v Sibiri" [Missionary Activity of Russian Orthodox Church in Siberia]. *Vopr. nauch. ateizma* 37 (1988): 187-201.

2755 Mal'tsev, G.P. *"Spasaia korabl' very"* ["Rescuing the Ship of Faith"]. Novosibirsk: Zap.-Sib. kn. izd-vo, 1981. 103 pp.

2756 Mal'tsev, Iu.S. "K istorii khristianstva v Srednei Azii epokhi rannego i razvitogo srednevekov'ia" [History of Christianity in Middle Asia in Epoch of Early and Developed Middle Ages]. *III Vsesoiuznaia konferentsiia vostokovedov "Vzaimodeistvie i vzaimovliianie tsivilizatsii kul'tur na Vostoke".* M., 1988. T. I. Pp. 95-97.

2757 Malushkov, V.G. "K voprosu o ponimanii cheloveka i obshchestva (islam-skogo) v trudakh iranskogo filosofa A. Shariati" [On the Question of Conception of Man and [Islamic] Society in the Works of Iranian Philo-sopher A. Shariati]. *Problemy etiki v filosofskikh ucheniiakh stran Vostoka.* M., 1986. Pp. 23-48.

2758   Malygin, K.A. *Prozrenie*: Ateist. besedy [Enlightenment: Atheistic Talks].
       Kuibyshev: Kn. izd-vo, 1988. 96 pp. Bibl. pp. 94-95.

2759   Malygina, N.N. "Ateisticheskaia problema smysla i tseli zhizni v sovre-
       mennoi bor'be idei" [Atheistic Problem of Life's Meaning and Goals in
       Contemporary Struggle of Ideas]. *Sotsial'no-eticheskie problemy povysheniia
       effektivnosti ateisticheskogo vospitaniia v mnogonatsional'nom regione.*
       Frunze, 1987. Pp. 34-40.

2760   Malyshev, A.A. "Kritika religioznykh vozzrenii na problemy ekologii" [Criti-
       cism of Religious Outlooks on the Problem of Ecology]. *Aktual'nye
       problemy nauchno-ateistichskogo vospitaniia molodezhi.* M., 1987. Pp.
       159-162.

2761   Malyshev, M.A. "Problema smerti v filosofii 'neschastnogo soznaniia'" [The
       Problem of Death in Philosophy of "Unhappy Consciousness"]. *Filos.
       nauki* 5 (1989): 51-59.

2762   Malyshev, M.A. "Problema smerti v istorii nravstvenno-religioznoi mysli"
       [The Problem of Death in the History of Moral-Religious Thought].
       Otnoshenie cheloveka k irratsional'nomu. Sverdlovsk, 1989. Pp. 167-197.

2763   Malyshev, N. "Vnachale dolzno byt' delo" [At First Ought to be a Cause].
       Agitator 22 (1987): 52-54.

2764   Malyshev, N.M. *Povyshenie trudovoi i obshchestvennoi aktivnosti trudia-
       shchikhsia - vazhnoe uslovie preodoleniia religioznykh predrassudkov* [The
       Increase of Labour and Public Activity of Workers - Important Condition
       for Overcoming Religious Prejudices]. M.: Znanie RSFSR, 1988. 40 pp.
       Bibl: p. 39.

2765   Malyshev, N.M. *V nevole ptitsy ne letaiut* [In Captivity Birds do not Fly].
       Novosibirsk: Zap.-Sib. kn. izd-vo, 1985. 80 pp.

2766   Malyshev, N.M. "Vovlechenie veruiushchikh v obshchestvennuiu zhizn',
       vliianie sotsial'noi aktivnosti na ikh soznanie i povedenie" [Involving
       Believers in Public Life, Influence of Social Activity on Their Conscious-
       ness and Behaviour]. *Aktual'nye problemy nauchno-ateisticheskogo
       vospitania molodezhi.* M., 1987. Pp. 147-154.

2767   Malysheva D.B. "Islam (do nachala XX veka)" [Islam (Before the XXth
       Century)]. *Vopr. istorii* 11 (1980): 97-110.

2768 Malysheva, D.B. "Islamskii faktor' v politike zapadnoevropeiskikh gosudarstv" ["Islamic Factor" in the Politics of Western European States]. *"Islamskii faktor" v mezhdunarodnykh otnosheniiakh v Azii (70-e - pervaia polovina 80-kh gg.).* M., 1987. Pp. 174-186.

2769 Malysheva, D.B. "Molodezh' i islam v arabskikh stranakh" [Youth and Islam in Arab Countries]. *Rabochii klass i sovrem. mir* 3 (1988): 122-131.

2770 Malysheva, D.B. *Religiia i obshchestvenno-politicheskoe razvitie arabskikh i afrikanskikh stran, 70-80-e gody* [Religion and Socio-Political Development of Arab and African Countries in the 70s-80s]. M.: Nauka, 1986. 228 pp. Summary in English. Bibl.: pp 222-226. For reviews see items 5150-5151.

2771 Mamaeva, E.B. "Istoriografiia istorii tserkvi na Urale perioda feodalizma" [Historiography of Church History in Urals in the Period of Feudalism]. *Istoriografiia obshestvennoi mysli dorevoliutsionnogo Urala.* Sverdlovsk, 1988. Pp. 109-113. Bibl.: pp. 112-113.

2772 Mamedov, A.K. "Filosofiia religii Kanta" [Kant's Philosophy of Religion]. *Religii mira, 1986.* M., 1987. Pp. 170-192.

2773 Mamedov, A.K. "Kritika Kantom matafizicheskikh pritiazanii khristianskoi teologii" [Kant's Critique of Metaphysical Claims of Christian Theology]. *Aktual'nye problemy ateisticheskogo vospitaniia i kritika religioznoi ideologii.* M., 1983. Pp. 35-39.

2774 Mamedov, A.M. *Islam i problemy sotsialno-kul'turnogo razvitiia arabskikh stran* [Islam and Problems of Socio-Cultural Development of Arab Countries]. Baku: Elm, 1986. 134 pp. Annot. bibl.: pp. 130-133. For review see item 5152.

2775 Mamedov, A.M. "Kritika religioznoi kontseptsii sotsial'noi spravedlivosti" [Criticism of Religious Conception of Social Justice]. *XXVII s'ezd KPSS i aktual'nye problemy sotsial'noi spravedlivosti.* Baku, 1987. Pp. 80-87.

2776 Mamedov, A.M. "Sovremenyi islam: sushchnost' musul'manskikh kontseptsii sotsial'noi spravedlivosti" [Contemporary Islam: The Essence of Moslem Conception of Social Justice]. *Kommunist Azerbaidzhana* 9 (1986): 80-87.

2777 Mamedov, A.S. *Svobodomyslie prosvetitelei Azerbaidzhana* [Free-Thinking of Azerbaijan's Enlighteners]. Baku: Azerneshr, 1987. 142 pp. Bibl.: pp. 137-141.

2778   Mamedov, D.R. "Internatsional'noe i natsional'noe v ateisticheskom vospitanii molodezhi" [International and National in Atheistic Upbringing of Youth]. *Aktual'nye problemy teorii i praktiki kommunisticheskogo vospitaniia studencheskoi molodezhi.* Tbilisi, 1980. Pp. 385-388.

2779   Mamedov, M.D. *Islam i sovremennaia ideologicheskaia bor'ba* [Islam and Contemporary Ideological Struggle]. Baku: Znanie AzSSR, 1983. 54 pp. (V pomoshch' lektoru / Resp. i Bakin. org. o-va "Znanie").

2780   Mamedov, M.D. "O kharaktere religioznosti i sekuliarizatsii v usloviiakh sotsializma" [On the Character of Religiousness and Secularization under Socialism]. *Izv. AN AzSSR. Ser. istorii, filosofii i prava* 2 (1982): 94-100. Summary in Azerbaijan.

2781   Mamedov, M.D. *Sotsial'nyi progress i religiia* [Social Progress and Religion]. Baku: Elm, 1985. 195 pp. In Azerbaijan.

2782   Mamedov, M.D. *Voprosy ateisticheskogo vospitaniia v usloviiakh NTR i razvitogo sotializma* [Problems of Atheistic Education under NTR and Developed Socialism]. Baku: Znanie AzSSR, 1982. 53 pp. (V pomoshch' lektoru / O-vo "Znanie" AzSSR). In Azerbaijan.

2783   Mamedov, M.D. et al. *Obshchestvo, religiia i ateizm* [Society, Religion and Atheism]. Baku: Azerneshr, 1985. 258 pp. In Azerbaijan.

2784   Mamedova, Zh. "Mif o 'probleme islama' v SSSR" [Myth About "The Problem of Islam" in USSR]. *Kommunist Azerbaidzhana* 6 (1986): 71-76.

2785   Mammaev M.M. "O vliianii islama na srednevekovoe izobrazitel'noe tvorchestvo narodov Dagestana" [Influence of Islam on Medieval Decorative Arts of Daghestan Peoples]. *Khudozhestvennaia kul'tura srednevekovogo Dagestana.* Makhachkala, 1987. Pp. 101-127.

2786   Mandzhavidze, D.A. "Gruzinskaia tserkov' i nekotorye voprosy ekonomi-cheskogo razvitiia Vostochnoi Gruzii v XVII-nachale XVIII vv." [Georgian Church and Some Questions of Economic Development of Eastern Georgia in XVIIth-Early XVIIIth C.]. *Istoriko-istochnikovedcheskie issledovaniia.* Tbilisi, 1988. Pp. 26-32. In Georgian. Summary in Russian.

2787   Mannai-ool M.Kh. "Bor'ba s religioznymi perezhitkami v Tuvinskoi ASSR" [Struggle with Religious Survivals in Tuva ASSR]. *Stroitel'stvo sotsializma i utverzhdenie nauchno-materialisticheskogo, ateisticheskogo mirovozzreniia (v regionakh rasprostraneniia lamaizma).* M., 1981. Pp. 158-165.

2788 Mantatov, V.V.; Iangutov, L.E. "Kritika osnovnykh printsipov filosofskogo obosnovaniia buddizma" [Criticism of the Fundamental Principles of Buddhism's Philosophical Basis]. *Nauch. dokl. vyssh. shk. Filosof. nauki* 2 (1984): 107-15.

2789 Manuilova, D.E. "Baptistskaia obshchina 20 let spustia" [Baptist Community 20 Years Later]. *Protestantskie organizatsii v SSSR.* M., 1989. Pp. 93-105.

2790 Manuilova, D.E. "Issledovaniia mirovozzrencheskikh orientatsii studentov kak uslovie effektivnosti prepodavaniia ateizma" [Research of World Outlook Orientations of Students as Condition of Effectiveness of Teaching Atheism]. *Prepodavanie nauchnogo ateizma v vuze.* M., 1988. Pp. 36-43.

2791 Manuilova D.E. "Izuchenie mirovozzrencheskoi orientatsii kak uslovie effektivnosti nauchno-ateisticheskogo vospitaniia" [Research of World Outlook Orientation as Condition of Effectiveness of Scientific-Atheistic Education]. *Aktual'nye problemy obespecheniia effektivnosti nauchno-ateisticheskoi raboty.* Cheboksary, 1986. Pp. 105-109.

2792 Manuilova, D.E. *Tserkov' i veruiushchii* [Church and Believer]. M.: Politizdat, 1981. 77 pp. (B-ka ateista). For review see item 5153.

2793 Manzanov, G.E. "Problemy ateisticheskogo vospitaniia shkol'nikov" [Problems of Atheistic Education of Schoolboys]. *Aktual'nye problemy nauchno-ateisticheskogo vospitaniia molodezhi.* M., 1987. Pp. 118-123.

2794 Marash, Ia.N. Ispol'zovanie pamiatnikov kul'tovogo iskusstva v ateisticheskoi propagande [Use of Monuments of Ecclesiastical Art in Atheistic Propaganda]. Minsk: Polymia, 1980. 40 pp., illus. Bibl.: pp. 38-39.

2795 Marash, Ia.N. *Politika Vatikana i katolicheskoi tserkvi v Zapadnoi Belorussii (1918-1939)* [The Policy of Vatican and Catholic Church in Western Belorussia (1918-1939)]. Minsk: Belarus', 1983. 96 pp. Annot. bibl.: pp. 93-95. For review see item 5154.

2796 Marchenko, A.V. "O edinstve ateisticheskogo i nravstvennogo vospitaniia" [On the Unity of Atheistic and Moral Education]. *Vopr. ateizma* 24 (1988): 85-90.

2797   Marchenko, N.G. "Sovremennye ideologicheskie i politicheskie aktsii po vozrozhdeniiu unii v zapadnykh oblastiakh Ukrainy]. [Contemporary Ideological and Political Actions for Revival of Uniate Church in Western Regions of Ukraine]. *Kritika sovremennoi katolicheskoi i protestanskoi teologii.* M., 1989. Pp. 113-133.

2798   Mardiev, Sh. "Podbirat' kliuch k serdtsu kazhdogo" [To Fit the Key to the Heart of Everyone]. *Part. zhizn',* Tashkent. 6 (1985): 71-75.

2799   Marem'ianin, Iu.P.; Chechulin, A.A. "Problemy sovershenstvovaniia ateisticheskogo vospitaniia v usloviakh aktivizatsii aktsii ideologicheskikh diversii protiv SSSR" [Problems of Perfection of Atheistic Education in the Conditions of Activization of Acts of Ideological Diversions against USSR]. *Nauchnyi ateizm, religiia i sovremennost'.* Novosibirsk, 1987. Pp. 147-160.

2800   Mar'ianov, B. "Kosmicheskie issledovaniia i vera v boga" [Cosmic Researches and Faith in God]. *Nauka i religiia* 2 (1983): 16-20.

2801   Mar'ianov, B.M. *Krushenie legendy: Protiv klerikal. fal'sifikatsii tvorchestva A.S. Pushkina* [Downfall of a Legend: Against Clerical Falsification of A.S. Pushkin's Works]. L.: Lenizdat, 1985. 119 pp.

2802   Mariniuk, V.I. "Gnoseologicheskie i psikhologicheskie aspekty formirovaniia nauchnogo mirovozzreniia" [Gnosiological and Psychological Aspects of Forming Scientific World Outlook]. *Vopr. ateizma* 17 (1981): 71-78.

2803   Marinov, G. "Samokritichnaia ispoved'" [Self-Critical Confession]. *Nauka i religiia* 4 (1982): 59-61; 6 (1982): 59-60.

2804   Markelova, T.A. "Muzyka i religiia" [Music and Religion]. *Muzei v ateisticheskoi propagande.* L., 1988. Pp. 89-102.

2805   Markevich, S. "Frantsuzy otstaivaiut svetskii kharakter obrazovaniia" [French Defend the Secular Character of Education]. Ateisticheskie chteniia. 18 (1989): 9-12.

2806   Markevich, S. *Sovremennaia khristianskaia demokratiia* [Contemporary Christian Democracy]. Transl. from Polish. M.: Politizdat, 1982. 287 pp.

2807 Markov, S.M. *Zachem cheloveku ispoved'?* [For What Does a Man Need Confession?]. Kishinev: Kartia Moldoveniaske, 1981. 105 pp. In Moldavian.

2808 Markovich, V.I. "O khristianizatsii gortsev Severo-Vostochnogo Kavkaza i khrame Datuna v Dagestane" [On Conversion to Christianity of Mountain-Dwellers of North-Eastern Caucasus and of Datun Temple in Daghestan]. *Khudozhestvennaia kul'tura srednevekovogo Dagestana.* Makhachkala, 1987. Pp. 37-48.

2809 Markovin, V.I. "Sentinskii khram i ego izuchenie" [The Study of Sentin Temple]. *Voprosy srednevekovoi arkheologii Severnogo Kavkaza.* Cherkessk, 1988. Pp. 8-32.

2810 Marks Karl i dr. *O religii* [On Religion]. Vil'nius: Mintis, 1982. 413 pp. In Lithuanian. For review see item 5155.

2811 Marr, N.Ia. "Bogi iazycheskoi Gruzii po drevne-gruzinskim istochnikam" [Gods of Pagan Georgia According to Old Georgian Sources]. *Tr. Tbil. un-ta.* 1987. T. 266. Pp. 7-35.

2812 "...Marshal Stalin doveriaet tserkvi" ["...Marshal Stalin Trusts the Church"]. *Agitator* 10 (1989): 26-30.

2813 Martirosov, G. "Kul'tura, ateizm i religiia" [Culture, Atheism and Religion]. *Kommunist Belorussii* 11 (1984): 70-77.

2814 Martishina, N.I. "Iz praktiki ateisticheskogo vospitaniia molodezhi Omskoi oblasti" [From the Practice of Atheistic Upbringing of Youth of Omsk Oblast]. *Aktual'nye problemy nauchno-ateisticheskogo vospitaniia molodezhi.* M., 1987. Pp. 56-60.

2815 Martynenko, N.I. *Kommunisticheskaia moral' i religiia* [Communist Morals and Religion]. M.: Znanie RSFSR, 1983. 40 pp. (V pomoshch' lektoru / O-vo "Znanie" RSFSR, Nauch.-metod. sovet po propagande nauch. ateizma). Bibl.: p. 35.

2816 Martynov, A.S. "Buddizm i dvor v nachale dinastii Tan (VII-VIII vv.)" [Buddhism and the Court at the Beginning of Tang Dynasty (VIIth-VIIIth C.)]. *Buddizm i gosudarstvo na Dal'nem Vostoke.* M., 1987. Pp. 91-108.

2817 Martynov, A.S. "Gosudarstvo i religiia na Dal'nem Vostoke" [State and Religion in the Far East]. *Buddizm i gosudarstvo na Dal'nem Vostoke.* M., 1987. Pp.3-48.

2818 Martynov, A.S. "Konfutsianskaia utopiia v drevnosti i v srednevekov'e" [Confucian Utopia in Antiquity and in the Middle Ages]. *Kitaiskie sotsial'nye utopii.* M., 1987. Pp. 10-57.

2819 Martynov, A.S. "Opisanie lam-proritsatelei u G.Ts. Tsybikova i u Khe Linia" [Description of Lam-Prophets by G.Ts. Tsybikov and He Lin]. *Vostoko-vednye issledovaniia v Buriatii.* Novosibirsk, 1981. Pp. 103-110.

2820 Martynov, A.S.; Porshneva, E.B. "'Ucheniia' i religii v vostochnoi Azii v period srednevekov'ia" ["Teachings" and Religion in Eastern Asia in the Middle Ages]. *Narody Azii i Afriki* 1 (1986): 79-101. Summary in English, p. 101.

2821 Marzamukhamedov, M.; Ezeev, B. *Sokrovishcha chelovecheskogo geniia: Nasledie musul'man. kul'tury v SSSR* [The Treasure of Human Genius: The Legacy of Moslem Culture in the USSR]. M.: Novosti, 1985. [52] pp., illus. In Farsi.

2822 Mashchenko, S.T. "K kharakteristike evoliutsii sekty 'istinnopravoslavnye khristiane'" [On Characteristics of The Evolution of the Sect "True Orthodox Christians"]. *Vopr. ateizma* 17 (1981): 143-150.

2823 Mashero, V. "Krepka li pozitsiia?" [Is the Position Strong?]. *Kommunist Belorussii* 7 (1988): 86-87.

2824 Maslennikov, V. "Oblomki drevnei pravdy" [Debris of the Ancient Truth]. *Nauka i religiia* 9 (1989): 36-39.

2825 Maslov, Iu. "Uchenie dzhainov" [Studies of Jains]. *Aziia i Afrika segodnia* 10 (1980): 59-61.

2826 Maslov, V.V. "Vliianie novogo obraza zhizni na protsess sekuliarizatsii v sfere pravoslavnoi obriadnosti" [The Influence of New Way of Life on the Secularization Process in Orthodox Ceremonial]. *Vopr. ateizma* 22 (1985): 105-112.

2827 Maslova, A.[G]. "Gumanisticheskaia sushchnost' marksistskogo ateizma" [Humanist Essence of Marxist Atheism]. *Nauka i religiia* 12 (1982): 26-30.

2828 Maslova, A.G. *Gumanizm i ateizm* [Humanism and Atheism]. M.: Politizdat, 1981. 64 pp. (B-ka ateista).

2829 Masse, *Islam* [Islam]. Transl. from French. 3rd ed. M.: Nauka, 1982. 191 pp. Name and geographical indices: pp. 182-190.
Published also in:
Dushanbe: Irfon, 1984. 240 pp. In Tajik. Index: pp. 229-239.

2830 *Mat' Varvara* [Mother Barbara]. M.: Novosti, [1989]. 39 pp., illus. (Zhen. vzgliad). In English. Published also in: French, German and Spanish.

2831 Matias, D.[M]. "Ateisticheskaia propaganda v raionnoi pechati" [Atheistic Propaganda in Regional Press]. *Kommunist Belorussii* 10 (1980): 69-75.

2832 Matias, D.M. *Ekumenicheskoe dvizhenie i sovremennyi katolitsism* [Ecumenical Movement and Contemporary Catholicism]. Minsk: Znanie BSSR 1984. 19 pp. (Material v pomoshch' lektoru / O-vo "Znanie" BSSR, Sektsiia ateist. vospitaniia). Bibl.: p. 19.

2833 Matias, D.M. *Khristianskoe chelovekoliubie. V chem ego smysl?* [Christian Love of Fellow-Men. In What Meaning?]. Minsk: Belarus' 1984. 63 pp. Annot. bibl.: pp. 61-62.

2834 Matias, D.M. *Religiia i ateizm o nravstvennom dostoinstve cheloveka* [Religion and Atheism on Moral Virtue of Man]. Minsk: Belarus', 1985. 95 pp. Annot. bibl.: pp. 92-94.

2835 Matsarina, L. "Uchityvaia dukhovnye zaprosy" [Considering Spiritual Needs]. *Nauka i religiia* 2 (1982): 11-13.

2836 Matsiutskii, S.P. *Neprivorotnoe zel'e* [Not Love-Philtre]. Kiev: Znanie UkSSR, 31 pp. (Ser. 5 "Nauchno-ateisticheskaia" / O-vo "Znanie" UkSSR; No 1). In Ukrainian. Bibl.: pp. 31-32.

2837 Matveev, K. "Maronity vchera i segodnia" [Maronites Yesterday and Today]. *Nauka i religiia* 7 (1985): 58-60.

2838   Matveev, O. "Budda - stranitsy zhizni i fragmenty ucheniia" [Buddha - Pages of Life and Fragments of Studies]. *Vetnam* Khanoi. 9 (1989): 38-39.

2839   Matviichuk, N.M. *Obychai liudei zlonravnykh* [Customs of Depraved People]. Kiev: Molod', 120 pp., illus.

2840   Matzhidov, R.M. "Rol' ateisticheskoi propagandy v utverzhdenii dukhovno-nravstvennykh tsennostei sotsialisticheskogo obraza zhizni" [The Role of Atheistic Propaganda for Affirmation of Spiritual-Moral Values of Socialist Way of Life]. *Izv. AN TadzhSSR.* Otd-nie obshchestv. nauk 3 (1984): 30-37. Summary in Tajik.

2841   Mavleev, E.V. "Mifotvorchestvo izobrazitel'nogo iskusstva" [Mythical Creation of Fine Arts]. *Zhizn' mifa v antichnosti.* M., 1988. Ch. I. Pp. 200-214.

2842   Mavliutov, R.R.; Madzhidov, R.M. *Islam* [Islam]. Dushanbe: Irfon, 1980. 110 pp. In Tajik.

2843   Mavrina, N.A. "K voprosu ob istorii rasprostraneniia lamaizma v Zapadnoi Sibirii" [On the Problem of the History of Dissemination of Lamaism in Weastern Siberia]. *Molodye ychenye i spetsialisty Kuzbassa v X piatiletke.* Kemerovo, 1981. Pp. 144-147.

2844   Mazalova, V.P. *Ateizm i ego fal'sifikatory* [Atheism and Its Falsifiers]. M.: Politizdat, 1984. 79 pp. (B-ka ateista).
       Published also in:
       Kishinev Kartia Moldoveniaske, 1986. 155 pp. (Besedy s veruiushchimi), in Moldavian.

2845   Mazalova, V.P. *Katolitsizm - chetvert' veka spustia posle II Vatikanskogo sobora* [Catholicism - A Quarter of a Century After the IInd Vatican Council]. M.: Znanie, 1989. 64 p. (Novoe v zhizni, nauke, tekhnike. Nauch. ateizm; 2/1989). Bibl.: P. 64.

2846   Mazalova, V.P. "Osnovnye napravleniia i metody teologicheskoi interpretatsii marksistsko-leninskogo ateizma i ikh nesostoiatel'nost'" [Basic Directions and Methods of Theological Interpretations of Marxist-Leninst Atheism and Their Groundlesness]. *Nauchnyi ateizm, religiia i sovremennost'.* Novosibirsk, 1987. Pp. 26-56.

2847 Mazalova, V.P. "Politicheskii aspekt katolicheskoi kritiki ateizma" [Political Aspect of Catholic Criticism of Atheism]. *Vopr. nauch. ateizma* 33 (1985): 121-132.

2848 Mazalova, V.P. "Vatikan obsuzhdaet problemy ateizma" [Vatican Discusses Problems of Atheism]. *Vopr. nauch. ateizma* 28 (1981): 276-284.

2849 Mazhitov, N.A. "O sisteme religioznykh verovanii rannikh bashkir" [The System of Religious Beliefs of Early Bashkirs]. *Mirovozzrenie narodov Zapadnoi Sibirii po arkheologicheskim i etnograficheskim dannym.* Tomsk, 1985. Pp. 83-84.

2850 Mazin, A.I. *Traditsionnye verovaniia i obriady Evenkov-Obochonov (konets XIX-nach XX v.)* [Traditional Beliefs and Rituals of Evenk-Obochon (End XIXth-Early XXth C.)]. Novosibirsk: Nauka. Sib. otd-nie, 1984. 201 pp., illus. Annot. bibl.: pp. 106-111.

2851 Mazitova, N.A. "Izuchenie islama v Kazani v XIX v." [Study of Islam in Kazan in XIXth. C.]. *Islam v istorii narodov Vostoka* M., 1981. Pp. 189-196. Annot. bibl.: pp. 195-196.

2852 Mazitova, N.A. "M.A. Mashanov i problemy issledovaniia islama v Kazani v kontse XIX-nachale XX v." [M.A. Mashanov and Problems of Islam's Research in Kazan in the End of XIXth-Early XXth C.]. *Istoriografiia Irana novogo i noveishego vremeni.* M., 1989. Pp. 89-98.

2853 Mazokhin, V. "Aktual'nye problemy ateisticheskoi propagandy" [Actual Problems of Atheistic Propaganda]. *Nauka i religiia* 4 (1980): 19-20.

2854 Mazokhin, V. "Nemetskomu soiuzu svobodomysliashchikh - 75 let" [75th Anniversary of the German Union of Free-Thinkers]. *Nauka i religiia* 12 (1980): 51-53.

2855 Mazurchuk, Iu.A. *Religiia i ideologicheskaia bor'ba* [Religion and Ideological Struggle]. L.: Znanie RSFSR, 1982. 16 pp. (V pomoshch' lektoru / O-vo "Znanie" RSFSR, Leningr. org.).

2856 Mchedlov, M.[P]. "Novoe i staroe v religioznoi filosofii" [New and Old in Religious Philosophy]. *Nauka i zhizn'* 9 (1982): 105-111.

2857 Mchedlov, M.P. "O sovremennykh protsessakh v religii" [Contemporary Processes in Religion]. *Vopr. filosofii* 2 (1984): 141-155. Summary in English, pp. 173-174.

2858 Mchedlov, M.P. *Politika i religiia* [Politics and Religion]. M.: Sov. Rossiia, 1987. 253 pp.

2859 Mchedlov, M.[P]. "Politika i religiia: traditsii i sovremennost'" [Politics and Religion: Traditions and Contemporaneity]. *Agitator* 16 (1987): 39-42.

2860 Mchedlov, M.[P]. "Religiia i politika: traditsii i sovremenost'" [Religion and Politics: Traditions and Contemporaneity]. *Nauka i religiia* 1 (1985): 24-28.

2861 Mchedlov, M.P. "Religiia i politika: traditsionnoe i novoe" [Religion and Politics: Traditional and New]. *Vopr. nauch. ateizma* 36 (1987): 4-23.

2862 Mchedlov, M.[P]. "Religiia i sovremennost'" [Religion and Contemporaneity]. *Nauka i zhizn'* 6 (1982): 60-66.

2863 Mchedlov, M.P. *Religiia i sovremennost'* [Religion and Contemporaneity]. M.: Politizdat, 1982. 272 pp.
      Published also in:
      M.: Progress, [1987]. 237 pp. In English. For review see items 5156-5162.

2864 Mchedlov, M.P. "Religiia, tserkov', politika" [Religion, Church, Politics]. *Kommunist* 14 (1982): 90-101.

2865 Mchedlov, M.P. *Sovremennye sotsial'nye dvizheniia i religiia* [Contemporary Social Movements and Religion]. M.: Znanie, 1985. 64 pp. (Novoe v zhizni, nauke, tekhnike. Nauch. ateizm; 3). Bibl.: p. 64.

2866 Mchedlova, E.M. "Burzhuaznoe svobodomyslie v sovremennoi Frantsii" [Bourgeois Freethinking in Contemporary France]. *Molodezh' i tvorchestvo: sotsial'no-filosofskie problemy.* M., 1988. Ch. I. Pp. 152-155.

2867 Mchedlova, E.M. "Kul'turnoe prosveshchenie kak sredstvo ateisticheskogo vospitaniia" [Cultural Enlightenment as Means of Atheistic Education]. *Dukhovnyi mir sovremennogo cheloveka.* M., 1987. Pp. 13-15.

2868 *Medetsina. Filosofiia. Ateizm:* Tez. Dokl. Nauch. Konf., Apr. 1984 [Medicine. Philosophy. Atheism. Theses of Lectures of Scientific Conference, Apr. 1984]. Ed.: I. Zaksas. Vil'nius: [S.n.], 1984. 64 pp. In Lithuanian.

2869 *Medetsina. Filosofiia. Gumanizm. Ateizm* [Medicine. Philosophy. Humanism. Atheism]. Ed.: O. Rachkauskene. Vil'nius: [S.n.], 1985. 60 pp. In Lithuanian.

2870 Medvedev, A.B. "Bibleiskii obraz cheloveka i zadachi sovremennogo ateizma" [Biblical Image of Man and Tasks of Contemporary Atheism]. *Otnoshenie cheloveka k irratsional'nomy*. Sverdlovsk, 1989. Pp. 96-116.

2871 Medvedev, I.V. "V tiskakh religioznogo obskurantizma" [In the Clutches of Religious Obscurantism]. *Argumenty*. M., 1988. Pp. 129-143.

2872 Medvedev, O.P. "Dzog-chen: Ob odnom ortodoksal. napravlenii tibet. buddizma" [Dzog-Chen: On an Orthodox School of Tibetan Buddhism]. *Narody Azii i Afriki* 6 (1989): 50-54. Summary in English.

2873 Medvedeva, E.A. "O roli islama v natsional'no-osvoboditel'nom dvizhenii" [Islam's Role in National-Liberation Movement]. *Mirovoi revoliutsionnyi protsess: Probl. i issled.* 4 (1982): 69-75.

2874 Medvedko, L.I.; Germanovich, A.V. *Imenem Allakha...: Politizatsiia islama i islamizatsiia politiki* [In the Name of Allah...: Politicization of Islam and Islamisation of Politics]. M.: Politizdat, 1988. 255 pp. For review see item 5163.

2875 Medvedko, L.I.; Germanovich, A.[V]. *Islam i osvoboditel'naia bor'ba* [Islam and Liberation Struggle]. M.: Novosti, 1983. 35 pp., in old Arab pagination. In Arabic. Published also in: English and French.

2876 Medyntseva, A.A. "Oklady 'korsunskikh' ikon iz Novgoroda" [Frameworks of "Korsun" Icons from Novgorod]. *Sov. arkheologiia* 4 (1988): 67-77. Bibl.: p. 77. Summary in English.

2877 Meerovskii, B.V. "Kritika klerikal'nykh kontseptsii religioznoi svobody" [Criticism of Clerical Conceptions of Religious Freedom]. *Problema svobody cheloveka v sovremennoi ideologicheskoi bor'be*. Riga, 1987. Pp. 179-187.

2878 Meerovskii, B.V.; Nikonov, K.I. "V poiskakh 'antropologicheskikh konstant' religii" [In the Search of "Anthropological Constants" of Religion]. *Problemy cheloveka v sovremennoi religioznoi i misticheskoi literature*. M., 1988. Pp. 18-26.

2879   Mefodii, mitropolit. "Zemnye dela tserkvi" [Earthly Affairs of the Church].
       Novoe vremia 24 (1988): 26.

2880   Meier, M.S. "O sootnoshenii svetskoi i dukhovnoi vlasti v osmanskoi
       politicheskoi sisteme v XVI-XVIII vv." [Correlation of Secular and
       Spiritual Authority in Osmanli Political System in XVIth-XVIIIth C.].
       Islam v istorii narodov Vostoka. M., 1981. Pp. 51-62. Annot. bibl.: pp.
       61-62.

2881   Meikshane, D.A. *Teoriia i praktika ateisticheskogo vospitaniia: Psikhol.
       aspekty* [Theory and Practice of Atheistic Education: Psychological
       Aspects]. Riga: Zvaigzne, 1983. 104 pp. In Latvian. Bibl.: pp. 100-103.
       Published also in 1986, 140 pp., in Russian.

2882   Meilakh, M. "'Chetvertyi put' Georgiia Giurdzhieva" [George Ghiurdzhiev's
       "Fourth Way"]. *Nauka i religiia* 9 (1989): 48-51.

2883   Meister, V. "Kak voznikla ideia zagrobnogo vozdaianiia" [How Occured the
       Idea of Recompense Beyond the Grave]. *Nauka i religiia* 10 (1980):
       32-34.

2884   Meitarchiian, M.B. "Rol' M. Bois v izuchenii zoroastriiskogo pogrebal'nogo
       obriada" [The Role of M. Boys in the Study of Zoroastrian Funeral
       Ceremony]. *Kul'tura i iskusstvo narodov Vostoka.* M., 1987. Pp. 68-69.

2885   Mekhtiev, A.Sh. "Zaiditskie podsekty" [Zaidit Subsects]. *Izv. AN AzSSR.* Ser.
       istorii, filosofii i prava 4(1985): 49-55. Summary in Azerbaijan.

2886   Mekhtiev, M.F. "Perestroika i ateisticheskoe vospitanie molodezhi" [Peres-
       troika and Atheistic Upbringing of Youth]. *Aktual'nye voprosy ateistiches-
       kogo vospitaniia molodezhi.* Baku, 1988. Pp. 28-38. In Azerbaijan.
       Summary in Russian.

2887   Melik-Gaikazova, N.N. "Katolicheskaia tserkov' vo V'etname" [Catholic
       Church in Vietnam]. *Narody Azii i Afriki* 1 (1988): 101-108.

2888   Melikhov, S.T. "Iz opyta ateisticheskoi raboty partiinykh organizatsii
       avtonomnykh respublik Severnogo Kavkaza (1917-1941 gg.)" [From the
       Experience of Atheistic Work of Party Organizations of Autonomous
       Republics of Northern Caucasus (1917-1914)]. *Izv. Sev.-Kavk. nauch.
       tsentra vyssh. shk. Obshchestv. nauki.* Rostov n/D. 2 (1987): 57-66.

2889 Melikoff, I. "O sredneaziatskom proiskhozhdenii sufizma Anatolii" [On Middle Asian Origins of Sufism of Anatolia]. *Sov. tiurkologiia* 5 (1988): 22-28. Annot. bibl.: pp. 27-28.

2890 Melikov, S.T. *Istinnoe litso 'slug allakha'* [The True Face of "Servants of Allah"]. Ordzhonikidze: Ir, 1987. 175 pp.

2891 Melikov, S.[T]. "Poniatie klassa i natsii v islame" [The Notion of Class and Nation in Islam]. *Lit. Osetiia.* Ordzhonikidze, 1987. Pp. 103-106.

2892 Melikset-bek, L.L. "Sekta 'Novyi Izrail'' i ee reaktsionaia sushchnost'" [The Sect "New Israel" and Its Reactionary Essence]. *Iz istorii religii i ateizma v Gruzii.* Tbilisi, 1988. Pp. 40-51. In Georgian. Summary in Russian.

2893 Melkumian, E.S. "'Islamskii faktor' v deiatel'nosti Soveta sotrudnichestva arabskikh gosudarstv Persidskogo zaliva" ["Islamic Factor" in the Activity of the Council of Cooperation of the Arab States in the Persian Gulf]. *"Islamskii faktor" v mezhdunarodnykh otnosheniiakh v Azii (70-e - pervaia polovina 80-kh gg.).* M., 1987. Pp. 88-101.

2894 Melkusova, G. "Kritika bogoslovskogo ponimaniia roli religii v obshchestve" [Criticism of Theological Interpretation of the Role of Religion in Society]. *Aktual'nye problemy ateisticheskogo vospitaniia i kritika religioznoi ideologii.* M., 1981. Pp. 73-79.

2895 Mel'nichenko, B.N. "Buddiiskaia obshchina i gosudarstvo v traditsionnom tailandskom obshchestve XV-XIX vv." [Buddhist Community and State in Traditional Thailand Society of the XVth-XIXth C.]. *Buddizm i gosudarstvo na Dal'nem Vostoke.* M., 1987. Pp. 204-226.

2896 Mel'nik, V.I. *Evoliutsiia sovremennogo piatidesiatnichestva* [Evolution of the Contemporary Pentecostalism]. L'vov: Vishcha shk. Izd-vo pri L'vov. un-te, 1985. 160 pp. Annot. bibl.: pp. 152-159.

2897 Mel'nik, V.I. "K kritike ekstremizma i fanatizma v sovremennom piatide-siatnichestve" [Criticism of Extremism and Fanaticism in Contemporary Pentecostalism]. *Vopr. ateizma* 18 (1982): 106-113.

2898 Mel'nik, V.I. *Piatidesiatnichestvo: novye tendentsii* [Pentecostalism: New Tendencies]. Kiev: Znanie UkSSR, 1988. 48 pp. (Ser. 5, Nauchno-ateisticheskaia / O-vo "Znanie" UkSSR; No 8. In Ukrainian.

2899 Mel'nikov, G.P. "Znachenie khristianizatsii Chekhii i ee vneshne-politicheskii aspekt v cheshskoi khronistike vtoroi poloviny XVI v." [Importance of Czech's Conversion to Christianity and Its Foreign Political Aspect in Czech Chronology of the Late XVIth C.]. *Slaviane i ikh sosedi. Mezhdunarodnye otnosheniia v epokhu feodalizma.* M., 1989. Pp. 108-124.

2900 Menabdishvili, T.I. *Kritika ideologii sovremennogo sektantstva* [Criticism of the Ideology of Contemporary Sectarianism]. Tbilisi: Sabchota Sakartvelo, 1981. 132 pp. In Georgian.

2901 Menabdishvili, T.I. *Reaktsionnyi kharakter sektantskoi morali* [Reactionary Character of Sectarian Morals]. Tbilisi: Metsniereba, 1983. 71 pp. In Georgian. Summary in Russian.

2902 Menkes, E. "Kandidat ot Armageddona" [Candidate from Armageddon]. *Nauka i religiia* 9 (1987): 60-62.

2903 Merkis, A.I. "Esli est' o'bekt issledovaniia" [If There is an Object for Research]. *Nauka i religiia* 8 (1982): 21-23.

2904 Meshcheriakov, A.N. *Drevniaia Iaponiia: buddizm i sintoizm: Probl. sinkretizma* [Ancient Japan: Buddhism and Shintoism: Problems of Syncretism]. M.: Nauka, 1987. 192 pp., illus. Summary in English. Bibl.: pp. 180-185. Index: pp. 186-190.

2905 Meshcheriakov, A.N. "Legendy iz 'Nikhon reiki'" [Legends from "Nihon Ryoki"]. *Narody Azii i Afriki* 3 (1981): 126-134.

2906 Meshcheriakov, A.N. "O nekotorykh osobennostiakh ranneiaponskogo buddizma" [Some Features of Early Japanese Buddhism]. *Drevniaia Indiia: Ist.-kul't. sviazi.* M., 1982. Pp. 219-227.

2907 Meshcheriakov, A.N. "Sintoistskii zmei i ranneiaponskii buddizm: problema kul'turnoi adaptatsii" [Shinto Snake and Early Japanese Buddhism: Problem of Cultural Adaptation]. *Buddizm. Istoriia i kul'tura.* M., 1989. Pp. 119-128.

2908 Meshcherskii, N.A. "K datirovke zakliuchitel'nogo nachala Evangeliia ot Marka" [To the Dating of Ev. Mrk].* *Pales. sb.* 28 (1986): 110-111. Summary in English.

2909 Mesters, E. "Vypolniaem svoiu missiiu" [We Fulfill Our Mission]. *Religiia v SSSR* 1 (1987): EM 1 - EM 2.

2910 *Mesto religii v obshchestvenno-politicheskoi zhizni stran Blizhnego i Srednego Vostoka* [The Place of Religion in Socio-Political Life in the Countries of the Near and Middle East]. [Ed.: Z.Z. Abdullaev]. Baku: AGU, 1985. 86 pp. Part of the text in Azerbaijan.

2911 Metelitsa, L.B.; Brisov, E.M. "Burzhuaznaia religioznaia propaganda po voprosam meditsiny i biologii - odno iz napravlenii sovremennoi psikhologicheskoi voiny" [Bourgeois Religious Propaganda on the Question of Medicine and Biology - One of the Trends of Contemporary Psychological War]. *Sov. meditsina* 11 (1985): 3-8.

2912 Metelitsa, L.B.; Brisov, E.M. "O roli meditsiny v ateisticheskom vospitanii" [Medicine's Role in Atheistic Education]. *Sov. zdravokhranenie* 6 (1983): 28-33.

2913 Metkin, A. "Delegatsiia Vsemirnogo islamskogo kongressa v Sovetskom Soiuze" [Delegation of the World Islamic Congress in Soviet Union]. *Religiia v SSSR* 2 (1988): AM 1-AM 3.

2914 *Metodologicheskie voprosy istorii razvitiia srednevekovoi filosofii narodov Zakavkaz'ia* [Methodological Questions of History of Development of Medieval Philosophy of Peoples of Transcaucasus]. Ed.: Z.B. Geiushev.: Baku: Elm, 1982. 239 pp.

2915 Metreveli, M.G. "Druzy Sirii i Livana" [Druse of Syria and Lebanon]. *Soobshch. AN GSSR* T. 112, 1 (1983): 193-196. Summaries in English and Georgian.

2916 Metreveli, M.G. "Interpretatsii islamskoi religii i sotsializma gosudar-stvennymi i politicheskimi deiateliami arabskikh stran" [Interpretation of Islamic Religion and Socialism by State and Political Dignitaries of Arab Countries]. *Novaia i noveishaia istoriia stran Blizhnego Vostoka.* Tbilisi, 1989. Pp. 120-126. In Georgian. Summary in Russian.

2917 Metreveli, M.G. *Obshchina druzov* [Druse Community]. Tbilisi: Metsniereba, 1987. 109 pp. In Georgian. Summary in Russian. Bibl.: p. 104-108.

2918 Mezentsev, V.[A]. "'Chudesa tam, gde v nikh veriat'" ["Miracles are There, Where They are Believed"]. *Nauka i religiia* 1 (1987): 36-39.

2919 Mezentsev, V.[A]. "Goroskopy, goroskopy..." [Horoscopes, Horoscopes...].
      Nauka i religiia 1 (1986): 56-59.

2920 Mezentsev, V.A. *O sueveriiakh - v ser'ez* [On Superstitions - In Earnest].
      M.: Sov. Rossiia, 1989. 240 pp.

2921 Mezentsev, V.A. *Riadom s zagadkoi* [Alongside with the Riddle]. M.: Mol.
      gvardiia, 1980. 176 pp., illus.

2922 Mezentsev, V.A. *Sueveriia i nauka* [Superstitions and Science]. M.: Znanie
      RSFSR, 1983. 39 p. (V pomoshch' lektoru / O-vo "Znanie" RSFSR,
      Nauch. metod. sovet po propagande nauch. ateizma). Bibl. p. 36.

2923 Mezentsev, V.A. *V tupikakh mistiki* [In Impasses of Mysticism]. M.: Mosk.
      rabochii, 1987. 176 pp., illus. Bibl.: p. 175.

2924 Mezentseva, O.V. "Kontseptsiia 'illiuzornosti mira' Shankary i neovedantizm"
      [Shankar's Conception of "Illusionist World" and Neovedantism]. *Ratsiona-
      listicheskaia traditsiia i sovremennost'*. M., 1988. Kn. 1. Pp. 225-244.

2925 Mezentseva, O.V. "Mesto i rol' induizma v ideologii dvizheniia bkhudan"
      [Place and Role of Hinduism in the Ideology of the Bhudan Movement].
      Religiia i obshchestvenaia zhizn' v Indii. M., 1983. Pp. 207-234. Bibl.: pp.
      231-234.

2926 Mezentseva, O.V. *Rol' induizma v ideologicheskoi bor'be sovremennoi Indii*
      [Role of Hinduism in Ideological Struggle of Contemporary India]. M.:
      Nauka, 1985. 175 pp. Bibl.: pp. 136-143.

2927 Mezhidov, D.D. et al. *Internatsionalizatsiia obshchestvennoi zhizni i preodole-
      nie perezhitkov proshlogo v Checheno-Ingushetii* [Internationalization of
      Public Life and Overcoming Survivals of the Past in Checheno-Ingush].
      Groznyi: Chech.-Ing. kn. izd-vo, 1984. 55 pp.

2928 Michell, D.; Rikard, R. *Fenomeny knigi chudes* [Phenomenons of the Book
      of Miracles]. [Transl. from English]. M.: Politizdat, 1988. 294 pp., illus.

2929 *Mif i deistvitel'nost'* [Myth and Reality]. Comp.: D. Gegeshidze. Tbilisi:
      Ganatleba, 1986. 58 pp. (Vydaiushchiesia mysliteli o religii i ateizme). In
      Georgian.

2930 *Mify, kul'ty, obriady narodov zarubezhnoi Azii* [Myths, Cults and Rituals of Peoples of Foreign Asia]. Ed.: N.L. Zhukovskaia. M.: Nauka, 1986. 256 pp., illus.

2931 Migovich, I.I. *Klerikal'nyi natsionalizm na sluzhbe antisovetizma* [Clerical Nationalism in the Service of Anti-Sovietism]. M.: Zanie, 1987. 64 pp. (Novoe v zhizni, nauke, tekhnike. Nauch. ateizm; 3/1987). Bibl.: p. 60.

2932 Migovich, I.I. "Osobennosti uniatskoi interpretatsii katolicheskoi filosofii" [Peculiarities of Uniate Interpretation of Catholic Philosophy]. *Vopr. ateizma* 23 (1987): 112-119.

2933 Migovich, I.I. *Pravda ob unii* [Truth about Uniate Church]. Kiev: Politizdat Ukrainy, 1988. 79 pp. In English.

2934 Migovich, I.I. *Prestupnyi al'ians: O soiuze uniat. tserkvi i ukr. burzhuaz. natsionalizma* [Criminal Alliance: On the Union of the Uniate Church and Ukainian Bourgeois Nationalism]. M.: Politizdat, 1985. 190 pp. For reviews see items 5173-5174.

2935 Migovich, I.I. *Reaktsionnaia sushchnost' klerikal'nogo natsionalizma* [Reactionary Essence of Clerical Nationalism]. Kiev: Politizdat Ukrainy, 1984. 293 pp. (Kritika ideologii i politiki antikommunizma). In Ukrainian. Bibl.: pp. 285-292.

2936 Migovich, I.I. *Uniatskaia tserkov' i ukrainskii burzhuaznyi natsionalizm* [Uniate Church and Ukrainian Bourgeois Nationalism]. Kiev: Vishcha shkola. 1981. 142 pp. (Ateist. b-chka studenta). In Ukrainian.

2937 Migovich, I.I. *Uniatskaia tserkov' - vrag kul'turnogo progressa* [Uniate Church - Enemy of Cultural Progress]. Kiev: Rad. shk., 1982. 189 pp. In Ukrainian. Bibl.: pp. 187-188.

2938 Migovich, I.I. "Uniatsko-natsionalisticheskii al'ians v antisovetskikh ideologicheskikh diversiiakh" [Uniate-Nationalist Alliance in Anti-Soviet Ideological Diversions]. *Argumenty, 1987*. M., 1987. Pp. 71-91.

2939 Mikaelian, N.R. "Nekotorye aspekty kontseptsii neobuddizma B.R. Ambedkara i osobennosti neobuddiiskogo dvizheniia v Indii" [Some Aspects of Conception of Neobuddhism of B.R. Ambedkar and Features of Neobuddhist Movement in India]. *Obshchestvennaia mysl' Indii. Proshloe i nastoiashchee.* M., 1989. Pp. 97-117.

2940   Mikaelian, N.[R]. "Prozelitizm v sovremennoi Indii" [Proselytism in Contemporary India]. *Aziia i Afrika segodnia* 3 (1983): 57-59.

2941   Mikhailenko, I.I. "Nekotorye problemy nauchno-materialisticheskogo vospitaniia studentov tekhnicheskikh vuzov" [Some Problems of Scientific-Materialist Education of Students of Technical Institutions of Higher Education]. *Atual'nye problemy nauchno-ateisticheskogo vospitaniia molodezhi.* M., 1987. Pp. 105-107.

2942   Mikhailov, T.M. *Buriatskii shamanizm: istoriia, struktura i sotsial'nye funktsii* [Buriat Shamanism: History, Structure and Social Functions]. Novosibirsk: Nauka. Sib. otd-nie, 1987. 288 pp., illus. Annot. bibl.: pp. 265-276.

2943   Mikhailov, T.M. *Iz istorii buriatskogo shamanizma: (S drevneishikh vremen po XVIII v.)* [History of Buriat's Shamanism: (From Ancient Times up to XVIIIth C.)]. Novosibirsk: Nauka. Sib. otd-nie, 1980. 320 pp. For review see item 5175.

2944   Mikhailov, T.M. *Priroda i chelovek v shamanizme mongol'skikh narodov* [The Nature of Man in Shamanism of Mongol People]. Novosibirsk: [S.n.], 1983. 5 pp.

2945   Mikhailov, T.M. "Razvitie massovoi ateisticheskoi raboty v Buriatskoi ASSR" [Development of Mass Atheistic Work in Buriat ASSR]. *Stroitel'stvo sotsializma i utverzhdenie nauchno - materialistichesko, ateisticheskogo mirovozzreniia (v regionakh rasprostraneniia Lamaizma).* M., 1981. Pp. 128-144.

2946   Mikhailov, T.M. "Religiia i ateizm v sisteme sovetskogo obraza zhizni" [Religion and Atheism in the System of Soviet Way of Life]. *Problemy sotsialisticheskogo obraza zhizni, potrebnostei, biudzheta vremeni naseleniia.* Ulan-Ude, 1988. Vyp. 1. Pp. 8-11.

2947   Mikhailov, T.M. "Sovetskii obraz zhizni i rost massovogo ateizma" [Soviet Way of Life and Growth of Mass Atheism]. *Velikii Oktiabr' i razvitie buriatskogo naroda.* Ulan-Ude, 1987. Pp. 153-168.

2948   Mikhailova, L.B. "Problema tserkovnogo kanona v drevnerusskoi ikonopisi XI-XVII vekov" [The Problem of Church Canon in Old Russian Icon Painting in XIth-XVIIth Centuries]. *Filosofsko-esteticheskie problemy drevnerusskoi kul'tury.* M., 1987. Ch. 1. Pp. 87-104.

2949 Mikhailova, L.V. *Katolicheskaia tserkov' i rabochii klass FRG* [Catholic Church and Worker's Class in FRG]. M.: Nauka, 1980. 46 pp. For review see item 5176.

2950 Mikhailova, V.P. "Simvolicheskaia kontseptsiia mifa [Symbolic Conception of Myth]. *Filosofiia: istoriia i sovremennost'*. M., 1988. Pp. 79-85.

2951 Mikhailovskaia, M.I. "Sotsial'no-klassovaia sushchnost' teologicheskoi interpretatsii ekologicheskikh problem" [Socio-Class Essence of Theological Interpretation of Ecological Problems]. *Voprosy filosofii i sotsiologii*. L., 1980. Pp. 102-106.

2952 Miknovskii, D.V. *Iskusstvo v ateisticheskom vospitanii* [Art in Atheistic Education]. L.: Lenizdat, 1980. 70 pp. (V pomoshch' propagandistu nauch. ateizma). Bibl.: pp. 68-69.

2953 Mikulichus, V. "Rozhdestvo Khristovo v Litve" [Christmas in Lithuania]. *Religiia v SSSR* 12 (1988): 1-3.

2954 Mikul'skaia, L.A.; Pkhidenko, S.S. *Rol' dukhovnykh interesov lichnosti v preodolenii religioznykh perezhitkov* [The Role of Spiritual Interests of Individual in Overcoming Religious Survivals]. Kiev: Znanie UkSSR, 1982. 46 pp. (Ser. 5 "Nauchno-ateisticheskaia" / O-vo "Znanie" UkSSR; No 6). In Ukrainian. Bibl.: pp. 43-44.

2955 Mikul'skii, D.[V]. "'Afganskaia problema' v krivom zerkale musul'manskoi pressy" ["Afghan Problem" in Distorting Mirror of Moslem Press]. *Molodezh'. Religiia. Ateizm.* 4 (1988): 63-75.

2956 Mikul'skii, D.V. "'Assotsiatsiia Brat'ev-musul'man' v Egipte i ee sotsial'no-politicheskaia doktrina" ["Moslem-Brotherhood" in Egypt and Its Socio-Political Doctrine]. *Vopr. nauch. ateizma* 36 (1987): 125-140.

2957 Mil'kov, V.V. "Cherty mirovozzreniia volkhvov" [Outlook Traits of Magicians]. *Istoricheskie traditsii filosofskoi kul'tury narodov SSSR i sovremennost'*. Kiev, 1984. Pp. 110-116.

2958 Miloshevich, M. "V usloviiakh ateizatsii obshchestvennoi zhizni" [Conditions of Atheismation of Social Life]. *Nauka i religiia* 9 (1981): 54-55.

2959 Miloslavskii, G.V. "Soderzhanie poniatiia 'islamskii faktor' v sovremennykh mezhdunarodnykh otnosheniiakh" [The Content of the Notion "Islamic

Factor" in Contemporary International Relations]. *"Islamskii faktor" v mezhdunarodnykh otnosheniiakh v Azii (70-e - pervaia polovina 80-kh gg.).* M., 1987. Pp.29-39.

2960 Miloslavskaia, T.P. "Deiatel'nost' 'Brat'ev-musul'man' v stranakh Vostoka" [The Activity of "Moslem-Brotherhood" in the Countries of Orient]. *Islam v strankh Blizhnego i Srednego Vostoka.* M., 1982. Pp. 7-24.

2961 Miloslavskaia, T.P. "Nachal'nyi etap deiatel'nosti assotsiatsii 'Brat'ev-musulman'" [Initial Stage of Activity of "Moslem Brotherhood"]. *Religii mira: Istoriia i sovremennost'. Ezhegodnik 1982.* M., 1982. Pp. 86-98.

2962 Milovidov, V.F. "Isoricheskie sud'by raskola i staroobriadchestvo" [Historical Fates of the Schism and Old Belief]. *Vopr. nauch. ateizma* 25(1980): 99-117.

2963 Milovidov, V.F. "Kritika sovremennoi mistiki" [Criticism of Contemporary Mysticism]. *Vopr. nauch. ateizma* 32 (1985): 126-139.

2964 Mindadze, N.R. "K voprosu prorochestva v gornykh raionakh Vostochnoi Gruzii" [On the Problem of Prophecy in Mountainous Regions in Eastern Georgia]. *Materialy po etnografii Gruzii.* Tbilisi, 1987. T. 23. Pp. 174-181. In Georgian. Summary in Russian.

2965 Mindlin, I.B. *Ateizm i religiia v trudakh G.V. Plekhanova* [Atheism and Religion in G.V. Plekhanov's Works]. M.: Nauka, 1984. 124 pp. (Nauch.-ateist. ser.).

2966 Minkiavichius, Ia.V. "Katolicheskaia teologiia i nauchno-tekhnicheskaia revoliutsiia" [Catholic Theology and Scientific-Technical Revolution]. *Vopr. nauch. ateizma* 28 (1981): 125-142.

2967 Minkiavichius, Ia.[V]. *Religiia i natsional'nye traditsii* [Religion and National Traditions]. Vil'nius: Znanie LitSSR, 1980. 23 pp. (Maerial dlia lektora / O-vo "Znanie" LitSSR).

2968 Minkiavichius, Ia.[V]. "Religiia i tserkov' v natsional'noi zhizni naroda [Litvy]" [Religion and Church in National Life of People (of Lithuania)]. *Nauka i religiia* 12 (1982): 31-33.

2969 Minkiavichius, Ia.V. "V kontekste real'nogo bytiia" [In the Context of Real Mode of Life]. *Nauka i religiia* 10 (1989): 6-7, 13.

2970 Min'ko, L.I.; Khudash, L.S. "Miroponimanie i verovaniia" [World Outlook and Beliefs]. *Obshchestvennyi, semeinyi byt i dukhovnaia kul'tura naseleniia Poles'ia.* Minsk, 1987. Pp. 232-242.

2971 Min'kovetskii, D.I. *Idu k liudiam* [I Go to People]. Kiev: Politizdat Ukrainy, 1983. 87 pp. In Ukrainian.

2972 *Mir. Obshchestvo. Chelovek* [World. Society. Man]. [Comp.: R. Ozolas]. Vil'nius: Mintis, 1980. 198 pp., illus. In Lithuanian.

2973 *Mir cheloveka* [Man's World]. [Comp.: A. Romanov]. M.: Mol. gvardiia, 1983. 191 pp., illus. Republished in 1986 and published in an enlarged ed. in 1987, 223 pp.

2974 Mirnanashvili, K.G. "Religioznoe znachenie rybolovnykh setei" [Religious Meaning of Fishing Nets]. *Materialy po etnografii Gruzii.* Tbilisi, 1987. T. 23. Pp. 232-236. In Georgian. Summary in Russian.

2975 Miroliubov, I. "Posle raskola" [After the Schism]. *Daugana* 4 (1989): 68-75.

2976 Mironov, B.N. "Ispovednye vedomsti - istohcnik o chislennosti i sotsial'noi strukture pravoslavnogo naseleniia Rossii XVIII - pervoi poloviny XIX v." [Confessional Registers - Source of Strength and Social Structure of Orthodox Population of Russia in XVIIIth-Early XIXth C.]. *Vspomogatel'nye istoricheskie distsipliny* 20 (1989): 102-117.

2977 Mirinova, M.M.; Nikandrov, S.P. "Kritika antikommunisticheskikh kontseptsii religioznoi prirody dukhovnoi kul'tury" [Criticism of Anti Communist Conception of Religious Nature of Spiritual Culture]. *Sb. nauch. tr. / Leningr. gos. in-t kul'tury im. N.K. Krupskoi.* 1986. T. 108. Pp. 147-156.

2978 Miroshnik, N. "...I dukha priglasiat" [...and Ghost They will Invite]. *Zhurnalist* 11 (1984): 68-69.

2979 Miroshnikova, E.M. "Kritika sovremennoi katolicheskoi kontseptsii truda - vazhnoe uslovie formirovaniia nauchno-ateisticheskogo mirovozzreniia molodezhi" [Criticism of Contemporary Catholic Conception of Labour - Important Condition for Forming Youth's Scientific-Atheistic World Outlook]. *Nauchnyi ateizm: ideal i mirovozzrenie.* Perm', 1988. Pp. 113-120.

2980   Mishutis, P. *Sistema ateisticheskogo vospitaniia v Sovetskoi Litve (1960-1977
       gg.)* [System of Atheistic Education in Soviet Lithuania (1960-1977)].
       Transl. from Lithuanian. Vil'nius: Mintis, 1985. 202 p.

2981   Mitin, A.N. *Obriad kreshcheniia i ateisticheskoe vospitanie* [Baptism
       Ceremony and Atheistic Education]. M.: Znanie, 1988. 23 pp. (V
       pomoshch' propagandistu i organizatoru ateist. raboty).

2982   Mitin, A.N. *V plenu mistiki i mnimykh tsennostei* [In the Captivity of
       Mysticism and Imaginary Values]. M.: Mosk. rabochii, 1981. 80 pp.
       (Besedy o religii).

2983   Mitin, A.N.; Doroshin, V.D. *Ot religioznykh illiuzii - k ateizmu* [From
       Religious Illusions - to Atheism]. M.: Mosk. rabochii, 1984. 95 pp.

2984   Mitina, V.I.; Khorol'skaia, T.A. "Kritika irratsionalisticheskoi interpretatsii
       lichnosti v khristianskoi antropologii" [Criticism of Irrational Interpretation
       of Individual in Christian Anthropology]. *Vopr. obshchestv. nauk* 63
       (1985): 103-109. Annot. bibl.: pp. 108-109.

2985   Mitirov, A.G. "Ob osobennostiakh lamaistskoi kul'tovoi praktiki kalmykov"
       [Features of Lamaist Religious Practice of Kalmyks]. *Voprosy istorii
       lamaizma v Kalmykii.* Elista, 1987. Pp. 58-70.

2986   Mitiukova, K.D. "Vsesoiuznaia nauchno-teoreticheskaia konferentsiia 'Islam i
       politika'" [All-Union Scientific-Theoretical Conference "Islam and
       Politics"]. *Izv. AN TadzhSSR.* Ser.: Filosofiia, ekonomika, pravovedenie 4
       (1988): 73-74.

2987   Mitrokhin, L.[N]. "Besedy ob ateisticheskom nasledii Marksa" [Talks on
       Marx's Atheistic Heritage]. *Nauka i religiia* 4 (1983): 23-27; 6 (1983):
       11-14; 8 (1983): 22-27; 10 (1983): 19-23; 12 (1983): 10-14; 2 (1984):
       16-20; 5 (1984): 18-23.

2988   Mitrokhin, L.N. "Filosofy i religiia" [Philosophers and Religion]. *Vopr.
       filosofii* 9 (1989): 16-35. Summary in English, p. 174.

2989   Mitrokhin, L.N. "Indiiskie istoriki o roli inkvizitsii v Goa v nasazhdenii
       ideologii katolitsizma v Indii XVI-XIX vv." [Indian Historians on the Role
       of the Inquisition in Goa in Spreading Catholic Ideology in India, XVIth-
       XIXth C.]. *Obshchestvennaia mysl' Indii: Proshloe i nastoiashchee.* M.,
       1989. Pp. 179-203. Annot. bibl.: pp. 201-203.

2990 Mitrokhin, L.[N]. "Marksisty i khristiane" [Marxists and Christians]. *Kommunist* 7 (1989): 100-111.

2991 Mitrokhin, L.N. "Metodologicheskii aspekt issledovaniia religioznoi morali" [Methodological Aspect of Research of Religious Morals]. *Vopr. nauch. ateizma* 34 (1986): 26-43.

2992 Mitrokhin, L.N. "Religiia i natsiia" [Religion and Nation]. *Nauka i religiia* 3 (1989): 2-3.

2993 Mitrokhin, L[N]. "Religiia i perestroika" [Religion and Perestroika]. *Zhurnalist* 4 (1989): 11-14.

2994 Mitrokhin, L.N. *Religii 'novogo veka'* [Religion of "The New Age"]. M.: Sov. Rossiia, 1985. 157 p. Bibl.: p. 156. For reviews see items 5177-5178.

2995 Mitrokhin, L.[N]. "Religiia v sisteme kul'tury" [Religion in Cultural System]. *Nauka i religiia* 8 (1987): 14-17; 10 (1987): 3-5; 1 (1988): 22-25.

2996 Mitrokhin, L.N. *Religioznye 'kul'ty' SShA* [Religious "Cults" in USA]. M.: Znanie, 1984. 64 pp. (Novoe v zhizni, nauke, tekhnike. Nauch. ateizm; 6). Annot. bibl.: p. 62-63.

2997 Mitrokhin, L.[N]. "Sotsialisticheskaia deistvitel'nost' i religiia" [Socialist Reality and Religion]. *Nauka i religiia* 11 (1987): 40-43.

2998 Mitrokhin, L.N. "Sotsial'no-psikhologicheskaia priroda 'religii novogo veka'" [Socio-Psychological Nature of "The Religion of the New Age"]. *Vopr. nauch. ateizma* 32 (1985): 46-77.

2999 Miuller, R. "'Slovo o polku Igoreve' - proizvedenie iazycheskoe ili khristianskoe?' ["The Lay of Igor's Host" - a Pagan or Christian Work?]. *Religiia v SSSR* 5 (1987): MT 1-MT 3.

3000 Mkrtychev, T.K. "Eshche raz k voprosu o chetyrekhrukoi bogine na l've v rannesrednevekovom iskusstve Srednei Azii [Again on the Question of Fourhanded Goddess on the Lion in the Early Medieval Art of Middle Asia]. *Tezisy konfrentsii aspirantov i molodykh nauchnykh sotrudnikov.* M., 1987. T. 1. Pp. 32-33.

3001 Mochalov, I.I. "K 125-letiiu so dnia rozhdeniia V.I. Vernadskogo: V.I. Vernadskii i religiia" [125th Anniversary of V.I. Vernadskii's Birthday:

V.I. Vernadskii and Religion]. *Vopr. istorii estestvoznaniia i tekhniki* 2 (1988): 36-44. Bibl.: p. 44. Summary in English.

3002 Moiseev, N.N. "V zone neopredelennosti" [In the Zone of Uncertainty]. *Nauka i religiia* 2 (1989): 2-4.

3003 Moiseeva, A.P. *Russkaia dukhovnaia kul'tura i ateizm* [Russian Spiritual Culture and Atheism]. Tomsk: Izd-vo Tom. un-ta, 1987. 183 pp.

3004 Moiseeva, T.M. "Etnograficheskie kollektsii MAE v ateisticheskom vospitanii" [Ethnographic Collections of MAE in Realm of Atheistic Education]. *Muzei v ateisticheskoi propagande.* L., 1980. Pp. 22-30.

3005 Mokhov, V.P. "O nekotorykh sotsial'no-psikhologicheskikh problem ateisticheskogo vospitaniia molodykh rabochikh sovkhozov" [On Some Social-Psychological Problems of Atheistic Education of Young Sovkhoz Workers]. *Aktual'nye problemy nauchno-tekhnicheskogo vospitaniia molodezhi.* M., 1987. Pp. 91-94.

3006 Molchanov, V.K.; Segura, K.Kh. *Moia vera svobodna* [My Faith is Free]. M.: Novosti, 1983. 95 pp., illus.
      Published also in 1983 in German and Spanish; in 1984 in Japanese; in 1985 in Danish, Dutch, Finnish, Norwegian, Polish, Swedish and Turkish.

3007 Molchanov, V.V. *Massovaia mistifikatsiia: pop-kul'tura i sueverie* [Mass Mystification: Pop-Culture and Superstition]. L.: Lenizdat, 1987. 111 pp. (Mify i real'nost': na frontakh ideol. bor'by). Bibl.: p. 110.

3008 Moldakasov, R.; Boleev, K. "Rol' spetsseminara v nauchno-ateisticheskoi podgotovke studentov-fizikov [Role of Special Seminary in Scientific-Atheistic Preparation of Students-Physicists]. *Aktual'nye voprosy metodiki prepodavaniia fiziki v insitute i shkole.* Alma-Ata, 1981. Pp. 27-31.

3009 Moliakov, I.Iu. "Kriticheskii analiz pravoslavnogo modernizma" [Critical Analysis of Orthodox Modernism]. *Istoriia khristianizatsii narodov Srednego Povolzh'ia. Kriticheskie suzhdeniia i otsenka.* Cheboksary, 1988. Pp. 94-101.

3010 Moliakov, I.Iu. "Kritika prorochestva - odin iz aspektov ateisticheskoi kontrpropagandy" [Criticism of Prophecy - One of the Aspects of Atheistic Counterpropaganda]. *Aktual'nye problemy obespecheniia effektivnosti nauchno-ateisticheskoi raboty.* Cheboksary, 1986. Pp. 109-117.

3011 Mollaeva, M. "Usilit' vnimanie ateisticheskomu vospitaniiu" [To Increase Attention to Atheistic Education]. *Turkmenistan kommunisti* 12 (1987): 46-55. In Turkmen.

3012 *Molodezh', religiia, ateizm* [Youth, Religion, Atheism]. M.: Mol. gvardiia, 1984 -
[Vyp.1]. 1984, 222 pp., illus.
Vyp. 2. 1985, 184 pp. Bibl.: pp. 182-183.
Vyp. 3. 1986, 216 pp. For reviews see items 5179-5181.

3013 *Molodezhi - ateisticheskuiu ubezhdennost'* [Atheistic Consciousness - to Youth]. [Comp.: I.Iu. Sapozhnikova]. Omsk: [S.n.], 1984. 64 pp. (Ateizm / TsK VLKSM).

3014 *Molodezhi ob ateizme* [To Youth on Atheism]. Polit. textbook. V.K. Tancher; V.A. Zots; A.M. Chernii et al. Kiev: Molod', 1984. 255 pp. Annot. bibl.: pp. 249-254. In Ukrainian.

3015 Molovidov, V.F. *Staroobriadchestvo i sotsial'nyi progress* [Old Belief and Social Progress]. M.: Znanie, 1983. 64 pp. (Novoe v zhizni, nauke, tekhnike. Nauch. ateizm; 9). Bibl.: p. 63. Annot. bibl.: p. 51.

3016 Momina, M.A. "O proiskhozhdenii grecheskoi triodi" [On the Origin of Greek Service Book]. *Palest. sb.* 28 (1986): 112-120. Summary in English.

3017 Mongush, M.V. "Istoriia tuvinskikh monastyrei po arkhivnym materialam" [History of Tuva Monasteries According to Archives]. *Istoriia i filologiia drevnego i srednevekovogo Vostoka.* M., 1987. Pp. 172-191.

3018 Mor, Kh. "Katolicheskie 'instituty sovershenstva' v proshlom i nastoiashchem" [Catholic "Institutes of Perfection" in the Past and Present]. *Vopr. nauch. ateizma* 28 (1981): 285-295.

3019 Moravskii, Z. *Vatikan izdali i vblizi* [Vatican from Afar and Close By]. Transl. from Polish O. Sokolova. M.: Progress, 1981. 319 pp.

3020 Mordasova, I.V. "O sotsial'nykh i gnoseolgicheskikh korniakh very v sud'bu" [On Social and Gnosiological Roots of Faith in Fate]. *Sotsial'no-filosofskie aspekty kritiki religii* L., 1980. Pp. 137-152.

3021   Mordvintsev, V.F. "Ispanskii perevod 'Enkhiridiona' i inkvizitsiia" [Spanish Translation of "Enchiridion" and the Inquisition]. *Erazm Rotterdamskii i ego vremia.* M., 1989. Pp. 169-184.

3022   Morina, L.G. "Vliianie razvitiia nauchnoi kartiny mira na modernizatsiiu religioznogo miroponimaniia" [Influence of Development of Scientific Picture of the World on Modernization of Religious World Outlook]. *Filosofskii analiz iavlenii dukhovnoi kul'tury: Teoret. i ist. aspekty.* M., 1984. Pp. 76-82.

3023   Morkeliunas, A. "Pri vzaimnom uvazhenii" [With Mutual Respect]. *Nauka i religiia* 6 (1981): 32-33.

3024   Moroz, O.P. *Ot imeni nauki: O sueveriiakh XX veka* [In the Name of Science: Superstitions of the XXth Century]. M.: Politizdat, 1989. 304 pp. For reviws see items 5182-5183.

3025   Morozova, L.E. "Pravoslavnaia tserkov' i natsional'no-osvoboditel'naia bor'ba russkogo naroda v XVI-XVII vv." [Orthodox Church and National-Liberation Struggle of the Russian People in the XVIth-XVIIth C.]. *Vopr. nauch. ateizma* 37 (1988): 140-150.

3026   Morozova, L.[E]. "Rol' pravoslaviia v otechestvennoi istorii" [The Role of Orthodoxy in Fatherland's History]. *Obshchestv. nauki* 6 (1988): 217-227.

3027   Moshchenko, N.T. *Nauchno-ateisticheskaia propaganda - vazhnoe sredstvo kommunisticheskogo vospitaniia trudiashchikhsia* [Scientific-Atheistic Propaganda - Important Means of Communist Education of Workers]. Alma-Ata: Znanie KazSSR , 1982. 24 pp. Bibl.: pp. 22-24.

3028   Moskalenko, A.T. "Modernizm i fundamentalizm v teologii sovremennykh khristianskikh sekt" [Modernism and Fundamentalism in Theology of Contemporary Christian Sects]. *Nauchnyi ateizm, religiia i sovremennost'.* Novosibirsk, 1987. Pp. 90-124.

3029   Moskalenko, A.T.; Chechulin, A.A. "Teoreticheskoi razrabotke voprosov nauchnogo ateizma - dolzhnoe vnimanie" [Due Attention to Theoretical Working Up of Problems of Scientific Atheism]. *Izv. Sib. otd-niia AN SSSR.* No 9: Ser. istorii, filologii i filosofii 2 (1986): 70.

3030 Moskalets, V.P. *Religioznyi kul't: osobennosti funktsionirovaniia i puti preodoleniia* [Religious Cult: Functioning Features and Ways of Overcoming]. Kiev: Nauk. dumka, 1987. 118 pp. Annot. bibl.: pp. 113-17.

3031 Motiashov, V. "Potrebitel'stvo, asketizm ili... ?" [Consumption, Asceticism or... ?]. *Nauka i religiia* 11 (1981): 57-59.

3032 Motsia, A. "Khristiane nekreshchenoi Rusi" [Christians of Nonbaptized Rus']. *Nauka i religiia* 1 (1988): 29-31.

3033 Movsumova, L.D. "Islam i zhenshchina" [Islam and Woman]. *Trudy konferentsii molodykh uchenykh Akademii nauk "Velikii Oktiabr' i sovremennnost': aktual'nye problemy obshchestvovedeniia"*. Baku, 1988. Pp. 19-20.

3034 Movsumova, L.D. "O putiakh povysheniia effektivnosti ateisticheskogo vospitaniia zhenshchin" [On Ways of Raising the Effectiveness of Atheistic Education of Women]. *Izv. AN AzSSR*. Ser. istorii, filosofii i prava 3 (1986): 102-108. Summary in Azerbaijan.

3035 Movsumova, L.D. "Osobennosti zhenskoi religioznosti" [Features of Woman's Religiosity]. *Izv. AN AzSSR*. Ser. istorii, filosofii i prava 2 (1989): 99-105. Summary in Azerbaijan.

3036 Mozgovoi, I.P. "Evoliutsiia pravoslavno-bogoslovskikh vozzrenii na kul'turnoe nasledie proshlogo" [Evolution of Orthodox-Theological Outlooks on Cultural Heritage of the Past]. *Politicheskoe soznanie trudiashchikhsia v usloviiakh perestroiki: poisk, opyt, puti formirovaniia*. Chernovtsy, 1988. Pp. 128-131.

3037 Mozgovoi. I.P. "Rol' nauchnogo ateizma v osvoenii kul'turnogo naslediia proshlogo" [The Role of Scientific Atheism in Assimilation of Cultural Heritage of the Past]. *Vopr. ateizma* 24 (1988): 109-115.

3038 Mozgovoi, I.P. "Sovremennoe pravoslavie o printsipe preemstvennosti v kul'ture" [Contemporary Orthodoxy on the Principle of Continuity in Culture]. *Vopr. ateizma* 25 (1989): 117-124.

3039 Mozheiko, I. "Khoziain zamka Alamut i ego nasledniki" [The Owner of the Castle Alamut and His Heirs]. *Nauka i religiia* 7 (1987): 59-64.

3040 Mshvelidze, M.D. "Narodnye obychai i obriady v den' Vozneseniia v Kartli" [Popular Customs and Rituals in the Ascension Day in Kartli]. *Istoriia religii i ateisticheskaia propaganda.* Tbilisi, 1987. Kn. 11. Pp. 85-93. In Georgian. Summary in Russian.

3041   "Muftii Talgat Tadzhuddin o mezhdunarodnoi islamskoi konferentsii" [Mufti Talgat Tadjuddin on International Islamic Conference]. *Religiia v SSSR* 12 (1988): 1-4.

3042   Mukasov, S. "Rol' traditsii svobodomysliia v dukhovnoi kul'ture kirgizskogo naroda" [The Role of the Tradition of Freethinking in Spiritual Culture of Kirghiz People]. *Dukhovnyi mir sovremennogo cheloveka.* M., 1987. Pp. 130-131.

3043   Mukhamedkhodzhaev, A.K. "K kharakteristike osnovnykh problem rannego sufizma" [On Characteristics of Basic Problems of Early Sufism]. *Izv. AN TadzhSSR.* Ser.: Filosofiia, ekonomika, pravovedenie 2 (1987): 15-20. Summary in Tajik.

3044   Mukhametshin, R.M. "Idei svobodomysliia v dorevoliutsionnom tvorchestve G. Ibragimova" [Ideas of Freethinking in Pre‾Revolutionary Works of G. Ibrahim]. *Iz istorii formirovaniia i razvitiia svobodomysliia v dorevoliu-tsionnoi Tatarii.* Kazan', 1987. Pp. 79-91. Bibl.: pp. 89-91.

3045   Mukhammad-Sadik Mukhammad-Iusuf. "'Islam - i vera, i obraz zhizni'" [Islam - both, Faith and Way of Life]. *Zvezda Vostoka* 12 (1989): 137-146.

3046   Mukhammad-Sadik Mukhammad-Iusuf. "My - za dobro i spravedlivost'" [We are for Good and Justice]. *Nauka i religiia* 11 (1989): 15-20.

3047   Mukhatov, T.D. "Priroda i struktura obshchestvennogo mneniia po voprosam religii i ateizma" [Nature and Structure of Public Opinion on the Questions of Religion and Atheism]. *Nauchnyi ateizm i obshchestvennoe mnenie.* M., 1987. Pp. 15-43.

3048   Mukhsimov, A. *Sotsialisticheskii obraz zhizni i ateisticheskoe vospitanie* [Socialist Way of Life and Atheistic Education]. Tashkent: Uzbekistan, 1986. 21 p. (Ser. "Istoriia"; No 7).

3049   Mukhtorov, A. "Kara-Timbinskoe 'chudo': Razoblachenie legendy o 'Muimuborak' v XIX v." [Kara-Timbin "Miracle": Exposure of the Legend About "Muimuborak" in the XIXth C.] *Pamir* 1 (1987): 130-137.

3050 Muminov, Kh.; Isava, F.A. "Izobrazhenie zhivotnykh v doislamskoi poezii kak otrazhenie doislamskikh verovanii i predstavlenii arabov " [Representation of Animals in Pre-Islamic Poetry as Reflection of Pre-Islamic Beliefs and Arabs Conception]. *III Vsesoiuznaia konferentsiia vostokovedov "Vzaimodeistvie i vzaimovliianie tsivilizatsii kul'tur na Vostoke".* M., 1988. T. 1. P. 21.

3051 Munavvarov, Z. "Skol'ko v mire musul'man?" [How Many Moslems are there in the World?]. *Aziia i Afrika segodnia* 10 (1989): 41.

3052 Murashova, V.[I].; Khmel'nitskaia, A.[P]. "...I ekskursii tozhe" [...And Excursions As Well]. *Agitator* 3 (1983): 59-61.

3053 Murashova, V.I.; Khmel'nitskaia, A.P. *Iskusstvo ubezhdat'* [The Art of Convincing]. M.: Politizdat, 1981. 64 pp. (B-ka ateista).

3054 Murashova, V.[I].; Khmel'nitskaia, A.[P]. "Kak ispol'zovat' khudozhestvennuiu literaturu v ateisticheskoi rabote" [How to Use Belles-Lettres in Atheistic Work]. *Agitator* 17 (1981): 56-58.

3055 Murashova, V.I.; Khmel'nitskaia, A.P. *S dumoi o cheloveke* [Concern About Man]. M.: Politizdat, 1986. 80 pp. (B-ka ateista).

3056 Murshudli, G.D. *Chto takoe svoboda sovesti* [What Freedom of Conscience Means]. Baku: Azerneshr, 1986. 44 pp. (B-ka ateista). In Azerbaijan. Bibl.: p. 43.

3057 Murtuzaliev, S.I. "Konstantinopol'skaia patriarkhiia v sisteme upravleniia pravoslavnym naseleniem Bolgarii v XV-XVI vekakh" [Patriarchate of Constantinople Administrating the Orthodox Population in Bulgaria in XVth-XVIth Centuries]. *V nauch.-prakticheskaia konf. molodykh uchenykh Dagestana "Molodezh' i obshchestvennyi progress".* Makhachkala, 1981. P. 18.

3058 Murtuzalieva, S. "Bor'ba idei i svoboda sovesti" [Struggle of Ideas and Freedom of Conscience]. *Sov. Dagestan* 2 (1981): 49-55.

3059 Murtuzalieva, S. "Uchityvaia mestnye osobennosti" [Taking into Consideration Local Features]. *Sov. Dagestan* 5 (1982): 46-50.

3060 Musaev, B.K. *Iz glubiny vekov* [From Ancient Days]. Nal'chik: El'brus, 1987. 66 pp. In Karachaev-Balkar.

3061   Musaeva, M.K. "Obriady vyzyvaniia dozhdia i solntsa u khvarshin v XIX-
       nach. XX v." [Ritual for Calling Out the Rain and Sun by Hvarshin in
       XIXth-Early XXth C.]. *Kalendar' i kalendarnye obriady narodov Dages-
       tana.* Makhachkala, 1987. Pp. 99-104.

3062   Mushirovskii, V.M.; Stokolos, N.G. *Muzei nauchnogo ateizma v Rovno:*
       Putevoditel' [Museum of Scientific Atheism in Rovno: Guide]. L'vov:
       Kameniar, 1985. 62 pp., illus. In Ukrainian. Bibl.: pp. 61-62.

3063   Muskhelishvili, N.L.; Shaburov, N.V. *Problema paradoksa i analiz soznaniia*
       [The Problem of Paradox and Analysis of Consciousness]. M.: Mezhved.
       nauch. sovet po voprosam "Soznanie", 1987. 80 pp. Bibl.: pp. 59-80.

3064   Muslimov, M. "Esli byt' otkrovennym.." [If to be Frank...]. *Sov. Dagestan* 4
       (1988): 26-30.

3065   Muslimov, S.Sh. "O formirovanii nauchno-ateisticheskoi ubezhdennosti
       studencheskoi   molodezhi   Dagestana"   [Forming   Scientific-Atheistic
       Consciousness of Students of Daghestan]. *Izv. Sev.-Kavk. nauch. tsentra
       vyssh. shk. Obshchestv. nauki* 4 (1983): 65-68.

3066   Muslimov, S.Sh. *Ot svobodomysliia k nauchnomu ateizmu: protsess sekulia-
       rizatsii i ateizatsii obshchestvenogo soznaniia narodov Severnogo Kavkaza*
       [From Free-Thinking to Scientific Atheism: Process of Secularization and
       Atheisation of Public Consciousness of the Peoples of Northern
       Caucasus]. Rostov n/D: Izd-vo Rost. un-ta, 1987. 176 pp. Annot. bibl.:
       pp. 167-175. For review see item 5184.

3067   Muslimov, S.[Sh]. "Otkrovennyi razgovor" [A Frank Talk]. *Nauka i religiia* 4
       (1984): 8-10.

3068   Muslimov, S.[Sh]. "Prismotrimsia k sebe po vnimatel'nei" [To Look Upon
       Oneself Attentively]. *Nauka i religiia* 7 (1988): 5-6.

3069   Muslimov, S.[Sh]. "S tochki zreniia lektora..." [From Lecturer's Point of
       View...]. *Sov. Dagestan* 5 (1987): 32-35.

3070   Muslimov, S.[Sh]. "So studencheskikh let" [Since Students Years]. *Nauka i
       religiia* 6 (1981): 16-17.

3071   Muslimov, S.Sh. "Sootnoshenie stikhiinogo i soznatel'nogo v protsesse
       ateisticheskogo vospitaniia" [Correlation of Spontaneous and Conscious in

the Process of Atheistic Education]. *Nauch. dokl. vyssh. shk. Nauch. kommunizm* 3 (1986): 105-111.

3072 Muslimov, S.[Sh]. "V poiskakh ubeditel'nosti: Nekotorye ostrye vopr. ateist. propagandy" [In the Search of Persuasiveness: Some Acute Problems of Atheistic Propaganda]. *Sov. Dagestan* 6 (1983): 34-43.

3073 Mustafaev, G.I. *Chemu uchit nauchnyi ateizm* [What Does Scientific Atheism Teach]. Baku: Azerneshr, 1986. 43 pp. (Ser. "B-ka ateista"). In Azerbaijan.

3074 Mustafaev, G.I. "XXVII s'ezd KPSS i ateisticheskoe vospitanie" [XXVIIth Congress of the CPSU and Atheistic Education]. *Aktual'nye voprosy ateisticheskogo vospitaniia molodezhi.* Baku, 1988. Pp. 3-16. In Azerbaijan. Summary in Russian.

3075 Mustafaeva, M.G. "Mezhnatsional'noe obshchenie, internatsionalistskoe i ateisticheskoe vospitanie" [Relations Between Nations, Internationalistic and Atheistic Education]. *Vopr. nauch. ateizma* 26 (1980): 51-66.

3076 Mustafaeva, M.G. "Osobennosti formirovaniia obshchestvennogo mneniia vokrug shariatsko-adatskikh traditsii v mnogonatsional'nom regione" [Features of Forming Public Opinion Around Shariat-Adats Traditions in Multi-National Region]. *Nauchnyi ateizm i obshchestvennoe mnenie.* M., 1987. Pp. 80-92.

3077 Mustafaeva, M.G. *Radi druzhby na Zemle* [For the Sake of Friendship in the World]. M.: Politizdat, 1983. 62 pp. (B-ka ateista).

3078 Mustafaeva, M.G.; Mustafaev, M.B. "Voprosy sotsial'no-psikhologicheskogo povedeniia lichnosti" [Problems of Socio-Psychlogical Behaviour of Individual]. *Izv. Sev.-Kavk. nauch. tsntra vyssh. shk. Obshchestv. nauki.* Rostov n/D. 2 (1987): 95-99.

3079 *Musul'mane v bor'be za mir* [Moslems in the Struggle for Peace]. M.: Progress, [1988]. 271 pp. In English and French.

3080 '*Musul'mane v bor'be za mir*', *mezhdunarodnaia islamskaia konf. (1986; Baku).* ["Moslems in the Struggle for Peace", Islamic International Conference (1986; Baku)]. Baku: [S.n.], 16 pp. Published also in French and Pharsee.

3081   *Musul'mane v SSSR* [Moslems in USSR]. M.: Novosti, 1989. 46 pp., illus. In English. Published also in Arabic, French and Turkish.

3082   *Musul'manskaia organizatsiia Azerbaidzhanskoi SSR* [The Moslem organization in the Azerbaijan SSR].* Baku, Iazychi, [1986]. 38, 30 pp. Parallel text, in   Arabic, Azerbaijan, English, French and Russian.

3083   *Musul'manskii mir, 950-1150* [Moslem World, 950-1150]. Transl. from English. Ed.: V.V. Naumkin. M.: Nauka, 1981. 312 pp. For review see item 5185.

3084   *Muzei istorii religii i ateizma.* Leningrad. Putevoditel' [Museum of the History of Religion and Atheism. Leningrad. Guide]. L.: Lenizdat, 1981. 144 pp., illus.

3085   *Muzei v ateisticheskoi propagande* [Museum in Atheistic Propaganda]. [Ed.: R.F. Filippova]. L.: GMIRIA, 1980. 116 pp.
       Published also in 1981, 148 pp., illus.; 1982, 113 pp.; [1987], 125 pp.

3086   Muzhukhoev, M.B. "Proniknovenie khristianstva k vainakham" [Penetration of Christianity in Vainahs]. *Etnografiia i voprosy religioznykh vozzrenii chechentsev i ingushei v dorevoliutsionnyi period.* Groznyi, 1981. Pp. 23-45.

3087   Muzikiavichius, A.A., et al. *Netserkovnye confesii: raznobrazie i skhozhest'* [Nonchurch Confessions: Variety and Similarity]. Vil'nius: [S.n.], 1989. 81 pp. In Lithuanian. Bibl.: pp. 78-80.

3088   Myl'nikov, A.S. *Chaianiia i ozhidaniia narodnye* [Popular Aspirations and Expectations]. L.: Znanie RSFSR. Leningr. org. Leningr. Dom nauch. ateizma, 1988. 32 pp. (V pomoshch' lektoru).

3089   Myslek, V. "Religiovedenie v sovremennoi shkole" [Study of Religion in Contemporary School]. *Nauka i religiia* 7 (1988): 32-33.

3090   *Mysli o religii* [Thoughts of Religion]. [Comp.: Kh.A. Alikulov]. Tashkent: Uzbekistan, 1987. 133 pp., illus. Annot. bibl.: pp. 123-133.
       Published also in: 1988, 117 pp., in Uzbek. For review see item 5186.

3091   *Na neprimirimykh pozitsiiakh* [On Uncompromising Positions]. [Comp.: E.P. Kovnatskii]. Groznyi: Chech.-Ing. kn. izd-vo, 1985. 104 pp.

3092 "Na perekrestke mnenii" [On the Cross-Roads of Opinions]. *Nauka i religiia* 6 (1989): 6-9.

3093 *Na puti k svobode sovesti* [On the Way to the Freedom of Conscience]. M.: Progress, 1989. 494 pp. (Perestroika: glasnost', demokratiia, sotsia- lizm).

3094 Nabiev, G. *Ateisticheskoe znachenie novykh sovetskikh obriadov* [Atheistic Importance of the New Soviet Ceremonies]. Tashkent: Znanie UzSSR, 1985. 22 pp. (V pomoshch' lektoru / O-vo "Znanie" UzSSR. Ser. obshchestv. -polit.). In Uzbek.

3095 Nabiev, G. *Nravstvennyi ideal i nauchnyi ateizm* [Moral Ideal and Scientific Atheism]. Tashkent: Uzbekistan, 1985. 30 pp. (Vopr. kom. morali; No 8). In Uzbek.

3096 Nabiev, R.A. "K voprosu o nauchno-ateisticheskikh vzgliadakh N.E. Fedoseeva" [On the Question of N.E. Fedoseev's Scientific-Atheistic Views]. *Deiatel'nost' fedoseevskikh kruzhkov po rasprostraneniiu marksizma v Rossii*. Kazan', 1989. Pp. 35-37.

3097 "Nadezhznyi i postoiannyi pomoshchnik" [Reliable and Constant Helper]. *Nauka i religiia* 7 (1983): 16-18.

3098 Nadiradze, L.I. "I.Iu. Krachkovskii kak perevodchik Korana: k interpretatsii termina 'fai'" [I.Iu. Krachkovskii as Translator of Koran: On Intepretation of the Term "Fay'"]. *Problemy arabskoi kul'tury*. M., 1987. Pp. 207-212. Bibl.: p. 212.

3099 Nadol'skii, R.V. *Ateisticheskie besedy i disputy* [Atheistic Talks and Disputes]. Minsk: Znanie BSSR, [1983]. 18 pp. (Material v pomoshch' lektoru / Pravl. o-va "Znanie" BSSR. Nauch.-metod. sovet po propagande nauch. ateizma). Bibl.: p. 18.

3100 Nadol'skii, R.V. *Baptizm v proshlom i nastoiashchem* [Baptism in the Past and Present]. Minsk: Belarus', 1987. 62 pp. Annot. bibl.: p. 61.

3101 Nadzhafov, M. *O propagande nauchnogo ateizma* [Propaganda of Scientific Atheism]. Baku: Znanie AzSSR, 1980. 56 pp. (V pomoshch' lektoru / O-vo "Znanie" AzSSR). In Azerbaijan.

3102   Nadzhimov, G. "Vazhnyi aspekt ateisticheskogo vospitaniia" [Important Aspect of Atheistic Education]. *Kommunist Uzbekistana* 11 (1988): 69-72.

3103   Nagle, L.Ia. "Deiatel'nost' raionnykh obshchestvennykh organizatsii po ateisticheskomu vospitaniiu" [The Activity of Regional Public Organizations in Atheistic Education]. *Vopr. nauch. ateizma* 28 (1981): 245-251.

3104   "Nagliadno, obrazno, emotsional'no" [Visually, Figuratively, Emotionally]. *Nauka i religiia* 7 (1982): 8-12.

3105   Nagornaia, L.K. "O kategorii 'ateisticheskogo soznanie'" [Category of "Atheistic Consciousness"]. *Zakonomernosti formirovaniia obshchestvennogo soznaniia.* Barnaul, 1984. Pp. 110-116.

3106   Naidakova, V.Ts. "O naznachenii elementov narodnosti v buddiiskoi misterii tsam" [Setting Elements of National Characters in Buddhist Mystery Tzam]. *Etnicheskaia istoriia i kul'turno-bytovye traditsii v Buriatii.* Ulan-Ude, 1984. Pp. 136-148.

3107   Nakkash, A.Kh. "Ali Abd ar-Razik i formirovanie svetskogo techeniia v traktovke gosudarstva i vlasti v islame" [Ali Abd al-Razik and Forming Secular Movement in the Treatment of State and Authority in Islam]. *Tezisy konferentsii aspirantov i molodykh nauchnykh sotrudnikov.* M., 1987. T. 1. Pp. 81-84.

3108   Nakkash, A.Kh. "Khaled Mukhammad Khaled: ot svetskogo gosudarstva k gosudarstvu islama" [Halid Muhammad Halid: From Secular State to the State of Islam]. *Konferentsiia molodykh uchennykh "Arabskii mir: ekonomika, politika, ideologiia".* M., 1987. Pp. 73-76.

3109   Nakonechnyi, R.A. *Antikommunisticheskaia napravlennost' soiuza ukrainskogo burzhuaznogo natsionalizma i religii* [Anti Communist Direction of the Union of Ukrainian Bourgeois Nationalism and Religion]. Kiev: Znanie UkSSR, 1981. 18 pp. (B-chka v pomoshch' lektoru "Kritika reakts. sushchnosti ukr. burzhuaz. natsionalizma" /O-vo "Znanie" UkSSR). In Ukrainian. Bibl.: p. 18.

3110   Nakonechnyi, R.A. "Kritika osnov soiuza burzhuaznogo natsionalizma i klerikalizma" [Criticism of Fundamentals of the Union of Bourgeois Nationalism and Clericalism]. *Vopr. ateizma* 25 (1989): 17-23.

3111 Nalbandian, V.S. "Mir i ego budushchee v predstavlenii Grigora Narekatsi" [The World and Its Future in Gregory Narekaci's Conception]. *Ist-filol. zhurn.* 3 (1988): 29-44. In Armenian. Summary in Russian.

3112 Narbaev, K. *Nauka i religiia* [Science and Religion]. Tashkent: Znanie UzSSR, 1984. 27 pp. (V pomoshch' lektoru / O-vo "Znanie" UzSSR. Ser. obshchestv.-polit.). In Uzbek. Bibl.: p. 27.

3113 Narmatov, E. *Iskusstvo i ateisticheskoe vospitanie* [Art and Atheistic Education]. Tashkent: Uzbekistan, 1983. 24 pp. (Vopr. kom. morali; No 7). In Uzbek.

3114 *Narodnoe antitserkovnoe dvizhenie v Rossii XII veka: Dokumenty Prikaz Tainykh del o raskol'nikakh, 1665-1667 gg.* [Popular Anti-Church Movement in Russia of the XIIth Century: Documents of the Secret Police on Schismatics, 1665-1667]. Comp.: V.S. Rumiantseva. M.: In-t istorii SSSR, 1986. 243 pp.

3115 Narskii, I.S. "Kant i religiia" [Kant and Religion]. *Kant. sb.* 8 (1983): 3- 12.

3116 Nashchokina, M.V. "Khramy-pamiatniki russkoi voinskoi slavy" [Temple-Monuments of Russian Military Glory]. *Pamiatniki Otechestva* 1 (1988): 143-149.

3117 Nasibov, A. "Ateisticheskaia propaganda - vazhnoe napravlenie ideologiches-koi raboty" [Atheistic Propaganda - Important Trend of Ideological Work]. *Kommunist Azerbaidzhana* 5 (1986): 80-85.

3118 *Nastol'naia kniga ateista* [Atheist's Handbook]. [Ed.: S.D. Skazkina]. 6th revised and enlarged ed. M.: Politizdat, 1981. 448 pp., illus.
Published as 7th ed. in 1983; 8th ed. in 1985; 9th ed. in 1987; and in: Vil'nius: Mintis, 1986. 446 pp. illus. In Lithuanian. For review see item 5187.

3119 *Natsional'naia kul'tura i religiia* [National Culture and Religion]. Ed.: N.A. Trofimchuk. M.: Aon, 1989. 145 pp.

3120 *Nauchno-Ateisticheskie issledovaniia v muzeiakh:* Sb. nauch. tr. [Scientific Atheistic Researches in Museums]. Ed.: S.A. Kuchinskii. L.: GMIRIA, 1984. 155 pp., illus.
Published also in:
1987. 148 pp., illus. Ed.: E.A. Snigireva.

1988. 147 pp., illus. E.: V.A. Khrshanov.

3121   *Nauchnyi ateizm* [Scientific Atheism]. [A.F. Okulov; R.G. Baltanov; V.I. Garadzha et al]. 2nd revised and enlarged ed. Erevan: Aiastan, 1980. 382 pp. In Armenian. Bibl.: pp. 368-380.
Published also in:
Baku: Maarif, 1981. 324 pp. In Azerbaijan.

3122   *Nauchnyi ateizm* [Scientific Atheism]. Textbook. Ed.: M.P. Mchedlova. M.: Politizdat, 1988. 303 pp. (Dlia sistemy polit. ucheby). Bibl.: pp. 297-300. For review see item 5188.

3123   *Nauchnyi ateizm: ideal i mirovozzrenie* [Scientific Atheism: Ideal and World Outlook]. [Ed.: M.F. Kalashnikov]. Perm': PGPI, 1988. 148 pp.

3124   *Nauchnyi ateizm i ateisticheskoe vospitanie* [Scientific Atheism and Atheistic Education]. [Ed.: E. Babosov]. Minsk: Belarus', 1983.
Vyp. 1. 1983. 159 pp.

3125   *Nauchnyi ateizm i obshchestvennoe mnenie* [Scientific Atheism and Public Opinion]. [Ed.: R.A. Lopatkin]. M.: AON, 1987. 141 pp.

3126   *Nauchnyi ateizm, religiia i sovremennost'* [Scientific Atheism, Religion and Contemporaneity]. Ed.: A.T. Moskalenko. Novosibirsk: Nauka. Sib. otd-nie, 1987. 334 pp.

3127   *Nauka okryliaet, religiia prinizhaet* [Science Inspires, Religion Humiliates]. Sci. ed.: A. Zafesov. Maikop: Krasnodar. kn. izd-vo. Adyg. otd-nie, 1984. 176 pp. In Adigei.

3128   Naumkin, V.V. "K voprosu o khassa i ama: Tradits. kontseptsiia 'elity' i 'massy' v musul'manstve" [On the Question of Khassa and Amma: Traditional Conception of "Elite" and "Masses" in Muhammedanism]. *Islam v istorii narodov Vostoka*. M., 1981. Pp. 40-50. Bibl.: pp. 49-50.

3129   Naumov, N.A. "Mirovozzrencheskaia funktsiia nauchnogo ateizma i kritika teologicheskoi interpretatsii nauchnoi kartiny mira" [World Outlook's Function of Scientific Atheism and Criticism of Theological Interpretation of the Scientific Picture of the World]. *Problemy istorii religii i ateizma*. Cheboksary, 1981. Pp. 19-30.

3130 Nazarenko, A.V.; Ronin, V.K. "Nauchnaia konferentsiia 'Vvedenie khristianstva u narodov Tsentral'noi i Vostochnoi Evropy. Kreshchenie Rusi' [Moskva, mart 1988]" [Scientific Conference "Introduction of Christianity to the Peoples of Central and Eastern Europe. Baptism of Rus'"]. *Istoriia SSSR* 6 (1988): 196-199.

3131 Nazarov, R. "Puti preodoleniia religiozno-natsionalisticheskikh predrassudkov" [Ways of Overcoming Religious-Nationalistic Prejudices]. *Sbornik trudov Republikanskoi nauchno-prakticheskoi konferentsii molodykh uchenykh i spetsialistov (12-14 aprelia 1989 g.).* Dushanbe, 1989. Sektsiia "Obshchestvennye nauki". Pp. 97-99.

3132 Nazarova, N. "Efiopskaia tserkov'" [Ethiopan Church]. *Aziia i Afrika segodnia* 7 (1982): 56-59. Summary in English, Suppl. p.6.

3133 Nazarova, N. "Indiiskie khristiane" [Indian Christians]. *Aziia i Afrika segodnia* 6 (1980): 59-60.

3134 Nazarova, N. "Koptskaia tserkkov'" [Coptic Church]. *Aziia i Afrika segodnia* 8 (1981): 58-60.

3135 *Ne ustupai polia t'me* [Don't Give Up Fields to Ignorance]. [Comp.: P.N. Dovgaliuk]. Kiev: Politizdat Ukrainy, 1983. 326 pp. In Ukrainian.

3136 Nechai, S. "Produmanno, ubeditel'no, kompetentno" [Considered, Convincing, Competently]. *Nauka i religiia* 12 (1980): 10-13.

3137 Nechitailo, Z.F. "Nauchno-tekhnicheskaia revoliutsiia kak faktor utverzhdeniia materialisticheskogo mirovozzreniia" [Scientific-Technical Revolution as Factor of Affirmation of Materialistic Outlook]. *Vopr. ateizma* 17 (1981): 27-35.

3138 Nefedov, A.N. *Na drevnem Makovtse: Troitse-Sergieva lavra: legendy i real'nost'* [In Ancient Makovts: Trinity-Sergius Monastery: Legends and Reality]. M.: Mosk. rabochii, 1987. 110 pp.

3139 Nefedova, N.P. "Lektsionnaia [nauchno-ateisticheskaia] propaganda: itogi i perspektivy" [Based on Lectures [Scientific-Atheistic] Propaganda: Results and Perspectives]. *Vopr. nauch. ateizma* 34 (1986): 146-156.

3140 Negmati, A.E. _Zemledel'cheskie kalendarnye prazdniki drevnikh tadzhikov i ikh predkov_ [Agricultural Calendar Holidays of the Ancient Tajiks and Their Ancestors]. Dushanbe: Donish, 1989. 127 pp.

3141 Negoitsa, P. "Za stenami Vatikana: Sovremen. katolitsizm i vyzovy vremeni" [Behind Vatican's Walls: Contemporary Catholicism and Challenge of the Time]. _Novoe vremia_ 7 (1989): 16-19; "Episkop iz Ekona protiv papy rimskogo" [Bishop from Ekon against Pope]. 9 (1989): 20-22; "Lichnaia diplomatiia papy" [Pope's Personal Diplomacy]. 10 (1989): 25-26.

3142 Neiachenko, R.V. "Vnedrenie v byt novykh obriadov i obychaev kak sostavnaia chast' ateisticheskogo vospitaniia" [Introduction into the Way of Life of New Ceremonies and Customs as a Component Part of Atheistic Education]. _Sotsialisticheskii obraz zhizni naseleniia Kalmytskoi ASSR: opyt, problemy, zadachi, sovershenstvovaniia_. Elista, 1987. Pp. 122-129.

3143 Neklessa, G. "Pechat' i propaganda ateizma" [The Press and Propaganda of Atheism]. _Kommunist Uzbekistana_ 6 (1989): 84-89.

3144 "Nekotorye voprosy kritiki religiozno-idealisticheskikh kontseptsii kul'tury" [Some Questions of Criticism of Religious-Idealistic Conceptions of Culture]. T.V. Artem'eva, et al. _Ideologicheskaia bor'ba i molodezh'_. L., 1987. Pp. 127-136.

3145 Nekrasov, S.M. _Zaveshchennaia pamiat'_ [Bequeathed Memory]. M.: Politizdat, 1989. 95 pp. (B-ka ateista).

3146 Nemira, L. "V kraiu Nairskom" [In the Land of Nair]. _Nauka i religiia_ 8 (1989): 24-27.

3147 Nemirovskaia, L.Z. "Formirovanie i razvitie u studentov interesa k nauchno-ateisticheskoi problematike" [Forming and Developing Students' Interest Toward Scientific-Atheistic Problematics]. _Prepodavanie nauch-nogo ateizma v vuze_. M., 1988. Pp. 23-36.

3148 Nenashev, M.I.; Shauro, E.A. _Obshchestvenno-politicheskoe i religioznoe soznanie molodykh mozambiktsev_ [Socio-Political and Religious Consciousness of Young Mozambiques]. M.: AN SSSR. In-t Afriki, 1989. 112 pp. Summary in Portuguese.

3149 Nepesov, T. "Kritika islama v tvorchestve Berdy Kerbabaeva" [Criticism of Islam in Berda Kerbabaev's Works]. *Izv. AN TSSR.* Ser. obshchestv. nauk 5 (1988): 48-56. In Turkmen. Summary in Russian.

3150 *Neprostye istiny* [Not Simple Truths]. [Comp.: N.V. Aivazova; P.A. Emelin]. M.; Sov. Rossiia, 1986. 96 pp.

3151 *Nesostoiatel'nost' sotsial'nykh doktrin tserkvi* [Groundlessness of Social Doctrines of the Church]. [M.N. Boldizhar et al]. Uzhgorod: Karpaty, 1988. 168 pp. In Ukrainian.

3152 Nessel'shtraus, Ts.G. "O probleme sinteza iskusstv v kul'tovom zodchestve srednevekov'ia" [The Problem of Synthesis of Art in Ecclesiastical Architecture of the Middle Ages]. *Problemy vzaimodeistviia iskusstv v khudozhestvennoi kul'ture zarubezhnnykh stran.* L., 1987. Pp. 33-45.

3153 Nesterchuk, V.P. "Struktura, soderzhanie i funktsii nauchno-ateisticheskogo mirovozzreniia" [Structure, Content and Functions of Scientific-Atheistic World Outlook]. *Izv. AN AzSSR.* Ser. istorii, filosofii i prava 2 (1988): 99-105.

3154 Nesterenko, A.D. "O prirode very i ee sootnoshenii s ubezhdeniem" [Nature of Faith and Its Correlation with Conviction]. *Vestn. Khar'k. un-ta* 208 (1981): 22-28.

3155 Nesterkin, S.P. "Psikhologicheskie osnovy srednevekovogo chan'-buddizma" [Psychological Bases of Medieval Ch'an-Buddhism]. *Psikhologicheskie aspekty buddizma.* Novosibirsk, 1986. Pp. 144-156.

3156 Nevecheria, S.A.; Tarasova, O.P. "Rol' problemnoi didaktiki v formirovanii optimisticheskogo mirovozzreniia studentov v protsesse izucheniia kursa nauchnogo ateizma" [The Role of Problematic Didactics in Formation of Optimistic Outlook of Students in the Process of Studying the Course of Scientific Atheism]. *Vestn. Khar'k. politekhn. in-ta* 228 (1985): 111-114.

3157 Nevelev, M.Iu. *Kontseptsiia very* [Conception of Faith]. M.: Prometei, 1989. 83 pp. (Author's ed.).

3158 Nevskii, A.N. "Osobennosti ateisticheskogo vospitaniia sredi sektantov" [Features of Atheistic Education Among Sectarians]. *Vopr. nauch. ateizma* 29 (1982): 32-42.

3159   Nezhnyi, A.[I]. "Strasti po krasnomu khramu" [Strong Feelings at the Red Temple]. *Ogonek* 28 (1989): 17-21.

3160   Nezhnyi, A.I. *Vzgliad so Sviatoi gory* [The View from the Holy Mountain]. M.: Pravda, 1989. 48 pp. (B-ka "Ogonek").

3161   Nguen Khung Khau. "Nekotorye aspekty filosofskogo ucheniia tkhien-buddizma Vinitaruchi" [Some Aspects of Philosophical Teaching of Vinitharuchi Thien-Buddhism School]. *Problemy etiki v filosofskikh ucheniiakh stran Vostoka.* M., 1986. Pp. 103-116.

3162   Nigmatova, D,; Shermatova, G. *Sotsialisticheskaia kul'tura i ateisticheskoe mirovozzrenie* [Socialist Culture and Atheistic World Outlook]. Tashkent: Uzbekistan, 1988. 22 pp. (Besedy o nauke; No 13). In Uzbek.

3163   Niiazi, A.Sh. "Traditsionnye musul'manskie religioznye deiateli i ikh rol' v Narodnoi Respublike Bangladesh" [Traditional Moslem Religious Dignitaries and Their Role in the People's Republic of Bangladesh]. *Narody Azii i Afriki* 4 (1988): 25-36.

3164   Nikiforov, A.V.; Khomutskii, F.A. "Internatsional'noe vospitanie v kurse nauchnogo ateizma" [International Education in the Course of Scientific Atheism]. *Dialektika sistemno-kompleksnogo podkhoda v internatsional'nom vospitanii molodezhi.* Alma-Ata, 1988. Pp. 62-66.

3165   Nikiforova, B.Z. *Krizis religii v sovremenom kapitalisticheskom mire* [Crisis of Religion in Contemporary Capitalist World]. L'vov: Vishcha shk. Izd-vo pri L'vov. un-te, 1986. 76 pp. (Ateist. b-chka studenta).

3166   Nikiforova, B.Z. "O spetsifike religioznosti molodezhi v kapitalisticheskikh stranakh]. [Specific Character of Youth's Religiosity in Capitalist Countries]. *Nauch. ateizm i ateist. vospitanie* 1 (1983): 77-84.

3167   Nikiforova, B.[Z]. "Odno iz tysiach" [One of Thousands]. *Nauka i religia* 4 (1983): 60-61.

3168   Nikishov, S.I. *Aktual'nye problemy propagandy ateizma v razvitom sotsialisticheskom obshchestve* [Actual Problems of Atheistic Propaganda in Developed Socialist Society]. M.: Znanie, 1982. 63 pp. (Novoe v zhizni, nauke, tekhnike. Ser. "Nauchnyi ateizm"; 5). Bibl.: p. 62.

3169 Nikishov, S.I. *XXVI s'ezd KPSS o polticheskikh spekuliatsiiakh na religioznykh chuvstvakh veruiushchikh* [XXVIth Congress of the CPSU on Political Speculations on Religious Feelings of Believers]. M.: Znanie RSFSR, 1981. 39 pp. (B pomoshch' lektoru / Pravl. o-va "Znanie" RSFSR, Nauch.-metod. sovet po propagande ateist. znanii). Bibl.: p. 35.

3170 Nikitin, A. "Kto napisal 'Troitsu Rubleva'?" [Who Painted "Rublev's Trinity"?]. *Nauka i religiia* 8 (1989): 44-48; 9 (1989): 40-43.

3171 Nikitin, A. "Pravoslavie: spornye stranitsy" [Orthodoxy: Disputable Pages]. *Nauka i religiia* 6 (1988): 3-8.

3172 Nikitin, D. "Angliiskaia [protestantskaia] missiia za Baikalom" [Anglican [Protestant] Mission in Trans Baikal]. *Baikal* 5 (1988): 135-137.

3173 Nikitin, D. "Islam na Mal'divakh" [Islam on the Maldives].* *Aziia i Afrika segodnia* 10 (1983): 60-61. Summary in English, suppl., p. 6.

3174 Nikitin, D. "Khristianstvo na ostrove Bali" [Christianity in Bali]. *Aziia i Afrika segodnia* 10 (1982): 61-63.

3175 Nikitin, D. "Koptskaia tserkov': Iz glubiny vekov" [Coptic Church: From Remote Ages]. *Aziia i Afrika segodnia* 5 (1983): 60-61.

3176 Nikitin, D. "Pravoslavnyi monastyr' na Sinae" [Orthodox Monastery in Sinai]. *Aziia i Afrika segodnia* 6 (1988): 49-52. Summary in English, suppl., p. 6.

3177 Nikitin, T.N.; Ronskaia, T.V. "O podgotovke katolicheskogo dukhovenstva dlia balkanskikh stran v XVII-XVIII vv." [Training Catholic Clergy for Balkan States in XVIIth-XVIIIth Centuries]. *Obshchestvo i gosudarstvo na Balkanakh v srednie veka*. Kalinin, 1980. Pp. 149-155.

3178 Nikitin, V. "Kreshchenie Rusi i otechestvennaia kul'tura" [Baptism of Rus' and Native Culture]. *Znamia* 8 (1988): 162-170.

3179 Nikitin, V. "Novyi sviatoi Gruzinskoi Pravoslavnoi Tserkvi" [New Saint of Georgian Orthodox Church]. *Religiia v SSSR* 4 (1988): 1 VN-3VN.

3180 Nikitin, V.N. "Issledovanie kategorii nauchnogo ateizma kak sredstvo povysheniia ideino-teoreticheskogo urovnia prepodavaniia nauchnogo ateizma" [Research of Categories of Scientific Atheism as Means for

Raising Ideological-Theoretical Level of Teaching Scientific Atheism].
*Aktual. vopr. metodiki prepodavaniia obshchestv. nauk i kom. vospitaniia
studentov* 5 (1987): 36-43.

3181   Nikitin, V.N. *Pogovorim o smysle zhizni* [Let's Talk About the Purport of
Life]. L.: Znanie RSFSR, 1980. 16 pp. (V pomoshch' lektoru / O-vo
"Znanie" RSFSR, Leningr. org.). Bibl.: p. 16.

3182   Nikolaev, R.V. "Solnechnyi kon'" [Solar Horse]. *Skifo-sibirskii mir: Iskusstvo i
ideologiia.* Novosibirsk, 1987. Pp. 154-158.

3183   Nikolaeva, E.Ia. "K voprosu o khristianstve na Bosfore" [The Problem of
Christianity in Bosphorus]. *Nauchno-ateisticheskie issledovaniia v muzeiakh.*
L., 1988. Pp. 14-16.

3184   Nikolaevskii, I. "'Gosudarstvo bez territorii'" [State Without Territory]. *Aziia
i Afrika segodnia* 9 (1983): 38-39.

3185   Nikolov, I. "Svoboda sovesti v Narodnoi Respublike Bolgarii" [Freedom of
Conscience in People's Republic of Bulgaria]. *Vopr. nauch. ateizma* 27
(1981): 134-150.

3186   Nikol'skii, N.[M]. "Gosudarstvennaia tserkov' krepostnoi epokhi" [State
Church in Serfdom Era]. *Khristianstvo i Rus'.* M., 1988. Pp. 93-110.

3187   Nikol'skii, N.M. *Istoriia Russkoi tserkvi* [History of the Russian Church]. 3rd
ed. M.: Politizdat, 1983. 448 pp., illus. (B-ka ateist. lit.). Bibl.: pp.
436-439.
Republished in 1985, and as 4th ed. in 1988.
Published also in:
Tallin: Eesti raamat, 1988. 352 pp. In Estonian. For review see item
5189.

3188   Nikonov, K.I. *Kritika antropologicheskogo obosnovaniia religii* [Criticism of
Anthropological Substantiation of Religion]. M.: MGU, 1989. 192 pp.
(Ateizm). Bibl.: pp. 187-191.

3189   Nikonov, K.I. *Religioznye kontseptsii cheloveka v sovremennoi bor'be idei*
[Man's Religious Conceptions in Contemporary Struggle of Ideas]. M.:
Znanie, 1986. 64 pp. (Novoe v zhizni, nauke, tekhnike. Nauch. ateizm;
7/1986). Bibl.: p. 63.

3190 Nikonov, K.I. *Sovremennaia khristianskaia antropologiia* [Contemporary Christian Anthropology]. M.: MGU, 1983. 184 pp. Bibl.: pp. 177-184. For review see item 5190-5192.

3191 Nikonov, K.I.; Tazhurizina, Z.A. *Kritika ideologicheskikh osnov pravoslavnogo monashestva* [Criticism of Ideological Foundations of Orthodox Monasticism]. M.: Znanie, 1982. 64 pp. (Novoe v zhizni, nauke, tekhnike. Ser. "Nauch. ateizm"; 3). Bibl.: p. 63.

3192 Nikulin, A.A. "Problemy povysheniia effektivnosti antireligioznoi propagandy v usloviakh mnogonatsional'nogo goroda" [Problems of Raising Effectiveness of Antireligious Propaganda in Multinational Town]. *Stanovlenie i razvitie dukhovnoi kul'tury razvitogo sotsializma.* Tashkent, 1981. Pp. 172-178.

3193 Nimaev, R.D. "Khramy Bon" [Bon Temples]. *V Vsesoiuznaia shkola molodykh vostokevedov.* M., 1989. T. 1. Pp. 63-64.

3194 Nirsha, V.M. "Shikhabuddin Sukhravardi i ego traktat 'Dary poznanii'" [Shihabuddin Suhrawardi and His Treatise "The Gifts of Cognition"]. *Obshchestv. nauki v Uzbekistane* 12 (1987): 49-52.

3195 Nitskute, Iu. "Issledovanie po katolicheskoi etike" [Research According to Catholic Ethics]. *Uchen. zap. vuzov LitSSR.* Problemy 36 (1987): 125.

3196 Niunka, V.Iu. *Sovremennyi Vatikan* [Vatican Today]. M.: Znanie, 1980. 64 pp. (Novoe v zhizni, nauke, tekhnike. Ser. "Nauch. ateizm"; No 9).

3197 Nogoibaev, B.N. "XXVII s'ezd KPSS o roli povysheniia sotsial'noi i trudovoi aktivnosti v ateisticheskom vospitanii trudiashchikhsia" [XXVIIth Congress of the CPSU on the Role of Increasing Social and Labour Activity in Atheistic Education of Workers]. *Sotsial'no-eticheskie problemy povysheniia effektivnosti ateisticheskogo vospitaniia v mnogonatsional'nom regione.* Frunze, 1987. Pp. 17-25.

3198 Nogoibaev, B.[N]. *Vera i deistvitel'nost'* [Faith and Reality]. Frunze: Kyrgyzstan, 1981. 66 pp. (B-chka ateista). In Kirghiz.

3199 Norovsambuu, S. "Mesto nauchnogo ateizma v sisteme kommunisticheskogo vospitaniia trudiashchikhsiia" [The Place of Scientific Atheism in the System of Communist Education of Workers]. *Stroitel'stvo sotsializma i utverzhdenie nauchno-materialisticheskogo, ateisticheskogo mirovozzreniia (v regionakh rasprostraneniia lamaizma)*. M., 1981. Pp. 120-127.

3200   Nosova, G.A. "Obriad kreshcheniia: traditsii i sovremennost'" [Ritual of Baptism: Traditions and Contemporaneity]. *Vopr. nauch. ateizma* 34 (1986): 234-257.

3201   Nosova, G.A. "S chem sviazan obriad kreshcheniia" [With What is the Ritual of Baptism Linked]. *Agitator* 16 (1988): 58-60.

3202   Nosovich, N.V. "Khristianskaia filosofiia istorii i sotsial'naia aktivnost' lichnosti" [Christian Philosophy of History and Social Activity of Individual]. *Muzei v ateisticheskoi propagande*. L., 1988. Pp. 24-36.

3203   Nosovich, V.I. *Edinstvo nravstvennogo i ateisticheskogo vospitaniia* [Unity of Moral and Atheistic Education]. Tallin: Znanie ESSR, 1984. 29 pp. (V pomoshch' lektoru / O-vo "Znanie" ESSR).

3204   Nosovich, V.[I]. "Marksistskii ateizm i moral'" [Marxist Atheism and Morals]. *Kommunist Estonii* 12 (1980): 53-58.

3205   Nosovich, V.I.; Vimmsaare, K.A. *Molodezh', nravstvennost', ateizm* [Youth, Morals, Atheism]. Tallin: Eesti raamat, 1986. 160 pp. In Estonian.

3206   Novichenko, N.R. *Sovremennaia pravoslavnaia propoved'* [Contemporary Orthodox Sermon]. Kiev: Znanie UkSSR, 1989. 46 pp. (Ser. 5 Nauchno-ateisticheskaia / O-vo "Znanie" UkSSR; No 8). In Ukrainian. Bibl.: p. 44.

3207   Novik, E.S. *Obriady i fol'klor v sibirskom shamanstve* [Rituals and Folklore in Siberian Shamanism]. M.: Nauka, 1984. 304 pp. (Vsled po fol'kloru i mifologii Vostoka). Bibl.: pp. 280-293. Summary in English. For review see item 5193.

3208   Novikov, M.P. *Ateizm v dukhovnoi zhizni obshchestva* [Atheism in the Spiritual Life of Society]. M.: Znanie, 1984. 63 pp. (Novoe v zhizni, nauke, tekhnike. Nauch. ateism; 5). Bibl.: p. 62.

3209   Novikov, M.[P]. "Pravoslavie i sovremennost'" [Orthodoxy and Contemporaneity]. *Agitator* 3 (1982): 40-42.

3210   Novikov, M.P. "Prepodavanie nauchnogo ateizma - vazhneishee sredstvo ateisticheskogo vospitaniia studentov [Teaching Scientific Atheism - Most

Important Means for Atheistic Education of Students]. *Prepodavanie nauchnogo ateizma v vuze.* M., 1988. Pp. 14-23.

3211 Novikov, M.P. *Rol' nauchnogo ateizma v formirovanii aktivnoi zhiznennoi pozitsii* [The Role of Scientific Atheism in Forming Active Vital Position]. M.: Znanie, 1980. 12 pp. (V pomoshch' lektoru).

3212 Novikov, M.P. "Vvedenie khristianstva na Rusi s tochki zreniia obshches-tvennogo progressa" [Introduction of Christianity into Rus' from the Point of View of Social Progress]. *Vopr. nauch. ateizma* 37 (1987): 9-19.

3213 Novikov, M.[P].; Tazhurizina, Z. "Ateizm i razvitie dukhovnoi kul'tury" [Atheism and Development of Spiritual Culture]. *Nauka i religiia* 4 (1983): 28-30; 6 (1983): 15-18.

3214 Novikova, G.L. "Nabory skandinavskikh iazycheskikh amuletov" [Collection of Scandinavian Pagan Amulets]. *XI Vsesoiuznaia konferentsiia po izucheniiu istorii, ekonomki, litaratury i iazyka Skandinavskikh stran i Finliandii.* M., 1989. T. 1. Pp. 153-155.

3215 Novikova, O.A. "K voprosu o vospriiatii smerti v srednie veka i Vozrozhdenie" [The Problem of Perception of Death in the Middle Ages and Renaissance]. *Kul'tura srednikh vekov i novogo vremeni.* M., 1987. Pp. 51-59.

3216 Novinskaia, M.I. "Religioznoe soznanie i sud'by marksizma v SShA" [Religious Consciousness and Marxism's Fates in USA]. *Rabochii klass i sovremen. mir* 4 (1988): 84-86.

3217 *Novoe myshlenie i svoboda sovesti: voprosy i otvety* [New Thinking and Freedom of Conscience: Questions and Answers]. M.: Znanie, 1989. 61 pp. (Novoe v zhizni, nauke, tekhnike. Nauch. ateizm; 11/1989).

3218 Novokhatskaia, L.P. "Reshenie natsional'nogo i religioznogo voprosov v SSSR i utverzhdenie nauchnogo mirovozzreniia" [The Solution of National and Religious Problems in USSR and Affirmation of Scientific World Outlook]. *Vopr. ateizma* 23 (1987): 33-39.

3219 Novosel'tsev, A.P. "Khristianstvo, islam i iudaizm v stranakh Vostochnoi Evropy i Kavkaza v srednie veka" [Christianity, Islam and Judaism in the Countries of Eastern Europe and Caucasus in the Middle Ages]. *Vopr. istorii* 9 (1989): 20-35.

3220   Novosel'tsev, A.P. "Priniatie khristianstva drevnerusskim gosudarstvom kak zakonomernoe iavlenie epokhi" [Assumption of Christianity by Ancient Russian State as Natural Occurrence of the Era]. *Istoriia SSSR* 4 (1988): 97-122.

3221   Novosel'tsev, V. "Ateisticheskoi propagande - nastupatel'nost'" [Offensiveness to Atheistic Propaganda]. *Agitator* 20 (1982): 57-58.

3222   Novruzov, P. "Rybokhvostye bozhestva" [Fishtailed Deities]. *Nauka i religiia* 8 (1985): 22-24.

3223   *Novye tendentsii v ideologii i deiatel'nosti katolitsizma v SSSR i problemy ateisticheskogo vospitaniia* [New Tendencies in Ideology and Activity of Catholicism in USSR and Problems of Atheistic Education]. Ed.: S.V. Krauialis. Vil'nius: [S.n.], 1983. 133 pp.

3224   *Novye tendentsii v russkom pravoslavii: voprosy i otvety* [New Tendencies in Russian Orthodoxy: Questions and Answers]. Comp.: S.I. Ivanenko. M.: Znanie RSFSR, 1989. 81 pp. Bibl.: p. 81.

3225   Nuikin, A. "Gospod' bog i 'intellektualy' XX veka" [God and "Intellectuals" of the XXth Century]. *Ural* 5 (1986): 158-170.

3226   Nuikin, A. "Vera est' nravstvennost'?" [Does Faith Mean Morality?]. *Molodoi kommunist* 1 (1988): 29-37.

3227   Nuraliev, Iu.N. *Uraza i zdorov'e* [Uraza and Health]. Dushanbe: Irfon, 1983 47 pp. In Tajik.

3228   Nurmagambetov, K. "Islam kak orudie burzhuaznoi propagandy" [Islam as a Tool of Bourgeois Propaganda]. *Part. zhizn' Kazakhstana* 12 (1986): 73-77.

3229   Nurulkhakov, K. "Edinstvo internatsional'nogo i ateisticheskogo vospitaniia" [Unity of International and Atheistic Education]. *Kompleksnyi podkhod v ateisticheskom vospitanii.* Dushanbe, 1988. Pp. 31-44. Bibl.: pp. 43-44.

3230   Nurulkhakov, K. *Islam i natsional'nye otnosheniia* [Islam and National Relationships]. Dushanbe: Irfon, 1985. 43 pp. In Tajik.
Published also in: 1987. 111 pp. In Tajik.

3231 Nurullaev, A.A. "K voprosu o vzaimosviazi natsional'nogo i religioznogo" [The Question on National and Religious Intercommunication]. *Natsional'nye problemy v sovremennykh usloviiakh.* M., 1988. Pp. 230-243.

3232 *O boge li spor?* [Is the Argument About God?]. [Comp.: V.A. Alekseev]. M.: Sov. Rossiia, 1987. 123 pp.

3233 *O edinstve internatsional'nogo i ateisticheskogo vospitaniia* [On the Unity of International and Atheistic Education]. Ed.: A.G. Kuchiev. Ordzhonikidze: SONII, 1983. 142 pp.

3234 *O khristianskom prazdnike 'Paskha' i novykh sovetskikh prazdnikakh i obriadakh* [On Christian Feast "Easter" and New Soviet Holidays and Ceremonies]. [Comp.: I.N. Romanov]. M.: [S.n.], 1984. 20 pp. (Metod. material v pomoshch' propagandistu / O-vo "Znanie". Tsentr. Dom nauch. ateizma). Bibl.: pp. 19-20.

3235 *O sovremennom pravoslavii* [Orthodoxy Today]. [Ed.: I.V. Bachurin]. Saratov: Izd-vo Sarat. un-ta, 1989. 40 pp.

3236 *O svobode sovesti* [Freedom of Conscience]. [Comp.: I.A. Malakhova]. M.: Sov. Rossiia, 1987. 90 pp. For review see item 4962.

3237 *O vere i neverii* [Faith and Lack of Faith]. [Comp.: M.M. Skibitskii]. M.: Politizdat, 1982. 239 pp., illus. (B-ka ateist. lit). Bibl.: pp. 230-238. For review see item 5196.

3238 *Ob ateizme i religii* [Atheism and Religion]. [N.P. Andrianov]. L.: Lenizdat, 1987. 71 pp. (B-chka politinformatora "Vopros-otvet").

3239 Obichkina, E. "Evangelie ot Robesp'era" [The Gospel from Robespierre]. *Nauka i religiia* 8 (1989): 11-15.

3240 Oblival'naia, A. "Borot'sia za cheloveka" [To Struggle for Man]. *Kommunist Kirgizstana* 8 (1984): 68-72.

3241 *Obriadnost' i mirovozzrenie* [Rites and World Outlook]. Ed.: S. Krauialis. Vil'nius: Otd. propagandy i agitatsii TsK KP Litvy, In-tut nauch. ateizma AON pri TsK KP Litvy, 1988 -
Vyp. 1. Muzikiavichius, A. *Prichiny sokhraneniia i puti preodoleniia religioznogo obriada kreshcheniia* [Causes of Preservation and Ways of Overcoming the Religious Ritual of Baptism]. 1988. 92 pp.

Vyp. 2. Muzikiavichius, A.; Skirtun, Ia. *Sostoianie i prichiny zhivuchesti obriada venchaniia* [Condition and Reasons of Stability of Wedding Ceremony]. 1989. 77 pp.

3242 *Obriady i kul'ty drevnego i srednevekovogo naseleniia Dagestana* [Rituals and Cults of the Ancient and Medieval Population of Daghestan]. [Ed.: M.A. Aglarov]. Makhachkala: Dag. fil. AN SSSR, 1986. 155 pp., illus.

3243 *Obriady i verovaniia narodov Karelii* [Rituals and Beliefs of the Peoples' of Karelia]. Ed.: A.P. Konkka et al. Petrozavodsk: 1988. 158 pp., illus.

3244 *Obshchepartiinoe, obshcheproletarskoe delo* [Allparty, Allproletarian Matter]. Comp.: B.M. Mar'ianov. M.: Sov. Rossiia, 1983. 125 pp. Bibl.: pp. 123-124.

3245 Ochirov, D.D. *Ot religioznoi very k ateizmu* [From Religious Faith to Atheism]. Ulan-Ude: Buriat. kn. izd-vo, 1981. 95 pp. Annot. bibl.: pp. 89-94.

3246 Ochkauri, T.A. *Pogrebal'nye obriady v Kartli v proshlom i nastoiashchem* [Funeral Rituals in Kartli in the Past and Present]. Tbilisi: Metsniereba, 1987. 67 pp. In Georgian. Summary in Russian. Bibl.: pp. 63-64.

3247 Ochnauri, A.A. *Kalendar' gruzinskikh narodnykh prazdnikov* [Calendar of Georgian Popular Holidays]. Tbilisi: Metsniereba, 1988. 212 pp. In Georgian. Summary in Russian. Index: pp. 201-208.

3248 Odilov, N.F. *Kommunizm i sovremennyi islam* [Communism and Contemporary Islam]. Dushanbe: Irfon, 1986. 47 pp. In Tajik.

3249 Odintsov, M.[I]. "Drugogo raza ne bylo..." [There Was Not Another Time...]. *Nauka i religiia* 2 (1989): 8-9.

3250 Odintsov, M.[I]. "Zhrebii pastyria: Stseny i dokumenty is zhizni patriarkha Tikhona" [The Fate of a Pastor: Scenes and Documents from Patriarch Tikhon's Life]. *Nauka i religiia* 1 (1989): 38-41; 4 (1989): 16-20; 5 (1989): 18-21; 6 (1989): 34-40.

3251 Odintsov, M.I. "Kritika religioznykh predstavlenii o sushchnosti patriotizma" [Criticism of Religious Notions on the Essence of Patriotism]. *Aktual'nye problemy nachno-ateisticheskogo vospitaniia molodezhi.* M., 1987. Pp. 132-135.

3252 Oganesian, N.O. "Global'naia strategiia islama: osnovopologaiushchie prin-
tsipy i konechnye tseli" [Global Strategy of Islam: Basic Principles and
Ultimate Aims]. *Vestn. obshchestv. nauk* 1 (1989): 16-22. Summary in
Armenian.

3253 Oganesian, N.O. "Ob antiimperialisticheskoi i antisotsialisticheskoi poten-
tsiiakh islama" [Islam's Antiimperialist and Antisocialist Potentialities].
Vopr. vostokovedeniia 3/4 (1987): 278-286. Summary in Armenian.

3254 Oganesian, S. "Antropnyi printsip Vselennoi s tochki zreniia nauki i religii"
[Anthropian Principle of the Universe from the Point of View of Science
and Religion]. *Po lenin. puti.* Erevan. 9 (1987): 81-86.

3255 Oganiants, B.G. "Problema ateisticheskogo vospitaniia v strukture mirovozzrencheskoi podgotovki studentov" [The Problem of Atheistic Education
in the Structure of Preparation Students' World Outlook]. *Mirovozzrencheskaia napravlennost' uchebnogo protsessa v pedagogicheskom vuze.*
M., 1987. Pp. 147-152.

3256 Ogneva, E.V. *Ideologicheskaia bor'ba i voprosy svobody sovesti v sovremennykh usloviiakh* [Ideological Struggle and Problems of Freedom of
Conscience in Contemporary Conditions]. Kiev: Znanie UkSSR, 1980. 15
pp. (B-chka v pomoshch' lektoru "Probl. nauch. ateizma" / O-vo "Znanie"
UkSSR). In Ukrainian. Annotations in Russian. Bibl.: p. 15.

3257 Ognevaia, E.V. "Ateisticheskoe vospitanie kak proiavlenie sotsialisticheskoi
svobody sovesti" [Atheistic Education as Manifestation of Socialist
Freedom of Conscience]. *Vopr. ateizma* 18 (1982): 29-36.

3258 Ognevaia, E.V. "Pravoslavie i revoliutsiia" [Orthodoxy and Revolution]. *Vopr.
ateizma* 23 (1987): 81-87.

3259 Ogorodnik, I.V. *Utverzhdenie sotsial'nogo bessmertiia* [Confirmation of Social
Immortality]. Kiev: Znanie UkSSR, 1987. 48 pp. (Ser. 5 Nauchno-
ateisticheskaia / O-vo "Znanie" UkSSR; No 5). In Ukrainian. Annot.
bibl.: p. 47.

3260 Okhotina, N.A. "Izmeneniia v polozhenii Kievskoi mitropolii v usloviiakh
mongolo-tatarskogo iga" [Changes in the Status of Kievan Metropolitan
See under Mongol-Tatar Yoke]. *Religii mira.* M., 1989. Pp. 157-175.

3261   Okhrimenko, Iu.M. *Deval'vatsiia 'khristianskogo gumanizma'* [Devaluation of "Christian Humanism"]. Kiev: Vyshcha shk. Izd-vo pri Kiev. Gos. un-te, 1986. 80 pp. (Ateist. b-chka studenta). Bibl.: pp. 76-79.

3262   Okhrimenko, Iu.M. "Mediko-ateisticheskii aspekt sotsializatsii lichnosti v usloviiakh sovremennogo kapitalizma" [Medical-Atheistic Aspect of Socialization of Individual under Contemporary Capitalism]. *Filos. vopr. meditsiny i biologii* 13 (1981): 119-126.

3263   Okhrimenko, Iu.M. "Mediko-psikhologicheskii aspekt khristianskoi obriadnosti kak spetsificheskogo vida chelovecheskoi deiatel'nosti" [Medical-Psychological Aspect of Christian Ritual as Specific Form of Human Activity]. *Filos. vopr. meditsiny i biologii* 16 (1984): 23-31.

3264   Okhrimenko, Iu.[M]. "Tsena zemnogo schast'ia" [The Price of Earthly Happiness]. *Nauka i religiia* 6 (1983): 30-32.

3265   Okulov, A.[F]. "Ateisticheskoe vospitanie: opyt, problemy" [Atheistic Education: Experience, problems]. *Polit. Samoobrazovanie* 12 (1984): 45-52. Bibl.: p. 52.

3266   Okulov, A.F. "Nekotorye voprosy ateisticheskogo vospitaniia v sovremennykh usloviiakh" [Some Problems of Atheistic Education in Contemporary Conditions]. *Dialektika internatsional'nogo i natsional'nogo v razvitii obshchestvennoi mysli.* Kishinev, 1984. Pp. 30-38.

3267   Okulov, A.F. *Sotsial'nyi progress i religiia* [Social Progress and Religion]. M.: Mysl', 1982. 191 pp. Bibl.: pp. 187-190. Annot. bibl.: pp. 178-186. For reviews see item 5199-5201.

3268   Oleshchuk, Iu.F. "O politicheskoi aktivizatsii amerikanskoi tserkvi" [Political Activization of American Church]. *Rabochii klass i sovremen. mir* 2 (1989): 35-43.

3269   Olimova, S,; Olimov, M. "Otreshit'sia ot illiuzii: Tradits. obshchestvo i ateizm" [To Give Up Illusions: Traditional Society and Atheism]. *Kommunist Tadzhikistana* 9 (1989): 74-78.

3270   Ol'khov, O.P.; Ianev, I.G. *Preodolenie* [Overcoming]. Omsk: Kn. izd-vo, 1988. 111 pp. (V pomoshch' ateistu).

3271 Omel'chenko, O.A. "Tserkov' v pravovoi politike 'prosveshchennogo absoliu-tizma' v Rossii" [Church in Legal Policy of "Enlightened Absolutism" in Russia]. *Istoriko-pravovye voprosy vzaimootnoshenii gosudarstva i tserkvi v istorii Rossii.* M., 1988. Pp. 24-92.

3272 Omurova, T.O. "Puti povysheniia effektivnosti ateisticheskogo vospitaniia zhenshchin v Kirgizii v svete XXVII s'ezda KPSS [Ways of Raising the Effectiveness of Atheistic Education of Women of Kirghizia in the Light of XXVIIth Congress of the CPSU]. *Sotsial'no-eticheskie problemy povysheniia effektivnosti ateisticheskogo vospitaniia v mnogonatsional'nom regione.* Frunze, 1987. Pp. 70-78.

3273 Onishchenko, A.S. *Aktual'nye voprosy ateisticheskoi propagandy* [Actual Problems of Atheistic Propaganda]. Kiev: Znanie UkSSR, 1984. 48 pp. (Ser V "Nauchno-ateisticheskaia" / O-vo "Znanie" UkSSR; No 10). Annot. bibl.: p. 47.

3274 Onishchenko, A.S. "Formirovat', utverzhdat' nauchnoe mirovozzrenie" [To Form, Assert Scientific World Outlook]. *Kommunist Ukrainy* 4 (1988): 55-63.

3275 Onishchenko, A.[S]. "Novye argumenty v starom spore" [New Arguments in Old Dispute]. *Nauka i religiia* 5 (1988): 6-8.

3276 Onishchenko, A.S. "Osnovnye napravleniia, formy i metody ateisticheskoi kontrpropagandy" [Fundamental Directions, Forms and Methods of Athei-stic Counterpropaganda]. *Vopr. nauch. ateizma* 34 (1986): 118-128.

3277 Onishchenko, A.S. *Prichiny sokhraneniia i osobennosti proiavleniia religioznosti v sovremennykh usloviiakh* [Motives of Preservation and Features of Manifestation of Religiousness in Contemporary Conditions]. M.: Znanie, 1980. 15 pp.
Pubished also in:
Dushanbe: Znanie TadzhSSR, 1980. 17 pp.

3278 Opalko, N.I. *Ateisty s iunykh let* [Atheists Since Youth]. Kiev: Znanie UkSSR, 1988. 48 pp. (Ser. 5 Nauchno-ateisticheskaia / O-vo "Znanie" UkSSR; No 6). In Ukrainian.

3279 *Opisi imushchestva novgorodskogo Sofiiskogo sobora XVIII-nachala XIX v.* [Distraint of Sophie Cathedral of Novgorod in VIIIth-XIXth Centuries].

[Comp.: E.A. Gordienko et al]. M.; L.: In-t istorii SSSR, 1988. 230 pp. Annot bibl.: pp. 47-49.

3280 *Opyt ateisticheskoi raboty sredi zhenshchin v respublikakh Srednei Azii* [Experience of Atheistic Work Among Women of Middle Asian Republics]. [Comp.: E.Z. Bairamov; L.E. Bairamova]. M.: [S.n.], 1985. 24 pp. (V pomoshch' propagandistu i organizatoru ateist. raboty / Vsesoiz. o-vo "Znanie", Tsentr. Dom nauch. ateizma). Bibl.: pp. 23-24.

3281 *Opyt raboty Domov nauchnogo ateizma Tadzhikskoi SSR* [Working Experience of the Houses of Scientific Atheism of Tadzhik SSR]. M.: Znanie, 1985. 99 pp. (V pomoshch' propagandistu i organizatoru ateist. raboty / Vsesoiuz. o-vo "Znanie", Tsentr. Dom nauch. ateizma).

3282 Orekhov, S.I. "Kliatva i prokliatie kak elementy religioznogo kul'ta" [Vow and Damnation as Elements of Religious Cult]. *Otnoshenie cheloveka k irratsional'nomu.* Sverdlovsk, 1989. Pp. 198-221.

3283 Oreshin, V. "Sovety po ateisticheskoi rabote" [Advices on Atheistic Work]. *Agitator* 6 (1983): 60-62.

3284 Orghish, V.P. *Antichnaia filosofiia i proiskhozhdenie khristianstva* [Ancient Philosophy and the Origin of Christianity]. Minsk: Nauka i tekhnika, 1986. 182 pp., illus. Bibl.: pp. 167-178. Name index: pp. 179-181.

3285 Orgish, V.P. "Drevnegrecheskaia filosofiia i khristianstvo. Kritika bogoslovskikh vozzrenii" [Ancient Greek Philosphy and Christianity. Criticism of Theological Outlooks]. *Nauch. ateizm i ateist. vospitanie* 1 (1983): 98-109.

3286 Orgish, V.P. *Drevniaia Rus':* Obrazovanie Kiev. gosudarstva i vved. khristianstva [Ancient Rus': Formation of Kievan State and Introduction of Christianity]. Minsk: Nauka i tekhnika, 1988. 150 pp., illus. Bibl.: pp. 143-147. Name index: pp. 148-149.

3287 Orlov, S.M. "Nagliadnost' i tekhnicheskie sredstva obucheniia v protsesse prepodavaniia nauchnogo ateizma" [Use of Visual Aids and Technical Means of Teaching in Process of Instruction Scientific Atheism]. *Prepodavanie nauchnogo ateizma v vuze.* M., 1988. Pp. 121-128.

3288 Orlova, A.S. "Metodologicheskie problemy tipologicheskogo analiza 'obezreli-gioznogo soznaniia'" [Methodological Problems of Typological Analysis of

"Irreligious Consciousness"]. *Filosofskii analiz iavlenii dukhovnoi kul'tury:* Teoret. i ist. aspekty. M., 1984. Pp. 82-88.

3289   Orlova, A.S. "O poniatii i tipakh nereligioznogo soznaniia" [Notions and Types of Irreligious Consciousness]. *Aktual'nye problemy ateisticheskogo vospitaniia i kritika religioznoi ideologii.* M., 1983. Pp. 39-43.

3290   Orlova, Zh.I. *Prezhde i teper'* [Before and Now]. Kiev: Veselka, 1981. 119 pp., illus. In Ukrainian.

3291   Osintseva, L.G. *Uteshiteli vechnost'iu* [Comforters of Eternity]. Cheliabinsk: Iuzh.-Ural. kn. izd-vo, 1987. 88 pp.

3292   Osipov, A.A. *Katekhizis bez prikras: Besedy byvshego bogoslova s veruiushchimi i neveruiushchimi o knige, izlagaiushchei osnovy pravoslav. very* [Catechism Without Embellishment: Talks of Former Theologian with Believers and Unbelievers about the Book, Expounding the Fundamentals of Orthodox Creed]. 2nd ed. M.: Politizdat, 1981. 271 pp., ilus. (B-ka ateist. lit.).

3293   Osipov, A.A. *Otkrovennyi razgovor s veruiushchimi i neveruiushchimi: razmyshleniia byvshego bogoslova* [Frank Talk with Believers and Unbelievers: Reflections of a Former Theologian]. 2nd revised and enlarged ed. L.: Lenizdat, 1983. 302 pp. Bibl. of A.A. Osipov's atheistic works: pp. 299-301.
Published also in:
Kiev: Politizdat Ukrainy, 1984. 266 pp. In Ukrainian. For review see item 5203.

3294   Osipov, Iu.M. "Buddizm i literatury stran Indokitaia" [Buddhism and Literature of Countries of Indo-China]. *III Vsesoiuznaia konferentsiia vostokovedov "Vzaimodeistvie i vzaimovliianie tsivilizatsii kul'tur na Vostoke".* M., 1988. T. 1. Pp. 107-109.

3295   Osipov, O.[P]. "S pozitsii uchenogo" [From a Scholar's Perspective]. *Nauka i religiia* 12 (1988): 14-15.

3296   Osipov. O.P. "Nekotorye puti sblizheniia natsional'nykh grupp i preodoleniia religioznykh perezhitkov" [Some Ways of Rapprochement of National Groups and Overcoming of Religious Survivals]. *Sovremennye eticheskie protsessy u narodov Zapadnoi i Iuzhnoi Sibiri.* Tomsk, 1981. Pp. 37-49.

3297   Osipova, L.F. "Znachenie obshchestvenno-politicheskoi praktiki v formirovanii
       nauchno-ateisticheskogo mirovozzreniia studentov" [Importance of Socio-
       Political Practice in Forming Student's Scientific-Atheistic World Outlook].
       Prepodavanie nauchnogo ateizma v vuze. M., 1988. Pp. 181-190.

3298   Osipovskii, E.G. "Otnoshenie sovremennoi protestanskoi teologii k marksiz-
       mu i ateizmu" [Attitude of Contemporary Protestant Theology Towards
       Marxism and Atheism]. *Kritika sovremennoi katolicheskoi i protestanskoi
       teologii*. M., 1989. Pp. 49-64.

3299   Osmanov, M.-N.O. "Dostoinstva russkogo perevoda korana, vypolnennogo
       akademikom I.Iu. Krachkovskim" [Merits of Russian Translation of Koran
       by Academician I.Iu. Krachkovskii]. *Pamiatniki istorii i literatury Vostoka:
       Period feodalizma*. M., 1986. Pp. 190-194.

3300   Osmanova, A.M. "Periodicheskaia pechat' i voprosy ateisticheskogo vospita-
       niia zhenshchin" [Periodical Press and Problems of Women's Atheistic
       Education]. *Kompleksnyi podkhod v ateisticheskom vospitanii*. Dushanbe,
       1988. Pp. 112-126. Bibl.: pp. 125-126.

3301   Osmanova, A.M. "Rol' periodicheskoi pechati v bor'be s religiozno-
       konservativnym obshchestvennym mneniem v Tadzhikistane" [The Role of
       Periodical Press in the Struggle with Religious-Conservative Public
       Opinion in Tajikistan]. *Nauchnyi ateizm i obshchestvennoe mnenie*. M.,
       1987. Pp. 63-79.

3302   *Osnovy nauchnogo ateizma* [Foundations of Scientific Atheism]. Comp.: Iu.A.
       Kalinin et al. Kiev: [S.n.], 1988. 231 pp. Bibl.: pp. 221-229.

3303   *Osnovy nauchnogo ateizma* [Foundations of Scientific Atheism]. [N.S.
       Gordienko; V.N. Nikitin; L.R. Kharakhorin, et al]. Tallin: Esti raamat,
       1980. 151 pp. In Estonian.
       Published also in:
       Tbilisi: Ganatleba, 1981. 243 pp. In Georgian.
       Erevan: Luis, 1982. 230 pp. In Armenian.
       3rd revised and enlarged ed., M.: Vyssh. shk., 1983. 199 pp. 4th. revised
       and enlarged ed.: 1989. 224 pp.
       Vil'nius: Mintis, 1986. 185 pp. In Lithuanian.
       Dushanbe: Irfon, 1988. 127 pp. In Tajik.

3304   *Osnovy nauchnogo ateizma* [Foundations of Scientific Atheism]. [Comp.: V.K.
       Tancher et al]. Kiev: UMKVO, 1989. 183 sheets, illus.

3305 Ostafeichuk, I. "Televidenie i radio: ateisticheskaia propaganda" [Television and Radio: Atheistic Propaganda]. *Kommunist Moldavii* 10 (1987): 84-87.

3306 Ostrovskaia, E.P. "Buddiiskii filosofskii traktat kak ob'ekt mezhkul'turnogo vzaimodeistviia" [Buddhist Philosophical Treatise as Object of Intercultural Reciprocity]. *III Vsesoiuznaia konferentsiia vostokovedov "Vzaimodeistvie i vzaimovliianie tsivilizatsii kul'tur na Vostoke"*. M., 1988. T. 1. Pp. 109-111.

3307 Ostrovskaia, L.V. "Istochniki dlia izucheniia otnosheniia sibirskikh krest'ian k ispovedi (1861-1904 gg.)" [Sources for Study the Attitude of Siberian Peasants Towards Confession (1861-1904)]. *Issledovaniia po istorii obshchestvennogo soznaniia epokhi feodalizma v Rossii*. Novosibirsk, 1984. Pp. 131-151.

3308 Ostrozhinskii, V.E. "Povyshenie effektivnosti sotsialisticheskoi obriadnosti v ateisticheskom vospitanii" [Raising the Effectiveness of Socialist Ceremonial in Atheistic Education]. *Vopr. nauch. ateizma* 29 (1982): 152-161.

3309 Ostrozhinskii, V.E. "Zhizneutverzhdaiushchaia aktivnost' materialisticheskogo mirovozzreniia" [Life-Asserting Activity of Materialist World Outlook]. *Kommunist Ukrainy* 3 (1985): 32-39.

3310 *Ot beregov Bosfora do beregov Efrata* [From the Banks of Bosphorus up to the Banks of Euphrates]. Ed.: D.S. Likhachev. M.: Nauka, 1987. 360 pp.

3311 *Otnoshenie cheloveka k irratsional'nomu* [Man's Attitude Towards Irrational]. Ed.: D.V. Pivovarov. Sverdlovsk: Izd-vo Ural. un-ta, 1989. 312 pp. (A. Ser. "Aktual. probl. filos. ateizma": Vyp. 1). Summary in English.

3312 *Otrechenie: Rasskazy byvshchikh veruiushchikh, porvavshchikh s religiei* [Renunciation: Stories of Former Believers, Who Broke Off with Religion]. [Comp.: V.L. Kharazov]. M.: Politizdat, 1982. 175 pp., illus. Published also in: Kishinev: Kartia Moldoveniaske, 1984. 187 pp. illus. In Moldavian.

3313 Otvety mitropolita Minskogo i Belorusskogo Filareta na voprosy redkollegii "Istoriko-filosofskogo ezhegodnika" [Metropolitan of Minsk and Belorussia Philaret's Answers to the Questions of Editorial Board of "Historic-Philosophical Annual"]. *Istoriko-filos. ezhegodnik*. M., 1988. Pp. 325-329.

3314 Otvety na voprosy veruiushchikh [Answers to Believers Questions]. [Ed.: R. Machidov]. Dushanbe: [S.n.], 1981. 34 pp. In Tajik. Vyp. 3. 1985. 32 pp. In Tajik.

3315 Ovchinnikov, S. "Preobrazhennyi Savl" [Transfigurated Savel]. Kuban' 11 (1989): 58-59.

3316 Ovchinnikov, V.G. Katolicheskaia tserkov' v Zapadnoi Afrike [Catholic Church in Western Africa]. M.: Nauka, 1982. 191 pp., illus. Bibl.: pp. 179-187. Name index: pp. 188-190. For review see item 5204.

3317 Ovchinnikov, V.G. "Pravoslavnaia tserkov' v istori nashei strany" [Orthodox Church in the History of Our Country]. Vopr. istorii 5 (1988): 111-121.

3318 Ovsienko, F.G. "Evoliutsiia katolicheskogo ucheniia o roli zhenshchiny v obshchestve, sem'e i brake" [Evolution of the Catholic Teaching on the Role of Woman in Society, Family and Marriage]. Vopr. nauch. ateizma 28 (1981): 163-182.

3319 Ovsienko, F.G. Evoliutsiia sotsial'nogo ucheniia katolitsizma [Evolution of Social Teaching of Catholicism]. M.: Izd-vo MGU, 1987. 256 pp. Bibl.: pp. 248-253. For review see item 5205.

3320 Ovsienko, F.[G]. "God devy Marii" [The Year of the Virgin Mary]. Nauka i religiia 3 (1988): 18-20.

3321 Ovsienko, F.G. Kriticheskii analiz katolicheskoi 'teologii truda' [Critical Analysis of Catholic "Theology of Labour"]. M.: Znanie, 1984. 63 pp. (Novoe v zhizni, nauke, tekhnike. Nauch. ateizm; 3). Bibl.: p. 62.

3322 Ovsienko, F.G. "Kriticheskii analiz ucheniia o cheloveke v sovremennoi katolicheskoi etike" [Critical Analysis of Studies about Man in Contemporary Catholic Ethics]. Gumanizm i religiia L., 1980. Pp. 18-34.

3323 Ovsienko, F.G. "Kritika metodologicheskikh osnov sotsial'nogo ucheniia katolitsizma" [Criticism of Methodological Foundations of Catholicism's Social Studies]. Vopr. nauch. ateizma 33 (1985): 50-71.

3324 Ovsienko, F.G. "Lichnost' i sotsial'noe razvitie v katolicheskoi 'antropologizirovannoi' teologii" [Individual and Social Development in Catholic "Anthropologicalized Theology"]. Vopr. nauch. ateizma 26 (1980): 109-130.

3325 Ovsienko, F.G. "Osveshchenie v kurse nauchnogo ateizma roli religii v sovremennoi politicheskoi i ideologicheskoi bor'be" [Elucidation in the Course of Scientific Atheism on the Role of Religion in Contemporary Political and Ideological Struggle]. *Prepodavanie nauchnogo ateizma v v uze.* M., 1988. Pp. 129-143.

3326 Ovsienko, F.G. *Problema cheloveka v filosofii katolitsizma* [The Problem of Man in Philosophy of Catholicism]. Kiev: Znanie UkSSR, 1986. 49 pp. (Ser. V, Nauchno-ateisticheskaia / O-vo "Znanie" UkSSR; No 1).

3327 Ovsienko, F.G. *Sotsial'no-eticheskoe uhenie sovremennogo katolitsizma* [Socio-Ethical Study of Contemporary Catholicism]. M.: Znanie, 1987. 64 pp. (Novoe v zhizni, nauke, tekhnike. Nauch. ateizm; 1/1987).

3328 Ozhegova, N.I. "Sintez iskusstva v srednevekovom khrame Birmy" [Arts' Synthesis in Burma's Medieval Temple]. *Narody Azii i Afriki* 6 (1988): 109-118.

3329 Paiusov, K.[A]. "Ateisticheskoe vospitanie v voinskom kollektive" [Atheistic Education in Military Collective]. *Kommunist Vooruzh. Sil.* 10 (1988): 25-32.

3330 Paiusov, K.A. *Razum protiv religii* [Reason against Religion]. M.: Voenizdat, 1986. 128 pp. For reviews see items 5206-5207.

3331 Pakarklis, P. *Atheism:* Sochineniia [Atheism: Works]. Vil'nius: Mintis, 1987. 599 pp., port. (Iz naslediia litov. filosofii). In Lithuanian. Bibl. of P. Pakarklis' works: pp. 531-552. Annot. bibl.: pp. 35-39. Index: pp. 553-598.

3332 Pakholik, U. "Voprosy sotsial'noi al'ternativy v entsiklike 'Laborem exercens' 'O chelovecheskom trude' 1981" [Problems of Social Alternative in Encyclical "Laborem Exercens" "On Human Labour" 1981]. *Vopr. nauch. ateizma* 36 (1987): 141-147.

3333 Palov, V.S. "Zapadnogermanskie klerikal'no-konservativnye kontseptsii profsoiuznogo dvizheniia i ikh obshchestvenno-politicheskie korni" [West German Clerical-Conservative Conceptions of Trade-Union Movement and Their Socio-Political Roots]. *Iz istorii politicheskoi bor'by v stranakh Zapadnoi Evropy v noveishee vremia.* Iaroslavl', 1986. Pp. 44-62.

3334 Pal'vanova, O.I. *Osobennosti ateisticheskogo vospitaniia zhenshchin v sovremennykh usloviiakh* [Features of Atheistic Education of Women in

Contemporary Conditions]. Ashkhabad: Ylym, 1988. 136 pp. Annot. bibl.: pp. 124-135.

3335   Pal'vanova, O.[I]. *Rol' trudovogo kollektiva v preodolenii religioznykh perezhitkov sredi zhenshchin* [Role of Labour Collective in Overcoming Religious Survivals among Women]. Ashkhabad: Ylym, 1983. 53 pp. For reviews see items 5208-5209.

3336   Pal'vanova, O.[I].; Khaidov, A. "'Sviatye mesta' - perezhitok proshlogo" ["Holy Places" - Survival of the Past]. *Izv. AN TSSR*. Ser. obshchestv. nauk 4 (1983): 37-41. Summary in English.

3337   "Pamiati Marty Anatol'evny Popovoi" [In Memory of Marta Anatol'evna Popova]. *Vestn. Mosk. un-ta*. Ser. 7. Filosofiia 2 (1981): 87, port.

3338   *Pamiatniki kul'tury i mirovozzrenie:* Ateist. ocherki [Cultural Monuments and World Outlook: Atheistic Essays]. Petrozavodsk: Kareliia, 1985. 159 pp.

3339   Panchenko, D.V. "Mifologicheskoe v platonovskom rasskaze ob Atlantide" [Mythological in Platonic Story on Atlantis]. *Zhizn' mifa v antichnosti* M., 1988. Ch. 1. Pp. 164-172.

3340   Pandre, R.V. *Ateisticheskaia podgotovka budushchego uchitelia* [Atheistic Preparation of the Future Teacher]. M.: Prosveshchenie, 1987. 127 pp.

3341   Pandzhikidze, T.I. *Bibliia - mif i deistvitel'nost'* [The Bible - Myth and Reality]. Tbilisi: Znanie GSSR, 1981. 32 pp. (O-vo "Znanie" GSSR; 29). In Georgian.

3342   Pandzhikidze, T.I. *Bibliia vchera, segodnia...* [The Bible Yesterday, Today...]. Tbilisi: Nakaduli, 1982. 179 pp. In Georgian.

3343   Pandzhikidze, T.I. *Iisus Khristos - legenda i deistvitel'nost'* [Jesus Christ - Legend and Reality]. Tbilisi: Ganatleba, 1987. 79 pp. In Georgian.

3344   Pandzhikidze, T.I. *Khristianstvo - proshloe i sovremennost'* [Christianity - the Past and Contemporaneity]. Tbilisi: Ganatleba, 1984. 219 pp. In Georgian.

3345   Pandzhikidze, T.I. *Po sledam religioznykh verovanii* [Along Footsteps of Religious Beliefs]. Tbilisi: Nakaduli, 1986. 239 pp., illus. In Georgian.

3346 Pandzhikidze, T.I. "Religiia: konets vtorogo tysiacheletiia" [Religion: End of the Second Millennium]. *Kommunist Gruzii* 3 (1983): 84-88.

3347 Pandzhikidze, T.I. *Sushchnost' religii i ateizma* [The Essence of Religion and Atheism]. Tbilisi: Subchota Sakartvelo, 1983. 229 pp. In Georgian.

3348 Panesh, E.Kh. "Nekotorye aspekty khristianizatsii adygov v svete mezhetnicheskikh kontaktov (Doislam. period)." [Some Aspects of Adygei Conversion to Christianity in the Light of Inter Ethnical Contacts (Preislamic Period)]. *III Vsesoiuznaia konferentsiia vostokovedov "Vzaimodeistvie i vzaimovliianie tsivilizatsii kul'tur na Vostoke."* M., 1988. T. 2. Pp. 32-33.

3349 Panich, T.V. "Mirozdanie v predstavlenii knizhnika XVII v." [The Universe in the Conception of XVIIth Century Scribe]. *Nauchnyi ateizm, religiia i sovremennost'.* Novosibirsk, 1987. Pp. 305-321.

3350 Panin, V.M. "Predposylki i osnovnye idei 'politicheskoi teologii' v FRG" [Pre-Requisites and Basic Ideas of "Political Theology" in FRG]. *Aktual'nye problemy ateisticheskogo vospitaniia i kritika religioznoi ideologii.* M., 1981. Pp. 42-49.

3351 Pankova, G.G. "Ideinye istoki 'teologii nadezhdy' Iu. Mol'tmana" [J. Moltmann's Ideological Sources of "Theology of Hope"]. *Dukhovnye tsennosti kak predmet filosofskogo analiza.* M., 1985. Pp. 124-129.

3352 Pankratov, I.Ia. "Razvitie form ustnoi propagandy v sisteme sredstv ateisticheskogo vozdeistviia" [Development of Forms of Oral Propaganda in the System of Means of Atheistic Influence]. *Problemy istorii religii i ateizma.* Cheboksary, 1980. Pp. 112-120.

3353 Pankratova, V.A. *Khristiane Karaly* [Karala Christians]. M.: Nauka, 1982. 174 pp. Summary in English. Bibl.: pp. 151-171.

3354 Panov, I.P.; Panov, M.I. *Nravstvennoe i ateisticheskoe vospitanie trudiashchikhsia* [Moral and Atheistic Education of Workers]. Krasnodar: Kn. izdvo, 1982. 127 pp.

3355 Panova, V.; Vakhtin, Iu. "Zhizn' Mukhammeda" [The Life of Muhammad]. *Nauka i religiia* 11 (1988): 54-58; 12 (1988): 34-38; 1 (1989): 52-55; 5 (1989): 56-59; 6 (1989): 56-61.

3356   Panova, V.S. *'Kolokol' Gertsena i Ogareva ob ateizme, religii i tserkvi* [Herzen and Ogarev's "Kolokol" (The Bell) on Atheism, Religion and Church]. M.: Mysl' 1983. 134 pp. Suppl.: "Kolokol's" Publications and Materials. Bibl.: pp. 119-133. For review see item 5210.

3357   Pantin, I. "Poisk nravstvennykh orientirov: Razdum'ia nad zametkami V. Tendriakhova 'Nravstvennost' i religiia'" [In the Search of Moral Guiding Lines: Thought on V. Tendriakov's Notes   on "Morals and Religion"]. *Nauka i religiia* 9 (1987): 49-50.

3358   Papuashvili, T.T. *Metody i formy nauchno-ateisticheskoi raboty* [Methods and Forms of Scientific-Atheistic Work]. Tbilisi, Znanie GSSR, 1980. 32 pp. (O-vo "Znanie" GSSR; 39). In Georgian.

3359   Parafeinik, N.I. "Povyshenie trudovoi aktivnosti molodezhi - vazhnyi faktor formirovaniia ee ateisticheskoi ubezhdennosti" [The Raising of Youth's Working Activity - Important Factor of Forming Atheistic Conviction]. *Vopr. ateizma* 24 (1988): 53-59.

3360   Paramo, P. "Sekty vyzyvaiut trevogu v Ispanii" [Sects Arouse Alarm in Spain]. *Argumenty.* M., 1988. Pp. 210-217.

3361   Paribok, A.V. "O buddiiskom poniatii 'pervoi ariiskoi lichnosti' v sviazi s simvolikoi vody v buddizme" [On Buddhist Concept of "First Aryan Personality" in Connection with the Symbolism of Water in Buddhism]. *Literatura i kul'tura drevnei i srednevekovoi Indii.* M., 1987. Pp. 150-162.

3362   Parkhomenko, N.T. *Sovetskaia obriadnost' - neot'emlemyi komponent sotsialisticheskogo obraza zhizni* [Soviet Ceremonial - Integral Component of Socialist Way of Life]. Kiev: Znanie UkSSR, 1982. 48 pp. (Ser. 5 "Nauchno-ateisticheskaia" / O-vo "Znanie" UkSSR; No 10). In Ukrainian. Bibl.: pp. 45-47.

3363   Parkhomenko, N.T. "Vliianie sovetskoi obriadnosti na preodolenie religioznosti v sfere semeino-bytovykh otnoshenii" [The Influence of Soviet Ceremonial on Overcoming Religiosity in the Sphere of Domestic-Everyday Relations]. *Vopr. ateizma* 21 (1985): 47-54.

3364   Parnov, E. "Tibetskie tsykly" [Tibetan Cycles]. *Novyi mir* 6 (1981): 198-215.

3365   Parnov, E.I. *Bogi lotosa* [The Gods of Lotus]. M.: Politizdat, 1980. 239 pp., illus. For reviews see items 5211-5214.

3366 Parnov, E.I. *Tron Liutsifera* [Lucifer's Throne]. M.: Politizdat, 1985. 303 pp., illus. For reviews see items 5215-5219.

3367 Pasha-zade, A. "Radi obshchego dela" [For the Sake of Common Cause]. *Kommunist Azerbaidzhana* 10 (1988): 82-87.

3368 Pasha-zade, A. "Otvergaia mech" [Repudiating the Sword]. *Novoe vremia* 49 (1987): 34-35.

3369 Pasha-zade, A.; Aliev, S. "Sataninskaia kniga" [The Satanic Verses]. *Aziia i Africa segodnia* 7 (1989): 12-15.

3370 Pashaeva, L.B. *Pozitivnye i negatiynye elementy v svadebnykh obychaiakh i obriadakh kurdov Gruzii* [Positive and Negative Elements of Marriage Customs and Rites of Georgian Kurds]. Tbilisi: Metsniereba, 1987. 50 pp. (Traditsiia i sovremennost'; No 20). Bibl.: pp. 44-48.

3371 Pashaeva, L.B. "Religiozno-kastovye zaprety v brake kurdov-ezidov Gruzii v proshlom" [Former Religious-Caste Bans in Weddings of Georgian Kurds-Ezids]. *Kavk. etnogr. sb.* Tbilisi, 1988. T. 7. Pp. 115-155. Bibl.: pp. 153-155.

3372 Pashchenko, V.A. "Ateizm kak tsennostnaia orientatsiia lichnosti" [Atheism as Valuable Orientation of the Individual]. *Vopr. ateizma* 17 (1981): 35-42.

3373 Pashchenko, V.A. *Nauchnyi ateizm kak dukhovnaia tsennost'* [Scientific Atheism as a Spiritual Value]. Kiev: Znanie UkSSR, 1983. 16 pp. (B-chka v pomoshch' lektoru "Probl. nauch. ateizma" / O-vo "Znanie" UkSSR). In Ukrainian.

3374 Pashkevich, P. "Arkhitektura pravoslavnykh tserkvei v Varshave v pervoi polovine XIX v." [Architecture of Orthodox Churches in Warsaw early XIXth Century]. *O prosveshchenii i romantizme: Sovetskie i pol'skie issledovaniia.* M., 1989. Pp. 165-179. Bibl.: pp. 176-179.

3375 Pashkov, V.I. "Nauchnyi ateizm v sisteme dukhovnogo mira molodezhi" [Scientific Atheism in the System of Youth's Spiritual World]. *Vopr. ateizma* 23 (1987): 27-33.

3376 Pashkov, V.M. "Protivopolozhnost' nauchnogo i religioznogo podkhodov k otsenke roli ateizma v dukhovnoi zhizni obshchestva i lichnosti" [Contrast Between Scientific and Religious Approaches in the Evaluation of the

Role of Atheism in the Spiritual Life of Society and the Individual]. *Vopr. ateizma* 25 (1989): 92-98.

3377 Pashkov, V.V. "Sovremennoe russkoe pravoslavnoe monashestvo kak forma asketizma" [Contemporary Russian Orthodox Monasticism as a Form of Ascetism]. *Molodezh' i tvorchestvo: sotsial'no-filosofskie problemy.* M., 1988. Ch. 3. Pp. 300-302.

3378 Pastukh, M.S. *Ubezhdennost' ateista:* Aktual. vopr. nauch.-ateist. vospitaniia molodezhi [Atheist's Conviction: Topical Problems of the Scientific-Atheistic Education of Youth]. Kiev: Molod', 1981. 111 pp.

3379 Pater, A. "Obshchee i osobennoe vo vzaimootnosheniiakh mezhdu tserkov'iu i gosudarstvom v sotsialisticheskom obshchestve" [The Common and Especial in Inter Relations Between the Church and the State in Socialist Society]. *Kritika sovremennoi katolicheskoi i protestanskoi teologii.* M., 1989. Pp. 92-103.

3380 Patina, T.V. "Konfessiia i etnos v Kenii" [Confession and Ethnic in Kenya]. *Sov. etnografiia* 5 (1987): 100-111.

3381 Pavliuk, V.V. *Psikhologiia sovremennykh veruiushchikh v usloviiakh sotsialisticheskogo obshchestva* [Psychology of Contemporary Believers in Socialist Society]. M., Znanie, 1980. 20 pp. (V pomoshch' lektoru).

3382 Pavlov, A.V. *Voina. Armiia. Religiia.* [War. Army. Religion]. M.: Voenizdat, 1988. 158 pp. For reviews see items 5222-5223.

3383 Pavlov, A.[V].; Khromov, A. "Tserkov' i problemy sokhraneniia mira" [The Church and Problems of Preservation of Peace]. *Kommunist Sov. Latvii* 6 (1988): 83-89.

3384 Pavlov, S.N. "O sovremennom sostoianii russkoi pravoslavnoi tserkvi" [Present Day Condition of the Russian Orthodox Church]. *Sotsiol. issled.* 4 (1987): 35-43. Bibl.: p. 43. Published also in: *Argumenty.* M., 1988. Pp. 73-90.

3385 Pavlova, O.I. *Amon fivanskii: Ranniaia istoriia kul'ta (V-XVII dinastii)* [Ammon of Thebes: Early History of the Cults (Vth-XVIIth Dynasties)]. M.: Nauka, 1984. 176 pp., illus. Annot. bibl.: pp. 108-148. Index: pp. 169-175.

3386 Pavlova, O.I. "Kul't Amona pri XI dinastii" [Amon's Cult under XIth Dynasty]. *Meroe* 3 (1985): 190-202, tables. Summary in English, p. 272.

3387 Pavlova, T.P. "'Islamskii faktor' v politike SShA (na rubezhe 80-kh godov)" ["Islamic Factor" in USA Politics (On the Eve of 80s)]. *"Islamskii faktor" v mezhdunarodnykh otnosheniiakh v Azii (70-e - pervaia polovina 80-kh gg.)*. M., 1987. Pp. 158-173.

3388 Pavlova, V.A. "Stanovlenie religioznogo mifa v protsesse razvitiia pervobytnogo mifologicheskogo kompleksa" [Formation of Religious Myth in the Process of Development of the Primordial Mythological Complex]. *Kritika religioznoi ideologii i problemy ateisticheskogo vospitaniia*. M., 1982. Pp. 89-96.

3389 Pavlun, Z.N. "Sem'ia kak ob'ekt ateisticheskogo vospitaniia" [Family as Object of Atheistic Education]. *Vopr. ateizma* 24 (1988): 72-79.

3390 Pazilova, V. "Dialog? Poka tol'ko znakomstvo!" [Dialogue? For the Time Being Acquaintance Only!]. *Nauka i religiia* 6 (1988): 30-31.

3391 Pazilova, V. "Mistika? Eto .. mistika" [Mysticism? Is... Mysticism]. *Nauka i religiia* 9 (1987): 8-9.

3392 Pazilova, V. "Vinovato li zerkalo?" [Is Mirror Guilty?]. *Nauka i religiia* 10 (1987): 40-41.

3393 Pchelin, N.G. "Deiatel'nost' missionerov v Kitae vo vtoroi polovine XVII-pervoi polovine XVIII vekov i ee otrazhenie v poslaniiakh frantsuzkikh missionerov kitaiskomu imperatoru Tsian'lunu" [The Activity of Missionaries in China in the Late XVIIth-Early XVIIIth Centuries and Its Reflection in the French Missionaries Messages to the Chinese Emperor Ch'ien Lung]. *Tezisy konferentsii aspirantov i molodykh nauhnykh sotrudnikov*. M., 1987. T. 1. Pp. 40-42.

3394 Pchelin, N.G. "O deiatel'nosti zapadnoevropeiskikh missionerov v Kitae vo vtoroi polovine XVII-1-voi polovine XVIII vv." [Activity of Western European Missionaries in China in Late XVIIth-Early XVIIIth Centuries]. *Deviatnadtsataia nauchnaia konferentsiia "Obshchestvo i gosudarstvo v Kitae"*. M., 1988. Ch. 2. Pp. 130-132.

3395 Pechiura, P.[I]. *Problema prazdnika* [The Problem of Holiday]. Vil'nius: Mintis, 1980. 80 pp. (Malaia ateist. seriia). In Lithuanian.

Published also in:
Kaunas: Shviesa, 1983. 93 pp. In Polish.

3396   Pechnikov, B. "Tevtonskii orden: anakhronizm ili ..?" [Teutonic Order: Anachronism or..?]. *Ateisticheskie chteniia* 17 (1988): 66-82.

3397   Pechnikov, V.D.; Konstantinov, V.N. "O vliianii nauchno-ateisticheskikh vzgliadov na sotsial'nuiu aktivnost' lichnosti" [Influence of Scientific-Atheistic Views on Individual's Social Activity]. *Filosofskie sotsiologicheskie problemy formirovaniia sotsial'noi aktivnosti lichnosti.* Vladimir, 1989. P. 146-154.

3398   Pekhota, G.I. "Kritika pravoslavno-bogoslovskikh predstavlenii o zhenshchine v proshlom i nastoiashchem" [Criticism of Orthodox- Theological Notions About Women in the Past and Present]. *Vopr. ateizma* 22 (1986): 78-85.

3399   Perelomov, L.S. "Rol' ucheniia Konfutsiia v stroitel'stve sotsializma s kitaiskoi spetsifikoi" [The Role of Confucius Teachings in the Building of Socialism with Chinese Specifics]. *III Vsesoiuznaia konferentsiia vostokovedov "Vzaimodeistvie i vzaimovliianie tsivilizatsii kul'tur na Vostoke".* M., 1988. T. 2. Pp. 148-149.

3400   Perelomov, L.S. "Simvol kitaiskoi natsii" [The Symbol of the Chinese Nation]. *Probl. Dal. Vostoka* 5 (1988): 87-97.

3401   Perelomov, L.S.; Abaev, N.V. "Buddizm v Kitae: istoricheskie traditsii i sovremennost'" [Buddhism in China: Historical Traditions and Contemporaneity]. *Probl. Dal'nego Vostoka* 3 (1980): 136-148.

3402   "Pereosmyslenie: za i protiv" [Reinterpretation: For and Against]. N.S. Gordienko; Y.M. Kobrin. *Nauka i religiia* 8 (1989): 5-9.

3403   *Perestroika i preodolenie religioznykh predrasudkov* [Perestroika and Overcoming of Religious Prejudices]. [G.R. Baldanova, et al.]. Kazan': Tatar. kn. izd-vo, 1988. 160 pp. Annot. bibl.: pp. 156-159.

3404   Peresun'ko, Iu. "Optina pustyn'" [Optin Pustyn Monastery]. *Otchizna* 10 (1989): 35-41.

3405   Peresun'ko, Iu.F. *Otvesti bedu!* [To Deflect Misfortune!]. M.: Mosk. rebochii, 1981. 80 pp.

3406 Pereverzev, V.E. "Ateisticheskaia rabota po mestu zhitel'stva" [Atheistic Work by Residence]. *Vopr. ateizma* 23 (1987): 39-43.

3407 Pereverzev, V.E. "Ateisticheskoe vospitanie rabochei molodezhi" [Atheistic Education of Working Youth]. *Vopr. ateizma* 19 (1983): 73-79.

3408 Pereverzev, V.E. *Metodika provedeniia vecherov-vstrech veruiushchikh i neveruiushchikh* [Methods of Conducting Evening-Meetings of Believers and Unbelievers]. Kiev: Znanie UkSSR, 1984. 16 pp. (V pomoshch' lektoru / O-vo "Znanie" UkSSR. Metodika lekts. propagandy i opyt metod. raboty). Bibl.: p. 16.

3409 Perfilova, T.B. "O kontaktakh Britanii s vostochnymi narodami Rimskoi imperii v oblasti religii" [British Contacts in the Realm of Religion with Oriental Peoples of the Roman Empire]. *Antichnaia grazhdanskaia obshchina.* M., 1986. Pp. 111-127.

3410 Perova, L. "'Ty dolzhen imet' strakh...'" ["You must Bear Fear"]. *Nauka i religiia* 8 (1981): 24-26.

3411 Pershin, S. "Pochemu tserkov' pokhozha na tserkov'" [Why Church is alike Church]. *Nauka i religiia* 3 (1985): 20-22.

3412 "Pervye itogi" [First Results]. *Nauka i religiia* 9 (1985): 2-4.

3413 Peskov, V.M. *Taezhnyi tupik* [Taiga Impass]. M.: Pravda, 1983. 48 pp. (B-ka "Koms. pravdy").

3414 Petliakov, P.A. *Kto i pochemu dobivalsia unii?* [Who and Why Was Striving for Uniate Church?]. Kiev: Znanie UkSSR, 1989. 16 p. (Ser. 5, Nauch. -ateist. / O-vo "Znanie" UkSSR; No 10). In Ukrainian.

3415 Petliakov, P.A. *Pravda ob avtokefalii* [Truth About Autocephalous]. [Transl. from Ukrainian]. Kiev: Politizdat Ukrainy, 1988. 68 pp. In English.

3416 Petliakov, P.A. *Uniatskaia tserkov' - orudie antikommunizma i antisovetizma* [Uniate Church - Tool of Anti Communism and Anti-Sovietism]. L'vov: Vishcha shk. Izd-vo pri L'vov. un-te, 1982. 168 pp.

3417 Petliakov, P.A.; Boldizhar, M.N. *'Dal'neishaia deiatel'nost' prekrashchaetsia...'* ["Further Activity is Discontinued..."]. L'vov: Kameniar, 1987. 131 pp. In Ukrainian.

3418 Petrash, Iu.G. *Nesviashchennaia 'sviatost"* [Unholy "Holiness"]. Tashkent: Uzbekistan, 1988. 70 pp. (Priroda, obshchestvo, chelovek).

3419 Petrash, Iu.[G]. "Perezhitki islama i ikh preodolenie" [Islam's Survivals and Their Overcoming]. *Kommunist Kirgizstana* 6 (1988): 61-66.

3420 Petrash, Iu.G. *Teni srednevekov'ia* [Shadows of the Middle Ages]. Alma-Ata: Kazakhstan, 1981. 150 pp., illus.

3421 *Petrashevtsy ob ateizme, religii i tserkvi* [Petrashevts on Atheism, Religion and Church]. [Comp.: F.G. Nikitina]. M.: Mysl', 1986. 269 pp. (Nauch.-ateist. b-ka). Annot. bibl.: pp. 233-257. Name index: pp. 258-267.

3422 Petrishchev, P.V. "K voprosu o roli pravoslavnoi tserkvi v obshchestvenno-politicheskoi zhizni Rossii: problemy marksistskogo analiza" [Problem of the Role of the Orthodox Church in the Socio-Political Life of Russia: Problems of Marxist Analysis]. *Voprosy teorii i praktiki nauchnogo ateizma.* M., 1988. Pp. 138-163.

3423 Petrov, N.N. "Kritika eticheskoi apologii 'bytiia boga', religii i tserkvi" [Criticism of Ethical Apologia of "God's Existence", Religion and Church]. *Problemy formirovaniia nauchno-ateisticheskogo mirovozzreniia v sotsialisticheskom obshchestve.* Samarkand, 198. Pp. 16-33.

3424 Petrov, S.B. "Vnereligioznye reguliativy khramostroitel'stva na Rusi" [Non-Religious Regulations for Temple Building in Rus']. *Molodezh' i tvorchestvo: sotsial'no-filosofskie problemy.* M., 1988. Ch. 3. Pp. 303-304.

3425 Petrova, A.V. "Istoki dzena i propoved' eskapizma" [Zen Sources and Sermon of Escapism]. *Problema cheloveka v sovremennoi religioznoi i misticheskoi literature.* M., 1988. Pp. 159-170.

3426 Petrovich, N.G. "Nesostoiatel'nost' illiuzornogo optimizma khristianskogo mirovozzreniia" [Groundlessness of Illusory Optimism of the Christian World Outlook]. *Aktual'nye problemy ateisticheskogo vospitaniia i kritika religioznoi ideologii.* M., 1981. Pp. 57-62.

3427 Petrukhanova, E.N. "Al-Khusein b. Mansur al-Khalladzh - vidnyi ideolog panteisticheskogo sufizma" [Al-Husein b. Mansur al- Hallaj - Prominent Ideologist of Pantheistic Sufism]. *Istoriia i traditsionnaia kul'tura narodov Vostoka.* M., 1989. Ch. 2. Pp. 30-42. Bibl.: pp. 39-42.

3428 Petrukhanova, E.N. "Sufiiskaia teoriia al-Khalladzha" [Al-Hallaj's Sufist Theory]. *V Vsesoiuznaia shkola molodykh vostokovedov.* M., 1989. T. 1. Pp. 64-65.

3429 Petrukhin, G. "Obratimsia k pervoistochniku: Razmyshleniia pisatelia-istorika, povodom dlia kotorykh iavilos' 1000-letie priniatiia khristianstva na Rusi" [Turning to Primary Sources: Reflections of a Writer-Historian on Occasion of 1000th Anniversary of the Adoption of Christianity in Rus']. *Kommunist Kirgizstana* 6 (1988): 92-96.

3430 Petrushenko, V.L.; Shcherbakov, G.N. *Vera v dukhovnom mire lichnosti* [Faith in the Spiritual World of the Individual]. L'vov: Vyshcha shk. Izd-vo pri L'vov. un-te, 1989. 96 pp. (Ateist. b-ka studenta). Bibl.: pp. 94-95.

3431 Petrushov, V.N. "O poniatii 'nauchnyi ateizm'" [Concept of "Scientific Atheism"]. *Voprosy filosofii i sotsiologii.* L., 1980. Pp. 87-91.

3432 *15-i vek Khidzhry dolzhen stat' vekom mira i druzhby mezhdu narodami* [15th Century of Hijri Should Be a Century of Peace and Friendship among Nations]. M.: Progress, 1982. 213 pp. In English. Published also in: Arabic and French.

3433 Pichikian, I.[R]. "Greko-baktriiskie altari khrama Oksa" [Greek-Bactrian Altars of the Temple of Oks]. *Inform. biull. / Mezhdunar. assots. po izucheniiu kul'tur Tsentr. Azii.* 12 (1987): 65-75.

3434 Pichikian, I.R.; Shelov-Kovediaev, F.V. "Grecheskie bozhestva v elli-nisticheskoi epigrafike i izobrazitel'nom iskusstve zapadnogo i vos-tochogo Irana" [Greek Deities in Hellenistic Epigraphy and Fine Arts of Western and Eastern Iran]. *Tretii Vsesoiuznyi simpozium po problemam ellinisticheskoi kul'tury na Vostoke, mai 1988 g.* Erevan, 1988. Pp. 68-70.

3435 Pikhoia, R.G. "Zametki na poliakh Ostrozhskoi Biblii iz sobraniia Ural'skogo universiteta - novyi istochnik po istorii obshchestvenno-politicheskoi mysli kontsa XVI v." [Marginal Notes of the Ostorozh Bible from the Collection of Urals University - New Historical Source of Socio-Political Thought of the Late XVIth Cenury]. *Obshchestvenno-politicheskaia mysl' dorevoliutsionnogo Urala.* Sverdlovsk, 1983. Pp. 20-27.

3436 Pikov, G.G. "Buddizm v gosudarstve kidanei" [Buddhism in the State of Kydan]. *Izv. Sib. otd-niia AN SSSR.* Ser. obshchestv. nauk 1 (1980): 149-155.

3437 Pimen, Patriarkh Moskovskii i vseia Rusi. "Programma miloserdiia" [The Programme of Mercy]. *Novoe vremia* 11 (1989): 22-23.

3438 Pimen (patriarkh Moskovskii i vseia Rusi). *Proizoshedshee 1000 let nazad kreshchenie Rusi vo mnogom opredelilo puti razvitiia narodov nashei strany* [Baptism of Rus' 1000 Years Ago, in many Respects Determined the Course of Development of the Peoples of Our Country]. M.: Novosti, [1988]. 32 pp., illus. (Avtoritet. mnenie). In English. Published also in: French and Spanish.

3439 Pimenov, A.V. "Iz istorii polemiki mimansy s buddiiskimi shkolami" [History of Mimana Polemics with Buddhist Schools]. *Buddizm. Istoriia i kul'tura.* M., 1989. Pp. 58-73.

3440 Piotrovskaia, I.L. "Koran o likhve-riba" [Koran on Lihve-Riba]. *Pis'mennye pamiatniki i problemy istorii kul'tury narodov Vostoka.* M., 1987. Ch. 1. Pp. 131-138.

3441 Piotrovskii, M.B. *Araviiskie korni Islama* [Arabian Roots of Islam]. M.: Nauka, 1986. 12 pp. In English. Published also in: *Narody Azii i Afriki* 2 (1987): 97-101.

3442 Piotrovskii, M.B. "Istoricheskie sud'by musul'manskogo predstavleniia o vlasti" [Historical Fates of the Moslem Notion of Power]. *Sotsial'no-politicheskie predstavleniia v islame: Istoriia i sovremennost'.* M., 1987. Pp. 6-20. Annot. bibl.: p. 18-20.

3443 Piotrovskii, M.B. "K voprosu o metodologii izucheniia islama" [Methodological Problem of the Study of Islam]. *Pis'mennye pamiatniki i problemy istorii kul'tury narodov Vostoka: XVI godich. nauch. sessiia LO IV AN SSSR.* M., 1982. Ch. 2. Pp. 123-129.

3444 Piotrovskii, M.B. "Kaili, abna', kaba'il' (iuzhnoaraviiskie verkhi VII v. i islam)" [Kayli, abna', kabail' (South Arabian Upper Crusts of the VIIth Century and Islam]. *Arabskie strany: Istoriia i sovremennost' (sotsial., ekon. i polit. probl.).* M., 1981. Pp. 221-226.

3445 Piotrovskii, M.B. "Mukhammed, proroki, lzheproroki, kahiny" [Muhammad, Prophets, False Prophets, Kahins]. *Islam v istorii narodov Vostoka.* M., 1981. Pp. 9-18. Annot. bibl.: pp. 16-18.

3446 Piotrovskii, M.B. "Prorocheskoe dvizhenie v Aravii VII v." [Prophetical Movement in Arabia in the VIIth Century]. *Islam: Religiia, obshchestvo, gosudarstvo.* M., 1984. Pp. 19-27. Annot. bibl.: pp. 25-27.

3447 Piotrovskii, M.B. "Skazaniia v Korane i v Biblii: preemstvennost' i razlichie" [Tales in Koran and in the Bible: Continuity and Difference]. *III Vsesoiuznaia konferentsiia vostokovedov "Vzaimodeistvie i vzaimovliianie tsivilizatsii kul'tur na Vostoke".* M., 1988. T. 1. Pp. 111-112.

3448 Piotrovskii, M.B. "Svetskoe i dukhovnoe v teorii i praktike srednevekovogo islama" [Laic and Spiritual in the Theory and Practice of Medieval Islam]. *Islam: Religiia, obshchestvo, gosudarstvo.* M., 1984. Pp. 175-188. Annot. bibl.: pp. 187-188.

3449 Pippert, U. "Vozvrat k religii" [Return to Religion]. *Amerika.* Vashington, 1989. No 394. Pp. 2-3, 31-33.

3450 Pisarchik, A.K. "O perezhitkakh kul'ta ivy u tadzhikov" [Survivals of the Cult of Willow by Tajiks]. *Proshloe Srednei Azii.* Dushanbe, 1987. Pp. 251-260.

3451 Pisarev, D.I. *D.I. Pisarev ob ateizme, religii i tserkvi* [D.I. Pisarev on Atheism, Religion and Church]. Comp.: E.I. Rozenberg. M.: Mysl', 1984. 416 pp., port. (Nauch.-ateist. b-ka). Annot. bibl.: pp. 376-400.

3452 Pismanik, M.G. *Dialog o vere* [Dialogue About Faith]. Perm': Kn. izd-vo, 1989. 222 pp., illus. Annot. bibl.: p. 221.

3453 Pismanik, M.G. "Etika ateisticheskogo vopitaniia" [Ethics of Atheistic Education]. *Vopr. nauch. ateizma* 35 (1986): 196-212.

3454 Pismanik, M.G. *Individual'naia religioznost' i ee preodolenie* [Individual Religiosity and Its Overcoming]. M.: Mysl', 1984. 205 pp. Annot. bibl.: pp. 182-204. For review see item 5225.

3455 Pismanik, M.G. *Kompleksnyi podkhod v individual'noi rabote s veruiushchimi* [Complex Approach in Individual Work with Believers]. M.: Znanie, 1981. 64 p. (Novoe v zhizni, nauke, tekhnike. Ser. "Nauch.-ateizm"; No 5).

3456 Pismanik, M.[G]. "Veruiushchii glazami sotsiologa" [Believer Through the Eyes of a Sociologist]. *Nauka i religiia* 7 (1987): 15.

3457 Pitirim, mitropolit Volokolamskii i Iur'evskii. "Opyt narodnogo dukha" [Experience of People's Spirit]. *Nashe nasledie* 4 (1988): 8-14.

3458 Pitirim, mitropolit Volokolamskii i Iur'evskii. "Ukloniat'sia ot otvetstvennosti Tserkov' ne mozhet" [The Church Can not Avoid Responsibility]. *Energiia: ekonomika, tekhnika, ekologiia* 6 (1989): 8-10.

3459 Pitsil', O.S. *Formirovanie ateisticheskogo obshchestvennogo mneniia na sele* [Forming Atheistic Public Opinion in the Village]. Kiev: Znanie UkSSR, 1981. 47 pp. (Ser. 5 "Nauchno-ateisticheskaia" / O-vo "Znanie" UkSSR; No 2). In Ukrainian. Bibl.: pp. 45-46.

3460 Pitsil', O.S. "Rol' trudovogo sel'skokhoziaistvennogo kollektiva v formirovanii ateisticheskogo obshchestvennogo mneniia mikrosredy" [The Role of Working Agricultural Collective in Forming Atheistic Public Opinion in Microenvironment]. *Vopr. ateizma* 17 (1981): 86-91.

3461 Piurveev, D.B. "Kul'tovoe zodchestvo kalmykov v XVII-XIX vv." [Religious Architecture of Kalmyks in XVIIth-XIX Centuries]. *Voprosy istorii lamaizma v Kalmykii.* Elista, 1987. Pp. 24-39.

3462 Pivovarov, D.V. "Irratsional'noe, sverkh'estestvennoe i predmet filosofskogo ateizma" [Irrational, Supernatural and the Subject of Philosophic Atheism]. *Otnoshenie cheloveka k irratsional'nomu.* Sverdlovsk, 1989. Pp. 9-38.

3463 Pivovarov, Iu.S. "Katolicheskaia i protestantskaia etika v sovremennom prave" [Catholic and Protestant Ethics in Contemporary Law]. *Problemy pravovoi i politicheskoi ideologii.* M., 1989. Pp. 155-181.

3464 Pivovarov, Iu.S. "O. fon Nell'-Broining kak teoretik 'sotsial'nogo katolitsizma'" [O. von Nell-Breuning as Theorist of "Social Catholicism']. *Istoriia politicheskoi mysli i sovremennost'.* M., 1988. Pp. 133-141.

3465 Pivovarov, Iu.S. "Tserkov' i gosudarstvo v istorii dorevoliutsionnoi Rossii" [Church and State in the History of Pre Revolutionary Russia]. *Istoriko-pravovye voprosy vzaimootnoshenii gosudarstva i tserkvi v istorii Rossii.* M., 1988. Pp. 120-144.

3466 Pkhidenko, S.S. *Ateizm i sotsial'naia aktivnost' lichnosti* [Atheism and Social Activity of the Individual]. Kiev: Znanie UkSSR, 1987. 47 pp. (Ser. 5, Nauch.-ateist. / O-vo "Znanie" UkSSR; No 6). In Ukrainian. Bibl.: p. 46.

3467 Plaksin, R.Iu. *Tikhonovshchina i ee krakh: Pozitsiia pravoslav. tserkvi v period Velikoi Okt. revoliutsii i grazhd. voiny* [The Movement of Tikhon Adherents and Its Failure: Position of Orthodox Church in the Period of the Great October Socialist Revolution and the Civil War]. [2nd revised and enlarged ed.]. L.: Lenizdat, 1987. 208 pp. Title of the 1st ed. *Krakh tserkovnoi kontrrevoliutsii, 1917-1923.* [Failure of Church Counterrevolution, 1917-1923].

3468 Platonov, K.K. *Chelovek i religiia* [Man and Religion]. Minsk: Nar. asveta, 1984. 143 pp., illus.

3469 Platonov, R.P. *Lozh' burzhuazno-klerikal'noi propagandy* [Lie of the Bourgeois Clerical Propaganda]. Minsk: Belarus', 1983. 64 pp. Bibl.: pp. 61-63. Annot. bibl.: pp. 59-60.

3470 Platonov, R.P. "Organizatsiia propagandy nauchnogo ateizma i povyshenie ee effektivnosti na osnove kompleksnogo podkhoda" [Organization of Propaganda of Scientific Atheism and Increasing Its Effectiveness on the Basis of Complex Approach]. *Vopr. nauch. ateizma* 25 (1980): 5-20.

3471 Platonov, R.P. *Propaganda ateizma:* Org., soderzh., rezul'taty [Propaganda of Atheism: Organization, Content, Results]. M.: Politizdat, 1985. 160 pp. For reviews see items 5226-5228.

3472 Platonov, R.[P].; Lensu, M. "Perestroika ateisticheskoi raboty - aktual'naia zadacha" [Perestroika of Atheistic Work - Actual Problem]. *Kommunist Belorussii* 2 (1982): 35-43.

3473 Platonov, V.G. "K istorii khudozhestvennykh traditsii staroobradchestva v Karelii" [History of Art Traditions of Old Belief in Karelia]. *Pravoslavie v Karelii.* Petrozavodsk, 1987. Pp. 97-101.

3474 Plekhanov G.V. *Ob ateizme i religii v istorii obshchestva i kul'tury:* Izbr. proizvedeniia [On Atheism and Religion in the History of Society and Culture: Selected Works]. Kiev: Politizdat Ukrainy, 1981. 327 pp. In Ukrainian.

3475 Pleshakov, A.R. "Ateisticheskoe vospitanie i formirovanie aktivnoi zhiznennoi pozitsii lichnosti" [Atheistic Education and Formation of Active Vital Position of Individual]. *Vopr. nauch. ateizma* 29 (1982): 111-125.

3476 Pleshkova, S.L. "Erazm Rotterdamskii i Lefevr d'Etapl'" [Erasmus of Rotterdam and Lefèbvre d'Étaples]. *Erazm Rotterdamskii i ego vremia.* M., 1989. Pp. 149-153.

3477 Pliguzov, A.I. "O razmerakh tserkovnogo zemlevladeniia v Rossii XVI veka" [Dimensions of Church Land-Ownership in XVIth Century Russia]. *Istoriia SSSR* 2 (1988): 157-163.

3478 Pliguzov, A.I.; Khoroshkevich, A.L. "Otnoshenie russkoi tserkvi v antior-dynskoi bor'be v XIII-XV vekakh" [Attitude of Russian Church in Anti-Horde Struggle in XIIIth-XVth Centuries]. *Vopr. nauch. ateizma* 37 (1988): 117-130.

3479 Plokhii, S.N. "Kongregatsiia propagandy very i uniatskie missionery na iugoslavskikh zemliakh vo vtoroi chetverti XVII v." [Congregation of Propaganda of Faith and Uniate Missionaries on Yugoslav Lands in Middle of XVIIth Century]. *Slaviane i ikh sosedi. Mezhdunarodnye otnosheniia v epokhu feodalizma.* M., 1989. Pp. 50-52.

3480 Plokhii, S.N. *Papstvo i Ukraina:* Politika rimskoi kurii na ukr. zemliakh v XVI-XVII vv. [Papacy and Ukraine: Politics of Roman Curia on Ukrainian Lands in XVIth-XVIIth Centuries]. Kiev: Vyshcha shk., 1989. 223 pp. Bibl.: pp. 207-218. Name index: pp. 219-221.

3481 Plokhii, S.N. "Vatikano-pol'skie otnosheniia 1648-1654 gg." [Vatican-Polish Relations, 1648-1654]. *Vopr. novoi i noveishei istorii* 33 (1987): 116-121.

3482 Plugin, V. "Andrei Rublev i Ivan Groznyi" [Andrei Rublev and Ivan the Terrible]. *Nauka i religiia* 7 (1989): 55-58.

3483 "Po sledam kel'tskikh bogov" [In the Footsteps of Celtic Gods]. *Ateisticheskie chteniia.* M., 1988. Pp. 195-203.

3484 Pochinskaia, I.V. "Osveshchenie nachal'nykh etapov staroobriadcheskogo knigopechataniia v istoriografii" [Illuminating in Historiography the First Stages of Old Belief Bookprinting]. *Istoriografiia obshchestvennoi mysli dorevoliutsionnogo Urala.* Sverdlovsk, 1988. Pp. 51-55.

3485 *Po tu storonu dobra i zla? Moral' i religiia v mire i v Latvii* [On the Other Side of Good and Evil? Morals and Religion in the World and in Latvia]. [Comp.: E. Freiberg]. Riga: Avots, 1989. 278 pp. In Latvian.

3486 Pochta, Iu.M. *Islam: istoki i sovremennost'* [Islam: Sources and Contemporaneity]. M.: Izd-vo Un-ta druzhby narodov, 1988. 85 pp.

3487 Pochta, Iu.M. "Islam i gosudarstvo" [Islam and State]. *Filosofskaia i obshchestvennaia mysl' stran Azii i Afriki.* M., 1981. Pp. 135-141.

3488 Pochta, Iu.M. *Islam i obshchestvo* [Islam and Society]. M.: Un-t druzhby narodov im. P. Lumumby, 1981. 14 pp. Bibl.: pp. 13-14.

3489 Pochta, Iu.M. *Sotsial'no-ekonomicheskie predposylki genezisa islama* [Socio-Economical Pre-Conditions of Islam's Genesis]. M.: Un-t druzhby narodov im. P. Lumumby, 1981. 36 pp. Bibl.: pp. 35-36.

3490 *Pod pokrovom kostela* [Under the Shroud of the Roman Catholic Church]. [Comp.: K. Strumskis]. Vil'nius: Mintis, 1983. 228 pp. In Lithuanian.

3491 *Pod predlogom religii* [On the Pretext of Religion]. [Ed.: I. Sakalauskas et al]. Vil'nius: Mintis, 1983. 167 pp. In Lithuanian.

3492 Podberezskii, I.V. "Indigenizatsiia katolitsizma na Filippinakh [Indigenization of Catholicism in the Philippines].* *Narody Azii i Afriki* (1986): 34-43. Summary in English, p. 219.

3493 Podberezskii, I.V. *Katolicheskaia tserkov' na Filippinakh* [Catholic Church in the Philippines]. M.: Nauka, 1988. 288 pp. Summary in English. Bibl.: pp. 280-283. Index: pp. 284-285.

3494 Podberezskii, I.V. "Kontekstualizatsiia katolitsizma na Filippinakh" [Contextualization of Catholicism in the Philippines].* *Narody Azii i Afriki* 6 (1987): 55-63. Summary in English, p. 215.

3495 *Podkhod tvorcheskii: slagaemye vysokoi effektivnosti ateisticheskogo vospitaniia* [Creative Approach: High Effective Components of Atheistic Education]. Comp.: E.S. Bystrov. L.: Lenizdat, 1986. 69 pp.

3496 Podlipa, Sh. "Burzhuazno-liberal'naia traktovka svobody sovesti" [Bourgeois-Liberal Interpretation of Freedom of Conscience]. *Vopr. nauch. ateizma* 36 (1987): 148-161.

3497 Podmazov, A.A. "Baptizm i adventizm v Latvii: krizisnye iavleniia i ikh prichiny" [Baptism and Adventism in Latvia: Crisis Occurrences and Their Causes]. *Protestantskie organizatsii v SSSR.* M., 1989. Pp. 106-111.

3498 Podmazov, A.A. *Sovremennaia religioznost': osobennosti, dinamika, krizisnye iavleniia* [Contemporary Religiosity: Features, Dynamics, Crisis Occurences]. Riga: Zinatne, 1985. 162 pp.

3499 Podmazov, A.A. "Spetsifika proiavleniia krizisa religii v razlichnykh konfessiiakh v Latvii" [Specifics of Manifestation of Crisis of Religion in Different Denominations in Latvia]. *Vopr. nauch. ateizma* 36 (1987): 233-249.

3500 Podoliak, V.A. "Missionerskaia propoved' v protestanskikh obshchinakh" [Missionary Sermons in Protestant Communities]. *Protestantskie organizatsii v SSSR.* M., 1989. Pp. 138-143.

3501 Podoliak, V.A. "Uchet spetsifiki sovremennoi religioznoi obriadnosti pri provedenii ateisticheskoi raboty" [Reckoning Specifics of Contemporary Religious Rituals when Conducting Atheistic Work]. *Vopr. ateima* 21 (1985): 85-91.

3502 Podoprigora, A.R. *Mirazhi 'potustoronnego' mira* [Mirages of "The Other" World]. Alma-Ata: Kazakhstan, 1984. 59 pp., illus. (Uchenye beseduiut s veruiushchimi).

3503 Podoprigora, A.R. *Paskha* [Easter]. Alma-Ata: Znanie KazSSR, 1980. 15 pp.

3504 Podoroga, V.A. "Problema 'kosvennogo' obshcheniia" [Problem of "Indirect" Contact]. *Dialektika obshcheniia: Gnoseol. i mirovozzrench. probl.* M., 1987. Pp. 78-110.

3505 Pokrovskii, N.[N]. "Ot 'Maiskogo tsvetka' k 'seilemskim ved'mam'" [From "May Flower" to "Salem Witches"]. *Nauka i religiia* 10 (1989): 23-26.

3506 Pokrovskii, N.N. *Chetvert' veka polevykh issledovanii staroobriadchestva vostoka Rossii. Obshchestvennoe soznanie, dukhovnaia kul'tura* [Quarter of a Century of Field Researches of Old Belief in Eastern Russia. Public Consciousness, Spiritual Culture]. Novosibirsk: [S.n.], 1988. 10 pp. In English.

3507 Poliakov, A.A. "Tserkov' i politika v period krizisa voennogo rezhima v Brazilii" [Church and Politics in the Period of Crisis of Military Regime in Brazil]. *Vopr. nauch. ateizma* 36 (1987): 96-109.

3508 Poliakova, E.A. "Some problems of Sufi studies"* *Islamic culture.* Hyderabad, 1987. Vol. 61. No 3. Pp. 73-89.

3509 Poliakova, E.Iu. "Severoirlandskii konflikt: religiia i politika" [North Ireland Conflict: Religion and Politics]. *Religii mira.* M., 1989. Pp. 35-52.

3510 Poliakova, M.V. "Vliianie kul'turnogo progressa na religiiu" [Influence of Cultural Progress on Religion]. *Chelovek i sotsial'nyi progress.* Izhevsk, 1982. Pp. 165-167.

3511 Poliakovskaia, M.A. "Zhizn' i smert' v ponimanii Dimitriia Kidonisa" [Life and Death in Dmitri Kidonis' Interpretation]. *Antichnaia i srednevekovaia ideologiia.* Sverdlovsk, 1984. Pp. 109-119.

3512 Polianovskii, G.P. *Kak vesti individual'nuiu rabotu s veruiushchimi* [How to Conduct Individual Work with Believers]. Tashkent: Uzbekistan, 1986. 30 pp. (B-chka ateista).

3513 Poliantsev, I.N. "Formirovanie ateisticheskoi ubezhdennosti u studencheskoi molodezhi" [Forming of the Atheistic Conviction of Students]. *Ideologi-cheskaia rabota partiinykh organizatsii Povolzh'ia.* Saratov, 1984. Pp. 117-121.

3514 Polishchiuk, Iu.D. *Intellektual'noe i emotsional'noe v ateisticheskom vospitanii* [Intellectual and Emotional in Atheistic Education]. Kiev: Znanie, 1980. 48 pp. (Ser. 5 "Nauchno-ateisticheskaia" / O-vo "Znanie" UkSSR; No 3). In Ukrainian. Bibl.: p. 48.

3515 Pollyeva, D.R. "Pravovye garantii svobody sovesti v SSSR i ateisticheskoe vospitanie molodezhi" [Legal Guarantees of Freedom of Conscience in USSR and Atheistic Upbringing of Youth]. *Aktual'nye problemy nauchno-ateistichskogo vospitaniia molodezhi.* M., 1987. Pp 190-195.

3516 Polonskaia, L.R. "Islam v istoricheskikh sud'bakh Pakistana" [Islam in Historical Fates of Pakistan]. *Vopr. istorii* 1 (1988): 88-99.

3517 Polonskaia, L.[R]. "Musul'manskie ideinye techeniia i kontseptsii" [Moslem Ideological Movements and Conceptions]. *Nauka i religiia* 6 (1983): 57-61.

3518   Polonskaia, L.R. "Religiia i ee vliianie na ideino-pliticheskuiu bor'bu v razvivaiushchikhsia stranakh Azii i Afriki" [Religion and Its Influence on Ideological-Political Struggle in Developing Countries of Asia and Africa]. *Natsional'no-osvoboditel'noe dvizhenie i ideologicheskaia bor'ba.* M., 1987. Pp. 148-181.

3519   Polonskaia, L.R. *Religiia v politicheskoi zhizni razvivaiushchikhsia stran Azii i Afriki* [Religion in Political Life of Developing Countries in Asia and Africa]. M.: Nauka, 1982. 9 pp. Published also in English.

3520   Polonskaia, L.R. "Sovremennye musul'manskie ideinye techeniia" [Contemporary Moslem Ideological Movements]. *Islam: problemy ideologii, prava, politiki i ekonomiki.* M., 1985. Pp. 6-25. Bibl.: pp. 24-25.

3521   Polonskaia, L.R. "Vtoraia mezhdunarodnaia konferentsiia po metodologii istorii religii" [The Second International Conference on Methodology of History of Religion]. *Religii mira: Istoriia i sovremennost'.* Ezhegodnik. 1982. M., 1982. Pp. 249-251.

3522   Polonskaia, L.[R].; Ionova, A.[I]. "Kontseptsiia 'islamskoi ekonomiki': Sots. sushchnost' i polit. napravlennost'" [The Conception of "Islamic Economics": Social Essence and Political Trend]. *Mirovaia ekonomika i mezhdunar. otnosheniia* 3 (1981): 113-119.

3523   Polonskaia, L.R.; Ionova, A.I. *Nekotorye voprosy aktivizatsii mezhdunarodnogo musul'manskogo dvizheniia* [Some Problems of Activization of Moslem International Movement]. M.: Znanie, 1980. 22 pp.

3524   Polonskaia, L.R., et al. *Islam na sovremennom Vostoke: problemy politiki, ideologii* [Islam in the Contemporary Orient: Problems of Politics, Ideology]. M.: [S.n.], 1980. 45 pp. (V pomoshch' leektoru / O-vo "Znanie" RSFSR, Nauch.-metod. sovet po propagande vnesh. politiki SSSR i mezhdunar. otnoshenii). Index of Moslem terms: pp. 41-43.

3525   Poltavcenko, T.M. *Kak voznikli khristianskie prazdniki* [How Christian Feasts Began]. Kishinev: Kartia Moldoveniaske, 1980. 76 pp. (Nauka i religiia). In Moldavian. Published also as an enlarged ed. in 1987, 102 pp., (Besedy s veruiushchimi).

3526 Polubichenko, L.V.; Kuznetsova, E.V. "Topologiia bibleizmov kak chast' angliiskoi literaturnoi traditsii" [Topology of Bibleism as a Part of English Literary Tradition]. *Vestn. Mosk. un-ta.* Ser. 9, Filologia 6 (1987): 20-26.

3527 Pomerants, G. "Paradoksy dzen" [Zen Paradoxes]. *Nauka i religiia* 5 (1989): 38-41.

3528 Ponomareva, L.V. *Ispanskii katolitsizm XX veka* [Spanish Catholicism of the XXth Century]. M.: Nauka, 1989. 285 pp., illus. Bibl.: pp. 278-284.

3529 Poor, I. "Dialektika sotrudnichestva" [Dialectics of Cooperation]. *Nauka i religiia* 11 (1982): 52-55.

3530 Popov, A.S. "K analizu sotsial'nogo znacheniia religii i ateizma" [Analysis of the Social Meaning of Religion and Atheism]. *Filos. nauki* 2 (1989): 11-17.

3531 Popov, A.S. "Kritika religioznogo podkhoda k voprosam kachestva zhizni" [Criticism of the Religious Approach to the Problems of Life's Quality]. *Dukhovnyi mir sovremennogo cheloveka.* M., 1987. Pp. 131-133.

3532 Popov, A.S. "Kritika religioznykh fal'sifikatsii aktual'nykh obshchestvennykh problem" [Criticism of Religious Falsifications of Contemporary Social Problems]. *Dukhovnye tsennosti kak predmet filosofskogo analiza.* M., 1985. Pp. 90-93.

3533 Popov, A.S. "Novye aspekty bogoslovskoi traktovki vzaimootnoshenii cheloveka s prirodoi" [New Aspects of Theological Treatment of Interrelations of Man with Nature]. *Vopr. nauch. ateizma* 26 (1980): 131-147.

3534 Popov, A.S. "Religiia i politika: 'soobshchaiushiesia sosydy' ili 'dva kontsa nesomknutogo kol'tsa'?" [Religion and Politics: "Communicating Vessels" or "Two Ends of an Unclosed Ring"]. *Filosofiia cheloveka: dialog s traditsiei i perspektivy.* M., 1988. Pp. 105-118.

3535 Popov, A.S. "Religioznye i nereligioznye storony soznaniia veruiushchikh" [Religious and Unreligious Sides of Believers Consciousness]. *Molodezh' i tvorchestvo: sotsial'no-filosofckie problemy.* M., 1988. Ch. 3. Pp. 306-308.

3536 Popov, A.S. *Sotsial'noe znachenie religii i ateizma: istoriia, sovremennost'* [Social Significance of Religion: History, Contemporaneity]. M.: Znanie,

1989. 63 pp. (Novoe v zhizni, nauke, tekhnike. Nauch. ateizm; 8/1989). Bibl.: pp. 61-62.

3537 Popov, A.S. "Sushchnost' teologicheskikh interpretatsii kontseptsii 'kachestva zhizni'" [Essence of Theological Interpretation of the Conception of "Life's Quality"]. *Kritika religioznoi ideologii i problemy ateisticheskogo vospitaniia.* M., 1980. Pp. 41-47.

3538 Popov, A.S. "Veruiushchie i ateisty: problemy dialoga" [Believers and Atheists: Problems of Dialogue]. *Vestn. Mosk. un-ta.* Ser. 7. Filosofiia 4 (1988): 68-77.

3539 Popov, A.S. "Vse li religioznye organizatsii v SShA prinimaiut segodnia uchastie v mirotvorcheskom dvizhenii?" [Are All Religious Organizations in USA Taking Part Today in the Peacemaking Movement?]. *Argumenty.* M., 1988. Pp. 218-221.

3540 Popov, A.S.; Kosolapova, O.R. "Aktual'nye problemy razvitiia ateisticheskoi teorii" [Actual Problems of Development of Atheistic Theory]. *Vestn. Mosk. un-ta.* Ser. 7. Filosofiia 5 (1987): 76-84.

3541 Popov, A.S.; Radugir, A.A. *Khristianskoe bogoslovie v poiskakh sotsial'nogo ideala* [Christian Theology in Search of the Social Ideal]. M.: Znanie, 1986. 64 pp. (Novoe v zhizni, nauke, tekhnike. Nauch. ateizm; 4). Bibl.: pp. 63-64.

3542 Popov, A.S.; Sitnova, L.I. "Kritika polozhenii papskoi entsikliki 'Trudom ruk svoikh' (1981 g.)" [Criticism of Papal Encyclical Tenet "By One's Own Hands" (1981)]. *Aktual'nye problemy nauchno-ateisticheskogo vospitaniia molodezhi.* M., 1987. Pp. 169-177.

3543 Popov, A.S.; Sitnova, L.I. "Osobennosti religioznoi interpretatsii aktual'nykh problem obshchestvennoi zhizni" [Features of Religious Interpretation of Actual Problems of Public Life]. *Vestn. Mosk. un-ta.* Ser. 7. Filosofiia 5 (1984): 64-74.

3544 Popov, L. "Chto pokazali issledovaniia" [What Researches Revealed]. *Agitator* 15 (1989): 58-60.

3545 Popov, L. "S ravnymi pravami pered zakonom" [Equal Rights Before the Law]. *Nauka i religiia* 11 (1980): 51-54.

3546 Popov, L.A. *Ateisticheskii potentsial russkoi literatury* [Atheistic Potential of Russian Literature]. M.: Prosveshchenie, 1988. 157 pp. For review see item 5229.

3547 Popov, L.A. *Byt', a ne kazat'sia: Pozitsiia ateista* [To Be, Not to Seem: Atheist's Position]. Tula: Priok. kn. izd-vo, 1989. 104 pp. Annot. bibl.: pp. 99-103.

3548 Popov, L.A. "O formirovanii ateisticheskikh ubezhdenii" [Forming Atheistic Convictions]. *Nauch. dokl. Vyssh. shk. Nauch. kommunizm* 6 (1985): 73-78.

3549 Popov, L.A. *Orientiry ateizma* [Guiding Lines of Atheism]. Tula: Priok. kn. izd-vo, 1983. 97 pp. Annot. bibl.: pp. 93-96.

3550 Popov, N.S. "K voprosu o religioznom dvizhenii v Mariiskom krae vo vtoroi polovine XIX-nachalo XX veka" [On the Problem of Religious Movement in Mari Territory Late XIXth-Early XXth Century]. *Arkheologiia i etnografiia Mariiskogo kraia* 7 (1984): 174-192.

3551 Popov, N.S. *O iazychestve* [Paganism]. Ioshkar-Ola: Mariiskoe kn. izd-vo, 1985. 97 pp., illus. In Mari.

3552 Popov, N.S. *Pravoslavie v Marriskom krae* [Orthodoxy in Mari Territory]. Ioshkar-Ola: Mariiskoe kn. izd-vo, 1987. 112 pp.

3553 Popov, V. "Vozniknovenie khristianstva na Rusi" [The Origin of Chistianity in Rus']. *Brat. vestn.* 1 (1988): 46-50.

3554 Popov, V.A. "K kharakteristiki traditsionnogo mirovozzreniia akanov" [Characteristics of Traditional World Outlook of Achaeans]. *Tr. In-ta etnografii im. Miklukho-Maklaia.* 1984. T. 113. Pp. 176-191. Summary in English.

3555 Popov, V.G. "Ateisticheskoe vospitanie kak pedagogicheskaia deiatel'nost'" [Atheistic Education as Pedagogical Activity]. *Filosofiia i pedagogika.* Sverdlovsk, 1988. Pp. 45-52. Bibl.: pp. 51-52.

3556 Popov, V.G. "Nauchno-ateisticheskii stil' myshleniia kak tsel' ateisticheskogo vospitaniia" [Scientific-Atheistic Style of Thinking as Aim of Atheistic Education]. *Sb. nauch. tr. / Sverdlov. ped. in-t.* 1980, 323. Pp. 52-66.

3557   Popova, L. "Narodnaia ikona i tserkov'" [Folk Icon and the Church]. *Nauka
       i religiia* 10 (1985): 39-41.

3558   Popova, M.A. *Freidizm i religiia* [Freudism and Religion]. M.: Nauka, 1985.
       200 Pp. For review see item 5230.

3559   Popovich, K.F. *Moldavskie klassiki o dukhovenstve i religii* [Moldavian
       Classics on Clergy and Religion]. 2nd revised ed. Kishinev: Lumina, 1983.
       103 pp. In Moldavian.

3560   Popovich, M.V. *Mirovozzrenie drevnikh slavian* [World Outlook of Ancient
       Slavs]. Kiev: Nauk. dumka, 1985. 167 pp. (Nauch.-popul. lit). Bibl.: pp.
       158-166.

3561   Porokhova, V. "Koran. Perevod smyslov" [Koran. Translation of Meanings].
       Nauka i religiia 7 (1989): 20-23; 9 (1989): 30-31; 11 (1989): 5; 12 (1989):
       54-55.

3562   Porshneva, E.B. "Narodnaia religioznaia traditsiia v Kitae XIX-XX vv."
       [Popular Religious Tradition in China in XIXth-XXth Centuries]. *Sotsia-
       l'nye organizatsii v Kitae*. M., 1981. Pp. 265-279.

3563   Porshneva, E.B. "Narodnye religioznye dvizheniia v srednevekovom Kitae"
       [Popular Religious Movements in Medieval China]. *Obshchestvennye
       dvizheniia i ikh ideologiia v doburzhuaznykh obshchestvakh Azii*. M., 1988.
       Pp. 64-78.

3564   Porshneva, E.B. "O meste 'gunfu' v narodnoi sektantskoi traditsii (na
       materiale buddiiskikh sekt)" [The Place of "Gunfu" in Popular Sectarian
       Tradition (on data of Buddhist sects)]. *Psikhologicheskie aspekty buddizma*.
       Novosibirsk, 1986. P. 131-136.

3565   Poshka, A. "Usiliia klerikalov zaderzhat' razvitie ateizma i sekuliarizatsii v
       burzhuaznoi Litve" [Clericals Efforts to Delay the Development of
       Atheism and Secularization in Bourgeois Lithuania]. *Ateistines minties
       raida lietuvoje*. Kaunas, 1988. Pp. 61-68. In Lithuanian. Summary in
       Russian.

3566   Posova, T.K. "Kosmogoniia rannego induizma" [Cosmogony of Early
       Hinduism]. *Narody Azii i Afriki* 4 (1988): 106-112.

3567 Pospelov, B.V. "Ideologiia religioznogo modernizma v Iaponii" [Ideology of Religious Modernism in Japan]. *Narody Azii i Afriki* 6 (198): 50-61. Summary in English, p. 252.

3568 Pospelov, B.[V]. "V poiskakh 'tret'ego puti'" [In the Search of "The Third Way"]. *Nauka i religiia* 6 (1984): 60-61.

3569 Pospelov, V.A. "Gumanisticheskie aspekty ateizma v razvitom sotsialisticheskom obshchestve" [Humanist Aspects of Atheism in Developed Socialist Society]. *Sotsial'no-filosofskie aspekty kritiki religii.* L., 1980. Pp. 3-12.

3570 Postnikov, V.A. "Franchesko Gvichchardini o religii i tserkvi" [Francesco Guicciardini on Religion and Church]. *Srednevekovyi gorod* 9 (1989): 97-107.

3571 Potapchuk, V.A. *Iskusstvo i religiia: tsennosti podlinnye i mnimye* [Art and Religion: True and Imaginary Values]. Alma-Ata: Kazakhstan, 1985. 70 pp., illus. (Uchenye beseduiut s veruiushchimi). Bibl.: p. 69.

3572 Potashinskaia, N.N. "Katolicheskaia tserkov' v 2000 g." [Catholic Church in the Year 2000]. *Religii mira.* M., 1987. Pp. 88-99.

3573 Potashinskaia, N.[N]. "Pered sudom inkvizitsii" [Before the Inquisition Court]. *Nauka i religiia* 4 (1985): 53-56.

3574 Potashinskaia, N.N. "Sotsial'no-ekonomicheskaia doktrina katolicheskoi tserkvi: otdel'nye aspekty" [Socio-Economical Doctrine of the Catholic Church: Separate Aspects]. *Religii mira.* M., 1989. Pp. 73-93.

3575 Poteonia, A.A. "O proiskhozhdenii nazvanii nekotorykh slavianskikh iazycheskikh bozhestv" [Origin of Names of Some Slav Heathen Deities]. *Slavianskii i balkanskii fol'klor.* M., 1989. Pp. 254-267.

3576 "Praktika, opyt, problemy" [Practice, Experience, Problems]. [T.K. Amangel'dyeva et al]. *Vopr. nauch. ateizma* 31 (1983): 206-221.

3577 "Pravda, skrytaia plashchanitsei" [Truth, Concealed by Shroud]. *Nauka i religiia* 6 (1989): 10-14.

3578 "Pravda o pravoslavnykh monastyriakh" [Truth About Orthodox Monasteries]. *Ateisticheskie chteniia.* M., 1988. Pp. 327-337.

3579 *Pravda o 'sviatykh mestakh'* [Truth About "Holy Places"]. [Ed.: S. Dzhuma-durdyev]. Ashkhabad: Ylym, 1986. 95 pp. In Turkmen.

3580 *Pravda pro uniiu: Dokumenty i materialy [1215-1951 gg.]* [Truth About Uniate Church: Documents and Materials (1215-1951)]. [Comp.: Iu.Iu. Slivka et al]. 3rd enlarged ed. L'vov: Kameniar, 1981. 448 pp. In Ukrainian.

3581 "Pravoslavie: spornye stranitsy" [Orthodoxy: Disputable Pages]. *Nauka i religiia* 6 (1988): 3-8.

3582 *Pravoslavie i kul'tura: Tserkov. pritiazaniia i ist. real'nost'* [Orthodoxy and Culture: Churches' Pretensions and Historical Reality]. Comp.: P.L. Kaushanskii et al. Kiev: Politizdat Ukrainy, 1987. 36 pp. Author and title index: pp. 32-35.

3583 *Pravoslavie i sovremennost'* [Orthodoxy and Contemporaneity]. [Ed.: B.A. Lobovik]. Kiev: Nauk. dumka, 1988. 336 pp.

3584 *Pravoslavie v Karelii: Istoriia i sovremennost'* [Orthodoxy in Karelia: History and Contemporaneity]. [Ed.: M.N. Bessonov]. Petrozavodsk: Kareliia, 1987. 156 pp. For review see item 5232.

3585 Pravotorov, V. "God ukhodiashchii - god griadushchii" [Departing Year - Coming Year]. *Nauka i religiia* 12 (1988): 2-4.

3586 Pravotorov, V. "'Samaia bol'shaia oshibka'" ["The Biggest Mistake"]. *Nauka i religiia* 11 (1987): 19-20.

3587 Pravotorov, V. "Vpervye..." [For the First Time...]. *Nauka i religiia* 9 (1989): 2-3.

3588 "Prazdniki fonarei" [Festivals of Lanterns]. *Nauka i religiia* 12 (1987): 42-43.

3589 *Predatel'stvo:* Fakty obviniaiut litov. burzhuaz. natsionalistov i relig. ekstre-mistov [Treason: Facts Accuse Lithuanian Bourgeois Nationalists and Religious Extremists]. [Comp.: A. Strumskis]. Vil'nius: Mintis, 1988. 128 pp. In Lithuanian.

3590 *Predvidenie kak forma nauchnogo poznaniia* [Foresight as a Form of Scientific Knowledge].   Ed.: A.K. Kadyrov. Tashkent: TashGU, 1985. 79 pp. Bibl.: pp. 77-78.

3591 Prebrazhenskii, K. "Zakat zhivogo solntsa" [Decline of the Living Sun]. *Nauka i religiia* 6 (1989): 15-18.

3592 *Prepodavanie nauchnogo ateizma v vuze* [Teaching of Scientific Atheism in Institution of Higher Education]. Ed.: M.P. Novikova. M.: Vyssh. shk., 1988. 223 pp.

3593 Presniakov, A.E. "Organizatsiia tserkvi na Rusi pri Vladimire" [Organization of the Church in Rus' under Vladimir]. *'Kreshchenie Rusi' v trudakh russkikh i sovetskikh istorikov.* M., 1988. Pp. 227-244.

3594 *Presviteriane* [Presbyterians]. *Brat. vestn.* 6 (1988): 37-39.

3595 Primakov, E.M. "Islam i obshchestvennoe razvitie zarubezhnogo Vostoka" [Islam and Social Development of the Foreign Orient]. *Religii mira: Istoriia i sovremennost'.* Ezhegodnik. 1982. M., 1982. Pp. 30-45.

3596 *Priniatie khristianstva narodami Tsentral'noi i Iugo-Vostochnoi Evropy i kreshchenie Rusi* [Adaptation of Christianity by the Peoples of Central and South-Eastern Europe and Baptism of Rus']. Ed.: G.G. Litavrin. M.: Nauka, 1988. 271 pp., illus.

3597 Priselkov, M.D. "O bolgarskikh istokakh khristianstva na Rusi" [Bulgarian Sources on Christianity in Rus']. *'Kreshchenie Rusi' v trudakh russkikh i sovetskikh istorikov.* M., 1888. Pp. 139-169.

3598 Privalov, K. "'Novye kul'ty' vo Frantsii" ["New Cults" in France]. *Nauka i religiia* 2 (1987): 58-61.

3599 Privalov, K. "S malykh let" [From Childhood]. *Nauka i religiia* 3 (1987): 58-60.

3600 Privalov, K. *Sekty: dos'e strakha* [Sects: Dossier of Fear]. M.: Politizdat, 1987. 191 pp., illus.

3601 *Problema cheloveka v sovremennoi religioznoi i misticheskoi literature* [Problem of Man in the Current Religious and Mystical Literature]. M.: [S.n.], 1988. 246 pp. Annot. bibl.: pp. 209-210.

3602 *Problemy ateisticheskogo vospitaniia* [Problems of Atheistic Education]. [Ed.: G.O. Charyev; K. Akmuradov]. Ashkhabad: Ylym, 1981. 163 pp. In Turkmen.

3603 *Problemy ateisticheskogo vospitaniia v usloviiakh Karachaevo-Cherkesii*
[Problems of Atheistic Education in Karachai-Cherkess]. [Ed.: R.A-Kh.
Dzhanibekova]. Cherkessk: Karachaevo-Cherkes. in-t. ekonomiki, istorii,
iaz. i lit., [1980]. 154 pp. Bibl.: pp. 124-153.

3604 *Problemy formirovaniia nauchno-ateisticheskogo mirovozzreniia v sotsialisticheskom obshchestve* [Problems of Forming Scientific Atheistic Outlook
in Socialist Society]. [Ed.: A.B. Bazarov, et al]. Samarkand: SamGU,
1980. 86 pp.

3605 *Problemy istorii religii i ateizma* [Problems of the History of Religion and
Atheism]. Ed.: G.E. Kudriashov. Cheboksary: ChGU, 1980. 153 pp.
Published also in 1981, 129 pp.

3606 *Problemy kul'tury v sovremennom zarubezhnom religiovedenii* [Problems of
Culture in Contemporary Foreign Study of Religion]. Ed.: Iu.A. Kimelev.
M.: INION, 1989. 188 pp. (Ser.: Probl. religii i ateizma za rubezhom).

3607 *Problemy nauchno-ateistichekogo vospitaniia studentov* [Problems of Scientific-
Atheistic Education of Students]. [Ed.: I. Machiulis]. Vil'nius: VGU, 1987.
141 pp. In Lithuanian and Russian.

3608 *Problemy obshchestvennogo soznaniia i kul'tury v razvivaiushchikhsia stranakh
Iugo-Vostochnoi Azii* [Problems of Public Consciousness and Culture in
Developing Countries of South-Eastern Asia]. Comp.: N.A. Tolmachev.
M.: VGBIL, 1985. 110 pp.

3609 *Problemy povysheniia effektivnosti ateisticheskogo vospitaniia* [Problems of
Increasing the Effectiveness of Atheistic Education]. [Ed.: E.G.
Filimonov]. M.: AON, 1985. 138 pp.

3610 *Problemy sovrshenstvovaniia ateisticheskoi raboty na sovremennom etape*
[Problems of Perfection Atheistic Work in Contemporary Stage]. [Comp.:
I.A. Malakhova]. M.: Znanie, 1984. 64 pp. (Novoe v zhizni, nauke,
tekhnike. Nauch. ateizm; 12). Bibl.: p. 63.

3611 Profeldova, A. "Klerikalizm v sisteme antikommunisticheskoi strategii
imperializma" [Clericalism in the System of Anti Communist Strategy of
Imperialism]. *Vestn. Mosk. un-ta. Ser. 12, Teoriia nauch. kommunizma* 3
(1988): 71-79.

3612 "Programma spetskursa 'Islamovedenie'" [Curriculum of Special Course of "Islamic Studies"]. Comp.: S.M. Prozorov et al. *Narody Azii i Afriki* 3 (1989): 106-116; 4 (1989): 107-116; 5 (1989): 112-122.

3613 Prokhorov, G.M. "Iz literaturnogo naslediia mitropolita Kipriana" [Literary Heritage of Metropolitan Kiprian]. *Slavianskie literatury*. M., 1988. Pp. 66-81.

3614 Prokof'ev, N.I. "Narodnoe, sotsial'no-soslovnoe i religioznoe v literature Drevnei Rusi" [National, Socio-Class and Religion in the Literature of the Ancient Rus']. *Lit. v shk.* 4 (1988): 12-16.

3615 Prokof'ev, V.Ia. "Nesostoiatel'nost' istolkovaniia suti mirovozzreniia v sovremennoi antropologicheskoi teologii" [Groundlessness of Interpretation of the Essence of World Outlook in Contemporary Anthropological Theology]. *Probl. filosofii* 79 (1989): 58-65.

3616 Prokoshina, E. "Kazimir Lyshchinskii - vydaiushchiesia myslitel'-ateist XVII veka" [Kazimir Lyshchinskii - Prominent Thinker-Atheist of the XVIIth Century]. *Ateistines minties raida lietuvoje*. Kaunas, 1988. Pp. 25-33.

3617 Proshin, G.G. *Chernoe voinstvo: Rus. pravoslav. monastyr'. Legenda i byl'* [Black Host: Russian Orthodox Monastery. Legend and Reality]. M.: Politizdat, 1985. 320 pp., illus. Published also in 1988, 351 pp., illus.

3618 Proshin, G.G. *Muzei i religiia* [Museum and Religion]. M.: Sov. Rossiia, 1987. 221 pp., illus.

3619 Prosvetov, A. "S krestom i tamtamom" [With Cross and Tom-Tom]. *Nauka i religiia* 9 (1980): 62-63.

3620 Protsenko, N.G. "Nekotorye aspekty nauchno-ateisticheskogo vospitaniia molodezhi" [Some Aspects of Scientific-Atheistic Upbringing of Youth]. *Aktual'nye problemy nauchno-ateisticheskogo vospitaniia molodezhi*. M., 1987. Pp. 67-70.

3621 Prozorov, S.M. "Istochniki 'Kitab al-milal va-n-ni-khal' ash-Shakhrastani po istorii musul'manskikh sekt" [Ash-Shahrastanis' Sources of "Kitab al-milal- va-n-ni-khal" on the History of Moslem Sects]. *Bartol'dovskie chteniia, 1981;* God piatyi. M., 1981. Pp. 71-72.

3622 Prozorov, S.M. "Istoriia islama v srednevekovoi musul'manskoi eresiografii" [History of Islam in Medieval Moslem Heresiography]. *Islam: Religiia, obshchestvo, gosuarstvo.* M., 1984. Pp. 83-86.

3623 Prozorov, S.M. "K istorii musul'manskoi dogmatiki: murdzhiity" [History of Moslem Dogmatics: Murdjiits]. *Islam v istorii narodov Vostoka.* M., 1981. Pp. 19-24. Annot. bibl.: pp. 23-24.

3624 Prozorov, S.M. "K voprosu o 'pravoverii' v islame: poniatie 'akhl as-sunna' (sunnity)" [Question of "True-Belief" in Islam: Concept of "Ahl al-Sunna" (Sunnites)]. *Problemy arabskoi kul'tury.* M., 1987. Pp. 213-318.

3625 Prozorov, S.M. "Klassifikatsiia musul'manskikh sekt po 'at-Tabsir fi-d-din' Abu-l-Muzaffara al-Isfara'ini" [Abu-l-Muzaffar al-Isfara'inis' Classification of Moslem Sects by "at-Tabsir fi-d-din"]. *Islam: Religiia, obshchestvo, gosudarstvo.* M., 1984. Pp. 96-101.

3626 Prozorov, S.M. "Neizvestnoe sochinenie po istorii religii v rukopisi iz sobraniia LO IV AN SSSR" [Unknown Work on the History of Religion in a Manuscript from the Collection of LO IV AN USSR]. *Pis'menye pamiatniki i problemy istorii kul'tury narodov Vostoka:* XV godich. nauch. sesiia LO IV AN SSSR. M., 1981. Ch. 2. Pp. 48-54.

3627 Prozorov, S.M. "Rukopis' sochineniia al-Fakhri (IX-XV v.) po istorii religii v sobranii LO IV AN SSSR" [Manuscript of al-Fahri (IXth-XVth Century) Work on the History of Religion in the Collection of LO IV AN USSR]. *Islam: Religiia, obshchestvo, gosudarstvo.* M., 1984. Pp. 102-110.

3628 Prussakova, N.G. "Kontseptsiia 'musul'manskoi natsii' i 'islamskogo gosudar-stva' v ideologii dvizhenia za obrazovanie Pakistana: Po rabotam ind. i pakist. publitsistov i istorikov" [Conception of "Moslem Nation" and "Islamic State" in Ideology of the Movement for Creation of Pakistan: Based on the Works of Indian and Pakistan Journalists and Historians]. *Islam v istorii narodov Vostoka.* M., 1981. Pp. 100-122. Annot. bibl.: pp. 120-122.

3629 Prussakova, N.G. "Vneshnepoliticheskii aspekt problemy musul'manskikh men'shinstv v mezhdunarodnykh otnosheniiakh" [Outer Political Aspects of the Problem of Moslem Minorities in International Relations]. *"Islamskii faktor" v mezhdunarodnykh otnosheniiakh v Azii (70-e - pervaia polovina 80-kh gg.).* M., 1987. Pp. 148-157.

3630   Pruzhinin, B.I. "'Zvezdy ne lgut', ili Astrologiia glazami metodologa" ["Stars Do Not Lie", or Astrology Through the Eyes of a Methodologist]. *Kriticheskii analiz nenauchnogo znaniia.* M., 1989. Pp. 48-71.

3631   Pshenichnyi S.A. "Otrazhenie bor'by khristianstva s iazychestvom po Povesti vremennykh let (Lavrent'ev. spisok) [Reflection of the Struggle of Christianity with Paganism by Russian Primary Chronicle (Lavrentian Text)]. *Otechestvennaia obshchestvennaia mysl' epokhi Srednevekov'ia.* Kiev, 1988. Pp. 151-161.

3632   *Psikhologicheskie aspekty buddizma* [Psychological Aspects of Buddhism]. [Ed.: V.V. Mantatov]. Novosibirsk: Nauka. Sib. otd-nie, 1986. 157 pp.

3633   Pubaev, R.E. "Buddologicheskie issledovaniia v Buriatii" [Buddhological Researches in Buriat]. *Obshchestv. nauki* 6 (1982): 186-191.

3634   Pubaev, R.E. "Istoriia buddiiskoi siddkhanty v osveshchenii Sumba-khambo v sochinenii 'Pagsam-Chzhonsan'" [History of Buddhist Siddhanta in Sumbha-Hambho Illumination in the Work "Pagsam-Chjonsan"]. *Buddizm i srednevekovaia kul'tura narodov Tsenral'noi Azii.* Novosibirsk, 1980. Pp. 40-53.

3635   Pubaev, R.E. *'Pagsam-Chzhonsan' - pamiatnik Tibetskoi istoriografii XVIII veka* ["Pagsam-Chjonsan" - Memorial of Tibetan Historiography of XVIIIth Century]. Novosibirsk: Nauka. Sib. otd-nie, 1981. 307 pp. Bibl.: pp. 276-286.

3636   Pubaev, R.E. "Tibetskii buddizm i ego rol' v istorii kul'tury narodov Tsentral'noi Azii v srednie veka" [Tibetan Buddhism and Its Role in the History of Culture of Central Asian Peoples in the Middle Ages]. *III Vsesoiuznaia konferentsiia vostokovedov "Vzaimodeistvie i vzaimovliianie tsivilizatsii kul'tur na Vostoke".* M., 1988. T. I. Pp. 113-114.

3637   Puchkov, P.I. "Etnos i religiia" [Ethnic Community and Religion]. *Etnicheskie protsessy v sovremennom mire.* M., 1987. Pp. 68-96.

3638   Pulatov, T. "Novgorod i Bukhara: simvoly very" [Novgorod and Bokhara: Symbols of Faith]. *Rodina* 8 (1989): 44.

3639   Purbueva, Ts.P. *'Biografiia Neidzhi-toina'* - *istochnik po istorii buddizma v Mongolii* ["Biography of Neyii-Toyin" - Source of History of Buddhism in Mongolia]. Novosibirsk: Nauka. Sib. otd-nie, 1984. 113 pp. The book contains also the biography of Neiji-Toina. Bibl.: pp. 102-109. Name index: pp. 110-112.

3640   Purbueva, Ts.P. "G.Ts. Tsybikov - issledovatel' mongol'skogo lamaizma" [G.Ts. Tsybikov - Researcher of Mongol Lamaism]. *Issledovaniia po istorii i kul'ture Mongolii.* Novosibirsk, 1989. Pp. 68-75. Bibl.: p. 75.

3641   Purevzhav, S. "Narodnaia revoliutsiia i otdelenie tserkvi ot gosudarstva v MNR" [People's Revolution and Separation of the Church from the State in Mongolian People's Republic]. *Stroitel'stvo sotsializma i utverzhdenie nauchno-materialisticheskogo, ateisticheskogo mirovozzreniia.* M., 1981. Pp. 32-40.

3642   Pushkarev, L.N. "Ateizm v obshchestvennoi bor'be Rossii v 60-kh gg. XIX v. (N.G. Chernyshevskii, I.A. Khudiakov, I.G. Pryzhov) [Atheism in Russia's Social Struggle in the 60s of the XIXth Century (N.G. Chernyshevsky, I.A. Khudiakov, I.G. Pryzhov)]. *Istoriograficheskie i istoricheskie problemy russkoi kul'tury.* M., 1983. Pp. 112-130.

3643   Pushkin, S.N. "Evoliutsiia vzgliadov sovremennogo russkogo pravoslaviia na tsivilizatsiiu" [Evolution of the Views of Contemporary Russian Orthodoxy on Civilization]. *Vopr. ateizma* 25 (1989): 112-116.

3644   Pushkin, S.N. "Nesostoiatel'nost' pravoslavnykh vzgliadov na tsivilizatsiiu" [Groundlessness of Orthodox Views on Civilisation]. *Sotial'no- filosofskie aspekty kritiki religii.* L., 1987. Pp. 131-141.

3645   Pushkina, T.A. "Ekumenicheskie vliianiia v bogoslovskoi interpretatsii nrav-stvennogo ideala" [Ecumenical Influences on Theological Interpretation of Moral Ideal]. *Nauchnyi ateizm: ideal i mirovozzrenie.* Perm', 1988. Pp. 82-88.

3646   Pustarnakov, V.F. "Zarozhdenie i razvitie filosofskoi mysli v predelakh religioznoi formy obshchestvennogo soznaniia epokhi Kievskoi Rusi" [Origin and Development of Philosophical Thought within the Limits of Religious Form of Social Consciousness in the Epoch of Kievan Rus']. *Otechestvennaia obshchestvennaia mysl epokhi Srednevekov'ia.* Kiev, 1988. Pp. 33-41.

3647 *Puti prozreniia* [The Ways of Enlightenment]. Sc. ed.: A.I. Utkin. Dnepropetrovsk: Promin', 1985. 102 pp.

3648 Puzanov, O.P. "Voobrazhenie kak faktor formirovaniia religioznogo nravstvennogo ideala" [Imagination as Forming Factor of the Religious Moral Ideal]. *Aktual'nye problemy ateisticheskogo vospitaniia i kritika religioznoi ideologii.* M., 1981. Pp. 27-31.

3649 Puzikov, V.P. *Illiuziia vechnoi zhizni: Dlia veruushchikh i neveruiushchikh* [Illusion of Eternal Life: For Believers and Unbelievers]. Simferopol': Tavriia, 1984. 95 pp.

3650 Puzikov, V.P. *Za fasadom sviatosti: Dlia veruiushchikh i neveruiushchikh* [Behind the Facade of Holiness: For Believers and Unbelievers]. Simferopol': Tavriia, 1987. 97 pp.

3651 Rabdanov, T. "Iubilei Bandido Khambo-lamy Erdyneeva" [Bandido Hambo-Lama Erdyneev's Anniversary]. *Religii v SSSR* 1 (1987): TR 1.

3652 Rabinovich, V.L. "Alkhmicheskii mif i khimery Sobora Parizhskoi bogomateri" [Alchemical Myth and Chimeras of Notre Dame de Paris]. *Kriticheskii analiz nauchnogo znaniia.* M., 1989. Pp. 72-90.

3653 Radchenko, V.A. *Obshchestvennoe mnenie v ateisticheskom vospitanii* [Public Opinion in Atheistic Education]. Kiev: Znanie UkSSR, 1986. 48 pp. (Ser. 5, Nauchno ateisticheskaia / O-vo "Znanie" UkSSR; No 9). In Ukrainian.

3654 Radchenko, V.A. "Sotsial'naia aktivnost' kak faktor formirovaniia ateisticheskoi napravlennosti obshchestvennogo mneniia" [Social Activity as Forming Factor of Atheistic Trend of Public Opinion]. *Vopr. ateizma* 24 (1988): 29-35.

3655 Radugin, A.A. "Irratsionalizm khristianskoi apologii religii" [Irrationalness of Christian Apology of Religion]. *Vestn. Mosk. un-ta. Ser. 7. Filosofiia* 4 (1982): 69-78.

3656 Radugin, A.A. "Kritika religioznoi filosofii i teologii v kurse 'Osnovy nauchnogo ateizma'" [Criticism of Religious Philosophy and Theology in the Course "Fundamentals of Scientific Atheism"]. *Prepodavanie nauchnogo ateizma v vuze.* M., 1988. Pp. 167-180.

3657 Radugin, A.A. *Personalizm i katolicheskoe obnovlenie* [Personalism and Catholic Renovation]. Voronezh: Izd-vo Voronezh. un-ta, 1982. 178 pp. Bibl.: pp. 173-177. For review see item 5233.

3658 Radzhapov, V. "Ateisty i veruiushchie v bor'be za mir" [Atheists and Believers in the Struggle for Peace]. *Agitator* 23 (1988): 53-54.

3659 Radzhapov, V. "Tam, gde zhivem" [There, Where We Live]. *Agitator* 23 (1985): 57-59.

3660 Ragauskas, I.[A]. "Budem zhit' bez tebia: Ateist i smert'" [Will Live Without You: Atheist and Death]. *Nauka i religiia* 4 (1982): 28-31.

3661 Ragauskas, I.A. *Stupaite, messa okonchena!* [Be Off, the Mass is Over!]. 6th ed. Vil'nius: Vaga, 1984. 437 pp. In Lithuanian.
      Published also in:
      Minsk: Belarus', 1981. 302 pp. In Belorussian.

3662 Ragimova, B.R. "Obshchinnye obriady i prazdniki samurskikh lezgin, sviazannye s narodnym kalendarem (konets XVIII-XIX v.)" [Community Rituals and Holidays of Samur Lezghin Linked with Popular Calendar (Late XVIIIth-XIXth Century)]. *Kalendar' i kalendarnye obriady narodov Dagestana.* Makhachkala, 1987. Pp. 64-70.

3663 Rakhmanova, I.B. "Bor'ba religii i ateizma v pervye gody sovetskoi vlasti" [Struggle of Religion and Atheism in the First Years of Soviet Power]. *Nauchnyi ateizm, religiia i sovremennost'.* Novosibirsk, 1987. Pp. 321-332.

3664 Rakhmatullaev, N. "Ob otnoshenii Ibn Sino k vostochnomu mistitsizmu" [Attitude of Ibn Sina toward Oriental Mysticism]. *Torzhestvo razuma.* Dushanbe, 1988. Pp. 138-146.

3665 Rakhmatullin, K.Kh. *Zvezdy: Nauka i sueveriia* [Stars: Science and Superstitions]. Alma-Ata: Kazakhstan, 1984. 64 p. (Uchenye beseduiut s veruiushchimi). For review see item 5234.

3666 Ramazanova, Z.B. "Obriady vyzyvaniia dozhdia i solntsa u laktsev v kontse XIX-nachale XX v" [Lakts' Rituals for Calling Rain and Sun Late XIXth-Early XXth Century]. *Kalendar' i kalendarnye obriady narodov Dagestana.* Makhachkala, 1987. Pp. 82-88.

3667 Ramm, B.Ia. "Issledovanie problem sovremennogo katolitsizma v literature 70-kh godov" [Research of the Problems of Contemporary Catholicism in the Literature of the 70s]. *Vopr. nauch. ateizma* 28 (1981): 309-323.

3668 Raneta, A.I. *Ideologicheskaia bor'ba v voprosakh svobody soznaniia* [Ideological Struggle on the Problems of the Freedom of Consciousness]. Kishinev: Znanie MSSR, 1981. 52 pp. (Material v pomoshch' lektoru / O-vo "Znanie" MSSR). Bibl.: pp. 51-52.

3669 Ranne, A. "'Upravitel' prekrasnogo sada'" ["Manager of the Beautiful Garden"]. *Nauka i religiia* 12 (1988): 20-21.

3670 Rapoport, Iu.A. "Sviatilishche vo dvortse na gorodishche Kalalygyr" [Sanctuary in the Palace of the Ancient Site Kalalygyr]. *Proshloe Srednei Azii.* Dushanbe, 1987. Pp. 140-148.

3671 Rapov, O.M. "Kogda khristianstvo prishlo na Rus'" [When Christianity Came to Rus']. *Priroda* 7 (1988): 58-67.

3672 Rapov, O.M. "Kogda proizoshlo kreshchenie Rusi, otmechennoe Konstan-tinopol'skim patriarkhom Fotiem?" [When Did the Baptism of Rus' Take Place, as Mentioned by the Patriarch of Constantinopole Photius?]. *Vneshniaia politika Drevnei Rusi.* M., 1988. Pp. 78-82.

3673 Rapov, O.M. "Kometa Galleia i datirovka kreshcheniia Rusi" [Halley's Comet and the Fixation of the Date of the Baptism of Rus']. *Istoriko-astronomicheskie issledovaniia.* 20 (1988): 147-166.

3674 Rapov, O.M. "O vremeni i obstoiatel'stvakh kreshcheniia naseleniia Novgoroda Velikogo" [Time and Circumstances of Baptism of the Popula-tion of the Great Novgorod]. *Vestn. Mosk. un-ta.* Ser. 8, Istoriia 3 (1988): 51-65.

3675 Rapov, O.M. *Russkaia tserkov' v IX-pervoi treti XII v. Priniatie khristianstva* [Russian Church in the IXth-Early XIIth Centuries. Adoptation of Chris-tianity]. M.: Vyssh. shk., 1988. 416 pp. Name index: pp. 409-415. For reviews see items 5235-5236.

3676 Rashkova, R.T. "Katolitsizm i sovremennaia kul'tura" [Catholicism and Contemporary Culture]. *Nauch. dokl. vyssh. shkoly. Filos. nauki* 2 (1981): 64-71.

3677   Rashkova, R.T. "Pod znakon devy Marii - k 2000 godu" [Under the Sign of the Virgin Mary - Towards the Year 2000]. *Argumenty* M., 1988. Pp. 11-25.

3678   Rashkova, R.T. "Politika Vatikana v oblasti kul'tury" [Vatican's Politics in the Realm of Culture]. *Vopr. nauch. ateizma* 34 (1986): 95-117.

3679   Rashkova, R.T. "Problema gumanizma v sovremennoi katolicheskoi filosofii kul'tury" [Problem of Humanism in Contemporary Catholic Philosophy of Culture]. *Gumanizm i religiia.* L., 1980. Pp. 3-18.

3680   Rashkova, R.T. "Problemy kul'tury v sovremennom katolitsizme" [Cultural Problems in Contemporary Catholicism]. *Vopr. nauch. ateizma* 28 (1981): 183-200.

3681   Rashkova, R.T. "Sekuliarizatsiia zapadnoevropeiskoi kul'tury v otsenke Vatikana" [Vatican's Estimation of the Secularization of West European Culture]. *Problemy formirovaniia svetskoi kul'tury v Zapadnoi Evrope.* L., 1987. Pp. 6-27.

3682   Rashkova, R.T. *Vatikan i sovremennaia kul'tura* [Vatican and Contemporary Culture]. M.: Politizdat, 1989. 416 pp., illus. Name index: pp. 386-415. For review see item 5237.

3683   Rassel, B. *Pochemu ia ne khristianin* [Why I Am Not a Christian]. [Comp.: A.A. Iakovlev]. M.: Politizdat, 1987. 334 pp. (B-ka ateist. lit.). Annot. bibl.: pp. 312-332. For reviews see items 5238-5239.

3684   Rassel, B, *Religiia i nauka* [Religion and Science]. Vil'nius: Mintis, 1982. 222 pp. In Lithuanian.

3685   Rassudova, R.Ia. "K istorii odezhdy sredneaziatskogo dukhovenstva" [History of the Garments of the Middle Asian Clergy]. *Pamiatniki traditsionno-bytovoi kul'tury narodov Srednei Azii, Kazakhstana i Kavkaza.* L., 1989. Pp. 170-179.

3686   Raushenbakh, B. "Skvoz' glub' vekov" [Through Remote Ages]. *Kommunist* 2 (1987): 99-105.

3687   Raushenbakh, B. "Vvedenie khristianstva - vazhnoe sobytie russkoi istorii" [Introduction of Christianity - Important Event In Russian History]. *Religiia v SSSR* 8 (1987): BR 1-BR 4.

3688   Razlogov, K.E. *Bogi i d'iavoly v zerkale ekrana* [Gods and Devils on the Screen]. M.: Politizdat, 1982. 224 pp., illus. For reviews see items 5240-5243.

3689   Razlogov, K.E. "Kino s tochki zreniia teologii" [Cinema From the Point of View of Theology]. *Vopr. nauch. ateizma* 30 (1982): 95-118.

3690   *Razum protiv mraka* [Reason Against Darkness]. [Comp.: E.P. Kovnatskii]. Groznyi: Chech.-Ing. kn. izd-vo, 1982. 76 pp.

3691   Razumovskii, O.S. "Sovremennaia fizika i teologiia" [Contemporary Physics and Theology]. *Nauchnyi ateizm, religiia i sovremennost'*. Novosibirsk, 1987. Pp. 56-75.

3692   Razuvaev, V. "Brat'ia razdelennye: Otnosheniia mezhdu Mosk. Patriarkhiei i Vatikanom ostaiutsia delikat. probl." [Divided Brothers: Relations Between Moscow Patriarchate and Vatican Remain a Delicate Problem]. *Novoe vremia* 45 (1989): 36.

3693   Razuvaev, V. "'Inoi altar' voodruziv': Chto stoit za novym rasskolom Rus. Pravoslav. Tserkvi na Ukraine" ["Erecting Different Altar": What Lies Behind the New Schism of the Russian Orthodox Church in Ukraine]. *Novoe vremia* 48 (1989): 37.

3694   Razuvaev, V. "U tserkvi tozhe net opyta...: Forum sviashchennosluzhitelei glazami ateista" [The Church as Well Does not Have Experience: Forum of Clergy Through Atheist's Eyes]. *Novoe vremia* 32 (1989): 38-39.

3695   Razuvaev, V. "V dni chinnykh torzhestv: Rus. Pravoslav. Tserkov' vstupaet v novyi etap svoei istorii" [In the Days of Ceremonious Celebrations: The Russian Orthodox Church Enters New Stage of Its History]. *Novoe vremia* 3 (1989): 36.

3696   *Razvitie ateisticheskoi mysli v Litve* [Development of Atheistical Thought in Lithuania]. Comp.: I. Zaksas. Vil'nius: [S.n.], 1986. 113 pp. In Lithuanian. Published also in:
         Kaunas: [S.n.], 1988, 135 pp., in Lithuanian. Part of the text in Russian.

3697   *Razviitie ateizma v usloviiakh zrelogo sotsialisticheskogo obshchestva* [Development of Atheism in Mature Socialist Society]. [Ed.: A. Balsus]. Vl'nius: Vil'n. gos. un-t, 1980. 116 pp. In Lithuanian.

3698 *Real'nost' i sueverie* [Reality and Superstition]. Ed.: A. Askarova. Tashkent: Fan, 1988. 60 pp. In Uzbek.

3699 Rebkalo, V.A. *Gumanizm real'nyi i mnimyi* [Real and Imaginary Humanism]. Kiev: Vyshcha shk. Izd-vo pri Kiev. gos. un-te, 1988. 80 pp. (Ateist. b-chka studenta). Bibl.: pp. 78-79.

3700 Red'ko, L.B. *Sovremennoe khristianskoe sektantstvo v Turkmenistane* [Contemporary Christian Sectarianism in Turkmenistan]. Ashkhabad: Znanie TSSR, 1984. 19 pp. (V pomoshch' lektoru / O-vo "Znanie" TSSR). Bibl.: p. 19.

3701 Regel'son, L.[L]. "Vybor" [Choice]. *Nauka i religiia* 5 (1988): 44-47.

3702 Regel'son, L.L. "K nauchnomu sporu o Turinskoi plashchanitse" [Scientific Dispute About the Shroud of Turin]. *Nauka i religiia* 6 (1989): 11-12.

3703 *Rekomendatsii po organizatsii i provedeniiu tsiklov lektsii i besed po nauchnomu ateizmu v svete reshenii XXVI s'ezda KPSS* [Recommendations for Organization and Conducting Cycles of Lectures and Talks on Scientific Atheism in the Light of the Resolutions of the XXVIth CPSU Congress]. Comp.: A.I. Abdusamedov. Tashkent: "Znanie" UzSSR, 1982. 25 pp. In Uzbek. Bibl.: p. 22-25.

3704 *Religii mira: Istoriia i sovremennost* Ezhegodnik [Religions of the World: History and Contemporaneity. Annual]. [Ed.: I.R. Grigulevich]. M.: Nauka, 1982 -
1982. 285 pp. Summary in English.
1983. 255 pp.
1984. 277 pp.
1985. 1986. 300 pp.
1986. 1987. 287 pp. Ed.: I.A. Kryvelev. For review see item 5244.

3705 *Religiia Afriki: Tradits. i sinkret. religii* [Religion of Africa: Traditional and Syncretic Religions]. [Ed.: An.A. Gromyko]. M.: Progress, 1987. 328 pp., illus. In Portuguese. Bibl.: pp. 304-318.

3706 "'Religiia bednykh'" [Religion of the Poor]. *Nauka i religiia* 12 (1987): 37.

3707 *Religiia i bor'ba idei v sovremennom mire* [Religion and the Struggle of Ideas in the Contemporary World]. M.: Znanie RSFSR, 1983. 47 p. (V pomoshch' lektoru / O-vo "Znanie" RSFSR, Nauch.-metod. sovet po propagande nauch. ateizma). Bibl.: p. 47.

3708 *Religiia i obshchestvennaia zhizn' v Indii* [Religion and Social life in India]. [Ed.: A.D. Litman et al]. M.: Nauka, 1983. 295 pp. For reviews see items 5245-5246.

3709 *Religiia i sovremennost'* [Religion and Contemporaneity]. [Comp.: I. Shloss]. Alma-Ata: Kazakhstan, 1985. 77 pp. In German.

3710 *Religiia i tserkov' v sovetskom obshcheste* [Religion and Church in Soviet Society]. [Comp.: V. Aleksandrov]. M.: Znanie, 1985. 20 pp.

3711 *Religiia - perezhitok proshlogo* [Religion - Survival of the Past]. [Ed.: A. Khaiydov]. Ashkhabad: Ylym, 1986. 98 pp. In Turkmen.

3712 *Religiia pervobytnogo obshchestva v svete sovremennykh dannykh* [Religion of Primitive Society in the Light of Contemporary Data]. Ed.: M.S. Butinova. L.: GMIRIA, 1984. 153 pp.

3713 *Religiia v bor'be mirovozzrenii i idei* [Religion in the Struggle of World Outlook and Ideas]. [Ed.: I. Zaksas et al]. Vil'nius: In-t. filosofii, sotsiologii i prava, 1980. 139 pp. In Lithuanian. Summary in Russian.

3714 *Religiia v politicheskoi zhizni SShA (70-e-nach. 80-e gg.)* [Religion in the Political Life of USA (70s-Early 80s)]. Ed.: M. Zamoshkin. M: Nauka, 1985. 225 pp. For review see item 5247.

3715 *Religiia v Sovetskom obshchestve: prichiny sokhraneniia i problemy preodoleniia* [Religion in Soviet Society: Causes of Preservation and Problems of Overcoming]. [Ed.: E.G. Filimonov]. M.: AON, 1989. 183 pp.

3716 "Religiia v stranakh Azii i Afriki" [Religion in the Countries of Asia and Africa]. *Narody Azii i Afriki* 1 (1980): 40-54.

3717 *Religioznaia obriadnost': soderzhanie, evoliutsiia, otsenki* [Religious Ritual: Content, Evolution, Appraisals]. [A.S. Onishchenko, et al]. Kiev: Vyshsha shk., 1988. 271 pp. Bibl.: pp. 258-266. Subject index: pp. 267-269.

3718 "Religioznoe obuchenie - byt' ili ne byt'?" [Religious Education - To Be or Not To Be?]. *Nauka i religiia* 9 (1989): 16.

3719 '*Religioznye deiateli za spasennie sviashchennogo dara zhizni ot iademoi katastrofy*', *vsemimaia konf. Moskva. 1982* ["Religious Personalities for Salvation of the Holy Gift of Life from Nuclear Catastrophe", World Conference. Moskow, 1982.]. M.: Novosti, 1982. 30 pp. Published also in: Arabic, English, French, German and Spanish.

3720 *Religioznye prazdniki i ateisticheskaia propaganda* [Religious Feasts and Atheistic Propaganda]. [Comp.: L. Miaesalu]. Tallin: Eesti raamat, 1980. 85 pp. In Estonian.

3721 *Religioznye predstavleniia v pervobytnom obshchestve* [Religious Notions in Primitive Society]. [Ed.: D.A. Krainov]. M.: INION, 1987. 261 pp.

3722 Renan, E. "Zhizn' Iisusa" [Life of Jesus]. *V mire knig* 8 (1989): 44-46; 9 (1989): 41-43; 10 (1989): 41-44.

3723 Rende, A.K. *Ateisticheskomu vospitaniiu - differentsirovannyi podkhod* [To Atheistic Education - Differentiated Approach]. Alma-Ata: Znanie KazSSR, 1981. 26 pp.

3724 Rende, A.K.; Shless, I.I. *Religiia i ideologichesaia bor'ba* [Religion and Ideological Struggle]. Alma-Ata: Znanie KazSSR, 1982. 36 pp. In German. Bibl.: pp. 35-36.

3725 Rerikh, E.I. "Kriptogrammy Vostoka" [Cryptograms of Orient]. *Pod'em* 2 (1989): 103-122.

3726 *Reshaetsia kompleksno* [It's Decided in a Complex Form]. [Comp.: V.V. Zybkovets]. M.: Sov. Rossiia, 1984. 96 pp.

3727 Reshetnikov, V.A. "Politika i religiia: problemy formirovaniia politicheskoi kul'tury molodezhi" [Politics and Religion: Problems of Shaping Youth's Political Culture]. *Teoreticheskie voprosy formirovaniia soznaniia sovetskoi molodezhi*. Barnaul, 1987. Pp. 105-115. Bibl.: pp. 114-115.

3728 Reshetnikov, V.A. "Problemy bor'by s klerikal'noi propagandoi" [Problems of Struggle with Clerical Propaganda]. *Aktual'nye problemy nauchno-ateisticheskogo vospitaniia molodezhi*. M., 1987. Pp. 166-169.

3729 Retiunskikh, L.T. "Otrazhenie sotsial'no-politicheskoi situatsii SShA v teologi Kharveia Koksa" [Reflection of Socio-Political Situation of USA in

Harvey Cox's Theology]. *Molodezh' i tvorchestvo: sotsial'no- filosofskie problemy.* M., 1988. Ch. I. Pp. 130-131.

3730 "Revoliutsiia i khristianstvo" [Revolution and Christianity]. *Nauka i religiia* 8 (1989): 10-11.

3731 Revunenkova, N.V. "Erazm i Kal'vin" [Erasmus and Calvin]. *Erazm Rotterdamskii i ego vremia.* M., 1989. Pp. 154-168.

3732 Revunenkova, N.V. "Gumanizm v konfessional'noi otsenke" [Humanism in Confessional Appraisal]. *Aktual'nye problemy izuheniia istorii religii i ateizma.* L., 1980. Pp. 130-139.

3733 Revunenkova, N.V. "Kritika gumanisticheskogo ucheniia o cheloveke v 'Nastavlenii' Zhana Kal'vina" [Criticism of Humanist Teaching about Man in John Calvin's "Institutes"]. *Gumanizm i religiia* L., 1980. Pp. 73-93.

3734 Revunenkova, N.V. "Rable i Kal'vin: bor'ba svetskoi i religioznoi kul'tury v epokhu Reformatsii" [Rabelais and Calvin: Struggle Between Laic and Religious Cultures During the Reformation]. *Problemy formirovaniia svetskoi kul'tury v Zapadnoi Evrope.* L., 1987. Pp. 64-90.

3735 Revunenkova, N.V. *Renessanskoe svobodomyslie i ideologiia Reformatsii* [Freethinking of the Renaissance and Ideology of Reformation]. M.; Mysl', 1988. 207 pp. Bibl.: pp. 195-204. Name index: pp. 205-206.

3736 Reznichenko, L.A. "Karlson protiv astrologov" [Carlson against Astrologists]. *Energiia: ekonomika, tekhnika, ekologiia* 7 (1989): 54-56.

3737 Reznichenko, V. "Sviataia smert' iz Buenos-Airesa" [Holy Death from Buenos-Aires]. *Nauka i religiia* 5 (1988): 25-27, 63.

3738 Reznikov, A. "Vifleemskaia zvezda - kometa Galleia?" [Bethlehem's Star - Halley's Comet?]. *Nauka i religiia* 10 (1986): 14-17.

3739 Reznikov, L.Ia. "Raskol sredi veruiushchikh severnogo Priladozh'ia" [Dissent among Believers of the Northern Side of Ladoga]. *Pravoslavie v Karelii.* Petrozavodsk, 1987. Pp. 73-84.

3740 Reznikov, L.Ia. *Valaam: krizis asketizma* [Balaam: Crisis of Asceticism]. L.: Lenizdat, 1986. 143 pp., illus.

3741 Rezvan, E.A. "Adam i banu adam v Korane (k istorii poniatii 'pervoc-helovek i chelovechestvo')" [Adam and Ibn Adam in Koran (History of the Notion "First Man and Humanity")]. *Islam: Religiia, obshchestvo, gosudarstvo.* M., 1984. Pp. 59-68.

3742 Rezvan, E.A. "Eticheskie predstavleniia i etiket v Korane" [Ethical Notions and Etiquette in the Koran]. *Etiket u narodov Perednei Azii.* M., 1988. Pp. 38-59.

3743 Rezvan, E.A. "Issledovaniia po terminologii Korana: 'Sura'; 'abd ('ibad. 'abid) [Allakh]'; 'umma'. 16:121/120" [Researches on Koran Terminology "Sura"; "Abd" (Ibad Abid) [Allah]; "Umma" 16:121/120]. *Problemy arabskoi kul'tury.* M., 1987. Pp. 219-231. Bibl.: pp. 230-231.

3744 Rezvan, E.A. "Koran i doislamskaia kul'tura" [Koran and Pre-Islamic Culture]. *Islam: Religiia, obshchestvo, gosudarstvo.* M., 1984. Pp. 44-58. Annot. bibl.: pp. 56-58.

3745 Rezvan, E.A. "Termin *daradzha* v Korane" [The Term *Daraja* in Koran]. *Sotsial'no politicheskie predstavleniia v islame: Istoriia i sovremennost'.* M., 1987. Pp. 69-80. Annot. bibl.: pp. 78-80.

3746 Riabova, I.T. "K voprosu o protsessakh sekuliiarizatsii v sotsialisticheskikh i kapitalisticheskikh usloviiakh" [Problem of Secularization Processes in Socialist and Capitalist Conditions]. *Kritika religioznoi ideologii i problemy ateisticheskogo vospitaniia.* M., 1980. Pp. 33-40.

3747 Riabushkin, N.V. "'Meditsinskie' temy sovremennykh bogoslovov (sovreme-nnaia teologiia i meditsina)" ["Medical" Themes of the Present Day Theologians (Contemporary Theology and Medicine)]. *Zdravokhranenie Ros. Federatsii* 11 (1980): 34-38.

3748 Riabushkin, N.V.; Tsaregorodtsev, G.I. *Nakazanie li bozh'e?* [Is It God's Punishment?]. M.: Politizdat, 1988. 319 pp., illus.

3749 Rimarenko, Iu.I. *Burzhuaznyi natsionalizm i klerikalizm* [Bourgeois Nationa-lism and Clericalism]. Kiev: Politizdat UkSSR, 1986. 140 pp. (Kritika ideologii i politiki antikommunizma). Annot. bibl.: pp. 135-139.

3750 Rimskii, V.P. "K probleme genezisa religii" [On the Problem of Genesis of Religion]. *Izv. Sev.-Kavk. Nauch. tsentra vyssh. shk. Obshchestv. nauki* 1 (1983): 55-60.

3751 Rishin, V.R. *Musul'manskii ektremizm - oruzhie imperializma* [Moslem Extremism - Weapon of Imperialism]. Tashkent: Uzbekistan, 1988. 39 pp. (Vopr. kom. morali; No 4). In Uzbek.

3752 Riumin, E.F. "S vysoty prozhitykh let" [From the Heights of Lived Years]. *Nauka i religiia* 11 (1984): 2-4.

3753 Rizhskii, M.I. *Bibleiskie proroki i bibleiskie prorochestva* [Biblical Prophets and Biblical Prophecies]. M.: Politizdat, 1987. 366 pp., illus. For review see item 5248.

3754 Rizhskii, M.[I]. "Bibleiskie proroki i prorochestva" [Biblical Prophets and Prophecies]. *Nauka i religiia* 3 (1985): 32-35; 4 (1985): 31-35; 5 (1985): 34-37; 9 (1985): 22-24; 11 (1985): 26-27; 12 (1985): 22-24.

3755 Robinson, A.N. "Simeon Polotskii - astrolog" [Simeon Polotskii - Astrologer]. *Problemy izucheniia kul'turnogo naslediia.* M., 1985. Pp. 177-184.

3756 Rodionov, M.A. *Golubaia busina na mednoi ladoni* [Blue Bead on Brazen Palm]. L.: Lenizdat, 1988. 144 pp., illus. (Razum poznaet mir). Bibl.: pp. 142-143. For review see item 5249.

3757 Rodionov, M.A. "Uchenie druzov v izlozhenii Sami Nasiba Makarima" [Druse's Teachings in Sami Nasiba Makarimas' Exposition]. *Islam: Religiia, obshchestvo, gosudarstvo.* M., 1984. Pp. 111-116.

3758 Rogachev, M.B. *Vremia protiv religii* [Time against Religion]. Syktyvar: Komi kn. izd-vo, 1986. 136 pp. Bibl.: pp. 124-136.

3759 Rogov, V.A. "Grekhovnoe i prestupnoe v prave Moskovskoi Rusi (ugolovnoe presledovanie eretichestva)" [Sinful and Felonious in the Law of Moscow Rus' (Criminal Persecution of Hereticism)]. *Istoriko-pravovye voprosy vzaimootnoshenii gosudarstva i tserkvi v istorii Rossii.* M., 1988. Pp. 11-23.

3760 Rogova, G.D. "Iz istorii ateisticheskoi propagandy v Adzharii" [History of Atheistic Propaganda in Adjar]. *Iz istorii religii i ateizma v Gruzii.* Tbilisi, 1988. Pp. 12-32. In Georgian. Summary in Russian.

3761 Rogova, G.D. "Sektantism v Gruzii (1921-1941)" [Sectarianism in Georgia (1921-1941)]. *Tr. Abkhaz. un-ta 1989.* T. 7. Pp. 9-17.

3762 Rogovaia, G.N. *Voidi v svetlyi mir* [Enter Into Bright World]. Kishinev: Kartia Moldoveniaske, 1987. 144 pp. In Moldavian.

3763 *Rol' khimicheskikh znanii v formirovanii nauchnogo mirovozzreniia* [The Role of Chemical Knowledge in Shaping Scientific World Outlook]. Comp.: A.G. Kochorva. Kishinev: Znanie MSSR, 1982. 51 pp. Bibl.: pp. 49-51.

3764 Rollan, R. "Zhizn' Ramakrishny" [The Life of Rama Krishna]. *Aziia i Afrika segodnia* 7 (1989): 56-61.

3765 Romanenko, B.P. *Voskhozhdenie: Ocherki o formirovanii ateist. mirovozzreniia rabochego klassa.* [Ascent: Essays on Forming Atheistic World Outlook of Workers Class]. L.: Lenizdat, 1989. 119 pp. Bibl.: pp. 117-118.

3766 Romanov, A.A. *Otkrytiia i sud'by: Vstrechi, besedy, razmyshleniia* [Discoveries and Fates: Meetings, Talks, Reflections]. M.: Sov. Rossiia, 1985. 158 pp.

3767 Romanov, I.N. *Sovremennaia ideologicheskaia bor'ba i zadachi ateisticheskogo vospitaniia* [Contemporary Ideological Struggle and Aims of Atheistic Education]. M.: Znanie, 1984. 22 pp. (V pomoshch' lektoru / Vsesoiuz. o-vo "Znanie", Tsentr. Dom nauch. ateizma).

3768 Romanov, L.N. "Iskusstvo i religiia" [Art and Religion]. *Sotsial'-no-filosofskie aspekty kritiki religii.* L., 1988. Pp. 42-62.

3769 Romanov, L.N. "K voprosu o filosofskikh istokakh muzykal'noi kul'tury rannego khristianstva" [Philosophical Sources of Musical Culture of Early Christianity]. *Muzei v ateisticheskoi propagande.* L., 1988. Pp. 81-89.

3770 Romanov, L.N. "K voprosu o vvedenii khristianstva na Rusi" [Introduction of Christianity into Rus']. *Muzei v ateisticheskoi propagande.* L., 1987. Pp. 104-115.

3771 Romanova, A.P. "Fenomenologicheskoe napravlenie v sovremennoi burzhuaznoi sotsiologii religii" [Phenomenological Direction in Current Bourgeois Sociology of Religion]. *Vopr. filosofii* 7 (1985): 135-142.

3772 Romanova, N.S. *Mirovozzrencheskaia funktsiia sotsialisticheskoi obriadnosti* [World Outlook's Function of Socialist Ceremonial]. Kiev: Nauk. dumka, 1987. 87 pp. Annot. bibl.: pp. 82-86.

3773 Romanova, N.S. "Znachenie sotsialisticheskoi obriadnosti dlia preodoleniia religioznogo mirovozzreniia" [The Importance of Socialist Ceremonial for Overcoming Religious Outlook]. *Vopr. ateizma* 21 (1985): 59-65.

3774 Romanova, S.A. "Ateisticheskoe vospitanie studentov vo vneuchebnoe vremia" [Students Atheistic Education in Non School-Hours]. *Aktual'nye problemy nauchno-ateisticheskogo vospitaniia molodezhi.* M., 1987. Pp. 110-114.

3775 Romanova, S.A. "Osobennosti formirovaniia pravoslavno-iazycheskogo sinkretizma Mari (XVI-XIX veka)" [Forming Features of Orthodox-Heathen Sincretism of Mari (XVIth-XIXth Centuries)]. *Istoriia khristianizatsii narodov Srednego Povolzh'ia. Kriticheskie suzhdeniia i otsenka.* Cheboksary, 1988. Pp. 42-48.

3776 Romanova, S.A. "Rol' trudovogo kollektiva v ateisticheskom vospitanii zhenshchin" [The Role of Labour Collective in Atheistic Education of Women]. *Aktual'nye problemy obespecheniia effektivnosti nauchno-ateisticheskoi raboty.* Chebokary, 1986. Pp. 55-60.

3777 Romanovich, V.V. *Lichnost' i religiia* [Individual and Religion]. Alma-Ata: Kazakhstan, 1982. 72 pp., illus. (Uchenye beseduiut s veruiushchimi). Bibl.: p. 71. For review see item 5250.

3778 Romanovich, V.V. *Religiia i zdorov'e* [Religion and Health]. Alma-Ata: Znanie KazSSR, 1980. 20 pp.

3779 Rostovtsev, M.I. "Gosudarstvo, religiia i kul'tura skifov i sarmatov" [State, Religion and Culture of the Scythians and Sarmatians]. *Vestn. dreev. istorii* 1 (1989): 192-210.

3780 Rotovskii, A.A. *Dukhovnost' ili bezdushnost'?.* Klerik. radiopropaganda i vopr. ideino-vospitat. raboty [Spirituality or Heartlessness? Clerical Radio Propaganda and the Problem of Ideological-Educational Work]. Kiev: Znanie UkSSR, 1989. 48 pp. (Ser. 5, Nauchno-ateisticheskaia / Znanie UkSSR; No 3). In Ukrainian.

3781 Rotovskii, A.A. *Klerikal'naia propaganda: tseli i sredstva* [Clerical Propaganda: Aims and Means]. Khar'kov: Prapor, 1988. 235 pp. Bibl.: pp. 230-233.

3782 Rotovskii, A.A. "Klerikal'no-antikommunisticheskaia radiopropaganda na SSSR: ideologicheskie funktsii, politicheskie raschety" [Clerical Anti-

Communist Radio Propaganda on USSR: Ideological Functions, Political Calculations]. *Vopr. nauch. ateizma* 36 (1987): 250-266.

3783   Rotovskii, A.A. *Klerikal'noe radioveshchanie v 'psikhologicheskoi voine'* [Clerical Broadcasting in the "Psychological War"]. Kiev: Politizdat Ukrainy, 1987. 167 pp. (Vopr. ideol. bor'by i kontrpropagandy). Annot. bibl.: pp. 163-166.

3784   Rotovskii, A.A. *Politika evangelizatsii: tseli mnimye i real'nye (Antikom. napravlennost' deiatel'nosti protestant. klerik. tsentrov)* [The Policy of Evangelisation: Imaginary and Real Aims (Anti-Communist Tendency of the Activity of Protestant Clerical Centres)]. Kiev: Znanie UkSSR, 1983. 45 pp. (Ser. 5 "Nauchno-ateisticheskaia" / O-vo "Znanie"UkSSR; No 3). In Ukrainian. Bibl.: p. 45. Annot. bibl.: p. 44.

3785   Rovnyi, B. "Uchit'sia ateizmu" [Study Atheism]. *Kommunist Kirgizstana* 4 (1988): 76-80.

3786   Rozenbaum, Iu.A. *Sovetskoe gosudarstvo i tserkov'* [Soviet State and Church]. M.: Nauka, 1985. 174 pp. (Ser. "Konstitutsiia SSSR. Lichnost' i pravo"). For review see item 5251.

3787   Rozenbaum, Iu.[A]. "Zakon o svobode sovesti" [The Law on Freedom of Conscience]. *Novoe vremia* 40 (1988): 24-26.

3788   Rozhnov, G. "'Eto my, gospodi!'" ["It is Us, O Lord!"]. *Ogonek* 38 (1989): 6-8.

3789   Rozhnov, V.E. *Proroki i chudotvortsy: Etiudy o mistitsizme* [Prophets and Miracle-Workers: Studies on Mysticism]. Kishinev: Kartia moldoveniaske, 1983. 266 pp., illus. In Moldavian.

3790   Rubakin, N.A. *Sredi tain i chudes* [Among Mysteries and Miracles]. Kishinev: Kartia moldoveniaske, 1980. 246 pp., illus. In Moldavian.

3791   Rubenis, A.A. *Drevnie znaki i simvoly* [Ancient Signs and Symbols]. Riga: Resp. metod. kab. po ucheb. zavedeniiam iskusstva i kul'tury LatvSSR, 1989. 60 pp., illus. In Latvian. Bibl.: p. 59.

3792   Rubenis, A.A. *Kritika osnovnykh printsipov protesantskoi neoortodoksii* [Criticism of Fundamental Principles of Protestant Neo Orthodoxy]. M.:

Znanie, 1983. 63 pp. (Novoe v zhizni, nauke, tekhnike. Ser. "Nauch. ateizm"; No 4).

3793 Rubtsova, N.A. "Liudi i bogi v stilistike 'Eneidy': elementy gimna v epizodakh poemy" [People and Gods in "Eneid's" Stylistics: Elements of Hymn in Poem's Episodes]. *Poetika drevnerimskoi literatury.* M., 1989. Pp. 53-67.

3794 Rubtsova, N.A. "Molitva i gimn v 'Iliade' Gomera" [Prayer and Hymn in Homer's "Iliad"]. *Vzaimosviaz' i vzaimovliianie zhanrov v razvitii antichnoi literatury.* M., 1989. Pp. 26-53.

3795 Rudaeva, A.V.; Lazareva, T.N. "Rol' Muzeia prirody KhGU v ateisticheskom vospitanii" [The Role of the Museum of Nature of the Khar'kov State University in Atheistic Education]. *Vestn. Khar'k. un-ta* 288 (1986): 99-100.

3796 Rudakova, N.M. *Protestantskoe sektantstvo i ateisticheskaia rabota* [Protestant Sectarianism and Atheistic Work]. Barnaul: Alt. kn. izd-vo, 1984. 55 pp. Fo review se item 5252.

3797 Rudinskii, F.M.; Shapiro, M.A. "Pravosoznanie grazhdan v sfere realizatsii svobody sovesti i praktika ee osushchestvleniia [Citizens' Legal Awareness Regarding the Realization of Freedom of Conscience and its Practical Implementation]. *Sov. gosudarstvo i pravo* 12 (1988): 22-31.

3798 Rudnev, V.A. *Obriady narodnye i obriady tserkovnye* [National Ceremonies and Church Ceremonies]. L.: Lenizdat, 1982. 159 pp. Bibl.: p. 158. For review see item 5253.

3799 Rudova, M.L. "Bodkhisatva Guan'in' v pamiatnikakh Dun'khuana" [Bodhisattva Guanyn in Monuments of Tunhuang]. *Tr. Gos. Ermitazha* 27 (1989): 57-60. Summary in English, p. 54.

3800 Rukavishnikova, N. "Khram Dzhagannatkha" [Jagannatha Temple]. *Nauka i religiia* 8 (1984): 60-63.

3801 Rumiantseva, M.G. "Ateisticheskii aspekt materialisticheskogo mirovozzreniia" [Atheistic Aspect of Materialistic Outlook]. *Faktor stanovleniia i sovershchenstvovaniia sotsializma: Ist.-ekon. i filos. aspekty.* Kazan', 1986. Pp. 32-36.

3802 Rumiantseva, T.G. *Kriticheskii analiz kontseptsii 'chelovecheskoi agressivnosti'*
      [Critical Analysis of the Conception of "Human Aggressiveness"]. Minsk:
      Izd-vo BGU, 1982. 128 pp. Bibl.: pp. 124-127.

3803 Rumiantseva, V.S. "Mezhdunarodnyi simpoziium o roli Russkoi pravoslavnoi
      tserkvi v istorii Rossii X-XVII vekov" [International Symposium on the
      Role of Russian Orthodox Church in the History of Russia of Xth-
      XVIIth Centuries]. *Istoriia SSSR* 6 (1988): 199-201.

3804 Rumiantseva, V.S. *Narodnoe antitserkovnoe dvizhenie v Rossii v XVII veke*
      [Popular anti-Church Movement in Russia in the XVIIth Century]. M.:
      Nauka, 1986. 264 pp., illus. Name index: pp. 251-263. For reviews see
      items 5254-5256.

3805 Ruml, V. "Vazhnyi uchastok lektsionnoi propagandy" [Important Sphere of
      Propaganda Based on Lectures]. *Nauka i religiia* 9 (1982): 51.

3806 Runeva, T.A.; Kolosnitsyn, V.I. "Razvitie esteticheskogo i preodolenie
      religioznogo mirootnosheniia v usloviiakh razvitogo sotsializma" [Deve-
      lopment of Aesthetic and Overcoming of Religious Outlook under
      Developed Socialism]. *Ekonomicheskie aspekty sotsialisticheskogo obraza
      zhizni.* Sverdlovsk, 1981. Pp. 91-96.

3807 Rusinov, V.N. "'Skazanie o Meletii Antiokhiiskom' i spory po tserkovno-
      obriadovym voprosam na Rusi v XIII-XVI vekakh" ["The Tale of Meletii
      from Antioch" and Disputes on Church-Ritual Problems in Rus' of the
      XIIIth-XVIth Centuries]. *Ideologiia i kul'tura feodal''noi Rossii.* Gor'kii,
      1988. Pp. 35-47. Bibl.: pp. 45-47.

3808 *Russkaia ikona XIV-XVI vekov: Gos. ist. muzei, Moskva. Al'bom.* [Russian
      Icon of the XIVth-XVIth Centuries: Moscow State Historical Museum.
      Album]. Comp.: I.L. Kyzlasova. L.: Avrora, 1988. 27 pp., illus. Bibl.: p.
      24.

3809 *Russkaia pravoslavnaia tserkov'* [Russian Orthodox Church]. M.: Progress,
      1982. 255 pp., col. illus. In English.

3810 *Russkaia pravoslavnaia tserkov', X-XX vv* [Russian Orthodox Church, Xth-
      XXth Centuries]. [Ed.: A. Preobrazhenskii]. M.: Progress, 1988. 464 pp.,
      illus. In English. Name index: pp. 456-462. Published also in:
      M.: Progress and in Genoa: Edest, [1988]. 479 pp., illus. (Veka i liudi).
      In Italian.

3811 *Russkaia pravoslavnaia tserkkov': do i posle 1000-letnego iubileia* [Russian Orthodox Church, Before and After the 1000th Jubillee]. M.: Novosti, 1989. 78 pp., illus. (B-ka sputnika). In English. Published also in: Arabic, French, German and Spanish.

3812 *Russkii feodal'nyi arkhiv XIV-pervoi treti XVI veka* [Russian Feudal Archive of XIVth-Early XVIth Centuries]. [Ed.: V.I. Buganova]. M.: In-t istorii SSSR, 1986 -
[1]. 1986. 219 pp., illus. Annot. bibl.: pp. 44-50.
[2]. 1987 (1988). 458 pp.
[3]. 1987 (1988). Pp. 459-695.
[4]. 1988 (1989). Pp. 695-941, illus.

3813 *Russkoe pravoslavie: vekhi istorii* [Russian Orthodoxy: Landmarks of History]. [Sc. ed.: A.I. Klibanov]. M.: Politizdat, 1989. 720 pp. Name and subject index: pp. 702-720. For reviews see items 5257-5260.

3814 *Russkoe pravoslavie i ateizm v otechestvennoi istorii* [Russian Orthodoxy and Atheism in Home History]. [Ed.: L.I. Emeliakh]. L.: GMIRIA, 1988. 155 pp.

3815 Rustamov, Iu.I. *Islam i obshchestvennaia mysl' sovremennoi Turtsii* [Islam and Social Thought of Contemporary Turkey]. Baku: Elm, 1980. 160 pp. Bibl.: pp. 151-160.

3816 Rustamov, V.A. *Sovetkoe zakonodatel'stvo o religioznykh kul'takh* [Soviet Legislation on Religious Cults]. Tashkent: Uzbekistan, 1986. 22 pp. (B-chka ateista). Published also in: Uzbek.

3817 Rustamova, Ch.T. "K voprosu o sootnoshenii religioznogo, natsional'nogo i narodnogo v obriadovo-prazdnichnoi sfere" [On the Problem of Correlation of Religious, National and Popular in Ceremonial-Festive Sphere]. *Voprosy teorii i praktiki nauchnogo ateizma*. M., 1988. Pp. 96-118.

3818 Rustamova, Ch.T. "Razvitie sotsial'no-politicheskoi aktivnosti zhenshchin kak vazhneishee uslovie preodoleniia ikh religioznosi" [Development of Socio-Political Activity of Women as the Most Important Condition for Overcoming Their Religiosity]. *Aktual'nye problemy nauchno-ateisticheskogo vospitaniia molodezhi*. M., 1987. Pp. 101-104.

3819   Rutkevich, A.M. *Psikhoanaliz i religiia* [Psychoanalysis and Religion]. M.: Znanie, 1987. 64 pp. (Novoe v zhizni, nauke, tekhnike. Nauch. ateizm; 11/1987). Bibl.: p. 63.

3820   Ruzmetov, A.M.; Alimasov, V. *Narodnye universitety i ateisticheskoe vospitanie* [Popular Universities and Atheistic Education]. Tashkent: Uzbekistan, 1986. 38 pp. (Ser. "Ekonomika"; No 13). In Uzbek.

3821   Rybachuk, N.F. *Trud i formirovanie novogo cheloveka* [Labour and Shaping of a New Man]. Kiev: Nauk. dumka, 1986. 105 pp.

3822   Rybakov, B.A. "Gorodskoe iazychestvo Drevnei Rusi" [Urban Paganism of Ancient Rus']. *Trudy V Mezhdunarodnogo kongressa slavianskoi arkheologii, Kiev, 18-25 sent. 1985 g.* M., 1987. T. 1. Vyp. 1. Pp. 77-79.

3823   Rybakov, B.A. *Iazichestvo Drevnei Rusi* [Paganism of Ancient Rus']. M.: Nauka, 1987. 783 pp., illus. Republished in 1988. Sequel to *Iazychestvo drevnikh slavian*. For review see item 5261.

3824   Rybakov, B.A. *Iazychestvo drevnikh slavian* [Paganism of Ancient Slavs]. M.: Nauka, 1981. 607 pp., illus. For reviews see items 5262-5270.

3825   Rybakov, B.[A]. "Nachal'nye veka russkoi istorii" [First Ages of Russian History]. *Khristianstvo i Rus'*. M., 1988. Pp. 5-30.

3826   Rybakov, R.B. *Burzhuaznaia reformatsiia induizma* [Bourgeois Reformation of Hinduism]. M.: Nauka, 1981. 183 pp. Bibl.: pp. 171-179. Annot. bibl.: pp. 158-170.

3827   Rybakov, R.B. "Izuchenie induizma v Rossii i SSSR - itogi i perspektivy" [Study of Hinduism in Russia and USSR - Results and Perspectives]. *Drevnie kul'tury Srednei Azii i Indii*. L., 1984. Pp. 172-179. Bibl.: pp. 178-179.

3828   Rybin, V.A. "Sovremennye aspekty politizatsii islama" [Contemporary Aspects of Politicization of Islam]. *Izv. AN KirgSSR*. Obshchestv. nauki 2 (1988): 32-37.

3829   Rybina, N.V. "Kritika monastyrskoi deistvitel'nosti v proizvedeniiakh russkikh pisatelei kontsa XIX veka" [Criticism of Monastery's Reality in the Works of Russian Writers Late XIXth Century]. *Pravoslavie v Karelii*. Petrozavodsk, 1987. Pp. 62-72.

3830   Rydlevski, G. "Osnovnye problemy veroispovednoi politiki v PNR [Funda-
       mental Problems of Creed Policy in Polish People's Republic]. *Argumenty.*
       M., 1988. Pp. 181-193.

3831   Ryskel'dieva, L.T. "Buddizm i poiski 'podlinnoi svobody" [Buddhism and
       Searches of "Genuine Freedom"]. *Problemy sotsial'nogo razvitiia v istorii
       filosofii.* M., 1982. Pp. 32-35.

3832   Ryskel'dieva, L.T. "O poniatii 'dkharma' v buddizme" [The Notion of
       "Dharma" in Buddhism]. *Problemy bytiia i poznaniia v istorii zarubezhnoi
       filosofii.* M., 1982. Pp. 27-35.

3833   Ryskel'dieva, L.T. "O poniatii 'dkharma' v buddizme makhaiany" [The
       Notion of "Dharma" in Mahayan Buddhism]. *Orientalistika v Kirgizii.*
       Frunze, 1987. Pp. 93-105.

3834   Ryskel'dieva, L.T. "O probleme soznaniia v filosofii buddizma" [The Problem
       of Consciousness in Philosophy of Buddhism]. *Filosofiia cheloveka: dialog
       s traditsiei i perspektivy.* M., 1989. Pp. 66-76.

3835   Ryskel'dieva, L.T. "Ob osnovnom filosofskom poniatii buddizma" [Funda-
       mental Philosophical Concept of Buddhism]. *Vsesoiuznye filosofskie
       chteniia molodykh uchenykh "XXVI s'ezd KPSS i aktual'nye problemy
       marksistsko-leninskoi filosofii."* M., 1982. Pp. 29-32.

3836   Ryspaev, B. "'Sozdavat' svetlyi schastlivyi byt'" ["To Create Bright and Happy
       Way of Life"]. *Nauka i religiia* 4 (1981): 6-9.

3837   Rza-Kulizade, S.D. "Rol' Ibn Sino v razvitii srednevekovogo svobodomysliia"
       [The Role of Ibn Sina in Development of Medieval Free Thinking].
       Torzhestvo razuma. Dushanbe, 1988. Pp. 101-106.

3838   *S obochin na svetlyi put'* [From Side to Bright Road]. [Comp.: D.M.
       Koretskii]. Kiev: Politizdat Ukrainy, 1984. 182 pp. In Ukrainian.

3839   Saakadze, D."Islamskia revoliutsiia' i kurdski vopros" ["Islamic Revolution"
       and the Problem of Kurds]. *Kommunist Gruzii* 8 (1989): 85-91.

3840   Saakian, A.S. "Armianskii variant srednevekovogo ikonopochitaniia"
       [Armenian Version of Medieval Icon Worship]. *Ist.-filol. zhurn.* 2 (1987):
       150-159. In Armenian. Summary in Russian.

3841   Sabanchiev, Kh.-M.A. "Otechestvennaia istoriografiia religioznykh verovanii balkartsev vo 2-oi polovine XIX-nachale XX veka" [Native Historiography of Religious Beliefs of Balkars Late XIXth-Early XXth Century]. *Izv. Sev.-Kavk. nauch. tsentra vyssh. shk. Obshchestv. nauki* 3 (1988): 58-66.

3842   Sabov, A.D. "Kakuiu pozitsiiu zanimaiut katolicheskaia i protestanskaia tserkvi v kapitalisticheskikh stranakh po problemam iadernogo razoruzheniia?" [What Position Do the Catholic and Protestant Churches in Capitalist Countries Occupy on the Problems of Nuclear Disarmament?]. *Argumenty.* M., 1988. Pp. 222-223.

3843   Sabov, A.D. "Religiia gneva" [Religion of Anger]. *Argumenty.* M., 1988. Pp. 27-58.

3844   Sadykov, A. *Svobodomyslie v ucheniiakh srednevekovykh myslitelei Vostoka* [Freethinking in Teachings of Medieval Thinkers of Orient]. Dushanbe: Irfon, 1984. 21 pp. In Tajik.

3845   Sadykova, N.S. "O deiatel'nosti Muzeia istorii narodov Uzbekistana po ateisticheskomu vospitaniiu trudiashchikhsia" [Activity of the Museum of History of Uzbekistan People in Atheistic Education of Workers]. *Obshchestv. nauki v Uzbekistane* 8 (1986): 39-41.

3846   Saenko, N.I. "Metodika ispol'zovaniia mestnogo materiala v lektsiiakh po nauchnomu ateizmu" [Methods of the Use of Local Material in Lectures on Scientific Atheism]. *Vopr. ateizma* 20 (1984): 19-24.

3847   Safronova, E.S. "Buddizm na Zapade i ego rol' v sovremennoi ideologicheskoi bor'be" [Buddhism in the West and its Role in the Contemporary Ideological Struggle]. *Voprosy teorii i praktiki nauchnogo ateizma.* M., 1988. Pp. 220-230.

3848   Safronova, N.A. *Uniatskaia tserkov' i fashizm* [Uniate Church and Fascism]. 2nd. enlarged and revised ed. L'vov: Vishcha shkola. Izd-vo pri L'vov. un-te, 1981. 14 pp. In Ukrainian. Bibl.: pp. 62-63.

3849   Sagalaev, A.M. "Faktory obrazovaniia religioznogo sinkretizma u uraloaltaiskikh narodov [Forming Factors of Religious Syncretism in Ural-Altai Peoples]. *Smena kul'tur i migratsii v Zapadnoi Sibiri.* Tomsk: 1987. Pp. 72-75.

3850 Sagalaev, A.M. *Mifologiia i verovaniia altaitsev: tsentr.-aziat. vlianiia* [Mythology and Beliefs of Altai People: Central Asiatic Influence]. Novosibirsk: Nauka. Sib. otd-nie, 1984. 121 pp. Bibl.: pp. 105-115.

3851 Sagalaev, A.M. "O zakonomernostiakh vospriiatiia mirovykh religii tiurkami Saiano-Altaia" [On Conformity of Perception of World Religions by Saian-Altai Turkic People]. *Genezis i evoliutsiia etnicheskikh kul'tur Sibiri.* Novosibirsk, 1986. Pp. 155-179. Annot. bibl.: pp. 172-179.

3852 Sagalaev, A.M. "Udarnye instrumenty v ritualakh lamaizma i iuzhnosibirskogo shamanstva" [Percussion Instruments in the Rituals of Lamaism and South Siberian Shamanism]. *Sov. etnografiia* 5 (1981): 117-124.

3853 Saidaliev, A. *Starost' i religiia* [Old Age and Religion]. Tashkent: Uzbekistan, 1989. 30 pp. (Marksizm-leninizm; No 3). In Uzbek.

3854 Saidbaev, T.S. *Dialogi ob Islame* [Dialogues on Islam]. Tashkent: Fan, 1988. 74 pp. For review see item 5271.

3855 Saidbaev, T.S. *Islam: istoriia i sovremennost'* [Islam: History and Contemporaneity]. M.: Znanie, 1985. 64 p. (Novoe v zhizni, nauke, tekhnike. Nauch. ateizm; 11). Suppl.: "Kompleksnyi podkod - neobkhodimoe uslovie effektivnosti ateisticheskogo vospitaniia" [All-embracing approach - necessary condition for effective atheistic education]. L. Bashirov. Bibl.: p. 58.

3856 Saidbaev, T.S. *Islam i obshchestvo: Analiz izmenenii roli i funktsii religii v sotsialisticheskom obschestve* [Islam and Society: Analysis of Changes of the Role and Functions of Religion in Socialist Society]. M.: [S.n.], 1980. 49 pp. Bibl.: pp. 48-49.

3857 Saidbaev, T.S. *Islam i obshchestvo: Opyt ist.-sotsiol. issled.* [Islam and Society: Experience of an Historic-Social Research]. 2nd enlarged ed. M.: Nauka, 1984. 302 pp. Bibl.: pp. 284-301.

3858 Saidov, N.Kh. *Sistema nauchno-ateisticheskogo vospitaniia v usloviiakh razvitogo sotsializma* [The System of Scientific-Atheistic Education under Developed Socialism]. Tashkent: Fan, 1982. 156 pp. Bibl.: pp. 144-155. For review see item 5272.

3859 Saidov, N.Kh. *Za nastupatel'nyi ateizm* [To an Offensive Atheism]. Tashkent: Uzbekistan, 1984. 111 pp. (B-ka ateista). In Uzbek. Bibl.: p. 111.

3860   Saidullaev, P. *Rol' sredstv massovoi informatsii v ateisticheskom vospitanii* [The Role of Means of Mass Information in Atheistic Education]. Tashkent: Znanie UzSSR, 1982. 25 pp. (V pomoshch' lektoru / O-vo "Znanie" UzSSR. Ser. obshchestv.-polit.). In Uzbek.

3861   Saidullaev, P. *Sotsialisticheskii obraz zhizni kak faktor ateisticheskogo vospitaniia truzhenikov sela* [Socialist Way of Life as a Factor of Atheistic Education of Village Toilers]. Tashkent, Znanie UzSSR, 1983. 20 pp. (V pomoshch' lektoru / O-vo "Znanie" UzSSR. Ser. obshchestv.-polit.). In Uzbek.

3862   Sakalauskas, I. "Ateisticheskoe vospitanie: posledovatel'nost' i tselenapravlennost'" [Atheistic Education: Consistency and Purposefulness]. *Kommunist.* Vil'nius. 12 (1986): 64-68.

3863   Sakalauskas, I. "Ateizm v sovremennykh usloviiakh" [Atheism in Present Day Conditions]. *Ateistines minties raida lietuvoje.* Kaunas, 1988. Pp. 7-13. In Lithuanian. Summary in Russian.

3864   Sakalauskas, I. "Nelegkii dialog" [Difficult Dialogue]. *Kommunist.* Vil'nius. 6 (1988): 72-75.

3865   Sakharov, A. "Tserkov' v period feodal'noi razdroblennosti" [The Church in the Period of Shattered Feudalism]. *Khristianstvo i Rus'.* M., 1988. Pp. 47-67.

3866   Sakharov, A.; Zimin, A.; Grekulov, E. "Tserkovnaia reforma i raskol" [Church Reform and Schism]. *Khristianstvo i Rus'.* M., 1988. Pp. 68-81.

3867   Sakharov, A.N. "Mezhdunarodnye aspekty kreshcheniia Rusi" [International Aspect of Baptism of Rus']. *Vestn. AN SSSR* 10 (1988): 122-133.

3868   Sakharov, S.I. *Sovremennye religioznye prazdnestva, obychai i ikh ideologicheskaia sushchnost'* [Contemporary Religious Feasts, Customs and Their Ideological Essence]. Tbilisi: Sabchota Sakartvelo, 1980. 226 pp. In Georgian.

3869   Saksanov, T. *Religioznye predrassudki* [Religious Prejudices]. Tashkent: Meditsina, 1981. In Uzbek.

3870   Saksonov, T. *Rol' istoricheskikh pamiatnikov v ateisticheskoi propagande* [The Role of Historic Monuments in Atheistic Propaganda]. Tashkent:

Uzbekistan, 1982. 32 pp. (Ser. "Marksizm-leninizm" / O-vo "Znanie" UzSSR; No 7). In Uzbek.

3871 Salenek, A.A. "Ateisticheskoe vospitanie v svete perestroiki" [Atheistic Education in the Light of Perestroika]. *Aktual'nye voprosy formirovaniia nauchno-materialisticheskogo mirovozzreniia trudiashchikhsia.* Tashkent, 1989. Pp. 150-156.

3872 Salidzhanova, N.S. "Nekotorye osobennosti ateisticheskogo vospitaniia molodezhi respublik Srednei Azii" [Some Features of Atheistic Upbringing of Youth of Middle Asian Republics]. *Aktual'nye problemy nauchno-ateisticheskogo vospitaniia molodezhi.* M., 1987. Pp. 98-100.

3873 Saltykov, G. "Musul'mane v Kitae" [Moslems in China]. *Nauka i religiia* 9 (1981): 59-63.

3874 Samarina, M.S. "'Novaia zhizn'" Dante i Bernard Klervosskii" [Dante's "New Life" and Bernard Klervosskii]. *Vestn. Leningr. un-ta.* Ser. 2, Istoriia, iazykoznanie, literaturovedenie 3 (1989): 91-93.

3875 Samokhvalov, N.I. "O znachenii ateisticheskogo vospitaniia v formirovanii marksistsko-leninskogo mirovozzreniia" [Importance of Atheistic Education in Shaping Marxist-Leninist Outlook]. *Nauch. kommunizm* 6 (1986): 36-43.

3876 Samostiak, A.K. "Vozvrashchenie k istine: Vospominaniia b. sviashchennika" [Return to the Truth: Reminiscences of a Former Priest]. *Nauka i religiia* 1 (1984): 29-31; 2 (1984): 26-29.

3877 Samozvantseva, N.V. "Formirovanie predstavlenii ob istorii v buddiiskoi traditsii Indii" [Forming of Conceptions about History in India's Buddhist Tradition]. *Buddizm: Istoriia i kul'tura.* M., 1989. Pp. 152-168.

3878 Sangilov, M. "Ateisticheskoe vospitanie v sem'e" [Atheistic Education in the Family]. *Kommunist Uzbekistana* 12 (1987): 68-70.

3879 Sapelkina, E.V. "Razoblachenie politicheskogo klerikalizma - aktual'naia zadacha ateisticheskkoi propagandy" [Exposure of Political Clericalism - Pressing Problem of Atheistic Propaganda]. *Vopr. ateizma* 24 (1988): 122-127.

3880 Sapronenko, V.V. *Dukhovnye potrebnosti i pravoslavie* [Spiritual Needs and Orthodoxy]. Stavropol': Kn. izd-vo, 1985. 96 pp. Bibl.: pp. 93-95.

3881 Sapronenko, V.[V]. "'Kreshchenie Rusi': Sushchnost' i posledstviia" ["Baptism of Rus'": Essence and Consequences]. *Stavropol'e* 1 (1988): 104-112.

3882 Saprykin, S.Iu. "Khramovye ob'edineniia Pontiiskoi Kappadokii" [Temples Union of Pontus Cappadocia]. *Tretii Vsesoiuznyi simpozium po problemam ellenisticheskoi kul'tury na Vostoke, mai 1988 g.* Erevan, 1988. Pp. 74-76.

3883 Saprykin, V.A. *Aktual'nye problemy nauchno-ateisticheskogo vospitaniia v usloviiakh goroda* [Actual Problems of Scientific-Atheistic Education in Town]. M.: Znanie, 1986. 64 pp. (Novoe v zhizni, nauke, tekhnike. Nauch. ateizm; 6/1986). Bibl.: p. 63-64.

3884 Saprykin, V.[A]. "Ateisticheskoe vospitanie v kollektive" [Atheistic Education in Collective]. *Agitator* 8 (1983): 34-36.

3885 Saprykin, V.A. "Nauchno-ateisticheskoe vospitanie v trudovom kollektive" [Scientific-Atheistic Education in Working Collective]. *Part. zhizn' Kazakhstana* 6 (1983): 47-54.

3886 Saprykin, V.A. *Sotsialisticheskii kollektiv i ateisticheskoe vospitanie: Opyt, sistema, problemy* [Socialist Collective and Atheistic Education: Experience, System, Problems]. M.: Politizdat, 1983. 175 pp. For reviews see items 5273-5274.

3887 Saprykin, V.A. *Urbanizatsiia. Ateizm. Religiia.: Probl. formirovaniia nauch.-materialist. mirovozzreniia v usloviiakh sots. goroda* [Urbanization. Atheism. Religion.: The Problem of Shaping Scientific-Materialist Outlook in a Socialist Town]. Alma-Ata: Kazakhstan, 1981. 287 pp., illus. For reviews see items 5275-5276.

3888 Saprykin, V.A. *Urbanizatsiia i ateisticheskoe vospitanie* [Urbanization and Atheistic Education]. Kiev: Politizdat Ukrainy, 1985. 175 pp. Bibl.: pp. 168-174.

3889 Saprykin, V.[A]. "Veruiushchie v sovremennom gorode" [Believers in Contemporary Town]. *Nauka i religiia* 2 (1987): 6-9.

3890 Saradzhian, P.A. "Vopros sotsial'noi spravedlivosti v ideologii ismailizma" [The Problem of Social Justice in the Ideology of Ismailism]. *Strany i narody Blizhnego i Srednego Vostoka.* 15 (1989): 223-238. In Armenian. Summary in Russian.

3891 Sardachuk, P.D. *Stupeni zrelosti* [Stages of Maturity]. M.: Politizdat, 1985. 79 pp. (B-ka ateista). For review see item 5277.

3892 Sardachuk, P.D. *Vospitanie ateisticheskogo mirovozzreniia* [Education of Atheistic World Outlook]. Kiev: Politizdat Ukrainy, 1982. 127 pp. In Ukrainian. Annot. bibl.: pp. 125- 126.

3893 Sarianidi, V.I. "Protozoroastriiskii khram v Margiane i problema vozniknoveniia zoroastrizma" [Proto Zoroastrian Temple in Marghian and the Problem of the Origin of Zoroastrianism]. *Vestn. drev. istorii* 1 (1989): 152-169. Summary in English.

3894 Sarkisian, A.A. *Antiklerikal'naia mysl' v Armenii v seredine XIX veka* [Anticlerical Thought in Armenia in the Middle of XIXth Century]. Erevan: Izd-vo Erev. un-ta, 1983. 54 pp. In Armenian.

3895 Sarkisian, A.A. *Khristianskii gumanizm - illiuzii i deistvitel'nost'* [Christian Humanism - Illusions and Reality]. Erevan: Luis, 1987. 96 pp. In Armenian.

3896 Sarkisian, A.[A]. "Problemy religii i natsii v armianskom svobodomyslii serediny XIX veka" [Problems of Religion and Nation in Armenian Free Thinking in the Middle of XIXth Century]. *Po lenin. puti* 12 (1988): 51-57.

3897 Sarkisian, A.A. *Religioznyi modernizm v tupike* [Religious Modernism in Impasse]. Erevan: Aiastan, 1984. 55 pp. In Armenian.

3898 Sarv, Kh.; Vladykin, V. "O mestakh zhertvoprinosheniia tipa sviashchennoi roshchi u estontsev i privolzhskikh finnov" [Places of Sacrifices of the Sacred Grove Type by Estonians and Volga Finns]. *Etnograafiamuuseumi aastaraamat* 36 (1988): 138-155. In Estonian. Summaries in German and Russian.

3899 Sarychev, V.V. "Otnoshenie baptistov k sluzhbe v armii: istoriia i sovremennost'" [Baptists' Attitude Towards the Service in the Army: History and Contemporaneity]. *Aktual'nye problemy nauchno-ateisticheskogo vospitaniia molodezhi*. M., 1987. Pp. 136-140.

3900 Sattarov, K. *Fol'klor i ateisticheskoe vospitanie* [Folklore and Atheistic Education]. Tashkent: Fan, 1988. 61 pp. In Uzbek.

3901 Sattarov, M.[M]. "Ob ateisticheskom nasledii V. Khuluflu" [V. Huluflu's Atheistic Heritage]. *Izv. AN AzSSR*. Ser. istorii, filosofii i prava. Baku, 1988. Pp. 3-10. In Azerbaijan. Summary in Russian.

3902 Sattarov, M.M.; Azizova, Z.S. "Azerbaidzhanskie sovetskie ateisty 1920-30-kh godov o proiskhozhdenii i sushchnosti obriada magerram (mukharrem)" [Azerbaijan Soviet Atheists of the 1920-30s on Origin and Essence of Muharram Ritual]. *Izv. AN AzSSR*. Ser. istorii, filosofii i prava 4 (1985): 95-102. Summary in Azerbaijan.

3903 Sattarov, M.M.; Dzhalilov, M.F. *Besedy ob ateizme* [Talks on Atheism]. Baku: Azerneshr, 1980. 118 pp. In Azerbaijan.

3904 Sattarov, M.M.; Dzhalilov, M.F. "Edinstvo internatsional'nogo i ateisticheskogo vospitaniia" [The Unity of International and Atheistic Education]. *Izv. AN AzSSR*. Ser. istorii, filosofii i prava 4 (1987): 114-121. In Azerbaijan. Summary in Russian.

3905 Satybekova, S.K.; Azimov, K.A. "K voposu o mirovozzrencheskoi sushchnosti sufiiskikh poniatii" [Problem of the Nature of the World Outlook of Sufist Conceptions]. *Vestn. AN KazSSR* 7 (1986): 47-53.

3906 Satyshev, V.E. "Politiko-pravovye vozzreniia presviterianskoi partii perioda angliiskoi burzhuaznoi revoliutsii" [Political-Legal Outlooks of Presbyterian Party in the Period of English Bourgeois Revolution]. *Aktual'nye problemy istoriko-pravovoi nauki* 3 (1988): 115-130.

3907 Saukh, P.Iu. *Ateizm i religiia o schast'e i meste cheloveka v mire* [Atheism and Religion on Man's Happiness and Place in the World]. Dnepropetrovsk: Promin', 1989. 183 pp.

3908 Saukh, P.Iu. *Dukhovnyi mir lichnosti i ateizm* [Spiritual World of the Individual and Atheism]. Kiev: Znanie UkSSR, 1986. 49 pp. (Ser. 5, Nauch.-ateist. / O-vo "Znanie" UkSSR; No 10). Annot. bibl.: pp. 48-49.

3909 Saukh, P.Iu. *Kategorii nauchnogo ateizma: Filos.-metodol. analiz* [Categories of Scientific Atheism: Philosophic-Methodological Analysis]. L'vov: Vyshcha shk., 1988. 216 pp., illus. For review see item 5278.

3910 Saukh, P.Iu. *Naidi svoe schast'e* [Find Your Happiness]. Kiev: Politizdat Ukrainy, 1986. 68 pp. (Besedy s veruiushchimi). Bibl.: pp. 66-67. In Ukrainian.

3911 Saukh, P.Iu. *Nauchno-tekhnicheskii progress i religiia* [Scientific-Technical Progress and Religion]. Kiev: Znanie UkSSR, 1982. 32 pp. (Ser. 5 "Nauchno-ateisticheskaia" / O-vo "Znanie" UkSSR; No 4). In Ukrainian. Bibl.: pp. 29-31.

3912 Saukh, P.Iu. "Pravoslavnaia moral': metodologicheskie printsipy ee kritiki" [Orthodox Morals: Methodological Principles of Its Criticism]. *Vopr. ateizma* 22 (1986): 85-92.

3913 Saukh. P.Iu. *Sovremennaia nauka i bor'ba ateisticheskogo i religioznogo miroponimanii* [Contemporary Science and the Struggle of Atheistic and Religious Outlooks]. L'vov: Vyshsha shk. Izd-vo pri L'vov. gos. un-te, 1987. 88 pp. (Ateist. b-chka studenta).

3914 Savateev, A.D. "Musul'manskaia intelligentsiia i obshchestva Tropicheskoi Afriki" [Moslem Intelligenstia and Societies of Tropical Africa]. *Puti evoliutsii i obshchestvennaia rol' sovremennoi afrikanskoi inteligentsii: poiski, tendentsii, perspektivy.* M., 1988. Pp. 129-134.

3915 Savchenko, A.V. *Kollektsiia ibaditskikh rukopisei nauchnoi biblioteki L'vovskogo gosudarstvennogo universiteta im. I.Ia. Franko* [Collection of Ibadit Manuscripts of the Scientific Library of L'vov's State University in the Name of I.Ia. Franko]. Kiev: [S.n.], 1988. 26 pp. Bibl.: pp. 21-22. Index: pp. 23-24.

3916 Savchenko, D.V. "Rol' sredstv massovoi informatsii i propagandy v formirovanii ateisticheski orientirovannogo obshchestvennogo mneniia" [The Role of Means of Mass Information and Propaganda in Shaping Atheistic Orientated Public Opinion]. *Nauchnyi ateizm i obshchestvennoe mnenie.* M., 1987. Pp. 43-62.

3917 Savchenko, L.V. "Molodezhnaia pressa i ateisticheskaia propaganda" [Youth Press and Atheistic Propaganda]. *Aktual'nye problemy nauchno-ateisticheskogo voapitaniia molodezhi.* M., 1987. Pp. 45-49.

3918 Savchenko, P.D. "Liuteranskaia tserkov'" [Lutheran Church]. *Brat. vestn.* 3 (1987): 47-53.

3919 Savel'ev, S.N. *Ideinoe bankrotstvo bogoiskatel'stva v Rossii v nachale XX veka* [Ideological Bankruptcy of God Seeking in Early XXth Century Russia]. L.: Izd-vo Leningr. un-ta, 1987. 184 pp. For review see item 5279.

3920 Savel'ev, S.N. "Russkoe bogoiskatel'stvo v nachale XX veka" [Russian God Seeking in the Early XXth Century]. *Filos. nauki* 8 (1989): 91-93.

3921 Savel'ev, S.N. *V mire razocharovanii, nedezhd i illiuzii* [In the World of Disappointments, Hopes and Illusions]. L.: Znanie RSFSR, 1982. 16 pp. (V pomoshch' lektoru / O-vo "Znanie" RSFSR. Leningr. org.).

3922 Savel'eva, L.P. "Deiatel'nost' missionerov v Novoi Zelandii v pervoi polovine XIX veka i ikh rol' v kolonizatsii strany" [Missionaries Activity in New Zealand Early XIXth Century and Their Role in Colonization of the Country]. *Problemy istorii Okeanii.* Irkutsk, 1987. Pp. 4-35.

3923 Savitskas, G.A. "Prichiny netraditsionnoi religioznosti v sovremennom amerikanskom obshchestve" [Reasons for Nontraditional Religiosity in Contemporary American Society]. *Dukhovnye tsenosti kak predmet filosofskogo analiza.* M., 1985. Pp. 116-120.

3924 Savostina, E.A. "Mif i kul't geroia" [Myth and Hero Cult]. *Zhizn' mifa v antichnosti.* M., 1988. Ch. 1. Pp. 98-115.

3925 Sazykin, A.G. "Antishamanskaia propoved' trekh buddiiskikh sviatykh" [Antishamanist Sermon of Three Buddhist Saints]. *Istoriografiia i istochnikovedenie istorii stran Azii i Afriki.* 11 (1988): 154-172.

3926 Sedov, Iu. "Islam vykhodit iz mechetei" [Islam Leaves Mosques]. *Novoe vremia* 36 (1987): 12-13.

3927 Sedov, V.V.; Chernetsov, A.V. "Slavianskoe iazychestvo kak problema mezhdistsiplinarnogo izucheniia" [Slav Heathenism as Problem of Interdisciplinary Study]. *Vest. AN SSSR* 12 (1981): 76-81.

3928 Segizbaev, O.A. *Narodnoe samosoznanie i religiia* [Popular Self-Consciousness and Religion]. Alma-Ata: Kazakhstan, 1984. 71 pp.

3929 Segizbaev, O.S. "Vklad Chokana Valikhanova v domarksovskii ateizm i filosofskii materializm" [Chokan Valihanov's Contribution in Premarxist Atheism and Philosophical Materialism]. *Chokan Valikhanov i sevremennost'.* Alma-Ata, 1988. Pp. 87-89.

3930 Seidakhmatov, K. *Kalendarnye poniatiia kirgizov* [Calendar Notions of Kirghiz]. Fruunze: Kyrgyzstan, 1987. 68 pp., illus. In Kirghiz. Bibl.: pp. 65-66.

3931 Seliverstova, N.A. "Rol' fakul'tativa po nauchnomu ateizmu v formirovanii nauchno-materialisticheskogo mirovozzreniia studentov" [Facultative Role on the Subject of Scientific Atheism in Shaping Students' Scientific-Materialist Outlook]. *Aktual. vopr. metodiki prepodavaniia obshchestv. nauk i kom. vospitaniia studentov* 5 (1987): 123-128.

3932 Sem, Iu.A. "Mifologicheskie predstavleniia nanaitsev o prirode i cheloveke" [Nanaians' Mythological Notions on Nature and Man]. *Genezis i evoliutsiia etnicheskikh kul'tur Sibiri.* Novosibirsk, 1986. Pp. 30-44.

3933 Semchenko, A.T. "Katolicheskii 'opyt orientatsii': 'chelovek-massy' na puti k 'spaseniiu dushi'" [Catholic "Orientation Experience": "Man-Masses" on the Way to "Salvation of the Spirit"]. *Problemy cheloveka v sovremennoi religioznoi i misticheskoi literature.* M., 1988. Pp. 77-88.

3934 Semenkin, N.S. *Filosofiia bogoiskatel'stva* [Philosophy of God Seeking]. M.: Politizdat, 1986. 175 pp. For reviews see items 5280-5282.

3935 Semenov, V. "Pod flagom 'zashchity islama'" [Under the Flag of the "Defence of Islam"]. *Mezhdunarodnaia zhizn'* 1 (1987): 36-44.

3936 Semenova, I.I. "Nekotorye voprosy formirovaniia internatsional'noi sotsialisticheskoi kul'tury v protsesse ateisticheskogo vospitaniia" [Some Problems of Shaping International Socialist Culture in the Process of Atheistic Education]. *Vopr. nauch. kommunizma* 61 (1985): 107-113.

3937 Semenova, L.A. "Fatimidskii ismailizm v sovremennom zapadnom islamo-vedenii" [Fatimit Ismailism in Contemporary Western Study of Islam]. *Islam v istorii narodov Vostoka.* M., 1981. Pp. 25-39. Annot. bibl.: pp. 37-39.

3938 Semenova, L.A. "O polozhenii dukhovenstva na Blizhnem Vostoke v kontse XII v." [Status of Clergy in the Near East in the Late XIIth Century]. *Bartol'dovskie chteniia, 1982:* God shestoi. M., 1982. P. 60.

3939 Semenova, L.N. "Tserkovnye preobrazovaniia v pervoi chetverti XVIII v." [Church Reforms in Early XVIIIth Century]. *Vopr. nauch. ateizma* 25 (1980): 130-150.

3940 Semenovker, V.N. "Metodologicheskie aspekty sovershchenstvovaniia nauchno-ateisticheskoi deiatel'nosti" [Methodological Aspects of the Perfection of

Scientific-Atheistic Education]. *Nauch. dokl. vyssh. shkoly. Filos. nauki* 6 (1981): 122-125.

3941 Sementsov, V.S. *Bkhagavadviga v traditsii i v sovremennoi nauchnoi kritike* [Bhagavad-Gita in Tradition and in Contemporary Scientific Criticism]. M.: Nauka, 1985. 236 pp. Bibl.: pp. 137-141. Annot. bibl.: pp. 125-135.

3942 Seraia, N.S. "Ob ateisticheskoi ubezhdennosti i kriteriiakh ee otsenki" [Atheistic Conviction and Criterions of Its Evaluation]. *Vopr. ateizma* 18 (1982): 67-72.

3943 Serdobol'skaia, L.A. *Nauchno-ateisticheskaia propaganda i sovremennost'* [Scientific-Atheistic Propaganda and Contemporaneity]. M.: Znanie RSFSR, 1984. 39 pp. (V pomoshch' lektoru / O-vo "Znanie" RSFSR, Nauch.-metod. sovet otd-niia po propagande nauch. ateizma). Bibl.: p. 38.

3944 Serebriakov, Iu.G. "Osobennosti proiavleniia religioznykh prazdnikov v usloviiakh sela i ikh uchet v ateisticheskoi rabote" [Features of the Display of Religious Feasts in Village and Their Consideration in Atheistic Work]. *Problemy istorii religii i ateizma.* Cheboksary, 1980. Pp. 51-57.

3945 Serebrianyi, S.D. "Rammokhan Rai: religiia i razum" [Rammohan Roy: Religion and Reason]. *Ratsionalisticheskaia traditsiia i sovremennost'.* M., 1988. Kn. I. Pp. 202-224.

3946 Serebrovskii, V. "Misteriia 'Tsam'" ["Tsam" Mystery]. *Dekor. iskusstvo SSSR* 1 (1982): 32-34.

3947 Sereda, G.V. "Kritika pravoslavnogo ponimaniia natsional'nogo samo-soznaniia" [Criticism of Orthodox Conception of National Selfconscious-ness]. *Filosofskii analiz iavlenii dukhovnoi kul'tury: Teoret. i ist. aspekty.* M., 1984. Pp. 64-69.

3948 Sergienko, E. "O sueveriiakh, mode i vospitanii" [Superstitions, Fashion and Education]. *Nauka i religiia* 12 (1980): 36-38.

3949 Severchuk, I.P. "Sovershenstvovanie ateisticheskoi lektsionnoi propagandy v Ukrainskoi SSR" [Perfection of Atheistic Propaganda Based on Lectures in the Ukrainian SSR]. *Vopr. nauch. ateizma* 34 (1986): 157-166.

3950 Severchuk, I.[P]. "Velenie vremeni" [Call of Time]. *Nauka i religiia* 1 (1981): 10-12.

3951 Shaburov, N.V. "Vospriatie germetizma ideologami rannego khristianstva (Laktantsii i Avgustin)" [Perception of Hermetism by Ideologists of Early Christianity (Lactantius and Augustine)]. *Meroe* 3 (1985): 243-252. Summary in English, p. 275.

3952 Shachkov, V.N. *Legendy zhivut na zemle* [Legends Live on the Earth]. Kirov: Volgo-Viat. kn. izd-vo Kirov. otd-nie, 1989. 112 pp.

3953 Shadnev, K.K. "K kritike kontseptsii burzhuaznykh 'sovetologov'-islamovedov" [Criticism of Conceptions of Bourgeois "Sovietologists"-Islamists]. *Obshchestv. nauki v Uzbekistane* 5 (1987): 47-52.

3954 Shaidaeva, G. "Religiia i nravstvennost': illiuziia garmonii" [Religion and Morals: Illusion of Harmony]. *Sov. Dagestan* 1 (1989): 75-78.

3955 Shakhnovich, M.I. *Bibliia v sovremennoi bor'be idei* [Bible in the Contemporary Struggle of Ideas]. L.: Lenizdat, 1988. 340 pp., illus.

3956 Shakhnovich, M.I. *Chelovek vosstaet protiv boga* [Man Revolts against God]. Kiev: Molod', 1984. 143 pp., illus. In Ukrainian. Published also in 2nd enlarged ed. in:
L.: Det. lit. Leningr. otd-nie, 1986, 175 p., illus.
Tashkent: Iulduzcha, 1987, 287 pp., illus. In Uzbek.

3957 Shakhnovich, M.I. *Kritika religioznykh istolkovanii ekologicheskikh problem* [Criticism of Religious Interpretations of Ecological Problems]. M.: Znanie, 1985. 64 pp. (Novoe v zhizni, nauke, tekhnike. Nauch. ateizm; 1). Bibl.: p. 64.

3958 Shakhnovich, M.I. "Ne obozhestvliat', a ochelovechit'" [Not to Deify, But to Humanize]. *Nauka i religiia* 10 (1986): 3-5.

3959 Shakhnovich, M.I. *Primety vernye i suevernye* [True and Superstitious Signs]. L.; Lenizdat, 1984. 190 pp., illus. For review see item 5283.

3960 Shakhnovich, M.M. "Ateisticheskoe vospitanie molodezhi i ideologicheskaia bor'ba" [Atheistic Upbringing of Youth and the Ideological Struggle]. *Aktual'nye problemy nauhno-ateisticheskogo vospitaniia molodezhi.* M., 1987. Pp. 65-67.

3961   Shakhnovich, M.M. "Kritika teologizatsii ucheniia Epikura" [Criticism of Theologization of Epicurean Teachings]. *Aktual'nye problemy izucheniia istorii religii i ateizma.* L., 1980. Pp. 116-130.

3962   Shakhnovich, M.M. "Osovnye etapy antichnogo ateizma" [Basic Stages of Ancient Atheism]. *Sotsial'no-filosofskie aspekty kritiki religii.* L., 1988. Pp. 3-19.

3963   Shakhnovich, M.M. "Sovremennaia 'khristianizatsia' filosofii Epikura" [Contemporary "Conversion to Christianity" of Epicurean Philosophy]. *Religii mira, 1986.* M., 1987. Pp. 155-169.

3964   Shakhnovich, M.M. "Tema 'Zarozhdenie kritiki religii na Drevnem Vostoke' v peredvizhnykh vystavkakh" [The Theme of the "Origin of the Criticism of Religion in the Ancient Orient" in Mobile Exhibitions]. *Muzei v ateisticheskoi propagande.* M., 1988. Pp. 138-149.

3965   Shakhrastani, M. A.-K. *Kniga o religiiakh i sektakh* [The Book on Religions and Sects]. Transl. from Arabic. M.: Nauka, 1984- (Pamiatniki pis'mennosti Vostoka).
       Ch. 1. *Islam* [Islam]. Transl. and introduced by S.M. Prozorova. 1984. 270 pp. Summary in English. Bibl.: pp. 245-248. Annot. bibl.: pp. 184-238. Indices: pp. 249-268.

3966   Shakirov, G.Sh. *Kosmonavtika na sluzhbe ateizma* [Astronautics in the Service of Atheism]. Tashkent: Znanie UzSSR, 1984. 21 pp. (V pomoshch' lektoru / O-vo "Znanie" UzSSR. Ser. obshchestv.-polit.).

3967   Shakirov, G.Sh. "Mesto ateisticheskogo vospitaniia v sisteme kommunist-icheskogo vospitaniia" [The Place of Atheistic Upbringing in the System of Communist Education]. *Sb. nauch. tr. Tashk. un-t.* 710 (1983): 68-74.

3968   Shakirov, U. *Sotsial'naia aktivnost' lichnosti i preodolenie religioznosti* [Social Activity of Individual and Overcoming of Religiosity]. Tashkent: Uzbekistan, 1988. 40 pp. (Marksizm-leninizm / O-vo "Znanie" UzSSR; No 7). In Uzbek.

3969   Shakirov, U. *Trud i ateisticheskoe vospitanie* [Labour and Atheistic Education]. Tashkent: Znanie UzSSR, 1982. 27 pp. (V pomoshch' lektoru / O-vo "Znanie" UzSSR. Ser. obshchestv.-polit.). In Uzbek. Bibil.: p. 26.

3970 Shalaev, Iu.M. "Religioznaia forma obshchestvennogo soznaniia i drugie perezhitki proshlogo v soznanii i povedenii liudei pri sotsializme" [Religious Forms of Public Consciousness and Other Survivals of the Past in Consciousness and Behaviour of People under Socialism]. *Voprosy sotsialisticheskogo obshchestvennogo soznaniia.* Tomsk, 1982. Pp. 75-88.

3971 Shalaev, Iu.M. "Sovetskii obraz zhizni i ateizm" [Soviet Way of Life and Atheism]. *Problemy dukhovnoi zhizni sotsialisticheskogo obshchestva.* Omsk, 1984. Pp. 87-104.

3972 Shalaev, Iu.M. *Vospitat' ateista* [To Educate an Atheist]. Omsk: Kn. izd-vo, 1986. 110 pp. (V pomoshch' ateistu).

3973 Shalgimbaev, D.; Moshchenko, N. "Tsennye traditsii" [Valuable Traditions]. *Nauka i religiia* 3 (1983): 36.

3974 Shalgimbaev, D. *Religiia i deti* [Religion and Children]. Alma-Ata: Mektep, 1985. 58 pp. In Kazakh.

3975 Shalygina, O.V. "Problema cheloveka v ekzistentsial'noi teologii" [The Problem of Man in Existentialist Theology]. *Molodezh' i tvorchestvo: sotsial'no-filosofskie problemy.* M., 1988. Ch. 1. Pp. 127-129.

3976 Shamanov, I.M. "Perezhivanie drevnetiurkskikh (rannikh) form religioznykh vozzrenii i etnicheskaia istoriia karachaevtsev i balkartsev" [Experience of Ancient Turkic (Early) Forms of Religious Views and Ethnic History of Karachai and Balkar Peoples]. *Voprosy sovetskoi tiurkologii.* Ashkhabad, 1988. Ch. 2. Pp. 204-208.

3977 Shamaro, A. "Kerzhatskie tropy" [Kerjak Paths]. *Nauka i religiia* 1 (1984): 23-28.

3978 Shamaro, A. "'Moi brilliantiki'" ["My Brilliants"]. *Nauka i religiia* 7 (1987): 12-14.

3979 Shamaro, A. "Na perelome: Tserkov. sobor 1917-1918 gg." [Turning Point: Church Synod 1917-1918]. *Nauka i religiia* 11 (1987): 13-16; 12 (1987): 38-42.

3980 Shamaro, A. "Po sovetu Maksima Gor'kogo" [On the Advice of Maxim Gorky]. *Naka i religiia* 6 (1987): 52-53.

3981 Shamaro, A. "Pochemu 'troeruchitsa'" [Why "Threehanded"]. *Nauka i religiia* 12 (1984): 26-29.

3982 Shamaro, A. "Son Tamerlana" [Tamerlane's Dream]. *Nauka i religiia* 8 (1984): 24-27.

3983 Shamaro, A. "Zhitie nesostoiavshegosia patriarkha" [Life of a Not Made Up Patriarch]. *Nauka i religiia* 6 (1988): 35-37.

3984 Shamaro, A.A. *Iskusstvo pod egidoi tserkvi: istina protiv apologetiki* [Art Under the Aegis of the Church: Truth against Apologetics]. M.: Znanie, 1981. 64 pp. (Novoe v zhizni, nauke, tekhnike. Ser. "Nauch. ateizm"; No 7). Bibl.: pp. 62-63.

3985 Shamaro, A.A. *Metodika nauchno-ateisticheskogo osveshcheniia pamiatnikov russkogo tserkovnogo zodchestva v ekskursiiakh* [Scientific-Atheistic Method of Shedding Light at Excursions on Monuments of Russian Church Architecture]. M.: Znanie, Tsentr. Dom nauch. ateizna, 1987. 46 pp.

3986 Shamaro, A.A. *Pamiatniki arkhitektury proshlogo v ateisticheskom vospitanii* [Monuments of Architecture of the Past in Atheistic Education]. M.: Znanie, 1985. 64 pp. (Novoe v zhizni, nauke, tekhnike. Nauch. ateizm; 2). Bibl.: p. 61. Annot. bibl.: pp. 62-63.

3987 Shamaro, A.A. "Pamiatniki tserkovnogo zodchestva v ateisticheskom vospitanii" [Monuments of Church Architecture in Atheistic Education]. *Vopr. nauch. ateizma* 30 (1982): 262-284.

3988 Shamaro, A.A. *Pravoslavie i russkaia kul'tura: tserkovnye pritiazaniia i istoricheskaia real'nost'* [Orthodoxy and Russian Culture: Churches' Claims and Historical Reality]. M.: Znanie, 1980. 64 pp. (Novoe v zhizni, nauke, tekhnike. Ser. "Nauch. ateizm"; No 12). Bibl.: pp. 62-63.

3989 Shamaro, A.A. *Russkoe tserkovnoe zodchestvo: simvolika i istoki* [Russian Church Architecture: Symbolism and Sources]. M.: Znanie, 1988. 64 pp. (Novoe v zhizni, nauke, tekhnike. Ser.: Nauch. ateizm; 1988, 10). Bibl.: p. 61.

3990 Shamaro, A.A. *Taina inokini Dosifei* [Secret of The Nun Dosifei]. M.: Sov. Rossiia, 1984. 188 p., illus. For review see item 5284.

3991 Shamenova, K.[Sh]. *Ateisticheskoe vospitanie sel'skoi molodezhi* [Atheistic Upbringing of Village Youth]. Frunze: Kyrgyzstan, 1985. 54 pp. (B-chka ateista). In Kirghiz.

3992 Shamenova, K.[Sh]. "Molodezhi - ateisticheskuiu ubezhdennost'" [Atheistic Conviction for Youth]. *Kommunist Kirgizstana* 9 (1988): 107-111.

3993 Shamenova, K.Sh. "Povyshenie sotsial'noi aktivnosti molodezhi - neobkhodimoe uslovie ateisticheskogo vospitaniia" [The Rise of Youth Social Activity - Necessary Condition for Atheistic Upbringing]. *Aktivizatsiia chelovecheskogo faktora v svete reshenii XXVII s'ezda KPSS*. Frunze, 1988. Pp. 75-78.

3994 Shamenova, K.[Sh]. "Programma KPSS (novaia redaktsia) o zadachakh ateisticheskogo vospitaniia" [Programme of the CPSU (New Edition) on the Tasks of Atheistic Education]. *Materialy IX Mezhrespublikanskoi nauchnoi konferentsii molodykh uchenykh, 27-29 oktiabria 1987 g.* Frunze, 1988. Pp. 429-431.

3995 Shamenova, K.Sh. *Rol' estestvennonauchnyk znanii v ukreplenii ateisticheskikh ubezhdenii molodezhi* [The Role of Knowledge of Natural Sciences in Strengthening of Youth Atheistic Conviction]. Frunze: Ilym, 1988. 59 pp.

3996 Shamenova, K.[Sh]. "Rol' sotsialisticheskoi dukhovnoi kul'tury v razvitii massovogo ateizma" [Role of Socialist Spiritual Culture in the Development of Mass Atheism]. *Dukhov. kul'tura i sotsial. progress*. Frunze, 1980. Pp. 76-80.

3997 Shamukhamedov, Sh.Sh.; Ergashev, A.E. *O vrede 'urazy'* [On the Harm of "Uraza"]. Tashkent: Meditsina UzSSR, 1987. 16 pp. In Uzbek.

3998 Shangina, L.I. "Sverkh'estestvennoe kak fenomen religioznogo soznaniia" [Supernatural as a Phenomenon of Religious Consciousness]. *Vopr. ateizma* 20 (1984): 98-106.

3999 Shapiro, I. "Iudaizm v SSSR" [Judaism in USSR]. *Nauka i religiia* 9 (1980): 38-39.

4000 Shaposhnikov, L.E. *Ideologiia slavianofil'stva i sovremennoe pravoslavie* [Ideology of Slavophilism and Contemporary Orthodoxy]. M.: Znanie, 1985. 64 pp. (Novoe v zhizni, nauke, tekhnike. Nauch. ateizm; 4). Bibl.: p. 64.

4001   Shaposhnikov, L.E. "Metody vozdeistviia russkoi pravoslavnoi tserkvi na molodezh'" [Methods of the Influence of Russian Orthodox Church on Youth]. *Filosofsko-sotsiologicheskie problemy obrazovaniia.* Gor'kii, 1979. Pp. 102-110.

4002   Shaposhnikov, L.E. *Pravoslavie i filosofskii idealizm* [Orthodoxy and Philosophical Idealism]. Gor'kii: Volga-Viat. kn. izd-vo, 1986. 144 pp. For reviews see items 5285-5286.

4003   Shaposhnikov, L.E. "Pravoslavnoe bogoslovie i filosofskaia apologiia religii (konets XVIII-XX v.)" [Orthodox Ideology and Philosophical Apologia of Religion (Late XVIIIth-XXth Centuries)]. *Filos. nauki* 5 (1989): 41-50.

4004   Shaposhnikov, L.E. *Pravoslavnyi modernizm o dvizhushchikh silakh sotsial'nogo protsessa* [Orthodox Modernism on the Driving Forces of Social Process]. M.: Znanie, 1988. 64 pp. (Novoe v zhizni, nauke, tekhnike. Nauch. ateizm; 1/1988).

4005   Shaposhnikov, L.E. "Problema 'kachestva zhizni' v sovremennom pravoslavii" [Problem of "Quality of Life" in Contemporary Orthodoxy]. *Nauch. dokl. vyssh. shkoly. Filos. nauki* 1 (1980): 84-90.

4006   Shaposhnikov, L.E. "Sotsial'no-filosofskie vzgliady M.M. Taraeeva i sovremennoe pravoslavnoe bogoslovie" [M.M. Taraeev's Socio-Philosophical Views and Contemporary Orthodox Theology]. *Nauch. dokl. vyssh. shkoly. Filos. nauki* 3 (1982): 114-123.

4007   Shaposhnikova, L. "Mudrost' vekov" [Wisdom of Ages]. *Nauka i religiia* 10 (1989): 27-31.

4008   Sharabiddinov, I.; Abdullaev, M.A. *Novye obychai i obriady - vazhnyi faktor ateisticheskogo vospitaniia* [New Customs and Ceremonies - Important Factor of Atheistic Education]. Tashkent: Uzbekistan, 1986. 32 pp. (Ser. "Kul'tura"; No 13). In Uzbek.

4009   Sharakhmatuloev, D. "O sotsial'nykh faktorakh sokhraneniia vliianiia islama na naselenie Tadzhikistana" [Social Factors of Preservation of Islam's Influence on Tajikistan Population]. *Voprosy teorii i praktiki nauchnogo ateizma.* M., 1988. Pp. 28-49.

4010   Sharevskaia, B.I. "Afrikanskie uchenye o religioznykh verovaniiakh v Tropicheskoi Afrike" [African Scholars on Religious Creeds in Tropical

Africa]. *Religii mira: Istoriia i sovremennost'*. Ezhegodnik. 1982. M., 1982. Pp. 227-242.

4011 Sharikova, N.N. "Mesto i rol' ateizma v sisteme dukhovnoi kul'tury sotsialisticheskogo obshchestva" [Place and Role of Atheism in the System of Spiritual Culture of Socialist Society]. *Formirovanie dukhovnoi kul'tury lichnosti v usloviiakh uskoreniia sotsial'no-ekonomicheskogo razvitiia.* Tashkent, 1988. Pp. 13-21.

4012 Sharikova, N.N. "Preodolenie religioznykh perezhitkov v protsesse formiro-vaniia kommunisticheskoi nravstvennosti" [Overcoming of Religious Survivals in the Forming Process of Communist Morality]. *Stanovlenie i razvitie dukhovnoi kul'tury razvitogo sotsializma.* Tashkent, 1981. Pp. 164-172.

4013 Sharipov, A. "Otnoshenie Abubakara Razi k religii" [Abu Bakr Al-Razis' Attitude Towards Religion]. *Izv. AN TadzhSSR.* Ser. Filosofiia, ekonomika, pravovedenie 3 (1986): 24-30. Summary in Tajik.

4014 Sharipov, U. "Izmyshleniia burzhuaznykh ideologov o polozhenii islama v SSSR" [Fabrications of Bourgeois Ideologists on the Condition of Islam in the USSR]. *Kommunist Tadzhikistana* 8 (1985): 72-77.

4015 Sharipova, R.M. "Dvizhenie islamskoi solidarnosti. Osnovnye teoreticheskie kontseptsii" [The Movement of Islamic Solidarity. Basic Theoretical Conceptions]. *'Islamskii faktor' v mezhdunarodnykh otnosheniiakh v Azii (70-e-pervaia polovina 80-kh gg.).* M., 1987. Pp. 60-66.

4016 Sharipova, R.M. *Panislamizm segodnia: Ideologiia i praktika Ligi islamskogo mira* [Pan-Islamism Today: Ideology and Practice of the League of Moslem World]. M.: Nauka, 1986. 140 pp. Bibl.: pp. 137-136. For review see item 5288.

4017 Sharipova, R.M.; Nadzhip, E.E. "Dvizhenie islamskoi solidarnosti" [The Islamic Solidarity Movement]. *'Islamskii faktor' v mezhdunarodnykh otnosheniiakh v Azii (70-e-pervaia polovina 80-kh gg.).* M., 1987. Pp. 67-76.

4018 Sharshembaev, T. *Zhizn' i religiia* [Life and Religion]. 2nd revised ed. Frunze: Mekten, 1983. 49 pp. In Kirghiz.

4019 Shashkov, A.T. "Izuchenie uralo-sibirskogo staroobriadchestva vtoroi poloviny XVII-nachala XVIII v. v otechestvennoi istoriografii" [Study in Native Historiography of Ural-Siberian Old Belief in Late XVIIth-Early XVIIIth Century]. *Istoriografiia obshchestvennoi mysli dorevoliutsionnogo Urala.* Sverdlovsk, 1988. Pp. 31-43.

4020 Shaskol'skii, I.P. "Tretii krestovyi pokhod shvedskikh rytsarei na vostochnye berega Baltiki (1293 g.)" [Third Crusade of Swedish Knights on the Eastern Shores of the Baltic Sea (1293)]. *Srednie veka* 52 (1989): 130-145.

4021 Shatunova, L.G. "Istoricheskaia transformatsiia kul'ta ikon v protsesse khristianizatsii narodov Srednego Povolzh'ia" [Historical Transformation of the Cult of Icons in the Process of Conversion to Christianity of Peoples of Middle Side of Volga]. *Istoriia khristianizatsii narodov Srednego Povolzh'ia. Kriticheskie suzhdeniia i otsenka.* Cheboksary, 1988. Pp. 69-76.

4022 Shatunova, L.G. "Puti preodoleniia ikonopochitaniia" [Ways of Overcoming Icon Worship]. *Aktual'nye problemy obespecheniia effektivnosti nauchno-ateisticheskoi raboty.* Cheboksary, 1986. Pp. 117-121.

4023 Shchapov, Ia.N. "Tserkov' v sisteme gosudarstvennoi vlasti Drevnei Rusi. Desiatina i ee proiskhozhdenie" [Church in the System of State Power of Ancient Rus'. Desiatina and Its Origin]. *'Kreshchenie Rusi' v trudakh russkikh i sovetskikh istorikov.* M., 1988. Pp. 245-257.

4024 Shchedrin, A.T. *Vazhnyi rezerv povysheniia effektivnosti propagandy nauchno-ateisticheskikh znanii* [Important Reserve of Raising Effectiveness of Propaganda of Scientific-Atheistic Knowledge]. Kiev: Znanie UkSSR, 1984. 14 pp. (V pomoshch' lektoru / O-vo "Znanie" UkSSR. Sredstva nagliadnosti v lekts. propagande).

4025 Shchedrin, V.K. *Kritika religioznoi morali* [Criticism of Religious Morals]. Kiev: Znanie UkSSR, 1980. 48 pp. (Ser. 5 "Nauchno-ateisticheskaia"; No 2). In Ukrainian. Bibl.: pp. 47-48.

4026 Shchedrin, V.K. *Svoboda sovesti v sovremennoi ideologicheskoi bor'be* [Freedom of Conscience in Contemporary Ideological Struggle]. Kiev: Vishcha shk. Izd-vo pri Kiev. un-te, 1984. 73 pp. (Ateist. b-chka studenta). Bibl.: pp. 70-72.

4027 Shchedrovitskii, D.V. "'Dozhd' rannii i pozdnii'" [Early and Late Rain]. *Arkhaicheskii ritual v fol'klornykh i ranneliteraturnykh pamiatnikakh.* M., 1988. Pp. 201-220.

4028 Shchennikova, L.A. "Zaprestol'naia ikona Uspenskogo sobora s izobra-zheniem 'Bogomateri Korsunskoi'" [Altar Icon of the Image of "Korsunsk Mother of God" in Uspensk Cathedral]. *Gos. muzei Mosk. Kremlia* 5 (1987): 8-23.

4029 Shcherbakova, G.N. "Dal'neishee uglublenie kritiki modernizatsii religioznoi very" [Further Deepening of Criticism of the Modernization of Religious Faith]. *Vopr. ateizma* 18 (1982): 84-91.

4030 Shcherbakova, G.N. "Nesostoiatel'nost' konfessional'nykh obosnovanii 'istinnoi' very v sovremennoi ideologicheskoi bor'be" [Groundlessness of Confe-ssional Basis of the "True" Faith in Contemporary Ideological Struggle]. *Vopr. ateizma* 17 (1981): 114-122.

4031 Shcherbatskoi, F.I. *Izbrannye trudy po buddizmu* [Selected Works on Buddhism]. [Transl. from English]. Comp.: A.N. Zelinskii et al. M.: Nauka, 426 pp., port. Part of the text in English.

4032 Shcheulov, I.V. *Fizicheskoe sovershenstvo - dukhovnoe bogatstvo* [Physical Perfection - Spiritual Richness]. Kiev: Politizdat Ukrainy, 1983. 127 pp. Bibl.: pp. 120-124.

4033 Shebikova, V. "Katolicheskaia tserkov' i ee programma religioznogo vos-pitaniia v sem'e" [Catholic Church and Its Programme of Religious Education of the Family]. *Vopr. nauch. ateizma* 35 (1986): 286-293.

4034 Shelli, P.B. *Triumf zhizni* [Life's Triumph]. M.: Mysl', 1982. 256 pp., illus. (Nauch. ateist. b-ka).

4035 Shepetis, L.[K]. "Ateisticheskoe vospitanie: bol'she realizma" [Atheistic Education: More Realism]. *Kommunist.* Vil'nius. 1 (1988): 6-15.

4036 Shepetis, L.K. "Ateisticheskomu vospitaniiu - deistvennost' i nastu-patel'nost'" [Efficacy of and Offensiveness to Atheistic Education]. *Vopr. nauch. ateizma* 32 (1985): 35-43.

4037   Shepetis, L.[K]. "Rol' trudovogo kollektiva v ateisticheskom vospitanii" [The
       Role of Labour Collective in Atheistic Education]. *Polit. samoobrazovanie*
       4 (1981): 36-44.

4038   Sherdakov, V.N. "Gde konchaetsia religioznost' i nachinaetsia ateizm?"
       [Where Does Religiosity End and Atheism Start?]. *Sotsiol. issled.* 4
       (1987): 44-49. Published also in *Argumenty*. M., 1988. Pp. 91-101.

4039   Sherdakov, V.N. *Illiuziia dobra: Moral. tsennosti i relig. vera* [Illusion of
       Good: Moral Values and Religious Faith]. Politizdat, 1982. 287 pp.
       Published also in:
       Kishinev: Kartia moldoveniaske, 1986. 222 pp. In Moldavian.

4040   Sherdakov, V.N. "Moral'nye tsennosti sotsializma i religiia" [Moral Values of
       Socialism and Religion]. *Vopr. nauch. ateizma* 35 (1986): 52-81.

4041   Sherdakov, V.N. *Nravstvennyi ideal i ateisticheskoe vospitanie* [Moral Ideal
       and Atheistic Education]. M.: Znanie, 1985. 64 pp. (Novoe v zhizni,
       nauke, tekhnike. Ser. "Nauch. ateizm"; 12). Bibl.: p. 64.

4042   Sherr, E.S. "Islam v Efiopii: Istoriia i sovremennost'" [Islam in Ethiopia:
       History and Contemporaneity]. *Narody Azii i Afriki* 5 (1988): 73-84.
       Summary in English, pp. 218-219.

4043   Sherr, E.[S]. "Islam v Somali i Efiopii" [Islam in Somalia and Ethiopia].
       Aziia i Afrika segodnia 1 (1988): 57-59.

4044   Sherr, E.S. "Somali: religiia i politika" [Somalia: Religion and Politics].
       Narody Azii i Afriki 4 (1987): 47-55.

4045   Shershneva, S.V. "Sekuliarizatsiia v SShA i ee protivorechiia" [Secularization
       in USA and Its Contradictions]. *Problemy formirovaniia svetskoi kul'tury v
       Zapadnoi Evrope*. L., 1987. Pp. 27-41.

4046   Shevchenko, Iu. "Katolikos vsekh armian Vazgen I prizyvaet: spokoistvie,
       zakonnost', dostoinstvo!" [Catholicos of All Armenians Vozghen I
       Appeals: Order, Lawfulness, Dignity!]. *Novoe vremia* 30 (1988): 26-27.

4047   Shevchenko, S.I. "Iz opyta ateisticheskogo vospitaniia molodezhi" [From the
       Experience of Atheistic Upbringing of Youth]. *Vopr. nauch. ateizma* 28
       (1981): 252-258.

4048 Shevchenko, V.N. "Religioznoe chuvstvo kak produkt obshchestvennoi deiatel'nosti" [Religious Feeling as a Product of Public Activity]. *Filos. vopr. meditsiny i biologii* 17 (1985): 116-124.

4049 Shevchuk, V.A. "Vozrozhdenie i reformatsiia v ukrainskoi kul'ture XV-XVII vv." [Rebirth and Reformation in Ukrainian Culture in XVth-XVIIth Centuries]. *Filos. i sotsiol. mysl'* 8 (1989): 75-88.

4050 Shevelev, V.V. *Dobroe slovo* [A Good Word]. M.: Politizdat, 1984. 160 pp. For review see item 5289.

4051 Shevelev, V.[V]. "V neskol'kikh chasakh ezdy ot Orenburga..." [A Few Hours Journey from Orenburg...]. *Nauka i religiia* 6 (1980): 24-26.

4052 Sheveleva, M.N. "Chteniia, posviashchennye 1000-letiiu kreshcheniia Rusi" [Readings, Dedicated to 1000th Anniversary of Rus' Baptism]. *Vestn. Mos. un-ta.* Ser. 9, Filologiia 6 (1988): 60-63.

4053 Sheviakov, D.P. "Formirovanie ateisticheskoi ubezhdennosti studentov v vuzakh kul'tury" [Forming Atheistic Conviction of Students in Institutions of Higher Cultural Education]. *Aktual. vopr. metodiki prepodavaniia obshchestv. nauk i kom. vospitaniia studentov* 5 (1987): 57-62.

4054 Sheviakov, D.P. "Kritika khristianskikh kontseptsii istorii kul'tury" [Criticism of Christian Conceptions of History of Culture]. *Sb. nauch. tr. / Leningr. gos. in-t kul'tury im. N.K. Krupskoi.* 1986. T. 108. Pp. 157-169.

4055 Shevtsova, L.F. "O nekotorykh novykh veianiiakh v politike katolicheskoi tserkvi" [Some New Trends in the Policy of the Catholic Church]. *Rabochii klass i sovrem. mir* 1 (1980): 71-79.

4056 Shevtsova, L.F. *Sotsializm i katolitsizm:* (Vzaimootnosheniia gosudarstva i katol. tserkvi v sots. stranakh) [Socialism and Catholicism: Interrelations of State and Catholic Church in Socialist Countries]. M.: Nauka, 1982. 215 pp. Annot. bibl.: pp. 208-214.

4057 Shifman, I.Sh. "Istoricheskie korni koranicheskogo obraza Allakha" [Historical Roots of Koranic Image of Allah]. *Problemy arabskoi kul'tury.* M., 1987. Pp. 232-237.

4058   Shifman, I.Sh. Kul'tura drevnego Ugarita (XIV-XIII vv. do n. e.) [Culture of
       Ancient Ugarit (XIVth-XIIIth Centuries B.C.]. M.: Nauka, 1987. 236 pp.,
       illus. Summary in English. Bibl.: pp. 197-208. Index: pp. 212-234.

4059   Shifman, I.Sh. "O nekotorykh ustanovleniiakh rannego islama" [Some Ascer-
       tainments of the Early Islam]. Islam: Religiia, obshchestvo, gosudarstvo.
       M., 1984. Pp. 36-43.

4060   Shifman, I.Sh. Vetkhii zavet i ego mir [Old Testament and Its World]. M.:
       Politizdat, 1987. 239 pp., illus. Bibl.: pp. 218-219. Subject and name index:
       pp. 226-238.

4061   Shil'diashov, I.M. "Ob izuchenii sinkreticheskikh elementov v religii" [Study
       of Syncretic Elements in Religion]. Nauchnyi ateizm, religiia i sovre-
       mennost'. Novosibirsk, 1987. Pp. 196-206.

4062   Shil'diashov, I.M. Religiia v Sibiri i ateisticheskoe vospitanie [Religion in
       Siberia and Atheistic Education]. Novosibirsk: Nauka. Sib. otd-nie, 1982.
       207 pp. Name index: pp. 204-206. For review see item 5290.

4063   Shilnitsev, N.M. Pravda o sekte innokent'ebtsev [Truth About the Innokenteb
       Sect]. Kishinev: Znanie MSSR, 1980. 27 pp. (Material v pomoshch'
       lektoru / O-vo "Znanie" MSSR. Ser. "Obshchestv.-polit. nauki")
       (Znanie-narodu / ...).

4064   Shilov, N.V. "Kul'turno-bytovye protsessy v mordovskom sele v preodolenie
       religioznykh perezhitkov" [Cultural-Social Processes in Mordovian Village
       and Overcoming of Religious Survivals]. Tr. / NII iaz., lit., istorii i
       ekonomiki pri Sovete ministrov Mord. ASSR. Saransk, 1987. Vyp. 89. Pp.
       119-137. Bibl.: pp. 135-137.

4065   Shilova, L.B.; Evseev, A.I.; Fatiev, N.I. "Aktual'nye voprosy ateisticheskoi
       kontrpropagandy na sovremennom etape" [Actual Problems of Atheistic
       Counterpropaganda in Contemporary Stage]. Ideologicheskaia bor'ba i
       molodezh'. L., 1987. Pp. 118-127.

4066   Shinkarev, V.N. "Predstavleniia tibeto-birmanskikh narodov o sud'be" [Notion
       of Fate by Tibet-Burmese People]. Istoricheskaia dinamika rasovoi i
       etnicheskoi differentsiatsii naseleniia Azii. M., 1987. Pp. 184-192.

4067   Shinkaruk, V. "Istoriia dukhovnoi kul'tury i religiia" [History of Spiritual
       Culture and Religion]. Nauka i religiia 10 (1985): 12-14.

4068 Shiravov, K.Z. *O marali kommunisticheskoi i religioznoi* [On Communist and Religious Morals]. Makhachkala: Dag. kn. izd-vo, 1984. 60 pp. (Sots. obraz zhizni i religiia).

4069 Shirinian, M.S. "Kratkaia redaktsiia drevnearmianskogo perevoda 'Tserkovnoi istorii' Sokrata Skholastika" [Short Edition of Old Armenian Translation of "Ecclesiastical History" by Socrates the Scholastic]. *Vizant. vremennik.* 1982. V. 43. Pp. 231-241.

4070 Shirinkina, T.G. "Ateisticheskoe vospitanie kak faktor formirovaniia kommunisticheskogo soznaniia" [Atheistic Education as Forming Factor of Communist Consciousness]. *Voprosy sotsialisticheskogo obshchestvennogo soznaniia.* Tomsk, 1982. Pp. 182-186.

4071 *Shirokim frontom* [On Wide Front]. [Comp.: E.Ia. Komissarov]. M.: Sov. Rossiia, 1984. 96 pp.

4072 Shirokova, N.S. *Kel'tskie druidy* [Celtic Druids]. L.: LGU, 1984. 70 pp.

4073 Shkhagoshev, Sh.A. *Predrassudki ne vechny* [Prejudices are not Eternal]. Nal'chik: El'rus, 1986. 126 pp.

4074 Shkolenko, Iu.[A]. "Kosmos bez boga" [Cosmos Without God]. *Nauka i religiia* 110 (1987): 8-11.

4075 Shkolenko, Iu.A. *Ot sootvoreniia do nashikh dnei:* (Kak i kuda razvivaiutsia religiia i ateizm) [From the Creation to Our Days: How and Where Religion and Atheism Develop]. M.: Znanie, 1989. 64 pp. (Novoe v zhizni, nauke, tekhnike. Nauch. ateizm; 4/1989). Annot. bibl.: pp. 59-60.

4076 Shlaifer, N.E. *Svoboda lichnosti i istoricheskii determinizm* [Freedom of Individual and Historical Determinism]. M.: Vysch. shk., 1983. 96 pp. Bibl: pp. 94-95.

4077 Shless, I.I.; Rende, A.K. *Religiia i ideologicheskaia bor'ba* [Religion and the Ideological Struggle]. Alma-Ata: Kazakhstan, 1983. 40 pp. In German. Bibl.: pp. 38-39.

4078 Shmargunova, E.I. *Kak podgotovit' i prochitat' lektsiiu na temu 'Nravstvennoe soderzhanie ateizma'* [How to Prepare and Read a Lecture on the Theme "Moral Content of Atheism"]. Minsk: Znanie BSSR, 1980. 24 pp.

(Material v pomoshch' lektoru / Pravl. o-va "Znanie" BSSR, Nauch.-metod. sovet po propagande nauch. ateizma). Bibl.: pp. 23-24.

4079 Shmargunova, E.I. "Kritika nravstvennogo dokazatel'stva bytiia boga" [Criticism of Moral Evidence of God's Existence]. *Nauch. ateizm i ateist. vospitanie* 1 (1983): 50-59.

4080 Shmelev, V.D. "Ateisticheskie idei 'Kritiki chistogo razuma'" [Atheistic Ideas of "Criticism of Pure Reason"]. *Kant. sb.* 8 (1983): 26-33.

4081 Shmelev, V.D. "Ateisticheskii smysl kantovskogo transtsendental'nogo ideala" [Atheistic Meaning of the Kantian Transcendental Ideal]. *Kant. sb.* 11 (1986): 70-81.

4082 Shodiev, D.; Vorob'ev, B. "Formirovat' ateisticheskuiu ubezhdennost'" [To Shape Atheistic Conviction]. *Kommunist Tadzhikistana* 3 (1988): 69-79.

4083 Shodiev, R. "Obshechelovecheskie normy morali i islam" [Common to All Mankind Morals and Islam]. *Problemy formirovaniia nauchno-ateist-icheskogo mirovozzreniia v sotsialisticheskom obshchestve.* Samarkand, 1980. Pp. 34-37.

4084 Shokhin, B.K. "Buddiiskaia versiia drevnei sankkh'ia-iogi" [Buddhist Version of Sankhya Yoga]. *Istoriko-filos. ezhegodnik.* M., 1987. Pp. 165-184.

4085 Shokot'ko, V.A. "O prichinakh sushchestvovaniia religioznykh perezhitkov u chasti molodezhi Slovakii" [Reasons for the Ongoing Existence of Religious Survivals by some of the Slovakian Youth]. *Vopr. ateizma* 18 (1982): 134-142.

4086 Shpak, Z.V. *Antigumanizm ideologii uniatstva i natsionalizma* [Antihumanism of the ideology of the Uniate Church and Nationalism]. Kiev: Znanie UkSSR, 1988. 48 pp. (Ser. 5, Nauchno-ateisicheskaia / O-vo "Znanie" UkSSR; No 7). In Ukrainian.

4087 Shpak, Z.V. *Ateizm i nravstvennyi ideal lichnosti* [Atheism and Moral Ideal of Individual]. Kiev: Znanie UkSSR, 1984. 49 pp. (Ser. 5 "Nauchno-ateisticheskaia" / O-vo "Znanie" UkSR; No 9). In Ukrainian. Annot. bibl.: p. 49. Published also in:
Kiev: Nauk. dumka, 1987. 123 pp. Annot. bibl.: pp. 117-122.

4088 Shpak, Z.V. *Naucho-ateisticheskoe vospitanie kak faktor utverzhdeniia nravst-venogo ideala stroitelia kommunizma* [Scientific-Atheistic Education as Affirming Factor of the Moral Ideal of the Builder of Communism]. Kiev: Znanie UkSSR, 1981. 16 pp. (B-chka v pomoshch' lektoru "Probl. nauch. ateizma" / O-vo "Znanie" UkSSR). In Ukrainian. Annot. in Russian. Bibl.: p. 16.

4089 Shtaerman, E.M. *Sotsial'nye osnovy religii Drevnego Rima* [Social Fundamentals of Religion of Ancient Rome]. M.: Nauka, 1987. 320 pp. Annot. bibl.: p. 308.

4090 Shtiuka, V.[G]. "Dukhovnoe osvobozhdenie cheloveka i svoboda sovesti" [Spiritual Liberation of Man and Freedom of Conscience]. *Kommunist Moldavii* 3 (1988): 65-71.

4091 Shtiuka, V.G. *Obshchestvo i religiia* [Society and Religion]. Kishinev: Kartia Moldoveniaske, 1980. 108 pp. (Nauka i religiia). In Moldavian.

4092 Shuba, A.V. "Modernizatsiia pravoslavno-bogoslovskoi interpretatsii natsional'-nykh otnoshenii" [Modernization of Orthodox-Theological Interpretation of National Relations]. *Vopr. ateizma* 18 (1982): 113-119.

4093 Shuba, A.V. *Natsional'nye otnosheniia v SSSR i sovremennyi religioznyi modernizm: Na materialakh russ. pravoslaviia* [National Relations in USSR and Contemporary Religious Modernism: Based on Materials of Russian Orthodoxy]. Kiev: Znanie UkSSR, 1983. 46 pp. (Ser. 5 "Nauchno-ateisticheskaia" / O-vo "Znanie" UkSSR; No 5). In Ukrainian. Bibl.: pp. 43-45.

4094 Shuba, A.V. *Pravoslavie i traditsii natsional'noi kul'tury* [Orthodoxy and Traditions of National Culture]. Kiev: Znanie UkSSR, 1989. 48 pp. (Ser. 5, Nauch.-ateist. / O-vo "Znanie" UkSSR; No 9). In Ukrainian.

4095 Shuba, A.V. *Religioznye verovaniia i natsional'nye otnosheniia* [Religious Beliefs and National Relations]. Kiev: Politizdat Ukrainy, 1985. 62 pp. (Bcscdy s veruiushchimi). In Ukrainian. Bibl.: pp. 59-61.

4096 Shuba, A.V. "Uchet natsional'nykh osobennostei v ateisticheskoi rabote" [Accountableness of National Features in Atheistic Work]. *Vopr. ateizma* 24 (1988): 42-48.

4097   Shuba, A.V.; Efremov, Iu.M. *Kritika bogoslovskikh fal'sifikatsii istorii vvedeniia khristianstva na Rusi* [Criticism of Theological Falsifications of the History on Introduction of Christianity into Rus']. Kiev: Znanie UkSSR, 1984. 14 pp. (V pomoshch' lektoru / O-vo "Znanie" UkSSR. Probl. nauch. ateizma). In Ukrainian.

4098   Shuba, A.V.; Solon'ko, N.V. "Edinstvo internatsional'noi i ateisticheskoi funktsii sotsialisticheskikh traditsii, prazdnikov i obriadov" [Unity of International and Atheistic Function of Socialist Traditions, Holidays and Ceremonies]. *Vopr. ateizma* 21 (1985): 34-40.

4099   Shubas, M. "Tekhnicheskii progress i religiia" [Technical Progress and Religion]. *Kommunist.* Vil'nius. 9 (1982): 41-46.

4100   Shugurov, L.M. "Rol' iazyka religii v fiksatsii i vyrazhenii religioznogo soznaniia" [The Role of the Language of Religion in Fixation and Expression of Religious Consciousness]. *Aktual'nye problemy ateisticheskogo vospitaniia i kritika religioznoi ideologii.* M., 1981. Pp. 31-37.

4101   Shukurov, A.M. *Islam, obychai i traditsii* [Islam, Customs and Traditions]. Baku: Azernesher, 1981. 74 pp. In Azerbaijan.

4102   Shukurov, A.M. *Sotsial'nyi progress i ateizm* [Social Progress and Atheism]. Baku: Znanie AzSSR, 1982. 50 pp. (V pomoshch' lektoru / O-vo "Znanie" AzSSR). In Azerbaijan.

4103   Shukurov, N. *Osnovy nauchnogo ateizma* [Fundamentals of Scientific Atheism]. Ashkhabad: Magaryf, 1988. 143 pp. In Turkmen.

4104   Shukurov, N. *Zarozhdenie religii* [Origin of Religion]. Ashkhabad: Turkmenistan, 1986. 116 pp. In Turkmen.

4105   Shukurov, Sh. "Ob iskusstve islama" [The Art of Islam]. *Dekor. iskusstvo SSSR* 12 (1988): 36-37.

4106   Shulembaev, K.Sh. *Ateizm i nravstvennyi progress* [Atheism and Moral Progress]. Alma-Ata: Znanie KazSSR, 1984. 31 pp. In Kazakh.

4107   Shulembaev, K.Sh. *Obraz zhizni. Religiia. Ateizm:* (Obshchee i osobennoe v obraze zhizni i rel. verovaniiakh kazakhov i vopr. ateist. vospitaniia) [Way of Life. Religion. Atheism: (Common and Particular in the Way of Life

and Religious Beliefs of Kazakhs and Problems of Atheistic Education)].
Alma-Ata: Kazakhstan, 1983. 263 pp. For review see item 5292.

4108　Shultmanis, A.K. *Povyshenie deistvennosti nauchnogo ateizma* [Increase of
Effectiveness of Scientific Atheism]. Riga: Znanie LatvSSR, 1983. 21 pp.
(Material v pomoshch' lektoru / O-vo "Znanie" LatvSSR, Nauch.-metod.
sovet po propagande nauch. ateizma) (Znanie - narodu / ...). In Latvian.
Annot. in Russian. Bibl.: pp. 20-21.

4109　Shurygin, Ia.I. *Kazanskii sobor* [Kazan Cathedral]. L.: Lenizdat, 1987. 191
pp., illus. Bibl.: pp. 187-188.

4110　Shurygin, Ia.I.; Kondrat'ev, V.I. *Ogon' i tlen: Ocherki ob iskusstve i religii*
[Fire and Decay: Essays on Art and Religion]. L.: Lenizdat, 1985. 110
pp., illus. Bibl.: pp. 108-109.

4111　Shvarev, Iu.I. *Korni pustotsveta: Besedy po istorii religii* [The Roots of Barren
Flower: Discussions on the History of Religion]. L.: Lenizdat, 1988. 127
pp. Bibl.: pp. 124-125.

4112　Shvarev, Iu.I. *Kriticheskie besedy ob apostol'skikh mifakh* [Critical Discussions
About Apostolic Myths]. Voronezh: Tsentr.-Chernozem. kn. izd-vo, 1981.
107 pp., illus.

4113　Shvarev, Iu.I. *Molodym o religii i ateizme* [To Young People on Religion
and Atheism]. Voronezh: Tsentr.-Chernozem. kn. izd-vo, 1988. 112 pp.

4114　Siamashvili, G. "Idei moral'noi religii Kanta v tvorchestve Tolstogo i
Dostoevskogo" [Ideas of Kant's Moral Religion in the Works of Tolstoy
and Dostoevsky]. *Iubileinaia sessiia filosofskogo seminara Tbilisskogo
gosudarstvennogo universiteta, posviashchennaia 200-letiiu "Kritiki
prakticheskogo razuma" Kanta, 18-19 marta 1988 g.* Tbilisi, 1988. Pp.
47-50. Summary in Georgian.

4115　Sidikhmedov, V.Ia. "Son razuma rozhdaet chudovishch: O sueveriiakh v
Kitae" [The Sleep of Reason Gives Birth to Monsters: Superstitions in
China]. *Probl. Dal'nego Vostoka* 4 (1989): 176-184.

4116　Sidorenko, L. "Dlia vsekh i kazhdogo" [For All and Everyone]. *Nauka i
religiia* 12 (1982): 10-13.

4117   Sidorov, A.I. "Arianstvo v svete sovremennykh issledovanii" [Aryanism in the Light of Contemporary Research]. *Vestn. drev. istorii* 2 (1988): 86-97. Summary in English.

4118   Sidorov, A.I. "Manikeistvo v izobrazhenii Avgustina (De heresibus, 46)" [Manichaeanism in Augustine's Representation (De Heresibus, 46)]. *Vestn. drev. istorii* 2 (1983): 145-161. Summary in English.

4119   Sidorov, A.I. "Nekotorye zamechaniia k biografii Maksima Ispovednika" [Some Remarks on Biography of Maximos the Confessor]. *Vizant. vremennik.* 1986. T. 47. Pp. 109-124.

4120   Sidorov, V.P. "Formirovanie khristianskogo sotsializma v Rossii" [Shaping Christian Socialism in Russia]. *Sotsial'no-filosofskie aspekty kritiki religii.* L., 1987. Pp. 113-130.

4121   Siiabov, A.G. "Kritika antimarksistskikh fal'sifikatsii polozheniia musul'man v SSSR" [Criticism of Anti-Marxists Falsifications on Moslem's Situation in USSR]. *Vopr. ateizma* 23 (1987): 124-127.

4122   Siksai, A.A. *Otkrylennye idealom* [Inspired by Ideal]. Uzhgorod: Karpati, 1986. 136 pp. In Hungarian.

4123   Silagadze, A.B. *Problemy nauchnogo ateizma v svete reshenii XXVI s'ezda KPSS* [Problems of Scientific Atheism in the Light of Resolutions of the XXVIth Congress of the CPSU]. Tbilisi: Znanie GSSR, 1982. 32 pp. (Nauch. ateizm / O-vo "Znanie" GSSR; 29). In Georgian.

4124   *Siloi znanii i ubezhdenii* [By Force of Knowledge and Persuasion]. [Ed.: A.I. Utkin]. Dnepropetrovsk: Promin', 1986. 78 pp.

4125   "Sil'van. Poucheniia" [Silvan. Exhortation]. *Kavkaz i Vizantiia* 5 (1987): 115-144.

4126   Simakin, S.A. "Animisticheskie verovaniia kachinov" [Animistic Beliefs of Cochins]. *Sov. etnografiia* 2 (1988): 120-126.

4127   Simakin, S.A. "K voprosu o spetsifike birmanskogo buddizma" [The Problem of Specific Character of Burmese Buddhism]. *Aktual'nye problemy ideologii i kul'tury stran Vostoka.* M., 1982. Pp. 91-100.

4128 Simonov, R.A. "Kalendarno-astronomicheskie tablitsy Norovskoi psaltyri" [Calendar-Astronomical Tables of Norov Psalter]. *Iazyk i pis'mennost' srednebolgarskogo perioda* M., 1982. Pp. 93-102.

4129 Simonova-Gudzenko, E.K. "O poiavlenii boginii Amaterasu v iaponskom panteone" [Appearance of the Goddess Amaterasu in the Japanese Pantheon]. *Sov. etnografiia* 1 (1988): 98-109.

4130 Sinitsyn, A.Iu. "Kul't predkov i etnicheskie stereotipy povedeniia birmantsev" [The Cult of Ancestors and Ethnic Stereotypes of Burmese Conduct]. *Sov. etnografiia* 3 (1989): 102-109.

4131 Siradze, R. "Zhizn' Georgiia Mtatsmideli" [The Life of George Mtatsmideli]. *Kommunist Gruzii* 8 (1989): 67-74.

4132 Siukiianen, L.R. "Kontseptsiia musul'manskoi formy pravleniia i sovremennoe gosudarstvovedenie v stranakh Arabskogo Vostoka" [Conception of Moslem Form of Governing and Contemporary State Authority in the Countries of the Arab Orient]. *Sotsial'no-politicheskie predstavleniia v islame: Istoriia i sovremennost'*. M., 1987. Pp. 45-68.

4133 Siukiianen, L.R. *Musul'manskoe pravo: Vopr. teorii i praktiki* [Moslem Law: Problems of Theory and Practice]. M.: Nauka, 1986. 256 pp. For review see item 5293.

4134 Sizonenko, V.B. "Nauchno-tekhnicheskii progress - ob'ektivnyi faktor formirovaniia dialektiko-materialisticheskogo mirovozzreniia" [Scientific-Technical Progress - Objective Shaping Factor of Dialectic-Materialistic World Outlook]. *Vopr. ateizma* 23 (1987): 21-27.

4135 Sizonenko, V.B. "Puti povysheniia effektivnosti ateisticheskogo vospitaniia molodezhi v usloviiakh sovershenstvovaniia sotsializma" [Ways for Increasing the Effectiveness of Atheistic Upbringing of Youth under the Conditions of Perfection of Socialism]. *Vopr. ateizma* 24 (1988): 65-72.

4136 Skachkov, A.Ia. "Smysl zhizni i nravstvennyi ideal cheloveka" [The Meaning of Life and Man's Moral Ideal]. *Nauchnyi ateizm: ideal i mirovozzrenie*. Perm', 1988. Pp. 41-49.

4137 Skibitskii, M.M. *Mirovozzrenie, estestvoznanie, teologiia* [World Outlook, Natural Science, Theology]. M.: Politizdat, 1986. 223 pp., illus.

4138   Skibitskii, M.M. *'Nauchnyi kreatsionizm':* pretenzii i deistvitel'nost' ["Scientific
        Creation": Pretensions and Reality]. M.: Znanie, 1987. 64 pp. (Novoe v
        zhizni, nauke, tekhnike. Nauch. ateizm; 8/1987). Bibl.: p. 64.

4139   Skibitskii, M.M. "Prometeev ogon'" [Prometheus Fire]. *Nauka i religiia* 9
        (1982): 27-29.

4140   Skibitskii, M.M. *Sovremennaia teologiia i estestvoznanie: mif o soiuze i
        deistvitel'nost'* [Contemporary Theology and Natural Science: Myths about
        Agreement and Reality]. M.: Znanie, 1983. 64 pp. (Novoe v zhizni,
        nauke, tekhnike. Nauch. ateizm; 6). Bibil.: p. 63.

4141   Skibitskii, M.M. *Sovremennoe estestvoznanie i religiia* [Contemporary Natural
        Science and Religion]. M.: Zanie, 1980. 64 pp. (Novoe v zhizni, nauke,
        tekhnike. Ser. "Nauch. ateism"; No 7).

4142   Skibitskii, M.[M]. "Sovremennoe estestvoznanie i teologiia: mif o soiuze i
        deistvitel'nost'" [Contemporary Natural Science and Theology: Myths
        about Agreement and Reality]. *Polit. samoobrazovanie* 6 (1983): 106-112.

4143   Skibitskii, M.M. "Sovremennyi fideizm i estestvoznanie" [Contemporary
        Fideism and Natural Science]. *Vopr. nauch. ateizma* 34 (1985): 79-94.

4144   Skopenko, V.S. "Kritika ekstremistskih proiavlenii sredi molodykh posledo-
        vatelei Soveta tserkvei EKhB" [Criticism of Extremist Manifestations
        among Young Followers of the Council of Churches EHB]. *Vopr. ateizma*
        25 (1989): 37-44.

4145   Skorbatiuk, I. "Buddizm v Koree" [Buddhism in Korea]. *Aziia i Afrika
        segodnia* 9 (1981): 59-61.

4146   Skrynnikov, R.[G]. "Patriarkh Germogen" [Patriarch Ghermoghen]. *Nauka i
        religiia* 11 (1988): 51-53.

4147   Skrynnikov, R.G. "Uchrezhdenie patriarshestva v Rossii" [Establishment of
        the Patriarchate in Russia]. *Vopr. nauch. ateizma* 25 (1980): 80-98.

4148   Skrynnikova, T.D. *Lamaistskaia tserkov' i gosudarstvo. Vneshniaia Mongoliia,
        XVI-nach. XX v.* [Lamaist Church and State. Outer Mongolia, XVIth-
        Early XXth Centuries]. Novosibirsk: Nauka. Sib. otd-nie, 1988. 103 pp.
        Bibl.: pp. 89-96.

4149 Skrynnikova, T.D. "Mongol'skie terminy sakral'nosti pravitelia (XIII v.)" [Mongol Terms of Sacramentality of the Ruler (XIIIth Century)]. *V Mezhdunarodnyi kongress mongolovedov (Ulan-Bator, sentiabr' 1987)*. M., 1987. 1. Istoriia, ekonomika. Pp. 126-132. Bibl.: p. 132.

4150 Skrynnikova, T.D. "Povinnosti shabinarov v Mongolii" [Shabinars' Duties in Mongolia]. *Pis'mennye pamiatniki i problemy istorii kul'tury narodov Vostoka: XV godich. nauch. sessiia LO IV AN SSSR*. M., 1981. Ch. I(1). Pp. 153-157.

4151 Skrynnikova, T.D. "Rol' buddizma v formirovanii politicheskikh idei v Mongolii (XIII-XVII vv.)" [The Role of Buddhism in Shaping Political Ideas in Mongolia (XIIIth-XVIIth Centuries)]. *Metodologicheskie aspekty izucheniia istorii dukhovnoi kul'tury Vostoka*. Ulan-Ude, 1988. Pp. 124-132.

4152 Skrynnikova, T.D. "Rol' Chzhebtszun-damba-khtukhty v tserkovnoi organizatsii mongol'skogo lamaizma XVII v." [The Role of Chjebtsun Damba Htuhta in Church Organization of Mongol Lamaism of the XVIIth Century]. *Buddizm i srednevekovaia kul'tura narodov Tsentral'noi Azii*. Novosibirsk, 1980. Pp. 18-32.

4153 Skrynnikova, T.D. "Sakral'nost' pravitelia v predstavleniakh mongolov XIII v." [Sacrality of Monarch in Concepts of Mongols of XIIIth Century].* *Narody Azii i Afriki* 1 (1989): 67-75. Summary in English.

4154 "Slagaemmye dukhovnogo bogatstva" [Components of Spiritual Wealth]. [Comp.: V. Evseev et al]. *Nauka i religiia* 1 (1984): 2-4.

4155 Slastenko, E.F.; Shakhvorostov, M.A. *Ateizm i nravstvennaia kul'tura lichnosti* [Atheism and Spiritual Culture of the Individual]. Kiev: Znanie UkSSR, 1984. 31 pp. (Ser. 5 "Nauchno-ateisticheskaia" / O-vo "Znanie" UkSSR; No 5). In Ukrainian. Annot. bibl.: pp. 30-31.

4156 Slavov, S. "Eticheskaia kontseptsiia bogomol'stva" [Ethical Conception of Devoutness]. *U istokov obshchnosti filosofii kul'tur russkogo, ukrainskogo i bolgarskogo narodov*. Kiev, 1983. Pp. 57-67.

4157 Slesarev, A.A. "Konkretno-sotsiologicheskoe issledovanie urovnia religioznosti i ateizatsii studencheskoi molodezhi tekhnicheskogo vuza" [Concrete-Sociological Research of the Level of Religiosity and Dissemination of Atheism among Students of Technical Institution of Higher Education].

Gumanitarizatsiia obrazovaniia v tekhnicheskikh vuzakh. M., 1989. Pp. 157-165.

4158   Sliunchenko, V.G. *Polotskii Sofiiski sobor:* ist.-arkhit. ocherk [Polotsk Cathedral of Sofia: Historic-Architectural Essay]. Minsk: Polymia, 1987. 48 pp., illus.

4159   "'Sluzhit' i pomogat'"" ["Serve and Help"]. *Nauka i religiia* 7 (1987): 54-55.

4160   Smagina, E.B. "Manikheiskaia estetika" [Manichaeist Aesthetics]. *Kul'tura i iskusstvo narodov Vostoka.* M., 1987. Pp. 93-94.

4161   Smirnov, A.F. "Traditsii ateizma i svobodomysliia v revoliutsionnom dvizhenii Rossii" [The Traditions of Atheism and Freethinking in Russia's Revolutionary Movement]. *Vopr. nauch. ateizma* 36 (1987): 268-294.

4162   Smirnov, B. "Sankkh'ia i ioga" [Sankhya and Yoga]. *Nauka i religiia* 7 (1987): 48-50; 8 (1987): 30-31; 10 (1987): 30-31.

4163   Smirnov, Iu. "Arkhitektura rituala bez rituala" [Architecture of Ritual Without Ritual]. *Dekor. iskusstvo SSSR* 10 (1988): 18-19.

4164   Smirnov, V. "Moskovskii seminar sluzhitelei tserkvei evangel'skikh khristian-baptistov: prizyv k edinstvu" [Moscow Seminary of Evangelist Christian-Baptists Clergy: Appeal for Unity]. *Religiia v SSSR* 2 (1988): VS 1-VS 3.

4165   Smirnova, A.I. "Demograficheskoe povedenie i religioznyi ideal" [Demographic Behaviour and Religious Ideal]. *Nauchnyi ateizm: ideal i mirovozzrenie.* Perm', 1988. Pp. 67-74.

4166   Smirnova, E.S. *Moskovskaia ikona XIV-XVII vekov: Al'bom* [Moscow Icon of XIVth-XVIIth Centuries: Album]. L.: Avrora, 1988. 319 pp. Bibl.: pp. 311-319.

4167   Smirnova, N.A. "Tomas Kranmer i nachalo anglikanskoi reformatsii v XVI veke" [Thomas Cranmer and the Beginning of Anglican Reformation in XVIth Century]. *Iz istorii drevnego mira i srednevekov'ia.* M., 1988. Pp. 76-94.

4168   Smolin, G.A. "Inozemnye religii v Guanchzhou IX v." [Foreign Religions in Guanchjou in IXth Century]. *Strany i narody Vostoka* 23 (1982): 76-90.

4169 Smyr, G.V. *Nekotorye problemy ateisticheskogo vospitaniia naseleniia Abkhazskoi ASSR* [Some Problems of Atheistic Education of the Population of Abkhazian ASSR]. Sukhumi: Alashara, 1984. 75 pp. Annot. bibl.: pp. 72-75. In Abkhaz.

4170 Snesarev, G.[P]. "Khazret Ali" [Hazret Ali]. *Nauka i religiia* 10 (1983): 31-34.

4171 Snesarev, G.P. *Khorezmskie legendy kak istochnik po istorii religioznykh kul'tov Srednei Azii* [Khoresm Legends as Sources of History of Religious Cults of the Middle Asia]. M.: Nauka, 1983. 212 pp.

4172 Snesarev, G.[P]. "Pakhlavan Makhmud" [Pahlavan Mahmud]. *Nauka i religii* 12 (1983): 24-28.

4173 Snesarev, G.[P]. "Sheikh Iusuf Khama'dani" [Sheikh Yusuf Hamadani]. *Nauka i religiia* 12 (1984): 30-32.

4174 Snigireva, E.A. "Sotsial'no-psikhologicheskii analiz velikopostnykh bogosluzhenii" [Socio-Psychological Analysis of Lenten Divine Services]. *Sotsial'no-filosofskie aspekty kritiki religii.* L., 1988. Pp. 101-157.

4175 Snisarenko, A.B. *Tretii poias mudrosti:* Blesk iazych. Evropy [The Third Girdle of Wisdom: Brightness of Europe's Paganism]. L.: Lenizdat, 1989. 291 pp. Bibl.: p. 277.

4176 Soboleva, L.S. "K voprosu o fol'klorizatsii obrazov Borisa i Gleba v dukhovnykh stikhakh" [Folklorist Representation of the Images of Boris and Gleb in Spiritual Verses]. *Publitsistika i istoricheskie sochineniia perioda feodalizma.* Novosibirsk, 1989. Pp. 132-144.

4177 Sogomonian, M. "Formirovanie ateisticheskogo mirovozzreniia v usloviiakh nauchno-tekhnicheskogo progressa" [Shaping of Atheistic World Outlook under the Conditions of Scientific-Technical Progress]. *Po lenin. puti.* Erevan. 2 (1988): 63-68.

4178 Sokhadzc, A.K. "Vopros izucheniia iazycheskikh kul'tovykh pamiatnikov v gornoi chasti Vostochnoi Gruzii v trudakh V.V. Bardavelidze" [The Problem of Study in B.B. Bardavelidze's Works the Heathen Cult Monuments in the Mountainous Part of Eastern Georgia]. *Materialy po etnografii Gruzii.* Tbilisi, 1987. T. 23. Pp. 160-166. In Georgian. Summary in Russian.

4179 Sokhraniaeva, T.V. "Edinstvo ateisticheskogo i nravstvennogo vospitaniia" [The Unity of Atheistic and Moral Education]. *Aktual'nye problemy ateisticheskogo vospitaniia i kritika religioznoi ideologii.* M., 1983. Pp. 11-16.

4180 Sokhraniaeva, T.V. "Kul'tura i ateizm" [Culture and Atheism]. *Dukhovnye tsennosti kak predmet filosofskogo analiza.* M., 1985. Pp. 94-98.

4181 Sokirianskaia, R.M. *Rol' ateisticheskogo vospitaniia v formirovanii vsestoronne razvitoi lichnosti* [The Role of Atheistic Education in Shaping of an All-Round Developed Individual]. Kiev: Znanie UkSSR, 1981. 15 pp. (B-chka v pomoshch' lektoru "Probl. nauch. ateizma" / O-vo "Znanie" UkSSR). In Ukrainian. Bibl.: p. 15.

4182 Sokolov, A. "Evangel'skie khristiane-baptisty: tsifry i fakty" [Evangelical Christian-Baptists: Figures and Facts]. *Religiia v SSSR* 6 (1987): AS 1-AS 2.

4183 Sokolov, B.V. "K voprosu ob istochnikakh romana Mikhaila Bulgakova 'Master i Margarita'" [On the Question of Sources of Mikhail Bulgakov's Roman "Master and Margarita"]. *Filos. nauki* 12 (1987): 54-64.

4184 Sokolova, E.I. *Tserkov' na Rusi X-XIII v.: problemy, zadachi, itogi issledovaniia v sovetskoi istoriografii (60-80-e gg)* [Church in Rus' in Xth-XIIIth Centuries: Problems, Tasks, Results of Researches in Soviet Historiography (60s-80s)]. M.: INION AN SSSR, 1988. 56 pp. (Ser.: metodol. probl. istorii). Bibl.: pp. 50-56.

4185 Sokolova, I.M. "Reznaia ikona 'Sniiatie so kresta'" [Carved Icon "Taking off the Cross"]. *Gos. muzei Mosk. Kremlia* 5 (1987): 58-67.

4186 Sokolova, M.A. "Alzhirskie ulemy-reformatory v bor'be za natsional'nuiu nezavisimost' i vozrozhdenie arabo-musul'manskikh tsennostei" [Algerian Ulama-Reformers in the Struggle for National Independence and Revival of Arab-Moslem Values]. *V Vsesoiuznaia shkola molodykh vostokovedov.* M., 1989. T. 3. Pp. 28-29.

4187 Sokolovskii, I.F. "Problema vzaimootnosheniia tserkvi i gosudarstva v mirovozzrenii A.S Khomiakova" [The Problem of Interrelations of Church and State in A.S. Khomiakov's World Outlook]. *Vopr. nauch. ateizma* 37 (1988): 209-225.

Published also in *Sotsial'no-filosofskie aspekty kritiki religii.* L., 1987. Pp. 95-113.

4188 Sokolovskii, S.B. "Minnonity v SShA" [Mennonites in USA]. *Religii mira.* 1986. M., 1987. Pp. 67-87.

4189 Solov'ev, A. "Kto takie kopty" [Who Are Copts]. *Nauka i religia* 12 (1985): 53-56.

4190 Solov'ev, E.Iu. *Nepobezhdennyi eretik: Martin Liuter i ego vremia* [Invincible Heretic: Martin Luther and His Time]. M.: Molodaia gvardiia, 1984. 288 pp., illus. Bibl.: p. 287.
Published also in: Riga: Avots, 1988. 298 pp., illus. In Latvian. Bibl.: pp. 295-297. For reviews see items 5294-5295.

4191 Solov'ev, O.F. "Masonstvo v Rossii" [Freemasonry in Russia]. *Vopr. istorii* 10 (1988): 3-25.

4192 Solov'ev, V.S. *Ateizm v sisteme vospitatel'noi raboty* [Atheism in the System of Educational Work]. Ioshkar-Ola: Mariiskoe kn. izd-vo, 1983. 71 pp.

4193 Solov'ev, V.S. *Po puti dukhovnogo progressa:* Nekotorye itogi povtor. sotsiol. issled. probl. byta, kul'tury, nats. traditsii, ateizma i verovanii naseleniia Mar. ASSR [On the Way of Spiritual Progress: Some Results of Repeated Sociological Research of the Problem of Way of Life, Culture, National Traditions, Atheism and Faiths of the Population of the Mari ASSR]. Ioshkar-Ola: Mar. kn. izd-vo, 1987. 161 pp.

4194 Solov'ev, V.S. "Pogrebal'nyi obriad rannesrednevekovskogo Tokharistana" [Burial Ritual of Early Medieval Toharistan]. *Proshloe Srednei Azii.* Dushanbe, 1987. Pp. 157-164.

4195 Solov'ev, V.S. *Sochineniia v dvukh tomakh* [Works in two Volumes]. M.: Mysl', 1988. T. 1. 892 pp. T. 2. 824 pp. For review see item 5296.

4196 Solov'cv, V.S.; Khlebnikov, E.A. *Ateisticheskaia rabota na sele* [Atheistic work in the Village]. M.: Profizdat, 1987. 64 pp. (B-chka prof. aktivista agroprom. kompleksa). Bibl.: p. 63.

4197 Solov'ev, Vl. "Sud'ba Pushkina" [Pushkin's Fate]. *Iunost'* 6 (1989): 56-60.

4198   Soninbaiar, Sh. "O sochineniiakh mongol'skikh avtorov na tibetskom iazyke
        po khronologii buddizma v Tibete i Mongolii" [Works of Mongol Authors
        in Tibetan Language According to Buddhism's Chronology in Tibet and
        Mongolia]. *Istochnikovedenie i tekstologiia pamiatnikov srednevekovykh
        nauk v stranakh Tsentral'noi Azii.* Novosibirsk, 1989. Pp. 163-170.

4199   *Sostoianie religioznosti i ateisticheskogo vospitaniia v regionakh traditsionnogo
        rasprostraneniia islama* [The State of Religiosity and Atheistic Education
        in Regions of Traditional Dissemination of Islam]. [Comp.: L.A. Bashirov
        et al]. M.: AON, 1989. 166 pp.

4200   *Sotsializm i religiia* [Socialism and Religion]. Kommunist 4 (1988): 115-123.

4201   *Sotsial'naia politika KPSS - moshchnoe sredstvo formirovaniia novogo
        cheloveka, utverzhdeniia sotsialisticheskogo obraza zhizni* [Social Policy of
        the CPSU - Powerful Means for Shaping New Man, Affirmation of
        Socialist Way of Life]. M.: INION, 1987. 47 pp. (Ser. "Aktual. probl.
        sovershchenstvovaniia sotsializma" / AN SSSR, INION). Bibl.: pp. 40-47.

4202   *Sotsial'naia rol' ateizma v Litve (1919-1940 gg.)* [Social Role of Atheism in
        Lithuania (1919-1940]. Vil'nius: Znanie, 1984. 36 pp. In Lithuanian.

4203   *Sotsial'no-filosofskie aspekty kritiki religii* [Socio-Philosophical Aspects of
        Criticism of Religion]. [Ed.: Ia.Ia. Kozhurin]. L.: GMIRIA, 1980. 153 pp.
        Published also in:
        1982, 140 pp.
        1983, 165 pp.
        1984, 135 pp.
        1985,   45 pp. illus.
        1986, 155 pp.
        1987, 155 pp.
        1988 (1989), 158 pp., ed.: S.A. Kuchinskii.

4204   *Sotsial'no-filosofskie aspekty religii* [Socio-Philosophical Aspects of Religion].
        Ed.: Ia.Ia. Kozhurin. L.: GMIRIA, 1981. 158 pp.

4205   *Sotsial'no-ideologicheskie funktsii nauchnogo ateizma* [Socio-Ideological
        Functions of the Scientific Atheism]. M.: [S.n.], 1981. 120 pp.

4206   *Sotsial'no-politicheskie predstavleniia v islame: Istoriia i sovremennost'*
        [Socio-Political Notions in Islam: History and Contemporaneity]. [Ed.:
        I.M. Smilianskaia et al]. M.: Nauka, 1987. 119 pp.

4207 *Sotsial'no-psikhologicheskie aspekty kritiki religii* [Socio-Psychological Aspects of Criticism of Religion]. [Ed.: Ia.Ia. Kozhurin]. L.: GMIRIA, 1986. 148 pp.

4208 *Sovershenstvovanie ateisticheskogo vospitaniia pri zrelom sotsializme* [Perfection of Atheistic Education Under Mature Socialism]. [Ed.: G.I. Mustafaev et al]. Baku: AzGU, 1985. 85 pp. In Azerbaijan and Russian.

4209 "Sovershenstvovat' nauchno-ateisticheskoe vospitanie" [To Perfect Scientific-Atheistic Education]. [Editorial]. *Part. zhizn'* 6 (1985): 63-67.

4210 *Sovet po ateizmu deistvuet* [The Council on Atheism Acts]. Comp.: G.I. Kriazhevskikh. L.: Lenizdat, 1985. 136 pp.

4211 *Sovetskii obraz zhizni i formirovanie nauchno-materialisticheskogo, ateisticheskogo mirovozzreniia* [Soviet Way of Life and Forming Scientific-Materialistic, Atheistic World Outlook]. M.: Znanie, 1981. 16 pp. (V pomoshch' agitatoru i politinformatoru. Ateist. vospitanie; Ser. 5. Vyp. 1). Bibl.: p. 16.

4212 *Sovetskii obraz zhizni i formirovanie nauchno-materialisticheskogo ateisticheskogo ubezhdeniia* [Soviet Way of Life and Forming Scientific-Materialistic Atheistic Convictions]. M.: Znanie, 1980. 16 pp. (V pomoshch' agitatoru. Ateist. vospitanie; Vyp. 1). Bibl.: p. 16.

4213 *Sovremennaia ideologicheskaia bor'ba i islam* [Contemporary Ideological Struggle and Islam]. [Ed.: G.I. Mustafaev et al]. Baku: AzGU, 1986. 96 pp. In Azerbaijan. Summary in Russian.

4214 *Sovremennaia religioznost': sostoianie, tendentsii, puti preodoleniia* [Contemporary Religiosity: Condition, Tendencies, Ways of Overcoming]. [Ed.: A.S. Onishchenko et al]. Kiev: Politizdat Ukrainy, 1987. 265 pp. Annot. bibl.: pp. 259-4. For review see item 5297.

4215 *Sovremennyi katolitsizm: filosofiia, ideologiia, politika* [Contemporary Catholicism: Philosophy, Ideology, Politics]. Vil'nius: Mintis, 1981. 214 pp. In Lithuanian.

4216 *Sovremennyi Vatikan* [Contemporary Vatican]. [Comp.: P.I. Filatova]. Dushanbe: Znanie TadzhSSR, [1985]. 13 pp. (V pomoshch' lektoru / O-vo "Znanie" TadzhSSR). Bibl.: p. 13.

4217   Springis, K.Ia. *Nebo, zemlia i ad* [Heaven, Earth and Hell]. Riga: Avots, 1985. 166 pp., illus. In Latvian.

4218   Sretenskii, L.V. "Nauchnyi ateizm v sisteme filosofii i obshchestvoznaniia" [Scientific Atheism in the System of Philosophy and Social Sciences]. *Metodologicheskie problemy sovremennoi nauki*. Iaroslavl', 1980. Pp. 45-64.

4219   Sretenskii, L.V. "Partiinost' sovremennogo nauchnogo ateizma" [Party Spirit of Contemporary Scientific Atheism]. *Aktual'nye metodologicheskie problemy nauchnogo poznaniia*. Iaroslavl', 1982. Pp. 80-87.

4220   Stakhovskii, Z. "Protivorechivyi balans: K itogam tret'ego vizita papy Ioanna Pavla II v Pol'shu" [Contradictory Balance: Results of the Third Visit to Poland of Pope John Paul II]. *Nauka i religiia* 10 (1987): 59-60.

4221   Stankaitis, Iu.[Iu]. "Ateisticheskie ubezhdeniia - faktor aktivnoi zhiznennoi pozitsii" [Atheistic Convictions - Factor of Active Vital Position]. *Kommunist.* Vil'nius. 12 (1987): 81-85.

4222   Stankaitis, Iu.Iu. *Kriticheskaia otsenka osnovnykh polozhenii katolicheskoi etiki v literature litovskikh burzhuazno-klerikal'nykh filosofov* [Critical Appraisal of Basic Catholic Ethics in the Literature of Lithuanian Bourgeois-Clerical Philosophers]. Vil'nius: [S.n.], 1981. 24 pp. (Material v pomoshch' lektoru / Muzei ateizma LitSSR). In Lithuanian. Bibl.: p. 24.

4223   *Stanovlenie i razvitie massovogo ateizma v zapadnykh oblastiakh Ukrainskoi SSR* [Creation and Development of Mass Atheism in Western Regions of Ukrainian SSR]. [Iu.Iu. Slivka et al]. Kiev: Nauk. dumka, 1981. 255 pp. In Ukrainian.

4224   Starchenkov, G.I. "Turtsiia: islamskii faktor v svetskom gosudarstve" [Turkey: Islamic Factor in Laic State]. *Narody Azii i Afriki* 2 (1988): 25-34.

4225   Starchenkov, G.I. "'Islamskii bum' i aktivizatsia islama v sovremennoi Turtsii" ["Islamic Boom" and Activization of Islam in Contemporary Turkey]. *III Vsesoiuznaia konferentsiia vosotokovedov "Vzaimodeistvie i vzaimovliianie tsivilizatsii kul'tur na Vostoke".* M., 1988. T. 2. Pp. 165-167.

4226   Starkova, K.B. "Istoriia i istoriografiia v Biblii" [History and Historiography in the Bible]. *Istoriia i traditsionnaia kul'tura narodov Vostoka.* M., 1989. Ch. 2. Pp. 3-18.

4227 Starkova, K.B. "'Stranstvie Avraama' (1 Q-Gen Ap XXI, 8-20)" ["Abraham's Wandering"]. *Palest. sb.* 28 (1986): 69-73. Summary in French.

4228 Starostina, Iu.[P]. "Buddizm i magiia" [Buddhism and Magic]. *Aziia i Afrka segodnia* 4 (1982): 58-61.

4229 Starostina, Iu.P. "Nekotorye aspekty modernizatsii etiki buddizma tkheravady" [Some Aspects of Modernization of Ethics of Theravada Buddhism]. *Problemy etiki v filosofskikh ucheniiakh stran Vostoka.* M., 1986. Pp. 82-103.

4230 Starostina, Iu.P. *Sovremennyi buddizm i problemy sotsial'no-ekonomicheskogo razvitiia v Iuzhnoi i Iugo-Vostochnoi Azii* [Contemporary Buddhism and Problems of Socio-Economical Development in South and South-Eastern Asia: Scientific-Analytical Review]. M.: INION. 1985. 102 pp. (Ser. "Sovrem. probl. sotsial. razvitiia i ideologiia stran Azii, Afriki i Latin. Ameriki" / AN SSSR, INION). Bibl.: pp. 95-101.

4231 Startsev, V.I. "Rossiiskie masony XX veka" [Russian Freemasons of the XXth Century]. *Vopr. istorii* 6 (1989): 33-50.

4232 Stebleva, I.V. "Sinkretizm religiozno-mifologicheskikh predstavlenii domu-sul'manskikh tiurkov" [Syncretism of Religious-Mythological Concepts of Pre Moslem Turks]. *III Vsesoiuznaia konferentsiia vostokovedov "Vzaimo-desitvie i vzaimovliianie tsivilizatsii kul'tur na Vostoke.* M., 1988. T. 1. Pp. 179-180. Published also in *Narody Azii i Afriki* 4 (1989): 51-56. Summary in English: pp. 219-220.

4233 Steniaev, O. "Voskresnaia shkola" [Sunday School]. *Nauka i religiia* 9 (1989): 17-18.

4234 Stepaniants, M.T. "Istoricheskie sud'by sufizma" [Historical Destinies of Sufism]. *Vopr. filosofii* 6 (1980): 101-112. Summary in English, p. 187.

4235 Stepaniants, M.T. *Filosofskie aspekty sufizma* [Philosophical Aspects of Sufism]. M.: Nauka, 1987. 192 pp. Summary in English. Bibl.: pp. 85-89. Annot. bibl.: pp. 74-84. For reviews see items 5298-5300.

4236 Stepaniants, M.T. *Musul'manskie kontseptsii v filosofii i politike (XIX-XX vv.)* [Moslem Conceptions in Philosophy and Politics (XIXth-XXth Centuries]. M.: Nauka, 1982. 248 pp. Summary in English. Bibl.: pp. 226-237. Name and terms index: pp. 238-243. For review see item 5301.

4237 Stepaniants, M.T. "'Musul'manskoe vozrozhdenchestvo'" ["Moslem Revivability"]. *Narody Azii i Afriki* 3 (1983): 20-29. Summary in English, pp. 220-221.

4238 Stepaniants, M.T. "Sufiiskie elementy v filosofii Ibn Sino" [Sufiist Elements in Ibn Sina Philosophy]. *Torzhestvo razuma.* Dushanbe, 1988. Pp. 61-65. Bibl.: pp. 64-65.

4239 Stepanov, A.Ia. "Ateisticheskaia propaganda v zerkale obshchestvennogo mneniia" [Atheistic Propaganda in the Mirror of Public Opinion]. *Nauchnyi ateizm i obshchestvennoe mnenie].* M., 1987. Pp. 129-140.

4240 Stepanov, A.Ia. "Ateisticheskoe prosveshchenie - programmnaia ustanovka KPSS" [Atheistic Instruction - Programmed Directive of the CPSU]. *Revoliutsionnoe mirovozzrenie i zadachi sovershenstvovaniia sotsializma.* Petrozavodsk, 1987. Pp. 116-126.

4241 Stepanov, A.Ia. *Na putiakh dukhovnogo voskhozhdeniia:* (Religiia i atheism v Karelii) [On the Ways of Spiritual Ascent: (Religion and Atheism in Karelia)]. Petrozavodsk: Kareliia, 1982. 152 pp. Bibl.: pp. 150-152.
Published also as 2nd revised and enlarged ed. in 1986, 168 pp.

4242 Stepanov, A.Ia. "Ob obriadnosti, sviazannoi s rozhdeniem detei" [On Ritual, Connected with Childbirth]. *Pravoslavie v Karelii.* Petrozavodsk, 1987. Pp. 144-145.

4243 Stepanov, A.Ia. "Shkola i pravoslavnaia tserkov'" [The School and Orthodox Church]. Petrozavodsk, 1987. *Pravoslavie v Karelii.* Pp. 36-45.

4244 Stepanov, P. "K 1000-letiiu russkoi pravoslavnoi tserkvi" [1000th Year of Russian Orthodox Church]. *Kuban'* 6 (1988): 56-65.

4245 Stepanov, P. "Religiia, ateizm i sovremennaia ideologicheskaia bor'ba" [Religion, Atheism and Contemporary Ideological Struggle]. *Kuban'* 2 (1985): 82-88.

4246 Stepanov, P.M. *Chudesa bez chudes* [Miracles Without Miracles]. Krasnodar: Kn. izd-vo, 1984. 176 pp.

4247 Stepanov, P.M. *Russkoe pravoslavie: pravda i vymysly* [Russian Orthodoxy: Truth and Fabrications]. Krasnodar: Kn. izd-vo, 1988. 96 pp.

4248 Stepanov, R.N. "Nekotorye nabliudeniia otnositel'no sovremennykh protsessov v islame (na primere Egipta)" [Some Observations Concerning Contemporary Processes in Islam (on Egypt's Example)]. *Islam v istorii narodov Vostoka.* M., 1981. Pp. 182-188. Annot. bibl.: pp. 187-188.

4249 Stepanov, R.N. "Sovremennaia interpretatsiia kharaktera vzaimootnoshenii nauki i religii kak odna iz form apologii islama" [Contemporary Interpretation of the Character of Interrelation of Science and Religion as one of Islam's Form of Apologia]. *Aktual'nye problemy izucheniia istorii religii i ateizma.* L., 1981. Pp. 23-38.

4250 Stepinskii, M.A. "Esteticheskie aspekty ateizma i voprosy nauchno-ateisticheskogo vospitaniia molodezhi" [Aesthetic Aspects of Atheism and Problems of Scientific-Atheistic Upbringing of Youth]. *Nauch. tr./* Kurskii ped. in-t. 1981. T. 211. Pp. 60-72.

4251 Sternin, A. "Zvezda i krest: Zametki lektora-zhurnalista" [Star and Cross: Remarks of a Lecturer-Journalist]. *Pod'em* 6 (1986): 127-133.

4252 Stetskevich, M.S. "Istoriko-religiovedcheskii analiz serii angliiskikh graviur pervoi treti XIX veka iz sobraniia GMIRiA" [Historic-Religious Analysis of a Series of English Engravings of the Early XIXth Century From GMIRiA Collection]. *Muzei v ateistichekoi propagande.* L., 1988. Pp. 60-81.

4253 Stetskevich, T.A. "E.A. Beliaev i sovetskoe islamovedenie" [E.A. Beliaev and Soviet Studies of Islam]. *Islam v istorii narodov Vostoka.* M., 1981. Pp. 147-153.

4254 Stetskevich, T.[A]. "Ekspozitsiia rasskazyvaet ob islame" [Exhibition Narrates about Islam]. *Nauka i religiia* 10 (1982): 41-45.

4255 Stetskevich, T.A. "Islam i svobodmyslie narodov Vostoka" [Islam and Free Thinking of Peoples of the Orient]. *Muzei istorii religii i ateizma.* Putevoditel'. L., 1981. Pp. 93-110.

4256 Stetskevich, T.A. "Istoriia islama v muzeinoi ekspozitsii" [History of Islam in Museum Exhibition]. *Muzei v ateisticheskoi propagande.* L., 1988. Pp. 119-130.

4257 Stetskevich, T.[A]. "Problemy islamovedeniia na stranitsakh zhurnala 'Nauka i religiia" [Islam Studies on the Pages of the Journal "Nauka i religiia"].

Aziia i Afrika segodnia 9 (1984): 54-55. Summary in English, suppl., p. 5.

4258   Stoiko, I.M. *Formirovanie ateisticheskoi ubezhdennosti* [Shaping Atheistic Conviction]. L'vov: Vishcha shk. Izd-vo pri L'vov. gos. un-te, 1986. 173 pp.

4259   Stokialo, V.A. *Kritika fal'sifikatsii katolicheskimi ideologami istoricheskogo materializma* [Criticism of Catholic Ideologist's Falsifications of Historical Materialism]. Kiev: Vishcha shkola, 1980. 215 pp. Bibl.: pp. 202-213.

4260   Stoliarov, A.A. "Gierokl, Ammonii et alii" [Heracles, Ammon et ali]. *Antichnaia filosofiia: spetsificheskie cherty i sovremennoe znachenie.* Riga, 1988. Pp. 56-59.

4261   Stoliarova, I.A. "Propaganda ateizma v ekskursii po gosudarstvennomu muzeiu gorodskoi skul'ptury" [Propaganda of Atheism in Conducted Tours in the State Museum of Urban Sculpture]. *Muzei v ateisticheskoi propagande.* L., 1980. Pp. 50-58.

4262   Stolovich, L. "Razgovor ob iskusstve i religii" [Conversation about Art and Religion]. *Nauka i religiia* 7 (1989): 5-8, 19.

4263   Storchevaia, T.G. "O buddizme Zapadnogo kraia" [Buddhism of the Western Land]. *Novoe v izuchenii Kitaia.* M., 1987. Ch. 1. Pp. 77-90. Bibl.: pp. 89-90.

4264   Strakhov, A.B. "O vozmozhnom uchastii iuzhnykh slavian v khristianizatsii Rusi" [Possible Participation of Southern Slavs in the Baptism of Rus']. *Slaviane i ikh sosedi.* M., 1988. Pp. 28-30.

4265   Stratii, Ia.M. "Renessansno-gumanisticheskie predstavleniia o sushchnosti cheloveka i o smysle ego zhizni v dukhovnoi kul'ture Ukrainy vo vtoroi polovine XVI-pervoi polovine XVII v." [Renaissance-Humanistic Idea on the Essence of Man and on the Meaning of his Life in Spiritual Culture of Ukraine Late XVIth-Early XVIIth Century]. *Otechestvennaia obshchestvennaia mysl' epokhi Srednevekov'ia.* Kiev, 1988. Pp. 289-300.

4266   Strautmane, T.L. *Moralizuiushchaia revoliutsionnost' ili revoliutsionnaia moral'?* [Moralised Revolutionary Character or Revolutionary Morals?]. Riga: Znanie LatvSSR, 1983. 23 pp. (Material v pomoshch' lektoru / O-vo "Znanie" LatvSSR, Nauch.-metod. sovet po propagande nauch.

ateisma) (Znanie narodu /...). In Latvian. Annotations in Russian. Bibl.: pp. 22-23.

4267 Strautmane, T.L. "Popytki liuteranskoi tserkvi v Latvii modernizirovat' religioznoe uchenie o morali" [Attempts of Lutheran Church in Latvia to Modernize Religious Teachings on Morals]. *Izv. AN LatvSSR* (1982): 51-60.

4268 Strautmane, T.L. *Sushchnost' i kritika religioznogo gumanizma* [The Essence and Criticism of Religious Humanism]. Riga: Znanie LatvSSR, 1980. 24 pp. (Material v pomoshch' lektoru / O-vo "Znanie" LatvSSR, Nauch.-metod. sovet po propagande nauch. ateizma) (Znanie narodu / ...). In Latvian. Annot. in Russian. Bibl.: pp. 23-24.

4269 *Stroitel'svo sotsializma i utverzhdenie nauchno-materialistichekogo, ateisticheskogo mirovozzreniia (v regionakh rasprostraneniia lamaizma)* [Building of Socialism and Affirmation of Scientific-Materialistic, Atheistic Outlook (in Regions of Dissemination of Lamaism)]. [Ed.: V.D. Timofeev, et al]. M.: Mysl', 1981. 176 pp.

4270 Sufianova, S.S. "Estestvenno-nauchnye predposylki ateisticheskogo vospitaniia" [Natural-Scientific Premises of Atheistic Education]. *Problemy formirovaniia nauchno-ateisticheskogo mirovozzreniia v sotsialisticheskom obshchestve.* Samarkand, 1980. Pp. 44-48.

4271 Suglobov, G.A. *O svychaiakh - obychaiakh i religioznykh obriadakh* [On Habits - Customs and Religious Rituals]. M.: Sov. Rossiia, 1987. 134 pp.

4272 Suglobov, G.A. *Voinu o vrede religii:* Vopr. i otvety [To Soldier on the Harmfulness of Religion: Questions and Answers]. M.: Voenizdat, 1984. 63 pp.

4273 *Sufizm v kontekste musul'manskoi kul'tury* [Sufism in the Context of Moslem Culture]. Ed.: N.I. Prigarina. M.: Nauka, 1989. 341 pp.

4274 Suiarko, V.A. *Ateizm i religiia v sovremennoi bor'be idei* [Atheism and Religion in Contemporary Struggle of Ideas]. Kiev: Vishcha shk., 1984. 81 pp. (Ateist. b-chka studenta).

4275 Suiarko, V.A. "Mezhdunarodnoe kommunisticheskoe i rabochee dvizhenie o dialoge i sotrudnichestve s truiashchimisiia veruiushchimi" [International

Communist and Workers Movement on Dialogue and Cooperation with Believing Workers]. *Vopr. ateizma* 17 (1981): 3-11.

4276 Suiarko, V.A. "Nastupatel'naia aktivnost' nauchnogo ateizma" [Offensive Activity of Scientific Atheism]. *Vopr. ateizma* 23 (1987): 67-74.

4277 Suiarko, V.A. "Razrabotka KPSS kontseptsii ateisticheskoi deiatel'nosti dolgovremennogo znacheniia" [Elaboration of the CPSU Conception of Importance of Atheistic Activity of a Long Duration], *Vopr. ateizma* 24 (1988): 11-18.

4278 Sukhikh, A.A. "K voprosu ob izmenenii otnosheniia sovremennogo bogosloviia k nauke" [The Problem of Change of Attitude of Contemporary Theology Toward Science]. *Vopr. obshchestv. nauk* 78 (1989): 88-92.

4279 Sukhov, A.D. *Ateisticheskie traditsii v russkoi filosofii* [Atheistic Traditions in Russian Philosophy]. M.: Znanie, 1989. 64 pp. (Novoe v zhizni, nauke, tekhnike. Nauch. ateizm; 3/1989). Bibl.: p. 63.

4280 Sukhov, A.D. "Ateizm ideologov revoliutsionnogo narodnichestva" [Atheism of Ideologists of Revolutionary Populism]. *Vopr. nauh. ateizma* 25 (1980): 170-185.

4281 Sukhov, A.D. *Ateizm peredovykh russkikh myslitelei* [Atheism of Front-Rank Russian Thinkers]. M.: Mysl', 1980. 228 pp., illus. For reviews see items 5304-5305.

4282 Sukhov, A.D. "Ch. Valikhanov - religioved i kritik religii" [Ch. Valikhanov - Student and Critic of Religion]. *Chokan Valikhanov i sovremennost'.* Alma-Ata, 1988. Pp. 126-128.

4283 Sukhov, A.D. "O sotsial'noi determinatsii i orientatsii obshchestvennogo soznaniia v Kievskoi Rusi" [Social Determination and Orientation of Public Consciousness in Kievan Rus']. *Otechestvennaia obshchestvennaia mysl' epokhi Srednevekov'ia* Kiev, 1988. Pp. 29-33.

4284 Sukho, A.D. "Problemy issledovaniia istorii russkogo ateizma" [The Problems of Research of the History of Russian Atheism]. *Istoricheskie traditsii filosofskoi kul'tury narodov SSSR i sovremennost'.* Kiev, 1984. Pp. 264-271.

4285 Sulatskov, A.A. *Liki baptizma* [Faces of Baptism]. Alma-Ata: Kazakhstan, 1982. 360 pp. For review see item 5306.

4286 Sulimova, T.S. "Nesostoiatel'nost' musul'manskikh interpretatsii obshchestven-nogo razvitiia i sotsial'nogo ideala" [Unfoundedness of Moslem Interpreta-tion of Public Development and Social Ideal]. *Vest. Mosk. un-ta.* Ser. 12, Teoriia nauch. kommunizma 1 (1989): 70-77.

4287 Sulimova, T.S. "O vliianii kontseptsii 'islamskogo vozrozhdeniia' na formiro-vanie obshchestvennogo soznaniia molodezhi arabskikh stran" [Influence of Conception of "Islamic Revival" on Shaping Public Consciousness of Youth of Arab Countries]. *Sovremennaia ideolo- gicheskaia bor'ba i molodezh'.* M., 1987. Pp. 102-113.

4288 Sultangalieva, A.K. "Evoliutsiia idei 'islamskogo edinstva' v istorii arabskoi mysli (kon. XIX - 80-e gody XX vv.)" [Evolution of the Idea "Islamic Unity" in the History of Arab Thought (End XIXth - 80s of the XXth Centuries)]. *V Vsesoiuznaia shkola molodykh vostokovedov.* M., 1989. T. 3. Pp. 24-26.

4289 Sultanov, F.M. "Pobeda sotsializma v SSSR - osnova preodoleniia religio-znosti" [The Victory of Socialism in USSR - Basis for Overcoming Religiosity]. *Iz istorii formirovaniia i razvitiia svobodomysliia v dorevoliutsionnoi Tatarii.* Kazan', 1987. Pp. 97-110. Bibl.: pp. 109-110.

4290 Sultanov, R.I. "Genezis ucheniia o svobode voli v srednevekovom islame" [Genesis of the Teaching of Free Will in Medieval Islam]. *Moral', obshchestvo, lichnost'* 3 (1981): 67-88.

4291 Sultanov, R.I. "Kasb i problema svobody v musul'manskoi filosofii istorii" [Kasb and the Problem of Freedom in Moslem Philosophy of History]. *Vopr. filosofii* 3 (1983): 127-133.

4292 Sultanov, R.I. "Ob izuchenii nachal'noi stadii islama" [Study of Islam's Initial Stage]. *Metodologicheskie problemy izucheniia istorii filosofii zarubezhnogo Vostoka.* M., 1987. Pp. 135-154. Bibl.: pp. 152-154.

4293 Sultanov, T.I. "Vzgliady pozdnesrednevekovykh musul'manskikh avtorov na istoricheskuiu nauku" [Views of Late Medieval Moslem Authors on Historical Science]. *Narody Azii i Afriki* 1 (1988): 50-57.

4294 *Sumerki bogov* [Twilight of the Gods]. Preface by A.A. Iakovlev. M.: Politizdat, 1989. 397 pp. (B-ka ateist. lit.). Annot. bibl.: pp. 345-393. Name index: pp. 394-397. For review see item 5307.

4295 Surapbergenov, A.S. *Religiia i moral'* [Religion and Morals]. Alma-Ata: Kazakhstan, 1984. 54 pp. In Uighur.

4296 Surguladze, I.K. *Astral'naia simvolika v gruzinskom narodnom ornamente* [Astral Symbolism in Georgian Folk Ornament]. Tbilisi: Metsniereba, 1986. 208 pp., illus. In Georgian.

4297 Surguladze, I.K. "Prostranstvennye aspekty v mifologicheskikh i religioznykh predstavleniiakh gruzin" [Spacial Aspects in Mythological and Religious Notions of Georgians]. *Materialy po etnografii Gruzii.* Tbilisi, 1987. T. 23. Pp. 133-159. In Georgian. Summary in Russian.

4298 Surguladze, I.K. *Sviatoi Georgii v gruzinskikh religioznykh verovaniiakh* [Saint George in Georgian Religious Beliefs]. Tbilisi: Metsniereba, 1983. 9 pp. Annot. bibl.: p. 9.

4299 Surkhasko, Iu.Iu. "Proiavleniia dvoeveriia v traditsionnoi semeinoi obriadnosti karel" [Manifestation of Dual Belief in Traditional Family Ritual of Karels]. *Pravoslavie v Karelii.* Petrozavodsk, 1987. Pp. 46-61.

4300 Surkhasko, Iu.Iu. *Semeinye obriady i verovaniia karel, konets XIX-nach. XX v.* [Family Rituals and Beliefs of Karels, Late XIXth-Early XXth Century]. L.: Nauka. Leningr. otd-nie, 1985. 172 pp., illus. Bibl.: pp. 164-170.

4301 Surovegina, N.A. "Edinstvo politicheskogo i ateisticheskogo vospitaniia v vuze" [Unity of Political and Atheistic Education in Institutions of Higher Education]. *Ideino-vospitatel'naia rabota v vuze.* Kalinin, 1987. Pp. 83-91.

4302 Sushanlo, F.M. *Buddizm v istorii narodov srednevekovoi Kirgizii* [Buddhism in the History of Peoples of Medieval Kirghizia]. Novosibirsk: [S.n.], 1983. 5 pp.

4303 Sushanlo, M.Ia. "Islam i khueitszu /dungane / Kitaia" [Islam and Hueitsu (Dungan) of China]. *III Vsesoiuznaia konferentsiia vostokevedov "Vzaimodeistvie i vzaimovliianie tsivilizatsii kul'tur na Vostoke".* M., 1988. T. 1. Pp. 130-131.

4304 Sushko, K.I. *Vse moglo byt' inache: Vstrechi s veruiushchimi i neveruiushchimi* [All Could Be Differently: Meetings with Believers and Nonbelievers]. Dnepropetrovsk: Promin', 1984. 86 pp.

4305 Sventsitskaia, I.[S]. "'Na potekhu Rimu' [For the Fun of Rome]. *Nauka i religiia* 9 (1986): 4-6.

4306 Sventsitskaia, I.S. *Ot obshchiny k tserkvi* [From Community to Church]. M.: Politizdat, 1985. 224 pp.

4307 Sventsitskaia, I.[S]. "Pergament iz mogily monakha" [Parchment from Monk's Grave]. *Nauka i religiia* 4 (1989): 42-43.

4308 Sventsitskaia, I.S. *Ranee khristianstvo: stranitsy isorii* [Early Christianity: Pages of History]. M.: Politizdat, 1987. 336 pp. (B-ka ateist. lit.). Name index: pp. 327-334. Republished in 1988 and 1989.

4309 Sventsitskaia, I.S. *Tainye pisaniia pervykh khristian* [First Christian Secret Writ]. M.: Politizdat, 1980. 198 pp. Name index: pp. 191-196. 2nd ed. published in 1981, 288 pp.

4310 Sverdlov, B. "'Volshebnyi fonar'" i vremia" ["Magic Lantern" and Time]. *Nauka i religiia* 5 (1981): 27-28.

4311 Sverdlov, M.B. "Sotsial'no-ekonomicheskie predposylki priniatiia khristianstva na Rusi" [Socio-Economic Pre-Conditions of Adoption of Christianity in Rus']. *Vopr. nauch. ateizma* 37 (1988): 20-29.

4312 *Svet nashego dnia* [Light of Our Day]. Uzhgorod: Karpati, 103 pp. In Moldavian.

4313 Svetlov, G.E. "Istoriia novykh religioznykh dvizhenii Iaponii v trudakh Murakani Sigeesi" [History of Japan's New Religious Movements in Murakani Sigysi Works]. *Narody Azii i Afriki.* 2 (1986): 166-167.

4314 Svetlov, G.E. *Put' bogov* [The Way of the Gods]. M.: Mysl', 1985. 240 pp., illus. Bibl.: pp. 233-239. For reviews see items 5308-5311.

4315 "Svezhii veter semnadtsatogo goda" [Fresh Wind of 1917]. [Comp.: M. Odintsov]. *Nauka i religiia* 11 (1989): 2-4.

4316 Sviderskii, Iu.Iu. *Bor'ba Iugo-Zapadnoi Rusi protiv katolicheskoi ekspansii v X-XIII vv.* [The Struggle of South-Western Rus' against Catholic Expansion in Xth-XIIIth Centuries]. Kiev: Nauk. dumka, 1983. 127 pp. In Ukrainian.

4317 *Svoboda sovesti* [Freedom of Conscience]. [A.A. Kruglova]. Minsk: Belarus', 1986. 79 pp. (Sov. Belorussiia). In English. Published also in French and German.

4318 *Svoboda sovesti: zakon i zhizn'* [Freedom of Conscience: The Law and Life]. Nauka i religiia 9 (1989): 10-16.

4319 *Svoboda sovesti v SSSR: Sotsial'nye garantii* [Freedom of Conscience in the USSR: Social Guarantees]. Ed. A.N. Kalaganov. Kazan': Izd-vo Kazan. un-ta, 1989. 79 pp.

4320 *Svobodomyslie i ateizm v burzhuaznoi Litve* [Freethinking and Atheism in Bourgeois Lithuania]. [Comp.: I. Sakalauskas]. Vil'nius: Mintis, 1986. 109 pp. In Lithuanian.

4321 *Svobodomyslie i ateizm v drevnosti, srednie veka i v epokhu Vozrozhdeniia* [Freethinking and Atheism in Ancient Times, Middle Ages and Renaissance]. [Ed.: A.D. Sukhova]. M.: Mysl', 1986. 285 pp., illus. For reviews see items 5312-5313.

4322 Sychev, V.F. *SShA i musul'manskii mir* [USA and Moslem World]. Dushanbe: Irfon, 1989. 285 pp. Summary in English. Bibl.: pp. 270-282.

4323 Sychev, V.F. "Vliianie 'islamskogo faktora' na mezhdunarodnye otnosheniia" [The Influence of "Islamic Factor" on International Relations]. *"Islamskii faktor" v mezhdunarodnykh otnosheniiakh v Azii (70-e-pervaia polovina 80-kh gg.).* M., 1987. Pp. 40-47.

4324 Sypacheva, T.A. "Religioznyi nravstvennyi ideal kak sotsial'no-psikhologicheskii fenomen" [Religious Moral Ideal as Socio-Psychological Phenomenon]. *Nauchnyi ateizm: ideal i mirovozzrenie.* Perm', 1988. Pp. 49-57.

4325 Syrodeeva, M. "Religiia i natsionalizm" [Religion and Nationalism]. *Kommunist* 13 (1988): 75-76.

4326 Tabakaru, D.N. "Ateisticheskoe vospitanie naseleniia v sovremennykh usloviiakh" [Atheistic Education of Population in Contemporary Conditions]. *Problemy kommunisticheskogo vospitaniia trudiashchikhsia v Moldavskoi SSR.* Kishinev, 1987. Pp. 213-221.

4327 Tabakaru, D.N. *Baptizm i 'nebesnyi Khanaan'* [Baptism and "Divine Hanaan"]. Kishinev: Kartia Moldoveniaske, 1980. 83 pp. (Nauka i religiia). In Moldavian. Published also in 1984, 112 pp. For review see item 5314.

4328 Tabakaru, D.N. *Beseduia s veruiushchimi* [Discussing with Believers]. Kishinev: Kartia Moldoveniaske, 1980. 64 pp. In Moldavian. For review see item 5314.

4329 Tabakaru, D.N. "Formirovanie ateisticheskogo mirovozzrenia trudiashchkhsia" [Shaping Atheistic Outlook of Workers]. *Kommunist Moldavii* 8 (1985): 47-52.

4330 Tabakaru, D.[N]. "Kritika ideologii religioznogo sektantstva" [Criticism of Ideology of Religious Sectarianism]. *Kommunist Moldavii* 11 (1981): 67-73.

4331 Tabakaru, D.N. "Utverzhdenie ateizma v Moldavskoi SSR" [Assertion of Atheism in Moldavian SSR]. *Narodnye traditsii i sovremennost'*. Kishinev, 1980. Pp. 6-15.

4332 Tadzhieva, G. "Antireligioznye idei v ustnom tvorchestve naroda kak forma svobodomysliia" [Antireligious Ideas in Peoples' Oral Creation as a Form of Freethinking]. *Iz istorii sotsial'no-filosofskoi mysli narodov Vostoka.* Frunze, 1989. Pp. 104-119.

4333 Tadzhikova, K.Kh. *Islam: mirovozzrenie, ideologiia, politika* [Islam: World Outlook, Ideology, Politics]. Alma-Ata: Kazakhstan, 1989. 175 pp. In Kazakh.

4334 Tafaev, G.I.; Alekseev, B.L. "Nekotorye osobennosti nauchno-ateisticheskogo vospitaniia sredi posledovatelei pravoslaviia" [Some Features of Scientific-Atheistic Education among Followers of Orthodoxy]. *Istoriia khristianizatsii narodov Srednego Povolzh'ia. Kriticheskie suzhdeniia i otsenka.* Cheboksary, 1988. Pp. 116-121.

4335 Tailor, E.B. *Pervobytnaia kul'tura* [Primitive Culture]. Transl. from English. M.: Politizdat, 1989. 573 pp., illus. (B-ka ateist. lit.). Name index: pp. 525-556.

4336 Tairov, S. *Islam i natsional'no-osvoboditel'noe dvizhenie arabskikh narodov* [Islam and National Liberation Movement of Arab People]. Tashkent: Znanie UzSSR, 1985. 24 pp. (V pomoshch' lektoru / O-vo "Znanie" UzSSR. Ser. obshchestv.-polit.). In Uzbek.

4337 Taiyrov, A. *Religiia i moral'* [Religion and Morals]. Alma-Ata: Kazakhstan, 1987. 47 pp. In Kazakh.

4338 Taksil', L. *Sviashchennyi vertep* [Sacred Den]. Erevan: Aiastan, 1981. 607 pp. In Armenian. Published also in:
Kiev: Politizdat Ukrainy, 1985. 544 pp.
Minsk: Belarus', 1987, 510 pp.
2nd ed. M.: Politizdat, 1988. 528 pp., illus. Republished in 1989.

4339 Taksil', L. *Zabavnaia bibliia* [Amusing Bible]. 2nd ed. Kiev: Politizdat Ukrainy, 1984. 411 p. In Ukrainian. Published also in:
Minsk: Belarus', 1988, 414 pp., annot. bibl.: pp. 404-412.

4340 Taksil', L. *Zabavnoe evangelie, ili Zhizn' Iisusa* [Amusing Gospel, or the Life of Jesus]. Minsk: Belarus', 1989. 383 pp.

4341 Taktakishvili, D.D. *Modernizm v gruzinskom pravoslavii* [Modernism in Georgian Orthodoxy]. Tbilisi: Metsniereba, 1985. 58 pp. In Georgian. Summary in Russian.

4342 Talipov, K.T.; Syroezhkin, K.L. "Religiia v SUAR: vozrozhdenie, sovremennoe sostoianie, sotsial'naia rol'" [Religion in SUAR: Revival, Contemporary Condition, Social Role]. *Vestn. AN KazSSR* 11 (1989): 67-74.

4343 Talymov, L. "Oproverzhenie" [Denial]. *Nauka i religiia* 6 (1988): 26-29; 7 (1988): 34-37.

4344 Tamginskii, I.I. "Iaponia: Religiozno-polit. dvizhenie Soka Gakkai - Komeito" [Japan: Religious-Political Movement of Soka Gakkai - Komeyto]. *Religii mira: Istoriia i sovremennost'*. Ezhegodnik 1982. M., 1982. Pp. 99-119.

4345 Tancher, V.K. *G.V. Plekhanov - propagandist nauchnogo ateizma* [G.V. Plekhanov - Propagandist of Scientific Atheism]. Kiev: Znanie UkSSR, 1981. 48 pp. (Ser. 5 "Nauchno-ateisticheskaia" / O-vo "Znanie" UkSSR; No 7). Bibl.: p. 48.

4346 Tancher, V.K. "Nauchnyi ateim: problemy teorii i zadachi praktiki" [Scientific Atheism: Theoretical Problems and Practical Tasks]. *Vopr. ateizma* 24 (1988): 3-11.

4347 Tancher, V.K. "O povyshenii effektivnosti nauchno-ateisticheskoi propagandy" [Rising Effectiveness of Scientific-Atheistic Propaganda]. *Nauch. dokl. vyssh. shk. Nauch. kommunizm* 1 (1982): 81-84.

4348 Tancher, V.K. "Problemy razvitiia teorii nauchnogo ateizma" [Problems of Development of the Theory of Scientific Atheism]. *Vopr. ateizma* 18 (1982): 3-15.

4349 Tancher, V.K. *Poblemy teorii nauchnogo ateizma* [Problems of Theory of Scientific Atheism]. Kiev: Vishcha shk. Izd-vo pri Kiev. un-te, 1985. 208 pp. Annot. bibl.: pp. 199-207.

4350 Tancher, V.K. *Religiia i sovremennyi mir: Probl. sotsial.-polit. modernizma v rus. pravoslavie* [Religion and Contemporary World: Problems of Socio-Political Modernism in Russian Orthodoxy]. Kiev: Znanie UkSSR, 1985. 48 pp. (Ser. V "Nauchno-ateisticheskaia" / O-vo "Znanie" UkSSR; No 2). Annot. bibl.: pp. 47-48.

4351 Tancher, V.K. "Sovershenstvovat' nauchno-ateisticheskoe obuchenie i vospitanie studencheskoi molodezhi" [To Perfect Scientific-Atheistic Teaching and Upbringing of Students]. *Vopr. ateizma* 20 (1984): 3-10.

4352 Tancher, V.K. "Velikii Oktiabr' i pobeda nauchnogo mirovozzreniia v SSSR" [The Great October and the Victory of Scientific Outlook in USSR]. *Vopr. ateizma* 23 (1987): 3-8.

4353 Tansykbaeva, S.I. "Rol' musul'manskikh dukhovnykh soslovnykh grupp v obshchestvennoi zhizni Pakistana" [The Role of Moslem Clergy Groups in Pakistan's Social Life]. *III Vsesoiuznaia konferentsiia vostokovedov "Vzaimodeistvie i vzaimovliianie tsivilizatsii kul'tur na Vostoke"*. M., 1988. T. 2. Pp. 169-172.

4354 Tarasevich, I.S.; Kuklev, A.A. "Religioznoe mirovozzrenie narodov Severa, Sibiri i Dal'nego Vostoka kak forma obshchestvennogo soznaniia i nekotorye osobennosti ego proiavleniia v praktike sotsial'no-ekonomicheskogo razvitiia regiona" [Religious Outlook of Peoples from the North, Siberia and Far East as a Form of Public Consciousness and Some Features of Its Manifestations in the Practice of Socio-Economic Development of the Region]. *Novaia sotsial'naia tekhnologiia osvoeniia Severa, Sibiri i Dal'nego Vostoka*. Sverdlovsk, 1989. Pp. 263-302.

4355 Tarasov, A.A. *Sovest'* [Conscience]. Mosk. rabochii, 1985. 241 pp., illus. (Iunost' - tvoi bol'shoi mir).

4356 Tarasov, Iu.V. "Antigumannost' ucheniia i praktiki Russkoge pravoslaviia" [Anti Humanity in the Teaching and Practice of Russian Orthodoxy]. *Vopr. ateizma* 22 (1986): 38-45.

4357 Tarasov, Iu.V. "Ateisticheskoe vospitanie - deistvennoe sredstvo realizatsii gumanizma" [Atheistic Education - Effective Means of Realization of Humanism]. *Vopr. ateizma* 24 (1988): 102-108.

4358 Tarasov, L.M. *Chudo v zerkale razuma* [Miracle in the Mirror of Reason]. L.: Lenizdat, 1989. 254 pp., illus.

4359 Tarasov, O.Iu. "Nekotorye aspekty sravnitel'nogo izucheniia religioznoi narodnoi zhivopisi Rossii, Dunaiskikh kniazhestv i Transil'vanii XVII-XIX vekov" [Some Aspects of Comparative Study of Religious Folk Painting of Russia, Danube Principalities and Transylvania of XVIIth-XIXth Centuries]. *Sov. slavianovedenie* 2 (1989): 47-62. Bibl.: pp. 61-62.

4360 Tarasov, V. "Simvol i deistvitel'nost'" [Symbol and Reality]. *Aziia i Afrika segodnia* 3 (1988): 54-56.

4361 Taratunskii, F.S. *Nravstvennaia svoboda i otvetstvennost'* [Moral Freedom and Resonsibility]. Minsk: Belarus', 1980. 63 pp.

4362 Tarba, I.D. *Aktual'nye problemy nauchno-ateisticheskoi propagandy* [Actual Problems of Scientific-Atheistic Propaganda]. Sukhumi: Alashara, 1987. 12 pp. In Abkhazian.

4363 Tarba, I.D. *O sisteme nauchno-ateisticheskogo vospitaniia v Abkhazskoi ASSR* [The System of Scientific-Atheistic Education in Abkhazian ASSR]. Sukhumi: Alashara, 1985. 41 pp. In Abkhazian.

4364 Tarbeev, V.A. *Pod zelenym flagom* [Under Green Banner]. Tashkent: Uzbekistan, 1984. 39 pp. (Ser. "Marksizm-leninizm"; No 11). In Uzbek.

4365 Tartarashvili, V.G. "Musul'manskoe dukhovenstvo v russko-iranskikh politicheskikh vzaimootnosheniiakh (XIX v.)" [Moslem Clergy in Russian-Iranian Political Interrelationships (XIXth C.)]. *Istoriia religii i ateisticheskaia propaganda*. Tbilisi, 1987. Kn. 11. Pp. 35-49. In Georgian. Summary in Russian.

4366   Tashchuk, V.G. *Ateizm i nravstvennyi mir molodezhi* [Atheism and Youth's Moral World]. Kishinev: Kartia Moldoveniaske, 1987. 199 pp. Bibl.: p. 198.

4367   Tashchuk, V.G. *Religioznye tainstva: chto kroetsia za nimi?* [Religious Mysteries: What is Concealed Behind Them?]. Kishinev: Kartia Moldoveniaske, 1984. 138 pp., illus. Annot. bibl.: pp. 134-137.

4368   Tashlanov, T. *Beseda c molodezh'iu* [Talk with Youth]. Tashkent: Uzbekistan, 1989. 101 pp., illus. In Uzbek.

4369   Tashlanov, T. *Natsional'nye i religioznye obriady* [National and Religious Ceremonials]. Tashkent: Uzbekistan, 23 pp. (B-ka Ateista). In Uzbek.

4370   Tavrizian, G.M. "Istoriia, filosofiia, istoriia filosofii v svete 'khristianskogo ekzistentsializma' G. Marselia" [History, Philosophy, History of Philosophy in G. Marcel's "Christian Existentialism"]. *Problemy marksistsko-leninskoi ideologii istorii filosofii.* M., 1987. Pp. 170-186.

4371   Tazhurizina, Z.A. *Ateizm i svobodomyslie v dukhovnoi zhizni russkogo naroda* [Atheism and Free Thinking in Spiritual Life of Russian People]. M.: Znanie, 1986. 64 pp. (Novoe v zhizni, nauke, tekhnike. Nauch. ateizm; 9/1986). Bibl.: pp. 63-64.

4372   Tazhurizina, Z.A. "Ateizm kak iavlenie dukhovnoi kul'tury" [Atheism as an Event of Spiritual Culture]. *Dukhovnaia kul'tura sotsializma i ideologiia.* Saransk, 1984. Pp. 85-96.

4373   Tazhurizina, Z.A. *Idei svobodomysliia v istorii kul'tury* [Ideas of Free Thinking in the History of Culture]. M.: Izd-vo MGU, 1987. 224 pp. For reviews see items 5315-5317.

4374   Tazhurizina, Z.A. "Rol' seminarov v aktivnom usvoenii nauchnogo ateizma studentami" [The Role of Seminaries in Active Mastering of Scientific Atheism by Students]. *Prepodavanie nauchnogo ateizma v vuze.* M., 1988. Pp. 52-61.

4375   Tazhurizina, Z.A. "Slushaia vologodskikh ekskursovodov" [Listening to Guides of Vologodsk]. *Nauka i religiia* 3 (1984): 25-28.

4376   Tazhurizina, Z.A. *Tvorcheskaia sushchnost' ateizma* [Creative Essence of Atheism]. M.: Znanie, 1981. 64 pp. (Novoe v zhizni, nauke, tekhnike. Ser. "Nauch. ateizm"; No 2).

4377   Tazhurizina, Z.[A].; Nikonov, K. "Chto takoe starchestvo?" [What is Senility?]. *Nauka i religiia* 6 (1981): 34-37.

4378   Teiiar de Sharden P'er. *Fenomen cheloveka* [Phenomenal Occurrence of Man]. M.: Nauka, 1987. 240 pp.

4379   Tel'nov, V.V. *Pod prikrytiem religii* [Under the Cover of Religion]. Alma-Ata: Znanie KazSSR, 1988. 42 pp.

4380   Temirov, A.K. "Formirovanie ateisticheskogo obshchestvennogo mneniia - vazhnoe uslovie neitralizatsii vliianiia religioznoi mikrosredy" [Shaping Atheistic Public Opinion - Important Condition for Neutralization of the Influence of Religious Microenvironment]. *Sotsial'no-etichesie problemy povysheniia effektivnosti ateisticheskogo vospitaniia v mnogonatsional'nom regione.* Frunze, 1987. Pp. 41-47.

4381   Tendriakov, V. "Nravstvennost' i religiia" [Morals and Religion]. *Nauka i religiia* 2 (1987): 5-7; 3 (1987): 5-7; 4 (1987): 51-53; 6 (1987): 22-24; 7 (1987): 9-11.

4382   *Teoreticheskie osnovy ateisticheskogo vospitaniia molodezhi* [Theoretical Foundations of Youth's Atheistic Upbringing]. [Ed.: S.S. Sobolev]. M.: [S.n.], 1980. 131 pp.

4383   *Teoriia i praktika nauhnogo ateizma* [Theory and Practice of Scentific Atheism]. Ed.: I. Garadzha. M.: Mysl', 1984. 236 pp.
        Published also in:
        Askhabad: Turkmenistan, 1985. 292 pp. In Turkmen. For review see item 5318.

4384   Tepsina, A.N. *Filosofiia religii K. Iaspersa* [K. Jasper's Philosophy of Religion]. L.: Izd-vo LGU, 1982. 152 pp.

4385   Terbish, L. "Uchenie o 'kolese vremeni' v Mongolii" [Teaching about "The Wheel of Time" in Mongolia]. *Vopr. istorii estestvoznaniia i tekhniki* 4 (1989): 93-95.

4386 Terekhina, G.P. "Teiiar de Sharden i protestantskaia teologiia" [Teilhard de Chardin and Protestant Theology]. *Kritika religioznoi ideologii i problemy ateisticheskogo vospitaniia.* M., 1982. Pp. 51-58.

4387 Terekhova, V.A. "Spetsifika religioznogo mifa" [Specific of Religious Myth]. *Aktual'nye problemy ateisticheskogo vospitaniia i kritika religioznoi ideologii.* M., 1983. Pp. 44-48.

4388 Terent'ev, A.A. *Dzhaiskie predstavleniia o sushchnosti cheloveka* [Dzhai Notion About the Essence of Man]. Novosibirsk: [S.n.], 1983. 4 pp.

4389 Tereshchenko, Iu.I. "Ateizm i moral'" [Atheism and Morals]. *Kommunist Ukrainy* 7 (1989): 73-79.

4390 Tereshchenko, Iu.I. "Dialektika kriticheskogo i pozitivnogo v ateisticheskoi kontrpropagande" [Dialectics of the Critical and Positive in Atheistic Counterpropaganda]. *Vopr. ateizma* 25 (1989): 44-50.

4391 Tereshchenko, Iu.I. *Edinstvo nauchnogo ateizma i kommunisticheskoi morali* [Unity of Scientific Atheism and Communist Morality]. Kiev: Vishcha shk., 1983. 97 pp. (Ateist. b-chka studenta). In Ukrainian.

4392 Tereshchenko, Iu.I. *Mnimye tsennosti religioznoi morali* [Imaginary Values of Religious Morals]. Kiev: Politizdat Ukrainy, 1985. 156 pp. In Ukrainian. Annot. bibl.: pp. 150-155.

4393 Tereshchenko, Iu.I. "Patriotizm: aktual'nyi aspekt nauchnogo ateizma" [Patriotism: Actual Aspect of Scientific Atheism]. *Kommunist Ukrainy* 9 (1985): 85-92.

4394 Tereshchenko, Iu.I. "Problemy aktualizatsii nravstvennogo soderzhaniia nauchnogo ateizma" [Problems of Actualization of Moral Content of Scientific Atheism]. *Vopr. ateizma* 24 (1988): 79-85.

4395 Teteruk, S.F. *O dobre i zle* [On Good and Evil]. Kiev: Politizdat Ukrainy, 1982. 71 pp. (Besedy s veruiushchimi). In Ukrainian.

4396 Teteruk, S.F. *Vozvrashchennaia vesna* [Returned Spring]. Kiev: Veselka, 1986. 103 pp., illus. In Ukrainian.

4397 Tetevina, E.G. "Problemy ateisticheskogo vospitaniia molodezhi" [Problems of Atheistic Upbringing of Youth]. *Sotsial'no-eticheskie problemy povyshenia effektivnosti ateisticheskogo vospitaniia v mnogonatsional'nom regione.* Frunze, 1987. Pp. 47-55.

4398   Tevialis, Iu.V. "Rabota raionnogo komiteta partii s trudiashchimisia-veruiushchimi" [The Work of Regional Party Committee with Workers-Believers]. *Veruiushchii v usloviiakh perestroiki.* M., 1989. Pp. 66-77.

4399   Tevzadze, G, "Kant o morali ateista" [Kant on Atheist's Morals]. *Iubilei-naia sessiia Filosofskogo seminara Tbilisskogo gosudarstvennogo universiteta, posviashchennaia 200-letiiu "Kritiki prakticheskogo razuma" Kanta, 18-19 marta 1988 g.* Tbilisi, 1988. Pp. 3-8. In Georgian. Summary in Russian.

4400   Tevzadze, G.; Gegeshidze, D.; Gordeznani, R. "Religioznaia filosofiia" [Religious Philosophy]. *Sovremennaia burzhuaznaia filosofiia.* Tbilisi, 1988. Pp. 359-423. In Georgian.

4401   *Tezisy respublikanskoi nauchno-metodicheskoi konferentsii 'Uluchshenie ateisticheskogo vospitaniia molodezhi uchebnykh zavedenii', Grodno, 24-25 dek. 1987 g.* [Theses of Republican Scientific-Methodical Conference "Improvement of Atheistic Upbringing of Youth of Educational Institutions", Grodno, 24-25 Dec.,1987]. Ed.: G.A. Martirosov. Grodno: Grodn. gos. un-t, Grodn. opor. punkt In-ta nauch. ateizma AON pri TsK KPSS, 1987. 185 pp.

4402   Tidikas, R.I. *Nravstvennoe znachenie ateisticheskogo vospitaniia* [Moral Significance of Atheistic Education]. Vil'nius: Znanie LitSSR, 1980. 18 pp. (Material dlia lektora / O-vo "Znanie" LitSSR). In Lithuanian. Bibl.: pp. 17-18.

4403   Tidikas, R.I. "Perestroika i katoliki Litvy" [Perestroika and Lithuania's Catholics]. *Veruiushchii v usloviiakh perestroiki.* M., 1989. Pp. 48-66.

4404   Tidikas, R.I. *Struktura i funktsii protsessa vospitaniia nauchno-ateisticheskikh ubezhdenii* [The Structure and Functions of Educational Process of Scientific-Atheistic Convictions]. Vil'nius: M-vo vysh. i sred. spets. obrazovaniia LitSSR, 1980. 47 pp. In Lithuanian. Bibl.: pp. 45-46.

4405   Tikhonova, G.Iu. "K voprosu ob evoliutsii religii v sotsialisticheskom obshchestve" [On the Problem of Evolution of Religion in Socialist Society]. *Dukhovnyi mir sovremennogo cheloveka.* M., 1987. Pp. 118-120.

4406 Tikhonova, T.P. "Mesto islama v nereligioznoi kontseptsii arabizma Saty Al'-Khusri" [The Place of Islam in Sati Al'-Husri's Nonreligious Conception of Arabism]. *Religii mira: Istoriia i Sovremennos'*. Ezhegodnik 1982. M., 1982. Pp. 72-85.

4407 Timchenko, I.[P]. "Ateisticheskaia rabota sredi zhenshchin" [Atheistic Work among Women]. *Agitator* 9 (1983): 39-41.

4408 Timchenko, I.P. *Zhenshchina, religiia, ateizm* [Woman, Religion, Atheism]. Kiev: Politizdat Ukrainy, 1981. 151 pp. Annot. bibl.: pp. 145-149. For reviews see items 5319-5320.

4409 Timchuk, M.N. *Edinstvo trudovogo i ateisticheskogo vospitaniia* [Unity of Working and Atheistic Education]. Kiev: Politizdat Ukrainy, 1985. 97 pp. In Ukrainian.

4410 Timofeev, I. "Rol' islama v obshchstvenno-politicheskoi zhizni stran zarubezhnogo Vostoka" [The Role of Islam in Socio-Political Life of Countries of Foreign Orient]. *Mirovaia ekonomika i mezhdunar. otnosheniia* 5 (1982): 51-63.

4411 Timoshin, L. "Etot 'stranyi mir Khare Krishna" [This "Strange World of Hare Krishna"]. *Nauka i religiia* 1 (1983): 52-57; 2 (1983): 59-63.

4412 Timoshin, L. "'Messiia dolzhen byt' bogache vsekh'" ["Messiah Must be All Rich]. *Nauka i religiia:* 11 (1982): 59-63.

4413 Timoshin, L. "'Moisei' Berg: 'Pastyrstvo flirtuiushchei rybki'" ["Moses" Berg: "Pastoral of a Flirting Fish"]. *Nauka i religiia* 9 (1983): 57-60; 10 (1983): 54-57.

4414 Timoshin, L. "Saientologiia: fantastiku - v biznes" [Scientology: Fantastics - into Business]. *Nauka i religiia* 2 (1985): 58-62; 4 (1985): 57-60.

4415 Timoshin, L. "Vunderkind iz 'Missii bozhestvennogo sveta'" [Infant Prodigy from "The Mission of Divine Light"]. *Nauka i religiia* 12 (1985): 44-48.

4416 Tipsina, A.N. "Formirovanie ateisticheskoi ubezhdennosti studentov pri izuchenii obshchestvennykh nauk" [Shaping Students Atheistic Conviction when Studying Social Sciences]. *Aktual. vopr. metodiki prepodavaniia obshchestv. nauk i kom. vospitaniia studentov.* L., 1987. Vyp. 5. Pp. 10-18.

4417   Titov, Iu.N.   "Protsess ogosudarstvleniia tserkvi v XVIII-XIX vv." [The
       Process of Church Integration into State System in XVIIIth-XIXth
       Centuries]. *Vopr. nauch. ateizma* 37 (1988): 173-186.

4418   Titov, Iu.P.   "Revoliutsionnye tribunaly v bor'be s tserkovnoi kontrrevoliutsiei"
       [Revolutionary Tribunals in the Struggle with Church Counter Revolu-
       tion]. *Istoriko-pravovye voprosy vzaimootnoshenii gosudarstva i tserkvi v
       istorii Rossii.* M., 1988. Pp. 147-168.

4419   Titov, N.Iu.   "Soslovnye problemy vzaimootnoshenii gosudarstva i tserkvi v
       period absoliutizma" [Class Problems in State and Church Interrelations
       under Absolutism]. *Istoriko-pravovye voprosy vzaimootnoshenii gosudarstva i
       tserkvi v istorii Rossii.* M., 1988. Pp. 93-109.

4420   Titov, S.K.   "Nekotorye aspekty vzaimodeistviia religioznoi ideologii i
       massovogo soznaniia (na materiale XV-XVI v.)" [Some Aspects of
       Reciprocity of Religious Ideology and Mass Consciousness (on Data of
       XVth-XVIth Century)]. *Problemy sotsial'nogo poznania.* Novosibirsk, 1981.
       Pp. 77-86.

4421   Tiulina, E.V.   "Kosmologicheskie predstavleniia v pominal'nom rituale
       Ekoddishta Shraddkhi" [Cosmological Notions in Ekoddishta Shraddha
       Funeral Ritual]. *Narody Azii i Afriki* 3 (1988): 44-53.

4422   Tiulina, E.V.   "Otrazhenie drevneindiiskikh kosmologicheskikh predstavlenii v
       pominal'noi obriadnosti" [Reflection of Ancient Indian Cosmological
       Notions in Funeral Rituals]. *Kul'tura i iskusstvo narodov Vostoka.* M.,
       1987. Pp. 101-102.

4423   Tivanenko, A.V.   *Drevnie sviatilishcha Vostochnoi Sibiri v epokhu kamnia i
       bronzy* [East Siberian Ancient Sanctuaries in the Stone and Bronze Ages].
       Novosibirsk: Nauka. Sib. otd-nie, 1989. 202 pp., illus. Bibl.: pp. 184-200.

4424   Tivanenko, A.V.   "Kul'tovye kompleksy kochevykh plemen gruppy dunku"
       [Religious Complexes of Nomadic Tribes of the Duncu Group]. *Tsybiko-
       vskie chteniia.* Ulan-Ude, 1989. Pp. 122-124.

4425   Tizhina, A.N.   "Problemy modernizatsii khristianstva v filosofii K. Iaspersa"
       [The Problem of Modernization of Christianity in K. Jasper's Philosophy].
       Sotsial'no-filosofskie aspekty kritiki religii. L., 1980. Pp. 41-57.

4426 Tkachenko, A.A. "Problema very i formirovanie ateisticheskikh ubezhdenii" [The Problem of Faith and Shaping Atheistic Convictions]. *Vopr. ateizma* 17 (1981): 19-27.

4427 Tkachenko, A.A. "Vo imia chego nam nuzhen mirovozzrencheskii dialog s veruiushchimi?" [In the Name of What do we Need a Dialogue About World Outlook with Believers?]. *Filos. i sotsiol. mysl'* 1 (1989): 28-44.

4428 Tkachenko, N.G.; Masan, A.N. "Papskoe podtverzhdenie dogovora Rigi s livonskimi feodalami o 'gotskom' prave 1225 g." [Papal Confirmation of Riga Agreement with Livonian Feudals on "Gothic" Law of 1225]. *Vestn. Mosk. un-ta.* Ser 8, Istoriia 1 (1988): 76-81.

4429 Tkachenko, N.V. "Modernistskoe istolkovanie otnosheniia 'chelovek - bog' v sovremennom pravoslavii" [Modernist Interpretation of Attitude "Man - God" in Contemporary Orthodoxy]. *Vopr. ateizma* 22 (1986): 71-77.

4430 Tkachenko, N.V. "Razvitie kul'tury myshleniia kak faktor ateisticheskogo vospitaniia molodezhi" [Development of Culture of Thought as Factor of Youth's Atheistic Upbringing]. *Aktual'nye problemy nauchno-ateisticheskogo vospitaniia molodezhi.* M., 1987. Pp. 70-74.

4431 Tkacheva, A.A. *Induistskie misticheskie organizatsii i dialog kul'tur* [Hindu Mystical Organizations and Dialogue of Cultures]. M.: Nauka, 1989. 139 pp. Summary in English. Bibl.: pp. 127-135.

4432 Tkacheva, A.[A]. "Guru, ucheniki, ashrany" [Guru, Pupils, Ashrans]. *Aziia i Afrika segodnia* 8 (1983): 58-61. Summary in English, suppl., p. 6.

4433 Tkacheva, A.A. "Sootnoshenie idei dukhovnoi obshchnosti religii i induistskogo messianstva v mirovozzrenii M.K. Gandi" [Interrelation of the Idea of Spiritual Community of Religion and Hinduist Messianism in M.K. Gandhi's World Outlook]. *Obshchestvennaia mysl' Indii. Proshloe i nastoiashchee.* M., 1989. Pp. 23-37.

4434 Tkacheva, A.[A]. "Vverkh po lestnitse, vedushchei v nikuda" [Up the Stairs Leading to Nowhere]. *Nauka i religiia* 8 (1988): 36-37.

4435 Tkacheva, V.I. "Problemy 'smysla zhizni' v sovremennom russkom pravoslavii" [The Problems of the "Meaning of Life" in Contemporary Russian Orthodoxy]. *Aktual'nye problemy izucheniia istorii religii i ateizma.* L., 1980. Pp. 25-32.

4436 Tofan, G.K. *Iz t'my* [From Darkness]. Uzhgorod: Karpati, 1983. 55 pp. In Ukrainian. Published also in 1984, in Moldavian.

4437 Toibi, A.D. "Khristianstvo i marksizm" [Christianity and Marxism]. *Daugava* 4 (1989): 96-103.

4438 Tokarev, S.A. *Istoriia religii* [History of Religion]. M.: Progress, [1989]. 413 pp. (B-ka studenta). In English. Bibl.: pp. 396-408. Subject index: pp. 409-413.
      Published also in Spanish and jointly with Delhi: Peoples Publishing House; Jaipur: Radjastan Peoples Publishing House, [1989]. 526 pp. in Hindu.

4439 Tokarev, S.A. "Kalendarnye obychai i obriady" [Calendar Customs and Ceremonials]. *Ateisticheskie chteniia* 1 (1988): 36-47.

4440 Tokarev, S.A. "O kul'te gor i ego mesto v istorii religii" [The Cult of Mountains and Its Place in the History of Religion]. *Sov. etnografiia* 3 (1982): 107-113.

4441 Tokarev, S.A. *Religiia v istorii narodov mira* [Religion in the History of Peoples of the World]. 4th revised and enlarged ed. M.: Politizdat, 1986. 576 pp., illus. (B-ka ateist. lit.). Bibl.: pp. 558-568.

4442 Tokarev, S.[A]. "Zhertvoprinosheniia" [Sacrifice]. *Nauka i religiia* 4 (1981): 32-35.

4443 Tokarev, V. "Khadzh: traditsiia i sovremennost'" [Hadj: Tradition and Contemporaneity]. *Aziia i Afrika segodnia* 5 (1987): 53-55.

4444 Tokbergenov, A. *Problemy nauchno-ateisticheskogo vospitaniia molodezhi* [Problems of Youth's Scientific Atheistic Upbringing]. Alma-Ata: Mekter, 1987. 117 pp. In Kazakh.

4445 Tokzhigitov, M.Zh. *Islam i ego modernizm* [Islam and Its Modernism]. Alma-Ata: Znanie KazSSR, 1983. 36 pp. In Kazakh.

4446 Tolstaia, S.M. "Terminologiia obriadov i verovanii kak istochnik rekonstruktsii drevnei dukhovnoi kul'tury" [Terminology of Rituals and Beliefs as a Source of Reconstruction of Ancient Spiritual Culture]. *Slavianskii i balkanskii fol'klor.* M., 1989. Pp. 215-229. Bibl.: pp. 228-229.

4447 Tolstoi, I. "Russkie dukhobortsy" [Russian Dukhobors]. *Chto s nami prois-khodit?* Vyp. 1 (1989): 193-237.

4448 Tolstoi, N. "Kreshchenie Rusi i russkaia kul'tura" [The Baptism of Rus' and Russian Culture]. *Novoe vremia* 24 (1988): 24-25.

4449 Tolstov, S.V. "Severnaia Irlandiia: Natsional'no-religioznyi aspekt ol'sterskogo krizisa" [Northern Ireland: National-Religious Aspect of Ulster Crisis]. *Vopr. novoi i noveishei istorii* 34 (1988): 103-115.

4450 Tomas,G.; Morgan-Uitts, M. "Chtoby ne nastal Armageddon" [May Armageddon not Come]. *Nauka i religiia* 8 (1988): 58-63.

4451 Tomashevich, O.V. "Aziatskie bogi v Drevnem Egipte" [Asiatic Gods in Ancient Egypt]. *III Vsesoiuznaia konferentsiia vostokovedov "Vzaimodeistvie i vzamovliianie tsivilizatsii kul'tur na Vostoke"*. M., 1988. T. 1. Pp. 40-41.

4452 Tomashevich, O.V. "Boginia Neit - okhranitel'nitsa mertvykh" [The Goddess Neyth - Protectress of the Dead]. *Meroe* 3 (1985): 227-238, tables. Summary in English, p. 274.

4453 Tomashevich, O.V. "Egipetskie bogi za predelami doliny Nila (ranee i staroe tsarstvo)" [Egyptian Gods Beyond the Nile Valley (Earliest and Old Kingdoms)]. *V Vsesoiuznaia shkola molodykh vostokovedov.* M., 1989. T. 1. Pp. 76-78.

4454 Tomilina, N.E. "Znachenie dostizhenii meditsiny dlia razvitiia ateisticheskogo miroponimaniia" [The Importance of the Achievement of Medicine for Development of the Atheistic Outlook]. *Dukhovnye tsennosti kak predmet filosofskogo analiza.* M., 1985. Pp. 98-103.

4455 Topilina, V.M. "Moldavskaia pravoslavnaia tserkov' v nachale XX veka" [Moldavian Orthodox Church at the Beginning of XXth Century]. *Kommunist Moldavii* 2 (1988): 79-86.

4456 Torchinov, E.A. "Buddizm i formirovanie dal'nevostochnogo istoriko-kul'turnogo areala" [Buddhism and Forming of Far Eastern Historic-Cultural Abode]. *Dvadtsataia nauchnaia konferentsiia "Obshchestvo i gosudarstvo v Kitae".* M., 1989. Ch. 1. Pp. 94-97.

4457 Torchinov, E.A. "Daosizm i imperatorskaia vlast' v traditsionnom Kitae" [Taoism and Imperial Power in Traditional China]. *Obshchestvennye dvizheniia i ikh ideologiia v doburzhuaznykh obshchestvakh Azii.* M., 1988. Pp. 44-51.

4458   Torchinov, E.A. "Daosskaia utopiia v Kitae na rubezhe drevnosti i srednevekov'ia (II-VI vv.)" [Taoist Utopia in China of Ancient and Middle Ages (IInd-VIth Centuries)]. *Kitaiskie sotsial'nye utopii.* M., 1987. Pp. 104-124.

4459   Torchinov, E.A. "Daossko-buddiiskoe vzaimodeistvie" [Taoist-Buddhist Reciprocity]. *Narody Azii i Afriki* 2 (1988): 45-54.

4460   Torchinov, E.A. "Etika i ritual v religioznom daosizme" [Ethics and Ritual in Religious Taoism]. *Etika i ritual v traditsionnom Kitae.* M., 1988. Pp. 202-235. Bibl.: pp. 233-235.

4461   Torchinov, E.A. "O psikhologicheskikh aspektakh ucheniia pradzhnia-paramity" [Psychological Aspects of Prajna-Paramita Teachings]. *Psikhologicheskie aspekty buddizma.* Novosibirsk, 1986. Pp. 47-69.

4462   Torchinov, E.A. "Retseptsiia buddizma v Kitae kak primer mezhkul'turnogo vzaimodeistviia" [Practice of Buddhism in China as Example of Inter-cultural Reciprocity]. *III Vsesoiuuznaia konferentsiia vostokovedov "Vzaimodeistvie i vzaimovliianie tsivilizatsii kul'tur na Vostoke.* M., 1988. T. 1. Pp. 131-133.

4463   Torchinov, E.A. "Teoretiko-metodologicheskii aspekt izucheniia daossko-buddiiskogo vzaimodeistviia" [Theoretical-Methodological Aspect of Study of Taoist-Buddhist Reciprocity]. *Deviadnadtsataia nauchnaia konferentsiia "Obshchestvo i gosudarstvo v Kitae".* M., 1988. Ch. 1. Pp. 124-127.

4464   Torchinov, E.A. "Traktat Ge Khuna 'Baotsu-tszy' kak istochnik po izucheniiu daosizma perioda Liu-chao" [Che Hun's "Baotsa-Tzu" Treatise as a Study Source of Taoism of the Liu Ch'i Period]. *Aktual'nye problemy izucheniia istorii religii i ateizma.* L., 1980. Pp. 139-153.

4465   Torchinov, E.A. "Tszun-mi o shkolakh khinaiany i makhaiany" [Tzun-mi on the Schools of Hinayana and Mahayana]. *Tsybikovskie chteniia.* Ulan-Ude, 1989. Pp. 124-126.

4466   *Traditsionnye i sinkreticheskie religii Afriki* [Africa's Traditional and Syncretical Religions]. Ed.: An.A. Gromyko et al. M.: Nauka, 1986. 588

pp., maps. (Religiia v XX v.). Summary in English. Annot. bibl.: pp. 525-560. Index: pp. 562-582. For review see item 5321.

4467 *Traditsionnye verovaniia i byt narodov Sibiri, XIX nach-XX v.* [Traditional Beliefs and Way of Life of the People of Siberia, XIXth Early-XXth Century]. Ed.: I.N. Gemuev et al. Novosibirsk: Nauka. Sib. otd-nie, 1987. 204 pp., illus.

4468 *Tri besedy ob ateisticheskom vospitanii* [Three Talks on Atheistic Education]. Perm': Kn. izd-vo, 1982. 79 pp. (Razgovory po dusham).

4469 "Tri vzgliada na odnu problemu" [Three Views of the Same Problem]. M. Kh. Titma; G.I. Naan; K. Paula. *Nauka i religiia* 12 (1989): 2-6.

4470 Trimingen, D.S. Sufiiskie ordeny v islame [The Sufi Orders in Islam].* Transl. from English. M.: Nauka, 1989. 328 pp. Bibl.: pp. 256-272. Annot. bibl.: pp. 209-253, Index: pp. 303-327. Transl. of the edition: *The Sufi orders in Islam* / J. Spencer Trimingham (Oxford, 1971).

4471 Trofimchuk, N.A. *Klerikal'naia radiopropaganda - orudie 'psikhologicheskoi voiny'* [Clerical Radio-Propaganda - Tool of "The Psychological War"]. M.: Znanie, 1988. 64 pp. (Novoe v zhizni, nauke, tekhnike. Nauch. ateizm; 7/1988). Bibl.: pp. 63-64.

4472 Trofimchuk, N.[A]. "Zalog uspekha" [Pledge of Success]. *Nauka i religiia* 8 (1984): 10-11.

4473 Trofimenko, A.P. *Vselennaia: tvorenie ili razvitie?* [The Universe: Creation or Evolution?]. Minsk: Belarus', 1987. 160 pp. Annot. bibl.: p. 160.

4474 Trofimov, Ia.F. *Khristianskie mify o 'kontse sveta'* [Christian Myths on "The End of the World"]. Alma-Ata: Kazakhstan, 1982. 70 pp., illus. (Uchenye beseduiut s veruiushchimi). Bibl.: p. 69.

4475 Trofimov, Ia.F. *Sovremennaia khristianskaia propoved': Sushchnost' i tendentsii* [Contemporary Christian Preaching: Essence and Tendencies]. Alma-Ata: Kazakhstan, 1986. 101 pp. Bibl.: p. 100.

4476 Trofimova, N.V. "Ideino-esteticheskie funktsii retrospektivnoi istoricheskoi analogii i bibleiskikh tsitat v 'Kazanskoi istorii'" [Ideological-Aesthetic Functions of Retrospective Historical Analogy and Biblical Quotations in "The History of Kazan"]. *Literatura Drevnei Rusi*. M., 1988. Pp. 68-82.

4477 Trofimova, Z.P. "Problema gumanizma na stranitsakh amerikanskogo zhurnala 'Religioznyi gumanizm'" [The Problem of Humanism in the Pages of the American Journal "Religious Humanism"]. *Vopr. filosofii* 10 (1987): 134-139.

4478 Trofimova, Z.P.; Dmitrieva, N.K. "Lektsii ob ateisticheskom vospitanii" [Lectures about Atheistic Education]. *Prepodavanie nauchnogo ateizma v vuze.* M., 1988. Pp. 96-111.

4479 Troianovskii, I.A. *Katolicheskaia tserkov' v SSSR* [Catholic Church in USSR]. M.: Novosti, 1984. 60 pp., illus. In English. Published also in French, German, Portuguese, Spanish, Vietnamese and in 1987 republished in Spanish.

4480 Troianovskii, I.A. *Sovetskoe gosudarstvo i tserkov': pravda i domysly* [Soviet State and Religion: Truth and Conjectures]. M.: Znanie, 1980. 12 pp.

4481 *Troitsa Rubleva: Antologiia* [Andrei Rublev's Trinity: Anthology]. 2nd revised and enlarged ed. Comp.: G.I. Vzdornoy. M.: Iskusstvo, 1989. 205 pp., illus. Bibl.: pp. 129-132.

4482 Tronina, G.I. *Emotsional'nost' v ateisticheskoi propagande* [Emotional in Atheistic Propaganda]. Izhvesk: Udmurtiia, 1989. 111 pp. Bibl.: pp. 109-110. Annot. bibl.: p. 108.

4483 Tronina, G.I. "Formirovanie kommunisticheskogo nravstvennogo ideala v protsesse ateisticheskogo vospitaniia molodezhi" [Forming of Communist Moral Ideal in the Process of Youth's Atheistic Upbringing]. *Nauchnyi ateizm: ideal i mirovozzrenie.* Perm': 1988. Pp. 121-129.

4484 Trubarov, A.A. "Nauchno-ateisticheskie aspekty izucheniia istorii Parizhskoi Kommuny" [Scientific-Atheistic Aspects of the Study of the History of the Paris Commune]. *Aktual'nye problemy nauchno- ateisticheskogo vospitaniia molodezhi.* M., 1987. Pp. 115-118.

4485 Trubitsin, V.A. "Rol' trudovogo kollektiva v ateisticheskom vospitanii mass" [The Role of Working Collective in Atheistic Education of Masses]. *Nauch. ateizm i ateist. vospitanie* 1 (1983): 153-157.

4486 Truevtsev, K.M. "Natsionalizm i religiia v soznanii intelligentsii arabskikh stran Afriki" [Nationalism and Religion in the Consciousness of Intelligentsia of Africa's Arab Countries]. *Puti evoliutsii i obshchestvennaia rol' sovremennoi afrikanskoi intelligentsii: poiski, tendentsii, perspektivy.* M., 1988. Pp. 211-217.

4487   Truska, L. "Tserkovnoe zemlevladenie v Litve v poslednei chetverti XVIII v." [Church Land-Ownership in Lithuania Late XVIIIth Century]. *Lieituvos istorijos metrastis.* Vilnius, 1988. Pp. 41-63. In Lithuanian. Summary in Russian.

4488   Tsaregorodtsev, G.I. "Shamany, znakhari, vrachi..." [Shamans, Witch- Doctors, Doctors...]. *Nauka i religiia* 8 (1988): 8-10.

4489   Tsaturian, S.A. *Transformatsiia otnosheniia russkogo pravoslaviia k Armiano-grigorianskoi tserkvi v XIX veke* [Transformation of Attitude of the Russian Orthodoxy Towards Armenian-Gregorian Church in the XIXth Century]. Erevan, Znanie ArmSSR, 1988. 23 pp.

4490   Tsekhanskaia, K.V. "Peiotizm - sovremennaia religiia severoamerikanskikh indeitsev" [Peiotism - Contemporary Religion of North American Indians]. *Religii mira.* M., 1989. Pp. 94-106.

4491   *Tsel' zhizni - zhizn'* [Life's Aim - is Life]. Comp.: [L.A. Velichanskaia]. M.: Sov. Rossiia, 1984. 527 pp. (Khudozh. i publitsist. b-ka ateista). Annot. bibl.: pp. 432-486. Name index: pp. 487-525.

4492   Tserbaev, T.A. "Nekotorye metodologicheskie problemy filosofsko-sotsiologicheskogo analiza religioznogo kul'ta" [Some Methodological Problems of Philosophic-Sociological Analysis of Religious Cult]. *Problemy istorii religii i ateizma.* Cheboksary, 1981. Pp. 92-103.

4493   *Tserkov' v sovremennom mire: Novye religii segodnia* [The Church in Contemporary World: New Religions Today]. Comp.: L. Miaesaln. Tallin: Esti raamat, 1983. 103 pp.

4494   Tsikhistavi, N. "'...Chtoby vse liudi spaslis' i prishli k urazumeniiu istiny...': Iz istorii khristianstva v Gruzii" ["...Let All People be Saved and Comprehend the Truth...": History of Religion in Georgia]. *Lit. Gruziia* 9 (1989): 206-213.

4495   Tsikvadze, R.I. *Ateisticheskie aspekty gruzinskikh traditsii* [Atheistic Aspects of Georgian Traditions]. Tbilisi: Sabchota Sakartvelo, 1985. 90 pp. In Georgian.

4496   Tsinoldr, F. "Uchityvaia opyt proshlogo" [Taking into Account Experience of the Past]. *Nauka i religiia* 8 (1983): 58-60.

4497   Tsinoldr, F. "Vazhnyi uchastok" [Important Sphere]. *Nauka i religiia* 12 (1980): 50-51.

4498   Tsitsiashvili, A.Ia.; Gabidzashvili, O.D. *Iudaizm i sionizm: Kritika ideologii i polit. praktiki* [Judaism and Zionism: Criticism of Ideology and Political Practice]. Tbilisi: Izd-vo Tbil. un-ta, 1982. 123 pp. In Georgian.

4499   Tskoerebebov, Z.L. "Sakral'nyi smysl tsifry '7' i ee sviaz' s astral'nymi i soliarnymi kul'tami v irano-skifo-alanskoi mifologicheskoi traditsii" [Sacral Meaning of the Number "7" and Its Connection with Astral and Solar Cults in Iranian-Scythian-Alan Mythological Traditions]. *Izvestiia. Akad. nauk GSSR. Iugo-Oset. NII.* Tbilisi, 1986. Vyp. 30. Pp. 59-70.

4500   Tsurkan, I.M. *Ateizm i molodezh'* [Atheism and Youth]. Kishinev: Kartia Moldoveniaske, 1980. 174 pp. In Moldavian. Bibl.: pp. 170-173.

4501   Tsurkan, I.M. *Sotsial'nyi progress i ateizm* [Social Progress and Atheism]. Kishinev: Shtiintsa, 1980. 186 pp. Summary in English. Annot. bibl.: pp. 178-183. For review see item 5322.

4502   Tsveig, S. *Sovest' protiv nasiliia* [Conscience Against Violence]. M.: Mysl', 1986. 238 pp., illus. republished in 1988.
       Published also in: Kiev: Politizdat Ukrainy, 1988. 390 pp. For review see item 5323.

4503   Tsvetkov, G.V. "K voprosu o spetsifike prepodavaniia kursa 'Osnovy nauchnogo ateizma' v khudozhestvennom vuze" [On the Problem of Specific Character of the Teaching the Course "Fundamentals of Scientific Atheism" in Art Institute of Higher Education]. *Aktual. vopr. metodiki prepodavaniia obshchestv. nauk i kom. vospitaniia studentov* 5 (1987): 62-68.

4504   Tsvetkov, G.V. *Ot bezreligioznosti k ateisticheskoi ubezhdennosti* [From Nonreligiosity to Atheistic Conviction]. L.: Znanie RSFSR, 1983. 16 pp. (V pomoshch' lektoru / O-vo "Znanie" RSFSR, Leningr. org.). Bibl.: pp. 15-16.

4505   Tsvetkov, V. "Propoved' soglasiia" [The Sermon of Consent]. *Nauka i religiia* 1 (1980): 22-23.

4506 Tsvik, I.Ia. *Religiia i dekadenstvo v Rossii* [Religion and Decadence in Russia]. Kishinev: Shtiintsa, 1985. 191 pp. Annot. bibl.: pp. 179-189. Summaries in English and French.

4507 Tsybenko, O.N.; Simonchik, A.N. *Pravda i vymysel o vvedenii khristianstva na Rusia* [Truth and Fabrication on Introduction of Christianity into Rus']. L'vov: Vishcha shk. Izd-vo pri L'v on. un-te, 1987. 71 pp. (Ateist. b-ka studenta).

4508 Tsybikzhapov, V.B. *Religiia i ateisty na sele* [Religion and Atheists in the Village]. Ulan-Ude: Buriat. kn. izd-vo, 1983. 53 pp. Annot. bibl.: pp. 47-52.

4509 Tul'pe, I.A.; Shershova, N.V. "Antiklerikalizm v russkoi zhivopisi vtoroi ploviny XIX veka" [Anticlericalism in Russian Painting in the Late XIXth Century]. *Russkoe pravoslavie i ateizm v otechestvennoi istorii.* L., 1988. Pp. 118-133.

4510 Tul'pe, I.A.; Smirnov, M.Iu. "Rol' lektorsko-propagandistskoi praktiki v podgotovke spetsialistov po nauchnomu ateizmu" [The Role of Lecturing-Propagandist Practice for Preparation of Specialists in Scientific Atheism]. *Aktual. vopr. metodiki prepodavaniia obshchetv. nauk i kom. vospitaniia studentov* 5 (1987): 128-132.

4511 Turdaliev, K. "Kontseptsiia 'islamskogo obshchestva' v ideologii shiizma (Irak)" [The Conception of "Islamic Society" in Shiist Ideology (Iraq)]. *Zarubezhnyi Vostok: osobennosti ideologii i politiki.* Tashkent, 1985. Pp. 84-99.

4512 Tur'ev, F.M. *Triasina: Rasskaz o cheloveke, porvavshem s religiei* [Quagmire: Story About a Man, who Broke off with Religion]. Syktyvkar: Komi kn. izd-vo, 1983. 40 pp.

4513 Turilov, A.A.; Chernetsov, A.V. "K izycheniiu 'otrechennykh' knig" [Study of "Repudiated" Books]. *Estetvennonauchnye predstavleniia Drevnei Rusi.* M., 1988. Pp. 111-140.

4514 Tursunov, A. *Chelovek i mirozdanie: vzgliad nauki i religii* [Man and the Universe: Scientific and Religious Views]. M.: Sov. Rossiia, 1986. 206 pp.

4515 Tursunov, A. "Islam i nauka" [Islam and Science]. *Nauka i religiia* 5 (1989): 6-8; 7 (1989): 24-25.

4516   Tutik, L.S. "GDR: dvizhenie za mir i uchastie v nem veruiushchikh (80-e
       gody)" [GDR: Peace Movement and Believers Participation in It (in the
       80s)]. *Voprosy germanskoi istorii.* Dnepropetrovsk, 1989. Pp. 204-112.

4517   Tutik, L.S. "Istochniki po istorii protestantizma i ikh osobennosti" [Sources
       on History of Protestantism and Their Peculiarities]. *Voprosy germanskoi
       istorii. Analiz istochnikov i ikh ispol'zovanie.* Dnepropetrovsk, 1984. Pp.
       58-67.

4518   Tutik, L.S. "Kontseptsii sotsial'nykh vzaimootnoshenii v osveshchenii
       protestantskoi literatury FRG" [Conceptions of Social Interrelations in
       Interpretation of FGR Protestant Literature]. *Voprosy germanskoi istorii.
       Revoliutsionnye i demokraticheskie dvizheniia novogo i noveishego vremeni.*
       Dnepropetrovsk, 1986. Pp. 79-86.

4519   Tutik, L.S. "Sovetskaia istoriografiia o protestantizme FRG" [Soviet
       Historiography on FRG Protestantism]. *Voprosy germanskoi istorii:
       Istoriogr. probl. germ. istorii v novoe i noveishee vremia.* Dnepropetrovsk,
       1980. Pp. 80-85. Bibl.: pp. 84-85.

4520   Tvardovskaia, V.A. "Religiozno-nravstvennaia utopiia F.M. Dostoevskogo"
       [F.M. Dostoevsky's Religious-Moral Utopia]. *Vopr. nauchnogo ateizma* 37
       (1988): 226-236.

4521   Tven, M. *Dnevnik Adama* [Adam's Diary]. M.: Politizdat, 1981. 295 pp.,
       illus. (B-ka ateist. lit.). Republished in 1982.
       Published also in:
       Vil'nius: Vaga, 1983. 413 pp. illus. In Lithuanian.
       Kiev: Politizdat Ukrainy, 1985. 312 pp. illus. In Ukrainian.
       Erevan: Aiastan, 1987. 374 pp., illus. In Armenian. For review see item
       5324.

4522   Tveritina, O. "Chuzhaia zhizn'?" [Someone Else's Life]. *Nauka i religiia* 9
       (1987): 16-18.

4523   *1000-letie kreshcheniia Rusi* [1000th Year of Baptism of Rus']. [Ed.: Iu.P.
       Zuev]. M.: AON, 1989. 120 pp. Bibl.: p. 119.

4524   "1000-letie kreshcheniia Rusi - vydaiushcheesia sobytie otechestvennoi i
       mirovoi istorii" [1000th Year of Baptism of Rus' - Outstanding Event of
       Native and World's History]. *Vopr. istorii* 5 (1988): 102-110.

4525 "Tysiacheletie kreshcheniia Rusi i problema dialoga Zapad-Vostok" [Millenium of Baptism of Rus' and the Problem of West-East Dialogue]. E.B. Rashkovskii; M.A. Batunskii; A.V. Zhuravskii et al. *Narody Azii i Afriki* 5 (1989): 79-92. Summary in English, p. 221.

4526 "U istokov frantsuzskogo ateima" [By the Sources of the French Atheism]. *Ateisticheskie chteniia*. M., 1988. Pp. 89-97.

4527 *Ubezhdaiushchee slovo* [Convincing Word]. [Comp.: A.I. Iaromenok]. Kiev: Politizdat Ukrainy, 1986. 72 pp. In Ukrainian.

4528 Ubushieva, S.I. *Ateisticheskaia propaganda v Kalmykii* [Atheistic Propaganda in Kalmyk]. Elista: Kalm. kn. izd-vo, 1986. 71 pp. Annot. bibl.: pp. 64-70. For review see item 5325.

4529 *Uchennye beseduiut s veruiushchimi. Seriia.* [Scientists Discuss with Believers. Serial]. Alma-Ata: Kazakhstan, 1977-1986. For review see item 5326.

4530 *Uchet osobennostei obydennogo soznaniia veruiushchikh v ateisticheskoi rabote* [Taking into Consideration in Atheistic Work the Ordinary Features of Believers Consciousness]. Comp.: V.G. Shadurskii. Kiev: Znanie, 1987. 33 pp. Bibl.: p. 32.

4531 Udal'tsova, Z.V. "Filostorogii - predstavitel' ereticheskoi tserkovnoi istorografii" [Philostroghy - Representative of Heretical Church Historiography]. *Vizant. vremennik*. 1983. T. 44. Pp. 3-17.

4532 Udam, Kh. "'Novoe tvorenie' v sufizme" ["New Creation" in Sufism]. *Uchen. zap. Tart. un-ta, Tr. po vostokovedeniiu* 6, Vyp. 558 (1981): 98-106. Summary in English.

4533 Ugrinovich, D.M. *Aktual'nye voprosy ateisticheskogo vospitaniia* [Actual Problems of Atheistic Education]. M.: Znanie RSFSR, 1981. 40 p. (V pomoshch' lektoru / O-vo "Znanie" RSFSR, Nauch.-metod. sovet po propagande nauch. ateizma). Bibl.: p. 38.

4534 Ugrinovich, D.M. "Kul'tura i religiia" [Culture and Religion]. *Vopr. nauch. ateizma* 30 (1982): 8-29.

4535 Ugrinovich, D.M. "Lektsiia kak vazhnaia forma prepodavaniia nauchnogo ateizma" [Lecture as Important Form for Teaching Scientific Atheism]. *Prepodavanie nauchnogo ateizma v vuze*. M., 1988. Pp. 44-51.

4536 Ugrinovich, D.[M]. "Metamorfozy protestantskogo modernizma" [Metamorphoses of Protestant Modernism]. *Nauka i religiia* 2 (1981): 55-57.

4537 Ugrinovich, D.M. *Psikhologiia religii* [The Psychology of Religion]. M.: Politizdat, 1986. 352 pp. Subject and name index: pp. 345-350. For reviews see items 5327-5329.

4538 Ugrinovich, D.[M]. "Religiia kak sotsial'noe iavlenie" [Religion as Social Occurrence]. *Nauka i religiia* 8 (1982): 17-21; 10 (1982): 16-18.

4539 Ugrinovich, D.M. *Rol' iskusstva v formirovanii ateisticheskogo mirovozzreniia* [The Role of Art in Shaping Atheistic World Outlook]. M.: Znanie, 1983. 63 pp. (Novoe v zhizni, nauke, tekhnike. Nauch. ateizm; 5). Bibl.: p. 60.

4540 Ugrinovich, D.M. "Sotsial'no-psikhologicheskie aspekty religioznogo utesheniia i nekotorye voprosy ukrepleniia ateisticheskogo soznaniia" [Socio-Psychological Aspects of Religious Consolation and Some Problems of Strengthening Atheistic Consciousness]. *Voprosy filosofii* 3 (1986): 61-71. Summary in English, p. 174.

4541 Ugrinovich, D.M. "Sovremennaia anglo-amerikanskaia sotsiologiia religii (osnovnye napravleniia i problemy)" [Anglo-American Contemporary Sociology of Religion (Basic Trends and Problems)]. *Vopr. nauch. ateizma* 27 (1981): 274-307.

4542 Ugrinovich, D.[M]. "U istokov iskusstva i religii" [By the Sources of Art and Religion]. *Nauka i religiia* 12 (1981): 37-42; 1 (1982): 32-37.

4543 Ugrinovich, D.[M]. "Vera bezreligioznaia i religioznaia" [Nonreligious and Religious Belief]. *Nauka i religiia* 2 (1985): 12-15.

4544 Ugrinovich, D.M. *Vvedenie v religiovedenie* [Introduction to Studies of Religion]. 2nd enlarged ed. M.: Mysl', 1985. 270 pp. The title of the 1st ed.: *Vvedenie v teoreticheskoe religiovedenie* [Introduction to Theoretical Studies of Religion]. Subject index: pp. 262-269. For reviews see items 5330-5331.

4545 Ukolova, V.I. *'Poslednii rimlianin' Boetskii* [Boethius "The Last Roman"]. M.: Nauka, 1987. 160 pp. For review see item 5332.

4546 Ukolova, V.I. "Tserkov' i eresi v Zapadnoi Evrope (V-XV vv.)" [The Church and Heresy in Western Europe (Vth-XVth Centuries)]. *Nauchnyi ateizm, religiia i sovremennost'.* Novosibirsk, 1987. Pp. 207-239.

4547 Ul'ianovskii, V.I. *Religiia i dukhovnoe nasledie proshlogo* [Religion and Spiritual Legacy of the Past]. Kiev: Znanie UkSSR, 1989. 48 pp. (Ser. 5, Nauchno-ateisticheskaia / "Znanie" UkSSR; No 7). In Ukrainian.

4548 Ul'ianovskii, V.[I]. "Sviatoi tsarevich Dmitrii i paradoksy istoriografii" [Saint Tsarevich Dimitry and Paradoxes of Historiography]. *Nauka i religiia* 6 (1981): 42-43.

4549 Ul'masov, R.U. "Obshchstvennoe mnenie kak faktor protivodeistviia vrazhdebnoi islamskoi propagande iz-za rubezha" [Public Opinion as Counteraction to the Inimical Islamic Propaganda from Abroad]. *Nauchnyi ateizm i obshchestvennoe mnenie.* M., 1987. Pp. 92-112.

4550 Umardzhnov, O. *Kompleksnyi podkhod k ateistichekomu vospitaniiu* [Complex Approach to Atheistic Education]. Tashkent: Uzbekistan, 1980. 23 pp. (Besedy o nauke; No 23). In Uzbek.

4551 Umarov, I. *Filosofskie i eticheskie vzgliady Ainulkuzata* [Ainulkuzats' Philosophical and Ethical Views]. Dushanbe: Irfon, 1984. 62 pp.

4552 Umarov, M. *Iavliaetsia li Koran sviashchennoi knigoi?* [Is the Koran a Holy Book?]. Tashkent: Uzbekistan, 1984. 101 pp. (B-ka ateista). In Uzbek.

4553 Umarov, S.Ts. *Evoliutsiia osnovnykh techenii islama v Checheno-Ingushetii* [Evolution of Islam's Basic Trends in Checheno-Ingush]. Groznyi: Chech.-Ing. kn. izd-vo, 1985. 32 pp.

4554 Umarov, S.Ts.; Shamilova, M.Sh. *Miuridizm pered sudom vremeni* [Miuridism Before the Trial of Time]. Groznyi: Chech.-Ing. kn. izd-vo, 1984. 48 pp.

4555 Umnov, L.S. *Byt i religiia* [Existence and Religion]. Alma-Ata: Znanie KazSSR, 1980. 20 pp. Bibl.: pp. 19-20.

4556 Umralina, G.R. "Sotsialisticheskii obraz zhizni i voprosy ateisticheskogo vospitaniia v mnogonatsional'nom regione" [Socialist Way of Life and Problems of Atheistic Education in Multinational Region]. *Sotsial'no-eticheskie problemy povysheniia effektivnosti ateisticheskogo vospitaniia v mnogonatsional'nom regione.* Frunze, 1987. Pp. 56-62.

4557 Uniatstvo: nasil'stvennoe vnedrenie, zakonomernost' krakha [Uniate Church: Forcible Inculcation, Destined to Failure]. [P.L. Irotskii; S.M. Biskup; A.V. Vozniak et al]. Kiev: Politizdat Ukrainy, 1983. 199 pp. In English.

4558 Uniatstvo i klerikal'nyi antikommunizm [Uniate Church and Clerical Anti-Communism]. [Ed.: A.S. Onishchenko]. Kiev: Politizdat Ukrainy, 1982. 301 pp. In Ukrainian. Annot. bibl. pp. 290-299.

4559 Uniatstvo i ukrainskii burzhuaznyi natsionalizm [Uniate Church and Ukrainian Bourgeois Nationalism]. [Ed.: S.M. Vozniak]. Kiev: Nauk. dumka, 1986. 252 pp. In Ukrainian.

4560 Ural'skie sotsiologicheskie chteniia, 4-e. Perm' 1982. 'XXVI s'ezd KPSS i aktual'nye problemy sotsial'noi politiki partii': Sektsiia: 'Probl. formirovaniia nauch.-materialist. ateist. mirovozzreniia sov. liudei' [The 4th Urals Sociological Readings, Perm'. 1982. "XXVIth Congress of the CPSU and Actual Problems of Party's Social Policy": Section: "Problems of Shaping Scientific-Materialist, Atheistic World Outlook of Soviet People"]. Perm': [S.n.], 1982. 51 pp.

4561 Usenova, M.M. Sem'ia i religiia [Family and Religion]. Alma-Ata: Mektep, 1986. 254 p.

4562 Ushakov, V.A. "Islamskii faktor' vo vneishei politike Irana" [The "Islamic Factor" in Iran's Foreign Policy]. "Islamskii faktor" v mezhdunarodnykh otnosheniiakh v Azii (70-e-pervaia polovina 80-kh gg.). M., 1987. Pp. 124-140.

4563 "Usilivaetsia kontrol' za sobliudeniem prav veruiushchikh" [Control on Observance of Believers Rights is Strengthening]. Religiia v SSSR 7 (1987): LK 1-LK 2.

4564 Usmanov, M.A. Dogmaty i obriady islama [Islam's Dogmas and Rituals]. Alma-Ata: Kazakhstan, 1980. 142 pp. In Uighur.

4565 Usmanov, M.[A]. "Kak sozdavalsia Koran" [How the Koran was Created]. Nauka i religiia 9 (1980): 32-37.

4566 Usmanov, M.A. "Musul'manskoe dukhovenstvo v khanstvakh Dzhuchieva Ulusa XIV-XVI vv." [Moslem Clergy in Djuchiev Ulus Khanates of XIVth-XVIth Centuries]. Bartol'dskie chteniia, 1982: God shestoi. M., 1982. Pp. 68-69.

4567 Usmanov, M.A. "Nekotorye metodologicheskie voprosy izucheniia modernizatsii sovremennogo islama" [Some Methodological Problems of Study of
the Modernization of Contemporary Islam]. *Vopr. nauch. ateizma* 26
(1980): 254-267.

4568 Usmanov, M.A. *Prichiny zhivuchesti islamskoi religii v regionakh traditsionnogo ee rasprostraneniia v SSSR* [Reasons for Islam's Tenaciousness in
Regions of Its Traditional Dissemination in USSR]. M.: Znanie, 1980. 11
pp. (V pomoshch' lektoru).

4569 Usmanov, M.A. *Reaktsionnaia sushchnost' islama i ateisticheskoe vospitanie*
[Reactionary Essence of Islam and Atheistic Education]. Tashkent:
Uzbekistan, 1986. 20 pp. (B-chka ateista). Published also in Uzbek.

4570 Usmanov, M.[A]. "Soderzhanie Korana" [The Content of the Koran]. *Nauka
i religiia* 10 (1980): 27-31.

4571 Usmanov, N. "Poleznye tochki sotrudnichestva" [Useful points for Collabo-
ration]. *Kommunist Uzbekistana* 6 (1989): 47-48.

4572 Uspenskii, V.L. "Buddiiskii kanon v Mongolii" [Buddhist Canon in Mongo-
lia]. *III Vsesoiuznaia konferentsiia vostokovedov "Vzaimodeistvie i vzaimovliianie tsivilizatsii kul'tur na Vostoke"*. M., 1988. T. 1. Pp. 135-136.

4573 Ustavshchikov, S. "Pravoslavnaia tserkov' na Eniseiskikh zemliakh" [Orthodox
Church on Enisei Lands]. *Enisei* 3 (1988): 65-70.

4574 Ustinenko, V.P. *Vospitanie ateisticheskoi ubezhdennosti* [Upbringing Atheistic
Conviction]. Kiev: Vishcha shk., 1986. 80 pp. (Ateist. b-chka studenta).

4575 Ustinov, A.P. "Ateizm v sisteme esteticheskogo vospitaniia" [Atheism in the
System of Aesthetic Education]. *Aktual'nye problemy obespecheniia
effektivnosti nauchno-ateisticheskoi raboty*. Cheboksary, 1986. Pp. 48-54.

4576 Ustinov, A.P. "Mesto sovetskoi intelligentsii v sisteme ateisticheskogo
vospitaniia trudiashchikhsia" [The Place of Soviet Intelligentsia in the
System of Atheistic Education of Workers]. *Kritika religioznoi ideologii i
problemy ateisticheskogo vospitaniia*. M., 1980. Pp. 17-26.

4577 Ustinov, A.P. "Rasshirenie i uprochenie sotsial'nykh sviazei lichnosti -
vazhneishee uslovie effektivnosti ateisticheskogo vospitaniia" [Broadening
and Strengthening of Individual's Social Relations - Most Important

Condition for Effectiveness of Atheistic Education]. *Aktual'nye problemy ateisticheskogo vospitaniia i kritika religioznoi ideologii.* M., 1981. Pp. 10-17.

4578　Utanov, S. "Bol'she nauchnosti - osnova nashei raboty" [More Scientifically - Foundation of Our Work]. *Kommunist Uzbekistana* 9 (1989): 68-71.

4579　Utkin, A.I. *Antinarodnaia sushchnost' uniatstva* [Anti-Popular Essence of the Uniate Church]. Kiev: Vishcha shk. Izd-vo pri Kiev. un-te, 1983. 79 pp. (Ateist. b-ka studenta). In Ukrainian. Annot. bibl.: pp. 75-78.

4580　Utkin, A.I. *Antisovetizm pod flagom 'zashchity religii'* [Anti-Sovietism under the Banner of "Defence of Religion"]. Kiev: Znanie UkSSR, 1987. 48 pp. (Ser. 5, Nauch.-ateist. / O-vo "Znanie" UkSSR; No 8). Bibl.: pp. 47-48.

4581　Utkin, A.I. *Uniia: put' predatel'stva i pozora* [Uniate Church: The Way of Treachery and Disgrace]. Uzhgorod: Karpaty, 1987. 176 pp. In Ukrainian.

4582　Utkina, L.M. "Izobrazhenie i master. K ikonografii obraza Artemidy v tvorchestve mastera Pana" [Image and the Master. Iconography of the Image of Artemis in the Work of Master Pan]. *Zhizn' mifa v antichnosti.* M., 1988. Ch. 1. Pp. 140-146.

4583　Uvarov, P.Iu. "Bor'ba tendentsii v noveishei istoriografii Katolicheskoi ligi kontsa XVI v." [Struggle of Tendencies in the Newest Historiography of Catholic League at the End of XVIth Century]. *Srednie veka* 51 (1988): 181-200.

4584　*Uzhgorodskii muzei ateizma* Putevoditel [Uzhgorod Museum of Atheism. Guide]. [Comp.: O.V. Olag et al]. Uzhgorod: Karpati, 1985. 62 pp., illus. Parallel text: Ukrainian-Russian. Summaries in: English, Hungarian, Slovak.

4585　"V predverii 1000-letiia" [On the Threshold of 1000th Anniversary]. *Novoe vremia* 15 (1988): 42-43.

4586　Vagabov, M.M. "Modernizm v zarubezhnom islame" [Modernism in Islam from Abroad]. *Nauch.-prakticheskaia konf. molodykh uchenykh Dagestana "Molodezh' obshchestvennyi progress".* Makhachkala, 1981. P. 27.

4587 Vagabov, M.V. *Islam i problemy formirovaniia ateisticheskogo mirovozzreniia molodezhi* [Islam and the Problems of Shaping Atheistic Outlook of Youth]. Makhachkala: Daguchpedgiz, 1988. 120 pp.

4588 Vagabov, M.V. *Islam i sem'ia* [Islam and Family]. M.: Nauka, 1980. 174 pp. Annot. bibl.: pp. 169-173. For reviews see items 5333-5334.

4589 Vagabov, M.V. *Islam i voprosy ateisticheskogo vospitaniia* [Islam and Problems of Atheistic Education]. M.: Vysh. shk., 1984. 167 pp. Bibl.: pp. 155-159. Annot. bibl.: pp. 160-166.

4590 Vagabov, M.V. *Perezhitki islama i nekotorye osobennosti i formy ikh proiavleniia v sotsialisticheskom obshchestve* [Islam's Survivals and Some Features and Forms of Their Manifestation in Socialist Society]. Tashkent: [S.n.], 1983. 34 pp. (V pomoshch' lektoru / O-vo "Znanie" UzSSR. Ser. "Obshchestveno-politicheskaia").

4591 Vagabov, M.V. *Perezhitki islama v semeinykh otnosheniiakh i prichiny ikh sokhraneniia* [Islam's Survivals in Family Relations and Reasons for Their Preservation]. M.: Znanie, Tsentr. Dom nauch. ateizma, 1989. 18 pp. (V pomoshch' lektoru-propagandistu).

4592 Vagabov, M.[V]. "Za granitsami semeinykh traditsii" [Behind the Limits of Family Tradition]. *Nauka i religiia* 3 (1984): 11-13.

4593 Vagabov, M.V.; Vagabov, N.M. *Islam i voprosy ateisticheskogo vospitaniia* [Islam and Problems of Atheistic Education]. M.: Vyssh. shk., 1988. 272 pp. For reviews see items 5335-5337.

4594 Vagabov, N.M. *Musul'manskii konfessionalizm v proshlom i nastoiashchem* [Moslem Confessionalism in the Past and Present]. Makhachkala: Dag. kn. izd-vo, 1985. 96 pp.

4595 Vagarshian, V.L. "Islam i natsionalizm v zapadnykh kontseptsiiakh razvitiia arabskikh stran (1950-1960-e gg.)" [Islam and Nationalism in Western Conceptions of Development of Arab Countries (1950s-1960s)]. *Problemy sovremennoi sovetskoi arabistiki*. Erevan, 1988. Vyp. 1. Pp. 87-92.

4596 Vagner, G. "U kolybeli drevnerusskogo iskusstva" [By the Cradle of Ancient Russian Art]. *Iskusstvo* 6 (1988): 59-64.

4597   Vaishvila A. "Shiluva: legendy i deistvitel'nost'" [Shilute: Legends and Reality]. *Nauka i religiia* 6 (1981): 29-31.

4598   Vaishvila, A. *Shiluvskii mif* [Shilutean Myth]. 2nd revised and enlarged ed. Vil'nius: Mintis, 1985. 83 pp., illus. (Besedy s veruiushchimi). In Lithuanian.

4599   Vakhabov, A. *Musul'mane v SSSR* [Moslems in the USSR]. M.: Novosti, 1980. 88 pp., illus. In English. Published also in Pharsee.

4600   Vakhidov, U.F. "Formirovanie i ispol'zovanie obshchestvennogo mneniia v preodolenii religioznoi obriadnosti" [Forming and Using of Public Opinion in Overcoming Religious Rituals]. *Zakonomernosti sotsial'no-ekonomicheskogo razvitiia obhchestva na sovremennom etape.* Tashkent, 1987. Pp. 142-151.

4601   Vakhtangadze, M.K. "Doislamskaia plemennaia organizatsiia i musul'-manskaia umma" [Pre-Islamic Tribal Organization and Moslem Umma]. *V Vsesoiuznaia shkola molodykh vostokovedov.* M., 1989. T. 1. Pp. 14-16.

4602   Vakradze, A.T. "Polozhitel'noe i otritsatel'noe teologicheskoe myshlenie v filosofii Vl. Solov'eva" [Positive and Negative in Theological Thought of Vl. Solovev's Philosophy]. *Areopagiticheskie razyskaniia.* Tbilisi, 1986. Pp. 87-110. In Georgian. Summaries in Russian and English.

4603   Valeev, F.T.; Valeev, B.F. "O reliktakh doislamskikh verovanii v religioznom mirovozzrenii zapadnosibirskikh tatar" [Relics of Pre-Islam Beliefs in Religious Outlook of West-Siberian Tatars]. *Mirovozzrenie narodov Zapadnoi Sibirii po arkheologicheskim i etnograficheskim dannym.* Tomsk, 1985. Pp. 38-40.

4604   Valeev, R.M. "G.S. Sablukov i otechestvennoe islamovedenie v 60-80-kh godakh XIX v." [G.S. Sablukov and Native Islam Study in the 60s-80s of XIXth Century]. *Istoriografiia Irana novogo i noveishego vremeni.* M., 1989. Pp. 13-24.

4605   Valeska fon Rok. "'...Vyshe nogu, i bud' slaven gospod'!'" ["... Foot Higher, and Glory to God!"]. *Argumenty .* M., 1988. Pp. 195-206.

4606   Valieva, D.V. *Mnimye druz'ia islama* [Imaginary Friends of Islam]. Tashkent: Fan, 1986. 86 pp. In Uzbek.

4607 Val'kova, L.V. "Mesto Saudovskoi Aravii v musul'manskom mire" [Saudi Arabia's Place in the Moslem World]. *"Islamskii faktor" v mezhdunarodnykh otnosheniiakh v Azii (70-e-pervaia polovina 80-kh gg.).* M., 1987. Pp. 102-113.

4608 Val'kova, L.V. "Rol' islama vo vneshnei politike Saudovskoi Aravii v 60-70-e gody" [The Role of Islam in Saudi Arabia's Foreign Policy in the 60s-80s]. *Islam v istorii narodov Vostoka.* M., 1981. Pp. 86-99. Annot. bibl.: p. 99.

4609 Val'kova, L.V. *Saudovskaia Araviia: neft', islam, politika* [Saudi Arabia: Oil, Islam, Politics]. M.: Nauka, 1987. 255 pp. Bibl.: pp. 244-248. Name index: pp. 249-251.

4610 Vaniushin, N.A. *Svoboda sovesti i religioznyi ekstremizm* [Freedom of Conscience and Religious Extremism]. Barnaul: Alt. kn. izd-vo, 1988. 143 pp. For review see item 5338.

4611 Varichev, E.S. *Pravoslavnaia tserkov': Istoriia i sotsial. sushchnost'* [Orthodox Church: History and Social Essence]. M.: Sov. Rossiia, 1982. 191 pp.

4612 Varichev, E.S. "Sotsialisticheskii obraz zhizni i voprosy ateisticheskogo vospitaniia" [Socialist Way of Life and Problems of Atheistic Education]. *Sb. nauch. tr. / NII kul'tury* 115 (1982): 30-44.

4613 Varlamov, I. "Deviatyi vizit papy" [Pope's Ninth Visit]. *Novoe vremia* 22 (1988): 11.

4614 Varshalomidze, D.R. et al. *Ateizm. Religiia. Sovremennost'* [Atheism. Religion. Contemporaneity]. Batumi: Sabchota Adzhara, 1986. 47 pp. In Georgian.

4615 Varshavskii, S.; Zmoiro, I. "Voino-Iasenetskii: dve grani odnoi sud'by" [Voino-Iasenetskii: Two Brinks of One Destiny]. *Zvezda Vostoka* 4 (1989): 102-111.

4616 Vasiakin, S.A. "Vliianie printsipov dzen-buddizma na sovremennye techeniia zapadno-evropeiskoi zhivopisi" [The Influence of Zen Buddhist Principles on Western European Contemporary Trends in Painting]. *Estetika: Teoriia, istoriia, praktika.* M., 1092. Pp. 138-139.

4617   Vasilenko, R.P. "Etruski i khristianskaia religiia" [Etruscans and Christian Religion]. *Antich. mir i arkheologiia* 5 (1983): 15-26.

4618   Vasilenko, V.A. "Pedagogicheskie idei v drevneindiiskikh 'Zakonakh Manu'" [Pedagogical Ideas in Ancient Indian "Laws of Manu"]. *Ocherki istorii shkoly i pedagogicheskoi mysli drevnego i srednevekovogo Vostoka.* M., 1988. Pp. 66-81. Bibl.: pp 80-81.

4619   Vasil'ev, A. "Islam v sovremennom mire" [Islam in Contemporary World]. *Mezhdunar. zhizn'* 10 (1981): 56-64.

4620   Vasil'ev, A. "L'intégrisme islamique et l'Egypte"* *L'Afrique du Nord: developpement contemporain* * M., 1988. Pp. 10-24.

4621   Vasil'ev, A.V. *Po sledam 'sviatykh' prestuplenii: Ateist. ocherki* [Along the Footsteps of "Sacred" Crimes: Atheistic Essays]. M.: Mol. gvardiia, 1988. 159 pp., illus. For review see item 5337.

4622   Vasil'ev, A.V.; Komarov, P.M. "Smena vlasti v Dzhordanville" [Change of Power in Jordanville]. *Argumenty, 1987.* M., 1987. Pp. 29-41.

4623   Vasil'ev, B.V. *O mode, kreste i ubezhdeniiakh* [On Fashion, Cross and Convictions]. L.: Znanie RSFSR, 1982. 17 pp. (V pomoshch' lektoru / O-vo "Znanie" RSFSR, Leningr. org.).

4624   Vasil'ev, Iu.M.; D'iakova, O.V. "Pogrebal'nyi obriad pokrovskoi kul'tury v svete letopisnykh i etnograficheskikh dannykh" [Burial Ritual of Shroud Culture in the Light of Chronicles and Ethnographical Data]. *Voprosy arkheologii Dal'nego Vostoka SSSR.* Vladivostok, 1987. Pp. 67-79. Bibl.: pp. 78-79.

4625   Vasil'ev, L. "Islam: napravleniia, techeniia, sekty" [Islam: Direction, Trend, Sects]. *Aziia i Afrika segodnia* 1 (1980): 58-61; 2 (1980): 54-57.

4626   Vasil'ev, L.S. "Etika i ritual v traktate 'Li tszi'" [Ethics and Ritual in "Li Tzy" Treatise]. *Etika i ritual v traditsionnom Kitae.* M., 1988. Pp. 173-201. Bibl.: p. 201.

4627 Vasil'ev, L.S. *Istoriia religii Vostoka* [History of Religions of the Orient]. M.: Vyssh. shk., 1983. 368 pp. 2nd revised and enlarged ed. was published in 1988, 416 pp. For reviews see items 5339-5340.

4628 Vasil'ev, L.S. "Konfutsii" [Confucius]. *Vopr. istorii* 3 (1989): 89-105.

4629 Vasil'ev, M.A. "Bogi Khors i Semargl vostochnoslavianskogo iazychestva" [The Gods Hors and Semargl of East Slavonic Paganism]. *Religii mira.* M., 1989. Pp. 133-156.

4630 Vasil'ev, V.A. *Nauka i religioznyi modernizm* [Science and Religious Modernism]. Minsk: Belarus', 1981. 63 pp. Annot bibl.: pp. 61-62.

4631 Vasil'eva, A.[V]. "Ateizm: dukhovnost' i vysota nravstvennykh idealov" [Atheism: Spirituality and the Height of Moral Ideals]. *Bibliotekar'* 6 (1988): 31-35.

4632 Vasil'eva, A.V. "Mesto religii v obshchestvennom soznanii osvobodivshchikhsia stran" [The Place of Religion in Social Consciousness of Liberated Countries]. *Sotsial'no-ekoonomicheskie problemy osvobodivshchikhsia stran.* M., 1987. Pp. 231-232.

4633 Vasilevskaia, N.S. "Sotsial'no-ekonomicheskaia politika razvitogo sotsialisticheskogo obshchestva kak faktor upravleniia protsessom formirovaniia massovogo ateisticheskogo soznaniia" [Socio-Economical Policy of the Developed Socialist Society as a Directional Factor of the Process of Forming Mass Atheistic Consciousness]. *Razvitoi sotsializm. Problemy teorii i upravleniia.* Iaroslavl', 1985. Pp. 79-86.

4634 Vasilevskaia, N.S.; Stretenskii, L.V. "Rol' i mesto issledovatel'skoi raboty studentov v vuzovskoi sisteme ateisticheskogo vospitaniia" [The Role and Place of Students' Researh Work in the Institutions of Higher Education System of Atheistic Education]. *Prepodavanie nauchnogo ateizma v vuze.* M., 1988.Pp. 190-202.

4635 Vasilevskaia, V.G. "'Kreshchenie Rusi' po vizantiiskim i arabskim istochnikam" ["Baptism of Rus'" by Byzantine and Arab Sources]. *"Kreshchenie Rusi" v trudakh russkikh i sovetskikh istorikov.* M., 1988. Pp. 72-106.

4636 Vasilevskis, E.[B]. "Vol'nodumnoe mirovozzrenie Aleksandrasa Grishkiavichiusa" [Alexandras Grishkiavichius Free Thinking Outlook]. *Ateistines minties raida lietuvoje.* Kaunas, 1988. Pp. 34-40. In Lithuanian. Summary in Russian.

4637   Vasilevskis, E.B. "Materializm i ateizm K. Lyshchinskogo i zapadno-evropeiskaia filosofskaia mysl' XVI-XVII vv. Sravnitel'nyi analiz" [K. Lyshchinsky's Materialism and Atheism and West-European Philosophical Thought of XVIth-XVIIth Centuries. A Comparative Analysis]. *Filoso-fskaia i obshchestvenno-politicheskaia mysl' Belorussii i Litvy.* Minsk, 1987. Pp. 225-240.

4638   Vasneva, T.[M]. "Formirovanie ateisticheskogo mneniia molodezhi v mnogonatsional'nom trudovom kollektive" [Forming Youth's Atheistic Opinion in Multi National Working Collective]. *Kommunist Tadzhikistna* 12 (1986): 75-80.

4639   Vasneva, T.M. "Psikhologicheskie faktory religioznosti i ateisticheskoe vospitanie molodezhi" [Religiosity's Psychological Factors and Youth's Atheistic Upbringing]. *Kompleksnyi podkhod v ateisticheskom vospitanii.* Dushanbe, 1988. Pp. 98-111. Bibl.: pp. 110-111.

4640   Vasneva, T.M. "Religioznye otnosheniia i normativno-reguliruiushchaia funktsiia religii" [Religious Relations and Religion's Normative-Adjustment Function]. *Izv. AN TadzhSSR. Ser. Filosofiia, ekonomika, pravovedenie* 1 (1986): 26-32. Summry in Tajik.

4641   Vazgen I Verkhovnyi patriarkh i katolikos vsekh armian. *Blago mira - v liudskom edinenii* [The Good of the World - in Peoples Unity]. M.: Novosti, 1988. 22 pp., illus. Published also in Spanish.

4642   Vdovichenko, P.I. *Sovremennaia ideologicheskaia bor'ba i religiia* [Contem-porary Ideological Struggle and Religion]. Minsk: Znanie BSSR, 1984. 21 pp. (Material v pomoshch' lektoru / Pravl. o-va "Znanie" BSSR, Nauch.-metod. sektsiia ateist. vospitaniia). Bibl.: pp. 20-21.

4643   Vdovina, L.N. *Krest'ianskaia obshchina i monastyr' v Tsentral'noi Rossii v pervoi polovine XVIII v.* [Peasant Community and Monastery in Central Russia Early XVIIIth Century]. M.: Izd-vo Mosk. un-ta, 1988. 213 pp., tables.

4644   "Vecher voprosov i otvetov" [An Evening of Questions and Answers]. *Nauka i religiia* 1 (1983): 28-30.

4645 Veinberg, I.P. "Voina i mir v vospriiatii avtorov bibleiskikh knig perioda vozniknoveniia blizhnevostochnykh derzhav (seredina I tysiacheletiia do n.e.)" [War and Peace in the Perception of Authors of Biblical Books in the Period of the Rise of Near Eastern Powers (Middle of the I Millennium B.C.)]. *Meroe* 4 (1989): 49-63.

4646 Veish, Ia.Ia. *Analiticheskaia filosofiia i religioznaia apologetika* [Analytical Philosophy and Religious Apologetics]. Riga: Zinatne, 1989. 203 p. For review see item 5341.

4647 Veish, Ia.Ia. *Sovremennyi khristianskii sotsializm* [Contemporary Christian Socialism]. Riga: Znanie LatvSSR, 1982. 23 pp. (Material v pomoshch' lektoru / O-vo "Znanie" LatvSSR, Nauch.-metod. sovet po propagande nauch. ateizma) (Znanie narodu / ...). In Latvian. Annot. bibl.: p. 23.

4648 Velichko, O.I. *Politicheskii katolitsizm i rabochee dvizhenie v Avstrii, 1918-1984* [Political Catholicism and Workers Movement in Austria, 1918-1984]. M.: Nauka, 1985. 222 pp. Bibl.: pp. 210-217. Name index: pp. 218-221. For review see item 5342.

4649 "Velikaia frantsuzskaia revoliutsiia i tserkov': Iz dekretov revoliutsionnogo pravitel'stva" [The Great French Revolution and Religion: Decrees of Revolutionary Government]. *Ateisticheskie chteniia.* M., 1989. Vyp. 18. Pp. 2-5.

4650 Velikaia, N.N.; Vinogradov, V.B. "Doislamskii religioznyi sinkretizm u vainakhov" [Pre-Islamic Syncretism by Vainahs]. *Sov. etnografiia* 3 (1989): 39-48. Summary in English, p. 174.

4651 *Velikii uchitel' - zhizn'* [Life - is a Great Teacher]. [Comp.: D. Repshene]. Vil'nius: Mintis, 1985. 204 pp. (Besedy s veruiushchimi). In Lithuanian.

4652 Velikovich, L.N. *Chernaia gvardiia Vatikana* [The Black Guard of Vatican]. M.: Mysl', 1980. 231 pp., illus. Annot. bibl.: pp. 221-230. 2nd enlarged ed. was published in 1985, 371 pp., illus., annot. bibl.: pp. 258-269.

4653 Velikovich, L.N. *Katolitsizm v sovremennom mire* [Catholicism in Contemporary World]. M.: Znanie, 1981. 64 pp. (Novoe v zhizni, nauke, tekhnike. Ser. "Nauch. ateizm"; No 11). Bibl.: p. 63.

4654	Velikovich, L.N. *Kritika klerikal'nykh kontseptsii voiny i mira* [Criticism of Clerical Conception of War and Peace]. M.: Znanie, 1986. 64 pp. (Novoe v zhizni, nauke, tekhnike. Nauch. ateizm; 2). Bibl.: p. 63.

4655	Velikovich, L.N. "Metamorfozy 'Obshchestva Iisusa'" [Metamorphoses of "Jesus Society"]. *Novoe vremia* 46 (1980): 28-30.

4656	Velikovich, L.N. *Religiia v sovremennoi ideologicheskoi bor'be* [Religion in Contemporary Ideological Struggle]. M.: Mosk. rabochii, 1981. 128 pp. (B-chka propagandista i politinformatora).

4657	Velikovich, L.N. *Soremennyi kapitalizm i religiia* [Contemporary Capitalism and Religion]. M.: Politizdat, 1984. 238 pp., illus. For review see item 5343.	Published also in:
Erevan: Aiastan, 1987. 294 pp., illus. In Armenian.

4658	Venda, V.F. *Obyknovennaia psikhologiia 'neobyknovennykh chudes'* [Ordinary Psychology of "Unusual Miracles"]. M.: Znanie, 1988. 64 pp. (Novoe v zhizni, nauke, tekhnike. Ser.: Nauch. ateism; 1988, 11).

4659	Ventura, A. "Protestantizm i kapitalizm" [Protestantism and Capitalism]. *Stanovlenie kapitalizma v Europe*. M., 1987. Pp. 198-210.

4660	Verbitskaia, V.V. "Realizatsiia khristianskikh poniatii v tvorchestve Kirilla Turovskogo. Priamye i perenosnye znacheniia" [Realization of Christian Concepts in Cyril Turov's Creative Work. Direct and Figurative Meanings]. *Materialy XXVII Vsesoiuznoi nauchnoi studencheskoi konferentsii "Student i nauchno-tekhnicheskii progress"*. Novosibirsk, 1989. Filologiia. Pp. 34-39.

4661	*Veril...*[I Believed...]. [Comp.: P. Pechiura]. Vil'nius: Mintis, 1981. 135 pp. (Malaia ateist. ser.). In Lithuanian. Published also in:
Riga: Avots, 1986. 154 pp. In Latvian.

4662	"Verit'... no vo chto?" [To Believe... But in What?]. *Molodoi kommunist* 8 (1989): 32-44.

4663	Verkhovskii, L. "Iisus perezhil Golgofu?" [Jesus Experienced Golgotha?]. *Nauka i religiia* 6 (1989): 13-14.

4664	Verna, V.V. "Etichese antinomii religioznogo ucheniia Avgustina: K voprosu interpretatsii probl. gumanizma v sisteme relig. mirovozzreniia"

[Ethical Antinomies of Augustine's Religious Teaching: Interpretation Problem of Humanism in the System of Religious World Outlook]. *Vestn. Mosk. un-ta.* Ser. 7. Filosofiia 4 (1983): 60-68.

4665 Vernan, Zh.-P. *Proiskhozhdenie drevnegrecheskoi mysli* [The Origin of Ancient Greek Thought]. Transl. from French. M.: Progress, 1988. 223 pp. Name index: pp. 220-222.

4666 Vershinskaia, A.A.; Man'kov, A.G. "Tserkov' i gosudarstvo v Rossii pervoi poloviny XVII v." [The Church and State in Russia Early XVIIth Century]. *Vopr. nauh. ateizma* 25 (1980): 118-129.

4667 *Veruiushchii v usloviiakh perestroiki* [Believer under Perestroika]. M.: AON, 1989. 138 pp.

4668 Veselov, V.I.; Vladimir, A.L. *Za shirmoi sviatosti* [Behind the Screen of Holiness]. Donetsk: Donbass, 1981. 103 pp.

4669 Veshchikov, A. "Ne v ladakh s faktami: O nekotorykh zarubezh. fal'sifikatsiiakh polozheniia pravoslav. tserkvi do revoliutsii" [At Odds with Facts: Some Foreign Falsification on the Situation of Orthodox Church before the Revolution]. *Nauka i religiia* 6 (1980): 36-38.

4670 Vezhichanina, O.S. *Muzei istorii religii i ateizma* [Museum of History of Religion and Atheism]. Dnepropetrovsk: Promin', 1988. 24 pp., illus.

4671 Vezhichanina, O.S. et al. *Dnepropetrovskii muzei istorii religii i ateizma: Krat. putevoditel'* [Dnepropetrovsk Museum of History of Religion and Atheism: A Short Guide]. Dnepropetrovsk: Promin', 1980. 29 pp., illus.

4672 Viakhtre, L. "O sootnoshenii estonskogo narodnogo kalendaria i srednevekovykh tserkovnykh kalendarei" [Correlation of Estonian Popular Calendar and Medieval Church Calendars]. *Etnograafiamuuseumi aastaraamat* 37 (1989): 167-178. In Estonian. Summaries in German and Russian.

4673 Viatkin, Ia. "Taro: kliuch ot zakrytogo khrama" [Taro: The Key of the Closed Temple]. *Nauka i religiia* 1 (1989): 48-51.

4674 Vidmantas, E. *Katolicheskaia tserkov' i natsional'nyi vopros vo vtoroi polovine XIX v.-nachale XX v. v Litve* [Catholic Church and National Problem in Lithuania, Late XIXth-Early XXth Centuries]. Vil'nius: Mokslas, 1987. 143

p. In Lithuanian. Summary in Russian. Bibl.: pp. 123-139. Name index: pp. 140-142.

4675 Vileitene, L.[B]. "Vliianie ateizma i sekuliarizatsii obshchestva na protsess modernizatsii sotsial'noi doktriny katolitsizma" [Influence of Atheism and Secularization of Society on the Modernization Process of Social Doctrine of Catholicism]. *Ateistines mintes raida lietuvoje.* Kaunas, 1988. Pp. 100-107. In Lithuanian. Summary in Russian.

4676 Vileitene, L.B.; Kruglov, A.A.; Prokoshina, E.S. "Razvitie nauchnogo ateizma v Sovetskoi Belorussii" [The Development of Scientific Atheism in Soviet Belorussia]. *Tr. AN LitSSR.* Ser., Obshchestv. nauki 1987. T. 2. Pp. 10-15. Summary in Lithuanian.

4677 Vilnite, O.T. *Kritika protestantskikh kontseptsii cheloveka* [Criticism of Protestant Conception of Man]. Riga: Znanie LatvSSR, 1981. 40 pp. (Material v pomoshch' lektoru / O-vo "Znanie" LatvSSR, Nauch.-metod. sovet po propagande marksistsko-leninskoi filosofii) (Znanie - narodu / ...). Bibl.: p. 39.

4678 Vimmsaare, K.[A]. "Ateisticheskoe vospitanie v obshchestve razvitogo sotsializma" [Atheistic Education in Society of Developed Socialism]. *Kommunist Estonii* 8 (1981): 51-57.

4679 Vimmsaare, K.A. *Evoliutsiia liuteranstva: Martin Liuter i nashe vremia* [Evolution of Lutheranism: Martin Luther and Our Times]. Tallin: Eesti raamat, 1985. 168 pp., illus. In Estonian. Bibl.: pp. 159-165.

4680 Vimmsaare, K.A. *Ravnodushie - eto khorosho ili plokho?* [Indifference - Is it Good or Bad?]. Tallin: Eesti raamat, 1981. 156 pp., illus. In Estonian. Bibl.: pp. 148-155.

4681 Vinogradov, A.I. *Metodika ateisticheskoi propagandy* [Method of Atheistic Propaganda]. M.: Znanie, 1985. 63 pp. (Novoe v zhizni, nauke, tekhnike. Nauch.-ateizm; 6). Bibl.: p. 60.

4682 Vinogradov, V.B. "Pogrebenie znakharki-charodeike v pozdnesrednevekovom ingushskom sklepe" [Burial of a Sorceres-Enchantress in Late Medieval Ingush Crypt]. *Etnografiia i voprosy religioznykh vozzrenii chechentsev i ingushei v dorevoliutsionnyi period.* Groznyi, 1981. Pp. 58-67.

4683 Vinogradoov, V.B. et al. *Religioznye verovaniia v dorevoliutsionnoi Checheno-Ungushetii* [Religious Beliefs in Pre-Revolutionary Checheno-Ingush]. Groznyi: ChIGU, 1981. 111 pp.

4684 Vinogradova, N.M. "Netraditsionnye religii i molodezh' v SShA" [Nontraditional Religions and Youth in USA]. *Aktual'nye problemy nauchno- ateisticheskogo vospitaniia molodezhi.* M., 1987. Pp. 184-189.

4685 Vinogradova, N.M.; Nevshupa, A.M. "Nekotorye aspekty kritiki netraditsionnykh religii v kurse 'Nauchnogo ateizma'" [Some Aspects of Criticism of Nontraditional Religions in the Course "Scientific Atheism"]. *Tezisy dokladov i vystuplenii na Vsesoiuznoi konferentsii "nauhnye osnovy kritiki nemarksistskikh kontseptsii v kursakh obshchestvennykh distsi- plin", 12-15 okt. 1988 g.* Odessa, 1988. Pp. 90-91.

4686 Vinogradova, T.N. "Bor'ba ispanskikh gumanistov protiv bogoslovskogo obosnovaniia pokoreniia indeitsev Ameriki" [The Struggle of Spanish Humanists Against Theological Basis of Subjugation of America's Indians]. *Gumanism i religiia.* L., 1980. Pp.106-123.

4687 Vinokur, A. "Kreshchenie Rusi: fakty i mify " [Baptism of Rus': Facts and Myths]. *Dal. Vostok* 6 (1988): 155-158.

4688 Vinokurov, V.V. "Problema cheloveka v 'estestvennoi teologii' i krizis srednevekovoi metafiziki" [The Problem of Man in "Natural Theology" and the Crisis of Medieval Metaphysics]. *Filosofiia cheloveka: dialog s traditsiei i perspektivy.* M., 1988. Pp. 34-52.

4689 Virtmane, V. *Popytki sovremennogo khristianstva prevratit' sem'iu v 'domashnuiuiu tserkov'* [Attempts of Contemporary Christianity to Convert Family into a "Home Church"]. Riga: Znanie LatvSSR, 1981. 28 pp. (Material v pomoshch' lektoru / O-vo "Znanie" LatvSSR, Nauch.-metod. sovet po propagande nauch. ateizma) (Znanie narodu / ...). In Latvian. Annot. in Rusian. Bibl.: pp. 26-27.

4690 Vishev, I.V. "Kritika osnovnykh khristiansko-teologicheskikh versii transtsendentnogo lichnogo bessmertiia" [Criticism of Basic Christian Theological Versions of Transcendental Individual Immortality]. *Vopr. nauch. ateizma* 26 (1980): 237-253.

4691   Visitaev, S.B. "O kul'turologicheskom analize religii" [Cultural-Logical Analysis of Religion]. *Izv. Sev.-Kavk. nauch. tsentra vyssh. shk. Obshchestv. nauki* 1 (1983): 42-46.

4692   Visitaev, S.B. "Religiia kak spetsificheskaia sfera deiatel'nosti" [Religion as Specific Realm of Activity]. *Izv. Sev.-Kavk. nauch. tsentra vyssh. shk. Obshchestv. nauki* 1 (1981): 34-38.

4693   Vistunov, E.I. *Priglashenie v zapadniu* [Invitation into Trap]. L.: Lenizdat, 1984. 173 pp., illus.

4694   Vistunov, E.I.; Tiutriumov, M.I. *Litsa bez masok* [Faces without Masks]. L. Lenizdat, 1980. 167 pp. For review see item 5344.

4695   Viullenberg, G. "Eto mnenie ne sootvetstvuet 'veroucheniiu'" [This Opinion Does not Correspond to the "Dogma"]. *Argumenty*. M., 1988. Pp. 206-210.

4696   *Vkladnaia kniga Troitse-Sergieva monastyria* [Supplementary Book of the Trinity-Sergius Monastery]. Comp.: E.N. Khitina et al. M.: Nauka, 1987. 439 pp. For review see item 5345.

4697   Vladimirov, A.L.; Solomka, A.P. *Prodannaia sovest'* [Sold Conscience]. Donetsk: Donbas, 1984. 85 pp.

4698   Vladimir, S.V.; Volkov, V.A. *Razum protiv dogmy* [Reason against Dogma]. M.: Nauka, 1982. 165 pp., illus. (Nauch. ateist. ser.).

4699   Vlasov, V.[G]. "Drevnerusskaia agronomiia i khristianstvo" [Ancient Russian Agronomics and Christianity]. *Nauka i zhizn'* 9 (1989): 44-49.

4700   Vlasov, V.G. "Khronologicheskie vekhi khristianizatsii na Rusi" [Chronological Landmarks of Conversion to Christianity of Rus']. *Vopr. nauch. ateizma* 37 (1988): 50-73.

4701   *Vliianie islamskogo faktora na mezhdunarodnye otnosheniia v Azii i Severnoi Afrike i politika Zapada na sovremennom etape* [Influence of Islamic Factor on International Relations in Asia and Northern Africa and the Policy of the West in Contemporary Stage]. Ed.: L.R. Polonskaia. M.: IV, 1985. 103 pp.

4702   Voinov, V.V.; Privalov, Iu.A. "Mif" [Myth]. *Probl. filosofii* 82 (1989): 41-49.

4703 Volgina, N.S. "Ateisticheskaia teoriia v sisteme sotsial'nogo poznaniia" [Atheistic Theory in the System of Social Cognition]. *Sotsial'noe poznanie i ego osobennosti.* Kalinin, 1983. Pp. 75-81.

4704 Volkogonov, D.A. "Stalin i religiia" [Stalin and Religion]. *Nauka i religiia* 2 (1989): 10-11.

4705 Volkov, S.V. "Buddiiskie monastyri v Koree IV-X vv." [Buddhist Monasteries in Korea, IVth-Xth Centuries]. *Buddizm: Istoriia i kul'tura.* M., 1989. Pp. 190-202.

4706 Volkov, S.V. *Ranniaia istoriia buddizma v Koree: (Sangkha i gosudarstvo)* [The Early History of Buddhism in Korea (Sanga and the State)]. M.: Nauka, 1985. 152 pp., illus. Summary in English. Bibl.: pp. 135-152. For review see item 5346.

4707 Volodin, A.I. "A.I. Gertsen: o svoeobrazii ego otnosheniia k religii" [A.I. Herzen: Originality of His Attitude Towards Religion]. *Vopr. nauch. ateizma* 30 (1982): 173-199.

4708 Volodin, A.I. *Problemy religii i nauki v ideinom tvorchestve A.I. Gertsena* [The Problems of Religion and Science in A.I. Herzen's Ideological Works]. M.: Znanie, 1987.64 pp. (Novoe v zhizni, nauke, tekhnike. Nauch. ateizm; 7/1987).

4709 Volodin, A.I. "'V istorii voznikaiut strannye paralleli...': (Ob odnom pochti zabytom epizode iz istorii bor'by s religiei v Rossii 60-kh godov XIX v.)" ["In History Strange Parallels Occur...": (One Nearly Forgotten Episode from the History of Struggle with Religion in Russia in the 60s of the XIXth Century)]. *Vopr. nauch. ateizma* 25 (1980): 283-302. Suppl.: "Stat'i P.L. Lavrova po voprosam mifologii, religii i ateizma v 'Entsiklopedicheskom slovare'" [P.L. Lavrov's Articles on the problems of Mythology, Religion and Atheism in "Encyclopaedia"].

4710 Volozov, V.B. "Buddy i Bodkhisattvy v iaponskoi kul'ture epokhi Kheian (IX-XI vv.)" [Buddhas and Bodhisattvas In Japan's Culture of the Heian Period (IXth-XIth Centuries)]. *Kul'tura i iskusstvo narodov Vostoka.* M., 1987. Pp. 18-19.

4711 Vol'pe, M.L. "Eskhatologicheskie predstavleniia afrikantsev" [African's Eschatological Notions]. *Narody Azii i Afriki* 4 (1988): 50-58.

4712   Volynskaia, N.M. "Brakhmanskoe obuchenie v Drevnei Indii" [Brahmin
       Teaching in Ancient India]. *Ocherki istorii shkoly i pedagogicheskoi mysli
       drevnego i srednevekovogo Vostoka.* M., 1988. Pp. 81-91. Bibl.: p. 91.

4713   *Voprosy ateisticheskogo vospitaniia molodezhi* [Problems of Atheistic
       Upbringing of Youth]. Ed.: O. Gabidzashvili. Tbilisi: Izd-vo Tbil. un-ta,
       1985. 223 pp. In Georgian.

4714   *Voprosy ateizma* [Problems of Atheism]. [Ed.: M. Mamedov]. Baku: Elm,
       1980. 185 pp. In Azerbaijan.

4715   *Voprosy ateizma* [Problems of Atheism]. [Ed.: V.K. Tancher]. Kiev: Visha
       shkola. Izd-vo pri Kiev. un-te. Appears since 1966.
       Vyp. 17. "Ateizm i religiia v sovremennoi bor'be idei" [Atheism and
       Religion in Contemporary Struggle of Ideas]. 1981. 151 pp.
       Vyp. 18. "XXVI s'ezd KPSS i problemy nauchnogo ateizma" [XXVIth
       Congress of the CPSU and Problems of Scientific Atheism]. 1982. 143
       pp.
       Vyp. 19. "Ateisticheskoe vospitanie molodezhi" [Atheistic Upbringing of
       Youth]. 1983. 136 pp.

4716   "Voprosy Ioanna Bogoslova" [Divine John's Questions]. [Transl. From Old
       Church Slavonic by E. Lazareva]. *Nauka i religiia* 11 (1989): 35-37.

4717   *Voprosy istorii lamaizma v Kalmyki* [History of Lamaism in Kalmyk]. [Ed.:
       N.L. Zhukovskaia]. Elista: KNIIFE, 1987. 132 pp.

4718   *Voprosy istorii religii i ateizma v Gruzii* [Problems of History of Religion and
       Atheism in Georgia]. Tbilisi: Metsniereba. Appears since 1968. In
       Georgian.
       [Kn. 6]. 1980. 123 pp.
       Renamed *Istoriia religii i ateisticheskaia propaganda v Gruzii* [History of
       Religion and Atheistic Propaganda in Georgia].
       [Kn. 7]. 1982. 74 pp. Summary in Russian.
       [Kn. 9]. 1985. 103 pp. Summary in Russian.
       Renamed *Iz istorii religii i ateizma v Gruzii* [From the History of Religion
       and Atheism in Georgia].
       [Kn. 10]. 1986. 115 pp. Summary in Russian. [Ed.: V. Chkhaidze].
       [Kn. 11]. 1987. 102 pp. Summary in Russian.
       [Kn. 12]. 1988. 102 pp. Summary in Russian.

4719 *Voprosy nauchnogo ateizma* [Problems of Scientific Atheism]. [Ed.: P.K. Kurochkin]. M.: Mysl'. Appears since 1966.
Vyp. 25. "Ateizm, religiia, tserkov' v istorii SSSR" [Atheism, Religion, Church in the History of USSR]. 1980. 341 pp.
Vyp. 27. "Svoboda sovesti v sotsialisticheskom obshchestve" [Freedom of Conscience in Socialist Society]. 1981. 335 pp. Bibl.: pp. 322-331.
Vyp. 28. 1981. 334 pp.
Vyp. 29. "Literatura po nauch. ateizmu, izd. v SSSR v 1976-1980 g." [Literature on Scientific Atheism Published in USSR in 1976-1980]. 1982. 304 pp. For review see item 5347.
Vyp. 30. "Ateizm, religiia i kul'tura" [Atheism, Religion and Culture]. 1982. 333 pp.

4720 *Voprosy nauchnogo ateizma v sisteme partiinoi ucheby* [Problems of Scientific Atheism in the System of Party Studies]. [Comp.: L.V. Markin]. Erevan: Aiastan, 1987. 347 pp. In Georgian. Published also in: L.: Lenizdat, 1982., 319 pp.

4721 *Voprosy - otvety. Srednii Ural v dvenadtsatoi piatiletke* [Questions - Answers. Middle Ural in the Twelfth Five Year Plan]. Sverdlovsk: Sred.-Ural. kn. izd-vo, 1987. Vyp. 9. "Ateizm i religiia" [Atheism and Religion]. [Comp.: E.I. Kirillova]. 1989. 96 pp.

4722 *Voprosy teorii i praktiki nauchnogo ateizma* [Problems of Theory and Practice of Scientific Atheism]. [Ed.: E.G. Filimonov]. M.: AON, 1988. 232 pp.

4723 Vorob'ev, B. "Veriu v cheloveka!" [I Have Faith in Man]. *Molodaia gvardiia* 1 (1987): 226-235.

4724 Vorob'ev, M.V. "Buddiiskaia obriadnost' v Iaponii v VI-VII vv. (Po 'Nikhongi')" [Buddhist Ceremonial in Japan in VIth-VIIth Centuries (By "Nihongi")]. *Pis'mennye pamiatniki i problemy istorii kul'tury narodov Vostoka: XXII godich. nauch. ses. LO IV AN SSSR.* M., 1989. Ch. 1. Pp. 76-81.

4725 Vorob'ev, M.V. "Buddiiski sutry v Iaponii v VII veke (Po 'Nikhongi')" [Buddhist Sutras in Japan in VIIth Century (By "Nihongi")]. *Pis'mennye pamiatniki i problemy istorii kul'tury narodov Vostoka.* M., 1987. Ch. 1. Pp. 81-84.

4726 Vorob'ev, M.V. "Buddizm v Iaponii v VI-VII vv." [Buddhism in Japan in VIth-VIIth Centuries]. *Uchen. zap. Leningr. un-ta.* 1988. No 422. Ser. Vostokoved. nauk. Vyp. 30. Pp. 184-193.

4727 Vorob'eva-Desiatovskaia, M.I. "O terminakh 'khinaiana' i 'makhaiana' v rannei buddiiskoi literature" [Terms "Hinayana" and "Mahayana" in Early Buddhist Literature]. *Buddizm. Istoriia i kul'tura.* M., 1989. Pp. 74-83.

4728 Voronchanina, N.I. *Islam v obshchestvenno-politic/heskoi zhizni Tunisa* [Islam in Socio-Political Life of Tunis]. M.: Nauka, 1986. 192 pp. Summary in English. Bibl.: pp. 187-190. For review see item 5348.

4729 Voronin, L.E. *Adventizm i reformizm* [Adventism and Reformism]. Stavropol': Kn. izd-vo, 1983. 112 pp.

4730 Voronkova, L.P. *Kritika filosofskoi dogmatiki pravoslavia* [Criticism of Philosophical Dogmatics of the Orthodoxy]. M.: Znanie, 1984. 63 pp. (Novoe v zhizni, nauke, tekhnike. Nauch. ateizm; 8). Bibl.: p. 61.

4731 Voronkova, L.P. *Kritika teologicheskikh kontseptsii sekuliarizatsii* (Evolutsiia amer. protestantizma) [Criticism of Theological Conceptions of Secularization (Evolution of American Protestantism)]. M.: Znanie, 1987. 63 p. (Novoe v zhizni, nauke, tekhnike. Nauch. ateizm; 9/1987). Bibl.: p. 56.

4732 Voronkova, L.P. "Mirovozzrenie P.A. Florenskogo" [P.A. Florenskii's World Outlook]. *Vestn. Mosk. un-ta.* Ser. 7, Filosofiia 1 (1989): 70-81.

4733 Vorontsov, G.V. "Formirovanie ateisticheskoi ubezhdennosti - vazhneishaia zadacha ateisticheskogo vospitaniia studencheskoi molodezhi" [Shaping of Atheistic Conception - Most Important Task of Atheistic Education of Students]. *Aktul. vopr. metodiki prepodavaniia obshchestv. nauk i kom. vospitaniia studentov.* L., 1987. Vyp. 5. Pp. 3-9.

4734 Vorontsov, V.G. *Massovyi ateizm: stanovlenie i razvitie* [Mass Atheism: In the Making and Development]. L.: Lenizdat, 1983. 183 pp., illus. Bibl.: pp. 181-182.

4735 Vorontsov, V.G.; Andrianov, N.P. *Ateisticheskoe vospitanie lichnosti* [Atheistic Education of Individual]. L.: Lenizdat, 1987. 56 pp.

4736 Voroshilov, A.S. *Baptizm kak on est': Sekta baptistov glazami sotsiologa* [Baptism as It is: Baptist Sect in the Eyes of a Sociologist]. Rostov n/D: Kn. izd-vo, 1983. 111 pp. For review see item 5349.

4737 Voroshilov, A.S. "Poniatie 'religioznost'" i ee kriterii" [Notion of "Religiosity" and Its Criterions]. *Izv. Sev.-Kavk. nauch. tsentra vyssh. shk. Obshchestv. nauki* 1 (1983): 51-55.

4738 *Vospitanie ateista.* Sov. zakonodatel'stvo o relig. kul'takh [Upbringing of an Atheist. Soviet Legislation on Religious Cults]. [Transl. by G.G. Furov]. Tskhinvali: Iryston, 1986. 38 pp. (V pomoshch' agitaturu i politinformatoru). In Osset.

4739 *Vospitat' ateista* [Educate an Atheist] [Comp.: R.N. Danil'chenko; Z.A. Tazhurizina]. M.: Mysl', 1988. 430 pp., illus. (B-ka dlia roditelei).

4740 *Vospityvaem ateistov* [We Educate Atheists: Essays and articles]. Kazan': Tatar. kn. izd-vo, 1983. 80 pp. In Tatar.

4741 *Vospityvat' ubezhdennykh ateistov* [Educating Convinced Atheists]. Tashkent: Esh gvardiia, 1984. 70 pp. In Uzbek.

4742 Vovk, O.L. *Iad pod sladkim medom:* Kritika emigrant. klerikal'nonatsionalist. kontseptsii [Poison Under Sweet Honey: Criticism of Emigrant Clerical-Nationalist Conceptions]. L'vov: Kameniar, 1984. 131 pp. In Ukrainian.

4743 Vovk, O.L. *Klerikal'no-natsionalisticheskie popytki vozrozhdeniia uniatskoi tserkvi na Ukraine* [Clerical-Nationalistic Attempts to Revive the Uniate Church in Ukraine]. Kiev: Znanie UkSSR, 1982. 15 pp. (B-chka v pomoshch' lektoru "Kritika reakts. sushchnosti ukr. burzhuaz. natsionalizma" / O-vo "Znanie" UkSSR). In Ukrainian. Annot. in Russian. Bibl.: p. 15.

4744 Vovk, O.L. *Mesto i rol' natsionalisticheskikh klerikalov v planakh reaktsii* [The Place and the Role of Nationalist Clericals in the Plans of the Reaction]. Kiev: Nauk. dumka, 1984. 140 pp. In Ukrainian. Annot. bibl.: pp. 136-139.

4745 Vovk, O.L.; Kokshinskii, O.A. *Iudaizm v reaktsionnykh planakh sionizma* [Judaism in the Reactionary Plans of Zionism]. Simferopol': Tavriia, 1987. 140 pp.

4746   *Vozgoritsia fakel razuma* [The Torch of Reason will Flare Up]. [Comp.: B.N. Konovalova]. M.: Sov. Rossiia, 1986. 494 pp. (Khudozh. i publitsist. b-ka ateista). Annot. bibl.: pp. 470-491. For reviews see items 5350-5351.

4747   Vozniak, N.V.; Vozniak, S.M. "'Khristianskii' natsionalizm uniatstva - orudie antikommunizma" ["Christian" Nationalism of Uniate Church - Tool of Anti-Communism]. *Vopr. ateizma* 17 (1981): 106-114.

4748   Vozniak, S.M. *Antikommunisticheskaia napravlennost' soiuza ostatkov uniatstva i ukrainskogo burzhuaznogo natsionalizma* [Anti-Communist Trend of the Union of Remainders of Uniate Church and Ukrainian Bourgeois Nationalism]. Kiev: Znanie UkSSR, 1984. 16 pp. (V pomoshch' lektoru / O-vo "Znanie" UkSSR. Probl. nauch. ateizma). In Ukrainian. Bibl.: p. 16.

4749   Vozniak, S.M. "Kto razygrivaet 'uniatskuiu kartu'?" [Who Raffles "Uniate's Card"?]. *Kommunist Ukrainy* 10 (1989): 67-77.

4750   Vozniak, S.M. *Uniatskii klerikalizm - dukhovnoe orudie antikommunizma* [Uniate Clericalism - Spiritual Tool of Anti-Communism]. Kiev: Znanie UkSSR, 1982. 48 pp. (Ser. 5 "Nauch.-ateisticheskaia" / O-vo "Znanie" UkSSR; No 3). In Ukrainian. Bibl.: pp. 46-48.

4751   Vozniak, S.M. *Uniatstvo na sluzhbe antikommunizma* [Uniate Church in the Service of Anti-Communism]. L'vov': Visshcha shk. Izd-vo pri L'vov. un-te, 1988. 87 pp. (Ateist. b-ka studenta). In Ukrainian.

4752   Vozniak, S.M. *Uniatstvo - orudie klerikal'nogo antikommunizma* [Uniate Church - Tool of Clerical Anti-Communism]. Kiev: Znanie UkSSR, 1987. 47 pp. (Ser. 5, Nauchno-ateisticheskaia / O-vo "Znanie" UkSSR; No 3). In Ukrainian. Bibl.: p. 46.

4753   "'Vremia blagopriiatno...': Beseda so sviashchennosluzhitelem Rus. pravoslv. tserkvi" ["Time is Favourable...": Conversation with a Priest of Russian Orthodox Church]. *Sotsiol. issled.* 4 (1988): 38-49.

4754   *Vsesoiznaia buddologicheskaia konf. (1987; Moskva).* [All Union Buddhological Conference (1987; Moscow)]. M.: Nauka, 1987. 258 pp.

4755   *Vsesoiuznye filosofskie chteniia molodykh uchennykh 'XXVI s'ezd KPSS i aktual'nye problemy marksistsko-leninskoi filosofii' (4-8 maia 1984 g.)* [All-Union Philosophical Readings of Young Scientists "XXVIth Congress

of the CPSU and Actual Problems of Marxist-Leninist Philosophy" (4-8 May, 1984]. M.: [S.n.], 1984.
Vyp. 10. *K. Marks i sovremennost': filosofiia, sotsiologiia, ideologiia* [K. Marx and Contemporaneity: Philosophy, Sociology, Ideology]. 1984. 212 pp.

4756   *Vstan', chelovek!* [Man, Get Up!]. [Comp.: A.I. Volodina; B.M. Shakhmatova]. M.: Sov. Rossiia, 1986. 527 pp. (Khudozh. i publitsist. b-ka ateista). Annot. bibl: pp. 426-511. Name index: pp. 512-526. For review see item 5352.

4757   Vud-starshii, Dzh. "Religiia i politika. 1984 god" [Religion and Politics. 1984]. *Argumenty* 1987. M., 1987. Pp. 149-164.

4758   *Vvedenie khristianstva na Rusi* [Introduction of Christianity into Rus']. [Ed.: A.D. Sukhov]. M.: Mysl', 1987. 304 pp., illus. Name index: pp. 275-285. For reviews see items 5353-5357.

4759   *Vvedenie khristianstva na Rusi: Ist.* ocherki [Introduction of Christianity into Rus': Historical Essays]. [Ed.: Iu.Iu. Kondufor]. Kiev: Nauk. dumka. 1988. 256 pp., illus. Annot. bibl.: pp. 221-253.

4760   *Vvedenie khristianstva u narodov Tsentral'noi i Vostochnoi Evropy. Kreshchenie Rusi* [Introduction of Christianity by People of Central and Eastern Europe. Baptism of Rus']. [Ed.: N.I. Tolstoi]. M.: Nauka, 1987. 63 pp.

4761   *Vvedenie v religiovedenie* [Introduction to Studies of Religion]. [Comp.: A. Ribelis]. Vil'nius: Mintis, 1981. 181 pp. In Lithuanian. For reviews see items 5358-5359.

4762   Vyblaia, L.I. *Tsena doveriia: Ocherki na ateist. temy* [The Price of Trust: Essays on Atheistic Themes]. Dnepropetrovsk: Promin', 1982. 127 pp.

4763   Vygovskii, L.A. *Ateizm i formirovanie dukhovnykh potrebnostei lichnosti* [Atheism and Forming Individual's Spiritual Needs]. Kiev: Znanie UkSSR, 1984. 32 pp. (Ser.5 "Nauchno-ateisticheskaia" / O-vo "Znanie" UkSSR; No 6). In Ukrainian. Bibl.: pp. 31-32.

4764   Vylegzhanin, Iu.N. "Kriticheskii analiz religioznoi fal'sifikatsii poznaniia" [Critical Analysis of Religious Falsification of Cognition]. *Dukhovnye tsennosti kak predmet filosofskogo analiza.* M., 1985. Pp. 138-142.

4765 Vylegzhanin, Iu.N. "Problema kul'tury v khristianskoi ideologii" [The Problem of Culture in Christian Ideology]. *Dukhovnyi mir sovremennogo cheloveka.* M., 1987. Pp. 247-249.

4766 *Vyshe effektivnost' ateisticheskogo vospitaniia* [Higher Effectiveness of Atheistic Education]. Alma-Ata: Znanie KazSSR, 1981. 21 pp.

4767 "Za mir i spravedlivost' na Blizhnem Vostoke. Sessiia v Echmiadzinskom monastyre" [For Peace and Justice in the Near East. Session in the Echmiadzinsk Monastery] *Religiia v SSSR* 6 (1987): LI 1-LI 2.

4768 Zaborov, M.A. "Ioannity" [Joannites]. *Vopr. istorii* 9 (1984): 92-102.

4769 Zabraniuk, A.P. 'Khristianskii sotsializm' S.N. Bulgakova i osvoboditel'noe dvizhenie v Rossii v nachale XX v." [S.N. Bulgakov's "Christian Socialism" and Liberation Movement in Russia, Early XXth Century]. *Filosofiia i osvoboditel'noe dvizhenie v Rossii.* L., 1989. Pp. 184-195.

4770 Zabraniuk, A.P. "Reaktsionnaia sotsial'naia rol' pravoslavnogo provident-sializma v kontse XIX-nachale XX veka" [Reactionary Social Role of Orthodox Providentialism at the End of XIXth-Early XXth Century]. *Sotsial'no-filosofskie aspeky kritiki religii.* L., 1980. Pp. 123-137.

4771 Zabroda, E.P. "Sotsial'no-psikhologicheskie mekhanizmy obshcheniia v religioznykh soobshchestvakh" [Socio-Psychological Relations Mechanism in Religious Fellowships]. *Filos. vopr. meditsiny i biologii* 18 (1986): 116-123.

4772 Zadorozhniuk, I.E. "Antropologicheskie osnovy sovremennogo mistitsizma" [Anthropological Foundations of Contemporary Mysticism]. *Problema cheloveka v sovremennoi religioznoi i misticheskoi literature.* M., 1988. Pp. 147-159.

4773 Zadorozhniuk, I.E. "Grazhdanskaia religiia v SShA" [Civic Religion in USA]. *Religii mira.* 1986. M., 1987. Pp. 48-66.

4774 Zadorozhniuk, I.E. "'Grazhdanskaia religiia' v SShA: kontseptsii R. Bellakha i real'nost'" ["Civic Religion" in USA: R. Bellah's Conceptions and Reality]. *Vopr. nauch. ateizma* 36 (1987): 57-74.

4775 Zadorozhniuk, I.E. "Ob ideinom soderzhanii kontseptsii 'grazhdanskoi religii'" [Ideological Content of the Conception "Civic Religion"]. *Sotsiol. issled.* 4 (1983): 165-167.

4776 Zadorozhniuk, I.E. "Protestantizm v obshchestvennoi zhizni Kanady" [Protestantism in Social Life of Canada]. *SShA. Ekonomika, politika, ideologiia* 11 (1988): 30-35.

4777 Zafesov, A.Kh. Naguchev, Kh.I. *Islam v Adygee* [Islam in Adigei]. Maikop: Krasnodar. kn. izd-vo. Adyg. otd-nie, 1989. 143 pp. In Adigei.

4778 Zaglada, A.A. "Metodologicheskie aspekty kritiki sovremennogo pravoslaviia" [Methodological Aspects of Criticism of Contemporary Orthodoxy]. *Vopr. ateizma* 22 (1986): 51-58.

4779 *Zagovor protiv razuma* [Conspiracy against Reason]. [Comp.: M.M. Skibitskii]. M.: Znanie, 1986. 63 pp. (Novoe v zhizni, nauke, tekhnike. Nauch. ateizm; 10/1986). Bibl.: pp. 62-63.

4780 Zagumennov, B. "Shankara v uchenie dzhniana-iogi" [Shankara in Jinyana-Yoga Teachings]. *Aziia i Afrika segodnia* 10 (1988): 54-57.

4781 Zaikovskaia, T.V. "Traditsionnye verovaniia i predstavleniia grekov Adzharii" [Traditional Beliefs and Conceptions of Adjar Greeks]. *Sov. etnografiia* 2 (1989): 105-115.

4782 Zainulabidov, M-G.B. *Ateisticheskaia rabota na sele: Opyt, problemy* [Atheistic Work in the Village: Experience, Problems]. Makhachkala: Dag. kn. izd-vo, 1986. 77 pp.

4783 Zaitsev, A.I. "Mif: religiia i poeticheskii vymysel" [Myth: Religion and Poetic Fantasy]. *Zhizn' mifa v antichnosti.* M., 1988. Ch. 1. Pp. 278-286.

4784 Zaitsev, A.I. "Svoboda voli i bozhestvennoe rukovodstvo v gomerovskom epose" [Free Will and Divine Guidance in Homeric Epos]. *Vestn. drev. istorii* 3 (1987): 139-142. Summary in French.

4785 Zaitsev, V.[A]. "Na slovakh - odno, v zhizni - drugoe" [In Words - One Thing, in Life - Another]. *Agitator* 2 (1988): 55-58.

4786 Zaitsev, V.A. *Belomorskii Sever: religiia, svobodomyslie, ateizm* [White Sea's North: Religion, Free Thinking, Atheism]. Arkhangel'sk: Sev.-Zap. kn. izd-vo, 1983. 208 pp. Annot bibl.: pp. 199-207.

4787 Zakharov, M.F. *Ateisticheskuiu ubezhdennost' - molodezhi* [Atheistic Conviction - to Youth]. Simferopol': Tavriia, 1981. 62 pp.

4788 Zakharov, M.F. "K voprosu o edinstve internatsional'nogo i ateisticheskogo vospitaniia" [The Problem of Unity of International and Atheistic Education]. *Nauch. kommunizm* 4 (1989): 52-55.

4789 Zakharova, N.A. "Kritika pravoslavnogo ponimaniia istorii kak vzaimodeistviia svobody cheloveka i bozhestvennogo predopredeleniia" [Criticism of Orthodox Interpretation of History as Interaction of Freedom of Man and Divine Predestination]. *Kritika religioznoi ideologii i problemy ateisticheskogo vospitaniia.* M., 1982. Pp. 29-35.

4790 Zakharova, N.A. "Ob odnoi iz popytok modernizatsii pravoslavnoi filosofii istorii" [One of the Attempts of Modernization of Orthodox Philosophy of History]. *Filosofskii analiz iavlenii dukhovnoi kul'tury. Teoret. i ist. aspekty.* M., 1984. Pp. 58-64.

4791 Zakharova, N.S. "Rol' sotsial'nykh funktsii esteticheskogo ideala v formirovaniia nauchno-materialisticheskogo ateisticheskogo mirovozzreniia" [The Role of Social Functions of Aesthetic Ideal in Forming Scientific-Materialist Atheistic Outlook]. *Nauchnyi ateizm: ideal i mirovozzrenie.* Perm', 1988. Pp. 94-100.

4792 Zakhidov, A. "Kritika burzhuaznykh interpretatsii 'svobodomysliia' narodov rannesrednevekovoi Srednei Azii" [Criticism of Bourgeois Interpretations of "Free Thinking" of Peoples of Early Medieval Central Asia]. *Filosofskoe nasledie narodov Srednei Azii i bor'ba idei.* Tashkent, 1988. Pp. 77-99.

4793 Zakovich, N.M. *Ateisticheskaia napravlennost' sovetskikh prazdnikov i obriadov* [Atheistic Direction of Soviet Holidays and Ceremonials]. Kiev: Znanie UkSSR, 1985. 48 pp. (Ser. 5 "Nauchno-ateisticheskaia" / O-vo "Znanie" UkSSR; No 11). In Ukrainian. Bibl.: pp. 45-47.

4794 Zakruzhnyi, M.G. "Praktika planirovaniia ateisticheskoi raboty" [Practice of Planning Atheistic Work]. *Nauch. ateizm i ateist. vospitanie* 1 (1983): 149-153.

4795 Zaks, I.M. *Kto sozdal garmoniiu mirozdaniia?* [Who Created the Harmony of the Universe?]. Kaunas: Shviesa, 1980. 56 pp. In Polish.

4796 Zaksas, I.[M]. "Antiklerikal'naia mysl' v burzhuaznoi Litve" [Anticlerical Thought in Bourgeois Lithuania]. *Ateistines minties raida lietuvoje.* Kaunas, 1988. Pp. 48-60. In Lithuanian. Summary in Russian.

4797 Zaksas, I.[M]. "Bessmerten trud i podvig cheloveka" [Immortal Are Man's Labour and Exploit]. *Kommunist.* Vil'nius. 5 (1981): 40-45.

4798 Zaksas, I.M. *Katolitsizm i ekzistentsializm* [Catholicism and Existentialism]. Vil'nius: Mintis, 1983. 198 pp. In Lithuanian. Summaries in German and Russian. Bibl.: pp. 193-197.

4799 Zaliubovina, G.T. "Kul't Poseidona i konsolidatsiia ioniiskogo etnosa vo II-nachale I tysiacheletia do n.e." [Poseidon's Cult and Consolidation of Ionic Ethnic Community in the IInd-Early Ist Century B.C.]. *Problemy issledovanii antichnykh gorodov.* M., 1989. Pp. 47-48.

4800 Zameleev, A.F. "Bibleiskie osnovy istoriosofii Povesti vremennykh let" [Biblical Fundamentals of Historiosophy of the Russian Primary Chronicle]. *Otechestvennaia obshchestvennaia mysl' epokhi Srednevekov'ia.* Kiev, 1988. Pp. 147-151.

4801 Zamaleev, A.F. *Filosofskaia mysl' v srednevekovoi Rusi (XI-XVI vv.)* [Philosophical Thought in Medieval Rus' (XIth-XVIth Centuries)]. L.: Nauka. Leningr. otd-nie, 1987. 247 pp., illus. Bibl.: pp. 242-245.

4802 Zamaleev, A.F.; Zots, V.A. *Bogoslovy ishchut boga: Filos.-ateist. ocherki po istorii khristian. teologii* [Theologians Search God: Philosophical- Atheistic Essays on the History of Christian Theology]. Kiev: Molod, 1980. 166 pp. Annot. bibl.: pp. 146-152.

4803 Zamoiskii, L.P. "Tri shaga v mir masonov" [Three Steps into the World of Masons]. *Argumenty.* M., 1988. Pp. 145-179.

4804 Zamoiskii, L.P. *Za fasadom masonskogo 'khrama'* [Beyond the Facade of Masonic "Temple"]. M.: Progress, [1989]. 170 pp. In English.

4805 Zaoiiako, A.P. "Sotsial'no-psikhologicheskie usloviia sushestvovaniia netraditsionnykh religii" [Socio-Psychological Conditions of the Existence of Nontraditional Religions]. *Molodezh' i tvorchestvo: sotsial'no-filosofskie problemy.* M., 1988. Ch. 3. Pp. 304-306.

4806 Zarginava, T.G. "Sotsialisticheskaia obriadnost' kak faktor ateisticheskogo vospitaniia" [Socialist Ceremonial as Factor of Atheistic Education]. *Vopr. nauch. ateizma* 34 (1986): 224-232.

4807 Zarian, A.K. "Ikonograficheskie problemy simvoliki khachkarov i mitraizma" [Iconographical Problems of Symbolism of Hachkars and Mithraism]. *Ist. -filol. zhur.* 1 (1989): 202-219. In Armenian. Summary in Russian.

4808 Zaripov, M.M. "Rol' Kazanskogo universiteta v razvitii svobodomysliia sredi tatar (seredina XIX v.)" [The Role of Kazan University in Development of Free Thinking among Tatars (Middle XIXth Century)]. *Iz istorii formirovaniia i razvitiia svobodomysliia v dorevoliutsionnoi Tatarii.* Kazan', 1987. Pp. 52-57. Bibl.: pp. 56-57.

4809 *Zarubeznyi Vostok: religioznye traditsii i sovremennost'* [Foreign Orient: Religious Traditions and Contemporaneity]. [Ed.: L.R. Polonskaia]. M.: Nauka, 1983. 264 pp.

4810 Zaruda, V.T. *Zhiznennaia pozitsiia i religioznaia vera* [Vital Position and Religious Faith]. Kiev: Politizdat Ukrainy, 1983. 151 pp. In Ukrainian. For review see item 5360.

4811 Zav'ialova, I. "Danila Moskovskii i Danilov monastyr'" [Danila of Muskovy and Danil's Monastery]. *Nauka i religiia* 6 (1988): 12-13.

4812 "Zavisit ot liudei..." [Depends on People...]. *Nauka i religiia* 2 (1980): 14-17.

4813 Zelenina, V.N. "Istoricheskaia evoliutsiia reguliativnoi funktsii religii" [Historical Evolution of Religion's Adjustment Function]. *Problemy istorii religii i ateizma.* Cheboksary, 1980. Pp. 44-51.

4814 Zelenina, V.N. "O reguliativnom vozdeistvii religii na soznanie i povedenie veruiushchikh" [On Religion's Adjustment Influence on Believers Consciousness and Behaviour]. *Aktual'nye problemy ateisticheskogo vospitaniia i kritika religioznoi ideologii.* M., 1981. Pp. 37-42.

4815 Zelenkov, B.I. "Ateisicheskaia ubezhdennost' i formirovanie patriotizma i internatsionalizma u molodezhi" [Atheistic Conviction and Forming Youth's Patriotism and Internationalism]. *Molodezh'-88.* M., 1989. Pp. 230-236.

4816 Zelenkov, B.I. "Preemstvennost' v ateistichekom vospitanii" [Continuity in Atheistic Education]. *Aktual'nye problemy nauchno-ateisticheskogo vospitaniia molodezhi.* M., 1987. Pp. 17-28.

4817 Zelenkov, B.I. "Problemy uchastiia komsomola v formirovanii ateisticheskoi ubezhdennosti molodezhi" [Problems of Komsomol Participation in Shaping Youth's Atheistic Conviction]. *Komsomol i formirovanie politicheskoi kul'tury molodezhi.* M., 1988. Pp. 138-153.

4818 Zenina, L. "Tenri - religiia sovremennoi Iaponii" [Tenrikyo - Religion of the Present Day Japan]*. *Aziia i Afrika segodnia* 3 (1980): 60-61.

4819 Zerkalov, A. "Voland. Mefistofel' i drugie: Zametki o 'teologii' romana M. Bulgakova 'Master i Margarita'" [Voland. Mephistopheles and Others: Remarks on "Theology" of M. Bulgakov's Roman "The Master and Margarita"]. *Nauka i religiia* 8 (1987): 49-51; 9 (1987): 27-29.

4820 Zgerskii, D. "Voina edinovertsev" [War of Coreligionists]. *Novoe vremia* 5 (1989): 8-9.

4821 Zhambulov, D.A. *Islam i nauka* [Islam and Science]. Alma-Ata: Znanie KazSSR, 1982. 38 pp.

4822 Zhardzin, A. "Otnoshenie kardinala Stefana Vyshinskogo k deiatel'nosti pol'skoi kontrrevoliutsi v 1980-1981 gg.: (Obshchestv.-polit. mysl' i polit. praktika)" [Cardinal Stephen Vyshinskii's Attitude Towards the Activity of Polish Counterrevolution in 1980-1981: (Socio-Political Thought and Political Practice)]. *Katolicheskaia tserkov' v PNR v 80-kh godakh.* M., 1988. Pp. 161-183.

4823 Zharikov, A. "O sviazi religioznogo s natsional'nym" [On the Causation of Religion with Nationality]. *Rol' sredstv massovoi informatsii v sovershenstvovanii mezhnatsional'nykh otnoshenii.* M., 1989. Ch. 2. Pp. 63-67.

4824 Zharinov, V.M. "Opyt uchastiia veruiushchikh Pol'shi v sotsialisticheskom stroitel'stve" [Experience of Poland's Believers Participation in Socialist Building]. *Nemarksistskie kontseptsii sotsializma v svete novogo politicheskogo myshleniia.* M., 1989. Pp. 114-116.

4825 Zhdanov, N.V. "'Organizatsiia ob'edinennykh musul'manskikh natsii'?" ["Organization of United Moslem Nations"?]. *Argumenty, 1987.* M., 1987. Pp. 43-69.

4826 Zhdanov, N.V; Ignatenko, A.A. *Islam na poroge XXI veka* [Islam on the Threshold of XXIst Century]. M.: Politizdat, 1989. 351 pp., illus. For review see item 5361.

4827 "Zhenshchina, sem'ia, religiia" [Woman, Family, Religion]. *Nauka i religiia* 3 (1988): 15-17.

4828 Zherbin, A.S. "Khristianizatsiia Karelii v XII-XVI vekakh" [Karelia's Conversion to Christianity in XIIth-XVIth Centuries]. *Pravoslavie v Karelii.* Petrozavodsk, 1987. Pp. 25-35.

4829 Zherebina, T.V. "Perezhitki kul'ta prirody u nekotorykh narodov Sibiri" [Survivals of the Cult of Nature by Some Siberian People]. *Nauchno-ateisticheskie issledovaniia v muzeiakh.* L., 1987. Pp. 51-70.

4830 Zherebtsov, Iu.V. "Kamennyi rel'ef u sela Khaliarta kak kul'tovyi ob'ekt lamaizma" [Stone Relief by Haliarta Village as Religious Object of Lamaism]. *Tsybikovskie chteniia.* Ulan-Ude, 1989. Pp. 55-57.

4831 Zhernevskaia, I.I. *Chasha piatogo angela* [Angel's Fifth Chalice]. L.: Lenizdat, 1985. 239 pp., illus. (Razum poznaet mir).

4832 Zhivogliad, I.[N]. "Ateisticheskomu vospitaniiu - nauchnyi podkhod" [To Atheistic Education - A Scientific Approach]. *Part. zhizn' Kazakhstana* 2 (1985): 66-69.

4833 Zhivogliad, I.N. *Selo, religiia i ateizm* [Village, Religion and Atheism]. Alma-Ata: Kazakhstan, 1985. 182 pp. For review see item 5362.

4834 Zhivogliad, I.N.; Prikhod'ko, L.S. "Protestantskie obshchiny v Karagandinskoi i Kustanaiskoi oblastiakh" [Protestant Communities in Karaganda and Kustanai Regions]. *Protestanskie organizatsii v SSSR.* M., 1989. Pp. 126-137.

4835 Zhivov, V.M. "'Mistagoniia' Maksima Ispovednika i razvitie vizantiiskoi teorii obraza" [Confessor's Maxime "Mystagogue" and Development of Byzantine Theory of Sacred Image]. *Khudozhestvennyi iazyk srednevekov'ia.* M., 1982. Pp. 108-127.

4836 *Zhizn' mifa v antichnosti* [The Life of Myth in Antiquity]. [Ed.: I.E. Danilova]. M.: Sov. khudozhnik, 1988.
      Ch. 1. "Doklady i soobshcheniia" [Papers and Communications]. 305 pp., illus.
      Ch. 2. "Diskussiia, summaries of the articles".* Pp. 306-464.

4837 "Zhizn' sviatogo Issy, Nailuchshego iz Synov Chelovecheskikh" [The Life of St. Issa. The Best of Human Sons]. [Preface by E. Lazareva]. *Nauka i religiia* 7 (1989): 59-62; 8 (1989): 21-23, 34.

4838 Zhol', K.K. *Sravnitel'nyi analiz indiiskogo logiko-filosofskogo naslediia* [Comparative Analysis of Indian Logical-Philosophical Legacy]. Kiev: Nauk.-dumka, 1981. 208 pp. Suppl.: Fragmenty iz tvorcheskogo naslediia / F.I. Shcherbatskoi. Bibl.: pp. 200-207.

4839 Zhol', K.K.; Merezhinskaia, E.Iu. *Nauka. Religiia. Obshchestvo* [Science. Religion. Society]. Kiev: Politizdat Ukrainy, 1986. 159 pp. Bibl.: pp. 152-158.

4840 Zhol', K.K.; Vydrin, D.I. *Kuda bredet piligrim: Vost. religii, kul'tura, molodezh'* [Where To Does the Pilgrim Drag Himself Along: Oriental Religions, Culture, Youth]. Kiev: Molod', 1988. 231 pp., illus.

4841 Zholkver, N. "Novyi oblik khristianskikh demokratov?" [New Aspect of Christian Democrats?]. *Novoe vremia* 23 (1988): 20-22.

4842 Zhosan, G.P. *Adventizm i vtoroe prishestvie* [Adventism and Doomsday]. Kishinev: Kartia Moldoveniaske, 1980. 139 pp. (Nauka i religiia). In Moldavian. Published also in 1984, 126 pp., in Russian.

4843 Zhuk, A.P. *Stanovlenie nauchno-ateisticheskoi mysli v Sovetskoi Belorussii* [Creation of Scientific-Atheistic Thought in Soviet Belorussia]. Minsk: Izd-vo BGU, 1981. 135 pp. Bibl.: pp. 128-134.

4844 Zhukovskaia, N.L. "Buddiisko-shamanskii sinkretizm u mongolov i buriat" [Buddhist-Shamanist Syncretism of Mongols and Buriats]. *Aktual'nye problemy istorii religii i ateizma*. Cheboksary, 1982. Pp. 22-31.

4845 Zhukovskaia, N.[L]. "Chetki" [Rosary]. *Nauka i religiia* 3 (1985): 38-39.

4846 Zhukovskaia, N.[L]. "Iaponiia: traditsii i vera" [Japan: Traditions and Faith]. *Nauka i religiia* 5 (1985): 57-60.

4847 Zhukovskaia, N.[L]. "Lamaizm" [Lamaism]. *Aziia i Afrika segodnia* 6 (1983): 58-61.

4848 Zhukovskaia, N.[L]. "Odin den' v monastyre Iamadera" [One Day in Yamadera Monastery]. *Aziia i Afrika segodnia* 4 (1985): 59-61.

4849 Zhukovskaia, N.L. "Problemy lamaizma v trudakh sovetskikh i mongol'skikh uchenykh" [Problems of Lamaism in the Works of Soviet and Mongol Scientists]. *Stroitel'stvo sotsializma i utverzhdenie nauchno-materialisticheskogo, ateisticheskogo mirovozzreniia (v regionakh rasprostraneniia lamaizma)*. M. 1981. Pp. 52-72.

4850 Zhuravskii, A.V. *Khristianstvo i islam: sotsiokul'turnye problemy: 8 dialoga* [Christianity and Islam: Socio-Cultural Problems: 8 Dialogues]. M.: Nauka, 1990. 128 pp. Bibl.: pp. 117-123. Name index: pp. 124-127.

4851 Ziborova, R.I. "Ateisticheskaia aktivnost' studentov" [Students Atheistic Activity]. *Sotsial'naia aktivnost' cheloveka: filosofskii analiz*. Krasnodar, 1986. Pp. 211-225.

4852 Ziiatov, A. *Nauka i religiia o morali* [Science and Religion on Morals]. Tashkent: Znanie UzSSR, 1982. 24 pp. (B pomoshch' lektoru / O-vo "Znanie" UzSSR. Ser. obshchetv.-polit.). In Uzbek.

4853 Ziiatov, A. *Sotsialisticheskii obraz zhizni i formirovanie ateisticheskogo mirovozzreniia* [Socialist Way of Life and Forming of Atheistic World Outlook]. Tashkent: Uzbekistan, 1986. 30 pp. (Ser. "Marksizm-leninizm"; No 10). In Uzbek.

4854 Zimak, Z.O. *Ideino-politicheskaia i nravstvennaia napravlennost' ateisticheskogo vospitaniia molodezhi* [Ideological-Political and Moral Trend of Atheistic Education of Youth]. Minsk: Znanie BSSR, 1982, 18 pp. (V pomoshch' lektoru / "Znanie" BSSR, Nauch.-metod. sovet po propagande nauch. ateizma). Bibl.: pp. 17-18.

4855 Zinchenko, L.P.; Kirikov, O.I. "Priobshchenie studentov k prakticheskoi ateisticheskoi rabote" [Joining Students in Practical Atheistic Work]. *Vopr. ateizma* 20 (1984): 67-73.

4856 Zivs, S. "Kak izrail'skie ravviny opravdyvaiut genotsid" [How Israeli Rabbis Justify Genocide]. *Argumenty i fakty* 41 (1983): 5.

4857 Zlotina, T.V. "Russkii chelovek XVIII stoletiia i vol'nodumstvo" [Russian Man of the XVIIIth Century and Free-Thinking]. *Dukhovnyi mir sovremennogo cheloveka*. M., 1987. Pp. 180-182.

4858 Zmeev, Iu.N. *Pod fal'shivoi vyveskoi: Estestvoznanie, religiia, ateizm* [Under False Sign: Natural Sciences, Religion, Atheism]. Simferopol': Tavriia, 1987. 129 pp.

4859 Zmeev, Iu.N. *Sotvorenie ili evoliutsiia: O bibleis. i nauch. kartine mira* [Creation or Evolution: Biblical and Scientific Picture of the World]. Kiev: Politizdat Ukrainy, 1988. 94 pp. (Besedy s veruiushchimi). In Ukrainian.

4860 Znamenskaia, E.S. "Nekotorye aspekty vzaimosviazi sotsial'noi spravedlivosti s protsessom stanovleniia i preodoleniia religii" [Some Aspects of Inter-communication of Social Justice with the Process of Creation and Over-coming of Religion]. *Dukhovnyi mir sovremennogo cheloveka.* M., 1987. Pp. 115-118.

4861 Znamenskaia, E.S. "Ponimanie sushchnosti sotsial'noi spravedlivosti v sovremennom russkom pravoslavii" [Understanding the Essence of Social Justice in Contemporary Russian Orthodoxy]. *Molodezh' i tvorchestvo: sotsial'no-filosofskie problemy.* M., 1988. Ch. 3. Pp. 298-300.

4862 Zol'nikova, N.D. "Bor'ba za kontrol' nad sibirskoi prikhodskoi obshchinoi i institut tserkovnykh starost" [Struggle for Control over Siberian Parochial Community and the Institute of Churchwardens]. *Issledovaniia po istorii obshchestvennogo soznaniia epokhi feodalizma v Rossii.* Novosibirsk, 1984. Pp. 87-102.

4863 Zol'nikova, N.D. "O nekotorykh zakonodatel'nykh istochnikakh po istorii tserkovnoi reformy Petra I" [Some Legislative Sources on History of Peter I Church Reforms]. *Literatura i klassovaia bor'ba epokhi pozdnego feodalizma v Rossii.* Novosibirsk, 1987. Pp. 105-114.

4864 Zol'nikova, N.D. "Prikhodskoe dukhovenstvo XVIII v., po zhalobam sibir-skogo naseleniia [Parochial Clergy of the XVIIIth Century, According to Complaints of Siberian Population]. *Nauchnyi ateizm, religiia i sovre-mennost'.* Novosibirsk, 1987. Pp. 266-289.

4865 Zolotova, N. "Kabinet nauchnogo ateizma" [Cabinet of Scientific Atheism]. *Agitator* 13 (1986): 62-63.

4866 Zolotukhin, S.A. "Otnoshenie studencheskoi molodezhi k religii i ateizmu" [Students Attitude Towards Religon and Atheism]. *Aktual'nye problemy nauchno-ateisticheskogo vospitaniia molodezhi.* M., 1987. Pp. 107-109.

4867   Zolotukhina-Abolina, E.V.; Slepakov, V.S. "Fenomen 'sviatosti' v religioznom
       i ateisticheskom soznanii" [Phenomenon of "Holiness" in Religious and
       Atheistic Consciousness]. *Izv. Sev.-Kavk. nauch. tsentra vyssh. shk.
       Obshchestv. nauki* 1 (1984): 46-50.

4868   Zots, V.A. "Ateisticheskii potentsial novoi sotsialisticheskoi obriadnosti"
       [Atheistic Potential of the New Socialist Ceremonial]. *Vopr. ateizma* 21
       (1985): 10-20.

4869   Zots, V.A. "Ateizm i dukhovnaia kul'tura sotsialisticheskogo obshchestva"
       [Atheism and Moral Culture of Socialist Society]. *Vopr. filosofii* 7 (1981):
       29-37. Summary in English, p. 186.

4870   Zots, V.A. *Ateizm i dukhovnoe nasledie proshlogo* [Atheism and Spiritual
       Legacy of the Past]. Kiev: Znanie UkSSR, 1983. 44 pp. (Ser. 5 "Nauchno-
       ateisticheskaia" / O-vo "Znanie" UkSSR; No 9). Bibl.: p. 44. In
       Ukrainian.

4871   Zots, V.A. *Ateizm i progress kul'tury* [Atheism and the Progress of Culture].
       Kiev: Rad. shk., 1985. 199 pp., illus. In Ukrainian.

4872   Zots, V.A. *Ateizm i religiia v sovremennoi ideologicheskoi bor'be* [Atheism
       and Religion in Contemporary Ideological Struggle]. Kiev: Vishcha shk.
       Izd-vo pri Kiev. un-te, 1986. 96 pp. Bibl.: pp. 94-95.

4873   Zots, V.A. *Ateizm v sisteme tsennostei dukhovnoi kul'tury* [Atheism in the
       System of Values of Spiritual Culture]. Kiev: Znanie UkSSR, 1980. 48 pp.
       (Ser. 5 "Nauchno-ateisticheskaia" / O-vo "Znanie" UkSSR; No 1). In
       Ukrainian. Bibl.: p. 48.

4874   Zots, V.A. *XXVII s'ezd KPSS o sovershenstvovanii ateisticheskogo vospitaniia*
       [XXVIIth Congress of the CPSU on Perfection of Atheistic Education].
       Kie: Znanie UkSSR, 1986. 48 pp. (Ser. 5, Nauch.-ateist. / O-vo "Znanie"
       UkSSR; No 7). In Ukrainian. Annot. bibl.: p. 47.

4875   Zots, V.A. *Edinstvo internatsional'nogo i ateisticheskogo vospitaniia* [Unity of
       International and Atheistic Education]. M.: Znanie, 1983. 64 pp. (Novoe v
       zhizni, nauke, tekhnike. Nauch. ateizm; 7). Bibl.: p. 63. Annot. bibl.: pp.
       61-62.

4876   Zots, V.A. "I v russkom slove otlilos'" [And in Russian Word it was Cast...].
       Argumenty, 1987. M., 1987. Pp. 93-113.

4877 Zots, V.A. "Kritika bogoslovskikh kontseptsii sverkh'estestvennogo prois-khozhdeniia kul'tury" [Criticism of Theological Conceptions of Supernatural Origin of Culture]. *Vopr. ateizma* 17 (1981): 99-106.

4878 Zots, V.A. *Kul'tura. Religiia. Ateizm* [Culture. Religion. Atheism]. M.: Politizdat, 1982. 158 pp. For reviews see items 5363-5364.

4879 Zots, V.A. "Kul'turnoe nasledie, pravoslavie, sovremennost'" [Cultural Legacy, Orthodoxy, Contemporaneity]. *Filos. i sotsiol. mysl'* 4 (1989): 18-25. Summary in English, p. 127.

4880 Zots, V.A. *Pravoslavie i kul'tura: fakty protiv domyslov* [Orthodoxy and Culture: Facts against Conjectures]. Kiev: Politizdat Ukrainy, 1986. 223 pp., illus. Annot. bibl.: pp. 210-221. For review see item 5365.

4881 Zots, V.A. *Schast'e iskat' na zemle: Ob opyte ateist. vospitaniia trudiashchikhsia* [Seek on the Earth Happiness: Experience of Atheistic Education of Workers]. Donetsk: Donbas, 1983. 73 pp.

4882 Zots, V.A. "Traditsii i novatorstvo ateisticheskoi raboty" [Traditions and Innovation of Atheistic Work]. *Vopr. ateizma* 24 (1988): 18-24.

4883 Zots, V.A.; Solon'ko, N.V. *Religiia. Mistika, Sovremennost'* [Religion. Mysticism. Contemporaneity]. Kiev: Znanie UkSSR, 1988. 47 pp. (Ser. 5, Nauchno-ateisticheskaia / O-vo "Znanie" UkSSR; No 12). In Ukrainian. Bibl.: pp. 46-47.

4884 Zubar', V.M.; Pavlenko, Iu.V. *Khersones Tavricheskii i rasprostranenie khristianstva na Rusi* [Kherson Tavricheskii and Dissemination of Christianity in Rus']. Kiev: Nauk. dumka, 1988. 206 pp., illus. Bibl.: p. 205.

4885 Zubenko, L.A. "Emotsional'no-psikhologicheskaia storona fenomena zhenskoi religioznosti" [Emotional-Psychological Side of Phenomenon of Woman's Religiosity]. *Obshchestvennoe soznanie i voprosy formirovaniia nauchnogo mirovozzreniia.* M., 1980. Pp. 68-82.

4886 Zubkov, M.F. "Istoriia masonstva v stranakh Tsentral'noi i Vostochnoi Evropy" [History of Freemasonry in Central and East European Countries]. *Vopr. istorii* 12 (1988): 127-133.

4887   Zubov, A.B. "Khristianstvo i 'dukh feodalizma'" [Christianity and the "Spirit of Feudalism"]. *Narody Azii i Afriki* 1 (1989): 110-116. Summary in English, pp. 203-204.

4888   Zuderman, B.V. ...*Naidet li veru na zemle?: Povestvovanie khristianina Very Evangel'skoi* [...Will He Find Faith on the Earth?: Narration of a Christian of Evangelist Creed]. Vladivostok: Dal'nevost. kn. izd-vo, 1989. 112 pp.

4889   Zuev, G.N. "O nekotorykh aspektakh vzaimosviazi voenno-patrioticheskogo i ateisticheskogo vospitaniia molodezhi" [Some Aspects of Interrelation of Military-Patriotic and Atheistical Upbringing of Youth]. *Nauch. kommunizm* 4 (1989): 42-48.

4890   Zuev, Iu.[P]. "'Den' vos'moi': Evoliutsiia sotsial.-polit. pozitsii Rus. pravoslav. tserkvi" ["The Eight Day": Socio-Political Evolution of the Position of Russian Orthodox Church]. *Nauka i religiia* 6 (1988): 14.

4891   Zuev, Iu.P. *Ot stradaniia - k schast'iu* [From Suffering - to Happiness]. Kishinev: Kartia Moldoveniaske, 1982. 112 pp. In Moldavian.

4892   Zuev, Iu.P. "Religioznye ob'edineniia i veruiushchie v usloviiakh demokrati-zatsii sovetskogo obshchestva" [Religious Unions and Believers under the Conditions of Democratization of Soviet Society]. *Filos. nauki* 4 (1988): 13-22.

4893   Zuev, Iu.P. "Rol' nauchno-materialisticheskogo [ateisticheskogo] mirovozzre-niia v formirovanii aktivnoi zhiznennoi pozitsii lichnosti" [The Role of Scientific Materialist [Atheistic] World Outlook in Forming Active Vital Position of the Individual]. *Vopr. nauch. ateizma* 35 (1985): 97-107.

4894   Zuev, Iu.P. *Sotsial'no-istoricheskii protsess i kritika ego bogoslovskoi interpre-tatsii* [Socio-Historical Process and Criticism of Its Theological Interpre-tation]. M.: Znanie, 1986. 64 pp. (Novoe v zhizni, nauke, tekhnike. Nauch. ateizm; 8/1986). Bibl.: p. 54.

4895   Zuev, Iu.[P]. "Uchityvaia novye real'nosti" [Taking into Consideration New Realities]. *Nauka i religiia* 12 (1987): 17-18.

4896   Zuev, Iu.P. "Vzgliad s rasstoianiia v 1000 let" [View from a Space of 1000 Years]. *Molodoi kommunist* 7 (1984): 39-45.

4897 Zuev, Iu.[P].; Timofeev, V. "Simpozium v Brno" [Symposium in Brno]. *Nauka i religiia* 4 (1983): 54-56.

4898 Zulikh, I. "Dollar blagoslovliaet bol'shoe shou 'moralistov'" [Dollar Blesses the Big Show of "Moralists"]. *Argumenty*, 1987. M., 1987. Pp. 179-183.

4899 Zvereva, G.I. "Presviterianskaia tserkov' i problemy natsional'nogo razvitiia Shotlandii v XX v. [Presbyterian Church and Problems of Scotland's National Development in the XXth Century]. *Religii mira*. M., 1989. P.p 53-72.

4900 Zybkovets, V. "Rabota prodolzhaetsia" [The Work Continues]. *Nauka i religiia* 8 (1985): 2-3.

4901 Zyrianov, P.N. *Pravoslavnaia tserkov' v bor'be s revoliutsiei 1905-1917 gg.* [Orthodox Church in the Struggle against Revolution, 1905-1917]. M.: Nauka, 1984. 224 pp. Nam,e index pp. 220-223. For reviews see items 5366-5368.

REVIEWS

* Abaev, N.V. *Chan-buddizm i kul'tura psikhicheskoi deiatel'nosti v srednevekovom Kitae* [Cha'n-Buddhism and the Culture of Psychical Activity in Medieaval China]. Cited above as item 223.

4902 Artiunov, S. "Novoe o chan-buddizme [New on Ch'an-Buddhism]. *Aziia i Afrika segodnia* 5 (1984): 64.

4903 Perelomov, L.S.; Saltykov, G.F. // *Narody Azii i Afriki* 3 (1985): 204-206.

* Abaev, N.V. *Chan-buddizm i kul'turno-psikhologicheskie traditsii v srednebekovom Kitae* [Ch'an-Buddhism and Cultural-Psychological Traditions in Mediaeval China]. Cited above as item 224.

4904 Pubaev, R. "Litsom k Vostoku" [Face to East]. *Pravda Buriatii* July, 12, 1989.

4905 Smirnov, V.A.; Zhambaldagbaev, N.Ts. // *Filos. nauki* 12 (1989): 135.

* Abaev, S. *Ateizm i vospitanie novogo cheloveka* [Atheism and Education of the New Man]. Cited above as item 230.

4906 Reipnazarov, S. "Aktual'nnnaia tema" [Actual Theme]. *Sov. Karakalpakiia* Oct. 23, 1982.

* Abdullaev, G.B. et al. *Estestvoznanie protiv idealizma i religii* [Natural Sciences Against Idealism and Religion]. Cited above as item 246.

4907 Mustafaeva, M.G. // *Izv. Sev.-Kavk nauch.· tsentra vyssh. shk. Obshchestv. Nauki* 4 (1984): 107-108.

* Abu Khamid-al-Gazali. "Voskreshenie nauk o vere" [Resurrection of Sciences About Faith]. Cited above as item 274.

4908 // *Narody Azii i Afriki* 6 (1981): 194-198.

* Akhmedov, A. *Islam v sovremennoi ideino-politicheskoi bor'be* [Islam in the Contemporary Ideological-Political Struggle]. Cited above as item 303.

4909 Ionova, A. "Islamskoe reshenie?" [Islamic Solution?]. *V mire knig* 4 (1986): 83-84.

* Akhmedov, A. *Sotsial'naia doktrina islama* [Islam's Social Doctrine]. Cited above as item 304.

4910 Avsent'ev, A. // *Stavrop. pravda* Sept. 7, 1982.

4911 Avsent'ev, V.V. // *Vopr. filosofii* 5 (1984): 170.

4912 Ionova, A. "Musul'manskie teorii obshshestvennogo razvitiia" [Moslem Theories of Social Development]. *Aziia i Afrika segodnia* 4 (1983): 63.

* Akmuradov, K. *Ateisticheskoe vospitanie sel'skogo naseleniia na sovremennom etape* [Villager's Atheistic Education in the Contemporary Period]. Cited above as item 325.

4913 Sar'ev, B.; Khydyrov, T. "Dlia sel'skikh ateistov" [For Rural Atheists]. *Turkm. iskra* Jan. 9, 1986.

* Akmuradov, T.A. *Formirovanie nauchno-materialisticheskogo mirovozzreniia trudiashchikhsia* [Shaping Workers' Scientific-Materialist World Outlook]. Cited above as item 5833.

4914 Boltaev, M.N. // *Obshchestv. nauki v Uzbekistane* 3 (1987): 66.

4915 Shakirov, V. et al. "Vazhnyi aspekt perestroiki soznaniia liudei" [Important Aspect of Restructuring Peoples' Consciousness]. *Kommunist Uzbekistana* 4 (1988): 92-94.

* Alekseev, N.A. *Rannie formy religii tiurkoiazychnykh narodov Sibiri* [Early Forms of Religion of the Turkic Language People of Siberia]. Cited above as item 354.

4916 Sunguchaev, Ia. "Prochtut s pol'zoi" [Will Benefit from Reading]. *Sov. Khakasiia* Nov. 21, 1981.

* Aliev, R.Ia. *Islam v kontseptsiiakh 'natsional'nogo sotsializma'* [Islam in Conceptions of "National Socialism"] Cited above as item 370.

4917 Mamedov, A. "Arabskie strany: islam v ideologii i politike" [Arab Countries: Islam in Ideology and Politics]. *Kommunist Azerbaidzhana* 6 (1988): 84-85.

* Alimbaev, A.A. *Ateizm sovetskogo rabochego klassa* [Atheism of Soviet Workers Class]. Cited above as item 379.

4918 Urazalin. B. // *Part. zhizn' Kazakhstana* 8 (1986): 88.

* Andreev, M.V. *Marksisty i khristiane:* Dialog [Marxists and Christians: A Dialogue]. Cited above as item 404.

4919 Sukhov, A. // *V mire knig* 11 (1983): 78-79.

* Andrianov, N.P. *Obraz zhizni - tvorchestvo:* Sotsial.-gumanist. tsennost' ateizma [Way of Life - Creative Work: Socio-Humanist Value of Atheism]. Cited above as item 415.

4920 Nefedova, N. // *Polit. Samoobrazovanie* 7 (1986): 136-137.

* Andriashvili, R.I. *Perezhitki islama v Gruzii* [Islam's Survivals in Georgia]. Cited above as item 422.

4921 Esitashvili, Sh. "Islam v Gruzii" [Islam in Georgia]. *Kommunist Gruzii* 4 (1985): 94-95.

* *Antikommunisticheskaia sushchnost' uniatsko-natsionalisticheskoi fal'sifikatsii istorii ukrainskogo naroda* [Anti-Communist Essence of Uniate-Nationalist Falsifications of the History of the Ukrainian People]. Cited above as item 441.

4922 Giatenko, P.; Chernyshev, V. "Fal'sifikatoram neimetsia" [Want of Falsifiers]. *Pravda Ukrainy* July 9, 1985.

* *Apokrify drevnikh khristian* [Ancient Christian Apocryphy]. Cited above as item 449.

4923 // *Znamia* 3 (1990): 238-239.

* Arestov, V.N.; Shudrik, I.A. *Iad s dostavkoi na dom* [Home Delivery of Poison]. Cited above as item 462.

4924 Polikarpov, V. // *Krasnoe znamia* Kharkov. Apr. 8, 1987.

* *Argumenty* [Arguments]. Cited above as item 463.

4925   Krupa, G. // *Belgor. pravda* March 3, 1981.

4926   Lenskii, A. "Soldaty istiny" [Soldiers of Truth]. *Znamia truda* Krasnovodsk, Jan 20, 1981.

* Aripov, M.K. *Sotsial'nyi ideal islama* [Islam's Social Ideal]. Cited above as item 464.

4927   Bitson, G. "Illiuziia i real'nost' ideala" [Illusion and Reality of Ideal]. *Kommunist Uzbekistana* 8 (1989): 93-95.

* Arsenkin, V.K. *Krizis religioznosti i molodezh'* [Crisis of Religiosity and Youth]. Cited as item 5834.

4928   Alekseev, V.; Pishchik, Iu. "Vernyi orientir" [True Guiding Line]. *Koms. pravda* Oct. 11, 1985.

4929   Dolia, V.E.; Pavlovskii, O.A. // *Nauch. dokl. vyssh. shk. Filos. nauki* 6 (1985): 177-179.

4930   Gegeshidze, D. "Ob ateisticheskom vospitanii molodezhi" [Youth's Atheistic Upbringing]. *Kommunist Gruzii* 4 (1985): 91-93.

4931   Gott, V.S.; Bolotin, I.S. "Molodezh' i budushchee religii" [Youth and Religions' Future]. *Sov. pedagogika* 10 (1985): 127-129.

4932   Mezentsev, V. "'Bor'bu ... postavit' nauchnee'" ["Place the Struggle Scientifically"]. *Molodoi kommunist* 9 (1985): 101-103.

4933   Rudakova, N. "Ateisticheskomu vospitaniiu - nauchnuiu osnovu" [Scientific Basis for Atheistic Education]. *Alt. pravda* Oct. 11, 1984.

* *Ateisticheskie chteniia* [Atheistic readings]. Cited above as item 499.

4934   Titovich, S. "Sborniki 'Ateisticheskie chteniia'" [Collections of "Atheistic readings"]. *Vospitanie shkol'nikov* 6 (1964): 76.

* *Ateisticheskii slovar'* [Dictionary of Atheism]. Cited above as item 9.

4935   Belov, A.; Nevinitsyn, A. // *Polit. samoobrazovanie* 6 (1984): 136-139.

4936   Iam, K.E. // *Nauch. dokl. vyssh. shk. Filos. nauki* 2 (1985): 177-179.

*   *Ateisticheskoe vospitanie* [Atheistic Education]. Cited above as item 505.

4937   Rakhimov, O. "Na osnove nauchnogo ateizma" [On the Basis of Scientific Atheism]. *Krasnaia zvezda* Apr. 20, 1982.

*   *Ateisticheskoe vospitanie: poisk, problemy* [Atheistic Education: Search, Problems]. Cited above as item 506.

4938   Kharazov, V. "Ateizm, kakim emu byt'?" [Atheism, What Kind Should it Be?]. *Sov. Moldavia* Nov. 19, 1988.

4939   Tazhurizina, Z. "Gumanisticheskie tseli ateisticheskogo vospitaniia" [Humanist Aims of Atheistic Education]. *Kommunist Moldavii* 7 (1980): 93-95.

*   *Ateisticheskoe vospitanie: Vopr. i otvety* [Atheistic Education: Questions and Answers]. Cited above as item 508.

4940   Bairanov, E. "Prodiktovano vremenem" [Dictated by the Time]. *Maryiskaia pravda* Nov. 6, 1984.

4941   Valiev, Sh. "Novaia kniga po ateizmu" [New Book on Atheism]. *Andizh. pravda* March 21, 1984.

*   *Ateisticheskoe vospitanie shkol'nikov* [Atheistic Upbringing of Schoolboys]. Cited above as item 510.

4942   Tikhonov, A. "Ateisticheskoe vospitanie trebuet znanii" [Atheistic Education Demands Knowledge]. *Nar. obrazovanie* 7 (1987): 94-95.

*   *Ateisty Kubani rasskazyvaiut* [Kuban's Atheists Recount]. Cited above as item 516.

4943   Vasil'ev, A. "Chitaia knigi ob opyte ateisticheskogo vospitaniia..." [Reading Books on the Experience of Atheistic Education...]. *Polit. samoobrazovanie* 7 (1985): 138-142.

*   *Ateizm i dukhovnaia kul'tura* [Atheism and Spiritual Culture]. Cited above as item 519.

4944 Gordenko, A.T. "Ateizm i kul'turnyi progress obshchestva" [Atheism and Cultural Progress of the Society]. *Kommunist Ukrainy* 11 (1986): 92-93.

* *Ateizm i religiia v Litve* [Atheism and Religion in Lithuania]. Cited above as item 525.

4945 Pechiura, P. // *Sov. Litva* July 18, 1985.

* *Ateizm v SSSR* [Atheism in USSR]. Cited above as item 529.

4946 Berdysheva, T.M. "Problemy stanovleniia i razvitiia ateizma v SSSR" [Problems of Creation and Development of Atheism in USSR]. *Vestn. Mosk. un-ta.* Ser. 7, Filosofiia 2 (1988): 72-74.

4947 Popov, L. // *Polit. samoobrazovanie* 5 (1988): 107-110.

4948 Popov, L. "Voskhozhdenie k ateizmu" [Ascent to Atheism]. *Orl. pravda* Nov. 13, 1986.

* Avksent'ev, A.V. *Islam na Severnom Kavkaze* [Islam in Northern Caucasus]. Cited above as item 537.

4949 Sovlamak, V. "Pravda ob Islame" [Truth About Islam]. *Sov. Dagestan* 6 (1984): 70-71.

* Avksent'ev, A.V.; Mavliutov, R.R. *Kniga o Korane* [The Book on the Koran]. Cited above as item 538.

4950 Dzhegutanov, E. "Kak otkryvaetsia 'zakrytaia kniga'" [How "The Closed Book" Opens]. *Stavrop. pravda* June 26, 1984.

4951 Gadzhiev, S.M. // *Izv. Sev.-Kavk. nauch. tsentra vyssh. shk. Obshchestv. nauki* Rostov n/D. 3 (1981): 101.

* Babii, A.I. *Pravoslavie v Moldavii* [Orthodoxy in Moldavia]. Cited above as item 555.

4952 Gutsu, V. "Pravoslavie v Moldavii: vchera i segodnia" [Orthodoxy in Moldavia: Yesterday and Today]. *Sov. Moldaviia* June 16, 1988.

* Babii, A.I. et al. *Preodolenie religii i utverzhdenie ateizma v Moldavskoi SSR* [Prevailing Over Religion and Confirming Atheism in Moldavian SSR]. Cited above as item 556.

4953 Vasilesku, G. "Sovremennaia religiia i ateizm" [Contemporary Religion and Atheism]. *Sov. Moldaviia* Dec. 23, 1983.

* Babosov, E.M. *Istina i bogoslovie* [Truth and Theology]. Cited above as item 560.

4954 Lensu, M.; Platonov, R. "Istina i mirovozzrenie" [The Truth and World Outlook]. *Kommunist Belorussi* 2 (1989): 89-91.

4955 Zots, V.A. // *Filos. nauki* 7 (1989): 142.

* Babosov, E.M. *Nauchno-tekhnicheskaia revoliutsiia i utverzhdenie ateisticheskogo mirovozzreniia* [Scientific-Technical Revolution and Affirmation of the Atheistic World Outlook]. Cited above as item 561.

4956 Rakhimov, O. "Na osnove nauchnogo ateizma" [On the Basis of Scientific Atheism]. *Krasnaia zvezda* Apr. 20, 1982.

* Baimuradov, N. *Leninskii printsip· svobody sovesti i ego osushchestvlenie v Tadzhikistane* [Leninist Principles on the Freedom of Conscience and Its Implementation in Tajikistan]. Cited above as item 124.

4957 Filatova, P.S. "S uchetom mestnykh uslovii" [Taking into Consideration Local Conditions]. *Kommunist Tadzhkistana* March 7, 1981.

* Bairamov, E.Z. *Zabroshennye chetki* [Abandoned Rosaries]. Cited above as item 582.

4958 Semenov, V. "Razgovor idet otkrovennyi" [The Talk is Frank]. *Tashauz. pravda* Aug. 29, 1986.

* Bakanurskii, G.L. *Lozhnye doktriny, reaktsionnaia politika* [False Doctrines, Reactionary Policy]. Cited above as item 596.

4959 Babii, A. "Zloveshchii al'ians" [Ominous Alliance]. *Sov. Moldaviia* Oct. 23, 1982.

4960   Ruvinskii, L. "Iudeiskie klerikaly i sionizm" [Judaic Clericals and Zionism]. *Znamia kommunizma* Odessa. Sep. 2, 1982.

  *   Balagushkin, E.G. *Kritika sovremennykh netraditsionnykh religii* [Criticism of Contemporary Nontraditional Religions]. Cited above as item 607.

4961   Vinokur, A. "Vo imia istiny" [In the Name of Truth]. *Dal'nyi Vostok* 2 (1987): 155-158.

  *   Barmenkov, A.I. *Svoboda sovesti v SSSR* [Freedom of Worship in USSR]. Cited above as item 635.

4962   Kalinin, V. "V storone ot real'nosti" [Aside of Reality]. *Novyi mir* 7 (1988): 257-259.

  *   Barzdaitis, I.I. *Obshchestvennaia rol' religii* [Social Role of Religion]. Cited above as item 639.

4963   Deksnis, B. "Znachitel'nyi etap razvitiia ateizma v Litve" [Important Stage of Development of Atheism in Lithuania]. *Kommunist.* Vil'nius. 1 (1981): 87-90.

  *   Barzdaitis, I.I. *Traditsii ateizma v Litve* [Tradition of Atheism in Lithuania]. Cited above as item 640. For review see item 4963.

  *   Basilov, V.N. *Izbranniki dukhov* [Chosen by Spirits]. Cited above as item 644.

4964   Alekseev, V.P. // *Vopr. istorii* 4 (1986): 115-116.

4965   Demidov, S. "Pod grokhot bubna" [Under Tambourine's Crash]. *Znamia Okriabria* May 22, 1985.

4966   Demidov, S. // *Turkm. iskra* June 22, 1985.

4967   Vainshtein, S.I. // *Izv. Sib. otd-niia AN SSSR* 1986. No 14. Ser. istorii, filologii i filosofii. Vyp. 3. Pp. 67-68.

4968   Vinokur, A. "U istokov religii" [By the Sources of Religion]. *Dal'nyi Vostok* 5 (1986): 154-157.

* Begun, V.Ia. *Rasskazy o 'detiakh vdovy'* [Tales about "Widow's Children"]. Cited above as item 662.

4969 Pashneva, E. "V teni masonskikh lozh" [In the Shadow of Masonic Lodges]. *Zhurnalist* 11 (1984): 35.

* Beliaev, V.P. *Ia obviniaiu!* [I Accuse!]. Cited above as item 674.

4970 Chubar, B. "Galan prodolzhaet bor'bu" [Galan Continues to Struggle]. *V mire kinig* 1 (1981): 64-65.

4971 Eremin, D. "Vo imia spravedlovosti i schast'ia" [In the Name of Justice and Happiness]. *Znamia* 9 (1980): 249-250.

* Belov, A.V. *Klerikal'nyi antikommunizm* [Clerical Anti-Communism]. Cited above as item 690.

4972 Maiat, E.E. // *Filos. nauki* 2 (1988): 121-124.

* Belov, A.V. *Ne delai sebe kumira* [Don't Make an Idol for Yourself]. Cited above as item 692.

4973 Alekseev, A. // *Molodoi kommunist* 5 (1986): 95-97.

4974 Popov, A. // *Polit. samoobrazovanie* 12 (1985): 131-133.

* Belov, A.V. *Sviatye bez nimbov* [Saints Without Nimbuses]. Cited above as item 697.

4975 Vladimirov, V. "Sviattsy pod mikroskopom" [Church Calendar under Microscope]. *V mire knig* 3 (1984): 82-83.

* Berezkin, Iu.E. *Golos diavola sredi snegov i dzhunglei* [Devil's Voice Amidst Snow and Jungles]. Cited above as item 707.

4976 Lobach, V. "'Golos diavola' i 'Golubaia busina'" ["Devil's Voice" and "Blue Bead"]. *Andizh. pravda* June 24, 1988.

* Bois, M. *Zaroastriitsy* [Zoroastrians]. Cited above as item 759.

4977 Khlopin, I.N. // *Izv. AN TSSR.* Ser. Obshchestv. nauk 1 (1989): 84-87.

* Bolotin, I.S. *Tupiki klerikal'nogo natsionalizma* [Impasses of Clerical Nationalism]. Cited above as item 768.

4978 Sherdakov, V.N. // *Nauch. kommunizm* 7 (1989): 125-127.

4979 Tavadov, G.T. "Religiia i natsionalizm" [Religion and Nationalism]. *Vest. Mosk. un-ta.* Ser. 12. Teoriia nauch. kommunizma 1 (1989): 86-87.

* Bongard-Levin, G.M. *Drevneindiiskaia tsivilizatsiia* [Ancient Indian Civilization]. Cited above as item 781.

5980 Vasil'kov, Ia.V.; Neveleva, S.L.; Rudoi, V.I. // *Narody Azii i Afriki* 1 (1981): 203-208.

5981 Vigasin, A.A. // *Vest. drev. istorii* 4 (1981): 153-155.

* Boriskin, V.M. *Ateizm i tvorchestvo* [Atheism and Creative Work]. Cited above as item 786.

4982 Iasterbov, I. // *Sov. Mordoviia* Feb. 25, 1987.

* Borisov, N.[S]. *Russkaia tserkov' v politicheskoi bor'be XIV-XV vv.* [Russian Church in Political Struggle in XIVth-XVth Centuries.]. Cited above as item 789.

4983 Borisov, N.S.; Khoroshev, A.S. "Po povodu odnoi retsenzii" [On the Occasion of a Review]. *Vopr. istorii* 10(1989): 153-158.

4984 Kuchkin, V.A.; Floria, B.N. "O profesional'nom urovne knig po istorii russkoi tserkvi" [Professional Level of Books on the History of Russian Church]. *Vopr. istorii* 11 (1988): 144-156.

* Brazhnik, I.I. *Pravo. Religiia. Ateizm* [Law. Religion. Atheism]. Cited above as item 813.

4985 Pollyeva, D.R. // *Izv. vuzov.* Pravovedenie 2 (1985): 85-87.

4986 Zadoroznik, I.E. // *Sov. gosuarstvo i pravo* 2 (1986): 138-141.

* *Buddizm, gosudarstvo i obshchestvo v stranakh Tsentral'noi i Vostochnoi Azii v srednie veka* [Buddhism, State and Society in Central and Eastern Asian Countries in the Middle Ages]. Cited above as item 836.

4987 Maliavin, V.V. // *Narody Azii i Afriki* 5 (1985): 193-199.

* *Buddizm i srednevekovaia kul'tura narodov Tsentral'noi Azii* [Buddhism and Medieval Culture of Peoples of Central Asia]. Cited above as item 839.

4988 Kuznetsov, V.S. // *Izv. Sib. otd-niia AN SSSR* 1984. No 14. Ser. istorii, filologii i filosifii. Vyp. 3. Pp. 71-73.

4989 Serrebriany, S.D. // *Narody Azii i Afriki* 5 (1981): 220-228.

* *Buddizm i traditsdionnye verovania narodov Tsentral'noi Azii* [Buddhism and Traditional Beliefs of Peoples of Central Asia]. Cited above as item 840. For review see item 4988.

* Budov, A.I. *Religioznye illiuzii na poroge zhizni* [Religious Illusions at Life's Threshold]. Cited above as item 844.

4990 Kuprianova, T. // *Nar. obrazovanie* 12 (1980): 92-93.

4991 Ponomareva, F. "Formiruia lichnost'" [Shaping a Personality]. *Mosk. komsomolets* March 31, 1981.

* Chibirov, L.A. *Drevneishie plasty dukhovnoi kul'tury osetin* [Ancient Layers of Osetins Spiritual Culture]. Cited above as item 926.

4992 Basilov, V.N. // *Sov. etnografiia* 5 (1986): 166-167.

4993 Vinogradov, V.B.; Baranichenko, N.N. // *Izv. Sev.-Kavk. nauch. tsentra Vyssh. shk.* Obshchestv. nauki 3 (1985): 99-100.

* Chukhina, L.A. *Chelovek i ego tsennostnyi mir v religioznoi filosofii* [Man and His Valuable Universe in Religious Philosophy]. Cited above as item 941.

4994 Kuz'mina, T.A. // *Vopr. filosofii* 3 (1983): 160-163.

4995 Markov, V. "Kritika religiozno-filosofskikh uchenii o cheloveke" [Criticism of Religious-Philosophical Teachings about Man]. *Izv. AN LatSSR* 3 (1981): 150-153.

4996 Vilnite, O. "Kritika predstavlenii o cheloveke v religioznoi filosofii" [Criticism of the Conception of Man in Religious Philosophy]. *Kommunist. Sov. Latvii* 5 (1981): 101-104.

*   *D.I. Pisarev ob ateizme, religii i tserkvi* [D.I. Pisarev on Atheism, Religion and Church]. Cited above as item 954.

4997   Kozhurin, Ia.Ia.; Goshevskii, V.O. "Novaia knniga o vydaiushchemsia russkom ateiste" [New Book on a Prominent Russian Atheist]. *Religii mira.* 1986. M., 1987. Pp. 366-369.

*   Demianov, A.I. *Religioznost' [Religiosity].* Cited above as item 997.

4998   Bogatov, V.V.; Tonkikh, A.S. // *Vestn. Mosk. un-ta.* Ser. 7, filosofiia 2 (1986): 87-3rd of the cover.

*   Dobren'kov, V.I. *Sovremennyi protestantskii teologicheskii modernizm v SShA* [Contemporary Protestant Theological Modernism in USA]. Cited above as item 1044.

4999   Kilunov, A.F. // *SShA. Ekonomika, politika, ideologiia* 3 (1982): 126-127.

5000   Mchedlov, M.P. // *Vopr. filosofii* 9 (1981): 176-179.

5001   Ugrinovich, D.M. // *Nauch. dokl. vyssh. shk.* Filos. nauki 1 (1982): 182-184.

*   Dobruskim, M.E. *Religiia i ateizm v evropeiskikh sotsialisticheskikh stranakh* [Religion and Atheism in European Socialist Countries]. Cited above as item 1047.

5002   Antonenko, V.G. // *Nauch. kommunizm* 3 (1988): 123-125.

*   Doroshenko, E.A. *Shiitskoe dukhovenstvo v sovremennom Irane* [Shiites Clergy in Contemporary Iran]. Cites above as item 1068.

5003   Ionova, A.; Luk'ianov, A. "Dukhovenstvo v strukture iranskogo obshchestva" [Clergy in the Structure of Iranian Society]. *Aziia i Afrika segodnia* 9 (1986): 64.

5004   Plastun, V.N. // *Narody Azii i Afriki* 4 (1986): 185-189.

*   *Drevnie obriady, verovaniia i kul'ty narodov Srednei Azii* [Ancient Rites, Beliefs and Cults of Middle Asia Peoples]. Cited above as item 1076.

5005   Berdyev, M.S. // *Izv. AN TSSR.* Ser. Obshchestv. nauk 6 (1989): 88-90.

* Dzhabbarov, I. *Ot nevezhestva k massovomu ateizmu* [From Ignorance to Mass Atheism]. Cited above as item 1116.

5006 Ismailov, B.; Egamberdiev, N. "Na puti k massovomu ateizmu" [On the Way to Mass Atheism]. *Kommunist Uzbekistana* 10 (1986): 94-96.

* Dzhabbarov, I.M. *Bogi, sviatye i liudi* [Gods, Saints and People]. Cited above as item 1117.
For review see item 5006.

* Dzhabbarov, I.M. *Dukhovnyi mir* [Spiritual World]. Cited above as item 1118.

5007 Khairullaev, M.; Aripov, M. "Protivorechiia i bogatstvo dukhovnogo mira cheloveka" [Contradictions and Wealth of Man's Spiritual World]. *Kommunist Uzbekistana* 7 (19890; 91-93.

* Eingorn, I.D. *Ocherki istorii religii i ateizma v Sibiri* [Studies of History of Religion and Atheism in Siberia]. Cited above as item 1156.

5008 Moskovskii, A.S.; Moskalenko, A.T. // *Izv. Sib. otd-niia AN SSSR* 1983. No 6. Ser. Obshchestv. nauk. Vyp. 2. P. 142.

5009 Sedov, K.I. // *Vopr. istorii* 10 (1985): 138-139.

* Eliade, M. *Kosmos i istoriia* [Cosmos and History]. Cited above as item 1164.

5010 Karasev, L.V. "Nado li boiat'sia istorii?" [Is it Necessary to Fear History?]. *Filos. nauki* 10 (1989): 120-125.

* Emeliakh, L.I. *'Zagadki' khristianskogo kul'ta* ["Mysteries" of Christian Religion]. Cited above as item 1178.

5011 Zazorina, T. "Rasseivaia kadil'nyi chad" [Scattering Censer's Fumes]. *Smena* Oct. 5, 1985.

* Ershov, V.P. *Rodniki poznaniia* [Springs of Knowledge]. Cited above as item 1225.

5012 Tsyganov, N.V. "Tsennyi opyt ateisticheskogo vospitaniia" [Valuable Experience of Atheistic Education]. *Vech. sred. shkola* 2 (1982): 79-80.

5013 Vlas'ev, G. "Ateizm i kraevedenie" [Atheism and Study of Local Lore, History and Economy]. *Leninskaia pravda* June 25, 1981.

   * Evsiukov, V.V. *Mifologiia kitaskogo neolita* [Mythology of China's Neolithic Age]. Cited above as item 1239.

5014 Antonova, E.V.; Sagalaev, A.M.; Kriukov, M.V. // *Narody Azii i Afriki* 6 (1989): 176-185.

   * Fedosik, V.A. *Tserkov' i gosudarstvo* [The Church and the State]. Cited above as item 1257.

5015 Min'ko, L. "U istokov odnogo al'iansa" [By the Sources of one Alliance]. *Kommunist Belorussii* 2 (1980): 92-93.

   * Filimonov, E.G. *Khristianskoe sektantstvo i problemy ateisticheskoi raboty* [Christian Sectarianism and the Problems of Atheistic Work]. Cited above as item 1279.

5016 Iarotski, P. "Kharakter krizisa khristianskogo sektantstva" [Character of the Crisis of Christian Sectarianism]. *Pravda Ukrainy* Jan. 9, 1982.

   * Filist, G.M. *Vvedenie khristianstva na Rusi* [Introduction of Christianity into Rus']. Cited above as item 1301.

5017 Gorbatskii, A. "Rus', mechem kreshchennaia" [Rus' by Sword Baptized]. *Zaria* Feb. 15, 1989.

5018 Korzun, M. "Drevniaia Rus': ot faktov - k predstavleniiam" [Ancient Rus': From Facts - to Imaginations]. *Kommunist Belorussii* 2 (1989): 91-92.

   * *Filosofiia. Religiia. Kul'tura* [Philosophy. Religion. Culture]. Cited above as item 1307.

5019 Kocharli, F. "Religiozno-filosofskie elementy v burzhuaznom mirovozzrenii" [Religious-Philosophical Elements in Bourgeois World Outlook]. *Kommunist Azerbaidzhana* 8 (1983): 99-101.

5020 Mitrokhin, L.N. // *Vopr. filosofii* 6 (1984): 163-166.

   * *Filosofiia i religiia na Zarubezhnom Vostoke* [Philosophy and Religion in Foreign Orient]. Cited above as item 1308.

5021   Agadzhanian, A.S. // *Narody Azii i Afriki* 4 (1986): 174-181.

5022   Panfilova, T.B. // *Vopr. filosofii* 9 (1986): 165-167.

*   *Filosofskie kontseptsii katolitsizma* [Philosophical Conceptions of Catholicism]. Cited above as item 1310.

5023   Shlegeris, A. "Ne tol'ko vshir, no i vglub'" [Not Only in Width, but in Depth as Well]. *Komunist.* Vil'nius. 12 (1987): 96-99.

*   *Filosofskie voprosy buddizma* [Philosophical Problems of Buddhism]. Cited above as item 1313.

5024   Cherevko, K. "Buddizm kak filosofskaia sistema" [Buddhism as Philosophical System]. *Aziia i Afrika Segodnia* 3 (1986): 64.

5025   Safronova, E.S. // *Narody Azii i Afriki* 3 (1986): 197-198.

*   Franko, I.Ia. *O Vatikane, unii i katolitsizme* [On Vatican, Uniate Church and Catholicism]. Cited above as item 5840.

5026   Slivka, Iu. "Kameniar protiv uniatstva" [Kameniar Against the Uniate Church]. *Pravda Ukrainy* July 14, 1982.

*   Frezer, D.D. *Zolotaia vetv'* [The Golden Bough]. Cited above as item 1351.

5027   Alekseev, V.P. // *Narody Azii i Afriki* 6 (1981): 219-221.

5028   Arutiunov, S.A. "K novomu izdaniiu 'Zolotoi vetvi'" [New Edition of "The Golden Bough"]; Kryvelev, I.A. "Ob istoriko-religioznykh vzgliadakh Dzh. Frezera" [J. Frazer's Historic-Religious Views]. *Sov. Etnografiia* 2 (1982): 139-147.

5029   Evsiukov, V.V. // *Izv. Sib. otd-niia AN SSSR* 1983. No 6. Ser. Obshcheastv. nauk. Vyp. 2. Pp. 147-149.

5030   Grigulevich, I. "U istokov religii" [By the Sources of Religion]. *Kommunist* 10 (1981): 126-127.

5031   Ugrinovich, D. "Magiia i religiia" [Magic and Religion]. *V mire knig* 7 (1981): 71-72.

* Furman, D.E. *Religiia i sotsial'nye konflikty v SShA* [Religion and Social Conflicts in USA]. Cited above as item 1357.

5032 Pankin, A. // *Novyi mir* 1 (1982): 266-267.

5033 Samkova, E.D. // *Sotsial. issled.* 2 (1982): 231-232.

5034 Voina, A.V. // *SShA. Ekonomika, politika, ideologiia* 10 (1981): 100.

5035 Zadorozhniuk, I.E. // *Vopr. filosofii* 3 (1982): 160-161.

* Furman, D.E. et al. *Religiia v politicheskoi zhizni SShA* [Religion in the Political Life of USA]. Cited above as item 1359.

5036 Borisiuk, V.I. "Tserkov' i politika" [The Church and Politics]. *SShA. Ekonomika, politika, ideologiia* 8 (1986): 108-109.

5037 Pankin, A. // *Novyi mir* 3 (1987): 271.

5038 Salmin, A.M. // *Sotsial. issled.* 2 (1986): 211-214.

5039 Zhilina, E.V. // *Vopr. filosofii* 12 (1986): 155-156.

* Gaidis, A.A. *Katolicheskii klerikal'nyi antikommunizm* [Catholic Clerical Anti-Communism]. Cited above as item 1387.

5040 Deksnis, B. "Klerikalnyi antikommunizm: pretenzii i deistvitel'nost'" [Clerical Anti-Communism: Claims and Reality]. *Komunist.* Vil'nius. 9 (1983): 85-88.

* Gapochka, M.P. *Materializm protiv fideizma* [Materialism against Fideism]. Cited above as item 5842.

5041 Babosov, E.M. // *Vopr. filosofii* 9 (1981): 174-176.

5042 Ezrin, G.I. // *Nauch. dokl. vyssh. shkoly filos. nauki* 6 (1981): 170-172.

5043 Grekov, L.I. // *Vopr. istorii estestvoznaniia i tekhniki* 1981. Vyp. 4. Pp. 138-139.

5044 Novik, I.B. "Issledovanie filosofskikh osnov ateizma" [Research of Philosophical Bases of Atheism]. *Vestn. Mosk. un-ta.* Ser. 7. Filosofiia 4 (1982): 94-96.

* Gerasimchuk, A.A. *Chelovek i priroda* [Man and Nature]. Cited above as item 1458.

5045 Girusov, E.V.; Starostin, V.I. // *Nauch. dokl. vyssh. shkoly filos. nauki* 3 (1982): 189.

* Glagolev, V.S. *Religiozno-idealisticheskaia kul'turologia* [Religious-Idealistical Culturology]. Cited above as item 5843.

5046 Kuprin, B.A. // *Vopr. filosofii* 1 (1987): 164-166.

5047 Velikovich, L.N. // *Nauch. dokl. vyssh. shk. Filos. nauki* 3 (1986): 175-177.

* Gordienko, N.S. *Ateizm i religiia v sovremennoi bor'be idei* [Atheism and Religion in Contemporary Struggle of Ideas]. Cited above as item 1525.

5048 Anan'eva, E. "Stavka na religiiu" [Count on Religion]. *Rud. Altai* Apr. 5, 1985.

5049 Chernysheva, N.A. // *Nauch. dokl. vyssh. shk. Filos. nauki* 4 (1984): 187-188.

5050 Popov, A.; Trofimov, Z. "Ateizm i religiia v sovremennom mire" [Atheism and Religion in Contemporary World]. *Polit. samoobrazovanie* 4 (1984): 139-143.

* Gordienko, N.S. *'Kreshchenie Rusi'* [Baptism of Rus']. Cited above as item 1531.

5051 Strel'nik, N. // *Penz. pravda* May 15, 1986.

5052 Vinokur, A. "Fakty protiv mifov" [Facts against Myths]. *Tikhookean. zvezda* Dec 11, 1984.

* Gordienko, N.S. *Osnovy nauchnogo ateizma* [Foundations of Scientific Atheism]. Cited above as item 1534.

5053 Meerovskii, B.V. // *Vopr. flosofii* 11 (1989): 171-174.

* Gordienko, N.S. *Sovremennoe russkoe pravoslavie* [Contemporary Russian Orthodoxy]. Cited above as item 1538.

5054 Shaposhnikov, L.E. // *Filos. nauki* 10 (1988): 126-127.

5055 Zhirovov, B. "Sopostavliaia s proshlym" [Confronting with the Past]. *Pravda* Dec 7, 1987.

* Grekova, T.I. *Bolezn' i smert' - zlo ili blago?* [Illness and Death - Evil or Blessing?]. Cited above as item 1571.

5056 Iag'ia, N.S.; Ruzin, R.P. // *Zdravokhranenie Ros. federatsii 6 (1985): 47.*

* *Grigulevich, I.R. Inkvizitsiia* [Inquisition]. Cited above as item 1587.

5057 Klibanov, A. "Tsennye trudy po istorii katlicheskoi tserkvi" [Valuable Works on the History of Catholic Church]. *Obshchestv. nauki* 4 (1984): 221-224.

* Grigulevich, I.R. *Proroki 'novoi istiny'* [Prophets of "The New Truth"]. Cited above as item 1593.

5058 Kryvelev, I.A. // *Sov. etnografiia* 1 (1986): 140-142.

* Grigulevich, I.R. *Tserkov' i oligarkhiia v Latinskoi Amerike* [The Church and Oligarchy in Latin America]. Cited above as item 1595.

5059 Andronova, V.P. // *Latin Amerika* 9 (1982): 138-140.

5060 Vinogradov, V.m.; Torshin, M.P. // *Novaia i noveishaia istoriia* 6 (1982): 185-187.

* Gubman, B.L. *Sovremennaia katolicheskaia filosofiia* [Contemporary Catholic Philosophy]. Cited above as item 1616.

5061 Porok, A.A. // *Filos. nauki* 1 (1989): 141-142.

* *Gumanizm i religiia* [Humanism and Religion]. Cited above as item 1630.

5062 Danilova, M.M.; Tazhurazina, Z.A. // *Nauch. dokl. vyssh. shkoly Filos. nauki* 4 (1982): 172-174 |

* Gurevich, P.S. *Vozrozhden li mistitsizm?* [Is Mysticism Revived?]. Cited above as item 1652.

5063 Vinokur, A. "Vo imia istiny" [In the Name of Truth]. *Dal'nyi Vostok* 2 (1987): 155-158.

* Gurov, Iu.S. *Ot bezrazlichiia - k ubezhdennosti* [From Indifference - To Conviction]. Cited above as item 1658.

5064 Pavlova, T. "Problemy ateisticheskogo vospitaniia molodezhi" [Problems of Youth's Atheistic Upbringing]. *Nar. obrazovanie* 2 (1984): 92.

* *Ia ateist* [I am an Atheist]. Cited above as item 1675.

5065 Leonov, A. "Ateisty po ubezhdeniiu" [Atheists by Conviction]. *Pravda* Nov. 10, 1980.

5066 Popov, L. // *Polit. samoobrazovanie* 6 (1981): 124-125.

* Iablokov, I.N. *Religiia* [Religion]. Cited above as item 1677.

5067 Rakhimov, O. "Na osnove nauchnogo ateizma" [On the Basis of Scientific Atheism]. *Krasnaia zvezda* Apr. 20, 1982.

* Iakas, P. *Chego katolichestvo ne dalo Litve?* [What Did Catholicism Not Give Lithuania?]. Cited above as item 1680.

5068 Sakalauskas, I. // *Litva lit.* 1 (1987): 181.

* Ignatovich, A.N. *Buddizm v Iaponii* [Buddhism in Japan]. Cited above as item 1763.

5069 Goregliad, V.N.; Torchinov, E.A. // *Narody Azii i Afriki* 5 (1988): 201-203.

* Ionova, A.I. *Islam v Iugo-Vostochnoi Azii* [Islam in South-Eastern Asia]. Cited above as item 1784.

5070 Efimova, L. "Ideinaia evoliutsiia islama" [Islam's Ideological Evolution]. *Aziia i Afrika segodnia* 7 (1982): 60.

5071 Stepaniants, M.T. // *Narody Azii i Afriki* 2 (1982): 173-176.

* Ippolitova, V.A. *Pole deiatel'nosti ateista* [Atheists' Sphere of Action]. Cited above as item 5845.

5072 Vasil'ev, A. "Chitaia knigi ob opyte ateisticheskogo vospitaniia..." [Reading Books about the Experience of Atheistic Education...]. *Polit. samoobrazovanie* 7 (1985): 138-142.

* *Iskusstvo i religiia v istorii filosofii* [Art and Religion in the History of Philosophy]. Cited above as item 1806.

5073 Babii, A.I.; Karaeva, L.K. // *Izv. AN SSSR*. Ser. obshchestv. nauk 3 (1982): 78-79.

5074 Emel'ianov, B. et al. "Iskusstvo i religiia: istoriko-filosofskii aspekt" [Art and Religion: Historic-Philosophical Aspect]. *Kommunist Moldavii* 1 (1983): 95-96.

* *Islam* [Islam]. Cited above as item 1807.

5075 Pochta, Iu.M. // *Narody Azii i Afriki* 4 (1987): 173-180.

* *Islam v istorii narodov Vostoka* [Islam in the History of Peoples of Orient]. Cited above as item 1816.

5076 Malashenko, A.V. // *Narody Azii i Afriki* 3 (1982): 166-171.

* *Islam v politicheskoi zhizni stran sovremennogo Blizhnego i Srednego Vostoka* [Islam in Political Life of Contemporary Near and Middle Eastern Countries]. Cited above as item 1817.

5077 Manucharian, A. "Aktivizatsiia islama na Blizhnem i Srednem Vostoke" [Islam's Activization in Near and Middle East]. *Po lenin. puti* Erevan, 6 (1987): 93-96.

* *Islam v sovremennoi politike stran Vostoka* [Islam in Contemporary Politics of Countries of the Orient]. Cited above as item 1819.

5078 Roshchin, M. "Islam i politika" [Islam and Politics]. *Aziia i Afrika segodnia* 6 (1987): 62.

* *Islam v SSSR* [Islam in the USSR]. Cited above as item 1820.

5079 Smirnov, Iu. "Sovremennyi islam i praktika nauchnogo ateizma" [Contemporary Islam and the Practice of Scientific Atheism]. *Pamir* 6 (1984): 121-125.

* *Istoriia i teoriia ateizma* [History and Theory of Atheism]. Cited above as item 1832.

5080 Gabinskii, G.A. // *Nauch. dokl. vyssh. shk. Filos. nauki* 2 (1983): 170-174.

* Iulina, N.S. *Teologiia i filosofiia v religioznoi mysli SShA XX veka* [Theology and Philosophy in Religious Thought of USA in the XXth Century]. Cited above as item 1840.

5081 Zadorozhniuk, I.E. // *Filos. nauki* 6 (1987): 117-120.

* Ivakin, A.A. *Chto takoe schast'e* [What Happiness Is]. Cited above as item 1854.

5082 Chakenov, B. "O neveroiatnoi interpretatsii avtorskoi idei" [An Unbelievable Interpretation of Author's Idea]. *Prostor* 3 (1987): 181-183.

* *Kak byla kreshchena Rus'* [How Rus' was Baptized]. Cited above as item 1905.

5083 "Novaia kniga Politizdata" [Politizdat's New Book]. *Tuvin. pravda* Sep. 16, 1988.

* Kapustin, N.S. *Osobennosti evoliutsii religii* [Peculiarities of Religion's Evolution]. Cited above as item 1955.

5084 Knyshenko, Iu.B. // *Izv. Sev.-Kavk. nauch. tsentra vyssh. shk. Obshchestv. nauki* 4 (1985): 99-100.

5085 Shevchenko, M.D. // *Vopr. filosofii* 7 (1985): 166-167.

* *Karmannyi slovar' ateista* [Atheist's Pocket Dictionary] Cited above as item 57. (5th. ed.)

5086 Mukhtarov, G. // *Sov. Nakhichevan'* Jan. 7, 1986.

* Karpov, N.B. *Ateisticheskie i antiklerikal'nye idei v tvorchestve G.I. Uspenskogo* [Atheistic and Anticlerical Ideas in G.I. Uspenskii's Works]. Cited above as item 1975.

5087 Shal'nev, B. "Pravda neravnodushnogo slova" [Truth of Not Indifferent Word]. *Leninskoe znamia* Lipetsk, Jan. 9, 1983.

* *Katolitsizm i svobodomyslie v Latinskoi Amerike v XVI-XX vv.* [Catholicism and Free Thinking in Latin America in XVIth-XXth Centuries]. Cited above as item 1997.

5088 Ianchuk, I.I. // *Novaia i noveishaia istoriia* 6 (1981): 180-182.

* *Katolitsizm v Belorussii* [Catholicism in Belorussia]. Cited above as item 1998.

5089 Martirosov, G. "Katolitsizm bez maski" [Catholicism without Mask]. *Kommunist Belorussii* 1 (1988): 93-95.

5090 Popov, B. "Posobie, kotorogo zhdesh'" [Textbook, which one is Waiting For]. *Grodn. pravda* April 24, 1987.

* Keiper, F.B.Ia. *Trudy po vediiskoi mifologii* [Works on Vedas Mythology]. Cited above as item 2010.

5091 Shokhin, V.K. // *Narody Azii i Afriki* 3 (1987): 187-193.

* Kenin-Lopsan, M.B. *Obriadovaia praktika i fol'klor tuvinskogo shamanstva* [Ceremonial Practice and Folklore of Tuva's Shamanism]. Cited above as item 2012.

5092 Moldavskii, D. "Dobaviv eshche odin istochnik" [Adding Yet Another Source]. *Vopr. lit.* 12 (1987): 210-213.

* Khachaturov, K.A. *'Eretiki' i inkvizitory* ["Heretics" and Inquisitors]. Cited above as item 2024.

5093 Gvozdev, Iu. *Teologiia osvobozhdeniia* [Theology of Liberation]. *Kn. obozrenie* Aug. 12, 1988. (No 33). P. 14.

5094 Markushin, V. // *Krasnaia zvezda* Aug. 5, 1988.

5095 Popov, A.S. // *Latin. Amerika* 1 (1989): 132-134.

* Khazratkulov, M. *Doislamskie verovaniia* [Pre-Islamic Beliefs]. Cited above as item 2057.

5096 Iusupov, Sh. "Vzgliad na sotsial'no-filosofskuiu literaturu" [A Glance at Socio-Philosophical Literature]. *Kommunist Tadzhikistana* 12 (1988): 86-88.

* *Khrestomatiia po istorii ateizma Litvy* [Reader on the History of Atheism of Lithuania]. Cited above as item 2072.

5097 Michiulis, I. "A my podumali..." [But we Thought...]. *Kommunist.* Vil'nius. 12 (1989): 94-97.

* *Khristianstvo i ego sotsial'naia funktsiia v Litve* [Christianity and Its Social Function in Lithuania]. Cited above as item 2073.

5098 Machianskas, F. "Khristianstvo i obshchestvennoe razvitie" [Christianity and Social Development]. *Kommunist.* Vil'nius.11 (1986): 100-104.

5099 Zaksas, I. // *Sov. Litva* May 12, 1987.

* *Khristianstvo i lamaizm u korennogo naseleniia Sibirii* [Christianity and Lamaism of Siberia's Native Population]. Cited above as item 5844.

5100 Mongush, Z. "Novye knigi o Tuve" [New Books on Tuva]. *Tuvin. pravda* July 31, 1983.

* *Khudozhestvennaia i publitsisticheskaia-biblioteka ateista* [Atheist's Libary of Belles-Lettres and Socio-Political Journalism]. Cited above as item 5845.

5101 Nikonenko, S. "'Na pochve iskusstva'" ["On Art's Ground"]. *V mire knig* 11 (1985): 76-77.

5102 Osipov, A. "Tsel' zhizni - zhizn'" [Life's Aim - is Life]. *Uchit. gazeta* Apr. 13, 1985.

* Kichanova, I.M. *Svetit putevodnaia zvezda* [Guiding Star Shines]. Cited above as item 2099.

5103 Anisimov, S.F. // *Filos. nauki* 10 (1989): 142.

* Kimelev, Iu.A.; Poliakova, N.L. *Nauka i religiia* [Science and Religion]. Cited above as item 2106.

5104   Matveev, V.I. // *Filos. i sotsiol. mysl'* 1 (1989): 121-122.

* Kirabaev, N.S. *Sotsial'naia filosofiia musul'manskogo Vostoka* [Social Philosophy of the Moslem Orient]. Cited above as item 2109.

5105   Kapustin, B.G. // *Vopr. filosofii* 12 (1988): 162-164.

* Kirinenko, M.G. *Svoboda sovesti v SSSR* [Freedom of Conscience in USSR]. Cited above as item 2118.

5106   Rudinskii, F.M. // *Sov. gosudarstvo i pravo* 8 (1987): 145-147.

* Klimovich, L.I. *Kniga o Korane, ego proiskhozhdenii i mifologii* [Book about Koran, Its Origins and Mythologies]. Cited above as item 2149.

5107   Aleksandrov, E.; Krutikhin, M. "Pravda o glavnoi knige islama" [The Truth about Islam's most Important Book]. *Kommunist Vooruzh. Sil* 11 (1987): 91-92.

* Kobishchanov, Iu.M. *Istoriia rasprostraneniia islama v Afrike* [History of Dissemination of Islam in Africa]. Cited above as item 2169.

5108   Demin, P. // *Aziia i Afrika segodnia* 2 (1988): 64.

* Kolesnikova, A.P. *Oprokinutoe nebo* [Overturned Heaven]. Cited above as item 2198.

5109   Sternin, A. "Udacha ateista" [Atheist's Success]. *Kommuna* Sep. 5, 1987.

* Kolodnyi, A.N. *Ateisticheskoe ubezhdennost' lichnosti* [Atheistic Conviction of Individual]. Cited above as item 2200.

5110   Zots, V.A. // *Vopr. filosofii* 8 (1984): 169.

* Korzun, M.S. *Russkaia pravoslavnaia tserkkov' na sluzhbe ekspluatatorskikh klassov X v. - 1917 g.* [Russian Orthodox Church in the Service of Exploiter Classes, Xth C. - 1917]. Cited above as item 2277.

5111   Danilova, M.M. // *Religii mira, 1986* M., 1987. Pp. 272-277.

5112 Matsias, D.M. // *Vestn. Belorus. un-ta.* Ser. 3, Istoriia, filosofiia, nauch. kommunizm, ekonomika, pravo 3 (1988): 72-73.

* Kostenko, N.A. *Ateizm i nravstvennost'* [Atheism and Morals]. Cited above as item 2293.

5113 Prokof'ev, V.I. // *Sib. ogni* 7 (1983): 174-175.

5114 Rizhskii, M.I. // *Izv. Sib. otd-niia AN SSSR*, No 3, Ser. istorii, filologii i filosofii Vyp. 1. Pp. 70-72.

5115 Zots, V.A. // *Vopr. filosofii* 7 (1984): 166-167.

* Koval'skii, N.A. *Imperializm. Religiia. Tserkov'* [Imperialism. Religion. Church]. Cited above as item 2312.

5116 Istiagin, L. "Sila i slabost' politicheskogo klerikalizma" [Strength and Weakness of Political Clericalism]. *Mirovaia ekonomika i mezhdunar. otnosheniia* 6 (1987): 144-147.

5117 Krasikov, A. "Religiia i ugroza iadernoi katastrofy" [Religion and the Threat of Nuclear Catastrophe]. *Pravda* Feb. 26, 1987.

5118 Zemlianoi, S. // *Kommunist* 7 (1987): 124-125.

* Kozarzhevskii, A.Ch. *Istochnikovedcheskie problemy rannekhristianskoi literatury* [Problems of Study of Sources of Early Christian Literature]. Cited above as item 2324.

5119 Trofimova, M.K. // *Vestn. drev. istorii* 1 (1989): 215-216.

* Kozin, A.P. *Religioznye verovaniia v svete nauchnoi medetsiny* [Religious Beliefs in the Light of Scientific Medicine]. Cited above as item 2335.

5120 Buzhenko, T. "Ateizm v rakurse meditsiny" [Atheism in Foreshortened Medicine]. *Raduga* 10 (1984): 173-175.

* Krasnikov, N.P. *Pravoslavnaia etika* [Orthodox Ethics]. Cited above as item 2355.

5121 Popov, L. // *Polit. samoobrazovanie* 1 (1983): 142-144.

5122 Popov, L. "Tsennosti podlinnye i mnimye" [Genuine and Imaginary Values]. *Orl. pravda* Sep. 1, 1981.

* Krianev, Iu.V. *Khristianskii ekumenizm* [Christian Ecumenism]. Cited above as item 2380.

5123 Iarotskii, P.L. // *Vopr. filosofii* 10 (1980): 183-184.

* Kriuchkov, N.I.; Mikhailov, T.M. *Preodolenie religioznykh perezhitkov Buriatii* [Overcoming Religious Survivals of Buriat]. Cited above as item 2400.

5124 Safronova, E. "V pomoshch' ateistu" [Aid for Atheist]. *Pravda Buriatii* June 8, 1988.

* Kryvelev, I. *Khristos: mif ili deistvitel'nost'?* [Christ: Myth or Reality?]. Cited above as item 2418.

5125 Arkhangel'skii, A. "Iz proshlogo o vechnom" [From the Past about Eternal]. *Novyi mir* 12 (1988): 244-248.

5126 Nikonov, K.I.; Tazhurizina, Z.A. "Mif i deistvitel'nost': legendarnoe i istoricheskoe v obraze Iisusa Khrista" [Myth and Reality: Legendary and Historical in the Image of Jesus Christ]. *Vestn. Mosk. un-ta.* Ser. 7, Filosofiia 3 (1989): 85-87.

* Kryvelev, I.A. *Bibliia* [The Bible]. Cited above as item 2424.

5127 Vinokur, A. "Nauka protiv mifa" [Science against Myth]. *Birobidzh. zvezda* Aug. 31, 1982.

5128 Vinokur, A. "V svete analiza" [In the Light of Analysis]. *Dal'nyi Vostok* 10 (1982): 155-157.

* Kuchinskii, S.A. *Ateizm i nravstvennyi ideal* [Atheism and the Moral Ideal]. Cited above as item 2434.

5129 Danilov, G. // *Belgor. pravda* Oct. 14, 1982.

* Kuchinskii, S.A. *Chelovek moral'nyi* [Moral Person]. Cited above as item 2436.

5130 Ermakova, M.K. "O vzaimosviazi ateizma i nravstvennosti" [Correlation of Atheism and Morality]. *Vech. sred. shk.* 1 (1988): 72-74.

* Kuroedov, V.A. *Religiia i tserkov' v Sovetskom gosudarstve* [Religion and Church in Soviet State]. Cited above as item 2484.

5131 Antonova, O. "Na konstitutsionnoi osnove" [On Constitutional Basis]. *Sov. kul'tura* Feb. 9, 1982.

5132 Evgrafov, F. "Sovetskoe gosudarstvo i tserkov'" [Soviet State and the Church]. *Gorkov. pravda* Feb. 13, 1982.

5133 Fedorov, S. "Pravda protiv lzhi" [Truth against Lie]. *Leninskii put'* Samarkand. Dec. 15, 1981.

5134 Karpushin, V. "Gosudarstvo i tserkov'" [State and the Church]. *Pravda* Dec. 1, 1981.

5135 Klochkov, V. "Gosudarstvo i tserkov' v SSSR" [State and the Church in USSR]. *Komuunist* 4 (1982): 119-121.

5136 Neitman, M. "Pravdu ne skroesh'" [Truth can not be Hidden]. *Zabaikal. rabochii* Apr. 9, 1982.

5137 Svetlichnyi, I. "O religii i gosudarstve" [On religion and State]. *Aviatsiia i kosmonavtika* 2 (1982): II.

5138 Tumanova, K. "Dlia vas, popagandisty" [For You, Propagandists]. *Put' k kommunizmu* Jan. 14, 1982.

5139 Vinokur, A. "Svoboda sovesti" [Freedom of Conscience]. *Birobidzh. zvezda* Apr. 7, 1982.

* Kuvakin, V.A. *Religioznaia filosofiia v Rossii* [Religious Philosophy in Russia]. Cited aove as item 2500.

5140 Kostyleva, T.V.; Iakovleva, A.M.; Iakovlev, E.G. // *Nauch. dokl. vyssh. shkoly Filos. nauki* 1 (1982): 186-188.

5141 Maslin, M.A.; Fedorkin, N.S. "Issledovanie religioznoi filosofii v Rossii i sovremennost'" [Research of Religious Philosophy in Russia and Contemporaneity]. *Vestn. Mosk. un-ta.* Ser. 7, Filosofiia 3 (1981): 69-72.

5142   Semenkin, T.V.; Serbinenko, V.V. // *Vopr. filosofii* 1 (1982): 167-170.

   *   Kuz'min, A.G. *Padenie Peruna* [The Fall of Perun]. Cited above as item
       2505.

5143   Kozhinov, V. "Vzgliadyvaias' v russkuiu istoriiu" [Looking at Russian
       History]. *Kn. obozrenie* Apr. 13, 1990. (No 15), p. 5.

5144   Men'shikov, A. "Khristianstvo i my" [Christianity and We]. *Nar. obrazovanie*
       11 (1989): 166-167.

   *   Kuzmitskas, B.Iu. *Filosofskie kontseptsii katolicheskogo modernizma*
       [Philosophical Conceptions of Catholic Modernism]. Cited above as item
       2517.

5145   Genzelis, B.K. // *Vopr. filosofii* 11 (1983): 169-170.

   *   *Lamaizm v Buriatii* [Lamaism in Buriat]. Cited above as item 2538.

5146   Nesterenko, Iu. "Ideologiia ekspluatatorov" [Exploiter's Ideology]. *Zabaik.
       rabochii* Jan. 13, 1984.

   *   Lamont, K. *Illiuziia bessmertiia* [Illusion of Immortality]. Cited above as item
       2539.

5147   Bushkova, G. "Zhizn' interesna i bogata schast'em" [Life is Interesting and
       Rich with Happiness]. *Nauka i religiia* 8 (1985): 15-18.

   *   Lobovik, B.A. *Religioznoe soznanie i ego osobennosti* [Religious
       Consciousness and Its Peculiarities]. Cited above as item 2646.

5148   Dolia, V.E. "Problemy izucheniia religioznogo soznaniia" [Problems of Study
       Religious Consciousness]. *Kommunist Ukrainy* 2 (1988): 90-92.

   *   Machianskas, F.P. *Obshchestvennye vzgliady V. Kopsukasa* [Social Views of
       V. Kapsukas]. Cited above as item 2695.

5149   Ermalavichius, Iu. "Ego tvorcheskoe nasledie po prezhnemu aktual'na" [His
       Creative Legacy is Actual as Before]. *Kommunist. Vil'nius.* 1 (1980):
       103-104.

* Malysheva, D.B. *Religiia i obshchestvenno-politicheskoe razvitie arabskikh i afrikanskikh stran* [Religion and Socio-Political Development of Arab and African Countries]. Cited above as item 2770.

5150 Polonskaia, L. "Politizatsiia religii" [Politicization of Religion]. *Aziia i Afrika segodnia* 11 (1986): 156-157.

5151 Zviagel'skaia, I. // *Aziia i Afrika segodnia* 2 (1987): 64.

* Mamedov, A.M. *Islam i problemy sotsial'no-kul'turnogo razvitiia arabskikh stran* [Islam and Problems of Socio-Cultural Development of Arab Countries]. Cited above as item 2774.

5152 Malashenko, A. "Nauka, obshchestvo i islam" [Science, Society and Islam]. *Aziia i Afrika segodnia* 8 (1987): 63-64.

* Manuilova, D.E. *Tserkov' i veruiushchii* [Church and Believer]. Cited abve as item 2792.

5153 Tsyganov, N.V. "Ateisticheskie znaniia - uchiteliu" [Atheistic Knowledge - to Teacher]. *Vech. sred. shkola* 1 (1983): 75-76.

* Marash, Ia.N. *Politika Vatikana i katolicheskoi tserkvi v Zapadnoi Belorussii (1918-1939)* [The Policy of Vatican and Catholic Church in Western Belorussia (1918-1939)]. Cited above as item 2795.

5154 Zimak, Z. "Oblichaia katolitsizm" [Exposing Catholicism]. *Kommunist Belorussii* 10 (1984): 93-96.

* Marks Karl i dr. O religii *[On Religion]*. Cited above as item 2810.

5155 Machiulis, I. "Osnovopolozhniki nauchnogo kommunizma o religii i ateizme" [The Founders of Scientific Communism on Religion and Atheism]. *Kommunist. Vil'nius* 9 (1982): 74-77.

* Mchedlov, M.P. *Religiia i sovremennost'* [Religion and Contemporaneity]. Cited above as item 2863.

5156 Demin, A. // *Aviatsiia i kosmonavtika* 1 (1983): 27.

5157 Garadzha, V.I. // *Vopr. filosofii* 10 (1983): 159-161.

5158   Krianev, Iu. // *Pravda* Feb. 9, 1983.

5159   Niunka, V. // *Kommunist.* Vil'nius 7(1983): 87-92.

5160   Popov, A.; Trofimova, Z. "Ateizm i religiia v sovremennom mire" [Atheism and Religion in Contemporary World]. *Polit. samoobrazovanie* 4 (1984): 139-143.

5161   Radzhapov, V. "Religiia i sovremennost'" [Religion and Contemporaneity]. *Agitator* 17 (1983): 52.

5162   Tiurin, Iu.Ia. // *Sotsiol. issled.* 4 (1983): 191-192.

    *   Medvedko, L.I.; Germanovich, A.V. *Imenem Allakha...* [In the Name of Allah...]. Cited above as item 2874.

5163   Salem, S. "Trevogi musul'manskogo mira" [Alarms of the Moslem World]. *Probl. mira i sotsializma.* Praga. 8 (1989): 88-89.

    *   *Mify narodov mira* [Myths of Peoples of the World]. Cited above as item 81.

5164   Erofeev, V. "Kul'tura i predanie" [Culture and Tradition]. *Lit. obozrenie* 1 (1983): 65-70.

5165   Evsiukov, V.; Komissarov, S. "Sviazi vremeni" [Time Connections]. *Sib. ogni* 5 (1984): 157-163.

5166   Fedorenko, N. / *Lit. gazeta* May 20, 1981. p. 15.

5167   Fedorov, G. "V mire bogov i geroev" [In the World of Gods and Heroes]. *Novyi mir* 8 (1982): 262-265.

5168   Kabo, V.R. // *Sov. etnografiia* 6 (1981): 152-155.

5169   Leites, N. "Vse o mife" [All about Myth]. *Vopr. lit.* 4 (1982): 214-222.

5170   Mirimanov, V. "Universal'noe issledovanie mirovoi mifologii" [Universal Research of World's Mythology]. *Iskusstvo* 8 (1981): 69-70.

5171   Preobrazhenskii, V.S. // *Izv. AN SSSR. Ser.* geogr. 5 (1989): 133-134.

5172   Strokan', S. // *Bakin. rabochii* Feb. 2, 1983.

  *   Migovich, I.I. *Prestupnyi al'ians* [Criminal Alliance]. Cited above as item
      2942.

5173   Kolodnyi, A.N. "Antinarodnyi al'ians uniatstva i natsionalizma" [Antipopular
      Alliance of the Uniate Church and Nationalism]. *Raduga* 8 (1986):
      128-131.

5174   Timofeev, V.D.; Fomichenko, V.V. // *Vopr. filosofii* 1 (1986): 169-170.

  *   Mikhailov, T.M. *Iz istorii buriatskogo shamanizma* [History of Buriat's
      Shamanism]. Cited above as item 2943.

5175   Kocheshkov, N.V. // *Izv. Sib. otd-niia AN SSSR 1985.* No 9. Ser. Istorii,
      filologii i filosofii. Vyp. 2. Pp. 57-88.

  *   Mikhailova, L.V. *Katolicheskaia tserkov' i rabochii klass FRG* [Catholic
      Church and Worker's Class in FRG]. Cited above as item 2949.

5176   Vasin, V.G. "Klerikalizm protiv rabochego dvizheniia" [Clericalism against
      Workers Movement]. *Rabochii klass i sovrem. mir* 1 (1981): 178-180.

  *   Mitrokhin, L.N. *Religiia 'novogo veka'* [Religion of "The New Age"]. Cited
      bove as item 2994.

5177   Geevskii, I.A. "Bum kul'tov" [Boom of Cults]. *SShA. Ekonomika, politika,
      ideologiia* 3 (1987): 118.

5178   Vinokur, A. "Vo imia istiny" [In the Name of Truth]. *Dal'nyi Vostok* 2
      (1987): 155-158.

  *   *Molodezh', religiia, ateizm* [Youth, Religion, Atheism]. Cited above as item
      3012.

5179   Ozhigova, L.I.; Ozhigov, B.A. "Osnovy formirovaniia ateisticheskoi
      ubezhdennosti" [Foundations of Forming Atheistic Conviction]. *Vech. sred.
      shk.* 4 (1985): 79-80.

5180   Ozhigova, L.I.; Ozhigov, B.A. "V bor'be za ateisticheskie ubezhdeniia" [In
      the Struggle for Atheistic Convictions]. *Vech. sred. shk.* 4 (1987): 76-78.

5181   Tikhonov, M. "Vospityvat' ubezhdeniem" [Educating by Persuasion]. *V mire knig* 4 (1985): 86.

   *   Moroz, O.P. *Ot imeni nauki* [In the Name of Science]. Cited above as item 3024.

5182   // *Priroda* 3 (1980): 123.

5183   Ulybkin, I. "Ot imeni nauki" [In the Name of Science]. *Priuk. pravda* Oct. 29, 1989.

   *   Muslimov, S.Sh. *Ot svobodomysliia k nauchnomu ateizmu* [From Free Thinking to Scientific Atheism]. Cited above as item 3066.

5184   Gamzaev, Sh.G.; Khanbabaev, K.M. // *Izv. Sev.-Kavk. nauch. tsentra vyssh. shk. Obshchestv. nauki* 3 (1988): 110-112.

   *   *Musul'manskii mir* [Moslem World]. Cited above as item 3083.

5185   Kurkchi, A. "Vostok: iz srednevekov'ia v sovremennost'" [The Orient: From the Middle Ages to Contemporaneity]. *Novyi mir* 9 (1982): 262-265.

   *   *Mysli o religii* [Thoughts of Religion]. Cited above as item 3090.

5186   Veliev, Sh. "Novye knigi o religii i ateizme" [New Books on Religion and Atheism]. *Andzh. pravda* Feb. 2, 1989.

   *   *Nastol'naia kniga ateista* [Atheist's Handbook]. Cited above as item 3118.

5187   Neitman, M. "Poleznoe posobie po ateizmu" [Useful Aid on Atheism]. *Zabaik. rabochii* Aug 12, 1982.

   *   *Nauchnyi ateizm* [Scientific Atheism]. Cited above as item 3122.

5188   Meerovskii, B.V. // *Vopr. filosofii* 11 (1989): 171-174.

   *   Nikol'skii, N.M. *Istoriia Russkoi tserkvi* [History of the Russian Church]. Cited above as item 3187.

5189   Vinokur, A. "Sumerki bogov" [God's Twilight]. *Dal'nii Vostok* 9 (1984): 155-156.

* Nikonov, K.I *Sovremennaia khristianskaia antropologiia* [Contemporary Christian Anthropology]. Cited above as item 3190.

5190 Kuznetsova, I.D. // *Vopr. filosofii* 5 (1985): 168-170.

5191 Meerovskii, B.V. // *Nauch. dokl. vysh. shk. Filos. nauki* 2 (1985): 184-186.

5192 Tazhurizina, Z.A. "Ateisticheskaia kritika religioznogo ucheniia o cheloveke" [Atheistic Criticism of Religious Teaching about Man]. *Vestn. Mosk. un-ta.* Ser. 7. Filosofiia 5 (1984): 100-103.

* Novik, E.S. *Obriady i fol'klor v sibirskom shamanstve* [Rituals and Folklore in Siberian Shamanism]. Cited above as item 3207.

5193 Starstev, A.F. // *Izv. Sib. otd-niia AN SSSR.* Ser. istorii, filologii i filosofii. Novosibirsk, 1989. Vyp. 1. Pp. 75-76.

* *O religii i tserkvi* [On Religion and Church]. Cited above as item 178.

5194 Kalugin, Iu. "Nestareiushchee ideinoe oruzhie" [Non Aging Ideological Weapon]. *V mire knig* 5 (1982): 63.

* *O religii islama* [On Islamic Religion]. Cited above as item 84.

5195 Faseev, K. "Spravochnik-slovar' po islamu" [Reference Book on Islam]. *Kommunist Tatarii* 10 (1982): 92-95.

* *O svobode sovesti* [Freedom of Conscience]. Cited above as item 3236. For review see item 4962.

* *O vere i neverii* [Faith and Lack of Faith]. Cited above as item 3237.

5196 Pishchik, Iu. "Prometeev ogon' razuma" [Prometheus' Fire of Reason]. *Polit. samoobrazovanie* 10 (1983): 142-144.

* Okulov, A.F. *Leninskoe ateisticheskoe nasledie i sovremennost'* [Leninist Atheistic Heritage and Contemporaneity]. Cited above as item 182.

5197 Kosolapova, O.R. "Lenin i sovremennye problemy nauchnogo ateizma" [Lenin and Contemporary Problems of Scientific Atheism]. *Vestn. Mosk. un-ta.* Ser. 7. Filosofiia 1 (1988): 70-72.

5198 Krianev, Iu. "Ateizm i kul'tura" [Atheism and Culture]. *Pravda* June 19, 1987.

 * Okulov, A.F. *Sotsial'nyi progress i religiia* [Social Progress and Religion]. Cited above as item 3267.

5199 Iablokov, I.N. // *Vopr. filosofii* 3 (1984): 169.

5200 Krianev, Iu. "Religiia i sovremennost'" [Religion and Contemporaneity]. *Pravda* Feb. 9, 1983.

5201 Popov, A.; Trofimov, Z. "Ateizm i religiia v sovremennom mire" [Atheism and Religion in Contemporary World]. *Polit. samoobrazovanie* 4 (1984): 139-143.

 * *Organizatsiia i metodika ateisticheskogo vospitaniia* [Organization and Methodics of Atheistic Education]. Cited above as item 89.

5202 Figlevskii, M. "Uchityvaia vozrostnye sposobnosti" [Taking into Consideration Age Group Abilities]. *Doshk. vospitanie* 11 (1987): 89-90.

 * Osipov, A.A. *Otkrovennyi razgovor s veruiushchimi i neveruiushchimi* [Frank Talk with Believers and Unbelievers]. Cited above as item 3293.

5203 Kondrashev, G. "Tsennoe ateisticheskoe nasledie" [Valuable Atheistical Legacy]. *Zvezda* 11 (1983): 185-186.

 * Ovchinikov, G.S. *Katolicheskaia tserkov' v Zapadnoi Afrike* [Catholic Church in Western Africa]. Cited above as item 3316.

5204 Kucherenko, G.S. // *Novaia i noveishaia istoriia* 4 (1983): 193-195.

 * Ovsienko, F.[G]. *Evoliutsiia sotsial'nogo ucheniia katolitsizma* [Evolution of Social Teaching of Catholicism]. Cited above as item 3320.

5205 Nemirovskaia, L.Z. // *Vopr. filosofii* 2 (1989): 170.

 * Paiusov, K.A. *Razum protiv religii* [Reason against Religion]. Cited above as item 3330.

5206 // *Aviatsiia i kosmonavtika* 2 (1987): 30-31.

5207 Suglobov, G. "Ateisticheskoe vospitanie voinov" [Soldiers' Atheistic Education]. *Kommunist Vooruzh. Sil* 24 (1986): 82-83.

* Pal'vanova, O. *Rol' trudovogo kollektiva v preodolenii religioznykh perezhitkov sredi zhenshchin* [Role of Labour Collective in Overcoming Religious Survivals among Women]. Cited above as item 3335.

5208 Saryev, B.S. "Ateizm v kommunisticheskom vospitanii" [Atheism in Communist Education]. *Izv. AN SSSR*. Ser. obshchestv. nauk 5 (1983): 89-91.

5209 Saryev, B.[S]. "Puti preodoleniia religioznykh perezhitkov" [Ways of Overcoming Religious Survivals]. *Turkm. iskra* Nov. 20, 1983.

* Panova, V.S. *'Kolokol' Gertsena i Ogareva ob ateizme, religii i tserkvi* [Herzen and Ogarev's "Kolokol" on Atheism, Religion and Church]. Cited above as item 3356.

5210 Kozlov, N.S. "Kniga ob ateisticheskom i antiklerikal'nom nasledii" [Book on Atheistic and Anticlerical Legacy]. *Vestn. Mosk. un-ta*. Ser. 7. Filosofiia. 2 (1986): 83-84.

* Parnov, E. *Bogi lotosa* [The Gods of Lotus]. Cited above as item 3365.

5211 Belousov, R. "Misteriia Gimalaev - mnimaia i podlinnaia" [Mystery of Himalayas - Imaginary and Genuine]. *Lit. gaz.* Dec. 2, 1981. P. 15.

5212 Linnik, Iu. "Zov Gimalaev" [Summons of Himalayas]. *Oktiabr'* 3 (1982): 205-207.

5213 Suteev, V. // *Lit. obozrenie* 5 (1982): 81-82.

5214 Zerkalov, A. "Pod sen'iu Gimalaev" [Under the Protection of Himalayas]. *Znanie - sila* 8 (1981): 38.

* Parnov, E.I. *Tron Liutsifera* [Lucifer's Throne]. Cited above as item 3366.

5215 Arab-Ogly, E. "Prizraki istorii" [History's Spectres]. *V mire knig* 12 (1985): 82-83.

5216 Bestuzhev-Lada, I. "Zagovor tenei" [Conspiracy of Shadows]. *Sov. kul'tura* Aug. 6, 1985. P. 5.

5217   Ponomarev, N. // *Izvestiia* July 18, 1985. Mosk. vech. vyp.

5218   Tokarev, L. "Besovskii khorovod" [Devilish Round Dance]. *Lit. gazeta* Sep. 25, 1985. P. 15.

5219   Vinokur, A. "Satana tam pravit bal" [The Satan Rules there over the Ball]. *Tikhookean. zvezda* May 25, 1985.

   *   Pashchik, Iu.B. *Stanovlenie ateizma K. Marksa i F. Engel'sa* [K. Marx and F. Engels' Realization of Atheism]. Cited above as item 184.

5220   Kolonitskii, P. // *Polit. samoobrazovanie* 3 (1985): 142-144.

5221   Madzhidov, R. "V arsenal propagandista" [In Propagandist's Arsenal]. *Kommunist Tadzhikistana* Feb. 11, 1984.

   *   Pavlov, A.V. *Voina. Armiia. Religiia* [War. Army. Religion]. Cited above as item 3382.

5222   Davydov, V. "Voina. Armiia. Religiia" [War. Army. Religion]. *Kommunist Vooruzh. Sil* 5 (1089): 94-95.

5223   Sergeev, E. "'Krestonostsy' XX veka" ["Crusaders" of the XXth Century]. *Aviatsiia i kosmonavtika* 12 (1989): 37-38.

   *   Pechiura, P.[I]. *Pochitanie ognia* [Worship of Fire]. Cited above as item 5852.

5224   Butene, F. "Stranitsa iz istorii religii" [A Page from the History of Religion]. *Kommunist. Vil'nius* 10 (1983): 92-93.

   *   Pismanik, M.G. *Individual'naia religioznost' i ee preodolenie* [Individual Religiosity and Its Overcoming]. Cited above as item 3454.

5225   Bokarev, P. // *Tamb. pravda* Jan. 12, 1985.

   *   Platonov, R.P. *Propaganda ateizma* [Propaganda of Atheism]. Cited above as item 3471.

5226   Grebennikov, R. "V tselostnom edinstve" [Integrity in Unity]. *Sov. Belorussiia* Jan. 14, 1986.

5227 Lensu, M.; Molochko, A. "O putiakh sovershenstvovaniia propagandy ateizma" [Ways of Perfection the Propaganda of Atheism]. *Kommunist Belorussii* 1 (1986): 93-96.

5228 Rusetskii, A.; Novitskii, V. // *Neman* 9 (1986): 170-171.

* Popov, L.A. *Ateisticheskii potentsial russkoi literatury* [Atheistic Potential of Russian Literature]. Cited above as item 3546.

5229 Meshcheriakov, V. "Kakov veruiushchi?" [What is Believer Like?]. *Vopr. lit.* 7 (1989): 236-243.

* Popova, M.A. *Freidizm i religiia* [Freudism and Religion]. Cited above as item 3558.

5230 Zadorozhniuk, I.E. "Novye raboty po psikhologii religii" [New Works on Psychology of Religion]. *Psikhol. zhurn.* T. 9. 6 (1988): 159-163.

* *Pravoslavie: Slovar' ateista* [Orthodoxy: Atheist's Dictionary]. Cited above as item 92.

5231 Ulybin, I. "Vse o pravoslavii" [All on Orthodoxy]. *Priok. pravda Nov. 11, 1988.*

* *Pravoslavie v Karelii* [Orthodoxy in Karelia]. Cited above as item 3584.

5232 Korshunov, V. "Pomnit' proshloe, znat' nastoiashchee" [To Remember the Past, to Know the Present]. *Sever* 11 (1987): 119-120.

* Radugin, A.A. *Personalizm i katolicheskoe obnovlenie* [Personalism and Catholic Renovation]. Cited above as item 3657.

5233 Kanterov, I.Ia.; Popov, L.A. // *Nauch. dokl. vyssh. shk. Filos. nauki* 3 (1983): 188-189.

* Rakhmatullin, K.Kh. *Zvezdy: Nauka i sueveriia* [Stars: Science and Superstition]. Cited above as item 3665.

5234 Zharmagambetov, N. "V pomoshch' ateistam" [Aid for Atheists]. *Turg. nov'* Aug. 1, 1984.

* Rapov, O.M. *Russkaia tserkkov'...* [Russian Church...]. Cited above as item 3675.

5235 Krianev, Iu.; Pavlova, T. "'Kreshchenie Rusi': fakty i interpretatsiia" [Baptism of Rus': Facts and Interpretation]. *Kommunist* 12 (1989): 124-127.

5236 Mezin, S.A. // *Voprosy istorii* 1 (1990): 165-168.

* Rashkova, R.T. *Vatikan i sovremennaia kul'tura* [Vatican and Contemporary Culture]. Cited above as item 3682.

5237 Zamoiskii, L. "Verit' v cheloveka" [To Believe in Man]. *Lit. gaz.* Sept. 6, 1989. P. 14.

* Rassel, B. *Pochemu ia ne khristianin* [Why I Am Not a Christian]. Cited above as item 3683.

5238 Andreeva, I.S. // *Filos. nauki* 9 (1988): 125-126.

5239 Zots, V. "Prioritety gumanizma" [Priorities of Humanism]. *Raduga* 11 (1989): 165-167.

* Razlogov, K.E. *Bogi i d'iavoly v zerkale ekrana* [Gods and Devils on the Screen]. Cited above as item 3688.

5240 Grigulevich, I. "V zerkale ekrana" [In the Mirror of Screen]. *Sov. kul'tura* May 5, 1983. P. 5.

5241 Iutkevich, S. "'Skvoz' zemliu v ad...'" ['Through Earth into the Hell...']. *Lit. gaz.* Dec. 14, 1983. P. 8.

5242 Shaternikova, M. // *Iskusstvo kino* 9 (1983): 137-138.

5243 Tolstykh, V.I. // *Vopr. filosofii* 4 (1984): 164-167.

* *Religii mira* [Religions of the World]. Cited above as item 3704.

5244 Zadorozhniuk, I.E. // *Novaia i noveishaia istoriia* 6 (1983): 187-189.

* *Religiia i obshchestvennaia zhizn' v Indii* [Religion and Social Life in India]. Cited above as item 3708.

5245 Kochetov, A.N. // *Narody Azii i Afriki* 2 (1985): 207-210.

5246 Vinokur, A. "Nash sosed - Indiia" [Our Neighbour - India]. *Dal'nyi Vostok* 3 (1985): 148-152.

* *Religiia v politicheskoi zhizni SShA* [Religion in the Political Life of USA]. Cited above as item 3714.

5247 Novinskaia, M.I. // *Vopr. istorii* 4 (1987): 135-137.

* Rizhskii, M.[I]. *Bibleiskie proroki i bibleiskie prorochestva* [Biblical Prophets and Biblical Prophecies]. Cited above as item 3753.

5248 Marakhinin, V.V. // *Izv. Sib. otd-niia AN SSSR.* Ser. istorii, filologii i filosofii 2 (1989): 54.

* Rodionov, M.A. *Golubaia busina na mednoi ladoni* [Blue Bead on Brazen Palm]. Cited above as item 3756.

5249 Lobach, V. "'Golos d'iavola' i 'Golubaia busina'" ["Devil's Voice" and "Blue Bead"]. *Andizh. pravda* June 24, 1988.

* Romanovich, V.V. *Lichnost' i religiia* [Individual and Religion]. Cited above as item 3777.

5250 Razumova, L. "Nesostoiatel'nost' bibleiskikh prorochestv" [Groundlessness of Biblical Prophecies]. *Leninskoe znamia* Petropavlovsk. Jan. 13, 1983.

* Rozenbaum, Iu.A. *Sovetskoe gosudarstvo i tserkov'* [Soviet State and Church]. Cited above as item 3786.

5251 Avak'ian, S.A. // *Sov. gosudarstvo i pravo* 8 (1987): 147-149.

* Rudakova, N.M. *Protestantskoe sektantstvo i ateisticheskaia rabota* [Protestant Sectarianism and Atheistic Work]. Cited above as item 3796.

5252 Vasil'ev, A. "Chitaia knigi ob opyte ateisticheskogo vospitaniia..." [Reading Books on the Experience of Atheistic Education...]. *Polit. samoobrazovanie* 7 (1985): 138-142.

* Rudnev, V.A. *Obriady narodnye i obriady tserkovnye* [National Ceremonies and Church Ceremonies]. Cited above as item 3798.

5253 Maksimov, L. "Oshibki v khoroshei knige" [Mistakes in a God Book]. *Nauka i religiia* 6 (1984): 21.

  * Rumiantseva, V.S. *Narodnoe antitserkovnoe dvizhenie v Rosii..* [Popular Anti-Church Movement in Russia..]. Cited above as item 3804.

5254 Abramov, A.I. // *Istoriia SSSR* 4 (1989): 180-183.

5255 Batser, M. "Vzgliad v minuvshchuiu epokhu" [View into a Past Epoch]. *Sever* 8 (1987): 119-120.

5256 Pokrovskii, N.N. "Issledovanie ob ideinoi bor'be v Rossii XVII veka" [Research on Ideological Struggle in Russia of the XVIIth Century]. *Vopr. istorii* 9 (1988): 151-155.

  * *Russkoe pravoslavie: vekhi istorii* [Russian Orthodoxy: Landmarks of History]. Cited above as item 3813.

5257 Iu. B. "Bez predvziatosti" [Without Prejudice]. *V mire knig* 10 (1989): 44.

5258 // *Lit. obozrenie* 7 (1989): 67.

5259 Popov, A. "Russkoe pravoslavie v kontekste istorii" [Russian Orthodoxy in Historical Context]. *Kommunist* 14 (1989): 120-123.

5260 Sakharov, A.N. "Dolgoe molchanie narusheno" [Long Silence is Infringed]. *Pravda* June 20, 1989.

  * Rybakov, B.A. *Iazychestvo Drevnei Rusi* [Paganism of Ancient Rus']. Cited above as item 3823.

5261 Rusanova, I.P.; Timoshchuk, B.A. // *Sov. arkheologiia* 2 (1988): 260-264.

  * Rybakov, B.A. *Iazychestvo drevnikh slavian* [Paganism of Ancient Slavs]. Cited above as item 3824.

5262 Arutiunov, S.A. // *Sov. etnografiia* 4 (1982): 154-161.

5263 Begunov, Iu.K. "Drevneslavianskoe iazychestvo i russkaia kul'tura" [Ancient Slav Paganism and Russian Culture]. *Rus. lit.* 4 (1983): 211-216.

5264 Chlenov, A. "Stikhiia slavianskogo iazychestva" [Element of Slavonic Paganism]. *V mire knig* 4 (1982): 62-63.

5265 Dediukhin, B. "Glubiny pamiati narodnoi" [Depths of Popular Memory]. *Volga* 9 (1982): 131-143.

5266 Epifantsev, V. "Romantika iazycheskoi stariny" [Romance of the Olden Times Paganism]. *Brian. rabochii* Dec. 1, 1981.

5267 Plitchenko, A. // *Sib. ogni* 1 (1982): 175-176.

5268 Rogov, A.I. // *Istoriia SSSR* 5 (1982): 186-189.

5269 Sakharov, A.N. "Istoricheskie puti vostochnogo slavianstva" [Historical Ways of Oriental Slavonic People]. *Vopr. istorii* 4 (1984): 120-137.

5270 Ugrinovich, D.M. // *Vopr. filosofii* 1 (1983): 165-166.

 * Saidbaev, T.S. *Dialogi ob islame* [Dialogues on Islam]. Cited above as item 3854.

5271 Isakov, R. // *Fergan. pravda* Feb. 16, 1989.

 * Saidov, N.Kh. *Sistema nauchno-ateisticheskogo vospitaniia v usloviiakh razvitogo sotsializma* [The System of Scientific-Atheistic Education under Developed Socialism]. Cited above as item 3858.

5257 Pirmatov, K.; Tadzhiev, S. "Kniga o problemakh i praktike ateisticheskogo vospitaniia" [Book on Problems and Practice of Atheistic Education]. *Part. zhizn' Tashkent.* 10 (1983): 93-94.

 * Saprykin, V.A. *Sotsialisticheskii kollektiv i ateisticheskoe vospitanie* [Socialist Collective and Atheistic Education]. Cited above as item 3886.

5273 Popov, L. // *Polit. samoobrazovanie* 12 (1984): 129-131.

5274 Timofeev, V. "Kollektiv i ateisticheskoe vospitanie" [The Collective and Atheistic Education]. *Part. zhizn'* 7 (1984): 77-79.

 * Saprykin, V.A. *Urbanizatsiia. Ateizm. Religiia* [Urbanization. Atheism. Religion]. Cited above as item 3887.

5275 Filimonov, E.G.; Filist, G.M. // *Nauch. dokl. vyssh. shkoly. Filos. nauki* 6 (1982): 177-180.

5276 Shulembaev, K. "Poleznoe issledovanie po ateizmu" [Useful Research on Atheism]. *Kazakhst. pravda* Sep. 19, 1981.

* Sardachuk, P.D. *Stupeni zrelosti* [Stages of Maturity]. Cited above as item 3891.

5277 Figlevskii, M. "Nachinaia s detskogo sada" [Starting from Kindergarten]. *Doshk. vospitanie* 5 (1986): 71-72.

* Saukh, P.Iu. *Kategorii nauchnogo ateizma* [Categories of Scientific Atheism]. Cited above as item 3909.

5278 Filonenko, M.V. // *Filos. dumka* Kiev. 6 (1988): 114-115.

* Savel'ev, S.N. *Ideinoe bankrotstvo bogoiskatel'stva v Rossii v nachale XX veka* [Ideological Bankruptcy of God Seeking in Early XXth Century Russia]. Cited above as item 3919.

5279 Kurganskaia, V.D. "Neskol'ko zamechanii k analizu bogoiskatel'stva" [Some Remarks on the Analysis of God Seeking]. *Vestn. Mosk. un-ta.* Ser. 7, Filosofiia 5 (1988): 70-71.

* Semenkin, N.S. *Filosofiia bogoiskatel'stva* [Philosophy of God Seeking]. Cited above as item 3934.

5280 Abramov, A.N. // *Filos. nauki* 10 (1987): 125-126.

5281 Dmitriev, N.K.; Babaev, Iu.V. "Bogoiskatel'stvo kak raznovidnost' religioznoi filosofii" [God Seeking as Variety of Religious Philosophy]. *Vestn. Mosk. un-ta.* Ser. 7, Filosofiia 6 (1987): 75-77.

5282 Guseva, A.V. // *Vestn. Leningr. un-ta.* Ser. 6, Istoriia KPSS, nauch. kommunizm, filosofiia, pravo 2 (1987): 124-125.

* Shakhnovich, M.I. *Primety vernye i suevernye* [True and Superstitious Signs]. Cited above as item 3959.

5283 "Ateisticheskie ocherki" [Atheistic Essays]. *Nauch. shk.* 4 (1986): 75-77.

* Shamaro, A.A. *Taina inokini Dosifei* [Secret of the Nun Dosifei]. Cited above as item 3990.

5284 Tazhurizina, Z. "Naedine s istoriei" [Alone with History]. *Sov. kul'tura* Sep. 4, 1985. P. 6.

* Shaposhnikov, L.E. *Pravoslavie i filosofskii idealizm* [Orthodoxy and Philosophical Idealism]. Cited above as item 4002.

5285 Akulinin, V.N.; Ermichev, A.A. // *Vestn. Leningr. un-ta.* Ser. 6, Istoriia KPSS, nauch. kommunizm, filosofiia, pravo 2 (1987): 123-124.

5286 Gordienko, N.S. // *Filos. nauki* 2 (1987): 124-125.

* Sharifov, V.; Khushkadamov, D. *Slovar'-spravochnik ateista* [Atheist's Dictionary-Reference Book]. Cited above as item 105.

5287 Khazratkulov, M. // *Kommunist Tadzhkistana* 2 (1987): 96.

* Sharipova, R.M. *Panislamizm segodnia* [Pan-Islamism Today]. Cited above as item 4016.

5288 Katin, Z. // *Aziia i Afrika segodnia* 5 (1987): 63-64.

* Shevelev, V.V. *Dobroe slovo* [A Good Word]. Cited above as item 4050.

5289 Dorozhkina, V. "Slovo dobroe i nuzhnoe" [Good and Necessary Word]. *Tamb. pravda* June 24, 1984.

* Shil'diashov, I.M. *Religiia v Sibiri i ateisticheskoe vospitanie* [Religion in Siberia and Atheistic Education]. Cited above as item 4062.

5290 Sukhanov, A. // *Sib. ogni* 4 (1983): 174-175.

* Shpazhnikov, G.A. *Religii stran Iugo-Vostochnoi Azii* [Religion of Countries of South-Eastern Asia]. Cited above as item 108.

5291 Zasedateleva, L.B. // *Sov. etnografiia* 4 (1982): 167-169.

* Shulembaev, K.Sh. *Obraz zhizni. Religiia. Ateizm* [Way of Life. Religion. Atheism]. Cited above as item 4107.

5292 Nysanabev, A. "Interesnoe issledovanie" [Interesting Research]. _Part. zhizn' Kazakhstana_ 12 (1983): 85-86.

* Siukiianen, L.R. _Musul'manskoe pravo_ [Moslem Law]. Cited above as item 4133.

5293 Saidov, A.Kh. // _Sov. gosudarstvo i pravo_ 5 (1988): 151-152.

* Solov'ev, E.Iu. _Nepobezhdennyi eretik: Martin Liuter..._ [Invincible Heretic: Martin Luther...]. Cited above as item 4190.

5294 Shmelev, V.D.; Chertikhin, V.E. // _Vopr. filosofii_ 5 (1986): 160-164.

5295 Shteklia, A. // _Kommunist_ 14 (1985): 126.

* Solov'ev, V.S. _Sochineniia v dvukh tomakh_ [Works in two Volumes]. Cited above as item 4195.

5296 Nosov, A. // _Novyi mir_ 6 (1989): 270-271.

* _Sovremennaia religioznost'..._ [Contemporary Religiosity...]. Cited above as item 4214.

5297 Samsonov, S.I. "Sovremennaia religioznost' i ee izuchenie" [Contemporary Religiosity and Its Study]. _Vestn. Mosk. un-ta._ Ser. 7, Filosofiia 5 (1988): 71-72.

* Stepaniants, M.T. _Filosofskie aspekty sufizma_ [Philosophical Aspects of Sufism]. Cited above as item 4235.

5298 Khazratkulov, M. // _Kommunist Tadzhikistana_ 9 (1989): 94-95.

5299 Khazratkulov, M. // _Vopr. filosofii_ 2 (1989): 168-169.

5300 Olimov, K. "Issledovanie po sufizmu" [Research on Sufism]. _Izv. AN TadzhSSR._ Ser.: Filosofiia, ekonomika, pravovedenie 2 (1988): 69-71.

* Stepaniants, M.T. _Musul'manskie kontseptsii v filosofii i politike_ [Moslem Conceptions in Philosophy and Politics]. Cited above as item 4236.

5301 Efimova, L. "Islam i sovremennost'" [Islam and Contemporaneity]. _Aziia i Afrika segodnia_ 2 (1984): 62-63.

* *100 otvetov veruiushchim* [100 Answers to Believers]. Cited above as item 116.

5302 Grekov, V. "Tsennyi spravochnik" [Valuable Reference Book]. *Belogor. pravda* Sep. 17, 1980.

5303 Konstantinova, M.K. "Dlia besed o religii i sueveriiakh" [For Talks on Religion and Superstitions]. *Vech. sred. shkola* 2 (1981): 80.

* Sukhov, A.D. *Ateizm peredovykh russkikh myslitelei* [Atheism of Front Rank Russian Thinkers]. Cited above as item 4281.

5304 Krianev, Iu.V. // *Nauch. dokl. syssh. shkoly. Filos. nauki* 5 (1981): 180-182.

5305 Skibitskii, M.M. // *Vopr. filosofii* 10 (1981): 183-184.

* Sulatskov, A.A. *Liki baptizma* [Faces of Baptism]. Cited above as item 4285.

5306 Kosenko, V. // *Zaria kommunizma* Oct. 19, 1983.

* *Sumerki bogov* [Twilight of the Gods]. Cited above as item 4294.

5307 Kerimov, V.I. // *Vopr. filosofii* 7 (1989): 169-170.

* Svetlov, G.E. *Put' bogov* [The Way of the Gods]. Cited above as item 4314.

5308 Cherevko, K.E. // *Sov. etnografiia* 5 (1987): 171-172.

5309 Dzharylgasinova, R.Sh. // *Rasy i narody* 16 (1986): 252-253.

5310 Latyshev, I.A. // *Narody Azii i Afriki* 1 (1987): 197-200.

5311 Vasil'ev, V.A. "Rol' sinto v obshchestvenno-politicheskoi zhizni Iaponii" [The Role of Shinto in Socio-Political Life of Japan]. *Probl. Dal'nego Vostoka* 4 (1985): 179-182.

* *Svobodomyslie i ateizm v drevnosti, srednie veka i v epokhu Vozrozhdeniia* [Freethinking and Atheism in Ancient Times, Middle Ages and Renaissance]. Cited above as item 4321.

5312 Biazrova, T.T.; Zlotina, T.V.; Petrov, S.B. // *Filos. nauki* 7 (1987): 123-125.

5313 Krianev, Iu. "Ateizm i kul'tura" [Atheism and Culture]. *Pravda* June 19, 1987.

   * Tabakaru, D.N. *Baptizm i 'nebesnyi Khanaan'* [Baptism and "Divine Hanaan"]. Cited above as item 4327.

5314 Gol'denberg, M. "Argumentirovanno i doveritel'no" [Argumentative and Confiding]. *Kommunist Moldavii* 10 (1982): 93-95.

   * Tabakaru, D.N. *Beseduia s veruiushchimi* [Discussing with Believers]. Cited above as item 4328.

      For review see item 5314.

   * Tazhurizina, Z.A. *Idei svobodomysliia v istorii kul'tury* [Ideas of Free Thinking in the History of Culture]. Cited above as item 4373.

5315 Shaposhnikov, L.E. "Ob otnoshenii ateizma k dukhovnomu naslediiu" [On Atheism's Attitude towards Spiritual Legacy]. *Vestn. Mosk. un-ta.* Ser. 7, Filosofiia 5 (1988): 68-70.

5316 Voronkova, L.P.; Tychinina, G.P. "Mirovozzrencheskaia orientatsiia molodezhi i traditsii svobodomysliia" [World Outlook Orientation of Youth and Traditions of Free Thinking]. *Vestn. Mosk. un-ta.* Ser. 7, Filosofiia 1 (1989): 95-3rd cover p.

5317 Zlotina, T.B.; Petrov, S.B. // *Filos. nauki* 7 (1988): 125-127.

   * *Teoriia i praktika nauchnogo ateizma* [Theory and Practice of Scientific Atheism]. Cited above as item 4383.

5318 Machiulis, I. "Aktual'nye problemy nauchnogo ateizma" [Actual Problems of Scientific Atheism]. *Kommunist.* Vil'nius 1 (1985): 94-96.

   * Timchenko, I.P. *Zhenshchina, religiia, ateizm* [Woman, Religion, Atheism]. Cited above as item 4408.

5319 Zots, V.A. // *Vopr. filosofii* 11 (1982): 171.

5320 Zots, V.[A]. "Zhenshchina i religiia" [Woman and Religion]. *Pravda Ukrainy* March 18, 1982.

* *Traditsionnye i sinkreticheskie religii Afriki* [Africa's Traditional and Syncretical Religions]. Cited above as item 4466.

5321 Borisov, N. "Religii v Afrike" [Religions in Africa]. *Aziia i Afrika segodnia* 2 (1987): 62-63.

* Tsurkan, I.M. *Sotsial'nyi progress i ateizm* [Social Progress and Atheism]. Cited above as item 4501.

5322 Bardash, I. // *Sel. khoz-vo Moldavii* 11 (1981): 53.

* Tveig, S. *Sovest' protiv nasiliia* [Conscience against Violence]. Cited above as item 4502.

5323 Vasilevskii, A. "Tsveig protiv nasiliia" [Zweig against Violence]. *Novyi mir* 9 (1988): 261-264.

* Tven, M. *Dnevnik Adama* [Adam's Diary]. Cited above as item 4521.

5324 Nadein, V. "Sud smekha" [Laughter's Court]. *V mire knig* 10 (1981): 65.

* Ubushieva, S.I. *Ateisticheskaia propaganda v Kalmykii* [Atheistic Propaganda in Kalmyk]. Cited above as item 4528.

5325 Sidorkin, I. "Opyt, ne poteriavshchii znachimost'" [Experience, which Did not Lose Its Significance]. *Tiechin gerl* (Svet i stepi). 1 (1989): 106-108.

* *Uchenye beseduiut s veruiushchimi* [Scientists Discuss with Believers]. Cited above as item 4529.

5326 Ashikbaeva, S. "Dlia veruiushchikh i ateistov" [For Believers and Atheists]. *Kazakhst. pravda* June 4, 1986.

* Ugrinovich, D.M. *Psikhologiia religii* [The Psychology of Religion]. Cited above as item 4537.

5327 Maiat, E.; Skibitskii, M. // *Polit. samoobrazovanie* 11 (1987): 140-143.

5328 Okulov, A.F. // *Vopr. filosofii* 6 (1988): 169.

5329 Zadorozhniuk, I.E. "Novye raboty po psikhologii religii" [New Works on Psychology of Religion]. *Psikhol. zhurn.* T. 9. 6 (1988): 159-163.

* Ugrinovich, D.M. *Vvedenie v religiovedenie* [Introduction to Studies of Religion]. Cited above as item 4544.

5330 Skibitskii, M.M. // *Filos. nauki* 6 (1987): 113-115.

5331 Zhelnov, M.V. "Aktual'nye voprosy religiovedeniia" [Actual Problems of Studies of Religion]. *Vestn. Mosk. un-ta.* Ser. 7, Filosofiia 4 (1987): 89-91.

* Ukolova, V.I. *'Poslednii rimlianin' Boetskii* [Boethius "The Last Roman"]. Cited above as item 4545.

5332 Var'iash, O.I. // *Srednie veka* 52 (1989): 354-356.

* Vagabov, M.V. *Islam i sem'ia* [Islam and Family]. Cited above as item 4588.

5333 Kovnatskii, E.P. // *Izv. Sev.-Kavk. nauch. tsentra vyssh. shkoly. Obshchestv. nauki* 4 (1981): 96-97.

5334 Magomedov, A.M.; Mustafaeva, M.G. // *Vopr. filosofii* 6 (1982): 168-169.

* Vagabov, M.V.; Vagabov, N.M. *Islam i voprosy ateisticheskogo vospitaniia* [Islam and Problems of Atheistic Education]. Cited above as item 4593.

5335 Masharipov, R. "Islam i ateizm" [Islam and Atheism]. *Khorezm. pravda* Aug. 10, 1989.

5336 Mustafaev, M.B. // *Izv. Sev.-Kavk. nauch. tsentra vyssh. shk. Obshchestv. nauki* 3 (1989): 101-102.

5337 Valiev, Sh. "Novie knigi o religii i ateizme" [New Books on Religion and Atheism]. *Andizh. pravda* Feb. 2, 1989.

* Vaniushin, N.A. *Svoboda sovesti i religioznyi ekstremizm* [Freedom of Conscience and Religious Extremism]. Cited above as item 4610.

5338 Anatol'ev, M. // *Alt. pravda* Aug. 6, 1988.

* Vasil'ev, A.V. *Po sledam 'sviatykh' prestuplenii* [Along the Footsteps of "Sacred" Crimes]. Cited above as item 4621.

For review see item 5337.

* Vasil'ev, L.S. *Istoriia religii Vostoka* [History of Religions of Orient]. Cited above as item 4627.

5339 Arutiunov, S.A.; Svetlov, G.E.; Furman, D.E. // *Narody Azii i Afriki* 6 (1984): 173-184.

5340 Ialkabov, B. "Istoriia religii" [History of Religion]. *Maryiskaia pravda* Aug. 15, 1984.

* Veish, Ia.Ia. *Analiticheskaia filosofiia i religioznaia apologetika* [Analytical Philosophy and Religious Apologetics]. Cited above as item 4646.

5341 Markov, V. "Analitiko-lingvisticheskaia filosofiia i teologiia pritiazhenie i ottalkivanie" [Analytic-Linguistic Philosophy and Theology of Attraction and Repulsion]. *Izv. AN LatSSR* 11 (1989): 138-139.

* Velichko, O.I. *Politicheskii katolitsizm i rabochee dvizhenie v Avstrii* [Political Catholicism and Workers Movement in Austria]. Cited above as item 4648.

5342 Istiagin, L.G. "Avstriia: evoliutsiia sotsial'nogo klerikalizma" [Austria: Evolution of Social Clericalism]. *Rabochii klass i sovrem. mir* 4 (1987): 187-189.

* Velikovich, L.N. *Sovremennyi kapitalizm i religiia* [Contemporary Capitalism and Religion]. Cited above as item 4657.

5343 Nevinitsyn, A. // *Polit. samoobrazovanie* 6 (1986): 139-142.

* Vistunov, E.I.; Tiutriumov, M.I. *Litsa bez masok* [Faces without Masks]. Cited above as item 4694.

5344 Shakh, M. // *Zvezda* 11 (1981): 222.

* *Vkladnaia kniga Troitse-Sergieva monastyria* [Supplementary Book of the Trinity-Sergius Monastery]. Cited above as item 4696.

5345 Kuchkin, V.A. "Tsennyi istochnik po istorii Rossii XIV-XVIII vv" [Valuable Source on Russia's History of the XIVth-XVIIIth Centuries]. *Vopr. istorii* 5 (1989): 165-167.

* Volkov, S.V. *Ranniaia istoriia buddizma v Koree* [The Early History of Buddhism in Korea]. Cited above as item 4706.

5346 Nikitin, A.V. // *Izv. Sib. otd-niia AN SSSR.* 1987. No.3: Ser. istorii, filologii i filosofii Vyp. I. Pp. 62-63.

* *Voprosy nauchnogo ateizma* [Problems of Scientific Atheism]. Vyp. 29. Cited above as item 4719.

5347 Krianev, Iu. "Religiia i sovremennost'" [Religion and Contemporaneity]. *Pravda* Feb. 9, 1983.

* Voronchanina, N.I. *Islam v obshchestvenno-politicheskoi zhizni Tunisa* [Islam in Socio-Political Life of Tunis]. Cited above as item 4728.

5348 Roshchin, M.Iu. // *Narody Azii i Afriki* 2 (1989): 194-197.

* Voroshilov, A.S. *Baptizm kak on est'* [Baptism as It is]. Cited above as item 4736.

5349 Evglevskii, A.A.; Astapenko, G.P. // *Izv. Sev.- Kavk. nauch. tsentra vyssh. shk. Obshchestv. nauki* 2 (1984): 101-102.

* *Vozgoritsia fakel razuma* [The Torch of Reason will Flare Up]. Cited above as item 4746.

5350 Frolova, T. // *Sov. pedagogika* 2 (1988): 134-135.

5351 Pankeev, I. "Ne obkhodit' molchaniem" [Not to Pass Over in Silence]. *Uchit. gazeta* Sep. 29, 1987.

* *Vstan', chelovek!* [Man, Get Up!]. Cited above as item 4756.

5352 Krianev, Iu. "Ateizm i kul'tura" [Atheism and Culture]. *Pravda* June 19, 1987.

* *Vvedenie khristianstva na Rusi* [Introduction of Christianity into Rus']. Cited above as item 4758.

5353 Kerimov, V. "Put' v 1000 let" [Way into 1000 Years]. *Pravda* May, 30, 1988.

5354 // *Kn. obozrenie* 3 (1988): 7.

5355 Krianev, Iu; Pavlova, T. "'Kreshchenie Rusi': fakty i interpretatsiia" ["Baptism of Rus'": Facts and Interpretation]. *Kommunist* 12 (1989): 124-127.

5356 Melamed, S.M. // *Prepodavanie istorii v shk.* 2 (1989): 153-157,

5357 V'iugin, D. "Esli khotite znat' kak krestili Rus'" [If You Want to Know how Rus' was Baptized]. *Komunist Kirgizstana* 8 (1988): 93-95.

   * *Vvedenie v religiovedenie* [Introduction to Studies of Religion]. Cited above as item 4761.

5358 Genzelis, B. "Tsennyi trud po ateizmu" [Valuable Work on Atheism]. *Sov. Litva* Dec. 25, 1981.

5359 Matsiavichius, I. "Nauchnyi marksistskii ateizm i marksistskoe religiovedenie" [Scientific Marxist Atheism and Marxist Studies of Religion]. *Kommunist.* Vil'nius, 6 (1982): 88-95.

   * Zaruda, V.T. *Zhiznennaia pozitsiia i religioznaia vera* [Vital Position and Religious Faith]. Cited above as item 4810.

5360 Chernyshov, V.S. // *Kommunist Ukrainy* 3 (1985): 94-95.

   * Zhdanov, N.B.; Ignatenko, A.A. *Islam na poroge XXI veka* [Islam on the Threshold of XXIst Century]. Cited above as item 4826.

5361 Zviagel'skaia, I.; Naumkin, V. "Islam vo vzaimozavisimom mire" [Islam in Interdependent World]. *Kommunist* 1 (1990): 122-126.

   * Zhivogliad, I.N. *Selo, religiia i ateizm* [Village, Religion and Atheism]. Cited above as item 4883.

5362 Makotchenko, V.; Bondarenko, Iu. // *Leninskii put'.* Kustanai, Oct. 19, 1985.

   * Zots, V.A. *Kul'tura. Religiia. Ateizm* [Culture. Religion. Atheism]. Cited above as item 4878.

5363 Grigulevich, I.R. // *Vopr. filosofii* 11 (1983): 162-164.

5364   Lobovik, B.A. "Zhizneutverzhdaiushchaia sila nauchnogo ateizma" [Vital Strength of Scientific Atheism]. *Kommunist Ukrainy* 7 (1983): 94-95.

*   Zots, V.A. *Pravoslavie i kul'tura: Fakty protiv domyslov* [Orthodoxy and Culture: Facts against Conjectures]. Cited above as item 4880.

5365   Manokha, A. "Khranitel' kul'tury - narod" [People are Custodians of Culture]. *Pravda Ukrainy* Sep. 19, 1986.

*   Zyrianov, P.N. *Pravoslavnaia tserkov' v bor'be s revoliutsiei 1905-1917 gg.* [Orthodox Church in the Struggle against Revolution 1905-1917]. Cited above as item 4901.

5366   Emeliakh, L.I. // *Istoriia SSSR* 6 (1986): 166-168.

5367   Goriushkin, L.M. // *Izv. Sib. otd-niia AN SSSR*. 1986. No 3: Ser. istorii, filologii i filosofii Vyp. I. Pp. 56-58.

5368   Lozhkin, V.V. // *Vopr. istorii KPSS* 9 (1985): 138-140.

DISSERTATIONS

5369 Abdukhalikov, S. "Sovetskoe zakonodatel'stvo o religioznykh kul'takh kak faktor povysheniia effektivnosti ateisticheskogo vospitaniia" [Soviet Legislation on Religious Cults as Factor of Increasing the Effectiveness of Atheistic Education]. Dissertation. Tashk. gos. un-t im. V.I. Lenina. Tashkent, 1987.

5370 Abdulkhakim, Abdullatif Mokhammed. "Kommunisticheskie i rabochie partii arabskikh stran o meste i roli islama v sovremennom natsional'no-osvoboditel'nom dvizhenii" [Communist and Workers Parties of the Arab Countries on the Place and Role of Islam in Contemporary National-Liberation Movement]. Dissertation. AN BSSR, Ins-t filosofii i prava. Minsk, 1987.

5371 Abdunazarov, Kh. "Deiatel'nost' Kompartii Tadzhikistana po ateisticheskomu vospitaniiu trudiashchikhsiia (1917-1980 gg.)" [Activity of Communist Party of Tajikistan in Atheistic Education of Workers (1917-1980)]. Dissertation. Tadzh. gos. un-t im. V.I. Lenina. Dushanbe, 1986.

5372 Agapova, N.G. "Razvitie teorii ateisticheskogo vospitaniia v dokumentakh i resheniiakh KPSS" [Development of Theory of Atheistic Education in Documents and Resolutions of the CPSU]. Dissertation. MGU im. M.V. Lomonosova. M., 1986.

5373 Aivazova, N.V. "Rol' obshchestva 'Znanie' v formirovanii nauchno-materialisticheskogo, ateisticheskogo mirovozzreniia trudiashchikhsiia v sovremennykh usloviakh" [The Role of the Society "Znanie" in Forming Scientific-Materialist, Atheistic World Outlook of Workers in Contemporary Conditions]. Dissertation. MGU im. M.V. Lomonosova. M., 1984.

5374 Akhadov, A.F. "Islam v sovremennom Azerbaidzhane, ego modernizatsiia i preodolenie" [Islam in Contemporary Azerbaijan, Its Modernization and Overcoming]. Dissertation. AN AzSSR, In-t filosofii i prava. Baku, 1987.

5375 Akhmedzhanov, B.A. "Kritika klerikal'noi fal'sifikatsii polozheniia islama i musul'man v Sovetskom Uzbekistane" [Criticism of Clerical Falsification

553

of the Situation of Islam and Moslems in Soviet Uzbekistan]. Dissertation. Tashk. gos. un-t im V.I. Lenina. Tashkent, 1987.

5376 Akhundova, N.Ch. "Rol' islama v obshchestvenno-politicheskoi zhizni Siriiskoi Arabskoi Respubliki (1963-1982 gg.)" [The Role of Islam in Social-Political Life of Syrian Arab Republic (1963-1982]. Dissertation. Azerb. gos. un-t im. S.M. Kirova. Baku, 1987.

5377 Akimbaev, S.N. "Izmenenie politicheskoi orientatsii musul'manskogo dukhovenstva v peiod stroitel'stva sotsializma v Kirgizii (1917-1937 gg.)" [Change of Political Orientation of Moslem Clergy in the Period of Building Socialism in Kirghizia (1917-1937)]. Dissertation. Kaz. gos. un-t im. S.M. Kirova. Alma-Ata, 1985.

5378 Akinchitis, I.I. "Evoliutsiia soznaniia novykh pokolenii veruiushchikh v sovetskom obshchestve" [Evolution of Consciousness of New Generations of Believers in Soviet Society]. Dissertation. Akad. obshchestv. nauk pri TsK KPSS. M., 1988.

5379 Aknazarov, Kh.Z. "Osobennosti islama v dorevoliutsionnom Kazakhstane i kritika ego ideologii" [Islam's Features in Pre-Revolutionary Kazakhstan and Criticism of Its Ideology]. Dissertation. AN AzSSR, In-t filosofii i prava. Baku, 1986.

5380 Akulinin, V.N. "Problema spetsifiki filosofii v religiozno-idealisticheskoi kontseptsii vseedinstva" [The Problem of Philosophy's Specificity in Religious-Idealistic Conception of Allunity]. Dissertation. LGU im. A.A. Zhdanova. L., 1987.

5381 Alekseev, L.P. "Klerikal'no-antikommunisticheskii kharakter ideologii i praktiki iegovizma" [Clerical-Anti-Communist Character of the Ideology and Practice of Jehovism]. Dissertation. Tashk. gos. un-t im. V.I. Lenina. Tashkent, 1987.

5382 Alekseev, N.A. "Rannie formy religii i Shamanizm tiurkoiazychnykh narodov Sibirii" [Early Religious Forms and Shamanism of Turkic Language People of Siberia]. Dissertation. AN SSSR, In-t etnografii im. N.N. Miklukho-Maklaia. M., 1986.

5383 Aliev, V.M. "Islam i azerbaidzhanskoe prosveshchenie" [Islam and Azerbaijan Enlightenment]. Dissertation. Azerb. gos. un-t im. S.M. Kirova. Baku, 1987.

5384 Alimbaev, A.A. "Stanovlenie ateizma i formirovanie nauchno-materia-listicheskogo mirovozzreniia rabochego klassa" [Creation of Atheism and Forming Scientific-Materialist World Outlook of Workers Class]. Dissertation. AN AzSSR. In-t filosofii i prava. Baku, 1988.

5385 Alimov, Z.Z. "Deiatel'nost' Tatarskoi oblastnoi partiinoi organizatsii po ateisticheskomu vospitaniiu trudiashchikhsia (1965-1985 gg.)" [Activity of Tatar Oblast' Party Organization in Atheistic Education of Workers (1965-1985]. Dissertation. Kazan. gos. un-t im. V.I. Ul'ianova-Lenina. Kazan', 1985.

5386 Allakhverdiev, K.V. "Soderzhanie i etapy razvitiia iranskoi revoliutsii 1978-1979 gg." [The Content and Development Stages of Iranian Revolution of 1978-1979]. Dissertation. MGU im. M.V. Lomonosova. M., 1985.

5387 Andreeva, O.V. "Kritika anglo-amerikanskoi burzhuaznoi istoriografii sovremennogo polozheniia pravoslavnoi religii i tserkvi v SSSR" [Criticism of Anglo-American Bourgeois Historiography of the Present Day Situation of the Orthodox Religion and Church in the USSR]. Dissertation. Un-t druzhby narodov im. Patrisa Lumumby. M.: Un-t druzhby narodov, 1987.

5388 Andronova, V.P. "Politicheskaia rol' katolicheskoi tserkvi i religii v Latinskoi Amerike (seredina 60-kh - 80-e gg.)" [Political Role of Catholic Church and Religion in Latin America (middle 60s-80s)]. Dissertation. AN SSSR, In-t Latin. Ameriki. M., 1988.

5389 Androsov, V.P. "Kontseptsiia nirishvara v drevneindiiskoi filosofsko-religioznoi traditsii" [Nirishvara Conception in Ancient Indian Philosophical-Religious Tradition]. Dissertation. AN SSSR. In-t vostokovedeniia. M., 1982.

5390 Antsipovich, N.V. "Svobodomyslie i ateizm v Zapadnoi Belorussii, 1919-1939" [Free-Thinking and Atheism in Western Belorussia, 1919-1939]. Dissertation. AN BSSR. In-t filosofii i prava. Minsk, 1988.

5391 Arestov, V.N. "Religioznyi ekstremizm: soderzhanie, prichiny i formy proiavleniia, puti preodoleniia" [Religious Extremism: Content, Motives and Forms of Manifestation, Ways to Overcome]. Dissertation. AN UkSSR, In-t filosofii. Kiev, 1984.

5392 Aroian, G.A. "Kritika sovremennykh bogoslovskikh kontseptsii vzaimo-
otnoshenia nauki i religii" [Criticism of Contemporary Theological
Conception of Interrelation of Science and Religion]. Dissertation. AN
UkSSR, In-t filosofii. Kiev, 1985.

5393 Artem'ev, A.I. "Sistemno-kompleksnnyi podkhod v ateisticheskom vospitanii"
[System-Complex Approach in Atheistic Education]. Dissertation. Akad.
obshchsestv. nauk pri TsK KPSS. M., 1986.

5394 Ashnokova, L.M. "Filosofskii analiz osnovnykh podkhodov k reshenii
problemy proiskhozhdeniia zhizni" [Philosophical Analysis of the Basic
Approaches Toward Resolution of the Problem of the Origin of Life].
Dissertation. MGU im. M.V. Lomonosova. M., 1986.

5395 Ataeva, M.[F]. "Usloviia i prichiny vosproizvodstva religioznosti sredi sel'skoi
molodezhi" [Conditions and Causes of Recurrence of Religiosity among
Rural Youth]. Dissertation. Akad. obshchestv. nauk pri TsK KPSS. M.,
1989.

5396 Azimov, A. "Mesto islama v ideologii natsional'no-osvoboditel'nogo dvizheniia
narodov Blizhnego Vostoka na sovremennom etape" [Place of Islam in
the Ideology of National-Liberation Movement of the People of Near
East in the Contemporary Stage]. Dissertation. Tashk. gos. un-t im. V.I.
Lenina. Tashkent, 1987.

5397 Azizova, Z.S. "Razvitie ateisticheskoi mysli v Sovetskom Azerbaidzhane
(1920-30-e gg.)" [Development of Atheistic Thought in Soviet Azerbaijan
(1920-30s)]. Dissertation Azerb. gos. un-t im. S.M. Kirova. Baku, 1987.

5398 Bagranovskii, A.E. "Religioznye otnosheniia" [Religious Relations]. Dissertation. MGU im. M.V. Lomonosova. M., 1988.

5399 Baikabilova, R. "Osobennosti religioznosti sredi zhenshchin-uzbechek i puti
sovershenstvovaniia ateisticheskoi, vospitatel'noi raboty sredi nikh"
[Religiosity Peculiarities Among Uzbek Women and Ways of Perfection
of Atheistic Work in Their Midst]. Dissertation. Tashk. gos. un-t im. V.I.
Lenina. Tashkent, 1988.

5400 Bakaeva, E.P. "Lamaizm v Kalmykii XVII-nachala XX vv." [Lamaism in
Kalmyk, XVIIth-Early XXth Centuries]. Dissertation. An SSSR. In-t
etnografii im. N.N. Miklukho-Maklaia. M., 1986.

5401 Bakani, M.V. "Mesto i sotsial'naia funktsiia religioznykh traditsii v sisteme gruzinskikh natsional'nykh traditisii" [Place and Social Function of Religious Traditions in the System of Georgian National Traditions]. Dissertation. Tbil. gos. un-t. Tbilisi, 1988.

5402 Bakanurskii, G.L. "Iudeiskii klerikalizm" [Judaic Clericalism]. Dissertation. MGU im. M.V. Lomonosova. M., 1986.

5403 Baltanova, G.R. "Kriticheskii analiz sovremennogo burzhuaznogo islamo-vedeniia" [Critical Analysis of the Current Bourgeois Islamic Studies]. Dissertation. MGU im. M.V. Lomonosova. M., 1984.

5404 Baranichenko, N.N. "Doislamskie verovaniia i kul'ty v istoricheskikh siste-makh obshchestvennykh otnoshenii vainakhov" [Pre-Islamic Creeds and Cults in Historical Systems of Vainakhs' Social Relations]. Dissertation. MGU im. M.V. Lomonosova, Ist. fak. M., 1985.

5405 Bashirov, A.M. "Ideologicheskie, filosofskie aspekty sufizma v osveshchenii angliiskogo vostokovedeniia (konets XIX-nach. XX v.)" [Ideological, Philosophical Aspects of Sufism in the Light of English Oriental Studies (Late XIXth-Early XXth C.)]. Dissertation. AN AzSSR, In-t. filosofii i prava. Baku, 1981.

5406 Bazilenko, I.V. "Istoriia vozniknoveniia bakhaizma: Bekha-Ulla (1817-1892 gg.) i ego uchenie" [History of Origin of Bahaism: Baha Ulla (1817-1892) and His Teaching]. Dissertation. LGU im. A.A. Zhdanova. L., 1988.

5407 Bedirov, M.N. "Ateisticheskoe vospitanie uchashchiksia mnogonatsional'noi shkoly" [Atheistic Upbringing of Pupils of Multinational School]. Disser-tation. Mosk. gos. ped. in-t im. V.I. Lenina. M., 1985.

5408 Bekov, K. "Mukhammad Shakhristani - istorik religii i filosofii" [Muham-mad Shahristani - Historian of Religion and Philosophy]. Dissertation. AN TadzhSSR. Otd. filosofii. Dushanbe, 1988.

5409 Beliakova, E.G. "Effektivnost' ateisticheskoi propagandy kak filosofsko-sotsiologicheskaia problema" [Effectiveness of Atheistic Propaganda as Philosophic-Sociological Problem]. Dissertation. Akad. obshchestv. nauk pri TsK KPSS. M., 1989.

5410 Berdysheva, T.M. "Issledovanie problem religii i ateizma v sovetskoi literature 20-30-kh godov" [Research of Problems of Religion and

Atheism in Soviet Literature of the 20s-30s]. Dissertation. MGU im. M.V. Lomonosova. M., 1988.

5411 Biletskaia, L.V. "Funktsii kategorii 'vera' i 'ubezhdenie' v formirovanii nauchno-ateisticheskogo mirovozzreniia lichnosti" [Functions of the Categories "Faith" and "Conviction" in Forming Individual's Scientific-Atheistic World Outlook]. Dissertation. AN UkSSR. In-t filosofii. Kiev, 1988.

5412 Bogdanenko, R.V. "Nauchno-tekhnicheskii progress v sotsialisticheskom obshchestve kak faktor sekuliarizatsii" [Scientific-Technical Progress in Socialist Society as Factor of Secularization]. Dissertation. Akad. obshchestv. nauk pri TsK KPSS. M., 1988.

5413 Boitsova, O.Iu. "Katolicheskii neomodernizm G. Kiunga" [G. Kewing's Catholic Neo-Modernism]. Dissertation. MGU im. M.V. Lomonosova. M., 1988.

5414 Bondar', N.I. "Formirovanie i razvitie traditsionnoi dukhovnoi kul'tury kubanskogo kazachestva" [Forming and Development of Traditional Spiritual Culture of the Kuban Cossacks]. Dissertation. AN SSSR. In-t etnografii im. N.N. Miklukho-Maklaia. Leningr. chast'. L., 1988.

5415 Boriak, E.A. "Traditsionnye znaniia, obriady i verovaniia ukraintsev, sviazannye s tkachestvom (seredina XIX-nachalo XX v.)" [Traditional Knowledge, Rites and Beliefs of Ukrainians, Connected with Weaving (Middle XIXth- Early XXth C.)]. Dissertation. AN SSSR. In-t etnografii im. N.N. Miklukho-Maklaia. Leningr. chast'. L., 1989.

5416 Borshcheva, N.M. "Problemy ateizma i religii v sovetskom iskusstve" [Problems of Atheism and Religion in Soviet Art]. Dissertation. MGU im. M.V. Lomonosova. M., 1988.

5417 Botnar', I.F. "Rol' islamskogo faktora v politicheskoi zhizni Turtsii (70-e - pervaia polovina 80-kh. godov XX v.)" [The Role of the Islamic Factor in the Political Life of Turkey (70s - Early 80s of the XXth C.)]. Dissertation. MGU im. M.V. Lomonosova. M.: Nauka, 1987.

5418 Bratchikova, E.K. "Siiskoe evangelie kontsa XVII veka i tvorcheskie printsipy russkikh miniatiuristov v osvoienii zapadno-evropeiskoi khudozhestvennoi traditsii" [Siisk Gospel of the Late XVIIth Century and Creative

Principles of Russian Miniaturists in Mastering West-European Art Traditions]. Dissertation. LGU im. A.A. Zhdanova. L., 1988.

5419 Brudzin'ski, V. "Katolicheskaia kontseptsiia voiny i mira" [Catholic Conception of War and Peace]. Dissertation. Akad. obshchsestv nauk pri TsK KPSS. M., 1989.

5420 Bukhnovets, I.A. "Antinarodnaia deiatel'nost' pravoslavnoi tserkvi v Severnoi Bukovine i bor'ba progressivnykh sil kraia protiv sotsial'no-ekonomicheskogo i politicheskogo gneta dukhovenstva (1774-1918 gg.)" [Anti-Popular Activity of the Orthodox Church in Northern Bukovina and the Struggle of Progressive Forces of the Krai against Socio-Economical and Political Oppression of the Clergy (1774-1918)]. Dissertation. L'vov. gos. un-t im. I. Franko. L'vov, 1987.

5421 Bunina, Z.B. "Rabochie katolicheskie organizatsii v antifrankistskom dvizhenii Ispanii" [Workers Catholic Organizations in Spain's Anti-Francist Movement]. Dissertation. Institut mezhdunarodnogo rabochego dvizheniia AN SSSR. M., 1986.

5422 Buraev, D.I. "Tibetskie istochniki o proiskhozhdenii i roli religii bon v stanovlenii Tibetskogo gosudarstva VII-IX vv." [Tibetan Sources on the Origin and Role of Bon Religion in Creation of the State of Tibet VIIth-IXth Centuries]. Dissertation. AN SSSR, In-t vostokovedeniia, Lening. ot-nie. L., 1987.

5423 Buriakovskii, A.Z. "Kritika noveishikh khristianskikh kontseptsii istorii" [Criticism of the Newest Christian Conceptions of History]. Dissertation. LGU im A.A. Zhdanova. L., 1987.

5424 Burkov, V.V. "Funktsii sredstv massovoi informatsii v bor'be s burzhuazno-klerikal'noi propagandoi" [Functions of the Means of Mass Information in the Struggle with Bourgeois-Clerical Propaganda]. Dissertation. LGU im. A.A. Zhdanova. L., 1987.

5425 Burnis, Z.Iu. "Katolicheskaia etika v Litve v 1920-1940 godakh" [Catholic Ethics in Lithuania in 1920-1940]. Dissertation. Vil'n. un-t im. V. Kapsukasa. Vil'nius, 1984.

5426 Chekal', L.A. "Sotsial'naia priroda i gnoseologicheskie osobennosti illiuzorno-kompesatsionnoi funktsii religioznogo soznaniia" [Social Nature and Gnosiological Features of Illusory-Compensatory Function of Religious Consciousness]. Dissertation. AN UkSSR, In-t filosofii. Kiev, 1989.

5427 Chertov, O.V. "Gumanizm 'oksfordskikh reformatorov'" [Humanism of "Oxford Reformers"]. Dissertation. LGU im. A.A. Zhdanova. L., 1988.

5428 Chesnokova, O.I. "Problemy filosofii religii Gegelia" [Problems of Hegel's Philosophy of Religion]. Dissertation. LGU im. A.A. Zhdanova. L., 1986.

5429 Dagvadorzh, D. "Kriticheskii analiz lamaistskoi kontseptsii cheloveka" [Critical Analysis of Lamaist Conception of Man]. Dissertation. MGU im. M.V. Lomonosova. M., 1988.

5430 Danilov, S.V. "Zhertvoprinosheniia zhivotnykh v ritualakh drevnikh plemen Zabaikal'ia kak istochnik po istorii religioznykh verovanii skotovod-cheskikh narodov" [Sacrifice of Animals in the Rituals of Ancient Transbaikal Tribes as Historical Source of Religious Beliefs of Cattle-Breeding People]. Dissertation. Kemer. gos. un-t. Kemerovo, 1988.

5431 Davliatbekov, N. "Osveshchenie religii i verovanii naseleniia verkhov'ev reki Piandzh v trudakh russkikh dorevoliutsionnykh issledovatelei" [Interpretation of Religion and Faith of the Population of the Upper Piandzh Riverhead in the Works of Russian Pre-Revolutionary Researchers]. Dissertation. AN TadzhSSR, In-t istorii im. A. Donishe. Dushanbe, 1986.

5432 Davydova, N.A. "Ideino-politicheskaia rol' buddiiskoi sangkhi v Shri Lanke i Tailande posle vtoroi mirovoi voiny" [Ideological-Political Role of Buddhist Sanga in Sri Lanka and Thailand after the Second World War]. Dissertation. AN SSSR, In-t vostokovedeniia. M.: Nauka, 1988.

5433 Delekov, L.A. "Avesta v sovremennoi nauke" [Avesta in Contemporary Science]. Dissertation. Mosk. gos. ped. in-t im. V.I. Lenina. M., 1986.

5434 Demchenkova, N.M. "Deiatel'nost' Kommunisticheskoi partii Belorussii po sovershenstvovaniiu form i metodov ateisticheskogo vospitaniia trudia-shchikhsia, 1971-1980" [Activity of the Communist Party of Belorussia in Perfection of Forms and Methods of Atheistic Education of Workers 1971-1980]. Dissertation. Belorus. gos. un-t im. V.I. Lenina. Minsk, 1987.

5435 Demeter, N.G. "Semeinaia obriadnost' tsygan Kelderari: (konets XIX-XX vv.) [Family Rites of Kelderary Gipsies: [(End XIXth-XXth Centuries)].

Dissertation. AN SSSR. In-t etnografii im. N.N. Miklukho-Maklaia. M., 1988.

5436 Denisova, L.V. "Obriad kak forma religioznoi deiatel'nosti" [Rite as a Form of Religious Activity]. Dissertation. Leningr. gos. ped. un-t im. A.I. Gertsena. L., 1988.

5437 Deriugin, S.V. "Teologiia osvobozhdeniia i revoliutsionnye protsessy v Latinskoi Amerike (70-e - 80-e gody)" [Theology of Liberation and Revolutionary Processes in Latin America (70s - 80s)]. Dissertation. AN SSSR. In-t mezhdunar. rabochego dvizheniia. M., 1989.

5438 Diatroptov, P.D. "Rasprostranenie khristianstva v Severnom Prichern.-mor'e" [Dissemination of Christianity in Northern Part of the Black Sea]. Dissertation. Mosk. gos. ped. in-t im. V.I. Lenina. M., 1988.

5439 Diuranov, A.A. "Filosofsko-eticheskii analiz problemy cheloveka v buddizme" [Philosophic-Ethical Analysis of the Problem of Man in Buddhism]. Dissertation. LGU. L., 1989.

5440 Dobretsova, V.V. "Bor'ba Kommunisticheskoi partii Zapadnoi Ukrainy protiv burzhuaznogo natsionalizma i klerikalizma, 1919-1939 gg" [The Struggle of the Communist Party of Western Ukraine against Bourgeois Nationalism and Clericalism, 1919-1939]. Dissertation. In-t istorii partii pri TsK Kompartii Ukrainy, fil. In-ta marksizma-leninizma pri TsK KPSS. Kiev, 1986.

5441 Dochanashvili, E.I. "Mtskhetskaia rukopis' i problema genezisa drevnegru-zinskoi versii bibleiskikh knig" [Mtshet Manuscript and the Problem of the Origin of Ancient Georgian Version of Scriptures]. Dissertation. Tbil. gos. un-t. Tbilisi, 1989.

5442 Dolgintseva, V.A. "Studencheskaia obriadnost' kak faktor formirovaniia nauchno-materialisticheskogo, ateisticheskogo mirovozzreniia" [Student Ceremonial as Forming Factor of Scientific-Materialist, Atheistic World Outlook]. Dissertation. AN UkSSR. In-t filosofii. Kiev, 1988.

5443 Dovbenko, V.M. "Filosofskii analiz sotsial'no-psikhologicheskogo aspekta religioznogo otchuzhdeniia" [Philosophical Analysis of Socio-Psychological Aspect of Religious Alienation]. Dissertation. AN UkSSR. In-t filosofii. Kiev, 1987.

5444 Dubman, E.L. "Tserkovno-monastyrskie feodaly v Simbirsko-Samarskom
      Povolzh'e v XVII-nachale XVIII v." [Church-Monastery Feudals in Simbir-
      Samarsk on the Volga in XVIIth-Early XVIIIth C.]. Dissertation.
      Kuibyshev. gos. ped. in-t im. V.V. Kuibysheva. Kuibyshev, 1986.

5445 Dudarenok, S.M. "Ateizm v razvitom sotsialisticheskom obshchestve"
      [Atheism in Developed Socialist Society]. Dissertation. LGU im. A.A.
      Zhdanova. L., 1984.

5446 Dudko, D.M. "Problemy verovanii iranoiazychnykh narodov Vostochnoi
      Evropy I tys. do n. e. - pervoi poloviny I tys. n. e. v otechestvennoi i
      zarubezhnoi istoriografii" [Problems of Beliefs of Iranianspeaking People
      of Eastern Europe in the First Millennium B.C. - Early First Milleniun
      A.D. in Native and Foreign Historiography]. Dissertation. AN SSSR. In-t
      vostokovedeniia. M., 1989.

5447 Dudyeva, T.K. "Ob'ektivnye usloviia i sub'ektivnye faktory povysheniia
      effektivnosti ateisticheskoi raboty" [Objective Conditions and Subjective
      Factors of the Rise of Effectiveness of Atheistic Work]. Dissertation.
      Akad. obshchestv. nauk pri TsK KPSS. M., 1988.

5448 Durmanova, E.A. "Deiatel'nost' Moskovskoi oblastnoi partiinoi organizatsii
      po atesticheskomu vospitaniiu trudiashchikhsia v usloviiakh razvitogo
      sotsializma" [Activity of Moscow District Party Organization in Atheistic
      Education of Workers in Conditions of Developed Socialism]. MGU im.
      M.V. Lomonosova. M., 1983.

5449 Dustov, D.K. "Rol' Kumskogo teologicheskogo tsentra v obshchestvenno-
      politicheskoi zhizni Irana (20 - 80-e gody XX v." [The Role of Qum
      Theological Center in Iran's Socio-Political Life (20s - 80s XXth C.)].
      Dissertation. AN SSSR. In-t vostokovedeniia. M., 1989.

5450 Dzhabarova, M. "Ateisticheskoe vospitanie kak faktor vozrastaniia sotsial'-
      noi aktivnosti zhenshchin" [Atheistic Education as Factor of Increase of
      Woman's Social Activity]. Dissertation. Tashk. politekh. un-t im. Abu
      Raikhana Beruni. Tashkent, 1989.

5451 Dzhanabi, M.M.T. al'. "Osobennosti sovremennykh islamskikh politicheskikh
      dvizhenii" [Peculiarities of Contemporary Islamic Political Movements].
      Dissertation. MGU im. M.V. Lomonosova. M., 1984.

5452 Dzhavadova, G.K. "Ateisticheskoe nasledie M.F. Akhundova i sovremennost'" [M.F. Akhundov's Atheistic Legacy and Contemporaneity]. Dissertation. Azerb gos un-t im. S.M. Kirova. Baku, 1987.

5453 Dzhomardzhidze, S.D. "Deiatel'nost' Kommunisticheskoi partii Gruzii po ateisticheskomu vospitaniiu molodezhi (1971-1980 gg)" [Activity of the Communist Party of Georgia in Atheistic Upbringing of Youth (1971-1980)]. Dissertation. In-t istorii partii pri TsK KP Gruzii, fil. In-ta marksizma-leninizma pri TsK KPSS. Tbilisi, 1984.

5454 Efremova, G.S. "Rol' dukovenstva v obshchetvenno-politicheskoi zhizni Irana v 60-70-kh godakh XX veka" [The Role of the Clergy in Socio-Political Life of Iran in the 60s-80s of the XXth Century]. Dissertation. MGU im. M.V. Lomonosova, In-t stran Azii i Afriki. M., 1985.

5455 Elkanidze, M.M. "'Makhavamsa' kak pamiatnik buddiiskoi ideologii drevnei Shri Lanki" ["Mahavamsa" as Memorial of Buddhist Ideology of the Ancient Sri-Lanka]. Dissertation. AN SSSR, In-t vostokovedeniia. M.: Nauka, 1988.

5456 Embulaeva, L.S. "Protestantizm o vzaimootnoshenii cheloveka i obshchestva" [Protestantism on Interrelations of Man and Society]. Dissertation. Akad. obshchestv. nauk pri TsK KPSS. M., 1989.

5457 Enukov, V.V. "Pogrebal'nyi obriad slavian Smolenskogo Podneprov'ia i Vitebskogo Podvin'ia" [Burial Ritual of Slavs of Smolensk by Dnieper and of Vitebsk Podvinia]. Dissertation. MGU im. M.V. Lomonosova. M., 1987.

5458 Falikov, B.Z. "Sotsial'no-politicheskie aspekty nekotorykh religioznykh dvizhenii v SShA" [Soci-Political Aspects of Some Religious Movements in USA]. Dissertation. AN SSSR, In-t SShA i Kanady. M., 1986.

5459 Farin'ia Khorkhe Dora Eusebiia. "Filosofskii analiz katolicheskoi antropologii" [Philosophical Analysis of Catholic Anthropology]. Dissertation. AN UkSSR. In-t filosofii. Kiev, 1988.

5460 Fedorov, I.O. "Uniatskaia politika Vatikana v Zapadnoi Belorussii v dovoennye gody (1919-1939)" [Uniate Policy of Vatican in Western Belorussia in Pre-War Years (1919-1939)]. Dissertation. Belorus. gos. un-t im. V.I. Lenina. Minsk, 1985.

5461 Fedutinov, Iu.Iu. "Islam v obshchestvenno-politicheskoi zhizni stran Zapadnoi Afriki" [Islam in Socio-Political Life in the Countries of Western Africa]. Dissertation. AN SSSR. In-t Afriki. M., 1988.

5462 Fernandes Dominges, R.R.S. "Obshchee i osobennoe v politike Kommunist-icheskoi partii Kuby po otnosheniiu k religii i tserkvi" [Common and Especial in the Policy of Cuban Communist Party Toward Religion and Church]. Dissertation. LGU im. A.A. Zhdanova. L., 1986.

5463 Filimonov, E.G. "Evoliutsiia khristianskogo sektantstva v sotsialisticheskom obshchestve" [The Evolution of Christian Sectarianism in Socialist Society]. Dissertation. MGU im. M.V. Lomonosova. M., 1985.

5464 Filipovich, L.A. "Filosofskii analiz pravoslavno-bogoslovskoi kontseptsii nravstvennykh kachestv cheloveka" [Philosophical Analysis of Orthodox-Theological Conception of Man's Moral Qualities]. Dissertation. AN UkSSR. In-t filosofii. Kiev, 1989.

5465 Filippova, M.I. "Burzhuaznoe islamovedenie SShA (50-80-e gg.) ob obshchest-vennykh funktsiiakh islama" [USA Bourgeois Islamic Studies (50s-80s) on Social Functions of Islam]. Dissertation. AN SSSR. In-t vostokovedeniia. M., 1988.

5466 Fokina, L.A. "Khristianizatsiia Drevnei Rusi v kontekste obshchestvennogo progressa" [Conversion to Christianity of Ancient Rus' in the Context of Social Progress]. Dissertation. MGU im. M.V. Lomonosova. M., 1989.

5467 Fokina, L.A. "Kriticheskii analiz antropologicheskoi tendentsii v russkom pravoslavii kontsa XIX - nachala XX veka" [Critical Analysis of Anthro-pological Tendency in Russian Orthodoxy Late XIXth - Early XXth Century]. Dissertation. LGU im. A.A. Zhdanova. L., 1987.

5468 Fominykh, E.V. "Proekty tserkovnykh preobrazovanii v Rossii v nachale XX veka" [Projects of Church Reforms in Russia Early XXth Century]. Dissertation. LGU im. A.A. Zhdanova. L., 1987.

5469 Frolova, E.A. "Problema very i znaniia v arabskoi filosofii" [The Problem of Faith and Knowledge in Arab Philosophy]. Dissertation. AN SSSR. In-t filosofii. M., 1985.

5470 Gabuniia, S.L. "Baskskie pogrebal'nye obriady i ikh gruzinskie paralleli" [Basques Burial Rites and Their Georgian Counterpart]. Dissertation. AN

SSSR. In-t etnografii im. N.N. Maklukho-Maklaia. Leningradskaia chast'. L., 1988.

5471 Gaidarov, G.I. "Teoreticheskie i metodologicheskie problemy preodoleniia perezhitkov morali islama" [Theoretical and Methodological Problems of Overcoming Moral Survivals of Islam]. Dissertation. Azerb. gos. un-t im. S.M. Kirova. Baku, 1986.

5472 Gaidis, A.A. "Kriticheskii analiz filosofsko-mirovozzrencheskikh osnov katolicheskogo klerikal'nogo antikommunizma" [Critical Analysis of Philosophic-World Outlook Foundations of Catholic Clerical Anti-Communism]. Dissertation. In-t filosofii i prava AN LitSSR. Vil'nius, 1984.

5473 Gal'skii, K.E. "Bor'ba Kompartii Ukrainy protiv reaktsionnoi ideologii i antinarodnoi praktiki ukrainskogo burzhuaznogo natsionalizma i uniatstva (1945-1986)" [The Struggle of the Communist Party of Ukraine against Reactionary Ideology and Anti-Popular Practice of Ukrainian Bourgeois Nationalism and Uniate Church (1945-1986)]. Dissertation. In-t istorii pri TsK KP Ukrainy. Kiev, 1987.

5474 Garadnai, Ia. "Teoriia sotsial'noi spravedlivosti v doktrine katolitsizma" [Theory of Social Justice in the Doctrine of Catholicism]. Dissertation. Akad. obshchhestv. nauk pri TsK KPSS. M., 1989.

5475 Gavrilov, I.E. "Mezhkhristianskie kontakty Moskovskoi patriarkhii kak faktor evoliutsii sovremennogo russkogo pravoslaviia" [Interchristian Contacts of the Moscow Patriarchate as Evolution Factor of Contemporary Russian Orthodoxy]. Dissertation. Leningr. gos. ped. in-t im. A.I. Gertsena. L., 1988.

5476 Gavriushenko, A.A. "Filip Melankhton: gumanist i reformator (1517-1524 gg.)" [Philip Melanchthon: Humanist and Reformer (1517-1524)]. Dissertation. Khark. gos. un-t im. A.M. Gor'kogo. Khar'kov, 1988.

5477 Gerasimova, K.M. "Etnosotsial'naia osnova sinkretizma kul'tovoi sistemy lamaizma" [Ethnosocial Basis of Syncretism of the Cult System of Lamaism]. Dissertation. AN SSSR. In-t etnografii im. N.N. Miklukho-Maklaia. M., 1989.

5478 Glebov, G.I. "Deiatel'nost' Kommunisticheskoi partii po osushchestvleniiu leninskoi politiki v otnoshenii religii i tserkvi, 1917-1925 gg." [Activity of the Communist Party in Realization of Leninist Policy Toward Religion and Church, 1917-1925]. Dissertation. MGU im. M.V. Lomonosova. M., 1985.

5479 Glomozda, K.E. "Kritika sovremennykh burzhuaznykh kontseptsii vvedeniia khristianstva v Drevnei Rusi" [Criticism of Contemporary Bourgeois Conception on Introduction of Christianity in Ancient Rus']. Dissertation. In-t istorii AN UkSSR. Kiev, 1986.

5480 Goliak, V.A. "Sotsialisticheskii trud kak faktor formirovaniia nauchno-ateisticheskogo mirovozzreniia" [Socialist Work as a Forming Factor of Scientific-Atheistic Outlook]. Dissertation. AN UkSSR. In-t filosofii. Kiev, 1983.

5481 Golobin, V.M. "Partiinoe rukovodstvo ateisticheskim vospitaniem sel'skoi molodezhi, 1971-1980 g" [Party Guidance in Atheistic Upbringing of Rural Youth, 1971-1980]. Dissertation. L'vov. gos. un-t im. I. Franko. L'vov, 1988.

5482 Golovko, L.V. "Osobennosti formirovaniia nauchno-ateisticheskogo mirovozzreniia studencheskoi molodezhi" [Peculiarities of Forming Scientific-Atheistic World Outlook of Students]. Dissertation. MGU im. M.V. Lomnosova. M., 1986.

5483 Golub', V.F. "Kritika 'bogoiskatel'skikh' fal'sifikatsii demokraticheskikh idei russkoi progressivnoi literatury" [Criticism of "God Seekers" Falsifications of Democratic Ideas of Russian Progressive Literature]. Dissertation. MGU im. M.V. Lomonosova. M., 1986.

5484 Grigorenko, A.Iu. "Svobodomyslie na Rusi kontsa XV - nachala XVI veka" [Free-Thinking in Rus' Late XVth - Early XVIth Century]. Dissertation. LGU im. A.A. Zhdanova. L., 1987.

5485 Grigorian, K.G. "Bor'ba peredovoi armianskoi obshchestvennosti protiv katolicheskoi propagandy v Zapadnoi Armenii v 30-70-e gody XIX veka" [The Struggle of Armenian Progressive Public Opinion against Catholic Propaganda in Western Armenia in the 30s - 70s of the XIXth Century]. Dissertation. AN ArmSSR. In-t istorii. Erevan, 1985.

5486 Guchinova, E.-B.M. "Sovremennye semeinye obriady kalmykov" [Contemporary Family Rituals of Kalmyks]. Dissertation. AN SSSR. In-t etnografii im. N.N. Miklukho-Maklaia. M., 1989.

5487 Gur'ianova, N.S. "Krest'ianskii antimonarkhicheskii protest v staroobriad-cheskoi eskhatologicheskoi literature perioda pozdnego feodalizma" [Peasant Anti-Monarchist Protest in Old Beliefs Eschatologic Literature in the Late Feudalism]. Dissertation. AN SSSR, Sib. otd-nie. In-t istorii, filologii i filosofii. Novosibirsk, 1985.

5488 Gurvits, M.M. "Venesuel'skaia sotsial-khristianskaia partiia KOPEI: istoriia, ideologiia, politika" [Venezuelan Social-Christian Party KOPEI: History, Ideology, Policy]. Dissertation. AN SSSR. In-t Latin. Ameriki. M., 1986.

5489 Guseva, A.V. "Problema soznaniia v filosofii vseedinstva" [The Problem of Consciousness in Philosophy of the Allunity]. Dissertation. LGU im. A.A. Zhdanova. L., 1988.

5490 Iagodzinski, Ia. "Katolicheskaia kontseptsiia khristianskoi Evropy" [Catholic Conception of Christian Europe]. Dissertation. Akad. obshchestv. nauk pri TsK KPSS. M., 1988.

5491 Iakh'iaev, M.G. "Islam kak sotsial'nyi fenomen sotsialisticheskogo obshche-stva" [Islam as a Social Phenomenon of Socialist Society]. Dissertation. Akad. obshchestv. nauk pri TsK KPSS. Kaf. ideol. raboty. M., 1988.

5492 Iakovenko, S.G. "Bretskaia tserkovnaia uniia: politicheskie i ideologicheskie aspekty (vtoraia polovina XVI v)" [Bretsk Uniate Church: Political and Ideological Aspects (Late XVIth C.)]. Dissertation. AN SSSR. In-t istorii SSSR. M., 1988.

5493 Ianchenko, L.V. "Kritika esteticheskoi kontseptsii sovremennogo russkogo pravoslaviia" [Criticism of Aesthetic Conception of Contemporary Russian Orthodoxy]. Dissertation. AN UkSSR. In-t filosofii Kiev, 1988.

5494 Iasinskii, E. "Problemy preodoleniia vliianiia katolicheskoi tserkvi na molodezh' v PNR" [Problems of Overcoming the Influence of Catholic Church on Youth of the Polish Peoples Republic]. Dissertation. Akad. obshchestv. nauk pri TsK KPSS. M., 1988.

5495 Ignat'ev, I.P. "Kriticheskii analiz sovremennykh psevdovostochnykh religioz-nykh kul'tov" [Critical Analysis of Contemporary Pseudo-Oriental Reli-gious Cults]. Dissertation. LGU im. A.A. Zhdanova. L., 1986.

5496 Il'in, V.N. "Anabaptizm v Anglii v XVI veke" [Anabaptism in England in the XVIth Century]. Dissertation. MGU im. M.V. Lomonosova. M., 1987.

5497 Iurtaev, V.I. "Islamskoe dvizhenie v kontse 70-kh - nachale 80-kh gg. i studenchestvo" [Islamic Movement in the Late 70s - Early 80s and Students]. Dissertation. AN SSSR. In-t vostokovedeniia. M., 1985.

5498 Iuzhakova, T.P. "Formirovanie nachal'nykh ateisticheskikh prestavlenii i poniatii u mladshikh shkol'nikov v protsesse obucheniia" [Formation of Initial Atheistic Notions and Concepts of Junior Schoolboys in the Process of Education]. Dissertation. Cheliab. gos. un-t. Cheliabinsk, 1986.

5499 Ivanov, A.I. "Sotsiologicheskii analiz religioznosti v trudovom kollektive i zadachi ateisticheskogo vospitaniia" [Sociological Analysis of Religiosity in Labour Collective and Tasks of Atheistic Education]. Dissertation. MGU im. M.V. Lomonosova. M., 1988.

5500 Kalashian, A.G. "Ateisticheskie vzgliady Nazareta Tagevariana" [Nazareth Tagevarian's Atheistic Views]. Dissertation. Tbil. gos. un-t. Tbilisi, 1988.

5501 Kalita, L.V. "Ateisticheskoe vospitanie molodezhi v trudovom kollektive" [Atheistic Upbringing of Youth in Labour Collective]. Dissertation. AN BSSR. In-t filosofii i prava. Minsk, 1987.

5502 Kalmykov, S.K. "Filosofsko-sotsiologicheskii analiz sovremennogo mistitsizma" [Philosophic-Sociological Analysis of Contemporary Mysticism]. Dissertation. Akad. obshchestv. nauk pri TsK KPSS. M., 1988.

5503 Kanterov, I.Ia. "Kriticheskii analiz filosofsko-teologicheskikh interpretatsii nauchnogo ateizma" [Critical Analysis of Philosophic-Theological Interpretation of Scientific Atheism]. Dissertation. MGU im. M.V. Lomonosova, Filos. Fak. M., 1986.

5504 Kapustin, N.S. "Osobennosti evoliutsii religii" [Peculiarities of Religion's Evolution]. Dissertation. Rost n/D. gos. un-t. Rostov n/D, 1988.

5505 Kapustina, M.I. "Problema sootnoshenii kul'tury i religii" [The Problem of Correlation of Culture and Religion]. Dissertation. LGU im. A.A. Zhdanova. L., 1986.

5506 Kavlelashvili, A.K. "Ateisticheskie vzgliady Niko Nikoladze" [Atheistic Views of Niko Nikoladze]. Disertation. Tbilis. gos. un-t. Tbilisi, 1986.

5507 Kazakov, M.M. "Religiozno-politicheskaia bor'ba v seredine i vtoroi polovine IV veka v Rimskoi imperii" [Religious-Political Struggle in the Middle and Late IVth. Century in Roman Empire]. Dissertation. Mosk. gos. ped. in-t im. V.I Lenina. M., 1988.

5508 Khachatrian, A.S. "Ideologiia i deiatel'nost' zarubezhnykh armianskikh tserkvei" [Ideology and Activity of Armenian Churches Abroad]. Dissertation. MGU im. M.V. Lomonosova. M.: MGU, 1986.

5509 Khadzhiev, Ia. "Deiatel'nost' Kompartii Turkmenistana po ateisticheskomu vospitaniiu naseleniia v 70-80-e gody" [Activity of Turkmenistan Communist Party in Atheistic Education of the Population in the 70s-80s]. Dissertation. In-t istorii partii pri TsK Kompartii Ukrainy, fil. In-ta marksizma-leninizma pri TsK KPSS. Kiev, 1988.

5510 Khaidarova, M.S. "Formirovanie i razvitie musul'manskogo prava v Arabskom khalifate (VII-XIII vv.)" [The Formation and Development of Moslem Law in Arab Caliphate (VIIth-XIIIth Centuries)]. Dissertation. AN SSSR. In-t gosudarstva i prava. M., 1985.

5511 Kamshik, P. "Inzhenerno-tekhnicheskaia intelligentsiia kak ob'ekt ateisticheskogo vospitaniia" [Engineering-Technical Intelligentsia as Object of Atheistic Education]. Dissertation. MGU im. M.V. Lomonosova. M., 1987.

5512 Khevecheria, S.A. "Optimizm nauchnogo ateizma" [Optimism of Scientific Atheism]. Dissertation. LGU im. A.A. Zhdanova. L., 1986.

5513 Khrapova, N.Iu. "Mesto i rol' Altaiskoi dukhovnoi missii v protsesse kolonizatsii i khoziaistvennogo osvoeniia Gornogo Altaia (1828-1905 gg.)" [The Place and Role of the Altai Religious Mission in the Process of Colonization and Economical Mastery of Gorno-Altai (1828-1905)]. Dissertation. Tom. gos. un-t im. V.V. Kuibysheva. Tomsk, 1989.

5514 Khul', Z. "Kriticheskii analiz istolkovaniia problemy 'chelovek - priroda' v sovremennoi katolicheskoi filosofii v Pol'she" [Critical Analysis of Interpretation of the Problem "Man - Nature" in Contemporary Catholic Philosophy in Poland]. Dissertation. AN UkSSR. In-t filosofii. Kiev, 1989.

5515 Khzhanovskii, K. "Katolicheskaia tserkov' v Pol'she i krest'ianstvo" [Catholic Church in Poland and Peasantry]. Dissertation. Akad. obshchestv. nauk pri TsK KPSS. M., 1988.

5516 Kimelev, Iu.A. "Sovremennaia zapadnaia filosofiia religii: osnovnye formy, napravleniia i tendentsii v 1970-1980-e gody" [Contemporary Western

Philosophy of Religion: Basic Directions, Forms and Tendencies in 1970s-1980s]. Dissertation. AN SSSR. In-t filosofii. M., 1989.

5517   Kirabaev, N.S. "Sotsial'naia filosofiia musul'manskogo srednevekov'ia" [Social Philosophy of Moslem Middle Ages]. Dissertation. MGU im. M.V. Lomonosova. M.: Un-t druzhby narodov, 1988.

5518   Kirikov, O.I "Kriticheskii analiz dogmaticheskikh obosnovanii pravoslavnoi kontseptsii 'makrodiakoni'" [Critical Analysis of Dogmatic Substantiation of Orthodox Conception "Macrodeaconate"]. Dissertation. AN UkSSR. In-t filosofii. Kiev, 1988.

5519   Klimov, V.V. "Filosofsko-sotsiologicheskii analiz osnovnykh napravlenii uniatsko-natsionalisticheskikh fal'sifikatsii dukhovnoi kul'tury" [Philosophical-Sociological Analysis of the Basic Directions of the Uniate-Nationalist Falsifications of Spiritual Culture]. Dissertation. AN UkSSR. In-t filosofii. Kiev, 1986.

5520   Kniazev, V.M. "Poniatie kul'tury: protivopolozhnost' dialektiko-materialisticheskogo i religiozno-antropologicheskogo podkhodov" [The Concept of Culture: In Contrast to Dialectic-Materialistic and Religious-Anthropological Approaches]. Dissertation. Ural. gos. un-t im. A.M. Gor'kogo. Sverdlovsk, 1984.

5521   Kobelianskaia, L.S. "Nauchno-ateisticheskii analiz religioznykh predstavlenii o smysle zhizni" [Scientific-Atheistic Analysis of Religious Notions about Meaning of Life]. Dissertation. AN UkSSR. In-t filosofii. Kiev, 1986.

5522   Kodymova, L. "Vospitanie ateisticheskoi ubezhdennosti u studencheskoi molodezhi" [Education of Atheistic Conviction of Students]. Dissertation. MGU im. M.V. Lomonosova. M., 1987.

5523   Kodzoev, B.A. "Partiinoe rukovodstvo povysheniem roli intelligentsii v internatsional'nom i ateisticheskom vospitanii trudiashchikhsia v 1959-1970 gg." [Party Guidance in Raising the Role of Intelligentsia in International and Atheistic Education of Workers in 1959-1970]. Dissertation. Mosk. gos. ped. in-t im. V.I. Lenina. M., 1985.

5524   Kolodni, A.N. "Ateizm kak forma mirovozzrencheskogo znaniia i samosoznaniia lichnosti" [Atheism as Form of World Outlook Knowledge and Individual's Self Consciousness]. Dissertation. AN UkSSR. In-t filosofii. Kiev, 1987.

5525 Kondratik, L.I. "Etapy i faktory stanovleniia ateisticheskogo soznaniia lichnosti v sotsialisticheskom obshchestve" [Stages and Factors in the Making of Individual's Atheistic Consciousness in Socialist Society]. Dissertation. AN UkSSR. In-t filosofii. Kiev, 1988.

5526 Kornev, V.I. "Buddizm Tkheravady i ego rol' v obshchestvennoi zhizni stran Iuzhnoi i Iugo-Vostochnoi Azii" [Theravadin Buddhism and Its Role in Social Life of South and South-Eastern Asian Countries]. Dissertation. AN SSSR. In-t vostokovedeniia. M., 1985.

5527 Korovikov, A.V. "Differentsiatsiia islamskogo dvizheniia i usilenie v nem ekstremistskikh tendentsii v 1967-1985 godakh" [Differentation of Islamic Movement and Strengthening in its Extremist Tendencies in 1967- 1985]. Dissertation. AN SSSR. In-t vostokovedeniia. M.: Nauka, 1988.

5528 Korrea Orsegera, S.M. "Problemy sovershenstvovaniia ateisticheskogo vospitaniia kubinskikh zhenshchin" [Problems of Perfection of Atheistic Education of Cuban Women]. Dissertation. LGU im. A.A. Zhdanova. L., 1986.

5529 Kosedovskii, Ia. "Ideologicheskaia ekspansiia katolicheskoi tserkvi v otnoshenii rabochego klassa PNR (80-e gody)" [Ideological Expansion of Catholic Church Toward Workers Class of Polish People's Republic (in the 80s)]. Dissertation. Akad. obshchestv. nauk pri TsK KPSS. M., 1988.

5530 Koval'chuk, S.N. "Filosofskaia problematika v protestantskom modernizme SShA" [Philosophical Problematics in Protestant Modernism in USA]. Dissertation. AN SSSR. In-t filosofii. M., 1988.

5531 Kozhokin, M.M. "Khristiansko-demokraticheskoe dvizhenie v burzhuaznoi Pol'skoi respublike (1918-1926 gg.)" [Christian-Democratic Movement in Polish Bourgeois Republic (1918-1926)]. Dissertation. MGU im. M.V. Lomonosova. M., 1988.

5532 Krapivin, M.Iu. "Partiinoe rukovodstvo bor'boi komsomola protiv religiozno-klerikal'nykh vliianii na molodezh' (Okt. 1917-1925 gg.)" [Party Guidance in Komsomol's Struggle against Religious-Clerical Influence on Youth (Oct. 1917-1925)]. Dissertation. Leningr. gos. ped. im-t im. A.I. Gertsena. L., 1988.

5533 Krashchenko, T.B. "Sotsial'no-psikhologicheskie aspekty vozniknoveniia, funk-tsionirovaniia i preodoleniia religioznogo soznaniia" [Socio-Psychological

Aspects of the Origin, Functioning and Overcoming of Religious Consciousness]. Dissertation. Mosk. in-t nar. khoz-va im. G.V. Plekhanova. M., 1986.

5534 Krasiuk, V.F. "Formirovanie ateisticheskogo mirovozzreniia trudiashchikhsia Belorussii v nachale XX veka" [Forming Atheistic World Outlook of Workers of Belorussia Early XXth Century]. Dissertation. AN BSSR. In-t filosofii i prava. Minsk, 1984.

5535 Krasovskaia, L.M. "Evoliutsiia nravstvennoi doktriny sovremennogo katolitsizma" [Evolution of Moral Doctrine of the Contemporary Catholicism]. Dissertation. MGU im. M.V. Lomonosova. M., 1987.

5536 Kruglova, G.A. "Kritika religiozno-idealisticheskikh kontseptsii vzaimodeistviia obshchetsva i prirody" [Criticism of Religious-Idealistic Conceptions of Interaction of Society and Nature]. Dissertation. Belorus. gos. un-t im. V.I. Lenina. Minsk, 1987.

5537 Kudriantsev, V.A. "Problema kul'tury v religioznom ekzistentsializme Paulia Tillikha" [The Problem of Culture in Paul Tillich's Religious Existentialism]. Dissertation. MGU im. M.V. Lomonosova. M., 1986.

5538 Kukhna, M. "Pol'skaia intelligentsiia i katolicheskaia tserkov'" [Polish Intelligentsia and the Catholic Church]. Dissertation. Akad. obshchestv. nauk pri TsK KPSS. M., 1988.

5539 Kulishova, T.A. "Deiatel'nost' partiinykh organizatsii Ukrainy po ateisticheskomu vospitaniiu rabochego klassa (1971-1980 gg.)" [Activity of Party Organizations of Ukraine in Atheistic Education of Workers Class (1971-1980)]. Dissertation. Kiev. gos. un-t im. T.G. Shevchenko. Kiev, 1987.

5540 Kuptsova, S.V. "Kriticheskii analiz sovremennykh teologicheskikh interpretatsii evoliutsii organicheskoi prirody i antropogeneza" [Critical Analysis of Contemporary Theological Interpretations of Evolution of Organic Nature and Anthropogeny]. Dissertation. MGU im. M.V. Lomonosova. M., 1986.

5541 Kurbanov, V.A. "Ateisticheskii aspekt internatsionalizatsii obshchestvennoi zhizni pri razvitom sotsializme" [Atheistic Aspect of Internationalisation of Social Life under Developed Socialism]. Dissertation. Azerb. gos. un-t im. S.M. Kirova. Baku, 1984.

5542 Kurganskaia, V.D. "Religiozno-filosofskoe soznanie v Rossii nachala XX v. kak sotsial'no-politicheskii fenomen" [Religious-Philosophic Consciousness in Russia Early XXth C. as Socio-Political Phenomenon]. Dissertation. MGU im. M.V. Lomonosova. M., 1987.

5543 Kusakin, A.A. "Stanovlenie i razvitie massovogo ateizma na Dal'nem Vostoke SSSR" [Formation and Development of Mass Atheism in the Far East of the USSR]. Dissertation. Leningr. gos. ped. in-t im. A.I. Gertsena. L., 1983.

5544 Kushnir, S.L. "Kriticheskii analiz sovetologicheskikh kontseptsii polozheniia religii i tserkvi v SSSR" [Critical Analysis of Sovietological Conceptions of the Position of Religion and Church in the USSR]. Dissertation. MGU im. M.V. Lomonosova. M., 1987.

5545 Kuz'min, B.V. "Indifferentnoe otnoshenie k religii i ateizmu sredi rabotaiush-chei molodezhi i puti formirovaniia ateisticheskoi ubezhdennosti" [Indifferent Attitude Towards Religion and Atheism among Working Youth and Means of Forming Atheistic Consciousness]. Dissertation. AN UkSSR. In-t filosofii. Kiev, 1986.

5546 Kuznetsov, V.S. "Religioznyi ekstremizm v baptizme: mekhanizmy nasazhd-eniia, osobennosti proiavleniia, puti preodoleniia" [Religious Extremism in Baptism: Spreading Mechanism, Manifestation Features, Ways of Overcoming]. Dissertation. AN UkSSR. In-t filosofii. Kiev., 1988.

5547 Kvapish, Ryshard. "Kriticheskii analiz ideologicheskikh i politicheskikh kontseptsii katolicheskogo ob'edineniia PAKS" [Critical Analysis of Ideological and Political Conceptions of Catholic Association PAX]. Dissertation. Akad. obshchestv. nauk pri TsK KPSS. M., 1988.

5548 Larionova, I.V. "Partiinaia i komsomol'skaia pechat' - vazhneishee sredstvo ateisticheskogo vospitaniia molodezhi" [Party and Komsomol Press - Most Important Means of Atheistic Upbringing of Youth]. Dissertation. MGU im. M.V. Lomonosova. M., 1987.

5549 Lebedev, S.N. "Sovremennyi dzen-buddizm" [Contemporary Zen-Buddhism]. Dissertation. Mosk. un-t. M., 1981.

5550 Leshan, V.E. "Novye tendentsii v evoliutsii religioznogo sektantstva" [New Tendencies in Evolution of Religious Sectarianism]. Dissertation. Akad. obshchestv. nauk pri TsK KPSS. M., 1985.

5551 Leshkanin, I. "Kritika revizionistskikh i opportunisticheskikh izvrashchenii nauchnogo ateizma" [Criticism of Revisionist and Opportunist Distortions of Scientific Atheism]. Dissertation. MGU im. M.V. Lomonosova. M., 1986.

5552 Levchenko, N.I. "Metodizm i antirabovladel'cheskoe dvizhenie v SShA (1830-1861 gg.)" [Methodism and Anti-Slavery Movement in the USA (1830-1861)]. Dissertation. AN SSSR. In-t vseobshch. istorii. M., 1988.

5553 Lomidze, B.G. "Ateisticheskii kharakter marksistsko-leninskogo ponimaniia cheloveka" [Atheistic Character of Marxist-Leninist Understanding of Man]. Dissertation. Tbil. gos. un-t. Tbilisi, 1989.

5554 Lotys, Zbignev. "Kontseptsiia estestvennogo prava i sovremennaia ideologicheskaia bor'ba" [Conception of Natural Law and Contemporary Ideological Struggle]. Dissertation. Rost. gos. un-t. im. M.A. Suslova. Rostov n/D, 1988.

5555 Lubchinskii, A.K. "Sotsialisticheskaia obriadnost' kak faktor preodoleniia nravstvennykh ustanovok religii i utverzhdeniia kommunisticheskoi morali" [Socialist Ceremonial as Factor for Overcoming Religious Moral Aims and Confirmation of Communist Morality]. Dissertation. AN UkSSR. In-t filosofii. Kiev., 1986.

5556 Luchshev, E.M. "Materialisticheskoe i ateisticheskoe soderzhanie estestvenno-nauchnoi propagandy v Rossii vo vtoroi polovine XIX veka" [Materialist and Atheistic Content of Natural-Scientific Propaganda in Russia Late XIXth Century]. Dissertation. LGU im. A.A. Zhdanova. L., 1984.

5557 Mageria, O.P. "Internatsionalizatsiia sovetskikh prazdnikov i obriadov kak obshchestvenno-istoricheskaia zakonomernost'" [Internationalization of Soviet Holidays and Ceremonials as Socio-Historical Regularity]. Dissertation. Kiev. gos. un-t im. T.G. Shevchenko. Kiev, 1988.

5558 Makharadze, M.K. "Filosofskoe soderzhanie areopagitiki" [Philosophical Content of Areopagitica]. Dissertation. Tbil. gos. un-t. Tbilisi, 1988.

5559 Maksimov, N.V. "Rol' pravosoznaniia v formirovanii ateisticheskogo mirovoz-zreniia" [The Role of Lawconsciousness in the Shaping of Atheistic World Outlook]. Dissertation. LGU im. A.A. Zhdanova. L., 1984.

5560 Mamedov, E.S. "Tsarizm i vysshee musul'manskoe soslovie Zakavkaz'ia" [Tsarism and the Highest Moslem Gentry of Transcaucasus]. Dissertation. Azerb. gos un-t im. S.M. Kirova. Baku, 1987.

5561 Mamedov, M.M. "Obydennoe religioznoe soznanie i osobennosti ego evoliu-tsii v usloviiakh razvitogo sotsializma" [Ordinary Religious Consciousness and Features of Its Evolution under Developed Socialism]. Disesrtation. AN AzSSR. In-t filosofii i prava. Baku, 1985.

5562 Marchenko, A.V. "Kriticheskii analiz eticheskikh vzgliadov predstavitelei bogoiskatel'stva v Rossii kontsa XIX - nachala XX veka" [Critical Analysis of Ethical Views of Representatives of God Seekers in Russia Late XIXth - Early XXth Century]. Dissertation. Kiev. gos. un-t im. T.G. Shevchenko. Kiev, 1989.

5563 Mardanov, R.S. "Vzaimoobogashchenie natsional'nykh kul'tur kak faktor formirovaniia ateisticheskoi ubezhdennosti trudiashchikhsia" [Mutual Enrichment of National Cultures as Forming Factor of Atheistic Conviction of Workers]. Dissertation. Tashk. gos. un-t im. V.I. Lenina. Tashkent, 1987.

5564 Mardonova, A. "Arkhaicheskie obriady i verovaniia gissarskikh tadzhikov" [Archaic Rites and Beliefs of Gissar Tajiks]. Dissertation. AN SSSR. In-t etnografii im. N.N. Miklukho-Maklaia. Leningr. chast'. L., 1989.

5565 Mar'iasov, A.G. "Vneshniaia politika i diplomatiia Islamskoi Respubliki Iran (1979-1983 gg.)" [Foreign Policy and Diplomacy of the Islamic Republic of Iran (1979-1983)]. Dissertation. Diplomat. akad. MID SSSR. M., 1985.

5566 Martines Kasanova, M. "Sotsial'noe znachenie religioznogo sinkretizma v katolitsizme na Kube" [Social Importance of Religious Syncretism in Catholicism in Kuba]. Dissertation. AN UkSSR. In-t filosofii. Kiev, 1987.

5567 Martyniuk, E.I. "Vlianie religioznykh predstavlenii na pravosoznanie veruiushchikh v SSSR" [Influuence of Religious Notions on Believers Sense of Justice in the USSR]. Dissertation. MGU im. M.V. Lomono-sova. M., 1988.

5568 Matiukhina, A.A. "'Vostochnaia politika' Vatikana na sovremennom etape" ["Oriental Policy" of Vatican in Contemporary Stage]. Dissertation. LGU. L., 1989.

5569 Mendelova, E. "Rol' isskustva v formirovanii religioznogo i ateisticheskogo mirovozzreniia" [The Role of Art in Shaping Religious and Atheistic World Outlook]. Dissertation. MGU im. M.V. Lomonosova. M., 1989.

5570 Migovich, I.I. "Kritika ideologii i politicheskoi praktiki uniatskogo klerikal'nogo natsionalizma" [Criticism of Ideology and Political Practice of Uniate Clerical Nationalism]. Dissertation. Akad. obshchestv. nauk pri TsK KPSS. M., 1986.

5571 Mirashvili, N.Sh. "Svetskie motivy v tvorchestve Sofroniia Ierusalimskogo" [Secular Motifs in Sophrony of Jerusalem Creative Work]. Dissertation. Tbil. gos. un-t. Tbilisi, 1988.

5572 Miroshnikova, E.M. "Kritika sovremennogo katolicheskogo prozelitizma" [Criticism of the Current Catholic Proselytism]. Dissertation. Leningr. gos. un-t im. A.I. Gertsena. L., 1986.

5573 Mirova, S. "Sotsial'nye i sotsial'no-psikhologicheskie faktory vosproizvodstva traditsii islama i shariata v otnoshenii k zhenshchine" [Social and Socio-Psychological Factors in Reproduction of Traditions of Islam and Shariat in Relation to Woman]. Dissertation. Akad. obshchestv. nauk pri TsK KPSS. M., 1989.

5574 Mirrakhimov, M. "Rol' sovetskoi obriadnosti v preodolenii religioznykh traditsii" [The Role of Soviet Ceremonial in Overcoming Religious Traditions]. Dissertation. Akad. obshchestv. nauk pri TsK KPSS. M., 1987.

5575 Moiseeva, A.I. "Traditsii svobodomysliia i ateizma v russkoi dukhovnoi kul'ture" [Traditions of Free Thinking and Atheism in Russian Spiritual Culture]. Dissertation. MGU im. M.V. Lomonosova. M., 1988.

5576 Moliakov, I.Iu. "Kriticheskii analiz roli Biblii v sovremennoi ideologicheskoi bor'be" [Critical Analysis of the Role of the Bible in Contemporary Ideological Struggle]. Dissertation. LGU im. A.A. Zhdanova. L., 1986.

5577 Mongush, M.V. "Lamaism v Tuve" [Lamaism in Tuva]. Dissertation. AN SSSR. In-t etnografi im. N.N. Miklukho-Maklaia. M., 1989.

5578 Montero, Kh.Kh. "Posledovatel'noe povedenie Kompartii Kuby printsipov marksizma-leninizma po religioznomu voposu" [Consistent Conduct of the Communist Party of Cuba in Marxist-Leninist Principles on the Religious Problem]. Dissertation. AN UkSSR. In-t filosofii. Kiev, 1986.

5579 Morina, L.G. "Znachenie leninskogo printsipa edinstva filosofii i estestvoznaniia dlia ateisticheskogo vospitaniia" [The Significance of Leninist Principle of Unity of Philosophy and Science for Atheistic Education]. Dissertation. MGU im. M.V. Lomonosova. M., 1985.|

5580 Movsumova, L.D. "Sotsial'no-ekonomicheskie i dukhovnye sekuliarizatsii zhenshchin v usloviiakh sotsializma" [Socio-Economic and Spiritual Secularization of Women under Socialism]. Dissertation. AN AzSSR. In-t filosofii i prava. Baku, 1987.

5581 Mukasov, S.M. "Traditsii svobodomysliia v dukhovnoi kul'ture kirgizskogo naroda" [Traditions of Free Thinking in Spiritual Life of Kirghizian People]. Dissertation. MGU im. M.V. Lomonosova. M., 1987.

5582 Mukhatov, T.D. "Obshchestvennoe mnenie kak faktor ateisticheskogo vospitaniia: metodologicheskie i prakticheskie problemy" [Public Opinion as Factor of Atheistic Education: Methodological and Practical Problems]. Dissertation. Akad. obshchestv. nauk pri TsK KPSS. M., 1987.

5583 Muradov, M.K. "Deiatel'nost' Kommunisticheskoi partii Azerbaidzhana po ateisicheskomu vospitaniiu trudiashchikhsia (1971-1975 gg.)" [Activity of the Communist Party of Azerbaijan in Atheistic Education of Workers (1971-1975)]. Dissertation. Azerb. gos. ped. in-t im. V.I. Lenina. Baku, 1986.

5584 Murtuzaliev, S.I. "Bolgarskii narod i osmanskaia politika islamizatsii (vtoraia polovina XV-XVI v.)" [Bulgarian People and Ottoman Policy of Islamization (Late XVth-XVI th C.)]. Dissertation. Institut slavianovedeniia i balkanistiki AN SSSR (Dagestanskii gosudarstvennyi universitet im. V.I. Lenina). 1986.

5585 Muslimov, S.Sh. "Obshchee i osobennoe v stanovlenii i razvitii nauchnomaterialisticheskogo, ateisticheskogo miroponimaniia narodov Severnogo-Kavkaza" [Common and Particular in Creation and Development of Scientific-Materialist, Atheistic World Outlook of People of Northern Caucasus]. Dissertation. AN AzSSR. In-t filoofii i prava. Baku, 1987.

5586 Muzhukhoev, M.B. "Srednevekovye kul'tovye pamiatniki Tsentral'nogo Kavkaza kak istoricheskii istochnik" [Medieval Religious Monuments of Central Caucasus as Historical Sources]. Dissertation. AN SSSR. In-t arkheologii. M., 1985.

5587 Muzikiavichius, A. "Prichiny sokhraneniia i osobennosti funktsionirovaniia religioznoi obraidnosti v sotsialisticheskom obshchestve" [Reasons of Preservation and Features of Functioning of Religious Ritual in Socialist Society]. Dissertation. Akad. obshchestv. nauk pri TsK KPSS. M., 1989.

5588 Nakani, M.V. "Mesto i sotsial'naia funktsiia religioznykh traditsii v sisteme gruzinskikh natsional'nykh traditsii" [Place and Social Function of Religious Traditions in the System of Georgian National Traditions]. Dissertation. Tbil. gos. un-t. Tbilisi, 1988.

5589 Nakkash, A.Kh. "Problema vlasti v islame. Istoricheskaia evoliutsiia arabskikh musul'manskikh kontseptsii" [The Problem of Power in Islam. Historical Evolution of Arab Moslem Conception]. Dissertation. AN SSSR. In-t vostokovedeniia. M., 1987.

5590 Nasrullaev, Kh. "Sushchnost' prisposobleniia ideologii islama i taktiki musul'manskogo dukhovenstva v sovremennykh usloviiakh" [The Essence of Adaptation of Ideology of Islam and Tactics of Moslem Clergy in Contemporary Conditions]. Dissertation. Tashk. gos. un-t im. V.I. Lenina. Tashkent, 1987.

5591 Nechaev, M.G. "Kontrrevoliutsionnaia deiatel'nost' tserkvi v period podgotovki i provedeniia Velikoi Oktiabr'skoi sotsialisticheskoi revoliutsii i grazhdanskoi voiny na Urale (1917-1919 gg.)" [Counterrevolutionary Activity of the Church in the Period of Preparation and Conducting the Great October Socialist Revolution and Civil War in Urals (1917-1919)]. Dissertation. Ural. gos. un-t im. A.M. Gor'kogo. Sverdlovsk, 1988.

5592 Nemirovskaia, L.Z. "Religiia i gumanizm v mirovozzrenii Tolstogo" [Religion and Humanism in Tolstoi's World Outlook]. MGU im. M.V. Lomonosova. M., 1988.

5593 Nesterov, S.P. "Kon' v kul'takh tiurkoiazychnykh plemen Tsentral'noi Azii v epokhu srednevekov'ia" [Horse in the Cults of Turkic Tribes of the Central Asia in the Middle Ages]. Dissertation. AN SSSR, Sib. otd-nie. In-t istorii, filologii i filosofii. Novosibirsk, 1986.

5594 Nguen Khyu Vui. "Sotsial'nye funktsii religii v usloviiakh neokolonial'nogo obshchestva" [Social Functions of Religion in Neocolonial Society]. Dissertation. Mosk. un-t. M., 1981.

5595 Nifontov, A.V. "Deiatel'nost' Kompartii Moldavii po ateisticheskomu vospitaniiu trudiashchikhsia v period mezhdu XXIII i XXV s'ezdami KPSS" [Activity of the Communist Party of Moldavia in Atheistic Education of Workers in the Period Between the XXIIIrd and XXVth Congresses of the CPSU]. Dissertation. MGU im. M.V. Lomonosova. M., 1989.

5596 Nikifirov, A.V. "Genezis i evoliutsiia eskhata-khiliasticheskikh predstavlenii adventizma sed'mogo dnia i puti ikh preodoleniia" [Genesis and Evolution of Eschato-Hiliastics of Seventh Day Adventism and Means of Overcoming Them]. Dissertation. Leningr. ped. in-t im. A.I. Gertsena. L., 1986.

5597 Nosovich, V.I. "Sushchnost', struktura i funktsii religioznoi psikhologii" [The Essence, Structure and Functions of Religious Psychology]. Dissertation. MGU im. M.V. Lomonosova. M., 1989.

5598 Novichenko, N.R. "Filosofsko-sotsiologicheskii analiz sovremennoi propovednicheskoi deiatel'nosti Russkoi pravoslavnoi tserkvi" [Philosophic-Sociological Analysis of Contemporary Preaching Activity of Russian Orthodox Church]. Dissertation. AN UkSSR. In-t filosofii. Kiev, 1989.

5599 Nueshi Mursi Abdessattar. "Ideinye kontseptsii i obshchestvenno-politicheskaia praktika dvizheniia 'brat'ia musul'man', (1928-1949 gg.) - period Khasana al'-Banny" [Ideological Conceptions and Socio-Political Practice of "Moslem Brotherhood" Movement, (1928-1949) - in the Period of Hasan al-Banna]. Dissertation. AN SSSR In-t vostokovedeniia. M., 1989.

5600 Odintsov, M.I. "Kritika kontseptsii 'khristianskogo patriotizma' Russkoi pravoslavnoi tserkvi" [Criticism of Conception of "Christian Patriotism" of the Russian Orthodox Church]. Dissertation. Akad. obshchestv. nauk pri TsK KPSS. M., 1987.

5601 Oleinikova, T.N. "Ateisticheskoe vospitanie starsheklassnikov v istorii pedagogiki i shkoly Kazakhskoi SSR, 1946-1980 gg." [Atheistic Education of Senior Schoolboys in the History of Pedagogy and School in the

Kazakh SSR, 1946-1980]. Dissertation. Kaz. ped. in-t im. Abaia. Alma-Ata, 1986.

5602   Oleksiuk, M.M. "Kritika antikommunisticheskikh kontseptsii i politicheskoi deiatel'nosti uniatstva" [Criticism of Anti-Communist Conceptions and Political Activity of the Uniate Church]. Dissertation. AN UkSSR. In-t filosofii. Kiev, 1985.

5603   Osipovskii, E.G. "Kontseptsiia ateizma v sovremennoi protestantskoi teologii" [Conception of Atheism in Contemporary Protestant Theology]. Dissertation. Akad. obshchetsv. nauk pri TK KPSS. M., 1989.

5604   Ovcharenko, V.S. "Politika Islamskoi Respubliki Iran v oblasti kul'tury i obrazovaniia" [Politics of Islamic Republic of Iran in the Realm of Culture and Education]. Dissertation. AN SSSR. In-t vostokovedeniia. M., 1988.

5605   Ovsienko, F.G. "Kriticheskii analiz teoreticheskikh osnov sotsial'noi doktriny katolitsizma" [Critical Analysis of Theoretical Foundations of Social Doctrine of Catholicism]. Dissertation. Akad. obshchetsv. nauk pri TsK KPSS. M., 1988.

5606   Panibratsev, A.V. "Filosofskie kursy Feofilakta Lopatinskogo v Moskovskoi slaviano-greko-latinskoi akademii (Pervaia chetvert' XVIII v.)" [Philosophical Courses of Pheophilact Lopatius in Slav-Greek-Latin Academy (Early XVIIIth C.]. Dissertation. MGU im. M.V. Lomonosova. M., 1989.

5607   Pantsulaia, T.U. "Sotsial'naia pozitsiia sovremennogo gruzinskogo pravoslaviia" [Social Position of Contemporary Georgian Orthodoxy]. Dissertation. Tbil. gos. un-t. Tbilisi, 1988.

5608   Papuashvili, T.T. "Osnovnye formy i metody ateisticheskogo vospitaniia v protsesse stroitel'stva kommunisticheskogo obshchestva" [Main Forms and Methods of Atheistic Education in the Process of Building Communist Society]. Dissertation. Tbil. gos. un-t. Tbilisi, 1986.

5609   Parinova, O.V. "Osobennosti stanovleniia ateisticheskogo soznaniia studencheskoi molodezhi" [Peculiarities of Creating Atheistic Consciousness of Students]. Dissertation. Leningr. gos. ped. in-t im. A.I. Gertsena. L., 1986.

5610   Pasechnik, M.S. "Samolikvidatsiia uniatskoi tserkvi - zakonomernoe sledstvie ee antinarodnoi deiatel'nosti" [Self Liquidation of the Uniate Church -

Natural Consequence of Its Anti-Popular Activity]. Dissertation. L'vov. gos. un-t im. I. Franko. L'vov, 1986.

5611 Pater, A. "Protsess normalizatsii otnoshenii i problema dialoga tserkvi i gosudarstva v PNR" [The Process of Normalization of Relations and the Problem of Dialogue of the Church and State in Polish People's Republic]. Dissertation. Akad. obshchetsv. nauk pri TsK KPSS. In-t nauch. ateizma. M., 1989.

5612 Patsukova, L.A. "Analiz latinoamerikanskimi marksistami evoliutsii katoli-tsizma na kontinente (60-e - 80-e gg.)" [Analysis by Latin American Marxists of Evolution of Catholicism on the Continent (60s - 80s)]. Dissertation. MGU im. M.V. Lomonosova. M., 1989.

5613 Pavliashvili, K.D. "Politika Vatikana 20-50kh godov XVII-go stoletiia po otnosheniiu k Gruzii i Iranu" [Politics of Vatican in the 20s-50s of the XVIIth Century towards Georgia and Iran]. Dissertation. AN GSSR. In-t istorii, arkheologii i etnografii im. I.A. Dzhavakhishvili. Tbilisi: Metsnie-reba, 1989.

5614 Pavlova, T.P. "Metodologicheskie problemy otsenki protsessa khristianizatsii Drevnei Rusi" [Methodological Problems of the Estimation of the Process of Conversion to Christianity of Ancient Rus']. Dissertation. MGU im. M.V. Lomonosova. M., 1988.

5615 Perova, L.N. "Strakh kak komponent religiozno-psikhologicheskogo komp-leksa" [Fear as a Component of Religious-Psychological Complex]. Dissertation. LGU. L., 1988.

5616 Petrishchev, P.V. "Problemy marksistskoi otsenki roli pravoslaviia v istorii Rossii" [The Problem of Marxist Estimation of the Role of Orthodoxy in the History of Russia]. Dissertation. Akad. obshhetsv. nauk pri TsK KPSS. M.. 1988.

5617 Petrov, S.B. "Ispol'zovanie kul'tovykh pamiatnikov v ateisticheskom vospitanii" [Use of Worship Monuments in Atheistic Education]. Dissertation. MGU im. M.V. Lomonosova. M., 1988.

5618 Petrova, M.A. "Khudozhestvennoe i religioznoe vospriiatie kul'tovogo isskustva" [Artistic and Religious Perception of Cult's Art]. Dissertation. LGU im. A.A. Zhdanova. L., 1985.

5619 Petrovich, M.G. "Optimizm kak sushchestvennaia cherta ateisticheskogo mirovozzreniia" [Optimism as Essential Trait of Atheistic World Outlook]. Dissertation. MGU im. M.V. Lomonosova. M., 1986.

5620 Pkhidenko, S.S. "Vzaimosviaz' preodoleniia religioznykh interesov i formirovaniia ateisticheskogo soznaniia i povedeniia lichnosti" [Correlation of Overcoming Religious Interests and Forming Atheistic Consciousness and Behaviour of Individual]. Dissertation. AN UkSSR. In-t filosofii. Kiev, 1983.

5621 Pleshakov, A.R. "Nauchno-ateisticheskoe vospitanie i formirovanie aktivnoi zhiznennoi pozitsii" [Scientific-Atheistic Education and Forming Active Vital Position]. Dissertation. Akad. obshchestv. nauk pri TsK KPSS. M., 1987.

5622 Poplavskaia, N.N. "Ukrainskaia antiklerikal'naia satira XVIII v." [Ukrainian Anti-Clerical Satire in XVIIIth C.]. Dissertation. AN UkSSR. In-t lit. im. T.G. Shevchenko. Kiev, 1988.

5623 Povarkova, T.A. "Rimsko-katolicheskaia tserkov' i gosudarstvo v PNR" [Roman-Catholic Church and State in Polish People's Republic]. Dissertation. MGU im. M.V. Lomonosova, filos. fak. M.: MGU, 1987.

5624 Pshizova, S.N. "Katolicheskaia tserkov' i rabochee dvizhenie Italii v 80-e gody" [Catholic Church and Workers Movement in Italy in the 80s]. Dissertation. MGU i. M.V. Lomonosova. M., 1989.

5625 Pubaev, R.E. "'Pagsam-Chzhonsan' - pamiatnik tibetskoi istoriografii XVII veka" ["Pagsam-Chjonsan" - Monument of Tibetan Historiography of the XVIIIth Century]. Dissertation. AN SSSR. In-t vostokovedeniia. Leningr. otd-nie. L., 1982.

5626 Pupysheva L.A. "Voprosy ateizma v trudakh M.M. Filippova (1858-1903 gg.)" [Questions of Atheism in the Works of M.M. Filippov (1858-1903)]. Dissertation. LGU im. A.A. Zhdanova. L., 1986.

5627 Radugin, A.A. "Sovremennyi katolicheskii irratsionalizm" [Contemporary Catholic Irrationalness]. Dissertation. MGU im. M.V. Lomonosova. M., 1986.

5628 Rapov, O.M. "Russkaia tserkov' v IX-pervoi treti XII v. Priniatie khristian-stva" [Russian Church in IXth-Early XIIth C. Taking Up Christianity]. Dissertation. MGU im. M.V. Lomonosova. Gos. kom. SSSR po nar. obrazovaniiu. M., 1989.

5629 Revenko, L.V. "Sootnoshenie religioznogo i nravstvennogo soznaniia veruiu-shchikh v sotsialisticheskom obshchestve" [Correlation of Religious and Moral Consciousness of Believers in Socialist Society]. Dissertation. MGU im. M.V. Lomonosova. M., 1987.

5630 Rimskii, V.P. "Problema sootnosheniia mifa i religii" [The Problem of Correlation of Myth and Religion]. Dissertation. Rost. n/D gos. un-t im. M.A. Suslova. Rostov n/D, 1985.

5631 Rogozhnikova, T.P. "'Zhitie Stefana Permskogo' Epifaniia Premudrogo" [Ephiphanius the Wise 'The Life of Stephen of Perm']. Dissertation. LGU im. A.A. Zhdanova. L., 1988.

5632 Rotovskii, A.A. "Ideologicheskie diversii protestantskikh antikommu nisticheskikh klerikal'nykh tsentrov i problemy ateisticheskoi kontrpropagandy" [Ideological Diversions of Protestant Anti-Communist Clerical Centres and Problems of Atheistic Counter Propaganda]. Dissertation. AN UkSSR. In-t filosofii. Kiev, 1985.

5633 Rumiantsev, M.G. "Metodologicheskie voprosy ateisticheskoi napravlennosti nauchnogo mirovozzreniia" [Methodological Problems of Atheistic Trend of Scientific World Outlook]. Dissertation. Kazan. gos. un-t im. V.I. Ul'ianova-Lenina. Kazan', 1986.

5634 Rustamova, Ch.T. "National'noe i internatsional'noe v sovetskoi obriad-nosti" [National and International in Soviet Ceremonial]. Dissertation. Akad. obshchestv. nauk pri TsK KPSS. M., 1988.

5635 Rybakov, R.B. "Burzhuaznaia reformatsiia induizma" [Bourgeois Reformation of Hinduism]. Dissertation. AN SSSR. In-t vostokovedeniia. M., 1981.

5636 Rybnikova, G.I. "Kritiicheskii analiz teologicheskoi kontseptsii V. Pannen-berga" [Critical Analysis of Theological Conception of V. Pannenberg]. Dissertation. MGU im. M.V. Lomonosova. M., 1988.

5637 Ryskel'dieva, L.T. "Poniatie 'dkharma' v buddizme makhaiany" [Concept of "Dharma" in Buddhism of Mahayana]. Dissertation. Mosk. un-t. M., 1982.

5638   Rysov, B.N. "Nesosoiatel'nost' pravoslavno-bogoslovskoi interpretatsii razvitiia
       samobytnoi kul'tury vostochnykh slavian" [Groundlessness of Orthodox
       Theological Interpretation of Development of Original Culture of Oriental
       Slavs]. Dissertation. AN UkSSR. In-t filosofii. Kiev, 1985.

5639   Sabo, P. "Sovremennaia katolicheskaia antropologiia" [Contemporary Catholic
       Anthropology]. Dissertation. Akad. obshchestv. nauk pri TK KPSS. M.,
       1989.

5640   Safronova, E.S. "Sinto i buddizm v srednevekovoi Iaponii" [Shinto and
       Buddhism in Medieval Japan]. Dissertation. AN SSSR. In-t etnografii. M.,
       1982.

5641   Sagalaev, A.M. "Lamaistskie elementy v mifologii i traditsionnykh kul'takh
       altaitsev" [Lamaist Elements in Mythology and Traditional Cults of Altai
       People]. Dissertation. AN SSSR. In-t etnografii. L., 1981.

5642   Salaev, L.N. "Religioznyi ekstremizm v sektantskikh ob'edineniiakh i puti ego
       preodoleniia" [Religious Extremism in Sectarian Communities and Ways
       of Its Overcoming]. Dissertation. MGU im. M.V. Lomonosova. M., 1986.

5643   Savel'ev, S.N. "Ideinoe bankrotstvo bogoiskatel'stva v Rossii v nachale XX
       veka" [Ideological Bankruptcy of God Seeking in Russia Early XXth
       Century]. Dissertation. LGU im. A.A. Zhdanova. L., 1987.

5644   Savitskii, A.L. "Gumanisticheskaia napravlennost' panteizma Sebast'iana
       Franka" [Humanist Direction of Sebastian Franks' Pantheism]. Disser-
       tation. LGU. L., 1988.

5645   Sedova, R.A. "Povesti o moskovskom mitropolite Petre v drevnerusskoi
       literature XIV-nach. XV vekov" [Stories about Metropolitan Peter of
       Moscow in Ancient Russian Literature XIVth-Early XVth Centuries].
       Dissertation. AN SSSR. In-t rus. lit. (Pushkinskii Dom). L., 1988.

5646   Seliverstova, N.A. "Metodologicheskoe znachenie leninskoi teorii otrazheniia
       dlia nauhnogo ateizma" [Methodological Importance of Leninist Theory of
       Reflection for Scientific Atheism]. Dissertation. LGU im. A.A. Zhdanova.
       L., 1984.

5647   Semenkin, N.S. "Filosofiia neopravoslaviia" [Philosophy of Neo Orthodoxy].
       Dissertation. Akad. obshchestv. nauk pri TsK KPSS. M., 1988.

5648 Semenova, T.N. "Znachenie leninskikh printsipov preodoleniia religii dlia teorii i praktiki nauchnogo ateizma" [Importance of Leninist Principles on Overcoming Religion for the Theory and Practice of Scientific Atheism]. Dissertation. MGU im. M.V. Lomonosova. M., 1986.

5649 Serebriakov, F.F. "Kriticheskii analiz kontseptsii 'sotsial'nogo sluzheniia' sovremennogo russkogo pravoslaviia" [Critical Analysis of the Conception of "Social Service" of the Contemporary Russian Orthodoxy]. Dissertation. MGU im. M.V. Lomonosova. M., 1987.

5650 Sereda, G.V. "Kritika bogoslovskogo ponimaniia natsional'nogo samosoz-naniia" [Criticism of Theological Comprehension of National Self-Consciousness]. Dissertation. MGU im. M.V. Lomonosova. M., 1986.

5651 Shadiev, K.K. "Kritika kontseptsii burzhuaznoi sovetologii o polozhenii islama v respublikakh Srednei Azii" [Criticism of Conception of Bourgeois Sovietology on the Position of Islam in the Middle Asian Republics]. Dissertation. AN UzSSR. In-t istorii. Tashkent, 1987.

5652 Shadurskii, V.G. "Gnoseologicheskii analiz roli zdravogo smysla v miropo-nimanii veruiushchego" [Gnosiologic Analysis of the Role of Common Sense in Believers World Outlook]. Dissertation. AN UkSSR. In-t filosofii. Kiev, 1986.

5653 Shapiev, B. "Sootnoshenie natsional'nogo i religioznogo v obychaiakh i traditsiiakh" [Correlation of National and Religious in Customs and Traditions]. Dissertation. Tashk. gos. un-t im. V.I. Lenina. Tashkent, 1988.

5654 Shaposhnikov, L.E. "Kritika analogii pravoslaviia v 'filosofii vseedinstva'" [Criticism of Orthodox Analogy in "Philosophy of All Unity"]. Disserta-tion. AN UkSSR. In-t filosofii. Kiev, 1987.

5655 Sharabidinov, I. "Internatsionalizatsiia obshchestvennoi zhizni kak faktor sekuliarizatsii semeino-bytovykh otnoshenii" [Internationalisation of Social Life as Factor of Secularization of Family-Daily Life Relations]. Dissertation. AN UzSSR. In-t filosofii i prava im. I.M. Muminova. Tashkent, 1989.

5656 Sharifkhodzhaev, M. "Podgotovka studentov pedagogicheskikh institutov k nauchno-ateisticheskoi vospitatel'noi rabote so starsheklassnikami" [Prepa-ration of Students of Pedagogical Institutes for Scientific-Atheistic

Educational Work with Senior Pupils]. Dissertation. APN SSSR, NII obshch. probl. vospitaniia. M., 1987.

5657   Shaub, I.Iu. "Kul'ty i religioznye predstavleniia naseleniia Bosfora VI-IV vekov do n.e." [Cults and Religious Notions of the Population of Bosphorus in VIth-IVth Centuries B.C.]. Dissertation. AN SSSR. In-t arkheologii, Leningr. otd-nie. L., 1987.

5658   Shcherbakova, G.N. "Logiko-gnoseologicheskii analiz sootnoshenii istiny i very" [Logical-Gnosiological Analysis of Correlation of Truth and Faith]. Dissertation. L'vov. gos un-t im. I. Franko. L'vov, 1986.

5659   Shchulembaev, K.Sh. "Stanovlenie i razvitie nauchno-ateisticheskogo mirovoz-zreniia trudiashchikhsia v protsesse utverzhdeniia sotsialis- ticheskogo obraza zhizni" [Formation and Development of Workers Scientific-Atheistic World Outlook in the Process of Assertion of Socialist Way of Life]. Dissertation. Akad. obshchestv. nauuk pri TsK KPSS. M., 1985.

5660   Shil'diashov, I.M. "Religiia i ateisticheskoe vospitanie v Sibiri (konets 1950-kh - seredina 1970-kh gg.)" [Religion and Atheistic Education in Siberia (Late 1950s - Middle 1970s)]. Dissertation. AN SSSR, Sib. otd-nie. In-t istorii, filologii i filosofii. Novosibirsk, 1986.

5661   Shpak, V.T. "Kriticheskii analiz sovremennykh burzhuaznykh interpretatsii filosofskogo i ateisticheskogo naslediia ukrainskikh revoliutsionnykh demokratov" [Critical Analysis of Contemporary Bourgeois Interpretation of Philosophic and Atheistic Legacy of Ukrainian Revolutionary Democrats]. Dissertation. AN UkSSR. In-t filosofii. Kiev, 1987.

5662   Sidor, M. "Vospitanie nauchno-ateisticheskogo mirovozzreniia uchashcheisia molodezhi" [Upbringing of Scientific-Atheistic World Outlook of Pupils]. Dissertation. AN BSSR. In-t filosofii i prava. Minsk, 1988.

5663   Sidorenko, M.N. "Deiatel'nost' partiinykh organizatsii Urala po ateistiches-komu vospitaniiu trudiashchikhsia v 1959-1965 godakh" [Activity of Party Organizations of the Ural in Atheistic Education of Workers in 1959-1965]. Dissertation. Ural. gos. un-t im. A.M. Gor'kova. Sverdlovsk, 1987.

5664   Sirota, E.B. "Obostrenie politicheskoi bor'by v Tsentral'noi Amerike i pozitsiia katolicheskoi tserkvi (1970-1980 gg.)" [Exacerbation of Political Struggle in Central America and the Position of Catholic Church (1970-1980)]. Dissertation. Mosk. gos. ped. in-t im. V.I. Lenina. M., 1989.

5665 Siukiiainen, L.R. "Musul'manskoe pravo. Voprosy teorii i praktiki" [Moslem Law. Questions of Theory and Practice]. Dissertation. AN SSSR. In-t gosudarstva i prava. M.: Nauka, 1987.

5666 Skibitskii, M.M. "Kriticheskii analiz otnosheniia sovremennogo khristianstva k estesvoznaniiu" [Critical Analysis of Attitude of Contemporary Christianity toward Natural Sciences]. Dissertation. Akad. obshchestv. nauk pri TsK KPSS. M., 1989.

5667 Smirnov, M.Iu. "Voprosy voiny i mira v sovremennoi khristianskoi ideologii" [The Problems of War and Peace in Contemporary Christian Ideology]. Dissertation. LGU im. A.A. Zhdanova. L., 1986.

5668 Smirnov, N.A. "Kritika religii i tserkvi v filosofskom uchenii Didro" [Criticism of Religion and Church in Philosophic Teachings of Diderot]. Dissertation. AK BSSR. In-t filosofii i prava. Minsk, 1987.

5669 Sogomonian, M.K. "Svobodomyslie Matteosa Mamuriana" [Free Thinking of Mattheos Mamurian]. Dissertation. Tbil. gos. un-t. Tbilisi, 1987.

5670 Sakhraniaeva, T.V. "Ateizm i dukhovnaia kul'tura" [Atheism and Spiritual Culture]. Dissertation. MGU im. M.V. Lomonosova. M., 1986.

5671 Sokoliuk, N.M. "Podgotovka studentov doshkol'nogo fakul'teta pedagogi-cheskogo vuza k ateisticheskomu vospitaniiu starshikh doshkol'nikov" [Training of Students of Pre-School Pedagogical Faculty of Institute for Higher Education for Atheistic Upbringing of Senior Pre-School Pupils]. Dissertation. Mosk. gos. ped. in-t im. V.I. Lenina. M., 1986.

5672 Sokurenko, E.G. "Chelovek i priroda v sovremennoi khristianskoi teologii" [Man and Nature in Contemporary Christian Theology]. Dissertation. MGU im. M.V. Lomonosova. M., 1986.

5673 Solodkova, O.L "Katolicheskie missionery na sluzhbe kolonial'noi ekspansii evropeiskikh stran v Iuzhnoi Azii v seredine XVI-nachale XVII v." [Catholic Missionaries in the Service of Colonial Expansion of European Countries in South Asia in the Middle XVIth-Early XVIIth C.]. Disser-tation. AN SSSR. In-t vostokovedeniia. M., 1988.

5674 Solov'ev, V.S. "Nauchnyi ateizm i formirovanie novogo cheloveka" [Scien-tific Atheism and Shaping of a New Man]. Dissertation. Akad. obshchestv. nauk pri TsK KPSS. M., 1987.

5675   Solov'eva, O.L. "Kriticheskii analiz problemy very v russkom pravoslavii" [Critical Analysis of the Problem of Faith in Russian Orthodoxy]. Dissertation. AN BSSR. In-t filosofii i prava. Minsk, 1987.

5676   Sudarev, I.N. "Problemy voiny i mira v politike sovremennogo Vatikana" [The Problems of War and Peace in the Politics of Contemporary Vatican]. Dissertation. Diplomat. akad. MID SSSR. M., 1987.

5677   Sultangalieva, A.K. "Evoliutsiia idei 'islamskogo edinstva' v istorii arabskoi mysli (konets XIX v. - 80-e gody XX v.)" [Evolution of the Idea of "Islamic Unity" in the History of Arab Thought (Late XIXth C. - 80s of the XXth C.)]. Dissertation. AN SSSR. In-t vostokovedeniia. M., 1988.

5678   Suvorov, N.A. "Nauchno-ateistichekoe vospitanie uchashchikhsia IX-X klassov pri obuchenii istorii SSSR" [Scientific-Atheistic Upbringing of Pupils of IXth-Xth Grades during Teaching the History of USSR]. Dissertation. APN SSSR, NII soderzh. i metodov obucheniia. M., 1985.

5679   Staran'chak, Iu. "Kriticheskii analiz problemy svobody i osvobozhdeniia truda v katolicheskoi filosofii Pol'shi" [Critical Analysis of the Problem of Freedom and Emancipation of Labour in the Catholic Philosophy of Poland]. Dissertation. Kiev. gos. un-t im. T.G. Shevchenko. Kiev, 1985.

5680   Stepanov, R.N. "Sovremennyi islam i nauka" [Contemporary Islam and Science]. Dissertation. Leningr. un-t. Filos. fak. L., 1981.

5681   Stetsenko, V.I. "Voinstvuiushchii ateizm v sisteme aktivnoi zhiznennoi pozitsii studencheskoi molodezhi" [Militant Atheism in the System of Active Vital Position of Students]. Dissertation. L'vov. gos. un-t im. I. Franko. L'vov, 1985.

5682   Tabutsadze, O.A. "Osobennosti religioznosti sel'skogo naseleniia Gruzii i zadachi ateisticheskogo vospitaniia na sovremennom etape" [Peculiarities of Religiosity of Georgian Rural Population and the Tasks of Atheistic Education in Contemporary Stage]. Dissertation. Tbil. gos. un-t. Tbilisi, 1988.

5683   Tadzhieva, M.U. "Deiatel'nost' partiinykh organizatsii proizvodstvennykh kollektivov Uzbekistana po ateistichskomu vospitaniiu v sovremennykh usloviiakh" [Activity of Party Organizations of Productive Collectives of Uzbekistan in Atheistic Education in Contemporary Conditions]. Dissertation. Tashk. gos. un-t im. V.I. Lenina. Tashkent, 1988.

5684 Taktakishvili, D.D. "Religioznyi modernizm i gruzinskoe pravoslavie" [Religious Modernism and Georgian Orthodoxy]. Dissertation. Tbil. gos. un-t. Tbilisi, 1989.

5685 Tatishvili, I.M. "Khattsko-khettskie stroitel'nye rituay" [Hatto-Hittite Building Rituals]. Dissertation. Tbil. gos. un-t. Tbilisi, 1988.

5686 Temisov, A.K. "Preodolenie konservativnogo obshchestvennogo mnenia kak faktor povysheniia effektivnosti ateisticheskogo vospitaniia" [Overcoming of Conservative Public Opinion as Factor for Increasing Effectiveness of Atheistic Education]. Dissertation. Tashk. gos. un-t im. V.I. Lenina. Tashkent, 1989.

5687 Terekhova, V.A. "Spetsifika religioznoi mifologii" [Specificity of Religious Mythology]. Dissertation. MGU im. M.V. Lomonosova. M., 1987.

5688 Tetevina, E.G. "Osobennosti sovershenstvovaniia sistemy ateisticheskogo vospitaniia studenchestva v regionakh traditsionnogo rasprostraneniia islama" [Peculiarities of Perfection of the System of Atheistic Education of Students in the Regions of Traditional Dissemination of Islam]. Dissertation. Tashk. gos. un-t im. V.I. Lenina. Tashkent, 1987.

5689 Tikhonova, G.Iu. "Novye tendentsii v ideologii russkogo pravoslaviia 80-kh godov" [New Tendencies in the Ideology of Russian Orthodoxy of the 80s]. Dissertation. MGU im. M.V. Lomonosva. M., 1988.

5690 Titov, N.Iu. "Tserkov' v politicheskoi sisteme Rossii pervoi poloviny XIX v." [Church in the Political System of Russia Early XIXth C.]. Dissertation. MGU im. M.V. Lomonosova. M., 1985.

5691 Titovets, A.A. "Nauchno-ateisticheskaia mysl' Sovetskoi Belorussii (20-e-nach. 60-kh gg." [Scientific-Atheistic Thought of Soviet Belorussia (20s-Early 60s)]. Dissertation. AN BSSR. In-t filosofii i prava. Minsk, 1989.

5692 Tkachenko, N.V. "Gnoseologicheskie i sotsial'no-psikhologicheskie usloviia vosproizvodstva religii v sotsialisticheskom obshchestve" [Gnoseological and Socio-Psychological Conditions of Reproduction of Religion in Socialist Society]. Dissertation. AN UkSSR. In-t filosofii. Kiev, 1987.

5693 Tokareva, E.S. "Italianskoe katolicheskoe dvizhenie v usloviiakh fashistskoi diktatury (1926-1943)" [Italian Catholic Movement under Fascist

Dictatorship (1926-1943)]. Dissertation. AN SSSR. In-t vseobshch. istorii. M., 1988.

5694 Tomashevich, N.I. "Razvitie politicheskoi kul'tury veruiushchikh v usloviiakh demokratizatsii sovetskogo obshchestva" [Development of Political Culture of Believers in the Conditions of Democratization of Soviet Society]. Dissertation. Akad. obshchestv. nauk pri TsK KPSS. M., 1989.

5695 Tomilina, N.V. "Ateisticheskoe znachenie dostizhenii meditsiny" [Atheistic Significance of Achievements in Medicine]. Dissertation. MGU im. M.V. Lomonosova. M., 1986.

5696 Trikhonova, G.Iu. "Novye tendentsii v ideologii russkogo pravoslaviia 80-kh godakh" [New Tendencies in the Ideology of Russian Orthodoxy of the 80s]. Dissertation. MGU im. M.V. Lomonosova. M., 1988.

5697 Tserbaev, T.O. "Religioznyi kul't: filosofsko-sotsiologicheskii analiz" [Religious Cult: Philosophic-Sociological Analysis]. Dissertation. Akad. obshchestv. nauk pri TsK KPSS. M., 1987.

5698 Tsikvadze, R.I. "Ateisticheskie aspekty gruzinskikh natsional'nykh traditsii" [Atheistic Aspects of Georgian National Traditions]. Dissertation. Tbil. gos. un-t. Tbilisi, 1984.

5699 Tskhovrebov, Z.L. "Kosmologiia osetinskogo Nartovskogo eposa" [Cosmology of the Osetin Nartov Epos]. Dissertation. AN SSSR. In-t etnografii im. N.N. Miklukho-Maklaia. M., 1989.

5700 Tutikova, O.I. "Nauchno-ateisticheskoe vospitanie uchashchikhsia PTU v usloviiakh uskoreniia sotsial'no-ekonomicheskogo razvitiia sovetskogo obshchestva" [Scientific-Atheistic Education of Students of PTU in Conditions of Acceleration of the Socio-Economic Development of Soviet Society]. Dissertation. Mosk. gos. ped. in-t im. V.I. Lenina. M., 1987.

5701 Udalkin, A.I. "Razvitie natsional'nykh otnoshenii i protsess sekuliarizatsii v sovetskom obshchestve" [Development of National Relations and the Process of Secularization in Soviet Society]. Dissertation. Akad. obshchestv. nauk pri TsK KPSS. M., 1989.

5702 Umarzhonov, O.M. "Osobennosti proiavleniia religioznosti u liudei preklonnogo vozrasta i rabota po povysheniiu ikh obshchestvennoi aktivnosti" [Manifestation Features of Religiosity by Old Age People and

Work for Increasing their Public Activity]. Dissertation. Tashk. gos. un-t im. V.I. Lenina. Tashkent, 1989.

5703 Umralina, G.R. "Edinstvo ateisticheskogo i internatsional'nogo vospitaniia kak uslovie ikh effektivnosti v mnogonatsional'nom i mnogokonfessional'nom regione" [Unity of Atheistic and International Education as Condition of their Effectiveness in Multi National and Multi Confessional Region]. Dissertation. Tashk. gos. un-t im. V.I. Lenina. Tashkent, 1988.

5704 Usenova, M.M. "Sotsialisticheskaia sem'ia kak faktor formirovaniia ateisticheskogo mirovozzreniia lichnosti" [Socialist Family as Shaping Factor of Atheistic World Outlook of Individual]. Dissertation. Tash. gos. un-t im. V.I. Lenina. Tashkent, 1988.

5705 Usmanov, S.M. "Khristianskaia demokratiia i politicheskaia bor'ba v Chili (70-kh-nach. 80-kh gg.)" [Christian Democracy and Political Struggle in Chile (70s-early 80s)]. Dissertation. AN SSSR. In-t Latin. Ameriki. M., 1985.

5706 Vagarshian, V.L. "Islam i arabskii natsionalizm v zapadnoi istoriografii poslevoennogo perioda" [Islam and Arab Nationalism in Western Historiography of the Post War Period]. Dissertation. AN SSSR. In-t vostokovedenia. M., 1988.

5707 Vakhidov, S. "Sotsial'no-istoricheskie prichiny sokhraneniia vliianiia islama na rabochikh korennoi natsional'nosti i problemy ateisticheskoi raboty v trudovom kollektive" [Socio-Historical Causes of Preservation of Islam's Influence on Workers of Indigenous Nationality and Problems of Atheistic Work in Workers Collective]. Dissertation. Akad. obshchestv. nauk pri TsK KPSS. M., 1989.

5708 Vasetskaia, E.N. "Kriticheskii analiz religiozno-idealisticheskoi filosofii vseedinstva" [Critical Analysis of Religious-Idealistical Philosophy of All-Unity]. Dissertation. MGU im. M.V. Lomonosova. M., 1988.

5709 Vasilenko, R.P. "Etruriia i Rim. Vliianie v oblasti religioznykh predstavlenii i kul'ta" [Etruria and Rome. Influence in the Realm of Religious Notions and Cult]. Dissertation. Mosk. gos. ped. in-t im. V.I. Lenina. M., 1988.

5710 Vazirov, Z. "Sotsial'no-politicheskie i nravstvenno-religioznye ucheniia v filosofskoi sisteme futuvvata" [Socio-Political and Moral-Religious

Teachings in the Philosophical System of Futuvvata]. Dissertation. AN KazSSR. In-t filosofii i prava. Alma-Ata, 1981.

5711 Velichko, O.I. "Rabochii klass i politicheskii katolitsizm Avstrii v novcishee vremiia" [Workers Class and Political Catholicism in Austria in the Newest Time]. Dissertation. AN SSSR. In-t mezhdunar. rabochego dvizheniia. M., 1986.

5712 Vershchagina, A.V. "Religioznoe sektantstvo i ego otritsatel'noe vliianie na byt i kul'turu veruiushchkh" [Religious Sectarianism and Its Bad Influence on Believers Way of Life and Culture]. Dissertation. AN BSSR. In-t iskusstvovedeniia, etnografii i fol'klora. Minsk, 1988.

5713 Vertelesh, Z. "Kriticheskii analiz vliianiia sotsial'no-politicheskoi doktriny rimsko-katolicheskoi tserkvi na formirovanie mirovozzreniia pol'skoi molodezhi" [Critical Analysis of the Influence of Socio-Political Doctrine of Roman-Catholic Church on Forming World Outlook of Polish Youth]. Dissertation. Vysch. koms. shk. pri TsK VLKSM. M., 1986.

5714 Vinokurov, V.V. "Poniatie nauki v sovremennoi katolicheskoi filosofii" [The Concept of Science in Contemporary Catholic Philosophy]. Dissertation. MGU im. M.V. Lomonosova. M., 1986.

5715 Vlasova, O.E. "Deiatel'nost' partiinykh organizatsii Srednego Povolzh'ia po ateisticheskomu vospitaniiu trudiashchikhsia" [Activity of Party Organizations of Middle Volga Region in Atheistic Education of Workers]. Dissertation. Mosk. gos. ped. in-t im. V.I. Lenina. M., 1984.

5716 Voitov, V.E. "Kul'tovo-pominal'nye sooruzheniia VI-VIII vv. na territorii Mongolii" [Religious-Funeral Buildings of VIth-VIIIth Centuries on the Territory of Mongolia]. Dissertation. AN SSSR. In-t arkhelogii. M., 1989.

5717 Vonova, A.I. "Islam v Iugo-Vostochnoi Azii: problemy sovremennoi ideinoi evoliutsii" [Islam in South-Eastern Asia: Problems of Contemporary Ideological Evolution]. Dissertation. AN SSSR. In-t vostokovedeniia. M., 1980.

5718 Voronkova, L.P. "Evoliutsiia protestantskoi kul'turologii" [Evolution of Protestant Cultureology]. Dissertation. Mosk. gos. ped. in-t im. V.I. Lenina. M., 1989.

5719 Vovk, O.L. "Zarubezhnye ukrainskie klerikal'no-natsionalisticheskie tsentry v antisovetskoi politike Vatikana (60-80-e gody)" [Ukrainian Clerical-Nationalist Centres from Abroad in Anti-Soviet Policy of Vatican (60s-80s)]. Dissertation. Uzhgor. gos. un-t. Uzhgorod, 1986.

5720 Voz'niak, M. "Problema ateizma v Pol'she" [The Problem of Atheism in Poland]. Dissertation. LGU im. A.A. Zhdanova. L., 1986.

5721 Vygovskii, L.A. "Rol' nauchnogo ateizma v formirovanii dukhovnykh potrebnostei lichnosti" [The Role of Scientific Atheism in Forming Spiritual Needs of the Individual]. Dissertation. AN UkSSR. In-t filosofii. Kiev, 1989.

5722 Zadorozhnaia, M.Ia. "Rol' sovetskikh prazdnikov v ateistichekom vospitanii" [The Role of Soviet Holidays in Atheistic Education]. Dissertation. Akad. obshchestv. nauk pri TsK KPSS. M., 1988.

5723 Zagalda, A.A. "Metodologiia nauchnogo ateizma: stanovlenie i sushchnost'" [Methodology of Scientific Atheism: Origin and Essence]. Dissertation. AN SSSR. In-t filosofii. Kiev., 1988.

5724 Zagidullin, D.N. "Deiatel'nost' Bashkirskoi oblastnoi partiinoi organizatsii po ateisticheskomu vospitaniiu trudiashchikhsia (1917-1937)" [Activity of Bashkir Oblast Party Organization in Atheistic Education of Workers (1917-1937)]. Dissertation. Ural. gos. un-t im. A.M. Gor'kogo. Sverdlovsk, 1984.

5725 Zainitdinova, A.N. "Sovetskaia periodicheskaia pechat' kak faktor ateisticheskogo vospitaniia" [Soviet Periodical Press as Factor of Atheistic Education]. Dissertation. Tashk. gos. un-t im. V.I. Lenina. Tashkent, 1989.

5726 Zakaras, V.K. "Bibleiskie istoki polovoi morali khristianstva" [Biblical Sources on Sexual Morals of Christianity]. Dissertation. AN BSSSR. In-t filosofii i prava. Minsk, 1988.

5727 Zakharov, A.A. "Obshchie tendentsii politizatsii katolitsizma v 80-e gg." [Common Tendencies in Politicization of Catholicism in the 80s]. Dissertation. MGU im. M.V. Lomonosova. M., 1986.

5728 Zakharova, N.A. "Kritika pravoslavnogo ponimaniia roli cheloveka v istoricheskom protsesse" [Criticism of Orthodox Conception of the Role of Man in Historical Process]. Dissertation. MGU im. M.V. Lomonosova. M., 1987.

5729 Zembrovskii, Ia. "Genezis i filosofskie osnovaniia religiozno-misticheskoi kontseptsii svobody N. Berdiaeva" [Genesis and Philosophical Foundations of Religious-Mystical Conception of Freedom of N. Berdiaev]. Dissertation. MGU im. M.V. Lomonosova. M., 1987.

5730 Zhardzina, A. "Kriticheskii analiz politicheskoi teologii Stefana Vyshinskogo" [Critical Analysis of Stephan Vyshinski's political Theology]. Dissertation. Akad. obshchestv. nauk pri TsK KPSS. M., 1988.

5731 Zhukova, G.G. "Religioznaia kontseptsiia slavianofilov i sovremennaia bor'ba idei" [Religious Conception of Slavophils and Contemporary Struggle of Ideas]. Dissertation. MGU im. M.V. Lomonosova. M., 1987.

5732 Zlotina, T.V. "Desakralizatsiia form obshchestvennogo soznaniia Rossii XVIII stoletiia" [Desacralization of Forms of Social Consciousness in Russia of the XVIIIth Century]. Dissertation. MGU im. M.V. Lomonosova. M., 1989.

5733 Zniatov, O. "Internatsionalizatsiia dukhovnoi zhizni i byta kak faktor preodoleniia islamskikh traditsii i utverzhdeniia novykh sotsialisticheskikh obriadov" [Internationalization of Spititual Life and Way of Life as Factor for Overcoming Islamic Traditions and Affirmation of New Socialist Ceremonials]. Dissertation. Tashk. gos. un-t im. V.I. Lenina. Tashkent, 1989.

CENSORED RELIGIOUS PUBLICATIONS

5734   *Bibliia* [The Bible]. M.: Mosk. patriarkhiia, 1983. 1372 pp., illus., maps. A jubilee ed. dedicated to 1000th anniversary of baptism of Rus'. was published in 1988, 1376 pp., illus.

5735   *Bibliia.* Kanonicheskie [The Bible. Canonical]. M.: Tserkov' khristian-baptistov sed'mogo dnia, 1981. 304 pp., maps.

5736   *Bogoslovskie trudy* [Theological Works]. M.: Mosk. patriarkhiia. 21 (1980): 241 pp., illus.

5737   *Chasoslov* [The Book of Hours]. M.: Mosk. patriarkhiia, 1980. 352 pp. In Old Church Slavonic and Russian.

5738   *Chin panikhidy* [Funeral Rite]. Novozybkov: Staroobriad. arkhiepiskopiia, 1984. 60 pp., illus.

5739   *Chinovnik arkhiereiskogo sviashchenosluzheniia* [Functional for Bishop's Religious Service]. M.: Mosk. patriarkhiia, 1982. In Old Church Slavonic and Russian. Published since 1982.
Kn. 1. 1982. 252 pp., illus.
Kn. 2. 1983. 175 pp., illus., music.

5740   *Chteniia i evangeliia* [Readings and Gospels]. [S.l.]: Liturg. komis., 1983. 398 pp. In Latvian.

5741   *Drevnepravoslavnyi kalendar'* [Ancient Orthodox Calendar]. Novozybkov: [S.n.], [1988].
1988. 80 pp., illus.
1989. 81 pp., illus.

5742   *Dukhonye razmyshleniia* [Spiritual Meditations]. M.: Tserkov' khristian adventistov sed'mogo dnia, 1986. 109 pp., illus. Transl. from English.

5743 *Estonskaia evangelichesko-liuteranskaia tserkov'* [Estonian Evangelic-Lutheran Church]. Tallin: Konsistoriia EELTs, 1983. 52 pp., illus. In Estonian.

5744 *Evangelicheskie pesni* [Evangelical Songs]. Elgava: Elgav. evang. khrist. obshchina letnego prazdnika, 1981. 270 pp. In Latvian.

5745 *Evangel'skie khristiane-baptisty v SSSR* [Evangelist Christian-Baptists in USSR]. M.: Vsesoiuz. sovet evang. khristian-baptistov, 1979. 103 pp., illus. Parallel text in Russian and English.

5746 Evlogii, arkhimandrit. "Osnovy pravoslavnogo monashestva" [Fundamentals of Orthodox Monasticism]. *Zhurn. Mosk. patriarkhii* 9 (1987): 74-75.

5747 *Gruzinskaia pravoslavnaia tserkov'* [The Georgian orthodox Church].* [Comp.: M.V. Tarkhnishvili]. M.: Mosk. patriarkhiia, 1983. 26 pp., illus. Parallel text in English, French, German and Russian.

5748 *Izbrannye kanony* [Selected Canons]. Novozybkov: Drevnepravoslav. Arkhiepiskopiia, [1987]. 128 pp.

5749 *Kalendar'* [Calendar]. M.: Religioz. o-vo khoral. sinagogi. In Yiddish and Russian.
(5741) 1979-1980. 1979. 42 pp., illus.
(5742) 1981-1982. 1981. 38 pp.
(5744) 1983-1984. 1983. 40 pp., illus. Publ. by Mosk. khoral. sinagoga.
(5745) 1984-1985. 1984. 39 pp., illus.
(5746) 1985-1986. 1985. 40 pp., illus.

5750 *Kalendar'* [Kalendar]. Echmiadzin: Sv. Echmiadzin. In New, Old and Armenian Style. In Armenian.
1981. 223 pp., illus.
1982. 231 pp., portr., illus.
1983. 222 pp.
1984. 223 pp., illus.

5751 *Kalendar' evangelicheskoi tserkvi... Litovskoi SSR* [Calendar of Evangelist Church of Lithuanian SSR]. Vil'nius: Evangel. liuteran. konsistoriia. Published since 1956. In Lithuanian.
...na 1982 g. 1982. 68 pp., illus.
...na 1983 g. 1983. 77 pp., illus.
...na 1984 g. 1984. 80 pp., illus.
...na 1985 g. 1985. 70 pp., illus.

5752 *Kalendar' ev.-liut. tserkvi Latvii.* [Calendar of Evangelist-Lutheran Church of Latvia]. Published since 1956. In Latvian.
1981 god. 1980. 192 pp., illus.
1982 god. 1981. 204 pp., illus.
1983 god. 1982. 183 pp., illus.
1984 god. 1983. 202 pp., illus.
1985 god. 1984. 177 pp., illus. Up to 1983 place and publisher are not mentioned. Since 1984 the publication mentions Riga: Konsistoriia ev.-liut. tserkvi Latvii.

5753 *Kalendar' evangel'skikh khristian-baptistov* [Calendar of Evangelist Christian-Baptists]. M.: Vsesoiuz. sovet evang. khristian-baptistov. Published since 1970.
1981. 1981. 96 pp., illus.
1982. 1982. 96 pp., illus.
1983. 120 pp., illus.
1984. 119 pp.
1985. 116 pp.
1988. 120 pp.
1989. 96 pp.

5754 *Kalendar' evreiskikh religioznykh prazdnikov i postov* [Calendar of Jewish Religious Holidays and Fasts]. M.: Religioz. o-vo Mosk. khor. sinagogi. In Yiddish and Russian.
...na 1980-1981 gg. (5741). 1980. 45 pp., illus.

5755 *Kalendar' gruzinskoi tserkvi* [Calendar of Georgian Churvh]. Tbilisi: Gruz. katolikos. Published since 1946. In Georgian.
1980. 1980. 423 pp., illus.
1981. 1981. 414 pp., illus.
1982. 1982. 415 pp., illus.
1983. 1983. 424 pp., illus.
1984. 1984. 399 pp., portr., illus.
1985. 1985. 526 pp., illus.
1989. 1989. 486 pp., illus.

5756 *Kalendar' Latviiskogo obshchestva baptistov* [Calendar of Latvian Baptist Society]. Riga: Bratstvo Latv. o-va baptistov. In Latvian.
1982. 1982. 70 pp., illus.
1984. 1984. 88 pp.
1985. 1985. 89 pp., illus. [Comp.: I. Tervits].

5757 *Kalendar' pravoslavnoi tserkvi* [Calendar of Orthodox Church]. M.: Mosk.
      patriarkhiia; Riga: Rizh. eparkhiia. In Latvian.
      1982 g. 1981. 33 pp.
      1983 g. 1982. 50 pp.

5758 *Kalendar' pravoslavnoi tserkvi* [Calendar of Orthodox Church]. M: Mosk.
      patriarkhiia; Tallin: Est. episkopstvo. In Estonian.
      1982. 1981. [36] pp., portr.

5759 *Kalendar' tserkvi khristian-adventistov sed'mogo dnia* [Calendar of the Church
      of Christian-Seventh Day Adventists]. M: [S.n.].
      ...na 1983 god. 1982. 72 pp.
      ...na 1984 god. 1983. 113 pp.
      ...na 1985 god. 1984. 136 pp.
      ...na 1988 god. 1987. 80 pp.
      ...na 1989 god. 1988. 49 pp., illus.

5760 *Kanonizatsiia sviatykh* [Canonization of the Saints]. Ed.: Mitropolit Krutitski
      i Kolomenski Iuvenalii. M.: Mosk. patriarkhat, 1988. 174 pp., illus.

5761 *Kanonik* [The Book of Canons]. Novozybkov: [S.n.], 1988.
      Ch. 1. 160 pp.

5762 *Katolicheskii kalendar'-spravochnik* [Catholic Calendar-Reference Book].
      Kaunas; Vil'nius: Litov. r.-k. episkopat. In Lithuanian.
      ...na 1982 god. 1982. 151 pp., illus.
      ...na 1983 god. 1983. 240 pp., illus.
      ...na 1985 god. 1985. 288 pp., illus.

5763 *Koran* [Koran]. Kazan': [S.n.], 1984. 575 pp. in old Arabian pagination, illus.
      In Arabic.

5764 Lebedev, L. *Kreshchenie Rusi, 988-1988* [Baptism of Rus', 988-1988]. M.:
      Mosk. Patriarkhiia, 1987. 170 pp., illus.

5765 *Lektsionarii* [Readings from Holy Writ]. Riga: Rizh. kuriia metropolii.
      Published since 1982. In Latvian and Latin.
      T. 5. *Obychnye obedni s XXIV po XXXIV nedeli* [Ordinary Mass from
      XXIVth to XXXIV Week]. 1984. 418 pp.

5766 *Liturgicheskii molitvennik* [Liturgical Prayer-Book]. 2nd revised ed. Kaunas:
      Vil'nius: Litov. r.k. episkopat, 1984. 624 pp., illus. In Lithuanian.

5767 Liuter, M. *Malyi Katekhizis* [The Small Catechism]. Tallin: Konsistoriia est. evangel.-liuteran. tserkvi, 1983. 43 pp., illus. In Estonian.
Published also in:
Riga: Latv. evang.-liter. tserkov'. konsistoriia, 1983. 16 pp. In Latvian.
Vil'nius: Evangel. liuter. konsistoriia, 1985. 35 pp., illus. In Lithuanian.

5768 *L'vovskii tserkovnyi sobor:* Dokumenty i materialy, 1946-1981 [L'vovs' Church Synod: Documents and Materials, 1946-1981]. M.: Mosk. patriarkhiia, 1982. 224 pp., illus. Annot. bibl.: pp. 39-40. Bibl.: pp. 207-220.
Published also in:
L'vov: Ekzarkhat vsei Ukrainy, 1984. 216 pp., illus. In Ukrainian.
M.: Mosk. patriarkhiia, 1983. 224 pp., illus. In English.

5769 Makarii, arkhiepiskop. *Pravoslavie na Ukraine* [Orthodoxy in Ukraine]. Kiev: Ukraina, 1980. 64 pp., illus. In Ukrainian. Published also in English.

5770 "Materialy k "'Bogoslovsko-tserkovnomu slovariu'" [Material for "Theologic-Church Dictionary"]. *Bogoslovskie trudy* 28 (1987): 344-352.

5771 *Mezhdunarodnaia konf. religioznykh deiatelei za sokhranenie sviashchennogo dara zhizni ot iadernoi katastrofy. Moskva.* 1982 [International Conference of Religious Dignitaries for Preservation of the Holy Gift of Life from Nuclear Catastrophy. Moscow. 1982]. M.: Mosk. patriarkhiia, 1983. 224 pp., illus. In English and Russian.

5772 "Mezhdunarodnaia tserkovno-istoricheskaia konferentsiia, posviashchennaia 1000-letiiu Kreshcheniia Rusi. Kiev, 21-28 iiulia, 1986 goda" [International Church-Historical Conference Dedicated to 1000th Anniversary of Baptism of Rus'. Kiev, July 21st-28th, 1986]. *Bogoslovkie trudy* 28 (1987): 7-229.

5773 *Mineia* [Mineya]. M.: Mosk. patriarkhiia. Oktiabr', 1980. 60 pp., illus.
Noiabr', 1980. Ch. 1. 1980. 440 pp., illus. Ch. 2. 1981. 554 pp., illus.
Dekabr', 1982. Ch. 1. 1982. 576 pp., illus. Ch. 2. 1982. 504 pp., illus.
Ianvar', 1983. Ch. 1. 1983. 592 pp., illus. Ch. 2. 1983. 559 pp., illus.
Mart, 1984. Ch. 1. 1984. 421 pp., illus. Ch. 2. 1985. 399 pp., illus.
Mai, 1987. Ch. 3. 1988. 520 pp., illus.
Iiul', 1988. Ch. 3. 1988. 416 pp., illus.
Avgust, 1989. Ch. 1. 1989. 448 pp., illus

5774 *Misale R.* [Readings from Holy Writ]. Riga: Rizh. kuriia metropolii, 1982- In Latvian. Published since 1982.

T. 1. *Period pered Rozhdestvom. Period Rozhdestva* [Readings before Christmas and during Christmas]. 1982. 227 pp.

T. 2. *Obychnyi liturgicheskii period s I po XI nedeliu* [Ordinary Liturgical Period from Ist to XIth Week]. 1983. 464 pp.

T. 3. *Period Posta. Period Paskhi* [Readings during the Fast and Easter]. 1983. 506 pp.

T. 4. *Obychnoe liturgicheskoe vremia v period s XII po XXIII nedeliu* [Ordinary Liturgical Period from XIIth to XXIIIrd Week]. 1983. 472 pp.

T. 6. *Chteniia is Sviashchennogo Pisaniia* [Readings from the Holy Writ]. 1985. 544 pp.

5775 *Molitvennye pesni* [Prayer Songs]. 2nd. revised and enlarged ed. Vil'nius: Taurage: Evang. liuter. konsistoriia, 1982. 392 pp. In Lithuanian.

5776 *Moskovskii Danilov monastyr'* [The Moscow monastery of St. Daniel].* M: Izd. Mosk. Patriarkhii, 1988. 64 pp., illus. Parallel text in Russian and English.

5777 *Nastol'naia kniga presvitera* [Presbyters' Reference Book]. M.: Vsesoiuz. sovet evang. khristian-baptistov, 1982.
[Vyp. 1]. 248 pp. Bibl.: pp. 238-246.
Vyp. 2. 1987. 240 pp. Bibl.: pp. 149-152.

5778 *Nastol'naia kniga sviashchennosluzhitelia* [Priests' Reference Book]. M.: Mosk. patriarkhiia, 1977 - Published since 1977.
T. 4. 1983. 824 pp., illus.
T. 6. 1988. 880 pp., illus. *Tematicheskii material dlia propovedi* [Thematical Material for Sermon].
T. 8. 1988. 800 pp., illus. *Pastyrskoe Bogoslovie. Ranne Khristianskie Ottsy Tserkvi* [Pastoral Theology. Early Christian Church Fathers].

5779 *Nastol'nyi kalendar' sluzhitelia Tserkvi khristian adventistov sed'mogo dnia* [Desk Calendar for Priest of Christian Seventh Day Adventists]. M.: Tserkov' khristian adventistov sed'mogo dnia, 1980 -
1980. 143 pp., illus.
1981. 152 pp., illus.
1982. 127 pp., illus.
1983. 133 pp., illus.
1984. 211 pp., illus.
1987. 1. 65 pp., illus.; 2. 65 pp., illus.
1988. 1. 64 pp., illus.; 2. 65 pp., illus.

5780 *Novyi zavet* [New Testament]. Echmiadzin: Sv. Echmiadzin, 1981. 712 pp. In Armenian.

5781 *Novyi zavet gospoda nashego Iisusa Khrista* [New Testament of Our Lord Jesus Christ]. M.: Vsesoiuz. sovet evang. khristian-baptistov, 1980. 413 pp., illus., map. Republished in 1981; and in 1984, 365 pp., illus., map. Same ed. republished by Tserkov' Khristian-adventistov sed'mogo dnia, 1984.

5782 *Oktoikh* [Collection of Orthodox Church Songs]. M.: Mosk. patriarkhiia, 1980 - In Old Church Slavonic.
Glasy 1 - 4. 1980. 711 pp., illus.
Glasy 5 - 8. 1981. 672 pp., illus.
1982. 208 pp., music, illus. (Suppl).

5783 *50-letie mitropolita Tallinskogo i Estonskogo Aleksiia* [50th. Anniversary of Metropolitan of Tallin and Estonia Alexis]. Tallin: Est. Eparkh. upr., 1980. 59 pp., illus. In Estonian.

5784 *Posobie dlia propoveduiushhikh v pervoi chasti subbotnego bogosluzheniia na 1985 god* [Aid for Preachers in the First Part of Saturday's Divine Service]. M.: Tserkov' khristian-adventistov sed'mogo dnia, 1984. 152 pp.
...na 1988 god. 1987. 320 pp.
...na 1989 god. 1988. 191 pp., illus.

5785 *Pravoslavnye khramy Moskvy* [Moscow's Orthodox Places of Worship]. M.: Mosk. patriarkhiia, 1988. 176 pp., illus. Parallel text in Russian and English.

5786 *Pravoslavnyi molitvoslov i psaltyr'* [Orthodox Prayer and Psalter]. M.: Mosk. patriarkhiia, 1980. 256 pp. Republished in 1988 as a jubilee ed. on the occasion of 1000th anniverary of baptism of Rus'.

5787 *Pravoslavnyi tserkovnyi kalendar'* [Orthodox Church Calendar]. M.: Mosk. patriarkhiia. Published since 1951.
1980. 1979. 160 pp., illus.
1981. 1980. 80 pp., illus.
1982. 1981. 80 pp., illus.
1983. 1982. 80 pp., illus.
1984. 1983. 80 pp., portr., illus.
1985. 1984. 80 pp., illus.
1988. 1987. 96 pp., illus.
1989. 1988. 112 pp., illus.

5788   *Pravoslavnyi tserkovnyi kalendar'* [Orthodox Church Calendar]. Kiev: Ekzarkh
       vsei Ukrainy, Mitropolit Kievskii i Galitskii. In Ukrainian.
       ...na 1980 god. 1980. 50 pp., portr.
       ...na 1982 god. 1981. 50 pp., illus.
       ...na 1983 god. 1982. 60 pp., illus. Ekzarkhat vsei Ukrainy.
       ...na 1984 god. 1983. 60 pp., illus.
       ...na 1985 god. 1984. 60 pp., illus.

5789   *Pravoslavnyi terkovnyi kalendar'* [Orthodox Church Calendar]. Riga: Rizh.
       eparkhiia Mosk. patriarkhii. In Latvian and Russian.
       ...na 1984 god. 1983. 40 pp., illus.
       ...na 1985 god. 1984. 73 pp.

5790   *Pravoslavnyi tserkovnyi kalendar'* [Orthodox Church Calendar]. Mosk.
       patriarkhiia. Tallin: Est. eparkh. upr. Published since 1955. In Estonian.
       1981. 1980. [35] pp., portr.
       1985. 1984. 43 pp., portr., illus.

5791   *Prazdnichnye dni armianskoi apostol'skoi tserkvi dlia eparkhii, rokovodstvuiush-
       chikhsia starym stilem* [Holidays of Armenian Apostolic Church for
       Dioceses, Using the Old Style]. Echmiadzin: Sv. Echmiadzin.
       1983. 1982. 31 pp., illus.
       1984. 1983. 31 pp., illus.
       1985. 1984. 32 pp., illus.

5792   *Religioznyi kalendar' na 1403 g. khidzhry - 1982/1983 godu evropeiskogo
       letoischesleniia* [Religious Calendar for 1403 Hegira - 1982/1983 Years of
       European Calendar]. Comp.: Dukhov. upr. musul'man Evrop. chasti Sov.
       Soiuza i Sibiri. Ufa: [S.n.], 1983. 32 pp. In Tatar.

5793   *Rimskii missal* [Roman Missal]. Vil'nius; Kaunas: R. K. Episkopat. Published
       since 1966. In Lithuanian. Part of the text in Latin.
       Ch. 1 - 3. 1982. 675 pp.
       [T]. 2. 1982. 295 pp., illus.
       [T]. 9. 1982. 95 pp.

5794   *Russkaia pravoslavnaia tserkov'* 988-1988 [Russian Orthodox Church
       988-1988]. M.: Mosk. patriarkhiia. 1988, Comp.: A.S. Buevskii et al. Vyp.
       2. 112 pp., illus. Sequel to [Vyp.1], published in 1980. 255 pp. illus.

5795 *Sbornik dukhovnykh pesen evangel'skikh khristian-baptistov* [Collection of Spiritual Songs of Evangelist Christian Baptists]. M.: VSEKhB, 1981. 403 pp.

5796 *Sbornik dukhovnykh pesnopenii* [Collection of Spiritual Psalms]. 4th ed. M.: Tserkov' khristian-adventistov sed'mogo dnia, 1984. 368 pp.

5797 *Sbornik dukhovnykh statei* [Collection of Ecclesiastical Articles]. M.: Vsesoiuz. sovet evang. khristian-baptistov, 1980. 110 pp. Published also in: 1983. 167 pp. Bibl.: pp. 132-135, 153-156.

5798 *Sbornik Estonskoi evangelichesko-liuteranskoi tserkvi* [Collection of Estonian Evangelist Lutheran Church]. Tallin: [S.n.], 1983. 84 pp., illus. In Estonian.

5799 *Slav'te Gospoda!* Kniga molitvennik katolikam [Praise the Lord! Prayer Book for Catholics]. Riga: Kuriia Rizh. metropolii, 1981. 381 pp., illus. In Latvian.

5800 *Sluzhba sviatoi paskhi* [Service of the Holy Passover]. M.: Mosk. patriarkhiia, 1982. 60 pp. of old slav pagination, illus. In Old Church Slavonic.

5801 *Staroobriadcheskii drevlepravoslavnyi tserkovnyi kalendar'* [Old Belief Ancient Orthodox Calendar]. [S.l.]: Staroobriad. arkhiepiskopiia novozybkov., mosk. i vseia Rusi.
...na 1983 god. 80 pp., illus. and suppl.
...na 1984 god. 1983. 80 pp., illus., suppl.
...na 1985 god. 1984. 82 pp., illus. Published in Novozybkov: Novozybkov. staroobriad. arkhiepiskopiia.

5802 *Staroobriadcheskii tserkovnyi kalendar'* [Old Belief Church Calendar]. M.: Staroobriad. mosk. arkhiepiskopiia i vseia Rusi.
...na 1980 god. 1980. 87 pp., illus., plate.
...na 1981 god. 1981. 80 pp., illus., plate.
...na 1982 god. 1982. 81 pp., illus., plate.
...na 1983 god. 1983. 81 pp., illus., plate.
...na 1984 god. 1983. 80 pp., illus.
...na 1985 god. 1984. 81 pp., illus., portr.
...na 1988 god. 80 pp. Suppl. 64 pp., illus. Name index: pp. 50-55.
...na 1989 god. 113 pp.

5803 *Staroobriadcheskii tserkovnyi kalendar'* [Old Belief Church Calendar]. Vil'nius
i dr.: Vyssh. staroobriad. sovet LitSSR i dr.
...na 1981 g. 1981. 91 pp., illus., plate.
...na 1982 g. 1981. 84 pp., illus., plate. Name index: pp. 36-40.
...na 1983 g. 87 pp., illus., plate. Name index: pp. 37-41.
...na 1984 g. 1983. 89 pp., illus.
...na 1985 g. 1984. 112 pp., illus.
...na 1988 g. 1987. 117 pp., illus. Name index: pp. 43-46.
...na 1989 g. 1988. 113 pp., illus.

5804 *Sviashchennoe evengelie* [Holy Gospels]. M.: Mosk. patriarkhiia, 1984. 215
pp., illus. In Church Slavonic.

5805 *Tan'ia* [Mishna. Religious-Philosophic Collection]. M.: Mosk. Khor. i
Mar.-Roshch. sinagoga, 1989. 644 pp. In Hebrew.

5806 *Trebnik* [Prayer Book]. M.: Mosk. patriarkhiia 1980. In Old Church Slavonic.
Ch. A. 1980. 286 pp., illus.
Ch. B. 1980. 256 pp.
Ch. 3. 1984. 368 pp., illus.

5807 *Tserkovnyi kalendar'* [Church Calendar]. Riga: [S.n.]. In Latvian.
...na 1985 god. 1984. 139 pp.

5808 *Tysiacheletie Kreshcheniia Rusi* [A Thousand Years of Baptism of Rus']. M.:
Mosk. patriakhiia, 1988. 351 pp., illus. Summary in English.

5809 *Uspenskaia Pochaevskaia lavra* [Uspensk Pochaev Monastery]. M.: Mosk.
patriarkhiia, 1983. 16 pp., illus. Part of the text in English.

5810 Vazgen I Katolikos. *Nasha obednia* [Our Mass]. Echmiadzin, 1988. 59 pp.
In Armenian.

5811 Vazgen I, patriarkh armianskoi tserkvi. *Kondaki, propovedi, vystupleniia*
[Church Songs, Sermons, Speeches]. Echmiadzin: Sv. Echmiadzin. In
Armenian.
Kn. 4. 1983. 198 pp., illus.

5812 *Vsenoshchnoe bdenie. Liturgiia* [All-Night Vigil. Liturgy]. M.: Mosk.
patriarkhiia, 1982. 96 pp., illus.

5813 "Vstrecha General'nogo sekretaria TsK KPSS M.S. Gorbacheva s Patriarkhom Moskovskim i vseia Rusi Pimenom i chlenami Sinoda Russkoi Pravoslavnoi Tserkvi" [Meeting of the General Secretary of the CC of the CPSU M.S. Gorbachev with Moscow and All Russia Patriarch Pimen and Synod Members of Russian Orthodox Church]. *Zhurn. Mosk. patriarkhii* 7 (1988): 2-6.

UNCENSORED RELIGIOUS PUBLICATIONS

5814 *Amvon.* Pravoslav. zhurn. v pomoshch' katekhizatoru i missioneru [Pulpit. Orthodox Journal, Aid for Catechumen and Missionary]. Ed.: R. Vershillo. M., 1988- Irregular.
No 1-2, 1988.

5815 *BKhO.* Biul. khrist. obshchestvennosti [Bulletin of Christian Public Opinion]. Ed.: O. Shishkova; A. Ogorodnikov. M., 1987. Monthly.
No 1-6. 1987.
No 1-9. 1988.

5816 *Blagovest'.* Ezhcmcs. mezhprikhod. pravoslav. zhurn [Ringing of Church Bell. Monthly Inter-Parish Orthodox Journal]. Ed. A. Zelinskii. L., 1988-
No 1-9, 1988.

5817 *Chasha.* Nezavisimyi zhurn. ekumen. o-v SSSR [Chalice. Independent Journal of Ecumenical Society of USSR]. Ed.: M. Baizerman et al. M., 1988.
No 1-2. 1988.

5818 *Evangelist.* [Evangelist]. No details.

5819 *Khare Krishna.* Khronika dvizheniia soznaniia Krishny v SSSR [Hari Krishna. Chronicle of the Movement of Krishna Consciousness in USSR]. Ed.: I. Matushkin. M., 1988. Irregular.
No 1-8. 1988.

5820 *Khristianskie noviny.* Belorusskii informator-biulleten' [Christian Novelties. Belorussian Informant-Bulletin]. Ed. is not mentioned. [S.l.]
No 1. 1989.

5821 *Krug.* Det. khrist. i lit. zhurn [The Circle. Children's Christian and Literary Journal]. Ed.: O. Volchek; O. Komarova. L., 1988-
No 1. 1988.

5822 Nadezhda [Hope]. Ed.: Z.Krarhmal'nikova. Published in early 80s. Ed. was imprisoned in 1982.

5823 *Nevskii dukhovnyi vestnik.* Pravoslav. ezhemes. zhurn. [Nevskii Spiritual Herald. Orthodox Monthly Journal]. Ed.: A. Maksotskii. L., 1988-
No 1-5. 1988.

5824 *Pravoslavnaia dumka.* Izdanie pravoslavnoi molodezhi [Orthodox Dumka. Publication of Othodox Youth]. Ed. not mentioned. Minsk, 1988.
No 1. 1988.

5825 *Pravoslavnaia Rus'.* [Orthodox Rus']. No details.

5826 *Protestant.* Period. izd. evang. khristian-baptistov [Protestant. Periodical Publication of Evangelist Christian-Baptists]. Ed.: P. Abrashkin. Irregular. M., 1988.
No 1-2. 1988.

5827 *Russkii vestnik.* Khristiansko-patrioticheskii soiuz [Russian Herald. Christian-Patriotic Union]. Ed.: V. Osipov. M., 1989- Monthly.
No 1-2. 1989.

5828 *Slovo very.* Izd. soiuza khristian Litvy [The Word of Faith. Publication of the Union of Christian of Lithuania]. Ed.: E. Morkunas; Iu. Melekh. Vil'nius, 1989. In Russian.
No 1. 1989.

5829 *Vera.* Izdanie Belorusskikh katolikov [The Faith. Publication of Belorussian Catholics]. Ed. not mentioned. Minsk-Smolensk, 1988- Monthly.
No 1. 1988.

5830 *Vestnik Belorusskogo Katolicheskogo Dukhpastyrstva.* [The Herald of Belorussian Catholic Spiritual Pastoral]. Ed. not mentioned. Minsk, 1988-
Irregular.
No 1. 1988.

5831 *Voskresenie.* Izd. KhDO "Chelovek" [The Resurrection. Publication of KhDO "Chelovek"]. Ed.: V. Savitskii. L., 1988. Weekly.
No 1-28. 1988.

5832 *Vybor.* Lit-filos. zhurn. rus. khrist. kul'tury [Choice. Literary-Philosophical Journal of Russian Christian Culture]. Ed.: V. Aksiuchits. M., 1987.
No 1. 1987.
No 2-4. 1988.

ADDENDUM

5833 Akmuradov, I.A. *Formirovanie nauchno-materialisticheskogo mirovozzreniia trudiashchikhsiia* [Forming Workers' Materialist World Outlook]. Tashkent Uzbekistan, 1986. 158 pp. For reviews see items 4914-4915.

5834 Arsenkin, V.K. *Krizis religioznosti i molodezh'* [Crisis of Religiosity and Youth]. M.: Nauka, 1984. 264 pp. For reviews see items 4928-4933.

5835 Artykov, A.A. *XXVI s'ezd KPSS i ateisticheskoe vospitanie* [XXVIth CPSU Congress and Atheistic Education]. Tashkent: Uzbekistan, 1981. 32 pp. (Ser. "Marksizm-leninizm"; No 12). In Uzbek.

5836 *Ateisticheskaia rabota v massakh* [Atheistic Work with Masses]. Comp.: M. Mamet'iarov]. Alma-Ata: Kazakhstan, 1980. 91 pp. In Uigur.

5837 Badmazhapov, Ts.B. "O semanticheskoi interpretatsii buddiiskoi ikonografii" [Semantic Interpretation of Buddhist Iconography]. *Dvadtsataia nauchnaia konferentsiia "Obshchestvo i gosudarstvo v Kitae".* M., 1989. Ch. I. Pp. 98-101.

5838 Beliaev, I.P. "'Islamskie igry' protiv Sovetskogo Soiuza" ["Islamic Plays" against Soviet Union]. *Argumenty*. M., 1988. Pp. 103-127.

5839 Demi'anov, A.I. *Fakty protiv izmyshlenii: (Mif o 'rel. vozrozhdenii' v SSSR i ego nesostoiatel'nost')* [Facts against Fabrications: (Myth on "Religious Revival" in USSR and Its Groundlessness)]. Voronezh: Tsentr.-Chernozem. kn. izd-vo, 1989. 128 pp.

5840 Franko, I.Ia. O *Vatikane, unii i katolitsizme* [On Vatican, Uniate Church and Catholicism]. Kiev: Politizdat Ukrainy, 1981. 285 pp. In Ukrainian. For review see item 5026.

5841 Furman, D.E. "Iudaistskii klerikalizm i ego funktsii v Izraile" [Judaic Clericalism and Its Functions in Israel].* *Narody Azii i Afriki* 6 (1989): 27-39.

5842 Gapochka, M.P. *Materializm protiv fideizma* [Materialism against Fideism]. M.: Politizdat, 1980. 191 pp. For reviews see items 5041-5044.

5843 Glagolev, V.S. *Religiozno-idealisticheskaia kul'turologiia: ideinye tupiki* [Religious-Ideological Culturology: Ideological Impasses]. M.: Mysl', 1985. 222 pp. For reviews se items 5046-5047.

5844 Iastrebov, I.B. Novye tendentsii v sotsial'noi programme sovremennogo katolitsizma [New Tendencies in Social Programme of Contemporary Catholicism]. Dissertation. In-t filosofii, sotsiologii i prava AN LitSSR. Vil'nius, 1988.

5845 Ippolitova, V.A. *Pole deiatel'nosti ateista* [Atheist's Sphere of Action]. M.: Sov. Rossiia, 1983. 104 pp. For review see item 5072.

5846 *Khristianstvo i lamaizm u korrenogo naseleniia Sibirii* [Christianity and Lamaism of Siberia's Native Population]. L.: Nauka, 1983. 64 pp. For review see item 5100.

5847 *Khudozhestvennaia i publitsisticheskaia biblioteka ateista* [Atheist's Library of Belles-Lettres and Socio-Political Journalism]. M.: Sov. Rossiia, 1984-1985. For reviews see items 5101-5102.

5848 Kozha, A. "Religioznoe mirotvorchestvo v iadernyi vek" [Religious Peace-Making in Nuclear Age]. *Religiia v SSSR* 2 (1987): AK 1-AK 2.

5849 Makatov, I.A. *Islam i natsional'nye traditsii* [Islam and National Traditions]. Makhachkala: Dag. kn. izd-vo, 1984. 74 pp. (Sots. obraz zhizni i religia).

5850 Makatov, I.A. *Kritika popytok imperializma i musul'manskoi reaktsii ispol'zovat' religiiu v antisovetskikh tseliakh* [Criticism of Attempts of Imperialism and Moslem Reaction to use Religion for Anti-Soviet Goals]. M.: Znanie RSFSR. Sektsiia propagandy nauch.-ateist. znanii, 1988. 44 pp. Bibl.: p .43.

5851 Makatov, I.A. "Novyi podkhod neobkhodim" [New Approach is Necessary]. *Nauka i religiia* 8 (1988): 43-44.

5852 Makatov, I.A. "V ushcherb interesam obshchestva i lichnosti" [In Detriment of Interests of Society and Individual]. *Sov. Dagestan* 6 (1986): 37-44.

5853 Makatov, I.[A]. "Vera v znanie i znanie o vere: Zametki ateista" [Faith in Knowledge and Knowledge about Faith: Atheist's Remarks]. *Zvezda Vostoka* 8 (1988): 125-133.

5854 Metkin, A. "Delegatsiia Vsemirnogo islamskogo kongressa v Sovetskom Soiuze" [Delegation of the World Islamic Congress in the Soviet Union]. *Religiia v SSSR* 2 (1988): AM 1-AM 3.

5855 Pechiura, P.[I]. *Pochitanie ognia* [Worship of Fire]. Kaunas: [S.n.], 1983. 26 pp. In Lithuanian. For review see item 5224.

5856 Rozhnov, G. "'Eto my, gospodi!'" ['It's Us, o God!"]. *Ogonek* 38 (1989): 6-8.

5857 Sergeeva, N. "Izrail' vo vlasti ravvinata" [Israel in the Power of Rabbinate]. *Aziia i Afrika segodnia* 4 (1984): 27-29.

5858 Zmeev, Iu.N. "Voprosy estestvennonauchnogo obosnovania ateizma [Problems of Natural-Scientific Basing of Atheism]. *Vopr. ateizma* 23 (1987): 119-124.

SUBJECT INDEX